The Essential Flower Gardening Encyclopedia

The Essential Flower Gardening Encyclopedia

Published by Fog City Press
814 Montgomery Street
San Francisco, CA 94133 USA

Reprinted 2005, 2006

Chief Executive Officer: John Owen
President: Terry Newell
Publisher: Lynn Humphries
Design Manager: Helen Perks
Production Manager: Caroline Webber
Production Coordinator: Monique Layt
Sales Manager: Emily Jahn
Vice President International Sales: Stuart Laurence

Editorial Coordinators: Jessica Cox, Jennifer Losco
Project Editors: Helen Bateman, Ariana Klepac,
Mary Moody, Bronwyn Sweeney, Susan Tomnay
Designers: Melanie Feddersen i2i design, Kerry Klimmer, Lena Lowe,
Kylie Mulquin, Stephen Smedley
Consultants: Kenneth A. Beckett, Geoffrey Burnie,
Ruth Rogers Clausen, Jennifer Stackhouse

 A catalog record for this book is available from
the Library of Congress, Washington, D.C.

ISBN: 1 877019 66 6

Color reproduction by Bright Arts Graphics (S'pore) Pte Ltd
Printed by Kyodo Printing Co. (S'pore) Pte Ltd
Printed in Singapore

A Weldon Owen Production

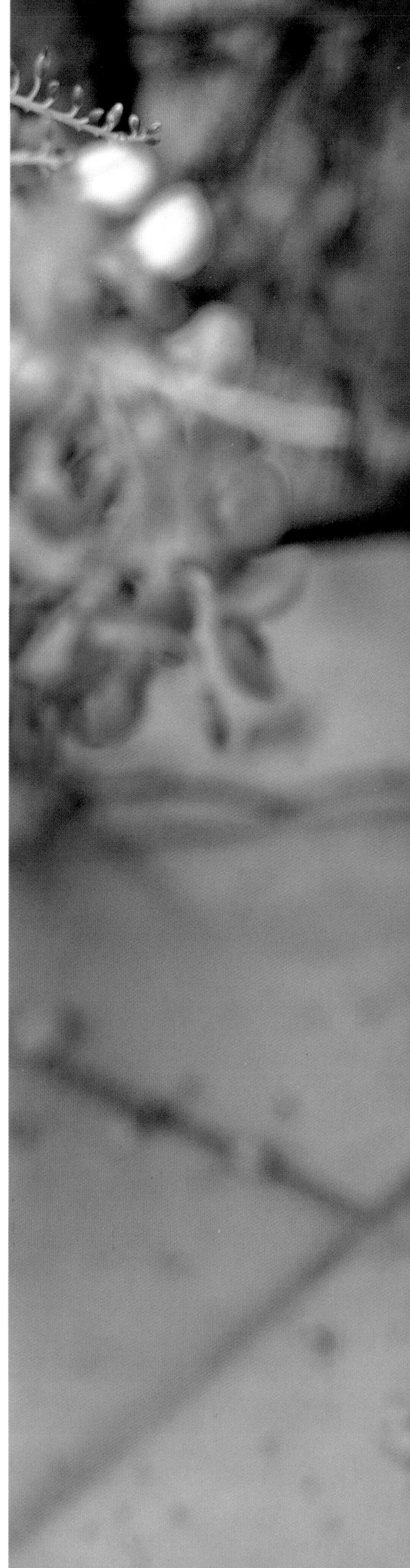

CONTENTS

PART ONE
THE ESSENTIALS OF FLOWER GARDENING

SECTION ONE
GARDENING WITH FLOWERS 10

Some Basic Botany 12
About Annuals 16
Perennial Favorites 22
Bountiful Bulbs 28

SECTION TWO
UNDERSTANDING YOUR GARDEN 32

Study the Soil 34
Your Local Climate 38
The Lay of the Land 40
Examine Your Exposure 42
Observe and Plan 44

SECTION THREE
PREPARATION AND PLANTING 46

Getting the Soil Ready 48
Adding Nutrients 50
Choosing the Right Plants 52
Planting Time 56
Growing Annuals 64
Propagating Perennials 68
Bulb Multiplication 74

SECTION FOUR
CARING FOR FLOWERS 76

Tools and Equipment 78
Mulching and Watering 84
Fertilizing for Good Growth 88
Pests, Diseases, Weeds 92
Pruning and Training 100
Preparing for Winter 104
Month by Month in the Flower Garden 108

SECTION FIVE
CREATING A FLOWER GARDEN 112

The Planning Stage 114
Great Design Ideas 118
Beds and Borders, Screens and Fillers 128
Creating a Cutting Garden 134
Making a Meadow Garden 136
Creating a Cottage Garden 140

SECTION SIX
PROBLEM-SOLVING WITH FLOWERS 146

Time-saving Gardening Tips 148
Handling Hillsides 154
Succeeding in the Shade 156
Turning Bogs into Beds 158
Growing a Water-wise Landscape 160

SECTION SEVEN
CONTAINER PLANTS 162

Considering Containers 164
Getting Started with Container Gardening 170
Flowers for Pots and Planters 174
Window Boxes and Hanging Baskets 180
Balconies, Courtyards, and Patio Gardens 184
Container Garden Primer 188
The Right Container Plant for the Right Place 194

SECTION EIGHT
HOUSEPLANTS 206

Houseplants at First Glance 208
Caring for Houseplants 214
Troubleshooting Houseplants 222
Houseplants in Your Home 226
Growing Plants Indoors 230
Creative Houseplant Displays 234
The Right Houseplant for the Right Place 238

SECTION NINE
BASIC GARDEN DESIGN 240

Color by Design 242
A Garden for the Senses 262
Landscaping with Plants 270
Solving Landscaping Problems with Plants
Special Plant Effects 280
Using Trees, Shrubs, and Vines 284

SECTION TEN
CREATIVE GARDEN DESIGN 290

Urban Solutions 292
Low-maintenance Gardens 298
Outdoor Living Areas 300
Contemporary and Avant-garde Designs 302

PART TWO
ENCYCLOPEDIA OF FLOWERS

HOW TO USE THIS ENCYCLOPEDIA 308

SECTION ONE
ORANGE-RED FLOWERS 310
Annuals 312
Bulbs 316
Climbers 320
Perennials 326
Shrubs 334
Trees 342

SECTION TWO
PINK FLOWERS 346
Annuals 348
Bulbs 356
Climbers 358
Perennials 362
Shrubs 378
Trees 388

SECTION THREE
PURPLE-BLUE FLOWERS 396
Annuals 398
Bulbs 402
Climbers 408
Perennials 414
Shrubs 436
Trees 450

SECTION FOUR
WHITE FLOWERS 452
Annuals 454
Bulbs 456
Climbers 464
Perennials 472
Shrubs 488
Trees 518

SECTION FIVE
YELLOW FLOWERS 536
Annuals 538
Bulbs 542
Climbers 548
Perennials 552
Shrubs 568
Trees 582

Glossary 587
Plant Hardiness Zone Maps 588
Index 591

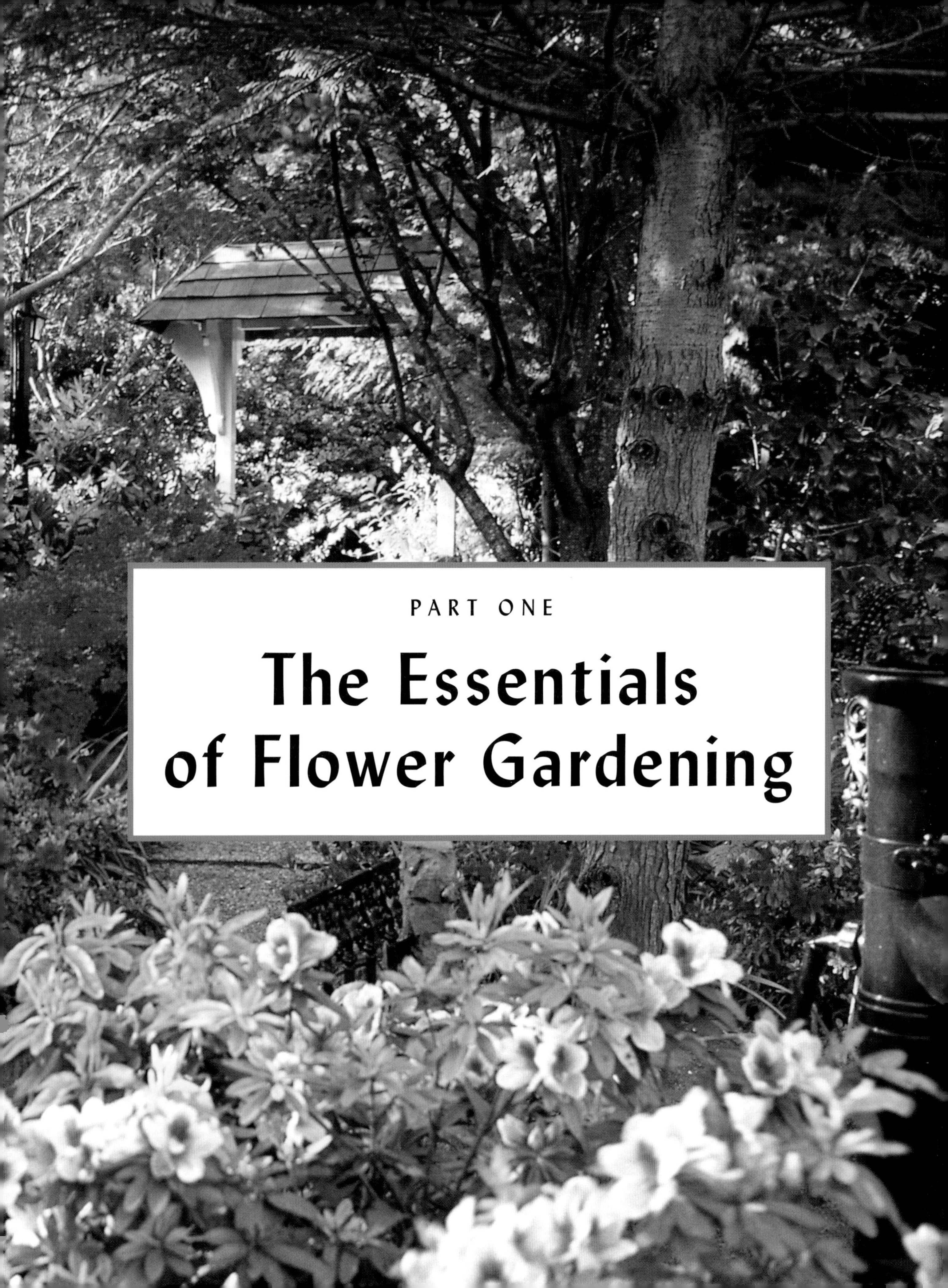

PART ONE

The Essentials of Flower Gardening

SECTION ONE

Gardening with Flowers

From the first dainty crocuses in early spring to fall's display of brightly colored asters, flowers provide an endless variety of forms in an ever-changing display throughout the growing season. Some evergreen perennials even provide interest in the coldest months, and you can bring certain annuals and bulbs indoors in containers for winter bloom. Flowers add color and beauty to your landscape—this chapter introduces you to the basics of flower gardening.

Some Basic Botany *12*

About Annuals *16*

Perennial Favorites *22*

Bountiful Bulbs *28*

Some Basic Botany

You will probably choose the annuals and perennials for your garden on the basis of the color and fragrance of their flowers. But don't forget to also consider their attractive leaves for those times when they aren't in bloom, and the many decorative seedpods or useful fruits that appear when flowering time is over.

Knowing a little basic botany will not only help you to identify and select the plants that are best suited for your garden. It will also help you to understand how your garden grows, so you can maintain your plants most effectively.

Root System

A plant's root system is vitally important, and certain root systems may be better suited to your soil than others. Roots help to hold the plant firm and stable in the soil and provide it with a system for absorbing water and nutrients. They may also act as storage organs (root vegetables do this), holding nutrients for use during times of vigorous growth or flowering.

Most annuals have a fibrous root system (made up of many fine and branching roots), which does not penetrate deep into the soil. Rather, it tends to remain quite shallow. Because this type of root system does not penetrate particularly deeply, you will need to pay special attention to the water requirements of such plants when rain is scarce.

Some plants, including many of the perennials, have strong central roots, called taproots, that travel straight down in search of water and nutrients. The taproot is a single, thick, tapering organ (a carrot, for example, is actually an enlarged taproot) with thin branch roots at the side. Taprooted plants can more easily withstand fluctuating soil moisture conditions, but many are more difficult to transplant because their roots tend to penetrate more deeply into the ground and can be very sensitive.

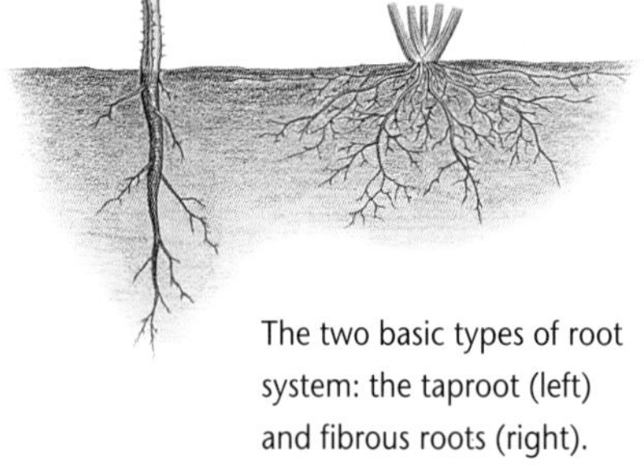

The two basic types of root system: the taproot (left) and fibrous roots (right).

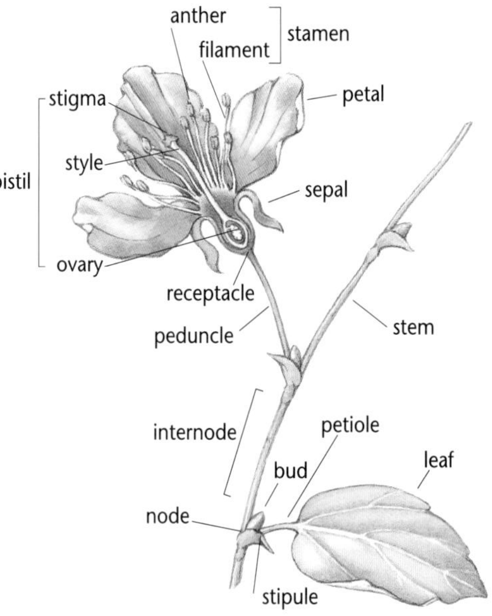

Knowing some of the common plant parts, identified here, will help you understand the descriptions you read in books and catalogs.

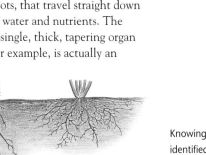

From petunias and flowering tobacco to showy stonecrop and sunflowers, a garden full of annuals and perennials offers a rich diversity of flower color, shape, texture, and smell.

Plant Stems

The stems of your annuals and perennials support the leaves, flowers, and seedpods, and also serve as pathways for movement of nutrients and water between roots and leaves. Just like roots, stems are storage organs, too. Bulbs and corms, from which tulips and gladioli grow, for example, are actually specialized storage stems.

Some plant stems are specially adapted for vegetative reproduction. Stolons (also known as rhizomes) are stems that travel horizontally along the soil surface. At certain intervals along the stolon, new shoots and roots will form, and these give rise to new plants. Sweet woodruff and sweet violets are examples of plants that produce stolons. Plants such as irises form new plants from underground stems, which are called rhizomes.

Simple leaf

Compound leaf

Lobed

Many perennials and some annuals can be propagated by stem cuttings. Swollen buds, or nodes, located along the stems are the sites for new growth. When you take stem cuttings from your plants to make new plants, the new root systems form underground at active nodes on the cutting. See "Propagating Perennials" on page 68 for more on taking cuttings.

Foliage

Among annuals and perennials, you will find every shape, texture, and color of leaf imaginable. Leaves that are whole and undivided, like those of marigolds and coneflowers, are called simple. Leaves divided into two or more parts on the same stalk are called compound. The lacy, finely divided leaves of yarrow, cosmos, and love-in-a-mist are compound leaves. Leaf shape ranges from the long, thin, linear leaves of irises to the eye-shaped, elliptical leaves of petunias and the almost circular nasturtium. They vary in their edges as well as their shapes. A leaf like forget-me-not with its smooth edge is called entire, those with jagged edges like lemon balm are toothed, and the wavy dusty miller leaf is lobed.

Toothed

Entire

Ovate

Linear

Leaves offer a tremendous variety of color, too. It's true that most leaves are green, but there are also the blue-grays of lavender and wormwood. Coleus is available in many brilliantly colored cultivars, with streaks of orange, red, green, and yellow. Leaves that are striped or blotched with different colors, like those of some geraniums, are called variegated. They also add color and interest to any planting.

This hybrid columbine flower will bring great pleasure to a gardener. But the real reason for its unusual beauty is attracting bees to pollinate it, so it will develop fruit, then seeds, and ultimately, new plants.

Flowers, Fruits, and Seeds

Most plants possess flowers, and those of annuals and perennials bloom in every imaginable color, fragrance, size, and shape. They range from the funnel-like petunia to the radiating coneflowers and daisies, the cup-shaped tulips and peonies to the snapdragons with their protruding lips. But this visual and olfactory feast is not designed for our benefit, but to attract bees, butterflies, and other pollinators to transfer pollen from the anther (the male part) of one flower to the stigma (the female part) of another flower of the same species. If the pollen fertilizes the egg inside the second flower's ovary, the result will be seeds.

The ovary ripens into a fruit, which contains the seeds. Plant fruits vary enormously, just like the flowers they come from. They can be fleshy, like apples, strawberries, and tomatoes; they can be dry fruits that open when they are finally ripe, such as stock, poppies, and lupines; or they can be dry fruits that don't open, such as sunflowers, corn, and all the nuts. When the fruits finally mature, and rot or dry, the seeds are released from the original plant; they can be spread by wind, water, birds, animals, and humans. If and when conditions are right, the seed will germinate and a new plant will begin to grow.

Plant Growth

A plant depends on light, moisture, temperature, oxygen and other gases, and nutrients, to germinate, grow, and thrive.

Start with the Seed

The first two things a seed needs to grow into a new plant are warmth and water. If the soil is too cold or too dry, the seed remains dormant. Warmth is usually more reliable than water. Soil temperatures don't change as rapidly as air temperatures, so once the soil is warm enough for growth to begin, it usually stays warm enough for growth to continue.

These coneflowers grow exuberantly until they are ready to bloom from midsummer onward. Such strong growth depletes the nutrients in the soil, so the edges of the clumps tend to be most vigorous.

Young seedlings thrive in warm, well-drained soil. By growing them indoors, you control moisture and heat and make sure conditions are just right.

Water is less dependable than warmth. If the soil dries out after germination begins, the young seedling soon dies. Soils with good structure increase the odds that the seed will germinate; the soil particles are fine enough to closely surround the seed, holding moisture against it.

Shoots and Roots

When the seed germinates, it puts out a temporary root, called the primary root, or radicle. The radicle stores some of the food that provides the energy the first aboveground shoot needs to push up through the soil (the rest of its food is in the seed leaves, which are the leaf-like parts attached to the shoot). The radicle also anchors the plant, so the shoot won't blow or wash away.

About the time the first shoot reaches the soil surface, lateral roots begin to grow from the radicle. Like the radicle, the lateral roots anchor the plant in the soil. Throughout most of the plant's life, the roots expand to counterbalance the aboveground parts of the plant. In many cases, the root mass is larger than that of the stems and leaves.

As roots grow, they produce chemical compounds that help make nutrients more soluble and therefore more available to the plant. Throughout their life, roots absorb water and dissolved nutrients from the soil. When they die, the roots add organic matter and nutrients to the soil.

The chemicals that roots produce and the dead cells they shed create an environment that soil microorganisms find attractive. They multiply more rapidly in the root zone than they do in the surrounding soil. As a result, organic matter breaks down faster, making nutrients more available in the soil that the roots touch. More roots encourage more organisms, which release more nutrients into the soil and promote more roots—a productive natural cycle.

Growth and Flowering

As plants grow, the water and nutrients the roots absorb flow up through the plant to the leaves and stems. During a process known as photosynthesis, the leaves and stems convert the water and nutrients to sugars; the sugars then flow down to the

This geranium has variegated leaves, which do not photosynthesize as effectively as all-green leaves.

roots to be stored as carbohydrates—food energy. Before it flowers and sets seed, the plant uses this energy for growth. While the stems and leaves are growing, the roots rapidly expand through the soil to reach water and nutrients. Once the plant flowers and the seed ripens, root growth slows as more energy is channeled to these demanding processes.

If the plant is an annual, it grows old and dies after the seed ripens. Its decaying roots, leaves, and stems return nutrients to the soil. If the plant is a perennial, it stores carbohydrates in its roots to use to start growing in the spring. Its leaves and stems die back and decay, adding nutrients to the soil to start the cycle over.

There are more than 250 species in the *Aster* genus; the New England aster, or *Aster novae-angliae*, is just one. Knowing the common and botanical names will help you obtain the plants you really want.

What's in a Name?

Botanical names can often tell you something about the plants they identify, such as the flower color or the growth habit. Listed below are some words that you may notice again and again in botanical names, along with their definitions.

Albus: white
Argenteus: silver
Aureus: golden yellow
Caeruleus: blue
Luteus: yellow
Nanus: dwarf
Palustris: swampy, marshy
Perennis: perennial
Prostratus: trailing
Purpureus: purple
Reptans: creeping
Roseus: rosy
Ruber: red
Sempervirens: evergreen
Speciosus: showy
Spinosus: spiny
Variegatus: variegated
Viridis: green
Vulgaris: common

Ajuga

Know Your Plant Names

One of the tricks to growing plants successfully is to learn their names. Members of your neighborhood plant society may understand common names, like bee balm for instance. But if you go to an out-of-town nursery and ask for bee balm, you may only get puzzled stares. Perhaps they call the plant Oswego tea, based on the fact that American pioneers used it as herbal tea. Alternatively, if you are looking for bee balm in a catalog, you may only find it listed under its botanical name, *Monarda didyma*.

You can see from this example that one plant can have a number of common names. Likewise, one common name can apply to several different plants. By getting to know botanical names, you will know exactly which plant you are talking about, planting, or ordering.

Scientists name plants with a system that gives each plant two names. Every naturally occurring plant that is able to reproduce is called a species, and each species is given a two-part name, for example, *Aster novae-angliae*, or New England aster. The word *Aster* indicates the genus (plural "genera") that includes all types of asters; *novae-angliae* refers to the particular type of aster called New England aster.

Species may be divided further into subspecies, varieties, and forms. These terms refer to variants of a species that occur in nature. Cultivars, on the other hand, are distinct horticultural types that are selected or produced by breeding under cultivation. For example, the plant *Lavandula angustifolia* 'Munstead' is a cultivar of English lavender. Cultivar names are always placed between single quotation marks. Cultivars are often mistakenly called varieties.

Sometimes plants from different species or genera will cross-pollinate, producing offspring that share the characteristics of both parents. These "new" plants are called hybrids. Hybrids may occur naturally or be man-made. An "x" in a plant's name (as in *Iris* x *germanica* var. *florentina*) usually indicates that the plant is a hybrid.

Botanical names can be easier to remember if you determine what they tell about the plant. Some refer to the person who discovered the plant or to what part of the world it was discovered in; others are descriptive. For instance, *Viola odorata* is the botanical name of sweet violet, which bears an especially fragrant flower.

About Annuals

One of the great joys of gardening comes from experimenting with different plants. Annuals offer some particularly exciting opportunities. If you're a beginner, you'll be gratified by the success you'll have with many of these easy-to-grow plants. As you gain more experience in flower gardening, you'll enjoy mixing all kinds of annuals with perennials, groundcovers, and other plants to create eye-catching combinations.

Part of the pleasure of growing annuals lies in their versatile natures. No matter where you live or what growing conditions you have to offer, you can find annuals that will thrive where you plant them.

Of course, annuals aren't just grown because they're practical and adaptable: They're beautiful, too! Their flowers come in a rich palette of colors that will suit every gardener's fancy. Some also offer handsome foliage. Others are treasured for their distinctive fragrance, their nostalgic associations, or their charm as cut flowers. And they are the greatest bargains in the gardening world: For the price of one container-grown perennial, you can buy enough annual seeds to fill an entire garden bed (and then save the seeds from those plants to grow more each season!). It's difficult to imagine a garden that wouldn't benefit from the addition of a few more annuals.

A restful corner has been lightened and brightened by the addition of annuals—cosmos and alyssum in the foreground, a dense row of larkspur encircling the stone bench in the background. Flowers in containers can be changed according to the season, and ever-popular daylilies give a vivid final note.

Create beautiful seasonal scenes by combining annuals with bulbs that bloom at the same time of the year, like these pansies and tulips.

Understanding Annuals

True annuals germinate, grow, flower, set seed, and then die all in one season. Their goal is to reproduce themselves. This is good news for the gardener, since it means that most annual plants will flower like mad to achieve their goal. Some of the best-known annuals—including petunias and marigolds, poppies and annual phlox—have achieved their great popularity because of their free-flowering nature. Even better news, if you use tricks such as deadheading (removing the spent flowers) to prevent seed formation, many annuals will step up flower production and continue to bloom well over an extended period until cold weather arrives.

The first hard frost usually kills the plants and signals the end of the bloom season for that year. Although you'll need to replant most annuals the following spring to get another show, some will sprout from seed dropped by this year's plants. See "Reseeding Annuals and Biennials" on page 21 for species that can return for years after just one planting.

Besides these true annuals, there are a number of perennial plants that are often thought of as annuals. These include tropical perennials, such as the many zonal geraniums, or perennials that will flower the first season from seed, such as four o'clocks (*Mirabilis jalapa*). These plants can live for years in frost-free climates, but, like true annuals, they meet their death at the hands of freezing temperatures in cold-winter climates. "Perennial Annuals" on page 18 lists some of the perennial plants that are normally grown as annuals.

Forget-me-nots (*Myosotis* spp.) are hardy annuals. You can sow them in early spring, or even in the preceding fall in mild areas.

Kinds of Annuals

Annuals are sometimes further separated into three groups—hardy, half-hardy, and tender—based on their cold tolerance. Some can withstand frost and freezing temperatures; some are quite delicate, and are quickly killed off by being planted out in such conditions. It's useful to know what kind of annuals you're growing because then you'll know how soon you can get away with planting your annuals in the spring. The catalog, seed packet, or plant tag should tell you if your plant is hardy, half-hardy, or tender.

Hardy Annuals Hardy annuals include forget-me-nots (*Myosotis* spp.), pansies, snapdragons, and other plants that can withstand several degrees of freezing temperatures. Almost all of these plants perform best during cool weather. They are often planted out in early spring by gardeners in cold-winter areas or in winter by gardeners in the South and West. Some hardy annuals, such as ornamental kale, are associated with cool fall weather.

Half-hardy Annuals Half-hardy annuals fit somewhere in the middle of hardy and tender. They will often withstand a touch of frost near the beginning or end of the gardening season. Many of the commonly grown annuals fit in this category.

A half-hardy designation is like yellow on a traffic signal: You need to use your judgment to decide when you can plant safely. If your spring has been a bit on the warm side and you're itching to plant—even though your average frost-free day has not yet arrived—you might just get away with planting half-hardy annuals. If you do, though, be prepared to cover them if cold night temperatures are predicted. Consider hedging your bets by planting out only part of your half-hardy seeds or transplants at one time; then wait a week or two to plant the rest.

Marigolds are generally classified as half-hardy annuals. They prefer warm weather but are able to survive a light frost in the fall.

Showy petunias bloom from early summer until fall and the first frost. No wonder they are so popular with gardeners, whether massed in beds and borders as here, or used as fillers in established plantings.

Tender Annuals Tender annuals, originally from tropical or subtropical climates, can't stand any degree of frost. More than that, they often grow poorly during cold weather and may be stunted by prolonged exposure to temperatures below 50°F (10°C). For best results, wait until late spring to plant tender annuals, such as celosia (*Celosia* spp.) and Joseph's coat (*Amaranthus tricolor*).

Biennials

Biennials have much in common with annuals, but they differ in one major respect: They take 2 years to complete their life cycle rather than the annuals' 1 year. The first year after sowing, they produce a leaf structure, building energy for the next year. The second year they flower, set seed, and die. Common garden biennials include sweet William (*Dianthus barbatus*), honesty (*Lunaria annua*), and foxglove (*Digitalis purpurea*).

Annuals in Your Garden

You could spend a lifetime exploring the rich diversity of annuals. With their range of colors, heights, habits, and bloom times, there are annuals for every purpose and every garden. If you're looking for exciting ways to enjoy these plants in your yard, here are some ideas to get started.

Many beginning gardeners draw their inspiration from public parks and gardens. Few American parks go without the summertime institution of brilliantly colored annuals laid out in formal blocks, rows, or patterns. These eye-catching displays tempt the first-timer to experiment with a few plants at home, almost inevitably lining up their annuals in rows.

Unfortunately, this mimicking of large public plantings is rarely satisfactory in a home garden, since the scale and budget are inevitably much reduced. When you have to pay for the plants, prepare the soil, and maintain the garden, large plantings usually aren't a realistic option. And the formal row arrangements that look fine in a public garden may look awkward and overly formal in a backyard setting.

Rows can be satisfactory for some purposes: along sidewalks leading to the front entrance, as a crisp edging to delineate paths and beds, or for formal displays to match a particular architectural theme. But many of us line things up simply because we don't trust our own design skills. A straight line seems like a safe bet, so we stop there and don't take it any further. But if you're willing to be a little more creative, you'll be amazed at all the fun ways you can add annuals to your landscape.

Annuals Alone

In some places, you may choose to go with a basic bed of annuals only. Plants that have been specially bred or exclusively selected for a certain height or color are ideal for this kind of design. These compact, uniform annuals, which inclue zinnias, dwarf marigolds, and scarlet sage (*Salvia splendens*), readily lend themselves to lines as well as to mass plantings of geometric shapes.

A single color of one annual—massed together—can make an eye-catching landscape accent. This kind of planting is useful for long-distance viewing (such as from the street), for marking drives or entry gates, or for drawing attention to a door or entryway. But keep in mind that color doesn't have to be shocking to attract attention. The standard American attention-getter—sheets of red geraniums or scarlet sage—definitely has a lot of room for improvement. Expanses of startling color may be exciting for a few weeks, but they aren't particularly easy on the nerves when you have to look at them for month after month. By varying the main color (such as different shades of red and pink) or by adding accents of complementary or contrasting tones (like very pale yellow marigolds with deep purple petunias), the picture becomes more pleasurable throughout the season. "Creating a Color-theme Garden" on page 122 has lots of great ideas you will be able to use to plan your bed and border plantings around your favorite flower colors.

Purple verbenas interweave with red geraniums, while yellow marigolds are grouped behind. The shifting masses of color look effective because plants of similar height have been chosen.

Perennial Annuals

You may be surprised to discover that some of the most popular annuals are actually perennials! The plants listed below are grown as annuals in most climates, but they can live for years in mild or frost-free areas.

Argyranthemum frutescens (marguerite)
Begonia Semperflorens-cultorum hybrid (wax begonia)
Bellis perennis (English daisy)
Catharanthus roseus (Madagascar periwinkle)
Dianthus chinensis (China pink)
Erysimum cheiri (wallflower)
Eustoma grandiflorum (prairie gentian)
Gazania hybrids (treasure flower)
Heliotropium arborescens (heliotrope)
Impatiens wallerana (impatiens)
Mirabilis jalapa (four o'clock)
Pelargonium x *hortorum* (zonal geranium)
Rudbeckia hirta (gloriosa daisy)
Salvia farinacea (mealy-cup sage)
Salvia splendens (scarlet sage)
Senecio cineraria (dusty miller)
Solenostemon scutellarioides (coleus)
Torenia fournieri (wishbone flower)
Verbena x *hybrida* (garden verbena)
Viola x *wittrockiana* (pansy)

Pansies

Annuals as Accents

Being fast-growing and relatively inexpensive, annuals are invaluable for providing quick color to new gardens. But don't forget that these yearly visitors can enhance an existing landscape as well. Repeated plantings of a particular type of annual or a certain color can give a note of continuity to the framework of shrubs and trees already established.

Experimenting with new colors and combinations allows a new twist on the theme each year, without the expense of changing the framework itself. Annual additions also enliven established borders of perennials. Purists may object to the inclusion of annuals in their herbaceous plantings (perennial-only plantings). But there's no law against it so why limit your options? While compact bedding plants may look awkward alongside larger perennials, many annuals have an airy grace that earns them a place among the most beautiful border plants. Foxgloves (*Digitalis purpurea*), hollyhocks (*Alcea rosea*), and black-eyed Susans (*Rudbeckia hirta*) are a few of the many annuals and biennials that make fine partners for perennials. As a bonus, long-blooming annuals can provide a steady supply of color to fill in as perennial companions come into and go out of flower.

Toadflax (*Linaria* spp.) is a fast-growing, bushy annual. It gives a long and colorful display, making it very useful as a bedding plant.

When deciding what to grow with your annuals, though, don't just stop with perennials. In an "everything goes" cottage garden, you can combine annuals with all kinds of other plants—bulbs, shrubs, grasses, herbs, trees, and whatever else looks good to you. There are no rules here; simply put each plant where it will thrive and complement its neighbors. Annual flowers are also a fun addition to a traditional vegetable garden, adding a bit of color or filling in after early-season crops are harvested. Some annuals, such as nasturtiums, sunflowers, and scarlet runner beans (*Phaseolus coccineus*), even have good flavor to match their good looks. For more fun ideas on incorporating annuals into your garden, see "Beds and Borders, Screens and Fillers" on page 128.

Combining different colors of the same plant adds variety and excitement to this mass planting of nemesia, a tender annual grown for its beautiful flowers.

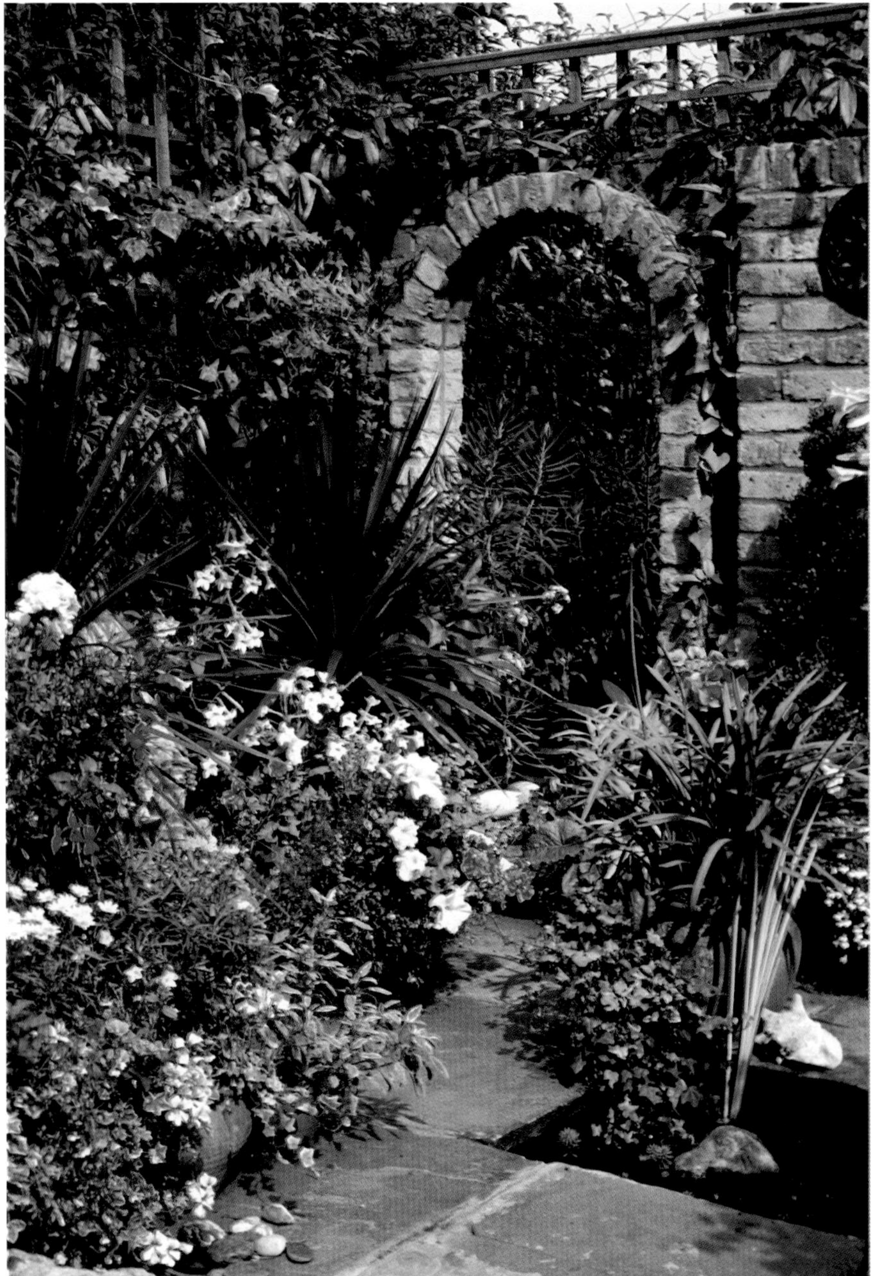

This patio garden with arch and pond has pots full of annuals scattered amongst shrubs, ornamental grasses, and vines. They work as brief, seasonal highlights, adding interest to the established design.

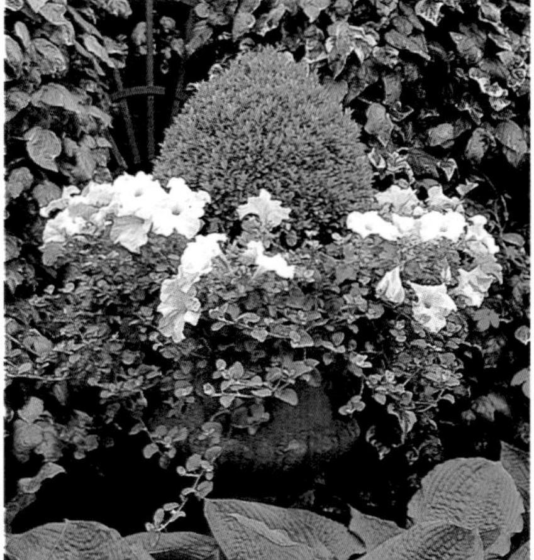

Annuals, such as the petunias and licorice plant (*Helichrysum petiolatum*) here, combine well with evergreen shrubs planted in containers.

Annuals in Containers

One of the easiest and most popular ways to bring excitement to any garden is with containers. These plantings may vary from year to year and even season to season. Pansies can dominate in cool weather, for instance, while ageratums or geraniums take over during the heat of summer.

A large pot or tub, overflowing with a carefully selected variety of flowering and foliage plants, is a classic way to show off annuals. Even with small containers, you can make hundreds of different combinations to liven up decks, patios, and balconies. You can have multiple pots that repeat the same theme throughout your garden, or change the plantings to set a new mood. Instead of combining several different plants in one container, group several smaller pots of individual plants. This is a good way to group colors, pick up predominant colors from nearby beds, or try out new color combinations. For more ideas, see "Getting Started with Container Gardening" on page 170.

Annuals for Scented Gardens

For many gardeners, fragrance is an important consideration when deciding which annuals to grow and where to put

If you enjoy fragrant flowers, tuck sweet peas and other scented annuals in your beds and borders. They make lovely fresh cut flowers, too.

Need a screen to block a view until you can put in a hedge or fence? Try tall annuals or biennials such as foxgloves (*Digitalis purpurea*).

them. Sweet alyssum (*Lobularia maritima*) smells of honey on a hot afternoon, while night-scented stock (*Matthiola longipetala* subsp. *bicornis*) wafts a sweet scent on an evening breeze. Scented blooms are also delightful in containers or beds sited near windows or outdoor sitting areas. If you usually spend your summer evenings outdoors, you might want to concentrate on evening-scented blooms; if you're only outdoors during the day, flowers that are fragrant during the evening may not be useful to you. "Flowers for Fragrance" on page 144 offers more tips on choosing scented flowers and foliage that are right for your needs and your garden.

Annuals for Cut Flowers

If you enjoy bringing your garden flowers indoors, consider starting a separate cutting garden. That way, you can have a generous supply of flowers for cutting without raiding your more visible displays. Annuals that are good for cutting produce lots of flowers and last well indoors; these include zinnias, snapdragons, cosmos, pot marigolds (*Calendula officinalis*), China aster (*Callistephus chinensis*), and rocket larkspur (*Consolida ambigua*). Scented flowers also make a delightful inclusion in any arrangement. So-called everlasting flowers—such as statice (*Limonium sinuatum*), globe amaranth (*Gomphrena globosa*), and strawflowers (*Bracteantha bracteata*)—are an important part of many cutting gardens, since their beauty lives on into the winter in dried arrangements. For more information on growing and harvesting annuals for arrangements, see "Creating a Cutting Garden" on page 134.

Annuals for Garden Challenges

Annuals are adaptable and quite easy to grow, making them the ideal solution for all kinds of challenges that your garden may throw at you. If you have just moved into a house, for example, you could fill the garden with annuals for a year or two while you decide on your long-term plans for the landscape. Or if you rent a home with a plot of ground, growing annuals will allow you to enjoy flower gardening without the more permanent investment in perennials. Annuals are great for city gardens, since they can make the most of compact spaces and give quick results in less-than-ideal growing sites. Tall annuals or biennials such as foxgloves and hollyhocks and annual vines such as morning glory are also excellent as temporary screens to hide unsightly views, objectionable fences, stumps, or neighbors' yards; see "Screens and Fillers" on page 132 for more ideas on using these plants effectively.

Reseeding Annuals and Biennials

Four-o'-clocks

Many gardeners count on self-sowing annuals and biennials for perennial pleasures. Far from being a nuisance, these reliable repeaters delight many gardeners with their perseverance and their ability to pop up in the most unexpected places. Exactly which plants will self-sow depends on your region, but the ones listed below are some of the most dependable reseeders.

- *Alcea rosea* (hollyhock)
- *Amaranthus caudatus* (love lies bleeding)
- *Calendula officinalis* (pot marigold)
- *Centaurea cyanus* (cornflower)
- *Cleome hasslerana* (cleome)
- *Consolida ambigua* (rocket larkspur)
- *Coreopsis tinctoria* (calliopsis)
- *Cosmos bipinnatus* (cosmos)
- *Digitalis purpurea* (foxglove)
- *Eschscholzia californica* (California poppy)
- *Helianthus annuus* (common sunflower)
- *Iberis umbellata* (annual candytuft)
- *Impatiens balsamina* (garden balsam)
- *Ipomoea tricolor* (morning glory)
- *Lobularia maritima* (sweet alyssum)
- *Lunaria annua* (honesty)
- *Mirabilis jalapa* (four o'clock)
- *Myosotis sylvatica* (forget-me-not)
- *Nicotiana alata* (flowering tobacco)
- *Nigella damascena* (love-in-a-mist)
- *Papaver rhoeas* (corn poppy)
- *Portulaca grandiflora* (rose moss)
- *Sanvitalia procumbens* (creeping zinnia)
- *Tanacetum parthenium* (feverfew)
- *Tithonia rotundifolia* (Mexican sunflower)
- *Tropaeolum majus* (nasturtium)
- *Verbascum bombyciferum* (mullein)
- *Zinnia angustifolia* (narrow-leaved zinnia)
- *Zinnia elegans* (zinnia)

Perennial Favorites

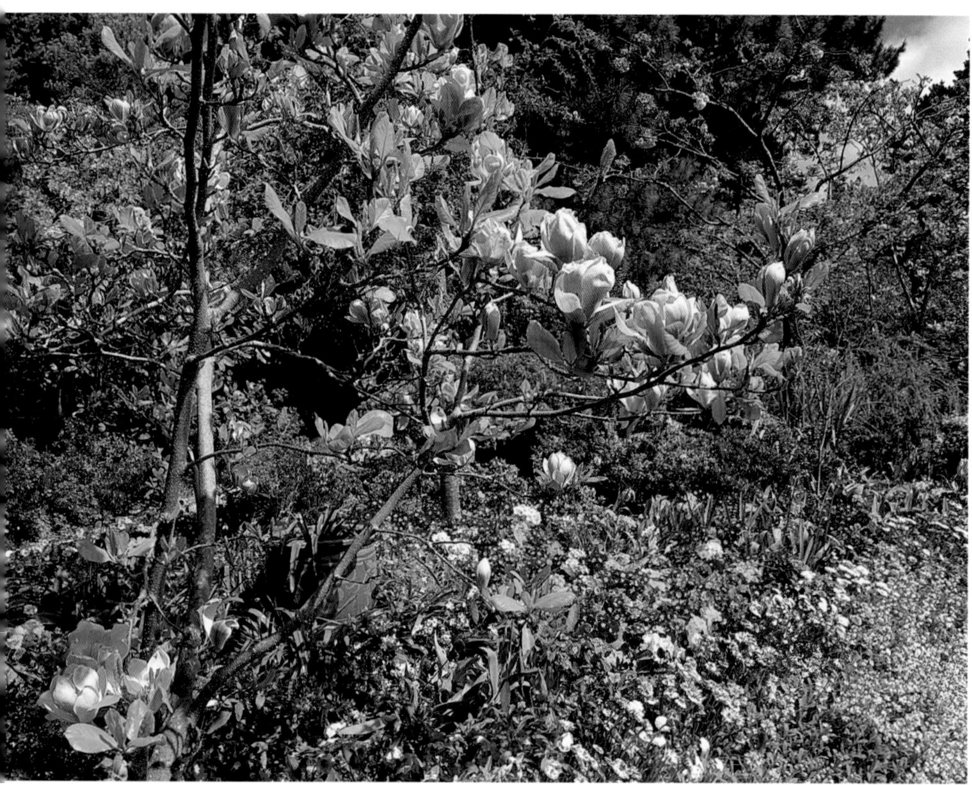

A spring border of perennials, which includes polyanthus primroses and paper daisies, makes an eye-catching display under the blossoms of an established magnolia tree.

Gardening with perennials is a joy that everyone can share. Whether your garden is large or small, sunny or shady, wet or dry, a wide variety of perennials will thrive there and provide you with beauty for years to come.

Hollyhocks are short-lived perennials. However, they make up for a brief life span by self-sowing so prolifically they are often grown as annuals.

Understanding Perennials

Let's begin by establishing just what we mean by "perennial." Perennial plants live and bloom for more than two growing seasons. Many will survive a decade or longer if planted in the right location; hardy perennials come back year after year, so you don't have to buy and replant them each spring. But even the short-lived plants are worth growing. For instance, blanket flowers (*Gaillardia* x *grandiflora*) bloom vigorously for a long portion of the summer, although they seldom return more than two years. Other perennials, such as columbines (*Aquilegia* spp.) and hollyhocks (*Alcea rosea*), have a short natural life span, but set seed that replaces the parent plant; the latter may be grown as an annual because of this. Occasionally, a biennial plant like foxglove (*Digitalis purpurea*) or sweet William (*Dianthus barbatus*), which normally grows foliage the first year and flowers the second, will live on for the third year. Despite their different life spans, you can call all these plants perennials. Most bulbs—including tulips, daffodils, hyacinths, and crocuses—are also perennials; they are discussed in greater detail in "Bountiful Bulbs" on page 28. Bulbs go dormant after flowering, freeing up space for annuals or maturing perennial plants to thrive.

Identifying perennials by their two-year life span may seem reasonably tidy, but the definition gets more complicated. This is because trees and shrubs are also perennials. However, they are exempted from our definition because they develop woody stems and limbs. With the exception of tree peonies (*Paeonia suffruticosa*) and a few other plants, perennial garden plants are herbaceous, which means they lack woody stems. In most cases, the foliage of perennials dies back down to the underground roots each dormant season. A few perennials, like rock cresses (*Arabis* spp.) and coral bells (*Heuchera* spp.), have evergreen foliage that persists through the winter.

Unlike annuals, most perennials only flower for a short while (days or weeks) each season. But many do offer attractive forms and foliage, so they look almost as good out of bloom as they do in bloom. Nor do they have to be replanted every year; these beauties come back on their

The arresting blues and architectural stature of delphiniums make them a fine accent when planted amidst red and white rose bushes.

own. They are cheaper than most trees and shrubs, and they're relatively simple to move or dig up and replace if you want to change the look and layout of your yard. Perennials are dependable and easy choices for beginners, and they come in enough variety to satisfy even the most experienced gardener.

Of the very many different types of perennials, dahlias are but one. These bulbs bloom from midsummer through fall in almost every color of the rainbow except blue. The bright yellow sunflowers are annuals.

Perennials in Your Garden

Now that you know what a perennial is, you can start to explore the many possibilities of incorporating them into your garden. With thousands of species and cultivars to choose from, there's a good chance that you'll find plenty of plant forms, leaf textures, and flower colors and shapes to fit the garden you have in mind. Any yard—large or small, sunny or shady—can be accented with perennials. A few clusters of perennial flowers will bring colorful highlights to drab corners; a garden full of perennials will become a landscape highlight. You can use perennials as accents, focal points, masses of color, or scenes of change.

Don't make the mistake of thinking that your flowering perennials should be separate from the rest of the landscape. To get the most enjoyment and the greatest effect from these plants, you first need to establish a garden size and shape that looks natural in your landscape and also fits in well with the existing elements, like buildings and trees. Then choose perennials with colors, textures, and forms that enhance your entire landscape. By combining your perennials with annuals, biennials, shrubs, and trees in the one glorious garden, you will be able to enjoy the benefits of each kind of plant while minimizing any of their drawbacks. For example, plant early-blooming perennials like irises and peonies with annuals like cleomes (*Cleome* spp.) and cosmos, which start blooming in early summer and carry on until frost. Use large sweeps of bold perennials in beds and borders beside the lawn, beneath openings in trees, and in front of hedges and shrub plantings. Put smaller clumps of dramatic perennials in strategic locations to highlight the entrance to walks, the location of a door, or the view from a window. Consider nesting a trio of three gold-centered, broad-leaved hostas (such as *Hosta* 'Gold Standard') at either side of the entrance of a woodland path. Or use a clump of common torch lilies (*Kniphofia uvaria*) to frame the top of a drive. A stand of irises is an attractive feature near a Japanese bridge in a water garden.

A clump of Siberian iris provides an elegant contrast to the bright green foliage of the trees behind and the splash of orange in front.

Seasonal Change

One of the most delightful features of perennials is their ability to change throughout the season—growing and spreading, passing into and out of bloom, and sometimes even coloring up nicely in fall or producing seed heads to stand over winter. The changeable quality of perennials can add life to an otherwise boring planting, such as a row of evergreens or a mass of annuals.

Succession of bloom is one reason the changeable nature of perennials is so appealing. By mapping out a garden plan and selecting the plants you will use carefully, you can have perennials blooming throughout the growing season, from early spring to late fall. You can arrange your garden so that there are some flowers, seed heads, or foliage of interest

A mixture of pink and white perennials—lilies, common rose mallow, and bellflowers—come into bloom in summer, amidst a background of purple and green foliage, to create a lovely show.

at any time during the growing season. Let the beauty of the flowers create a shifting sequence of harmonies and contrasts. Spring might be rich with purple violets and yellow primroses. In early summer, the garden could be ripe with red peonies and violet-blue Siberian iris (*Iris sibirica*). In late summer this might change to purple coneflowers (*Echinacea purpurea*), ivory chrysanthemums, and pink Japanese anemones (*Anemone* x *hybrida*).

Before and after the flowers, let the show continue with the beauty of foliage and form alone. Enjoy the excitement of watching the plants grow and thrive, from the first shoots to the much-anticipated blooms. Note how the flower stalks rise gracefully over the foliage or peep from between the stems. Watch the leaves late in the season, as they ripen to bronze or lemon, then disappear.

Perennial Style

Perennials look lovely when grouped into individual beds and borders, but they also make wonderfully flexible tools for decorating all parts of your landscape. Small perennials can enliven a deck or patio; others are large enough to screen your unsightly objects such as trash cans, which you don't want to see from the patio. Depending on where you place your perennials, you can make a small yard seem bigger or divide a large yard into intimate, comfortable spaces, or rooms. A winding path lined with foliage plants or flowers can create a little bit of mystery and lead people to a seat in the shade, a small sculpture, or a wonderful view.

Geometry and symmetry are the hallmarks of a formal garden where clipped borders of English lavender are planted under standard roses.

A spring bed of pink tulips and yellow primroses gives a display of vivid contrasting colors. The use of perennials or annuals under bulbs looks much more attractive than leaving the soil bare or mulched.

Perennials can be used to create flower gardens of many different moods, whether traditional or nontraditional in design style. This can include formal gardens, cottage gardens, herbaceous borders, island beds, and cutting gardens. They can also be used to make the most of the conditions your site has to offer with special gardens for meadows, woodlands, and rocky areas. Whether your site is dry or wet, sunny or shady, there's a garden style that's just right for you.

Formal Gardens

Historically, formal gardens were only found on large estates, where there was plenty of space to lay out vast geometric patternings of neatly clipped plants. But today, this style of garden is spreading into smaller yards. Formal beds mimic the prevailing angles of houses and patios, blending in where space is too limited to soften the scene with curving lines.

Formal gardens are usually laid out in squares or rectangles with low hedges of clipped boxwood, hollies, or other evergreens. Plant the beds symmetrically, using the same sequence of perennials and edging plants on either side of a central axis. Make your own patterns with lines, angles, and curving rows. Choose plants carefully—limit your selection to those perennials that will stay in place and keep a uniform height and neat appearance. Try new cultivars developed for their uniformity, such as 'Moonbeam' thread-leaved coreopsis (*Coreopsis verticillata* 'Moonbeam'), 'Stella de Oro' daylily, and 'Blue Clips' tussock bellflower.

If the classic formal garden is too rigid for your taste, you can always take a more modern approach. Plant sections of the garden with a touch of informality by maintaining the basic geometric shapes of the formal section but softening the angles with creeping and trailing edgers.

A cottage garden gives a loose, casual effect by the careful selection and positioning of plants.

Daylilies are hardy plants that produce showy, colorful blooms in a range of different climates.

Cottage Gardens

The classic cottage garden is an eclectic collection of plants, including perennials, annuals, herbs, and roses, allowed to ramble and intertwine. Cottage gardens usually are at least partially enclosed within walls, hedges, or fences, making them a natural choice for a small suburban house or a modern townhouse with an enclosed yard. You might allow the plants to spread unchecked or to self-sow, letting the seedlings arise where they may. For this to work well, though, you must be willing to do some pulling up and rearranging if the new arrivals pop up where they're not wanted. Unify the scene with a permanent focal point, such as a path that marches through the garden's center to a door, patio, or bench.

Perennial Borders

Borders are the most popular and versatile of all the ways to grow perennials. A border is a planting area that edges or frames another feature of the garden. It may separate the lawn from a hedge, fence, steps, deck, or wooded area; set off a path from the lawn or the driveway; or divide the vegetable garden from the lawn. Be sure to look at the transition areas in your property to find potential areas for borders.

Most perennial borders are designed to be viewed primarily from the front. It's best if you set the shorter plants in the foreground and the taller plants in the back. You can plant a border exclusively with perennials to produce what is known as an herbaceous border. Or add structure, excitement, and four-season interest by creating a mixed border of woody plants, bulbs, and annuals as well as perennials.

This border has an informal feel, with common thrift hanging over the pathway while lupines stand tall at the rear.

Island beds will be viewed from all sides. When planting them, it's a good idea to set the tallest annuals and perennials toward the center of the bed and the shorter ones along the outside.

Island Beds

Unlike borders, which are usually seen from one side, island beds are designed for you to walk around them and see them from all different angles. Because they are located away from structures like houses and fences, island beds are exposed to maximum sun and air penetration. As a result, plant stems are stockier and need less staking, and the garden tends to be healthier and easier to maintain.

Locate your island bed in some open situation, but don't just plunk the bed down in the middle of the lawn. Like a border, you must tie it in with existing permanent structures to make it look good. Use an island bed to create an oasis of color in the back corner of the yard, to echo the shape of shrub groupings elsewhere in the lawn, or as a "welcome garden" at the foot of the drive.

The Cutting Garden

Many perennials produce flowers and foliage that are ideal for indoor use in arrangements. You can snip a few flowers from your perennial borders, but if you take too many the garden will look bare. To have lots of flowers for picking, grow a utilitarian garden just for cutting. You don't need a fancy design or a particular shape—pick a suitable spot and line up your plants in rows, just as you would for vegetables. Cage the stems of floppy perennials like delphiniums and dahlias with a wire grid or stake to keep them supported and straight. Add annuals and bulbs to your cutting garden to round out your choice of materials for arrangements.

Meadow Gardens

Natural gardens combine the beauty of local wildflowers with an informal, often low-maintenance, design. The most popular of these are meadow gardens that feature durable, sun-loving flowers. If you don't have room for a whole meadow, you can easily create a meadow look in a smaller garden by using plenty of reliable cultivated perennials and then mixing in meadow flowers and grasses among them. Common perennials that are natural choices for most meadow gardens include butterfly weed (*Asclepias tuberosa*), New England aster (*Aster novae-angliae*), purple coneflower (*Echinacea purpurea*), and bee balm (*Monarda didyma*). Look in wildflower gardening books or check with local wildflower societies to find out which plants grow best in your area.

Once you've chosen the plants that will be in your meadow, you'll need to help them gain a roothold by preparing a good seedbed. You can't just scatter seed in a lawn or an open piece of ground and

ABOVE: Versatile, easy-to-grow clumps of orange coneflower can be used in formal or informal beds or borders, cottage gardens, and even meadows. BELOW: A meadow of wildflowers is an excellent option for brightening up out-of-the-way corners.

expect good results. You'll also need to keep the soil moist at the time when the seeds are germinating, and weed regularly for the first few years. Once the meadow is established, a yearly mowing in late winter will help control those woody plants that would otherwise overwhelm the perennial flowers. Beyond that, you can let these perennials grow and mingle as they will.

A bog garden is a great site for many kinds of irises. The flowers are beautiful in early summer, and the spiky leaves look good all season.

Container Gardens

Take a break from petunias and grow perennials in containers instead. Potted perennials are great as accents for steps, decks, and patios, especially in small gardens. Compact, long-blooming, and drought-tolerant perennials make natural choices for containers. Some perennials for containers include 'Stella de Oro' daylily and the Galaxy series of yarrow (*Achillea* 'Galaxy Series'). Or try spring-blooming bleeding heart (*Dicentra spectabilis*); when it goes dormant in the heat of summer, cover it with annuals. Containers dry out more quickly than gardens, so you may need to water daily during the hot, dry parts of the summer.

Start the spring season early with a container full of cold-tolerant primroses and daffodils, with a few pansies added to the mix as well.

Rock Gardens

Some perennials are particularly attractive grouped among rocks in a wall or rock garden. These are the plants that have evolved to grow best in full sun and soils that have exceptionally good drainage and low fertility. Some, such as perennial candytuft (*Iberis sempervirens*), wall rock cress (*Arabis caucasica*), and basket of gold (*Aurinia saxatilis*), cascade gracefully over the rock surface. Others, like the more petite Labrador violets (*Viola labradorica*) and primroses (*Primula* spp.), as well as a host of unusual alpine plants, nestle in between the rocks. All of these plants are delightful choices for planting on rocky slopes, in raised beds, or in the crevices of drystone retaining walls.

Bog Gardens

Some perennials have an affinity for wet ground and will thrive at the edge of a pond or in boggy or marshy areas. Perennials for low, moist areas include Japanese iris (*Iris ensata*), goat's beard (*Aruncus dioicus*), turtlehead (*Chelone* spp.), marsh marigold (*Caltha palustris*), and cardinal flower (*Lobelia cardinalis*).

If you already have a pond or wet spot, a bog garden is the solution. If you don't have a naturally wet area but enjoy bog plants, you can create your own bog. Dig a trench at least 12 inches (30 cm) deep and line it with a heavy plastic pond liner. Put a soaker hose on the top of the plastic and refill the trench with humus-rich soil. The open end of the hose should protrude slightly so that you can attach it to your garden hose and fill the "bog" with water. Repeat as necessary to keep the soil moist.

Woodland Gardens

If you have a wooded lot with lots of lovely, large trees, take advantage of their shade to create a woodland garden. To brighten the area in early spring (before the trees leaf out and shade the area), try early-blooming woodland wildflowers like wood anemone (*Anemone nemorosa*), wild columbine (*Aquilegia canadensis*), Virginia bluebell (*Mertensia virginica*), and common bleeding heart (*Dicentra spectabilis*). To extend the season of interest, add ferns and shade-tolerant perennials that retain their foliage all season. These include hostas, Lenten rose (*Helleborus orientalis*), Siberian bugloss (*Brunnera macrophylla*), Solomon's seal (*Polygonatum odoratum*), and lungwort (*Pulmonaria saccharata*).

Shady nooks provide a cool, peaceful refuge that hellebores like. Water them regularly for the first few years; after that, they'll tolerate dry shade.

Bountiful Bulbs

Beautiful and versatile, bulbs are one type of perennial that belong in every landscape. Many of the popular bulbs—including daffodils, crocus, hyacinths, and tulips—are traditionally associated with spring gardens. But with a little planning, you can have bulbs in bloom in your garden from late winter through midfall. And to fill the few months that bulbs aren't blooming outdoors, you can bring some types indoors and enjoy their vividly colored flowers all winter long.

Understanding Bulbs

There's a time and place in the garden for nearly every bulb. The dainty blooms of early bulbs such as crocus and snowdrops (*Galanthus* spp.) signal the beginning of the gardening season with their arrival. Daffodils, tulips, and other larger bulbs are the epitome of the spring garden, while gladioli, lilies, and others strut their stuff in the summer. Some, including fall crocus (*Colchicum autumnale*) and hardy cyclamen (*Cyclamen hederifolium*), flower very late, marking the transition to winter temperatures despite their fragile, spring-like appearance. If you choose carefully, you can have bulbs blooming in your garden nearly the whole year round!

Bulbs flower at different times because they are naturally adapted to different growing conditions. Learning a little about how bulbs grow and the various kinds of bulbs will help you to understand more about growing these colorful and versatile plants in your garden.

How Bulbs Grow

Over time, bulbs have developed in their own unique way to cope with particular environments. A bulbous plant stores energy and water below ground in an enlarged root or stem. This storage area allows the plant to grow and flower when the growing conditions are favorable and to ride out unfavorable weather in a dormant state.

Tulips, for example, evolved on the high plains of western Asia. Between the hot, dry summers and freezing winters, a tulip takes advantage of the two mildest seasons. It roots in fall, relying on late rains to pump moisture into the bulb.

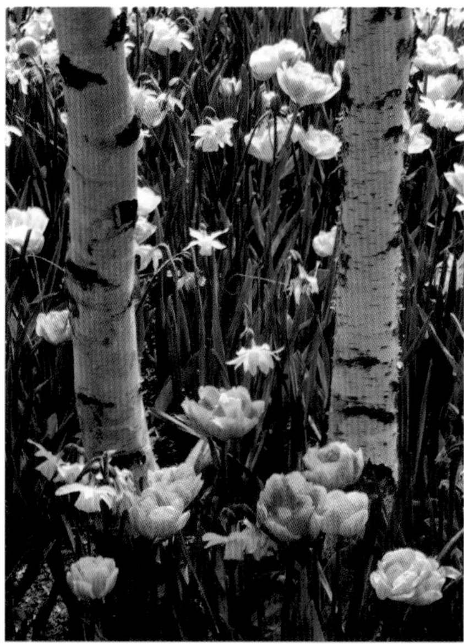

There are thousands of tulip cultivars, here planted with daffodils. They bloom at different times, so you can enjoy them all through spring.

Aboveground growth begins in early spring, often before cold weather has completely retreated. Melting snow waters the emerging buds, and bright sunshine stimulates the leaves to store energy

A dense planting of grape hyacinths creates a path of purple, broken only by groupings of multicolored tulips, yellow crown imperials, and white spring daisies.

Tulips rise above a carpet of red wallflowers. Make the most of your space by underplanting tall bulb flowers with low-growing annuals.

depleted by the flowering process. As hot, dry weather arrives, the bulb goes back into a dormant state.

Of course, bulbous plants come from environments all around the globe, so they don't all behave in the same manner. Some may be stimulated to grow by the return of the rainy season; others respond to the warmth of spring or summer. While you don't need to know exactly which conditions encourage a particular bulb to bloom, it's helpful to realize that all your bulbs will go through some kind of seasonal cycle of growth and dormancy. The individual entries in "Encyclopedia of Flowers," starting on page 306, explain the cycle for each bulb, so you'll know when to plant, when to expect flowers, and when to divide or move the bulbs you've chosen.

Kinds of Bulbs

The many different plants that have underground storage structures are grouped together under the general term "bulbs." But technically speaking, these underground structures take on several forms, which include true bulbs, corms, tubers, and rhizomes.

True Bulbs True bulbs, such as tulips, daffodils, lilies, and hyacinths, must reach a particular size before they can flower. A full-size bulb contains layers of food-storing scales surrounding a tiny flower, formed during the previous growing season. If it has sufficient water, nutrients, and light, the bulb will blossom reliably the first year; this makes true bulbs a good choice for beginning gardeners. Encouraging true bulbs—especially some tulips—to bloom in subsequent years can sometimes be a little trickier. The growing requirements are quite specific, and vary for different species, but most true bulbs are easy to grow and maintain for years.

bulb

True bulbs reproduce by two methods: by seed and by bulblets produced at the base of the mother bulb (or, in the case of some lilies, in the leaf axils of the stem).

Corms Corms, such as those of crocus or gladioli, resemble true bulbs on the outside. Cut one open, however, and you'll discover a major difference. The corm is solid—a reservoir full of energy without an embryonic flower inside. Under favorable conditions, a corm draws on its stockpile of food to produce leaves and flowers from growth buds on the top of the corm. As it grows, a corm exhausts its resources and often, but not always, grows a new corm to replace the old one. Corms also reproduce by forming small new corms, called cormlets or cormels, around the main corm.

corm

Tubers Like corms, tubers are solid storage structures. But unlike corms, which form roots only at the bottom, tubers can sprout roots from "eyes" (buds) scattered over their surface. The one tuber everyone knows is the potato. Most other tubers bear a resemblance to it, although some may be flatter or thinner. Caladiums and tuberous begonias grow from tubers. Dahlias grow from similar structures, which are called tuberous roots.

Most tubers originated in areas where summer temperatures are fairly warm and rainfall is plentiful. They can adapt to a whole range of conditions as long as they have warmth and sufficient moisture. Many will not survive in frozen ground, however, so it's important to remember to dig them up in fall and store them indoors over winter. Most tubers can be cut or broken into pieces to increase your stock of a plant; just make sure each piece has one or more eyes so it can produce new shoots.

tuber

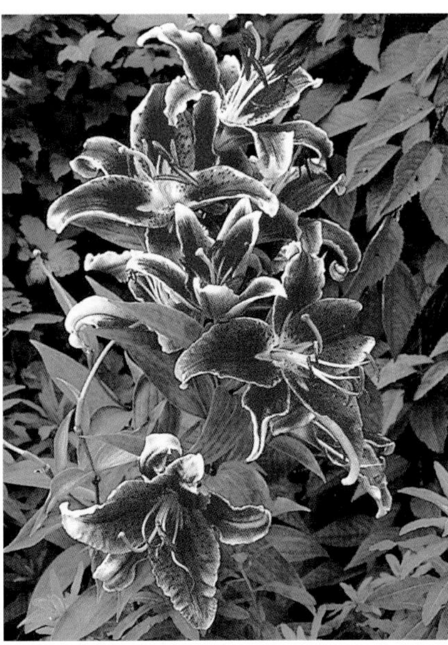

Lilies grow from scaly bulbs. You may notice that the bulbs have fleshy roots when you buy them; other bulbs shouldn't have roots.

Rhizomes A rhizome is a fleshy, creeping stem that is sometimes visible at ground level but is often hidden underground. Roots are produced on the undersides of each rhizome. Perhaps the most easily recognized rhizome belongs to the old-fashioned bearded iris; other examples include the tender cannas and calla lilies (*Zantedeschia aethiopica*).

To plant most rhizomes, place them horizontally just below the soil surface, so the roots can easily grow down into the soil. You can increase rhizomes very easily by simply cutting them into pieces and then replanting them.

rhizome

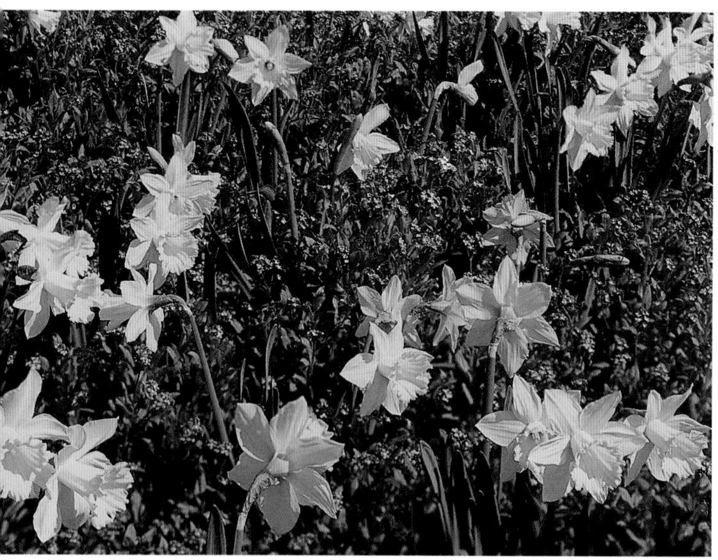

Daffodils are traditional favorites for adding color to spring gardens. Pair them with a carpet of forget-me-nots to add sparkle to beds and borders.

Later-blooming bulbs such as lilies and dahlias add height and color to mid- and late-season borders. "Beds and Borders, Screens and Fillers" on page 128 lists more ideas on using bulbs in flower gardens.

Bulbs for Flower Arrangements and for Fragrance

Madonna lilies (*Lilium candidum*), tuberoses (*Polianthes tuberosa*), hyacinths, along with some other bulbs, are renowned for the sweet fragrances that they offer. Their scents are delightful both outdoors and indoors. But be sure to use moderation when cutting these flowers for arrangements; a single bloom can pleasantly scent a room, but a mass of them can be overpowering.

Even without fragrance, many hardy and tender bulbs can be enjoyed indoors in arrangements, so make sure you include them in your cutting garden. Start the season with tulips and daffodils, followed by summer snowflake (*Leucojum aestivum*) and lilies, as well as gladioli and dahlias. In the South, you can even grow amaryllis (*Hippeastrum* hybrids) outdoors for cut flowers. "Creating a Cutting Garden" on page 134 offers more details for growing and handling bulbs for cutting.

Bulb Magic

Like annuals, bulbs are often used in masses in large-scale landscapes. While it's difficult to re-create those grand displays found in public parks when you have limited space and money, well-chosen bulbs can create equally stunning effects in many parts of the home garden.

Bulbs in Beds and Borders

It's hard to beat bulbs for early color. What could be more welcome to a winter-weary gardener than a patch of brightly colored crocus by the back door? While bulb flowers are pretty on their own, you can also combine them with other early-blooming perennials or shrubs to create stunning effects, such as a golden flood of daffodils beneath a blooming forsythia. Many spring-blooming bulbs enliven planted areas beneath trees before the trees have leafed out. The bulbs finish just as the shade-loving ferns, hostas, or annuals come into their own.

Bulbs are especially useful when tucked into perennial plantings, because they will get the bloom season off to an early start. And summer beds make a great place for showcasing tender bulbs, such as cannas and gladioli, among annuals or perennials.

TOP LEFT: Create a pretty spring picture by combining snowdrops with the lovely foliage of Italian arum. BOTTOM LEFT: Mix bulbs with annuals and perennials to create beautiful color-theme plantings. White tulips stand out in the midst of a silver-and-white garden, which looks crisp and clean all day long. RIGHT: Striking purple hyacinths—such as *Hyacinthus orientalis* ("Amethyst")— have a rich, sweet scent that will waft through your garden and linger in your house when used in flower arrangements.

Succulents are perfect plants for pots; they will thrive in hot conditions and don't need constant watering to survive.

Bulbs in Containers

Bulbs are perfect for pots, either alone to give a touch of spring color or combined with annuals or perennials for a longer season of interest. They can also be potted up in fall for later indoor pleasure. Tender bulbs, such as amaryllis and paperwhite narcissus, are very easy to grow and flower on the windowsill with little fussing. Hardy bulbs, such as tulips and hyacinths, need to be potted and chilled for several months to give them a condensed form of winter before bringing them inside. This process is known as "forcing," although the bulbs aren't forced to do anything except bloom a bit ahead of schedule, either in the house or on the patio. Depending on where you live, there are different methods of forcing bulbs; see "Bulb Multiplication" on page 74 for more detail.

Bulbs in Lawns and Woodlands

Naturalizing—planting bulbs in random, natural-looking drifts under trees, lawns, meadows, or unmanicured woodsy areas—is another fun way to add bulbs to your yard. Look for species and selections that are described as good for naturalizing; almost all daffodils and crocuses qualify, as do grape hyacinths (*Muscari* spp.), Siberian squill (*Scilla sibirica*), and Spanish bluebells (*Hyacinthoides hispanicus*). It's easy and low maintenance to do, and the results look better and better every year as the bulbs multiply to produce even more blooms.

Naturalized bulbs are often best in less high-visibility areas, where you can enjoy the blooms but not be bothered by the sight of the ripening leaves. Space bulbs in irregular patterns for the most natural look, and plant lots of them so you'll see them from a distance. More information on this process is in "Making a Meadow Garden" on page 136. Very early bulbs, such as spring crocus, are sometimes naturalized in lawns to provide color. You may have to put off the first spring mowing for a week or two to let the bulb foliage turn yellow, but after that you can mow as usual. Fall-blooming bulbs can also look good in grassy areas, but you'll have to stop mowing in late summer, as soon as you see the flower buds beginning to sprout from the soil.

Create a sea of spring color by planting some crocus in your lawn. They will spread and naturalize as the years pass, but be sure not to mow until the crocus leaves have yellowed.

Blooming Bulbs through the Year

With some planning, you can have bulbs blooming with your perennials from spring through fall. Below is an approximate bloom schedule for gardens in Zone 6. Zone 3 gardens are usually a good 2 weeks later; gardens in Zone 8 and warmer parts of Zone 7 are about 1 week earlier. (If you're not sure which zone you live in, check the Plant Hardiness Zone Maps starting on page 588.)

- Species crocus (including *Crocus tommasinianus*): early March
- Snowdrops (*Galanthus* spp.): early March
- Reticulated iris (*Iris reticulata*): early March
- Dutch crocus (*Crocus vernus* hybrids): late March
- Early daffodils: late March to early April
- Species tulips: April
- Grape hyacinths (*Muscari* spp.): mid-April
- Siberian squill (*Scilla sibirica*): mid-April
- Daffodils and narcissus: late April
- Hyacinths: late April
- Crown imperial (*Fritillaria imperialis*): late April
- Hybrid tulips: late April to May
- Giant onion (*Allium giganteum*): early summer
- Lilies: early to late summer
- Autumn crocuses (*Colchicum* and *Crocus* spp.): early fall to midfall
- Hardy cyclamen (*Cyclamen* spp.): fall or early spring

Crown imperials

SECTION TWO

Understanding Your Garden

You may have some idea of what you want from plants, but do you know what kind of growing conditions you have to give them? A new garden will get off to a successful start if you take stock of your growing conditions, including the soil, topography, and exposure of your garden, and your local climate. These factors will have a great effect in determining which flowers will grow well in your garden, as well as how and where you plant them.

Study the Soil 34

Your Local Climate 38

The Lay of the Land 40

Examine Your Exposure 42

Observe and Plan 44

Study the Soil

Gardening can be a breeze if you have deep, fertile soil that is rich in organic matter. But even if you don't (and very few gardeners do), you can still have a beautiful garden. Developing and then maintaining healthy garden soil is a critical part of establishing thriving annuals and perennials. You must balance the mineral and organic components of your soil to provide the air, water reserves, and nutrients needed by plants and other living organisms. You can improve the soil you have—by adding organic matter or building raised beds, for instance—and you can also look for plants that are adapted to your conditions. Either way, you'll need to know a few basic things about the soil you're starting with.

The soil in this lush spring garden obviously provides the right conditions for bluebells, forget-me-nots, and rhododendrons.

Soil Composition

Sand, silt, and clay—all the mineral elements that make up your soil—are categorized by size. Sands are the largest mineral particles. A coarse grain of sand can be as big as 1 millimeter in diameter; finer sand may dwindle down to one-tenth that size. Sand particles are found irregularly in the soil. They leave loose, air-rich pockets, called pore spaces, that allow water and dissolved nutrients to drain away. Consequently, sandy soils tend to be dry and infertile. Clay particles, the ultrafine elements, are about 1,000 times smaller than sand. They can pack together to make a tight, water- and nutrient-rich but poorly oxygenated soil. Between sand and clay are the medium-sized silt particles, from 0.05 to 0.002 millimeters in diameter. They are intermediate in their effects on water retention and aeration.

Soil Texture

Most soils are a mix of the three different particle groups. The ideal soil texture for most annuals and perennials is a loam, with a ratio of 40 percent sand, 40 percent silt, and 20 percent clay. Loam drains quickly, but not so quickly that plant roots cannot absorb water and nutrients. And the pores between the soil particles hold enough air for roots to be able to get enough oxygen for their needs.

As the percentages shift in any direction, gardening becomes more challenging. Loose sandy soils, which have at least 35 percent sand, don't hold water and nutrients well and so they'll need more frequent watering and fertilizing. You can pick plants that are adapted to drier, infertile soil. And remember, too, that these soils are good for slowing the growth rate of vigorous plants and reducing root or crown rots on susceptible plants. Tight, clayey soils hold water too well, becoming soggy, water-logged, and hard to work. They can be ideal for heavy feeding, moisture-loving perennials like astilbes, or for perennials grown in warm, dry climates; otherwise, you'll probably want to loosen the soil with organic matter or build raised beds

Sandy soil loses nutrients and water quickly.

Clayey soil drains slowly but holds nutrients well.

Silty soil can become packed and drain poorly.

Loamy soil, with its balance of sand, silt, and clay particles, is the most desirable soil type. It is usually well drained and often quite fertile.

to improve drainage. Silty soils have some characteristics of both extremes, but tend to be more like clay than like sand. If and how you want to amend silty soil will depend on what plants you'd like to grow.

Soil Structure

Another important characteristic of your soil is its structure. Soil structure refers to the way in which the sand, silt, and clay particles join together to form clumps (known as aggregates). A soil with high amounts of sand or clay will usually be too loose or too dense to support good plant growth. A well-balanced soil tends to form crumbly, granular clumps. Unlike soil texture, which is very difficult to change, soil structure can be improved by adding organic matter on a regular basis.

Organic Matter

Organic matter—basically the decaying remains of plant material such as leaves and grass, manure, and other animal products—is a critical component of all soils. Healthy soils usually have 5 percent organic matter or more. Soils that are high in organic matter tend to be dark brown or black and have a loose, crumbly feel and a nice earthy smell.

No matter what kind of soil you have, adding organic matter—in the form of compost, aged manure, chopped leaves, or other nutrient-rich materials—is the number-one way to make it suitable for a wide range of plants. Organic matter improves garden soil by loosening up heavy clays, improving water retention, promoting better drainage, and increasing fertility by retaining nutrients. Organic matter can hold up to twice its weight in moisture, slowly releasing water to plant roots and improving moisture retention in sandy soils (so you'll be able to water and fertilize less frequently). It encourages fine clay particles to clump together into larger soil aggregates, and this will improve soil aeration. It also encourages healthy populations of earthworms and other soil organisms, which in turn contribute nutrients and encourage root growth. All of these factors lead to vigorous, healthier plants that look great and are naturally more resistant to pest and disease problems. Organic matter is decomposing all the time, so you must add more to help replace the decaying particles and keep nutrient levels high.

If you have a soil that is clayey and tends to hold lots of water, the perfect solution is to grow moisture-loving plants such as astilbes.

The Ribbon Test

You can make a rough estimate of your soil's texture by making a ball of just-moist soil in your fist, then squeezing out a ribbon of earth between your thumb and index finger. Sandy soils will break up immediately. Clayey soils hold together, forming a ribbon 1 inch (2.5 cm) long or more. Loamy soils fall somewhere in between.

Soil Depth

The actual depth of your soil has an impact on root growth and this in turn affects what plants—deep- or shallow-rooting—will thrive in your garden. In some regions, the soil is a thin dust over bedrock. In others, thousands of years' worth of decayed prairie grasses have formed soils 6 feet (1.8 m) deep.

Compost is an invaluable source of organic matter and nutrients. Work it into the soil (top) or spread it on the surface as a mulch (bottom).

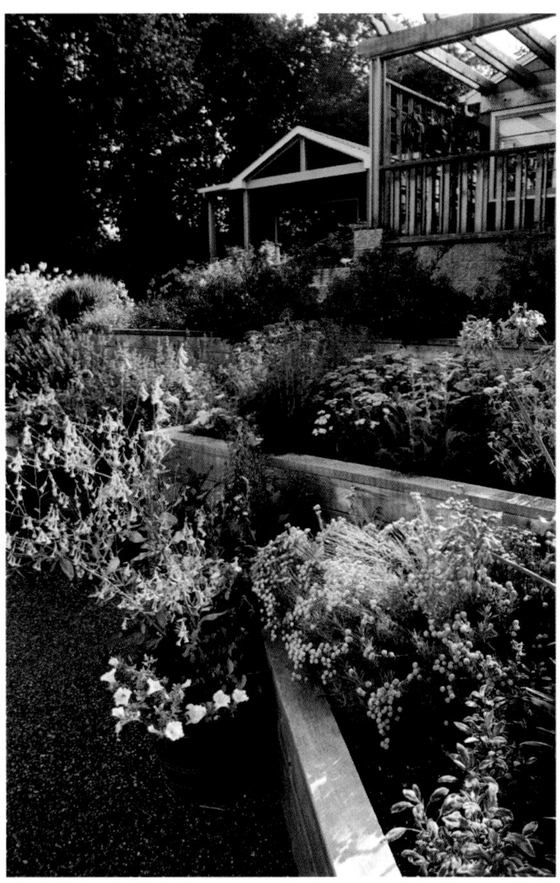

Perennials tend to have deeper roots than annuals, so if your soil is shallow, you could build raised beds to ensure good growth.

It's easy to tell which conditions you have—just dig down into the soil in your yard with a shovel. If you can go 2 feet (60 cm) without hitting a sheet of rock or a band of dense, tightly compacted soil, you'll be able to grow a wide range of annuals and perennials as well as vegetables, herbs, and other shallow-rooted plants with little trouble. Larger plants, like shrubs and trees, generally need soil that's at least 3 feet (90 cm) deep to have vigorous growth. Soils less than 2 feet (60 cm) deep are not as hospitable to root growth; they may also be prone to waterlogging, and often have fewer nutrients than deeper soils. If your soil is shallow, you may decide to build raised beds and fill them with a good soil to provide more area for root growth. A 6-inch (15-cm) high bed should accommodate most annual flowers; you'll need an 18- to 24-inch (45- to 60-cm) bed for perennials. (Raised beds can dry out quickly, though, so you may have to water them more often.) Or you could stick with more shallow-rooted plantings that are adapted to limited root zones.

Soil forms as solid bedrock weathers into smaller and smaller mineral pieces. Organic matter gives the soil surface a darker color.

Soil Organisms

There is abundant life in a healthy soil. Among the beneficial organisms are fungal mycelia, strands of fungus that run through the soil. They bind small soil particles into larger ones and improve soil structure. Beneficial bacteria can decompose organic and mineral elements, freeing nutrients for plants to use. Earthworms tunnel through the soil, consuming and breaking down organic matter, and leaving behind nutrient-rich castings. All of these organisms thrive in the same conditions that the roots of most plants prefer: a loose, moist, but well-drained soil with plenty of organic matter. Soil that is compacted, low in organic matter, or excessively wet is generally low in soil organisms, and your plants probably won't flourish there either.

Earthworms (left) and millipedes (above) are two soil organisms that play an important role in breaking down dead plant matter in the garden.

Soil Fertility

Fertility is the availability, not just the presence, of nutrients in the soil. In order to grow, plants draw large amounts of nitrogen, phosphorus, potassium, magnesium, calcium, and sulfur from the soil. They also require traces of iron, manganese, molybdenum, boron, chlorine, copper, zinc, and nickel. Many of these nutrients are released naturally for plants to use through mineral-rich rocks breaking down into soil.

Most plants grow best when the soil contains an ample supply of balanced nutrients, but some actually grow better if soil nutrients are low. Nitrogen-rich soils, for instance, will cause plants like yarrow and coreopsis to form lush, floppy growth that requires yearly staking. In the same conditions, nasturtiums will grow leaves at the expense of flowers. Grown in less fertile soil, the same plants do much better. Knowing the nutrient content

Coreopsis grows best in soil that isn't very fertile; too much nitrogen can cause weak stems.

of your soil will help you select the most appropriate plants for the conditions.

A soil test can tell you if your land has the right nutrients in the right balance for normal plant growth. If the results show that the pH is extreme or your soil is low in available nutrients, use an organic fertilizer to correct the problem. (This is discussed in greater detail in "Fertilizing for Good Growth" on page 88.) Use restraint when correcting a deficiency, though; too much fertilizer can easily be as bad as not enough. Follow the application rates given on the product label.

Soil pH

Soil pH—the measurement of your soil's acidity or alkalinity—is another factor that can determine which plants will grow well because pH affects the availability of nutrients in your soil. Chemically, pH is the measure of hydrogen ions in the soil. It is measured on a scale of 1 to 14, with 7 as neutral. Soils that have pH ratings below 7 are acidic, and as the pH drops, the soil becomes increasingly more acidic. Soils with pH ratings above 7 grow increasingly more alkaline. An acidic pH—5.5 to 6.5—is ideal for most of the flowering plants. But a few, such as pinks (*Dianthus* spp.) and baby's breath, need a soil that is more alkaline, or rich in limestone. Their ideal pH is slightly higher than neutral, at around 7.5.

You can determine your soil pH yourself with a simple home test available at your local garden center, or you can send a sample to a soil-testing laboratory for analysis. If the soil test shows you need to adjust the pH level, begin by adding extra compost when you are preparing the bed or applying a top-dressing. If that is not sufficient to moderate excess acidity, add some calcitic limestone (calcium carbonate) or dolomitic limestone (which contains both calcium and magnesium) for magnesium-deficient soils. Organic matter also helps lower the pH of overly alkaline soils. If it is not enough, you can also add powdered sulfur. The quantity of pH amendments you use will vary with how far you need to adjust the pH and what type of soil you have. For more on preparing soils for planting, see "Getting the Soil Ready" on page 48.

In most cases, it's best to choose annuals and perennials that will thrive in your soil conditions rather than to change the soil to fit the plants. If you really want to try to grow plants that need different conditions, consider grouping them in one bed, where you can more easily adjust the soil to fit their needs.

Flowers for Acid Soil

Here are just a few of the plants that tolerate or even appreciate acidic soil, which has a pH below 6.5.

Chrysanthemum spp. (chrysanthemums)
Convallaria majalis (lily-of-the-valley)
Lilium spp. (lilies)
Tagetes spp. (marigolds)

This garden bed of mostly annuals needs fertile, nutrient-rich soil. Annuals are the tourists of the flower garden; their short stay means they don't have much time to extract the nutrients they need to bloom.

Flowers for Alkaline Soil

If your soil's pH is on the high side (7.5 or higher), consider some of the following plants, which are naturally adapted to alkaline soil.

Ageratum houstonianum (ageratum)
Anemone x *hybrida* (Japanese anemone)
Antirrhinum majus (snapdragon)
Bergenia spp. (bergenias)
Cosmos spp. (cosmos)
Dianthus spp. (pinks)
Gypsophila paniculata (baby's breath)
Heuchera spp. (coral bells)
Paeonia spp. (peonies)
Verbascum spp. (mulleins)
Zinnia spp. (zinnias)

Peonies

Your Local Climate

To have healthy, vigorous perennials that will grow and thrive year after year with minimal care, you need to choose plants that are well adapted to your climate.

Understanding Hardiness Zones

Find out what hardiness zone you live in so you can choose the right plants for your area. The Plant Hardiness Zone Maps, from page 588, divide continental USA, Europe and Australasia into many different zones based on average minimum yearly temperatures. If you choose plants that are reportedly hardy in your zone, you can be fairly confident that those plants will survive an average winter in your area. To really be on the safe side, you may want to stick with plants that are hardy to at least one zone colder than yours. If you live in Zone 6, for instance, you can depend on perennials that are hardy to Zones 4 or 5.

Tulips, daffodils, grape hyacinths, and many other bulbs are ideally suited to Zones 4 to 8. They are a fast and easy way to add spring color.

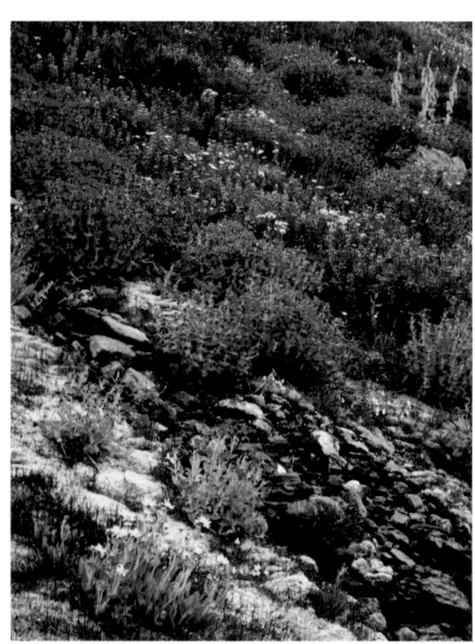

A garden in a cold climate will suit low-growing, hardy perennials adapted to alpine conditions.

You'll find that the plant entries in this book and in many other books and catalogs give a range of hardiness zones—such as "Zones 5 to 8"—for a particular plant. That's because cold temperatures aren't the only factor that determines if a plant will grow well in an area; heat can have a great effect, too. The upper limit of a plant's hardiness range will give you an idea of what kind of summer temperatures that plant can tolerate. If a plant is listed as hardy in Zones 5 to 8, for example, you could grow it in Zones 5, 6, 7, and 8; Zones 4 and lower would probably be too cold, and Zones 9 and 10 could be too hot.

Learning about Local Weather

Hardiness zones are helpful for narrowing down your plant choices, but they aren't foolproof guidelines. If you live in a large town or city, for instance, your local area may be significantly warmer than the hardiness map would predict. Elevated and open, exposed areas may get colder than other properties in the same zone. In cold areas, consistent snow cover provides fabulous insulation and may allow you to grow plants from warmer zones. For annuals and bulbs in particular, you will need to know the dates of the average first and last frosts in your area, to determine when it's safe to sow or transplant.

Knowing when and how much it rains in your area is very important if you want to choose plants that won't need regular watering. As a broad rule of thumb, most annuals and perennials need about 1 inch (25 mm) of rain each week during the growing season (spring and autumn). If your area doesn't get enough rain during the crucial growing months, you'll have to provide water for your plants or switch to water-wise landscaping.

Wind is another factor to consider. It can make your climate more severe than

A garden in the Southwest uses combinations of stone, cactus, and agave with flowering verbena.

Consider Your Climate

Understanding your climate will help you choose the annuals and perennials that are best adapted to the conditions available in your garden. This list of temperate and subtropical climates explains how your climate will influence the plants you can grow.

Cool summer and cold winter (Southern Canada and New England): You'll need to look for cold-hardy annuals and perennials that emerge after spring freezes subside and that bloom early enough to escape fall freezes.

Hot summer and cold winter (Midwest and Northeast): You can grow a wide range of annuals and perennials that are hardy and moderately heat-tolerant.

Cool summer but mild winter (Northwest coast): Many annuals and perennials will thrive and bloom here, flowering longer than they would in warmer areas.

Mild winter and hot summer (South Central and Southeast): These areas have enough cold for a dormant period, but their long, hot summers may stress annuals and perennials. If summer is humid, fungal diseases are more likely to plague susceptible plants, so look for disease-resistant cultivars. Winter rains may leave the soil wet for long periods, increasing the potential for rotting; consider growing plants in raised beds.

Arid climates (Southwest): Periods of drought can stress plant growth, so grow drought-tolerant plants in sunken beds with good irrigation. Salt buildup may damage plant roots; look for salt-tolerant species like sea lavenders (*Limonium* spp.).

Subtropical (Southern Florida and Texas): If a cold dormancy period is limited or lacking altogether, select suitable tropical and subtropical plants. Or if you want to grow more common annuals and perennials, you can take special measures, like planting in fall or giving plants a rest period by cutting foliage back.

you think. As you spend time in your yard, observe which direction the wind usually comes from. Is your yard exposed to strong winds, or is it fairly sheltered by trees, hills, or buildings? Strong winds may quickly dry out plants and erode bare soil. When it's cold, winds can draw water out of exposed plant tops and roots faster than it can be replaced, leading to severe damage or death. Yet wind can actually be an asset in very humid climates, where good air circulation becomes more important in preventing the development of plant diseases.

Where winds are strong or frequent, protect your gardens by locating them on the sheltered side of walls, solid fences, or hedges. In exposed areas with cold winter winds and no consistent snow cover, choose plants that are rated for at least one zone colder than yours to be safe. Or you could cover plants that are normally adapted to your zone with a generous layer of branches (or chopped leaves) for winter protection. See "Going with the Wind" on page 274 for more ideas.

California poppies, drought-tolerant and easy to grow, work well in Midwest wildflower gardens.

Sea lavender is a tough perennial that is quite adapted to sites with sandy or salty soil.

With its climate of mild winters and cool summers, the Northwest coast provides good conditions for gardening. Roses, rose campions, and spike speedwell will flower longer here than in warmer regions.

The Lay of the Land

The topography of your yard—whether it slopes or is uniformly flat—will influence how plants grow, when they bloom, how long the display lasts, and how you'll design your garden. Each kind of topography has its own advantages and disadvantages for gardening.

Gardening on a Flat Area

If your yard is as flat as a cornfield, you are faced with your own particular design opportunities and growing considerations. Actually preparing the site is usually fairly easy, since you don't have to worry much about soil erosion, although you may have drainage problems if your soil is high in clay. A major design challenge is often the lack of a background for your garden. As part of your landscape design, think about installing fences or planting shrubs and trees to "frame" your flower gardens. Another option is to regrade the site, creating gentle, natural-looking rises that will add visual interest.

If only part of your property is flat, be sure to reserve it for recreation—perhaps a barbecue area or a play area for children.

A wall covered with wisteria and golden chain tree provides a lovely, protective enclosure that will keep out harsh winds and wild weather.

Make the most of a flat section on an otherwise undulating or hilly site—use it for an entertaining area.

Gardening on a Hilltop

A garden on a hilltop will face different conditions from gardens just down the slope. The soil on a hilltop may be thin due to erosion, and is often very well drained. Hilltop sites are often windswept as well. Strong winds can topple tall plants, so you'll either need to stake your annuals and perennials or stick with shorter plants. Winds can also dry out plants quickly, so you may have to water more often. The stunning views available from many hilltop sites turn all of these problems into minor inconveniences, however. When planning a landscape for a hilltop site, you may want to design your flower gardens to frame a particularly nice view of the surrounding countryside. If excessive wind is a problem, you can decrease the velocity by setting a fence, hedge, or vine-covered trellis between the prevailing wind direction and your garden.

Terraced beds of stone or timber will allow you to create a garden on a sloping site. Then plant the beds out with petunias and salvias.

Gardening on a Slope

A hilly yard has great potential for interesting settings for your annuals and perennials. It also has more microclimates—the slight variations in growing conditions that will affect plant displays. In general, soils on slopes tend to be well drained, but the topsoil may be thin because of erosion. Flowering gardens on slopes are less prone to late-spring and early-fall frosts, as the cold air tends to settle down in the valley and the warm air rises up over the slope.

Slopes are ideal sites for rock gardens. If the slope isn't naturally rocky, you can add groupings of large boulders or layers of flat rock that resemble natural outcroppings. Leave pockets of soil between the rocks in which to grow small perennials like candytuft (*Iberis sempervirens*), sweet violets (*Viola odorata*), and primroses (*Primula* spp.), along with small bulbs and dwarf conifers.

If your site has a very steep slope, though, think twice before stripping the existing vegetation to plant a flower garden. The soil might wash away before most of the annuals and perennials can root and stabilize the slope. One way to handle slopes is by planting them with those plants that take root and spread aggressively, such as daylilies, ajuga (*Ajuga reptans*), and geraniums (*Geranium* spp.). Space the plants closely for more rapid stabilization of the bank, and use burlap or straw to hold the soil in place until the roots do their job.

If you don't want to rely on plants alone to control erosion, you can terrace the hill or install a retaining wall to moderate the slope. A beautiful rock or timber retaining wall will give your landscape interesting structure and let you grow plants that do not root strongly enough to survive on a slope.

Gardening in a Valley

At the base of a slope, flower gardens are more prone to late-spring and early-fall frosts. Frost and cold air will inevitably concentrate in low-lying areas, known as frost pockets, slowing or damaging spring growth and fall flowers. The same frost may miss plants growing in warmer areas slightly uphill. Gardeners in low-lying areas may want to wait a little later than others to remove protective winter mulches. And moisture will collect at the base of the slope too, just like frost. Valleys are rich in rainfall runoff and often have natural water features such as ponds and streams. Topsoil eroded from surrounding slopes tends to collect here, but if the soil is clayey, it may not drain well. A common way to deal with this drainage problem is to plant perennials in raised beds. If poor drainage is really a problem, you could install drainage tiles to channel the excess water into another area.

In valleys and flat terrain, the best solution if you have poor drainage is to actually use the moisture around any creeks, ponds, and lakes to your advantage. Let a bubbling brook or the reflective surface of a pond become the focus around which you plant water-loving plants. Clothe the banks with the flashiest of the moisture-lovers like red-spiked cardinal flowers (*Lobelia cardinalis*), Japanese primroses (*Primula japonica*), golden-flowered big-leaved ligularia (*Ligularia dentata*), or the plume-like, rose-red rodgersia (*Rodgersia pinnata*).

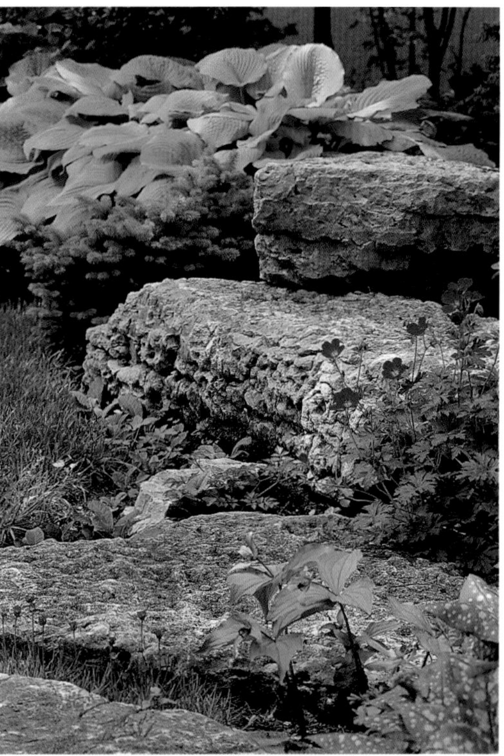

Use any rocks you find on your property as the framework for a raised rock garden or as a pathway of flagstones.

If you live in a valley, you may have a pond or even just a spot that always seems wet. This is where primroses, hostas, and irises will thrive.

Examine Your Exposure

Exposure refers to the amount of sun and shade that your yard receives in the course of the day. The exposure of different places on your property can vary widely, depending on where each garden bed is in relation to the house and also to other shade-casting features such as sheds, trees, and fences.

South-facing Sites

Locating a garden on the south side of your house (or a wall or fence) provides the maximum amount of light in the Northern Hemisphere. In cool Northern summers, many sun-loving annuals and perennials thrive against a south wall. But where summers are hot, all but the most heat- and drought-tolerant perennials may bake against south walls because of the high temperatures there.

Eastern Exposures

Many flowering plants thrive with an eastern exposure, such as that along the eastern edge of woods, on the east side of a steep hill, or against an east-facing wall. Plants on these sites receive up to a half day of direct light, and they're sheltered from the hot afternoon sun. This protection from strong afternoon rays prolongs bloom time where summers are hot. When you read a description that suggests afternoon shade for a particular plant—such as lady's mantle (*Alchemilla mollis*), cranesbills (*Geranium* spp.), or Japanese anemone (*Anemone* x *hybrida*)—try an eastern exposure.

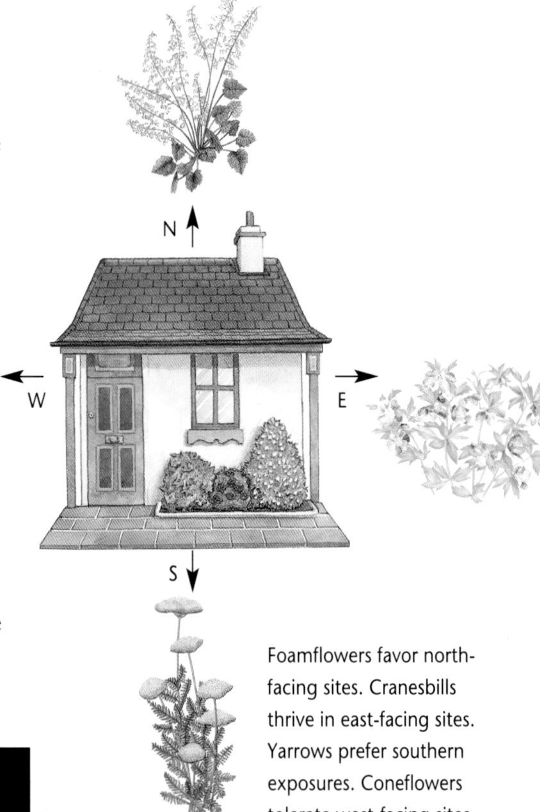

Foamflowers favor north-facing sites. Cranesbills thrive in east-facing sites. Yarrows prefer southern exposures. Coneflowers tolerate west-facing sites.

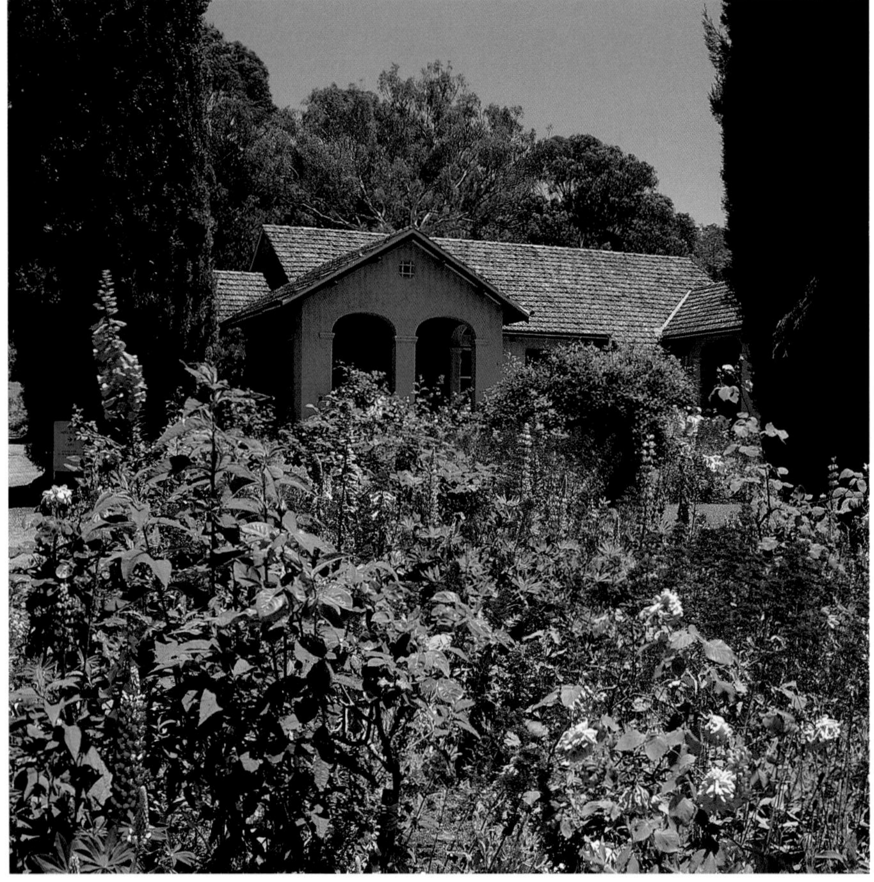

Each side of your house offers different growing conditions, called microclimates. The south side of the house will provide the maximum amount of light for your annuals and perennials, no matter the season.

West-facing Sites

Western exposures are a challenge for most plants. The site is generally cool and shady in the morning, but the temperature can change dramatically when strong sun hits it during the warmest part of the day. Shade-loving plants generally don't handle such extremes well; their leaves may turn brown or go off-color.

In the North of the continent, the temperature differences between morning and afternoon may be moderate enough not to harm plants, especially if a tree, fence, or outbuilding casts a little shade there in the afternoon.

In Southern gardens, try tough, drought-tolerant perennials that can take sun or partial shade, including blue false indigo (*Baptisia australis*), boltonia (*Boltonia asteroides*), patrinia (*Patrinia scabiosifolia*), Cupid's dart (*Catananche caerulea*), cushion spurge (*Euphorbia epithymoides*), daylilies (*Hemerocallis* spp.), common sundrops (*Oenothera tetragona*), violet sage (*Salvia* x *superba*), and coneflowers.

Coneflowers thrive in full sun but will also grow in light shade. They are tough and long-lived.

Northern Exposures

A garden set against a north-facing wall or fence or on the north side of a steep hill receives much less light and remains cool throughout the day. If the site is open (without large trees or buildings to the east or west), it will probably still be bright. A bright, evenly cool spot is ideal for most shade-loving plants; even those preferring full shade should grow well here. Try flowering and foliage annuals and perennials such as hostas, ferns, and lungworts (*Pulmonaria* spp.).

Understanding Sun and Shade

Identifying the direction that your property faces will give you a general idea of the growing conditions that you have to offer. But unless you have a totally flat, featureless lot, you'll also have to consider the shade cast by trees, shrubs, fences, hedges, trellises, sheds, the house next door, and any other structures.

How do you tell if a particular spot has full sun, partial shade, or full shade? Watch the spot regularly over the course of a day (check on it every hour or so), and note each time you check whether the spot is sunny or shady. Any site with less than 6 hours of direct sunlight throughout the day is shady. Annuals and perennials that prefer full sun need 6 hours or more of direct sunlight to grow well. A site that receives a few hours of morning or late afternoon sun but no direct midday sun is described as having partial shade. Many perennials that prefer full sun will tolerate partial shade.

A generally bright site that receives little direct sun but lots of filtered or reflected light is said to have light or dappled shade. Typically, this kind of shade occurs beneath high-branched deciduous trees (such as honey locusts [*Robinia pseudoacacia*]) that don't cast solid shadows. Full, dense, or deep shade is darker, and fewer plants grow well in it. The area under hemlocks or other such evergreens is in deep shade all year long. Plants growing under maples, beeches, and other densely branched deciduous trees are in full shade most of the summer.

Keep in mind that shade changes during the year, both because the angle of the sun changes in the sky and because deciduous trees grow and then shed their leaves. You may find that a site that is in full sun on July 1 is shaded by a nearby tree or building in April or October when the sun is much lower in the sky.

A maple tree provides deep shade during the heat of summer. In fall, its leaves color and drop, and it remains bare until the spring, providing temporary sunlight for wildflowers and bulbs.

The deep shade under a maple or oak disappears when the tree loses its leaves, and the ground below stays bright until mid- to late spring. Many of the spring wildflowers, including bluebells (*Mertensia virginica*) and foamflowers (*Tiarella* spp.), have adapted to readily take advantage of this temporary sun and bloom before the overhead trees leaf out. Spring-blooming bulbs that go dormant by the time the trees are fully leafed out are also good. Even if your yard is deeply shaded the rest of the season, you can probably enjoy masses of color in the spring and beautiful green and patterned foliage the rest of the year. For more specific advice on landscaping shady sites, turn to "Succeeding in the Shade" on page 156.

There's no need to despair if you have shade. Many colorful annuals and perennials, including cosmos, irises, hostas, and primroses, thrive in full or at least partial shade.

Observe and Plan

The trick to gardening with annuals and perennials is finding and combining plants that will thrive in your particular conditions.

To have a beautiful, healthy garden, you don't have to be born with a "green thumb." The real secret to creating a great-looking garden is a keen sense of observation. To determine what kind of growing conditions you have available—how much light, what kind of climate and topography, and what kind of soil—you need to live with your yard so you can choose the annuals and perennials that will grow and thrive there.

Starting from Scratch

If you've just built a new house, moved into a new development, or inherited a particularly uninspired all-lawn landscape, you may be staring at bare soil or a large expanse of grass where you want a garden to be located.

The best way to start a new landscape may be not to start it—at least for a year or so. If you can stand it, live with the landscape through one year. See where water puddles after storms or where it runs off quickly, taking valuable topsoil with it. Note where structures and trees cast shadows on your property, and how the shadows change throughout the seasons. See how traffic patterns develop: Where do you always walk to reach the car? Where do visitors and utility people tend to tread on their way to the door? Take note of these patterns, and incorporate them into your landscape plan.

As you install your new landscape, it's wise to start on the "hard" elements—like walls, fences, and paths—first. These give overall structure. This is also the best time to plan and install an automatic irrigation system if you need one. Once permanent elements are in place, then you can start planting. You may choose to plant a few beds of annuals for quick color during the first few seasons or just wait for the perennials to develop. Don't forget that annuals are great for filling in gaps in young perennial gardens!

Adapting an Existing Garden

In some ways, adapting an existing garden is more challenging than starting from scratch. Although your garden may have pleasant features like large trees or an established lawn to work with, you also have someone else's tastes to contend with and their mistakes to undo.

Enliven an established garden of trees and ivy with bergenia rather than pulling everything out.

Work on one project at a time, establishing different features gradually, such as a pergola that you can underplant with different perennials.

If you've lived with the garden for at least a year, you are probably very aware of its troublesome points. But don't try to convert the whole garden all at once. Instead, identify the elements you want to change, then work slowly, choosing a few (or one major one) to work on each year.

Annuals and perennials, being fast-growing and adaptable plants, can provide masses of seasonal color and beautiful foliage with just some basic care. If the existing plants are overgrown, dig them out, divide them, and replant the vigorous outer parts into enriched soil. If they are in the wrong spot, dig them up and move them in the spring.

Plant petunias for quick and easy color during the first few growing seasons in your garden.

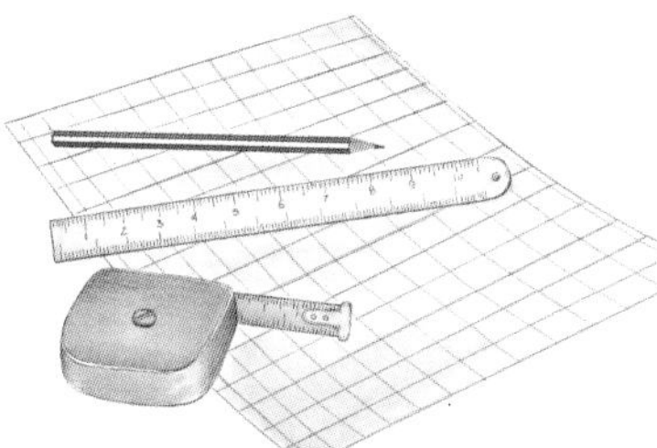

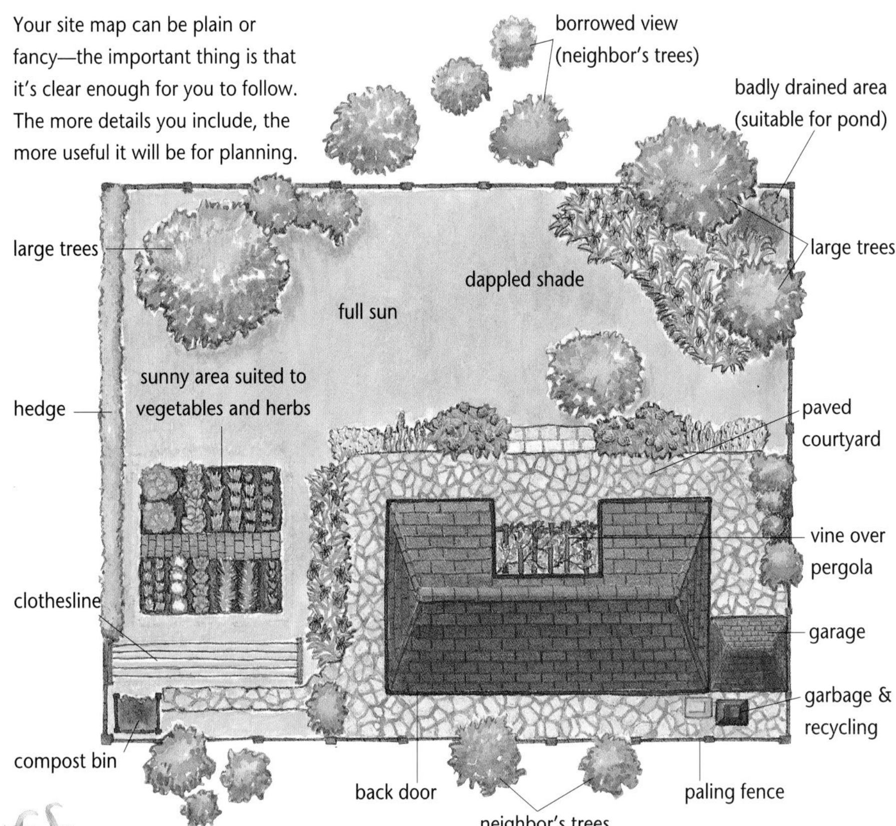

Your site map can be plain or fancy—the important thing is that it's clear enough for you to follow. The more details you include, the more useful it will be for planning.

Creating a Site Map

The easiest way to record everything you've learned about your site—the soil conditions, drainage, exposure, slope, and microclimates—is by making a site plan. It will show you the factors you'll need to consider when planning which plants you can grow and where you can put them. The more accurate your plan, the more useful it will be.

You'll need just a few simple tools: a 50- or 100-foot (15- or 30-m) tape measure, graph paper, a pencil, and a ruler. A second person is a big help. If you're by yourself, you may find measuring easier if you use a long (100 foot [30 m]) piece of string that is tied to a short, pointed stake at each end.

It's good to start with a survey map of your property. If you don't have one, draw a rough outline of the yard to scale: 1 inch (2.5 cm) on paper for each foot (30 cm) of garden space is a good scale for gardens shorter than 10 feet (3 m). Locate north with a compass or a local street map, and indicate it on your map. Draw outlines of your house, driveway, paths, and patios. Also sketch in sheds or garages, plus fences, hedges, and existing gardens.

Don't forget to mark any significant topographical features on your map, too. Include low areas (and whether or not they are wet), hilltops, and large boulders. Note which direction slopes face and whether slopes are gentle (easy to walk up or mow) or steep (hard to walk up).

Include trees and large shrubs on your map. If an area contains many trees and shrubs, outline it and mark it as woods. Note any other areas that get less than 6 hours of direct sun and whether they have light, partial, or dense shade. Also note areas that may be sunny in spring and shady once the trees leaf out.

Finally, look for good views that you'd like to preserve and bad views that you might want to screen out. Mark nice views with an arrow so you'll remember not to block them with tall perennials. Also indicate which windows you look out of to see your yard. Mark anything you'd like to screen, such as trash cans, and areas you don't want to mow, such as around posts and trees.

Make several photocopies of your finished map, so you'll be able to sketch in different landscaping ideas and test how they look before you start digging.

Make the Most of Microclimates

Each garden might have several unique growing areas, normally called microclimates. Shady nooks fit into this category. So do hot spots, like beds that get extra heat from walls or paving.

As you plan your plantings, look for these special spots where particular annuals and perennials may thrive. A sunny, south-facing bed along a brick terrace, for instance, could hold extra warmth for a great show of crocus and pansies in early spring. The same site, though, would probably be too hot for the pansies in summer, so you'd need to replace them with heat-tolerant annuals or perennials, such as the many types of daylily (*Hemerocallis* spp.), treasure flowers (*Gazania* hybrids), or sundrops (*Oenothera tetragona*).

SECTION THREE

Preparation and Planting

Careful planning will take you a long way toward a great-looking landscape. The next step is to follow through with good soil preparation, informed plant purchasing, and the right planting techniques to get those plants off and growing. This chapter will guide you through the process of preparing the site, acquiring your plants, and planting them, so that your flower garden stays healthy and beautiful all season long.

Getting the Soil Ready 48

Adding Nutrients 50

Choosing the Right Plants 52

Planting Time 56

Growing Annuals 64

Propagating Perennials 68

Bulb Multiplication 74

Getting the Soil Ready

Along with proper plant selection, preparing a planting bed so that it contains good, granular soil is critical to the success of your flower garden. If you do a thorough job at this stage, you will be rewarded by quicker plant establishment and less weeding later.

Timing

If possible, start digging your new garden a season or a year before you intend to do any planting. That way, you can do a really thorough job of preparing the soil, and the soil will have a chance to settle before you plant. If spring typically is too wet to work the soil in your area, dig the garden in fall instead. If you can't prepare the soil ahead of time, you can usually get the bed ready and start planting in the same season. See "Planting Time" on page 56 for suggestions on the best time to actually plant.

Making New Beds

When you're digging a garden bed in a lawn, begin by marking the bed outline with rope, a garden hose, or string and stakes. Strip off the sod with a flat spade by cutting long, spade-width strips across the width of the bed. Slide your spade under the strips to sever them from the soil. Roll up the turf as you go or remove it in rectangles, and take the bundles to the compost pile. As an alternative, you can kill the grass by covering it with black plastic. However, this can take several weeks or more than a month depending on the weather—the hotter it is outside, the faster the plastic works. Till in the turf when it has decayed.

Use a broadfork to prepare previously worked beds or to aerate compacted soil before planting.

Working the Soil

Once you've cleared the beds, it's time to break up the soil. Consider your choice of tools carefully. Decades ago, gardeners turned the soil with garden spades, forks, and other hand tools. In recent years, many have turned to rotary tillers. These machines can churn the top 5 to 6 inches (12.5 to 15 cm) of soil with much less effort on your part. But tillers aren't always the best choice. Excessive tilling, or tilling when the soil is too wet or too dry will break up the good, granular soil structure into tiny particles and lead to soil compaction. If you choose to use a rotary tiller, make sure you work the soil when it's evenly moist. For details on determining soil moisture, see "Squeeze Your Soil to Test Moisture."

Careful digging and regular additions of organic matter will help maintain a good, granular soil.

Preparing a Bed

1. Set out stakes and string to mark the area you're going to dig.

2. Remove the sod by stripping it off the soil with a spade.

3. If a soil test indicates the site is too acid, apply lime to the soil.

4. Spread a layer of compost over the area and dig it into the bed.

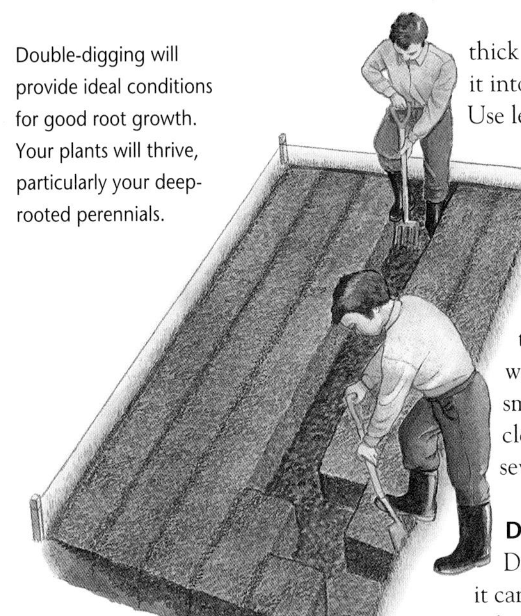
Double-digging will provide ideal conditions for good root growth. Your plants will thrive, particularly your deep-rooted perennials.

If you have a small garden and are willing to dig with hand tools, you can usually loosen the soil to a depth of up to 6 to 8 inches (15 to 20 cm), which is deep enough for annuals. Or you can make the bed 12 inches (30 cm) deep, which is better for the longer roots of perennials, if you double dig. Complete instructions on double-digging can be found below.

Add compost before planting so you can work it in throughout the bed. For a heavy clay or light sandy loam that is low in organic matter, lay a 4-inch (10-cm) thick layer over the entire area and work it into the top 8 inches (20 cm) of soil. Use less compost if you want to plant yarrows, artemisias, and other perennials that grow best in dry, sunny sites. Add more compost in warm climates—where organic matter seems to "burn up" in a few weeks—to compensate for the fast rate of decomposition. After working the soil, rake the surface to smooth it and break up any large clods. Then let the bed soil settle for several weeks before planting.

Work compost into the soil before planting to provide nutrients for healthy, steady growth.

Double-digging

Double-digging is hard work, but it can be worthwhile if you are gardening in heavy clayey soil or if you're growing perennials and want to encourage them to root extra deeply in drought-prone areas. Remove the sod and weed roots first. Starting at one end of the bed, dig a trench 12 inches (30 cm) wide and as deep as your spade across the width of the bed. Put all the topsoil you unearth into a wheelbarrow and move it to the far end of the garden. Now loosen up the exposed subsoil with a garden fork or your spade. Then back up to dig the next 12-inch (30-cm) wide strip. Shift that topsoil, with some added compost or other organic matter, into the first trench and then loosen the new area of subsoil. Continue in this fashion until you reach the far end of the bed. Finish the last strip with the topsoil from your wheelbarrow and rake the bed smooth. Once you've prepared the bed, avoid stepping on it; otherwise, you'll compact the soil and undo all your hard work. If you can't reach in from the sides to plant, lay a board across the soil and step on that. Remove it when you're done.

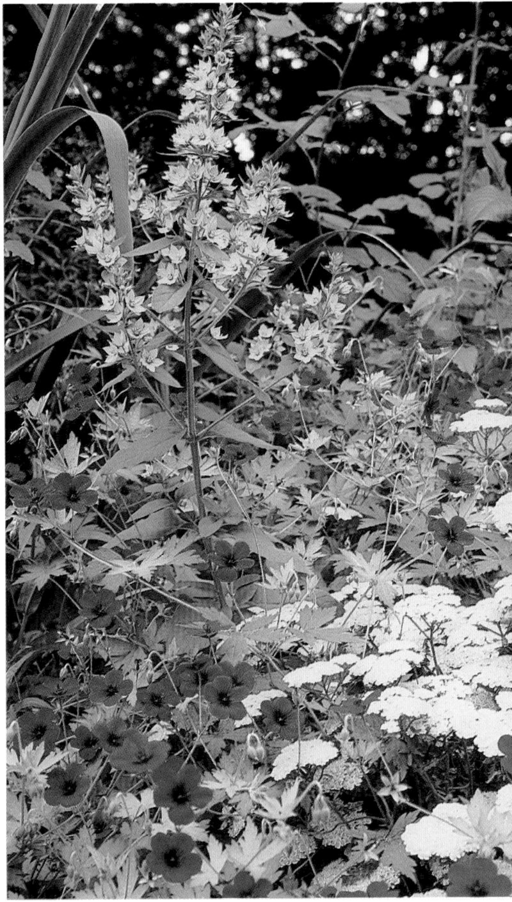
Loose, well-drained soil is the secret to success with cranesbills, yarrow, and yellow loosestrife.

Squeeze Your Soil to Test Moisture

Walking on or working wet soil can quickly destroy the porous, open structure you're trying so hard to build. So before you break out your shovel and work boots, try this simple test: Take a handful of soil and squeeze it. If moisture runs out between your fingers, the soil is too wet to work. If it does not, open your hand. The soil should be in a ball in your palm. If it will not cling together, it is too dry to work. In that case, water the bed thoroughly, let it sit for 24 hours, and evaluate again. If the soil stays in a ball, tap it lightly with a finger. If the soil breaks apart easily, it is ready to work. If it stays tight, it is still too wet. Wait a few more dry days and try again.

Adding Nutrients

As you prepare your new garden for planting, you should also think about adding any nutrients your plants may need. The right nutrients in the right balance will help ensure that your annuals and perennials get off to a good start.

Annuals as well as vegetables and herbs are heavy feeders, so if you're planning an edible garden, be sure to give your plants a nutrient boost.

Understanding Plant Nutrients

The availability of soil nutrients is as important to plant health and vigor as vitamins and minerals are to people. The nutrients that plants require to grow are called essential elements. Three of the essential elements plants need—carbon, hydrogen, and oxygen—come from the air. The other essential elements come from the soil.

The essential elements supplied by the soil are divided into two groups—macronutrients and micronutrients (also known as trace elements). Three macronutrients are especially critical—nitrogen, potassium, and phosphorus. These are the primary nutrients, represented on fertilizer bags in ratios tagged by their elemental initials: N, P, and K. Nitrogen (N) powers growth and protein formation; phosphorus (P) is essential for root and fruit development and for photosynthesis; and potassium (K) is crucial to root and flower development as well as water and sugar flow. All three of these nutrients must be present in the right balance for your annuals and perennials to grow and thrive. The secondary macronutrients—sulfur, calcium, and magnesium—are used in smaller amounts. Micronutrients include iron, molybdenum, manganese, zinc, chlorine, boron, copper, and nickel.

Plants use relatively large amounts of the macronutrients, much as humans use a lot of carbohydrates, proteins, and fats. They use smaller quantities of the micronutrients, much as humans need small amounts of vitamins and minerals. The difference in the amount plants use doesn't indicate a difference in how important the element is. All of them are essential, and a lack of just one affects how effectively plants can use the others. That's why balancing soil fertility is so important for good plant growth.

Fertilizers or Amendments?

The first step to choosing the right organic material is knowing the difference between a true fertilizer and a soil amendment. Fertilizer is a material that contains significant amounts of the chemical elements that plants need to grow, like nitrogen, phosphorus, and potassium. It may also contain material that improves the soil, such as organic matter. But its primary function is to add nutrients. Bloodmeal, bat guano, and greensand are examples of organic fertilizers.

An amendment is a material that physically improves the soil —usually its structure or its drainage—or enhances microbial activity. It may contain some nutrients, but not enough to be called a fertilizer. Compost, grass clippings, lime, and peat moss are examples of soil amendments.

The material you use really depends on what effect you want. Fertilizers are useful for correcting specific nutrient deficiencies and for providing a general nutrient boost during the growing season. Amendments are important for long-term soil health, since they add organic matter and humus. Using a balance of fertilizers and amendments will help ensure your plants have all the nutrients they need and help build soil humus as well.

Start with a Soil Test

Before you invest in a big bag of fertilizer, find out what's in your soil to start with. It may already contain everything your plants need to grow beautifully. You can use home test kits or you can send soil samples to a lab for testing before you plant. To have your

Lupines belong to the same family as peas and beans. These plants seldom need extra nitrogen.

Flowering plants can have very different nutrient needs. Group those with similar needs together, as in this border that includes verbena, sage, and sedum.

soil analyzed by a lab, contact your local Cooperative Extension agent, land-grant university, or professional soil-analysis laboratory for information or directions.

Applying Nutrients

How you actually apply organic nutrients to your garden depends on several factors. If you're starting a new bed, for instance, mix in potassium, phosphorus, and any other fertilizers or amendments (like lime or sulfur) recommended in the soil test results at the same time that you dig. Or better yet, add them to your compost pile, then add the compost to the soil—the abundant microorganisms in the compost help break down rock powders and other low-solubility fertilizers faster than the smaller, less-active populations in the soil do. Potassium and phosphorus are very important to encourage healthy roots that will keep perennials returning each year.

With that said, be aware that flowering plants can differ widely in their soil needs. Some, like California poppy (*Eschscholzia californica*), are well adapted to shallow, dry, infertile soil and may not flower well in deep, fertile conditions. Others, like astilbes (*Astilbe* x *arendsii*), will turn brown and crispy unless they have rich, evenly moist soil. Either buy plants that are adapted to the conditions your garden has to offer or be willing to put some work into creating the right conditions to fit the plants you want to grow. You can find out the soil and moisture needs of flowering plants by looking in gardening books and magazines or by referring to the individual entries in "Encyclopedia of Flowers," starting on page 306.

Adding gypsum will supply your soil with calcium and sulfur, but it won't change the soil pH.

Remember that annuals only last for a season, which means they don't have a great deal of time to extract slow-release fertilizers from the soil. Before planting them, mix a balanced fertilizer or compost into the soil to feed the microorganisms and provide a small, steady supply of nutrients to the annuals.

Once your annuals and perennials are established, you can supply them with nutrients by working fertilizer materials into the soil around the base of each plant and by mulching with organic materials like chopped leaves or compost. For more on fertilizer materials, see "Fertilizing for Good Growth" on page 88.

Choosing the Right Plants

Starting with healthy plants is a key step in having a naturally healthy garden. It's crucial, after all those hours spent planning your design, carefully deciding what to grow, and getting the soil ready, that you buy strong, problem-free plants and bulbs.

Buying from Local Retailers

A good local nursery or garden center—one that offers a variety of plants and takes good care of them—is a real treasure. Usually its staff members are good sources of information specific to your area, such as which plants grow well there. The nursery may even have a demonstration garden where you can see how plants look when fully grown and compare different cultivars.

Advantages and Disadvantages

One advantage of buying locally is that you can inspect plants and bulbs before buying them. Also, your plants won't have to suffer through shipping. Most nurseries and garden centers offer container-grown plants, which are easiest to handle. On the down side, the selection they have on sale may be limited, and the plants may be more expensive.

If you want a particular cultivar of a plant, you're most likely to find it via a mail-order source.

Buying by Mail

If you want unusual plants, don't have access to a local nursery, or want to get the best possible prices, mail-order sources provide limitless possibilities. Write for catalogs several months before you want to plant so you'll have time to compare selections and prices. Some catalogs have information on the virtues of specific plants and useful growing information.

A favorite pastime for the keen gardener is a trip to the local nursery to find new plants for the garden.

Advantages and Disadvantages

Catalog shopping is a fun way to while away dreary winter evenings, and it's convenient, too. You can learn about exciting new plants and often find good prices when you compare several catalogs. On the down side, you don't really know what you're paying for until you get it. Shipping stress can weaken even the strongest plants. If you get bareroot perennials (with roots that are wrapped in packing material), they'll need to be planted or potted up almost immediately.

Buying Tips

The best approach to ordering by mail is to ask gardening friends which catalogs they've ordered from and which they would buy from again. If you don't know anyone who gets annual or perennial catalogs, visit a library and get addresses and phone numbers from advertisements in recent gardening magazines.

When you order from a source for the first time, just buy a few plants and see how they look when they arrive. If you're happy with the quality for the price, order more; otherwise, shop elsewhere. Remember, if an offer sounds too good to be true, it probably is!

Inspect mail-order plants as soon as they arrive. If they are damaged, you should return them; contact the source right away to find out how to do so. Mail-order perennials are often shipped when they are dormant (not actively growing) and may look dead. Plant them anyway and water them well. If they don't produce any buds or new growth in a few weeks, contact the source.

If your plants were shipped in pots, water them as needed and keep them out of bright sunlight for the first few days. Mail-order plants may also arrive bareroot—without any pot or soil. If they're bulbs, they're happy that way; keep them cool and in the dark until you're ready to plant. Other bareroot plants need more attention; for best results, plant them within a couple days of their arrival.

Don't be swept away by the enormous choice of plants. Check they are healthy before buying.

To plant out a cottage garden, especially one on this scale, it's most cost-effective to buy by mail order.

Healthy Plant Checklist

A stressed, diseased, or pest-infested plant is a recipe for disappointing results. So before you pay for your purchases, take a minute to check them over carefully—following the points here—to make sure you're getting the best plants possible.

1. Look to see if the plant is tagged with its botanical and cultivar name. If not, or if it's labeled only by common name or color, chances are that it's not an improved type and you may not want it.

2. Test for root-bound plants, which may have been sitting around for a long time in a small pot. Give the plant a soft tug and see if the root ball pops out of the pot readily. If the roots are packed into a solid mass or circle around the inside of the pot, the plant is root-bound and may be slow to adapt to garden conditions.

3. Look at the roots. Firm, white roots are a sign of good health. If you can't pull the plant out of its pot to see the roots, check where the shoots emerge from the soil. Emerging stems should not be brown, soft, blemished, or wilted—these are symptoms of rots and other diseases.

4. Give the same thorough inspection to the stems and foliage. Look for signs of diseases such as brown or black leaf spots, white powdery mildew, or tiny orange spots of rust. You don't want to bring these problems home to infect plants in your garden.

5. Check the color of the foliage. If it is a deep and uniform color, the plant is most likely healthy and well fed.

6. Be on the lookout for weed shoots emerging through or near the crown (base) of the annual or perennial. Grasses and perennial weeds will reemerge and can invade your newly planted garden.

7. Last, check for insect pests. Look beneath the leaves, along the stems, in the shoot tips, and on the flower buds for soft-bodied aphids, cottony mealybugs, and hard-shelled scale insects. Spider mites, another common pest, will make leaves stippled or turn them yellow or bronze. If there are pests on one plant,

Different Ways to Buy Perennials

Perennials that are container grown may cost a bit more but they will give an instant effect in the garden.

Field-dug perennials are often quite mature and usually adapt quickly once planted in a new site.

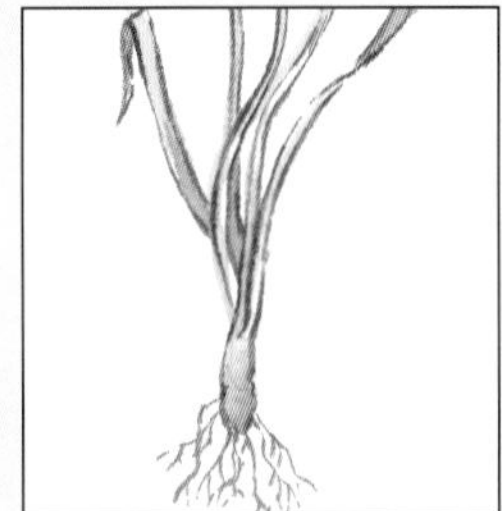

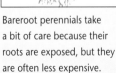

Bareroot perennials take a bit of care because their roots are exposed, but they are often less expensive.

Gently slide a plant from its pot to check the roots. Avoid plants with massed or circling roots.

Good-quality plants will have healthy white roots that are still growing through the soil ball.

they may be on every single plant in that greenhouse or garden center. Consider shopping elsewhere.

Buying Annual Transplants

Look for annuals that are fairly uniform and seem healthy. Avoid those that are wilted, as well as those with visible problems. (Review the "Healthy Plant Checklist" to get a good idea of the signs and symptoms to look for.) While wilted plants usually recover when watered, repeated wilting can stunt their growth and make them less likely to perform well in your garden over the season.

Another thing to consider is whether or not the plants are in bloom. If you're looking for specific flower colors, you may want to buy plants that already have some blooms. In most cases, though, you'll get the best growth from plants that aren't yet blooming. If you can only buy transplants that are already flowering, pinch off the flowers at planting time. It seems hard to do, but it will help your plants in the long run. They'll put their energy into making new roots and then quickly start producing bushy new growth and dozens of new flower buds.

Plants that look strong and healthy are likely to grow well. Weak, sickly plants may introduce pests and diseases into your garden.

Buying Perennials

There are several ways to sell the same perennial plant—in a container, bareroot, or field-dug. What follows are some specifications that will help you evaluate how to use your plant budget most wisely.

Container-grown Perennials

Perennials are most commonly sold in containers. Container-grown perennials are convenient and easy to handle. You can keep the pots in a warm, well-lit location until you are ready to plant. Then you can slide the root ball out and plant the perennials in the garden with minimal disturbance.

However, there is a catch. Horticultural researchers are finding that the roots tend to stay in the light, fluffy "soil" of synthetic potting mixes, rather than branching out into the surrounding garden soil. But you can avoid this problem by loosening roots on the outside of the ball and spreading them out into the soil as you plant. (For more information on planting, see "Planting Perennials" on page 58.)

Container-grown perennials come in different sizes, so their prices vary widely. Larger-sized pots, usually 1- and 2-gallon (4.5- to 9-liter) containers, are generally more expensive. The cost may be worthwhile if you need immediate garden impact. On the other hand, you can buy younger plants inexpensively in multicell packs or small pots. These sizes work fine if you don't mind waiting a year or more for them to fill out and bloom with abandon. In fact, young plants tend to become established in the garden faster than older ones, catching up to the bigger plants in a short time.

Garden mums, or chrysanthemums, are usually sold as container-grown perennials. Unless you want a particular flower color, it's best to buy perennials that aren't in bloom.

Bareroot Perennials

You will come across many species of dormant bareroot plants for sale early in the growing season. In late summer or early fall, you can also find bareroot items such as bearded irises, peonies, common bleeding heart (*Dicentra spectabilis*), and oriental poppies (*Papaver orientale*). You may choose to buy bareroot plants to save money—they are usually less expensive than large container-grown plants—or you may receive them unexpectedly. Mail-order companies often send plants bareroot to save on shipping and space. You open the box to find long spidery roots and—at best—a small tuft of foliage. These plants look more dead than alive, but looks can be deceiving. If you keep the roots moist and cool and plant them quickly and properly, most bareroot plants will recover and thrive.

When the plants arrive, tend to them promptly. Open the box to let some air in. The plants' roots should be wrapped in a protective medium like shredded newspaper, excelsior, or sphagnum moss. Be sure to keep this medium moist but not soggy.

Field-dug Perennials

You may be able to find a plant collector, hobbyist plant breeder, farmer, or nursery owner who will sell you mature plants dug from the field. If you handle the root ball carefully, you can move field-dug perennials much later in the summer than bareroot plants because the roots are protected by soil. Set the root ball, surrounded by soil, in a firm wooden flat or sturdy bucket. Cover it with a moist towel, damp peat moss, or compost to keep the roots and soil moist. Replant it as soon as you get home.

Avoiding Wild-collected Bulbs

Part of being a good shopper is knowing where the bulbs you buy are coming from. While much progress has been made in limiting the collection of species bulbs from the wild, some disreputable sources still gather the bulbs they sell from native habitats. You'll want to buy only from dealers that sell cultivated bulbs.

Dutch companies now label all of their bulbs with their source, and they supply that information in their catalog. American dealers are not required to inform their customers whether their bulbs were grown in production fields or collected from wild sources. However, most American sources actually do provide that information and are against taking plants from the wild.

Wild collection is not an issue with hybrids and cultivars, since these plants don't grow in the wild. But it can be a concern when you're buying species bulbs, including Grecian windflower (*Anemone blanda*), hardy cyclamen (*Cyclamen* spp.), winter aconite (*Eranthis hyemalis* and *E. cilicicus*), snowdrops (*Galanthus* spp.), snowflakes (*Leucojum* spp.), species daffodils (such as *Narcissus asturiensis*, *N. bulbocodium*, and *N. triandrus*), and sternbergia (*Sternbergia* spp.). Make sure you purchase only those bulbs you're sure are from cultivated stock. If you can't tell, ask the supplier or find another source.

Daffodils

Bulbs come in many shapes and sizes. Buy those that are plump and firm; avoid shriveled ones.

Buying Bulbs

High-quality, full-sized bulbs command top dollar, based on the amount of time and labor it takes to produce them, but you can rely on them for truly spectacular results. A higher price, however, doesn't always mean that one tulip or daffodil cultivar is better than another. New cultivars tend to be much more expensive than older ones that have been around for a while. New cultivars are fun to try, but the old standbys that have proven to be good performers through the years are usually both economical and dependable.

A top-quality bulb is firm to the touch (not mushy or squishy) and free of large blemishes or scars. Some bulbs, such as tulips and hyacinths, may have a trace of blue mold on them. A few small mold spots will not harm the bulb, but a noticeable layer may indicate that the bulb was stored improperly before being offered for sale, and is best avoided. Look for bulbs that show little or no root or shoot growth except for a pale growth bud at the top. (Lilies are an exception, since they often have fleshy roots attached.) It's wise to shop early in the season so you can get the bulbs before they dry out from sitting in a store for weeks.

Buy generous quantities of bulbs and plant them in drifts or large clumps for a dramatic spring show.

Planting Time

You have your plants, and you have a place to put them. Now you're ready to turn your dream garden into a reality. Although you may have been anticipating the moment of planting for months, don't rush when it arrives. Planting properly takes time and a lot of bending. Work slowly and deliberately to save wear and tear on your body and to get each plant settled as well as possible. Try not to compact the soil. Lay boards across the bed when you need to step in it. This spreads your weight across a broad area instead of concentrating it in one spot.

Planting Annuals

Planting time for annuals varies. In cold areas, it is around the average date of the last frost for your area. In tropical and subtropical areas, you can plant many annuals virtually all year round. But before you set them out in the garden, make sure your transplants, or seedlings, are "hardened off"—adjusted to outdoor conditions. For details on this important step, see "Handling Hardening Off."

Plants that like average, well-drained soil and full sun will be easy to care for if planted together.

Transplants that are in flower will take a little longer to get established and put on new growth.

If you want to tuck transplants in around existing plants, dig individual holes for each transplant.

When actually planting your annuals, check back to the instructions on the seed packets, plant labels, or entries in "Encyclopedia of Flowers," starting on page 306, for suggested information on spacing. If you live in a hot, dry climate or a very cool area that only has a short growing season, you may want to set the plants a little closer together so they'll shade the soil and fill in faster. In humid climates, use the suggested spacings or slightly wider spacings to allow good air circulation between plants; this will help minimize disease problems.

Step-by-Step Guide to Transplanting

1. Dig a hole, then carefully remove the plant from its container.

2. Set the plant in the hole so the base of the stem is level with the soil surface.

3. Gently firm down the soil around the base of the plant so it is stable.

4. Water the plant thoroughly with a fine spray to wet the soil around the roots.

When possible, set transplants out on a cloudy day so they'll be less prone to transplant shock. Use a trowel to dig a hole twice as big as the root mass. Tip the pot or cell pack on its side and gently slide the plant out of its container. Or, if the plant is growing in a peat pot, just tear off the upper rim of the pot and place the whole pot in the hole. Set each plant so the stem base is at the same level as it was in the pot. Fill around the roots with soil, firm the soil gently, and water thoroughly.

Handling Hardening Off

If you buy greenhouse-grown seedlings or raise your own indoors, they will need to be hardened off before they are ready for transplanting. This involves gradually exposing them to the harsher outdoor conditions: more sunlight, drying winds, and varying temperatures.

Start by moving seedlings outdoors on a nice day. Set shade-loving annuals in a sheltered, shady spot for 2 or 3 days before planting. Give sun-loving annuals about 1 hour of full sun, then move them into the shade of a fence or covered porch. (Take them in at night if frost threatens.) Lengthen the sun time each day, over a period of at least 3 days, until plants can take a full day of sun. Then you can plant them in the garden.

If you don't have a shady spot or if you work during the day and can't run home to shift flats of annuals, make a simple shelter with a section of lath fencing (sometimes called snow fencing). Support the section with bricks or blocks and slide your seedlings underneath. The laths will give a continuously shifting pattern of sun and shade. After 3 or 4 days, your seedlings should be in ideal condition for transplanting.

Protecting Young Plants

If temperatures are unseasonably warm, your transplants may like a few days of sun protection, especially during the afternoon. Use the lath fencing you used for hardening them off (see "Handling Hardening Off" for details), or shelter them with sheets of newspaper clipped to stakes or cages. Mist seedlings occasionally if they wilt, but don't add a lot of extra water to the soil; swampy soil is as bad as dry soil for tender roots.

If late frosts threaten, protect plants through the night with overturned cans, buckets, or clay flower pots. Floating row covers (weigh down the edges with rocks or boards) can provide a few degrees of frost protection and also protect young plants from birds and animal pests.

Sometimes, soil-dwelling caterpillars called cutworms will feed on seedlings at night, eating them off right at ground level. To protect young plants, you can surround them with a metal or cardboard collar. Slip sections of paper towel rolls over seedlings or open-ended soup or juice cans over transplants. Press the collar into the soil, so at least 1 inch (2.5 cm) is below the soil and several inches are left above. Remove after 2 to 3 weeks, or mulch over them and remove at the end of the season; paper collars will break down on their own.

Row covers can be handy for protecting tender seeds from frosts.

Sowing Seed in the Garden

Many popular annuals grow just as well from seed sown outdoors as they do from transplants, which have grown from seed sown indoors. Some even grow better from direct-sown seed because they like cool outdoor temperatures or because they don't respond well to transplanting. A few annuals in this easy-to-grow group include morning glories (*Ipomoea* spp.), California poppy (*Eschscholzia californica*), and rocket larkspur (*Consolida ambigua*). To find out if the annuals you want to grow can be direct-sown, check the seed packet or the individual entries in "Encyclopedia of Flowers," starting on page 306. These sources will also tell you the best time for sowing.

Direct-sowing is simple. First, get the soil ready for planting (as explained in "Getting the Soil Ready" on page 48). Sow medium-sized and large seeds individually or scatter them evenly over the surface. Try to space them ½ to 1 inch (12 to 25 mm) apart. If you have very small seeds, mix them with a handful of dry sand and distribute them over the seedbed.

Cover most seeds with a thin layer of fine soil or sand. If you're dealing with fine seeds, just pat them into the soil or tamp down the area with a board. After sowing, make sure the seedbed stays moist until the

Start your garden by setting out indoor-grown transplants, then direct-sow seeds around them.

Planting a Container-grown Perennial

1. Dig a planting hole that is larger than the root ball.

2. If desired, add a handful or two of compost to the hole.

3. Add enough water to just moisten the soil before planting.

4. Gently slide the perennial plant out of its container.

5. Use your fingers to loosen the soil mix around the roots.

6. Set the plant in the hole. Backfill with soil, then firm lightly.

seedlings are visible. If there isn't enough rainfall, water gently with a watering can, sprinkler, or fine hose spray. Covering the seedbed with a layer of floating row cover helps to keep the soil moist and protects the seed from drying winds, heavy rain, and birds. (Remove the cover once the seedlings emerge.)

If seedlings are crowded, you'll need to thin them out for good growth. Dig up and carefully transplant extra seedlings, or use scissors to cut off the stems of unwanted seedlings at ground level.

Planting Biennials

If you decide to grow biennial plants, such as foxgloves (*Digitalis purpurea*) and forget-me-nots (*Myosotis sylvatica*), you need a slightly different growing approach than if you were planting annuals. Most biennials will sprout well when sown outdoors. But if you sow them directly into the garden, their leafy, first-year growth will take up room without adding much interest to your flower display.

The easiest and most effective method is to set aside a temporary growing area (called a nursery bed) where your biennials can grow through the summer. Prepare your nursery bed just as you would any garden area, but site it in an out-of-the-way spot. Sow the biennial seeds directly into the bed in spring or summer and thin them as needed. Dig the plants up and move them to their final garden spots in late summer or early fall; they will be ready for bloom in the following spring or summer.

Large, double types of marigold are best grown from transplants.

Planting Perennials

Planting your perennials at the right time of year is an important factor in giving them a good start. Time your planting efforts so your new perennials will start growing in a period of abundant rainfall and moderate temperatures—usually spring or fall. In cool climates, like Zone 5 and colder, concentrate your planting efforts in spring. (If you aren't sure what zone you live in, see the Plant Hardiness Zone Maps starting on page 588.) Planting in spring allows the new plants enough time to establish strong root systems before winter arrives. You can take a chance with late-summer planting for very hardy or seasonally available perennials. In warmer climates with mild winters, such as Zones 9 and 10, plant in fall so perennials will be well established before the long, hot summer. In areas where summer isn't too hot and winter isn't too cold—Zones 6 through 8—you can plant perennials in fall or spring. If your climate has periods of drought, plant whenever there is abundant natural rainfall and temperatures are between about 40° and 70°F (4.4° and 21.2°C).

Plant Spacing

Before you actually plant the perennials, set them in place to see how they look.

A newly planted garden may look a little sparse at first, but don't despair—it will fill in surprisingly fast.

If you are grouping several of the same kind of plant, mark the outside edge of the mass on the soil surface with a hoe, a trickle of limestone, or a row of pegs. Then set the plants, still in pots, inside the markers. Move them into a natural-looking arrangement—clustered unevenly rather than lined out in geometrical rows. Be certain each plant has enough space. If you crowd plants, they will grow weakly and be more susceptible to disease.

Double-check spacings with a tape measure—measuring distances by eye is not always effective. Check lines and masses of a single species of perennial to be sure the spacing is even. Leave more space between the faster growers. Let difficult-to-move plants like peonies, blue false indigo (*Baptisia australis*), and gas plant (*Dictamnus albus*) have enough elbow room to mature to their full size. You can use tighter spacings for smaller, more slow-spreading plants like coral bells (*Heuchera* spp.), since they are easy to move when the plants need more room.

As you work out the spacings, decide if you want to leave some open areas here and there within the garden to let air circulate and sun penetrate. A more open garden lets you enjoy the attractive silhouettes of plants. However, a tightly packed garden will be an ocean of color and texture—a more intense display. Stand back and study the appearance of the bed from different angles to get some idea of how the finished garden will look. Readjust as needed. When you are satisfied, start planting.

Planting

In most cases you'll set new plants in the ground at the same depth at which they are growing presently. Replanting at the

Planting a Bareroot Perennial

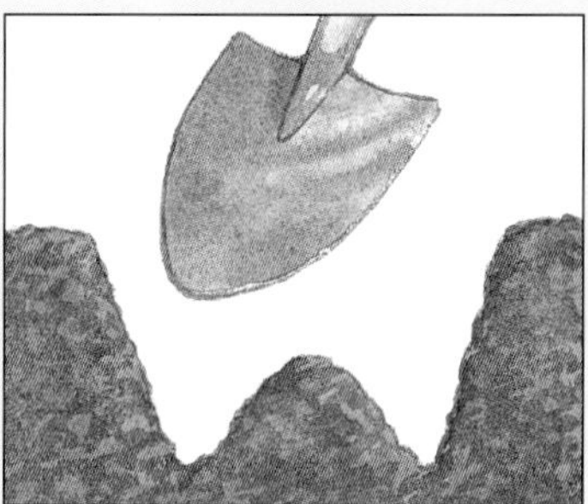

1. Dig a hole large enough to hold the roots without bending them.

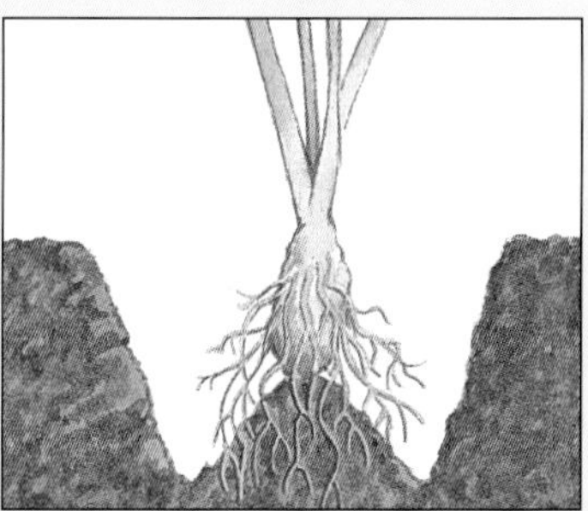

2. Set the crown in the hole. Spread the roots over the mound.

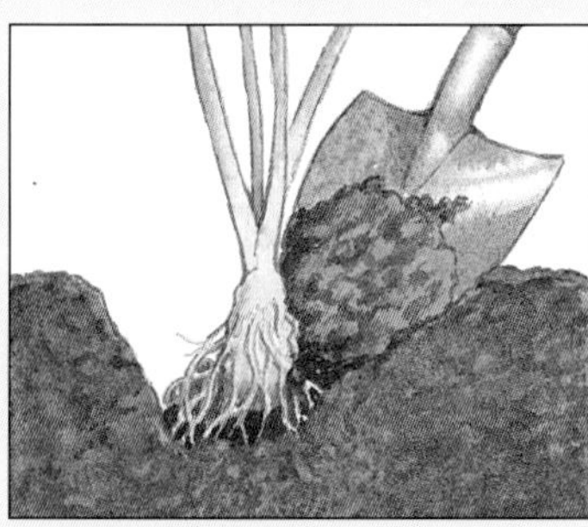

3. Backfill the hole with soil, firm gently, and water well.

same depth keeps the crown—the point from which shoots emerge—from being buried in damp soil, where it is likely to rot. However, if you have just prepared the soil, it will settle 1 to 2 inches (2.5 to 5 cm) over the coming months. In a new bed, plant the perennials slightly deeper so their roots and crowns do not stick up above the soil once it has settled. Exactly how you plant perennials depends on whether you are using container-grown, bareroot, or field-dug stock.

Container Plants If you are planting a potted perennial, you can easily see how low in the ground to plant it. Dig deeply enough so the surface of the container soil will be at the top of the hole (adjusting as necessary for new beds). Fill the hole with water to moisten the soil.

Now, get the plant ready for planting. Slip it out of the pot—most larger plants are root-bound enough to slide out quite easily. If not, you can gently squeeze the base of the plastic pot to loosen the root ball. Then break up the edges of the root ball so the roots will have more contact with the soil. Place in the hole and cover with soil to the crown.

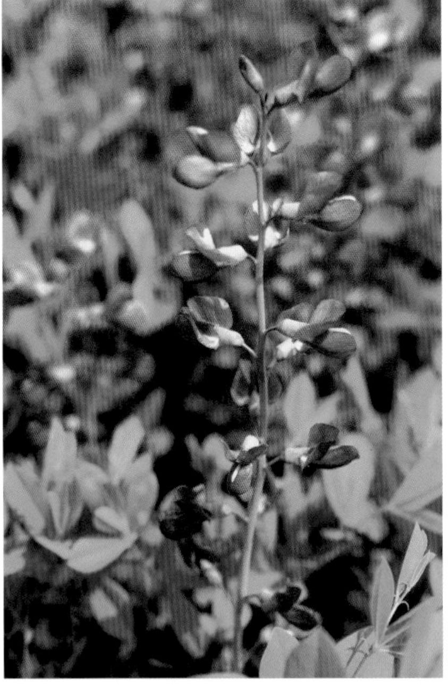
Some plants, like blue false indigo, can be tricky to move because of their deep root system.

Good soil preparation of beds and careful planting will give your plants every chance of success.

If the roots are wrapped around themselves, they may not break free and root into the soil. You will have to work them loose. You can quarter the roots of fibrous-rooted perennials like garden mums. Although the process may seem harsh, it will encourage new root growth. Make four deep slices, one on each side of the root ball, or make a single cut two-thirds up the center to divide the ball in half. Mound some soil in the center of the planting hole. Open the root quarters out from the cuts and spread them out over the mound. Cover the rest of the roots up to the crown. Don't try this technique on perennials with taproots like monkshoods (*Aconitum* spp.).

After planting, firm the soil gently around the plant, water it well, and mulch. Mulching your bed with organic materials like compost, straw, or shredded leaves will conserve moisture and reduce weed competition. (New beds are especially weed-prone, since turning the soil exposes weed seeds.) For more information on choosing and using mulches, see "Make the Most of Mulch" on page 84.

Field-dug Plants Plant your field-dug perennials that have a lot of soil still around the roots in a hole the same size as the root ball. If much of the soil has fallen off the roots, make the hole slightly larger so you can move the roots into the best position. Drench the hole with water and set in the perennial at the same depth it was growing. Work any exposed roots into the surrounding soil as you refill the hole, then firm the soil gently.

Bareroot Plants When you start with bareroot plants, you will have to take more time settling the plants into the

Best Bulbs for Naturalizing

Small bulbs tend to be the best choices for naturalizing: They bloom dependably, they're easy to plant, and they're usually relatively inexpensive. Daffodil bulbs tend to be large, but even they are often sold in bargain mixtures for naturalizing. Listed below are some of the bulbs that adapt well to naturalizing.

Allium moly (lily leek)
Anemone blanda (Grecian windflower)
Colchicum speciosum (showy autumn crocus)
Crocus spp. (crocus)
Galanthus nivalis (common snowdrops)
Hyacinthoides hispanicus (Spanish bluebells)
Leucojum aestivum (summer snowflake)
Muscari armeniacum (grape hyacinth)
Narcissus hybrids (daffodils)
Scilla sibirica (Siberian squill)

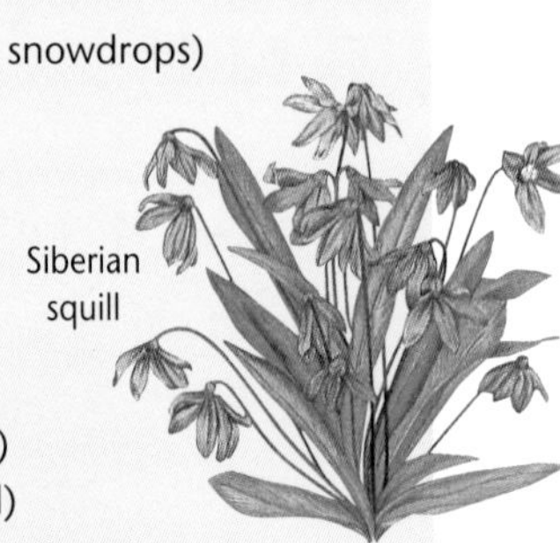
Siberian squill

ground. This process can be tricky the first few times, but be patient and don't be afraid to work with the roots. You'll soon get it right.

First, soak the roots in a bucket of lukewarm water for a few hours to prepare them for planting. If you don't have time to plant straight after obtaining your bareroot plants, keep the roots moist and store them, in their original package, in a cool location for a day or two. If you need to wait longer than that to plant, pot up the plants or set them into a nursery bed until you are ready. When you are ready to plant, identify how deeply the plants have been growing in the nursery. The aboveground portions—green foliage tufts, leaf buds, or dormant stems—usually emerge from the root system above the former soil line. Plant so these structures will stay slightly above the surface of the soil in your garden once it has settled. (Peonies are an exception, since their shoots will emerge through the soil from about 1 inch [2.5 cm] underground.)

Next, make a hole that is deep and wide enough to set the plant crown at the soil surface and stretch out the roots. Form a small mound of soil in the bottom of the hole. Set the root clump on it with the crown resting on top of the mound. Spread the roots gently in every direction and fill in around them with soil. Then firm the soil gently, water well, and apply a layer of mulch. Keep the soil evenly moist for the next few weeks.

Planting Bulbs

Planting bulbs requires some imagination on your part. After all, when you buy bulbs, you get a bunch of brown-wrapped packets of plant energy that have the potential to transform themselves into brilliantly colored crocus or daffodils. With proper planting and good care, your bulbs will be able to fulfill that potential.

To get your perennials off to a good start, plant when temperatures are moderate and rainfall abundant.

Plant drifts of polyanthus primroses with spring bulbs like daffodils, tulips, and Spanish bluebells.

When You Get Them Home

It's usually best to plant bulbs within a few days of buying them, so they'll have plenty of time to adapt to their new home and send out a good crop of roots. If you can't plant right away, store your bulbs in a cool, dark, and relatively dry place until you're ready for them.

Planting in Beds and Borders

Once you've prepared the soil, planting is easy—just dig the hole to the proper depth, pop in the bulb, and cover it with soil. The proper hole depth will vary, depending on what bulbs you're growing. A general rule of thumb is that the base of a bulb or corm should be planted 3 to 4 times as deep as the height of the bulb. For example, a crocus corm that measures 1 inch (2.5 cm) high should be planted 3 to 4 inches (7.5 to 10 cm) deep; a 2-inch (5-cm) high tulip bulb needs a hole 6 to 8 inches (15 to 20 cm) deep. If your soil is on the sandy side, plant a bit deeper. To find out the best planting depth for your bulbs, check the catalog description or packet label or refer to the individual entries in "Encyclopedia of Flowers," starting on page 306.

Set the bulb in the hole with the pointed growth bud facing upward. If you can't tell which side should be up—and it's often difficult with small bulbs such as Grecian windflowers (*Anemone blanda*)—set the bulb on its side or just drop it into the hole and hope for the

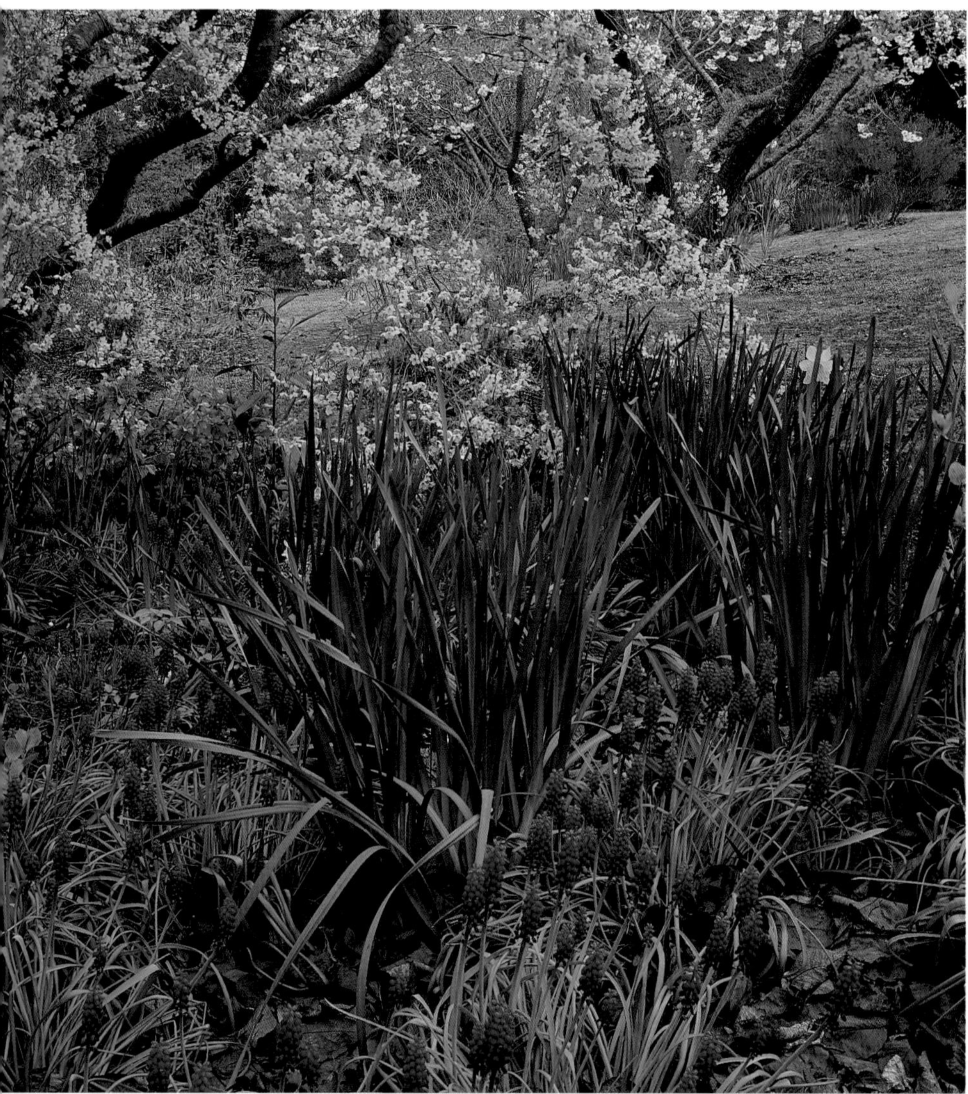

Naturalize grape hyacinths and daffodils under a spring-flowering tree. To plant bulbs in grass, especially large bulbs like daffodils, use a hand-held bulb planter or trowel to make individual holes.

best. Most bulbs have a strong will to grow, and they'll find a way to send up their shoots.

Space the bulbs so each one has ample room to grow. As a general rule when planting in beds and borders, you should leave 5 to 6 inches (12.5 to 15 cm) between large bulbs and 1 to 3 inches (2.5 to 7.5 cm) between small bulbs. Once you've got the spacing the way you want it, carefully replace the soil around the bulbs to refill the hole. Firm the soil by patting it with your hand or the back of a rake, then water the area well.

Planting in Grassy Areas

When you "naturalize" bulbs in a lawn or meadow, you don't have the luxury of preparing a nice, loose planting area all at once. Fortunately, the bulbs that grow well in these situations are pretty tough.

The easiest bulbs to plant are the small ones, such as crocus, Siberian squill (*Scilla sibirica*), and grape hyacinth (*Muscari armeniacum*). Simply get down on your hands and knees with a narrow trowel, dandelion digger, or garden knife. Insert the tool into the soil to lift up a flap of turf, or wiggle the tool back and forth to make a small hole. Insert the bulb, firm the soil and sod over it, and water in well.

For larger bulbs, it's often easier to use a shovel or spade to remove a larger patch of turf, about 1 foot (30 cm) square. Loosen the soil to the proper depth, plant the bulbs, replace the turf, and water. You can also buy special bulb planting tools to make individual holes for your large bulbs. Hand-held planters look like deep cookie cutters and work pretty much the same way. They are fairly inexpensive but can be very tiring to use. A similar type of planter that's mounted on a handle is a little easier to use, since you can push the cutting edge into the ground with your foot instead of your hand.

For easier planting, try an auger attachment that connects to a regular hand-held power drill. These tools can be hard to use around rocks and tree roots, but they will allow you to make many holes quickly and easily under most conditions.

Hand-held bulb planting tools

Special Care

Different bulbs have adapted to survive in very different conditions. Although most bulbs flower at spring time, that is not the case for all bulbs. So the time of year that you plant your bulbs is crucial if you want them to perform to their best.

When planting in masses, it's usually easiest to dig a large planting area that can hold many bulbs.

Spring Bulbs It's easy to add spring bulbs to your garden, but it does take a little advance planning. Mail-order catalogs of spring bulbs often arrive in spring to early summer, so you can decide what your garden needs and place your order for delivery in fall. Late summer and fall are also the times you'll find spring bulbs for sale at local garden centers. In Northern gardens, early to midfall is the best time to plant; in Southern areas, the planting season continues through early winter.

Spring Bulbs and Winter Chilling

Winter chilling is an important step in the life of most spring-blooming bulbs. If you live in a warm climate, where winter temperatures generally stay above freezing, you may find that some spring bulbs bloom poorly or don't bloom at all in the years after planting. Hybrid tulips commonly have this problem; some daffodils and crocus (below) also grow poorly without a chilling period.

To have a great show of blooms each year, look for species and cultivars that don't need much chilling. (Ask your neighbors, local garden center, or Cooperative Extension Service to recommend the bulbs that grow best in your area.) You can also look for "precooled" bulbs, or give new bulbs an artificial cold period by storing them in the vegetable drawer of your refrigerator for 6 to 8 weeks before planting them in early to midwinter.

Water spring bulbs just after planting and again as needed if the soil dries out in winter or spring. Scatter compost or balanced organic fertilizer over the soil when the new shoots appear in spring to provide a nutrient boost for healthy growth and good flower bud formation for next year.

Most spring bulbs thrive in full or partial sun (that is, at least 6 hours of sun a day). They are ideal for planting under deciduous trees, since the bulbs can bloom and their foliage ripen before the tree leaves expand fully and block the sunlight. Unless you're planning to plant new, replacement bulbs each year (as may be necessary with hybrid tulips), always allow the bulb leaves to wither away naturally after flowering. They may look unsightly, but if you cut off, pull off, or bundle the leaves together, the bulb won't store the energy it needs and it may bloom poorly or even die by the next year.

For a great show of hybrid tulips each year, pull them out after bloom and plant new tulips in fall.

Summer Bulbs Some summer bulbs—including lilies and ornamental onions (*Allium* spp.)—can live from year to year, so you'll plant them once and enjoy their blooms for years to come. These "hardy" bulbs are usually planted in fall for bloom the following summer, although lilies can also adapt to early-spring planting. The key is to plant them early enough so the root system can get established before warm weather promotes lush top growth.

Other summer bloomers are classified as "tender" bulbs. These cold-sensitive beauties may not be able to survive the winter in your area. Unless you live in a warm climate (roughly Zone 8 and south), you'll need to plant gladioli, cannas, dahlias, and other tender bulbs in spring to early summer and dig them up in the fall for winter storage indoors.

Fall Bulbs The trick with fall-flowering bulbs is remembering to plant them at the right time of year. Magic lilies and naked ladies are best planted in early summer, when the bulbs are dormant. Late summer or early fall, just before their bloom starts, is the best time for most other fall-flowering bulbs.

Like other bulbs, fall bloomers need to ripen their leaves fully to store enough food for good flowering. So live with their leaves until they wither away—don't cut or pull them off before they turn yellow. If you "naturalize" fall bulbs in grassy areas, you'll also need to remember to stop mowing as soon as you see the first flower buds emerging from the soil in late summer to early fall.

Growing Annuals

With just a few packets of seeds, you can grow enough plants to fill an entire garden with annual color.

Growing your own annual plants from seed is great fun—and easier than you might think. A single packet of seeds can produce dozens, or even hundreds, of plants for a fraction of the cost of buying transplants. Starting from seed also gives you a much greater variety of plants to choose from, since most retail sources only grow a few cultivars of the most popular annuals. Some annuals grow best when started indoors; others are tough enough to be planted right in the garden where you want them to grow.

Sowing Seed Indoors

Starting seed indoors takes some time and space, but it also gives the best results for many annuals. Tender annuals, such as globe amaranth (*Gomphrena globosa*) and impatiens, need the warm conditions to get a good start in life and can then begin blooming soon after you set them out in late spring. Other annuals—including dwarf morning glory (*Convolvulus tricolor*) and strawflowers (*Bracteantha bracteata*)—grow equally well when sown indoors or out, but they'll begin blooming earlier if you start them indoors. This time saving is important in Northern gardens and especially at high elevations, where growing seasons are short.

When you're not sure if you should start a particular plant from indoor-sown seed, check the seed catalog description or seed packet. You'll also find specific growing tips in the individual entries in "Encyclopedia of Flowers," starting on page 306. When you're ready to sow, follow these guidelines.

Choosing a Container

While suitable containers come in a wide variety of shapes and sizes, they generally fall into one of two types: open trays that can hold many seedlings or pots that hold just a few seedlings each. Both types work fine, but if you're sowing small quantities of several different annual seeds, you may find it easier to keep track of them in individual pots. Buy commercially made

Zinnias are adaptable annuals that can be grown successfully from seed started indoors or outdoors.

pots or trays (often called flats), or recycle milk cartons and margarine tubs. Just about any container will work, as long as it has drainage holes in the bottom.

For extra-easy transplanting, try preformed peat pots (available from most garden centers). At transplanting time, you can set the whole plant—pot and all—in the ground. The pot walls will break down, allowing the roots to spread out with no transplant shock. Peat pots are especially useful for starting seeds that are notoriously difficult to transplant, such as morning glories (*Ipomoea* spp.) and rocket larkspur (*Consolida ambigua*).

Picking a Growing Mix

For best results, buy a bag of commercial growing mix. Some gardeners select standard potting soil; others prefer mixes created specifically for seed starting. These mixes contain a balanced mixture of disease- and weed-free materials that will hold a good supply of moisture while letting excess water drain freely.

Choosing a Spot

For good growth, your seedlings will need the right temperatures and adequate light. Most annuals will sprout and grow well at average indoor temperatures (between 60° and 75°F [16° and 24°C]), so warmth usually isn't a problem. Finding a spot with enough light can be tricky, though. If your house is blessed with a sunroom or deep, sunny window sills, you can get good results growing seedlings there without providing extra light. Otherwise, you'll need to set up a simple light system to keep your seedlings happy and healthy. Garden centers as well as garden-supply catalogs sell lights in a variety of sizes and prices. Four-foot (1.2-m) fluorescent shop lights sold in home centers also provide excellent results, and they're generally much less expensive than grow lights.

Figuring Out Your Last Frost Date

When you're looking for guidelines on when to sow or plant annuals, you'll often find advice like "sow indoors 4 to 6 weeks before your last frost date" or "set plants out after the danger of frost has passed." That's fine, you may say, but how do I know when the last frost will be?

The answer is that you don't know exactly when your last spring frost will occur in a given year. But you can find out the average date of the last frost in your area by asking gardening friends or neighbors or calling your local Cooperative Extension Service office.

Remember that the last frost date is a guideline, not a guarantee. In any given year, frosts could end a week or two earlier than expected or—more important—sneak in a week or two later. Pay careful attention to weather forecasts around this time, and be prepared to protect tender plants if late frosts are predicted.

Knowing When to Sow

You can sow most seeds indoors in early spring, about 6 to 10 weeks before your last frost date, although some need to be started earlier or later. To find out the best timing for your particular seeds, check the seed packet or the individual entries in "Encyclopedia of Flowers," starting on page 306.

Getting Started

When you're ready to sow (or, even better, the night before), dump your seed-starting mix in a large bucket or tub and add some warm water to moisten it. Start

Annuals such as celosia are difficult to transplant, so it's best to plant the seed straight in the ground.

Seedlings need plenty of light for compact, bushy growth. Near a window is a good spot.

with a few cups of water and work the mix with your hands to help it absorb the moisture. Keep adding several cups of water at a time and working it into the mix until the mix feels evenly moist but not soggy. (If you squeeze a handful of mix and water runs out, it's too wet; add some more dry mix to get the balance right.)

Once the mix is moist, you can fill your chosen containers. Scoop the mix into each container and level it out to about ¼ inch (6 mm) below the upper edge of the container. Don't pack down the mix; just tap the filled container once or twice on your work surface to settle the mix and eliminate air pockets.

Flowering tobacco has very fine seeds. Don't cover the seeds, just press them into the mix.

Step-by-Step Guide to Planting Seeds

1. Sow the seed evenly over the moistened growing medium.

2. Press the seed lightly into the surface of the medium with a wooden block.

3. Cover the seed according to the packet directions; firm the mix lightly.

4. Carefully moisten the top of the growing medium with a fine mist of water.

5. Label the container so you'll remember what you planted.

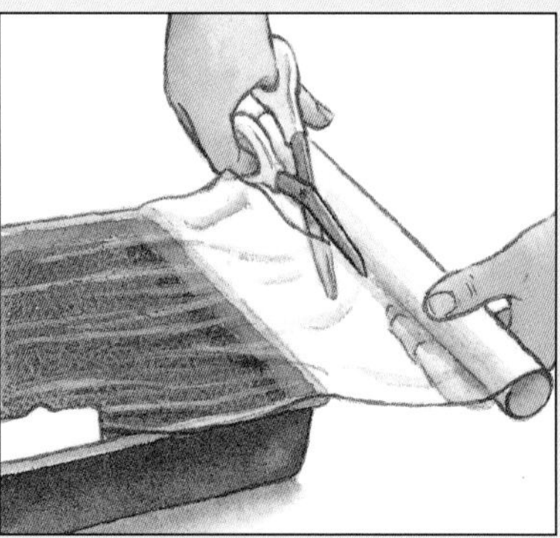

6. Cover with clear plastic until the seed begins to germinate.

Sowing the Seed

When you're sowing large seeds, such as four o'clocks (*Mirabilis jalapa*), use a pencil to make individual holes ½ to 1 inch (12 to 25 mm) apart. For small seeds, use a pencil to make shallow rows and sow as evenly as possible into the rows. Fine seeds, such as those of petunias and begonias, can be hard to sow directly from the packet. To distribute tiny seeds more evenly, mix them with a spoonful of dry sand and scatter the mixture over the surface of the mix with a saltshaker.

If the seeds need to be buried in order to germinate (this will be indicated on the seed packet or in the individual entries in "Encyclopedia of Flowers," starting on page 306), sprinkle the needed amount of dry mix over the seed. Fine seeds are usually not covered; just press them lightly into the surface of the mix with your fingers or the back of a spoon. Mist the surface lightly to moisten it.

Set the containers in a well-lit spot where you can check them daily. Covering them with glass, plastic lids, plastic bags, or plastic food wrap will help to keep the potting mix moist with condensation and reduce or eliminate the need to water. (This is especially important for small, surface-sown seeds, since they can dry out quickly.) Most seeds sprout in 1 to 3 weeks. Remove the glass or plastic covering as soon as you see seedlings appear.

Growing Healthy Seedlings

Once your seedlings have sprouted, move them to full light (if they're not there already). Place them on a sunny windowsill or under the lights you've set up. Hang the lights so they're about 4 inches (10 cm) above the seedlings. Keep the lights on 14 to 16 hours a day. An inexpensive timer can turn the lights on and off for you automatically.

Seedling pots tend to dry out quickly indoors. Water them every few days to keep the soil evenly moist. If possible, water them from the bottom by adding about ½ inch (12 mm) of water to the tray the pots are sitting in. (Do not let the pots sit in water continuously.) Watering carefully from the top is also an option.

If your seedlings start to get crowded after the two sets of true leaves have appeared, transplant them to a larger container or to individual pots.

Saving Seeds

Collecting and saving seed is a fun and easy way to preserve some of your favorite annuals and perennials (and save a bit of money, too!). You'll get the best results if you stick with seeds of nonhybrid plants. These seeds are likely to produce plants that resemble their parents. Seeds from hybrid plants—those specially bred or selected for special traits, such as color or flower form—often produce seedlings that look quite different. (You can usually tell if a plant is a hybrid by the name or the description on the seed packet or plant tag: Look for the word "hybrid" or the symbol "F1.")

Seeds of spring-blooming annuals, biennials, and perennials usually are ready by midsummer; later-blooming annuals can mature their seeds through the first few frosts. On a dry day, gather seeds from seedpods that are dry and brittle but not yet open. Plants from the daisy family, such as marigolds (*Tagetes* hybrids), produce their seeds directly at the stem tips; simply pull or brush these off the seed head into your hand. Store harvested seed in paper envelopes in a cool, dry, mouse-proof place over the winter, until you're ready to start them in spring; then sow them as you would purchased seed.

When your seedlings have produced two sets of true leaves—the ones that appear after the first "seed" leaves—they are ready to be transplanted to individual pots or cell packs. Fill the pots with moistened potting mix. Use a knife blade or the pointed end of a plant label to dig small clumps of seedlings out of the tray. Gently separate the seedlings, holding them by their leaves (not their fragile stems or roots). Make a depression in the new pot, lower the seedling roots into the hole, and carefully fill around the roots with the potting mix.

Set planted pots in a shallow tray of water until the soil surface looks moist. Then place the pots in a spot where they are shaded from full sun and keep them cool for a day or two before moving them back to the windowsill or their position under lights. Keep the soil evenly moist. Periodically apply a dose of liquid fertilizer (such as fish emulsion), following the manufacturer's directions for seedlings.

If you don't have the time or enough space to raise seedlings indoors, you can always try the wide variety of annuals that grow from seed planted in the garden. For more information, see "Sowing Seed in the Garden" on page 57.

A few types of zonal geranium will grow from seed sown indoors, but this is one of the few annuals that is usually propagated from cuttings.

Propagating Perennials

You can propagate perennials by a number of methods. Depending on which method you choose, you might end up with a few or a few hundred new perennials from a single plant. You will create several good-sized new plants from one large specimen by division. By taking stem or root cuttings, you can get dozens of new plants. Or start perennials from seed and you may end up with hundreds of plants from a single packet.

When you're considering a method, decide how important it is that the offspring resemble the parent plant. With vegetative methods of propagation, such as division, layering, and cuttings, you will obtain an exact clone of the parent plant in nearly every case. This is especially important when you want to propagate cultivars or hybrids, which usually produce variable offspring when grown from seed.

Open-pollinated plants are likely to vary from their parent plant, which was pollinated by bees.

Seed is a good way to propagate perennials when you want species or varieties. There are also a few cultivars that come true from seed. Use seed-grown plants in informal gardens where differences in height, foliage and flower color, and bloom time don't matter or can even be considered an advantage. When uniformity matters in a formal garden, a row, or an edging, use vegetatively propagated plants to get the best results.

Delphiniums can be propagated by a variety of methods—by cuttings, seeds, or division.

When you are looking for perennial seed, you will find two types: open-pollinated and hybrid seed. There are natural hybrids, such as the Lenten rose (*Helleborus* x *orientalis*), and there are commercial hybrids, the result of controlled breeding. Hybrids tend to be more uniform than open-pollinated plants, but they are not always as consistent as vegetatively propagated plants. If you buy the seed of a hybrid and want more of that plant, you must buy more seed from the company or propagate the originals vegetatively. It will not come true from seed that you collect from your own plants.

If you want a mass of English primroses, they are easy to grow from seed sown in the garden.

Another important issue in choosing a propagation method is how long each method takes to produce flowering plants. Perennial seedlings and (to a lesser extent) cuttings will take a season or more—sometimes several years—to reach flowering size. Even when they do flower, the display may be sparse until the plants reach a substantial size. If you want quick results, use the division method or choose fast-growing perennials that may flower during their first year of life if you start them early indoors. Divisions generally recover quickly and often bloom the same season they're planted. For fast-maturing cuttings, try asters and garden mums (*Chrysanthemum* x *morifolium*). Perennials that bloom from seed the first year after a winter sowing include 'Snow Lady' shasta daisy (*Leucanthemum* x *superbum* 'Snow Lady'), columbines, delphiniums, and purple coneflowers (*Echinacea purpurea*).

Perennials from Seed

Seed is an excellent method to use when propagating certain perennials. It's a great way to stretch a tight budget if you don't mind waiting for a show. Growing your own seedlings allows you to select unusual species and choice varieties that you can't usually buy at greenhouses and nurseries. However, if you buy seed of a cultivar, such as 'Goldsturm' coneflower (*Rudbeckia fulgida* 'Goldsturm'), the seedlings will be variable and may not all live up to the high performance values of vegetatively propagated stock.

Always use high-quality seed, packed for the current year. Buy from a reputable seed company that offers high germination rates. You can find out the rates from the percentage of viable (live) seeds listed on the package. If you have any seed left over from last year or any home-collected seed, try sprouting a few before you sow a whole packet. Roll the seeds in a moist paper towel and enclose the rolled towel in a plastic bag. Keep the bag warm and watch for germination in the next several weeks. If only half of the seeds sprout, you will know you need to sow twice as much seed to get the number of plants you want.

Sowing Seed

Just as wild and self-sowing perennials do naturally, you can sow seed directly outdoors in a well-prepared bed. Cover the seed to the depth indicated on the package in loose soil and keep the soil moist until the seedlings begin to emerge.

Although direct sowing is certainly the easiest technique, you will probably realize that it is not the most dependable. When planted directly into your garden, your seed can be eaten by birds or insects or attacked by fungi. It may get too cold or too hot, too wet or too dry. For a better survival rate and an earlier start than direct seeding offers you, start seedlings indoors under fluorescent lights or in a sunny, south-facing window.

Depending on the size of the seed and the speed of growth, with seed that is easy to germinate, you should start it indoors 6 to 12 weeks before the last spring frost. In warm climates, start fast-germinating seed in summer to set out in the cool of fall and winter.

Other perennials will take much longer to germinate. You may need to expose the seed to a chilling period by placing the sown seed in the refrigerator for a certain number of weeks. If a perennial needs special treatment, it will be indicated

A glassed-in verandah on the sunny side of the house is a good propagating spot for the colder months.

Potting-up Seedlings

1. Put some moist potting mix in the base of the new pot.

2. Squeeze the container gently to loosen the roots.

3. Carefully slide the plant from the container with its roots intact.

4. Center the plant in the new pot and fill in with moist potting mix.

The flexible stems of bellflowers make this plant well suited to being propagated by layering.

on the seed packet or in "Encyclopedia of Flowers," starting on page 306.

Sow your perennial seed in a sterile, peat-based seedling mix that has been thoroughly moistened. This lightweight medium encourages rooting while discouraging root diseases. Start seed in small individual pots or peat pots, or save space by sowing seed in rows in flats (shallow plastic or wooden trays). Sprinkle tiny seeds lightly on top of the seedling mix and press them gently into the surface. Push larger seeds down into the soil as deep as they are wide. Cover the container with clear plastic wrap to keep the soil evenly moist until the seeds germinate, but make sure the plastic doesn't touch the soil.

After sowing, keep the medium moist and between 60° and 75°F (15.5° and 30°C). Warmth-loving perennials will come up most quickly at the higher end of the temperature range while cool-season perennials may germinate faster at the lower end. Avoid rapid temperature changes, which can stunt growth.

Caring for Seedlings

When your seedlings emerge, move them into bright light and remove the plastic. Water as often as necessary to keep the soil moist and to prevent wilting. When you water, set the container of seedlings in a tray of water so the growing medium can soak up moisture without disrupting the seedlings. If you water from overhead, you may wash the seedlings away.

If you have sown seed in flats or trays, move seedlings to their own pots when they have two sets of true leaves in addition to the bottom set of fleshy seed leaves. You can move most perennials into 4-inch (10-cm) pots if you intend to plant them outdoors in a couple of weeks. If not, you should keep moving the plants up to larger containers to prevent roots from binding. This process is known as potting up. Feed the young plants lightly with compost tea or liquid seaweed. If the weather is cold or hot, leave the transplants indoors under lights or on the windowsill. If it is relatively mild, move the plants out into a cold frame or another sheltered area for hardening off before transplanting them into your garden beds. For more details on this, see "Handling Hardening Off" on page 57.

Layering

Some plants are easy to root while still attached to the mother plant, a technique called layering. Burying a section of the stem encourages roots to form at each buried leaf node (the place where a leaf joins the stem). Layering does take up some space, since you need to bury the attached stem close to the parent plant. You won't get many new plants from this method (usually only one per stem), and it can take weeks or months for the stem to root. But layering is easy to do and the resulting plants will be exact duplicates of the parent plant.

You can use this technique with plants that have flexible stems or a creeping habit and the ability to root at the leaf axils. Good candidates for layering include pinks (*Dianthus* spp.), cranesbills (*Geranium* spp.), wall rock cress (*Arabis caucasica*), snow-in-summer (*Cerastium tomentosum*), and bellflowers (*Campanula* spp.). Layering will not work on daylilies, ornamental grasses, hostas, irises, peonies, or other bushy perennials.

Simple Layering

Layering is a quick and easy way to propagate many types of perennial, especially those that naturally tend to creep along the soil. Spring is a good time to start a layer, although it can work any time during the growing season.

1. Select a flexible stem and bend it down to the soil.

2. Use a wire pin to secure the stem, then cover it with soil.

3. Dig up the rooted layer and transplant it to another spot.

How It Works

The first step to successful layering is finding a suitable stem. If the plant is upright, look for one or several long stems that bend easily to the ground; if the plant has a creeping habit, any stem is suitable. Leave the top three sets of leaves on the stem to nourish the plant, but remove the leaves from the stem for 2 to 7 inches (5 to 17.5 cm) below the top greenery. Strip the leaves from at least two nodes (leaf joints), carefully leaving the dormant buds undamaged. Bend the stem down and see where the stripped area will contact the soil. Loosen the soil in that area to about 4 inches (10 cm) deep and water it. Bury the stem in the loosened soil, holding it in place with a bent wire pin, and firm the soil over the stem. The stem should be buried 2 to 3 inches (5 to 7.5 cm) deep with the leafy tip still exposed. If you are layering an upright shoot, encourage the tip to return to its upright position by tying it to a stake pushed into the soil if necessary.

Keep the area moist and mulched while the buried stem roots. Depending on the temperature and species, it will take several weeks to several months. The easiest way to layer is to leave the plant in place until the following season. If you want faster results, check its progress by gently uncovering the stem and looking for roots or tugging lightly to see if the shoot has become more secure in the ground. Once the roots reach about 1 inch (2.5 cm) long you can cut the shoot free from the mother plant. Wait several weeks for more rooting, then dig up and transplant the new plant.

Division is the quick way to propagate perennials, and is especially suited to fibrous-rooted plants.

Reproduction by Division

Many perennials flower best when they're young, and their flower production drops as they mature. To keep them flowering well, you must divide them—dig them up and split the root mass into pieces. In addition to reviving older plants, division is the easiest and fastest technique for propagating perennials. It's also a good way to keep fast-spreading perennials under control, and you'll have lots of extra plants to share with friends and neighbors.

How often you need to propagate depends on why you're dividing. If you're using division to propagate, it depends on how many new plants you want and how fast the plant is growing. Divide annually to retard aggressive spreaders like bee balm (*Monarda didyma*), bigroot geranium (*Geranium macrorrhizum*), obedient plant (*Physostegia virginiana*), and yarrows. If you want to rejuvenate your perennials, you can divide them whenever flowering starts to decline. To keep performance high, you can divide asters and painted daisies (*Chrysanthemum coccineum*) every year or two. Some perennials, including peonies, daylilies, and astilbes, can go for years without division.

How to Divide

Begin dividing by digging up the root system. Shake off as much loose soil as possible and remove any dead leaves and stems. You may also want to wash most of the soil off the roots and crown so you can see the roots and buds clearly.

Perennials with fibrous roots, such as asters and garden mums (*Chrysanthemum* x *morifolium*), are the easiest to dig and divide. You can pull them apart with your hands or cut them with a spade. Others, like daylilies and astilbes, can grow woody with age. You may have to pry these roots apart with a crowbar or two garden forks

Step-by-step Division

Division is a fast and reliable way to propagate many clump-forming perennials, including daylilies and garden mums. It may not work well with more sensitive perennials, like sea hollies (*Eryngium* spp.) and gas plant (*Dictamnus albus*).

1. Use shears or your hands to divide the perennial clump into several smaller pieces.

2. Make sure each new piece has its own roots and some top growth.

3. Replant the pieces immediately, water them well, and apply a light layer of mulch.

Taking Stem Cuttings

1. Select a strong, young shoot. Use sharp pruning shears to make a clean cut just below a node.

2. Snip the leaves off the bottom half of the cutting, leaving 2 to 3 sets of leaves, with 2 to 3 leaf nodes exposed at the base.

3. Insert the bottom half of the prepared cutting into a container of moist, lightweight potting mix.

4. Cover with an upended jar or with plastic to hold in the moisture. Set in a bright place out of direct sun.

held back to back or cut them with a saw or ax. Discard the woody parts, which will not reroot well.

To renew an existing planting, slice the plant into halves, thirds, or quarters. Discard the old, woody growth from the center of the clump and replant the vigorous outer portions.

When you want to build a larger stock of new plants, you can divide perennials into smaller pieces. Just make sure you keep several buds or growing shoots on the sections you will replant. Look for the buds growing along the length of the roots or clustered together in a central crown.

Work compost and other soil amendments back into the soil before replanting. Reset divisions at the same level at which the original clump was growing.

Cuttings

Cuttings—small pieces of stem or root—are another way to propagate many perennials. Cuttings take more care than other methods, like layering and division. But if you like a challenge, you can use cuttings to create many new plants from your existing perennials. Cuttings are a good way to propagate perennials that are difficult to divide and cultivars that don't come true from seed.

Stem Cuttings

Stem cuttings are effective for propagating many kinds of perennials. Try perennials such as wall rock cress (*Arabis caucasica*), garden mums, common sneezeweed (*Helenium autumnale*), garden phlox (*Phlox paniculata*), pinks (*Dianthus* spp.), showy stonecrop (*Sedum spectabile*), and spike speedwell (*Veronica spicata*).

Taking Cuttings You should take stem cuttings when perennials are in vegetative growth, either in spring before blooming or after flowering is finished for the season. You should select a healthy medium-soft stem—one that is not soft, new growth or hard, old growth—from the lower portion of the plant, where shoots are more likely to root quickly. Cut the selected stems free with a sharp, clean knife or pair of shears.

Preparing the Cuttings Slice the stem into sections between 2 and 4 inches (5 to 10 cm) long, so that each cutting has two or three sets of leaves on the top and a couple of nodes (leaf joints) stripped of leaves on the bottom. These nodes will produce roots when you insert them into a pot of moist, sterile, peat-based growing mix.

Some stem cuttings, like those from blue false indigo (*Baptisia australis*), will root more easily if you dip their lower ends in a commercially available rooting hormone powder. However, if you find the right moisture, light, and warmth levels, most perennials will root without

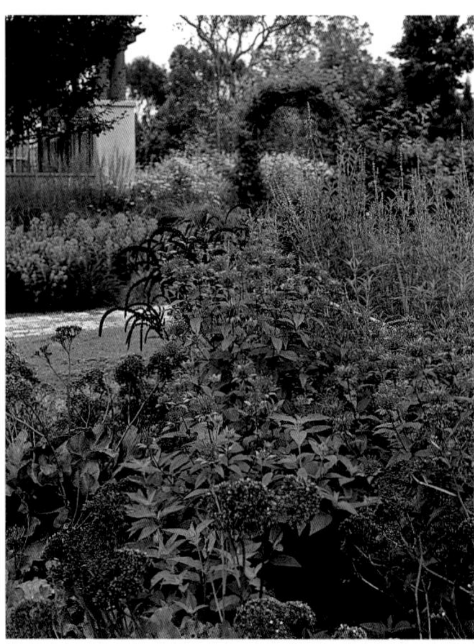
A good way to stop bee balm spreading and to produce new, healthy plants is to divide annually.

Root cuttings require a little extra care, but for delicate Japanese anemones, it will be worthwhile.

this treatment. Make a hole in the mix with a clean pencil and slide the cutting in. Firm the mix around it and water to settle the cutting into the soil.

Caring for Cuttings Cover the container with a clear plastic-wrap tent. Prop the plastic above the plant foliage to avoid rot. Keep the cuttings in a warm place and in indirect light until they root, which takes about 2 to 4 weeks. When they begin to grow, remove the plastic and move the plants into brighter light.

To determine if the cuttings have rooted, look to see if roots are emerging from the pot's drainage hole. You can also tug gently on the stem—if you meet resistance, the cuttings have rooted. Transplant the rooted cuttings into larger containers or a nursery bed to grow them to garden size.

Root Cuttings

Less common than stem cuttings, root cuttings are another way to produce new plants that are usually identical to the parent plant. Root cuttings are suitable for several kinds of perennials, including Siberian bugloss (*Anchusa azurea*), oriental poppies (*Papaver orientale*), Japanese anemones (*Anemone* x *hybrida*), and garden phlox (*Phlox paniculata*).

Take root cuttings from fall to early spring, while the parent plant is dormant. Carefully lift the plant from the garden and wash the soil from the roots. Using a sharp, clean knife, cut off a few pencil-thick roots near the crown. Cut each root into 2- to 4-inch (5- to 10-cm) pieces; make a straight cut at the top (the end closest to the crown) and a slanted cut at the bottom. Insert the cuttings into a pot filled with moist, sterile potting mix so the flat top of each cutting is level with or slightly below the surface. Place in a cold frame until they root and then pot them individually. Once the plants reach the desired size, move them into the garden.

Taking Root Cuttings

Root cuttings are a bit trickier to take than stem cuttings, but they can work just as well with a little care. As you collect the roots, place them in a plastic bag to protect them from drying winds. Use a clean, sharp knife to minimize damage to the root tissue as you prepare the cuttings, and make a note of which end of the root was closest to the crown so you don't plant the root cuttings upside down. Don't overwater.

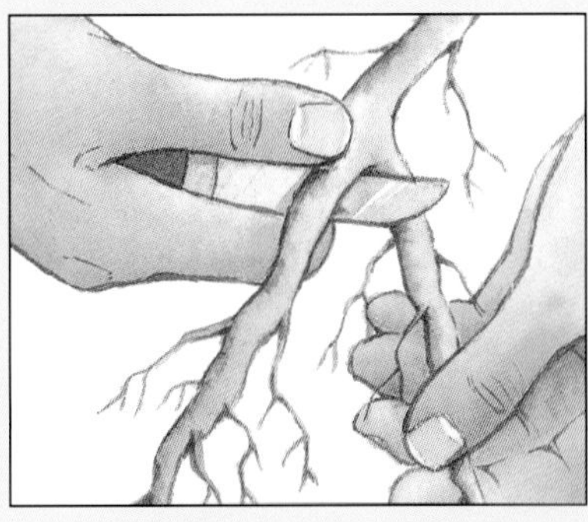

1. Cut a healthy, pencil-thick root piece.

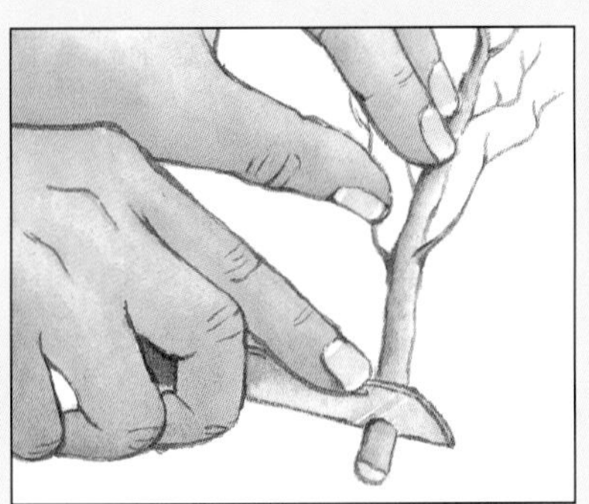

2. Make a straight cut at the end that was closest to the crown.

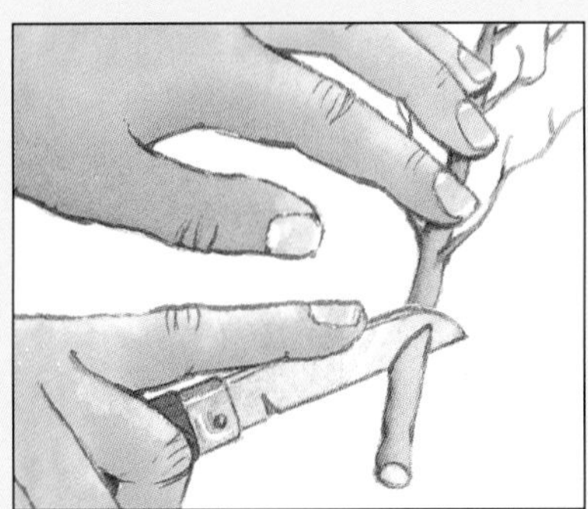

3. Make a sloping cut at the other end of the cutting.

4. Carefully insert cuttings, pointed end down, in a pot of potting mix.

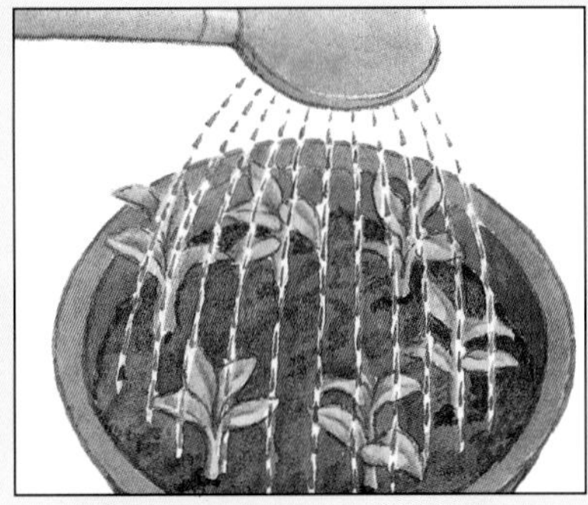

5. Keep cuttings evenly moist until they start to grow, then transplant.

Bulb Multiplication

You can increase your bulb plantings by using division or seeds to propagate the bulbs you already have. It takes a little longer to get flowers, but you can't beat the price!

Multiplication by Division

Division is the fastest and easiest way to propagate nearly all bulbs, corms, tubers, tuberous roots, and rhizomes. Besides being quite simple to do, division has another advantage: All the new plants that you create will be identical to the parent bulb, so you can easily increase your favorite colors and flower forms.

Bulbs and Corms

Some bulbs, such as tulips and daffodils, form small "bulblets" near their base. Gladioli and other corms produce similar offsets called "cormlets." With good care, both bulblets and cormlets can grow to full flowering size in a year or two.

To divide spring bulbs, lift the clump with a spade or digging fork after the foliage has died back in late spring. To divide gladiolus corms, lift them in late summer or fall, as the foliage turns yellow. Separate the bulblets or cormlets by gently pulling them away from the mother bulb or corm. Plant the bulblets or cormlets in a nursery bed or corner of the vegetable garden, where they can grow undisturbed for a few years. Water and fertilize them regularly. When the bulbs reach flowering size, move them to their final spot in the garden.

After the first year, tulip bulbs tend to divide into several smaller bulbs, which will not flower as well. Separate and replant them.

Tubers and Tuberous Roots

Division is also an effective way to increase tuberous-rooted plants, such as dahlias and tuberous begonias. The best time to divide is in spring, just after you bring these tender plants out of winter storage. Use a sharp knife to cut begonia tubers into two or three pieces, each with at least one growth bud. On dahlias, cut tuberous roots apart at the stem end, so each root has at least one bud.

Plant each new piece in a pot and set it under grow

Growing Lilies from Bulblets

1. Remove bulblets that form below the ground along the stem.

2. Grow them in pots for a year or two before planting them out.

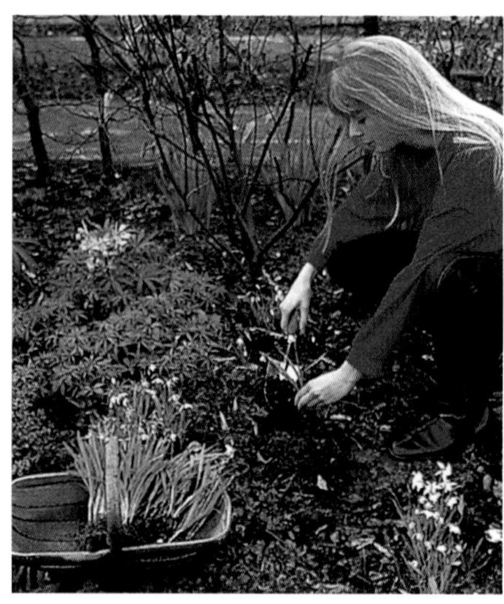

Unlike most bulbs, snowdrops can be divided while still in bloom in late winter and spring.

lights or in a greenhouse. Keep the temperature between 65° and 75°F (18° and 24°C). Water as needed so the potting soil stays evenly moist but not wet. (Don't fertilize newly cut bulbs—wait until they're growing in soil.) In a few weeks, you should have healthy new plants that are ready for transplanting into outdoor gardens and containers.

Rhizomes

Cannas and bearded irises are two common examples of plants that grow from rhizomes. Use a sharp knife, a spade (if the clump is really big), or your hands to pull or cut apart the rhizomes. Discard any old, woody pieces from the center of the original clump.

Divide canna clumps into pieces about 6 inches (15 cm) square, making sure that each has at least one growth bud. The best time to divide cannas is in spring, right before you plant them in pots or outdoors in the garden. Bearded irises, on the other hand, prefer to be divided just after they flower. Separate them into pieces with at least one "fan" of leaves on each. Trim the foliage back by at least half, and replant the irises into soil that you've enriched with compost, leaf mold, or well-rotted manure.

If you want lots of one kind of bulb, grow them from seed, but you'll wait a few years for flowers.

Growing Bulbs from Seed

You can also grow your bulbs from seed if you're really patient—you'll wait a few years for flowers. When they bloom, the seedlings may not look like the parent plant, which can be fun if you like surprises but disappointing if you want the exact color of the original.

Special Tips for Lily-lovers

Lilies, like other bulbs, produce bulblets that you can separate from the parent plant and grow into new plants of full flowering size. But there are some other special propagation techniques you can try.

Bulbils: Sometimes you may notice small, dark minibulbs (called "bulbils") growing along the stems of your lilies. This is common on tiger lilies and a few other types. Gently pull or twist the bulbils off the stem in late summer and plant them in pots or a nursery bed to grow to flowering size.

Scaling: Scaling is a technique you can use on all lilies. In fall, dig up the bulb you want to propagate and remove a few of the outer scales. Dust the broken edges of these scales with sulfur. Plant the scales in pots or trays, with their base just below the soil surface, and set them under lights or in a greenhouse. New bulblets will quickly form along the base of each scale. After a few weeks, gently pull off the bulblets, put them in the refrigerator for 2 months, and then plant them in pots or an outdoor nursery bed to grow. They can reach flowering size in as little as 2 years, depending on the species or hybrid you're growing.

The rhizomes of bearded irises are easily divided with a sharp knife, a garden spade, or your hands.

Gather seed in summer or fall, after your bulbs flower. Check the developing seedpods every few days, then collect the seeds as the seedpods begin to open. Sow the seed in well-drained seed-starting mix in pots or trays. Cover it with a thin layer of mix and set the containers in a cool, shaded place outdoors. Water as needed to keep the soil evenly moist.

When seedlings appear, move the containers to a sunny place. Continue watering until the seedlings die down. (Seedlings will go dormant for part of the year, just like their garden-grown parents.) Water sparingly until new growth appears again, then keep them evenly moist. Depending on the species you're dealing with, your baby bulbs may reach flowering size in as little as 1 year, although 3 to 5 years is more common.

SECTION FOUR

Caring for Flowers

Once your flowers are planted, you need to know how to keep them looking their best. Fortunately, there are some simple but effective steps you can follow to help promote the health of your garden. And remember, maintenance is easiest if you do it regularly, as this will keep little tasks from mushrooming into overwhelming ones.

Tools and Equipment *78*

Mulching and Watering *84*

Fertilizing for Good Growth *88*

Pests, Diseases, Weeds *92*

Pruning and Training *100*

Preparing for Winter *104*

Month by Month in the Flower Garden *108*

Tools and Equipment

When it comes to caring for your garden, the task will be made much simpler if you've got good tools to hand. Using the right tool makes any job easier, as you know if you've ever used a butter knife when you couldn't find the screwdriver or the heel of a shoe as a substitute for a hammer. But a shopping trip for garden tools can be so baffling that you may well decide to stick with the butter knife and shoe. When faced with a wall-long display of shovels, spades, forks, rakes, trowels, and cultivators, it can be hard to decide what tools, and which version of them, you need.

You may decide on a whole collection of garden tools, or just a few of the basics, depending on your needs and budget.

A Basic Tool Collection

Fortunately, most gardeners can get away with a half-dozen basic tools. You'll need a spade to turn the soil and a shovel for digging holes and for moving soil, sand, and amendments around. A spading fork is useful for turning the soil, working in amendments and green manures, turning compost, and dividing perennials. You'll also need a metal rake for smoothing the soil, a hoe for weeding, and a trowel for planting and transplanting. If you have a huge vegetable garden, you may want to get a rotary tiller, wheel hoe, or even a garden tractor to which you can attach various implements. Hand pruners may be necessary for pruning perennials. However, if you garden in containers, the only tools you'll need will be a trowel and hand cultivator.

Spades

A spade is used to turn soil, remove sod, or cut straight edges between lawns and beds. The square edge and flat blade also make spades handy for digging trenches.

To use, push the blade into the soil, resting your foot on the top rim of the blade and leaning your body weight onto it. Pull the handle back and down. When lifting, bend your knees before sliding one hand down the handle; if possible, brace the handle of the spade with your thigh.

Shovels

Shovels with pointed blades are handy for digging holes, whereas shovels with straight blades are the best type to use for scooping up loose materials such as sand, soil, gravel, or soil amendments. For good leverage, the handle should reach your shoulder at least; your nose is even better.

Good-quality tools can be expensive, but they are a pleasure to use and can last for many years.

When digging with a shovel, use your foot to push the blade into the soil. Use your legs and arms, not your back, to lift the load. Before tossing the load, turn your whole body, not just your upper torso, in the direction of the toss.

Forks

Spading forks and English garden forks are useful in many areas of the garden. Use them for turning heavy or rocky earth, working cover crops and organic matter into the soil, fluffing compost, aerating soil, lifting root crops, and dividing clumps of crowded perennials. A border fork is a smaller version of the spading fork. Pitchforks are for fluffing compost and moving piles of hay or straw, but not for digging.

To turn soil or work in organic matter, use your foot to push the tines into the soil, lift the fork, then dump the load with a twist of your arms and wrists. Avoid using a fork to pry rocks out of the soil or you'll bend the tines.

To fluff compost, dig the tines into the compost at a 45-degree angle and lift it with a slight toss. To aerate a lawn, use your foot to push the fork into the soil, then push the handle back and forth.

Separate perennial clumps by inserting the fork to loosen the center, then pull the crown apart with your hands.

A shovel is good for digging holes or scooping up loose materials like sand, soil, or bark chips.

A mattock is a handy tool for wrestling with hard, rocky soil or digging out stubborn stumps.

Choose from a range of different cultivators.

Broadforks

Also called U-bars or bio-forks, broadforks are used to loosen soil down to quite sizeable depths without actually turning it over like forks and spades do. However, broadforks don't loosen or aerate the soil as much as double-digging does. They're good tools to use if you don't want to mix poor-quality lower soil layers with the good, granular topsoil. Broadforks are also useful for cultivating beds with fragile soil structure, heavy soil that needs frequent loosening, or sandy soil that you don't want to over-aerate.

Rest your foot on the crossbar to which the tines are attached. Use your body weight to push the tines into the soil. If you're loosening the soil for planting, pull the handles toward you and push down so the tines lift out of the soil. To break up a hardpan, push the tines into the soil, then push and pull the handles back and forth.

Mattocks

Mattocks, also called grub hoes, are handy for removing stumps and breaking up hard or rocky soil that gets in the way of your landscaping plans. You can also use them to dig holes.

Use a swinging motion with the pick end to sever woody plant roots and to break up stony soil. Use the blade with a chopping motion for digging a hole or for prying rocks you've loosened with the other end.

Crowbars

A crowbar—also known as a caliche bar, pry bar, or axle rod—is a handy tool for prying large rocks, stumps, or pieces of broken concrete out of the ground. You can also use it to break up tight caliche soil (a soil type found in the Southwest), make holes in hard soil for garden stakes, or roll big rocks into place when building a stone wall.

When prying out a rock, use the edge of the hole or another rock as a fulcrum: Put the bar's tip under the heavy rock, rest the center of the bar on the fulcrum, and push down on the free end.

A trowel and hand cultivator are all you need for container gardens.

Trowels

Trowels are standard equipment for on-your-knees digging. Use a trowel when digging a hole for bulbs or transplants, making a furrow for seeds, or even weeding around small plants. Transplant trowels have narrow, cupped blades that are very handy for planting or working in small spaces.

Dig holes by using the trowel as a scoop to loosen and lift the soil. Or hold the handle in your fist with the face of the blade pointing toward you and dig by stabbing the soil and pulling back and up.

Rakes

A metal garden rake is an indispensable part of any garden tool collection. Use rakes for clearing stones, leaves, sticks, and other debris from beds and making a smooth surface for planting. Rakes are also handy for forming and shaping raised beds, working fertilizer into the soil, and spreading manure, compost, mulches, and other organic matter across the soil surface. If you're smoothing the soil before planting, work when the soil is slightly moist.

Both the tines and the back of the rake are useful for pushing and pulling soil and organic matter around.

A plastic or more durable metal rake is very useful.

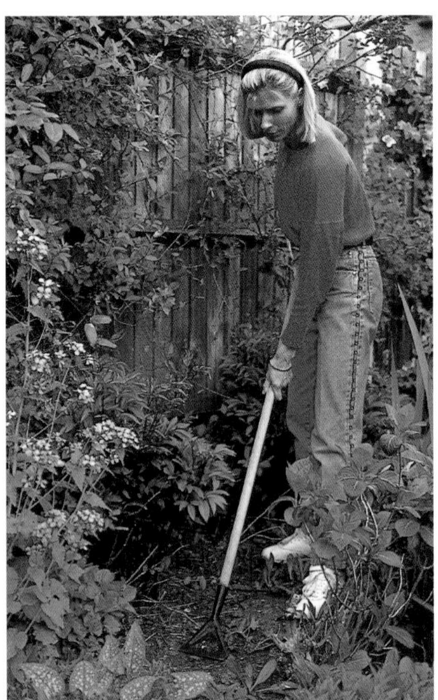

Hoes are handy for many tasks—laying out rows, digging furrows, and weeding around plants.

Cultivators

Depending on the type of cultivator, you can use it to loosen and aerate the soil, scratch in dry fertilizer, and pull out weeds. Hand-held cultivating tools are good for working around the base of plants and other small spaces. There are a number of different cultivators, each of which is used in a slightly different way.

Asian hand cultivators: These resemble a trowel with a pointed end. The blade curves into a scooped shape, making it useful for deep cultivating.

Cape cod weeders: This tool has an L-shaped blade; pull the blade along just below the surface for weeding and loosening the soil.

Dandelion weeders: Also called asparagus knives or fishtail weeders, these tools have a blade that resembles a forked tongue; use them to dig out weeds with long taproots and to harvest asparagus.

Hand cultivators: These very handy tools have three claw-like tines and either a short or long handle. Use them to work closely around plantings, rake weeds from the soil, or scratch in a side-dressing of dry fertilizer. Spring-toothed weeders are similar, but a spring gives the tines some bounce, making them more flexible.

Hand forks: Hand forks resemble small garden forks and can work the top 4 inches (10 cm) of soil or make holes for transplants. They're good for tight places.

Heart hoes: These hoes, also called one-prong cultivators, have a single C-shaped tine with a heart-shaped end. They let you work close to plants without doing damage. (A long-handled version may be called a biocultivator.)

Hotbed weeders: Hotbed weeders have a C-shaped blade that cuts along three of its edges, making them good for cutting small weeds in tight places.

Pavement weeders: These tools have an angled, pointed blade that you use to scrape between sections of sidewalk or driveway. (An old kitchen knife will work just as well.)

Hoes

Hoes are generally used for slicing weeds off at soil level, though they can have other uses, too. The eye hoe is designed for heavy digging and moving soil. Hoeing is easiest when the soil is slightly moist.

If you're using a standard pull or draw hoe—where the neck of the hoe curls back toward you—position your hands with your thumbs pointing up and pull the hoe toward you with a sweeping motion. If you use a push hoe—with the blade pointing away from you—hold the handle with your thumbs pointing down. Push it in front of you as you walk, with the blade just under the soil surface.

Rotary Tillers

Rotary tillers are most useful in medium to large vegetable gardens or annual flower beds. Use them for preparing bare soil for planting and for working in

A rotary tiller is most useful for cultivating bare soil in a large vegetable garden or annual flower bed.

A pair of hand pruners is invaluable for keeping your flowering plants trim, tidy, and in bloom.

amendments or green manure crops. Avoid using them to clear a sodded area; they can cause weed problems by chopping up the plants and perennial weed roots and spreading them through the soil. Till the soil only when a soil ball, made in your fist, easily falls apart when touched. Tilling when the soil is too wet or too dry can destroy soil structure.

Hand Pruners

Most gardeners of annuals and perennials will need little more than a pair of hand pruners. They are used to remove growth that's ¾ inch (18 mm) in diameter and smaller. Choose bypass pruners over anvil-type pruners: The latter tend to crush stems, while the scissor action of the former makes a cleaner cut. Ratchet-action hand pruners have also become more available and may be worthwhile for people with limited strength in their hands. However, don't be tempted to use the extra power to cut pieces larger than ¾ inch (18 mm); you may crush or tear the tissue left on the plant.

Carrying pruners in your pocket can be tough on your clothes and on you, too, if you forget they are there! A holster for your hand pruners is a wonderful accessory because it keeps them comfortably close at hand. With pruners at the ready, you're more likely to make a cut when you see the need.

If you find yourself using both hands to make a cut with your hand pruners, stop and reach for a pair of loppers. Loppers work best on cuts up to 1¾ inches (4.3 cm) in diameter. Choose wood handles (preferably ash) over metal ones for better shock absorption and pick bypass loppers over anvil loppers; the bypass version has the better cutting mechanism. Also look for models with a rubber disk that functions as a shock absorber when the tool snaps closed.

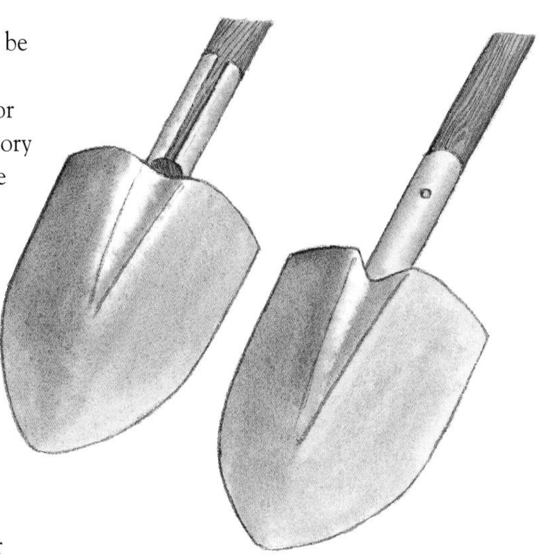

Avoid open-socket tools (left) that have the top of the blade partly wrapped around the handle. Solid-socket tools (right) are much more durable.

Buying Good Tools

There's nothing quite like the feel of working in your garden with a good-quality, well-constructed tool. Here are some things to consider as you shop for garden equipment, so you'll get the best tools for your money.

Cost

How much you spend on buying your tools depends on how long you want them to last. If you want to keep the tools for decades, get the best you can afford—$40 for a spade or hoe isn't unreasonable. If you're on a tight budget, if you plan to move in a few years and don't want the extra baggage, or if you leave your tools outside all the time, buy the bargain basement kind for about $15. Be warned, however, that cost-cutting on materials and design makes cheap tools more difficult to use than their more expensive counterparts. And cheap tools might not even make it through a season without bending or breaking.

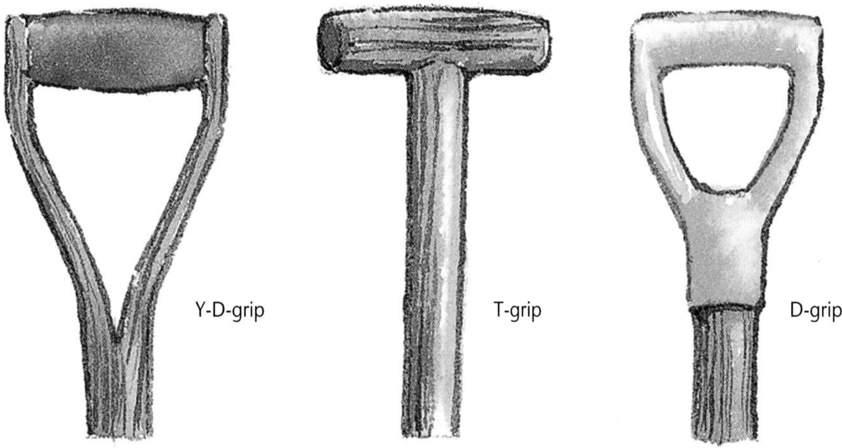

Tool handles come in several different styles of grip; choose the one that feels most comfortable to you.

If possible, choose tools with a handle length that is comfortable for you; this minimizes aches and pains.

Construction

When you go shopping for garden tools, read the labels carefully to see whether the metal part of a tool is stamped steel or forged steel. Forged steel is much stronger, but makes the tool cost 20 to 30 percent more than a stamped steel tool. If you want the item to last well, decide upon a forged steel product. If budget is an issue, consider the stamped steel tool.

Also investigate how the handle attaches to the metal part. Don't buy the tool if the metal wraps only partway around the handle; this construction, called open socket, leaves the wood exposed to water and mud, which can lead to rot. Also avoid tools where the handle is poked onto a spike at the top of the metal portion of the tool, then surrounded with a metal collar to keep the handle from splitting. Neither this type of construction, called tang and ferrule, nor open socket is durable and may only last a season or two. Instead, choose tools with metal that wraps all the way around the handle (called solid-socket construction) or has strips of metal bolted to the handle (known as solid-strap construction).

Handles

If you want a wooden handle, look for one made of white ash. Handles of spades and forks are sometimes made from hickory, but it's heavier and less flexible. The grain should run the length of the handle, without knots. Painted handles often hide low-quality wood; don't buy them.

Alternatives to wood are fiberglass or solid-core fiberglass. Both are stronger than wood; solid-core fiberglass is nearly unbreakable. Fiberglass adds about $8 to the cost of a tool, while solid-core fiberglass adds about $16. The additional cost is worth it if you want a tool that will last you for years and years.

Grips

If the end of the handle has a grip for you to hang on to, check how the grip is designed. Make sure it is fastened to the handle and not just slipped over it. Beyond that, the style you choose is a matter of preference (and availability). Try out a few to see which feels best.

Size

If you have a choice from the array of tools available, pick those with a handle length that feels most comfortable to you. Shovels should reach at least shoulder height; rakes can be even longer to give you a better reach. A hoe's handle should be long enough to let you stand upright when the blade is about 2 feet (60 cm) from your feet and just about flat on the ground. Short-handled tools, such as spades and forks, usually have 28-inch

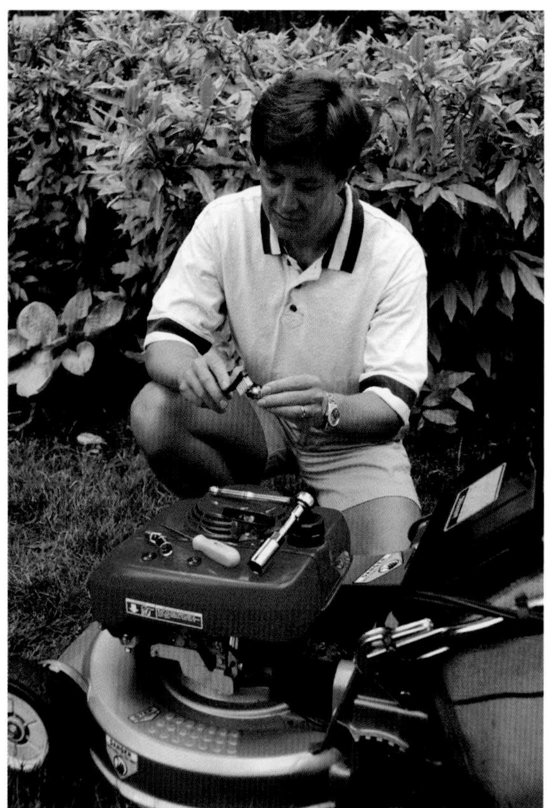

For dependable service, brush tools and equipment off after use and clean and oil them thoroughly before storing for winter.

(70-cm) handles, but tall gardeners should look for ones with 32-inch (80-cm) handles. For hand tools such as trowels, choose the length that feels comfortable in your hand. When buying a mattock or pick, choose a weight that you can lift and swing without strain.

Caring for Tools

Once you've gone to the trouble of buying good tools, it's worth a little extra effort to keep them in shape. Without proper care, even the best built and most expensive tool can get corroded and dull after a season or two, making it as unpleasant to use as the cheapest department-store tool. When you are ready to dig, you'll be glad of the few minutes you put into keeping your tools clean and sharp.

Keep Them Clean

It's pretty easy at the end of a hot and grimy day in the garden to justify putting the tools away dirty. And you can even get away with it a few times. But eventually the moist soil clinging to your tools will make them rust. And once you finally do get around to cleaning them, the dry soil is harder to get off than the moist soil would have been.

For that reason, it's a virtue to force yourself into the habit of cleaning your tools when you're done with them. This doesn't mean just scraping the shovel off with the trowel. For one thing, then you have to scrape the trowel off with the shovel, then the shovel off with the trowel again, and so on. Also, all that scraping of metal on metal damages tools.

Better alternatives include using a stick, wooden spoon, or paint stirrer to scrape off the clinging soil. Or try a long-handled, heavy-duty scrub brush that you put in a convenient spot in your shed. Another trick is to keep a tub of sharp sand around and dip the tool up and down in it until the soil comes off.

It's especially worthwhile to clean all your tools before storing them away for the winter. Clean off any soil, then use steel wool or a wire brush to remove any rust. Coat the metal with a light oil and hang the tools someplace where you can see and admire them all winter long.

Since your skin touches the handle the most, you may want to keep wooden handles smooth by sanding any rough spots. If you wish, apply varnish or another sealer (like tung oil) to protect the wood. If a handle breaks, pick up a replacement during your next trip to the hardware store; don't just try to tape the old one back together.

Keep Them Sharp

Your spade and hoe will do a better job for you if you keep them sharpened. You'll get the best results if you sharpen them briefly and often rather than making it a big job for the end of the year.

For most gardeners, a metal file is an adequate sharpening tool. Use a file that matches the contour of the tool's surface—a flat file for a flat-bladed hoe or spade and a half-round file for a curved shovel blade. The aim is to keep the angle of the existing edge but to thin it a bit and remove any nicks. If you have many tools, a whetstone or grindstone will do the job more quickly. If you don't want to sharpen them yourself, you can take your tools to someone who does it professionally. The best time to do this is in late fall, as you prepare your tools for storage. Sharpeners are often swamped with work in spring and they may not have time to do your tools as soon as you need them if you wait.

Oil and sharpen your hand pruners to keep them in good working order, so they give a nice, clean cut rather than crushing plant stems.

Mulching and Watering

Cocoa shells make an attractive mulch, but they break down quickly and need to be reapplied.

All plants need a certain amount of moisture—some more, some less—in order to grow. Watering with hoses, sprinklers, and watering cans will be necessary at certain times of the year, but there are other ways of making sure your plants don't go thirsty.

Make the Most of Mulch

Mulch is one way as it protects the soil, slowing evaporation and keeping it moist longer after each rain or watering. In fact, it is an important part of producing healthy plants in almost any climate. It helps keep out weeds by preventing weed seedlings from getting a foothold, and organic mulches add nutrients and organic matter to the soil as they decay.

If you use mulch on frozen soil during the winter, it will keep the earth evenly frozen; this reduces the rapid freezing-and-thawing cycles that can damage plant roots and push plant crowns out of the soil (a process known as frost heaving). In hot-summer climates, mulch will slow the rapid decay of organic matter added to the soil, so each application will last longer. In any climate, mulch can work double duty as an attractive background for your annuals and perennials.

Mulching with compost is a good way to add nutrients to your garden. It may be all you need to fertilize light feeders, such as common thrift (*Armeria maritima*), coreopsis (*Coreopsis* spp.), and yarrow (*Achillea* spp.). Compost mulch will conserve moisture, but unfortunately, it will not do much to squeeze out weeds.

As useful as mulch is in most gardens, there are situations when mulching can actually cause garden problems. If slugs and snails are your garden's major pests, an organic mulch can provide them with the cool, dark, moist conditions they prefer. If you're trying to garden in heavy, wet clay, mulch can slow evaporation even more, contributing to root rot.

However, in cold-climate areas with short growing seasons, mulch will keep the soil cool for longer in spring and give your plants a late start. In these areas, only mulch in summer after your plants have appeared and the soil has warmed up. Remove the mulch and compost it when you clean up the garden in fall.

If you mulch with uncomposted wood chips or sawdust, keep in mind that these materials can rob your plants of soil nitrogen as they decompose. If you must mulch with these woody materials, top-dress the soil with a high-nitrogen material like bloodmeal or cottonseed meal before adding the mulch.

Many organic materials are useful for mulching, including bark chips, compost, and leaves.

Choosing a Mulch

The time you take to choose the right mulch for your needs is time well spent. You want a mulch that looks good and is free of weeds. Cost and availability may also be important factors in your choice.

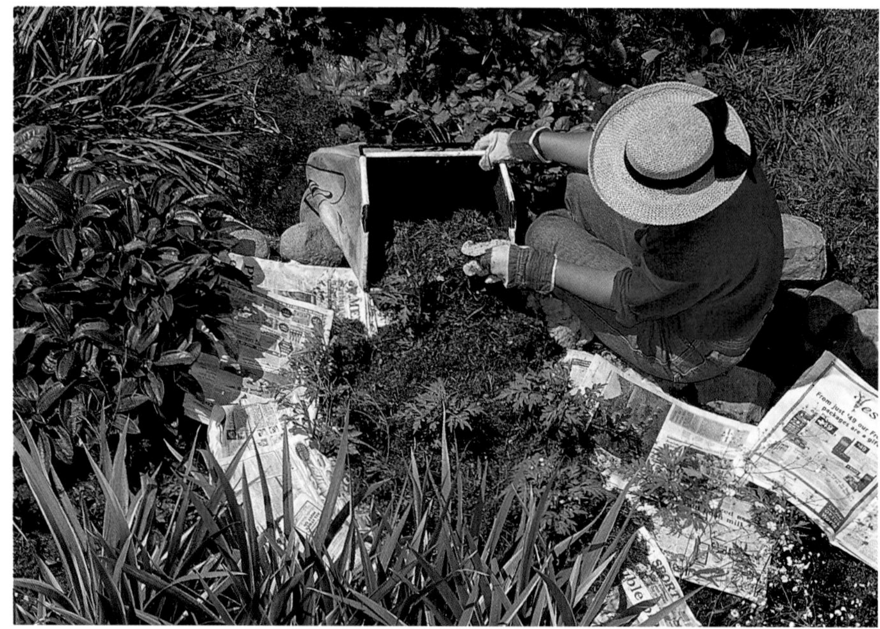

Newspaper is a cheap weed-suppressing mulch; cover with a decorative mulch to stop it blowing away.

Fallen leaves will provide a wealth of excellent organic material for mulching—and they're free!

Many kinds of organic mulches are available. Shredded leaves make a useful mulch and they are free, so the price is right. Grass clippings scattered around plantings are a good way to recycle your lawn waste. Cocoa bean hulls have an attractive dark color and chocolaty aroma but they are not widely available. Dark-colored, fine-textured, well-decomposed compost can act as a mulch, too; it also gives the soil a rich, healthy look as well as improving soil fertility.

Straw is a good mulch for vegetables, but it may look too utilitarian for most flower gardens. Chunks of shredded bark or wood chips may be suitable for large, bold perennials; they are hard to work without gloves, however, and will dwarf small, fine-textured annuals and creepers. Sections or shreds of newspaper are good placed under more attractive mulches. But do not use colored newspaper as some inks can be toxic.

Try to choose a mulch that won't pack down into dense layers. Dense layers of fine-textured or flat materials, like grass clippings or an extra thick coating of shredded bark, tend to shed water. Rain and irrigation water will run off the bed instead of trickling down into the soil. If you want to use these kinds of mulches, create air pockets between the particles by mixing in coarse, fluffy material like shredded leaves, small bark chunks, or ground corncobs.

If you use a mulch that won't pack down and your garden has well-drained soil, you can lay the mulch as much as 4 to 6 inches (10 to 15 cm) deep to get maximum weed control. On soils that tend to stay wet or in gardens that do not have a big weed problem, reduce the mulch layer to 2 to 3 inches (5 to 7.5 cm) deep. Leave 4 to 6 inches (10 to 15 cm) of unmulched ground around the base of each plant; this way, the crown stays drier and is less likely to rot.

All organic mulches will gradually decompose over a period of weeks or months, so you need to replace the mulch layer frequently to keep the soil covered. You will have to reapply softer mulches like compost or grass clippings more often than harder wood chips or shredded leaves, which decompose more slowly.

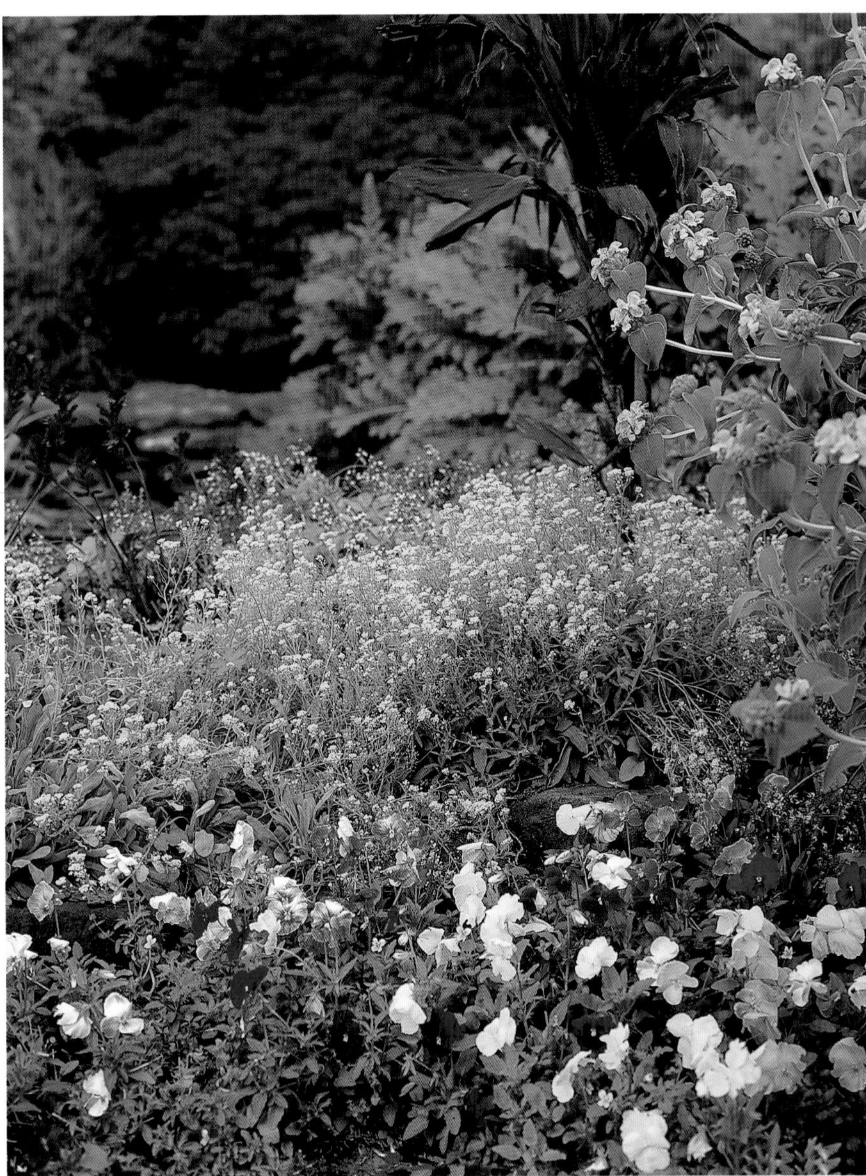

Your plants will grow lushly with an organic mulch to moderate soil temperatures and conserve moisture.

Watering Wisely

A garden that is actively growing and flowering will need a source of moisture at all times. If water is in short supply, flowers and flower buds are the first to suffer damage; if water is overly abundant, plant roots rot. You will have to fine-tune your watering depending on several factors, including the type of soil you have, the amount of natural rainfall, the plants you grow, and the stage of growth the plants are in.

Consider Your Soil

If you do not already know how moisture-retentive your garden soil is, find out. For instance, will it provide reserves of water for 1 week after a good drenching or will most of the moisture drain away within a day? To answer this question, water a portion of the garden thoroughly. After 48 hours, dig a small hole 6 inches (15 cm) deep. If the soil is reasonably water-retentive, the earth at the bottom of the hole will still be moist. If it is not, you can improve its water-holding capacity by working in lots of compost. This organic matter acts like a sponge, holding extra moisture reserves that plant roots can draw on. If you do add a great deal of organic matter, you can water less frequently. But when you do irrigate, water extra thoroughly to saturate the organic matter.

Keeping Track of Rainfall

Monitor the rainfall in your garden and vary your irrigation schedule accordingly. Overwatering can be as bad as underwatering, especially in heavier soils. You can tell how much rain has fallen if you leave out a rain gauge, which is like a narrow measuring cup with inches (millimeters) of rainfall marked on the side. If you don't want to buy a rain gauge, you can set a small, clean can out in an open part of the garden and use a ruler to measure how much rain water it collects. Check your gauge once a week to keep track.

A good rule of thumb to follow is that your garden should get 1 inch (25 mm) of water a week. This amount of water will wet the soil deeply and thus encourage roots to grow down farther underground. Of course, some annuals and perennials need more moisture and some need less, so you'll have to adjust your supplemental irrigation depending on the needs of your plants.

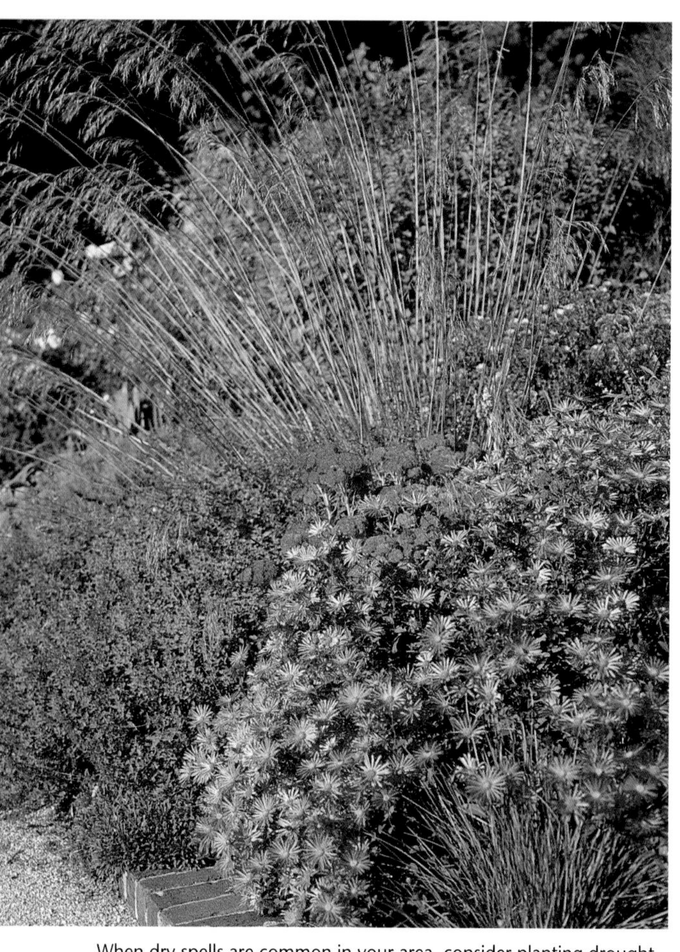

When dry spells are common in your area, consider planting drought-tolerant perennials such as asters, sedums, sages, and *Stipa* grass.

If natural rainfall is inadequate, water your plants regularly to promote healthy, vigorous growth.

Different Plants Have Different Needs

Some annuals and perennials thrive in moist soils. Others will grow weakly or rot where water is abundant. It's important to group plants with similar water needs together. Water more frequently if you grow plants that need evenly moist soil. These include delphiniums, astilbes, and

Unsure about your soil's moisture content? Check below the soil surface to see if the root zone is dry.

Whenever possible, avoid overhead watering. It wastes water and can encourage disease to spread.

the real moisture-lovers, bog plants such as Japanese primroses (*Primula japonica*) and marsh marigolds (*Caltha palustris*).

Let the soil dry out more between waterings for drought-tolerant plants, such as lavender, coneflowers (*Rudbeckia* and *Echinacea* spp.), torch lilies (*Kniphofia* hybrids), perennial candytuft (*Iberis sempervirens*), and Cupid's dart (*Catananche caerulea*). These plants will probably need no more than ½ inch (12 mm) of water per week.

Expect to coddle newly planted plants until their roots establish and spread far enough to support the plants. If the weather is warm and dry, you may have to water daily until a drenching rain comes. If the season is cool and rainy, you can let nature handle the irrigation.

Ways to Water

When rainfall is not sufficient for plant needs, you'll have to irrigate the plants in your garden. Supply moisture gently so it will seep down instead of running off. Whenever possible, use a drip or trickle irrigation system or a soaker hose that releases droplets of water onto the soil without wetting plant leaves. Keeping the leaves and flowers dry reduces disease problems. Also, letting the water trickle into the ground is efficient because little is lost by way of evaporation.

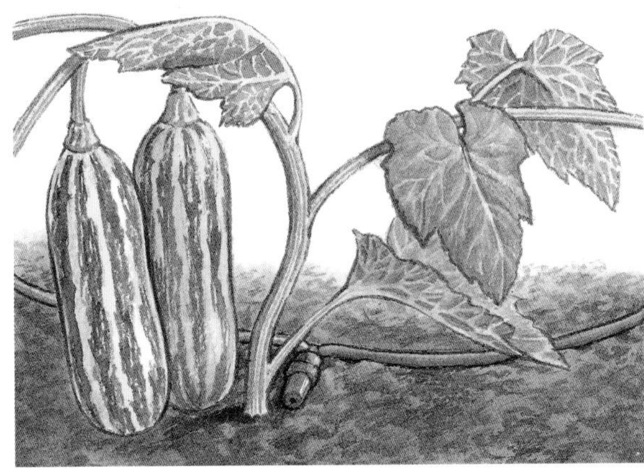

Drip irrigation systems with individual emitters will deliver a small but steady supply of water directly to the base of each plant.

Water conservation is even more effective if you organize your network of "leaky" tubes or soaker hoses so they irrigate only the annuals and perennials, not the weeds or open areas. But don't expect annuals and perennials to grow roots in areas of the garden that remain dry. Since the root spread of your plants may be limited to irrigated zones, be sure to soak the soil deeply in those areas where you do water so the root systems can grow big enough to support the plants.

You also can apply water to individual plants with a trickling hose or watering can. To reach extra deeply into the soil or to supply additional water to a wilting plant on a hot day, sink a water reservoir into the soil. This can be a plastic drainage tube, clay pot, or leaky plastic bucket filled with water. For slower release in sandy soils, plug the largest holes on pots and tubes and let the moisture slowly seep out of small, pin-prick openings.

Overhead sprinkling, which wastes lots of water through evaporation, is not a good choice for gardens. It waters weeds, helping them grow, and it wets foliage and flowers, increasing plant disease problems. Watering by hand is also inefficient as it will probably take hours, unless you've got a very small yard. Of course, for container gardens, watering by hand—either with a hose or a watering can—is the most realistic irrigation option.

How to Conserve Water

The following list gives ideas on how you can conserve water in your garden.

- Designate separate parts of the garden for plants with low, medium, or high water requirements and water them individually. Annuals will need more water than deep-rooted, established perennials.
- Insulate the soil surface with a thick layer of organic mulch.
- Work in plenty of compost to maintain your soil's organic matter. Organic matter holds water in the soil like a sponge.
- Eliminate weeds as soon as they appear.
- In dry climates, select plants that are drought-tolerant.
- If paths are included in the design of your garden, use gravel or pulverized bark to pave them. A living cover like grass will compete with your plants for moisture.

Fertilizing for Good Growth

Supplying your plants with the nutrients they need is a critical part of keeping them healthy and vigorous. How much fertilizer you should add to your garden will depend on how fertile the soil is and which plants you're growing.

The texture and natural fertility of your soil will have a great impact on how much and how often you need to add supplemental nutrients. A sandy soil will hold fewer nutrients than a clayey soil or a soil that's high in organic matter, so you'll need to fertilize a sandy soil more frequently.

Nutrient Needs

The amount and type of fertilizer you use in your garden, and how you apply it, will vary, depending on whether you're growing annuals or biennials, perennials or bulbs. Fertilizer requirements also vary depending on the type of perennial.

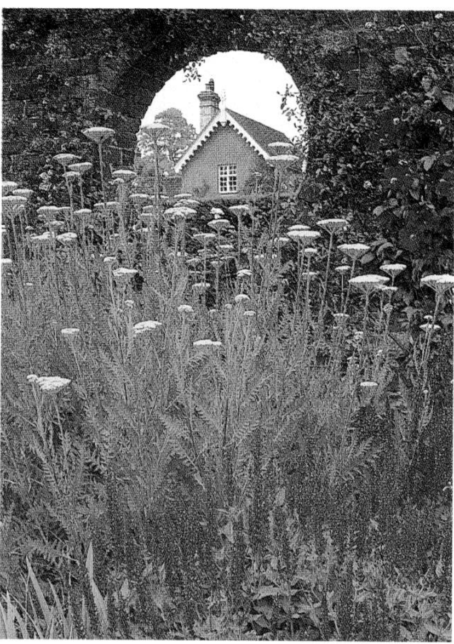

Yarrows and sages have similarly light nutrient needs, so it's a good idea to grow them together.

Annuals

Annuals grow quickly, so they need a readily available supply of nutrients for good flowering. In spring, scatter a 1- to 2-inch (2.5- to 5-cm) layer of compost over the bed and dig it in as you prepare the bed for planting. Or, if you're tucking annuals around perennials and other permanent plants, mix a handful of compost into each planting hole. If you don't have compost, you could also use a general organic garden fertilizer. Once or twice during the season, pull back the mulch and scatter some more compost or fertilizer around the base of each plant, then replace the mulch. For most annuals and biennials, this will provide all the nutrients they need.

For plants that appreciate extra fertility, such as wax begonias and sweet peas (*Lathyrus odoratus*), or for those that are looking a little tired by midsummer, a monthly dose of liquid fertilizer can provide a quick nutrient boost. Spray the leaves or water the plants with diluted fish emulsion or compost tea (made by soaking a shovelful of finished compost in a bucket of water for about a week, then straining out the soaked compost). Regular doses of liquid fertilizer (every 1 to 3 weeks) will also keep container plants healthy and vigorous.

Cosmos, like many annuals, will grow well with several applications of compost throughout the season.

Perennials

Perennials stay in the same place for years. Since you only have one chance (before planting) to get the soil into good shape, take time to prepare their beds well. Once they are established, most perennials—all but the heavy feeders—will grow happily with a light layer of compost applied once or twice a year.

Some perennials, such as yarrows (*Achillea* spp.), sages (*Salvia* spp.), and coreopsis (*Coreopsis* spp.), should receive no more than an annual layer of compost; otherwise, they will become leggy and topple over from too much fertilizer. But you may want to give other perennials a little fertility boost to encourage new growth or rejuvenation. Fertilize in spring as the plants begin growing, as well as after planting or dividing, and after deadheading or cutting back.

To meet the requirements of heavy feeders, or to encourage exceptional blooms from perennials such as pinks (*Dianthus* spp.), lilies, and delphiniums, use extra fertilizer. Push aside any mulch

Spring is a good time to fertilize spring- and fall-blooming bulbs. You may add bonemeal in fall.

or compost first. Add phosphorus and potassium, as well as any other nutrient recommended in your soil test results; see page 37. Apply them just as the plants begin setting flower buds. Scratch the fertilizer into the soil lightly with a hand cultivator, then replace the mulch.

Bulbs

Most bulbs will get along just fine without you having to add a lot of extra fertilizer. Working compost or other organic matter into the soil at planting time and using it as a mulch will provide much of the nutrient supply your bulbs need.

For top-notch growth, you can also sprinkle commercial organic fertilizer over the soil around the bulbs, following the package directions. Use a mix blended especially for bulbs if you can find one; otherwise, a general garden fertilizer is acceptable. Fertilize spring- and fall-flowering bulbs in spring. Summer-flowering bulbs usually grow best with several small applications of fertilizer in early- to midsummer.

Tuberous begonias, lilies, and other bulbs growing in pots benefit from weekly or bimonthly doses of liquid fertilizer. Spray the leaves or water the plants with diluted fish emulsion or compost tea.

Applying Fertilizers

When you fertilize, you can eliminate deficiencies by applying either liquid or dry fertilizer or both. If you decide to use a combination of fertilizers, make sure you don't apply more total nutrients than your plants need. Remember that too much fertilizer can be as bad as not enough, leading to weak stems, rampant, sprawling growth, and disease problems.

Perennials grow in the same place for years, so prepare the soil well and enrich it before planting.

A Sampler of Organic Fertilizers

A wide variety of organic materials is available for correcting nutrient deficiencies. Before you buy any fertilizer, check the label for information about the nitrogen, phosphorus, and potassium content. This is indicated by a series of three numbers, such as 5-10-5. This means that 100 pounds (45 kg) of a fertilizer with this formulation contains 5 pounds (2.25 kg) of nitrogen, 10 pounds (4.5 kg) of phosphorus, and 5 pounds (2.25 kg) of potassium. Use this information to compare the nutrient content of different fertilizers and to figure out how much of a given material you need to add to your garden based on your soil test results. Compost is one source of many plant nutrients. Listed below are other commonly used organic fertilizers, along with their nutrient content.

Bloodmeal: 12-0-0 to 14-0-0, contains nitrogen plus iron.

Bonemeal: 1-10-0, contains about 20 percent calcium. If processed with some meat or marrow, bonemeal can contain higher percentages of nitrogen.

Fish emulsion: 3-1-1 to 5-2-2, releases most of its nitrogen quickly. It is often sprayed onto leaves for a fast-acting nutrient boost.

Fish meal: 5-3-3, contains both immediately available nitrogen and a slow-release form of nitrogen that supplements the soil for up to 2 months.

Seaweed extract: 1-0.5-2.5, usually made from kelp, provides trace elements and natural growth hormones. Use liquid kelp as a foliar spray. Kelp meal is a concentrated form high in potassium and boron.

Liquid Fertilizers

Commonly used liquid fertilizers include fish emulsion, liquid seaweed, and compost tea. Use a single dose of liquid fertilizer for a quick but temporary fix of a nutrient shortage, or apply it every 2 weeks for a general plant boost. You can spray these materials directly onto the plants, which will absorb the nutrients through their foliage.

Applying Fertilizer

Scatter dry organic fertilizer evenly over the bed to slowly release nutrients.

Or apply the dry fertilizer in a ring around the base of each plant.

Spray liquid fertilizer on the leaves for an immediate nutrient boost.

Dry Fertilizers

Dry fertilizers are released to plants more slowly than liquid fertilizers. Scratch them into the surface of the soil in a circle around the perimeter of the plant's foliage, so the nutrients are released gradually as they dissolve in soil moisture. This encourages roots to extend outward.

Using Compost

Compost is a balanced blend of recycled garden, yard, and household wastes that have broken down into dark, crumbly organic matter. It is the key to success in any garden, being an excellent source of nutrients for your plants. The time you spend making compost and applying it to your garden will be more than returned by improved soil and plant health.

Creating Your Own Compost

Making compost is a lot like cooking—you mix together ingredients, stir them up, and let them "cook." But with a compost pile, the source of heat isn't electricity or gas—it's the activity of decomposer organisms like bacteria and fungi that live in soil and break down dead plant and animal tissues. These organisms work best when given warmth, moisture, plenty of oxygen, and a balance of carbon and nitrogen.

You can add a wide variety of materials to your compost. Vegetable scraps from the kitchen, grass clippings, fallen leaves, and soft plant trimmings are all good choices. If you have access to manure from animals such as chickens, rabbits, cows, or horses, you can add that also. There are some things you should avoid, including fats, bones, and meat scraps, which can attract scavengers to your pile. Also avoid composting manure from humans, dogs, and cats—this material can carry disease organisms.

Choose a shady, well-drained spot for your compost pile. For your convenience, put it as close to your garden as possible. If you're concerned that a loose compost pile would be unattractive, you can contain it in a bin. Make a homemade bin from wire fencing, wood, or concrete blocks, or buy a commercially available bin.

Keep your compost close to the garden so you can easily add trimmings or get finished compost.

Hot Composting

Hot composting takes some work, but it will provide you with high-quality compost in a matter of weeks. There are many different systems of hot composting, but they tend to have some elements in common. Most require building a large pile of different layers of high-nitrogen and high-carbon elements, along with some soil or finished compost to make sure the right decomposers are present. Turning or fluffing the pile every few days or weeks, to provide the decomposer organisms in the pile with oxygen, is another critical part of encouraging fast breakdown.

A wood-and-wire bin is a good way to keep your compost contained and easily accessible.

A yearly application of compost will supply all of the nutrients most perennials need to thrive.

To create a hot-compost pile, blend both soft and green (high-nitrogen) plant scraps, like lawn clippings, lettuce scraps, and dandelion leaves, with tough and brown (high-carbon) scraps, like fallen leaves, straw, and woody flower stalks. The moist, green items provide the decomposers with the nitrogen they consume as they break down the high-carbon materials.

Chop up the debris you plan to compost, and combine about 1 part of high-nitrogen elements with 2 parts high-carbon material in a pile about 3 feet (90 cm) high and wide. Pile up these elements in layers or just jumble them together. Add a shovelful of soil or finished compost in between each layer and enough water to keep the pile evenly moist. Turn the pile with a pitchfork every few days to add oxygen.

If all goes well, your compost should be ready in a few weeks. The material may break down more quickly in hot weather or more slowly in cold weather. When your compost is fairly cool and most of the original materials are unrecognizable, it is ready to use.

Cold Composting

Making "cold" compost is easier than making hot compost, but it takes longer. (A cold-compost pile won't really feel cold; it just doesn't get warm like a hot-compost pile.) Since the period of decomposition is extended up to a year or more, more nutrients can wash away in rainwater. You'll have to leave more space for the slower decomposing piles, and you'll have to wait much longer until it's ready. Cold compost will not heat up enough to kill seeds or disease organisms, so don't add mature weeds or diseased plant material to the pile.

To create a cold-compost pile, just choose a shady, well-drained place to drop your organic scraps. Let them build up to a pile about 3 feet (90 cm) wide by 3 feet (90 cm) high and then begin again in a new location. After a year or so, the original materials should be broken down, although the compost will probably still be fairly lumpy. Use the compost as it is, or screen out the lumps and leave them to break down for a while longer.

Using Compost

There are many different ways to add compost to your garden. If you are preparing a new bed, you can work it in as you dig. In an established garden, use compost as a mulch. As a general rule, cover the bed with 2 inches (5 cm) a year to maintain a fertile soil. Use more if you are growing moisture-loving perennials like astilbes; it will soak up and retain water. Use less around perennials such as yarrow that prefer drier, less-fertile soils. Compost breaks down gradually over the growing season—add more as needed.

If your compost supply is limited, spread a thin layer around each plant and top with a mulch.

Pests, Diseases, Weeds

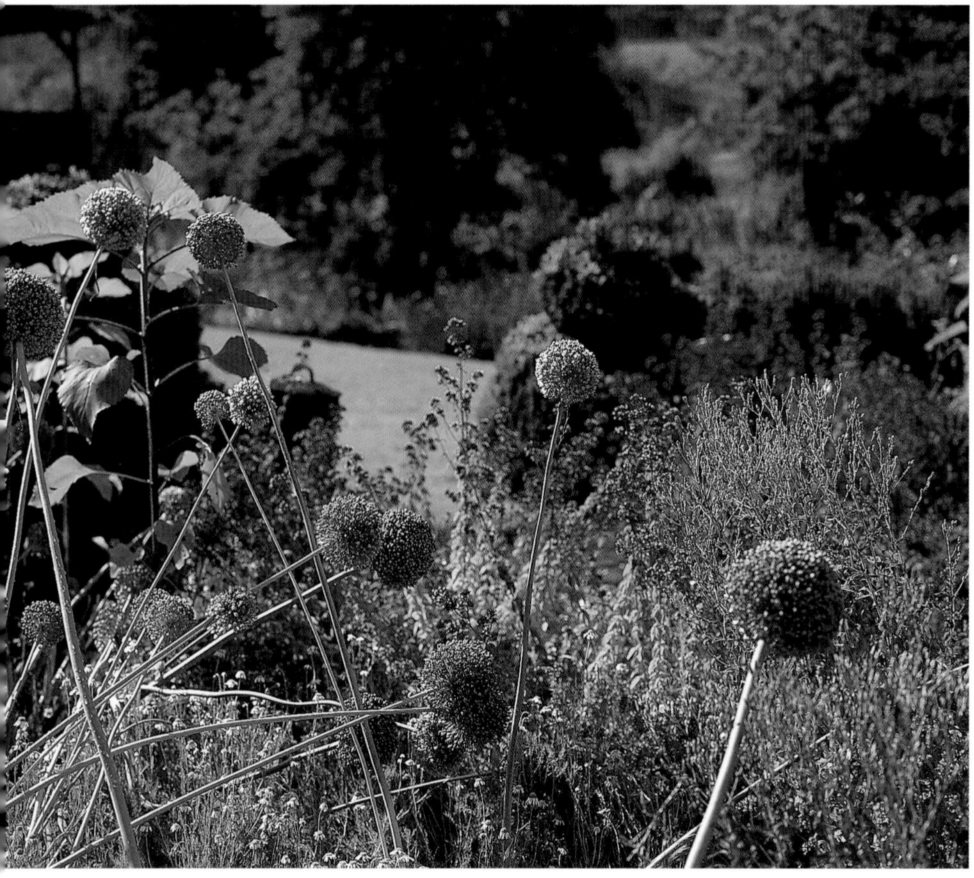

A healthy, vigorous garden, with plants that are not too crowded, is less inviting to pests and diseases.

Growing annuals and perennials will offer many pleasures as well as a few challenges—such as pests, diseases, and weeds. With good soil and good care, your plants will naturally be more resistant. Gardeners often notice that after several years of building up the soil, keeping the garden clean, and encouraging natural predators, insect and disease problems diminish from a constant battle to the occasional flare-up. And weeds can be kept under control by applying mulches. But it's important to be able to identify and handle any problems that do arise.

Prevention and Control

Generally, pests and diseases are not a big problem for annuals and perennials. You may never have to spray if you seek out the most disease-resistant species and cultivars and then plant them where they will thrive. Strong, healthy plants do not make easy targets for pests or diseases. Just as we are constantly exposed to cold and flu germs, plant pests, fungi, viruses, and bacteria are all around. They will infect weaker or stressed plants before harming vigorous ones.

Pests, diseases, and weeds are easiest to control if you catch them before they get out of hand. Inspect your garden regularly to help you spot problems before they spread. If you find a pest or disease problem, you'll need to properly identify it. Insect damage on your annuals and perennials can vary widely, depending on the pest causing the problem.

You need to figure out what's causing the damage in order to be able to choose the best control. Only then can you decide how to treat it: by handpicking, trapping, or by some other organically acceptable control.

If you use a commercial organic spray, always read the label first. Labels list important information on proper storage, target pests, and effective application. Even organic sprays and dusts can irritate skin or lungs, so wear protective clothing and gloves to be on the safe side.

Identifying Some Common Pests

Knowing about the most common pests to attack annuals and perennials will help you notice any infestations on your plants

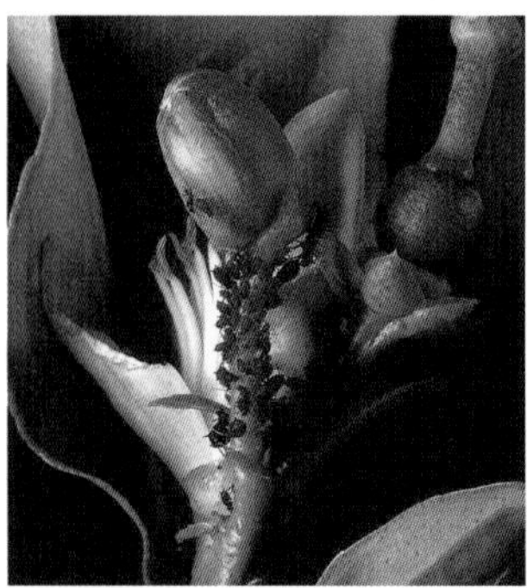

Aphids cling to leaves and buds.

Japanese beetles chew into leaves.

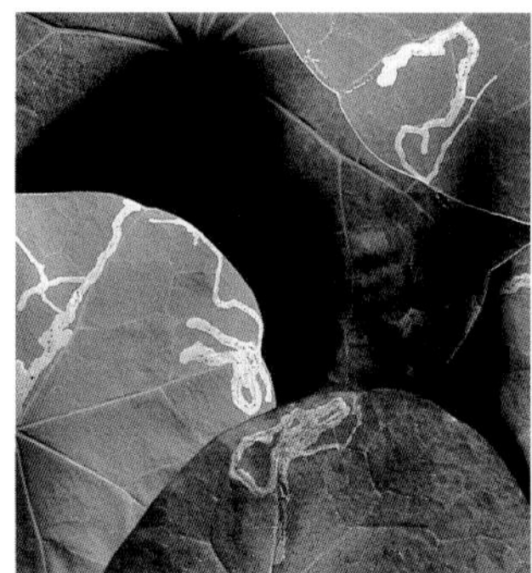

Leafminers leave trails inside leaves.

Spider mites build tiny webs.

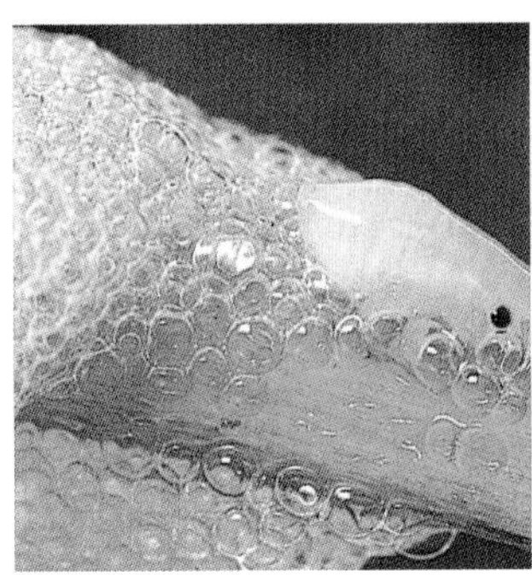
Spittlebugs suck the sap of plants.

Slugs chew large holes in leaves.

Thrips attack leaves and flowers.

Mealybugs attack stems and fruit.

and also be able to identify them. You can identify insects by the appearance of the larvae or adults and also by the kind of damage they do to the plant.

Aphids

Aphids are tiny, soft-bodied, pear-shaped insects that feed on a wide variety of annuals and perennials. They tend to cluster near the growing tips and on the undersides of leaves. Large groups of aphids can cause the foliage, flowers, or shoots of plants to twist, pucker, or drop, and they leave a trail of sugary excrement (called honeydew), which is sticky and often harbors a black, sooty mold. Aphids also can spread viral diseases as they feed.

Japanese Beetles

These shiny, metallic blue-green beetles with bronze wing covers feed on many different annuals and perennials, including hollyhocks (*Alcea rosea*), New York asters (*Aster novi-belgii*), foxgloves (*Digitalis* spp.), and purple coneflowers (*Echinacea purpurea*). They will eat the green part of leaves, so that only the leaf veins remain, and also chew on flowers. The grubs are white with brown heads; they feed mostly on lawn grass roots.

Leafminers

Leafminers are the tiny larvae of small flies. The larvae tunnel inside perennial foliage, leaving light-colored trails that you can see from the top of the leaf. They can be a problem on columbines (*Aquilegia* spp.), delphiniums, and garden mums (*Chrysanthemum* x *morifolium*).

Spider Mites

These tiny, spider-like pests will attack many perennials, especially when the weather becomes hot and dry. The brown, red, or green mites make very fine webs over plants and suck the plant sap from the underside of a leaf, causing it to curl and its upper surface to turn speckled, pale, and dull-looking.

Plant Bugs

Tarnished plant bugs are green or brown with yellow triangles on their forewings; four-lined plant bugs are yellowish green with four black stripes down their back. Both of these insects will leave irregular holes or sunken brown spots in the middle of leaves. They also cause distorted growth on the leaves or growing tips of many annuals and perennials.

Slugs and Snails

Slugs (slimy mollusks) and snails (slimy mollusks with a coiled shell on their back) can be a problem anywhere the soil stays damp, and this is especially a problem in shady gardens. They crawl up on annuals and perennials and chew ragged holes in the leaves, stems, and flowers. They can eat the entire plant in this way. They can also ruin young seedlings or transplants.

Thrips

Thrips are minute, quick-moving insects that feed on the flowers and leaves of several different kinds of plants. They give the affected plant tissue a pale, silvery look in damaged areas. Eventually the infected plant parts can wither and die.

Other Pests

You also may find mealybugs (slow-moving, soft-bodied insects hidden beneath a white, cottony shield) under leaves and along stems; leafhoppers (which look like tiny grasshoppers) on stems and leaves; borers (fat pink caterpillars), which tunnel down the leaves of bearded irises and eat large cavities into the rhizomes; and cutworms (fat, dark-colored caterpillars), which chew through the stems of young seedlings and transplants.

Local Wildlife

Squirrels can do a lot of damage to your bulbs.

Deer, rabbits, mice, and other animal pests can attack bulbs. All these animals may feast on both the flowers and the actual bulbs. You can try to discourage them by planting daffodil bulbs, which are poisonous and usually avoided by animals. Some people believe that the strong odor of crown imperial (*Fritillaria imperialis*) bulbs and plants repels voles, mice, and squirrels. Pet dogs and cats can be useful for discouraging local wildlife, but they may cause damage, too.

For more information on pests and diseases that attack specific flowering plants, go to the individual entries in "Encyclopedia of Flowers," starting on page 306.

Controlling Pests

Once you have figured out the identity of a problem-causing pest, you can choose the best method for controlling it.

Handpicking

If you only find a few pests among your annuals and perennials, you can pick them off the plants by hand and crush them under your heel. This is effective for large, slow-moving pests like snails and slugs, Japanese beetles, and cutworms, but not for small pests or large infestations.

Traps and Barriers

Avoid garden damage by catching pests in traps or deterring them with barricades. Sticky traps are very effective for some pests: Yellow sticky traps will attract aphids, while white traps will catch tarnished plant bugs. You can either buy pre-made sticky traps at a garden center or make your own by painting pieces of wood or cardboard the appropriate color and coating them with petroleum jelly. Hang the traps on stakes throughout your garden and clean or replace them as needed to keep them effective.

You can trap slugs and snails with a shallow container of beer set in the soil so the top rim is at ground level; they crawl in and drown. Surrounding plants with a ring of diatomaceous earth (a powdery material composed of tiny, spiny-shelled algae) will also keep slugs and cutworms at bay; renew the barrier after each rain.

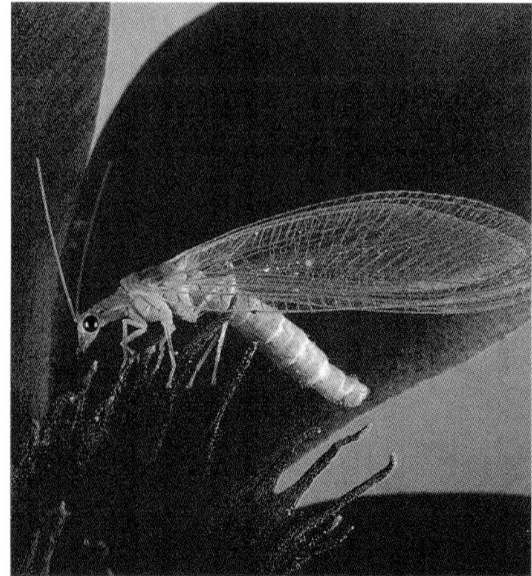

Adult lacewings feed on nectar and honeydew, but the larvae eat large numbers of insect pests.

Paper collars protect seedlings from cutworms.

To protect your bulbs from the local wildlife, it is possible to take preventive measures when planting where mice, voles, shrews, and squirrels are especially troublesome. Although it takes some doing, you can fashion bulb crates—a little like lobster traps—out of sturdy wire mesh. Choose mesh with a grid size of about 1 inch (2.5 cm). Small animals can sneak through larger mesh, while your bulb shoots may not be able to poke through smaller mesh. Dig a hole large enough to hold the crate, so the top is just below the soil surface. Place the crate in the hole and backfill with some of the soil you removed. Plant your bulbs in the crate, then fill the rest of the cage with soil and close the lid. Use the remaining soil to cover the lid and fill in around the rest of the cage.

Biological Controls

You can use biological weapons like *Bacillus thuringiensis* (BT), a bacterial disease, and milky disease to eliminate pests without harming people, animals, or beneficial insects. To control damage by many different kinds of caterpillars, spray or dust foliage with BT. (Don't use this material if you want to encourage butterflies in your garden, though; it will kill the larvae of attractive butterflies as well as those of other, unwanted insects.) Another bacterial disease, known as milky disease, attacks Japanese beetle grubs. Apply this granulated material over your lawn and water it into the soil, where it will infect the grubs.

Beneficial Insects

When you plant a number of different annuals and perennials, most of which produce nectar and pollen, you will attract many beneficial insects—such as lady beetle and lacewing larvae, praying mantids, and wasps—that eat or parasitize pests. In a healthy garden, natural populations of such insects will go a long way in keeping pests under control.

Organically Acceptable Insecticides

If, after you've tried other options, you still can't control a pest, you can try some of the less toxic insecticides that come from natural sources. These tend to break down faster than chemical pesticides and leave less environmental residue. Make sure you apply these products according to package directions and at the susceptible time in the pest's life cycle.

Insecticidal soaps, made of the potassium salts of fatty acids, will kill soft-bodied insects such as aphids, leafhoppers, mealybugs, and plant bugs. You can also

Praying mantids devour many other insects—pests and beneficials alike. They even eat each other.

Different plants are attacked by different pests or diseases. Foxgloves are susceptible to Japanese beetles, while poppies can get downy or powdery mildew.

spray with highly refined horticultural oils to coat plant leaves and to smother insects like aphids, mealybugs, leafminers, mites, and leafhoppers. Read the label carefully and apply only when the weather is cool. Before spraying a whole plant with either soap or oil, spray just a few leaves and wait a few days. If the leaves show any sort of damage, such as discoloring or spotting, find another control method.

Among the botanical insecticides, which are derived from plants, pyrethrins are effective on some beetles, caterpillars, aphids, and bugs. Rotenone will control beetles, borers, aphids, and red spider mites. Ryania is effective against beetles and caterpillars. Sabadilla, another botanical, is a powerful insecticide; use it as a last resort for tough pests like thrips. Botanical pesticides have broad-spectrum activity, meaning that they will harm beneficial as well as pest insects.

Identifying Some Common Diseases

Annuals and perennials that are sited in ideal growing conditions seldom suffer much from diseases. Sometimes, though, the weather or other influences beyond your control will provide the right conditions for fungal, bacterial, or viral diseases to attack your plants. Being aware of the most common diseases will help you take the appropriate prevention and control measures for your conditions.

Stunted Growth or Discolored Foliage

Diseases usually appear on particular species while ignoring others. If several different types of plants growing together have similar symptoms, you should suspect a nutrient deficiency, not a disease. Pale or yellow leaves may indicate a lack of nitrogen or iron. Mottled leaves may need

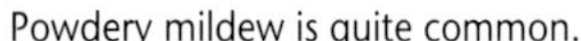
Powdery mildew is quite common.

Downy mildew has white spots.

Rust shows as light-colored spots.

Fungal wilts affect leaves and stems.

magnesium. Dark leaves with purple or red near the veins may lack phosphorus. Distorted growth and the death of young leaves and buds may indicate various micronutrient deficiencies.

The best approach to handling nutrient deficiencies is to take a soil test so you'll know what's missing and what you need to add. Sometimes, it's just a matter of adjusting the soil pH, so the nutrients that are already in your soil can become available to your perennials; more information on the nutrients that plants need can be found in "Adding Nutrients" on page 50. For a quick but short-term solution, spray the leaves of plants with fish emulsion or liquid seaweed. Working a good amount of compost into the soil before planting and using it as a mulch should keep your soil well stocked with a balanced supply of nutrients.

Fungal Diseases

Many different fungi attack annuals and perennials, causing a variety of symptoms. Rot fungi can affect perennial roots, crowns, stems, and flowers, usually making them turn soft and mushy. You will see rot most commonly on perennial roots growing in wet, heavy soil or on crowns planted too deeply in the garden. Among the most susceptible plants are baby's breath (*Gypsophila paniculata*), balloon flowers (*Platycodon grandiflorus*), coreopsis (*Coreopsis* spp.), delphiniums, irises, and garden phlox (*Phlox paniculata*).

Botrytis blight is a common fungal disease. It attacks flowers that open during wet weather, making them blacken and curl. Peonies, irises, and dahlias are especially susceptible.

Fungal leaf spots infect plants such as peonies, asters, daylilies, and columbines (*Aquilegia* spp.). The leaf spots disfigure foliage and, if not caught, can cause widespread defoliation and plant death.

Downy mildew and powdery mildew are fungal diseases that form a furry, white coating on the leaves of annuals and perennials like the different types of phlox, bee balm (*Monarda didyma*), asters, poppies (*Papaver* spp.), delphiniums, and dahlias. These diseases are unattractive and cause severely infected leaves to drop.

Rust diseases also attack annuals and perennials, including hollyhocks (*Alcea rosea*), garden mums (*Chrysanthemum* x *morifolium*), and asters. They turn the foliage a rusty color, often stunting growth and distorting leaf development.

Bacterial Diseases

Bacteria also can cause diseases that are characterized by wilting, rotting tissues,

This leaf has signs of iron deficiency, not disease.

Thin stems and cut back flowers after they've bloomed to minimize the chances of diseases developing.

Fungal and bacterial leaf spots affect foliage.

Mosaic produces yellow or white areas or streaks.

or root or lower-stem galls. Peonies and poppies can get a bacterial blight, which causes black spots on the leaves, flowers, and stems. Dahlias and baby's breath can be infected with bacterial crown gall, which stunts growth and can kill the plants. Coral bells (*Heuchera sanguinea*) can be attacked by a bacterial stem rot.

Viral Diseases

Viruses can cause perennial leaves or flowers to turn yellow or mottled yellow and green. They cause stunted growth and poor flowering or sudden wilting and death. Viruses are carried from plant to plant by sucking insects, such as aphids and leafhoppers, or by garden tools like pruning shears. Viral mosaic can attack dahlias, delphiniums, pinks (*Dianthus* spp.), peonies, and poppies. Aster yellows, which is a similar disease, infects baby's breath, balloon flowers, bellflowers (*Campanula* spp.), coreopsis, garden mums, and delphiniums.

Controlling Diseases

Good garden hygiene and proper plant selection go a long way toward preventing and controlling diseases. If you remove faded foliage in fall and cut back flowers after they bloom, you'll remove common sites of disease attack. If soilborne disease is a particular problem in your area, grow annuals and perennials in well-drained soil to reduce the likelihood of root diseases getting a start. Also, try not to damage the plant roots when you work the soil or weed.

Careful watering can help reduce disease outbreaks. Whenever possible, avoid wetting plant leaves. If foliage stays wet overnight, fungal spores may have time to germinate and attack leaves. Overhead watering and even walking through wet foliage can transfer disease from plant to plant. Use a ground-level irrigation system, like a trickle system or drip irrigation, and don't work in the garden when plants are still wet from a recent fall of rain.

If the weather is cold and wet or hot and humid—conditions that encourage disease—and if you grow susceptible plants, you may get an outbreak of disease in the garden. When a disease does strike, remove damaged plant parts promptly, before the disease can spread, and throw them away with the household trash. This can go a long way toward controlling diseases.

If your garden has had problems with diseases in past years, you may want to make a preventive treatment with ecologically acceptable, organic materials. Antitranspirants—leaf coatings that are ordinarily used to protect broad-leaved evergreens during winter—may reduce fungal disease problems. You can try dusting foliage with powdered sulfur to prevent mildew, rust, and leaf spots. A baking soda spray (1 teaspoon of baking soda to 1 quart [1 L] of water) can prevent and control some fungal problems. Compost tea and seaweed-based fertilizer sprays can also help prevent diseases. If a disease becomes rampant and even sprays do not help, replace the plant with something that is not susceptible—a different species or a resistant cultivar.

In most cases, diseases are not a big problem in the annual and perennial garden. Choosing the right plants for your conditions, preparing the soil thoroughly, and planting with the proper spacing all contribute to problem-free plants. Inspect new additions carefully for any signs of disease before setting them loose in the garden. If you have any doubts, consider throwing the plant away or, if that seems too drastic, plant it in an isolated spot in the yard. Move it into the garden if it seems all right at the end of the season. Dispose of it if it's diseased.

Using ecologically acceptable controls against plant disease problems means you don't destroy your garden's diversity.

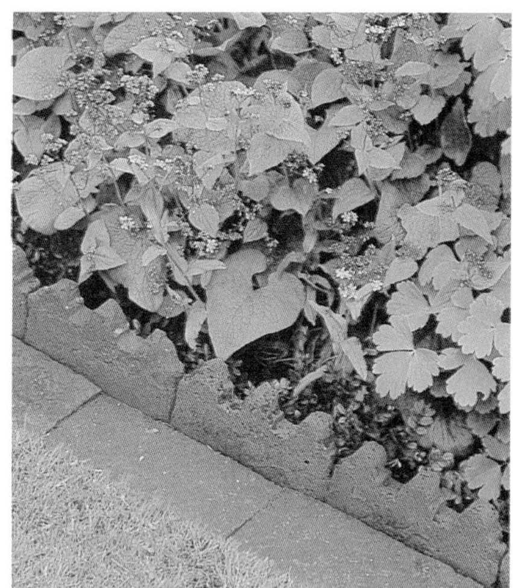

A mowing strip will stop the lawn from invading your plants and keep the garden looking neat.

Weed Them Out

Like pests and diseases, weeds can pop up in even the most well-cared-for gardens. The trick is to take care of the problem early, before the weeds get large enough to compete with your plants for space, light, water, and nutrients.

Perennial Weeds

Like the perennial flowers you're growing in the garden, perennial weeds will live for many years once they are established. What separates the unwanted weeds from the desirable plants is often the speed with which the weeds can spread. Many perennial weeds, like bindweed and Canada thistle, have creeping underground stems, called rhizomes. These rhizomes can spread quickly in the loose, rich soil of your flower garden, quickly engulfing your desirable plants. Other perennial weeds have long, tough taproots. If you break off the top of the plant, a new one will quickly sprout from the root.

Loosening the soil with a spading fork can make hand-pulling weeds a whole lot easier.

Thoroughly removing the roots of perennial weeds as you prepare the soil for planting will go a long way toward keeping these weeds at bay. Mulching and regular weeding will help prevent new perennial weeds from getting started.

If perennial weeds get out of control despite your best efforts, it's often easiest to just start the bed over. Dig up your good perennials and set them aside until you can dig through the bed and remove all the fleshy roots of the weeds. Before you replant your perennials, make sure their clumps are free of weed roots, too; otherwise, the weeds will have an easy time reinvading your garden.

Dandelions have deep, tough taproots that are difficult to remove. They also have fine, floating seeds that spread easily.

One of the most common weed problems in perennial gardens is lawn grass, which will creep in along the edges of beds and borders. Block invasion of grass by cutting along the garden's edge frequently with a sharp spade or edger and remove the errant sprigs of grass. Or take preventive action when you dig the bed: Add a metal, wood, stone, brick, or plastic edging to form a barrier around the perimeter of the garden. Sink the edging at least 4 to 6 inches (10 to 15 cm) deep to block creeping grass stems in their underground movement.

Annual Weeds

Annual weeds may not have the invasive roots of their perennial counterparts, but they will reproduce themselves hundreds of times over from seed, often growing fast and spreading far. The key to controlling annual weeds is to remove them from the garden before they set seed. Cut them off or scrape them out of the soil with a hoe or hand weeder. If the soil is soft or damp, you can easily pull the entire weed, root and all, by hand. Snip weeds with scissors if you think pulling will damage small or newly planted annuals and perennials that are nearby. Throw the weeds, as long as they are seed-free, into your compost pile.

How to Be Weed-wise

Weed control starts while you are preparing the bed for your new garden. Removing the sod from the area and composting it will remove many of the existing weeds. As you dig, keep an eye out for the long white roots of spreading weeds. Thoroughly remove any of these

Landscape fabrics make effective weed-proof covers. Lay over prepared soil, cut slits for planting, then cover with a mulch.

roots; if you leave even little pieces, roots can quickly sprout into new plants.

Once your annuals and perennials are well established, you can control most weeds if you mulch and weed conscientiously for the first year or two. By the third year, your perennial clumps should be well filled in, leaving little room for weed invasion.

Pulling and Digging Pulling gets rid of annual weeds well, especially if the soil is damp enough for the roots to come up easily. Just be sure not to toss weeds that reroot easily, such as purslane (*Portulaca oleracea*), on the ground. Always try to pull annuals before they begin to flower and set seed. If they have already started flowering, collect the pulled weeds in a bucket; don't leave them on the ground, since their seeds could still ripen, drop onto the soil, and germinate.

Digging is a slightly better choice for perennial weeds, assuming you get all of the buried portions of the plant. If you don't, these buried portions can quickly produce new weeds. Use hand tools to dig out small or shallow-rooted perennials. You may need a spading fork, spade, or shovel for tough, deep roots, like those of pokeweed (*Phytolacca americana*) and dandelion.

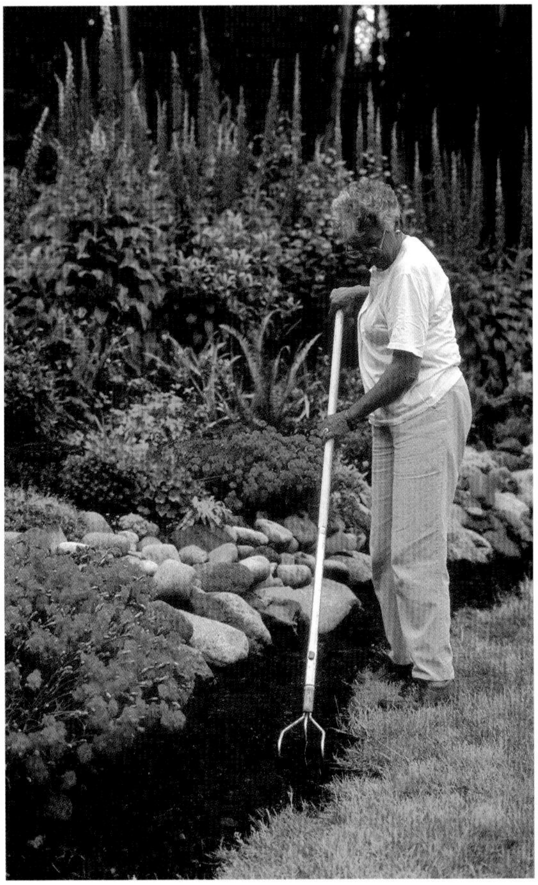

Hoeing flower gardens once or twice early in the season can control weeds until your plants fill in to cover the soil.

Hoeing and Tilling When the weeds are too numerous to pull up one by one, by hand, a sharp hoe is a good solution. In most cases, hoes are best for young or annual weeds. But you can also deal a damaging blow to some established perennials—primarily those with thin or soft stems—by forcing them to use their food reserves to replace the decapitated top growth.

There are several schools of thought about the best time to hoe. One says you should hoe when the soil is damp, so the roots pull out easily. Another says to hoe when the soil is dry, scraping the weeds off at the soil surface without disturbing the soil or digging up new weed seed. Most of us just hoe when we find time and inspiration. All of these approaches are reasonable. If you're trying to control perennial weeds, it's most important to hoe every 7 to 14 days to cut off the top growth before it starts sending food back down to the roots.

Removing weeds when they're small or preventing them from sprouting in the first place will make the job of weed control much easier.

Mowing Mowing doesn't get the roots, but it can keep all but the lowest-growing weeds from setting seed. And if you mow often enough (every week or two), it weakens perennials by making them use up their food reserves to replace the top growth you've removed.

Mowing works on woody shrubs and vines as long as the stems aren't too thick for the machine. For tall, tough weeds and tree seedlings no more than ¾ inch (18 mm) in diameter, use a heavy-duty string trimmer with a blade attachment. If you must control brush over a large area, consider renting a walk-behind tractor with a sickle-bar attachment.

Pruning and Training

Carefully pinching the growing tip out of clumping plants will promote bushy growth.

A pinch of this and a stake for that—these and other simple steps are the recipe for a neat-looking, flower-filled garden. The tips and techniques below can be used to promote sturdier stems and bigger or more abundant blooms throughout your flower garden.

Pinching

Pinching is a quick and easy technique that is useful for many kinds of annuals and perennials. Use it to:

- Promote bushy growth. Much like a heading cut, a well-placed pinch removes the stem tip bud. This generally encourages the remaining buds lower on the stem to grow, making the plant fuller.
- Reduce staking chores. Pinching also promotes sturdier stems, considerably reducing the need for staking to keep plants upright and looking good.
- Delay flowering. The best example is the traditional practice of pinching garden mums (*Chrysanthemum* x *morifolium*) to delay flowering until fall. Begin pinching them in spring and continue about every 2 weeks until July 4 in the South and mid-July in the North. Don't pinch later than that or your plants may not bloom.
- Discourage flowering altogether. Regular pinching can put off flowering on certain plants. This technique is commonly used to promote fresh new growth on herbs such as sweet marjoram, basil, and oregano, which otherwise can become stringy and tasteless once flowering begins. Use the same trick on coleus when you wish to promote the colorful leaves instead of the insignificant flowers.
- Extend the bloom season. Extend the bloom time of a mass planting by pinching only half of the plants or by giving half of them one less pinch than the rest. The less-pinched plants will bloom earlier, followed by the more-pinched plants.

The best time to pinch annuals is at planting time. Pinch perennials as they start their spring growth, when there are several sets of full leaves on each stem. Pinch annuals and perennials by taking tip growth away with your thumb and forefinger, normally down to the first full set of leaves below the tip; also pinch away dead or yellow stems or leaves. If the stems are too tough or wiry to break easily with your fingers, use scissors or a sharp pair of pruning shears to make a clean cut.

Pinching Precautions

There are a few situations where pinching may not be helpful. You can't, for instance, depend on pinching to make a plant shorter. Many annuals, perennials, and herbs that are pinched eventually attain the same height they would have grown to had they not been pinched—they're just fuller and sturdier.

Don't pinch plants that send up a single leafy stalk (like lilies) or leafless flowering stalks (like irises). Otherwise, you'll end up taking off the flower buds, and you'll be left with plain stalks sticking up out of the garden.

A midseason pinch works well to keep annuals such as impatiens and begonias from collapsing under their own weight—or flopping under a heavy rain—during a long growing season. Reach about one-third of the way into the plant on each

Pinch your garden mums to delay flowering until fall and to promote the largest number of blooms.

stem and pinch at a joint. The pinched plants may look slightly bedraggled initially. But after a few days, they'll be off and blooming again, only shorter now, more compact, and less likely to be damaged during a storm. Do a pinch like this in the early morning or on a cloudy day to keep the tender interior foliage from being scorched. Toss the trimmings in the compost pile or root them in potting soil to make new plants.

Disbudding

If you are growing dahlias, garden mums, or peonies, you may want to try disbudding to encourage fewer but larger flowers. This technique is easy—simply support the stem gently with one hand and rub or pinch off the unwanted side buds with your other hand. Each disbudded stem will bear one bloom that is larger and showier than normal. Disbudding is not necessarily a technique you'll use regularly, but it's fun to try if you want to have a few special, large blooms for display or use in arrangements.

The Don'ts of Deadheading

Despite the advantages of deadheading, you may have good cause to skip it on occasion. Spare the seedpods of perennials that you want to self-sow, like foxgloves (*Digitalis* spp.) and wild columbines (*Aquilegia canadensis*). You may also want to leave any attractive seedpods or cones alone; they can extend the beauty of certain perennials through the dormant season. Try this with the velvety black or orange-brown cones of coneflowers (*Rudbeckia* and *Echinacea* spp.), the glossy, dark seed clusters of blackberry lilies (*Belamcanda chinensis*), the dry, feathery plumes of astilbes, the russet pods of 'Autumn Joy' sedum (*Sedum* 'Autumn Joy'), and the papery "flowers" of Lenten roses (*Helleborus* x *orientalis*). You may also want to spare the plume-like seed heads of ornamental grasses that you grow with your annuals and perennials.

Pruning shears are handy for deadheading spent flowers that have thick or wiry stems.

Deadheading

Deadhead your annuals, perennials, and herbs by pinching off spent flowers. This practice keeps the blooms coming by directing the plant's energy back into more flowers (or into bulb formation) rather than into seed production. Deadheading also prevents plants that self-sow readily—like morning glories (*Ipomoea* spp.)—from seeding themselves throughout your garden. Don't use this technique if you want to collect the seed or if you are growing the plant for its decorative seed heads.

To deadhead, snap off faded blooms with your fingers or snip them off with pruning shears. On plants with terminal flowers, pinch the blooms back to a set of full leaves; as a result, you're likely to get additional flowers from the side buds. On plants with flowers that arise on a single, leafless stem—including hostas, poppies (*Papaver* spp.), pincushion flower (*Scabiosa caucasica*), and most bulbs—follow that stem down to its base and pinch it there.

Cutting Back

Cutting stems back with hand pruners, grass shears, or even string trimmers is a satisfying and worthwhile pruning project that you can do almost anytime.

Fall and Winter Trimming

If you like the garden to look tidy over winter, you could cut back all remaining perennials to just above ground level after the first frost. For winter interest, though, you may choose to leave ornamental grasses, evergreen perennials and herbs, and plants with interesting seed heads, like showy stonecrop (*Sedum spectabile*) and coneflowers (*Rudbeckia* spp.). You can wait until late winter to cut these plants back to just above the ground. Make sure

Deadhead poppies for rebloom, then leave the last flowers in place to allow the plants to self-seed.

If left untrimmed, sedums' dense blooms develop into seed heads that are ideal for winter interest.

you remove the old top growth before spring, or you may end up cutting off some of the new growth as well. If the plants get ratty and unattractive, you'll do no harm by cutting them back earlier.

Spring and Summer Trimming

Consider cutting back mat-forming perennials after they bloom. Shear the stems back by about half to encourage compact growth—and sometimes you may even get a second flush of bloom—on perennial candytuft (*Iberis sempervirens*), wall rock cress (*Arabis caucasica*), moss pinks (*Phlox subulata*), catmints (*Nepeta* spp.), and snow-in-summer (*Cerastium tomentosum*).

Cutting plants back by half in early summer can promote sturdier stems on many tall-growing plants, including asters, ironweeds (*Vernonia* spp.), great blue lobelia (*Lobelia syphilitica*), and tall native sunflowers (*Helianthus* spp.). Your fall garden will be graced with the later-than-normal flowers and your plants will resist the temptation to keel over when burdened with all those blooms. But do resist the urge to trim tall stems much after early summer or the plants may not have time to develop new flower buds before frost.

Another great use for cutting back is the old "cut and come again" trick. Shear off the top third of bushy, multistemmed plants after flowering, and you may get another flush of bloom later in the season. Try this on vigorously growing mints, coreopsis (*Coreopsis* spp.), bee balms (*Monarda* spp.), gaura (*Gaura lindheimeri*), and boltonia (*Boltonia asteroides*).

Staking

Staking takes a little effort to do properly, but the end result can be magnificent. Spend time in spring to put stakes around the plants you know tend to flop—like peonies, dahlias, and asters—and you'll save yourself the heartache of seeing their beautiful blooms sprawling in the mud after a summer storm.

Bamboo Stakes

Bamboo stakes are great for supporting upright, spiky plants such as snapdragons (*Antirrhinum majus*), foxgloves (*Digitalis* spp.), and delphiniums. Use stakes that are about two-thirds of the ultimate height of the stem. Place the stakes firmly in the ground when the plants are young, being careful not to insert them through the crowns of the plants. Attach soft fabric or yarn ties to the stakes and knot the loose ends around the stems as they grow.

To support bushy plants like yarrows (*Achillea* spp.) and baby's breath (*Gypsophila paniculata*), place 3 or 4 stakes around the clump so that the outer edges of the plant will cover them as the plant grows. String twine back and forth among the stakes to support the stems as they grow.

Pea Brush

Pea brush (also called pea staking) is another, far more casual-looking, option for supporting annuals and perennials with slender, floppy stems, like larkspur (*Consolida ambigua*) and asters. It's also a great way to recycle the woody prunings from trees and shrubs. However, as a precaution, you may want to let the prunings dry out in the sun for a week or so before using them as

What to Cut Back

Certain perennials benefit from cutting back. Give spring bloomers a trim after they flower to tidy them up for the rest of the season. Cut back summer bloomers after their first flush; some may bloom again later in the season. Here are some perennials that like being cut back.

Spring bloomers: rock cress (*Arabis caucasica*), creeping phlox (*Phlox stolonifera*), goat's beard (*Aruncus dioicus*).
Summer bloomers: Frikart's aster (*Aster* x *frikartii*), catmint (*Nepeta* x *faassenii*), Persian cornflower (*Centaurea dealbata*), common spiderwort (*Tradescantia* x *andersoniana*), common thrift (*Armeria maritima*), bellflowers (*Campanula* spp.), blanket flower (*Gaillardia* x *grandiflora*), sages (*Salvia* spp.), lavender cotton (*Santolina chamaecyparissus*), spotted lamium (*Lamium maculatum*), soapworts (*Saponaria* spp.), pincushion flower (*Scabiosa caucasica*).

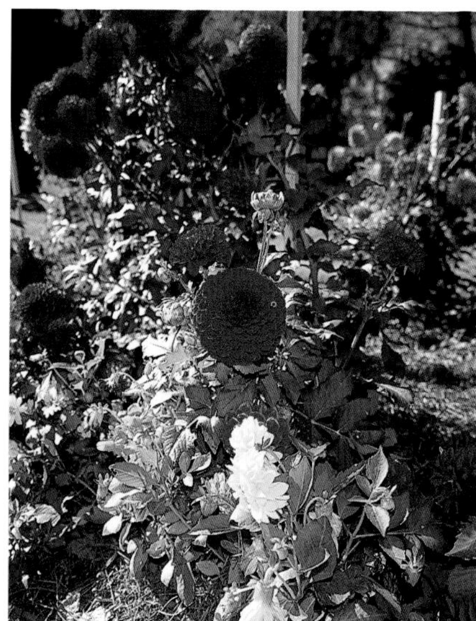

Individual wooden stakes help support the tall, bushy growth and heavy flowers of dahlias.

Careful placement of plants, followed by discreet staking, routine deadheading, and trimming back at season's end, will ensure a tidy yet bountiful garden.

Cages will help flower stems to grow straight.

stakes; if you stick fresh stems into the soil, some might actually take root!

In early spring, push the stem ends of small twiggy branches firmly into the ground around seedlings, annual transplants, or emerging perennial shoots. The tops of the twigs should be slightly shorter than the ultimate height of the plants they are supporting. As the leaves fill in and the plants approach full size, the staking becomes invisible.

Cages

Cages and other wire supports are useful for bushy annuals and perennials, like asters, peonies, and Japanese anemones (*Anemone* x *hybrida*). Set commercial ring or linking stakes either over or around emerging clumps, or make your own supports with pieces of wire-mesh fencing and wooden stakes.

Finally, if you find that you're doing entirely too much staking, check your soil's fertility. Columbines (*Aquilegia* spp.), spiderworts (*Tradescantia* spp.), and other annuals and perennials that grow well in lean to moderately fertile soils often grow tall and spindly when given too rich a diet. Hold off on the fertilizer and compost for a year or two.

Preparing for Winter

Once the flowers start to fade and you can feel a definite chill in the air, it's time for the last outdoor maintenance task of the season. By preparing your garden for winter, you will ensure that your annuals and perennials will be back again in the spring.

Fall Cleanup for Perennials

To help your perennials survive their winter ordeal, give all perennial beds a thorough watering before the ground freezes. Remove dead foliage and cut dead stems back to the ground. Compost garden debris unless it's diseased or full of seeds; if so, bury or dispose of it. After the first hard frost, give your beds a generous layer of mulch to protect plants from frost heaving and dramatic temperature changes. Use about 1 inch (2.5 cm) of heavy materials, like bark chips, or about 3 inches (7.5 cm) of light mulches, such as pine needles or chopped leaves. In particularly cold or exposed sites without dependable snow cover, also add an extra cover of light branches (those from pines or firs work well), pine needles, or (after the holidays) boughs from a discarded Christmas tree. You will have to remove this covering and pull the mulch back from around the base of the plants in early spring to let the soil warm up.

If fall is always a busy time for you and you never quite finish your garden cleanup, don't worry. Some plants, such as ornamental grasses and plants with interesting seedpods (including astilbes and blue false indigo [*Baptisia australis*]), are beautiful well into winter. You can leave these standing until early spring.

A layer of pine needles will protect your plants from the effects of extreme temperature changes.

While many plants have finished flowering by fall, love lies bleeding and certain sages are still in bloom.

Most of the garden won't look so tidy if it is not cut back, but it will get through the winter just the same. Standing stems actually help hold lightweight mulches in place through winter storms. Focus your cleanup time on any plants that showed signs of disease this year or in previous years; fall cleanup reduces the chance of future recurrence.

In spring, get into the garden early (when the soil dries out and no longer squishes underfoot) to cut remaining stems back before new spring growth starts. Otherwise, it will become a much more complicated and time-consuming task as you try to trim out the old growth without damaging the new shoots. If you've had problems in the past with certain plants, like mulleins (*Verbascum* spp.) and patrinia (*Patrinia scabiosifolia*), reseeding too prolifically, cut off their seed heads in the fall.

Annuals Ready for Winter

Before the first frost, take cuttings from or dig up any special annuals that you want to grow again next year and take them inside for the winter; see "Bringing Annuals Indoors" for more information. Also collect any seeds you want to save.

After the first hard frost, tender and half-hardy annuals usually turn brown; pull these out and toss them on the compost pile. Hardy annuals such as alyssum (*Lobularia maritima*) may keep blooming through several frosts; you can either pull them out in fall or wait until early spring. Foxgloves (*Digitalis* spp.), honesty (*Lunaria annua*), and other biennials usually make it through winter just fine, but a protective layer of mulch applied after the ground is frozen can help in severe-winter areas.

Handling Tender Bulbs

The final part of your gardening duties before winter sets in is to see to your tender bulbs, which seem to need more work than cold-hardy bulbs such as daffodils and crocus. With the latter, you just plant them once and enjoy them for years. With the former, you may have to dig or lift them for winter storage indoors. But when you consider the beautiful blooms you get in return, you'll probably agree that tender bulbs are worth a little extra effort.

Exactly what counts as a tender bulb? Well, it depends on what climate you live in, but bulbs that often spring to mind are those from tropical and subtropical climates. These include dahlias, tuberous begonias, gladioli, cannas, and caladiums. Some tender bulbs can take more cold than others. Cannas, for instance, may survive winters in areas as cold as Zone 7. Others, including tuberous begonias and caladiums, can survive over winter only in frost-free areas.

Astilbe seed heads can look attractive even after turning brown; consider leaving them for winter.

If you're not sure which bulbs are tender in your area, you can often figure it out by noting when you find them for sale. You'll generally find tender bulbs at local garden centers in late winter to midspring. You can also check catalog descriptions or refer to the individual plant entries in "Encyclopedia of Flowers," starting on page 306. In addition to information on each bulb's preferred climate, the plant entries also provide tips on how to handle each kind of bulb for indoor storage.

Once you learn the basics, you'll see that it's not difficult to keep your favorite tender bulbs from year to year.

Most annuals turn brown after the first frosts, but alyssum is hardy and will bloom a little longer.

Bringing Annuals Indoors

The first frost of fall doesn't have to signal the end of your annuals' bloom season. With just a little effort, you can enjoy their colorful flowers on your windowsills all winter.

Tender perennials that are usually grown as annuals usually adapt best to life indoors. These include coleus, geraniums (*Pelargonium* spp., both flowering and scented-leaf types), impatiens (including New Guinea types), wax begonias, and heliotrope (*Heliotropium arborescens*).

Overwintering these plants indoors allows you to keep them year after year, so you don't need to buy new ones each year. It's also a great way to preserve plants that have special traits, like especially good fragrance, an unusual flower form, or a striking color that you particularly like.

To overwinter annuals indoors, dig up whole plants before the first fall frost, cut them back by about one-third, and plant them in pots. Or take 3- to 5-inch (7.5- to 12.5-cm) cuttings from healthy, vigorous stems in mid- to late summer. Snip cuttings from non-flowering shoots if possible; otherwise, pinch off any flowers and flower buds. Remove the leaves from the lower half of the cutting and insert the bottom one-third of the stem into a pot of moist potting soil. Enclose the pot in a plastic bag and set it in a bright place out of direct sun. When cuttings are well rooted—usually in 3 to 4 weeks—remove the bag and move the pot to a sunny windowsill.

Whether you bring in whole plants or just cuttings, inspect them carefully first for any signs of pests or diseases. Avoid bringing in affected plants if possible. If you really want to save a special plant that has a problem, treat it as explained in "Pests, Diseases, Weeds" on page 92 or check the individual entries in "Encyclopedia of Flowers," starting on page 306.

During the winter, look after your annuals as you would any other houseplants. In the spring, move them back into the garden after the last frost date. Help them make the adjustment between indoors and outdoors by moving them out into the sunshine gradually; see "Handling Hardening Off" on page 57 for guidelines.

Lifting for Storage

Digging tender bulbs for indoor storage is just another part of routine fall-garden cleanup. When the bulb foliage turns yellow or brown, that's a good sign that the bulb is ready for storage. If the leaves stay green or if you don't have time to dig the bulbs when they are first ready, you can wait until just after the first frost. The cold temperatures will cause the leaves to turn black, but the bulbs are protected by the soil and should survive a light frost just fine. Don't wait any longer, though—get out and start digging, or your bulbs may get damaged by the increasingly cold temperatures.

Actually digging up the bulbs is simple. First, cut any tall stems back to about 6 inches (15 cm), so you can clearly see the base of the stem. Then carefully loosen the soil all the way around the plant. Use a trowel or hand fork to work around small bulbs and those growing in pots. (You can also turn whole pots over to dump out the soil and the bulbs at the same time.) A shovel or spading fork works better for big clumps, like dahlias and cannas.

Lilies can be planted in fall or you can wait until spring; at least prepare the bed in fall and mulch thickly.

Showy autumn crocuses flower in fall. The leaves die down but the corms don't need to be stored.

Once the soil is loose, you can lift the bulb easily. Shake off as much soil as you can from the bulbs, label them, and set them on newspaper in a cool, shady place, such as a garage, potting shed, or porch. Dust any cuts on the bulbs or tubers with sulfur and leave them to dry for several days. Keep the bulbs out of the hot sun and away from areas where squirrels, mice, and other animals can get at them; otherwise, the local wildlife may think you're providing a buffet lunch for them.

Storing

Once your bulbs have dried for a few days, you can store them. Some gardeners keep their bulbs in mesh bags (like the kind onions come in) or paper bags with a few holes punched in them for better air circulation. Others prefer to store bulbs in boxes of slightly damp wood shavings or peat moss to keep the bulbs from drying out too much over winter. The first year or two, try storing some bulbs each way and see what works best for you; then stick with that method. Either way, make sure you keep the bulbs labeled, since many look alike and it's easy to forget which is which.

Once the bulbs are packaged, you need to find a good storage spot. It should be dark to prevent the bulbs from sprouting and on the cool side—ideally about 50° to 60°F (10° to 16°C). Possible sites include

Gladioli are tender bulbs that must be lifted and stored over winter, to be replanted in the spring.

Lifting and Storing Tender Bulbs

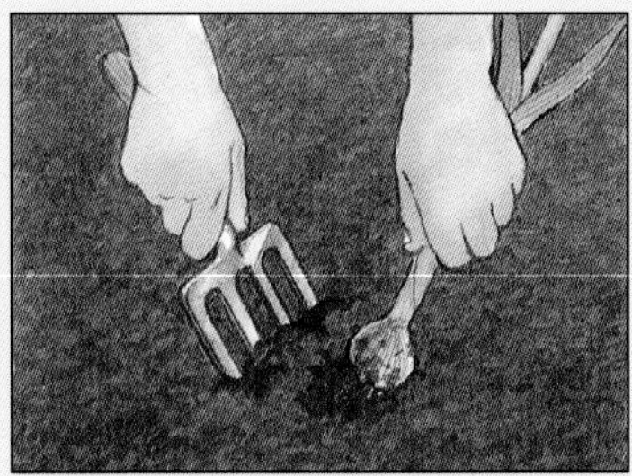

1. Use a garden fork to carefully lift the bulb from the ground.

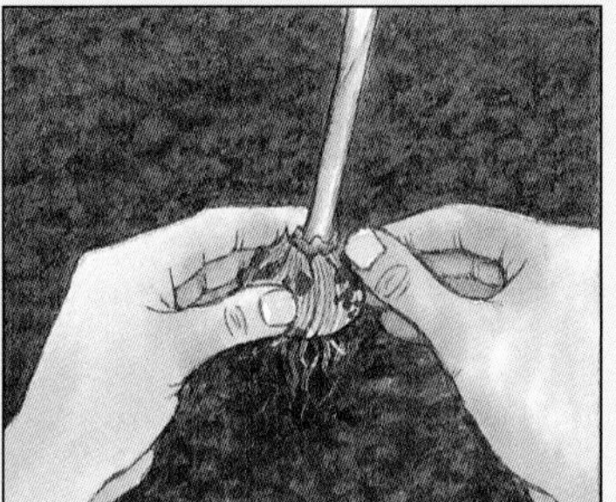

2. Brush off as much soil as you can from around the bulb and its roots.

3. Lay the bulbs out to dry in a sheltered spot for a few days.

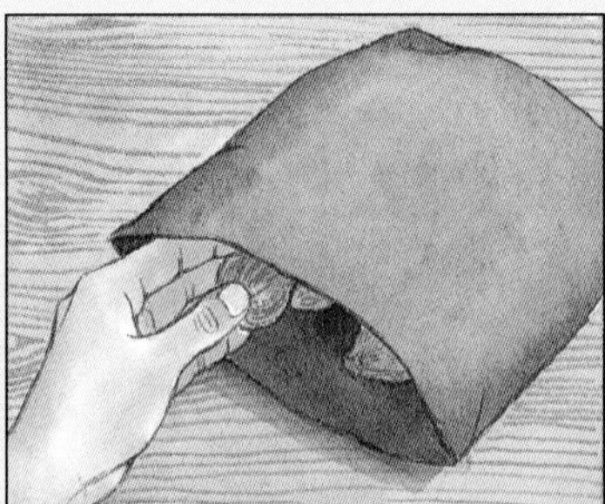

4. Store the bulbs in a bag or box and set them in a cool, dark place.

basement cupboards, insulated attics, crawl spaces, and attached garages that don't freeze. Experiment to find the best storage spot in your home.

During the storage period, check your bulbs every 3 to 4 weeks. Throw away any that are rotting. Sprinkle water on those that are starting to look shriveled. When spring arrives, retrieve your bulbs from storage and plant them in the garden or in pots as you would new store-bought bulbs. For suggested planting times, check the individual entries in the "Guide to Popular Perennials" on page 202.

When tuberous begonias are ready to grow in spring, they'll produce little green or pink shoots.

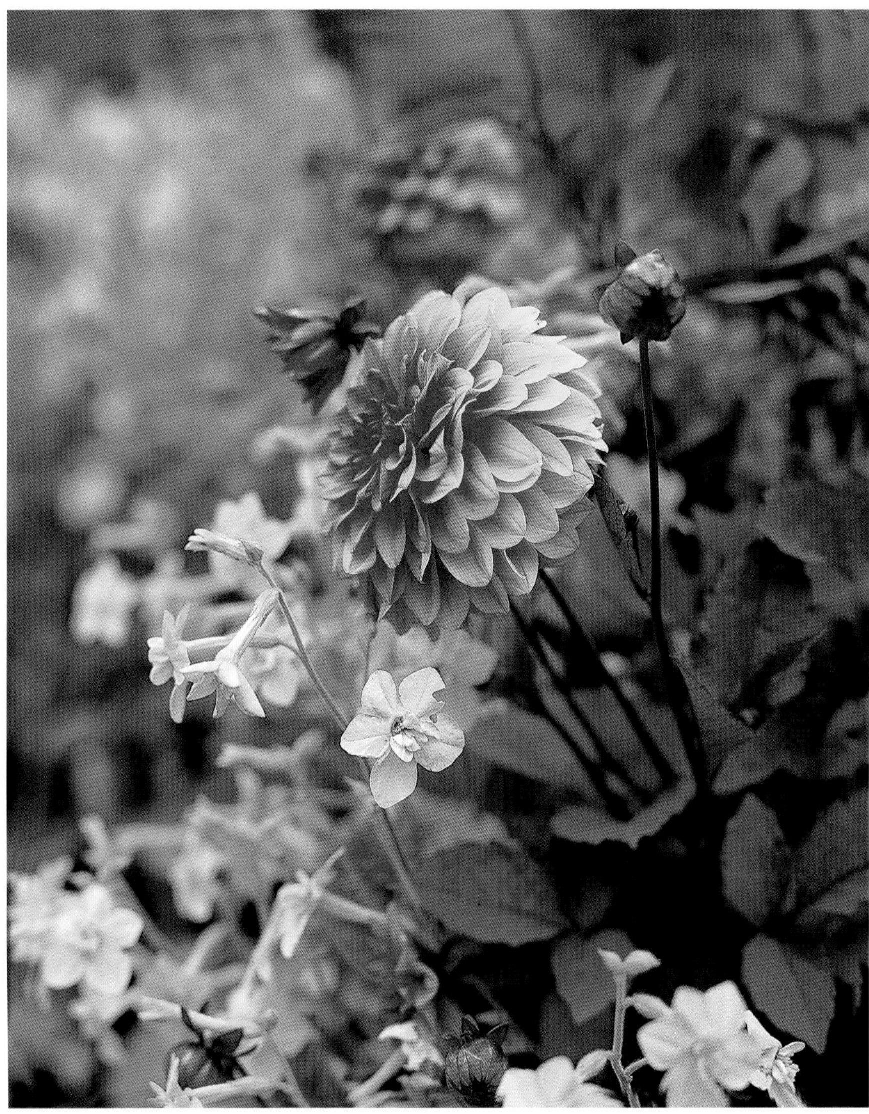

Buy new dahlia roots each year, or dig up your favorites in fall and store them indoors for the winter.

Month by Month in the Flower Garden

Like all bulbs, there is a right and a wrong time to plant ranunculus so they flower with the spring.

When is the best time to plant bulbs? When should you divide your perennials? What can you do in the garden on a cold November day? Even experienced gardeners sometimes forget what needs to be done in the garden and when to do it. In this section, you'll find a month-by-month calendar with handy reminders of the garden jobs that are appropriate for each month of the year.

This calendar is based on Zone 6, where the frost-free growing season is approximately late April to mid-October. If your garden is in a different zone, it's easy to adapt this calendar to fit your region. To find out which zone you're in, check the Plant Hardiness Zone Maps, starting on page 588.

In warmer climates (Zones 7 to 9), spring comes sooner, so do the March to May chores a month or two earlier (the warmer the climate, the sooner you can start) and wait until the first frost to do your fall cleanup. In Zone 10, ignore the fall cleanup and mulching information; keep weeding, watering, and watching for pests throughout the year.

In colder zones and at high elevations (where the frost-free season is more likely to be late May or early June to late August or early September), this calendar will be about a month ahead of you for much of the year. Wait a month to do your March to May chores, finish the September chores in August, and start your fall garden cleanup after the first frost.

January

Review any notes that you made in your notebook about last year's garden; transfer important reminders (such as plants that you want to move or divide) to a list or calendar for the upcoming year. Daydream about how you want to use your yard when the warm weather returns. Start or revise your new or existing garden plans (even if you need snowshoes or an umbrella to inventory your yard).

Take stock of stored tender bulbs and any seeds that you've collected; toss out any that aren't sound. Order summer bulbs and plants from mail-order catalogs soon to avoid the rush. During thaws, check the garden beds for plant heaving; replace the soil around any exposed roots.

February

On warm days (or when the snow melts), inventory the garden to list cleanup chores for next month. Plan a weeding session; warm days in February and March are great times for getting rid of winter annual weeds, such as chickweed.

March is a good time to turn last year's compost.

March

As weather permits, clean up stray leaves, winter debris, remaining stems, and anything left undone last fall. Cut back ornamental grasses. Try not to step in beds where the soil is still wet. When the forsythias begin to show their cheerful yellow flowers, pull some of the winter mulch off of your beds so the soil can warm up. Turn last year's compost pile so it will be ready to spread when the ground warms up. Start a new pile with the debris from your spring cleanup. Take soil tests.

Nemesia needs a long, cool growing period; know your last frost date and set transplants out after then.

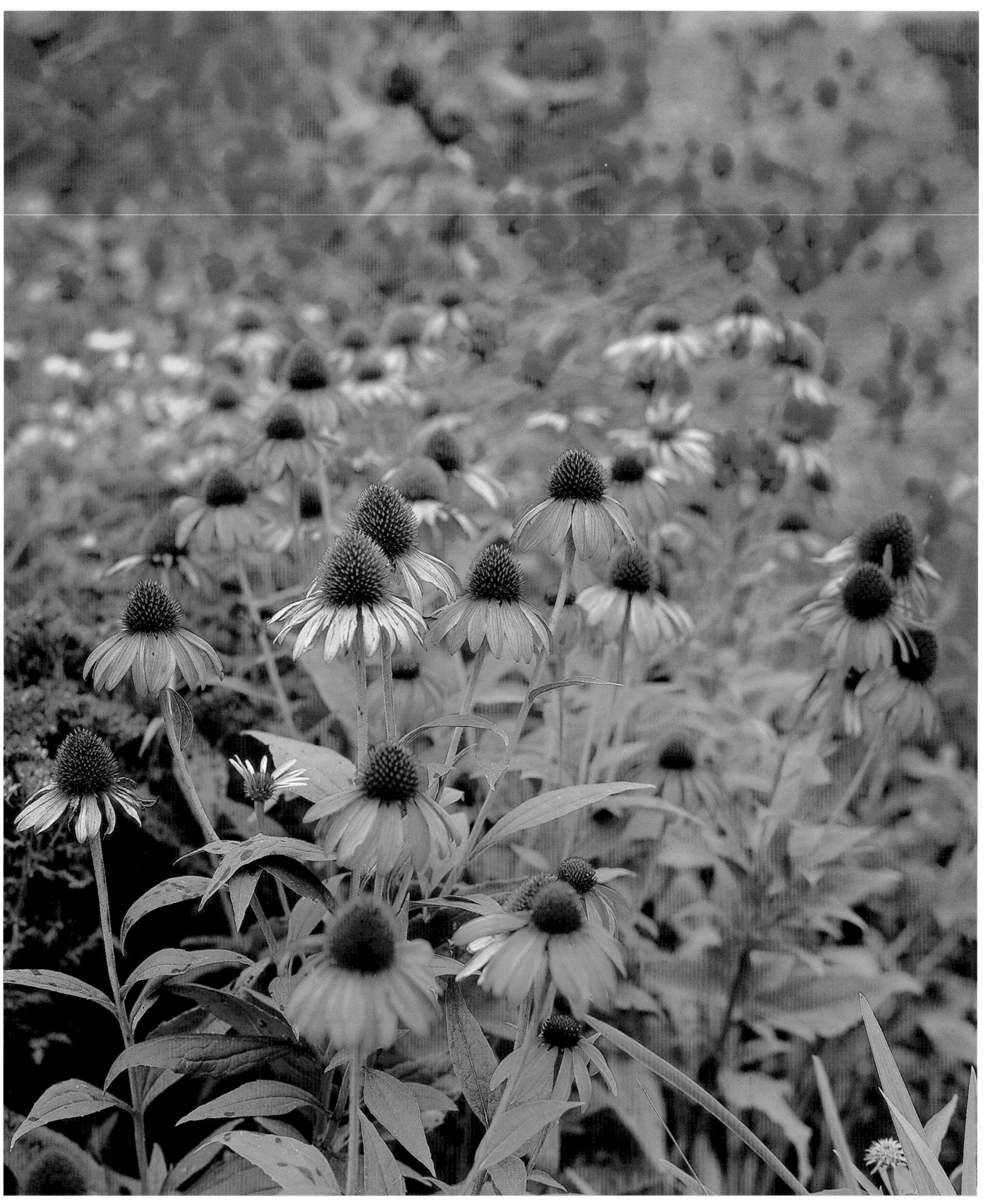

Perennials can be protected from frosts and extreme winter temperatures with a layer of mulch applied after the soil freezes. Start removing the mulch in March.

Thin the stems of garden phlox in May, before it blooms, to reduce the likelihood of powdery mildew.

Check out the garden shows that are held in your local area to get new garden design and planting ideas.

April

Finish your garden cleanup; pull up and discard any weeds. Dig over your annual garden beds, add plenty of compost, and include fertilizers as needed. Add any nutrients recommended by your soil test results in the general garden area, too. Start scouting for pests. In dry climates, set out drip irrigation systems for easy watering once the weather warms up.

As you enjoy your spring bulbs, jot down some notes to remind you what you want to add in the fall for next year. Top-dress bulb plantings with compost or balanced organic fertilizer for good blooms next year. Remove any spent flowers but leave the foliage until it dies back so bulbs can store enough energy to bloom next year. Side-dress clumps of emerging perennials with compost or well-rotted manure. Give annuals and any perennials that need rich soil—including phlox, delphiniums, and bee balms (*Monarda* spp.)—a little organic fertilizer. Divide summer- and fall-blooming perennials when the new shoots are about 3 inches (7.5 cm) tall.

May

Plant bareroot perennials and container-grown plants as you get them. Divide and replant spring-blooming perennials and crowded bulbs after they flower. Plant annuals, tender perennials, and tender bulbs (including dahlias and gladioli) outside once the danger of frost has passed. Add annuals to beds to hide the dying foliage of hardy bulbs. Replace and replenish mulch.

Pinch back perennials that tend to get leggy, such as New England asters (*Aster novae-angliae*) and garden mums (*Chrysanthemum* x *morifolium*). Thin out the weakest stems of clump-formers like garden phlox (*Phlox paniculata*). Pull or dig weed seedlings as soon as you spot them or they'll quickly get out of hand. Place wire ring stakes around peonies and other perennials that tend to flop; stake any tall flower stalks individually. If slugs or snails are a problem in your garden, set out shallow pans of beer to trap them; empty the traps regularly.

June

Walk through your garden regularly, both to enjoy it and to scout for problems. Remove and destroy diseased foliage. Stake annuals and perennials that need support if you didn't do it last month. Remove spent blossoms to prevent plants from self-seeding.

Watch the weather; water if rainfall is scarce. Wait until the top 1 to 2 inches (2.5 to 5 cm) of soil is dry, then water thoroughly. Container plantings may need daily watering during hot spells.

July

If you've kept up on your garden chores so far, you'll have earned a chance to relax just as the weather starts to heat up. Take some lemonade into the garden and make notes in your garden journal.

Water your perennials as needed. If the weather is very dry, consider watering the

Before you set out transplants of climbing annuals, be sure to install a support for the vines to climb on.

Foxglove penstemons should be divided every 4 to 6 years, after they have finished flowering in early fall.

compost pile, too; it will break down faster when evenly moist. Cut flowers for indoor arrangements in the morning, before the heat of the day. Remove spent flowers. Order spring bulbs this month or next to arrive in time for fall planting.

August

Now is the best time to move or divide oriental poppies (*Papaver orientale*), bearded irises, and—at the end of the month—peonies. Keep up the weeding, deadheading, pest patrol, and watering; remove all tattered or browning foliage. Cut flowers before they open fully for using in fresh arrangements, drying, or pressing. Cut leafy herbs for drying just when they start blooming.

September

September is often a dry month; monitor your soil and water as needed. Keep deadheading, weeding, and pest patrol. This is a good time to divide many perennials that have finished flowering, to dig up and rearrange plants in beds, and to plant container-grown perennials and shrubs. Keep them well watered until winter to promote good root development.

Start new beds. Plant a cover crop—such as winter rye—to protect the soil over winter (till it under before spring planting). Or dig in chopped leaves and garden wastes; they will decompose by spring. Now is a good time to get your soil tested and to correct pH imbalances.

October

To extend your flower display a bit, cover tender plants on nights when frost is expected. Dig and store tender bulbs (such as tuberous begonias, dahlias, caladiums, and gladioli) when their foliage turns yellow and withers. Pull annuals after frost and toss them in the compost pile, or leave them if they have interesting seed heads.

Cut back the dead stems and leaves of perennials or let them stand until spring for winter interest. Remove and destroy any diseased foliage. Rake leaves for the compost pile or till them into new beds. Chop leaves with the lawn mower for good winter mulch (but don't mulch yet).

Plant spring bulbs. Record where you planted them on your site map so you won't dig into them when you plant annuals in the spring. Water perennial beds (as well as new shrub and bulb plantings) thoroughly before they go dormant to help them survive through the cold winter months.

November

Mow wildflower meadows now or wait until late winter if you want to enjoy the seed heads and leave seeds for the birds.

Retrieve stakes and replace missing plant labels. Drain and store hoses; shut off and drain outdoor water taps. Take stock of your gardening tools. Toss out what's beyond salvaging and note what needs replacing; mend, clean, and oil the rest.

If you don't have a map of your garden, make one now or next month (before snow falls) for winter planning. After the ground freezes, add a thick layer of mulch. Cover plants that need extra protection with branches.

December

Make a wish list of garden supplies for holiday presents or a shopping list for favorite gardeners. Catch up on garden reading. Look through all the books and magazines that piled up over the summer for new design ideas and new plants you'd like to try. Buy or make a new calendar for next year's garden.

Rake fallen leaves off your lawn and save them for mulching your plants after the ground freezes.

SECTION FIVE

Creating a Flower Garden

This chapter summarizes some basic landscape design principles, to show how to combine different plants and design a garden that looks good the whole year round.

The Planning Stage *114*

Great Design Ideas *118*

Beds and Borders, Screens and Fillers *128*

Creating a Cutting Garden *134*

Making a Meadow Garden *136*

Creating a Cottage Garden *140*

The Planning Stage

For a garden to be effective, it has to match your site conditions, your style, the amount of time you can set aside for gardening, and the results you want from the garden. Ideally, it should also blend in with the topography and complement your house so everything looks like it belongs right where it is. A little thinking and planning will ensure you end up with a beautiful, healthy, easy-care garden. And knowing your personal goals will guide you through the planning process and ensure that you end up with the garden you want. Don't jump into creating a flower garden without sufficient planning.

Deciding Where to Plant

You may have your heart set on growing particular plants, in which case you'll have to choose a site on your property that's suitable. Your site choices are probably limited; you will need a spot that can provide the right amount of light and the right soil conditions for your plants. Alternatively, you may have decided where you want to have a garden and then pick the plants that are adapted to those growing conditions. Either way, the key is to match the plants to the place they're growing. Use the information you gathered for your site map (as explained in "Living with Your Garden" on page 45) to decide where that is. If you have a fairly flat site with moist but well-drained soil, you can plant a wide variety of annuals and perennials. But chances are good that you'll have at least one area in the yard with more challenging conditions, such as slopes or wet spots.

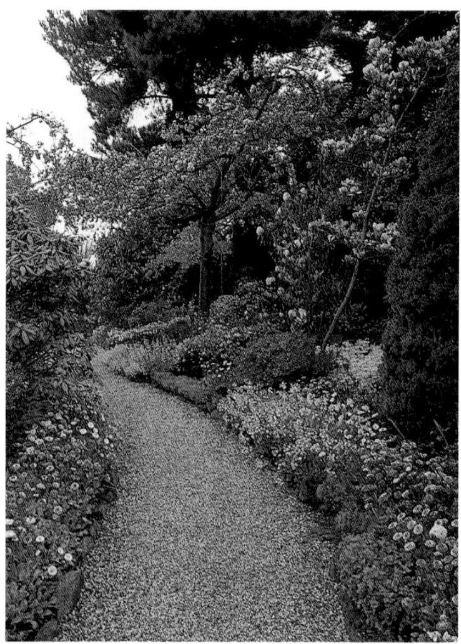

An underplanting of pink and white annuals perfectly complements a flowering cherry tree.

Creating the garden that you want will take planning, patience, and imagination—and it should be fun.

If you have a very difficult spot, you might decide to ignore it and limit your plantings to the most hospitable areas of the yard. Or you may choose to take up the challenge and plan a garden of annuals and perennials that are naturally adapted to those tough conditions. You may be pleasantly surprised to see how well-chosen plantings can turn a problem site into a pleasing garden area. You'll find specific suggestions for dealing with slopes, wet spots, and other difficult sites in "Problem-solving with Annuals and Perennials" starting on page 146.

If you don't have particular plants in mind, you have a lot more freedom in site selection. Here are some points to consider when deciding on a planting area.

- How much sun does it get? Many annuals and perennials thrive in full sun, but some adapt to or even need at least partial shade.
- What is the soil like? Is it loose and sandy, hard and clayey, very wet, very dry, or very rocky? There's an annual or perennial for just about every site, but fairly loose, well-drained soil that isn't too dry or rocky is ideal. If you're stuck with miserable, compacted clay soil, you could excavate the area and refill it with good topsoil. For very clayey, rocky, or wet sites, raised beds are another alternative.
- Is it easy to reach? A flower bed at the end of your driveway or by your mailbox may seem like a nice idea, but it could be a hassle to maintain—especially if you have to lug water out to it regularly. Try to keep plantings closer to the house, where you can reach them easily for any watering, grooming, and general maintenance.
- What's growing there now? Neglected areas will have to be cleared of weeds. If the area is currently a lawn, you'll need to remove the turf. Clearing out overgrown shrub plantings can be an even bigger task. However, just about any site can be prepared for planting if you're willing to put the time and effort into it.

Combine plants with similar needs so it's easier to keep them in top condition. Yarrow and torch lilies, for example, don't need regular watering.

How Big Should Your Garden Be?

A key part of planning a great-looking landscape is being realistic about how much time you have to spend on it. Digging up and planting the area is the most obvious chunk of time you'll spend in the garden. But you may be surprised at how much time you'll need to allow for the aftercare—the mulching, weeding, watering, fertilizing, staking, and pest and disease control that your chosen plants will need every year to look their best.

For example, you'll probably need to spend at least a few hours each month out in the yard to maintain a 200-square-foot (18.6 sq m) flower garden once it's been established. And that doesn't include any planning or preparation time. It also assumes you keep it mulched to discourage weeds and reduce the need for watering.

Your own garden may take more or less time, depending on the plants you choose, how immaculate you want them to look, and how carefully you've planned for your site. It's safest to start small, so plan your first garden a bit smaller than you think you want. Live with your first garden for a few years, and see how comfortable you are with the time you spend on it. As the plants become established, you'll have less watering and weeding to do, and you'll get a good idea of how much maintenance your garden really needs. Then, if you decide you want to expand, you'll have a more realistic feel for how much garden you can actually handle.

What's Your Style?

Deciding where and how big you want your perennial plantings to be are two important aspects of planning a practical garden. But not all gardening has to be practical; choosing a style for your garden is a chance to add a fun and personal touch to your yard.

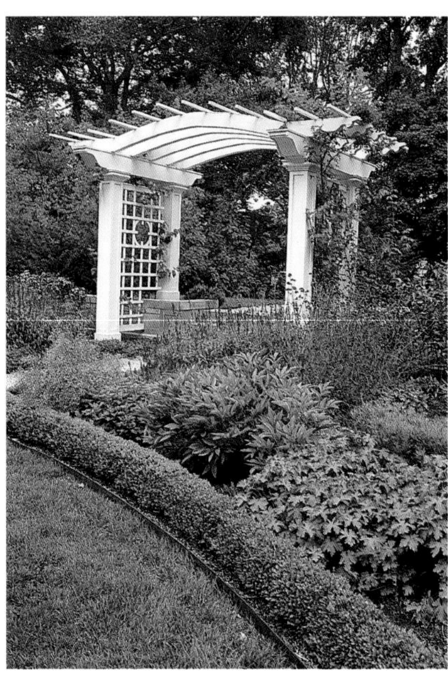
A clipped hedge is a common feature of formal gardens. But a slight curve, and the loose clumps of mealy-cup sage, adds a touch of informality.

Informal gardens tend to have curved lines and a variety of casual plantings.

Formal gardens are laid out with straight lines and symmetrical plantings.

One thing you'll want to consider is whether your landscape will have a formal or an informal feel. Formal landscaping uses straight lines, sharp angles, and symmetrical plantings with only a limited number of different plants. These kinds of landscapes often include features such as clipped hedges or brick walls to define different spaces in the garden. Formal designs tend to have a restful feel. But they may not be as restful for the gardener, since you will need to clip, stake, and weed on a regular basis to keep your plants and design looking perfect.

Informal landscapes use curving lines to create a more natural feeling. They tend to have few permanent features such as walls, although elements such as rustic split-rail fences and wood-chip paths add to the informal feel. These kinds of gardens generally include many different kinds of plants—trees, shrubs, herbs, and vines as well as annuals and perennials. They are relaxed and lively. Since the plants are free to spread, they tend to need less regular maintenance. You won't need to keep sharp edges on the beds, and a few weeds won't immediately be obvious and ruin the look of the garden.

Limiting your choices to a color theme can make shopping easier, and it creates an elegant look.

Zinnias

Plan Your Plant List

You probably already have some idea of what you want to grow in your garden. As you flip through books, magazines, and catalogs for more ideas, it's fun to make a wish list of plants you'd like to try. Along with the names, you'll also want to note the characteristics of each plant, including its light and soil needs, height, color, and bloom time.

If you have already chosen a site for your garden, the next step is to go through your list and select the plants that are adapted to the site. "Creating Great Combinations" on page 118 offers some tips on grouping your selections based on height, color, and bloom time; jot down a list of about 5 to 10 different plants. If you'd rather grow your annuals and bulbs for a particular purpose—for cutting, perhaps, or fragrance—you'll have to consider the needs of each plant you want to grow and then find a spot in your yard where it will thrive.

Your list will remind you what you're looking for as you browse through catalogs and shop at your local nursery. Check off the plants as you buy or order them, so that you won't forget and purchase the same plant twice by mistake!

Whether you choose a formal or informal landscape may depend on your personal style or the style of your house. It can be hard to mix informal and formal areas effectively; a simple solution is to choose one for harmonious landscaping.

Putting It All Together

By now you probably have lots of ideas and thoughts swirling around in your head. You know where and how big you want the garden to be and which plants you want to grow. In this section, you'll learn about the different techniques and steps you can use to organize your gardening ideas.

Try Out Your Ideas

Now head outside with a copy of your plant list and your site plan (the one you drew up with the help of "Creating a Site Map" on page 45). Outline the shape of the planting area with flexible hose or rope. Step back and walk around the yard to see how the dimensions look from several viewpoints (including the view through your windows). If you have trouble visualizing how the filled bed will look, use trash cans, filled leaf bags, or boxes to give the area some height and mass. Adjust the outline of the area until it looks balanced from all viewpoints.

Put Your Plan on Paper

Sketching garden designs will allow you to try out many different ideas, however unrealistic, without the hassle of physically digging up and moving existing plants. Your plan may simply be the outline of the bed with scrawled notes as to roughly where the plants will go. Or you may want to invest the time in drawing up a formal scale plan of the bed so you can make sure the garden will have just the right blend of colors, heights, and textures and so you'll know just what you need to buy.

To make a scale plan, measure the final outline of the bed decided on in "Try Out Your Ideas," and transfer the dimensions to paper. If your garden is small, you could

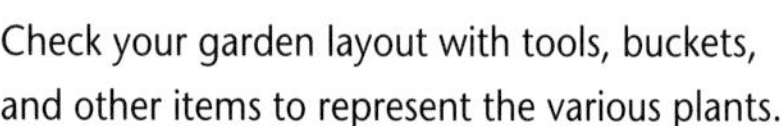

Check your garden layout with tools, buckets, and other items to represent the various plants.

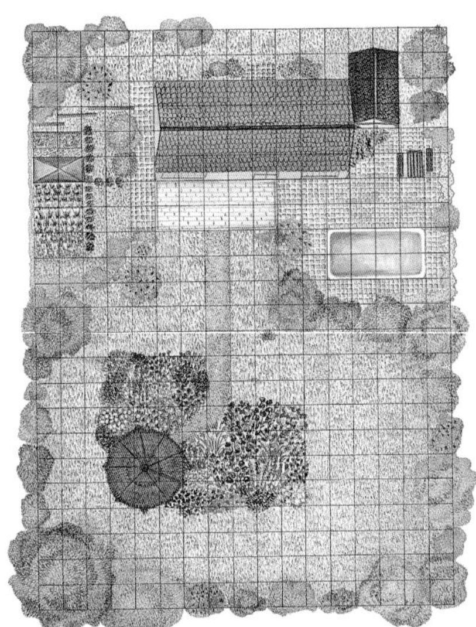

Planning is a fun wintertime activity that allows you to try out different design options. It can also help you spot possible problems before digging.

draw the area right onto your site map. In most cases, though, it's easier to draw each planting area on a separate piece of graph paper; that will give you more room to write. Choose the largest scale that allows your design to fit on one sheet: 1 inch (2.5 cm) on paper to 1 foot (30 cm) of planting area works well for gardens shorter than 10 feet (3 m). Mark the scale you are using on the page for future reference. Make several copies of this plan so you can try out different ideas.

Draw rough outlines on your base plan to show where each plant will go. Check heights to make sure you don't have tall plants at the front blocking short ones at the back, unless the short plants bloom before the tall plants fill out. If you have room, allow space for 3 or 5 plants of each type—a few different plants in large masses can have a more dramatic effect than many single plants. Mark dots (or small xs) within outlines to show locations of individual plants.

As you plan the layout, check the spread of each plant, which is listed in the individual plant entries starting on page 306. Leave enough room between plants so that each can mature to its full spread and overlap by no more than a few inches. If your budget is tight, space the perennials farther apart; you can increase them by division the following year, or fill the gaps with annuals and bulbs. Allow for some unplanted (mulched) space at the front of the bed so the plants can sprawl out a bit without flopping onto the lawn and creating a mowing headache.

Fine-tune Your Plan

If you really want to make sure your design is just right, you can make colored maps or overlays to help you visualize color combinations and different seasons. Make several copies of your scale plan, or use several sheets of tracing paper as overlays.

Use a different copy or overlay sheet for early spring, late spring/early summer, late summer, and fall; you may also want one for winter interest. Color the plants that bloom at each time. If you have old plant catalogs with color pictures, clip swatches of particular flowers and glue them inside the outline instead of just coloring. If foliage color is important, add the color as a thick outline surrounding the area of flower color. When you're satisfied that your design meets your needs, make a clean copy that includes plant names.

When doing your plan, add elements to liven up your plants with a focal point, such as a trellis.

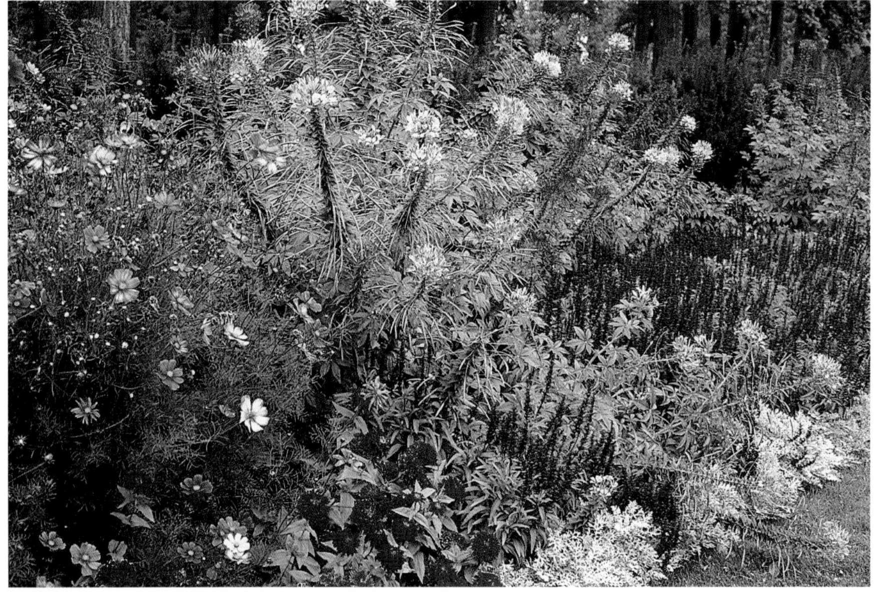

The time you spend planning what to grow will be worth it when your careful groupings of plants bloom.

Great Design Ideas

With so many wonderful annuals and perennials to choose from, it's hard to resist planting one of each. But if you buy them one by one and plop them in the ground wherever there's room, your garden will look like a plant collection—interesting, perhaps, but not beautiful. You'll need to figure out what you want to grow and where you want to grow it. Garden design is basically the process of refining your plant choices, placement, and combinations to get the best effect. This is what transforms a collection of individual plants into a pleasing composition, a good landscape design.

Part of the fun of landscaping with annuals and perennials is creating an ever-changing display. Working with living material, material that changes from week to week and season to season, makes designing a garden different from redecorating a room, even though it builds on the same principles of contrast, balance, texture, and color.

Design Rules

While designing a garden is a very personal and creative activity, it is a good idea to follow some basic design rules. These rules will give your finished garden a very polished or natural look. The key rules are to create balance and rhythm and to add a dominant feature to tie the garden together.

First, keep the garden in balance. Include plants with a mix of heights and sizes throughout your plantings. Don't plant all of the tall or massive flowers on one side, with a group of low, delicate plants at the other end. In formal gardens, you may balance one side of the garden by planting the same design on the other, making a mirror image. For an informal garden, you can vary the plantings, perhaps matching a large blue-flowered annual on one side with a lower-growing plant that has bright red flowers. In this case, you are balancing brighter color with larger size.

Second, create a rhythm, or a sense of continuity, throughout the entire garden. You can repeat groupings of the same plant or use other plants with identical colors or similar flower shapes. Let a middle-of-the-border plant drift from the foreground to the background, giving a sense of movement and uniting the different layers of the garden.

Third, establish a dominant feature. This focal point can be as simple as a spectacular long-blooming perennial. But since perennials come in and out of bloom fairly quickly, you will have to establish a new focus when the first bloom ends. For a more permanent accent, you can feature a path, sculpture, birdbath, or tree as your center of interest, and build the garden around it. This brings you back to the concept of making the annual and perennial garden part of the overall landscape. The annuals and perennials can brighten existing permanent structures, and the structures can bring stability and focus to the continually changing display of foliage and flowers.

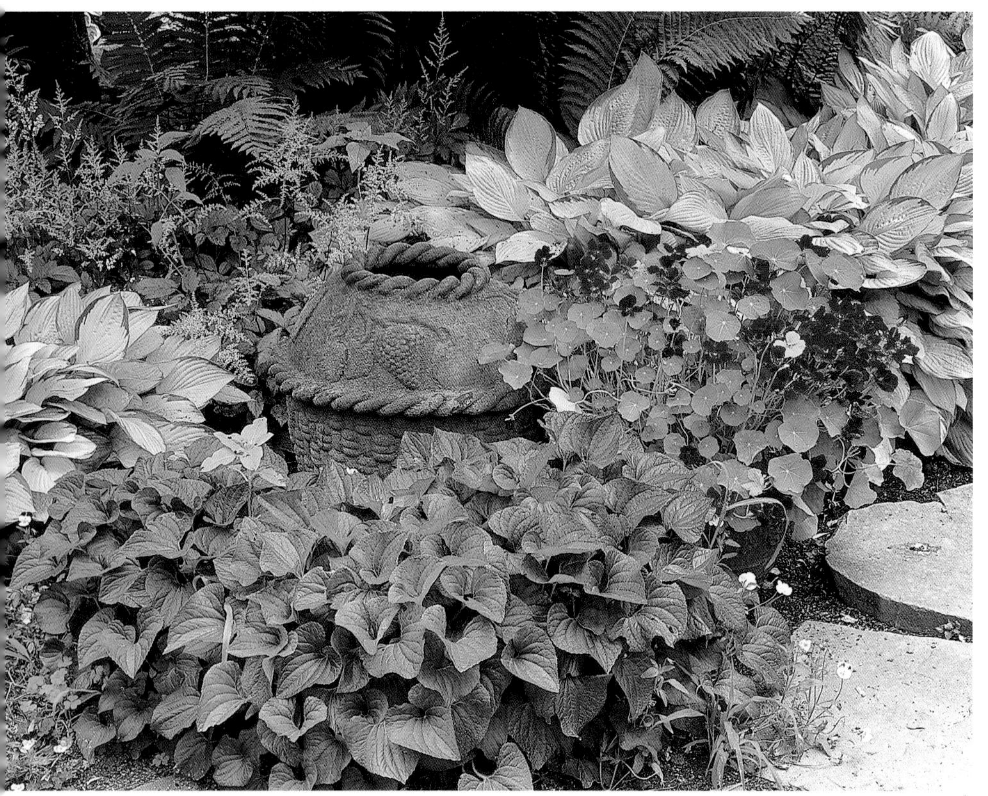

A lovely ceramic jar, nestled among hostas and nasturtiums, draws the attention of people strolling by.

Creating Great Combinations

When it comes to garden aesthetics, there are no hard-and-fast rules that can be applied. After all, our tastes in flowers are as individual as our taste in clothing. However, there are a number of general guidelines that will help you create good plant combinations. Great-looking gardens are basically sequences of many individual plant combinations. The best aren't just based on flower color and season of bloom; they consider the quality, color, and texture of each plant's leaves as well. Good combinations also feature different plant heights and forms: short, medium, or tall; mat-like, spiky, or rounded. Equally important is the overall texture—whether a plant is fine and delicate in appearance, like baby's breath (*Gypsophila* spp.), or coarse and dramatic, like peonies and ligularias (*Ligularia* spp.). You should also remember sunlight and soil requirements.

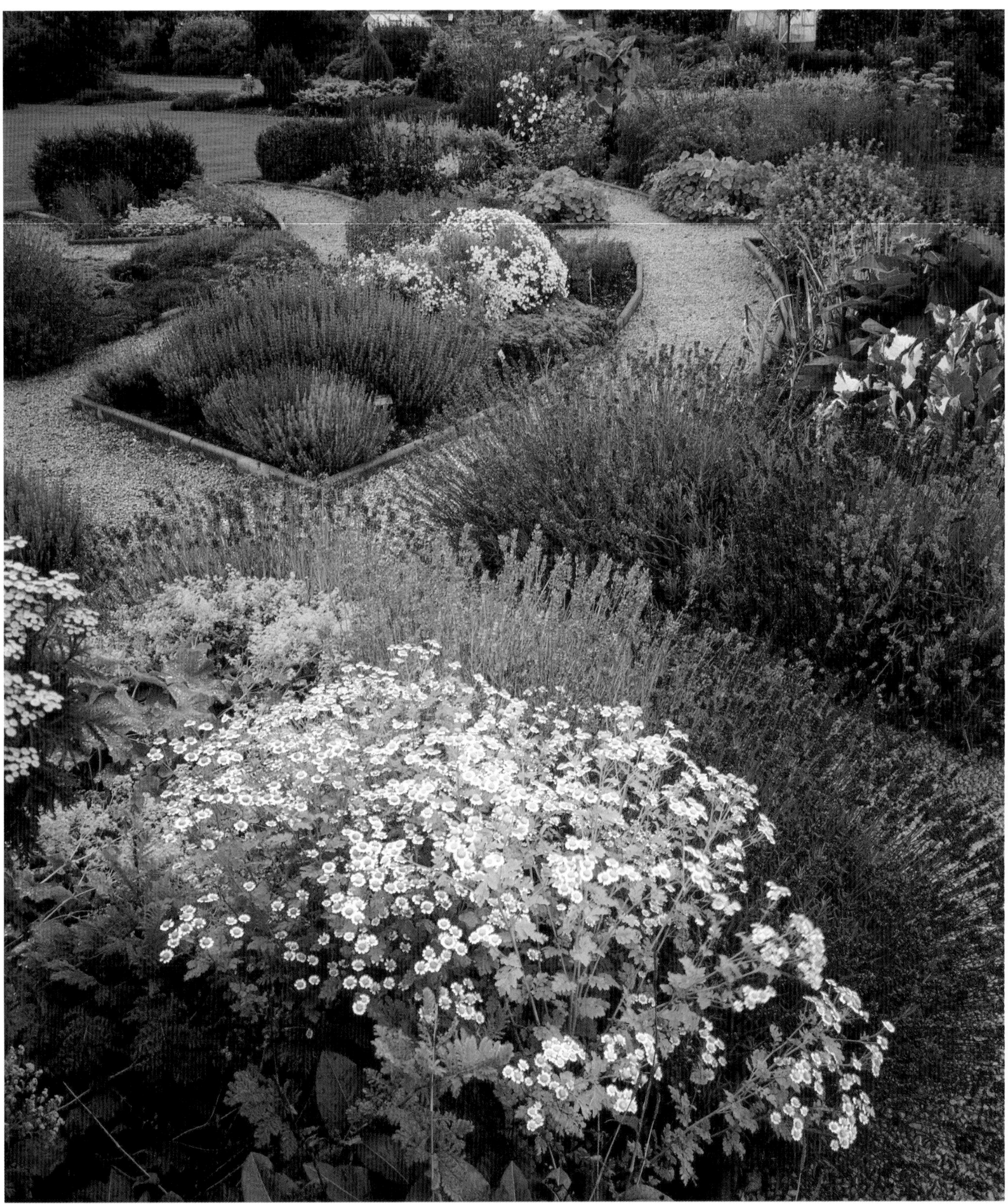

The lines created by gravel footpaths, weaving among beds of feverfew and lavender, create a sense of movement, inviting you to venture further into the garden. The plants form similarly rounded shapes and are of a similar height; this, along with the repetition of color, works to give rhythm and continuity.

Lilies, yellow loosestrife, butterfly bush, and bee balm like full sun but can tolerate light shade, too.

Choose Compatible Plants

The first step to any good combination is choosing plants that prefer the same growing conditions. You might think that cornflowers (*Centaurea cyanus*) would look charming with impatiens, for instance, but they probably won't grow well together; one needs full sun and the other prefers shade. Know the site conditions you have available, and stick with plants you know can thrive there.

To begin, group species that have similar light requirements. If your garden includes both lightly shaded and sunny areas, you have greater design freedom because you can pick from a wide range of suitable plants. Or if you want to blend some annuals and perennials that need partial shade in a sunny bed, you can plant them on the shaded north side of taller plants or in the filtered sunlight that reaches near the base of lanky plants. For instance, you could put Siberian bugloss (*Brunnera macrophylla*) in the northern shadow of a daylily. Or grow clumps of sweet violet (*Viola odorata*) below a tall purple coneflower (*Echinacea purpurea*).

You also need to consider the plants' preferred soil conditions and group those with similar needs. For instance, you can combine prairie-type plants, like thread-leaved coreopsis (*Coreopsis verticillata*), New York aster (*Aster novi-belgii*), and common sneezeweed (*Helenium autumnale*), in a well-drained soil that is not excessively fertile. Similarly, group plants that take a more moist, more fertile soil, like sun-loving delphiniums and garden phlox, or plants that prefer to grow in light shade, like astilbes, bleeding hearts (*Dicentra* spp.), and coral bells (*Heuchera* spp.).

Think about Bloom Time

A plant's bloom season is another important thing to consider. Annuals make great companions for bulbs, since the annuals can fill in the garden space left when the bulbs go dormant. But if you want plants to be in flower at the same time, look for annuals and perennials with similar bloom seasons.

Contrasts and Complements

Well-planned gardens balance contrast and similarity. Contrasting colors, sizes, or other design elements give a bold and stimulating effect. Use contrast to draw attention to a particular location and to add a lively feel. But overusing contrast—too many different textures or too many strong colors—can give your garden a jumbled, chaotic look.

Similarity—the absence of contrasts—increases the sense of harmony. Use subtle variations of related colors and gradual height transitions to create a soothing garden design. Too much similarity risks being uninteresting, so add a touch of contrast—a few perennials of different height, color, or texture—for balance.

Repetition acts as a bridge between similarity and contrast. Repeating similar elements will unify even the boldest designs. Exact, evenly spaced repetitions of particular plants or combinations create a formal look. Combine different plants with similar flower colors or leaf shapes to give an informal garden a cohesive but casual look.

The yellow of coneflowers makes a great contrast with the purple of mealy-cup sage. Both plants like the same conditions, too.

Large masses of plants in single colors add unity to this garden of pot marigolds, borage, rose campions, and poppies. The repetition of yellow and orange stands out most vividly amid the other colors.

Color Combinations

Colors have different qualities. Warm colors—those related to red, orange, or yellow—are bold. They are stimulating and stand out, grabbing your attention in a landscape. Cool colors—those related to violet, blue, or green—are more tranquil and appear to recede from the viewer. Pure hues—like true yellow, blue, and red—are more vibrant than lighter or darker versions of the same color. Mixing warm and cool colors will add depth and interest to your plantings.

Color combinations are very personal creations. While certain combinations and types of colors tend to create specific effects, only you can decide whether you like that particular effect. Some gardeners enjoy the lively result of mixing orange and yellow with purple or blue; others prefer the crisp look of whites or the restful feel of pale yellows, soft pinks, soothing blues, and silvers.

Combining similar flower colors in the garden creates a harmonious, balanced effect. Try grouping reds with oranges and yellows, yellows with greens and blues, or blues with purples and reds. Colors that share the same intensity of lightness or darkness are also similar; for instance, several different pastels—like pale blues, yellows, apricots, and pinks—blend more harmoniously than several pure hues. Place pale blues, soft pinks, lavender, and dark violet up close where the colors won't fade into the background.

If contrast and excitement are what you're after, choose complementary hues like yellow and violet, red and green, or blue and orange. Or place a light tint next to a very bright or dark shade of the same hue (try pale blue with intense blue or dark blue or pale pink next to fuchsia or a deep burgundy).

White and gray don't appear on the color wheel, but they play an important role in the garden. White has a split personality: It can be exciting or soothing. Bright white is surprisingly bold; it stands out starkly among bright and dark colors, and even holds its own in a group of soft pastels. A dash of pure white in a spread of harmonious colors is as dramatic as a dash of a bright complementary color. Cream and similar muted whites are softer; they blend well with everything.

Gray is the great unifier. Silvery or gray foliage works even better than green to soften the transition between two bold or complementary colors. Gray adds a certain drama of its own by contrasting with neighboring green foliage.

When you're deciding on colors for your garden, limit yourself to two main colors and possibly a third for accent. Also add some minor colors for small touches of diversity. If possible, match flower or foliage colors with the other elements in the landscape, like walkways, shutters, or flowers or berries on nearby shrubs. But keep the color scheme simple. If you use too many colors, the garden will look fragmented and chaotic.

Be especially careful about color compatibility. Colors have many different hues, and they don't all look good together. You will find that, typically, the following rules hold true:

- Warm and cool colors are a surefire combination when mixed together. Try blue and pink, green and red, blue and orange, or purple and yellow.

Rich red tulips are even more striking when partnered with a cool silvery gray.

- Take advantage of foliage color—add plants that have silver, blue, gold, or variegated leaves if they work well with surrounding flowers.
- Magenta is hard to mix, but it works with cream or pale yellow.
- Muted colors can look washed out against strong, clear tones. Stick with one or the other.
- Reddish blues may not work beside yellowish blues.
- Orange-pink flowers will clash next to purple-pink flowers.
- White flowers do not look good next to cream.
- Mix orange-red with scarlet, salmon with yellow, or pure pink with lavender only in cool climates or partially shady sites where the colors will stay vivid. In heat or full sun, these colors can fade to less compatible combinations.

As well as offering harmonious color, this group of chives and euphorbia has interesting texture.

Texture and Form Factors

Texture and form are as important as color in creating interesting combinations and landscapes. Masses of even-textured foliage can often tone down bold colors; dramatic leaf shapes can add extra zip to a pastel planting. Here are some other tips you can try to plan effective plantings:

- Balance rounded clump-formers, such as shasta daisies (*Leucanthemum* x *superbum*) and coreopsis, with spiky plants such as mulleins (*Verbascum* spp.), foxgloves (*Digitalis* spp.), and spike gayfeather (*Liatris spicata*).

Don't Forget Foliage

Flowers aren't the only source of color. Foliage comes in a surprising array of different greens, from the blue-green of California poppy (*Eschscholzia californica*) to the yellow-green of summer cypress (*Kochia scoparia*) or the deep green of geraniums. Fortunately, nearly all greens go well together and set off almost all flowers. As a background, it blends and harmonizes strong colors—such as reds, yellows, and oranges—that you probably wouldn't think to combine in an outfit. Pastel colors like soft pinks, blues, and yellows may look washed out against a light-colored shirt, but they never get lost against dark-green leaves.

Foliage can come in other colors, too. Silver-leaved plants such as dusty miller look great in almost any kind of garden. Yellowish leaves, such as those of golden feverfew or some coleus, can be pleasing with pinks and blues. You can add a bold spire of color with the blazing red leaves of Joseph's coat (*Amaranthus tricolor*) or a subtle accent with the bronzy leaves of wax begonias.

The muted shades of this mossy green garden are lifted by a blaze of purple at the entranceway.

- Contrast shiny leaves—like those of European ginger (*Asarum europaeum*) and bear's breech (*Acanthus mollis*)—with velvety or fuzzy leaves, such as those of lamb's ears (*Stachys byzantina*) or lungworts (*Pulmonaria* spp.).
- Contrast fine foliage, such as lacy fern fronds, with the smooth, broad leaves of hostas and similar plants.
- Include spiky leaves, like those of irises, gladioli, and blackberry lilies (*Belamcanda chinensis*); they'll stand out from mat-like or mounded plants long after their flowers fade.
- If you have a small garden that you'll see from a distance, use bold colors, bold textures, or bold shapes to make it appear larger and closer to the viewer.

Coordinating Heights and Habits

Mix annuals and perennials of varying heights to add visual interest to your garden design. Organize heights to progress from short to tall so no flowers will be hidden behind taller plants. If you view a garden from the front, put the tallest plants toward the back of the garden. Or with a bed that you see from

Flowers can have intriguing shapes and textures. Bells of Ireland has an unusual flower color, too.

all sides, cluster the tall plants near the center, and let the lower plants taper down in height toward the edges.

Many plants have shapes or growth habits that make them particularly useful for certain purposes. Low-growing plants like common thrift (*Armeria maritima*), pinks (*Dianthus* spp.), and coral bells (*Heuchera sanguinea*) have neat foliage and make attractive edgings. Try full or

A Combination Case Study

Once you start grouping plants with an eye for compatible heights, habits, and colors, you'll develop a feeling for which ones could look good together. But when you're a beginner, the idea of planning pleasing combinations may be a little intimidating.

To see how easy it can be, let's look at one simple combination and figure out why it works. We'll start with a patch of Madagascar periwinkle (*Catharanthus roseus*), with its flat, five-petaled, deep-pink blossoms. Behind that, we'll add a group of mealy-cup sage (*Salvia farinacea*) for its spikes of small, blue flowers. And to enhance this duo, let's tuck in a few plants of airy yellow cosmos (*Cosmos sulphureus*) toward the back.

Why does this trio work? First, all three annuals share the need for a sunny spot and perform best in the summer heat. The shape, texture, and height of each plant is different but compatible; the flower sizes and shapes also vary. Finally, the colors—pink, blue, and yellow—work well together; each contrasts with the other, but none is so strong that it overwhelms the others.

If you really like this combination, you could create a whole bed of just these three kinds of plants. Or you could expand it by adding other compatible plants—perhaps the blue-flowered, low-growing annual lobelia or a dramatic yellow Asiatic hybrid lily to serve as a focal point. Once you start trying out new flower and foliage combinations, the fun never ends!

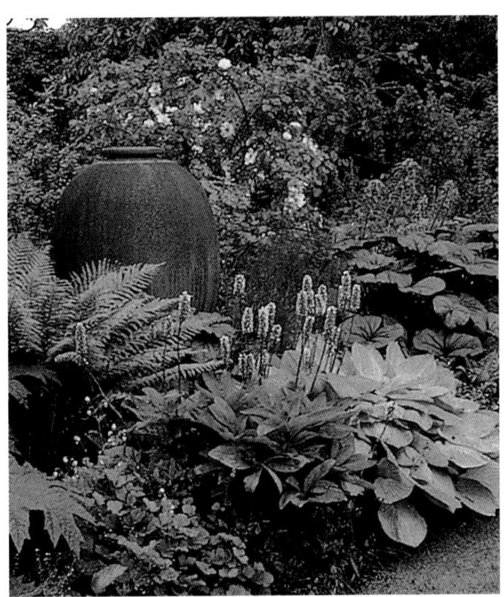

Fleeceflowers (*Polygonum* spp.) and other spiky plants look good with mounded plants like hostas.

tall types like goldenrod (*Solidago* spp.), boltonia (*Boltonia asteroides*), or black snakeroot (*Cimicifuga racemosa*) to hide unattractive views or to serve as a background for large beds and borders.

Some annuals and perennials are excellent groundcovers. They can squeeze out weeds, provide attractive foliage, and give you a more interesting alternative to English ivy. Use groundcovers by themselves, one species per bed, or blend several with different foliage textures and colors but similar growth rates. Try creeping phlox (*Phlox stolonifera*), ajuga (*Ajuga reptans*), spotted lamium (*Lamium maculatum*), forget-me-nots (*Myosotis sylvatica*), and sweet alyssum (*Lobularia maritima*), among others.

For visual interest, make the most of the graduating heights and varying forms of annuals and perennials.

Gardens based on purple and blue flowers are soothing—a perfect place to relax after a rough day.

Creating a Color-theme Garden

You can design beautiful gardens around a theme as simple as a single color. This may sound plain, but it's anything but that—color-theme gardens are attractive and dramatic additions to any landscape. Even gardens that are based on green leaves contain varying tints and shades, as well as textures and patterns, from the frosty blue-greens of some hostas to the deep glossy green of European wild ginger (*Asarum europaeum*). When you start including flower colors against the greens, you add an extra level of interest. Even if the flowers you choose are all in the same color group, the many different shades and tints create a mosaic of changing colors throughout the season.

Planning a color-theme garden starts by picking the color you want to work with. Try a monochrome (based on one flower color) border if you have a favorite color or love collecting flowers of a particular color. Or make a small monochromatic section part of a long mixed-color border, perhaps using silver foliage to separate it from flowers of other colors.

If you have a couple of unconnected small beds, you might want to try using a different color in each. Or choose a single color for the whole garden in each season: perhaps pink for spring, white for summer, and yellow for fall, or whatever colors appeal to you.

Gardens with lots of yellow flowers and foliage look cheerful and sunny, even on dreary days.

White gardens are especially charming at night, when the pale blooms reflect any available light.

Another option to consider is a two-color border. Blue and white is a classic combination. Or perhaps pinks and yellows are more to your liking. Yellow or chartreuse with maroon or burgundy is another popular color combination.

The key to creating a beautiful and effective color-theme garden is to pick the colors that you like and those that blend well with your house. White flowers, for instance, can look dirty against cream-colored siding, while bright pinks can clash with rusty orange brick.

If you're not sure how certain colors will look in a given setting, try growing the plants there in a container for a year. If the colors look good to you, go ahead and plan a full-scale garden; if they don't fit the bill, move the pot elsewhere, and try a different combination in that spot next year. You'll save yourself a lot of time and money this way, and you'll be more confident about the results.

In the sections below, you'll find more tips for planning gardens around some of the most popular colors.

Beautiful Blue Gardens

Blue is a popular color theme for annual and perennial plantings. Many beloved summer-blooming plants have blue flowers, including delphiniums, Siberian iris (*Iris sibirica*), bellflowers (*Campanula* spp.), and pincushion flower (*Scabiosa caucasica*). To extend the season, add blue-flowered shrubs, such as caryopteris (*Caryopteris* x *clandonensis*), and annuals such as ageratum and the intensely blue lobelia (*Lobelia erinus*).

For spring color, plant bulbs such as Spanish bluebells (*Hyacinthoides hispanicus*) and Siberian squills (*Scilla sibirica*). For even more choices, expand your list to include the many flowers in the blue-violet range.

Several plants offer bluish foliage; amethyst sea holly (*Eryngium amethystinum*) and blue false indigo (*Baptisia australis*) offer blue flowers as well. Many of the finest hosta cultivars—including 'Krossa Regal', 'Blue Giant', and 'Hadspen Blue'—have cool blue leaves that look super in shady gardens. Rue (*Ruta graveolens*) and blue fescue (*Festuca cinerea*) produce their best blues in full sun. Also include silver foliage, which is stunning in blue borders.

Pretty Pink Gardens

Pink is an easy choice for a color theme, since so many annuals, perennials, hardy bulbs, and flowering shrubs come in this color. Use pink flowers alone, or try a two-color combination of pink and red, pink and white, or pink and pale yellows. Pink foliage is hard to find, but purples—like purple garden sage (*Salvia officinalis* 'Purpurascens')—and silvers—such as lamb's ears (*Stachys byzantina*)—are perfect additions to pink borders.

Wonderful White Gardens

Elegant white theme gardens offer perhaps the widest range of flower choice, as so many annuals, perennials, hardy bulbs, and flowering shrubs and trees come in bright white, off-white, or cream.

All-white designs are sometimes known as "moon gardens" because the flowers almost glow under the light of a full moon. This effect can also be achieved under street lights in urban gardens or at the edge of a well-lit patio. Moon gardens include many plants with silver or gray foliage; they may also include flowers in the palest pastels, as these reflect moonlight almost as well as white. For gardens near the house, include fragrant types of white roses, lilies, and peonies, along with fragrant annuals such as sweet alyssum (*Lobularia maritima*) and flowering tobacco (*Nicotiana alata*).

Rousing Reds, Oranges, and Yellows

Hot-color borders are exciting and vibrant. Yellow gardens have a sunny, cheerful look and are fairly easy to arrange without fear of clashing colors. Reds and oranges make the loudest statements of the various color themes, but red flowers also have the greatest potential to clash with each other. Before planting a whole border of these bright colors, consider trying a small bed or part of a border first to see if you like the effect.

TOP: Red flowers look marvelous against green leaves. The contrast between the two is dynamic. BOTTOM: Mixing a variety of reds, yellows, and oranges can produce exciting combinations, too.

Attractive purple and silver foliage will remain long after the showy rose and clematis blooms are over.

Orchestrating All-Year Interest

You see your yard every day of the year, so make sure it's worth looking at. A good selection of spring-, summer-, and fall-blooming annuals and perennials, plus a few plants with evergreen leaves for winter interest, will give you a landscape that is truly attractive all year long. All-season interest starts with flower displays that spread beyond one season. Choosing plants for different seasons is easy: Look under "Flowering Time" in the individual plant entries starting on page 172.

Foliage and plant form are other features you can use to keep your garden looking beautiful as flowers come and go. From spring through fall, many annuals and perennials have leaves in attractive colors—like the maroon leaves of 'Palace Purple' heuchera (*Heuchera* 'Palace Purple')—or interesting shapes, such as the starry leaves of blood-red cranesbill (*Geranium sanguineum*). Unusual plant forms—such as the spiky leaves and flowers of hollyhock (*Alcea rosea*), foxgloves (*Digitalis* spp.), blackberry lily (*Belamcanda chinensis*), yuccas, and spike gayfeather (*Liatris spicata*)—add drama, especially next to mounds such as cushion spurge (*Euphorbia epithymoides*). Use different types of foliage and forms to add contrast, or repeat similar leaves and shapes to unify a planting scheme.

Your Spring Landscape

After a long, dreary winter, few things are more welcome than colorful spring flowers. In spring, Lenten rose (*Helleborus orientalis*) and crocuses bloom before most of the garden shrugs off winter. Plant early bulbs where you'll see them from windows or as you enter the house so you can enjoy their bright colors when it's cold outside. Many wildflowers and shade-loving plants bloom as trees leaf out, so spring is a good season to draw attention to areas that will be shady and green later on. Supplement early-blooming annuals and perennials with flowering shrubs and trees such as forsythias, azaleas, magnolias, dogwoods, flowering cherries, and crab apples.

A Wealth of Summer Color

As spring turns into summer, many old-fashioned annuals and perennials—including cornflowers, peonies, irises, and columbines (*Aquilegia* spp.)—reach their peak, making it an easy time to feature flowers. Supplement these with early summer shrubs and vines such as rhododendrons, roses, clematis, wisteria, and honeysuckle (*Lonicera* spp.).

Bulbs such as bluebells (*Hyacinthoides* spp.) blend beautifully with spring-flowering shrubs.

Cornflowers and corn poppies are easy-care, hardy annuals that will provide masses of color all summer.

As summer progresses, daisy-like annuals and perennials—including blanket flower (*Gaillardia* x *grandiflora*) and coreopsis (*Coreopsis* spp.)—take center stage. Good-looking foliage keeps up appearances where early perennials have finished blooming. Silver leaves make dramatic partners for hot- or cool-hued flowers; yellow, purple, or variegated foliage also attracts attention. Flowering shrubs for July and August include abelia (*Abelia* x *grandiflora*), butterfly bush (*Buddleia davidii*), and hydrangeas. Sourwood (*Oxydendrum arboreum*) and Japanese pagoda tree (*Sophora japonica*) are large trees that bloom prolifically in late summer, as does the large trumpet creeper vine (*Campsis* spp.).

Combinations for Fall

Asters, boltonia, and Joe-Pye weeds (*Eupatorium* spp.) keep blooming after fall frosts nip most annuals. As flowers fade, foliage brightens—and not just on trees or shrubs such as burning bush (*Euonymus alata*). Leaves of peonies and common sundrops (*Oenothera tetragona*) turn beautiful shades of red, balloon flower (*Platycodon grandiflorus*) and amsonia (*Amsonia* spp.) leaves turn bright yellow, and many ornamental grasses bleach to gold. Jack-in-the-pulpit (*Arisaema triphyllum*) and white baneberry (*Actaea pachypoda*) are perennials with dramatic berries that may last into fall.

Perennials for Winter Interest

After the leaves drop, attention turns to evergreen plants and those with seedpods or fruits. Perennials with showy winter seedpods include coneflowers, blue false indigo (*Baptisia australis*), blackberry lily (*Belamcanda chinensis*), and astilbes.

Many crab apples and shrubs such as viburnums, cotoneasters, and deciduous and evergreen hollies (*Ilex* spp.) display fruits well into winter. Ornamental grasses remain attractive for months; cut them to the ground when they look tattered to make way for spring's new growth.

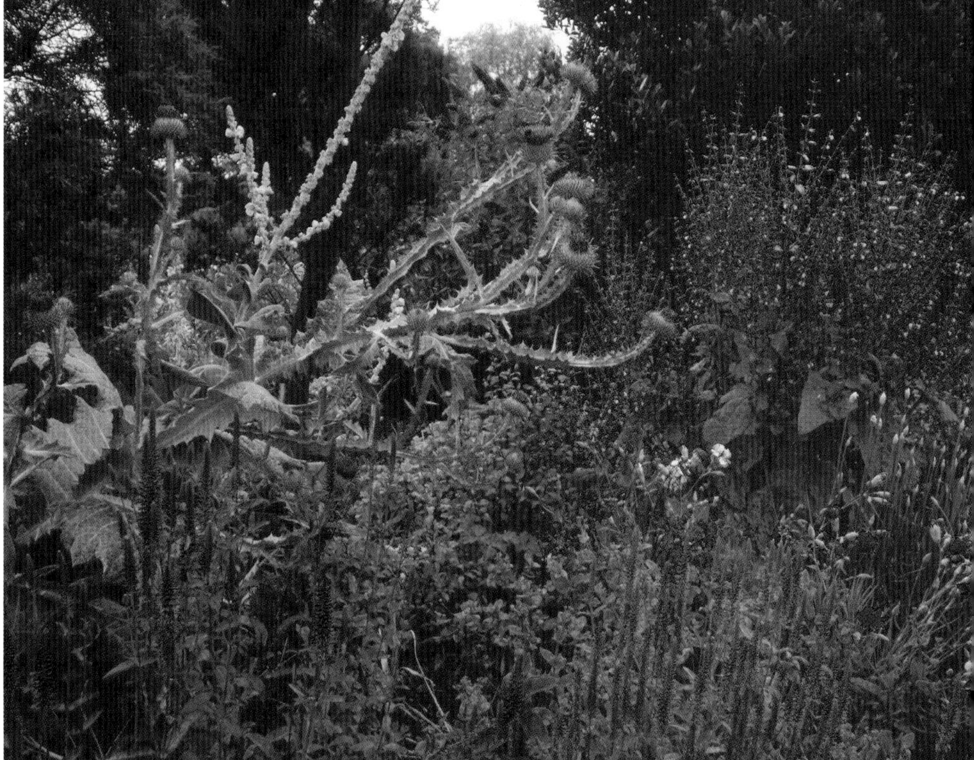
Plants such as this ornamental thistle can add a bold, architectural statement amid your plantings.

Beds and Borders, Screens and Fillers

Two of the most common ways to group annual and perennial plantings are as beds and borders. They also have another widely used function, to screen out ugly views or hide the old garden shed or the back fence that's seen better days. And annuals are the perfect solution for filling in empty spaces. When you're starting a new garden, one of the hardest parts of the process is waiting for all those empty patches of soil to fill in, and that's when annuals will come to the rescue.

This delightful lavender border combines the structure of a double border with the casual feeling from the lavender's sprawling growth.

Borders and Beds

Borders typically are long, rectangular areas that create a visual edge to a lawn or other part of the landscape. You can also design them with gentle curves for a more informal look. They are usually sited to be viewed from a distance and because they're usually seen from one side, borders generally have a distinct front and back, with taller plants located to the rear.

Generally, the longer a border is, the wider it should be—to a point. This will keep you from making awkward-looking squares. A rectangle extends the garden and maintains enough depth for varying plant heights. In a small suburban yard, you could make a border that is 4 feet (1.2 m) wide by 14 feet (4.2 m) long. Or in a larger yard, extend the border to 5 feet (1.5 m) wide by 21 feet (6.3 m) long. However, there is no reason why you can't make a border any length and width that you want, as long as it complements the existing structures.

If you want a really wide border, it's a good idea to put an access path of a couple of stepping stones through the middle so you can maintain all sections of the border without walking on the garden soil. If you want a border more than 3 feet (90 cm) wide in front of a hedge or wall, leave space behind it for a mulched or grassy access path so you can get to all parts of your border.

If a border must be small to fit a small yard, give it more power by placing it close to the house and using small but effective groupings of flowers. Especially in a small garden, every plant must be attractive for as long as possible, so look for plants that have a long bloom season and attractive foliage.

Multiple purple blooms on the stems of clustered bellflowers make this an excellent border plant.

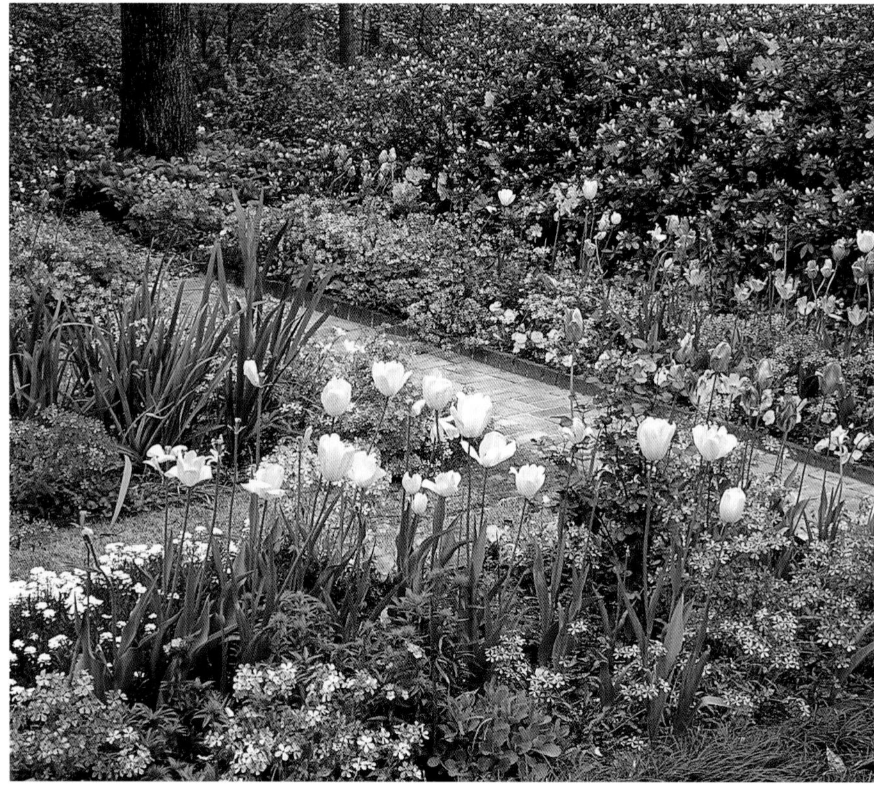

Borders of hybrid tulips interplanted with blue phlox mark a pathway through a woodland garden.

Beds come in many shapes and sizes. Try to choose a shape and style (formal or informal) that matches or balances nearby features in your yard. The front of the bed can curve even if the side up against the house must be straight. Keep the bed narrow enough to allow you to reach all the plants from outside the bed, or place stepping stones in it for easy access.

Beds surrounded by lawn are called islands; often these are oval or kidney shaped. They are a great way to add color and height to new property while you're waiting for the trees and shrubs to mature. Island beds are also useful for replacing the grass under trees, reducing the need for trimming and making mowing easier.

Like borders, beds are usually designed to be seen from a distance. And because island beds are often viewed from all sides, the design needs to look attractive all around, like a table centerpiece. Since there's no "back," put your tallest plants toward the middle and surround them with the lower plants.

As a general rule, make island beds three times as long as they are wide for the most natural effect. You also make one end wider than the other so you can grow taller flowers there. But be sure to balance the extra bed width by putting an appropriate group of bold plants in or near the narrower side. Since you can view an island bed from all sides, put the tallest plants in the center. If, on the other hand, you will view it primarily from one angle, perhaps from the house or patio, make the highest point in the back. Then you can add extra tiers of midborder plants and still have some low-growing annuals and perennials on the far side.

Flower beds of spring annuals, all of a similar height, are an easy and popular way to make a display.

Asiatic lilies, with their lovely large blooms, are good for adding height to beds and borders.

Perennial Plantings

Perennial borders may stretch along a driveway, walkway, fence, or the edge of woods, although they don't really have to "border" anything; borders may merely create the illusion of a boundary to a "room" within the landscape.

Perennial borders are sometimes just that—only perennials. But more and more gardeners are enjoying the benefits of mixing their perennials with other plants, including shrubs, small trees, hardy bulbs, annuals, and ornamental grasses. These plants complement perennials by adding extra height, texture, and color to the border. Shrubs, trees, grasses, and bulbs add year-round interest; annuals are brief but brilliant.

Perennial beds are often located closer to the house than borders, perhaps along the foundation or edging a patio. If you're going to put a bed where you'll see it all the time, choose your plants carefully for all-season interest. High-visibility beds will also need either some extra work or carefully chosen, low-maintenance plants to look their best all the time.

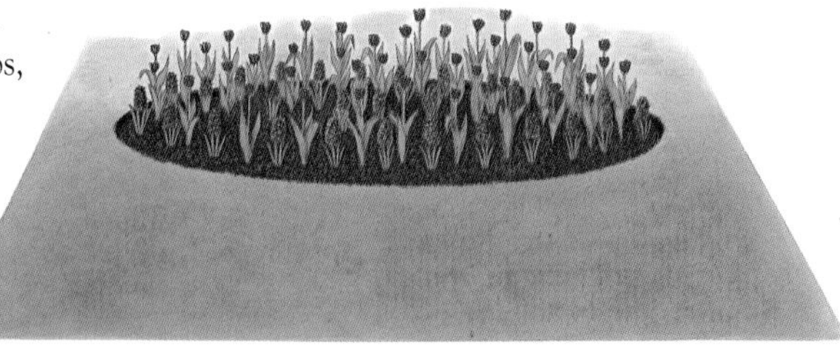

An island bed may become a feature, especially if filled with spring bulbs.

Annuals Alone

Flower beds are traditionally one of the most popular ways to display annuals. Setting aside separate beds for annual flowers is an easy way to go. Since you start with an empty area each year, spring

Bed and Border Planning Pointers

Borders and beds can be designed to feature one big seasonal show or to showcase long, overlapping seasons of bloom. If you have the room for several different beds or borders, it can be fun to arrange each one with a different bloom season. That way you will always have at least one bed that is loaded with lovely flowers.

In small gardens or in plantings that you see every day, it's worth planning for long bloom times, attractive foliage, and year-round interest. Here are some planning tips you can try:

- Include some spring-, summer-, and fall-flowering annuals and perennials in each planting area.
- Look for plants that have great-looking foliage all season, such as hostas, artemisias, and lady's mantle (*Alchemilla* spp.).
- Choose long-blooming species and cultivars, like wild bleeding heart (*Dicentra eximia*) and 'Moonbeam' coreopsis (*Coreopsis verticillata* 'Moonbeam'); they can bloom for 8 weeks or longer.
- Include a few plants with good-looking evergreen foliage to give interest during the colder months. Bergenias and some alumroots (*Heuchera americana*) often turn a lovely reddish color in the cool temperatures of fall and winter.

soil preparation is a snap—you simply clean up any debris left in the bed, scatter some compost over the top to add nutrients and organic matter, and dig or till to loosen the top layer of soil.

Formal Gardens Formal flower beds tend to have a simple, geometric shape—such as a square, rectangle, or circle—and a limited number of different plants. The simplest may contain a mass of just one annual, such as marigolds or geraniums. For a little more variety, you could combine two or three different annuals, planted in straight rows or patterns.

If you grow different annuals together, pick those with varying heights. Select one that's low and spreading—such as edging lobelia (*Lobelia erinus*) or sweet alyssum (*Lobularia maritima*)—for the outer edge. The plants for the inside of the bed should be taller, usually no more than about 2 feet (60 cm). If the bed is in a spot where you can see it from all sides, you might want to include a taller "focal point" annual, such as castor bean (*Ricinus communis*) or love lies bleeding (*Amaranthus caudatus*), as a dramatic accent in the center.

The key to success with a formal bed is uniformity: You want the plants to be evenly spaced and evenly developed. If you're growing a bed of just one kind of annual—all marigolds, let's say—you could sow seed over the prepared bed, thin the seedlings to an even spacing, and expect fairly uniform results. In most cases, though, you'll get the best results by starting with transplants. All of the plants will be at the same stage, so they'll start blooming at the same time, and you can set them out at the proper spacing to get a nice, even look.

Low-growing plants can soften the edges of paths and steps; just trim them back as needed.

Informal Gardens If you enjoy a more casual-looking garden, then an informal planting may be more your style. Informal gardens can be any shape you like, though they often have a flowing outline that curves around the base of shrubs or other structures. Informal plantings usually include at least three or four different annuals. As with formal plantings, the plants you choose for informal beds should have varying heights for visual interest. But you aren't limited to having to plant informal beds in masses or rows. You can set plants out in whatever drifts, masses, or groupings look good to you.

Starting an informal flower bed from transplants is a good idea if you have

For a formal look, try a classic single border. An edging strip and gravel path make for easy maintenance.

specific plant groupings in mind. Placing transplants just where you want them gives you the most control over which colors and plant heights are next to each other. If you plan to plant different annuals in separate drifts, you could also start from seed sown directly in the garden. Or if you want a really casual, meadow-like effect, you could mix all the seeds together and scatter them over the soil; for more tips on starting a meadow garden, see "Making a Meadow Garden" on page 136.

Annuals with Other Plants

Although they look wonderful by themselves, annuals also have a lot to offer in groupings with other plants. In borders predominantly planted with perennials, bulbs, and shrubs, you can use annuals as a formal or informal edging, suggesting a flowering necklace around the border. While the other plants come in and out of bloom, the annual edging adds consistent color through most of the season. Repeating the same annual edging in different flower beds is a good way to link the separate beds in a garden picture.

Of course, you can also add annuals to the inside of borders as well. While the compact, uniform annuals that are excellent for formal bedding can look stiff and awkward next to perennials, many other annuals have a looser, more graceful habit. In fact, annuals and biennials such as larkspur (*Consolida ambigua*), foxgloves (*Digitalis purpurea*), and Canterbury bells (*Campanula medium*) are so charming when mixed with perennials that they are often considered traditional parts of a perennial border. Tall annuals and biennials such as cosmos,

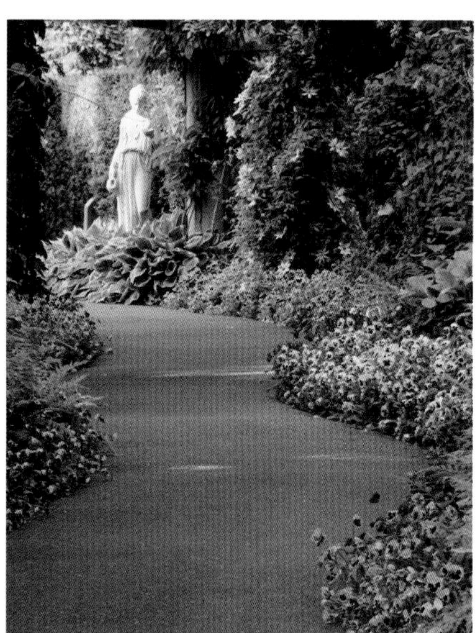
A border planted with vines and shrubs is enlivened with an edging of annuals like pansies.

A garden bed can be practical as well as pretty. Why not consider planting a bed of herbs?

For a Foundation

A foundation planting is similar to a bed; it's that small strip of soil that surrounds the house, and it may be the most misunderstood area in the garden. Evergreen shrubs are typically chosen for a foundation planting because they grow quickly and are "interesting" all year. But the plants that look just right in 5 years often take over the house in 15 or 20. Shrubs may need frequent pruning, and in cold areas they may be damaged by heavy, wet snow sliding off of the roof above.

Perennials, alone or with hardy bulbs and annuals, grasses, trees, vines, and shrubs, offer attractive and more colorful alternatives to a boring row of clipped evergreens. Well-chosen perennials won't drastically outgrow their location, and they're dormant when snow falls off the roof. Mixing perennials that have evergreen leaves—such as heart-leaved bergenia (*Bergenia cordifolia*) and perennial candytuft (*Iberis sempervirens*)—with hardy bulbs and ornamental grasses can create year-round appeal. Plus, perennials change continually through the season.

Foundation sites may have extreme growing conditions. Light levels and microclimates can vary dramatically on different sides of your house. Eaves may create a constant drought by blocking rainfall. At the drip line, the soil may be totally compacted by the impact of falling or dripping water. To cope with this, plan to cover the strip from the house to just past the roof edge with mulch. If this strip is too wide to be hidden behind a row of plants, plant drought-tolerant species that can take these tough conditions.

Choose the plants that can take the conditions and that look good to you. Include some fragrant flowers for a welcoming touch. Many herbs offer fragrant flowers or leaves, and are handy for cooking.

For a formal look, keep the lines straight with a pathway of bricks or square or rectangular flagstones and straight edges to plantings. For a less formal design, curve the edge of the bed to create a gentle, casual feel and to allow a few of the plants in front to sprawl a bit onto the path.

cleome, hollyhocks, and mulleins (*Verbascum* spp.) are ideal for adding height to the back of a mixed border. And shorter, airy annuals blend easily into border edgings; try plants like pot marigolds (*Calendula officinalis*), annual candytuft (*Iberis umbellata*), and annual baby's breath (*Gypsophila elegans*) with low-growing perennials and bulbs.

Screens

While the word "annual" commonly brings to mind compact, small plants like petunias and marigolds, there are a number of fast-growing annuals that can reach amazing heights of 6 feet (180 cm) or more in a single season. Tall-growing biennials and perennials may take a little longer, but they are just as effective at screening out an unpleasant view. Then there are the annual vines, with their twining stems that quickly cover trellises or fences for welcome shade and privacy. With these great plants to choose from, why spend another season staring at your neighbor's yard?

A row of sunflowers will make a cheerful cover-up.

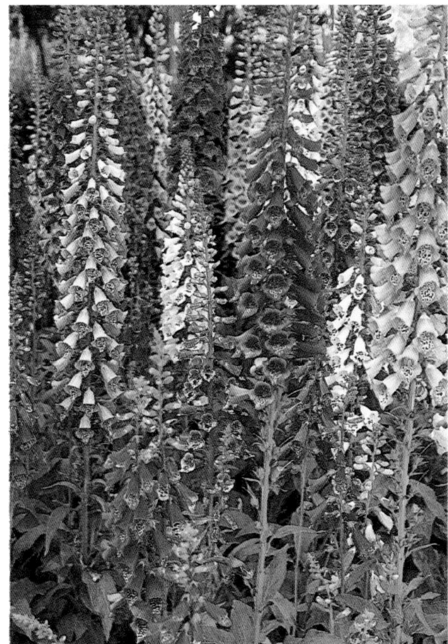

Common foxgloves are real showstoppers. Plant them thickly to make a lovely temporary fence.

Tall Annuals and Perennials

Grow tall annuals and perennials in your yard to block out or cover up unattractive features, such as dog runs, trash cans or clothesline poles. Or plant a row or mass of tall annuals to create a "neighbor-friendly" temporary fence that delineates your property line or separates different areas of your garden. Some top-notch tall plants include hollyhocks (*Alcea rosea*), sunflowers (*Helianthus annuus*), Mexican sunflower (*Tithonia rotundifolia*), the wide variety of foxgloves (*Digitalis* spp.), castor bean (*Ricinus communis*), delphiniums, and cardinal flowers (*Lobelia cardinalis*), and the spreading masses of goldenrod (*Solidago* spp.), spotted Joe-Pye weed (*Eupatorium maculatum*) and Queen-of-the-prairie (*Filipendula rubra*).

Annual Vines

A leafy curtain of annual vines is an ideal way to ensure privacy on a porch or patio without appearing to be unneighborly. Flowering vines also add a quaint, old-fashioned touch to the most ordinary, unsightly support. A cloak of morning glories can convert a ho-hum garden shed into a charming garden feature, while a mass of scarlet runner bean will accent an arch or liven up a lamppost.

Most annual vines cover territory in a hurry. You can easily train them to climb a wooden or wire trellis, chain-link fences, lattice work, or even strong twine. Tall wooden or bamboo stakes also make effective supports. While annual vines are usually lighter than woody vines (such as wisteria or trumpet creeper), they can put on a lot of growth in one season, so supply a sturdy support. Unlike clinging vines such as ivy, annual vines mostly climb with tendrils or twining stems, so don't expect them to scamper up a bare wall without assistance.

Morning glories (*Ipomoea tricolor*) have long been loved for their heart-shaped leaves and beautiful, trumpet-shaped flowers. The closely related moonflower (*Ipomoea alba*) is another popular vine; it offers large, white, heavily fragrant flowers that open in the evening. Besides being covered with clusters of colorful blooms, scarlet runner bean (*Phaseolus coccineus*) has the added bonus of edible beans. Other popular annual vines include cup-

Cup-and-saucer vine quickly covers fences or trellises, its blooms changing color with age.

The area under trees doesn't have to be dull. Plant annuals like pot marigolds and violas for season-long show and variety.

and-saucer vine (*Cobaea scandens*), black-eyed Susan vine (*Thunbergia alata*), sweet pea (*Lathyrus odoratus*), and hyacinth bean (*Lablab purpureus*).

Fillers

When you start any new garden, one of the hardest parts of the process is waiting for plants to fill in. This is especially true of perennial and shrub beds, since these plants can take 3 or 4 years to really get established and look like anything. New groundcover plantings can appear pretty sparse for the first few years, too. While you need to allow ample space for these plants to fill in as they mature, the bare soil in between is boring and empty, and it provides an open invitation for weeds to get started. And while mulch can suppress weeds, it doesn't add a great deal of excitement to a new planting. That's where filler annuals come in handy.

Fillers for Flower Beds

If you're looking for annuals to fill in around your new perennial plantings, choose those with a similar range of heights and colors as the perennials. Select a few short or trailing annuals for the front of the border, a few medium-sized plants for the middle of the border, and a few tall annuals for the back. While you could sow annual seed directly into the ground around the perennials, it's often easier to start with transplants of the annuals you want. Good filler annuals such as cleome (*Cleome hasslerana*) and cornflower (*Centaurea cyanus*) will drop seed and come back year after year. If your annuals do reseed, thin the seedlings to allow the expanding perennials room to develop.

Fillers for Groundcovers

Low-growing annuals such as rose moss (*Portulaca grandiflora*), baby blue-eyes (*Nemophila menziesii*), and sweet alyssum (*Lobularia maritima*) can be excellent fillers for young groundcover plantings. Use one kind of annual for a uniform effect. It's just as easy to scatter seed around the groundcover plants, although you could also set out annual transplants in the available spaces instead. While many low-growing annuals will self-sow, you may want to scatter some fresh annual seed over the planting for the first few springs until the groundcovers fill in.

Try a colorful planting of low-growing annuals to fill in the bare spots around new shrub plantings.

Low-growing pansies mix well with groundcovers such as ajuga and Japanese primrose.

Creating a Cutting Garden

If you enjoy having armloads of flowers to bring indoors for fresh arrangements, consider adding a cutting garden to your landscape. A cutting garden is simply one or more beds where you grow flowers to be used just for arrangements. You can collect beautiful blooms from your cutting garden without raiding your carefully planned displays in the rest of the yard.

Cutting Garden Basics

Few people have enough space to put a cutting garden truly out of sight, but the more removed it is, the less you'll worry about making it look nice. Some gardeners turn over a corner of their vegetable garden to cut flowers; others create separate cutting beds along a garage, in a sunny side yard, or in a sheltered corner of the backyard.

Wherever you put your cutting beds, you want them to be easy to reach and maintain. Be sure to prepare the soil well. Sow seeds or set out transplants just as you would for any garden, but there's no need to worry about too much planning or grouping specific heights and colors; just plant them in rows. With bulbs, plant hardy bulbs in fall and tender ones in spring after the soil has warmed enough.

Best Bulbs for Cutting

Listed below are some bulbs that make colorful, long-lasting cut flowers, arranged by bloom season; choose the ones you like best.

Spring Bloom
Allium spp. (ornamental onions)
Hyacinthus orientalis (hyacinth)
Leucojum aestivum (summer snowflake)
Muscari armeniacum (grape hyacinth)
Narcissus hybrids (daffodils)
Tulipa hybrids (tulips)

Summer Bloom
Canna x *generalis* (canna)
Gladiolus x *hortulanus* (gladiolus)
Lilium Asiatic hybrids (Asiatic lilies)
Lilium Trumpet hybrids (trumpet lilies)

Fall Bloom
Dahlia hybrids (dahlias)
Gladiolus x *hortulanus* (gladiolus)
Lilium Oriental hybrids (Oriental lilies)
Lycoris squamigera (magic lily)

Trumpet lily

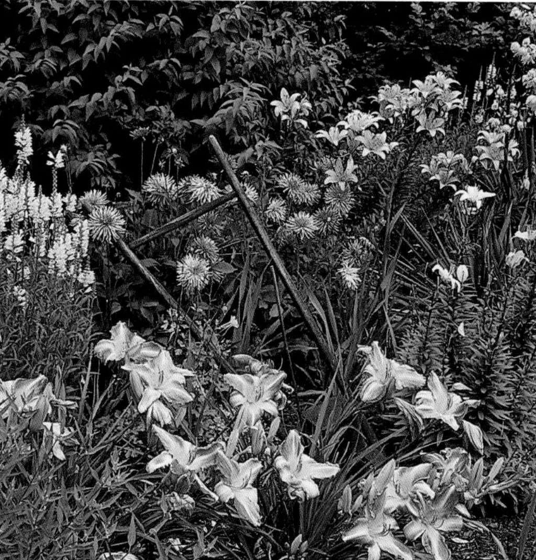
Beds full of perennials grown for cutting don't need lots of planning, but they still require all the care you would lavish on any other plants.

Mulch between the rows with a loose organic material (such as straw). Water as needed to keep the soil evenly moist for best growth and fertilize annuals that like extra nutrients. Stake floppy or long-stemmed flowers such as delphiniums, peonies, and baby's breath to keep the stems upright and the flowers clean.

Snipping tulips from regular beds is fine if you only do a few arrangements each season.

Foliage is a crucial part of many arrangements.

Japanese irises, with their gorgeous purple and yellow flowers atop elegant stems, make a lovely arrangement.

Choosing Plants for Cutting

Selecting plants for your cutting garden is much the same as choosing plants for any planting. Most importantly, you need to choose plants that will thrive in your growing conditions; if they aren't growing well, they won't produce many flowers. Here are some other things you'll want to consider when you're deciding what to include:

- If space is limited, concentrate on growing annuals and perennials in your favorite flower colors; if you have lots of room, plant a variety of colors to have lots of options.
- Grow plants with different shapes to keep your arrangements from looking monotonous. Include spiky flowers and foliage for height, flat or round flowers and leaves for mass, and small, airy flowers and leaves for fillers.
- Look for annuals and perennials with long stems. Dwarf or compact cultivars are great for ornamental plantings, but their stems are usually too short for easy arranging.
- Don't forget to include foliage—it adds body and filler to arrangements. Use leaves in subtle greens and silvers to emphasize individual flowers or colors; variegated leaves make striking accents.

Best Annuals for Cutting

Plan to sow some each of early-, mid-, and late-summer flowers to have a steady supply of blooms throughout the season. This list of suitable annuals for cut flowers shows their normal peak bloom season to help with your planning and planting.

Stocks

Antirrhinum majus (snapdragon; midsummer)
Calendula officinalis (pot marigold; early summer)
Callistephus chinensis (China aster; midsummer)
Centaurea cyanus (cornflower; midsummer)
Consolida ambigua (rocket larkspur; midsummer)
Cosmos bipinnatus (cosmos; late summer to fall)
Cosmos sulphureus (yellow cosmos; midsummer)
Dianthus barbatus (sweet William; early summer)
Gaillardia pulchella (blanket flower; midsummer)
Gypsophila elegans (annual baby's-breath; early summer)
Helianthus annuus (common sunflower; late summer)
Iberis umbellata (annual candytuft; early summer)
Lathyrus odoratus (sweet pea; early summer)
Matthiola incana (stock; early summer)
Rudbeckia hirta (black-eyed Susan; midsummer)
Tithonia rotundifolia (Mexican sunflower; late summer)
Viola x *wittrockiana* (pansy; early summer)
Zinnia elegans (zinnia; midsummer)

Tulips

The bright flowers and ferny foliage of cosmos are fine additions to arrangements in late summer.

There are so many annuals, perennials, and hardy bulbs to choose from when arranging flowers. To add something extra to your arrangements, include ornamental grasses in your cutting garden. They look great with both flowers and foliage. Spray their delicate flowers with lacquer or cheap hairspray to make them last longer.

Gathering Cut Flowers

The best time to collect cut flowers is when the buds are just opening, not when they are in full bloom. Collect them during a cool part of the day; morning is usually best. Take a bucket of lukewarm water and a sharp pair of clippers or a knife with you. If picking bulb flowers, choose those flowers with as few leaves as possible, so the bulbs can store enough energy for the next bloom season. As you snip the stem from the rest of the plant, make a sloping, rather than straight, cut; this opens up a little more room for the stems to absorb water. Plunge the cut flowers into the bucket immediately, so they are in water up to the base of the flower. (If you are cutting dahlias, sear the bottom of the stem with the flame from a match before putting it in the water.)

As you arrange the flowers, cut the stems to their final lengths under water so no air bubbles enter. Remove leaves that will be below the waterline in the finished arrangement. After arranging, fill the vase to the top with water; refill as soon as the level drops. You can also buy commercial preservatives to help extend the life of your blooms, or add a shot of lemon-lime soda, although the easiest method is simply to change the water every few days. Flowers will last longest in a cool room out of direct light.

Making a Meadow Garden

Meadows are informal blends of flowers and grasses growing in a sunny, open spot. They provide food and shelter for birds, beneficial insects, and butterflies. They also add a casual, country touch to any yard. Best of all, established meadows require little upkeep. But do bear in mind that what you see as a meadow garden may look like a patch of weeds to your neighbors. Discuss your plans with them and check local mowing ordinances in your area before you begin, to avoid any misunderstandings and complaints as you convert your lawn into a meadow.

Cut down on mowing time by replacing some lawn with a field full of California poppies and goldfields.

Steps to a Great-looking Meadow

Creating a vigorous, beautiful meadow involves more than simply shaking seeds out of a packet or can onto a grassy or dusty spot. For best results, you'll need to give your meadow the same care you'd use to start any garden. Prepare the soil well, choose the best-adapted annuals and perennials, and plant them properly. Just follow these simple steps:

1. Pick a site with well-drained soil and at least 6 hours of sun a day.

Fill in out-of-the-way places in your yard with prolific wildflowers to create a meadow garden.

2. In spring, summer, or fall, remove existing grasses and aggressive weeds; lawn grasses can spread vigorously and smother small, new plants. Skim off slices of turf with a spade. Compost the pieces of sod or use to fill holes in the remaining lawn.
3. Spread 1 to 2 inches (2.5 to 5 cm) of compost over the area, and dig or till it into the top 4 to 6 inches (10 to 15 cm) of soil. Use a rake to remove any rocks and smooth the soil.
4. Kill all weeds and reduce the bank of weed seeds in the soil to obtain a clean weed-free site.
5. In fall, set out your perennials, bulbs, and grasses and mulch them well. Their roots will be well established by spring, and your plants will be ready to put on great growth.
6. In spring, if you wish, rake away some mulch to sow annual wildflower seeds between the perennial meadow plants. Annuals will provide quick color the first year while the perennials are growing new roots and getting established.
7. Through the first growing season, water your meadow when the soil is dry to 1 to 2 inches (2.5 to 5 cm) deep to help the growing young plants establish.

Routine Meadow Maintenance

Mow your meadow once a year to keep it looking good and to keep weeds, shrubs, and trees from invading. Late fall to early winter, after plants have formed seeds, is the best time. If you want to feed the birds, leave seed heads standing until late winter or early spring; just be aware that they'll be harder to mow after winter rain and snow have beaten them down.

Cut the whole meadow to a height of about 6 inches (15 cm). Use a sickle-bar

Meadows are beautiful and low-maintenance, and they're ideal habitats for bees and butterflies.

Kill Weeds Before You Plant

To make a clean, weed-free site for your meadow garden, remove any perennial weeds, dig or till to loosen the soil, and rake the seedbed smooth. Then try one of the methods below:

Let exposed weed seeds germinate, then hoe or till the soil shallowly to remove the weeds that pop up.

Cover the soil with a sheet of thick, clear plastic during summer. The heat generated will kill any weed seeds.

mower for large areas; a string trimmer or hand clippers can handle small patches. A regular lawn mower won't work; it cuts too low. Leave trimmings in place so plants can self-sow, or collect them for your compost pile.

Aside from the yearly trim, your only maintenance is to dig out tree seedlings and aggressive weeds such as quack grass, poison ivy, bindweed, and burdock as soon as they appear. Established meadows don't require water, fertilizer, or mulch. As the plants get more established, your meadow garden will look different each year, but it will always be beautiful.

Wonderful Wildflower Meadows

Wildflower meadows are fairly easy and inexpensive to grow from seed, and their beautiful spread will provide a welcome visiting spot for the native butterflies, bees, and birds of your region. Evenly scatter a mixture of native wildflower and native grass seeds on the soil surface and rake them in. It's well worth the trouble to track down a mix of true natives; if you buy a "one-size-fits-all" mix, you'll be paying for some seed that won't grow where you live. Ask your Cooperative Extension Service or local botanical garden to recommend plants that will grow well in your area. It will take about 3 seasons for your wildflower meadow to completely fill in, though you should have some pleasing results in the first year.

Marvelous Annual Meadows

If you enjoy the easy, informal appearance of meadow gardens but don't want to wait a few years for perennial plants to get established, try planting an annual meadow. Many catalogs are now selling seed mixes of meadow annuals, containing colorful, easy-care plants like corn poppy (*Papaver rhoeas*), cornflower (*Centaurea cyanus*), California poppy (*Eschscholzia californica*), and calliopsis (*Coreopsis tinctoria*).

Most meadow annuals thrive in full sun and average soil, so choose a site with as much sun as possible. Prepare the soil as you would for any other annual garden. It's smart to prepare the site in fall so it will be ready for planting the following spring. When you are ready to plant, hoe the surface to clear off any weeds that have sprouted, then scatter the seed evenly over the surface. Rake the bed lightly to scratch the seed into the soil, then water the area well using a light spray. Keep the soil moist for 2 or 3 weeks, until the seedlings start growing.

A mixture of annuals, perennials, bulbs, and grasses creates an ever-changing scene.

Established annual meadows don't need a great deal of care; just hand pull any weeds you see. At the end of the

Black-eyed Susan cultivars in vivid red are a natural choice for inclusion in an annual meadow.

Grasses in the Flower Garden

As well as having a place in any meadow garden, ornamental grasses blend beautifully into many traditional flower borders. Annuals and perennials add vibrant colors to the more subtle, muted tones of many grasses. The grasses, in turn, supply all-season interest and soothing backgrounds for delicate flowers.

Choose companions for your grasses based on the growing conditions you have available. In sunny areas, good choices include garden mums, delphiniums, peonies, the many different types of poppy, shasta daisies (*Leucanthemum* x *superbum*), gas plant (*Dictamnus purpureus*), and lupines (*Lupinus* spp.). Under trees, plants like ferns, hostas, and lily-of-the-valley (*Convallaria majalis*) combine well with shade-loving sedges. In dry locations, colorful rock garden plants—including maiden pinks (*Dianthus deltoides*), wall rock cress (*Arabis caucasica*), and woolly yarrow (*Achillea tomentosa*)—are ideal with low-growing grasses. And in wet places, rushes (*Juncus* spp.) form naturally beautiful combinations with water-loving perennials such as blue flag (*Iris versicolor*) and Siberian iris (*Iris sibirica*).

Grasses look great with flowers in all parts of the garden. Spring bulbs such as daffodils, crocus, grape hyacinths, snowdrops, and tulips make a colorful display early in the season; as they fade, the fast-growing grasses neatly camouflage the dying bulb foliage. In semiwild areas, wildflowers combine beautifully with the less showy grasses, including broomsedge (*Andropogon virginicus*), tufted hairgrass (*Deschampsia caespitosa*), switch grass (*Panicum virgatum*), and prairie cord grass (*Spartina pectinata*).

season, mow or cut the plants to the ground as outlined above. While many meadow annuals will reseed themselves, the second and subsequent years seldom rival the beauty of the first; sowing a fresh mix of seed each year will provide the best results.

Naturalizing with Bulbs

The bulb equivalent of a meadow garden is known as naturalizing. Bulbs are planted in random, natural-looking drifts in grassy areas, under trees, or in woodlands. It's easy to do, and the results look better and better every year as the bulbs multiply to produce even more blooms. The result will be flowers that you plant once and enjoy forever, with no need for yearly fussing.

Deciding Where to Plant

Naturalized bulbs are often best in low-maintenance areas, where you can enjoy the blooms but not be bothered by the sight of the ripening leaves. Very early bulbs, such as spring crocus, are sometimes naturalized in lawns to provide color. You may have to put off the first spring mowing for a week or two to let the bulb foliage turn yellow, but after that you can mow as usual. Fall-blooming bulbs can also look good in grassy areas, but you'll have to stop mowing in late summer, as soon as you see the flower buds sprouting from the soil.

Thick grass may be too competitive for some bulbs, but a sparse lawn—especially under deciduous trees—is just the right environment to help bulbs take hold. The bulbs get plenty of spring sun and moisture before the trees leaf out, and the flowers add cheerful spring and/or fall color to otherwise drab areas. If you have many trees, you can combine sweeps of naturalized bulbs with shade-loving annuals, perennials, and shrubs to create a charming woodland garden with four-season interest.

To grow masses of wildflowers, find a native seed mix of plants that are sure to grow in your area.

Groundcovers make another great companion for naturalized bulbs. The leaves and stems of the groundcovers support the bulb flowers, provide an attractive backdrop, help to keep soil from splashing onto the blooms, and mask the ripening bulb leaves. In turn, the bulbs provide a pretty seasonal show of flowers to make the groundcovers more exciting.

Purple coneflowers, phlox, and thin-leaved sunflowers form a lovely, easy-care combination.

Start your meadow off in spring with naturalized bulbs, such as crocuses. The best planting technique for so many crocuses is to lift up large sections of sod, loosen the soil, plant the bulbs, then replace the sod.

Daffodils planted in grass will multiply over the years to provide a thick carpet of yellow.

Planting Naturalized Bulbs

The key to successful naturalizing is to plant your bulbs in natural-looking arrangements rather than in straight rows or patterns. It's usually best to place them randomly over the planting area by hand until the arrangement looks right to you. Don't just toss out handfuls of bulbs from a standing position; the bulbs may get bruised or damaged as they fall and be prone to pest and disease problems.

Many gardeners find that a narrow trowel is the easiest tool to use for planting small bulbs. You simply insert the trowel into the ground at an angle, lift up a flap of sod, tuck the bulb into the soil, and replace the flap. Or you can plant bulbs in groups by lifting up larger sections of sod, loosening the exposed soil, pressing the bulbs into the soil, and replacing the sod. (This technique works best with small bulbs such as crocus.) If you have lots of bulbs to plant, you may want to try using an auger attachment that connects to a power drill to dig many holes quickly and easily. (These attachments are usually sold in garden centers and through garden-supply catalogs.) For more information on bulb-planting techniques, see "Planting Bulbs" on page 61.

Marvelous Meadow Plants

The recipe for a magnificent meadow includes a blend of tough perennial flowers and noninvasive perennial grasses, with a scattering of annuals and a dash of daffodils and other naturalized spring bulbs for early color. Below you'll find some suggested flowers you can consider for your moist or dry site, along with some great meadow grasses.

Sneezeweed

Perennials for Dry Meadows

Achillea filipendulina (fern-leaved yarrow)
Asclepias tuberosa (butterfly weed)
Baptisia australis (blue false indigo)
Echinacea purpurea (purple coneflower)
Gaillardia x *grandiflora* (blanket flower)
Helianthus x *multiflorus* (perennial sunflower)
Liatris spicata (spike gayfeather)
Oenothera tetragona (common sundrops)
Rudbeckia fulgida (orange coneflower)
Solidago rigida (stiff goldenrod)

Perennials for Moist Meadows

Aster novae-angliae (New England aster)
Chelone glabra (white turtlehead)
Eupatorium maculatum (spotted Joe-Pye weed)
Eupatorium rugosum (white snakeroot)
Filipendula rubra (queen of the prairie)
Helenium autumnale (common sneezeweed)
Lobelia cardinalis (cardinal flower)
Physostegia virginiana (obedient plant)
Thermopsis caroliniana (Carolina lupine)

Great Grasses for Meadows

Andropogon virginicus (broomsedge)
Bouteloua curtipendula (side oats grammagrass)
Festuca spp. (fescues)
Schizachyrium scoparium (little bluestem)
Sporobolus heterolepis (prairie dropseed)

Blue grass

Creating a Cottage Garden

Perennials, annuals, shrubs, and trees combine in a charming cottage garden of purple and pink hues.

The tall, spiky flowers of foxgloves and the brilliant red of oriental poppies add a dramatic touch as feature flowers in a cottage garden.

The ultimate in informality, cottage gardens display a glorious riot of colors, textures, heights, and fragrances. Cottage gardens defy many gardening "rules": Plants are planted so they are packed closely together, with standard spacing ignored. Colors aren't organized into large drifts. Tall plants pop up in front of shorter ones. Flowers are allowed to flop over and grow through each other to create a delightful, casual mixture.

While cottage gardens may appear effortless and unorganized, they need to be planned, planted, and maintained just like any other flower garden. In this section, you'll learn the tricks to capturing the informal cottage garden effect without creating a messy-looking mixture.

Choosing a Site

Locate cottage gardens next to the house, especially by a door. If your front or side yard is small, you may want to devote the whole space to the garden. In this case, a gravel, brick, stone, or even cement path is essential; make it wide (at least 3 feet [90 cm]) to allow room for plants to spill out onto it.

Picking the Plants

To create a pleasing jumble rather than a chaotic mess, combine a variety of different flower shapes and sizes. Thinking of flowers in terms of their visual impact will help you get the right balance.

"Feature" flowers are the ones that first catch your eye; they have strong shapes—like spiky lupines (*Lupinus polyphyllus*) and massive peonies—or bright colors.

"Filler" flowers tend to be smaller and less obvious than feature plants. Baby's breath (*Gypsophila paniculata*) is a classic.

"Edgers" are low plants used in the fronts of beds or spilling over onto paths; think of thymes and catmint (*Nepeta* x *faassenii*).

These categories aren't rigid: Lavender and the flowers of lady's mantle (*Alchemilla mollis*) make nice fillers, but both are often used to edge paths as well. Rose campion (*Lychnis coronaria*) works as a filler, but if set among flowers with contrasting colors,

A mixed cottage border includes milky bellflowers, lamb's ears, and a feature planting of giant sea holly.

Delphiniums are traditional favorites, ranging from white through all shades of blue and purple.

its bright magenta flowers may stand out as a feature. The key is to use some flowers that serve each purpose, so you don't have all bright (and probably clashing) feature flowers, all small filler flowers, or all low edging plants.

As you choose plants for the garden, include some that have scented foliage or flowers (choosing fragrant plants is discussed in more detail below). It's also important to choose flowers that bloom at different times for a continuous display.

Perennials aren't the only plants you can grow in your cottage garden: Annuals, herbs, shrubs, vines, and bulbs all can have a place in your cottage garden, too. Old-fashioned roses, either shrub types or climbers, are a classic ingredient and an important source of fragrant flowers. Climbing roses or honeysuckles look great trained over a door or archway; let clematis climb up lampposts or railings.

Including unusual and unlikely plants is a cottage garden tradition of long standing. Accent yours with dwarf fruit trees, and tuck in some other edibles for surprise: Try colorful lettuces, curly parsley, red-stemmed 'Ruby' chard, and maroon-podded 'Burgundy' okra.

Shasta daisies, loosestrife, and rose mallow offer a harmonious variety of color, texture, and height.

Pretty Perennials for Cottage Gardens

These great cottage garden flowers have been favorites for years. Use feature flowers for bold colors and textures, edging plants to line the front, and filler flowers to tie the whole design together. You can discover more about the specific plants listed below by referring to "Encyclopedia of Flowers," starting on page 306.

Purple rock cress

Feature Flowers

Alcea rosea (hollyhock)
Campanula persicifolia (peach-leaved bellflower)
Delphinium x *belladonna* (Belladonna delphinium)
Dictamnus albus (gas plant)
Iris bearded hybrids (bearded iris)
Lilium hybrids (lilies)
Lupinus polyphyllus (garden lupine)
Paeonia lactiflora (common garden peony)
Papaver orientale (oriental poppy)
Phlox paniculata (garden phlox)
Verbascum chaixii (nettle-leaved mullein)

Edging Plants

Aubrieta deltoidea (purple rock cress)
Aurinia saxatilis (basket of gold)
Campanula portenschlagiana (Dalmatian bellflower)
Cerastium tomentosum (snow-in-summer)
Dianthus gratianopolitanus (cheddar pinks)
Euphorbia epithymoides (cushion spurge)
Heuchera sanguinea (coral bells)
Nepeta x *faassenii* (catmint)
Primula vulgaris (English primrose)
Pulmonaria saccharata (Bethlehem sage)

Filler Flowers

Alchemilla mollis (lady's mantle)
Aquilegia x *hybrida* (hybrid columbine)
Aster novae-angliae (New England aster)
Astrantia major (masterwort)
Centaurea hypoleuca (knapweed)
Centranthus ruber (red valerian)
Coreopsis verticillata (thread-leaved coreopsis)
Geranium sanguineum (blood-red cranesbill)
Gypsophila paniculata (baby's breath)
Leucanthemum x *superbum* (shasta daisy)
Lychnis coronaria (rose campion)
Patrinia scabiosifolia (patrinia)

The delicate blooms of peach-leaved bellflowers have long been a favorite in the cottage garden.

Gardening for Butterflies

A cottage garden is a mass of flowers, and that means that it can be a very attractive place for butterflies. Planting a landscape for butterflies is a great way to add an exciting element of moving color to your yard. Choosing and growing the right annuals and perennials will supply the food butterflies need throughout their lives. You'll also want to provide water and shelter to encourage the butterflies that arrive to stay.

Growing Food for Butterflies

To find out what plants the butterflies in your area like, look for them in nearby gardens, old fields, and at the edges of woods. Observe which flowers they prefer and where they stop to sun themselves. If you see a pretty butterfly sipping nectar from a particular flower, consider growing that plant. Imitating nature is the secret to successful butterfly gardening.

To have a great butterfly garden, you must get used to a few holes in the leaves of your plants. You need to let the caterpillars feed in order to keep the adult butterflies around. Many "flowers" listed for butterfly gardens—including violets, parsley, hollyhocks (*Alcea rosea*), and milkweeds (*Asclepias* spp.)—are really food sources (leaves) for the caterpillars.

Adult butterflies that are ready to lay eggs are attracted by the plants that will feed their developing larvae. Some adults also feed on flower nectar. Plants that have clusters of short, tubular, brightly colored flowers are especially popular. Many shrubs—including butterfly bush (*Buddleia davidii*) and abelia (*Abelia* x *grandiflora*)—are also natural choices.

Encourage thirsty butterflies with a water source.

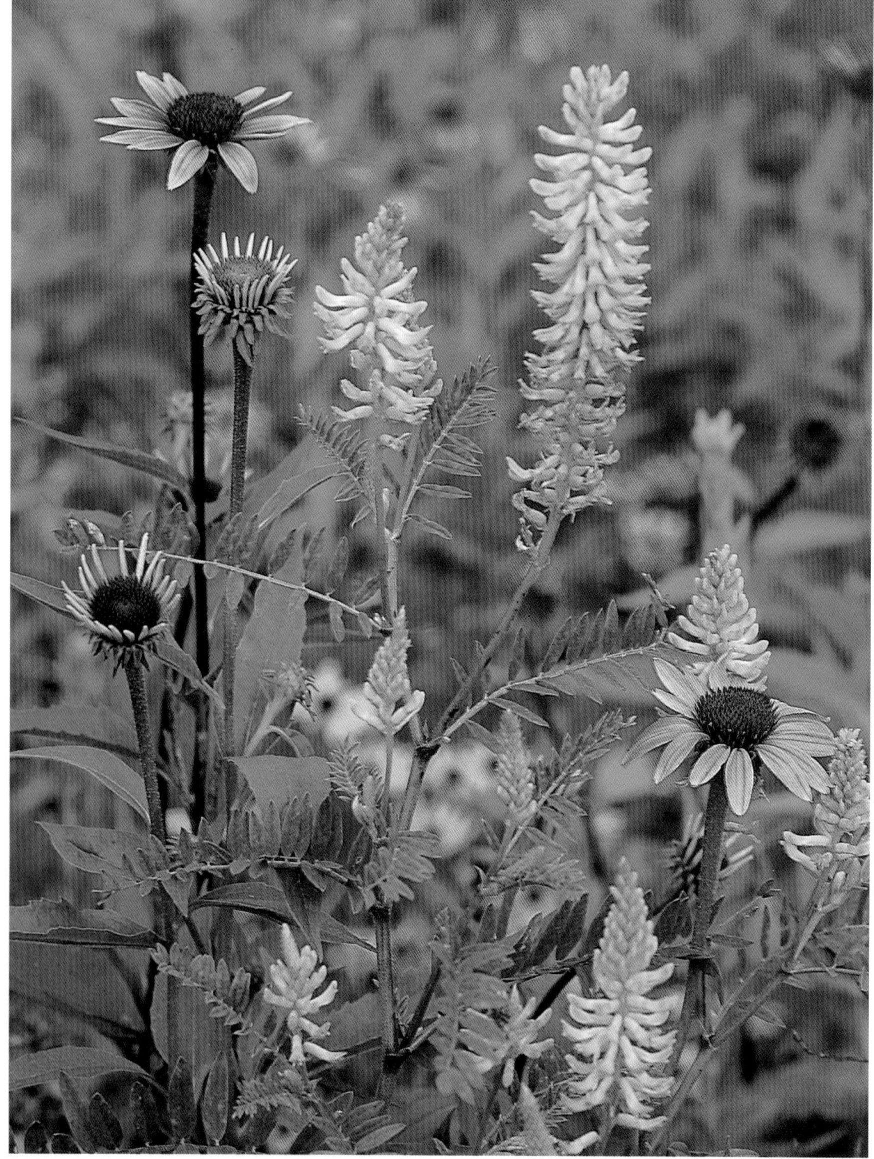

Growing local wildflowers will provide a food source for the butterfly species native to your area.

Orange coneflowers offer nectar for fritillaries and crescentspots, while the flowers of showy stonecrop are a magnet for tortoiseshells.

A variety of different plants in a sheltered, sunny spot is sure to attract the local butterflies. This walled garden is a fine example.

Just Add Water Butterflies are attracted to shallow puddles and muddy soil. Dig a small, shallow basin, line it with plastic, and cover it with sandy soil and gravel to form a butterfly-luring water source.

Diversify Your Yard Adding diversity to your landscape means creating different mini-environments as well as increasing the number of different plants you grow. Edge habitats—where woods meet lawn or meadows and lawn meets garden or shrub plantings—provide great environments for butterflies because they offer protection from predators. If you can, allow a corner of your yard to go wild; a tangle of brush offers perfect protection.

Most butterflies are fussy eaters, feeding on just one or a few plant types. To be sure your garden has what they want, grow a range of plants.

Arranging Your Butterfly Plantings

If you have an informal landscape, consider planting a meadow garden (as explained in "Making a Meadow Garden" on page 136). If you don't have room for a meadow, grow some of the many wildflowers that double as garden perennials, such as asters and coneflowers (*Echinacea* and *Rudbeckia* spp.). Scatter these plants throughout your landscape, or put several of them together in a special butterfly garden. Large splashes of color are easier for butterflies to find than a single plant, so group several plants of the same color together.

Providing a Safe Haven for Butterflies

Along with growing their favorite food and nectar plants, you can take a number of steps to encourage butterflies to stay in your yard.

Make a Spot for Sunbathing All butterflies like sun and dislike wind, so plant flowers in sunny spots with walls or shrubs as windbreaks. Set flat stones in a sheltered, sunny spot for butterflies to bask on.

Best Bets for Butterflies

Here are some beautiful perennials that are especially popular with butterflies. To learn more, look up the individual entries in "Encyclopedia of Flowers," starting on page 306.

Achillea filipendulina (fern-leaved yarrow)
Asclepias tuberosa (butterfly weed)
Aster novae-angliae (New England aster)
Astilbe x *arendsii* (astilbe)
Baptisia australis (blue false indigo)
Boltonia asteroides (boltonia)
Centranthus ruber (red valerian)
Dianthus gratianopolitanus (cheddar pinks)
Echinacea purpurea (purple coneflower)
Erigeron speciosus (daisy fleabane)
Eupatorium maculatum (spotted Joe-Pye weed)
Eupatorium rugosum (white snakeroot)
Gaillardia x *grandiflora* (blanket flowers)
Leucanthemum x *superbum* (shasta daisy)
Lupinus polyphyllus (garden lupine)
Monarda didyma (bee balm)
Phlox paniculata (garden phlox)
Rudbeckia fulgida (orange coneflower)
Scabiosa caucasica (pincushion flower)
Sedum spectabile (showy stonecrop)

Most butterflies have very specific tastes. By increasing the variety of plants to provide a smorgasbord of food and nectar sources, you will attract many different species from early spring through fall.

Avoid Using Pesticides One of the most important steps in having a butterfly haven is ensuring that you are creating a safe, pesticide-free habitat. Even organically acceptable pesticides such as rotenone and pyrethrin kill butterflies and their eggs and larvae. BT, a biological control used against many garden pests, is also fatal to the larvae of desirable butterflies. Use safer techniques such as handpicking and water sprays to remove pests from plants. If you don't want butterfly larvae to munch on your vegetable garden (carrots, celery, cabbage, broccoli, and parsley are a few of the preferred butterfly targets), protect those crops with floating row covers.

Gardening with Fragrance

Annuals and perennials with fragrant leaves and flowers have a place in any landscape, not just the cottage garden. There's nothing like the fresh scent of mint to perk you up after a long day. And who could resist resting on a cozy garden bench near a patch of peonies in full, fragrant bloom? In beds, borders, cottage gardens, and foundation plantings, mixing in some scented perennials will add an extra-special touch to your yard.

Heady, scented roses are a classic part of any fragrance garden. Whether in miniature, bush, or climbing form, they combine beautifully with annuals and perennials for extra color and even additional scents.

Fragrance in Flowers

When you mention fragrance in the garden, most people automatically think of flowers. Peonies and lilies are probably the most well known perennials, and among annuals, consider sweet William (*Dianthus barbatus*) or China pinks (*D. chinensis*), two carnation relatives noted for their spicy scents. Sweet alyssum (*Lobularia maritima*) is a common and easy-to-grow annual that's beloved for its fresh, honey-like fragrance. Mignonette (*Reseda odorata*) is an old-fashioned favorite with small, insignificant flowers but a powerful and delightful fragrance. There are many other plants that have pleasing scents as well; see "Favorite Fragrances" for more ideas.

Traditionally, scented flowers were grown close to the house so the fragrance could be appreciated through open doors and windows. But they're equally nice near outdoor eating areas and porches—any place where people linger. Raised planters are great for short, fragrant flowers so you don't have to get down on your hands and knees to enjoy the scents.

Many fragrant flowers are also visually beautiful, so you can enjoy looking at them and sniffing them as you walk around or work in the yard. Cutting these flowers for arrangements brings this pleasure indoors. A few annuals withhold their scents until the sun sets, then release their sweet perfume on the evening breeze. Night-scented stock (*Matthiola longipetala* subsp. *bicornis*), sweet rocket (*Hesperis matronalis*), and flowering tobacco (*Nicotiana sylvestris*) carry remarkably potent night scents.

Flowering tobacco dazzles by day, then fills the night with a wonderfully sweet fragrance.

Scented foliage and vivid flowers make bee balm an attractive inclusion in the garden. Plant it along a path to enjoy its scent when brushing past.

Fragrance in Foliage

A number of plants have fragrant foliage, but you need to touch these to smell them. Plant lavender and bee balm (*Monarda didyma*) where you'll brush against them as you walk by. Grow lemon balm (*Melissa officinalis*) near a garden seat or in a raised container so you can easily rub the leaves to release their delicious lemony odor. Wormwood (*Artemisia absinthium*) and rue (*Ruta graveolens*) leaves have pungent scents that some people find pleasing and others find disagreeable; try sniffing these plants before you buy them. Some annuals have fragrant leaves as well. Scented geraniums (including *Pelargonium tomentosum*, *P. crispum*, and *P. graveolens*) are noted for their aromatic leaves. When you rub them, they release scents resembling those of peppermint, lemons, roses, and many other plants. Annual herbs such as basil, anise, and dill also offer fragrant foliage.

Stock has a rich, spicy fragrance that is noticeable in the garden or in fresh arrangements indoors. One species even has a potent scent at night.

Fragrant Plants

The real key to having a scented garden that you enjoy is smelling plants before you buy them. The fragrance that a friend raves about may be undetectable or even unpleasant to you. Visit nurseries or public gardens when the plants you want are blooming, and sniff the flowers or foliage to see what you think. Different cultivars of the same plant may vary widely in their scents, so smell them all before you choose. "Favorite Fragrances" gives you some ideas of specific annuals and perennials that most gardeners agree are great additions to any scented garden.

To get the most pleasure from your fragrant plants, grow them where you will walk, sit, or brush by them often. Try them along the path to your front door, around a deck or patio, or in a foundation planting near open windows for your indoor enjoyment. Raised beds and container gardens are especially good spots for scented plants, since they'll be closer to your nose and easier to sniff.

Just as a bed of many different flower colors can look jumbled, a mixture of many strong fragrances can be distracting or even downright repulsive. As you plan your garden, try to arrange it with just a couple of scented plants in bloom at any given time. That way, you can enjoy different fragrances all through the season without being overwhelmed by too many at once.

Catmint has gray-green leaves that give off a pungent, minty smell—it's irresistible to cats.

Favorite Fragrances

Here is a list of a few easy annuals, biennials, and perennials that are commonly grown for their fragrance. Keep in mind that scents are subjective; what's pleasing to one person may be undetectable or offensive to another. If possible, try to sniff plants before you buy them to see if you like the fragrance. For complete growing information, see the individual entries starting on page 306.

Sweetpeas

Annuals and Biennials

Dianthus barbatus (sweet William)
Dianthus chinensis (China pink)
Erysimum cheiri (wallflower)
Heliotropium arborescens (common heliotrope)
Ipomoea alba (moonflower)
Lathyrus odoratus (sweet pea)
Lobularia maritima (sweet alyssum)
Matthiola incana (stock)
Mirabilis jalapa (four o'clock)
Nicotiana alata (flowering tobacco)
Petunia x *hybrida* (petunia)

Perennials for Fragrance

Centranthus ruber (red valerian)
Convallaria majalis (lily-of-the-valley)
Dianthus gratianopolitanus (cheddar pinks)
Hemerocallis hybrids (daylilies), mainly yellow types
Hyacinthus orientalis (hyacinth)
Iris bearded hybrids (bearded iris)
Lavandula angustifolia (lavender)
Lilium hybrids (lilies), especially regal lilies, trumpet hybrids, and oriental hybrids
Narcissus hybrids (daffodils)
Nepeta x *faassenii* (catmint)
Paeonia lactiflora (common garden peony)
Phlox paniculata (garden phlox)
Polygonatum odoratum (fragrant Solomon's seal)

The flowers and leaves of lavender are scented, and they retain their spicy fragrance after drying.

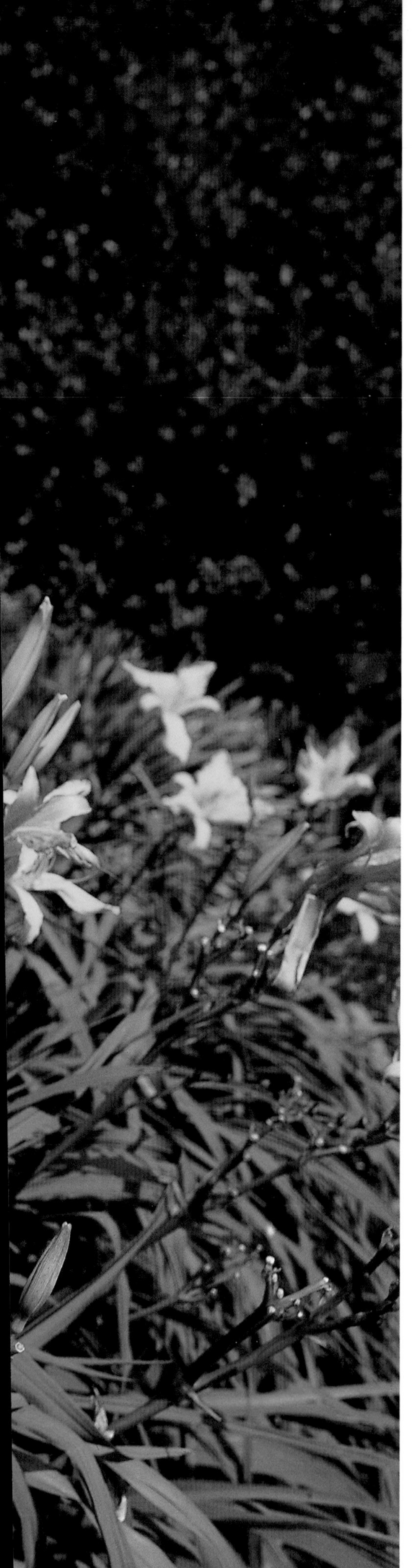

SECTION SIX

Problem-solving with Flowers

It's a rare property that doesn't have at least one difficult spot. Maybe it's a steep, hard-to-mow slope between the yard and the street. Or a dry, shady area under mature maple trees on the side of the house. Or a low, soggy spot that never really dries out, even in the heat of summer. Whatever the problem, some careful thought and plant selection can turn a difficult site into a beautiful landscape feature. This section gives you some ideas about how to solve your flower garden problems.

Time-saving Gardening Tips *148*

Handling Hillsides *154*

Succeeding in the Shade *156*

Turning Bogs into Beds *158*

Growing a Water-wise Landscape *160*

Time-saving Gardening Tips

No matter what kind of site you have, you probably have a problem that is common to most gardeners: a lack of time. With today's busy lifestyles, it is hard for many gardeners to find the time they'd like to spend keeping their yard looking great all year long. Even if you do have plenty of time to work in the garden, there are probably a number of chores—such as weeding or edging—that you tend to put off while you spend your time doing fun things, like planting.

The solution is good planning, so your garden doesn't become just another series of chores that must be done and it doesn't take more time than you have. No matter what kind of garden you want, you can tailor your landscape plans and plant choices to focus on maximum return for minimum effort. A few hours of careful planning and site preparation will cut down amazingly on maintenance. You'll spend less time working on your yard and have more time to enjoy it!

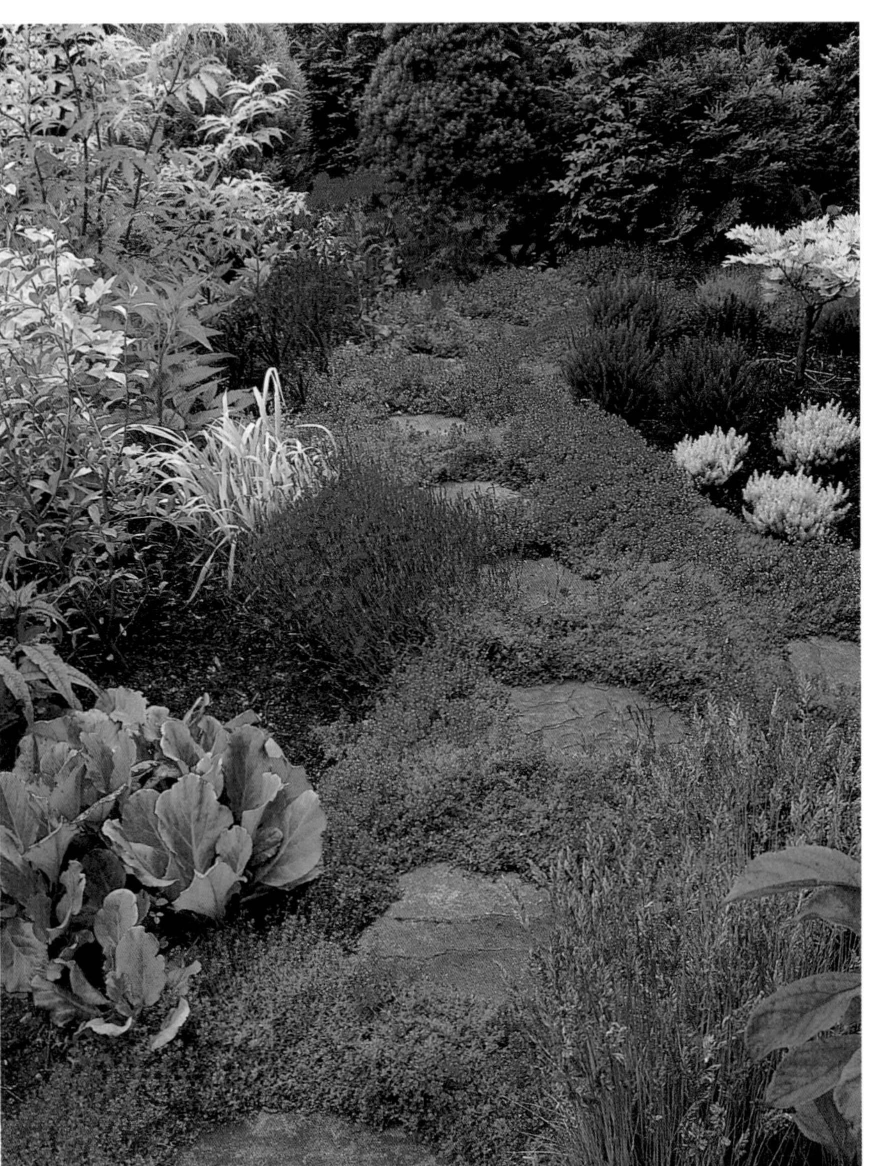

Eliminate mowing and trimming under trees by replacing grass with groundcovers and stepping stones.

If you're going to plant under trees, make sure you choose shade-loving annuals and perennials.

Picking plants that are adapted to the growing conditions you have to offer is a key part of creating a healthy, beautiful, easy-care garden. Many annuals and perennials can adjust to a wide range of different light and soil conditions; others are particularly well suited to certain challenging growing conditions.

What's the Most Work?

The key to low-maintenance landscaping is identifying your most bothersome gardening tasks. Which chores take the most time? Which do you like least? Landscape your yard to minimize the unpleasant chores so you can focus on the things you like most, whether it's fussing over a formal herb garden or sipping lemonade in the shade. Below are easy-care solutions to some of the most time-consuming landscape tasks.

Hand Trimming

Reduce hand trimming around tree trunks, fences, posts, and bird baths by replacing the grass there with hostas, daylilies, or other groundcovers.

Edging

If you hate doing the edges on the flower beds and loathe digging out the grass that invades from the lawn, install edging strips. Make sure the strips are level with or slightly below the top of the grass so you can mow over them.

Weeding

Minimizing weeding starts at planting time. First, be sure not to skimp on site preparation. Every weed you remove before you start means a whole bucketful of weeds you won't have to remove later. After planting, apply and maintain a good mulch cover. Check the mulch depth 3 or 4 times a year and add more if needed. You might have to remove a few weeds that sprout in the mulch occasionally, but they'll be easy to pull.

One of the best things you can do to cut down on weeding is to get in the habit of pulling weeds as soon as you see them. Otherwise, you give them a chance to spread or set seed and you'll end up with more work. Carry a basket, bag, or bucket with you every time you walk around the yard to collect pulled weeds. (They may reroot if you leave them on the soil.)

Mowing is just one of the many tasks involved in maintaining a lawn area. But there are alternatives.

Watering

If hauling hoses around the yard isn't your idea of fun, planning a water-wise garden will cut down on your watering chores. First, look for plants that thrive in your area without extra water. Fields, roadsides, graveyards, and abandoned lots are good places to get ideas of tough plants that can survive without supplemental watering.

The mulch that you use on finished plantings to keep weeds down will also help to keep the soil moist and reduce watering chores. If you must water, consider laying soaker hoses or drip irrigation systems; then you'll only have to hook up the hose or turn on the system when you need to water, instead of standing there watering by hand.

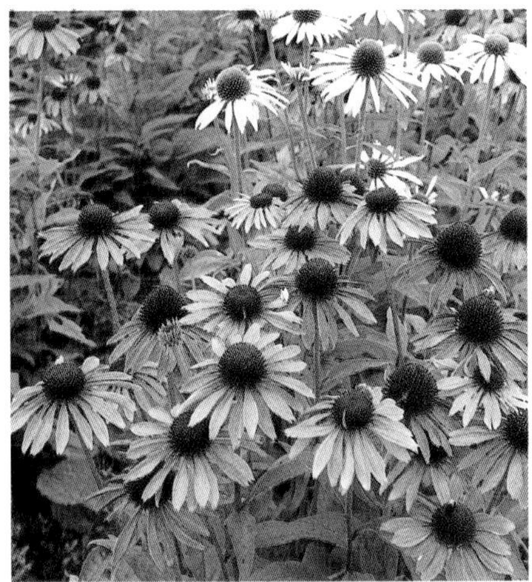

Choosing hardy, drought-tolerant perennials like purple coneflowers will reduce watering chores.

Reducing the Lawn Area

Lawn maintenance is probably the most routine and time-consuming part of caring for a traditional landscape. The obvious but surefire way to save on mowing time is to grow less grass. There are plenty of ways to cut down on mowing areas. Build a deck or patio. Line the area below the swing set with landscape fabric and cover it with bark nuggets. Eliminate grass from hard-to-mow areas and replace it with an easy-to-maintain mulch. In small gardens, urban areas, or dry climates, consider eliminating the lawn altogether. Annuals and perennials look great next to paving stones, bricks, cement pavers, or gravel.

All of these solutions have their place. But they don't cool things off the way a big area covered with plants can, and they just aren't as soothing to the eye. If you like growing things but want to mow less, a meadow garden, especially one of hardy local wildflowers, could be the answer; you'll find more information at "Making a Meadow Garden" on page 136. Or you could try groundcovers.

Great Groundcovers

Groundcovers are a fine alternative to lawns. They are also great for reducing trimming chores along walls and fences and under tree and shrub plantings.

Make mowing easier with edgings or pathways to prevent plants from sprawling onto the lawn.

For loads of color, it's hard to beat maiden pinks blooming all summer long in sunny spots.

You can find a groundcover that is ideally suited to just about any site and taste. They can come in the form of creeping vines, low-growing perennials, or clumpy shrubs. As well as having attractive deciduous or evergreen foliage, they may offer showy flowers and fruits. Some prefer shade, some like sun; others can take a bit of both. One thing most groundcovers can't take is foot traffic. Mulch or lawn is the best choice for heavily trampled areas.

Choosing Good Groundcovers Because there are so many terrific groundcovers to choose from, it can be hard to know where to start. Begin by identifying the conditions where you want the plants to grow: Is the site sunny or shady? Is the soil moist or dry? Then think about how tall the groundcover can grow; their heights can range from a few inches (centimeters) up to a few feet (a meter). If you're planting on a slope, you need to plant a fast-spreading, dense groundcover to prevent erosion. You will find growing information for some of the most popular ground covers in "Encyclopedia of Flowers," starting on page 306.

Lily-of-the-valley

Getting Started Just like lawns and meadows, groundcover plantings grow best in well-prepared soil. Remove any sod and weeds, and then loosen the soil thoroughly, working in a ½- to 1-inch (12- to 25-mm) layer of compost or other organic matter. Rake the surface smooth, and you're ready to plant.

A general rule of thumb for spacing is to set plants 1 to 3 feet (30 to 90 cm) apart; use the closer spacing for small or slow-growing species, and the farther one for larger plants or fast growers. At these spacings, most groundcovers will take about two years to form a solid carpet. If you want faster results, use closer spacings, but keep in mind that the project will then cost more, since you'll need to buy more plants.

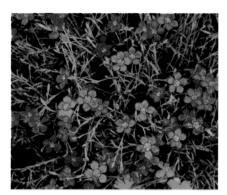

A mixture of different thymes makes a beautiful, fragrant, and useful groundcover for a sunny site.

Got It Covered

Many creeping vines and perennials make excellent groundcovers. Some are well adapted to life in spots that get plenty of filtered light but no direct sun, while others will take full sun.

Ajuga reptans (ajuga)
Antennaria dioica (pussy toes)
Asarum europaeum (European wild ginger)
Calluna vulgaris (heather)
Campanula portenschlagiana (Dalmatian bellflower)
Chamaemelum nobile (Roman chamomile)
Convallaria majalis (lily-of-the-valley)
Dianthus deltoides (maiden pink)
Galium odoratum (sweet woodruff)
Geranium sanguineum (blood-red cranesbill)
Hemerocallis hybrids (daylilies)
Hosta hybrids (hostas)
Lamium maculatum (spotted lamium)
Liriope spicata (creeping lilyturf)
Oenothera speciosa (showy sundrops)
Pachysandra procumbens (Allegheny pachysandra)
Pachysandra terminalis (Japanese pachysandra)
Phlox stolonifera (creeping phlox)
Saxifraga stolonifera (strawberry geranium)
Stachys byzantina (lamb's ears)
Thymus serpyllum (mother of thyme)
Tiarella cordifolia (foamflower)
Vancouveria hexandra (American barrenwort)
Waldsteinia fragarioides (barren strawberry)

Caring for Groundcovers Because some groundcovers can take a few years to completely cover the soil, mulch with straw, chopped leaves, or a similar light material to prevent erosion and suppress weeds. Or plant annuals in the bare spots. Water and weed regularly until the plants are established (usually by the end of the first season). For extra interest, try interplanting your groundcovers with spring bulbs like crocus and daffodils. The groundcovers will help to hide the ripening bulb foliage.

Quick and Easy Flowers

To some people, just the mention of low-maintenance landscaping conjures up images of gravel-covered front yards or expanses of boring green groundcovers. But there's no reason why low care has to mean no flowers. With a little planning, you can have "knock-your-socks-off" color and spend a minimum of time on routine maintenance.

The lifespan characteristics of the different groups of flowering plants (annuals, biennials, and perennials) will influence how much and what

Flower meadows are ideal for sunny spots. Fairly easy and inexpensive to grow from seed, they also attract a wide range of butterflies and bees to your garden.

kind of maintenance you'll need to put into the flowers you choose to grow.

Annuals live only one growing season. Since the parent plants die off at the end of the season, you need to replace them every year with seeds or transplants. Their strong points are that they're very easy to grow (even if you get a late start in spring planning and planting), they bloom for a long time, and they come in just about any color and height you want.

Hardy perennials come back year after year, so you don't have to buy and replant them each spring. But unlike annuals, most perennials only flower for a short while (days or weeks) each season. Many do offer attractive forms and foliage, however, so they look almost as good out of bloom as they do in bloom. Most bulbs go dormant after flowering, freeing up space for annuals or maturing perennial plants.

Biennials flower in the second year. Some, like pansies, are commonly grown as annuals. Some that reseed easily, like hollyhock (*Alcea rosea*), are as dependable as perennials. It takes some planning and patience to get a good show from most biennials, so they tend to be grown less frequently than annuals and perennials.

Combining them into one glorious garden lets you enjoy the benefits of each group while minimizing the drawbacks. Early-blooming perennials (like irises and peonies) combine well with annuals like cosmos and cleomes (*Cleome* spp.), which start blooming in early summer and carry on until frost.

Within each group you can find low-maintenance plants. The trick is to choose those that don't need special attention such as staking, indoor winter storage, or frequent pruning. Do look for plants that shrug off heat, scoff at drought, and laugh in the face of pests. And while adopting the low-maintenance option eliminates some touchy species, you'll still have more to choose from than you could ever hope to grow.

Hostas, the easy-care solution for shade, can be green, yellow, blue, or variegated in gold or white.

Easy Annuals
Annual flowers are great for low-maintenance gardens. They're easy to grow, as long as they get the light and water they need. They come in just about every color and height you'd want. They're cheap, so you get a big effect for a little money, and if one isn't healthy, you can toss it out without much anguish. In addition, you can plant most annuals as late as early summer if you don't get around to spring gardening as soon as you'd like.

You can grow your annuals from seed or buy transplants. Growing them from seed is less expensive and gives you a greater choice of cultivars. But you have to sow most annuals indoors 6 weeks before you move them outside, which means you have to worry about soil mixes, moisture, temperature, light, and all the other factors that influence success with seeds. Starting your own annuals indoors from seed can be fun and rewarding, but it's not the route to go if you really want minimal maintenance. Fortunately, many colorful, low-care annuals, such as marigolds and zinnias, are easy to start by sowing seeds directly where you want them to grow. Follow the information on the seed packets for sowing times and depths.

Buying transplants is much easier than starting seeds indoors, and it is still relatively inexpensive. Just figure out how many plants you need and head to the garden center around planting time. (For most annuals, this is around the average date of the last frost for your area. If you're not sure of your last frost date, ask your gardening neighbors or the local Cooperative Extension Service.)

As you pick through the stock, try to avoid buying plants that are already blooming—they'll only take longer to make new roots. Put back any that have discolored stems or leaves, holes in the leaves, or any other sign of either disease or insect damage. Don't buy annuals that are spindly or pale; look for compact, leafy, deep green plants. When possible, set transplants out on a cloudy day, so they'll be less prone to transplant shock.

Low-maintenance Perennials and Bulbs
Adding perennial plants to a low-maintenance landscape requires some thought. Compared to most annuals, perennials flower for a shorter period, so you have to figure out what will be blooming when and whether it will look good with its neighbors. They're more expensive, so you'll want to provide them with ideal conditions to keep them healthy and vigorous. And you have to plant early—sometimes the preceding fall—to get good color during the season.

Why take the trouble? Because well-chosen perennials, once established, come back year after year with little or no help from you. Some give a splash of color in the early spring, just when your late-winter depression verges on true dementia. Their successive bloom seasons give you an incentive to get outside and walk around the yard to see what's flowering. For some, perennials bring back fond memories of favorite people or places from the past.

Below are some tips for choosing perennials for your yard. "Caring for Annuals and Perennials" starting on page 76 will give you the details on maintaining your flowers.

Picking Easy-care Perennials If you really want to avoid lots of laboring, shun tall or floppy perennials, such

Dependable, Easy-care Perennials

Here's a list of some of the most trouble-free perennials you can grow. All of the plants below thrive in sun and average, well-drained soil with little fuss. You'll find complete information about growing all these plants in the individual plant entries starting on page 306.

Achillea filipendulina (fern-leaved yarrow)
Alchemilla mollis (lady's mantle)
Anemone x *hybrida* (Japanese anemone)
Armeria maritima (common thrift)
Asclepias tuberosa (butterfly weed)
Aster novae-angliae (New England aster)
Baptisia australis (blue false indigo)
Boltonia asteroides (boltonia)
Centranthus ruber (red valerian)
Coreopsis verticillata (thread-leaved coreopsis)
Echinacea purpurea (purple coneflower)
Echinops ritro (globe thistle)
Gaillardia x *grandiflora* (blanket flower)
Geranium sanguineum (blood-red cranesbill)
Hemerocallis hybrids (daylilies)
Iris sibirica (Siberian iris)
Leucanthemum x *superbum* (shasta daisy)
Liatris spicata (spike gayfeather)
Lilium hybrids (lilies)
Narcissus hybrids (daffodils)
Nepeta x *faassenii* (catmint)
Paeonia lactiflora (common garden peony), single-flowered cultivars
Physostegia virginiana (obedient plant)
Platycodon grandiflorus (balloon flower)
Rudbeckia fulgida (orange coneflower)
Sedum spp. (sedums)
Salvia x *superba* (violet sage)
Veronica spicata (spike speedwell)
Yucca filamentosa (Adam's needle)

Blanket flower

California poppy is an easy-to-grow annual for sunny gardens: just scatter the seed in a well-drained soil.

as hybrid delphinium (*Delphinium* x *elatum*) and baby's breath (*Gypsophila paniculata*), which will need staking. Also steer clear of tender perennials, such as canna (*Canna* x *generalis*) and dahlia (*Dahlia* spp.), that you will have to dig up and store over the winter. Unless you want to cover a large area, avoid those that spread, like lamb's ears (*Stachys byzantina*) and goutweed (*Aegopodium podagraria*). Pass up those that die out after a few years, like many perennial asters. And don't plant those that have a serious pest in your area, unless you can get a resistant cultivar.

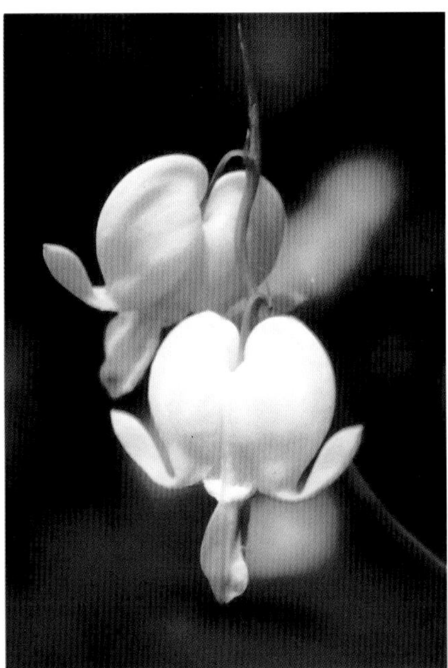
The delicate blooms and ferny foliage of bleeding heart are a lovely and hardy addition to a garden.

What's left? A lot, starting with dependable spring bulbs like crocus and daffodils; irises, if iris borer isn't a severe problem in your area; daylilies (there are thousands to choose from); and hostas, for shady areas. Try short cultivars of balloon flower (*Platycodon grandiflorus*) and bellflowers (*Campanula* spp.). Choose coreopsis (*Coreopsis* spp.) and other native wildflowers, especially in a natural garden. Be sure to include old-time favorites like bleeding heart (*Dicentra* spp.). And don't forget ornamental grasses like fountain grass (*Pennisetum alopecuroides*) and blue fescue (*Festuca cinerea*), great for their foliage and interesting seed heads.

Balloon flowers have saucer-shaped flowers. To avoid having to stake them, use short cultivars.

The list goes on. For more ideas, look at gardens that bloom even though you know no one bothers with them. And before you plant any perennial, research its growth requirements to be sure it suits your conditions.

Easy Annuals from Seed

Save the step of transplanting by sowing seeds of these tough annuals directly in the garden.

Calendula officinalis (pot marigold)
Centaurea cyanus (cornflower)
Cleome hasslerana (cleome)
Consolida ambigua (rocket larkspur)
Eschscholzia californica (California poppy)
Helianthus annuus (common sunflower)
Lathyrus odoratus (sweet pea)
Lobularia maritima (sweet alyssum)
Nigella damascena (love-in-a-mist)
Papaver rhoeas (corn poppy)
Portulaca grandiflora (rose moss)
Tagetes spp. (marigolds)

Oriental poppy

Handling Hillsides

Terraces or low walls can turn a troublesome slope into an eye-catching landscape feature.

With a little imagination and work, you can transform a sloping site from a maintenance headache into a landscape asset. Hillsides are awkward to mow and weed, so the best strategy is to cover them with plants that take care of themselves. Or, if you're willing to invest some time and money, you can build retaining walls or terraced beds that will safely and attractively support a wide range of beautiful annuals and perennials.

Plantings along walls (and even in the wall if possible) will soften the look of any hard edges.

Super Plants for Slopes

Grass is probably the most common groundcover used to hold the soil on slopes, but it isn't especially interesting, and it can be a real pain to mow every week. For an attractive and easy-care solution, replace the turf grass with tough, low-maintenance plants that look great and protect the soil, too. To get you started, "Great Groundcovers for Slopes" lists some of the most reliable options for sunny and shady sites.

Sunny Slopes

One good option where you have a sunny slope is planting a mixture of sun-loving groundcovers, taller spreading perennials (such as daylilies), and spreading shrubs, such as creeping juniper (*Juniperus horizontalis*). Or, if you like a casual look and you're willing to mow the slope once a year, consider turning it into a wildflower meadow. You'll find more information on planning and planting a meadow garden in "Making a Meadow Garden" on page 136.

Simple Planting on Steep Slopes

If you're turning a steep, grassy slope over to groundcovers, try this tip: Cover the area with black plastic for several weeks to kill the grass. Then remove the plastic and plant your groundcovers right into the dead sod. The sod will keep the soil from washing away while the groundcovers are establishing. Finish off the planting with a layer of mulch for good looks.

Building a rock garden is another great solution for a sunny, well-drained slope. Place large rocks at irregular intervals throughout the area. Bury each so that more than half is underground to keep it from rolling or washing away. Large, secure stones will give you a steady foothold so you can get

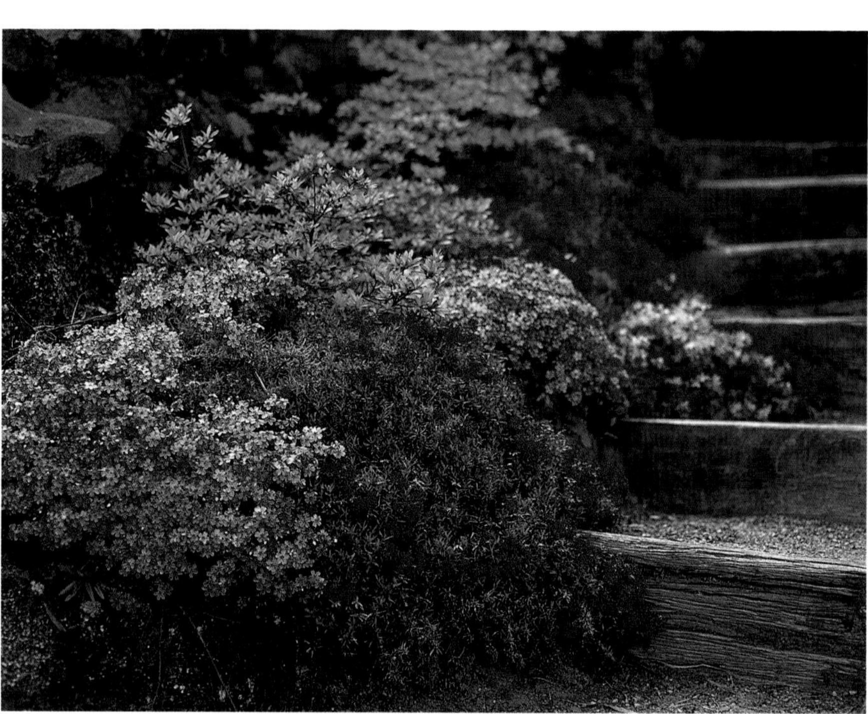

Slopes tend to be well drained and are natural sites for rock gardens. Choose drought-tolerant annuals and perennials with a low-growing, spreading habit, so they will cascade over the rocks and onto steps.

Thrift is adapted to harsh conditions, so its dense spread of flowers from late spring to summer offers great color for rock and wall gardens.

into the garden for occasional weeding. Between the stones, plant sprawling, sun-loving annuals and perennials, such as wall rock cress (*Arabis caucasica*), snow-in-summer (*Cerastium tomentosum*), and basket of gold (*Aurinia saxatilis*), with small hardy bulbs, such as crocus and reticulated iris (*Iris reticulata*).

Shady Slopes

On shady slopes, spreading species and hosta cultivars make great groundcovers, alone or combined with other annuals and perennials. Other good companions include lily-of-the-valley (*Convallaria majalis*), pachysandra (*Pachysandra terminalis*), and common periwinkle (*Vinca minor*). For extra interest, add spring-flowering bulbs to get early color from groundcover plantings.

If the slope is shaded by deciduous trees, create a woodland garden by combining groundcovers such as ajuga and European wild ginger (*Asarum europaeum*) with early-blooming wildflowers. Creeping phlox (*Phlox stolonifera*), wild bleeding heart (*Dicentra eximia*), and Allegheny foamflower (*Tiarella cordifolia*) are a few species that will bloom in spring before the trees leaf out fully and shade the area.

Establishing Plantings

Good soil preparation is a key part of successful slope landscaping. Remove the existing grass and weeds, and dig the soil to loosen it. If the slope is steep, you'll need to build temporary terraces before you plant. Long, flat boards anchored behind 2-foot (60-cm) spikes driven partly into the ground hold the soil in place for a year or two. Once plants have gotten established and filled in, you can remove the boards and spikes.

Set the plants into the ground as you would for any garden; see "Planting Time" on page 56 for details. Water well and add a thick mulch layer. Weed and water regularly for the first year to get the plants off to a good start; after that, they should need little care.

Terraces for Slopes

Constructing permanent terraces requires more time, effort, and money up front, but the terraces last for years and they will dramatically increase the variety of perennials you will be able to grow.

Low retaining walls (up to 2 feet [60 cm] high) are reasonably easy to construct from flat stones or lumber. But do consult a professional landscaper or builder for any wall that must be taller than 2 feet (60 cm): Large retaining walls must be well anchored on the slope and properly designed to take the weight of the soil they will hold. This keeps them from washing out, cracking, or tumbling down later. It's easier to make walls correctly than to repair them.

Fill finished terraces with good topsoil. After the soil settles for a few weeks, add a bit more if needed to level the top of the beds. Then plant your perennials. Keep in mind that terraces may dry out more quickly than regular in-ground beds, so you're better off looking for plants that can take dry conditions.

On gentle slopes, make shallow basins to trap moisture and minimize erosion. Terraces are a better option if you have to handle steep slopes.

Great Groundcovers for Slopes

Here are some tough and trouble-free perennials that adapt well to life on a sloping site. To learn more about specific plants, look them up in the individual plant entries starting on page 306.

Groundcovers for Sun

Cerastium tomentosum (snow-in-summer)
Dianthus gratianopolitanus (cheddar pinks)
Phlox subulata (moss phlox)
Sedum spurium (two-row sedum)
Stachys byzantina (lamb's ears)

Groundcovers for Shade

Ajuga reptans (ajuga)
Asarum europaeum (European wild ginger)
Epimedium x *rubrum* (red epimedium)
Galium odoratum (sweet woodruff)
Hosta hybrids (hostas, spreading types)
Lamium maculatum (spotted lamium)

Succeeding in the Shade

Shady nooks provide a cool, peaceful refuge for plants and people who can't take the hot summer sun. Shade-loving plants may not always glow with the vibrant colors of poppies and peonies, but they offer many wonderful possibilities to the open-minded gardener who wants to experiment with subtle shades and textures. Success in shady sites, as in any kind of garden, depends on careful planning and on choosing plants that grow happily in such conditions.

Single or double, white, pink, red, orange, or lavender—impatiens add vivid color to the shady garden.

Picking Your Plants

The two main factors that will determine which plants can grow well in your shade garden are how much light the garden gets and how much water is available.

Sites that get a few hours of direct sun or a full day of filtered light can support a wider range of plants than a spot that's in deep shade all day. Gardens under deciduous trees may get lots of sun until early summer, when the developing tree leaves begin to block the light. "Examine Your Exposure" on page 42 can help you figure out what type of shade you have. The individual plant entries starting on page 306 will tell you which kind of conditions each plant prefers.

Shady gardens can also vary widely in the amount of moisture that's available. Plants that grow well in moist woodland soils usually aren't happy in the dry shade under roof overhangs or shallow-rooted trees such as maples and beeches. In moist shade, you may need to seek out slug- and snail-resistant plants; some hostas that are less prone than others to slug damage include 'Blue Angel', 'Sum & Substance', 'Krossa Regal', *Hosta sieboldiana*, and *H. fortunei* 'Aureomarginata'.

To give your shade garden a strong start, thin out branches to admit more light, enrich and mulch the soil, and plant close to tree trunks, where there are few feeder roots to compete with your plantings.

As with planning any garden, look for perennials that are attractive as well as adaptable. Spring tends to be the primary bloom season in a shade garden, but you'll be seeing the plants all season long, so choose ones that also look good when they're not flowering. Along with all the varying shades of green, leaves come in many colors, including silvery blue, blue-green, yellow-green, and purple. Plants with multicolored (variegated) leaves are also good choices for adding sparkle to a shady corner. Hostas are available in many leaf colors and variegations, and they flower as well. Several species of lungwort (*Pulmonaria* spp.) offer silver-speckled leaves, along with pink-and-blue spring flowers. Ferns, lamiums (*Lamium* spp.), and hellebores (*Helleborus* spp.) are other natural choices for foliage interest. If you're gardening under shallow-rooted trees like maples and beeches, look for drought-tolerant shade-lovers like barrenworts (*Epimedium* spp.) and yellow archangel (*Lamiastrum galeobdolon* 'Herman's Pride'). And for extra color in summer, remember annuals such as impatiens and begonias and the colorful foliage of coleus and caladiums.

Make the most of early spring, before trees leaf out, with spring bulbs like Siberian squill.

Planning and Planting Tips

Take advantage of several strategies for succeeding in shade. First, direct traffic away from shallow-rooted trees and areas you wish to keep as deep shade so you can replace scraggly lawn with groundcovers. Use stepping stones or heavily mulched paths to guide visitors around planted areas. A bench on an informal stone patio makes an inviting destination and works well in the deepest shade or beneath the most shallow-rooted trees.

Second, enrich the soil with lots of organic matter. A good supply of organic matter may mean the difference between death and survival in shade, especially dry shade. If you are gardening under trees, you can't just till in the organic matter or dump a thick layer on the surface; either way, you'll harm the tree roots. Instead, try digging and then enriching individual planting pockets close to the tree trunk, where there are few feeder roots. Dig a hole about 8 inches (20 cm) in diameter for each plant and mix in a handful or two of compost; then plant as usual.

After planting, water the area thoroughly and apply a layer of mulch. In dry shade, water regularly until the plants are established, and plan on watering even mature plants during dry spells.

Shade gardens need less water because the drying sun doesn't beat down on them. But they also are perfect for fungal diseases that like humid, cool, dark conditions. For that reason, it's important to space shade plants at the distance recommended—or even wider—to get good air movement. When you do water, irrigate so you wet the soil rather than the leaves.

Slugs and snails, being very fond of moist areas, can be troublesome in shade gardens. If you're finding holes in your leaves (hostas are a favorite target), encircle the bed with a strip of copper edging to keep the pests out. Catch slugs that are already inside the bed by trapping them in fruit rinds set upside down on the soil surface; check traps and remove pests daily until the problem decreases. If they become a real problem, you may want to remove some or all of the mulch; despite all of its benefits, mulch also provides shelter for these troublesome pests.

The colorful foliage of coleus adds a bright touch.

Super Plants for Shade

Here's a list of just some annuals and perennials that will thrive in a shady garden. You'll find more information in the individual entries starting on page 306.

Annuals

Begonia Semperflorens-Cultorum hybrid (wax begonia)
Celosia cristata (celosia)
Impatiens wallerana (impatiens)
Lobelia erinus (edging lobelia)
Lunaria annua (honesty)
Myosotis sylvatica (forget-me-not)
Nicotiana alata (flowering tobacco)

Perennials

Actaea pachypoda (white baneberry)
Ajuga reptans (ajuga)
Aquilegia spp. (columbines)
Arisaema triphyllum (Jack-in-the-pulpit)
Asarum europaeum (European wild ginger)
Astilbe x *arendsii* (astilbe)
Bergenia spp. (bergenias)
Brunnera macrophylla (Siberian bugloss)
Cimicifuga racemosa (black snakeroot)
Dicentra eximia (fringed bleeding heart)
Epimedium x *rubrum* (red epimedium)
Helleborus orientalis (Lenten rose) (see below)
Hosta hybrids (hostas)
Iris cristata (crested iris)
Lamium maculatum (spotted lamium)
Polygonatum odoratum (fragrant Solomon's seal)
Pulmonaria saccharata (Bethlehem sage)
Smilacina racemosa (Solomon's plume)
Tiarella cordifolia (Allegheny foamflower)
Uvularia grandiflora (great merrybells)

Turning Bogs into Beds

Don't let a wet yard or soggy spot deter you from gardening in that area. Even a year-round spring or bog can be attractively landscaped with beautiful, easy-care annuals and perennials. You may decide to approach the area as you would any other garden, with a formal planting plan in mind. Or you may choose to go for an informal feel and create a casual-looking natural area.

Options for Organized Plantings

If your problem site is under water most of the year, go with the flow—leave it as a wetland or convert it into a small pond and plant annuals and perennials to cascade over its edges. Some of the most beautiful native plants, including cardinal flower (*Lobelia cardinalis*), white or pink turtleheads (*Chelone* spp.), queen of the prairie (*Filipendula rubra*), and some ferns, prefer to grow where their feet are wet. They look equally good in perennial beds and wild settings.

If you would like a more traditional flower bed or border where soil is constantly soggy, raise the level of the soil in the planting area at least 4 inches (10 cm). Adding a healthy dose of organic matter and bringing in additional soil to make raised beds can often transform a constantly wet site into an evenly moist site—the ideal condition for many classic garden flowers. If the bed is still soggy, even in summer—that is, the soil never gets dry enough to crumble when you squeeze some—and you don't want to raise the bed any higher, stick with the plants listed in "Plants That Like Wet Feet."

A bog garden is a great site for many kinds of iris, with their spiky leaves and beautiful flowers.

Building Raised Beds

One solution for poor drainage is to raise the plants above the existing soil. If you're planting trees and shrubs, build low, wide mounds of soil called berms and plant in those. If growing vegetables and flowers, construct raised beds that are about 6 inches (15 cm) high in cool climates or no more than 4 inches (10 cm) in warm climates (where raised beds can dry out quickly). If you make the beds 3 to 4 feet (90 to 120 cm) wide and leave a walkway between them, you can work the bed from either side without having to step on the soil (which can lead to compaction).

Create temporary raised beds in the vegetable garden by raking soil into broad,

Plants That Like Wet Feet

Here are some super perennials that will thrive in consistently moist soil. For more information, see the individual entries starting on page 306.

Arisaema triphyllum (Jack-in-the-pulpit)
Aruncus dioicus (goat's beard)
Asarum europaeum (European wild ginger)
Astrantia major (masterwort)
Brunnera macrophylla (Siberian bugloss)
Chelone spp. (turtleheads)
Eupatorium maculatum (spotted Joe-Pye weed)
Filipendula rubra (queen of the prairie)
Galium odoratum (sweet woodruff)
Iris sibirica (Siberian iris)
Ligularia dentata (big-leaved ligularia)
Lobelia cardinalis (cardinal flower)
Lysimachia punctata (yellow loosestrife)
Monarda didyma (bee balm)
Physostegia virginiana (obedient plant)
Polygonum affine (Himalayan fleeceflower)
Primula denticulata (drumstick primrose)
Smilacina racemosa (Solomon's plume)
Tradescantia x *andersoniana* (common spiderwort)
Trollius x *cultorum* (hybrid globeflower)

Diverting excess water into a pond or retaining basin can add an attractive feature to a garden.

Build raised beds with timber frames and good soil to turn a wet site into a well-drained garden.

flattened mounds. For more permanent beds in any part of the landscape, frame the beds with landscape timbers or wide boards secured with braces and anchored with metal stakes. Stone or brick can give beds a particularly attractive appearance for ornamental plantings. Fill the frame with organically enriched soil. When you add soil to build a berm or raised bed, be sure you're not covering the roots of existing trees or shrubs.

A Natural Solution for Soggy Sites

If you enjoy the informal feel of naturalistic landscaping, wet spots are a perfect place to "go wild." Healthy wetlands serve important ecological roles by purifying groundwater, replenishing the water table, and supporting a wide variety of plants and wildlife that would not normally be attracted to a garden.

A mixed planting of moisture-loving perennials can provide season-long interest in a wet spot. It's not really necessary to carefully plan out your plantings to ensure there are different heights, textures, and colors—just set your plants out in random order. Great blue lobelia (*Lobelia siphilitica*), swamp milkweed (*Asclepias incarnata*), marsh marigold (*Caltha palustris*), yellow flag (*Iris pseudacorus*), and blue flag (*Iris versicolor*) are a few colorful perennials that grow happily in constantly soggy soil. Angelica (*Angelica atropurpurea*), a native perennial herb, forms lush, leafy clumps and tall flower clusters in wet soil. Native cattails (*Typha latifolia*) thrive in standing water, but they may choke out everything else (which isn't a problem if you like them). Royal ferns (*Osmunda* spp.) and beech ferns (*Thelypteris* spp.) are also great additions for foliage interest.

If your soil is constantly moist but not saturated, your planting options expand dramatically. Most woodland plants and wildflowers prefer moist soil to dry soil. Many sun-loving wildflowers also grow happily in moist soil. If the area dries out enough to support grass, try a wet meadow, with rugged perennials like spotted Joe-Pye weed (*Eupatorium maculatum*) and New England asters (*Aster novae-angliae*). Cut the meadow with a string trimmer once a year (wear boots to keep your feet dry!) in late fall or early spring. You'll learn more about planning, planting, and also maintaining such areas in "Making a Meadow Garden" on page 136.

For more ideas, take a look at natural marsh, streamside, or pond habitats in your area to see what is thriving there and how it looks. You'll get lots of ideas about other plants that will grow well in your particular area and how you can arrange them. (Just remember to gather ideas and inspiration only from these wild, natural areas, not the plants themselves. In any case, many garden centers are expanding their selections to include water-garden plants, so you should have no trouble buying the plants you've decided upon.)

Accent a small wet spot with a clump of moisture-loving plants like these bright yellow primroses.

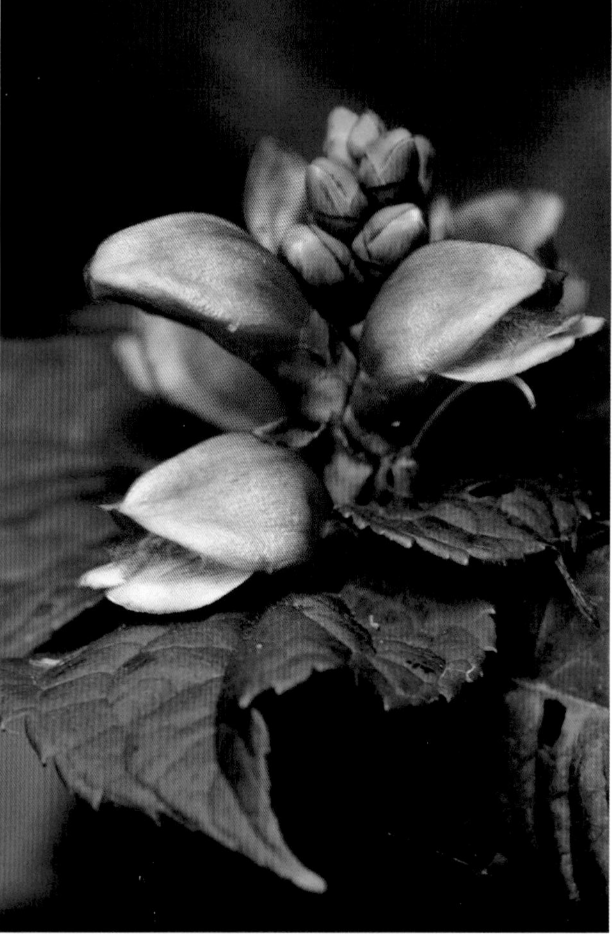
Turtleheads take their name from their unusual flower shape, like a turtle with its mouth open. And like their namesakes, they prefer moisture.

Growing a Water-wise Landscape

If you live where rainfall is scant or undependable or if your soil is so sandy that water runs right through, it makes sense to plan your landscape accordingly. You'll spend less time tinkering with your sunny garden if you choose plants that can take the heat. Consider the wide variety of fabulous flowers that thrive in full sun and can withstand dry spells. Using water-wise gardening techniques will also save you more than just water — it can save you time and money, too! Plus, you'll be spared the disappointment of watching poorly chosen plants wither and die as the heat and drought take their toll. Instead, you'll have a landscape that not only looks great but can weather tough conditions with little extra help from you.

Water-saving Basics

Water-wise gardening involves a two-part approach. One is keeping the rainfall that you do get in the soil or in storage, so it's available to plants when they need it. The other part is reducing the total amount of water that your garden needs to thrive.

Keeping Water Where You Need It

Good soil care is a key step in ensuring that moisture stays where plant roots can get it. Loose, crumbly soil can easily soak up rainfall that would just run off of beds that were compacted. Digging the soil thoroughly at planting time and keeping it loose by not walking on the beds will keep the soil in good shape.

Adding organic matter to your soil is another way to trap moisture. Organic matter is a natural sponge, soaking up water when it is available and releasing it later on to plant roots. Adding ample quantities of organic matter when preparing your soil before planting time will help plants withstand dry spells. Also use liberal quantities of mulch to replenish the supply of organic matter and to prevent moisture that is already in the soil from evaporating.

Channeling and storing rainfall are two other ways to reduce the need for supplemental watering. Regrading areas of your yard may help to keep rainfall from running off into the street, or at least slow down the water so that it has more chance to soak in. Building terraces (as explained in "Handling Hillsides" on page 154) is a great way to slow or stop runoff on sloping sites. Place a large plastic trash can (cut a hole in the lid to let water in) or commercially available rain barrel under a downspout to collect rainwater for later use.

At planting, set plants out in shallow depressions, so the crowns and the soil immediately around them are slightly below the normal soil level. Or use extra soil to form a shallow basin around each

Brilliant pot marigolds bloom from summer to fall, thriving in full sun and dry, average soils.

A water-wise landscape could include lamb's ears, yarrow, torch lilies, sedum, Russian sage, and grasses.

Plants for Hot, Dry Places

These plants don't mind heat and are happiest in soils that are very well drained and even sandy. Once established, they withstand extended dry spells. For more information on specific plants, check out the individual entries starting on page 306.

Turkestan onion

Annuals

Amaranthus caudatus (love lies bleeding)
Calendula officinalis (pot marigold)
Catharanthus roseus (Madagascar periwinkle)
Centaurea cyanus (cornflower)
Gaillarda pulchella (blanket flower)
Gomphrena globosa (globe amaranth)
Helianthus annuus (common sunflower)
Nicotiana alata (flowering tobacco)
Rudbeckia hirta (black-eyed Susan)
Sanvitalia procumbens (creeping zinnia)
Verbena x *hybrida* (garden verbena)

Perennials

Achillea filipendulina (fern-leaved yarrow)
Allium giganteum (giant onion)
Artemisia absinthium (common wormwood)
Asclepias tuberosa (butterfly weed)
Aubrieta deltoides (purple rock cress)
Aurinia saxatilis (basket of gold)
Baptisia australis (blue false indigo)
Catananche caerulea (Cupid's dart)
Centranthus ruber (red valerian)
Cerastium tomentosum (snow-in-summer)
Coreopsis verticillata (thread-leaved coreopsis)
Dianthus gratianopolitanus (cheddar pinks)
Echinacea purpurea (purple coneflower)
Echinops ritro (globe thistle)
Eryngium amethystinum (amethyst sea holly)
Euphorbia epithymoides (cushion spurge)
Gaillardia x *grandiflora* (blanket flower)
Helianthus x *multiflorus* (perennial sunflower)
Oenothera tetragona (common sundrops)
Perovskia atriplicifolia (Russian sage)
Rudbeckia fulgida (orange coneflower)
Salvia officinalis (garden sage)
Salvia x *superba* (violet sage)
Sedum spectabile (showy stonecrop)
Sedum spurium (two-row sedum)
Stachys byzantina (lamb's ears)
Verbascum chaixii (nettle-leaved mullein)
Yucca filamentosa (Adam's needle)

plant (new or already established) to collect and hold available water.

Reducing Overall Water Needs

Cutting down on the amount of water your yard actually needs is another important part of planning a water-wise landscape. Here are some ideas to try:

- Mulch, then mulch more! A thick layer of organic mulch will help hold moisture in the soil for plant roots.
- Reduce the size of your lawn. Lush lawns just aren't compatible with arid climates. Prairie and meadow gardens are adapted to drier conditions; once established, they don't need watering (see "Making a Meadow Garden" on page 136 for details).
- Group plants together in garden beds according to their water requirements. Locate thirsty plants closest to the house, rain barrel, or water faucet, where you can reach them easily. Landscape outlying areas with species that need little if any supplemental water; see "Plants for Hot, Dry Places."

If dry spells are common in your area, consider replacing lawn pathways with mulch or gravel.

- When planting, leave a little extra space between all plants so their roots can reach farther for water without competing with each other. (Mulch the bare soil between plants.)
- Block or moderate drying winds with a hedge or a windbreak. Or locate your garden on the sheltered side of an existing structure.
- If you must water, do it early or late in the day, preferably using drip systems or soaker hoses. "Mulching and Watering" on page 130 will tell you how to judge when your plants really need to be watered.

A generous layer of mulch will help moderate soil temperatures as well as conserve moisture.

HORTICO

SECTION SEVEN

Container Plants

Indoors and out, containers give you the freedom to move plants around, creating a constantly changing display of foliage and flowers. You can enjoy flower-filled planters on your patio or perhaps a colorful window box display outside your kitchen or living room. Be as imaginative as you like, arranging combinations for the greatest visual impact in your garden.

Considering Containers *164*

Getting Started with Container Gardening *170*

Flowers for Pots and Planters *174*

Window Boxes and Hanging Baskets *180*

Balconies, Courtyards, and Patio Gardens 184

Container Garden Primer *188*

The Right Container Plant for the Right Place *194*

Considering Containers

Nearly everyone can have a window box or two, even if they live high above the ground.

While all pots will hold plants, some are more effective than others, some more attractive, some better value, and some more appropriate to their mundane duties. Picking the right container can go a long way toward creating a good-looking, easy-care container garden.

Generally, plants can be grown in anything that will hold soil and allow proper drainage. Traditional containers include terracotta or clay pots, plastic pots, hanging baskets, wire baskets lined with sphagnum moss or fibrous liners, concrete planters, planter boxes, barrels, tubs, metal and enamelled containers, and bushel baskets. Some of these containers are much more durable than others. But there is no need to limit yourself to the purely traditional. Containers can be wooden wine crates, garbage bags filled with growing medium ("sausage gardens"), or even an old, broken coffee pot.

Containers can be either utilitarian or decorative, or a mixture of the two. When choosing a container you will need to consider whether the container will be in a highly visible location, or buried in a window box. And if it is to be visible, remember to coordinate the container color with the colors of the plants you select. While containers can be painted to create a totally different look or a less heat-absorbing surface, these may be unnecessary chores.

When you're shopping for a new pot or planter, it is important to consider the size of the container, the material the container is made from, as well as the container's drainage capabilities.

Select the Right Size

The container size that's right for your needs mostly depends on what plants you want to grow. Containers should be large enough to hold the minimum amount of container mix needed by your plants to grow in until they are mature or you repot them. For herbs, small to medium-sized vegetables, and flowering annuals and perennials, pots that hold about 2 to 4 gallons (9 to 18 l) of growing medium will work best. Small trees or shrubs can start out in 2- to 4-gallon (9- to 18-l) pots, but you'll probably need to move them to larger containers after their first season. Large vegetable plants, such as tomatoes and peppers, will be more productive if you give them plenty of room. Five-gallon (23-l) containers are a good size for peppers; full-sized tomatoes should have at least 10-gallon (45-l) pots.

If there's one general rule to follow when deciding what size pot to use, it's bigger is usually better. Small pots can really look out of scale and get lost when

Terracotta (clay) pots

What to Look for in a Container

How much space do you have and how do you want it to look over time? For small spaces, use smaller containers and avoid bigger plants with overly large leaves, flowers, and other features which can make the whole thing seem cramped.

Make sure there are enough drainage holes in the container or that it is made of a material that you could drill into or cut holes in.

Will your container mix be able to breathe? In most conditions porosity in a container is a plus, unless you live in a very dry climate where the container might dry out.

In colder climates, a container that retains heat and protects root systems against temperature extremes will prolong the life of your plants in the fall and allow you to plant earlier in the spring.

Extremes of temperature are bad news since they can cause pots to break open and spill out the plants and container mix. In very cold conditions, plastic can become brittle and terracotta pots can freeze and crack.

Your container is going to be full of wet mud. Will it be too heavy for your deck, balcony or roof? Will the cumulative weight of your containers be crushing? Will it be too heavy for you to move?

ABOVE LEFT: Bulbs in wickerwork baskets.
ABOVE RIGHT: The natural beauty of terracotta lends itself to effective window boxes and pots.

you set them down in the great outdoors. The bigger the pot, the better it will look in your overall garden design. Plus, the larger pots don't dry out nearly as fast as little ones, so you won't have to water them as often. However, one factor to bear in mind is weight—mature, well-watered plants in suitable containers can be very heavy. You may want to use lighter materials if you are going to rearrange your plants often or if you move home regularly. Use large pots sparingly if you're gardening on a balcony or rooftop. (In fact, you may want to have a structural engineer check out the stability of these areas before you set up any containers.)

Consider the Materials

The material that a container is made from can be just as important as its size. Each kind of material has advantages and disadvantages, depending on what you're growing and where you're growing it.

Clay and Terracotta

Containers made from clay or terracotta look very attractive, and they have the advantage of providing extra bottom weight so that taller plants won't blow over in the wind. However, containers made of terracotta and other porous materials can absorb water that may be needed by your plants, so they may need extra watering. If temperatures dip below freezing where you live, you will need to take extra care of terracotta containers. (There are now terracotta pots that are promoted as frost-resistant, so choose these if you can.)

When the growing season slows in the fall, you will need to empty, clean, and sterilize your terracotta pots, and store them where they won't be subject to freezing. If left filled through the winter, moisture can get into the soil, which will expand as it freezes and can crack the pot. If you do not relish these extra tasks, don't choose terracotta. Concrete is generally more durable for year-round growing than terracotta. Large clay and concrete containers can also be quite heavy to move.

Plastic and Fiberglass

For plants that you need to move inside in winter and outside in summer, a plastic or fiberglass container will be

The spiky and dramatic agave contrasts well with the tall, graceful lines of the mosaic pot.

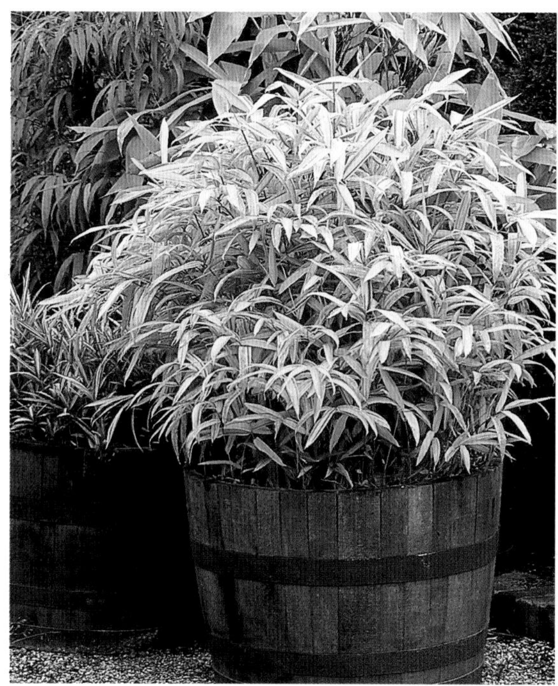

Tubs and barrels are ideal for planting trees and shrubs, or simply for large plantings.

much lighter than clay, concrete, or wood. Plastic containers also won't dry out as fast as those made of clay, and plastic is usually much less expensive. If you need to buy several large pots, this could be a major factor. The main disadvantage of plastic and fiberglass pots is that they are more likely to blow over in windy areas.

Wood

Wood falls in between plastic and clay in weight and porosity. It has the advantage of insulating the roots from overheating when the summer sun strikes the planter. However, wood can be a problem, since water has a rather unfortunate effect on many timbers. Cedar or redwood can be used without painting and are rot-resistant, but many chemically treated timbers should be avoided. You'll probably need to replace wooden planters every few years. If you like the look and insulating value of wooden planters but want to help them last longer, you could use plastic liners or set already-potted plants inside them.

Metal

From lead to cast-iron (plain, painted, or slightly rusted) to galvanized tin or wirework, metallic plant containers can look stunning. However, in hot climates, metal containers can really heat up, and make plants dry out very quickly.

Container Color

Whatever kind of container material you choose, look for pots and planters that are light-colored, especially if you live in a hot climate. Light-colored pots help to reflect the heat and keep the roots cool. Black pots are the worst choice in hot climates, since they can absorb enough heat to damage tender roots.

Drainage

The other important factor to consider when choosing a container is to make sure it has adequate drainage holes. Many gardeners place coarse rocks or broken pot shards in the bottom of pots to improve the drainage. This helps a little, but adequate drainage holes are the critical thing for healthy root growth and top-growth. Most commercially available pots and planters already have drainage holes in them. However, if you are creating your own containers from wood or recycled plastic buckets, make the drainage holes at least ½ inch (12 mm) in diameter. Drill at least six holes in medium-sized containers and more in larger ones.

What if you have a great-looking container that doesn't have drainage holes? You can still use it for outdoor growing if you're willing to give it a little extra attention. First, put a few blocks of wood in the base. Next, set in an already-potted plant so that it is resting on the wood blocks. The blocks will keep the plant roots from sitting in the water that collects in the base of the outer pot. Over time—and especially after heavy rains—however, the water level may rise to the level of the inner pot. During very wet weather, lift out the inner pot every day or two, and dump out any water that has collected in the pot; otherwise, your plants may suffer or even die.

You can make a container out of anything that will hold soil, including an old bathtub. However, don't forget to add drainage holes at the bottom.

Things to Avoid in a Container

One of the great things about container gardening is that you can put a plant in just about anything and call it a container. However, there are some types of container that it's best to avoid and some important points to note:

- Avoid containers that have a small opening at the top. This will limit air circulation in the container and make it very difficult for you to water the plant adequately.
- Containers with narrow bases have a tendency to tip over. Containers with wide, stable bases are best, especially for larger plants that can become top-heavy as they become full-grown.
- Do not use containers that have too few or no drainage holes.
- Terracotta pots dry out rapidly.
- Very shallow containers tend to dry out more quickly.
- Cheap plastic pots can deteriorate in ultraviolet sunlight.
- Glazed ceramic pots can be excellent choices, but make sure they have several drainage holes.
- In warm weather or in full sunlight, dark-colored pots can dry out the soil and overheat your plant.
- Avoid containers that claim to be biodegradable—they may degrade to the point that they spill out your plants and soil at an inconvenient moment.
- Avoid any container that has been used to store chemicals or any caustic materials.
- Beware of containers that are made from concrete or cement. Possible leaching of chemicals from the container might make the container mix extremely alkaline and might harm acid soil-loving plants such as camellias, azaleas, and rhododendrons.

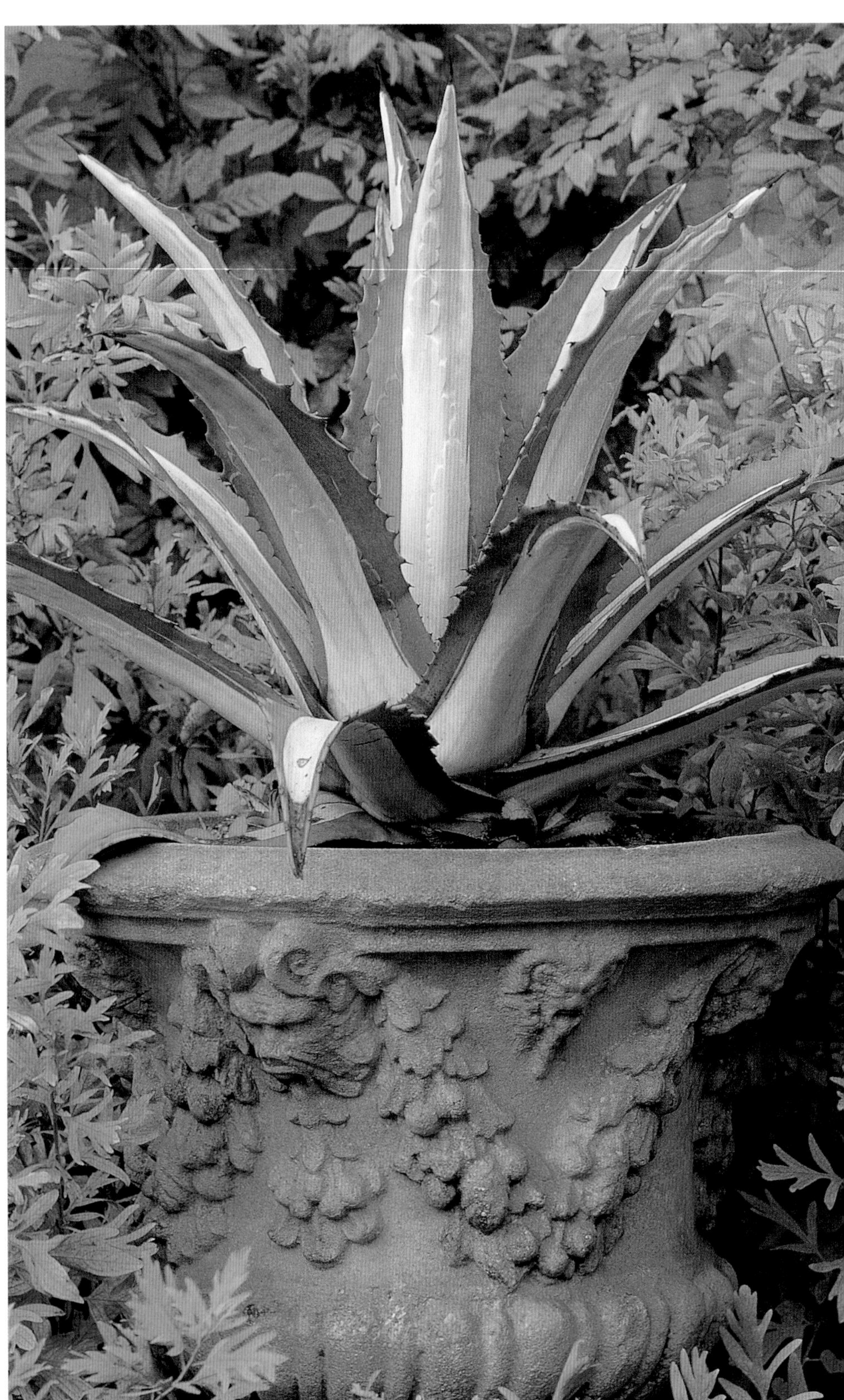

A special, large planter, such as a carved stone urn, can become a focal point for the whole garden.

Selecting Container Mixes

Once you've picked the perfect container, it's time to fill it with the best possible growing medium. While soil is just fine in the garden, it is a bad choice for plants in pots when used alone. The frequent watering demanded by container plants will cause most real soil to compact into a tight, brick-like mass (or if your garden soil is very sandy, it will dry out much too quickly in a container). The answer is to use a soil mix that is specially blended for plants in containers.

Since container plants have less soil for roots to grow in and to extract nutrients from, the soil must be carefully prepared. The container mix should be sterile (free from weeds and disease), be light enough to provide for air space (as well as allowing the container to be moved easily), and meet the needs of the individual plant to be grown.

Picking the Right Mix

Like "ideal" garden soil, a container mix should hold enough water for good root growth but allow excess water to drain out. It should also contain a balance of nutrients to steadily nourish a wide variety of plants for normal, healthy growth.

You can buy a variety of container mixes at your local garden center. Those that contain some amount of real soil are called soil-based mixes. These tend to feel heavy, and they generally hold more water. Soil-less mixes usually contain peat moss and/or vermiculite to hold moisture. These mixes usually feel very light and can dry out more quickly.

When you are faced with a row of different products at the garden center, it can be hard to choose which one to buy. If you grow a lot of one kind of plant (cacti or African violets, for instance), you may want to try a mix formulated especially for that type of plant. In most cases, though, an all-purpose container mix is fine. Buy a small bag and see how your plants grow in it.

Good drainage is important for healthy container plants, so look for a container mix that contains some perlite or bark.

Some gardeners get good results by purchasing a heavier mix and adding perlite or vermiculite to improve drainage, or adding peat to improve water retention. "Making Your Own Container Mixes" below offers recipes for blending your own customized container growing medium.

Using Commercial Container Mixes

For annuals, which will only live in their pots for one growing season, you can use any well-drained, commercial container mix. Most such mixes don't have any compost or soil in them—they are primarily composed of peat and usually some vermiculite (to absorb and hold water) and perlite (to improve drainage). If you use these soil-less mixes straight from the bag, you'll need to fertilize regularly.

Hyacinths

To improve a commercial soil-less mix for growing perennials, shrubs, and trees, you can add up to 20 percent compost or a combination of 10 percent compost and 10 percent garden soil. Both the compost and the soil provide slow-release nutrients and generally improve the ability of the mix to hold moisture and nutrients. And there's another big bonus when you add compost to your container mix—microorganisms in the compost will help prevent diseases and keep your plants healthy! Composted bark chips are also an excellent addition to keep the mix loose for good root growth.

If you need to keep your container mix as light as possible—for a large window box, for example—add the 20 percent compost but no soil. Instead, add some extra perlite (about 10 percent). Or, if you need the mix to be heavier to help prevent a taller shrub from blowing over in the wind, add some extra soil or sand to the container mix.

Making Your Own Container Mixes

Blending your own container mix from scratch is also a possibility for creating the perfect mix. It allows you to custom blend a variety of different ingredients to match the needs of your particular plants. Your main goal is to combine ingredients that have a variety of particle sizes so the mix is not too fine. You'll also always need to add some compost to provide slow-release nutrition and to help prevent diseases.

Making good container mix is an art, not a science. There are many different recipes that will give great results. The recipes given here are just guidelines, and your plants will still grow well if you need to use more or less of any ingredients.

Basic Container Mix

This simple blend will work well for a wide variety of container plantings.

4 parts peat moss (mixed thoroughly with ½ ounce [15 g] dolomitic limestone per gallon of peat)

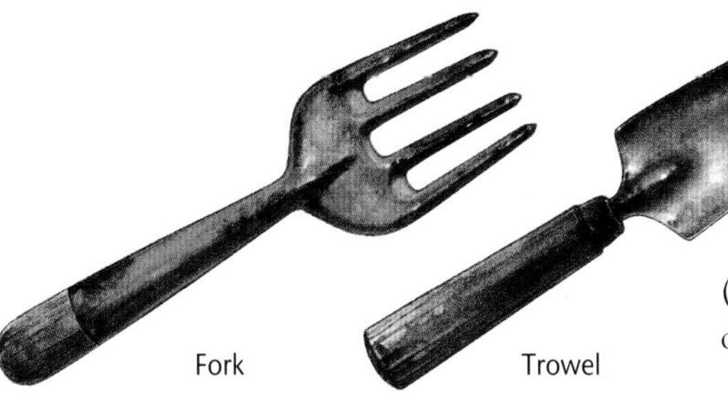

1 part compost (or ½ part compost and ½ part garden soil)

1 part perlite or vermiculite

Pile all of these materials in a large tub and use your hands or a shovel to mix them thoroughly. These materials can be very dusty, so it's a good idea to wear a dust mask during the mixing process.

Deluxe Container Mix

This blend is especially good for long-term plantings (including trees, shrubs, and perennials) in larger containers.

4 parts sphagnum peat

2 parts compost (or 1 part compost and 1 part garden soil)

1 part small bark chips (composted)

1 part perlite

Combine materials as you would for the basic mix. To each cubic foot (or 7½ gallons [34 l]) of mix, add the following slow-release organic fertilizers:

To get top performance from large containers, add compost and organic fertilizers to the mix.

4 ounces (110 g) of dolomitic limestone

4 ounces (110 g) of bonemeal (or 1 pound [500 g] of rock phosphate or colloidal phosphate)

1 pound (500 g) of greensand

2 ounces (55 g) of bloodmeal

2 ounces (55 g) of kelp meal

With this deluxe container mix, your plants will have plenty of nutrients to get off to a great start, and you shouldn't need to begin supplemental fertilizing until at least a month after you plant.

Fertilizing Potted Plants

Even the best mix can't provide all the nutrients that your container plants and houseplants will need. For a nutrient supplement, use a liquid fertilizer poured onto the container mix. You can use fish emulsion, seaweed extract, or a combination of the two. Each contains different nutrients. A list of useful organic fertilizers can be found in "A Sampler of Organic Fertilizers" on page 89.

For best growth, you should feed your outdoor container plants each week. Houseplants vary in their appetites. Some people feed houseplants with very diluted fertilizers each time they water, some use regular strength with every other watering, and some feed monthly. Whichever routine you choose, remember to cut back or stop fertilizing during the winter, when low light slows growth.

Overfertilizing can be as harmful as underfertilizing. An overfertilized plant produces weak, lanky growth that's susceptible to diseases and insects. And overfertilizing can make salts accumulate in the soil, creating conditions few roots like. The sure sign of salt buildup is a white crust on the soil surface or on the surface of clay pots. To get rid of it, pour water through the soil continuously (until water runs out the drain holes for a few minutes) to wash out the salt. For severe problems, move the plant to a new pot, or scrub the old pot to remove the salt crust; wash the pot and repot the plant in fresh soil.

How Much Do You Need?

If you need to fill more than a few small pots, it can be hard to decide how much mix to buy or blend. You need to do a little calculating, but that's a whole lot easier than lugging home more mix than you need or having to go back to the store for more.

Some containers are labeled by volume, usually given in gallons (liters). In this case, most of your work is done, especially if your mix is measured in gallons. (If the mix is measured in cubic feet, divide the number of cubic feet by 7.5 to get the number of gallons of mix.)

To find the volume of a square or rectangular pot, simply multiply the length and width by the height. Divide the number of cubic inches by 1,728 to get the number of cubic feet of soil you need. If your mix is measured in gallons, multiply the number of gallons by 7.5 to find the number of cubic feet.

To find the volume of a round pot, you first need to figure out the area of the top circle of the pot. Lay a ruler across the top of the pot to measure the diameter (how far it is from side to side). Now, divide that number by 2, multiply it by itself, and then multiply it by 3.14. Take that answer and multiply it by the height of the pot to find the number of cubic inches of mix the pot can hold. Divide the number of cubic inches by 1,728 to get the number of cubic feet of mix you need. If your container mix is measured in gallons, multiply the number of gallons by 7.5 to find out the number of cubic feet.

Getting Started with Container Gardening

The great thing about gardening in containers is the flexibility you get. Since the plants aren't rooted in the ground, you can place them exactly where you want them. You can create a miniature landscape filled with your favorite plants right around your deck or patio, where you get to relax and really enjoy their beauty and fragrance. If you live in a high-rise apartment building or condo where you have no ground for a garden, you can create a lush green oasis on a tiny balcony or outdoor stairway. City dwellers can grow large gardens entirely in containers on building rooftops. Even if you have nothing but a wall and windows to call your own, you can fill hanging baskets with trailing plants and pack window boxes full of flowers, herbs, and vegetables. In this chapter, you'll learn creative and exciting ways to use container plants to liven up your living spaces.

With plants in containers, you can rearrange and replace each pot as needed, maintaining a garden that always looks picture-perfect. While the plants are flowering, you can place the container where you'll see it best and enjoy it most. Then, as the blooms fade, you can retire the pot to the basement or garage until next year. Or, if your season permits, you can redo it with fresh plants and enjoy it all over again. For more ideas on displaying containers creatively, see "Planning Your Container Garden" below, and "Gardens for Small Spaces" on page 172.

Flowering shrubs such as camellias and roses are a great choice, since they bloom every year.

Grouping together many small pots of annuals and bulbs creates a colorful and stunning display.

In Northern areas, container growing has another big advantage—it allows you to grow all sorts of perennial plants that are not cold-hardy enough to live outdoors year-round. Camellias, for instance, are hardy outside only to Zone 8, where winter minimum temperatures average 10° to 20°F (–12° to –7°C). As container plants, however, you can grow them anywhere by moving them outside in the summer and indoors to a bright, cool sunroom or breezeway in winter. (Plus, they can bloom from November to April—a time when their splendid flowers will be especially welcome.) Fragrant orange and lemon trees are other tender plants Northerners can enjoy if grown in containers.

The fact is, you can grow practically any plant you want in a container—all kinds of flowers, bulbs, vegetables, and even small trees and shrubs. "Flowers for Pots and Planters" on page 174 is full of tips on choosing annuals, perennials, and bulbs for colorful containers all season long. If you have room for a large pot, you may want to try adding a few trees or shrubs to give height and year-round interest to your collection. If you select a potted tree or shrub that's evergreen or has attractive bark even when its leaves are gone, you'll get year-round enjoyment. Quick-growing sasanqua camellias (*Camellia sasanqua*) provide a deep green camouflage which pays dividends every fall with a wall of flowers. Container vines are good as they have the plus of providing quick shade or privacy for an exposed porch or patio.

Planning Your Container Garden

A container planting can be as simple as a single pot of flowers, or a larger pot with a combination of plants as lush and full as any garden border. You'll get the most enjoyment from your container plants when you choose and group them to fit in with the setting in your home or garden.

Choose the Right Size

Plants in single, small containers can look out of place all alone on a deck or patio. To get the best effect, you want your container plants to be in proper scale with the great outdoors. Whenever possible, opt for larger containers, at least 10 inches (25 cm) in diameter; generally the bigger, the better. (Large planters get very heavy, so be sure to place them where you want them before you fill them with container mix.) Using larger containers will cost a

Foliage Matters

When planning your container garden, consider the value of foliage. In some areas, flowers may be difficult to cultivate, but a host of beautiful foliage plants will more than compensate for the lack of colorful blooms. If your courtyard or balcony receives full or part-sun, foliage leaves will vary from limpid green to rich gold, and from silver to deep purple. In summer, these foliage plants will be at their most colorful and sumptuous. If your site is shaded, check the needs of foliage plants and select those that will adapt to the conditions.

In size, leaf shape, and color, foliage plants display wonderful diversity. Ferns themselves are a broad group of plants with a varied range of fronds. Growing them can be a most satisfying hobby. For color, consider croton (*Codiaeum variegatum*) or the ever-popular bromeliads. Consider, too, a variety of foliage textures, for example the polka dot plant (*Hypoestes phyllostachya*) with its striking leaf spots.

LEFT: Fortunately, nearly all greens—from blue-green to yellow-green—are agreeable colors that go well together and set off most flowers.

little more up front, but the plants will definitely grow better, you'll have to water less often, and the overall effect of the container garden will be better.

If you prefer to grow plants in smaller containers, group them together to create an eye-catching effect. It also makes the regular watering and maintenance much easier, since all the plants are in the same place. For extra interest, it's a good idea to vary the heights of plants in a group of pots. You can use short plants in smaller pots for the front and taller plants in the back. Or use bricks, plastic milk crates, or upside-down pots to vary the height of individual pots in a grouping.

Consider the Colors

To get the most enjoyment out of your container garden, don't forget to think about color combinations when you're buying the plants. Groupings usually look best when one or two colors dominate. For example, a yellow accent (maybe dwarf marigolds) works well with a group of blue flowers, such as ageratum. White is also a good accent color—it looks good with

A silver and white garden looks crisp and clean during the day, and the colors stand out at night.

If you're looking for can't-miss color, an orange and red combination might be the perfect accent for your courtyard or patio.

every color. Sweet alyssum (*Lobularia maritima*) is an excellent, white, trailing plant that always looks nice as it spills loosely over the sides of the pots. (It also has an outstanding sweet fragrance.)

A mixture of many different colors can look too "busy," but you can create an attractive grouping with several shades of the same color. You might, for instance, try red pansies with pink primroses or try light-blue petunias with deep-blue lobelia (*Lobelia erinus*). Plants with attractive silvery or green foliage, such as dusty miller (*Senecio cineraria*) or parsley, make great accents for these kinds of plantings.

Gardens for Small Spaces

Most of us live in cities, which means that many people have little or no ground space available for gardening. But with the right choice of plants and containers, you can transform a tiny courtyard, balcony, deck, or roof space into something that is every bit as colorful and satisfying as any large-scale garden plot.

In planning your container garden, think of it as a mini-landscape and apply the same design principles that you would to a large outdoor area. Depending on the space at your disposal, choose plants that will create pleasing contrasts as well as a sense of unity. You can achieve a satisfying balance with a mixture of blooms and foliage and by combining plants of different shapes, colors, and sizes. To add further variety, as well as a practical touch, to your container garden, you can, if the sun is right, even grow herbs, vegetables, and small fruit trees.

A Movable Garden

Even if you have an outdoor planted garden, some container plants can be used to supplement your in-ground plants, or act as feature elements of your landscape design. Containers have the advantage of flexibility—you need never get bored with a well-varied container garden. You can move pots around to create different displays, heights, and colors, or to give the plants extra shade or sun according to their needs or the season. You can also give special prominence to plants when they are flowering at their peak. Another advantage of a container garden is that you get a chance to grow, and to highlight, some exotic gems that might otherwise be lost in an open garden bed, or that need to be wintered in a greenhouse.

Balcony Gardens

A balcony is always above ground level often is the only garden available to people who live in apartments. Make sure that the balcony will safely support the weight of large containers and their soil. If your balcony is square or rectangular, choose containers that are firmly based

Annuals for an All-blue Container Garden

Blue theme container gardens have a cool, restrained look, but they're tricky to pull off successfully. Blue and green are such similar colors that blue flowers tend to blend into the background sea of green leaves.

Varying the different kinds of blue—from soft lavender-blue to bright sky-blue and deep cobalt-blue—is one way to add extra interest to a cool-color planting. Companion plants with silver or chartreuse leaves, such as dusty miller (*Senecio cineraria*) or golden feverfew (*Tanacetum parthenium* 'Aureum'), are also excellent additions.

The following list contains a few blue-flowered annuals you might want to include in your cool-color garden. For more information, see the entries in "Encyclopedia of Flowers" starting on page 306.

- Ageratum (*Ageratum houstonianum*)
- Browallia (*Browallia speciosa*)
- Cornflower (*Centaurea cyanus*)
- Rocket larkspur (*Consolida ambigua*)
- Edging lobelia (*Lobelia erinus*)
- Forget-me-not (*Myosotis sylvatica*)
- Baby-blue-eyes (*Nemophila menziesii*)
- Love-in-a-mist (*Nigella damascena*)
- Mealy-cup sage (*Salvia farinacea*)
- Wishbone flower (*Torenia fournieri*)
- Pansy (*Viola* x *wittrockiana*)

Baby-blue-eyes

and square. Troughs make excellent containers for balconies as their flat sides enable you to position them flush against the wall or front where they will not take up valuable space or be tripped over, and they are less likely to blow over in the wind than tall slender pots. Avoid too many small pots, or they will detract from the overall design.

What you can successfully grow depends on the direction your balcony faces. Those that receive gentle, early morning sun can grow many palms, ferns, azaleas, fuchsias and camellias. A shady balcony may receive plenty of light, but no direct sun. Here shade-loving plants would be the happiest. If your balcony is protected from wind, you will be able to create a delightful mini-jungle using many lush, foliage plants. Popular ferns, such as fishbone, Boston and hare's foot fern, make spectacular hanging basket plants. Trailing ivies and vines can be grown up walls or made to spill out of wall-containers or pots.

A balcony that gets good direct sun for several hours is perfect for those who want to grow colorful flowering annuals, herbs, citrus trees in tubs, and vegetables. Bay trees are especially attractive as containers plants; two or more, neatly clipped and in identical pots, could form the framework of a stylish semi-formal herb garden. In hot, dry areas, or whereit is difficult to water, consider someof the many succulents and silver-leaved plants that are able to withstand periods ithout water.

An extremely narrow balcony, viewed from a bedroom, could be transformed into a peaceful, oriental-style garden. Here you could cover the floor with stepping stones and pebbles and use a potted group of dwarf bamboos, one impressive bonsai, or a dwarf Japanese maple and a Japanese-inspired sculpture. A bamboo screen or blind could be used to hide an undesirable view.

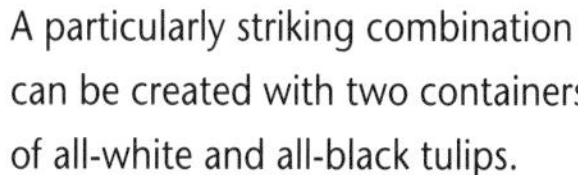

A particularly striking combination can be created with two containers of all-white and all-black tulips.

Roof Gardens

A roof-top container garden often solves the problem of space in a densely built environment. You will need to check the weight that your roof can safely hold, and make sure that there is adequate floor drainage, because your plants will need plenty of watering. The plants may also need protection from the wind, and here you may want to erect some screens or windbreaks, which can also be used to hide unattractive views

Stocks and browallia

First of all, put in climbing and trailing plants to soften the hard outlines of surrounding walls and to cover structures and increase their effectiveness as windbreaks. Next, pot up shrubs, colorful flowers and herbs. It's best to place the containers along the sides so that the weight is evenly distributed at the strongest part.

Decks

There is nothing like an above-ground timber deck for creating extra space, convenience and comfort. Decks are good for sloping sites, but also invaluable if your garden is shady, since often the extra height of the deck will give your plants longer hours of sunlight. A deck is an ideal place to grow culinary herbs, so that you can quickly snip them while you are cooking. Don't forget to raise all pots on feet or stands, so that excess moisture can drain away freely from the timber.

In a cool climate, a deck crowned with a covered pergola will keep the wet weather away from the house and provide a dry, year-round entertaining area. It will also create a warm micro-climate for tender plants, such as palms, tree ferns and some interesting foliage plants. The pergola joists will give you strong overhead support for suspending hanging baskets of Boston ferns, Christmas cactus and fuchsias.

Blues and purples look best in a position where you can see them up close. From a distance, they'll blend into the background.

Flowers for Pots and Planters

Nothing says summer like pots and planters filled to overflowing with lush foliage and beautiful blooms. Create your own colorful container gardens with a bounty of easy annuals and bulbs and dependable, long-blooming perennials.

Choosing a Container

Container possibilities are endless. You can buy commercially made plastic or clay containers or make your own out of old barrels, washtubs, or even buckets. Be creative; almost anything you can put drainage holes in—from clay drainage tiles to old leather work boots—can be pressed into service.

Solid-sided containers, such as plastic pots, hold water longer than porous clay. Plastics are great if your summers tend to be hot and dry, since you'll have to water less often. But if you live in a wet climate, or if you tend to overwater, porous pots are probably best. Plastic pots are lighter, making them easier to move, but they are more prone to blowing over. Clay pots are heavy and less likely to blow over, but they often crack when they do tip.

In windy areas or for tall plants, place rocks in the bottom of any pot to increase stability. Dark pots heat up in bright sun and dry out quickly; avoid black plastic pots for container gardens that are growing in full sun. For more information about types of containers, see "Considering Containers" on page 164.

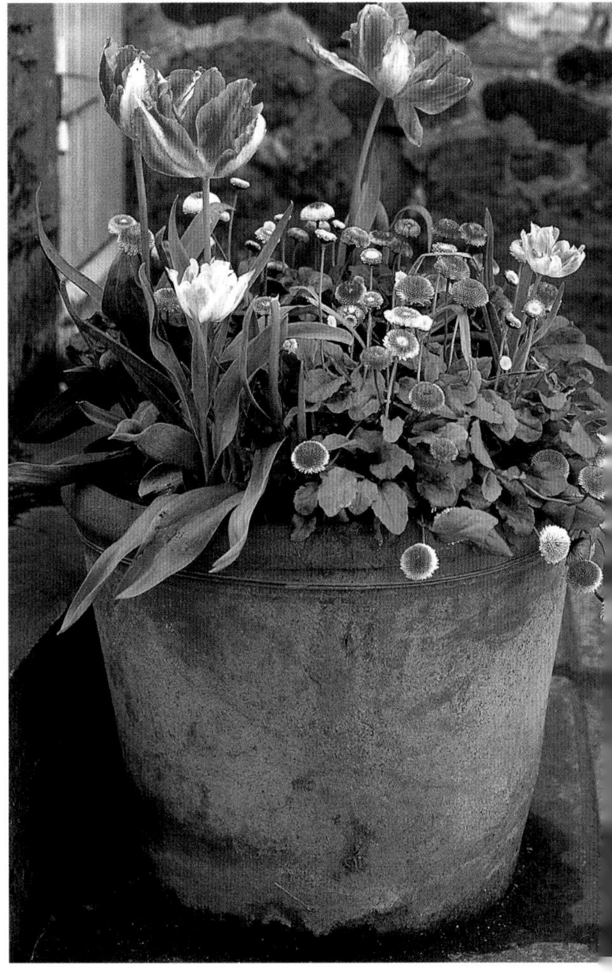

A combination of tall tulips and low-growing English daisies, both in pale pink tones, is an eyecatching combination.

Caring for Annuals and Perennials in Containers

Container plants share closer quarters than garden plants, so they need special care to stay lush and lovely. Large pots tend to provide the best conditions for growth, since they hold more soil, nutrients, and water, but they are also quite heavy if you need to move them. Pots or baskets that are about 8 inches (20 cm) deep can usually hold enough soil for good growth without getting too heavy. If you don't plan to move the planter, it can be as big as you want; containers as large as half-barrels will give you ample planting space for a wide variety of flowers.

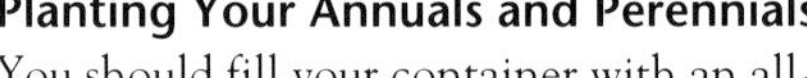

Planting Your Annuals and Perennials

You should fill your container with an all-purpose container mix purchased from your local nursery or garden center. You need to choose a growing medium that will hold some water but not too much. Straight garden soil isn't a good choice, but you can improve it by mixing 2 parts soil with 1 part finished compost (or peat moss) and 1 part perlite. Commercial container mixes are easy to use, and they can support a variety of different plants. Or you can use sterilized, premixed "soil-less" container mixes. These are free of soilborne diseases and they weigh much less than regular container mixes—an important consideration for rooftop gardeners and for plantings in large pots. Set your plants into the container mix, firm them in, and then water well.

Bees and Butterflies

Depending on where you choose to place your container annuals and perennials, you may like to give some consideration to the flying insects, especially bees and butterflies, that fragrant plants are likely to lure. Butterflies are attractive and welcome visitors to garden plots and outdoor container plants. They find a number of perennials particularly alluring. Butterfly bushes (*Buddleia* spp.) and butterfly weed (*Asclepias tuberosa*) are just two obvious examples of butterfly-bringing perennials. Other butterfly-attracting perennials are listed in "Best Bets for Butterflies" on page 143.

Bees are more problematic, because of the possibility, or the fear, of stings. Nevertheless, non-stinging honeybees play a greater role in pollination and the setting of seed than any other insect, and should be welcome viistors to the garden. Be careful, though, around the black-and-orange bumblebee, which can sting if disturbed.

Common sulfur butterfly and New England aster

Watering

Keeping the right water balance is a key part of successful container gardening. Some containers may need watering every day, others only once a week. A general rule is to wait until the top 1 inch (2.5 cm) of container mix is dry; then water well, until some comes out of the bottom. If the water seems to run right through the pot, put a tray or saucer underneath; empty any water that remains the next day. Very small pots, small and medium-sized clay containers, and hanging baskets dry out especially quickly; you may have to water these as often as twice a day.

If a pot or basket dries out completely, you still may be able to save the plants. Set the pot or basket in a larger container filled with water, let it sit there for an hour or two, and then set the pot or basket in a shady spot for a few hours until the plants perk up again. Then move the pot or basket back to its original spot, but be extra careful to keep the plants well watered from then on.

Fertilizing

Besides regular watering, the other key to lush-looking annuals and perennials is regular fertilizing. Since their rooting space is limited, annuals and perennials in containers need fertilizer much more often than plants growing in the ground. Give them a boost by watering them with diluted fish emulsion, liquid seaweed, or a balanced organic fertilizer; follow the instructions on the package to find out how often and how much fertilizer you should apply. You can also water the plants with compost tea (made by soaking a shovelful of finished compost in a bucket of water for about a week, then straining out the soaked compost).

Start in late spring by feeding once every 2 weeks, then check the containers in midsummer. If annuals and perennials look lush but aren't flowering well, change to fertilizing once every 3 weeks. If the plants begin to look somewhat spindly, start fertilizing every week. If the plants seem to be growing and flowering well, stick with the 2-week schedule.

Solving Challenges with Containers

With a little creativity, you'll find many different ways to use containers filled with annuals and perennials. If you can't kneel, or if you garden from a wheelchair, you can grow plants at a convenient height in raised planters. If your soil is too hard or rocky to dig, you can grow flowers in half-barrel planters instead of in the ground.

If you've got a shady spot that's just crying out for color, you can use potted annuals or perennials to create a rotating display: As flowers fade, move the shady pot to a sunnier spot and replace with a container that's robust from sunshine. Or tuck a few pots into a dull planting to add quick color. If space is really limited, you could create your own garden paradise on a rooftop or porch, or in a window box.

Containers can also make great garden accents. Choose bold, sculptural perennials such as yucca (*Yucca filamentosa*) for formal designs; mix different colors and cascading plants for a cottage look.

Annuals

Annuals make perfect container plants. They grow quickly, flower profusely, and provide a long season of good looks. Some also offer distinctive foliage, while others perfume the air with their sweet scents.

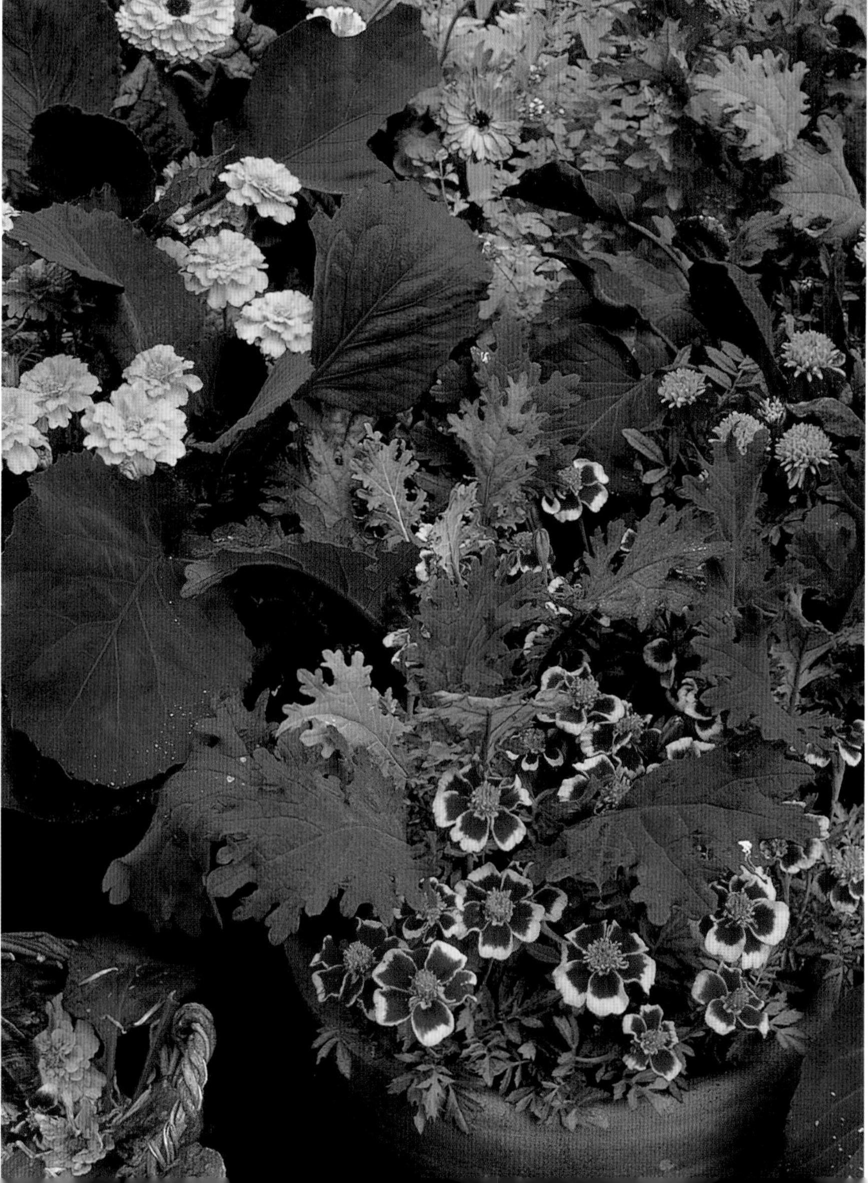

The orange-yellow of the marigolds and calendulas is a great complement to the purple-leaved ornamental cabbages and kale.

Groups of small and medium-sized containers create charming spots of movable color; large planters can showcase a stunning mix of colorful annuals in a relatively small space. Window boxes and hanging baskets are other options for displaying a wide range of flowering and foliage annuals.

You can insert small, individual pots of flowers, such as primulas, inside window boxes, for an instant display.

Choosing Annuals for Containers

While most annuals do extremely well in containers, the many compact cultivars of marigolds, petunias, impatiens, begonias, and ageratum are especially good. These annuals begin blooming early and put on a non-stop show of color all season long.

As with any kind of garden, the first step to planning successful container plantings is choosing plants that have similar growth needs, such as their light requirements. The amount of sun or shade your container garden receives is a major consideration for your choice of plants.

Most flowering annuals prefer plenty of sun. Sunny spots can support a wider range of colorful annuals, including treasure flower (*Gazania rigens*), mealy-cup sage (*Salvia farinacea*), and narrow-leaved zinnia (*Zinnia angustifolia*). Be sure you don't plant sun-lovers, such as marigolds, in the same container with shade-loving annuals, like coleus.

If you're planting a container for a shady spot, take care to select plants that thrive in shade. If you're looking for plants for a shady location, some of the best choices include flowering tobacco (*Nicotiana* spp.), bergenia (*Bergenia cordifolia*), wishbone flower (*Torenia fournieri*), impatiens (*Impatiens* spp.), wax begonias (*Begonia* Semperflorens-Cultorum hybrids), and monkey flower (*Mimulus* x *hybridus*).

Each cell pack or seed packet will come with a label that tells you if the plants prefer sun or part shade. However, be skeptical of those sun/shade ratings; labels sometimes say a particular plant can take part shade when it really requires full sun to grow well. To confirm plants' light needs, check their individual entries in "Encyclopedia of Flowers" starting on page 306.

When planning a container garden—whether it is a pot, hanging basket, window box, or planter—you also need to consider the ultimate height of the annuals you select. As a general guideline, try to choose annuals that are the same height or smaller than the height of the container; otherwise, the planting may look top-heavy.

When to Buy and What to Plant

Spring is when garden centers have the largest selection of annual flowers (and again in the fall for those of you in milder climates), and that's when you will probably want to fill most of your containers. Most annuals aren't frost-tolerant, so you should put them out after the danger of frost has passed. One major exception to this rule is the pansy. Pansies (and their cousins, Johnny-jump-ups [*Viola tricolor*]) are very fond of cool spring (and fall) weather; plant them outside just as soon as the garden centers get them in.

If you didn't get around to setting up your containers in spring, or if your pansy plantings are looking tired by midsummer, don't assume you're stuck with no flowers for the rest of the season. Grocery and discount stores often sell annuals only in the spring, but you can usually find some nice annuals at local garden centers later in the season.

Single-annual containers can be pleasing, but mixed plantings of three or four different annuals are even more exciting. While the plants you pick are up to you, there are some basic guidelines you can follow to create a successful container planting. First, select a "star" plant. Base your container planting around one centerpiece plant—perhaps a tall cleome, a tuberous begonia, or a bold love-lies-bleeding (*Amaranthus caudatus*). Then choose a "supporting cast" to complement the star plant and fill out the

Start Your Own Annuals

For an "instant" effect, you can buy and plant annuals that are already blooming. If you're not in a hurry, though, you can start your own; many kinds are easy to grow from seed. Growing your own annuals is also a good way to save money.

Some kinds of annuals, such as marigolds, mature quickly, so you can sow them directly into outdoor pots. Other annuals that are easy to grow from direct-sown seed include sweet alyssum (*Lobularia maritima*), nasturtiums (*Tropaeolum majus*), morning glories (*Ipomoea* spp.), and zinnias. Sweet alyssum is cold-tolerant, so you can plant the seed in early spring; for the rest, wait until after frost has passed.

Other annuals have very tiny seeds or might take a little longer before they start flowering, so they are best started indoors under lights. Check the instructions on the seed packets, and start the seeds the recommended number of weeks before your last spring frost so they'll start flowering shortly after you move them outside. If you live in an area with a long growing season, start another batch of plants in early summer; use these to replace tired container plantings in late summer or early fall in order to have an all-season display of flowers.

Nasturtiums

You can train lantana (*Lantana camara*) to grow upright into a stunning lollipop-shaped standard, or tree, form.

container. Try one or two with bold leaves or an upright habit—such as impatiens or snapdragons—and one or two that sprawl or trail—such as edging lobelia (*Lobelia erinus*) or creeping zinnia (*Sanvitalia procumbens*).

Growing Perennials in Containers

No matter what size or style of garden you have, growing perennials in pots can greatly expand your planting options. You will also discover how practical and versatile these movable gardens can be. Perennials work well in pots as long as you give them the growing conditions and routine care that they need. Plant several perennials in one pot or group several in individual containers. Top choices include those with a long season of bloom, such as the compact, golden orange 'Stella d'Oro' daylily. Other perennials that look especially good in containers are those with interesting foliage, such as hostas, ornamental grasses, lady's-mantle (*Alchemilla mollis*), heart-leaved bergenia (*Bergenia cordifolia*), and spotted lamium (*Lamium maculatum*). Try using some of these plants in large containers, mixed with annuals to provide constant color. Hardy bulbs also add spring color to containers.

Perennials need a little more care than annuals, as you don't just pull them out at the end of the season. Because they are growing in containers, they are much more susceptible to winter damage than plants growing in the ground. In Northern areas, you'll want to move container perennials to an unheated garage or cold basement to protect them from the alternate freezing and thawing cycles, which can damage or kill them. You'll need to water the pots lightly during winter.

Bulbs for Container Gardens

As you plan your container plantings, don't stop with common favorites like geraniums and petunias; liven them up with some colorful bulbs! Bulbs make excellent companions for annuals in pots, since the annuals usually root

Consider Flower Shape

Flowers come in all sorts of shapes and sizes. Plant breeders are constantly enhancing the shape of flowers to give us more ruffles and more petals—as well as larger blooms. And this feast isn't only available in the indoor plant range—your favorite annuals, bulbs, and perennials (even roses) are bred for brilliant blooms. You can't fail to notice the bold and brassy amaryllis (*Hippeastrum* hybrids), with their outsized, colorful trumpets sitting on top of a single stem, or the increasingly decorative shapes of the newer kinds of tulips.

But there are many other flowers that have evolved naturally—to catch the eye of particular insects, birds, or moths. Some of these are showy performers; others have to be viewed up close to reveal their magic. Take for instance the lovely mountain laurel (*Kalmia latifolia*), whose flattened bells are held in bunches. It is really only when you can look closely at each single blossom and bud that you fully realize its delicate beauty. Or you can grow a pot of lavender cotton (*Santolina chamaecyparissus*), with its tight, yellow balls seemingly floating atop the gray foliage during summer. Other plants form star-shaped flowers (such as bellflowers) or pea-like flowers, or the magnificent urn shapes of magnolias, while asters have a ring of petals radiating from the center to entice their pollinators to land. There is a diverse range of shapes that we can use for our container gardens.

Asters and bellflowers

Broad, shallow containers work well for displaying daffodils and other spring bulbs.

in the top soil layer while the bulbs are planted much deeper. The bulbs also benefit from the covering of annuals, which shade the soil and pot to some extent, keeping the bulbs cool. Some bulbs provide beautiful blooms; others provide eye-catching foliage. And there are bulbs for almost every exposure, from bright sunshine to dappled shade.

Container Bulbs through the Season

Pots of traditional spring-blooming bulbs—including hyacinths, tulips, and daffodils—are especially welcome early in the growing season. To coax them into bloom in pots, you need to give them a chilling period, as explained in "Growing Bulbs Indoors" on page 231. These spring bloomers combine beautifully with cool-season annuals, such as pansies, common stock (*Matthiola incana*), and English daisy (*Bellis perennis*).

When warm weather sets in, summer bulbs come into their glory. Asiatic lilies make a lovely show in early summer and look especially good with a cascade of annual blooms beneath them. Other great summer bulbs for pots include gladioli, crocosmia and Siberian iris (*Iris sibirica*).

For partially shady spots, tuberous begonias are among the most wonderful of potted bulbs. They bloom over a long period, in a wide range of colors and flower forms. Cascading types can look charming tumbling out of hanging baskets or over the sides of large containers. For extra excitement, grow tuberous begonias with shade-loving annual companions, such as coleus, fibrous begonias, browallia (*Browallia speciosa*), and wishbone flower (*Torenia fournieri*).

Extra Tulips and Daffodils

You may have noticed, with surprise and delight, some container displays of colorful blooming bulbs that seem to have more flowers than the container could possibly seem to accommodate. You may well think, on viewing such a prolific display, that your eyes are deceiving you. But the answer is simple—the bulbs have been double-, or even triple-planted. Rows of bulbs have been planted in a large container, one underneath the other.

Multiple-planting will not work very well with some bulbs. Tulips and daffodils and reticulated iris (*Iris reticulata*) are probably more responsive than most to this treatment. Hyacinths grow rather too profusely for planting in layers.

Bulbs will need to be chilled and then "forced" before being planted in layers. How to do this is explained in "Growing Bulbs Indoors" on page 231. To plant bulbs in layers, place the lower row, with the narrow side up, on a thick layer of container mix—fill the pot to a little over one-quarter of its capacity. Add more container mix until the bulbs are almost covered, with their tips just visible above the surface. Then place another row of bulbs with their bases in between the tips of the lower bulbs. Top up the container with more mix, until only the tips of the upper row are visible. Then sit back and wait for a profusion of flowers to appear.

Containers for Bulbs

For best results, choose a large pot that can hold an ample amount of container mix. Large pots will provide ample rooting room for your bulbs, and they tend to dry out less quickly than small pots. For lilies, choose a pot at least 10 inches (25 cm) wide and deep. Smaller bulbs can grow in slightly smaller pots, but they'll also do well in large containers. Big plants such as cannas need plenty of room; try them in large planters or half-barrels.

Fill the bottom of the container with a well-drained commercial container mix. Adjust the thickness of this layer to match the needs of the bulbs you're planting. Lily bulbs should sit deep enough to have 5 to 6 inches (12.5 to 15 cm) of container mix over their tops; set smaller bulbs so they're covered with 3 to 4 inches (7.5 to 10 cm) of mix. Fill the container with container mix to within an inch or two (2.5 to 5 cm) of the rim. You can also plant young annual plants into the pot as you normally would, firming them in well and then watering thoroughly.

A container packed full of variegated tulips adds a touch of spring to any part of the garden.

If you're growing pots of warmth-loving summer bulbs—like dahlias and liliums—you can get a head start on the season by starting them indoors. Plant them inside in 6- to 8-inch (15- to 20- cm) pots, 6 to 8 weeks before nighttime temperatures hit 50°F (10°C). Grow them under lights, in a greenhouse, or on a sunny porch or windowsill while you wait for the weather to warm up. When you're ready to set them out in their outdoor containers, remove the bulbs from their pot and plant them at the same depth they were growing. Then plant annuals around the sides, being careful not to damage the bulb shoots.

Caring for Container Bulbs

Throughout the season, keep a close eye on your containers to make sure the container mix doesn't dry out completely. In hot, dry weather, you may need to water every day, especially for small containers. Fertilize several times during the summer months to keep the plants growing vigorously. For more information on basic container maintenance, see "Caring for Annuals and Perennials in Containers" on page 174.

At the end of the season, dig out the bulbs or tubers of tender bulbs for winter storage. Shake off the soil and let the bulbs air dry for several days. Store them in labeled paper or mesh bags, or bury them in wood shavings, styrofoam packing material, or peat moss to prevent the bulbs from drying out too much. Check the bulbs monthly and sprinkle them lightly with water if they look shriveled. Or simply leave the bulbs in their pot and bring the whole pot indoors for winter storage in a cool basement.

Grasses for Containers

Many small and medium-sized grasses are attractive in pots, urns, and planters. Northern gardeners can enjoy spectacular grasses that are hardy only in Zones 8 and 9 by growing them outdoors in pots during the summer, then moving them to a cellar or cool greenhouse for the winter.

In very hot weather, check plants daily and water as needed to keep the container mix evenly moist. Since frequent watering leaches nutrients out of the mix, give container-grown grasses a topdressing of compost or organic fertilizer during the hotter summer months.

In mild climates, you can leave the containers outdoors all winter as long as you never let the soil dry completely. In colder regions, either store the containers indoors or tip them on their sides, so water can't collect and drown the roots. Then bury them beneath a pile of leaves, evergreen boughs, or similar materials.

When rescuing buried plants from outdoor storage in the spring, wait until all frosts are over before uncovering them. If the plants have started to grow, put them in a sheltered, shaded spot for a few days until the foliage has hardened enough for them to withstand sunlight.

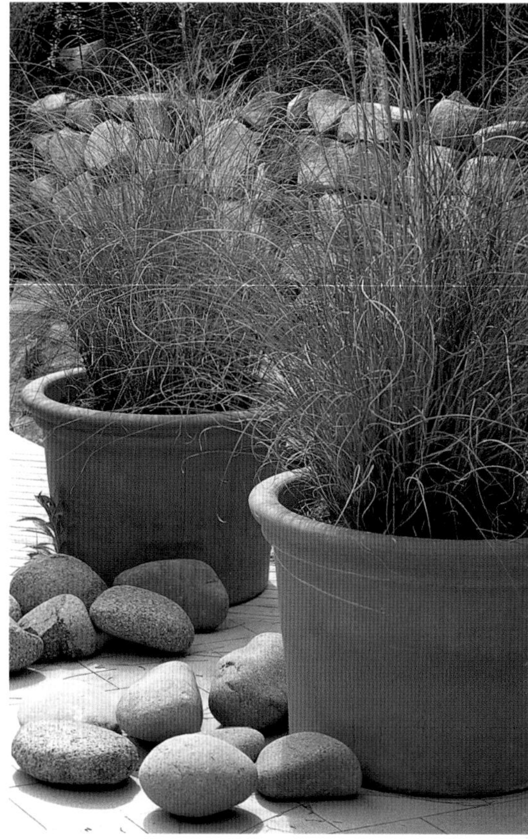

Ornamental grasses make exciting container plants. However, you may need to bring pots of cold-tender types indoors for the winter months.

Container Water Gardens

A small water garden adds a special sparkle to any collection of container plants. As a bonus, the open water will attract birds and even frogs and toads. You can use any large container—an old bathtub, half-whiskey barrel, or a special plastic tub sold complete with a filter and small fountain. Set the container on your patio or deck, or sink it into the ground for a natural pool effect.

A filter usually isn't necessary for a small water garden if you make sure you include a few oxygenating plants—such as *Elodea canadensis*—to help keep the water clear. Specialty nurseries sell these oxygenators, along with pygmy (dwarf) water lilies and other water plants suitable for a tub garden. Grow the plants in individual containers set down into the tub, so that you can replace them as needed or dismantle the garden for the winter in the North.

Always include a few fish in the container to control mosquito larvae. Goldfish are a great choice, and they're easy to overwinter indoors in a goldfish bowl or small aquarium.

Window Boxes and Hanging Baskets

Window boxes and hanging baskets are an excellent way to brighten up small spaces, such as windows, decks and patios, or porch railings.

When planting your window box, choose compact plants that won't block your view.

Window Boxes

Conventionally, boxes are placed on the exterior sills of windows. However, there is no reason why the trend to indoor gardening should not include the window box—why not arrange window boxes on the inside of your windows, using the wide range of flowering and foliage plants to make a striking display?

The Right Container

Window boxes can be made of metal (usually copper or lead), wood (redwood or cedar), terracotta, cement, or plastic. They can be simple, unadorned boxes or painted, stenciled, molded, or carved.

Many garden centers sell ready-made window boxes of plastic, wood, or metal, with special brackets that screw to the wall below the window to hold the box. Usually these boxes are not very large, so try not to overplant them; allow enough space for plants to grow larger through the season.

One of the secrets of creating a really good-looking window box is to keep the box in proportion to the window it decorates, so that it occupies about one-quarter of the height of a low window and about one-fifth the height of a tall one. Try to bear this in mind when choosing your window box container.

Building Your Own Window Boxes

If you build your own boxes, make them a little bigger than the typical garden-center sizes. A box about 8 inches (20 cm) wide and deep will give you enough additional soil for a range of plants to grow well. Be sure to put the box together with galvanized screws. Don't use nails—they won't hold as well as screws. It's also a good idea to reinforce the corners of the box to help them stay together.

Whether you choose to buy your window boxes or make your own, make

Creating a Window Box Display

You can improve the view from your window by simply planting a window box of beautiful flowers on the windowsill outside. Choose a container material that is in keeping with the style of your home. A simple material, such as terracotta, always looks good.

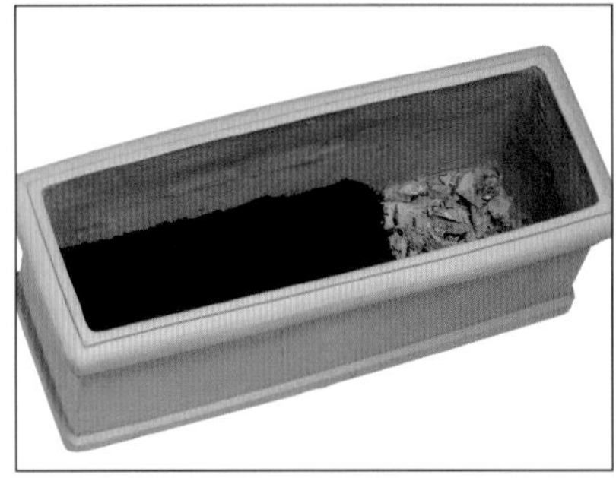

1. Line the window box with a layer of shards for good drainage. Add a 2-inch (5-cm) layer of container mix.

2. Arrange the plants in the window box to experiment with the design, until you are happy with the arrangement.

3. Plant the taller plants first and then the lower-growing plants. Firm the container mix around the plants.

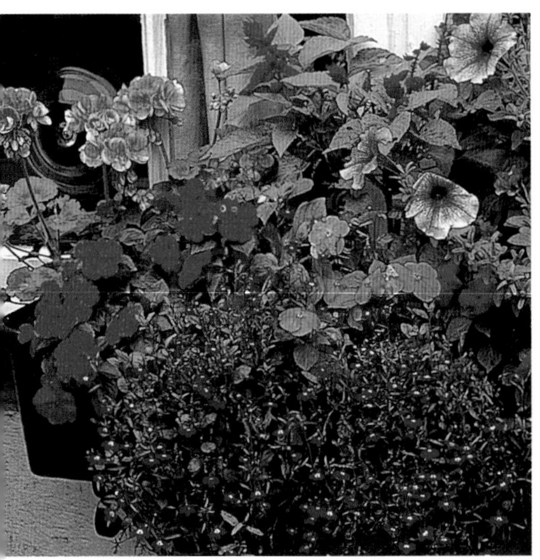

Window boxes attract lots of attention, so make sure you can reach them for regular grooming.

Fragrant Favorites for Window Boxes

If you want some powerful nighttime fragrance wafting into your bedroom from your window boxes, pick up a packet of evening-scented stock (*Matthiola longipetala* subsp. *bicornis*) seeds and plant some in a corner of each window box. The stock isn't a showy flower, but it has a strong, sweet scent that fills the air at night. Other good choices for fragrance include petunias, sweet alyssum (*Lobularia maritima*), 'Lemon Gem' marigold (*Tagetes tenuifolia* 'Lemon Gem'), scented geraniums (*Pelargonium* spp.), mignonette (*Reseda odorata*), stock (*Matthiola incana*), and night phlox (*Zaluzianskya capensis*).

sure that there are adequate drainage holes in the bottom, so excess water can run out.

Cachepots

Window boxes can be surprisingly flexible, particularly if you decide to follow the practice of cachepot gardening—the use of containers (usually utilitarian) within more decorative outer containers.

Using a cachepot can make both outdoor, as well as indoor, gardening very versatile. As one group of plants finishes its display, it can be replaced by others held in readiness for the purpose. These can be loosely placed in the window box or held in place with container mix, peat, sphagnum moss, or some other material that will hold moisture.

Cachepots can be especially useful when you are planting window boxes since they need to be strongly secured to your windowsill or ledge. They can also be rearranged very easily if your original planting ideas need a little fine tuning.

Securing Window Boxes

While a window box can be a superb addition to your home, a little planning is needed to make sure the project is trouble-free. The weight of plants, container mix, window box, and water can be quite substantial, and you need to be able to secure the window box and, at the same time, avoid having any moisture becoming trapped to damage the structure of your home. Allowing a gap of just half an inch (12 mm) lets air circulate and water escape.

Before you install your window boxes, fill one with soil and water it well. Then lift it carefully so you experience just how heavy it is: You need to use really sturdy supports to hold all that weight.

Since large window boxes can be cumbersome as well as heavy, you may want to secure them in such a way as they can be easily taken down from the window for cleaning and maintenance work.

Pay particular attention to supporting brackets as they can be under a lot of pressure and any loosening or damage has to be quickly repaired.

Picking the Plants

Top plant choices for window boxes include all of the low and medium-sized annuals, along with plenty of trailing plants, such as large periwinkle (*Vinca major*) and petunias. And if the window above the box will be open to let in the summer breezes, be sure to include some fragrant plants; see "Fragrant Favorites for Window Boxes" for ideas.

Planting Your Window Box

Once you've selected the plants for your window box, it's time to start planting.

If you are planting directly into the window box, add a drainage layer of about an inch or so of coarse gravel, terracotta chips, or other suitable drainage material. If the window box has few drainage holes, the drainage layer is of even greater importance.

Fill the window box about half full with premium-quality container mix, adding some slow-release fertilizer.

Plant the most upright-growing plants first, to provide a kind of design backbone to your planting scheme. Then fill in the intermediate spaces with lower-growing specimens, allowing enough space for your flowers to grow. Once you're happy with the appearance of your window box, water it thoroughly.

To maintain the look of your window box, check it regularly as it will need watering more often than similar flowers planted in the open garden.

Grow scented plants, such as herbs, in your window box. Not only are they practical, but the lovely fragrance will waft through the window.

To keep hanging baskets looking lush through the season, water them regularly, fertilize often, and pinch off any spent flowers.

Hanging Baskets

Bring your container gardens to new heights with hanging baskets. Baskets look terrific on porches, beside a doorway, or hanging on an arbor over a patio. You can buy hanging baskets already planted and ready to hang, or you can easily plant them yourself. Some gardeners develop a real passion for hanging baskets and a well-planted basket can be a truly spectacular sight. Hanging baskets do not necessarily have to be hung up particularly high. It's up to you to decide what is the best height to display your favorite plants.

Preparing the Basket

Many garden centers and hardware stores stock lightweight, plastic baskets complete with drainage saucers and supporting light chains—these are certainly the most convenient and cheapest baskets. To some they can look a bit hard-edged, but if you are planting so that the container is hidden, this won't matter too match.

There are other ready-made hanging baskets made of ceramic, terracotta, wood, or metal, but weight may become an issue with these.

The true hanging garden enthusiast usually prefers a moss basket—a wire frame lined with sphagnum moss or a layer of similar fibrous material to hold the container mix and plants. At a pinch you can use good quality burlap—doubled over if it seems a little thin. Some adventurous folk even plant through slits in the fiber at the sides of the basket.

It is best to use a galvanized or otherwise rust-proofed wire basket frame. Most container mixes that are specially sold for hanging baskets are peat-based, which may be very tricky to remoisten if they dry out. Add some standard mix containing loam or humus to aid moisture retention. Slow-release fertilizer added to the mix will give your plants a boost and reduce feeding later.

Plant evergreens, such as Boston fern (*Nephrolepis exaltata*), for a basket with year-round interest.

As your hanging basket settles down, you may notice water running from thinner sections of the fiber. One of the great advantages of moss basket gardening is that you can add reinforcement from the outside by poking an extra piece of fiber through the wire frame.

Picking Plants for Hanging Baskets

Hanging baskets are great for annuals that grow quickly and bloom spectacularly. However, if you grow varieties that need full sun, this adds to the natural tendency of hanging baskets to dry out fast. Baskets look best with a combination of low,

Color Theming

Petunias

You can create a color feast in your hanging basket by selecting plants of similar colors that will blossom at the same time. For example, an informal golden summer basket will be the result of planting English ivy (*Hedera helix*), pansies (*Viola* x *wittrockiana*), helichrysum (*Helichrysum petiolare*), and yellow snapdragon (*Antirrhinum* spp.). This combination will thrive in a semi-shaded position. Or, for a more dramatic look, try ivy-leafed pelargonium (*Pelargonium* spp.), rose moss (*Portulaca grandiflora*), and garden verbena (*Verbena* x *hybrida*) to create a red basket. This combination prefers a sunny site and will have a long flowering life.

If your hanging basket allows for planting at the side as well as the top, try planting red, white, and pink flowering begonias. They will grow into a compact ball that will last right through the summer.

bushy plants to fill the top and trailing plants to spill over the sides. Good bushy plants include tuberous begonias (*Begonia* Tuberhybrida hybrids), browallia (*Browallia* spp.), and vinca (*Catharanthus roseus*). Around the edge of the basket include cascading plants, such as petunias, annual lobelia (*Lobelia erinus*), sweet alyssum (*Lobularia maritima*), nasturtium (*Tropaeolum majus*), and mints (*Mentha* spp.). Plants that are both bushy and trailing, such as ivy geranium (*Pelargonium peltatum*) and fuchsia (*Fuchsia* x *hybrida*), look good when planted by themselves to fill a hanging basket.

Perhaps the most dramatic effect is achieved by a hanging basket that is richly planted with a single type of plant. This is certainly the easiest way to meet one of the basic requirements of hanging basket—and indeed all container—planting. Plants in the same container must share identical (or very similar) soil, water, light, and temperature requirements.

Hanging Baskets for Herbs

You don't have to limit your choice of plants to the conventional, flowering annuals. The dry, warm conditions that are characteristic of hanging baskets can suit many Mediterranean plants, particularly the cooking herbs.

As herbs will be picked quite often, it is best to hang a herb basket within easy reach of the kitchen. Herbs to try include oregano, thyme, basil, and lemon balm.

Planting and Caring for Hanging Baskets

Most hanging basket containers look like regular containers, and you plant them in basically the same way. However, hanging baskets dry out faster than other container plants, so it's a good idea to use a container mix that holds plenty of water. Adding extra vermiculite will help. It also helps to use larger baskets which are at least 12 inches (30 cm) in diameter, because these will dry out more slowly.

You can find a plant suitable for a hanging basket in any situation. Impatiens, or busy Lizzy, (*Impatiens wallerana*), is ideal for providing a burst of color to shady areas of the garden, such as under a veranda.

One of the keys to lush-looking containers is regular fertilizing. Give hanging baskets a boost by misting or watering them with liquid fertilizer, such as fish emulsion.

Because hanging baskets allow you to display concentrated plantings of your favorite plants, it is a good idea to plant them more densely than you would in the open garden or in more conventional containers. The tangled, intertwining effect of such dense plantings is part of the appeal of the hanging basket.

Since most hanging baskets have a rounded base, steady them by placing them in a flower pot or kitchen mixing bowl.

Garden centers sell brackets that let you hang baskets anywhere you choose on a wall or post. Make sure you choose sturdy brackets and fasten them securely; they have to hold a lot of weight.

The easiest way of watering hanging baskets that are out of reach is to get a long extension nozzle for your garden hose and simply lift the water to the height of the basket. Alternatively, you can hang the basket on a rope or chain that can be lowered, so that you can water it as you would any other container, and carry out other necessary maintenance work at the same time.

You won't need to water too much at first, when the plants are small. But as the plants grow, the basket may need watering at least once and possibly twice a day by the end of the season.

If your hanging baskets are drying out too quickly, consider using water-retaining pellets to help you even out the moisture highs and lows in this miniature ecosystem.

If you're going to be away from home, even for one night, move your baskets to a shady spot until you return, or ask a neighbor to water them for you.

Balconies, Courtyards, and Patio Gardens

Container plants are ideal for balconies, courtyards, patios, and other outdoor living areas. You can create many types of containerized gardens in these areas, even in the limited space of balconies. Whether your balcony is in a high-rise apartment or on the second floor of a suburban home, you can transform it quickly and simply into a peaceful patch of green.

Courtyards and patios are increasingly significant aspects of the modern lifestyle. As urban backyards become smaller, courtyards and patios are becoming popular as outdoor rooms, and are now home to everything from decorative trees, shrubs, and succulents to productive container vegetable and herb gardens.

Your Balcony Backyard

Just because you live in an apartment doesn't mean you have to be deprived of a garden. A clever use of containers can help you discover a lively new world. With a few containers brimming with colorful flowers, your balcony can become a relaxing area for entertaining. Dwarf trees and small shrubs can be used to create interesting effects on a small scale, and you can even be productive with vegetables and herbs in containers and flowering fruit trees. Here are some ways to transform your balcony into a lush, green space.

You can even grow a productive garden of fruits, herbs, and vegetables in the confined space of a balcony.

Getting Started

Before you start your balcony garden, there are some important factors to consider. The first and most obvious consideration is the amount of weight your balcony can bear. Most condominium balconies have concrete floors, but some city houses have timber floors which will not support the weight of concrete containers. It is best to avoid using heavy containers—use plastic and cedar wood where possible. Spread the load over a wide area and make sure brackets and hooks are capable of taking the weight of hanging pots or baskets.

Next, check the microclimate of your balcony. Note the direction the balcony faces and how much sun it receives. Some balconies are very sheltered and receive no direct sunlight or wind at all, while others have considerable wind exposure and scorching sunlight. Many balcony plants don't get much rain since they are situated beneath awnings, so you must ensure that the container mix is kept moist.

Balcony Design

Because balconies are usually small, space is a major design consideration. The main principle is to keep the design as simple as possible. The last thing you want is a cluttered, busy look. Using square or rectangular containers that suit the angles and edges of balconies will save space. And use hanging baskets, espaliered, and climbing plants to bring walls to life. One approach is to grow climbing plants on a trellis attached to the wall for that purpose. Don't forget to leave enough room for a small table and a couple of chairs.

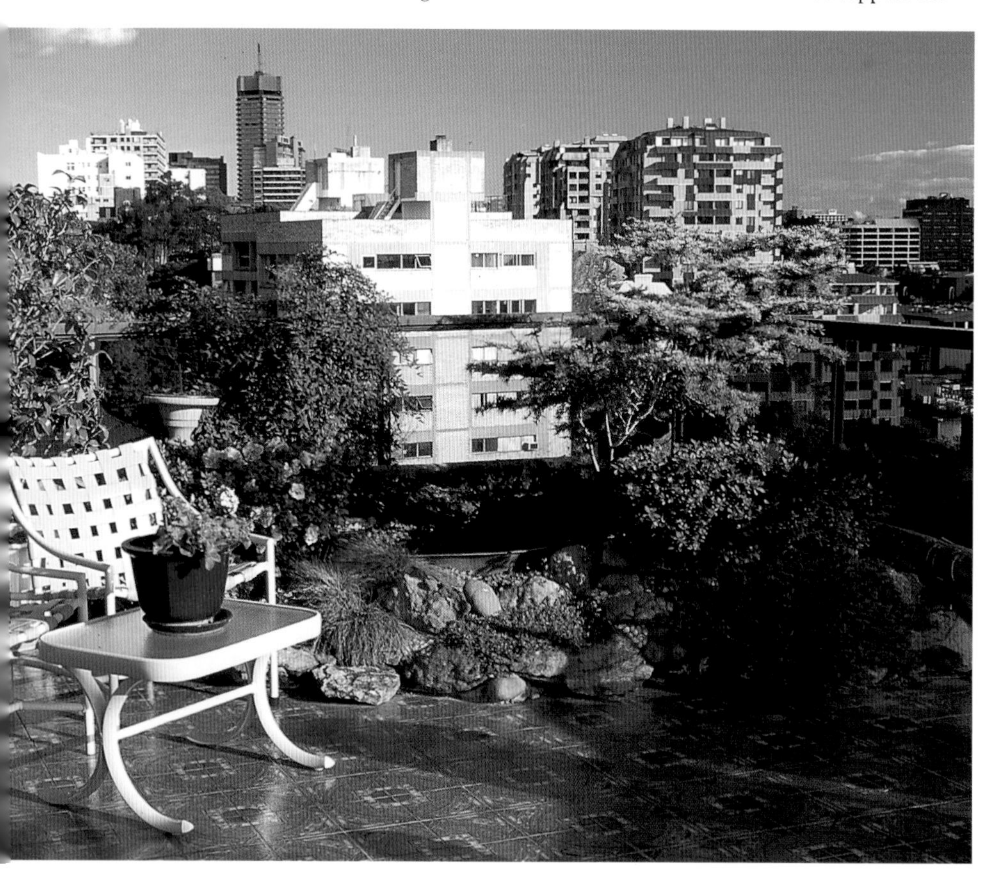

Rooftop gardens are often blasted by wind and sun, so select suitable plants for the conditions.

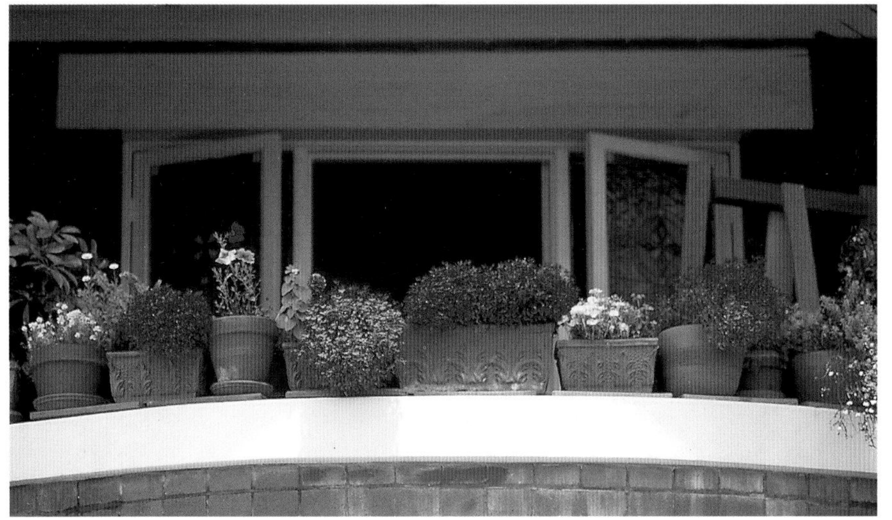

Be sure to use heavy, wide pots in windy areas, to prevent the pots from being blown over.

Courtyards and Patios

Courtyards are areas that adjoin the house or are discrete, enclosed areas inside a garden. They are natural extensions of the house and provide areas for entertaining, relaxing, or barbecuing.

Courtyards are not a recent invention and have been elements of gardens from early times. A courtyard provides a small, confined area in which to create a unique atmosphere. The limitations of courtyards are part of their appeal. The walls, hedges, or buildings that create the space for a courtyard also define its boundaries.

Patios are the ideal areas for everything from barbecues to formal lunches and dinner parties. Building a patio is an ideal way to create a separate, private room somewhere in the garden.

While some patios adjoin the house or are close to the kitchen, these days many patios are located in the backyard. You can place your patio under a large tree, in an area where there is an attractive view, or simply in the section of the yard that receives the most sun. In hot climates, you may wish to place the patio in a cool area surrounded by greenery.

You can partially enclose the patio by surrounding it with a formal clipped hedge, clipped balls of box (*Buxus* spp.), or well-placed large pots.

The biggest challenge when designing and constructing your ideal separate area is coming to terms with space limitations. The small scale of courtyards and patios makes attention to detail a priority.

Courtyard and Patio Design

Think carefully about the style and function of your courtyard or patio. Do you want it to have a formal or an informal style? With a formal look you can create a modern, minimalist style with a few container plants. But perhaps you prefer the informal texture, softness, and color of carefully selected plants.

A vine-covered trellis and collection of potted plants transform this corner into an inviting alcove.

Details are very important in small areas because mistakes are more obvious. Space should be carefully allocated and the selection of materials to be used is a major consideration. Avoid using too many plants in small spaces. You can use repeat plantings to give a clean, uncluttered appearance. Several large containers or planter boxes can be more eye-catching than a collection of small pots.

How to Decorate Courtyard Walls

Courtyard walls cry out for climbing plants. You can attach wire to a wall in any pattern and train a potted climber to flesh out the design. Diagonal patterns

Shape up Your Balcony, Courtyard, or Patio

Terracotta pots filled with clipped shapes or standards create truly elegant effects and may be used as dominant features. You can create an exquisite look in a small space by using several pots of clipped shrubs. Box (*Buxus* spp.) can be clipped into spheres, squares, or any shape you desire. It is cheaper to buy a large, unclipped box and shape it yourself than to buy one already shaped. But keep in mind that it does take several years to obtain a good shape—which accounts for the relatively high cost of clipped box.

Containers filled with box make great portable hedges or screens. They are ideal for separating your courtyard or patio from the rest of the garden in order to create a separate garden room.

Correct pruning is a must when shaping container plants. The aim is to have compact, solid growth. Make sure you have a good pair of hedge clippers. The general rule is to prune in late spring after new growth has appeared. The next new growth should be pruned in late summer or fall. The main aim of pruning the new tips is to encourage the stem to branch two or three times in order to create denser growth.

Planning your courtyard carefully will help you to transform your ideas into a workable design.

look good, but the choice is yours. The first step is to drill holes for galvanized roofing screws and then pull the wire tight between the screws to create the pattern. You might consider accentuating your climber's flowers and foliage by painting the wall a contrasting color.

A suitable climber for this treatment is star jasmine (*Trachelospermum jasminoides*), which has glossy, evergreen leaves and perfumed, white flowers. You could also use clematis, cup-and-saucer vine (*Cobaea scandens*), ivy, or bleeding glorybower (*Clerodendrum thomsoniae*).

A trellis is another way of attaching climbers to walls. Fix a square, rectangle, or arch of trellis to the wall, plant a climber at the base and train it over the trellis. Choose an evergreen like ivy that can be clipped as it grows to the shape of the trellis. A clever approach is to incorporate this structure into a *trompe-l'oeil*. Stephanotis is also recommended for a trellis design and it has a perfume to die for. Mandevillas are easy to grow and have large, showy flowers.

What to Plant Where

Every inch of space counts in courtyards, patios, and balconies and every plant should fulfil its purpose well. Correct positioning of plants according to their cultivation needs is of great importance, as small spaces will magnify any problems or errors. Remember to choose plants for their foliage as well as their flowers to ensure year-round appeal. Check the basic needs and features of plants in "Encyclopedia of Flowers," starting on page 306.

Sunny Balconies, Courtyards, and Patios

Colorful annuals are always eye-catching for sunny balconies. Scented geraniums (*Pelargonium* spp.) are ideal for container culture and provide bright color for weeks on end. Petunias and sages (*Salvia* spp.) are also good choices. Yuccas, heavenly bamboo (*Nandina domestica*), together with love-lies-bleeding (*Amaranthus caudatus*) will also grow well. For more plants that grow well in the sun, see "The Right Container Plant for the Right Place," starting on page 194.

Succulents are particularly suitable for really hot balconies and courtyards where it is difficult to get anything to grow. The huge range of leaf shapes and sizes enables you to have a variety of interesting mixes.

You need not be deprived of essential kitchen ingredients such as herbs if you have a small but sunny courtyard or balcony. Plant a selection of herbs in a large trough or pot. You could grow chives, parsley, marjoram, thyme, oregano, and rosemary. A large tub of salad greens is also an interesting approach for a balcony or courtyard. Choose loose-leafed varieties of lettuce so you can pick the leaves as required. If you have the space, why not grow a lemon tree in a pot?

Water Features for Balconies, Courtyards, and Patios

You can cool hot and sunny balconies, courtyards, and patios with a water feature. Water spheres are popular. The sphere, over which water trickles from the top, can be placed in its own dish and surrounded by pebbles. It is as much a sculpture as a water feature. Even a birdbath will provide the presence of water and perhaps create a cool bathing spot for local birds. A large water bowl with a lotus or waterlily planted in it makes a stylish feature, or you could even add a small fountain.

Wall fountains are favorite courtyard features as they enhance both the wall and its surroundings. Creative gardeners can enliven a small courtyard or patio by combining mosaic and water in a Moorish style. A mosaic may be created on the ground or on a wall, or you can decorate your containers. There are some wonderful tiles and pebbles around, and when pieces of broken crockery or other brightly colored objects are added, the outcome can be quite stunning.

This row of potted geraniums (*Pelargonium* spp.) forms a colorful, yet practical, privacy screen.

Shady Balconies, Courtyards, and Patios

There are many plants that grow well in shady positions. Impatiens gives displays of flowers for months on end, and there is a great color range. Bergenias (*Bergenia* spp.) give a good foliage display, as do ferns. For more shade-loving plants, see “The Right Container Plant for the Right Place,” starting on page 194.

Don't forget the importance of the containers themselves. A grouping of colorful pots can bring a shaded balcony, courtyard, or patio garden to life.

Windy Balconies, Courtyards and Patios

For windy positions you should select low, sturdy pots that will not be blown over easily. Use hardy, compact plants that are strong enough to withstand strong gusts of wind, such as glossy abelia (*Abelia* x *grandiflora*), lavender, and rosemary.

Even on the shadiest of patios, you can always find attractive plants to suit the site.

Scented Plants for Balconies, Courtyards, and Patios

Scented plants add another dimension to container gardens. By using a number of fragrant plants, you can create a “scent pocket” on your balcony or in a section of your courtyard. Here are some suggestions:

- Gardenia (*Gardenia augusta*)
- Sweet pea (*Lathyrus odoratus*)
- Lavender (*Lavandula angustifolia*)
- Lilies (*Lilium* hybrids)
- Magnolia (*Magnolia* spp.)
- Lemon balm (*Melissa officinalis*)
- Sweet cicely (*Myrrhis odorata*)
- Daffodils (*Narcissus* hybrids)
- Four-o'clocks (*Mirabilis jalapa*)
- Rosemary (*Rosmarinus officinalis*)
- Roses (*Rosa* spp.)

Plants for Hanging Baskets

Hanging baskets are ideal for balconies and courtyard walls. Hanging baskets bring attractive, colorful plants to eye level and have the advantage of saving valuable floor and ground space. Here are some suggestions for plants to grow in baskets:

- Ageratum (*Ageratum houstonianum*)
- Basket-of-gold (*Aurinia saxatilis*)
- Fuchsia (*Fuchsia* x *hybrida*)
- Treasure flower (*Gazania rigens*)
- Strawberries (*Fragaria* spp.)
- Nasturtium (*Tropaeolum majus*)
- Rock speedwell (*Veronica prostrata*)

Evening Stars

As twilight descends, your courtyard, patio or balcony takes on a very different aspect. It is transformed into another world in which the predominance of the visual gradually gives way to the scents and sounds of night. Many light-colored flowers and silver foliage look their best during this twilight transformation, while others actually open in a burst of activity. For nighttime fragrance consider the following plants:

- Moonflower (*Ipomoea alba*)
- Jasmine (*Jasminum* spp.)
- Chilean jasmine (*Mandevilla suaveolens*)
- Night-scented stock (*Matthiola bicornis*)
- Four-o'clocks (*Mirabilis jalapa*)
- Flowering tobacco (*Nicotiana* spp.)
- Stephanotis (*Stephanotis floribunda*)
- White-flowering star jasmine (*Trachelospermum jasminoides*)

Night-scented stock

Caring for Balcony, Courtyard, and Patio Plants

A good container mix is the key to success with pot plants for balconies, courtyards, and patios. For hot areas, make sure you purchase a container mix that will hold moisture. Adding water-storing granules to a container mix will assist with water retention. You can also buy mixes for specific purposes, such as those formulated especially for terracotta pots. Because of their porous nature, you should line the inside of terracotta or stone pots with black plastic. But don't line the bottom of the pot or drainage will be impeded.

Potted plants need regular feeding. Annuals benefit from fortnightly feeds of a soluble plant food at half strength. Add a slow-release fertilizer to shrubs.

Container Garden Primer

When planting groups of flowers in a container, ensure their light requirements are compatible.

In many ways, caring for container gardens is the same as for houseplants. They all need good soil, periodic fertilizing, and regular watering. However, the main difference is that outdoor containers are exposed to more light and more wind, so they'll need more water and more fertilizer to stay in top shape. And since they can't spread their roots to search out water and nutrients, container plantings are completely at your mercy for their needs.

To keep your container plants healthy, you'll have to pay attention to them at least every other day—maybe every day in midsummer. But if you set everything up carefully at the beginning, your plant care chores won't amount to more than a few minutes a day. There are a few techniques you can use to make your container plantings as low maintenance as possible.

Starting with large containers and using a rich, moisture-retentive potting mix are the two key steps to success. You'll find that large containers will look better than smaller pots, and they won't need to be watered as often. Plastic pots tend to lose water more slowly than clay pots, so they're a good choice for reducing your watering chores. (You'll find everything you need to know about containers in "Considering Containers" on page 164.)

Rich, organic soil is the foundation of any good garden. It is important to choose a commercial container mix that will provide good rooting conditions for your container plants. You can also learn how to blend your own potting mixes to create a growing medium that's perfectly suited to your plants and less expensive as well. (For more information, see "Selecting Container Mixes" on page 168.)

Once your container gardens are established, routine grooming, fertilizing, and watering will keep them growing strong. "Container Care," below, offers pointers on planting, pinching, and preventing pest problems to keep your container gardens in peak condition.

Container Care

You've got the pot, and you've got the soil—now it's time to get your container garden started! Planting containers is easy, and it's a fun chance to try out new flower and foliage combinations to create pleasing groupings. Once you have your potted plants settled in, you'll want to groom them occasionally to keep them looking their best through the season. You'll also want to keep an eye out for pest and disease problems so you can catch them before they get out of hand.

Use small stakes to keep weak-stemmed plants from sprawling.

Planting

There's no special trick to planting containers; simply do it just as you would garden beds, spacing transplants according to the instructions on the seed packets or the transplant labels. You can space them a little closer in containers if you want, but don't overdo it and try to put too many plants into one container. Remember, the container won't look full and lush immediately, but the little transplants will grow up quickly. It's more likely that you'll need to trim them back than worry about them looking too sparse.

Grooming

Through the season, a little regular pruning will keep all of your container plants looking first-rate. Once a week, grab a bucket and your garden shears and visit each of your container plantings. Snipping back long shoot tips on annuals and removing spent flowers on perennials will stimulate bushy growth and more flowering. Removing any damaged or dead leaves or branches will keep the plants looking fresh and healthy. Collect the clippings in the bucket for later composting.

If you've included taller plants in your containers, you may need to stake them to support their upright growth. You can buy bamboo stakes in various heights, or just use small branches pruned from shrubs in your yard. (If you save a little pile of branches when you prune in late winter, you'll have a perfect source of free material for staking. And the branches actually work better than the bamboo stakes because all of the side twigs help to support the plants better.)

Coping with Container Problems

Keeping your container gardens well watered and fertilized will go a long way toward keeping the plants healthy and vigorous. Insects tend to attack plants that are weak or stressed, so if you prevent the stress, you protect the plants.

Occasionally, though, conditions may be right for insects or diseases to attack even healthy-looking plants. Once a week or so, take a few minutes to really look at your plants and see if you notice any problems developing. Turn over a few leaves, and check the shoot tips for any indications of pests.

If bugs do show up, the same sprays that protect your houseplants will also work well outside. Spraying plants thoroughly with water will keep aphids and spider mite levels down. Insecticidal soap is generally recommended primarily to control soft-bodied insects (such as aphids), although it also works against tough customers like Japanese beetles. Just be sure you spray plants thoroughly, hitting both the tops and bottoms of all leaves. Soap sprays must hit the insects directly to be effective. Handpicking or flicking pests into a tub of soapy water also works well for larger insects, such as caterpillars. But be sure you know what you're killing—some very nasty-looking bugs are actually beneficial insects that prey on plant-eating pests.

If you have trouble with slug or snail damage (the usual symptoms are large holes in the leaves), sprinkle some finely crushed eggshells over the surface of the container mix in the pots. The snails and slugs will be deterred since they won't want to crawl over the rough edges of the eggshells. (As a bonus, the empty eggshells will provide a slow-release source of calcium, an important plant nutrient.)

Snails cannot reach hanging baskets, but are a problem for pots on the ground, wall baskets, and window boxes.

Diseases are seldom a problem on container plants. As long as there are holes in the bottom of the container, root rots due to poor drainage aren't too common. If you let the plants dry out often, the leaf tips may turn brown—make more effort to water regularly to prevent further damage. Pinch off and discard plant parts that show fuzzy, white or gray patches—signs of powdery mildew—or off-color spots. Brown or white scorched spots on indoor plants that you've recently moved outside for the summer indicate sunburn. Plants generally grow out of this damage, although they will be somewhat weakened for a while. To avoid this problem, follow the guidelines covered in "Inside Out and Outside In" on page 232.

LEFT: When planning container plantings, consider how they'll look through the whole season. Bulbs are great for spring, but you'll need to replace them with annuals for later color.

Japanese beetles feed on a wide range of edible plants and herbs, as well as ornamentals.

Watering Container Gardens

While providing enough light is your greatest concern for indoor plants, watering is usually the most critical factor outdoors. Plants growing in outdoor containers need more water as the season grows warmer and as they grow larger in relation to their pots. If you live in a windy location, containers dry out even more quickly.

Unlike plants growing in the ground, the roots of container plants have only a limited space from which to absorb water and nutrients. Plants in the ground may be stressed if they aren't watered during a drought, but they usually recover. If the soil in a container gets too dry, however, the plants may sicken and die.

Do not wait until plants are dry to water them—the container mix dries out it shrinks, leaving a gap for water to run through the pot. Peat-based mixes can also be difficult to remoisten.

Knowing How Much to Water

The rule for watering established container plants is to always wet the container mix thoroughly, until water runs out of the bottom of the pot. The exception to this is when your container plants are very young and haven't yet grown roots out into the container. In this case, water sparingly or less often until the top growth begins to be about the same size as the container. Once the plant is established, water it as you would your other plants.

Large pots tend to dry out more slowly than small pots, so they'll need watering less often.

Save Time with Self-watering Pots

When you're shopping for pots, you may find some labeled "self-watering." While these containers aren't totally self-watering—you do have to add water from time to time—they have a reservoir area built into the bottom to hold a supply of water. Some of these containers have a wick running down from the soil to the reservoir; others are designed so that a small column of soil extends down into the reservoir to soak up water as needed. There's usually a small hole in the side of the container where you can fill the reservoir and check the water level.

These pots tend to be a bit more expensive, but they definitely help to reduce the frequency of watering. If you want to place a container planting in a spot where it's difficult for you to check it daily, by all means consider using a self-watering pot.

Use Pure Water

Water that has a high salt content can harm your plants, if it is used over a long period. Sodium, calcium, and magnesium salts can cause damage to your plants that will first show in the leaves. Leaf speckling, leaf burn, and leaf fall can be caused by excessively salinated water.

Over time, salts can accumulate and show up as a white or tan crust at the edges of plant pots, or actually soak through clay or terracotta pots. Crust may also form on the soil surface and around the plant stems.

If your tap water is hard or salty, you will probably know about it already—you will have trouble getting soap to lather and doing your laundry. Use distilled or purified water instead of tap water. The increasing popularity of water purifiers means that pure water is available in many households. However, this is not practical for larger quantities of water in which case you may have to buy water in large capacity bottles.

It's generally not wise to keep saucers under pots, but they can help with pots that dry out quickly.

Do not use artificially "softened" water on your plants which merely replaces the magnesium and calcium salts with sodium. It is not actually pure water.

If your tap water is chlorinated, let it stand in a pan or bucket overnight before using it on your plants. Alternatively, fill your bucket with the hose nozzle set to a fine spray. Both methods disperse chlorine.

Choosing Equipment for Easier Watering

There are several pieces of equipment that are quite helpful in making container watering as easy and efficient as possible. A watering can will be fine if you have only one or two pots to water. But if you have a collection of many containers, you'll save a lot of time and energy by using a hose with a special attachment called a water breaker. The breaker provides a soft, steady flow that won't wash the soil out of the pots as you water. You can buy the breaker alone, or attached to a long-handled watering wand that lets you reach all of your pots and hanging baskets easily.

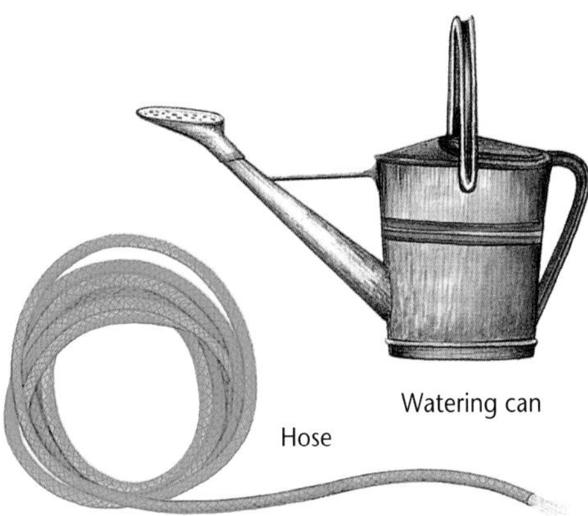

These wands usually come with a shut-off valve so you don't have to leave the hose running when you go to turn it on or shut it off—a very handy feature.

If you live in an apartment and don't have access to an outside faucet, you can buy special attachments for your kitchen faucet and special lightweight hoses that you can run from your kitchen out to your balcony or rooftop garden.

Reducing Watering Chores

Besides having the right equipment, there are also several things you can do to keep your watering chores to a minimum.

Use large pots. The bigger the pots you use, the less often you will need to water—since large pots dry out more slowly—and the better your container garden will look.

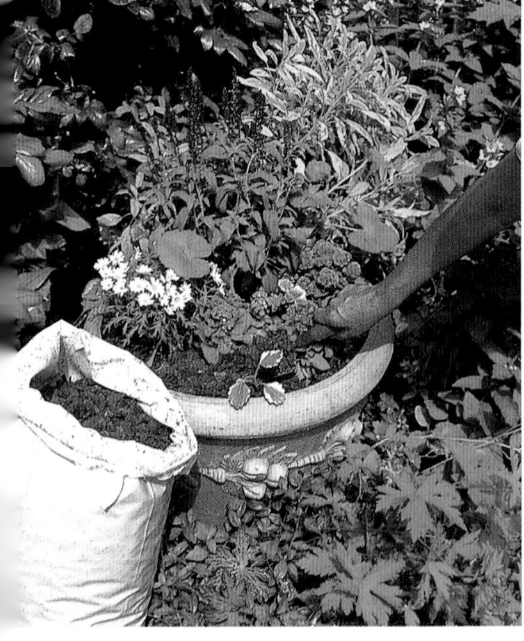

Covering exposed soil with mulch while plants are young keeps it from drying out as quickly.

Choose plastic or wood over clay. Clay pots dry out much faster than plastic or wood, so you may want to avoid using clay containers if you live in a hot, dry climate.

Arrange plants with similar watering needs into groups. This will make watering easier and reduce overall water loss.

Cover the soil with mulch. Mulching plants with shredded bark or grass clippings will help to reduce evaporation and keep moisture in the container mix.

Amend your container mix. Adding extra compost or vermiculite to the mix will help it hold more moisture. Or you may want to try the new synthetic water-absorbing polymers now on the market. These polymers aren't organic, but they are apparently nontoxic. You just combine the polymer granules with the container mix before planting, and the granules work by absorbing large amounts of water and holding it until the plant's roots need it.

Use a long-necked spout or wand if you are watering plants from the top. By doing this you can avoid splashing leaves and be able to direct water more carefully all over the surface of your container mix.

If you follow all of these tips and your plants are drying out so fast that they need watering twice a day, either move them to larger pots or prune them back to bring the top growth into better balance with the roots. (Pruning off older growth also helps to stimulate fresh new flowers on annuals and many perennials.)

Watering Wisdom

In general, you should not keep saucers under outdoor plants because they will fill up with water during rainstorms and could cause the soil to become waterlogged and the roots to rot. If you are concerned about pots leaving stains where they sit on your deck or patio, just set them up on small scraps of wood. (This is especially a good idea for large containers to ensure that water drains well from the bottom holes.)

There are two instances where it can be all right to put saucers under your outdoor plants. The first is when a plant should be moved to a bigger container and needs a little extra water until you have time to repot it. The other time you may want to use saucers is when you are going away for a day or two and want your plants to get by without extra watering. Water as normal and add some extra water to the saucers to sustain the plants; remove the saucers when you return.

Never water your plants with icy cold water, as it might shock the root system. It is safer to use tepid water.

Fungus and molds like cool, wet conditions. If you water in the mornings, you avoid leaving your plants wet all night and minimize fungal problems.

Shallow watering is no help, especially in hot conditions. Water deeply so that the entire soil mass is wet to encourage deeper root growth.

One soaking might not be enough for large pots. Wait until you see water running through the bottom of the pot.

A Quick Fix for Parched Plants

It's bound to happen—one day you accidentally skip a container while you're watering, and you come home the next day to find a pot of wilted plants. Before you throw the whole thing away, first try reviving the plants with a deep soaking.

Submerge the whole pot or basket in a large bucket or tub of water, and leave it there for an hour or two. Take it out and set or hang it in a cool, shady place for a day or two to see if the plants perk up. If they do revive, move the container back to its previous spot, and pay extra-careful attention to watering and fertilizing to help the plants make a full recovery.

Fertilizing Container Gardens

To keep your container plantings in great shape from spring through fall, you'll need to supply extra nutrients sometime during the growing season. You can choose from a variety of solid or liquid materials to fertilize your plants and flowers.

Choosing Fertilizers

Whether you should use organic or chemical fertilizers is a hot topic among gardeners. However, the choice you make has environmental implications that you might want to consider. Excess nitrogen and other chemical salts from inorganic fertilizers seep into groundwater and waterways, degrading the environment.

You can buy organic fertilizers, such as fish emulsion, bloodmeal, and bonemeal, at most local garden centers. Or you can combine these ingredients with wood ashes, coffee grounds, and other recyclable organic "wastes" to make your own organic fertilizer blends. See "A Sampler of Organic Fertilizers" on page 89 for more about organic fertilizers.

Whatever fertilizer you choose, be sure to read and thoroughly understand the instructions on labels and packaging so that you can apply just the right amount for the specific plants you are growing. If in any doubt, it is better to underfertilize plants. In fact, some experienced gardeners prefer to use fertilizer at half strength but twice as often.

A similar effect can be achieved by using slow-release fertilizers—chemical fertilizers that have been coated with a type of resin that breaks down and releases small doses of fertilizer over a longer period of time. Some gardeners mix in slow-release fertilizers at planting time and, for plants with limited nutrient needs, they may be enough to support the plant throughout its life. For other plants, further applications of liquid fertilizers throughout the growing season may still be needed.

Regular feedings with liquid fertilizer will keep annuals vigorous and blooming all season long.

Necessary Nutrients

Plants can't really tell the difference between an organic fertilizer and one made in a chemical factory. More important is the range of elements available to the plant and the balance between them. It may be a good idea to try out different fertilizers on various specimens of a plant, experimenting to find out which fertilizer produces the best results for you.

These days, chemical and many organic fertilizers will let you know the ratio of the most important elements plants need for healthy growth. The numbers represent the proportion by weight of the most important plant nutrients contained in the fertilizer: nitrogen (N), phosphorus (P), and potassium (K).

Nitrogen

Nitrogen is the most important element, since plants use it to build proteins, enzymes, chlorophyll, and hormones. Adequate nitrogen gives a plant healthy, green leaves and strong growth. Too little nitrogen results in a pale, slow-growing plant. Too much nitrogen can give you a plant that is very green and sappy, and attractive to pests and disease. Nitrogen is always on the move through the soil, atmosphere, and living things, and can be rapidly leached away in irrigation water. Therefore, it's the element most likely to be in short supply. Bloodmeal (12-1-1) can give your plants a quick jolt of nitrogen but you may prefer to use more balanced fertilizers such as fish emulsion (5-2-2) or cottonseed meal (7-2-2).

Organic fertilizers release nutrients slowly, promoting steady, healthy plant growth.

Phosphorus

Phosphorus is essential to the plant's metabolic processes, seed production, and root development. A phosphorus deficiency shows up as stunted growth, sometimes with a reddish or purplish cast to the leaves. Phosphorus becomes available to plants when there is plenty of water and organic matter, and the soil pH is close to neutral. Bonemeal (1-11-0) is the classic organic source for phosphorus.

Potassium

Potassium is necessary in fairly large quantities to regulate metabolic reactions within the plant, including photosynthesis. Some plants need potassium more than any other nutrient. A plant deficient in potassium might be soft and weak, and its leaf margins might appear scorched. There isn't much potassium in organic matter so if your plants need it, you should add granite dust or another rock powder.

Using Fertilizers

Meeting the nutrient needs of your container plants starts at planting time. Adding compost to commercial or homemade container mixes is one of the best things you can do to promote good root growth. Compost provides millions of live microorganisms, which feed on other organic fertilizers and make the nutrients available to your plants. (Organic fertilizers will still work in soils without compost, but they are much more effective with it.)

If you're growing annual flowers, herbs, and vegetables, mixing extra organic fertilizers into the compost-enriched soil is not really necessary. However, for long-term container plantings, such as perennials, shrubs, and trees, supplementing the container mix with kelp (seaweed) meal, greensand, and other organic nutrients will help ensure a steady supply of nutrients for the developing roots. "Making Your Own Container Mixes," on page 168, offers a recipe for a well-balanced, nutrient-enriched, deluxe growing medium that's great for the needs of these "permanent" plantings.

Once your plants are established, after a few weeks, it's time to start adding extra nutrients. Begin with a liquid fish product, using it at half the recommended strength every 2 weeks. Most fish fertilizers are higher in nitrogen than in potassium or phosphorus. This is fine until it's time for flowering plants to begin blooming. Then you may want to treat flowering plants to a handful of bonemeal (for extra phosphorus) and kelp meal or wood ashes (for plenty of potassium). Mix these materials with a little compost and scratch them into the soil surface.

You can keep feeding most container plants through late summer; after that, the cooler temperatures of fall will naturally slow their growth. For outdoor potted trees and shrubs, stop fertilizing by midsummer to give the new growth a chance to "harden up" before frost.

RIGHT: It is a good idea to add some compost to container perennials, shrubs, and trees every spring.

Successful Containers Start with Compost

Hopefully, you have enough space for a small compost pile. You just need an area that's at least 3 feet (90 cm) long, wide, and high. You can buy a commercial compost bin, build your own out of old pallets or chicken wire, or just heap the material in a pile. Good compost ingredients include most organic garden and kitchen wastes. Avoid oils, fats, and bones—all of which break down slowly and attract scavengers—and human and pet wastes, which carry diseases. Also avoid adding diseased or insect-infested materials.

Mix a balance of dry materials, such as leaves or shredded newspaper, with moist materials, such as grass clippings or vegetable peelings. The pile should feel damp but not soggy. If it's dry, add water; if it's too wet, mix in more dry material. Keep adding more materials as you gather them until the pile fills its space or bin. About once a week, use a pitchfork to turn over, or at least stir up, the mix. Eventually—after a few weeks or months—the original ingredients will break down into dark, crumbly compost. Before using the finished compost, sift it through ½-inch (12-mm) wire mesh to screen out any lumps that are left.

If you don't have the space for outdoor composting, try worm composting. You can keep worms in an indoor bin and feed them your food scraps to make a very rich compost. Several garden-supply catalogs offer bins, instructions, and even the worms themselves.

Of course, if you just need a little compost now and then, or if you need more than you can make, you can buy it in bags at your garden center. If your community has a composting program, you may also be able to get it at no charge from your local yard waste composting site.

If you want to turn your compost from a solid nutrient source into a quick-acting liquid fertilizer, make it into tea. Add one or two shovelfuls of compost (or farm manure) into a burlap or woven-mesh bag. Tie the bag securely and submerge it into a large bucket or barrel of water. Let it steep for 1 week, then remove the bag. Dilute the remaining liquid until it is the color of weak tea if you plan to spray or sprinkle it directly on your perennials, or use it full strength to drench the ground around the base of the plants.

Compost tea

The Right Container Plant for the Right Place

For successful container gardening, it is important to match plants with their preferred conditions. To help you make the best choices for the conditions you have, the following plant chart summarizes the specific needs of favorite flowering perennials, annuals, bulbs, groundcovers, trees, and shrubs. You can see at a glance exactly which plants prefer sun, and which prefer shade, and you can check if the plant will thrive in your particular climatic zone. In addition, the chart notes the main season of floral interest for the plant, as well as other useful comments to guide you in your plant choices.

Plant	Light Needs	Hardiness	Season of interest	Comments
PERENNIALS				
Woolly yarrow (*Achillea tomentosa*)	Full sun	Zones 3–7	Yellow flowers bloom from early to midsummer.	Ideal for low-maintenance containers.
Bicolor monkshood (*Aconitum* x *bicolor*)	Full sun to light shade	Zones 3–7	Dark blue or two-toned flowers bloom in summer and fall.	All parts of the plant are poisonous if ingested.
Azure monkshood (*Aconitum carmichaelii*)	Full sun to light shade	Zones 3–7	Blue flowers bloom in late summer and fall.	Dislikes disturbance once established.
White baneberry (*Actaea alba*)	Partial to full shade	Zones 3–9	Fuzzy white flowers bloom in spring; white berries occur in late summer to fall.	Plant in a large (2-foot/60-cm wide) container.
Ajuga (*Ajuga reptans*)	Full sun to partial shade	Zones 3–8	Blue or purple flowers bloom in spring or early summer.	Looks great growing under a Japanese maple (*Acer palmatum*).
Lady's-mantle (*Alchemilla mollis*)	Partial shade	Zones 3–9	Greenish-yellow flowers bloom in late spring.	Plant is especially pretty in a cool, moist, partly shady spot.
Peruvian lily (*Alstroemeria aurea*)	Full sun to partial shade	Zones 7–10	Orange or yellow flowers bloom throughout summer.	Achieves best performance after the third year.
Willow blue star (*Amsonia tabernaemontana*)	Full sun to partial shade	Zones 3–9	Blue flowers bloom in spring with some secondary shoots appearing in early summer.	Plant in a large (2-foot/60-cm wide) container.
Three-veined everlasting (*Anaphalis triplinervis*)	Full sun to partial shade	Zones 3–8	A profusion of white flowers in July, August, and September.	Flowers dry on the plant and last for weeks.
Italian bugloss (*Anchusa azurea*)	Full sun to light shade	Zones 3–8	Blue flowers bloom in late spring.	Plant in a large (2-foot/60-cm wide) container.
Grape-leaved anemone (*Anemone tomentosa* 'Robustissima')	Full sun to light shade	Zones 3–8	Pink flowers bloom in summer and fall.	Plant in a large (2-foot/60-cm wide) container.
Hybrid columbine (*Aquilegia* x *hybrida*)	Full sun to partial shade	Zones 3–9	Flowers of many colors, including yellow, red, purple, white, and pink, bloom in early summer.	In light shade, combine with wildflowers, ferns, and hostas in a large container.
Marguerite (*Argyranthemum frutescens*)	Full sun	Zones 7–10	White, pink, or yellow flowers bloom from spring to fall and in winter.	Plant in a large (2-foot/60-cm wide) container.
Thrift (*Armeria maritima*)	Full sun	Zones 4–8	Pink flowers bloom in spring and summer.	Drought-tolerant once established.

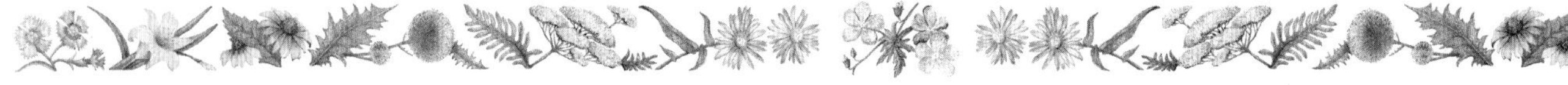

Plant	Light Needs	Hardiness	Season of interest	Comments
Butterfly weed (*Asclepias tuberosa*)	Full sun to light shade	Zones 3–9	Orange flowers bloom profusely in May and June.	The flowers attract butterflies.
Frikart's aster (*Aster* x *frikartii*)	Full sun to light shade	Zones 6–8	Lavender-blue flowers bloom from midsummer to fall.	Flowers are ideal for floral arrangements.
New England aster (*Aster novae-angliae*)	Full sun to light shade	Zones 3–8	The white, pink, rose, lavender and purple flowers bloom from summer through fall.	Plant in a large (2-foot/60-cm wide) container.
Astilbe (*Astilbe* x *arendsii*)	Full to partial shade	Zones 3–9	Red, pink, and white blooms in spring and early summer.	Pots may be placed in shallows of ponds during summer.
Dwarf Chinese astilbe (*Astilbe chinensis* var. *pumila*)	Partial shade	Zones 5–8	Pinkish-blue flowers bloom from mid- to late summer.	Flowers dry well and are good for winter arrangements.
Masterwort (*Astrantia major*)	Partial to full sun	Zones 6–9	Pink or white daisies bloom in early to late summer.	If plant is in full sun, ensure its roots are kept moist.
Rock cress (*Aubrieta deltoidea*)	Full sun to light shade	Zones 4–8	White, rose, or purple flowers bloom in early spring.	Ideal for hanging baskets or urns.
Basket-of-gold (*Aurinia saxatilis*)	Full sun	Zones 3–7	Brilliant yellow flowers bloom in early spring.	Avoid excessively hot and humid conditions.
Blue false indigo (*Baptisia australis*)	Full sun or partial shade	Zones 3–9	Deep blue flowers bloom in spring and early summer.	Plant in a large (2-foot/60-cm wide) container.
Heart-leaved bergenia (*Bergenia cordifolia*)	Partial shade	Zones 3–9	Pink, rose, or white flowers bloom in spring.	Avoid slug and snail damage by placing pot in a high place.
Siberian bugloss (*Brunnera macrophylla*)	Partial shade	Zones 3–8	Forget-me-not-blue flowers bloom in spring.	Plant in a large (2-foot/60-cm wide) container.
Carpathian harebell (*Campanula carpatica*)	Full sun to light shade	Zones 3–8	Blue-purple or white flowers bloom in early summer.	Looks great combined with yellow daylilies.
Dalmation bellflower (*Campanula portenschlagiana*)	Sun or partial shade	Zones 5–9	Blue-purple flowers bloom in spring and early summer.	Plant is ideal for window boxes or hanging baskets.
Cupid's dart (*Catananche caerulea*)	Full sun	Zones 4–9	Blue-purple flowers bloom in summer.	Plants may be short-lived in badly drained container mixes.
Knapweed (*Centaurea hypoleuca*)	Full sun	Zones 3–7	Pink flowers bloom in spring and early summer.	Remove faded flower heads to promote rebloom.
Red valerian (*Centranthus ruber*)	Full sun	Zones 4–8	Deep coral red flowers bloom in spring and summer.	Plants perform best in areas with dry summers.
Leadwort (*Ceratostigma plumbaginoides*)	Full sun to partial shade	Zones 5–9	Cobalt blue flowers appear from late summer until frost.	Plant in a large (2-foot/60-cm wide) container.
Pink turtlehead (*Chelone lyonii*)	Full sun to partial shade	Zones 3–8	Rosy pink flowers bloom from late summer into fall.	Plant in a large (2-foot/60-cm wide) container.
Lily-of-the-valley (*Convallaria majalis*)	Partial to full shade	Zones 2–8	Waxy, white flowers appear in spring.	Glossy, orange-red berries may appear in summer.

Plant	Light Needs	Hardiness	Season of interest	Comments
Hybrid delphinium (*Delphinium* x *elatum* hybrids)	Full sun	Zones 4–7	Flowers from white to true blue to lavender and purple appear in spring.	Plant in a large (2-foot/60-cm wide) container.
Garden mum (*Dendranthema* x *grandiflorum*)	Full sun to light shade	Zones 3–9	White, pink, red, gold, or yellow flowers bloom from summer through fall.	Plant in a large (2-foot/60-cm wide) container.
Cheddar pinks (*Dianthus gratianopolitanus*)	Full sun	Zones 3–9	White, rose, or pink flowers bloom from early to midsummer and often continue until frost.	Looks good cascading out of a hanging basket.
Cottage pinks (*Dianthus plumarius*)	Full sun	Zones 3–9	Fragrant white or pink flowers bloom from early to midsummer.	This sweet-scented plant is ideal for hanging baskets and window boxes.
Bleeding heart (*Dicentra spectabilis*)	Partial shade; full sun in Northern gardens	Zones 3–9	Pink flowers bloom in spring.	Combine with bulbs, primroses, and wildflowers for a spring display.
Leopard's bane (*Doronicum orientale*)	Full sun to shade	Zones 3–8	Bright yellow flowers bloom in spring and early summer.	Plant in a large (2-foot/60-cm wide) container.
Globe thistle (*Echinops ritro*)	Full sun	Zones 3–8	Steel-blue flowers bloom in midsummer.	Good drainage is essential, especially in winter.
Daisy fleabane (*Erigeron speciosus*)	Full sun or light shade	Zones 2–9	Flowers in white, pink, rose, or purple bloom in early to midsummer.	Hardy container plant.
Amethyst sea holly (*Eryngium amethystinum*)	Full sun	Zones 2–8	Steel-blue flowers bloom in summer.	Plant is extremely drought-tolerant once established.
Queen-of-the-prairie (*Filipendula rubra*)	Full sun to light shade	Zones 3–9	Peach-pink flowers bloom in late spring and early summer.	Plant in a large (2-foot/60-cm wide) container.
Blanket flower (*Gaillardia* x *grandiflora*)	Full sun	Zones 4–9	Yellow and orange flowers bloom throughout summer.	Drought-tolerant container plant.
Endres cranesbill (*Geranium endressi*)	Full sun to partial shade	Zones 4–8	Soft pink flowers bloom from early to midsummer.	The pale pink flowers become darker with age.
Baby's breath (*Gypsophila paniculata*)	Full sun to light shade	Zones 3–9	Masses of small, dainty, white flowers appear in summer.	Plant in a large (2-foot/60-cm wide) container.
Common sneezeweed (*Helenium autumnale*)	Full sun to light shade	Zones 3–8	Yellow flowers bloom in late summer and fall.	Plant in a large (2-foot/60-cm wide) container.
Lenten rose (*Helleborus* x *hybridus*)	Light to partial shade	Zones 4–8	Reddish purple, pink, or white flowers bloom from early winter through spring.	Established plants tolerate dry container mix and deep shade.
Daylilies (*Hemerocallis* hybrids)	Full sun to light shade	Zones 3–9	Orange, yellow, red, pink, buff, apricot, or green flowers appear from spring through summer.	Most modern hybrids need 8 hours of direct sunlight to flower well.
Coral bells (*Heuchera* spp.)	Full sun to light shade	Zones 3–8	White, red, purplish, or pink flowers bloom during summer.	Heat-tolerant container plant.

Plant	Light Needs	Hardiness	Season of interest	Comments
Hostas (*Hosta* hybrids)	Light to moderate shade	Zones 4–9	Purplish or white flowers appear in summer.	Avoid slug and snail damage by placing pot in a high place.
Perennial candytuft (*Iberis sempervirens*)	Full sun to light shade	Zones 3–9	White flowers bloom in early spring.	Shear after flowering to promote compact growth.
New Guinea impatiens (*Impatiens* New Guinea hybrids)	Full sun to filtered light	Zones 5–10	Orange, red, purple, lavender, or pink flowers bloom in summer.	Can bring pots indoors during winter.
Impatiens (*Impatiens wallerana*)	Partial to full shade	Zones 5–10	White, pink, red, orange, or lavender blooms from late spring until frost.	Good for window boxes and hanging baskets.
Crested iris (*Iris cristata*)	Partial shade	Zones 3–8	Lavender flowers bloom in midspring.	Looks great combined with ferns.
Shasta daisy (*Leucanthemum* x *superbum*)	Full sun	Zones 3–10	White flowers with bright yellow centers appear during summer.	Deadhead plants to promote continued bloom.
Spike gayfeather (*Liatris spicata*)	Full sun	Zones 3–9	Pinkish purple flowers bloom in midsummer.	Plants tend to flop in partial shade.
Creeping lilyturf (*Liriope spicata*)	Full sun to deep shade	Zones 5–10	Lavender to whitish flowers bloom mid- to late summer.	Drought-tolerant container plant.
Cardinal flower (*Lobelia cardinalis*)	Full sun to partial shade	Zones 2–9	Scarlet flowers bloom in late summer to fall.	Plant in a large (2-foot/60-cm wide) container.
Persian nepeta (*Nepeta mussinii*)	Full sun	Zones 3–8	Lavender-blue flowers bloom from spring to midsummer.	A relative of catnip, this plant may attract cats.
Showy sundrops (*Oenothera speciosa*)	Full sun to very light shade	Zones 3–8	White flowers bloom in summer.	Plant in a large (2-foot/60-cm wide) container.
Prickly pear (*Opuntia humifusa*)	Full sun	Zones 5–9	Yellow flowers with white stamens bloom in late spring or early summer.	Plant in a large (2-foot/60-cm wide) container.
Allegheny pachysandra (*Pachysandra procumbens*)	Partial to full shade	Zones 5–9	White or purplish flowers bloom in early spring.	Plant in a large (2-foot/60-cm wide) container.
Common garden peony (*Paeonia lactiflora*)	Full sun to light shade	Zones 2–8	Flowers from white, cream, and yellow to pink, rose, burgundy, and scarlet bloom from April to June.	Plant in a large (2-foot/60-cm wide) container.
Oriental poppy (*Papaver orientale*)	Full sun to light shade	Zones 2–7	Flowers in shades of pink through red bloom in summer.	Plant in a large (2-foot/60-cm wide) container.
Foxglove penstemon (*Penstemon digitalis*)	Full sun to light shade	Zones 4–8	White flowers with purple lines bloom from late spring to early summer.	Plant in a large (2-foot/60-cm wide) container.
Garden phlox (*Phlox paniculata*)	Full sun to light shade	Zones 3–8	Flowers of magenta to pink and white bloom from mid- to late summer.	Dense flower heads are fragrant and useful for cutting.

Plant	Light Needs	Hardiness	Season of interest	Comments
Obedient plant (*Physostegia virginiana*)	Full sun to light shade	Zones 3–9	Rose pink to lilac-pink flowers bloom in late summer.	Plant in a large (2-foot/60-cm wide) container.
Balloon flower (*Platycodon grandiflorus*)	Full sun to light shade	Zones 3–8	Rich blue flowers appear in summer.	Established plants are drought-tolerant.
Fragrant Solomon's seal (*Polygonatum odoratum*)	Partial to full shade	Zones 3–9	Pale green flowers in spring. Blue-black fruits in summer.	Plant in a large (2-foot/60-cm wide) container.
Japanese primrose (*Primula japonica*)	Light shade	Zones 4–8	Cultivars flower in pink, rose, red, purple, and white in late spring to early summer.	Place containers near the edges of ponds.
Polyanthus primrose (*Primula* x *polyantha*)	Light to partial shade	Zones 3–8	Flowers vary from white, cream, and yellow to pink, rose, red, and purple in spring and early summer.	Good hanging basket plant.
English primrose (*Primula vulgaris*)	Light to partial shade	Zones 4–8	Pale yellow flowers bloom in spring and early summer.	Plants may go dormant if container mix dries out in summer.
Pasque flower (*Pulsatilla vulgaris*)	Full sun to light shade	Zones 3–8	Purple flowers with yellow centers bloom from early to midspring.	Plant does not tolerate a soggy container mix.
Orange coneflower (*Rudbeckia fulgida*)	Full sun	Zones 3–9	Gold flowers with dark central cones bloom during summer and fall.	Drought-tolerant container plant.
Violet sage (*Salvia* x *superba*)	Full sun to light shade	Zones 4–7	Violet-blue flowers appear in early to midsummer.	Drought-tolerant container plant.
Pincushion flower (*Scabiosa caucasica*)	Full sun to light shade	Zones 3–7	Flowers in pink, red, purple, or blue hues bloom in summer.	Plants are sensitive to high temperatures.
Sedum (*Sedum spectabile*)	Full sun	Zones 3–9	Small bright pink flowers bloom in mid- to late summer.	Plant is extremely drought-tolerant.
Dusty miller (*Senecio cineraria*)	Semi-shade	Zones 7–9	Yellow flowers bloom in summer.	The silvery foliage looks good at night.
Solomon's plume (*Smilacina racemosa*)	Light to full shade	Zones 3–8	White flowers bloom in late spring.	Grow in a large (2-foot/60-cm wide) container.
Lamb's-ears (*Stachys byzantina*)	Full sun to light shade	Zones 4–8	Rose-pink flowers bloom in spring.	The silvery foliage looks good at night.
Stoke's aster (*Stokesia laevis*)	Full sun to light shade	Zones 5–9	Blue flowers bloom in summer.	Established plants tolerate dry conditions.
Allegheny foamflower (*Tiarella cordifolia*)	Light shade	Zones 3–8	White flowers bloom in midspring.	Ideal container plant for shady gardens.
Common spiderwort (*Tradescantia* x *andersoniana*)	Full sun to partial shade	Zones 3–9	Blue, purple, or white flowers appear in spring and summer.	Plants in dry containers go dormant in summer.
Great merrybells (*Uvularia grandiflora*)	Partial to full shade	Zones 3–8	Lemon-yellow flowers bloom in spring.	Spring sun is important for bloom, but plant needs summer sun.

Plant	Light Needs	Hardiness	Season of interest	Comments
Nettle-leaved mullein (*Verbascum chaixii*)	Full sun to light shade	Zones 4–8	Yellow flowers bloom in summer.	Plant in a large (2-foot/60-cm wide) container.
Spike speedwell (*Veronica spicata*)	Full sun to light shade	Zones 3–8	Pink, blue, or white flowers bloom in summer.	Plant in a large (2-foot/60-cm wide) container.
Sweet violet (*Viola odorata*)	Sun or shade	Zones 6–9	Purple flowers bloom in spring.	Perfume is sweet and quite strong.
ANNUALS				
Ageratum (*Ageratum houstonianum*)	Full or half-day sun	Zones 5–10	Lavender, blue, pink, or white flowers from early summer until frost.	Protect plant from hot midday sun.
Love-lies-bleeding (*Amaranthus caudatus*)	Full sun	Zones 6–10	Crimson flowers bloom from midsummer until frost.	Grow in a very large container, such as a half-barrel.
Snapdragon (*Antirrhinum majus*)	Full sun to light shade	Zones 6–10	Flowers bloom in wide range of colors, except true blue, in late summer.	Remove spent flower spikes to promote more flowers.
Wax begonia (*Begonia* Semperflorens-Cultorum hybrids)	Half-day of sun with shade in hottest hours	Zones 5–10	Small white, pink, or red flowers bloom from spring to fall.	Can bring pots indoors for winter.
Hybrid tuberous begonias (*Begonia* Tuberhybrida hybrids)	Half-day of sun or filtered sun	Zones 6–10	Flowers in all colors except blue bloom from summer until frost.	Reduce watering in fall and bring pots indoors before or just after the first frost.
English daisy (*Bellis perennis*)	Full sun to partial shade	Zones 3–9	White, pink, or red flowers bloom from April to June.	Looks great combined with forget-me-nots and spring bulbs.
Swan River daisy (*Brachyscome iberidifolia*)	Full sun	Zones 6–10	Blue, white or rose-colored flowers bloom from spring.	Excellent hanging basket plant.
Strawflower (*Bracteantha bracteatum*)	Full sun	Zones 5–10	White, pink, rose, orange, red, or yellow flowers from midsummer until frost.	The long-lasting flowers are ideal for drying.
Ornamental cabbage (*Brassica oleracea*)	Full sun to light shade	Zones 6–9	Leaves are marked with pink, purple, cream, or white in fall.	Looks good in window boxes.
Browallia (*Browallia speciosa*)	Full to filtered sun	Zones 6–9	White, blue, or lilac flowers bloom from summer.	Ideal for window boxes and baskets in partial shade.
Pot marigold (*Calendula officinalis*)	Full sun	Zones 4–9	Orange and yellow flowers bloom from summer to fall.	Flowers tend to close during cloudy weather and at night.
China aster (*Callistephus chinensis*)	Full sun	Zones 4–9	White, cream, pink, red, purple, or blue flowers bloom from late summer to frost.	Renew mix and change pot each year to minimize disease.
Madasgar periwinkle (*Catharanthus roseus*)	Full sun	Zones 5–10	White, rose, or pink flowers bloom throughout the year.	Tolerates heat, pollution, and drought.
Celosia (*Celosia cristata*)	Full sun	Zones 5–10	Flowers of red, pink, orange, or yellow bloom all summer.	Tricky to get started, but easy once plant is established.

Plant	Light Needs	Hardiness	Season of interest	Comments
Cornflower (*Centaurea cyanus*)	Full sun	Zones 5–9	White, blue, pink, purple, or red flowers bloom in summer.	Pinching off spent blooms can prolong the flowering season.
Cleome (*Cleome hasslerana*)	Full sun to light shade	Zones 4–10	White, pink, or lavender flowers from midsummer to midfall.	Plant in a large (2-foot/60-cm wide) container.
Rocket larkspur (*Consolida ambigua*)	Full sun	Zones 4–9	Purple-blue, rose, pink, or white flowers bloom from late spring through summer.	The spiky blooms make great cut flowers.
Dwarf morning glory (*Convolvulus tricolor*)	Full sun	Zones 5–10	Blue flowers with a yellow throat and a white central band bloom all summer.	Great for hanging baskets.
Coreopsis (*Coreopsis tinctoria*)	Full sun	Zones 6–10	Yellow flowers with maroon centers, plain yellow, or orange flowers bloom from midsummer until frost.	Cutting plants back by one third in summer can prolong flowering.
Cosmos (*Cosmos bipinnatus*)	Full sun to partial shade	Zones 4–10	White, pink, or red flowers bloom from late summer through fall.	Remove spent flowers to encourage more blooms.
Yellow cosmos (*Cosmos sulphureus*)	Full sun	Zones 4–10	Yellow, orange, or red blooms appear from late summer until frost.	Seed can be collected from mature flowers at the end of the season.
Sweet William (*Dianthus barbatus*)	Full sun to partial shade	Zones 6–9	Red, pink, or white flowers bloom from early to midsummer.	Start new plants each year for the best results.
China pink (*Dianthus chinensis*)	Full sun	Zones 6–9	White, pink, or red flowers appear through summer.	Fragrant container plant.
Wallflower (*Erysimum cheiri*)	Full sun to partial shade	Zones 6–9	Red, pink, or creamy white flowers bloom from midspring to early summer.	Fragrant container plant.
California poppy (*Eschscholzia californica*)	Full sun	Zones 6–10	Orange, yellow, white, pink, or red flowers appear from summer to fall.	Pinch off developing seedpods to prolong bloom.
Snow-on-the-mountain (*Euphorbia marginata*)	Full sun	Zones 6–9	Tiny flowers with white bracts appear in summer.	Cut stems leak a milky sap that can irritate mouth, eyes, and skin.
Prairie gentian (*Eustoma grandiflorum*)	Full sun to partial shade	Zones 6–9	White, cream, rose, and purple-blue blooms appear in summer.	Bring pot indoors for winter.
Blanket flower (*Gaillardia pulchella*)	Full sun	Zones 5–9	Red, yellow, or orange flowers bloom in summer.	Plant is heat- and drought-tolerant.
Treasure flower (*Gazania rigens*)	Full sun	Zones 6–10	The mainly red, orange, or yellow blooms appear from midsummer until frost.	For winter bloom, bring plants indoors before frost.

Plant	Light Needs	Hardiness	Season of interest	Comments
Globe amaranth (*Gomphrena globosa*)	Full sun	Zones 6–10	Magenta, pink, or white flowers from midsummer until frost.	Compact cultivars are best suited to container culture.
Licorice plant (*Helichrysum petiolatum*)	Full sun	Zones 6–10	Yellow-white flowers bloom in spring.	Great for window boxes and hanging baskets.
Annual candytuft (*Iberis umbellata*)	Full sun to partial shade	Zones 5–9	White, pink, pinkish-purple, rose, or red flowers appear from spring through midsummer.	In hot-summer areas, pull out plants after bloom.
Garden balsam (*Impatiens balsamina*)	Full sun to partial shade	Zones 5–10	White, pink, purple, rose, or red flowers appear from midsummer until frost.	Good container plants for shady areas.
Sweet pea (*Lathyrus odoratus*)	Full sun	Zones 6–10	Flowers in white, pink, red, or purple bloom from midspring into summer.	Provide a tepee of bamboo stakes for plant to climb on. Looks good in a hanging basket.
Annual statice (*Limonium sinuatum*)	Full sun	Zones 6–10	Flowers in white, pink, peach, red, orange, yellow, purple, and blue bloom in summer and early fall.	Flowers are pretty in dried or fresh arrangements.
Edging lobelia (*Lobelia erinus*)	Partial to full sun	Zones 5–10	Blue, violet, pink, or white flowers appear in summer.	Looks good in strawberry jar planters.
Sweet alyssum (*Lobularia maritima*)	Full sun	Zones 5–9	White, pink, or purple flowers appear from summer to fall.	Great for edging large containers.
Honesty (*Lunaria annua*)	Partial shade	Zones 7–10	Purple-pink flowers bloom in spring and early summer; followed by silvery seedpods.	Blooms are lightly fragrant.
Virginia stock (*Malcomia maritima*)	Full sun to partial shade	Zones 6–10	Purple, pink, or white flowers appear from midsummer until frost.	Ideal for window boxes.
Common stock (*Matthiola incana*)	Full sun	Zones 6–9	White, pink, red, yellow, or purple flowers appear in summer.	Fragrant container plant.
Monkey flower (*Mimulus* x *hybridus*)	Partial shade	Zones 5–9	Orange, yellow, or red blooms appear in summer.	Bring containers indoors to overwinter.
Four-o'clock (*Mirabilis jalapa*)	Full sun to partial shade	Zones 6–10	Flowers in white or shades of pink, magenta, red, and yellow appear from midsummer until frost.	Fragrant container plant. Flowers open in the late afternoon.
Forget-me-not (*Myosotis sylvatica*)	Partial shade to a half-day of sun	Zones 5–9	The tiny blue or pink, white-centered flowers bloom from May to June.	Can bloom in the first year if started early indoors.
Baby-blue-eyes (*Nemophila menziesii*)	Full sun to partial shade	Zones 5–9	Sky blue flowers with a white center bloom in summer.	Looks great trailing out of pots and planters.

Plant	Light Needs	Hardiness	Season of interest	Comments
Flowering tobacco (*Nicotiana* spp.)	Partial shade to full sun	Zones 6–10	White, pink, or red flowers bloom from summer until frost.	Plant in large (2-foot/60-cm wide) container.
Love-in-a-mist (*Nigella damascena*)	Full sun to partial shade	Zones 5–9	Blue, pink, or white flowers bloom in summer.	Established plants are care-free.
Iceland poppy (*Papaver nudicaule*)	Full sun	Zones 2–10	White, pink, red, orange, or yellow flowers bloom in early to midsummer.	Easiest to grow from seed sown directly into the container.
Corn poppy (*Papaver rhoeas*)	Full sun	Zones 4–9	Scarlet, red, white, pink, and bicolor flowers bloom during summer.	Remove spent blooms to extend the flowering season.
Petunia (*Petunia* x *hybrida*)	Full sun; tolerates half-day sun	Zones 6–10	Red, salmon, pink, deep purple, blue, yellow, orange cream, or white blooms appear from early summer.	Ideal for hanging baskets and window boxes.
Annual phlox (*Phlox drummondii*)	Full sun	Zones 6–10	Flowers of various colors, some with a contrasting eye, bloom from midsummer.	If plant stops flowering, cut back by half and water thoroughly.
Rose moss (*Portulaca grandiflora*)	Full sun	Zones 6–10	White, pink, red, orange, yellow, and magenta flowers bloom in summer and fall.	Ideal for hot, dry spots.
Black-eyed Susan (*Rudbeckia hirta*)	Full sun to light shade	Zones 3–10	Golden-yellow flowers bloom from summer into fall.	Flowers are excellent in fresh arrangements.
Mealy-cup sage (*Salvia farinacea*)	Full sun	Zones 6–9	Purple-blue flowers bloom from midsummer until frost.	Too much shade will lead to spindly growth and poor flowers.
Scarlet sage (*Salvia splendens*)	Full sun	Zones 6–10	Mostly red flowers bloom from early summer until frost.	Tall types bloom longer than dwarf cultivars.
Creeping zinnia (*Sanvitalia procumbens*)	Full sun	Zones 5–10	Yellow or orange flowers bloom from midsummer until frost.	Ideal for hanging baskets.
Coleus (*Solenostemon scutellarioides*)	High, indirect light to moderate shade	Zones 8–10	Pale blue flowers appear from late spring to early summer.	Dwarf types are ideal for window box culture.
Marigolds (*Tagetes* spp.)	Full sun to a half-day of sun	Zones 5–10	Yellow, orange, gold, cream, brown, or maroon blooms appear in summer.	Pinching off spent flowers prolongs bloom season.
Feverfew (*Tanacetum parthenium*)	Full sun to partial shade	Zones 4–9	White or yellow flowers bloom in early to midsummer.	Removing spent flower stalks will promote new leafy growth.
Mexican sunflower (*Tithonia rotundifolia*)	Full sun	Zones 5–10	Glowing orange flowers bloom in early summer.	Plant in a large (2-foot/60-cm wide container).
Wishbone flower (*Torenia fournieri*)	Partial shade	Zones 6–9	Purplish-blue flowers with a yellow throat bloom from summer to fall.	Bring pots indoors to enjoy the blooms during winter.

Plant	Light Needs	Hardiness	Season of interest	Comments
Nasturtium (*Tropaeolum majus*)	Full sun	Zones 5–9	Flowers in a range of colors appear from early summer through fall.	Tends to grow poorly in hot-summer areas.
Large periwinkle (*Vinca major*)	Light shade	Zones 5–9	Brilliant violet flowers bloom in spring.	Ideal for hanging baskets and window boxes.
Pansy (*Viola* x *wittrockiana*)	Partial shade	Zones 5–9	Pink, red, orange, yellow, blue, purple, and near-black flowers bloom in spring and fall.	Plants do not like hot weather.
Zinnia (*Zinnia* spp.)	Full sun	Zones 5–10	Flowers of nearly every color, except true blue, bloom from midsummer to frost.	Fertilize monthly and pinch off spent blooms.
Bulbs				
Star of Persia (*Allium christophii*)	Full sun	Zones 4–8	Metallic, lilac-pink flowers bloom in summer.	Striking in a container with tall ornamental grasses and sedums.
Grecian windflower (*Anemone blanda*)	Full sun to partial shade	Zones 5–8	Blue, pink, or white flowers bloom in mid- to late spring.	Ideal for window boxes.
Italian arum (*Arum italicum*)	Partial shade	Zones 6–10	Greenish-yellow flowers bloom in mid- to late spring.	Columns of reddish-orange berries appear in fall.
Showy autumn crocus (*Colchicum speciosum*)	Full sun to partial shade	Zones 4–9	Pink flowers bloom in late summer to early fall.	Corms may bloom before planting if planting is delayed.
Crocosmia (*Crocosmia* x *crocosmiiflora*)	Full sun	Zones 6–9	Red or orange flowers bloom in summer and early fall.	Foliage resembles that of gladiolus.
Hardy cyclamen (*Cyclamen hederifolium*)	Partial shade	Zones 5–9	Pink or white flowers bloom in early fall.	Grows well in containers placed under trees and shrubs.
Dahlias (*Dahlia* hybrids)	Partial to full sun	Zones 9–10	Red, orange, pink, purple, white, and yellow flowers bloom from midsummer through fall.	The dwarf cultivars are best for container gardening.
Crown imperial (*Fritillaria imperalis*)	Full sun	Zones 5–9	Yellow, orange, or red blooms appear in mid- to late spring.	Plant has a musky (skunk-like) odor.
Checkered lily (*Fritillaria meleagris*)	Partial shade	Zones 3–8	Flowers from white to deep purple bloom in spring.	Combine with daffodils for a pretty feature.
Common snowdrop (*Galanthus nivalis*)	Full sun to partial shade	Zones 3–9	White flowers bloom in late winter and early spring.	Established bulbs are trouble-free.
Spanish bluebells (*Hyacinthoides hispanica*)	Full sun to partial shade	Zones 4–8	White, pink, and purple-blue flowers bloom in spring.	One of the easiest of all spring bulbs to grow in containers.
Hyacinth (*Hyacinthus orientalis*)	Full sun	Zones 4–8	White, pink, red, orange, yellow, blue, and purple flowers bloom in spring.	Suitable for winter forcing indoors.
Reticulated iris (*Iris reticulata*)	Full sun	Zones 5–9	Blue, purple, or white flowers bloom in early spring.	Suitable for winter forcing indoors.

Plant	Light Needs	Hardiness	Season of interest	Comments
Siberian iris (*Iris sibirica*)	Full sun to partial shade	Zones 3–9	Summer flowers range from pure white to purple.	Head- and cold-tolerant.
Summer snowflake (*Leucojum aestivum*)	Full sun to partial shade	Zones 4–9	White flowers bloom in mid- to late spring.	Interplant with summer- and fall-blooming annuals.
Lilies (*Lilium* hybrids)	Full sun to partial shade	Zones 4–8	Lilies bloom in early summer in a huge variety of colors.	Dwarf hybrids are best for smaller containers.
Grape hyacinth (*Muscari armeniacum*)	Full sun to light shade	Zones 3–10	Purple-blue, white-rimmed flowers bloom in early spring.	Allow foliage to turn yellow before storing the pot, dry, over summer.
Daffodils (*Narcissus* hybrids)	Full sun to partial shade	Zones 4–8	The mostly yellow or white flowers bloom in spring.	For the best display, grow daffodils in a pot for a single season only.
Siberian squill (*Scilla sibirica*)	Full sun to partial shade	Zones 3–8	Deep blue flowers bloom in spring.	Established bulbs are trouble-free.
Tulips (*Tulipa* hybrids)	Full sun to partial shade	Zones 3–8	Flowers in orange, pink, purple, red, white, green, and yellow bloom in spring.	For a great display every year, plant new bulbs each fall.
Kaufmanniana tulip (*Tulipa kaufmanniana*)	Full sun to light shade	Zones 4–8	Pink, yellow, red, and white flowers bloom in early spring.	Can withstand considerable drought and shade.
GROUNDCOVERS				
Wall rock cress (*Arabis caucasica*)	Full sun	Zones 3–7	White flowers bloom in spring.	Plant smothered in clusters of fragrant flowers.
Mountain sandwort (*Arenaria montana*)	Full sun	Zones 4–8	White flowers with a yellow eye bloom in spring and early summer.	Ideal for trough culture.
Snow-in-summer (*Cerastium tomentosum*)	Full sun	Zones 2–7	White flowers bloom in spring and early summer.	Looks good in a hanging basket.
Hardy iceplant (*Delosperma cooperi*)	Full sun	Zones 7–9	Rosy purple flowers bloom from summer until frost.	Looks good cascading from hanging baskets and urns.
Sun rose (*Helianthemum nummularium*)	Full sun	Zones 6–8	Yellow, pink, or white flowers bloom in late spring and early summer.	Plant blooms for many weeks, although each flower lasts for only one day.
Yellow archangel (*Lamium galeobdolon*)	Partial to full shade	Zones 4–9	Yellow flowers bloom in late spring.	Ideal for hanging baskets.
Spotted lamium (*Lamium maculatum*)	Partial to full shade	Zones 3–8	Lavender-pink flowers bloom throughout summer.	Perfect for low-maintenance containers and hanging baskets.
Creeping Jenny (*Lysimachia nummularia*)	Full sun to full shade	Zones 3–8	Yellow flowers bloom throughout summer.	Grow in window boxes or hanging baskets.
Mazus (*Mazus reptans*)	Full sun to partial shade	Zones 5–8	Light blue-violet flowers bloom in spring and summer.	Ideal for a shallow container or trough.
Blue-eyed Mary (*Omphalodes verna*)	Partial shade	Zones 5–8	Lavender-blue flowers bloom in spring.	Mulch in hot climates to prolong bloom period.

Plant	Light Needs	Hardiness	Season of interest	Comments
Creeping phlox (*Phlox stolonifera*)	Partial to full shade	Zones 2–8	Lavender, pink, blue, or white flowers bloom in late spring.	Purple cultivars look good combined with yellow primroses.
Bethlehem sage (*Pulmonaria saccharata*)	Partial to full shade	Zones 3–8	Pink to medium blue flowers bloom in spring.	Foliage remains attractive all season unless in a dry mix.
Rock soapwort (*Saponaria ocymoides*)	Full sun	Zones 4–10	Bright pink flowers bloom in early to midsummer.	May be grown in a hanging basket.
Two-row stonecrop (*Sedum spurium*)	Light to partial shade	Zones 3–8	Flat, pink clusters of flowers appear in midsummer.	A tough, durable spreader for dry containers or hanging baskets.
Hens-and-chickens (*Sempervirum tectorum*)	Full sun	Zones 5–9	Small, purple-red, aster-like flowers bloom in summer.	Low-maintenance container plant.
Mother-of-thyme (*Thymus serpyllum*)	Full sun	Zones 4–7	Rose-purple flowers bloom in summer.	Combine in shallow containers with succulents.
Rock speedwell (*Veronica prostrata*)	Full sun	Zones 4–8	Deep blue flowers bloom in late spring.	Perfect for containers in sunny courtyards.
Barren strawberry (*Waldsteinia fragarioides*)	Partial shade	Zones 5–8	Yellow flowers bloom in late spring.	Grow in hanging baskets.
TREES AND SHRUBS				
Glossy abelia (*Abelia* x *grandiflora*)	Full sun	Zones 6–10	Pinkish-purple or white flowers in late spring to early summer.	Flowers are lightly fragrant.
Boxwood (*Buxus sempervirens*)	Full sun to partial shade	Zones 6–10	Tiny, pale green blooms appear in early spring.	Easy to clip into a variety of topiary shapes.
Heather (*Calluna vulgaris*)	Full sun to partial shade	Zones 5–7	Tiny, pinkish flowers bloom from late summer to fall.	Plant different cultivars together in a large container.
Camellia (*Camellia japonica*)	Partial shade	Zones 8–10	White, pink, or red flowers bloom in winter.	Plant in a large (2-foot/60-cm wide) container.
Sasanqua camellia (*Camellia sasanqua*)	Full sun	Zones 7–9	Pink, red, white, or lavender flowers bloom in fall.	Cultivars range from small sizes for hanging baskets to large types for tubs.
Hybrid bluebeard (*Caryopteris* x *clandonensis*)	Full sun	Zones 5–9	Purple-blue flowers bloom in mid- to late summer.	Ideal in a sheltered position near a sunny wall.
Smoke tree (*Cotinus coggygria*)	Full sun	Zones 5–9	Pink, purple, or gray plumes from midsummer to fall.	Water frequently until plants are established.
Rose daphne (*Daphne cneorum*)	Full sun	Zones 4–9	Pink flowers bloom in late spring, and sometimes in fall.	Keep container raised on feet to ensure good drainage.
Slender deutzia (*Deutzia gracilis*)	Full sun	Zones 5–9	White flowers bloom in late spring or early summer.	Prefers a moist, semi-shaded site, away from drying winds.
Fuchsia (*Fuchsia* x *hybrida*)	Filtered light	Zone 7	White, red, pink with violet, or purple flowers bloom in summer	Best planted alone in hanging baskets. Place away from winds.
Common gardenia (*Gardenia augusta*)	Partial shade	Zones 8–10	White flowers bloom in early to midsummer.	The creamy-white flowers are extremely fragrant.

SECTION EIGHT

Houseplants

Indoor plants depend on us to meet all their needs—adequate light, a suitable temperature range and level of humidity, and the right amount of water and nutrients. However, you can easily achieve good results if you select your plants wisely and take a little time to understand their basic requirements, as well as ensure you establish a routine to provide the necessary care and conditions.

Houseplants at First Glance *208*

Caring for Houseplants *214*

Troubleshooting Houseplants *222*

Houseplants in Your Home *226*

Growing Plants Indoors *230*

Creative Houseplant Displays *234*

The Right Houseplant for the Right Place *238*

Houseplants at First Glance

Most common houseplants are truly easy to grow if you understand their basic needs for light, water, and fertilizer. Even the blackest thumb can grow a drought-tolerant jade plant or ponytail palm. But why settle for just the most common, easiest plants when there is a wonderful world of colorful flowers, sparkling variegated leaves, dramatic cacti, and exotic orchids waiting for you to explore? Whatever time and skills you have and whatever the conditions in your home, there are dozens of beautiful houseplants that you can grow!

You need to start off by learning how to choose the right plants to suit the conditions in your home, as explained in "Buying the Best Plants" below. Once you bring your plants home, giving them the right amount of light is probably the single biggest key to keeping them healthy and happy. "Provide the Right Light" on page 210 will help you to understand how to estimate how much light each location receives, so you can pick the ideal location for each plant.

Many houseplants can grow just fine in the temperatures and humidity levels found in the average home, but some need special treatment. If you choose a fern that needs high humidity, for example, there are special techniques you can use to give it a more humid environment. "Humidity and Temperature" on page 212 will tell you what you need to know about these important factors.

Plant-shopping Guidelines

When you're looking for just the right plant for a particular spot, remember to keep these key points in mind:

- Decide where you want the new plant to grow and estimate the light level available in that location.
- Browse through the individual plant entries, starting on page 306, and make a list of plants you like that have light requirements that match the conditions you can provide. (Or you can check the tags on the plants as you shop to see if the ones you like can take the conditions you can offer.)
- Shop around for the best color and size selection and prices.
- Choose a well-shaped plant. When buying a flowering houseplant, also look for one that has plenty of buds, with just a few flowers beginning to open.
- Be sure there are no signs of insect or disease problems before you buy. You don't want to take home any problems that could spread to your other plants!

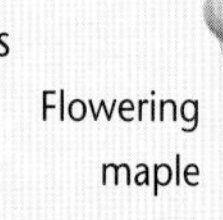

Flowering maple

Buying the Best Plants

Let's face it. If you're out shopping, you see a houseplant you like, and the price is right, you're probably going to bring it home. It may not be the best way to get the perfect plant to match the conditions in your home, but most of the time it works out just fine. Check the plant tag, or look up the plant in "Encyclopedia of Flowers," starting on page 306; then find a site in your home that can provide the right growing conditions.

If, on the other hand, you want a plant that will thrive in a particular location, you need to be more careful to choose just the right one. A little advance planning is especially helpful if you intend to buy a large (and therefore more expensive) plant.

Estimate the Light

Your first step in buying the right plant is to consider how much light is available in the location you've chosen. Unless you're planning to place the plant directly in front of a large south, east, or west window, you should avoid buying houseplants that need bright light or direct sun. Instead, stick with those that only need medium light. Flowering plants require more light than plants grown only for their attractive foliage, so if you're expecting flowers, it's especially important to be sure the plant gets enough light. If you have to place a plant well away from the windows, try to select one that can tolerate low light levels. (For details on estimating light levels, see "Provide the Right Light" on page 210.)

LEFT: When shopping for plants it is important to select plants that suit the conditions in your home. BELOW: It helps to combine houseplants that have similar light and watering requirements.

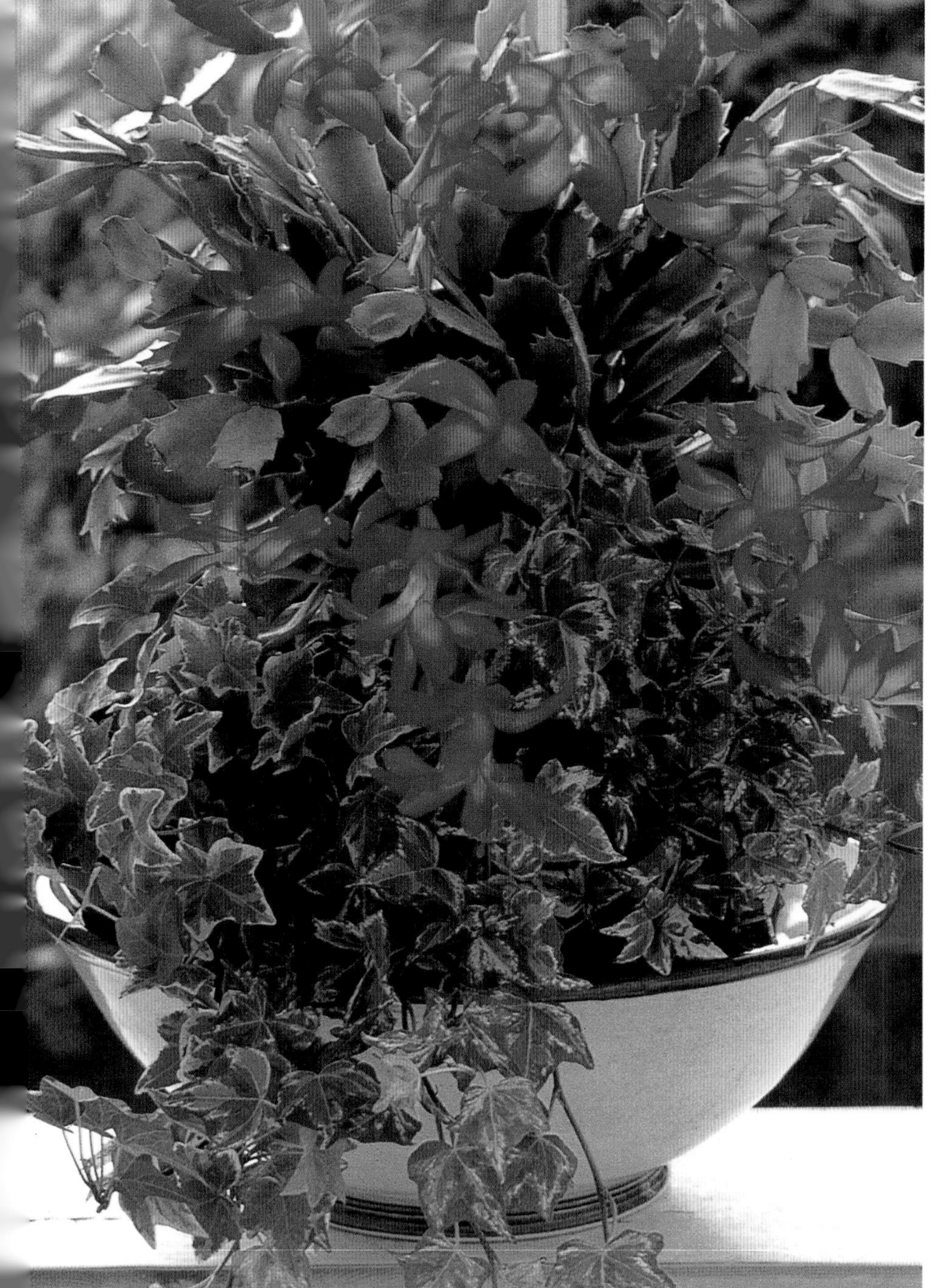

Do a Little Research

Once you've estimated the light levels available in the location you've chosen, turn to "The Right Houseplant for the Right Place" on page 238, and make a list of plants suitable for your chosen location Look up each of the plants listed in "Encyclopedia of Flowers," starting on page 306, and use the color photographs to help you decide which plants are most suitable for your needs. Jot down the names of your favorites.

Now that you know what you're looking for, you can shop around a little. Prices can vary a lot, especially for large plants, so it's worth investigating several sources; check out the garden centers, florists, and grocery stores in your area. Talk to the employees and find someone who can help you make a good plant selection.

When you've decided exactly which kind of plant you're going to buy and where you're going to buy it, look over all the plants of that type that the seller offers. Some plants will have a nicer overall shape than others; look for those that you find most appealing. Once you decide which plant you want, inspect it closely for any signs of insect or disease problems before you take it home. (For specific tips on identifying common problems, see "Handling Pests and Diseases" on page 222.)

Consider Flowering Habits

If you're buying a flowering plant, there are some factors to consider. First of all, be aware that many flowering houseplants are grown under special controlled conditions in commercial greenhouses and are not likely to rebloom for you next year unless you have a greenhouse or can give them special care. Some, such as Persian violet (*Exacum affine*), are actually annuals that won't live more than a year or so, even with the best care.

Even though they can be relatively short-lived, flowering plants are still a good choice for brightening up indoor spaces. Live flowering plants will last at least two to three times longer than cut flowers, and some—including florist's cyclamen (*Cyclamen persicum*), orchids, and African violets (*Saintpaulia* hybrids)—will bloom nonstop for many months. So go ahead and feel confident to bring flowering plants home to enjoy; just don't feel like it's your fault if they don't bloom again next year.

When you are choosing a flowering houseplant, always try to pick one that has lots of buds, with just a few already open. That way you'll get the maximum bloom time as the unopened buds bloom over the next several weeks.

Provide the Right Light

When you're growing plants indoors, light is the factor you need to consider most carefully. Indoor light—whether it comes from sunlight coming in through the windows or from artificial electric lights—is nowhere near as bright as the sunlight that plants receive when they're growing outdoors. The light in a room may seem almost as bright as sunlight, but in reality it's usually only about one-tenth as bright. (The brightness seems similar to us because the pupils in our eyes open wider to make the dim light appear brighter.)

Entrance halls look welcoming if decorated with plants. However, they are often low in light. Plan your displays using the most tolerant houseplants.

Healthy Plant Checklist

In the fun and frenzy of spring plant shopping, it's easy to overlook quality in the quest for getting the "perfect" plant. But as you choose, keep in mind that bringing home a stressed, diseased, or pest-infested plant is a recipe for disappointing results. Before you pay for your purchases, take a minute to check them over carefully—following the points here—to make sure you're getting the best plants possible.

1. **Peruse the plant.** It should be similar in size and color to other plants of the same type. Avoid plants that seem stunted or off-color.
2. **Look at the leaves.** Avoid plants that have yellowed leaves or brown tips (signs of improper watering). Carefully turn over a few leaves and check the undersides for signs of pest infestation. Avoid plants with tiny white insects that fly up when you move the leaves (whiteflies); clusters of small, pear-shaped insects (aphids); or yellow-stippled leaves with tiny webs underneath (caused by spider mites).
3. **Check the stems.** The stems should be stocky and evenly colored, with no visible cuts, bruises, or pests.
4. **Inspect the roots.** It's okay if a few roots are coming out of the drainage holes at the bottom of the container. However, masses of tangled roots indicate that the plant is long overdue for transplanting. Overgrown plants can be saved if you loosen or remove some of the matted roots at transplanting time, but it's better to start off with younger plants if you have a choice.

Most common houseplants have become popular precisely because they can tolerate the lower light conditions found inside our homes. As long as you know whether a plant prefers low, medium, or high light, you'll do just fine in providing the right conditions.

Find the Right Spot

South-facing windows let in the most light, and most houseplants will flourish there. Although east and west exposures don't provide as many hours of bright light as south windows, many bright-light lovers (and all plants that need medium light) will grow well in most east- or west-facing windows. Save north-facing windows for

low-light plants. To identify plants suitable for the varying light intensities in your home, see "The Right Houseplant for the Right Place" on page 238.

There are several things besides direction that affect the amount of light coming in through a window. A very large east-facing window might actually be brighter than a small, south-facing one. Shade from trees may make a west-facing window more like a northern one. Fortunately, most houseplants are very adaptable. Your plants should do fine, as long as you do your best to match the right plant to the right window.

If you're the type of person who feels more comfortable with a little more precision, you can buy an inexpensive light meter, which will measure the actual amount of light at any given spot. These meters usually measure light in units known as "foot-candles" and come with a chart that tells you how many foot-candles various plants require.

Place Plants Properly

Matching your plants to the best available windows is important, but placing each plant so it's right up near the glass is probably even more important than having the right window.

The intensity of light drops off very rapidly as it enters the room, so a plant even a few feet from the window will get only half as much light as it would if you kept it right next to the window.

If your windowsills are too narrow to hold plants, consider adding a shelf to make the sill wider, or place a table in front of the window so you can set plants on it. Keep the windows clean and remove any sheer curtains that might cut down the light intensity.

ABOVE LEFT: Sunrooms are not only attractive places for humans to relax, but they also provide the ideal conditions for a wide range of plants, being warm, light, and airy.

LEFT: Flower production takes lots of energy, so blooming plants generally need all the light that they can get. A sunny window is an ideal spot.

Move Plants to Manage Light Levels

There may be times when you want to position a plant in a spot that you know doesn't provide enough light for it. For example, say you buy a spectacular flowering azalea and you really want to keep it on the dining-room table where everyone can enjoy it. You can usually get away with this for a week or so; then you will need to move the plant back into the brighter light next to a window. Most plants won't suffer much from such a procedure. Obviously, the lower the plant's light needs, the longer it can tolerate a dim location.

Another way to keep plants thriving in low light locations is to rotate two plants between the dark location and a bright window every few weeks or so. That way you get to enjoy a plant right where you want it all the time, and the two plants will get enough light to thrive. This is how shopping malls and offices keep their plants looking so good: The plants are moved back to a greenhouse periodically to recuperate, then they go back to the mall or office.

By the way, placing a plant close to an incandescent light bulb doesn't help much, but there are other types of lights that work very well for growing houseplants if your window space is limited. For more information, see "Gardening under Lights" on page 228.

Is Your Plant Getting the Right Light?

If your plant isn't getting the right light, it may show symptoms that tell you it needs a new location. Sometimes, you may notice that plants growing in bright windows develop a yellowy tinge or white or brown patches on the leaves that get the most sun. This may mean the plant is getting too much light. This doesn't happen often with houseplants, but it could be a problem if you put a low-light plant like a Chinese evergreen (*Aglaeonema* spp.) directly in a south-facing window. If these symptoms occur, move the plant away from the window.

Aglaeonema 'Silver Queen'

The opposite problem—plants not getting enough light—is far more common. A plant trying to grow where there's not enough light will gradually become leggy and spindly, and its lower leaves may turn yellow and drop off. Or the plant may just sit, not putting out any new growth at all. If you notice that a plant is not growing, or if there's new growth but it looks weak and spindly, try moving the plant to a brighter location in your home.

Some plants, such as weeping fig (*Ficus benjamina*), may drop a lot of their leaves when you first bring them home. This is because they were probably grown outside in very bright light. When you move them to the much dimmer interior of your home, they simply don't need as many leaves because there isn't as much light, so they drop them. Don't be alarmed at this. Keep the plant in the brightest location you have, water it moderately, and wait for it to adjust. It should stop dropping leaves after a few weeks. If a plant continues to drop leaves or grow poorly, consider moving it to a brighter spot. Too often when houseplants grow poorly, people give them more water or fertilizer thinking that will solve the problem. Some plants do drop leaves when their soil is dry. But if the real cause is low light, extra water or fertilizer is the last thing they need.

Weeping fig

Humidity and Temperature

Although humidity levels and temperature levels are not as critical for good growth as light intensity or proper watering, they can have an effect on the health and vigor of your plants.

Handling Humidity

Almost all houseplants will grow better if you can give them higher humidity levels than those found in the average home. Indoor air is usually much drier than outdoor air, especially during the winter when heating systems drive away moisture. Summer air-conditioning also creates dry indoor air.

In general, plants with thin, delicate leaves tend to be more sensitive to low humidity, while plants such as Chinese evergreens (*Aglaeonema* spp.), with their thick, waxy leaves, can tolerate typical home humidity levels. There are some plants on the market, such as bird's nest fern (*Asplenium nidus*), that look great at the store (because they just came from a greenhouse) but usually grow poorly in most homes unless you provide extra humidity. Always check the label and avoid buying a plant that needs extra humidity, unless you just like it so much that you want to give it that extra care.

You can buy an inexpensive humidity gauge (at hardware stores) to monitor the water vapor in the air. Most plants thrive in humidity levels similar to those humans

A pebble tray—a shallow tray filled with pebbles and some water—is a great way to provide a more humid atmosphere for your indoor plants.

To provide extra humidity for indoor herbs, place a layer of pebbles in a bowl, add enough water to cover the pebbles, and set the pot on top.

like—around 40 to 60 percent humidity. It's more likely, however, that the humidity in your house is below this. In winter, in fact, it may be as low as only 10 or 20 percent (which is as dry as a desert!).

Symptoms of low humidity include brown leaf tips and edges and leaf curling. If you notice these signs, consider the following techniques for increasing humidity levels for your plants.

Grouping Plants One way to increase humidity is to cluster your houseplants together. This happens naturally when you place plants in groups near windows. As the leaves release water vapor, the extra moisture creates a more humid microclimate for the plants. Using clay pots instead of plastic also helps a little because water vapor evaporates from the sides of the clay pots.

Misting Some people like to mist their plants directly to increase humidity, and this does help a little. However, as soon as the mist evaporates, the humidity level will drop. Misting plants so heavily that water stands on the leaves is not good, either, since that can lead to disease problems. If you decide to mist, do it during daytime hours and do it lightly.

Pebble Trays A better choice than misting is to grow houseplants on trays containing pebbles and water. You can use any kind of saucers or shallow trays to hold the water—plastic cafeteria-type trays work well; even baking sheets are fine. Set the plants on a 1- to 2-inch (2.5- to 5- cm) layer of pebbles or gravel. Add enough water to bring the water level just below the top of the pebbles. (You don't want the bottom of the pots to be sitting in water.) Moisture will evaporate steadily from the trays and rise to increase humidity around the plants' leaves. This is a very effective way to raise humidity levels, and humidity-loving plants like ferns will definitely benefit if you grow them over these water-filled trays.

Grouping plants helps to keep the humidity levels adequate.

Humidifiers If you happen to have a room humidifier or an automatic humidifier installed in your heating or air-conditioning system, you'll be able to raise the humidity in the whole growing area of your home. Both you and your plants will be very comfortable year-round.

The Right Temperature

Most common houseplants prefer typical home temperatures of around 65°F (18°C) during the day and 55° to 60°F (12° to 15°C) at night. However, some need cooler temperatures during part of the year. Certain flowering plants, such as azaleas and camellias (*Camellia japonica*), won't bloom well unless you give them a period of cooler temperatures. Check the individual plant entries starting on page 306, to find out the temperature preferences of each kind of plant.

Defining Light Levels

What exactly do "high light," "medium light," and "low light" mean? Check the descriptions below to see which apply best to your available conditions.

- **High Light** Areas directly in front of most south-facing windows and large, unobstructed east or west windows. These locations will usually provide between 4 and 6 hours of direct sun per day.
- **Medium Light** Areas directly in front of unobstructed small or medium-sized east or west windows. Plants will also get medium light from partly shaded, large south, east, or west windows.
- **Low Light** North windows and other windows shaded by large trees, porches, buildings, or awnings. Low light also applies to all locations more than a few feet away from windows.

Caring for Houseplants

Well-designed containers can give you a garden's worth of beauty in a relatively small space.

All the elements of a houseplant's environment must be in balance to ensure continuing health and growth. An understanding of how the plant grows and how light, watering, and fertilizing affect plants will help you to determine which plants are right for your home.

Some people have trouble knowing how much to water their plants, and too much or too little water can spell trouble. But with the tips and techniques covered in "Watering Wisely" below, you'll know exactly when to water and when to wait.

The foundation of organic gardening is nutrient-rich, disease-preventing compost. You'll want to combine compost with slow-release organic fertilizers to feed your houseplants. In "Fertilizing for Healthy Growth" on page 216, you'll find out how to mix your own fertilizers using household wastes such as coffee grounds and wood ashes, along with products such as bonemeal and bloodmeal.

As your houseplants thrive, they will eventually outgrow their containers. "Potting and Repotting" on page 217 will tell you how to know when repotting is in order and exactly how to do it.

Another aspect of keeping your houseplants in peak condition is covered in "Grooming and Pruning" on page 218. This section covers basic plant pruning techniques that you can use to keep plants vigorous but still compact and well shaped.

When you find out how much fun and how rewarding it is to grow gorgeous, vigorous houseplants, you'll probably want to expand your collection. In "Making More Plants" on page 219, you'll learn all the basics of propagating your existing stock to fill every part of your home with lush and lovely houseplants.

Light

Light is as important as water to plants. Although a plant may not die through lack of light, it will not develop in the expected way. Windows facing north give an even light without direct sun throughout the year, while windows facing south give direct sunlight in winter, but less in summer. But during summer these windows are too hot for all plants except cacti. Plants should be placed at least 3 feet (90 cm) from the window to prevent heat damage.

Windows facing west and east give the most direct sun on a year-round basis. East-facing windows can become as hot in summer as south-facing windows. How much light a plant receives also determines how much care is needed. A houseplant receiving high light during summer needs to be watered and fed more regularly than during winter when the light is less intense and photosynthesis slows.

Watering Wisely

Next to getting the light levels right, watering is probably the most important aspect of houseplant care. You can't just water this plant once a week and that one twice a week; there are too many different factors that will affect how much water a plant needs. If you understand what those factors are and how they increase or decrease your plants' water requirements, then you'll know what to expect and be

A sunny south window is the perfect spot for cacti and succulents. A sunny east or west window could also be suitable.

better able to give each plant the right amount of water.

The major factors that will affect how much water a certain plant needs include:

The plant's particular moisture preference. The individual plant entries, starting on page 306, tell you if a plant needs dry conditions (as succulents and cacti do) or if it needs constantly moist soil (as many ferns prefer). Most houseplants fall in the middle and need a steady supply of moisture with the soil surface drying out between waterings.

Reticulated irises

The container the plant is growing in. Plants in terracotta or clay pots will dry out faster than those in plastic pots. Large plants growing in small pots will also need water more frequently. (That's one of the reasons plants need to be repotted into larger pots as they grow.)

The container mix the plant is growing in. Container mixes containing ample compost or peat moss will absorb and hold more moisture than mixes containing lots of sand.

The amount of light the plant gets. Plants growing in bright light need more water than those placed in dimmer areas.

The weather conditions. Plants will use much more water during bright, warm, summer periods when they are actively growing than in the winter, when the temperatures are cooler and the daylight hours are much shorter. They will also require very little water during sustained periods of cloudy weather.

Considering all these varying factors, it's easy to see why it's so important to check each plant's soil before you water.

When to Water

Your first clue about when to water should be the soil surface, which usually turns a lighter color when it's dry. If it's dark colored and damp, do not water.

If the surface is dry, you can use your finger to check the soil an inch or two (2.5 to 5 cm) below the surface. If you still feel moisture, wait a day or two and test again. When that top layer feels dry, it's the right time to water.

Another way to check soil moisture is to lift the pot. You can tell immediately if the plant feels really light and thus needs water or if it feels relatively heavy, in which case you should wait a few more days before you water.

This technique works especially well for small to medium-sized plants in lightweight plastic pots.

Some pots are just too big to lift, and the soil near the surface may dry out while there's still plenty of moisture deeper in the soil. Always check for moisture several inches deep in large pots; if you go only by whether the soil surface is dry, you could easily overwater. When in doubt, always underwater rather than risk giving too much water and thereby destroying the roots.

How to Water

Once you're sure a plant needs watering, water it thoroughly so a little water runs out into the saucer under it. When you apply more water than the soil can absorb, the excess flows out the bottom into the saucer. This flow of water through the soil, similar to what happens in the garden when it rains, serves an important function in container plants. As the water runs through the mix, it pushes out used air and allows fresh air to move into the spaces between the soil particles. (Plant roots need both water and air to thrive. That's why it's so important to have a loose, well-drained container mix and to always water thoroughly.)

Always use pots with drainage holes, and always put saucers under them. Without drainage holes, it's too easy to overwater and make the soil soggy. (The excess water trapped in a pot without drainage holes could cause the roots to rot and the plant to die.) And if you don't have a saucer under the plant, you'll be tempted to underwater to avoid having water run out the bottom and make a mess.

Occasionally when you water, you may notice that the water seems to be running rapidly through the soil and out the bottom without being absorbed by the soil. When this happens, you've let the soil get too dry. When container mix dries out, it shrinks away from the sides of the pot, leaving space where water can run right through. To water a dried-out pot, you need to set the entire pot in a bowl or sink full of water up to the pot's rim and let the soil slowly absorb the water. After the soil is thoroughly rewetted, let the pot drain, then return it to its saucer.

Signs of Overwatering and Underwatering

Overwatering is just as bad for your plants as underwatering—maybe even worse. When plants are too dry, their leaves will droop, so at least you have a clue that they need to be watered (although it's best to water just before leaves start to droop).

When plants are kept too wet, you may see the same symptom—drooping leaves—but it will be because the roots are rotted and the plant can no longer obtain the food and water it needs from the container mix. If this happens, your plant may or may not recover; your only hope is to reduce watering and cross your fingers.

Underwatered, wilted plants

Water-quality Considerations

Not all water is suitable for houseplants. The chlorine in our drinking water doesn't seem to harm plants, although some gardeners like to let tap water sit overnight so the chlorine evaporates. Fluorine, on the other hand, has been shown to cause slight damage to some plants. If you use city water that has fluorine added, then you might want to collect rainwater and use it. Home water softeners add salts to the water, so avoid using soft water; otherwise, the salts can build up to toxic levels in the soil.

If you have water that is naturally hard or alkaline, it may eventually cause the pH of the container mix to become too high. (pH is a measure of how acid or alkaline the soil is. A pH below 7.0 is acid; a pH above 7.0 is alkaline. Most plants grow best when the soil pH stays around neutral, between pH 6.0 to 7.5.) You can offset the effects of hard water by using compost in your container mix and adding vinegar to your watering solution once a month. (Use 1 tablespoon of vinegar per gallon [4.5 l] of water, and water as usual.) The pH level is more important for some plants than others; check the entries in "Encyclopedia of Flowers," starting on page 306, to find out if the plant you're growing has specific pH preferences for healthy growth.

Watering for Vacations

If you'll be away for more than a few days, there are several techniques you can use to get extra water to your plants. If you're only going to miss one of your usual watering days, you can water the plants thoroughly and add some extra water to the saucers. (While you shouldn't make a habit of leaving water standing in the saucers, it's okay to do it occasionally.)

If you're going to be gone for more than just a few days, you can set your plants up to be wick-watered. To do this, use a strip of nylon pantyhose, a rolled-up paper towel, or some other absorbent material for the wick. Insert one end of the wick into the bottom of the pot, making sure it makes good contact with the container mix, then run the other end into a container of water. Recycled margarine tubs with lids work well for small plants; just cut a hole in the lid, fill the tub with water, run the wick down through the hole, and set the plant on top of the reservoir. Capillary action will draw water up along the wick and into the container. (This method also works well year-round for plants that need constant moisture, such as gardenias and ferns.)

Fertilizing for Healthy Growth

If you want your houseplants to thrive, you have to give them food as well as water. The best organic fertilizers for houseplants are the same ones that work well outside—bloodmeal, bonemeal, and fish and seaweed products.

A wick-watering setup is a handy way to water plants if you're going on a long vacation.

A drip irrigation system is an easy and effective way to water your indoor container plants.

You can also use household "wastes" such as wood ashes and coffee grounds. But the first item on your fertilizer list should always be compost, which is the organic gardener's secret for success.

Compost is especially good for pot plants because it releases nutrients slowly over time, just the way plants growing in the wild receive their nutrients. Compost will never burn roots or cause major salt buildup like synthetic chemical fertilizers. Plus, compost doesn't just feed your plants—it prevents disease and improves the structure of the soil, so air and water can reach the roots better. Ample compost also helps the soil retain moisture, so you won't have to water as often. Compost also contains the major plant nutrients nitrogen, phosphorus, and potassium, plus minor nutrients and trace elements not provided by chemical fertilizers.

If you aren't already making your own compost, consider starting. It's easy. And if you can't make your own compost, check with your local government—many communities are now composting yard wastes and offering the compost free to anyone who wants it.

A Simple Program for Feeding Houseplants

Use compost whenever you pot up a new plant or re-pot an old one, adding up to 1 part compost for every 3 or 4 parts container mix. Each spring thereafter, take your plants to a sink or bathtub and water them heavily with warm water until water runs steadily out the bottom for a few minutes. This leaches out any harmful salts, which can build up over time. It's a good idea to do this once a year, but you should also do it anytime you notice a crusty deposit in the saucers or around the pot rims. Rinse the leaves thoroughly, too.

After you've completed the spring leaching treatment, add a ½- to 1-inch (12- to 25-mm) layer of fresh compost to all of the pots. (If there's not room in the pot, just wash away some of the soil with a hose.) Mix a small amount of a balanced organic fertilizer into the compost before you apply it to the pots. That should feed most plants well into midsummer. (Check the fertilizer packages for guidelines.)

Most houseplants will be getting much more light during the summer than in the winter, so a couple of months after the spring compost/fertilizer treatment, begin feeding them about once a month with a half-strength liquid fish fertilizer. The fish fertilizer contains plenty of nitrogen, the nutrient most likely to be in short supply. It also contains the other major plant nutrients—phosphorus and potassium—and important trace elements. Keep feeding the plants until growth slows in fall. Remember that too much fertilizer can be just as bad as too little. Go easy when you fertilize plants in dim locations, and don't fertilize at all during the short days of winter unless you have a plant that continues to grow actively then.

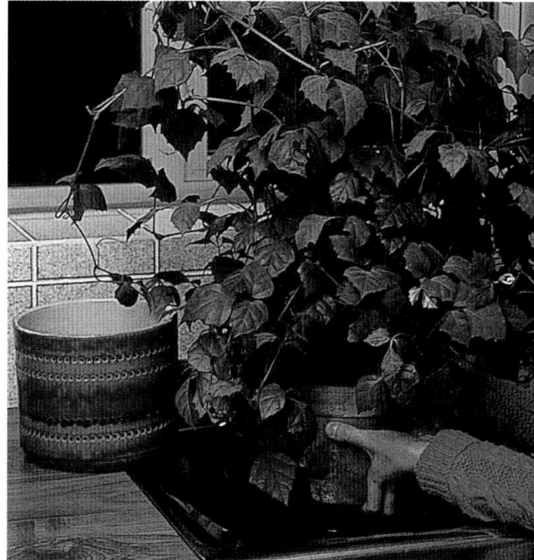

If you notice a white crust or buildup, run water through the soil to leach out the harmful salts.

Understanding Organic Fertilizers

The three major nutrients plants need most are nitrogen (N), phosphorus (P), and potassium (K). Fertilizer labels carry these "N-P-K" numbers, which tell you the percent of each nutrient. Bonemeal, for example, typically has a ratio of 1-11-0, meaning it contains 1 percent nitrogen, 11 percent phosphorus, and no potassium.

To keep plants happy, you want a balance of all three. It doesn't have to be exactly 5-5-5 or 2-2-2, but try to get the numbers as similar as possible. For flowering plants, switch to a formula with more of the middle number (phosphorus) when it's time for the plant to set flower buds, since this will stimulate flowering. Foliage houseplants generally prefer a high-nitrogen formula, such as 5-3-3.

You can buy balanced organic fertilizers, or you can mix your own. Listed here are some common organic fertilizer materials. To determine the N-P-K ratio, add up the percent of each nutrient in the ingredients, and divide by the total number of parts to get the N-P-K ratio of the mixture. Say you combine 2 parts bloodmeal (2 x 11-1-1 = 22-2-2) with 1 part bonemeal (1-11-0) and 2 parts wood ashes (2 x 0-2-8 = 0-4-16). Add up each part of the ratios, and you get 23-17-18. Divide each part of the ratio by 5 (since you're using 5 equal parts of fertilizer), and you'll see that the resulting mix has an N-P-K ratio of 4.6-3.4-3.6, a good balance.

Bloodmeal: 11-1-1
Bonemeal: 1-11-0
Coffee grounds: 2-0.3-0.2
Compost: 0.5-0.5-0.5 to 2-2-2
Cottonseed meal: 6-2-1
Fish emulsion: 4-1-1
Granite dust: 0-0-4
Greensand: 0-2-7
Kelp meal: 1-0.5-2
Manures: 1-1-1 (typically)
Phosphate rock: 0-3-0
Tea leaves: 4-0.5-0.5
Wood ashes: 0-2-8

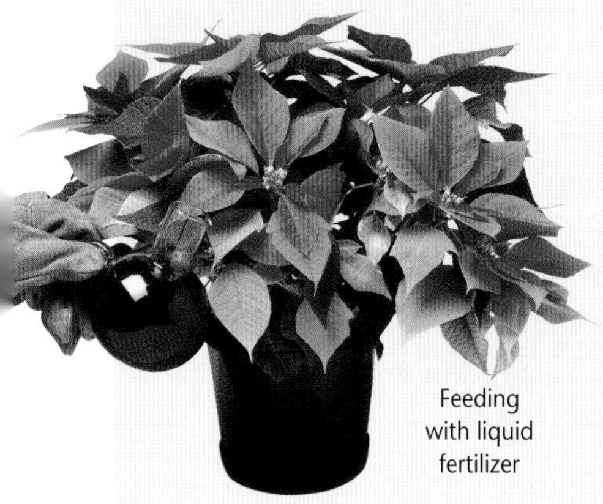

Feeding with liquid fertilizer

Potting and Repotting

Your houseplants will eventually need to be repotted, either because they grow too big for their pots or because they need to be moved into fresh container mix.

Generally, you should repot your plants about once every year or two in the spring or summer, when plants are actively growing. If they get too big for their pot, they can become "root-bound," which means they have grown so many roots that there's not enough container mix left to support further growth. Most (but not all) plants shouldn't be allowed to become root-bound. You can check to see how crowded the roots are becoming by lifting the plant and tapping the pot until it slips loose. Lift out the plant to examine the rootball. If you see lots of soil with some roots, all is well. But if you see mostly roots and little soil, it's time to repot.

How to Repot a Houseplant

You have a choice when you repot—you can move the plant to a larger pot size, or you can keep the plant in the same pot. If you want the plant to grow bigger and don't mind going to a larger container, choose a new pot that's 1 to 2 inches (2.5 to 5 cm) in diameter larger for small to medium-sized plants, or 4 to 6 inches (10 to 15 cm) larger for bigger plants. (If you move a small plant into a very big pot, you run a risk that the excess soil around the plant's roots will stay too wet and cause the roots to rot.)

When you're moving a plant to a larger pot, add some container mix to the bottom—enough so that the soil level will be an inch or two (2.5 to 5 cm) below the pot rim when you set in the plant to allow room for watering. Then remove the plant from the pot it's growing in. Holding the base of the pot in one hand, lift the plant slightly and tap around the rim with your other hand to loosen the pot. Carefully lift the plant out and set it on the soil in the new pot. Then add container mix around the edges, using a trowel or stick to gently settle the soil around the root ball. That's it—it's as easy as one, two, three.

If you see roots circling the outside of the root ball when you remove the plant from the container, it's time to do some repotting.

If you'd prefer to keep the same pot, remove the plant and shake away as much of the old soil from the roots as you can. If the plant's root ball is so dense and tangled that the soil won't shake loose, use a large knife to slice away an inch or two (2.5 to 5 cm) of the root ball on all sides and the bottom. Add fresh container mix to the bottom of the pot, then set the trimmed plant back in and add fresh soil in the space you created around the sides. This root pruning allows you to keep the plant to a manageable size. If the plant itself can be pruned, trim it back a bit to bring the top into better balance with the reduced roots. (See "Grooming and Pruning" below for details on pruning.)

If you're repotting a very large plant, you may want to ask someone to help you. Removing the plant will be easier if you lay the container on its side, then carefully pull out the plant.

Container Mixes

You can use any commercial container mix for most houseplants, but your plants will grow much better if you add some compost and slow-release organic fertilizers before you plant. If you want to blend your own growing mix, see "Selecting Container Mixes" on page 168 for some recipes. There are a few plants that prefer special container mixes. Cacti and succulents, for instance, appreciate extra sand for drainage, while African violets (*Saintpaulia* spp.) thrive with extra peat moss for acidity and moisture retention. The entries in "Encyclopedia of Flowers," starting on page 306, indicate if a plant has a preference.

Grooming and Pruning

It's natural for houseplants to lose some of their older leaves as they grow. Shrubby plants such as weeping fig (*Ficus benjamina*) may also shed leaves when they're moved to a new location, sometimes leaving a tangle of bare twigs in the center of the plant. If you spend a few minutes now and then trimming off these yellowing leaves or dead twigs, your houseplants will look much better.

Many houseplants don't require pruning beyond this grooming. If all of the leaves grow out from a single center or crown of the plant and there are no stems or branches (as on African violets

African violet

Repotting a Houseplant

Young, healthy plants grow quickly, and can soon fill their pots with roots. Once the roots have filled the pot, they can go through the drainage holes or over the surface of the soil. This makes the container mix dry out quickly. It's time to repot.

1. Choose a new pot that is slightly larger than the old one. Add a layer of container mix.

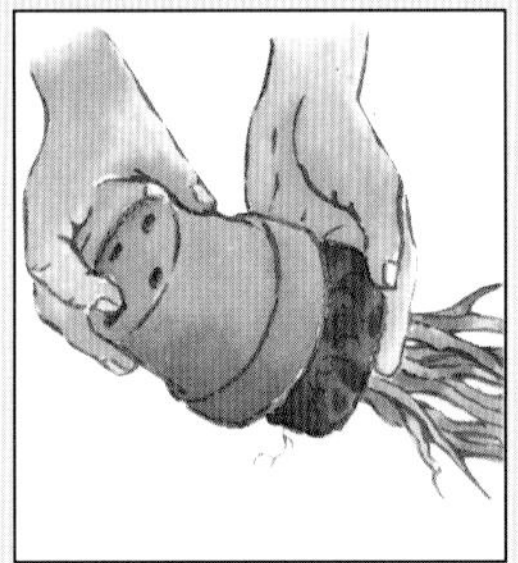

2. Carefully turn plant over onto one hand, and use the other to pull off the old pot.

3. Settle the plant at the same level in the new pot, and fill in around the sides with mix.

[*Saintpaulia* hybrids] and florist's cyclamen [*Cyclamen persicum*]), then you can't (and don't need to) prune the plant.

Trailing or vining plants (such as passionflowers [*Passiflora* spp.] or wandering Jew [*Zebrina pendula*]), on the other hand, benefit from pruning. Simply pinch or snip off unwanted leaves and stems with your fingers or scissors; use pruning shears to remove woodier stems cleanly.

There are three basic reasons to prune your houseplants, as follows:

Pruning for Shape Regular trimming improves a houseplant's appearance by eliminating any long, awkward stems or branches that grow out of proportion to the rest of the plant. Don't hesitate about this—cutting back gangly branches will help, not harm, the plant.

Pruning to Promote New Growth Pruning is also helpful to trailing plants, such as Swedish ivy (*Plectranthus australis*). Cutting back the growing tips causes the plant to put out more shoots and become bushier. You should always make your pruning cuts right above a side branch or leaf node (the spot where a leaf joins the stem). In many cases, the plant will produce two new stems from the cut point, leading to bushier, more attractive growth.

Pruning for Size Control Pruning is also helpful in keeping plants a manageable size. If a bushy plant, such as a citrus, has become larger than you want, you can prune it back hard, cutting off as much as a third of the leaves. In this way, you keep the top in balance with the roots without having to move the plant to a larger pot.

To find out special pruning needs, refer to the individual entries in "Encyclopedia of Flowers," starting on page 306.

Making More Plants

With just a few simple materials, you can propagate a wide variety of wonderful houseplants. Once you learn how to take cuttings, prepare air layers, divide plants, and propagate from runners, you'll have dozens of new plants to expand your collection or give away.

Some plants can be reproduced several different ways; others propagate best with one particular technique. To find out what's best for your houseplant, check the entries in "Encyclopedia of Flowers," starting on page 306.

Taking Stem Cuttings

It is possible to propagate most types of houseplants from stem cuttings. Remember to use very sharp secateurs, knives, or razor blades when making the cuts, since bruised or split stems may rot. It is a good idea to water the plant about 2 hours before taking cuttings, as this will ensure that the stems and leaves are moist. If you are taking cuttings from a flowering stem, gently pinch off the flowers first. Using hormone rooting powder on the cut end will speed up the process.

1. Select healthy, green growth and make a cut just above a leaf axil or node.

2. Trim the cutting just below the lowest leaf node and remove the lower leaves.

3. Make a hole with a stick in the container mix and plant the cutting in the new pot.

Taking Cuttings

Cuttings are pieces of stem (or sometimes just a single leaf) that can produce roots and grow into new plants. This is a fairly easy way to reproduce bushy or vining plants, such as ivies (*Hedera* spp.) and passionflowers (*Passiflora* spp.). Here's how:

1. Cut short pieces from the shoot tips of the plant, so there are about two nodes (those joints where the leaves come off the stem) below the three or four leaves on the shoot tip.
2. Remove the leaves from the two bottom nodes on the shoot.
3. Insert the base of the cutting in water or moist sand or vermiculite, so the two exposed nodes are covered. (You might want to try a few cuttings in each of these materials; different plants root better in some conditions than others.)
4. Slide a clear plastic bag over the pot of cuttings to keep the humidity high until the stems root.

Miniature roses bloom on new wood, so the plants will require regular trimming in order to promote fresh, new flowering growth.

Taking Leaf Cuttings

It is possible to propagate some plants by leaf cuttings. A whole leaf, together with some of the leaf stalk, is cut and then transplanted into slightly moist container mix. The new roots and shoots will develop from the cut end of the leaf stalk.

1. Remove a leaf and trim the leaf stalk to a length of about 1½ inches (3 cm).

2. Plant the leaf in the new pot, placing it in the soil at about a 45° angle.

3. Rest the leaf stalk against the side of the container to support the cutting.

5. It is best to place the cuttings in a warm, bright spot out of direct sunlight.

Some cuttings root very quickly; others will take weeks. You can tell when roots have formed because the plant will begin to send out new growth. When this happens, replant the rooted cuttings into regular container mix and fertilize them.

Leaf Cuttings for Even More Plants

It's hard to believe that a single leaf—or even just a small piece of a leaf—can turn into a new plant, but it's true. Succulents such as jade plant (*Crassula argentea*) and burro's tail (*Sedum morganianum*) will readily sprout new plants from single leaves that fall from the main plant, if you know what to do. Just stick the fat, fleshy leaves halfway into sandy container mix and water them as usual. Soon you'll have a handsome crop of new succulents.

Other plants are not quite as simple to grow from leaf cuttings, but cape primrose (*Streptocarpus* hybrids) and rex begonia (*Begonia rex*) leaves can be pinned onto moist container mix after you make small cuts through the larger veins on the leaf. Keep the leaf moist by covering the pot loosely with plastic wrap, and tiny plants will eventually form at the cuts.

African violet (*Saintpaulia* hybrids) plants can be propagated from the leaf and a little of the stem, or from the leaf alone. The new plant can form either at the base of the stem or from the midrib of the leaf blade. To propagate African violets, make a diagonal cut at the base of the leaf and place the cutting in a growing medium containing half peat and half sand.

Air Layering

With air layering you create a root system on a stem or branch as it grows in the air. It is best to begin air layers in spring or early summer that are detached in fall when growth is dormant.

Air layering is also good for preventing some plants from getting out of control. Dracaenas (*Dracaena* spp.), dumbcane (*Dieffenbachia amoena*), rubber tree (*Ficus elastica*), and some other plants gradually grow taller until they reach the ceiling. You can prune these plants by simply cutting them back, but here's how to return this type of plant to a manageable height while also gaining some new houseplants for your collection:

1. First, get some fibrous sphagnum moss. The stuff you want is coarse, stringy, and light-colored. Moisten the moss well.
2. Make a shallow cut across the trunk where you want new roots to form—about a third of the way through, at an angle.
3. Press a little moss into the cut, then take a large handful of the damp moss and wad it around the trunk at the cut point.
4. Wrap the moss tightly with plastic wrap so it's held firmly in a ball all around the trunk. Secure the plastic-wrapped ball of moss with tape or twine.
5. Check the moss every few weeks to be sure it's still moist (open wrapping and add water if it isn't), and watch for roots. Eventually they'll become visible through the plastic. Depending on the plant, it can take 8 to 12 weeks for the roots to form.
6. When they seem well formed, cut off the plant just below the new roots, and pot up your new shorter plant. Keep in a cool shaded position for a couple of weeks until the plant has had time to adjust to its new environment.

The now topless trunk will reshoot or, if you'd like even more plants, you can cut pieces off the trunk, lay them sideways in a fresh container of container mix, and just barely cover them with more mix. The pieces will sprout new shoots and turn into new plants. Keep the remaining trunk base in the pot, and water it lightly; it too will sprout new leaves.

It is a good idea to cover a container of cuttings with a plastic bag to provide extra humidity.

Dividing

Division is one of the easiest ways of propagating. Plants with multiple stems that arise from the base of the plant are usually propagated this way. Division of indoor foliage plants should be carried out during early spring.

Some houseplants grow from a center point but produce additional offshoots as they grow, expanding into larger and larger clumps. The popular aloe plant (*Aloe vera*) grows this way; so do asparagus fern (*Asparagus densiflorus*) and moses-in-a-boat (*Rhoeo spathacea*).

How to propagate by division:

- Remove the plant from its container.
- Carefully shake some of the soil away so that the roots can be easily seen.
- The rootball can now be divided by using a sharp knife or simply by pulling it apart with your hands. However, be careful not to damage the roots.
- Repot the divisions immediately into a good-quality container mix.
- Place the divisions in a shaded position for at least two weeks until the plant has had time to recover. Water when the soil surface appears dry.

Plantlets or Runners

A runner is a specialized stem that develops from the axil of the leaf at the crown of a plant, grows horizontally along the ground, and forms a new plant at one of the nodes—spider plants (*Chlorophytum comosum*) and piggyback plants (*Tolmiea menziesii*), along with strawberries, are the most commonly known examples of this type of plant. These are easily propagated by placing a small pot, containing a good-quality container mix, next to the parent plant. Without severing the runner, lay the plantlet on the container mix in the new pot and hold it in place with a bobby pin. Sever it from the parent plant when new growth appears.

Another approach is to remove the plantlet from the parent plant and place it in a good container mix. Enclose the pot in a plastic bag to provide humidity until the roots have formed.

Rooting Medium

The correct rooting medium will influence both the quantity of the cuttings that will root and the quality of the root system formed. A mixture of sand and peat moss is the most common combination. River sand only should be used and the best type is the sand used by plasterers in the building trade. The sand should be fine enough to hold some moisture but coarse enough to allow water to drain through.

Peat moss is actually the remains of aquatic, marsh, swamp, or bog vegetation that has been preserved underwater in a partially decomposing state. Peat moss is used in conjunction with sand to increase the water-holding capacity. When using peat moss you should take care not to overwater the plant, as this can cause the new roots to deteriorate.

A medium consisting of 2 parts sand to 1 part peat moss is the most effective for rooting plants. Half sand and half peat can be used, but take care not to overwater.

You can place plantlets from stem ends of the spider plant (*Chlorophytum comosum*) and set the base of the plantlet in a container of water. When new roots begin to form, move the plantlet to a new container.

Plant Hormones

Plant hormones are helpful in propagation by cuttings. When applied to cuttings, plant hormones encourage the production of plant roots and produce a greater number of evenly distributed roots. Plant hormones also shorten the time taken by the plant to root. Rooting hormones are widely available and come in a powder form. The end of the cutting is dipped into the powder before it is placed in the propagating medium.

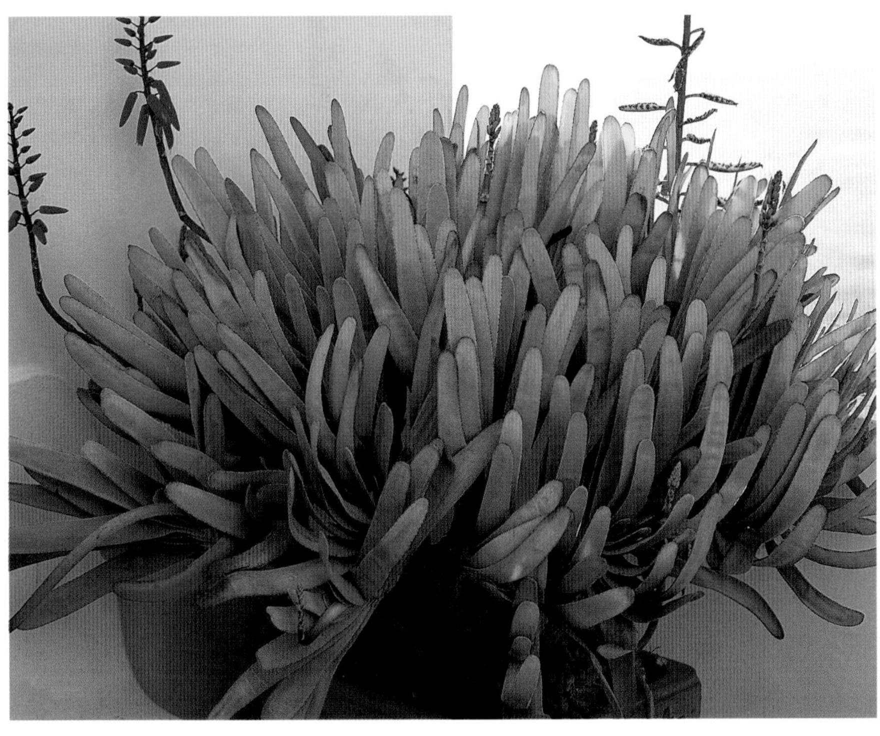

Aloe (*Aloe vera*) plants produce additional offshoots as they grow. You can remove and replant these offsets at any time.

Troubleshooting Houseplants

The best defense against pests and diseases is strong, healthy plants. And that's what you'll get using the techniques explained in this book. If pest or disease problems do show up on your plants, you'll find safe, nontoxic solutions below.

Handling Pests and Diseases

Outdoors, organic gardeners keep plants healthy by protecting and encouraging the natural balance between bad bugs and good bugs (the ones that prey on the bad guys). But plants growing indoors don't have any good bugs around to keep the pests in check, so sometimes the pests may multiply and cause problems. Indoor plants also face a few disease problems.

The most important thing you can do to prevent insect or disease outbreaks is to keep your plants healthy and vigorous: Give them sufficient light and fertilizer and the correct amount of water and humidity. For reasons scientists don't yet fully understand, pest insects are actually attracted to plants that are weak or stressed. Strong, organically grown plants are far less likely to have pest problems than plants that are weak and unhealthy.

The second important pest-prevention technique is to learn the symptoms of common houseplant problems and inspect your plants regularly. Most pests don't cause serious damage until they've been around awhile; if you spot an outbreak early, you can nip it in the bud (so to speak!).

Whiteflies are easy to identify because they will fly up into the air whenever you disturb the plant. Whiteflies multiply rapidly, so you'll have to spray them quickly, before they get out of control.

Common Houseplant Pests

The trick to handling pests is identifying them correctly, so you can choose the most effective control measure. Below you'll find descriptions of the pests you're most likely to encounter, along with suggested controls.

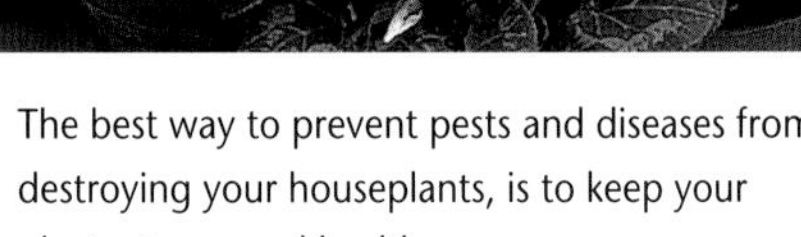

The best way to prevent pests and diseases from destroying your houseplants, is to keep your plants strong and healthy.

Sprayer

Aphids Aphids are small insects about 1/16 inch (2 mm) long. They may be white, green, black, brown, or orange in color, and may or may not have wings. They are often found in clusters on tip growth and flower buds. Rub off aphids by hand or prune out infested leaf tips. For serious infestations, take plants outside and blast them weekly with a strong spray of water, or use soap spray.

Fungus Gnats These are small, slow-moving, dark-colored insects that you may notice running across the soil or flying up into the air when you water. Controls usually aren't necessary. If you have many flies, you can drench the soil with Gnatrol, a microbial pesticide containing a bacteria that kills the larvae.

Mealybugs These look like tiny tufts of white cotton. They are usually found clustered in sheltered areas of stems or on the undersides of leaves. Apply rubbing alcohol to individual mealybugs using a cotton swab. Be persistent in inspecting plants and repeating treatment as needed.

Mites These bugs are about the size of a grain of salt. Leaves attacked by mites are stippled or mottled; flowers may be deformed. If you look closely, you can usually see fine webbing over the damaged areas. Webs don't necessarily mean the plant has mites; they may just be webs from small spiders. Leave those spiders to help you control the pests. Wash mites off with a strong spray of water. Insecticidal soap or oil sprays also control these pests.

Scales These insects live underneath a shell about 1/8 inch (3 mm) in diameter. Sticky specks appear on leaves. Check the leaves and stems above the sticky area for little bumps that can be rubbed off. Young scales are flat and semitransparent; they get darker and larger as they get older. Rub off scales by hand or spray with horticultural oil. Move plants outside in warm weather to allow natural enemies to control the scales.

Whiteflies These are tiny, white bugs about 1/16 inch (2 mm) in length. If you notice white specks flying up when you brush against a plant, you'll need to spray promptly. Use yellow sticky traps to capture adult flies. Spray with insecticidal soap or oil to control immature, wingless nymphs (which are usually found on the undersides of leaves).

Controlling Houseplant Pests

You can treat houseplant pests with just a few simple, nontoxic materials.

Sticky Traps Sticky traps are basically just pieces of cardboard or plastic (usually yellow and about the size of an index card) that are covered with an adhesive material. When flying pests, such as aphids and whiteflies, land on the trap, they get stuck. Hang a few traps around your houseplants, or attach them to the ends of stakes and insert the stakes into the plant pots.

Water Sprays A spray of plain old water is often enough to knock pests off your plants. You need a spray that's forceful enough to remove the pests but not strong enough to damage the plant. Wash the plant off in the shower, or take it outside and spray it thoroughly with your garden hose.

Insecticidal Soap Insecticidal soap is specifically formulated to kill pests such as aphids and mites without harming you or your plants. It's widely available in garden centers in both ready-to-use spray bottles or in a liquid concentrate that you mix with water. (The concentrate is much better value than the ready-mixed sprays.) If you have "hard" tap water, mix the soap with distilled water, or it won't work well. (You'll know you have hard water if soap makes a scummy ring in your bathtub.)

Horticultural Oil Horticultural oil works by smothering insects and eggs. It is also effective in helping prevent certain diseases, especially when combined with baking soda. The oil now comes in several grades, so be sure you buy the superior grade oil that is labeled for use directly on plant leaves. (Until recently, horticultural oil was less refined and could only be used on outdoor plants that were dormant and leafless during the winter, such as fruit trees.) Mix and apply oil sprays according to package directions.

Dealing with Diseases

Most popular houseplants aren't likely to have diseases—that's one of the reasons they're widely grown. Keeping plants healthy by providing good air circulation and adequate light, water, and fertilizer is your best defense against disease.

One common disease that may show up is powdery mildew. It causes distinctive, white powdery spots on the leaves of begonias and other susceptible plants. If you notice mildew or other suspicious spots on leaves, remove the infected leaves and spray the plant with either a sulfur solution or a homemade spray of baking soda and oil (follow the recipe in "Homemade Sprays for Pests and Diseases" below).

Keep in mind that these sprays only work to prevent the spread of disease, not to cure infected leaves. Always try to spray at the first sign of disease, and remove all infected leaves first. If a plant becomes severely damaged by disease, it may be best to discard it altogether.

Dumbcane

Diseases can also attack plant roots, where they are difficult to detect or treat. Sudden wilting or poor growth for no apparent reason are the main symptoms.

Be sure you aren't overwatering, as this can promote root disease. Try letting the plant dry out between waterings; it may recover. If it doesn't, throw it out and be careful not to overwater in the future.

Homemade Sprays for Pests and Diseases

Commercial organic pest and disease sprays are convenient, but it's also easy to mix your own. You'll find two easy recipes here.

Whenever you spray, always cover the top and bottom surfaces of every leaf. If the plant can be pruned, do it before you spray. Repeat the spraying a week or so after the first spray to catch any bugs you missed or to prevent any remaining disease spores from attacking. To avoid marking walls, floors, and furniture, always move plants to some place where you can clean up easily—perhaps your shower, kitchen sink, or laundry tub, or outdoors if the weather's warm—before you spray.

Soap-and-oil Pest Spray

For a homemade insecticidal soap spray, mix 1 cup of vegetable oil and 1 tablespoon of dish soap. When you need to spray, mix 1 to 2 teaspoons of this oil/soap stock with 1 cup of water. Homemade soap-and-oil sprays may have a slightly greater risk of burning leaves than a commercial spray; test them on a few leaves, then wait a few days to make sure no damage appears before spraying a whole plant.

Homemade Fungicide

Mix together 1 tablespoon of baking soda, 1 tablespoon of horticultural oil or vegetable oil, and a few drops of dish soap with 1 gallon (4.5 l) of water. Try to use this fungicide spray solution on your plants before the disease symptoms develop, or as soon as you notice a problem.

It's easy to overlook scales until plants are infested. Check leaves and stems frequently for tiny bumps.

For an aphid infestation, rub the aphids off with your fingers, or spray with water or soapy water.

Houseplant Troubleshooting Chart

Symptoms	Possible Problem	Suggested Treatments
Dying plants or seedlings	Too much fertilizer	Water thoroughly to flush excess fertilizer. Halt or severely reduce feeding program.
	Water-logged plants	Improve drainage. Halt or severely reduce watering. Repot.
Weak-looking, stunted, pale plants	Insect attack	Isolate plant. Try to identify insects. Remove insects; wash with soapy water. See "Common Houseplant Pests" on page 48.
	Water-logged plants	Improve drainage. Halt or severely reduce watering. Repot.
	Under-nourished plants	Feed regularly with complete fertilizer or specialized plant food.
Weak-looking, straggly plants	Not enough light	Move gradually into a position with better light. Provide artificial lighting if necessary.
	Overcrowded	Divide plants. Repot.
	Too much nitrogen	Reduce or halt feeding. Use a low- or no-nitrogen fertilizer.
	Water-logged plants	Improve drainage. Halt or severely reduce watering. Repot.
Fading, wilting plants	Not enough warmth	Check recommended temperature range for plant.
	Not enough moisture	Water, if badly wilted. Immerse in water for quick recovery. Check for causes of excessive drying such as heaters, air-conditioning vents, or drafts.
	Too much moisture	Improve drainage. Halt or severely reduce watering.
Slow plant growth	Not enough light	Move gradually into a position with better light. Provide artificial lighting if necessary.
	Too little water	Check plant's watering needs. Follow correct watering procedure.
	Too little fertilizer	Add liquid fertilizer every 2 to 3 weeks.
	Roots pot-bound	Repot.
	Natural dormancy in winter	Be patient. Wait for spring.
White crust on soil	Build-up of fertilizer salts	Remove crust, leaching salts by flushing with pure water.
Lower leaves turn yellow, but remain on plant	Too little fertilizer, particularly nitrogen	Add high-nitrogen fertilizer.
Base of stem is soft or mushy	Too much water, particularly in cold weather	Let soil surface dry out between waterings. Improve drainage. Repot if necessary. Add coarse sand to container mix to improve drainage.
	Fungal attack in damp, cold conditions	Isolate plant. Move to warmer situation. Allow it to dry. Repot if necessary.
Collapse of plant	Extreme heat or cold	Check for cause of change, such as window left open. Move to position with more moderate temperature.
	Gas fumes	Check for source of fumes. Remove carefully.
Brown-edged leaves	Too hot, too dry	Check recommended temperature range for plant. Immerse in a bucket of water and place out of direct sunlight.
	Container mix saturated with chemical salts	Water repeatedly to flush excess salts from container mix.
	Leaves have been splashed with strong chemicals or fertilizer	Rinse leaves with water. Take care that leaves are not splashed with unwanted chemicals.

Symptoms	Possible Problem	Suggested Treatments
Brown patches on stems and leaves	Die-back, fungal disease or other infection	Isolate plant. Remove affected leaves and stems and destroy. Check for other symptoms to diagnose infection.
Powdery mold on leaf surface	Powdery mildew	Remove affected parts and destroy. Move plant to airier position. For severe infestations, use a systemic insecticide.
Reddish-brown, powdery marks on leaf surfaces	Rust	Isolate plant, cut off affected areas and destroy. For severe infestations, use a systemic insecticide.
Speckled leaves	Virus infection	Destroy infected plants
Sudden loss of leaves	Rapid temperature or light change	Check recommended temperature range for the plant. If necessary, restore previous temperature or light conditions.
Bronzed or abnormally reddened leaves	Not enough heat	Check recommended temperature range for the plant. If necessary, move to a warmer, more sheltered position.
	Not enough phosphorus or potassium	Use higher phosphorus or potassium fertilizer.
Dry and brittle leaves	Too little water or low humidity	Follow the proper procedure for watering houseplants. Increase humidity.
Leaf drop	Too much sun	Move to a location with less light.
	Too much fertilizer	Halt fertilizer for 3 to 4 weeks.
	Too much water	Follow the proper procedure for watering your houseplants.
	Too little water	Follow the proper procedure for watering your houseplants.
	Exposure to cold or draft	Check the temperature. Control cold source.
Brown or yellow leaves	Occasional yellowing of lower, older leaves is natural	No treatment necessary.
Yellow or white ring and spots on leaves	Splashing cold water on foliage while watering	Water more carefully. Do not splash foliage.
Swellings on leaves, corky ridges, water-soaked spots that turn red or brown	Too much moisture absorbed from warm, moist soil and cool, moist air	Increase warmth. Lower humidity. Place pot where soil will not get warmer than surrounding air.
Yellowing between veins of young leaves, older leaves less severely affected	Too little iron or magnesium	Boost with trace element fertilizer.
Healthy leaves but no blooms	Not enough light	Move to a position with more light.
	Not enough warmth	Check recommended temperature range for plant. If necessary, move to a warmer position.
	Too much nitrogen	Reduce or halt feeding. Use a low- or no-nitrogen fertilizer.
	Plant is too young or a late-flowering variety	Some plants take years to flower and some varieties bloom much later than others. Be patient.
Bud drop	Too much heat or cold	Check for cause of change such as window left open. Move to position with more moderate temperature.
	Shock from moving from greenhouse to home	Check plant's growing requirements. Adjust growing conditions to restore previous conditions, if possible.
	Poor humidity	Increase humidity.
	Draft shock	Control source of draft, or move plant to another location.

Houseplants in Your Home

Houseplants can be so much more than just a spot of greenery on a windowsill. Use them to fill your home with sweet fragrances, such as those of orange blossoms and jasmine. Brighten up the dull days of winter with the brilliant flowers of amaryllis and long-lasting, exotic orchids. Grow lush tropical plants to decorate the living room, and raise tasty herbs for the kitchen.

However, it is important to learn how to select the right plants for your available space. Different areas around your home will be suitable for different kinds of plants. See "Microclimates in Your Home", below.

Even if your home doesn't have big, sunny windows, you can still enjoy growing houseplants by using electric lights to create a garden even in the darkest corner of your home. See "Gardening under Lights" on page 228, for more information.

Whatever ways you choose to bring plants into your home, they will bring you much pleasure. They are a source of living and changing beauty, providing color, form, and fragrance throughout the year.

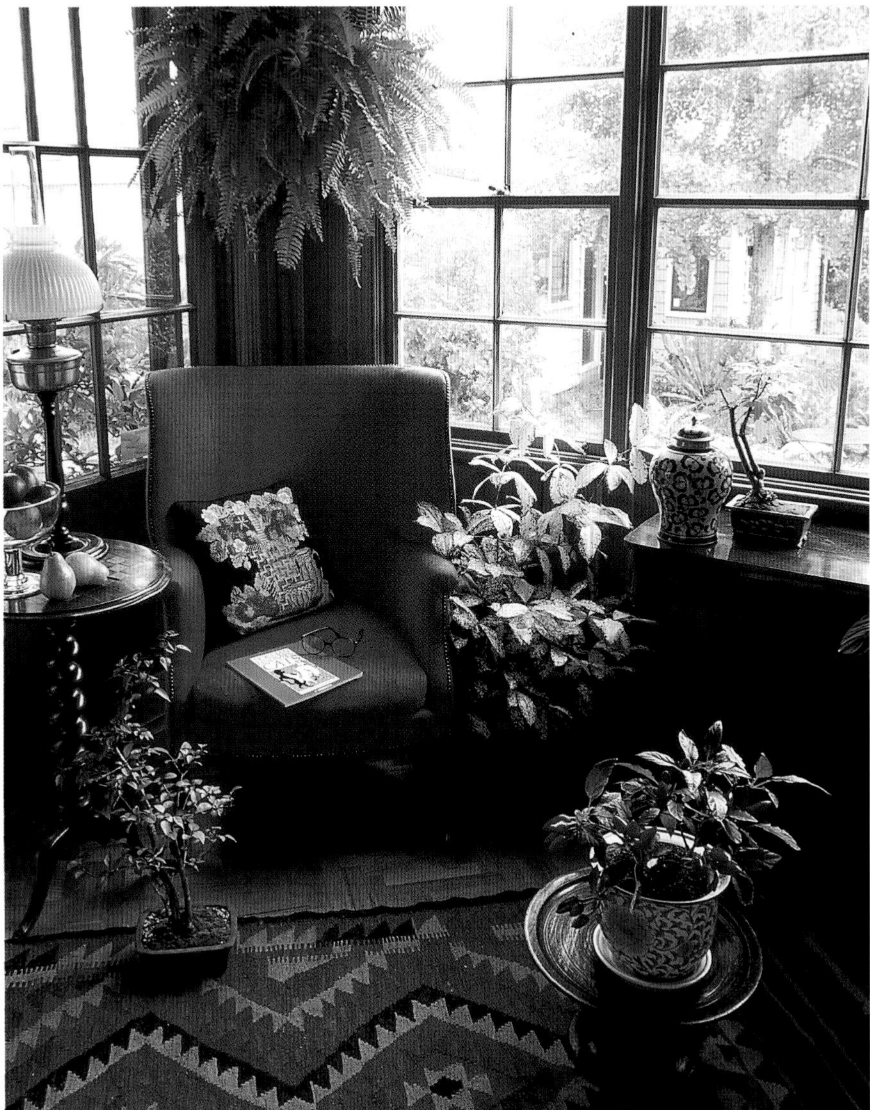

ABOVE: The two large windows in this room provide enough light for a variety of plants.

Microclimates in Your Home

Just as in the open garden, there is no single climate that covers every area in your home. Critical plant requirements—light, heat, moisture, and humidity—vary from room to room, and in different sections of each room, so it is worth the effort to find out where specific plants will grow best. However, remember that microclimates are not static—conditions vary with the season and with the ways in which you use your home.

Windows

When you are choosing a window for a particular plant, you have to consider more than the direction the window faces. A south-facing window opening onto a large, open area is going to provide your plants with a lot more light than it would if tall buildings, a shade tree or, worse, a mature evergreen were growing just outside.

Light intensity also varies with the season, from a maximum in summer, declining in fall to a minimum in winter, and then gradually increasing again in spring. Watch your plants for signs of light deficiency—pale, spindly growth and feeble looking leaves—during fall or early winter. If your plants are affected, gradually shift them to brighter windows.

Be careful, though. Moving a houseplant from a north-facing window directly to a sunny south-facing window can result in scorching. If a plant must be moved from low light to bright sunlight, place the plant to the side of the sunny

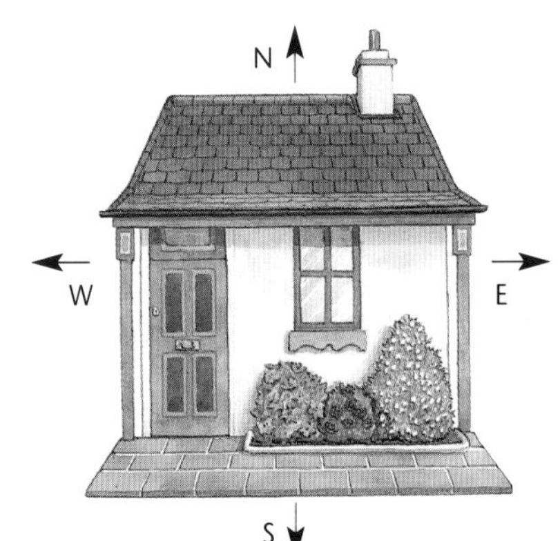

When placing houseplants, you need to consider the exposure of each window in your home, as well as features outside that may block the light.

window. After several weeks, move the plant into the direct sunlight.

Temperature

Temperature is a very important consideration, especially in those areas where air-conditioning and central heating are necessities in most homes. Most houseplants do not like rapid indoor temperature fluctuations and these often occur without us realizing it, especially in fall as cold fronts blow in.

A window above a heat vent or radiator may provide perfect light exposure but the temperature and humidity levels may be catastrophic for plants that like humid conditions and warm, but not hot, temperatures.

If you place a houseplant near a heater, when the heater kicks in, the temperature around that plant can increase very quickly and the warm air movement can rapidly dry out the foliage due to the warm air movement. *Ficus* trees can suddenly, and dramatically, shed their leaves when this happens.

Cyclamen

Winter holds another potential problem for houseplants—drafts. Plants that are kept inside during the winter months enjoy a warm environment. If a plant is located close to a frequently opened door or a cracked window, then temperatures can rapidly fluctuate every time the door opens. Such positioning may or may not be detrimental to plant health depending on the species.

Windowsills pose another problem due to heat buildup on sunny days and cold pockets on cold winter days. Monitor the temperature and choose hardy plants that tolerate these changing conditions.

Another problem area can be electrical appliances—especially televisions, VCRs, and stereos, which are likely to have plants placed nearby or even on them. These appliances produce heat and can rapidly heat up the air around your plants.

Humidity

Humidity is directly related to temperature. As temperature increases, the air is able to hold more water. Consequently, cool air tends to be dry. Most tropical plants come from the warm regions of the world and prefer high humidity. People, however, like to live in climate-controlled buildings with air-conditioning that actually reduces humidity. To combat this problem—especially with sensitive plants like ferns, orchids, and bromeliads—you can increase humidity by adding water to the air with humidifiers, and using other methods (see "Humidity and Temperature" on page 212).

RIGHT: Maidenhair ferns (*Adiantum* spp.), like most ferns, are tropical plants and like fairly high humidity. It is a good idea to provide extra moisture to the air in the room with a humidifier.

ABOVE: Flower production takes lots of energy, so blooming houseplants generally need all the light they can get.

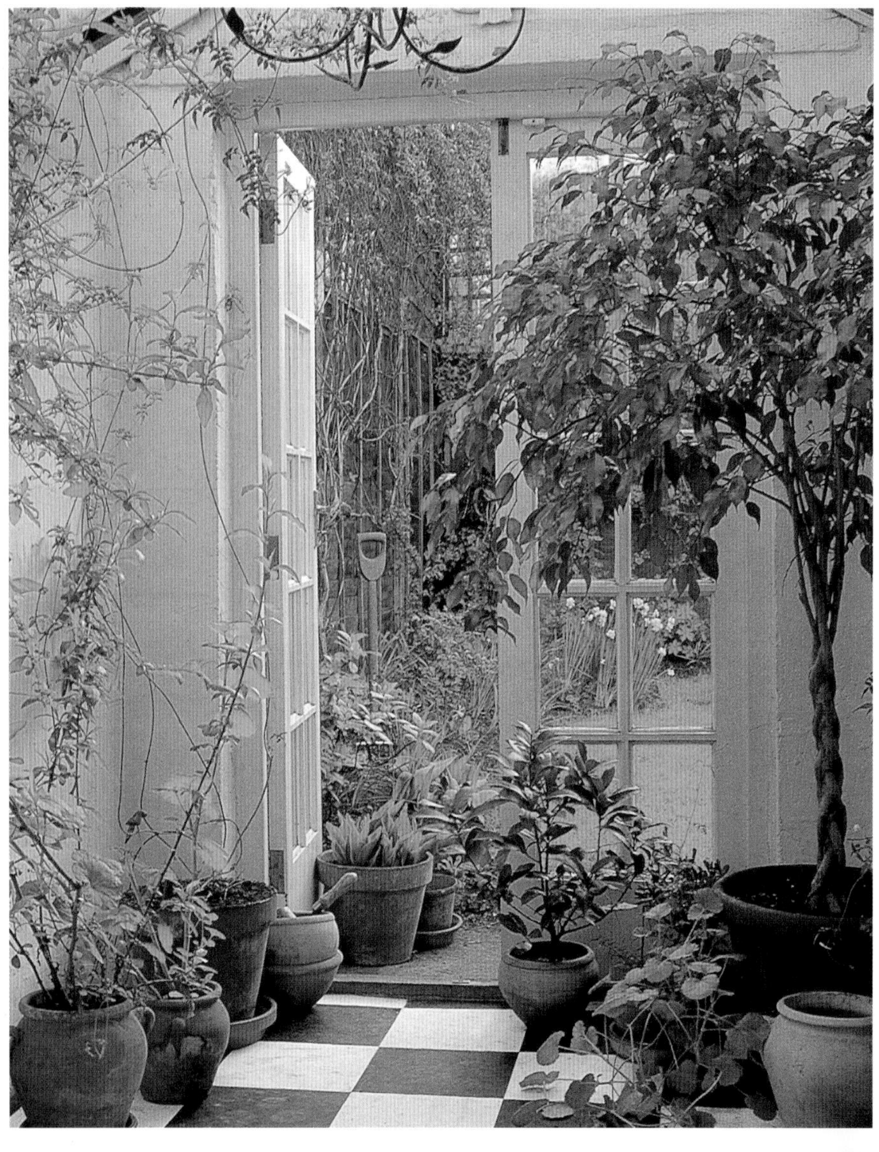

LEFT: A mixture of flowers and foliage adds a welcoming touch to a sunny entranceway.

Plants that require high humidity are best grown in terrariums or closed containers where it is possible to regulate the humidity (see "Creative Houseplant Displays" on page 234).

Bathrooms and kitchens, if they are sunny, often have a higher humidity than other areas of the home, and may be more suitable for humidity-loving houseplants.

Gardening under Lights

Even if your window space is limited, you can still have a colorful collection of houseplants—just set up your indoor garden under artificial lights. Besides allowing you to grow more plants, a well-designed light garden can really brighten up dark corners in the living room, kitchen, or other areas. There are two main kinds of lights to choose from—standard fluorescents (like those used in stores and offices) or special high-intensity discharge lights.

The light requirements for plants are often given as "low," "medium," or "high." Hold a hand between the source of light and the spot where a plant is to be set. The amount of shadow gives a rough measure of available light. If there is no shadow, or if it is very hard to see, low light exists. If the shadow is somewhat blurred, but definitely there, medium light exists. A sharp and distinct shadow indicates high light conditions.

A plant sitting in a sunny window receives less light than it would in a greenhouse or garden. A plant growing in a window gets most of its light from just one side and may grow in a lop-sided fashion toward the light. Turning the plant keeps it straight but it doesn't cure the lack of adequate light exposure.

Light duration greatly influences plants, as flowering and rest periods are triggered by particular daylengths. Actually it is the length of the dark period, or night, that controls the response. For instance, poinsettia blooms when given long nights. Blooming is prevented by a few minutes of light, given during the dark period. Some plants enter rest periods during the fall and winter in response to shortening days.

Fluorescent Lights

Fluorescent lights obviously aren't nearly as bright as sunlight, but they'll work fine to grow relatively short plants that only

A light setup can expand your houseplant options if your windows aren't bright enough for good growth.

LEFT: A sunny south-facing window is the perfect position for a collection of cacti and succulents. RIGHT: Most bromeliads thrive in sunny windows, but they can also adapt to bright north windows or fluorescent lights.

require low to medium light levels. Just be sure to keep your houseplants as close as possible to the lights for best growth.

The best size fixture of fluorescent light is one that holds two or four 48-inch (1.2-m) long bulbs. You can find "shop light" fluorescent fixtures and tubes at most hardware and home-supply stores. A two-tube, 4-foot (1.2-m) long setup complete with bulbs is quite affordable.

At your local garden center, you may also find more expensive fluorescent bulbs which are sold as "plant growth lights." Manufacturers claim that these lights are best for plant growth, but most research has concluded that these bulbs are really no better than the standard, and more inexpensive "warm white" or "cool white" bulbs that are widely available at most hardware stores.

High-intensity Discharge Lights

If you want to grow houseplants that are larger than about 1 foot (30 cm) tall under artificial light, you should consider using a high-intensity discharge (HID) light instead. HID lights use special sodium or metal halide bulbs, and they come in very bright-wattage ranges from 175 to 1,000 watts.

The 1,000-watt units are probably too intense for use anywhere except in a greenhouse or basement—you just wouldn't want to have such a bright light on in your living areas. But the 400-watt type is perfect for a spare corner in your living room or bedroom. It will provide an ample amount of light for a growing area about 6 feet (180 cm) square. HID lights are bright enough to grow virtually any plants you want—even large, sun-loving vegetables such as peppers and tomatoes. The lights aren't as bright as outdoor sunlight, but you can make up for some of the difference by leaving the lights on for up to 16 hours per day.

HID lights are generally available from specialty suppliers (such as those that sell equipment for greenhouse or hydroponic gardening). To find a source, look for ads in gardening magazines, or check your local phone book for greenhouse suppliers.

What about Light Bulbs?

Regular incandescent light bulbs don't work well for growing houseplants. Part of the reason for this is that the glow the bulbs give off doesn't provide the right wavelengths of light for good plant growth. The other reason is that they are very inefficient, releasing a lot of their energy as heat.

There are special "grow light" incandescent bulbs on the market, and these may help a little if you use them on a large plant in a dim corner. In general, though, you'll be spending a lot of money (for electricity and replacement bulbs) for little benefit. For best results, stick with fluorescent or high-intensity discharge (HID) lights.

Special Growing Guidelines

If you grow plants under electric lights (especially the brighter HID types), you'll need to fertilize regularly to keep up with the plants' growth. (Unlike outdoor or window plants, which slow down during cloudy weather, plants under lights keep growing steadily.)

To provide the right amount of light every day, you may want to buy a timer to automatically turn the lights on and off. Timers are available at hardware stores. Most experts suggest that you leave the lights on for 14 to 16 hours per day, unless you're growing day-length-sensitive flowering plants, such as Christmas cactus (*Schlumbergera bridgesii*) and poinsettia, which need short (12-hour) days to trigger flowering.

Poinsettia

Growing Plants Indoors

Whatever ways you choose to bring plants into your home, they will give you much pleasure. They are a source of living and changing beauty, providing color, form, and fragrance throughout the year. If flowers are your favorite, check out "Flowering Houseplants" below. "Growing Bulbs Indoors" on page 231 also has ideas on adding beautiful blooms to your home with amaryllis, paperwhite narcissus, and other easy-to-grow bulbs.

To keep your houseplants happy and healthy, consider giving them a summer vacation outdoors. When you bring them inside again in fall, you can also pot up garden plants such as rosemary, geraniums, and other tender herbs and flowers to enjoy indoors over winter and then move out again next spring. You'll find all the details on shifting plants around safely in "Inside Out and Outside In" on page 232.

The best place for most houseplants is in a sunny window but, for flowering houseplants, a high light position is usually mandatory.

Flowering Houseplants

Foliage houseplants are attractive and dependable, but it's really the brilliant colors and the fantastic fragrances of flowering plants that grab and hold the interest of houseplant-lovers of all levels. Flowering plants tend to demand a little extra care, but it's all worthwhile when you get to enjoy the beautiful blooms.

To get an idea of the wonderful plants you can pick from, stroll around any local greenhouse, or flip through "Encyclopedia of Flowers," starting on page 306. When you find a plant you simply must have, use the guidelines here to help keep it happy and vigorous.

Choose the Right Site

To grow flowering plants successfully, you must consider the available light levels carefully. If you put a foliage plant in a location where it gets less light than it would really like, it may still grow reasonably well. But without the necessary amount of light, a flowering plant will bloom poorly or may refuse to flower at all. Most flowering plants, such as hibiscus (*Hibiscus rosa-sinensis*), require high light—at least 4 hours of direct sun in a south window, for example. A few, such as the popular African violet (*Saintpaulia* hybrids), will flower in medium light levels, but almost none will bloom well in low light.

Generally, you should always give flowering plants your brightest windows. And if you can, move the plants outdoors for the summer. In many cases, a few months of brighter outdoor light will be enough for the plant to grow strong and set flower buds, even if you can only give it medium light during the rest of the year indoors. (Be sure to read "Inside Out and Outside In" on page 232 for information on how to safely move houseplants outside.)

Fertilize for Flowers

Besides giving them plenty of light, you'll also need to fertilize flowering houseplants carefully for the best blooms. To flower healthily, plants must have plenty of phosphorus, which is the middle number in the N-P-K rating you'll see on any bag or bottle of fertilizer. (If you're not clear on how the N-P-K ratings work, turn back to "Understanding Organic Fertilizers" on page 217 for a review.)

If you buy a plant that's already in flower, you don't need to worry about fertilizing it while it's blooming. But when

Try Moth Orchids for Months of Bloom

One of the best-kept secrets of indoor flower growing is the lovely moth orchid (*Phalaenopsis* hybrids). Orchids have a reputation of being difficult to grow, but these elegant hybrids will thrive easily in a warm spot, such as a windowsill.

They produce tall sprays of large, striped and spotted blooms in white, pink, yellow, green, and red.

The most amazing thing about colorful, winter-blooming moth orchids is that their graceful, arching flower sprays can last for many weeks. For the price of a bouquet of cut flowers (which only lasts a week or two) you can enjoy the beautiful blooms for up to several months at a time. Just water and fertilize them regularly, and give them a few weeks of cooler nighttime temperatures in the fall to set new flower buds.

Most cultivars of spring crocus respond well to forcing. You can pack many bulbs into one pot.

it finishes flowering, and if it's a kind that's likely to flower again for you (check the individual plant entries in "Encyclopedia of Flowers" starting on page 306, for that information), then you should begin feeding it. Give the plant a regular "balanced" fertilizer (one with roughly equal amounts of N, P, and K) as long as it's actively growing. Shortly before it's time for the plant to flower again, you should change to a fertilizer that contains extra phosphorus (such as a 5-7-4 fertilizer) to stimulate flowering.

Don't Expect Miracles

Despite your best care, there are some flowering houseplants that just simply refuse to bloom again the following year after you bring them home. Some plants may need special greenhouse conditions; others demand carefully maintained periods of light and darkness each day to repeat their colorful show.

Poinsettia (*Euphorbia pulcherrima*), Reiger begonia, and florist's cyclamen (*Cyclamen persicum*) are a few examples of houseplants that are difficult or nearly impossible to get to rebloom without a lot of fussing. (If you're not sure whether your plant will reflower, check the entry in "Encyclopedia of Flowers," starting on page 306.) If you really like looking at the leaves, you can keep these as foliage plants when they are done blooming; otherwise, discard them after flowering and buy replacements.

Growing Bulbs Indoors

Indoor bulbs are a terrific way to enjoy brilliant flowers and fragrance, especially during the winter months. You can even "force" some spring bulbs to flower early in order to enjoy their blooms ahead of time. Even though the process is called forcing, there's not much force involved. You simply provide a condensed version of the winter the bulbs would otherwise get when growing in the ground outdoors. All you have to do is pot them in the fall with pointed ends up and just the tips showing. Store them in a cool, dark place for several weeks (15 weeks for crocuses, 15 to 17 weeks for daffodils, 11 to 14 weeks for hyacinths, and 14 to 20 weeks for tulips), and keep them watered as needed. Then bring them inside to a bright windowsill. In a few weeks, you'll have beautiful bulbs blooming indoors even if there's still snow on the ground outdoors.

Bulbs for Forcing

Most spring bulbs can be forced, but some perform better in pots than others. Spring-blooming crocus, Siberian squill (*Scilla sibirica*), and reticulated iris (*Iris reticulata*) are very easy to chill and bring into bloom. A few tulips that perform especially well in containers include pale orange 'Apricot Beauty', plum purple 'Atilla', and some of the small, rock garden species (such as the lovely yellow-and-white *Tulipa tarda* and the yellow or bronze-pink *Tulipa batalinii*).

Tulips

Daffodils are also gratifyingly easy to force. Although the large, yellow, trumpet daffodils are traditional favorites, many gardeners also enjoy smaller, free-flowering cultivars such as 'Pipit', 'Hawera', and 'Tete-a-tete'. Hyacinths, too, usually perform well in pots; a few that are especially good include pale pink 'Lady Derby', darker pink 'Pink Pearl', deep

Easy Amaryllis

Amaryllis bulbs are easy to grow, and bloom year after year. Set potted amaryllis in a bright window and water lightly until they start growing—it takes just a few weeks for the flowers to open. Turn the plant regularly so the stalk won't become lopsided. Use a bamboo stake and a rubber band to hold the stalk once the giant flowers begin to open.

While amaryllis is flowering, you can move it to a table where everyone can enjoy it. When the flowers fade, cut off the stalk and return the plant to a bright window. During summer, put the potted plant outside in light shade. Water and fertilize, and let it grow to replenish the bulb. (You can continue growing it inside if you prefer.)

Before frost in the fall, bring the plant back inside and gradually reduce watering. As the leaves begin to die back, place the plant in a cool, dark area. The leaves will die down, and the bulb will go dormant. Don't water the plant during this period.

After a month or two, top-dress the pot with 1 inch (2.5 cm) of fresh mix and a teaspoon of bonemeal. Bring the plant back into a warm spot, water lightly until new growth begins, and then return it to a bright window and watch those wonderful flowers appear again!

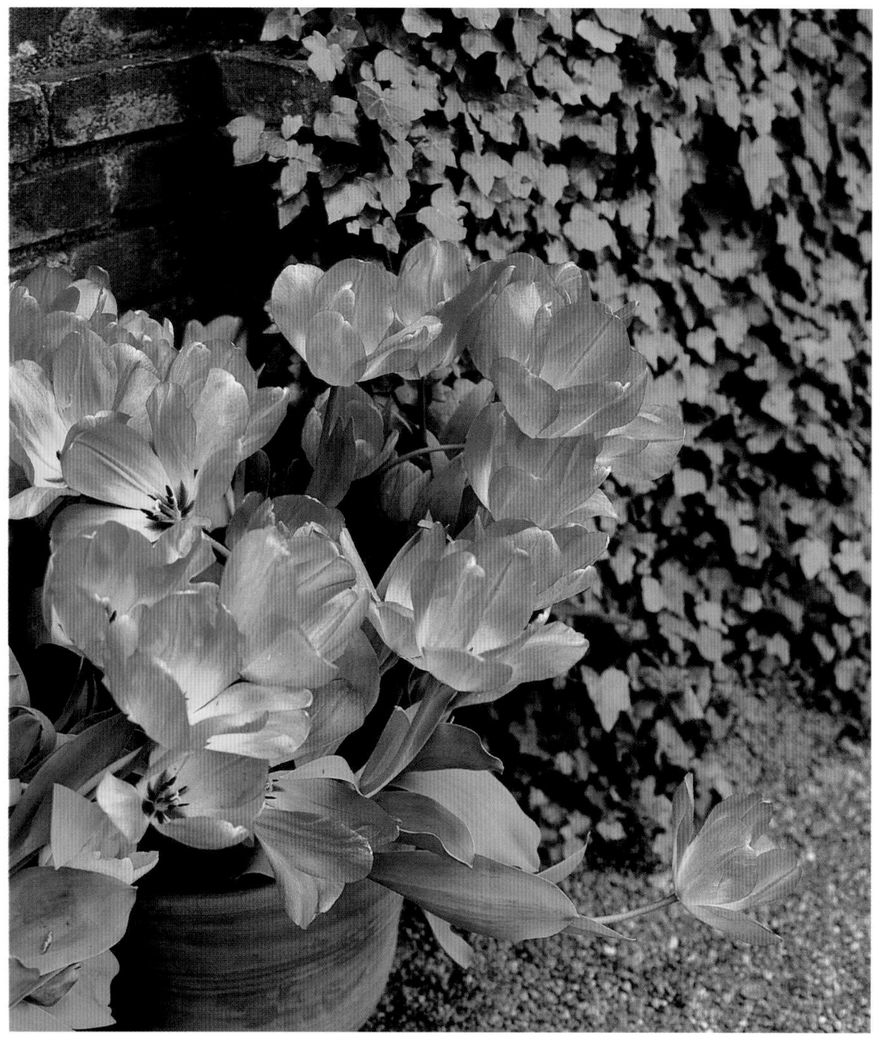

Pots dry out more quickly outdoors, so ensure you check them frequently to prevent wilting.

blue 'Blue Jacket', and salmon-pink 'Gypsy Queen'. Their sweet fragrance is ideal for curing a case of the winter blues!

For more ideas of bulbs to choose, check catalogs or garden-center bulb displays for the phrase "good for forcing." "Encyclopedia of Flowers," starting on page 306, also notes those bulbs that are particularly well suited for forcing.

Inside Out and Outside In

Just like people, many houseplants appreciate a vacation. Moving your houseplants outdoors for the summer months is a great way to keep them healthy and happy. When you bring them back in for the winter, you can also dig and pot up rosemary, geraniums, and other flowers and herbs for indoor enjoyment. To help your plants through these transitions, try the tips below.

Moving Indoor Plants Outside

Many indoor plants benefit from spending a summer outside. Flowering plants, which require bright light, will especially appreciate some time outdoors. If your plants have aphids, scales, or other pests, moving them outdoors can give beneficial insects a chance to attack the unwanted insects, solving your pest problems. If you have a large number of indoor plants, you may want to move the bright-light lovers outside for the summer and shift some medium-light plants to the brighter spots vacated by the high-light lovers.

Before moving plants outside, wait until the weather is warm and settled. Introduce indoor plants to outside sunlight gradually. If you don't, their leaves can show brown or white scorched spots.

To give your houseplants time to adjust, always place them in full shade when you first move them outside. After a few weeks in the shade, you can move the kinds that enjoy brighter light out from the shade to partial or full-sun locations.

Plants growing in the brighter, airier conditions of the great outdoors grow much faster than they do indoors, so they'll need more water and fertilizer than normal. Pay special attention to make sure they don't dry out; they may need daily watering when temperatures peak in summer. Check the individual entries in "Encyclopedia of Flowers," starting on page 306, to see if your particular plants have any special needs when they are living outdoors.

Bringing Outdoor Plants In

Many plants typically grown outside can also be enjoyed inside. Plants classified as "tender perennials" will keep on growing

To avoid sunburning your plants' leaves, always put indoor plants in a shaded spot for a while when you first move them outside.

Wax begonia

if you protect them from freezing temperatures by moving them indoors for the winter months.

Geraniums (*Pelargonium* spp.) are a perfect example. You can enjoy their colorful flowers or pleasant scents in the garden all summer, then bring them indoors in fall and keep them in a bright window. Other great plants for indoor growing include rosemary (*Rosmarinus officinalis*), wax begonias (*Begonia* Semperflorens-Cultorum hybrids), and coleus, just to name a few. You can even bring hot pepper plants inside to hold them over for the next year.

To move plants indoors, you can dig them up and set them in a pot. Usually you'll want to trim them back pretty hard to bring the top growth into balance with the now much smaller root ball. After they're potted up and trimmed, keep them well watered, and let them stay outside for a few weeks in part shade. This transition period will help them recover from the shock of being transplanted, so they can grow back nice and bushy. Be sure to bring any cold-tender plants inside as soon as frost is predicted.

If you'd rather have smaller plants (which fit better on windowsills), you can easily take root cuttings from many garden plants in summer or early fall. Cut off 3 or 4 inch (7.5 to 10 cm) long shoot tips, and remove all but two or three of the top leaves. Insert the bottom 2 to 3 inches (5 to 7.5 cm) of each cutting into a small pot of moist sand, vermiculite, or container mix, and cover the cuttings with a clear plastic bag to keep the humidity high. Place them in a warm, medium-bright location until they root and begin growing, then remove the plastic and move them to your brightest south windows for the winter. You can move the plants back out to the garden in spring, after all danger of frost has passed.

RIGHT: Geraniums make both excellent indoor and outdoor container plants.

When you bring any outdoor plants inside, there's always a chance you may bring in some pest problems as well. Once those pests are inside they can spread to your other plants quickly, since there are no natural enemies to keep them in balance. To minimize the chance of problems, inspect your plants carefully before you bring them in; refer back to "Common Houseplant Pests" on page 222 to remind yourself of what to look for and how to control any problems you find.

Certain garden plants are very susceptible to aphids when grown indoors. Hot peppers are a good example. If you find that aphids keep coming back even when you have sprayed the plant several times, it may be best just to enjoy that particular plant outdoors each summer and not try to keep it indoors. Or, if it's a plant you really love, you can order specific beneficial insects from mail-order suppliers and release them to munch on the aphids or other troublemakers.

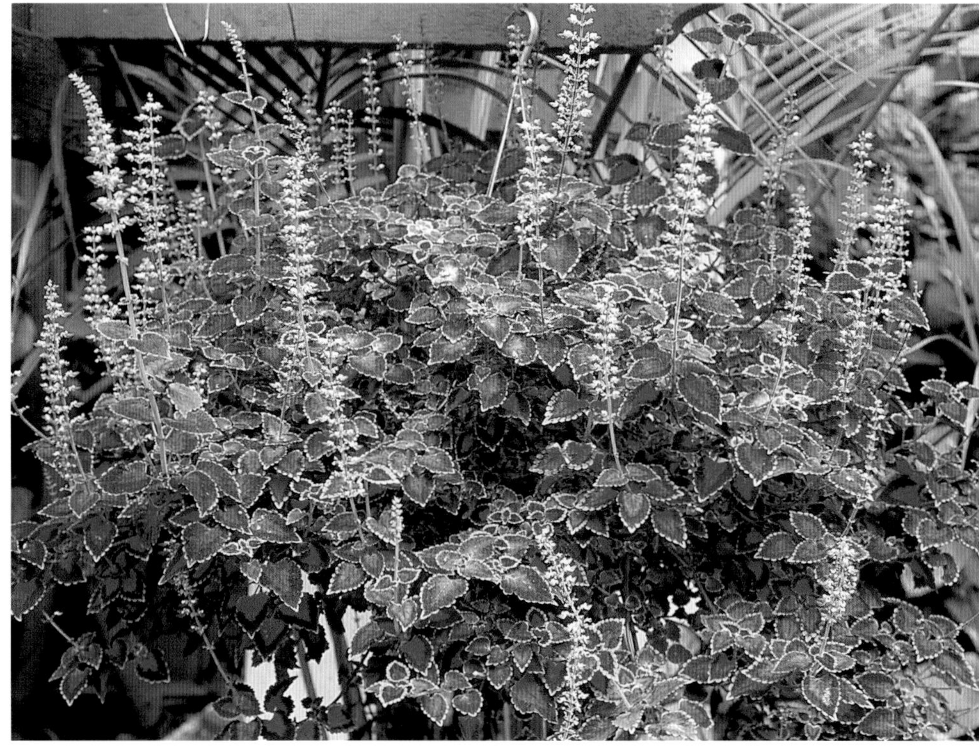
Bring coleus plants indoors during winter to brighten up the house with the colorful foliage.

Creative Houseplant Displays

There is no need to be limited in your choice of houseplants by the conventional. There are some amazing plants that can adapt to growing in your home—and a host of wonderful ways in which you can display them.

Terrariums, Dish, and Bottle Gardens

To get even more enjoyment out of your houseplant collection, you can create decorative groupings of colorful or unusual plants in terrariums, dish, or bottle gardens. These simple projects are fun, and they provide great, movable accents for any part of your home.

Try a Terrarium or Bottle Garden

Terrariums or bottle gardens are simply clear, glass containers in which you grow a group of plants. They work especially well for plants that require high humidity, such as ferns and insect-eating bog plants, such as Venus fly-traps. The moisture emitted by the leaves inside the glass container condenses and runs back into the soil.

Plants with patterned or variegated leaves, such as peperomias, look great in bottle gardens.

You can purchase beautiful, leaded-glass terrariums that resemble miniature conservatories, or you can use a container of virtually any shape. Old aquariums work particularly well, as do brandy snifters and recycled, clear glass wine jugs.

Next, decide what type of plants you want to grow. Tropical plants that like warm temperatures and high humidity, such as miniature gloxinias (*Sinningia* hybrids), polka dot plant (*Hypoestes phyllostachya*), ferns, and mosses, are generally a good choice. If you have a cool room, you could select a group of temperate woodland plants that like shade, humidity, and cool temperatures. Just be sure all the plants you choose like reasonably similar conditions. And unless you're using a large container, choose plants that won't grow very big.

Once you've chosen your container and selected your plants, place 1 inch (2.5 cm) of coarse sand or gravel in the bottom. Then add several inches of container mix and set in your plants. If you're planting

Making a Dish Garden

Dish gardens are an excellent way to display a collection of low-growing cacti or succulents. You can create a miniature desert landscape with these plants in a wide, shallow dish. Dish gardens look great displayed in the center of a coffee table.

1. Take a wide, shallow container and line it with about 1 inch (2.5 cm) of gravel. Cover the gravel with a 1-inch (2.5-cm) layer made up of half sand and half soil-based container mix.

2. While the plants are still in their original pots, place them in the dish and move them around to experiment with the design, until you are happy with the arrangement.

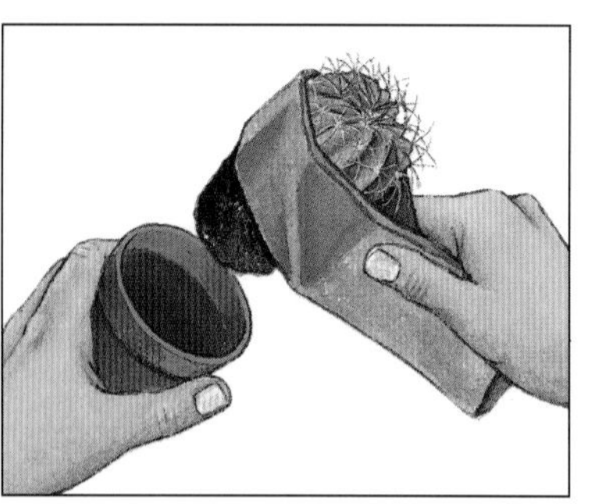

3. A good way to remove cacti from their original pots, without getting pricked by the spines, is to fold a piece of paper around the cactus and use this as a "handle" to lift the plant out.

4. Place the plants in the dish in your desired arrangement. Fill the dish with container mix by pouring the mix gently around the plants' roots.

ABOVE: You can train vines around various frames made from wire, bamboo, plastic, or rattan. Here jasmine is trained around a hoop-shaped wire.

LEFT: A stunning effect can be created by topiaries. Small-leaved, evergreen plants are most suitable for topiary training.

in a bottle with a small opening, you may need to use special long-handled tools to slide plants into the container. Water the plants to settle them into the mix.

Give the finished terrarium whatever light level the plants you selected require. However, be aware that the clear glass sides of the container will trap considerable heat, so keep the terrarium out of direct sunlight. And don't over-water—there are no drainage holes, and the container traps and recycles most of the moisture that evaporates from the soil and leaves. You may have to water only once a month, especially while the plants are small.

Dish Gardens

A dish garden is any open container in which you grow several different plants to create a miniature garden. This technique works especially well for smaller kinds of cacti and succulents, which grow well in a wide, shallow dish. As with the terrarium, you should choose relatively small plants, with shallow root systems, that all share similar requirements.

If you plant a dish garden of cacti or succulents, use a special cactus container mix, or make your own by mixing equal parts of standard container mix and sand. For other plants, standard, all-purpose container mix should work fine.

You can also decorate your dish garden with stone chippings, gravel, or even colored glass or tiny seashells. Many nurseries and garden centers stock these materials. Aquarium dealers also have a good selection of colored pebbles.

Training Houseplant Topiaries

Topiary is the art of training plants to a particular shape. It's actually quite easy, and there are many houseplants that adapt well to topiary training. There is a vast array of suitable shapes, so you can continually experiment with new topiaries to add to your houseplant collection.

Setting Up Standards

The simplest topiaries are known as "standards." To create a standard, you train a single-stemmed plant up a long stake, then trim the tip of the plant to form a round ball on top of the stem. One of the best houseplants to train as a standard is myrtle (*Myrtus communis*). It grows slowly in medium light, so you can enjoy the plant for many years. Plus, the leaves have a sweet fragrance when cut or crushed.

Training Plants to Topiary Forms

You can also make topiary by training an ivy, jasmine, or other vining plant onto a special wire form. Circles and heart shapes are common, but you can find them in a practically unlimited range of other shapes, too. To train a plant to a form, simply insert the form in the pot, then fasten the stems to whatever part of the form you

Top Picks for Topiaries

Many plants can adapt to life as a topiary, but some tend to be better-suited than others. You want a plant that will grow fast enough to give you results fairly quickly, but not so fast that it will outgrow its shape without weekly trimming. Here's a sampling of some of the best choices for indoor topiary projects.

English ivy (*Hedera helix*)
Lantana (*Lantana camara* or *L. montevidensis*)
Lavender (*Lavandula* spp.)
Myrtle (*Myrtus communis*)
Rosemary (*Rosmarinus officinalis*)
Scented geraniums (*Pelargonium* spp.)

Ivy

want to cover. Use coated wire or soft string ties to secure the plant's stems to the form as they grow.

Maintaining a Topiary

Care for topiaries the same way you would regular plants of the same kind. The only extra thing you need to do is trim the plant regularly to maintain the shape. Fast-growing plants may need trimming every few weeks to keep their shape; slower-growing species may only need clipping once or twice a year.

Hydroponics at Home

Hydroponics is the art of growing plants in water or another medium rather than soil. Some gardeners experiment with hydroponics inadvertently when cuttings of certain plants start growing roots after they have been a while in a vase or jar of water. More elaborate hydroponics systems are either active or passive.

Active hydroponics systems work by actively passing a nutrient solution over your plant's roots. The engine required to pump nutrient solution to your plants need be nothing more complex than a small aquarium water pump.

Passive hydroponics systems provide plants with nutrients through a capillary or wick system. Working like an oil lamp, the wick draws nutrient solution from the reservoir to the growing medium and roots.

You can grow bulbs in hyacinth glasses. Place the bulb in the top of the glass and fill it with water until it just touches the bulb.

Hydroponic gardening is so different to conventional forms of gardening that it can take a bit of experimentation until you feel comfortable but, once you have started, you may find it a flexible system for growing virtually any kind of plant.

Hydroponics kits are now available at many nurseries and garden centers and there are specialist hydroponics stores where you can get advice and support.

Many types of palm are slow-growing, and can take several years to reach their maximum height.

Exotic Plants

Are you looking for houseplants that fit the style of your home, or plants that explore some of the more unusual areas of houseplant gardening? You can add a special touch to your home with exotics such as palms, orchids, cacti and succulents, and other unusual plants.

Palms

Palms add a wonderful, tropical feeling to the indoor garden. They are bold houseplants that command attention. Palms suited to indoor cultivation are slow-growing while young, or have a small mature size. Some of the best palms for growing indoors include parlor palm (*Chamaedorea elegans*), a small palm, never taller than 3 feet (90 cm); bamboo palm (*Chamaedorea erumpens*), taller, forming clumps of smooth, slender stems; miniature date palm (*Phoenix roebelinii*), an elegant palm with dark green, glossy fronds and a textured trunk; and kentia palm (*Howea forsterana*) which has a slender trunk and a crown of dark-green, drooping, feather-shaped fronds. Check with your local garden center for other species of palms that are suitable for the indoors.

Orchids

Orchids are extremely popular and, with more than 35,000 kinds available, they are the largest family of flowering plants on earth—wild orchids grow everywhere except the Arctic and Antarctic. The popularity of orchids is no doubt due to the huge variety of flower colors and shapes. Orchids can be white, red, orange, yellow, green, purple, brown and even blue.

While some orchids can be expensive and difficult to cultivate, there are many others that are well within the average budget and no more difficult to grow than any other flowering plant.

Two easy orchids for the beginner are Dendrobium hybrids and Phalaenopsis

RIGHT: Showy cattleya orchids are among the most recognizable types. They can adapt to intermediate temperatures and medium light.

hybrids. Both of these orchids come in a wide variety of colors, but you will be most likely to find purple, pink, lavender, and white. Phalaenopsis orchids (sometimes called "moth orchids" because of the shape) are striped or spotted as well.

As you become more experienced at growing orchids, and learn how to meet their needs in your home, you may want to branch out into named varieties and rare species types. This is part of the fun of orchid culture and judicious selection will guarantee that something is in bloom all year long. Serious growers buy their plants from professional orchid breeders. For further information about orchids, see "Encyclopedia of Flowers," starting on page 306.

Carnivorous Plants

Carnivorous plants can be fun to grow and are of special interest to children, who find these specimens fascinating.

Pitcher plants (*Sarracenia* spp.) are flowering plants that use their leaves, shaped like pitchers, to trap insects. The pitchers produce nectar on the top of the plant to attract insects. The insides of the pitchers are lined with downward-pointing hairs that are used to prevent the insect from escaping once it is in the pitcher. The juices that are contained in the bottom of the leaf eventually digest the insect.

Venus fly-traps (*Dionaea muscipula*) supplement their nutrient intake by catching insects. They are low-growing, rosette-shaped plants with leafy stalks topped with two rounded, hinged blades. The leaves are touch-sensitive, so when an insect touches the leaves, the hinges snap shut and trap the insect.

Sensitive Plants

There are some plants that are sensitive to touch. If you simply touch them with a finger, the fern-like leaves will close up and droop on contact, reopening after several minutes. Sensitive plant, or touch-me-not (*Mimosa pudica*), is one of the most popular and widely available varieties. It has attractive balls of pink flowers, as well as the sensitive leaflets. It is easy to raise from seed if you can't find plants at your garden center.

Venus fly-traps are moisture-loving plants, and are ideal for terrarium or bottle garden culture.

Cacti and Succulents

There are so many varieties of cacti and succulents that at first the range can seem bewildering. Cacti and succulents have adapted to growing in the arid and semi-arid regions of the world. Their leaves have become smaller and their stems larger in order to store water and, in almost all cacti, the leaves have completely disappeared so that only the thickened green stems remain. Where they have not disappeared, the leaves may be thickened or insulated with coverings of hair, wax, or fleshy scales.

Cacti and succulents can be excellent houseplants for they are both adaptable and tough. They are suited to wide variations in temperature and can survive a certain amount of neglect. They need plenty of light; a bright, warm, south window is satisfactory for many. A window greenhouse is ideal and can accommodate many plants.

Because cacti and succulents can survive in relatively small amounts of soil, they can live in small pots. You can even combine an interesting collection of several types in one container. Large pot size can make moisture control difficult and may actually harm your plants.

There are many varieties of cacti and succulents and, as the plants differ in family, they also differ in physical characteristics in an enormous variety of form and color. Some unusual cacti include the bishop's cap (*Astrophytum myriostigma*), the old man cactus (*Cephalocereus senilis*), and the feather cactus (*Mammillaria plumosa*). The wax vine (*Hoya carnosa*) has clusters of waxy, delicately fragrant flowers. Many cacti and succulents will flower in a spectacular fashion when the growing conditions are ideal. Their brilliant flowers are often surprisingly large compared to the size of the plant.

An indoor succulent and cacti garden can be easy to maintain, as the plants tolerate a fair amount of drought.

The Right Houseplant for the Right Place

The key to growing houseplants successfully is matching your plants to the growing conditions they prefer. To help you make the best choices for your home, the following chart summarizes the specific needs of common flowering houseplants. You can see at a glance exactly which plants grow in low light, which need bright light, and which prefer cooler temperatures or need extra humidity to thrive. (For fuller definitions of low, medium, and high light conditions, see "Defining Light Levels" on page 213 for an explanation.) Pick the plants that will thrive in the growing conditions your home has to offer.

Flowering Houseplant	Light Needs	Water Needs	Comments
Flowering maples (*Abutilon* hybrids)	High	Moist; drier in winter	Keep at 50°–60°F (10°–16 °C) at night. Pinch shoot tips and fertilize for bushy growth and best flowering.
Chenille plant (*Acalypha hispida*)	Medium to high	Evenly moist	Needs warmth and high humidity.
Lipstick vine (*Aeschynanthus* hybrids)	Medium	Moist; drier in winter	Good for hanging baskets.
Flamingo flowers (*Anthurium* spp.)	Medium	Constantly moist	Must have warmth and high humidity.
Flowering begonias (*Begonia* spp.)	Medium	Allow to dry slightly between waterings	Discard Reiger types after flowering, as they will not usually rebloom next season.
Bougainvilleas (*Bougainvillea* spp.)	High	Allow to dry between waterings; water less after flowering	Needs warmth indoors; grow outdoors in summer.
Ornamental pepper (*Capsicum annuum*)	High	Evenly moist	Grow plants in the garden in summer and move them inside to a warm spot for the winter.
Chrysanthemums (*Chrysanthemum* spp.)	High	Moist	Prefer cool temperatures. Discard or plant outside after bloom.
Citrus (*Citrus* spp.)	High	Allow to dry slightly between waterings	Outstanding winter fragrance and fruit if you keep the plants outside for the summer.
Clivia (*Clivia miniata*)	Medium to high	Moist in summer, drier in winter	Keep cool (40°F [4°C]) in fall. Long-lived, reliable bloomer.
Coffee plant (*Coffea arabica*)	High	Constantly moist and high humidity	Needs a warm spot. Seldom produces flowers or beans when grown indoors.
Cigar plant (*Cuphea ignea*)	High	Allow to dry between waterings	Blooms readily.
Florist's cyclamen (*Cyclamen persicum*)	Medium to high	Evenly moist	Prefers cool nights. Blooms over a long period, but may not rebloom.
Crown of thorns (*Euphorbia milii*)	High	Allow to dry between waterings	Easy to grow.
Poinsettia (*Euphorbia pulcherrima*)	High	Allow to dry slightly between waterings	Prefers cool nights. May not rebloom.
Gardenia (*Gardenia jasminoides*)	High	Evenly moist with high humidity	Keep plants warm. 'Prostata' blooms more readily than standard types.
Hibiscus (*Hibiscus rosa-sinensis*)	High	Evenly moist	Keep plants warm. Hibiscus may grow to 6 feet (180 cm) tall.

None of the plants in this chart is difficult to grow if you provide the right conditions. If you're just getting started, though, you might want to try some of the plants that have a leaf symbol (❧) after their name. These are some of the easiest houseplants you can grow. They can tolerate some neglect, they're not fussy about how they're watered, and they're not particularly susceptible to pests or diseases. These plants are also easy to find: You'll find them at almost any garden center or grocery store. Once you've gained confidence, you can start looking for more challenging kinds in specialty catalogs and greenhouses.

Flowering Houseplant	**Light Needs**	**Water Needs**	**Comments**
Amaryllis (*Hippeastrum* hybrids) ❧	Medium; high when flowering	Moist while in active growth	Keep bulbs warm to start new growth after the rest period. Amaryllis will rebloom every year with minimal care. Keep the plant cool while in bloom, so flowers last longer.
Wax vine (*Hoya carnosa*) ❧	Medium to high	Allow to dry between waterings	Very durable vining plant.
Jasmines (*Jasminum* spp.)	High	Evenly moist	Jasmines generally prefer warmth, but some need a cool period in fall to flower. Superb fragrance. Prune after bloom season.
Kalanchoe (*Kalanchoe blossfeldiana*)	High	Allow to dry between waterings	Thrives in average to cool temperatures. May not rebloom.
Orange jasmine (*Murraya paniculata*) ❧	Medium to high	Evenly moist	Easy to grow, with superb fragrance.
Orchids	Ranges from low to high	High humidity; allow to dry between waterings	Moth orchids have very long-lasting flowers.
Sweet olive (*Osmanthus fragrans*)	High	Allow to dry slightly between waterings	Plants prefer cool conditions. The small flowers have superb fragrance.
Oxalis (*Oxalis* spp.)	High	Evenly moist	Some types require a dormant (rest) period after flowering.
Passionflowers (*Passiflora* spp.)	Very high	Keep moist while growing	Plants need warmth. Many types are fragrant; robust vines will require a trellis.
Geraniums (*Pelargonium* spp.)	High	Allow to dry between waterings	Geraniums can take average to cool temperatures. Grow them outside in summer. There are many types of geranium with scented or patterned leaves.
African violets (*Saintpaulia* hybrids)	Medium	Allow to dry slightly between waterings	Keep African violets warm. They make excellent long-blooming houseplants.
Christmas cactus (*Schlumbergera bridgesii*) ❧	Medium to high	Moist while blooming; then drier	Requires long, dark nights and cool temperatures in fall to set flower buds.
Gloxinias (*Sinningia* hybrids)	Medium to high	Keep moist and provide high humidity	Gloxinias prefer warmth, but they appreciate a cool rest period after flowering.
Jerusalem cherry (*Solanum pseudocapsicum*)	High	Keep moist	Keep plants cool. May grow to 4 feet (120 cm) tall.
Stephanotis (*Stephanotis floribunda*)	High	Keep moist	Vining plants produce clusters of fragrant star-like flowers.
Cape primrose (*Streptocarpus* hybrids)	Medium	Keep moist	Cape primrose offers a long period of colorful bloom.

SECTION NINE

Basic Garden Design

Garden color comes from plants—from their flowers, fruit and foliage—and from other elements in the landscape, such as paths, paving and even the house. Color can be used with restraint or exuberance, and may vary from season to season. In the following pages, we examine the major plant colors, then look at how they can be combined successfully in a garden.

Color by Design *242*

A Garden for the Senses *262*

Landscaping with Plants *270*

Solving Landscaping Problems with Plants *274*

Special Plant Effects *280*

Using Trees, Shrubs, and Vines *284*

Color by Design

Color can be used in your garden in many ways, from the simple formality of an all-green garden, to calming blues and purples, sunny yellows, and vibrant yellows and oranges.

Green

Few monochromatic garden schemes work as well as peaceful green. Green hues are the most restful to look at and are the kindest of all colors, visually. The Italians were the first to make decorative use of the all-green garden, notably in the symmetrical, Renaissance gardens where carefully pruned trees were used to create formal avenues and vistas. Clipped hedges were used to link the villa and garden structurally and to divide the garden into compartments. Classical ornaments were some of the decorative features used in these gardens. Only a limited variety of plants was used and you can imitate this inventiveness on a smaller domestic scale.

Foliage for Food

In Medieval monastic gardens, plants were grown both for their beauty and for use as kitchen crops or herbs. The modern garden, with its often restricted space, is ideal for reviving this style of mixed gardening. Vegetables and herbs can be as decorative as flowering plants, and look particularly effective when planted in an all-green garden. Here you can experiment with different plant combinations and really enjoy (as well as feed) yourself. With its dramatic sculptural shape, angelica *Angelica archangelica* is an herb to be used boldly. Group three or four together for height at the back of a border. Make use of the aromatic bay *Laurus nobilis* with its dense, rich green foliage that will tolerate close clipping—the bay has always been popular for hedges and topiary.

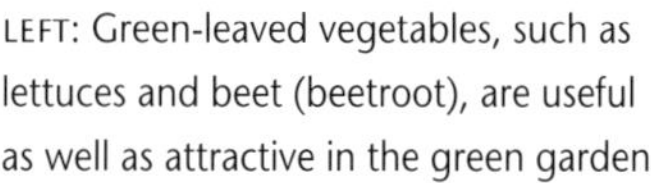

Grape vine

LEFT: Green-leaved vegetables, such as lettuces and beet (beetroot), are useful as well as attractive in the green garden.

Leafy perennials, such as rhubarb, cabbages, spinach and chard, can be fitted in between existing plantings, while ornamental, edible foliage plants, such as fennel and lovage, can be used as features. Paths can be edged with small, frilly lettuces and parsley. Thyme has always been a popular foliage plant and taller types can be clipped as very dwarf hedges. Marjoram and oregano are good edging plants that will quickly spill over the edges of paths or fill bare patches between paving and steps. Perhaps tuck in some variegated mint for a change of texture. And don't forget a grape vine, which can be grown against a wall or over a pergola, creating a ceiling of greenery and dangling clusters of decorative green fruit.

ABOVE: Green herb garden with lemon balm *Melissa officinalis*, thyme *Thymus* spp. and rosemary *Rosmarinus officinalis*.
LEFT: Garden alcove with standard *Robinia pseudoacacia* 'Mop Top' and Monterey cypress *Cupressus macrocarpa* hedge.

Go Tropical

If a lush, green tropical look is for you, then an abundance of carefully chosen evergreens planted at different levels will help create the mood of a tropical garden—even in a temperate climate. Rich, verdant greens, bold foliage forms and textures become all-important, as do the movement and form of shadows. Retain any existing trees to provide structure to the landscape and shelter for any large-leaved plants that may become damaged by wind. Beneath them you can grow a colony of shade-loving ferns, clumps of aspidistras or bold masses of hostas. Both the windmill palm *Trachycarpus fortunei* and the Japanese banana *Musa basjoo* are reasonably hardy, tropical-looking specimens for warm, sheltered spots. Groves of *Cordyline australis* and tree ferns such as *Dicksonia antarctica* will definitely add a touch of class, especially when viewed against the light. For a pool-side setting, plant the arum lily *Zantedeschia aethiopica* 'Green Goddess' for its large, glossy leaves and exotic, green-tinged flowers. However, for enhancing a water feature it is hard to beat *Gunnera manicata* with its fabulous, giant leaves. Last but not least, don't forget to include some climbers.

BELOW: Subtropical green garden featuring cabbage trees *Cordyline* spp., bromeliads, mondo grass *Ophiopogon* spp. and crotons *Codiaeum* spp.

Foliage Plants for a Tropical Retreat

Adiantum pedatum (American maidenhair)
Cordyline australis (New Zealand cabbage tree)
Dicksonia antarctica (soft tree fern)
Dryopteris filix-mas (male fern)
Fatsia japonica (Japanese aralia)
Hosta spp. (hostas)
Matteuccia struthiopteris (ostrich fern)
Musa basjoo (Japanese banana)
Phormium tenax (New Zealand flax)
Phyllostachys spp. (medium-sized bamboos)
Polystichum setiferum (soft shield fern)
Tetrapanax papyrifer (rice-paper plant)
Trachycarpus fortunei (windmill palm, chusan palm)

Variegated

Variety creates interest in the garden and this can be highlighted with the decorative use of foliage with contrasting, variegated leaf color. With evergreen or prolonged display, variegated leaves are invaluable when seasonal flowers have disappeared, especially toward the end of summer.

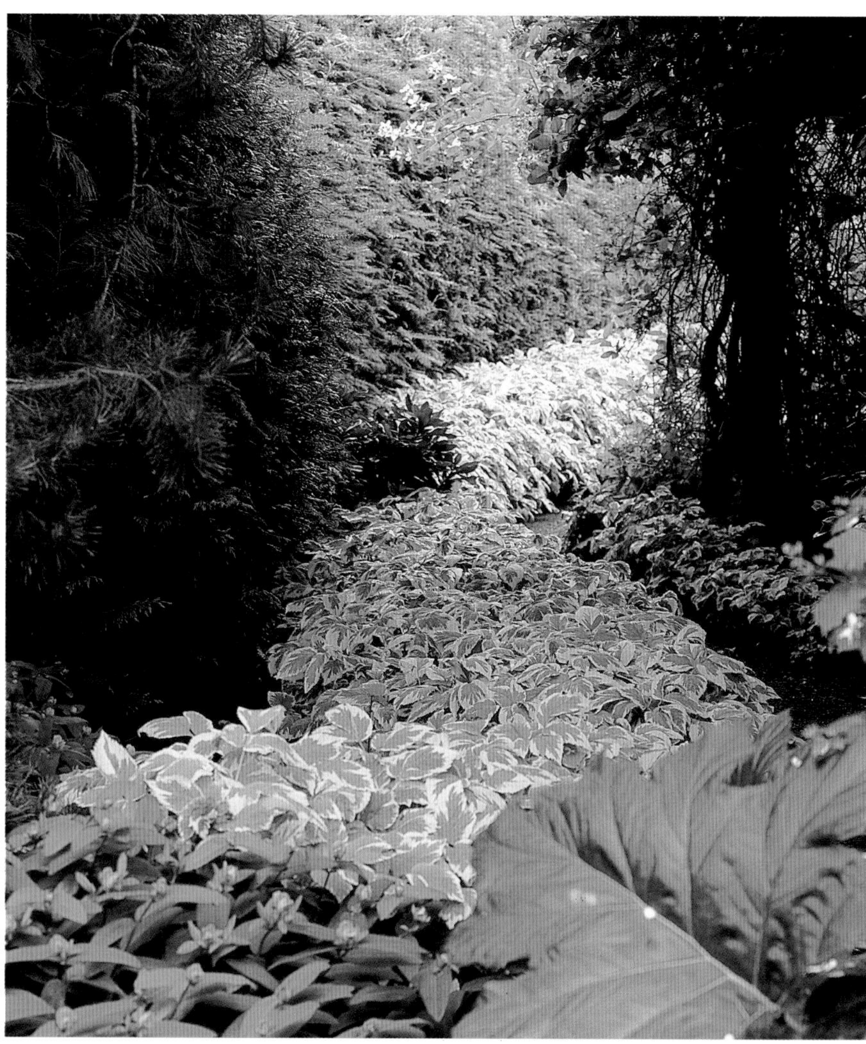

Using Variegated Plants

Hostas are among the most beautiful and useful foliage plants and many have variegated leaves—they are even lovelier when grown in dappled shade and are ideal for moist, woodland-type areas. Use them in masses as an edging to highlight a winding pathway, or plant them together with waterside plants.

Don't overlook the endless possibilities of the variegated ivies that will lighten a dark corner even through the bleaker months. They can also be used as groundcovers in places where grass won't survive and may be trained over fences, archways or sheltered walls as well as unsightly sheds. Ivies can also be trained on wire frames to produce topiary features. Smaller-leaved cultivars of *Hedera helix* produce a wide range of attractive variegations in gold, cream and silver. These can be trained horizontally along the front of a border or rock garden to form a dainty hedge.

It's hard to beat the variegated phormiums for sheer design, strong visual impact and individuality. They form large clumps of long, leathery, swordlike leaves and the eye is naturally drawn to them. Use them as focal points to entryways, pools, courtyards and rock gardens, as well as set among perennials.

ABOVE: A sea of variegated ivy among acanthus.
BELOW LEFT: Choose giant hostas for creating drama in a mixed planting, or alone as an accent.

Create positions in your garden to suit your favorite variegated plants. If you like arum lilies, tuck in a few clumps among your shrubs. Lush, broad-leaved plants can be set off against the striped spear-like leaves of *Iris pallida* 'Variegata'. For flower arrangers, the intricately patterned leaves of *Arum italicum* and the white-splashed leaves of *Zantedeschia elliottiana* can be picked for indoor arrangements.

Variegated Grasses

Although you don't want to overdo the use of variegated leaves in your garden

ABOVE: Caladiums are invaluable for summer color in shady beds and borders, especially in warm- and hot-summer areas.
RIGHT: Coleus are great for all-season color. Groups of mixed leaf plantings can look too busy, so grow them alone in masses.

design, as the effect can be very busy, you may want to experiment with some of the less invasive of the ornamental grasses. Often the most interesting forms have striking variations, especially cultivars of *Miscanthus sinensis*, such as 'Morning Light' and 'Variegatus.' 'Zebrinus' is a tall variety with horizontal bands of gold across the leaf blade, giving it the common name of zebra grass. It is a real eye-catcher and looks good in cottage gardens. All the above grasses are moderately frost-hardy and may also be used for waterside plantings.

Placing Variegated Plants

Variegated leaves are rarely as vigorous as their plain green counterparts, so it's often best to keep the plants out of direct sunlight. White-patterned plants, especially, are apt to be scorched in full sun. Use them to bring light and artistry to shaded places. Also, variegated plants tend to revert to plain green: If you see a green shoot, remove it straight away or it will eventually crowd out the variegated ones.

LEFT: Variegated ornamental grasses make wonderful garden accents, especially when used creatively in sculptural containers.

Variegated Foliage Plants

Arum italicum 'Marmoratum' (Italian arum)
Aspidistra elatior 'Variegata' (cast-iron plant)
Glechoma hederacea 'Variegata' (variegated ground ivy)
Hedera colchica 'Sulphur Heart' (Persian ivy)
Hedera helix varieties and cultivars (English ivy)
Hosta crispula
Hosta fortunei 'Albopicta'
Hosta fortunei 'Aureamarginata'
Hosta 'Moonlight'
Hosta 'Shade Fanfare'
Hosta undulata var. *univittata*
Iris pallida 'Variegata' (Dalmation iris)
Lamium maculatum (dead nettle)
Liriope muscari 'Variegata' (lily turf)
Melissa officinalis 'Aurea' (lemon balm)
Mentha suaveolens 'Variegata' (variegated apple mint)
Miscanthus sinensis 'Morning Light' (Japanese silver grass)
Miscanthus sinensis 'Variegatus'
Miscanthus sinensis 'Zebrinus' (zebra grass)
Phalaris arundinacea var. *picta* (gardener's garters)
Phormium tenax 'Variegatum' (flax)
Pleioblastus variegatus (bamboo)
Vinca major 'Variegata' (periwinkle)

Dead nettle

White

Many beautiful garden effects are achieved by using white flowers alone. Because they reflect so much light, white flowers appear almost luminous as dusk falls and seem to glow through the night. Make good use of this feature by growing white flowers to highlight paths, driveways and entrances, to create an impression of light. For quick results, advanced annual seedlings, such as candytuft, violas, petunias, primulas and lobelias, all come in white and are excellent for edging.

An all-white garden looks cool in the hottest weather. However, in masses, white can be a little overwhelming. Include some soft gray-leaved plants, such as some of the artemisias, lavender cotton *Santolina* spp. and mats of lamb's ears *Stachys byzantina*, to soften the impact of the bright whites. The occasional pale pastel-colored flowers, such as ivory tulips or creamy white roses, together with the odd patch of white-variegated foliage, add a complementary and subtle contrast.

Studying Form

Planning a white garden often involves choosing a framework of key plants.

Favorite White Flowers

- Azaleas
- Camellias
- Clematis
- Gardenias
- Moonflower (right)
- Jasmine
- Japanese anemones
- Lilies
- Lily-of-the-valley
- Petunias
- Roses
- Tobacco flowers
- Tulips
- Viburnum
- *Wisteria sinensis* 'Alba'

Climbers

Clothe walls and fences with *Clematis armandii* or *C. montana*. Climbing, white roses are another choice, perfect for adorning arches, pergolas and arbors. Against a warm, sunny wall Confederate jasmine gives you neat, evergreen foliage all year, and clusters of dainty, white, jasmine-like flowers in summer. It can also be used as a groundcover. Climbing hydrangea *Hydrangea petiolaris* is good for shady walls and fences.

Among the most magnificent of climbers is the white Chinese wisteria *Wisteria sinensis* 'Alba' with its long, vertical festoons of perfumed flowers. It does not always have to grow against a wall or support—it can be planted in the open as a standard and with careful pruning, will become more beautiful and shapely over time.

Flower Beds and Borders

Most gardeners find it easiest to grow their white flowers within a border. When planting herbaceous beds and borders, consider the height of the plants. By all means position the taller plants behind low-growers, but make sure that they are well displayed at their flowering

ABOVE: White annuals and perennials look stunning when planted with white-variegated foliage plants, such as hosta.

RIGHT: White poppies, white cosmos and sweet alyssum *Lobularia maritima*.

times. A border might include daisies, aquilegias, lilies, baby's breath, dahlias, carnations and some annuals. Clump-forming perennials, such as white campanulas, foxgloves and columbines, with their tall, elegant spires of flowers, look great when backlit by morning sun.

Designing with Shrubs

A number of shrubs of the same species planted in a row as a hedge or in groups provides good structural form to the garden. For instance 'Iceberg' roses, camellias, azaleas, viburnums and the double form of the gracefully arching *Spiraea cantoniensis* all make stunning white-flowering hedges.

A White, Scented Garden

Many white flowers are perfumed. You can create a romantic, white, scented garden within a "secret," or private, area of your garden surrounded or defined by hedges. Plan for a succession of scented, white bulbs from early spring with the honey-scented snowdrop and *Crocus chrysanthus*, then the exquisite lily-of-the valley, freesias and hyacinths, followed by the glorious summer lilies *Lilium candidum* and *L. regale*. *Galtonia candicans* will fill the garden with delicious fragrance from midsummer to early autumn. In warmer areas plant a border of heady gardenias and provide a comfortable garden seat to prolong the pleasure.

Night Scents

Famed for its evening fragrance, the tobacco plant *Nicotiana elata* can be placed at the back of the border. As soon as the sun goes down, it sends its rich sweet scent into the night air. Dame's rocket *Hesperis matronalis* var. *albiflora* is another favorite night-scented plant.

TOP: Black and white paved courtyard featuring standard white 'Iceberg' roses.
ABOVE: A silver and white garden looks crisp and clean during the day and also stands out at night.

Silver and Gray

Some of the most outstanding foliage plants have silver or gray leaves. The silvery color of certain plants' leaves is caused either by the reflection of light from millions of tiny hairs, or small beads of wax in leaves, which protect the plants from dehydration. Silver and gray plants harmonize beautifully with other colors, but a silver and gray theme by itself can look delicate and magical.

Silver and Gray Stunners

For a breathtaking sight, you can't beat the magnificent Colorado spruce *Picea pungens* 'Glauca', long regarded as one of the most highly desirable, silvery blue conifers. If you lack space, the smaller-growing 'Koster' will form a neat, conical shape with the same coloring and can be used for specimen and group planting. The slower-growing dwarf 'Montgomery' could become the star of your rock garden, especially through the long winter months. If you want something truly unusual, you could train the cascading *Cedrus atlantica* 'Glauca Pendula' over a timber support to display its fantastic curtains of silvery gray foliage.

One of the most statuesque of gray-leaved plants is the cardoon *Cynara cardunculus*—a close relative of the artichoke. It reaches 7 feet (2.1 m) and has large, silvery gray, deeply divided leaves. To be seen at its best it needs plenty of space, and it makes an outstanding addition to any silver garden scheme.

You could also include some of the aromatic lavenders, especially the silvery gray *Lavandula angustifolia* 'Hidcote'. This lavender has a neat, compact habit and is very popular in herb garden designs.

Silver and Gray Plants

Agave parryi (agave)
Artemisia absinthium 'Lambrook Silver' (common wormwood)
Artemisia ludoviciana 'Silver Queen' and 'Valerie Finnis' (silver king artemisia)
Artemisia 'Powis Castle'
Artemisia stelleriana 'Broughton Silver' (beach wormwood)
Buddleia alternifolia (fountain butterfly bush)
Cynara cardunculus (cardoon)
Echeveria spp. (echeveria)
Festuca glauca (blue fescue)
Lavandula angustifolia 'Hidcote' (English lavender)
Ruta graveolens 'Jackman's Blue' (rue)
Salvia officinalis (sage)
Santolina chamaecyparissus (lavender cotton)
Senecio cineraria (dusty miller)
Senecio viravira
Stachys byzantina (lamb's ears)
Verbascum olympicum (mullein)
Yucca rigida (yucca)
Yucca whipplei (our Lord's candle)

TOP: Cardoon, dusty miller, wormwood and ballota create a stunning silver-gray grouping.
RIGHT: Colorado spruce *Picea pungens* 'Glauca'.

FAR LEFT: Silvery gray lamb's ears *Stachys byzantina* look great when grown alone in masses.
LEFT: Create an elegant effect by combining artemisia and lamb's ears with blue-leaved pinks.

Artemisias have some outstanding gray and silver leaves—*Artemisia ludoviciana* and its cultivars 'Silver Queen' and 'Valerie Finnis' and *Artemisia absinthium* 'Lambrook Silver' are all great assets in a mixed, silver border. For a fine foliage contrast, tuck in some blue fescue *Festuca glauca.*

A beautiful specimen plant is the silvery green form of *Buddleia alternifolia*—a tall, deciduous shrub that can be trained as a standard to give a graceful, weeping effect that is further enhanced in summer with fragrant, lilac flowers.

Silver Succulents

Many succulent perennials with interesting, architectural qualities have silver or gray foliage. They are valuable in emphasizing structure in the garden and make dramatic focal points. *Agave parryi* is a good accent plant, forming rosettes of gray-blue, succulent leaves. When planted in rows, it makes a pleasing low hedge and looks beautiful against a softly colored sandstone wall.

Yucca rigida has 3-foot (90-cm) long, powdery blue leaves that form a rosette from the top of a trunk that grows to 6 feet (1.8 m) tall. It makes a dramatic landscape feature, especially near pools, and looks good planted with a small group of stemless *Y. whipplei*, which form a dense, almost globular clump of rigid, gray-green leaves. Both species bear spectacular, straight spikes of creamy white, waxy flowers in summer.

Small and Silver

Smaller plants can also be important accents, providing emphasis at ground level. They are best planted in groups of three or more to give the whole arrangement form.

Lavender cotton *Santolina chamaecyparissus*, with its lacy, silvery, aromatic foliage, makes an excellent low hedge. Because it is trouble-free and withstands close trimming, it is extremely popular for setting off the more solid greens of formal, clipped gardens and old-fashioned, herbal knot gardens.

Another well-loved border plant is lamb's ears *Stachys byzantina*, which creates a lovely mat of silvery, velvet-textured leaves and in summer bears spikes of small, pinkish or mauve flowers. The non-flowering form, *S. byzantina* 'Silver Carpet', is also popular.

For a dry, sunny spot, make use of the echeverias—striking silver-leaved succulents that can be used as groundcovers or rockery edging, or allowed to spill over urns or walls.

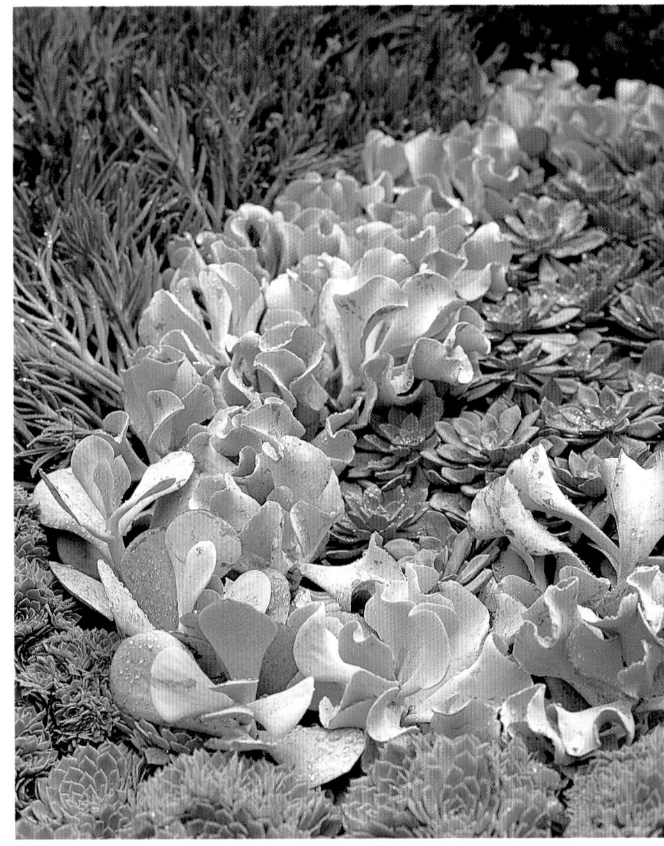

RIGHT: Silver-gray succulents make an eye-catching feature.

Red

If you like bursts of brilliance and visual drama in your garden, red flowers are for you. Red cannot help but make an impression and it is the easiest color to use for impact.

Mum

Begonia

Gerbera

Pansy

Daylily

Up Close and Personal

Red flowers seem to come forward. This can help create a feeling of intimacy in a small garden, or to lead the eye to the front door or a particular garden feature. Hot, vibrant reds often look better close to the house or in areas associated with various kinds of activity, such as the swimming pool or a terrace used for dining.

Watch the Tones

Scarlet reds with an orange undertone, and crimson reds with a blue pigment may clash violently, so try to keep the two colors apart in a flowering border.

Scarlet dahlias, verbenas, begonias, *Crocosmia* 'Lucifer', *Zinnia elegans* Dreamland Series and the firecracker plant *Russelia equisetiformis* all have tomato-red tones that work well together, particularly when they are used against plain green foliage.

Crimson red flowers, such as some of the darker red roses, tulips, dianthus and fuchsias, blend together. The plum-colored foliage of purple sage *Salvia officinalis* 'Purpurascens', varieties of *Heuchera* and the strappy leaves of the purple New Zealand flax will pick up the blue pigment of crimson red flowers and will enrich their setting.

Non-flowering Plants with Red Features

In all gardens, plants look more arresting if placed next to others with very different textures. Here are some fabulous plants with red features that will provide you with an interesting balance of texture and shape throughout the year.

Berberis thunbergii 'Red Pillar' is a small upright shrub to 4½ feet (1.35 m) with small, neatly rounded, reddish-purple leaves and glossy, red fruit. Although deciduous, this is a charming background shrub for a red flower border.

Dwarf capsicums or chilies *Capsicum* spp., with their bright, dangling red fruits, can be grown as ornamentals and add texture and variety in a group of red-flowering plants.

LEFT: Red maple *Acer rubrum*.

BELOW: The striking red stems of ruby chard.

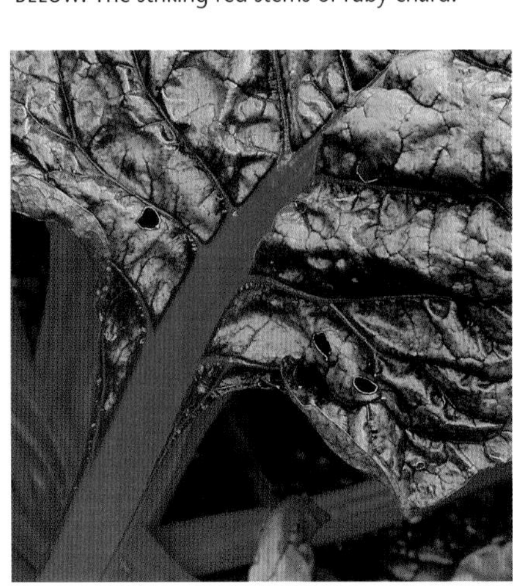

ABOVE: Joseph's coat *Amaranthus tricolor.*
TOP RIGHT: The stone path is a great foil to the massed planting of red flowers which includes petunias, geraniums, lobelias and begonias.
BOTTOM RIGHT: If you are looking for can't-miss color, then an all-red border may be the perfect accent for your garden.

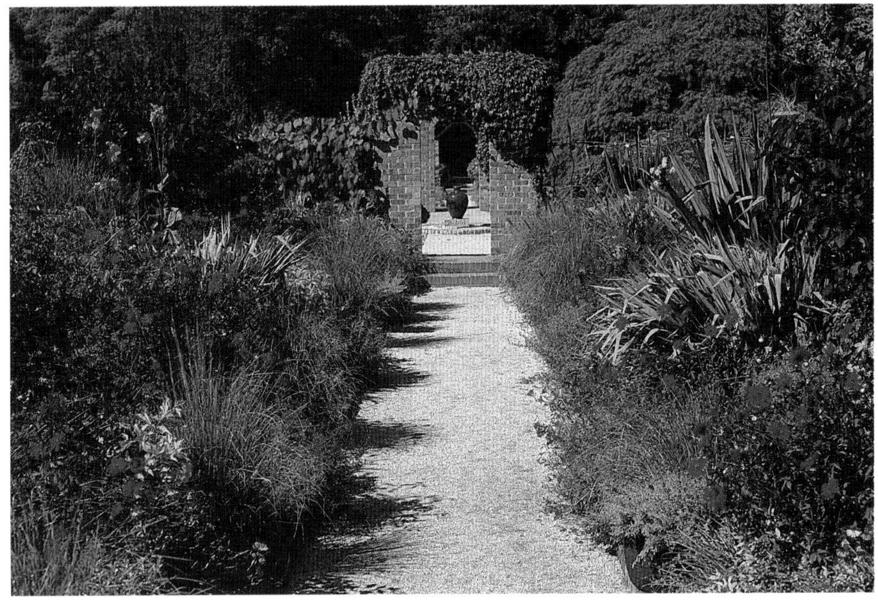

Cornus alba 'Sibirica' is a deciduous shrub with dark green leaves that turn red in autumn. But its outstanding feature is its bare, shiny, red branches that provide stunning color during the winter months.

Many of the cotoneasters will provide you with an abundance of small, glossy, red fruit in late autumn that may persist through winter.

Imperata cylindrica 'Red Baron' (syn. 'Rubra') is the Red Baron blood grass that provides great foliage contrast and should be sited where the sun can highlight its rich, vibrant color.

Nandina domestica 'Nana' is an excellent edging plant. Its leaves are red-tinged when young, and develop red tones when the cold weather arrives. It also has red berries in autumn and winter. 'Firepower' has bright red leaves.

New Zealand flax *Phormium tenax* 'Dazzler' is an outstanding feature, waterside or border plant with red, strap-like leaves edged with plum-purple.

Rheum palmatum 'Atrosanguineum' is an ornamental rhubarb with burgundy-red, emerging leaves that fade to dark green, but retain their reddish color underneath. Tall panicles of small, cherry-red flowers appear early in summer. This is especially beautiful as a waterside plant.

Ricinus communis 'Gibsonii' is a compact variety of the castor-oil plant. It has bronze foliage with red veins and striking red stems. An outstanding background plant for the red flower border, it also looks good framing billowing grasses.

Rosa rugosa has many fragrant, carmine-red flowers, but it is the large, tomato-shaped, red to orange-red hips that are its most stunning feature.

Blue and Purple

Blue is both brilliant and pure. It is one of the most intense colors, even when it is clouded into more purple and mauve tones. Blue flowers encompass a wide variety of tones and shades and are as infinite as the sky in their ability to reflect light in different ways. They are seldom one-colored and there are also many variations on blue within a single group, for example the delphiniums and hydrangeas, which come in every shade of blue and purple.

Open Up Your Space

Optically, blue is a receding color. It appears to move back, away from the viewer. You can exploit this effect by placing blue or mauve-blue flowers at a distance from the house or at the bottom of your garden to increase the sense of space. A beautiful backdrop to a fence or wall could be a curtain of blue trumpet vine *Thunbergia grandiflora* or the frost-hardy, mauve *Wisteria sinensis*. Blue-flowering climbers are also good for concealing swimming pool enclosures. They add a sense of calm, harmonize with most colors, and blend in with the distance. Pale blue or mauve flowers edging a garden walk will increase the feeling of length.

Create a Blue and Purple Garden Theme

If all the blue tones from gray to purple are included in your color scheme, as well as all the delightful blue-purple herbs, such as hyssop, borage and lavender, there are enough blues to fill an entire garden, or at least a whole section of your garden.

ABOVE LEFT: Blues and purples are perfect for a cool-color border. Plant blue and purple flowers and blue-green leaves together for best effect.
ABOVE: Columbines (*Aquilegia* spp.).

Favorite Blue Flowers

Anchusa azurea (Italian bugloss)
Borago officinalis (borage)
Campanula persicifolia (peach-leaved bellflower)
Centaurea cyanus (cornflower)
Cynoglossum amabile (Chinese forget-me-not)
Delphinium cultivars
Felicia amelloides (blue Marguerite)
Gentiana spp. (gentian)
Hydrangea macrophylla (hydrangea)
Iris cultivars
Myosotis spp. (forget-me-nots)
Nigella damascena (love-in-a-mist)
Polemonium caeruleum (Jacob's ladder)
Salvia farinacea (mealy cup sage)
Teucrium fruticans (bush germander)
Thunbergia grandiflora (sky flower)
Veronica prostrata (prostrate speedwell)
Veronica spicata (spike speedwell)

LEFT: *Felicia amelloides* with *Ajuga reptans*

RIGHT: Pathway bordered by catmint *Nepeta* spp.
BOTTOM: Purple-blue 'Damson' plums.

For starters, there are the innumerable violets and irises, columbines, cornflowers, verbenas and more.

Purple and lavender colors create stunning accents. They can be found in lilacs, lupins, asters, Canterbury bells, delphiniums and many of the sages.

Blue-green or gray leaves can be used to balance blue flowers and create a gentle drift of changing hues, like a misty seascape. For example, try the decorative leaves and bracts of Miss Willmott's ghost *Eryngium giganteum*, set among agapanthus and the spiky blue flowers of *Allium caeruleum*. The grayish green foliage of catmint, borage and cornflowers all work beautifully together. Mauve flowers can be emphasized by placing them against the silvery leaves of lavender cotton *Santolina* spp. or the leaves of cardoon *Cynara cardunculus*.

On the Wild Side

Use forget-me-nots to create a marvelous spring carpet effect below deciduous shrubs. Their soft blues will link different areas and, once established, they will self-sow for years to come.

For cooler climates, a favorite meadow plant is the perennial Jacob's ladder *Polemonium caeruleum*, which displays its erect, lavender-blue flowers in early summer. This is a beautiful old-fashioned plant that self-sows successfully in a wild garden.

The best location for naturalizing bulbs, such as bluebells, is beneath deciduous trees and, here, a romantic woodland glade can be created on either a small or large scale. Bulbs usually have the most impact when planted in masses of just one color. But if you want variety, you could plant together drifts of bulbs such as irises, bluebells and hyacinths, of varying hues from the palest blue to the deepest purple, for a wonderful, and often fragrant, effect.

ABOVE: Forget-me-nots *Myosotis* spp. are ideal for naturalizing under deciduous trees. They reseed prolifically, so if you don't want to deal with seedlings, shear off the developing seed heads.

LEFT: Sneezeweed cultivar *Helenium* 'Waldtraut'.
BELOW: Marigolds come in a range of oranges and yellows with either single or double flowers.

BELOW: Cottage garden with sunflowers, sweet peas, busy Lizzie and hollyhocks.

Yellow and Orange

Yellow is the color of sunshine and orange the dazzler. While yellow flowers seem to give the garden a feeling of airy lightness, orange flowers optically foreshorten distance, so that the color appears to leap out from its surroundings. Both yellow and orange are attention-seekers in the garden and create a bright and cheerful atmosphere.

Take a Tip from Nature

Nature provides us with a profusion of yellow-to-orange flowers, both cultivated and growing wild. For example, wonderfully scented wallflowers grow in a rich harmony of yellow, tawny gold, russet and orange. Daffodils and jonquils *Narcissus* spp. combine many shades of yellow, while the flowers of the pot marigold come in pale yellow to deep orange in both single and double varieties. Both the Californian poppy *Eschscholzia californica* and the Iceland poppy *Papaver nudicaule* come in a range of these tones from yellow and gold to orange. For later in the season, there is a wide variety of yellow and orange daylilies *Hemerocallis* hybrids and *Lilium* spp., including the flecked tiger lilies. The trailing annual, garden nasturtium *Tropaeoleum majus*, gives us various shades of yellow, gold, orange and orange-red flowers—gorgeous colors that can be picked up in nearby plantings.

Cream and Yellow

If you want to tone down your orange and yellow setting, add some creamy colored flowers. Cream flowers make great companions to most flower colors, but are particularly valuable in softening any harsh effects created by bright yellow and orange flowers. Here you could choose the lighter tones of orange and yellow plants, or add a few creamy or pale yellow roses. False Solomon's seal *Smilacina racemosa*, with its lemon-scented, creamy white, feathery plumes, is good in partial shade, grown between shrubs. For a bright, sunny position, silver- and gray-foliaged plants will blend well as background color.

At the Water's Edge

If you have a damp, low-lying area beside a pond or water garden, you could provide a congenial home for those plants that like to grow in permanently wet soil. Some of the best waterside plants have yellow flowers and clearly reflect their blooms in the calm water's surface. Plants such as *Ranunculus lingua*, yellow flag iris *Iris pseudocorus*, Japanese iris *Iris ensata*, candelabra primulas, ligularias and yellow loosestrife *Lysimachia punctata* are just the plants to cheer up a difficult wet area.

At the very edge of the water you could grow a bold, single clump of *Acorus calamus* 'Variegatus', a pretty grass with aromatic, bright green leaves to 4 feet (1.2 m) long with cream and white stripes. *A. gramineus* 'Ogon' is a smaller version with pale green and deep cream variegated leaves to 10 inches (25 cm) long.

Aquatic plants, such as water lilies, will further enhance the setting. Some of the *Nymphaea* cultivars come in clear, bright yellows and pale creamy yellows. The yellow floating heart *Nymphoides peltata*, best for frost-prone areas, has fringed, bright golden-yellow flowers that resemble miniature water lilies.

TOP: The gentle, pale yellow flowers of fern-leaved yarrow *Achillea filipendulina*. Plant at the front or middle of perennial borders, or with grasses in wildflower meadows.
LEFT: Water lily *Nymphaea* 'Pygmaea Helvola'.

A Yellow and Orange Cut Flower Garden

Many yellow and orange flowers are used for indoor flower arrangement. Traditionally a small portion of the country garden was set aside for cutting flowers. You may lack the space for such an area in your garden, but cut-flower plants can be grown in the flower border or, in the best tradition of a cottage-style garden, set among your vegetables. If you have the space, don't forget the fabulous sunflower for impact both in the garden and indoors.

Achillea spp. (yarrows)
Antirrhinum majus (snapdragon)
Calendula officinalis (pot marigold)
Dahlia cultivars (dahlias)
Erysimum cultivars (wallflowers)
Helenium cultivars (sneezeweed, Helen's flower)
Helianthus annuus (sunflower)
Hemerocallis spp. (daylilies)
Iris spp. bearded varieties
Kniphofia cultivars (red hot pokers)
Narcissus spp. (daffodils/jonquils)
Papaver nudicaule (Iceland poppy)
Ranunculus spp. (buttercups)
Tulipa spp. (tulips)

Pink

Charming, pink flowers are the flowers of romance, from the early-flowering cherry blossom and pink camellias to the later-flowering roses, peonies, lilies and nerines.

Pink Effects

Pink can be a warm color, when in the coral and salmon-pink range, or cool, when in the mauve-pink range. The cool pinks, that are linked with blue pigments, blend well with blue and purple flowers. When mixing different pinks, make sure you keep the tones closely related and use appropriate foliage to either heighten the effect, or to calm things down.

The glossy-leaved acanthus is a good foil to all pink flowers and bears its own flower spikes of pinkish purple. Peonies of all types have interesting divided leaves and are complemented by nearby plantings of green-leaved hostas.

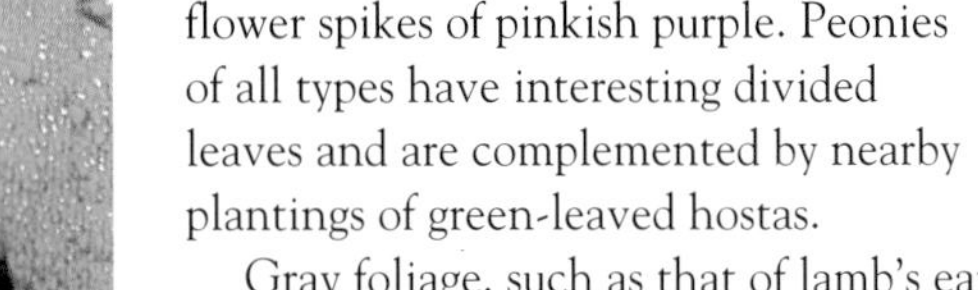

Gray foliage, such as that of lamb's ears *Stachys byzantina*, anthemis or lavender cotton, will highlight most pink flowers particularly well.

You can deepen mauve-pink flowers with purplish sage, feathery purple fennel or the plum-colored leaves of *Weigela florida* 'Foliis Purpureis'.

Hydrangeas that turn pink in alkaline soil, as well as frothy pink rhododendrons, are both excellent for brightening up partly shady areas of the garden.

An Enchanted Garden

An all-pink garden walk has an almost fairy-tale charm. Be adventurous with pink and grow old-fashioned roses extravagantly over arches and to curtain

TOP LEFT: Lilies add height and color to any flower bed or border. Combine them with mounding annuals, perennials or groundcovers that can shade the soil and keep the bulbs cool.
TOP RIGHT: Besides being a great garden accent, globe amaranth *Gomphrena globosa* dries well for dried flower arrangements.
LEFT: Old-fashioned pink roses are perfect for a romantic, scented, pink-themed garden.

Favorite Pink Flowers

Argyranthemum 'Bridesmaid', 'Mary Wootton', 'Vancouver' (Marguerite daisy)
Amaryllis belladonna (belladonna lily)
Armeria maritima (sea pink)
Camellia spp. (camellias)
Clematis 'Nelly Moser'
Daphne cneorum (rose daphne)
Deutzia x *elegantissima* 'Rosealind' (deutzia)
Dianthus spp. (carnations and pinks)
Dierama pulcherrimum (fairy's fishing rod)
Kalmia latifolia (mountain laurel)
Kolkwitzia amabilis 'Pink Cloud' (beauty bush)
Lavatera 'Barnsley' (mallow)
Magnolia liliiflora (lily magnolia)
Nerine bowdenii (pink spider lily)
Paeonia lactiflora (peony)
Prunus x *subhirtella* (flowering cherry)
Rhododendron spp. (rhododendrons and azaleas)
Rosa spp. (roses)
Syringa meyeri 'Superba' (lilac)
Weigela florida (old-fashioned weigela)

Mountain laurel

walls. Create a flowering backdrop of pink clematis, which can also be grown over large shrubs or small trees.

Include many of the irresistible pink flowers, such as camellias, peonies, carnations and pinks themselves (*Dianthus* spp.), but also include some perennials with architectural qualities. Show-stoppers such as the giant of the lily family *Eremurus robustus*, with its tall flower-spikes of pale pink, and clumps of pink Russell lupins are great accent plants for full sun. Other plants of distinction are the striking, plumelike, summer flowers of pink astilbes and *Sedum spectabile* with scalloped leaves and dusky pink flowers. Good background bedding plants include pink cosmos, poppies and the spider flower *Cleome hassleriana*. The showy pink turtlehead *Chelone obliqua* and some of the alliums are good for late summer, while pink cultivars of dahlia and *Aster novi-belgii* will carry their late summer flowers well into autumn.

ABOVE: Astilbes are perfect for moist shade gardens. Their airy plumes add grace and motion to the garden. Plant masses beside a pond where their blooms can be reflected in the water.

In the Shade

Pink flowers will brighten up a shady spot beneath deciduous trees and here you could add a few treasures such as the delightful *Cyclamen hederifolium*, with its heavily marbled, ivy-like leaves and sometimes scented, autumn flowers in shades of rose pink. The autumn crocus *Colchicum autumnale* also has flowers in shades of pink. The highly desirable pink trout lily *Erythronium revolutum*, with strongly mottled leaves and lilac-pink early summer flowers, multiplies easily when planted in partial shade around shrubs and trees.

ABOVE: Azaleas (*Rhododendron* spp.) come in a multitude of sizes and colors. These deep pink flowers are a spring favorite.

Combining Colors

Color is one of the principal contributors to a great-looking garden, but the best gardens aren't based on flower color alone. By using plants of different sizes, forms, colors and textures we achieve variety and interest when building up a complete garden picture.

Irises and daylilies

Color in the Garden

The basic, ever-present and most important color in the landscape is green. There are many diverse and subtle shades of green—from the palest lime to vibrant emerald. Some greens are dark, others more grayish, silvery or olive in tone. Consider also the color of your house, fence, walls, paving or other features when choosing your plant colors. Many trees and shrubs produce flowers in their season and although fleeting, these colors should also be taken into account.

Shrubs, especially the evergreens, are likely to be permanent parts of the landscape and will largely act as a long-term, leafy background to a garden setting. As a general rule, best results are achieved if strongly contrasting shrubs are not placed in close proximity, or the effect is jarring. A descending scale of leaf size or subtle variations of closely related colors are harmonious.

Bright-leaved or golden-foliaged plants give a garden vitality and can be used in shadowy areas of a garden to brighten and lighten them. For example *Sambucus racemosa* 'Plumosa Aurea' in a dull corner can bring a splash of light. *Robinia pseudoacacia* 'Frisia', with its rich yellow, pinnate leaves that turn orange-yellow in autumn, is also a valuable brightener.

For breathtaking autumn color there are some rich reds provided by deciduous plants, such as the Japanese maples and *Nyssa sylvatica*—both make outstanding specimen plants, and are best sited where they will catch the weak autumn light. The pretty, slow-growing *Acer palmatum* 'Sango-kaku' will provide a contrasting delicate tracery of amber-gold in autumn.

Use a variety of other forms to draw attention to a particular location or add a little light relief. You could introduce some good architectural plants such as the cordylines, palms, variegated phormiums and low-growing, symmetrical conifers to draw the eye to an entrance or a particular garden feature. Tall, vertical accent plants and stately conifers, no matter what color, are best grown as specimens to create eye-catching interludes in a garden plan or to attract attention to a vista.

A Palette of Flowers

Most gardeners find it easiest to grow flowers within a flower border. The border may include annuals, but mostly it is made up of perennials. Here you can truly paint with color, form, texture and line.

On the true color wheel, where red, blue and yellow are the primary colors, the colors that are opposite each other make the strongest contrast—green with red, or blue with yellow for example.

LEFT: A blue wall creates an appropriate backdrop for a grouping of blue-leaved cabbages and citrus-yellow blooms.
ABOVE: The yellow, nodding flowers of 'February Gold' daffodils look stunning paired with plants with yellow-variegated leaves.

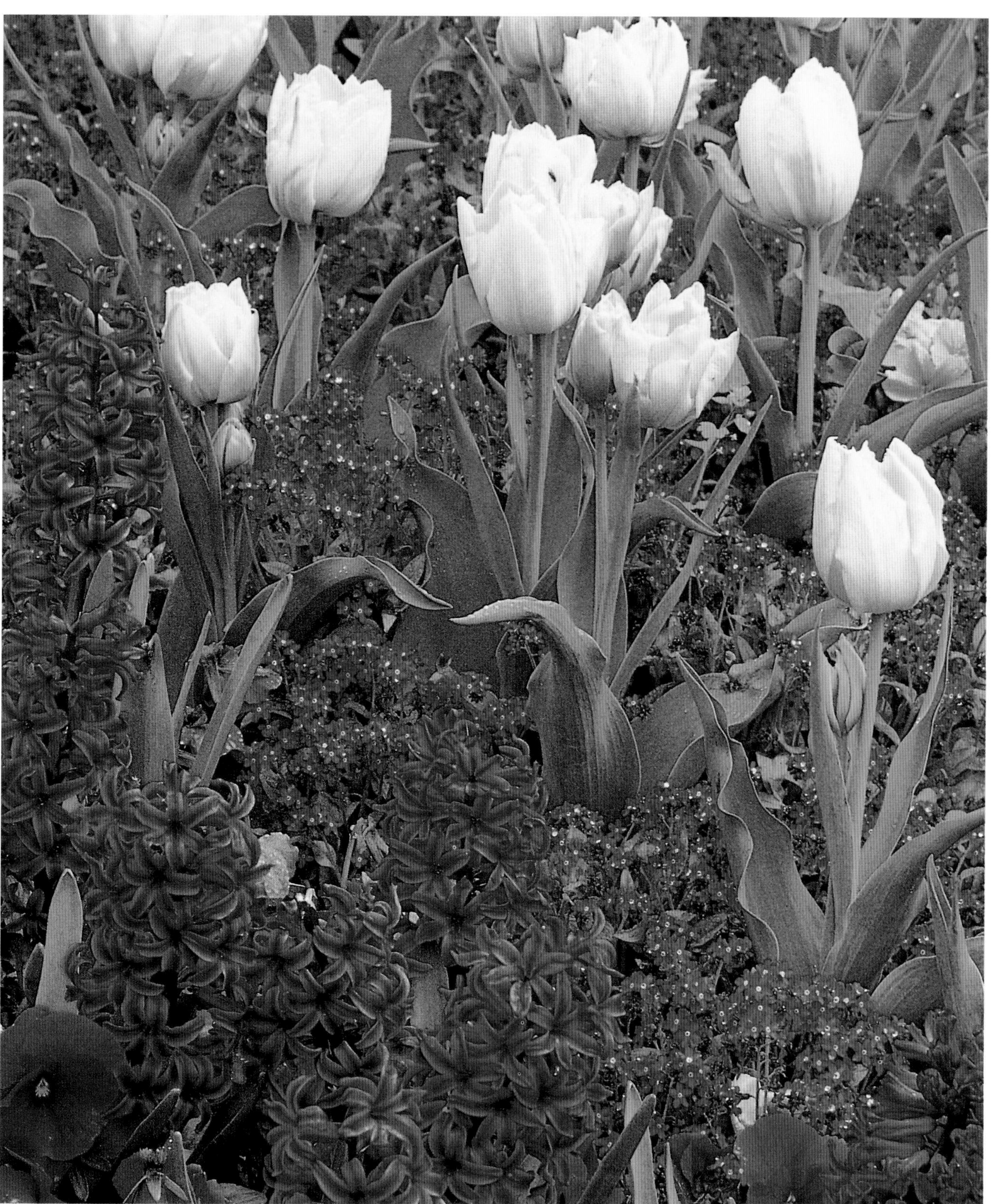

Purple and yellow are complementary colors on the color wheel, and therefore making an exciting, yet harmonious combination. Here low-growing purple hyacinths and velvety pansies are mixed with taller-growing yellow tulips.

Compare the same garden design but with two different color schemes—cool blue and purple on the left and hot yellow and orange on the right.

When colors share some of the same pigment—such as blue combined with its near-relative purple—the result is harmonious. But pair blue with lemon—its opposite on the color wheel—and the impact is more eye-catching.

Color combinations are personal. Some gardeners enjoy the result of mixing orange and yellow with purple or blue; others prefer crisp whites or the restful feel of pale yellows, soft pinks and silvers.

Combining similar flower colors with dark and light tones, quite close to each other, creates a pleasing effect. Try grouping reds with oranges and yellows; citrus-yellows with greens and blues; or blues with purple and reds. Colors sharing the same degree of lightness or darkness also work well; for instance, several different pastels, such as pale blues, pale yellows and pale pinks, blend more effectively than several pure hues.

White and gray don't appear on the color wheel, but they play an important role in the garden. White has a split personality: It can be exciting or soothing. Bright white is surprisingly bold; it stands out among both bright and dark colors, even in a group of soft pastels. A dash of pure white in a spread of harmonious colors is as dramatic as a dash of a bright complementary color. Cream and muted whites are softer; they tend to blend well with everything.

Gray is the great unifier. Silver or gray foliage works even more effectively than green to soften the transition between two complementary or bold colors. Gray adds a certain drama of its own by contrasting with neighboring green foliage. Gray-foliaged plants look particularly lovely with flowers of a pastel shade and those that are evergreen will hold the fort in winter.

Get Some Rhythm

Take a tip from garden designers and grow foliage plants in repeated groupings. Lush, green plants such as *Euphorbia characias* subsp. *wulfenii* and the architectural *Acanthus* spp. look good through all seasons and provide a link between different types of flowering plants. With its foamy, lime-green flowers, clumps of *Alchemilla mollis* are a charming, long-season companion to all neighboring plants.

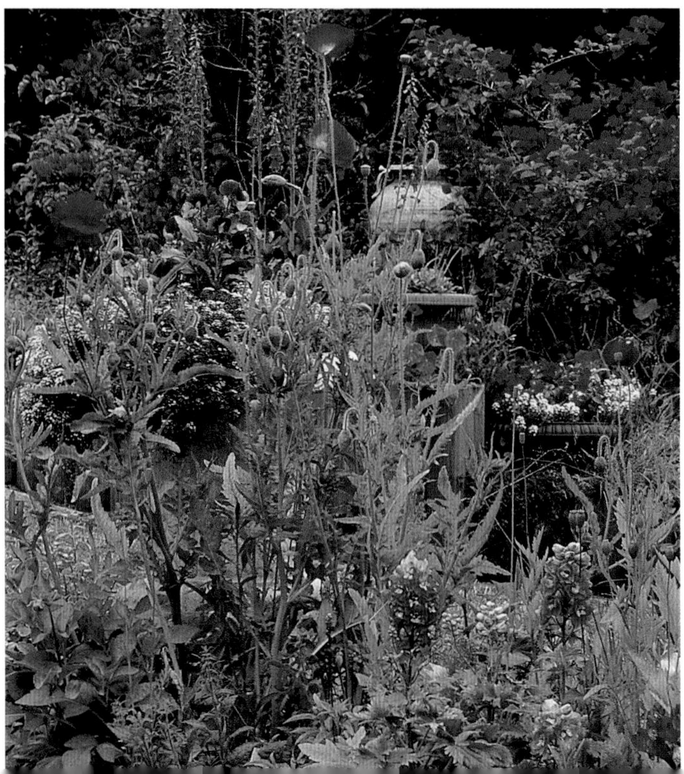

ABOVE: Green agave nestling among a riot of beefsteak plant *Iresine* spp.
RIGHT: Cottage garden with a mix of colorful annuals in the pink, blue and purple range, including delphinium, poppies, foxgloves and violets.

You could also include some spiky leaves, such as those of the irises and some of the variegated grasses, to provide definition and contrast.

Some Super Combinations

Color associations offer scope for creating very different and interesting effects. Don't be too timid, as you can easily move most perennials at almost any time of the year. After all, that's what gardening is all about—retaining our interest and enthusiasm by changing things about to suit our individual style and moods. Here are some color combinations you might like to try, bearing in mind that foliage color is just as important as flower color.

Combine crimson and pink flowers, but tone down the planting with plum-colored foliage, such as that of *Berberis thunbergii* 'Red Pillar'.

Create a theatrical, tropical effect with the coppery red *Ricinus communis* 'Gibsonii', underplanted with canna lilies with bold bronze or rich purple leaves, or the striking green and yellow 'Striata'. The flamboyant red, orange and apricot flowers look stunning.

White flowers and white-variegated leaves make excellent companions. Grow dozens of *Hosta undulata* var. *univittata* with their bold, white streaks with white violas and tulips to lighten a shady garden walk.

Plant out masses of blackish green *Ophiopogon planiscapus* 'Nigrescens' as a bold border to several prostrate junipers with silvery blue leaves, to create a beautiful carpet of contrasting foliage.

ABOVE: A soft, gentle, pastel effect created by white daisies, mauve irises and yellow wallflowers.

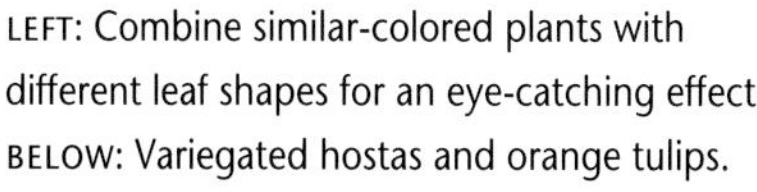

LEFT: Combine similar-colored plants with different leaf shapes for an eye-catching effect. BELOW: Variegated hostas and orange tulips.

For architectural contrast, but with harmonious color, grow the purple-leaved *Phormium tenax* 'Purpureum' with the slate-gray *Hosta sieboldiana* 'Elegans' around its base.

Imitate Claude Monet's planting at Giverny, France, and grow orange nasturtiums in front of violet-blue asters. And if you're lucky enough to have a red footbridge, drape it with purple wisteria.

For a charming, gray picture, use the glaucous foliage of some of the shrubby eucalypts with the silvery green, pinnate leaves of *Melianthus major*. Set this off with the bold, bronze-leaved *Rogersia podophylla* and some of the blue-leaved hostas, together with a substantial clump of *Ajuga reptans* 'Catlin's Giant' for a frilly, informal carpet.

For a late-season burst of fiery color, plant rudbeckias, sunflowers, heleniums, Turk's cap lilies, yellow and red dahlias, celosias, red hot pokers and *Monarda* 'Cambridge Scarlet'. These flowers all have complementary colors from the hot side of the spectrum, and they can all be picked for arrangements to warm up the house as the days get cooler.

A Garden for the Senses

With planning, and an eye for detail, you can design a garden that will appeal to all the five senses. To make a garden sensual, you need the right design elements, decorative features and plant selection.

Sight

Gardens are visually stimulating places. Plants contribute color from flowers, leaves and even bark, affecting the look of other plants nearby by contrasting or complementing them. The shifting patterns of light and dark, along with the season cycles, mean that gardens are constantly changing visually.

Hard landscaping features, such as walls, paths and even the choice of mulches, further enrich the visual impact of a garden. And, with carefully placed potted, topiarized or clipped plants you can bring an element of fun or perhaps mystery to even the simplest garden.

Even individual flowers can be visually stimulating due to their patterning, shape or size. Consider the amazingly detailed checkerboard pattern of a checkered lily, or the perfectly circular shape of a drumstick primula flower head.

Decide the Mood

It is possible to control the degree of visual stimulation a garden design provides by the way plants are selected and combined. Gardens with many different colored plants and surfaces can seem busy and complex. On the other hand, limiting the choice of plants, and therefore the number of color combinations, can subdue a garden, making it more peaceful and restful. By taking advantage of the seasonal changes plants undergo, you can have a garden that takes on different moods at different times of the year. For example, a garden that's full of color and contrast in spring may become a quiet, leafy, green oasis in summer.

The nodding flowers of checkered lilies *Fritillaria meleagris* add a charming touch to spring gardens. Naturalize them in wild areas.

Floral Pictures

Flowers provide immense visual variety and excitement. You can think of flowers as a living paint. They can provide a wash of color that enlivens a large area, or be daubs of color that create visual highlights. Unlike paint on a wall, however, flowers are usually seasonal. In addition, they vary in the length of their display. Flowers can last for just a day or for many months. Some even change color through the day, like the miraculous four o'clock *Mirabalis jalapa*, which opens a brilliant pink and then fades to yellow, or the rose of Sharon *Hibiscus mutabilis*, which opens rosy red and fades through pink and then to white.

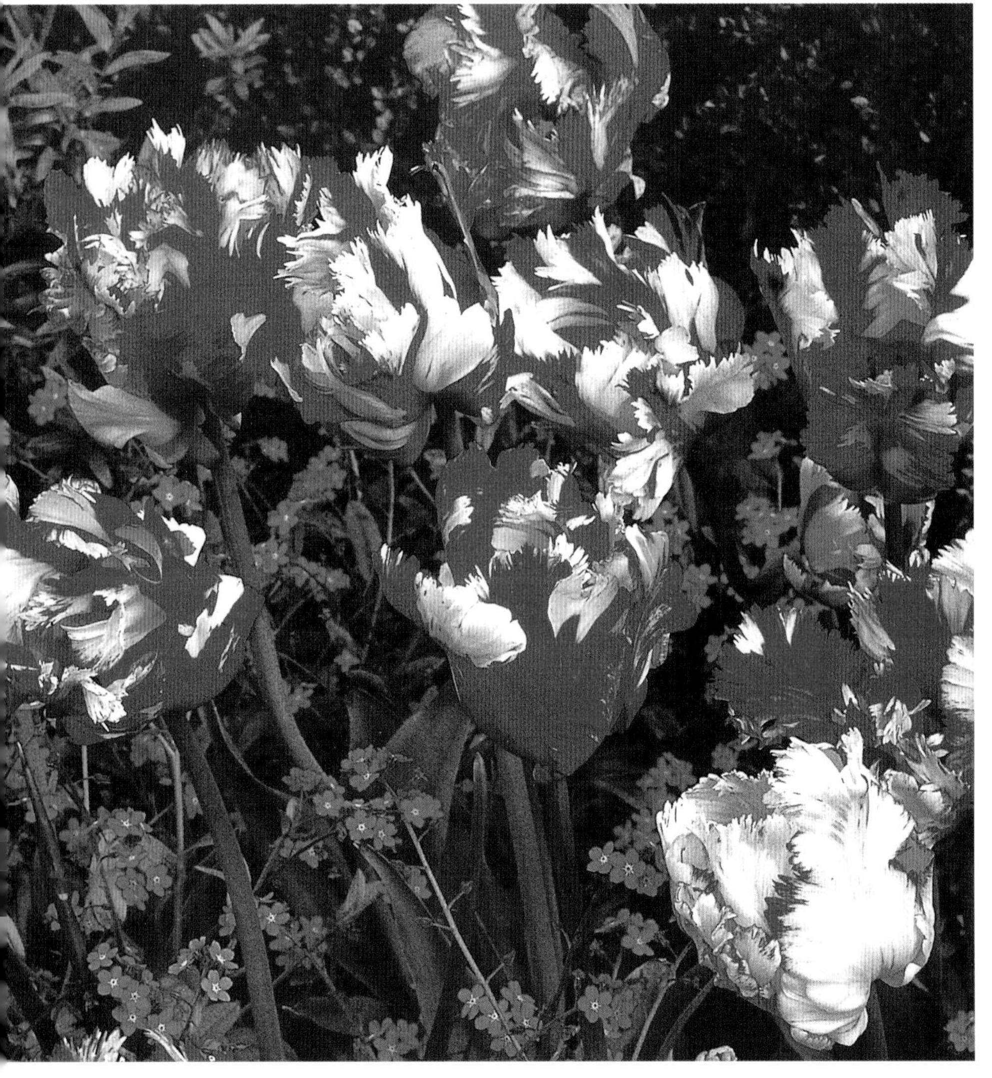

It's hard to match hybrid tulips for pure color power; here they team with forget-me-nots.

To get the most from plants when they flower, be aware of their flower color, the normal flowering season and how long it may last. Remember too that masses of a single color will have more visual impact than many different colors mixed together. If you are using annuals for colors, look for plants that offer single color selections so you can mix and match the color you want in your garden.

A stunning and classical effect can be achieved with a trompe l'oeil framed by a living vine.

Visual Tricks

As soon as two colors—whether they are on cushions on a sofa or flowers in a garden—are placed beside one another, they affect our perception. Dark colors, for example, will recede, while lighter colors will seem to stand out. In a garden, combining plants so that colors recede and others leap forward adds a sense of depth, even in a small space.

Other visual tricks in a garden are done to make a space seem larger or more varied than it really is. A long path, for example, can seem even longer if its sides are not parallel but are angled (so they would eventually converge). Our eyes perceive a path that appears longer than it actually is.

Garden mirrors or even ponds can also be used to fool the eye as they reflect parts of the garden, thereby making it appear larger. A mirror disguised as a gate will appear to lead to an as yet unexplored section of garden.

Painting a small panel or even an entire wall with an imaginary scene is a device known as trompe l'oeil, and it has been used in gardens for thousands of years. The painting may be a landscape that doesn't exist, such as a glimpse to an imagined view, or an ornament for which there isn't room, such as a fountain or statue.

To make the trompe l'oeil seem realistic, frame it with real plants. A painting that evokes a Tuscan landscape scene, for example, can be flanked by a pair of columnar cypress or junipers such as *Juniperus virginiana* 'Skyrocket'.

LEFT: Include some exotic and unusual flowers in your garden, such as this delightful Queen's tears *Billbergia nutans*.
RIGHT: The colorful patterns of peeling bark can be an attractive feature.

Touch

We "see" a garden through our hands and our feet, as well as with our eyes. We can even lie or sit in, on or among plants, to enjoy the texture of their leaves, or to soak up the warmth from sun-soaked paving.

Designing a garden to stimulate the sense of touch can bring a lot of pleasure, yet the way a garden feels is not often considered when it is being designed. To cater to your sense of touch in a garden, use a mix of plants and surfaces that will stimulate and excite.

If you're looking for something a little different to grow, with an unusual texture, try growing Turkestan onion *Allium karataviense*, with its bulbous flower heads. It looks great with silvery-leaved plants.

Planting for Comfort

One of the most important issues of touch is for something to feel good. Plants may feel pleasant to touch, or they can be a pain—quite literally. Those with sharp thorns or prickles can be touched in painful rather than pleasurable ways. Avoid using plants with prickles or sharp spines in places where you are likely to come in contact with them. Agaves beside the swimming pool or roses crowding next to the driveway are not going to feel good. However, thorny plants do have a place—they make excellent deterrents along boundaries.

The velvety-soft leaves of lamb's ears *Stachys byzantina* are popular with children.

In areas where you want to encourage people to touch and feel plants or where they may be brushed against accidentally, concentrate on selecting plants that feel good. When something feels comfortable, it also feels safe.

The concept of touch in a garden goes beyond plants to the other elements of the landscape. Burning hot paving under bare feet isn't a good feeling, neither are vast expanses of prickle-infested lawns or damp, slippery, mossed-over paths. Much cooler and more pleasant to touch are soft lawns or groundcovers.

Touchy-Feely Plants

Some plants just cry out to be touched, felt or patted. Plants with a rounded, cushiony shape or felty leaves ask to be stroked. Lamb's ears, such as the large-leaved *Stachys byzantina* 'Big Ears', has soft, gray leaves that feel felty to the touch. Baby's tears *Soleirolia soleirolii* (also called helxine) has tiny, green leaves that look and feel soft. This is a lovely soft groundcover for a shaded spot.

The curry plant *Helichrysum italicum*, with its small, soft, rounded leaves, feels good to touch. And, when you do brush or touch the leaves of the curry plant, they release a strong curry scent, therefore stimulating both your sense of smell and taste. Heighten the sense of touch by clipping the curry plant into a rounded shape that echoes the rounded shape of the aromatic leaves.

Other plants that lend themselves to the soft cushiony look and feel include

Feel-good Plants

Ferns (e.g. maidenhair fern *Adiantum aethiopicum*)
Lamb's ears *Stachys byzantina*
Lawn grasses (especially cool-season grasses)
Mondo grass *Ophiopogon japonicus*
Mosses
Sedums
Selaginella
Snow-in-summer *Cerastium tomentosum*
Spanish moss *Tillandsia usneoides*

lavenders, hebes, boxwood, some dwarf conifers and many small succulents. But plants aren't always as they seem. They can look soft and inviting, yet conceal a spiky nature, as do cleomes, which have small spines under their leaves.

It's not just leaves that feel good to touch. Many flowers are tempting to touch, too. The foaming flower heads of hydrangeas, for instance, seem to ask to be ruffled. The crape-like flowers of the crape myrtle *Lagerstroemia indica* need to be touched to see if they feel as well as look like crape.

Some plants that feel good to touch aren't usually considered as garden plants. Moss, for example, when it's growing on rocks, steps or under a woodland canopy, looks soft and inviting. If you have a moist, shaded area, think about using moss as a groundcover and turning the area into a moss garden—a traditional form of garden in Japan. Moss can be transplanted or encouraged to grow naturally. Painting bare rocks with plain yogurt or milk helps encourage mosses and algae to develop on the damp surfaces.

Walk Through

Plants that are good to feel aren't just encountered at ground level. Plants that trail over paths or cascade over archways are felt as they are brushed past. The effect is much like walking through a beaded curtain in a doorway—or perhaps a dense, tropical rainforest.

Evoke a feeling of a lush, tropical paradise by planting vines so they have to be pushed aside as you move through a garden or along a path.

The same effect can also be achieved with tall-growing plants that have cascading leaves or branches, such as tree ferns and dwarf palms, which have arching fronds, or weeping standards such as weeping elms and mulberries, that form a curtain of green branches.

A curtain of drooping purple wisteria is a delight to walk through.

The spines of the golden barrel cactus *Echinocactus grusonii,* which has the alternative common name of mother-in-law's seat.

Make a Point

Plants that are sharp and prickly also have a place in a garden to appeal to the senses—even if they are outside our normal comfort zone. The golden barrel cactus *Echinocactus grusonii* has a round shape that looks a bit like a squat stool. The sight of its armory of long, sharp spines, however, quickly puts any ideas of sitting on the barrel-shaped cactus seat well out of mind.

Smell

The way flowers or foliage smell has become an important element in plant choice in landscape design. Fragrant plants, such as herbs or sweetly scented flowers, are much in demand to delight our sense of smell.

Finding Fragrance

Always use your nose when you are selecting plants—after all, if there is a fragrant variety that fits the design brief, you may as well select it over a plant without scent. Roses, for example, may vary in their fragrance. Some have gorgeous heads of flowers but no scent. Rose growers list the choicest scented roses in their catalogs. If you are buying roses in winter or early spring while they are dormant, be guided by the catalog description to find a strongly scented rose.

Fragrant Foliage

When choosing plants for fragrance, smell leaves as well as flowers. Fragrant foliage provides months of scent. Herbs are an excellent source of fragrance and can be used in many garden situations. Thyme, for example, can be grown in cracks in paving, while chamomile is a fragrant alternative to lawn in cool to mild areas.

Foliage plants can even imitate floral fragrances. One of the most wonderful rose scents in the garden comes not from roses, but from the leaves of the shrubby rose geranium *Pelargonium graveolens*. There are also other scented geraniums, such as lemon and tutti frutti.

Other plants with fragrant, if slightly acrid, scents in their leaves include artemisias, lavenders, Marguerite daisies, marigolds and tomatoes.

Heady-scented roses are a classic part of a scented garden. Plant them over an archway or gate.

Harvest aromatic herbs lightly and often to release their fragrance and to keep the plants producing fresh, new growth.

Catching the Scent

Selecting a fragrant plant is only part of the task of introducing fragrance to your garden. Getting the most benefit from your perfumed plants means considering the position they are to grow in. There's no point in growing a perfumed plant in a part of the garden you rarely visit.

Instead, make sure that you plant perfumed plants near windows and doors that are often open. If there's no space in a garden bed, you can plant a perfumed plant in a container positioned near an entranceway. A row of scented shrubs along the front fence or near the gate is a delightful way to welcome visitors and

Fragrant Selections

A selection of the following shrubs in your garden ensures the air is filled with wonderful perfume throughout the year.

Winter sweet *Chimonanthus praecox*
Daphnes *Daphne* spp.
Mexican orange blossom *Choisya ternata*
Gardenias *Gardenia* spp.
Witch hazels *Hamamelis* spp.
Luculia *Luculia gratissima*
Port wine magnolia *Michelia figo*
Murraya *Murraya paniculata*
Osmanthus *Osmanthus fragrans*
Plumeria *Plumeria rubra*

will also be much appreciated by people walking by your home.

Enjoy the fragrance of plants inside, too, by picking a few sprigs of whatever's smelling great outside and bringing it indoors to scent the house. For long-term fragrance from the garden, turn fragrant plants into homemade potpourri by drying their leaves and petals.

Another smart place to grow fragrant plants is in a courtyard, so the scent is captured and held. If your garden design doesn't include a courtyard, position the fragrant plant against a wall, as this helps to confine the perfume.

Often, pungent or fragrant leaves have to be rubbed, crushed or brushed against before they will release a noticeable scent. It is important to position plants with fragrant foliage where they will be touched. Good locations include the edge of paths, gates or steps.

As well as growing perfumed shrubs or vines in the garden, use smaller, fragrant plants in pots as seasonal highlights so you can get close-up and take in their fragrance. Hyacinths grow well in pots and are decorative and fragrant. Also great for potted fragrance are dwarf sweet peas *Lathyrus odoratus*, dwarf wallflowers, narcissus and freesias.

Position a garden bench in a favorite part of the garden and surround it with fragrant lavender.

Night Fragrance

Some plants vary in the way they smell depending on the time of day. There is a group of plants that are more strongly scented in the evening than they are in the daytime. These plants intensify their scent at night in order to attract nocturnal insects, such as moths, as pollinators. These are plants to select to grow outside your outdoor dining area or under a bedroom window. They add an extra dimension to your garden by making it a place to visit and experience by night as well as by day.

Some interesting night-scented plants include nicotiana, many of the cestrums (some of which are so strongly scented as to be quite overwhelming) and the so-called queen of the night *Selenicereus grandiflorus*, a climbing cactus with large, white, fragrant flowers at night.

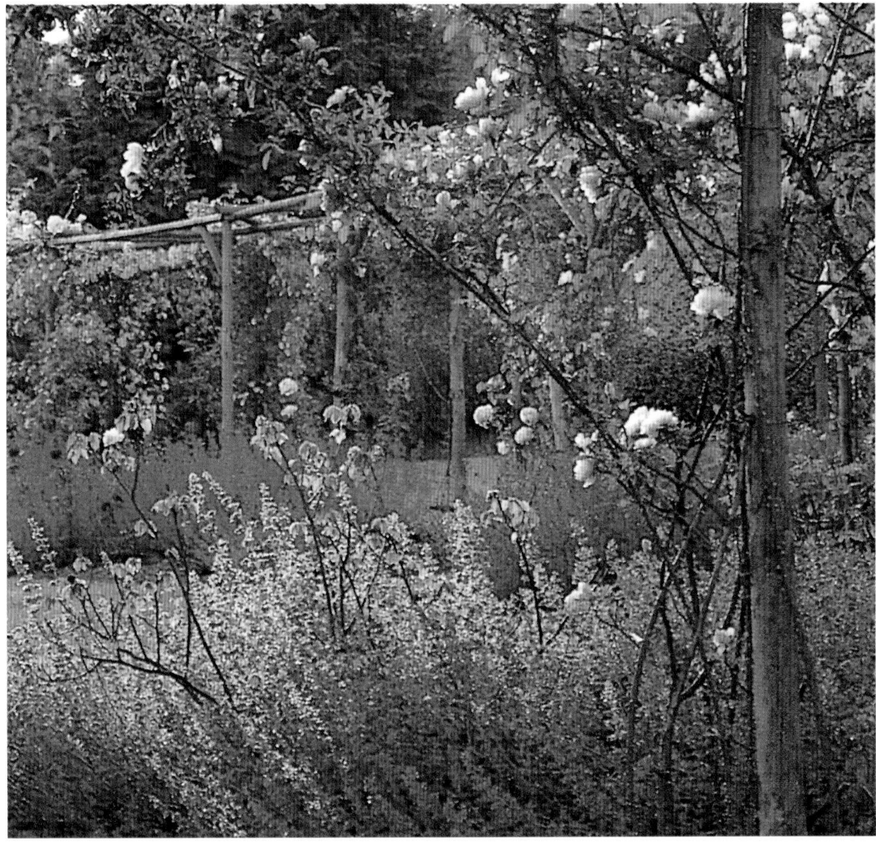

Catmints *Nepeta* spp. have gray-green leaves with a pungent, minty scent that cats love. They look wonderful with other perennials and shrubs.

Sound

Some people talk to their plants, but few gardeners listen to the sounds of plants when deciding what to grow. The sounds of plants are usually highlighted by the wind stirring their leaves or branches, but some plants explode and crackle as the heat triggers seedpods to burst open. Even the sound of dropping fruit on a path or the garage roof adds a different dimension to the garden. Falling walnuts, for example, can really crash down on a metal roof.

Sound in gardens is used to create an atmosphere or highlight a mood or a theme. Gentle sounds bring an air of calm and tranquillity, while more boisterous or unusual sounds can make a garden seem alive and exciting.

Pleasant sounds, such as the wind rustling through leaves, or splashing water, are also used to mask unwanted sounds of traffic, neighbors or passersby. It is impossible to use plants or even water features to completely block out unwanted noise (especially from nearby roads) but garden sounds can offer a welcome distraction.

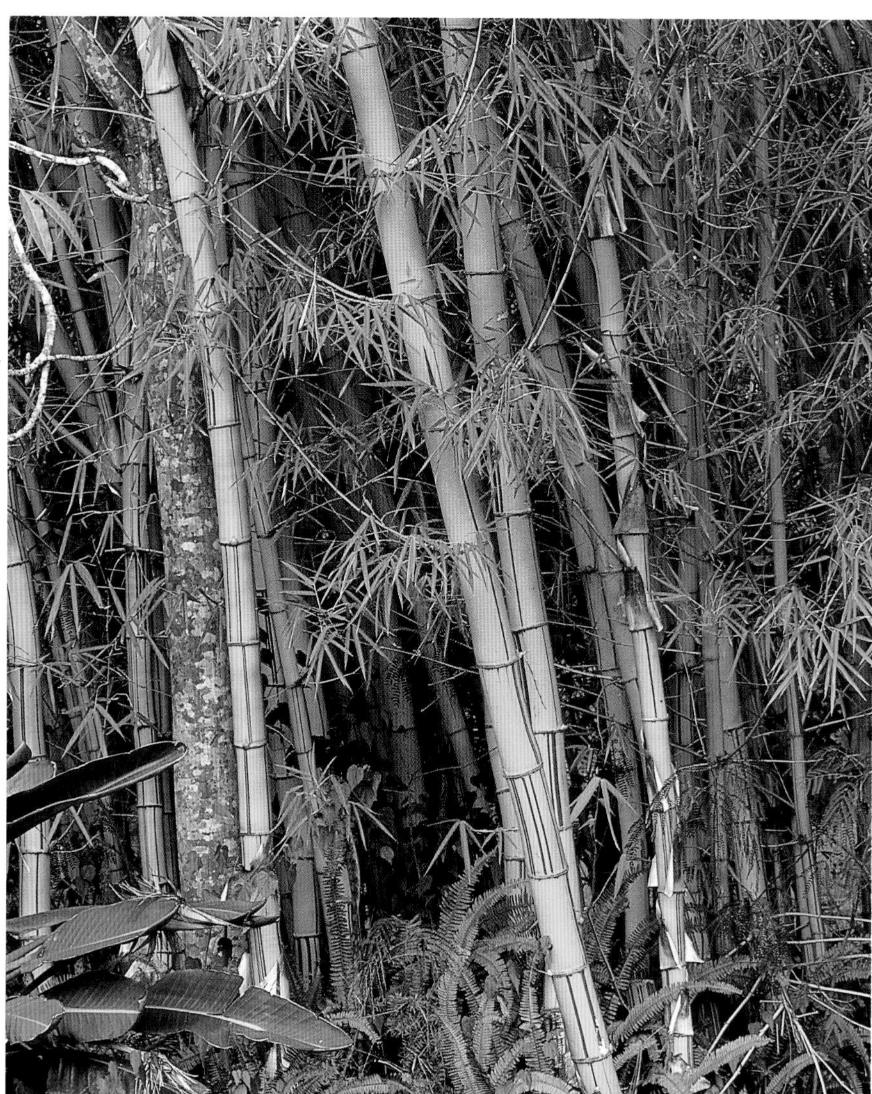

Plant painted bamboo *Bambusa vulgaris* 'Vittata', to hear the wind rustle through its leaves.

The crackling, dry, silvery seedpods of honesty *Lunaria annua* are great for dried arrangements.

The Sounds of the Wind

One of the best plant choices to bring sound to your garden is bamboo. The rustle of its leaves in even the slightest breeze brings an added dimension to any garden with an oriental theme. Select a clumping bamboo or grow bamboo in a large container. Some ideal choices are buddha's belly bamboo *Bambusa ventricosa*, painted bamboo *B. vulgaris* 'Vittata', with its beautifully marked golden stems, or hedging bamboo *B. multiplex* 'Alphonse Karr'.

If a running form of bamboo is planted, keep it confined with root barriers sunk at least 3 feet (1 m) into the ground to prevent its underground spread.

In a large garden, or for an avenue planting, enjoy the sighing, rushing sounds wind makes blowing through pine needles by growing a windbreak of pines. Some of the best sounds come from trees that are far too large for the average garden, such as Monterey pine *Pinus radiata* or the beautiful Mexican weeping pine *P. patula*, with its cascades of needles that also ripple in the wind.

You can also use the wind to set chimes or bells ringing that will add yet another layer of sounds to your garden.

Water Music

One of the best ways to introduce sound into a garden is with moving water. It can bubble, gurgle, splash, trickle or cascade, depending on the type of water feature. Create more varied sounds by lining the cascade or pool with pebbles. Add an oriental touch with the clunk of a *shishi odoshi*, a Japanese water feature made from bamboo, which rhythmically spills water into a small pond.

A water feature at the front gate can be used to set the scene and mark the transition from the street to the private space of your garden. People will feel a sense of arrival as soon as they open the garden gate and hear the sound of water.

Alternatively, use water in a courtyard where the noise will be magnified by the surrounding walls. Install a wall fountain or a pond with a fountain.

Water can also be used to transform part of a larger garden into an oasis or as a focal point for a small space. It is even possible to have a small, self-contained water feature on a deck or balcony.

Attracting Wildlife

Another source of garden sounds comes from birds and insects, attracted to gardens by plants, a birdbath or a feed table. As native habitat is reduced to isolated pockets or removed altogether from urban areas, the plants in gardens have become vital for the survival of native animals and insects.

ABOVE: The sound of crunching gravel underfoot is always satisfying and appealing.
LEFT: A water feature, such as a fountain or trickling water spout, is one of the most popular additions to a Japanese-style garden.

To make your garden wildlife-friendly, make sure that you plant groups of dense shrubs that will offer homes and shelter to small birds. Prickly evergreen shrubs make an excellent safe haven. Also ensure you select plants with their flowering or fruiting time in mind so that there is a succession of nectar-rich flowers in bloom during the year. Additional food also comes from seeds and fruit, so don't always prune away fruits and seeds that may offer food to native wildlife.

Don't overlook the sounds of frogs and toads, which can be attracted to live and breed in garden ponds or bog gardens.

Selecting Surfaces

As you or others move around a garden, there is interaction with surfaces. Loose surfaces, such as gravel, shingle and even cobblestones, bring a very different sound to your garden. The scrunch of gravel underfoot on a path or driveway can be a welcoming sound, or even alert you that visitors are approaching.

Landscaping with Plants

Most of us have some experience in applying design principles to completely human-made structures, usually the exteriors and interiors of buildings. Unless something goes wrong with the stability of the structure on which we are working, everything is under control and the materials we are working with more or less stay put.

However, when designing a landscape, we are working with materials that quite literally have lives of their own. As with decorating a room, however, understanding and, where necessary, enhancing the basic structure of the landscape is essential, since this is the foundation upon which all other garden work is built.

When starting a garden from scratch, beginners in landscape design can feel intimidated by the magnitude of the task in front of them, but whether you are designing the structure of a large garden, or putting together a group of plants in, say, a window box or trough, similar design considerations can apply—even if you are not always aware of them.

Whether in a container or the open garden, each design is literally unique. A design may be tall and dramatic, or low and rounded. It may be fan-shaped or triangular, circular, curving or completely asymmetrical and random looking. It may closely follow the boundaries of the space within which you're working, or meander, or cut diagonally across the space.

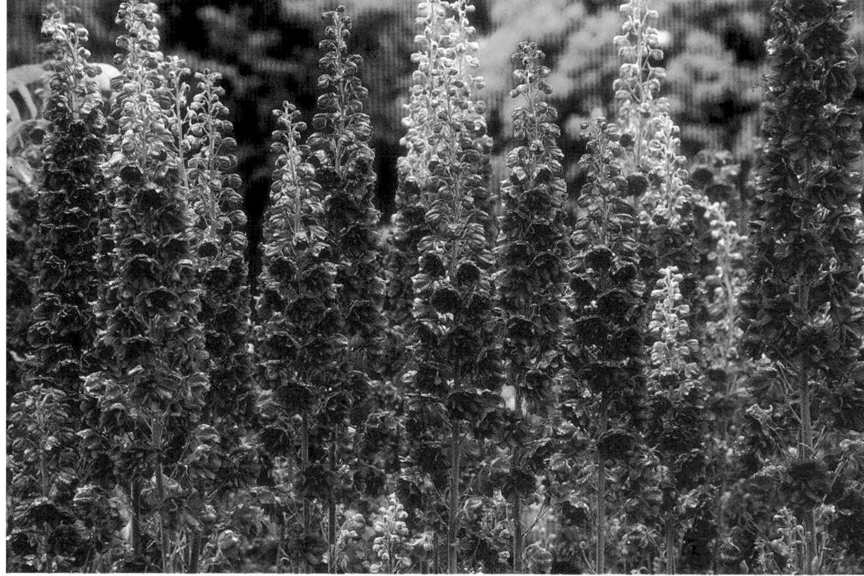

A mass planting of intensely blue-purple, upright-growing delphiniums makes an eye-catching display.

And you are not limited to exploring the space within side boundaries: The floor and ceiling of your garden—or the "garden rooms"—can also be modified.

You can change the ground levels of your site and try different surfaces, textures and colors. Ceilings can be represented by garden structures and the developing canopies of maturing trees as well as by the wilder-growing climbers, such as some roses, that will send their long canes shooting skyward.

Lilies

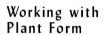

Working with Plant Form

When you consider plant forms, you are exploring and experimenting with the ways they can contribute to the overall structure of your landscape design.

Form refers to a plant's shape and growth habit—twining, upright-growing, pyramidal, rounded, vase-shaped, spreading, spiky or otherwise. While you can prune or train many plants to direct the shape they take, it will mean a lot less work for you if you select plants that naturally take the shape you want.

One useful approach may be to think of plants as performing one of three basic design roles: as vertical accents, as fillers for bulk and color, or as climbers and creepers, twining through other plants or cascading over retaining walls.

Blooms, fruits, variegated or unusually colored leaves and interesting growth habits can also contribute to these effects

LEFT: A garden path is framed by a wisteria-covered pergola. RIGHT: Virginia creeper *Parthenocissus tricuspidata.*

RIGHT: The attention-grabbing, red stems of *Cornus sericea* can grow to 7 feet (2 m) tall.

by attracting the eye and emphasizing the plant's structural roles.

Vertical accents include trees and shrubs, vines on trellises and tall, flowering plants (such as hollyhocks, delphiniums, irises and lilies), as well as the dramatic shapes of ornamental grasses, New Zealand flax and palms, and some tall cacti and other succulents.

Fillers are low-growing or mounding plants, and can range from small annuals, such as primulas and dwarf French marigolds, and perennials, including the various sages and Mexican daisies, to naturally mounding shrubs, such as some rhododendrons, aucuba, flowering quinces and many more.

Everybody has their own favorite vines and creepers, such as wisteria, some roses, ivies (choose docile cultivars), vinca, jasmine, nasturtiums, spider plant and others. A wall, a fence, the side of your house or an old tree can be suitable for growing beautiful climbing plants on. In small gardens, you may find that there is actually more vertical surface space than the total ground area.

With all forms of plants, the objective is to make optimum use of the resources available to you.

As with a conventional plant border, you will need to base your selection of wall plants and climbers not only on the colors and varieties that most please you but also on a range that will provide interest through the year.

Deciduous or Evergreen

Whether your trees and shrubs hold their leaves throughout the year, or shed them as the colder months approach, will determine an important part of the seasonal structure of your landscape.

Trees and shrubs that lose their leaves in autumn and produce new foliage in spring are called deciduous. They lose their leaves as they become dormant during winter with the result that, except for limited root growth, the plants' biological processes are suspended.

Deciduous trees and shrubs are popular and many have leaves that turn brilliant colors before they fall. They include oaks, maples, elms, liquidambars, dogwoods, ashes, viburnums and hydrangeas.

Camellia

Evergreen trees and shrubs hold most of their leaves throughout the year, but do not make the mistake of believing that they do not shed—they do lose some leaves all year round.

Popular evergreen trees include conifers, such as pines, cypresses, spruces and firs, as well as eucalypts, boxwood, most types of holly, and most rhododendrons, camellias and azaleas.

Complexities do arise, however, even within the same family of plants. For instance, although most hollies are evergreen, there are deciduous hollies. There are also deciduous and evergreen azaleas. In some cases, whether a tree or shrub loses its leaves will depend on just how cold it gets in winter where you live.

It has been common design practice to mark outer boundaries of the landscape with evergreen trees and shrubs, while positioning deciduous specimens in front

RIGHT: Include feature plants with stunning autumn foliage, such as this vibrant *Acer*.

This wooden archway frames a winding path that leads through to a hidden area of the garden.

of the evergreen background. This means that the center of the garden is sunnier during the coolest time of the year.

In larger gardens, there is a trend to mark internal divisions and screens in the garden as strongly as the outer boundaries.

Surprises and a sense of going on a journey are valuable elements in designing a garden, and planning for paths to turn corners and go through archways is a delightful way of guiding visitors through your garden. Plan paths so that they lead to a concealed feature such as a gazebo, water garden or simply a pleasant bench on which to sit.

Mature height is an important factor to consider when planning whether you will choose evergreen or deciduous trees and shrubs—the higher your maturing plant grows, the greater the shade it will cast. The amount of privacy you want or whether you need to screen an ugly view will also be factors in determining if you want evergreen cover or not.

A Framework of Plants

True plant lovers always delight in the possibilities involved in creating a new garden, but before beginning, it is wise to look at the garden's existing structure and surroundings.

Because of their size, any existing large trees will be important elements in your landscape design. If any plant has to be removed for any reason, usually the sooner this is done the better. Assess the visual impact of all existing plantings but pay particular attention to the mature trees and shrubs you want to keep. Try to imagine what other plants might be added for balance or to strengthen the visual framework of the site. If you are trying to move away from a rather bitsy mixture of plantings, you might consider planting additional specimens of plants that you like that are already doing well in your garden.

An existing row of mature trees or shrubs might provide enclosure along a busy street, but you might prefer to thin the row to create vistas from the street and openings to entice visitors to enjoy your garden—even from a distance.

Since the house is usually, but not always, the dominant design element around which you will be working, examine it closely for inspiration. Try to define the architectural style of the house. Also, because many homes combine elements of more than one style, look for the most prominent features, and the ones that you like most.

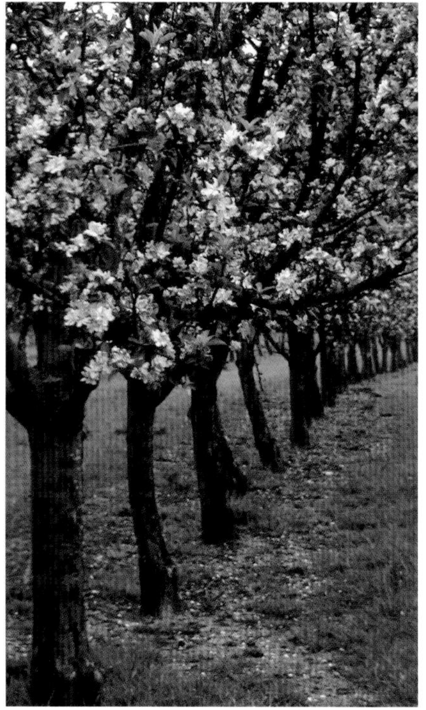

If there is a favorite bay window or a terrace that catches the sun in the morning, you may want to design vistas that extend these features into the garden, enhancing the view or highlighting a favorite tree or some other feature.

Larger, spreading trees along the borders provide screening yet avoid casting too much shade on the inner garden. Walls, arbors and columnar trees will give vertical structure to the garden, leaving more space for flower beds and other features in the garden's heart.

Feature Plants and Gap-fillers

For your initial planting, focus on landmark plants—the trees and shrubs that will grow to be the mature framework of your garden, or form the special features upon which the design of the landscape as a whole will focus. These will help give your garden a sense of structure. If you like roses and your garden offers the right conditions, they can provide a lovely theme for your garden, because they have so many different forms—bushes, small trees, climbers, ramblers—and grow quickly in suitable conditions. Other options include the wide range of hedging plants as well as evergreen and deciduous shrubs and trees.

Ivy

One rule to remember is to have taller plants toward the back of your viewing area, so that you create a sense of balance and flow as well as preventing smaller plants from being smothered and killed.

Foundation Planting

One area that is sometimes overlooked is the foundation planting—the parts of the garden that anchor the house and other structures to the landscape and create a sense of transition between the two.

When choosing foundation plants, consider how their forms can reinforce the

A row of blossoming trees in spring creates a superb, colorful garden "wall" or screen.

LEFT: Sealing-wax palm *Cyrtostachys renda* makes a stunning feature plant in a warm-climate or tropical garden. RIGHT: Japanese kerria *Kerria japonica.*

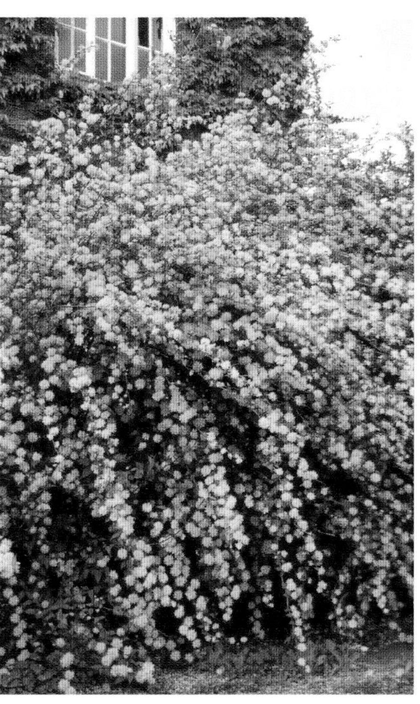

lines of your architecture. Columnar trees or tall grasses accentuate the height of the house and mirror vertical elements such as tall chimney stacks.

The horizontal lines of contemporary and ranch-style homes can be reinforced by spreading and weeping trees or low-growing shrubs; aim to complement rather than compete with the architecture.

Spreading trees and low shrub masses can balance strong vertical lines and make any building appear a part of the landscape, but it is important not to plant shrubs that cover the bottom of the house. This can create a boring, dense horizontal mass as well as problems with damp inside the house.

When planting shrubs beneath windows, and working with informal or semiformal design styles, look for plants with horizontal growth habits so that you do not have to hack upright-growing shrubs into flat-topped travesties of their natural selves.

You could create a low-maintenance foundation planting by planting a straight row of dwarf evergreens and surrounding them with a layer of mulch. With a little extra effort, you can combine a variety of plants for an interesting, dynamic planting scheme that is a pleasure to stroll by on your way in and out the door.

Foundation plantings have traditionally contained mostly evergreen conifers, such as yew and juniper, or broad-leaved evergreens, such as azaleas and boxwood. Evergreens do add color and hide the foundation all year, but deciduous shrubs have their place, too. Many species, including dwarf fothergilla *Fothergilla gardenii* and Japanese kerria *Kerria japonica*, offer year-round interest with brightly colored flowers, autumn leaf color or attractive stems.

When choosing foundation plants, look for flower colors to complement the colors of your house.

Although there is an enormous range of plants from which you might choose, try to limit your design to just a few different plant types, and plant multiple specimens of each. Not only will the design look better but you'll have fewer kinds of plant to maintain.

If you choose interesting species, you don't have to worry that the lack of diversity will be monotonous. Look for plants with attractive textures or growth habits or with interesting fruit, flowers, or bark—and remember to include groundcovers, trailing plants, climbers and vines to help fill in empty spaces and bind the different elements together.

Because climbing plants usually grow quickly, they can fill spaces while slower-growing plants mature. Some are very rapid growers and benefit from enriched soil at planting and feeding occasionally until well established.

When your main plantings have matured, you can thin out the temporary climbers and vines, using the clippings as cuttings to start them anew elsewhere.

Solving Landscaping Problems with Plants

There may be a landscape somewhere that has never had any substantial problems, but such perfection is not very likely. Every garden is the result of someone dealing with a range of problems in an intelligent and creative way.

Because home gardeners can now choose from a very wide range of plants and, in nature, plants have adapted to the most unlikely and extreme environments, careful plant selection can help you make a beautiful garden from what might seem a very difficult site.

Also, the chances are good that at least some of your problems are shared by your neighbors—you are unlikely to be alone. Local garden centers and plant stores will be only too familiar with the tales of woe you bring them. They will also stock plants that suit your site and be able to suggest remedies when things do go wrong. You may also find that local agricultural organizations, universities or colleges provide a horticultural advice service—perhaps available on the Internet.

Astilbe

One useful approach is to work with, not against, what you have. What seem to be hurdles in your garden can be overcome, especially if you are prepared to amend your plans so that you are working with natural conditions. This may also point your landscape in directions that you might not have considered otherwise.

Add color to a shady area with beautiful flowering plants such as hellebores *Helleborus* spp.

Take time to identify your garden's biggest drawbacks and observe what effect these are having. In a new garden, try not to make really major changes for the first year so that you can identify the pluses and minuses through every season.

If you have a few problems, try to prioritize them and do not attempt to solve all problems at once. Some will inevitably take several seasons to fix, while others may involve high costs. Professional advice and reconstruction or soil amendment may be needed in more extreme cases.

Going With the Wind

Very windy landscapes can have a rather unearthly appearance. Trees can be stunted or bent over, or even nonexistent, plants of any kind are difficult to establish and soil dries out quickly. In summer, plants can get blown down and in winter, winds add to the chill.

Use plants to build shelter. Consider planting a hedge or a sheltering belt of

Barriers, such as a fence, can reduce wind velocity for distances up to five times their height.

Trees and Shrubs for Wind Shelter

Plants can be a great alternative to a solid fence for dividing a property or blocking an unpleasant view. Open-branched trees are good dispersers of wind. These plants tolerate close planting to create an effective barrier or screen.

Araucaria heterophylla (Norfolk Island pine)
Cedrus spp. (cedars)
Cupressus spp. (cypresses)
Grevillea robusta (silky oak)
Ilex spp. (hollies)
Juniperus virginiana (eastern red cedar)
Lagunaria patersonii (Norfolk Island hibiscus)
Liquidambar styraciflua (liquidambar)
Melaleuca quinquenervia (broad-leaved paperbark)
Picea abies (Norway spruce)
Pinus spp. (pines)
Platanus orientalis (oriental plane tree)
Populus spp. (poplars)
Quercus palustris (pin oak)
Schinus molle (peppercorn tree)
Ulmus parvifolia (Chinese elm)

Holly

SHADY GARDEN CORNER You can lighten and brighten a shady area of the garden, such as a corner under an overhanging shade tree. First, paint the wall a pale color that will reflect light. Then plant a variety of golden-leafed, white-variegated or white-flowered plants.

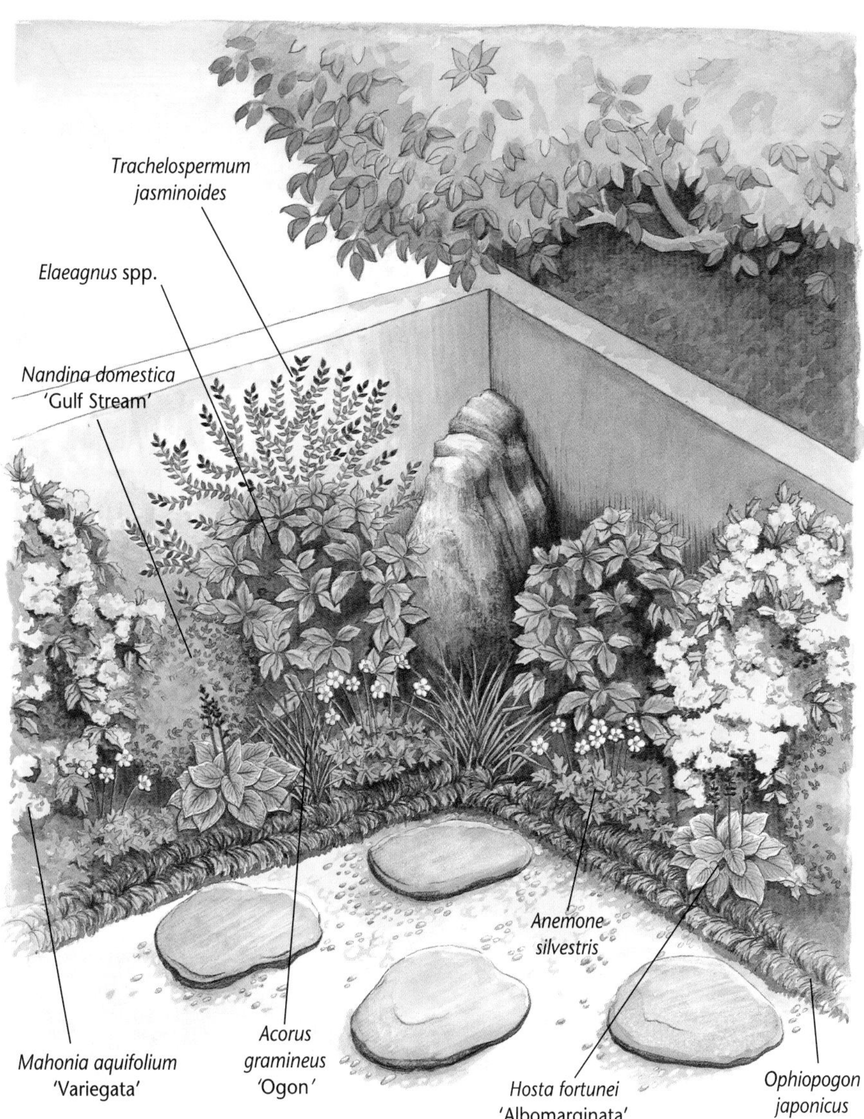

trees and shrubs across the windiest border of your garden. Plant barriers can be most effective in providing shelter from strong winds, because solid barriers such as a wall can cause wind eddying that can damage your plants.

Shelter plants may well need protection as they develop. Erect temporary screens of loose-weave hessian or heavy-duty shade cloth on posts, either as a single, large screen or as a broad cylinder around individual plants.

You can also use woven fence panels as a temporary shelter to protect a growing hedge or windbreak. When the fence's useful life is over, the hedge should be well established.

When planting shelter, resist the temptation to plant only the fastest-growing trees. They can get out of control and unless you plan to clip them regularly, you might find less unruly plants much easier in the long term.

In the Shade

Just about every garden has its shady spots, and it is important to know where they are before planting. As plants need light in order to produce food for growth, only a few hardy species will cope with almost total shade. Shade-loving plants tend to have larger foliage than sun-lovers—nature's way of compensating for the lack of light—and they often have smaller and paler flowers. Heavily shaded gardens will therefore not support a bright display of colorful flowers, but with good planning and the right selection of plants, it is possible to create an attractive and serene shade garden. The contrast between pale flowers and dark foliage in a shaded spot can be effective and striking, especially when plantings are massed and viewed from a distance.

Hostas, such as *Hosta ventricosta*, are ideal for season-long interest in a shady, moist situation.

There are several kinds of shady conditions. Beneath evergreen trees or beside high walls, there may be permanent shade. Other areas may have dappled shade for part of the day. There are seasonal variations, too, with the area under deciduous trees receiving more sunlight in winter. To ensure that you choose the right plants, identify the kind of shade that different areas receive: it's worth sketching shade patterns on a rough garden plan to get an overall picture. Shady areas under a tree or below a wall will usually be dry because the tree or wall provides shelter. The ground is often covered with debris such as dead leaves and twigs. And to compound the problem, tree roots make it difficult for other plants to establish themselves.

Groundcovers and ivies cope well with these conditions, as well as perennials such as foxgloves, hostas, bergenias, and lady's mantle. Bergenias are particularly valuable for shaded areas. Their large leaves are evergreen, and these tolerant plants will survive in even the most inhospitable conditions.

Begonias, astilbe, and *Dicentra* spp. are among the flowers that thrive in moist shaded positions. Another good choice is the hardy cyclamen (*Cyclamen hederifolium*), which flowers in fall and then bears deep green mottled leaves through the winter. For a more complete list of shade-loving flowers, see "Super Plants for Shade," on page 157.

Bethlehem sage

Shade that results from tree or shrub canopies can be lightened by judicious pruning. Broken or diseased branches should be removed first. Then, prune away low-hanging branches to raise the canopy. As you move further up the tree, remove branches that are crowded together and those that cross each other.

In a seaside dune garden, use plants such as sea holly *Eryngium amethystinum* to hold the sand in place.

Groundcovers such as blue lilyturf (*Liriope muscari*) and Japanese pachysandra (*Pachysandra terminalis*) will benefit from the additional light and water. Spring bulbs, such as daffodils, crocuses, and snowdrops, also thrive in partially shaded areas under trees. They bloom early, and then disappear as the site becomes more heavily shaded when the trees fill out with the approaching summer. Plant spring bulbs before winter to enjoy their colorful display and fragrance.

For very hilly areas of the garden that are hard to maintain, you can create level planting areas with a series of terraced beds.

Hills and Slopes

Steeply sloping ground can be a maintenance problem. However, mulch and the right selection of plants can turn slopes and hillsides into an attractive, and trouble-free, part of the garden.

A thick covering of mulch will help to conserve water and keep weeds at bay. Groundcovers and spreading plants will also keep the soil in place and soak up rain. If your site is really steep, you may also want to consider terracing to create a series of level planting areas. For details on how to create terraces, see "Terraces for Slopes," on page 155.

Another option is to set a series of stepping-stones in place through a sloping area. Plant creeping herbs such as thyme or chamomile in the gaps between the stones to add flowers and fragrance to the pathway.

An attractive solution to hilly sites is to create an informal meadow garden, with a profusion of wildflowers providing color and stabilizing the soil at the same time. For more information, see "Making a Meadow Garden" on page 136.

Coasting Along

Seaside gardens can have similar problems to merely windy gardens, but there are two additional problems—first, the wind that carries salt spray can be very damaging to plants and, second, sand can blow into the garden. However, coastal gardens are generally warmer than those inland in the same region and seaside gardens are usually frost-free.

Again, the solution is to develop shelter, but using salt-resistant plants. They will probably not grow as tall or lush as they might inland.

Mediterranean gardens are naturally at home on maritime sites in warmer climates, and in really sandy areas, think about a dune garden. Use grasses, sea hollies and other maritime plants to anchor the sand to one spot.

Wet Spots

Wet areas are generally caused by a high water table or poor drainage or both. You cannot do much about the first, other than to build up parts of your garden with raised beds, terracing and so on. If you excavate to change levels, you can develop contrasting wet and drier areas.

If an area suffers from poor drainage, you may need to consider installing a piped drainage system. Although this is quite an investment, it will resolve the problem once and for all. Alternatively—and more cheaply—you can improve the porous quality of the soil by adding compost, mulch, or bark.

Often water stands where soil has been compacted. Once the compacted layer has been broken up the water will run away more easily.

Some of the most attractive flowers actually prefer almost-constant moisture. So, rather than seeing soggy sites as a problem, select appropriate plants and maximize their potential. Foliage is a good indication of a plant's natural habitat, and plants with large, glossy leaves are usually best suited to moist or shady conditions.

Bee balm (bergamot)

Some plants thrive in moist soil; some prefer wet soil; while others, such as the water lilies, grow best with their roots actually in water. These are known as "aquatics." Very few bulbs enjoy wet soil, and most will rot if they become waterlogged. Trees and shrubs for wet conditions include *Amelanchier lamarckii*, birches, *Cornus alba*, mountain ash *Sorbus* spp., *Viburnum opulus* and willows (but be careful, because some are very vigorous). Herbaceous plants to choose from include astilbes, daylilies, hostas, ligularia, bee balm (bergamot), *Mimulus* (monkey flower) and primulas. For a list of flowers that thrive in moist conditions, see "Plants That Like Wet Feet" on page 158. And remember that you won't have to water your wet-site plants, so maintenance is easier.

Hot and Dry Sites

Positions in full sun, often on poor soil, tend to lose their reserves of moisture very quickly. By late spring, plants begin to wilt, growth stops and only the most drought-resistant plants survive.

Many silver-leaved species are particularly sensitive to winter wetness, but will get by comfortably in such a site. Select plant species that relish hot, dry conditions. Again, this might be the perfect site for a Mediterranean garden.

Purple loosestrife *Lythrum salicaria* 'Feuerkerze' is a perennial that is happiest in wet areas of the garden.

The prettiest of the Mediterranean shrubs have aromatic leaves, fragrant blooms and often have silver foliage. Sage, rosemary, several species of lavender, *Phlomis* and *Cistus* (rock roses) will all grow well here. Use them with dark evergreens such as dwarf juniper. Dry landscaping, or xeriscaping, enhances the arid effect. Consider gravel or grit as a mulch and set out rocks to accentuate the desert look.

Frost Pockets

The more sheltered a garden, the more likely it is to hold a frost pocket, especially if that area does not get direct sunlight. Some frost pockets can be created when new structures are built or maturing trees and shrubs cast more shade. If possible, let more light in and develop greater air circulation. A gap in a hedge or wall, for example, can allow more air flow.

Avoid planting vulnerable, frost-tender plants species in frost pockets. A plant may be trying to produce delicate spring blooms only to have buds and flowers killed or stunted by one cool night and a ground frost.

The Art of Concealment

Most of us share at least a part of our gardens with parked cars, garbage and compost bins, fuel tanks, woodpiles, gas and electric meters, utility wires and all the other paraphernalia of daily life. Few of these objects actually add beauty to the landscape but they can be disguised in various ways.

Sometimes designing a really spectacular focal point in your garden can distract attention from the more unsightly utility areas. More common, however, is the careful deployment of garden structures, such as screens (especially when covered with vines and other climbers), hedges, tall feature plants and other barriers.

A hot-color, summer border featuring crocosmia *Crocosmia* 'Lucifer', scarlet sage *Salvia splendens,* and marigolds *Tagetes patula* and *Tagetes erecta.*

Designing Beds and Borders

Before you plant your flower garden, think about the style of beds and borders that best suits your landscape and gardening style. Carefully planned flower beds will eliminate much of the drudgery and give you more time to enjoy your garden.

Allow enough space between and around flower beds to enable the lawn mower to fit comfortably so that you don't have to make a second pass to trim that extra few inches of grass. Remember, too, that formal beds with squared-off edges and corners require more maintenance than informal, free-flowing beds. Round corners and gentle curves make for easier mowing and help create a low-maintenance flower garden. For more ideas, go to "Beds and Borders, Screens and Fillers," starting on page 128.

Constructing Beds and Borders

Building a bed or border is easy if you start with a plan and follow a few simple rules. A successful border is largely a matter of good marriages between plants. Whether you use traditional perennials and annuals or shrubs with interesting foliage, the goal is the same: Combine plants whose colors and textures look good together, and plan for an extended season with a succession of bloom or foliage texture.

Start with the tall, long-lived plants that will give form to the border. Fill in with the low, more rambling plants and then add your special features—for example, bulbs that might have a brief but spectacular blooming season.

Make sure you locate plants with similar water, soil and light needs together. When designing islands of low-water plants, target those areas where summer irrigation would be difficult.

As well as being ideal for gardens with a Mediterranean theme, many culinary herbs combine well with ornamental shrubs and perennials. Sited alongside a patio or near the kitchen door, a bed of mixed flowers, herbs, vegetables and fruit can be very welcoming and attractive, as well as useful.

Edging Away

It can be tough to mow around or along beds and borders without cutting into the

Summer border edged with *Lavandula angustifolia* 'Dwarf White' and *L. angustifolia* 'Princess Blue'.

Bed and Border Tips

As with many gardening and landscaping tasks, a systematic approach makes things a little easier. These tips for creating your own garden beds and borders reflect the experience of many landscape designers and gardeners.

- Ask the "why?" question. What is this bed or border actually for? Why do you want it?
- Select your location. Determine its exposure (sun, part-sun or shade) and other growing conditions. Be wary of maturing trees and other changes that might affect your new garden.
- Measure and sketch your site dimensions and any special features with which you will have to deal.
- Choose a theme, taking account of the color or style of your home, or from the types of plant that do well in your area. You can also choose a theme to suit a particular use—to attract birds or butterflies, for instance.
- Go for a variety of blooming times. Look around your neighborhood and public gardens to see what is in bloom throughout the year.
- Plant densely for a fuller, lusher effect.
- Prepare your soil, mixing in generous amounts of compost or other soil amendment, and then smooth it out.
- Arrange the plants, still in their pots, on the soil and adjust as needed before planting. For one-sided viewing, place tall plants at the back, short to medium growers in the middle ground, and ground-huggers in the front. To view from all angles, put the tall plants in the middle and lower-growers around them.
- Plant in groups with several plants of the same kind together—odd numbers, such as threes or fives, usually seem to look best.
- Incorporate accent plants. Use dramatic plants (tall grasses or succulents, for example) as features throughout the bed or border, to act as a focal point.

'Red Baron' blood grass

Goldenrod

bedding plants. The more formal your landscape plans, the more neat edges and tidy boundaries matter.

If you look at photographs of old garden beds, the problem of neat edging was dealt with in a number of ways, including terracotta sections in a wide variety of "spaded" or decorative shapes arranged between path or lawn and bed or border. Wire hoops and miniature wire fences were also used.

Home gardeners have also edged with many different materials: timber, stone, brick and cement in formal or informal sections, laid loose or fastened or cast in place, perhaps with a bagged or painted finish to match pathways.

In more recent times, edging systems of metal and plastic have been developed that lie under the desirable lawn grass height so that they can be mown over. Your local garden center or hardware store will either stock edging products or be able to order them for you, and it seems that terracotta edging sections are rather coming back into fashion, especially for gardens surrounding older houses.

Edging with Plants

You can also use tough, ground-hugging plants along the front of your flower beds and borders. Edging plants are small, neat, compact plants used at the front of the border, in the same way that shrubs or fences define the back of the border.

Any plant can be used for edging if it can be kept within bounds of space and low height and suits the growing conditions in your bed or border. The job of edging plants is to frame or add contrast to surrounding borders, lawns or hardscapes by forming bands of color. They will also help conceal less than attractive garden edging materials of metal or plastic.

Once established, it is easy to keep your edges neat. Replace any dead or ragged plants, deadhead the flowers and prune the plants back a bit if they become unruly. If you keep your edging plants in good health, your whole landscape will appear neat, complete and well cared for.

Spiky plants, such as spike gayfeather, look wonderful contrasted with low, mounded plants.

Special Plant Effects

Many plants are more flexible in cultivation than we might at first think. Over the centuries, gardeners have trained plants to get the greatest possible benefit from them and, in doing so, have created a variety of distinctive garden forms and styles that may have a place in your landscape.

Fruit trees, such as apples, pears, apricots and plums, have been carefully cultivated to produce as much fruit as possible in the smallest space. It is possible to train these trees into shapes to fit almost any space. Keep this in mind as you plan planting schemes to enliven small side yards, cramped courtyards, tight property lines and landscape sites with walls and fences.

ABOVE LEFT: Two spiral boxwood *Buxus* spp. topiaries make a striking display at an entrance.
ABOVE RIGHT: A romantic "gateway" has been created by a topiarized yew *Taxus baccata* hedge.

Experiment with Espalier

Espalier is a training technique that turns a normally bushy plant into a flat, almost two-dimensional form. Although the technique requires persistent attention and fearless pruning, the results are tremendously rewarding. Use espalier training to cover a blank or nondescript wall, to create a leafy screen that gives privacy to a doorway, deck, patio or porch, or to grow faster-yielding fruit in a small space.

Before you choose the plants you want to train, think carefully about the exposure of the site where you plan to create the espalier. Training styles for espalier are limited only by your imagination. For a classical look, you might choose a formal U-shape, fan or interwoven Belgian fence pattern. Informal, free-flowing patterns are attractive, too, but they can be more difficult to train without having them look like a jumble of stems.

Espaliered trees take time to train and maintain. You'll have to shape them carefully, choosing the best main branches and manipulating them into the right position. Then you'll have to thin out side growth and errant shoots to maintain the purity of the pattern you've established. The stunning results, however, more than repay the extra work.

Topiary Tales

Training shrubs, trees and vines into fanciful shapes is another practice that carries pruning into the realm of sculpture. A single example of topiary can be a graceful focal point in a small garden; multiple figures can transform a larger space into a magical land, peopled with strange and wonderful creatures and shapes.

Evergreen, small-leaved plants are usually the plants of choice for garden topiary projects. Yews *Taxus* spp. and boxwoods *Buxus* spp. are traditional favorites for this type of pruning.

FAR LEFT: Espalier is a training technique to use to add charm and beauty to a narrow space.
LEFT: Carefully trained fruit trees can produce a unique and effective fence that is also productive.

For best results, start with a young or newly planted shrub; older shrubs may require more drastic pruning to get them into the shape you want and are not as resistant to disease.

Topiaries are generally trained into either geometric or representational forms. Geometric shapes, such as boxes and spheres, take less time, thought and planning, as evidenced by the abundance of these in residential landscapes.

For a more whimsical look, you may shape your topiary into a more unusual form, such as a boat, bird, giraffe, dog, chair or wishing well. If you plan to try a complicated figure, it's helpful to sketch out the final shape you want; then you can refer to the sketch as you prune. Try to keep the figure fairly simple; it can be hard to achieve and then maintain fine details.

Basic Bonsai

Bonsai is an art that attempts to replicate, in a container, the look of an old tree that has been shaped by time and the elements. The process of training these beautiful bonsai requires much time and patience, but the results can be stunning and gratifying.

Before you buy or begin a bonsai project, be aware that these plants will need some special care. Hardy bonsai normally prefer to be outdoors during the growing season. They enjoy the shelter of a lath house or some other shade-producing structure, where they will receive bright, indirect light and protection from the elements. One gust of wind can easily knock over small plants and undo months or years of care!

Bonsai generally grow in shallow pots, so you'll have to water them frequently—possibly as often as twice a day in hot weather—to keep the soil evenly damp. During the winter months, you'll need to protect bonsai from cold temperatures by bringing them indoors before the first frost, and keeping them on a sunny windowsill.

For more detailed information on the selecting, training, shaping, and maintaining bonsai plants, go to "Plants in Miniature," on page 282.

Pleaching

Pleaching is the interweaving of growing branches, vines and other climbing plants, and can be trained as a living wall or arbor as well as an avenue of trees.

Carefully selected trees are planted on a grid, like a small orchard. As they grow, the branches are pruned and trained along this grid, so that eventually the branch of one tree meets that of its neighbor. At this point, an incision is made in the bark of both branches and they are tied together. When these pleached branches mature to form substantial limbs, the trees are all connected together.

Pollarding

Pollarding is a way of imposing a formal look on a tree, and for controlling the size of an otherwise large-growing tree.

Lime trees *Linden* spp. are a popular tree for pleaching, as their young limbs are pliable and easily trained into the interlocked pattern. Pleaching is often used for avenues, as the technique creates a formal but pleasing effect.

In addition to creating a stylized appearance, the training technique known as pollarding can restrain the height of a large-growing tree, such as this mulberry *Morus* spp.

In winter, a pollarded tree is a trunk, topped by a rather clubbed head or very short limbs. In summer, a mass of vigorous shoots wildly bursts forth from the tree's head or limbs.

Deciduous, fast-growing trees that do not resent being pruned hard are ideal candidates for pollarding, for example chestnut, horse chestnut, linden, London plane tree, sycamore, eucalypt and willow.

You can create a pollarded tree by removing branches along the trunk of a young tree to give the tree a high head with at least 5 or 6 feet (1.5 or 2 m) of clear trunk.

A pollarded tree needs to be pruned every winter, or at least every second or third winter. Pruning is easy. Cut off all new stems back to within half an inch (1 cm) or so of where they grew the previous season.

Plants in Miniature

Bonsai is an artform, originally from China, but developed and refined in Japan, of reproducing in miniature, species of trees and shrubs that grow much larger in nature. Careful pruning and training of the roots and branches of bonsai plants prevents them growing to their natural size and can produce some beautiful and eye-catching shapes.

Bonsai are traditionally grown in shallow pots, which restrict the spread of the roots and so limit the size to which the plants can grow. Depending on the species, bonsai can be as small as a couple of inches (about 5 cm) tall or can grow to just over 3 feet (1 m). Bonsai plants can live for very long periods—often longer than their full-size counterparts.

Bonsai Styles and Effects

Experts often argue about the proper classification of bonsai styles. As with any long-established art or craft, new styles emerge and traditional forms are modified by innovative practitioners. You can get some idea of the variety of shapes and sizes from the pictures on these pages, or by looking through a specialist bonsai book. Some of the widely recognized styles are:

Japanese maple (*Acer palmatum*) is an attractive plant for bonsai, because the leaves turn a beautiful copper color during fall.

- "upright," in which the trunk of the tiny tree is either perfectly straight, or slightly bent to the right or the left;
- "slanting," where the trunk leans conspicuously;
- "cascading," in which the plant flows over the edge of its container and falls below its base; and
- "semi-cascading," where the end of the plant falls just over the edge of the container.

With upright bonsai, the plant, like most container plants, is placed in the center of its container. Slanting, cascading, and semi-cascading bonsai can differ in that often the plant is placed toward one end of a rectangular container and trained so that the foliage sweeps across the pot toward the other end.

Some of the best effects can be gained by growing three plants grouped together, or many of the same species almost filling the surface in the style of a mini forest. You can have lots of fun propagating plants for use in this way. Some plants, such as figs (*Ficus* spp.), have distinctive aerial roots, and you can expose these in what is known as root-over-rock or clinging-to-rock settings.

Moss, too, plays a very important role in a bonsai setting, and you'll find that it helps to keep the surface of these shallow containers moist, while also adding to their overall visual appeal.

Shaping Bonsai

Bonsai begins with pruning the branches and roots of the desired plant, in order to help restrict the growth of the plant. It is best to train and prune in early spring, just before new growth appears. Leaf pruning can be done throughout the season.

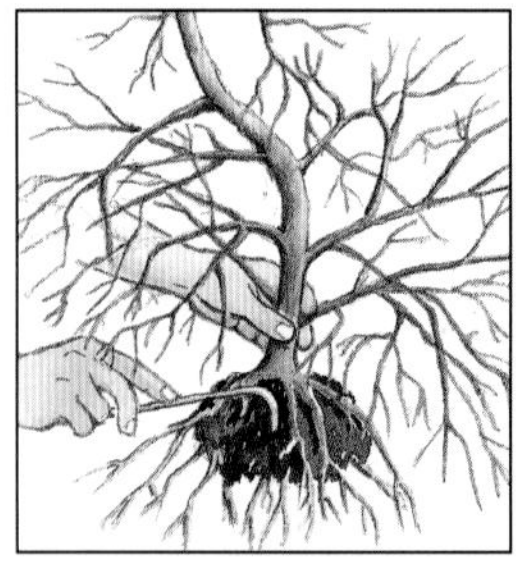

1. Remove plant from its pot and remove the excess container mix from the roots.

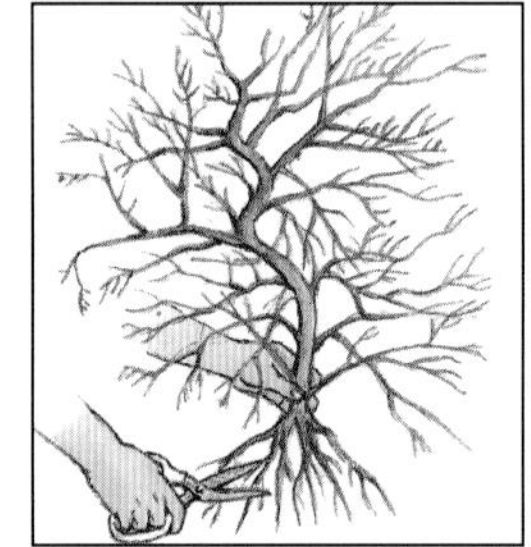

2. Prune the roots with clippers, to cut away about half the roots and any damaged growth.

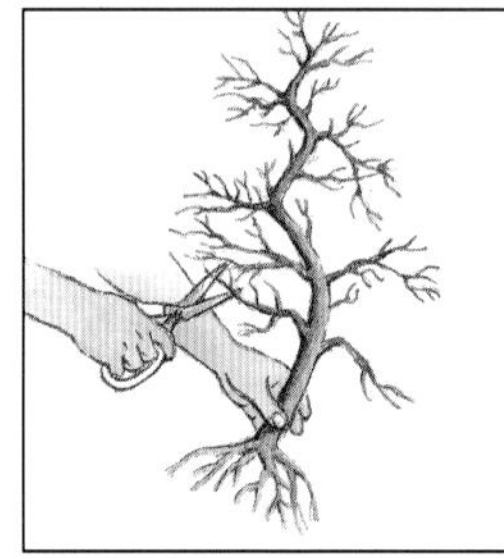

3. Prune the top of the plant to reveal the natural structure of the original plant.

Suitable Plants

You can grow bonsai from seeds or cuttings, but most bonsai are cultivated from young plants or trees, that are then pruned and shaped to produce the desired effect. Shrubs, such as azaleas, are generally more adaptable to different styles than tree species. In general, however, it's a good idea to base your idea of the finished product on the natural shape and style of the original plant. It takes an expert bonsai practitioner to mold a plant into a shape that is foreign to its original form.

Most sizable plants, deciduous and evergreen, can be grown as bonsai. Popular deciduous species include beeches (*Fagus* spp.), hawthorns (*Crataegus* spp.), and Japanese maple (*Acer palmatum*). Evergreen candidates for bonsai treatment include azaleas (*Rhododendron* spp.), camellias (*Camellia* spp.), junipers (*Juniperus* spp.), pines (*Pinus mugo* and *P. parvifolia*), spruces (*Picea* spp.), and boxwoods (*Buxus* spp.). Most species that are suitable for bonsai can be molded into upright and slanting forms and many are adaptable to other styles. Pines work well for both upright and slanting bonsai plants, while junipers can be used across the whole stylistic range.

If you are just starting out as a bonsai grower it is probably wise to begin with one of the easier to grow plants, such as Japanese maple or juniper. Both of these are relatively hardy and are more tolerant of inexpert handling than other species. Japanese maples are easy to grow from seed and are quick to give a good display.

Once you have selected the type of plant to work with, be sure to start with small specimens. If you start with a larger plant, you'll need to root prune it over time, getting the roots into successively smaller pots to control the growth.

Maintenance

To train a bonsai plant into the shape you desire, it is usually, but not always, necessary to wire the branches or stems to control the direction of their growth. This must be done carefully, in a way that does not cut into the plant and create permanent scars. It is important to realize that wiring is a temporary measure and that its purpose is to control the shape, but not the size, of the plant. More details on wiring and shaping plants can be found in "Training Bonsai" on page 78.

There are no hard and fast rules about watering bonsai. If the plants are kept outdoors, regular winter and fall rain will generally keep them adequately watered.

You can display your bonsai alone, or group them with other bonsai and container plants in rock gardens.

In warmer times, and in extended dry spells, they will need watering several times a week, or even daily. Exposure to drying winds, too, can necessitate extra watering. Do not water a plant for a day or two before wiring.

If your bonsai are grown from outdoor species, rather than from houseplants, you can take them indoors occasionally, but not for long periods. Frequent changes of environment can cause unnecessary stress and inhibit their healthy development. Bonsai respond best to a stable setting and a regular routine.

Regular year-round fertilizing is important for the health of your plants. More frequent feeding is advisable during the spring and summer months. Throughout most of the year, use a fertilizer that is not too rich in nitrogen, and, if possible, apply a nitrogen-free fertilizer in the fall. Too much nitrogen will encourage unsightly, spindly growth. Inquire at your garden center, or at a specialist bonsai nursery about the most appropriate food for your bonsai plants in different seasons.

A normal potting mix is quite suitable for most bonsai plants, especially if you are a bonsai beginner. One thing that you need to ensure is that the soil drains well. Specialist bonsai soil, which is available from specialist bonsai centers, is generally lighter than regular potting mix and contains less fertilizer. The extra fertilizer put into regular potting mix is designed to encourage larger growth in container plants.

You will need to repot your bonsai plants at regular, but not very frequent, intervals. This is in order to revitalize the soil and promote new root growth. Very small plants should be repotted every two or three years; larger ones every five years or so. Repotting also provides a good opportunity to prune a plant's roots. Late fall, when the plant has ceased growing for the season, is the best time to repot.

The word bonsai basically means "plant in a tray." There are many different styles of bonsai in Japan, named according to the overall shape, as well as the angle of the trunk in the container.

Using Trees, Shrubs, and Vines

The biggest investment in your garden landscape—in both time and money—is the selection, purchase and planting of trees, shrubs, and vines. Trees dominate the garden's landscape, and create a sense of calm and permanence. Shrubs and vines are hardworking plants, providing shade, privacy, or color to your garden.

Landscaping with Trees

Trees generally have a mature height ranging from 15–100 feet (4.5–30 m) or more. A small tree is defined as one that generally doesn't exceed 25–35 feet (7.5–10.5 m) in mature height. A medium-sized tree matures at 50–65 feet (15–19.5 m), and a large tree matures at 75–100 feet (22.5–30 m) or taller. Growing conditions, climate, competition with grass and other plants, mechanical or animal damage, and pollution can prevent a tree from reaching its mature height.

These versatile plants frame views, develop patterns for your landscape and unify your design. To get the most out of the trees you select, you should consider the following features and what they can add to your design.

Beauty

Trees serve as backdrops for other plants or garden features and as focal points, like large, living sculptures. You can use them to screen unwanted views and give you privacy. Your trees establish the walls and ceilings for your outdoor rooms. You can use them to soften the architecture of your house or to call attention to it.

Climate Control

By shading your house, trees keep things cool, reducing energy bills. (Don't plant evergreen trees for summer shade, though; they'll block the sun in winter, preventing passive solar heating of your house.) You can use trees as a windbreak, to intercept and buffer prevailing winds. If winter winds are your bane, needle-leaved evergreens are the best choice for a windbreak. If you live near a seacoast, choose salt-tolerant species to soften the sea winds.

Consider Growth Rates

Trees grow at different rates, ranging from less than 1 foot (30 cm) per year to several feet (about 1 m) per year. Species with a slow-to-medium growth rate, such as oaks, generally require less maintenance than fast-growing ones. Fast-growing trees, such as poplars and willows, are often short-lived, surviving only 20–30 years, and they also generally have weak wood, which is more susceptible to damage from wind, storms and pests.

Livability

Trees absorb noise and reduce glare, and they purify the air you breathe. Patios or play areas become more usable during hot summers when shaded by trees. Many trees have edible fruits that can feed your family or attract wildlife.

Consider Form and Function

When you select trees, use your landscape plan to help you decide what shape of tree to select and how each tree will function in the landscape. The arrangement of the branches gives each species of tree a distinctively shaped crown.

Most needle-leaved evergreens, such as pines and spruces, tend to have more symmetrical or rigid shapes than deciduous trees, such as oaks or maples. Needle-leaved evergreens often display the familiar conical or pyramidal "Christmas tree" look. Deciduous trees and broad-leaved evergreens can be many shapes, including round, vase-shaped and columnar.

Trees are often classified according to their intended use—as specimens, shade trees or street trees. Choose

LEFT: Full-moon maple *Acer japonicum* (top) and Japanese maple *Acer palmatum* (bottom).

LEFT: Black locust trees (*Robinia pseudoacacia*) provide dappled shade for a garden setting.
RIGHT: A water view is framed by the branches of a gum tree.

magnolia *Magnolia* x *soulangiana* is showy for a couple of weeks during spring when in flower, but fades into the background during the remainder of the year. A kousa dogwood *Cornus kousa*, on the other hand, bears showy flowers in spring, red fruits in autumn and attractive peeling bark in winter.

your landscape trees according to their function. For an upright, narrow screen, for example, you might select either a tree with a columnar shape or a pyramidal needle-leaved evergreen.

Specimen Trees

Specimen trees are showy in some way. They may put on an eye-catching display of flowers in spring, such as a flowering crab apple, or blaze with autumn color, such as *Acer rubrum* 'October Glory'. Or they may have unusually colored leaves, such as purple smoke tree *Cotinus coggygria* 'Royal Purple', or bright berries, such as American mountain ash *Sorbus americana*.

Specimen trees are valuable as focal points in a winter landscape. Fruits that hang on the branches after the leaves drop, such as the fruits of crab apples, add color to the winter landscape. Trees with attractive winter silhouettes, such as flowering dogwoods, also make good specimen trees.

Select a specimen tree with multiseasonal interest. A saucer

RIGHT: Deciduous trees make ideal companions for early bulbs. Here snowdrops grow under a forsythia.

Shade Trees

Shade trees may be showy, but it's their cooling effect that's important. A tree with a round or vase shape is ideal as a shade tree. Decide the location of a new shade tree with care: Make sure the tree's shadow will shade the area you intend it to.

If you want filtered shade or want to be able to grow grass under your tree, use a tree with small, fine leaves, such as a thornless honey locust *Gleditsia triacanthos* var. *inermis*, not one with a dense canopy of large, overlapping leaves, such as a Norway maple *Acer platanoides*.

The price of an advanced tree will not seem cheap, but it is a good investment. First you are paying for the growth the tree has achieved and, with the right care, trees will repay you by being the longest-lived and often the most maintenance-free plants in your landscape.

Street Trees

Street trees are tough species that withstand the difficult growing conditions along the street. They are heat- and pollution-tolerant, grow well in poor soils, and can stand drought. Their roots must grow in very limited spaces, and their crowns must fit under overhead utility lines. Street trees have to be neat: Look for trees that don't have messy fruit, falling twigs or large leaves that can block storm sewers.

In spite of these demands, a number of attractive trees are available for roadside planting. Among small trees, consider trident maple *Acer buergerianum*, thornless cockspur hawthorn *Crataegus crus-galli* var. *inermis* or golden-rain tree *Koelreuteria paniculata*. Suitable medium to large trees include thornless honey locust *Gleditsia triacanthos* var. *inermis*, Japanese pagoda tree *Sophora japonica* and silver linden *Tilia tomentosa*.

Landscaping with Shrubs

Shrubs can be used to add a touch of greenery at the foundation of the house, make a thick screen between neighbors, add seasonal color from flowers or fruit, or outline the garden rooms of a landscape design. Even in a well-planted landscape, shrubs sometimes go unnoticed. The glossy, dark green of common boxwood Buxus sempervirens makes an ideal backdrop for light-colored flowers, but few passersby appreciate the shrub. Instead, their eyes are drawn to the blossoms that the boxwood sets off.

Types of Shrubs

Shrubs are woody plants with multiple stems, ranging from a few inches (centimeters) tall to approximately 15 feet (4.5 m) when they reach maturity. Occasionally an individual shrub is trained to a single treelike stem, called a standard. And large shrubs are sometimes "limbed up" into small trees, by removing the lower branches.

Like trees, shrubs can be deciduous, evergreen or semi-evergreen. If all leaves drop each autumn, with new leaves each spring through summer, the shrub is deciduous. Deciduous shrubs, including such favorites as roses *Rosa* spp. and spireas *Spiraea* spp., often have attractive flowers. For heavy flower production, plant them in full sun.

Evergreen shrubs have leaves year-round, though each year some of the oldest leaves drop off and are replaced by new leaves. Shrubs with wide, often thick, leaves, such as camellias *Camellia* spp. and rhododendrons *Rhododendron* spp., are called broad-leaved evergreens. Shrubs with thin, narrow leaves, such as junipers *Juniperus* spp. and dwarf mugo pines *Pinus mugo* var. *mugo*, are classified as needle-leaved evergreens.

ABOVE: A planting of light-colored azaleas *Rhododendron* spp. helps to brighten up a shady area under trees.
LEFT: A fragrant combination of pink roses and lavender is ideal planted near a garden seat.

A few shrubs are semi-evergreen, holding some of their leaves well into the winter months.

Choosing and Using Shrubs

There are many ways to use shrubs creatively in your landscape. You can use them to define the border of your property, hide an exposed foundation on your house, or block an unwanted view. These useful plants can create privacy, show people where to walk, or just provide an attractive show throughout the year. They also filter noise, break the force of the wind, and provide shade. Of course you can plant a hedge composed of plants from a single species, but one of the most creative and ornamental ways to use shrubs in a landscape is in mixed plantings. Try combining deciduous and evergreen species, interplanting shrubs that bloom at different seasons, or adding flowering shrubs to a perennial border to create year-round interest.

Before making your selections, consider what you want the shrubs for and what season or seasons you need them to work for you. If you need to block the noise of traffic year-round, for example, plant evergreen shrubs, such as yews *Taxus* spp., hollies *Ilex* spp. or, in warm regions, camellias *Camellia* spp. If you need privacy only for summer barbecues, deciduous shrubs would be a fine choice.

Specimens

Shrubs make excellent specimen plants. Use them to highlight a special feature in your yard, such as the beginning of a path or the end of a border or patio. For specimens, look for shrubs that are attractive for as many months as possible. Many viburnums, for example, have attractive spring flowers, summer fruit and good autumn color.

Backdrops and "Walls"

You can use shrubs to mark the garden rooms or the parts of your landscape—to screen a quiet sitting area from an area designed for active play, or to wall utility areas off for trash or storage. You can also use shrubs as a backdrop for plantings of flowers. But if you use shrubs in this manner, look for ones that will complement but not compete with your flowers. Choose green shrubs such as boxwoods or junipers, for example, and avoid those with showy blossoms of their own.

Screens and Hedges

Shrubs are the perfect choice for hedges and screens, to block unattractive views or the sights and sounds of nearby neighbors and traffic. To calculate how many shrubs you need to buy for an effective hedge or screen, determine the mature spread of the species you've selected. Figure on spacing the shrubs closer together than their mature spread so that they'll form an unbroken line. For example, if a particular shrub has a mature spread of 5 feet (1.5 m), plan to space the plants 3–4 feet (90–120 cm) apart, depending upon how large they are when you buy them and how quickly you want a solid screen or hedge. Divide the total hedge length by the spacing you select to determine the number of shrubs you need to buy.

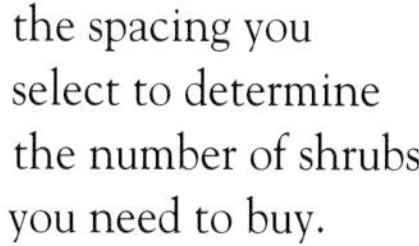

Hydrangea

Seasonal Attractions

In your landscape, shrubs can be utilitarian, but they can also be a focal point. Look for shrubs with multiseasonal interest—especially for use as accents or specimens. Oak-leaved hydrangea *Hydrangea quercifolia*, for instance, has interesting oak-leaf-shaped leaves that turn purple in autumn. Its showy clusters of off-white flowers dry on the plant and persist well into the winter. The peeling bark provides additional winter interest. The fruits on shrubs such as pyracanthas *Pyracantha* spp. and viburnums *Viburnum* spp. provide food for birds, while the plants serve as protective cover. Fruiting shrubs are also excellent for attracting wildlife.

Size Up Your Selections

If you want your shrubs to stay short, regular pruning will help to keep them in bounds. But a better approach is to choose shrubs that mature at the height you need. There are dwarf or miniature cultivars available of many popular shrubs. Dwarf cultivars of many trees—especially spruces *Picea* spp. and arborvitae *Thuja* spp.—are also commonly used as shrubs. Look for plants with names such as 'Prostrata', 'Nana', 'Compacta', 'Densa' and 'Pumila', but don't stop there. Be sure to verify mature height before you buy; compact forms of some trees and large shrubs may still be much larger than you want at maturity.

LEFT: Common box *Buxus sempervirens* is an ideal shrub for clipping into a formal hedge.

LEFT: Climbing plants can quickly grow to maturity to fill a garden landscape.

Landscaping with Vines

Vines, or climbers, are often used simply for the beautiful flowers and foliage they bring to the garden. Vines are functional as well: They are fast-growing and quickly lend an established look to the landscape. They can also soften or hide the harsh architectural lines of buildings, create or define garden spaces, provide privacy, screen unsightly views or noise, cover up ugly masonry, and break up the monotony of long fences and walls.

Types of Vines

While all vines twine or climb, there are three basic types of vines: annuals, herbaceous perennials and woody perennials. Most vines are fast growers, although some of the woody perennials may take a year or two to get established.

Annual vines, such as common morning glory *Ipomoea purpurea*, climb a lamppost or trellis in a hurry, making a good show in a single season. You'll need to replant annual vines each year, although some will self-sow. Some vines grown as annuals in cooler areas, including black-eyed Susan vine *Thunbergia alata*, are perennial in warmer climates.

Herbaceous perennial vines, such as crimson starglory *Mina lobata*, die back to the ground every winter and regrow in spring.

Hardy woody vines include familiar species such as clematis *Clematis* spp., honeysuckles *Lonicera* spp. and wisteria *Wisteria* spp. Most hardy woody vines are deciduous, dropping their leaves each autumn but leaving a woody stem from which new leaves, flowers and fruits grow the following year. Others, including wintercreeper euonymus *Euonymus fortunei* and English ivy *Hedera helix*, are evergreen.

Choosing and Using Vines

You can find a vine for any type of soil—fertile or poor, wet or dry—and any exposure from full sun to deep shade. Just as with trees and shrubs, the best course is to match the plant to your site rather than trying to alter your conditions to suit the plant. Most vines are adaptable plants and accept a wide range of growing conditions. A few vines require special conditions. Clematis, for example, need sun for good flower production but do best with cool roots, so plant them in full sun but shade their roots with a groundcover, low-growing perennial, or an organic mulch.

Climbing vines will soften the look of a raw, new fence or quickly screen an unsightly view. A hot, sunny porch becomes much more inviting when a trellised vine adds dappled shade. Vines trained on upright supports can fit in spaces too small for most trees and shrubs. They can be used as a vertical accent in flower or herb gardens or to mark the corners of an outdoor living area. Many vines also do well in containers on a deck or patio or in a courtyard garden.

Deciduous vines growing on the sunny sides of your house will shade the walls in summer, reducing your home's energy needs. Where garden banks are steep or grass is difficult to grow, evergreen vines make excellent groundcovers. Some vines, such as grapes and Chinese gooseberry *Actinidia chinensis*, also provide edible fruit for you or for wildlife.

Fast-growing Vines

Listed below are some particularly fast-growing vines that can cover a space quickly.

Actinidia spp. (kiwi fruit/Chinese gooseberries)
Ampelopsis brevipedunculata (porcelain ampelopsis)
Clematis maximowicziana (sweet autumn clematis)
Humulus lupulus (hops)
Mina lobata (crimson starglory)
Passiflora spp. (passionflowers)
Thunbergia alata (black-eyed Susan vine) pictured right

How Vines Climb

Vines either trail along the ground or climb appropriate supports. If you want your vines to climb, you'll need to know how they do it. Then you can choose an appropriate support for the vine you have in mind.

Some vines, such as passionflowers (*Passiflora* spp.) and sweet peas (*Lathyrus* spp.), climb by means of tendrils that grasp any objects they touch. These vines soon blanket a trellis or pergola, with little training. Vines that climb with tendrils need supports thin enough for their tendrils to grasp. Some tendrils will entwine themselves around supports, while others will loop around supports, then twine around themselves.

Other vines, such as wisterias, climb by twining their entire stems around supports. Twining vines need no encouragement to wrap themselves around a pole or porch post. These vines wrap themselves around slender supports, such as wires, railings or other vines, as well as around large objects such as columns and tree trunks.

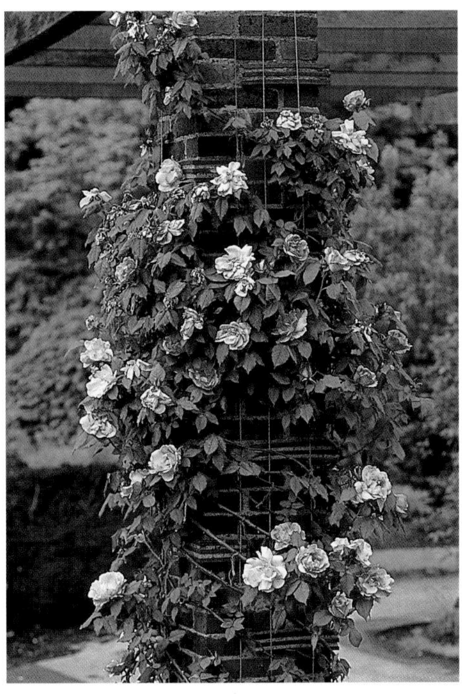

ABOVE: Large-flowered climbing rose, *Rosa* 'Lady Waterlow', disguises a brick column.
BELOW: Wisteria, Monet's garden, Giverny, France.

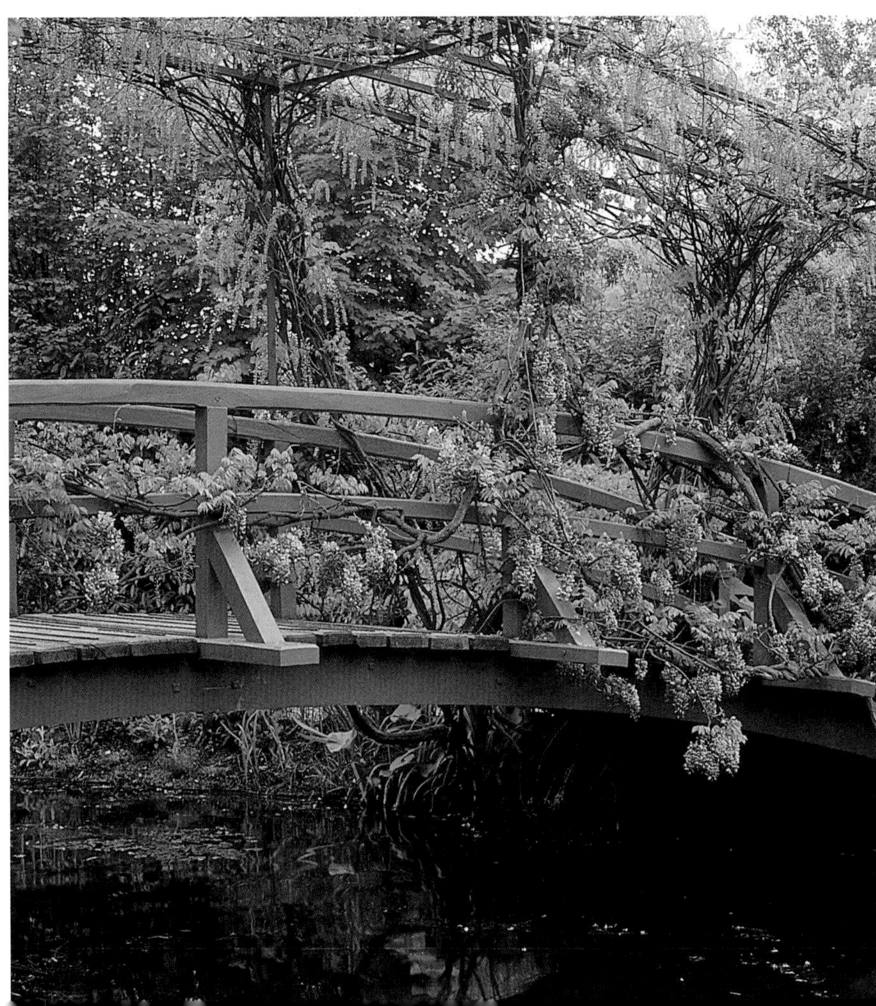

English ivy *Hedera helix*, wintercreeper euonymus *Euonymus fortunei* and climbing hydrangea *Hydrangea anomala* var. *petiolaris* use adhesive, aerial rootlets along their stems to cling to wood, brick, stone or other materials. Virginia creeper *Parthenocissus quinquefolia* and Boston ivy *P. tricuspidata* bear tendrils that end in adhesive discs.

A few plants, such as climbing roses, are often classified as vines even though they have no natural way to attach to a support. To help this type of vine climb, either weave its stems back and forth through a fence, trellis or arbor, or tie them to the support.

Climbing Supports for Vines

If you want your vines to grow upright, begin training them on supports as soon as you plant them. Use a structure big enough to support the mature plant, and put it in place before you plant the vine.

Buy or build freestanding supports that are constructed of sturdy, durable materials. Wood is a traditional and attractive choice for fan-shaped trellises, lattice panels, graceful arbors, or other supports. For longevity and durability, choose cedar or another naturally rot-resistant wood, or keep the support structure painted. Wire fencing framed with two-by-fours is a low-cost option that will give a vine years of sturdy support. Use galvanized or plastic-coated fencing to prevent rust. Copper or aluminum wire and tubing can also be fashioned into rustproof supports.

Training Vines

Use string to guide young vines to the structure you want them to climb. Fasten one end of the string to the support and tie the other end around a rock or a stick. Place the rock at the base of the plant, or poke the stick into the ground nearby, making sure to avoid the vine's rootball. Use string or soft fabric strips to tie vines to their supports until they begin to twine or cling by themselves.

SECTION TEN

Creative Garden Design

If you are seeking inspiration, you'll find it in the following pages. Any garden, whatever its size, from wide open spaces to the confines of a balcony or courtyard, can have style and a unifying theme. A garden may be designed with the wild, back-to-nature look of a meadow, or it can capture the simple lines found in classical design. Seek inspiration from the surroundings, the climate or a favorite place or era.

Urban Solutions *292*

Low-maintenance Gardens *298*

Outdoor Living Areas *300*

Contemporary and Avant-garde Designs *302*

Urban Solutions

Most of us live in cities, which means that many people have little or no ground space available for gardening. But with the right choice of plants and containers, your little patch can be as satisfying and as beautiful as any large-scale garden. Charming combinations and effects can be achieved and, if the sun is right, you can even grow herbs, vegetables and small fruit trees.

In a very small space, or a small, walled garden, don't bother to grow grass. Instead, transform the space into a delightful and secluded patio by laying paving stones, patterned brickwork, ceramic tiles, slate or even gravel. Once laid, a paved area needs less maintenance than grass, and plants can tumble over the edges without doing damage. And there is no lawn to mow.

A courtyard with low hedges of clipped boxwood surrounding beds of yellow and white irises.

Urban Garden Style

Every garden is different, and calls for its own design. Your garden design also reflects your personality and the relationship you want to have with your garden.

A small garden is usually viewed at close quarters from the house, so try to visually link the garden to the house, and keep it in harmony with the style of the interior.

The design of a contemporary house can be echoed with the use of contemporary or minimalist-looking paving material and bold clumps of architectural plants. In most modern gardens, and particularly in a small city garden, it is often better to include several of one plant of the same type and color, rather than a number of different varieties. Small, tufty grasses and sedges planted in masses look great in modern gardens, with pebbles or rocks and perhaps a modern sculpture. In an arid climate, cacti and succulents are a natural solution.

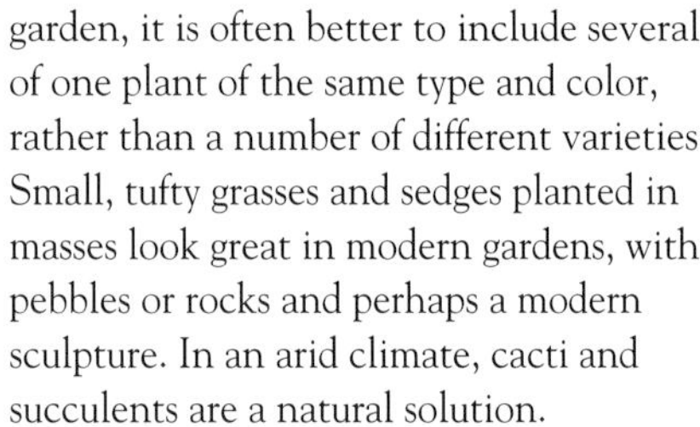

If you live in a traditional building with country-style furnishings, a sunny, town garden can be turned into a small, charming cottage garden. Use the existing beds for taller-growing plants and rambling roses, and place masses of colorful flowering plants in pots, tubs and urns.

A green foliage garden is both stylish and trouble-free, and ideal for a small, shady town garden, whether it is contemporary or traditional.

A tropical foliage theme can also be used to good effect in a small seaside garden where an outsized oriental day bed on a veranda could set off a collection of bold, tropical-looking plants. To provide visual interest, use contrasting leaf shapes, textures and variegated foliage, set at different levels in the garden. Bamboos, for example, could be used to create an

Spanish-inspired courtyard with square pond, ferns and topiarized boxwood in containers.

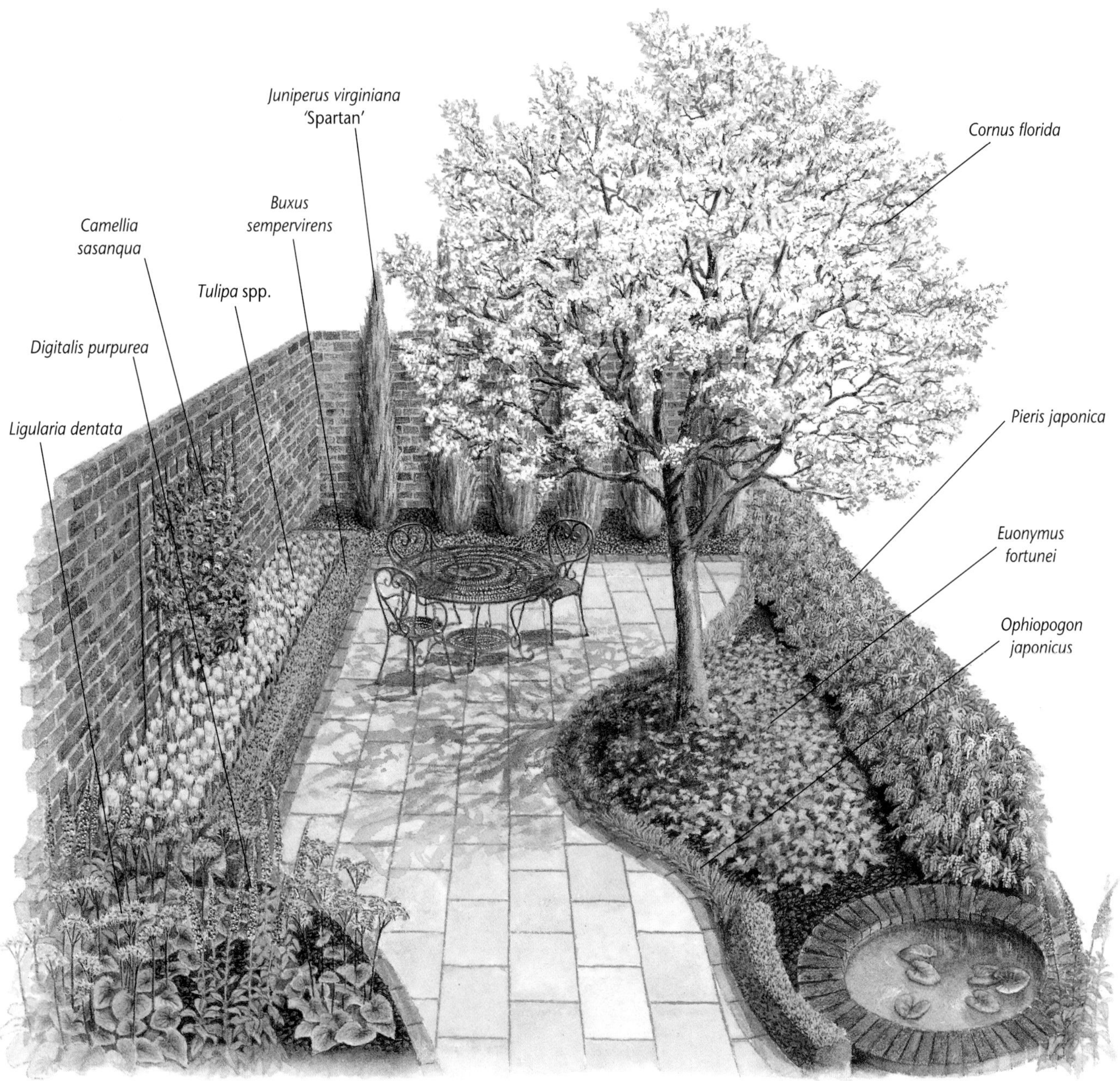

SUNNY COURTYARD WITH SHADE TREE This plan shows a paved, informal courtyard with a deciduous shade tree. A table and chairs are positioned in the shade of the tree. A shrub is espaliered along one wall and is edged with a low, boxwood hedge and infilled with spring bulbs. A row of narrow, evergreen conifers masks the rear boundary. Under the tree is a massed, low planting of groundcovers with taller shrubs behind. At the entrance to the courtyard is a water feature and a leafy planting with spire flowers.

effective vertical screen or a framework to the bold, kidney-shaped leaves of clumping ligularias. A tinkling water feature or an ornamental pot set among a profusion of green foliage will provide just the right focus to the lush jungle effects of the planting.

If terracotta tiles, pots, urns and a wall fountain appeal, and you have a climate to suit, you might like to create an informal Mediterranean-inspired garden. Here you can grow grapevines, wisteria, lavender, roses, citrus, vegetables and plenty of lush and undisciplined herbs to create a relaxing, rustic atmosphere. If a formal, Italian garden is more your style, clipped boxwood hedges are always impressive in a small garden. Pots of citrus or clipped bay trees will provide dramatic accents along walls or on terraces, and a strategically placed classic sundial, urn, fountain or statue will complete the picture.

An espaliered fruit tree, such as this pear, is a thing of beauty, and makes good use of space.

Wall Plants

In a small garden, you will probably have more wall space than ground space. Fences, walls, garages and railings provide the extra dimensions, so aim to cover them with climbing or trailing plants, such as wisteria, honeysuckle, clematis, climbing roses and solanum.

Espaliered plants, trained flat against walls, are ideal for making the most of space and, after the initial establishment period and the occasional removal of unwanted shoots, often prove far easier to manage in a small space than rampant climbers. Fruit trees are traditionally used, and when trained against a warm wall will crop prolifically, but sasanqua camellias are also beautiful, and their loose, pliable branches can be easily manipulated along a series of horizontal wires.

Although tall fences and trees prevent people from looking into your garden, or block out ugly views, they can cast a great deal of shade and give a restricted feeling. As an alternative, a small pergola clothed with grapevines, Virginia creeper or ivy will both screen you from nearby buildings and provide a shady private retreat.

Container Courtyard

Growing plants in containers is often the only successful way some people in cities can garden. It also gives greater flexibility to supplement the garden or to decorate windows, entrances, verandas and balconies with potted plants and hanging baskets. Smaller pots can be moved around to create different displays, heights and colors, or to give the plants extra sun or shade according to their needs. Another advantage of a container garden is that you get a chance to grow some exotic gems that might otherwise be lost in an open garden bed, or that need to be overwintered in a greenhouse. But the best thing is that they are movable. This gives you an opportunity to create new looks, move pots with the season, or show off flowering plants at their peak. On the whole, plain containers are the most successful and have the advantage of suiting a variety of plantings.

Growing plants in containers allows you to move the plants around to experiment with various combinations.

Balcony Gardens

A balcony is always above ground level and often is the only garden available to people who live in apartments. Make sure that the balcony will safely support the weight of large containers and their soil. If your balcony is square or rectangular, choose containers that are firmly based and square. Troughs make excellent containers for balconies as their flat sides enable you to position them flush against the wall or front where they will not take up valuable space or be tripped over. And if wind is a problem, troughs are less likely to blow over than tall slender pots. Avoid

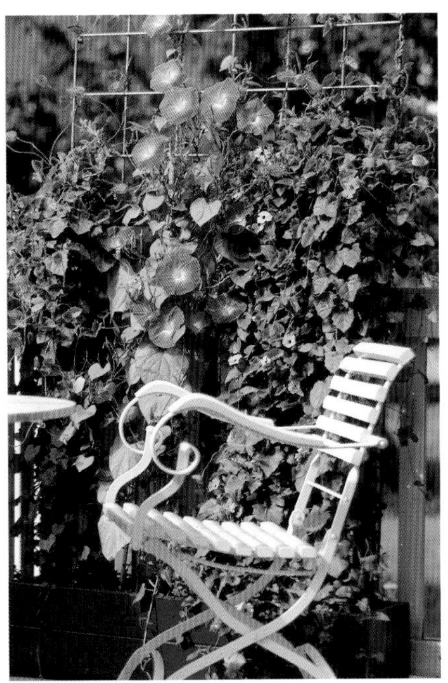

A balcony garden with a trellis covered in *Ipomoea tricolor* 'Heavenly Blue' and *Thunbergia.*

too many small pots, or they will detract from the overall design.

What you can successfully grow depends on the direction your balcony faces. Those that receive gentle, early morning sun can grow many palms, ferns, azaleas, fuchsias and camellias. A shady balcony may receive plenty of light, but no direct sun. Here shade-loving plants would be the happiest. If your balcony is protected from wind, you will be able to create a delightful mini-jungle using many lush, foliage plants. Popular ferns, such as fishbone, Boston and hare's foot fern, make spectacular hanging basket plants. Trailing ivies and vines can be grown up walls or made to spill out of wall-containers or pots.

A balcony that gets good direct sun for several hours is perfect for those who want to grow colorful flowering annuals, herbs, citrus trees in tubs, and vegetables. Bay trees are especially attractive as container plants; two or more, neatly clipped and in identical pots, could form the framework of a stylish semi-formal herb garden. In hot, dry areas, or where it is difficult to water, consider some of the many succulents and silver-leaved plants that are able to withstand periods without water.

An extremely narrow balcony, viewed from a bedroom, could be transformed into a peaceful, oriental-style garden. Here you could cover the floor with stepping stones and pebbles and use a potted group of dwarf bamboos, one impressive bonsai, or a dwarf Japanese maple and a Japanese-inspired sculpture. A bamboo screen or blind could be used to hide an undesirable view.

Roof Gardens

A roof-top garden often solves the problem of space in a densely built environment, and at very least you should be able to grow plants in containers. You will need to check the weight that your roof can safely hold, and make sure that there is adequate floor drainage, because your plants will certainly need plenty of watering. The plants may also need protection from the wind and here you may want to erect some screens or windbreaks. Try to position these screens to also hide unattractive views, and also make sure they are securely anchored to withstand the wind.

Petunias in hanging basket

First of all, put in climbing and trailing plants to soften the hard outlines of surrounding walls and to cover structures and increase their effectiveness as windbreaks. Next, pot up shrubs, colorful flowers and herbs. It's best to place the containers along the sides so that the weight is evenly distributed

This roof terrace has been transformed into a delightful, and private, outdoor living space.

at the strongest part. This is also probably the area where height is most needed to soften the straight lines of walls.

Decks

There is nothing like an above-ground timber deck for creating extra space, convenience and comfort. Decks are good for sloping sites, but also invaluable if your garden is shady, since often the extra height of the deck will give your plants longer hours of sunlight. A deck on the same level as internal floors makes entertaining easier and gardening a breeze if you want to relax outside in the evening after work. It's also an ideal place to grow culinary herbs, so that you can quickly snip them while you are cooking. Don't forget to raise all pots on feet or stands, so that excess moisture can drain away freely from the timber. If your deck is fairly high, make sure that the stairs leading to the rest of the garden are comfortable and wide enough to allow for the traffic of pot plants, gardening equipment and potting mixes.

In a cool climate, a deck crowned with a pergola and roofed in clear, plastic glazing material will keep the wet weather away from the house and provide a dry, year-round entertaining area. It will also create a warm micro-climate for tender plants, such as palms, tree ferns and some interesting foliage plants. The pergola joists will give you some strong overhead support for suspending hanging baskets of Boston ferns, Christmas cactus and fuchsias.

A lawn path winds its way through colorful, curved garden beds to the house's entrance.

Food at Your Fingertips

If your deck is large and sunny enough, it is possible to cultivate some fruit trees. In frost-free climates, citrus—such as kumquats, limes and lemons—make beautiful potted specimens, providing rich evergreen foliage, perfumed flowers and colorful fruit for the picking. Dwarf fruit trees such as apples, pomegranates and peaches can be also contained in large pots. Strawberries will tolerate a wide range of conditions and are the simplest fruit to grow in containers. They can also be hung in large baskets and will cascade decoratively down the sides.

Front Gardens

When designing with plants in the front garden, consider all the different angles from which they will be seen. Apart from being seen from the street, often the front garden is viewed from the upstairs or balcony. In a very small garden, think about the shapes you are creating. Boxwood hedges, for example, add impact by defining areas in an architectural way. These can be used in both traditional and contemporary garden plans. In a very small front garden, you could plan for a miniature boxwood-hedged garden to fit the shape of the land with an inner massed planting of one seasonal color, such as blue hyacinths for early spring, or white impatiens or petunias for most of summer.

Summer window box with a cascade of lobelias, pelargoniums, helichrysum and Marguerites.

An easy-care front garden could be made with a combination of soil and square paving blocks set in a geometrical design. In the squares of soil where some height is needed, grow lightly clipped bushes of myrtle, bay, rosemary, *Murraya* and lavender. In the foreground squares, put in some low-growing bushes of variegated thyme or creeping thyme if you want some groundcover. If you have a picket fence, tuck in some nasturtium seeds along the edge for a pretty cascade of leaves and flowers that will peep out onto the footpath.

Modern condos or townhouses often offer little opportunity for a distinctive garden, and the simplest treatment is usually the most effective. Sometimes there is just a small raised bed built into the design. Here a flower bed could look good, with a bold planting of

Standard fuchsia

canna lilies backed by a clump of papyrus *Cyperus papyrus*. Or you may prefer a planting of easy-care Marguerite daisies or daisy-flowered felicias. If there is a narrow side bed leading to the front door, a neat row of dwarf conifers such as *Thuja occidentalis* 'Smaragd' can give you an instant formal look. Or if you have no garden at all, you could place a matched pair of dwarf conifers either side of the front door, or a standard flowering plant, such as a fuchsia. An extremely narrow bed could support a climbing fig to give a rich curtain of green to a stark wall.

Window Boxes

Window boxes are a delightful way to decorate bare walls, balconies and small city houses with colorful bulbs, annuals, perennials or other small trailing plants. They are especially invaluable to the apartment-dweller, who may have no outside space at all for regular gardening. Boxes and troughs can be bought in different sizes. When buying a window box, also get the bolts, brackets and screws to fix it securely into position, so that it does not become dislodged during windy weather.

Frequently used culinary herbs are a natural choice for a sunny window box outside a kitchen window. Thyme, prostrate rosemary, mint, parsley, chives and basil are easy, decorative and all smell and taste good. If you don't get a lot of sun, concentrate on such herbs as mint, chervil, parsley, lemon balm and chives that can get along on a little less. They will all need a good potting mix and regular watering.

Recycling Materials

With any new projects, try to match materials as closely as possible with your building and its style. Recycled local materials are not only cheaper, they are often preferable, because they tend to blend with the design and color of your home and offer a foolproof a way of retaining the integrity of your garden design.

A gravel path with a circular brick pattern, and steps made from wooden railway sleepers.

Paving materials that echo the style of the house often look best in recycled materials. Old bricks, stone slabs, slate and old concrete slabs have a subtle weathered appearance and texture and are ideal for paved terraces and patios—often the main, permanent sitting areas in small gardens. Large slabs can act as stepping-stones and paths. Old bricks can also be used for sand-pits, barbecues, to define edges and as a raised sitting wall.

The appearance of some structures, such as pergolas, arches, privacy screens, fences, gates, seats and tables, can often be enhanced by using recycled timber that can be found at local timber yards.

Old railway sleepers are good for seats, raised beds, retaining walls or placed at intervals along a sloping pathway to make steps. They can also be laid relatively close together flush with the ground to form an effective and delightful rustic area of paving. A sturdy bridge over a pond or beautiful rounded river pebbles can easily be constructed using railway sleepers.

Wooden window boxes brimming with colorful *Pelargonium peltatum*, runner beans and petunias.

Low-maintenance Gardens

Just how much time can you devote to maintaining your new garden? Do you want to pay someone else to do it for you? It is possible to reduce or eliminate many of the maintenance chores that can make it much less of a pleasure.

Creating a low-maintenance garden doesn't mean settling for a second-best landscape. You can have a great-looking garden, except you won't have to spend nearly as much time as your neighbors do to keep your yard looking great.

A big part of making your garden low maintenance comes from working with the plants and conditions you have, rather than struggling to make poorly adapted plants grow.

Plants are healthiest, and require the least care from you, when they are well suited to the region and site where you plant them. In cool, humid regions, it's easy to grow woodland wildflowers in shady spots. In hot, dry areas, lavender cottons *Santolina* spp., penstemons and other heat- and drought-tolerant plants will thrive with little extra care.

A low-maintenance landscape does not mean exactly the same thing to every gardener. Maybe you hate mowing the lawn, but enjoy puttering in the flower garden. In that case, low maintenance would mean a small (or no) lawn, so you have more time for deadheading spent blossoms and pruning perennials.

Or maybe you find mowing relaxing but hate trying to keep up with ripe vegetables that must be harvested. In that case, low maintenance might mean a tomato patch surrounded by an acre of turf.

However, there are some principles that you can follow when designing your garden to reduce maintenance:

- Simple design
- Paving
- Small or no lawn areas
- No water features
- No plants that require clipping
- Reduce bedding plants and concentrate or shrubs or plants that self-sow
- Few pots or containers
- Choose low- or no-care plants
- Use native plants and plants you know do well in your area
- Use mulches for moisture control and to prevent weeds
- Install an underground irrigation system.

Make the most of a small site with a combination of paving and low-care plants, such as stonecrop.

Make an Anti-wish List

Planning a low-maintenance landscape is more than just deciding what you *do* want; it's also important to know what you definitely *don't* want. Take a realistic assessment of your landscape by picking up a notebook and a pencil and then taking a stroll around your yard. Jot down any problem areas—maybe it's that rocky patch in the backyard where nothing but weeds will grow; or perhaps it's the steep grassy bank along the sidewalk which is a real pain to mow.

Also look for high-maintenance elements that you may want to reduce or eliminate—perhaps you just can't stand the thought of clipping that privet hedge three times a year. Or maybe you enjoy having some fresh produce but are tired of tilling, weeding, and watering a huge vegetable garden every summer.

Add these notes to your "anti-wish" list. When you are finished, prioritize the list so that you can deal with those problems you find most annoying. That will help you form a practical action plan to converting your existing garden to a truly low-maintenance landscape.

Build raised beds to turn a wet site into a well-drained garden, so you can grow what you want.

For easy-care color all season long, fill your flower beds with a variety of self-sowing annuals.

Time-saving Trees and Shrubs

Once they're established, most trees and shrubs are the epitome of low-maintenance plants for your garden. You don't have to mow them, harvest them or pinch off their dead flowers. Most of the care they might require, such as pruning or raking, can wait until autumn or winter, when the rest of the garden is making few demands on your time.

However, it is important to avoid trees and shrubs with troublesome habits, such as brittle trees that drop twigs after every gust of wind. Others have messy fruit, such as practically any wild fig or the spiky, round seedpods of liquidambars.

Easy-care Lawns

Do you really need a lawn? If you do, you can reduce mowing chores by replacing some of the lawn with shrubs, trees or groundcovers—but don't plant trees and shrubs in your lawn, because you will actually increase your mowing difficulties.

Install mowing strips to cut down on edging chores and make maintenance easier by eliminating grass growing under or along fences and walls, on steep slopes, and under low-branching or shallow-rooted trees.

Quick Flower Gardens

The most important piece of advice for creating a low-maintenance flower garden is: Match the plants to your site. Most of the popular annuals do best in well-drained, enriched soil. Perennials and bulbs tend to be more forgiving, so if your conditions are less than ideal, consider selecting from these groups. Naturally adapted wildflowers are another good choice for difficult sites.

A strip of bricks set into the soil around a flower bed lets you mow right up to the edge.

Both formal and informal flower gardens can be low-maintenance if your plants are well chosen. Formal and semi-formal gardens rely on order and symmetry for their controlled look. Spread a thick layer of mulch both to keep weeds at bay and to retain moisture—this will save on weeding and watering time. Make sure, too, that you don't select plants for your formal garden that will self-sow or spread quickly. Otherwise, you'll be spending far too much time keeping the garden neatly cultivated.

Informal, or country, gardens are more forgiving in terms of maintenance. Select plants that will grow quickly and self-sow. Combine hardy perennials such as bee balm (*Monarda* spp.) with long-flowering, self-sowing annuals that provide color and variety. So-called invasives, such as Jerusalem artichoke (*Helianthus tuberosus*) can be useful to get an informal garden started quickly, but can be problematic later on when the garden is fully established.

When planning your low-maintenance flower garden, limit your plantings to three colors. Your garden will look better with its large blocks of color, and you won't have to spend time planning and designing the garden, selecting and placing a range of plants. White flowers and silver foliage are always handy to provide variety and contrast, and will separate conflicting colors such as orange and pink. A sea of blue flowers will make your garden look bigger.

Bulbs are ideal for a low-maintenance, informal garden. For best effect, plant them in drifts so that they seem to have grown naturally in the landscape. Once the bulbs have been planted and become established, your work is finished, and you will be rewarded with an annual display of color. Large numbers of small bulbs make maximum visual effect: One color, one kind is a good maxim. Bulbs are useful also for filling in otherwise difficult spaces such as beneath trees, around the edges of the garden, or on sloping banks.

Hollyhocks

Outdoor Living Areas

Today's gardens are often considered to be an extension of the house. Whether you have a large garden, or simply a balcony or small roof garden, you can create a delightful outdoor space for entertaining, activities or simply relaxing.

A garden landscape design is usually considered to be a success if it is beautiful in itself, and also enhances the visual appeal of the buildings set within it. However, your landscape can be even more attractive if it is also useful and functional, designed to meet the needs of family, friends and visitors.

With the high cost of interior floor space, outdoor living areas can add extra entertaining and living space. Even when not in use, well-planned, attractive decks and terraces, adjacent to the house, give a feeling of added space to interior rooms.

This gazebo, secluded among flowering trees and shrubs, is a delightful place to sit and relax.

Some homes have several outdoor living areas. Small terraces adjacent to bedrooms, bathrooms and dining rooms are becoming more and more popular. A daybed under a covered veranda provides a delightful place for summer sleepouts. Or, for the ultimate in outdoor living, a screened-off shower, spa or plunge bath can extend out into the garden from the bathroom.

A terrace or outdoor living area may also be placed well away from the house to take advantage of a striking view, breezes or the shade of an unusually beautiful tree.

Attractive, long-lasting outdoor furniture and accessories, such as water features, sculpture and container plants, can be useful to decorate and enrich outdoor living areas.

Terraces, Patios and Decks

Most outdoor living and entertaining areas include a terrace, patio, veranda or deck of some sort. Locate these features where they will receive breezes and afternoon shade during hot summer weather. If sun is a problem, plant some suitable shade or rig up overhead shading structures, such as sails or umbrellas.

Patios should be large enough to be useful. Small concrete slabs near the house are often rather cold and uninviting. Keep in mind the kinds of activities that will take place on your patio; it should be large enough to accommodate family and friends when entertaining. You may also need space for games, game tables and wheeled toys.

However, the patio can be made too large, so that it takes on the coldness of a parking lot. It's best to keep the size of your patio in scale with the size of your garden and house.

LEFT: Timber deck with outdoor setting under an umbrella, with containers of pickerel weed *Pontederia lancellata*.
RIGHT: Consider a wood-floored area for children's outdoor games.

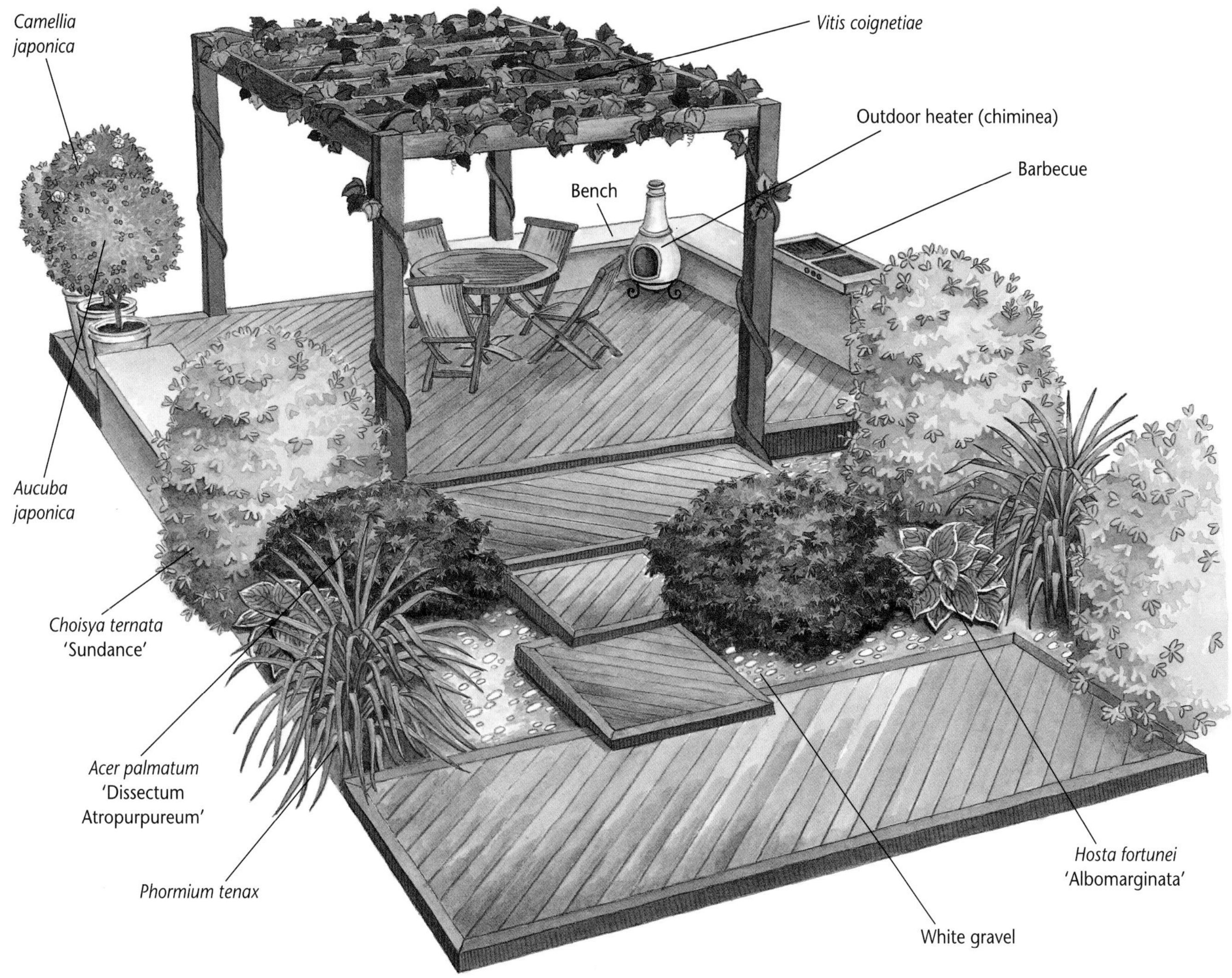

Outdoor living and entertaining areas are usually adjacent to the living areas of the house and can serve as a kind of transition between the interior of the house and the garden.

Children's Play Areas

Locate a children's play area close enough to the house so that adults can keep an eye on the kids. Sand piles and swing sets are popular, as are play houses, tree houses and paved areas for riding wheeled toys. Keep designs as simple as possible and make sure everything is easy to maintain. Consider how the area might be modified as children grow up and reused when the children no longer use it.

Active Sports and Recreation

Recreation or active sports areas, such as swimming pools or tennis courts, require considerable space, investment and planning. If such facilities are on your wish-list but will not be installed straight away, make them easier to build in the future by planning access and also leaving open lawn areas that can be easily removed when the time arrives. Spas, plunge pools and hot tubs require less space but still need careful planning.

OUTDOOR LIVING AREA This plan shows an outdoor living area under a pergola. An ornamental grapevine twines over the pergola, providing shade and shelter. (The grapevine grows out of the ground.) On either side of the pergola are two uncovered areas. Both of these have a low bench around a section, and the area on the right of the pergola has a raised barbecue. There are three large, potted plants on the left side of the pergola. Under the pergola cover is timber decking, which extends out to the garden via timber "stepping stones." Various low-growing plants, in contrasting colors, grow here. Around these plants and stepping stones is a groundcovering of white gravel.

Contemporary and Avant-garde Designs

One of the most important things about any landscape design is that it should feel right for its setting. How far is it stretching disbelief to build a natural-looking pond in the middle of a metropolis? Is it likely that your "authentic" rockery was left untouched when everything else between here and the horizon has been bulldozed? In the inner city, the standard suburban garden beds, trees and a large lawn can seem out of place or are just not possible.

Cities also tend to be crucibles where styles from all over the world are fused and used to generate new ideas. This is clearly apparent in architecture and interiors, so it would actually be rather surprising if it were not having an influence in landscaping and gardening.

This contemporary garden design shows the use of steel for pergolas, rather than the traditional wood.

Material Considerations

New materials, especially new sorts of surfaces, and old materials used in new ways, are transforming the ways we think about landscape design. One of the influences at work here is urban chic—straight lines (although round shapes, such as perfect circles, are also making inroads), minimalist plantings and adventurous use of textures, shapes and colors, often employing surprisingly basic materials. Urban gardens, both residential and commercial, are where contemporary garden design is most quickly evolving.

Modern materials such as concrete, glass, plastics, polymers and metals can be used by themselves, in combination with each other or blended with natural stone, terracotta and wood in building a landscape. Glass is being used as sheets, windows and as mirrors as well as being recycled as blocks or pebbles which can be used for paths and as a non-decaying mulch. Neon lighting and other exotic effects can be used to highlight the artificial nature of the landscape being created using, say, resin-bonded artificial marble or synthetic stone. Galvanized and stainless steel is being used in gardens—including as pavers and as cables joining elements of the garden together (or just holding it up). Quite a few designers also like having old iron in the landscape somewhere, rusting away. All these materials are available for structural work as well as for furniture, ornaments and other decorations.

Spectacular, blue-themed roof garden, pictured at night, showing neon strip lighting and other lighting effects.

The use of some less orthodox materials can depend on your climate, as well as personal taste. Metal surfaces can be interesting and attractive in warm or temperate Zones but where it gets very hot or very cold, they may be unsuitable, uncomfortable or even dangerous. Also, nothing dates quite so quickly as contemporary design—what was avant-garde last year can seem a bit tired now.

New materials are also being developed from recycling and the greater awareness of the environmental impact of waste products. Building and industrial materials are being recycled as landscaping materials in unprecedented volumes.

Japanese Influences

Since the late 19th century, Japanese-style gardens have played an important role in the development of Western gardens and landscape design. It's an influence that continues to be strong in 21st-century design. The influence of Japanese garden design principles and of their choice of traditional materials is strong in many contemporary garden designs. Modern designs that are inspired by traditional Japanese concepts reflect

LEFT: Green bamboo *Phyllostachys utilis*.
RIGHT: The restrained coolness and simplicity of Japanese design is shown in this garden featuring a *Pinus sylvestris*, timber gate, raked white gravel, stone bridge and rocks.

the idea of harmony and balance, which is probably the most important objective of Japanese garden design. Features, such as stones, gravel and water, that so often occur in modern designs, are integral parts of Japanese gardens where they are used to create spaces of beauty and, often, of great symbolism. Along with traditional plants and pruning techniques, these materials introduce movement and art to the landscape or are combined to form places for stillness and meditation, again ideas adapted from Japanese garden design through history.

The key to traditional Japanese garden design, and to many contemporary Western schemes, is not so much what specific material is used, but how it is used. Often the individual beauty of a single plant or garden feature is highlighted, as opposed to the Western taste for lush abundance and overall effect.

As important as the initial design is, so too is ongoing maintenance and the ways in which plants and garden features are shaped and trained. Plants must be kept sculpted and shaped properly if the original effect is to be preserved.

The principles and intention behind creating this sort of space can be applied to other types of gardens as well. However, many Japanese-style gardens in the West are mere overlays of quasi-Japanese elements on a landscape.

To build a satisfying garden, it is necessary to observe nature closely enough to be able to distil sights, sounds and fragrances and express them with absolute economy of means—a simple grouping of rocks, plants and water. The result must be an elegant balance of opposites: mass and emptiness, light and dark colors, smooth and rough textures, sound and silence, and revealing and hiding.

Closeup showing raked gravel in a Japanese garden, in the pattern of water ripples.

Flat Gardens

Flat gardens, or *hira-niwa*, are constructed without hills or water; the flat ground level symbolizes water. The ground is usually covered with pebbles, raked in circles and lines to give the impression of water ripples. These gardens contain stones, trees, stone lanterns and wells and are representative of the seaside or of grand lakes. Carefully selected and placed groups of stones symbolize islands; sometimes a waterfall is suggested by upright oblong stones. The garden design is very subtle; the placement of stones often suggests far-off lands and mystical locales.

Modern flat gardens also often contain wells and stone lanterns. The wells usually have a purpose in these gardens: namely purification of those who wish to observe the gardens. These wells are typically constructed from wood, and have either a pulley system or a large spoon for drawing out the water. Stone lanterns are not only ornamental, but also serve to illuminate the gardens at night.

Hill Gardens

The Japanese name for hill gardens, *tsukiyama-sansui*, means "hills and water": the foundations of a classic hill garden. Such a garden is like a three-dimensional picture. Whereas traditional gardens were viewed from only one point, modern gardens are designed with winding paths throughout them, to display the garden to full advantage. Usually these paths are made of carefully selected flat stones.

Water plays a very important role, and nearly every garden contains a waterfall and a pond. Waterfalls are an essential part of hill gardens, as they not only help

Oriental garden scene in autumn with maple tree *Acer* spp. with stunning orange leaf color, white summerhouse, stone lantern, path and pond.

water flow down the hill, they also provide great symbolism. They are usually constructed with two large stones, giving the appearance of great distance and size. They are often shaded by several tasteful bushes or trees which form a partial screen. The *ike*, or pond, is meant to represent a sea, lake or pond in nature. It is usually rimmed with stonework piling, and always contains an island.

Islands have great symbolic significance in Japanese hill gardens. The islands are built with rocks as their base and dirt piled neatly on top, in order for plants to grow. Sometimes a garden designer will include a bridge to an island. If so, often there will be a stone lantern or other object of reverence.

Irises

The general layout of this type of garden is designed to give the appearance of great distance and expansiveness, as if the whole world were contained in this one garden. Some have suggested that this is because there is so little space in Japan. A more philosophical viewpoint is that the creators of these gardens wish to present the essence of nature, or nature boiled down to its essential components.

Tea Garden

The modern form of Japanese tea garden is the one most well-known around the world. The Japanese tea garden plays an integral part in the tea ceremony, and as the ceremony has grown more elaborate through the years, so have the tea gardens. Japanese tea gardens now comprise two parts: the *soto-roji* (outer garden) and the *uchi-roji* (inner garden).

The outer section consists of a place where guests wait for the master to appear; the inner section contains the tea house itself. Stone lanterns light the pathway, which is made of either gravel or flat stones, between these two sections. The tea garden is usually made in a style similar to a hill garden, but is different in several respects.

First of all, the tea garden contains a wash basin, or *tsukubai*. The *tsukubai* is surrounded by *yaku-ishi* (literally "accompanying stones"), one in front, which is used for standing on, one on the right, and one on the left.

The basin itself can be any shape, as long as it can be easily used. In fact, broken stone lanterns are often put to use as new wash basins. The tea garden also contains a resting place, for breaks in the tea ceremony. This resting area was not in the original tea gardens. The resting place's principal purpose is to convey the spirit of *wabi*, or quiet solitude in nature.

While the outer garden contains deciduous plants and trees and is open and spacious, the inner garden is densely filled with evergreens, symbolizing its everlasting peace. The tea gardens of today have relatively few stones; flowering plants and extravagant designs are avoided, in favor of indigenous plants and materials found commonly along Japanese roads and in the countryside. Again, garden designers seek to find the essence of nature, and present it as a contemplative subject.

Contemporary Minimalism

The philosophy of minimalism, rooted simultaneously in classicism and modernism, has had a strong influence on architecture and interior and graphic design, as well as landscape. Minimalist gardens, with their emphasis on clean

Japanese-style garden with a bridge over a slate riverbed, with tea house on a patio in the background.

LEFT: Creative garden design with metal dish surrounded by clipped boxwood hedge. The metal dish is echoed in the metal strips on the painted magenta wall.
RIGHT: Japanese-style courtyard.

lines, pure form and a strong sense of place, are closely related to contemporary architecture and lifestyles.

New trends in more relaxed and ecologically aware planting have contributed greatly to the development of such green spaces, and the creative use of trees and hedges to define and control space is often an important design element.

The principle of "less is more" when applied to the garden can avoid it looking untidy and give it a feeling of space and a certain tranquillity. In addition, strong design can provide a clear guide as to what you need to do to build and maintain your garden—and what distractions you should avoid.

Minimalism in design has been reworked over the past few decades, and owes much to Japanese and European—especially Scandinavian—esthetics.

A minimalist garden can be a flexible space in which to play, work, read, relax, meditate, entertain, and so on—but one that always looks good. Key concepts relate to boldness, simplicity (even austerity) and cleanliness rather than fuss, mess and pointless elaboration. This can require a certain discipline, not least in being ruthless about what does—or, mostly, does not—fit in. Spaces are sharply defined and kept free of clutter.

When buying plants, for example, you will not choose nine different kinds and plant them any old way. It may be a new discipline and at first rather hard to do, but a group or line of nine specimens of the same plant—or three clusters of three—will certainly have much more design impact on your landscape and bring greater cohesion to your garden.

Avant Gardening

Traditional gardens are usually more popular with the public and most gardeners, but contemporary gardens are great places to find new ideas and inspiration for garden design.

Some of these ideas will inevitably fall by the wayside and it takes time to see which trends or fashions will prove influential, popular and long-lasting.

Split-level timber decks, for example, are becoming increasingly popular. Decks have been around for a long time but people have been cautious about where to put them. Now decks are being used much more often, whether to go up over a hill, over water and to create different levels. Another trend is the strong coordination, including color, of interior and exterior spaces.

Contemporary garden design is evolving all the time. Go to garden shows and see what new ideas appeal to you and how you can adapt them to your landscape.

Futuristic garden design with rill (small stream) that ends in a large round, metallic pool.

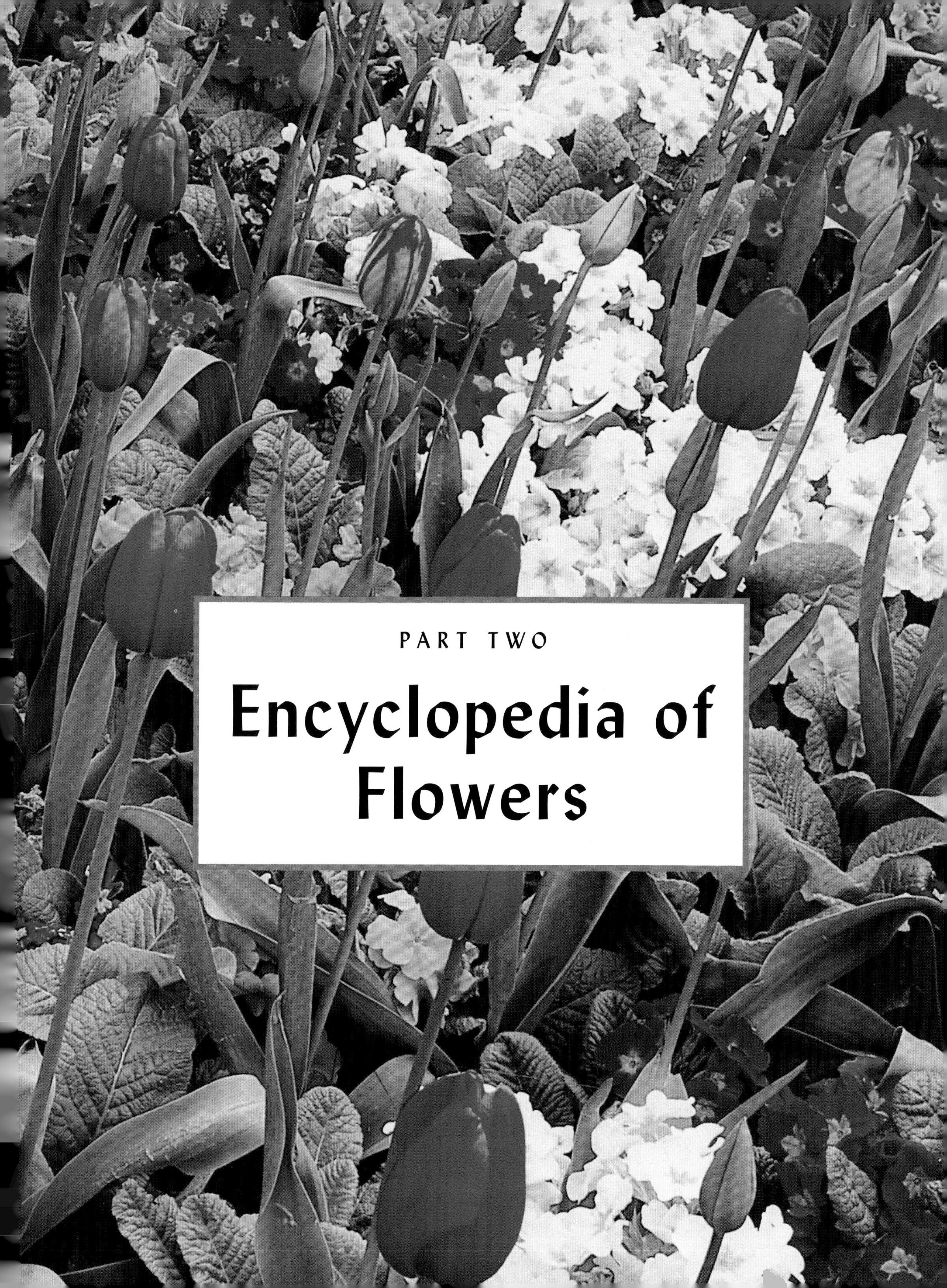

PART TWO

Encyclopedia of Flowers

How To Use This Encyclopedia

This encyclopedia has been divided into five color groups: orange-red, pink, purple-blue, white and yellow. Each color group is further divided into six plant types: annuals, bulbs, climbers, perennials, shrubs and trees. Within each of these groups entries are listed alphabetically by botanical name.

Sample Entry

All entries in the book contain the following information.

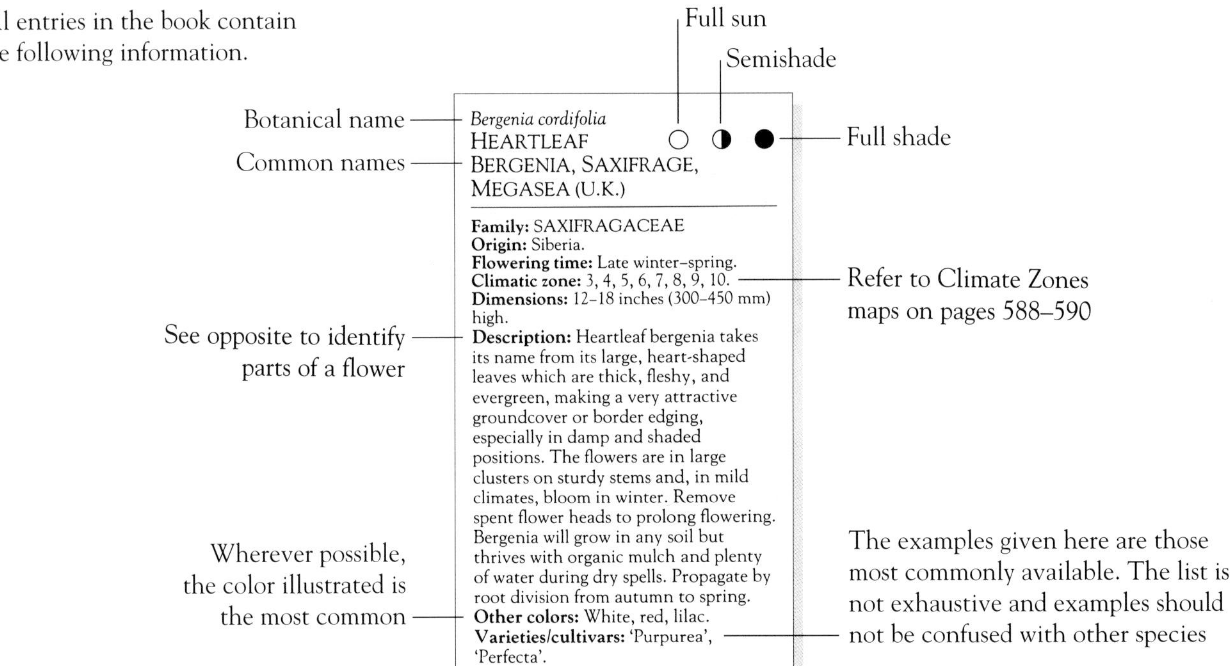

Full sun
Semishade
Full shade
Botanical name
Common names
See opposite to identify parts of a flower
Wherever possible, the color illustrated is the most common
Refer to Climate Zones maps on pages 588–590
The examples given here are those most commonly available. The list is not exhaustive and examples should not be confused with other species
Bergenia cordifolia
HEARTLEAF BERGENIA, SAXIFRAGE, MEGASEA (U.K.)
Family: SAXIFRAGACEAE
Origin: Siberia.
Flowering time: Late winter–spring.
Climatic zone: 3, 4, 5, 6, 7, 8, 9, 10.
Dimensions: 12–18 inches (300–450 mm) high.
Description: Heartleaf bergenia takes its name from its large, heart-shaped leaves which are thick, fleshy, and evergreen, making a very attractive groundcover or border edging, especially in damp and shaded positions. The flowers are in large clusters on sturdy stems and, in mild climates, bloom in winter. Remove spent flower heads to prolong flowering. Bergenia will grow in any soil but thrives with organic mulch and plenty of water during dry spells. Propagate by root division from autumn to spring.
Other colors: White, red, lilac.
Varieties/cultivars: 'Purpurea', 'Perfecta'.

Glossary

The glossary on page 587 explains many of the horticultural terms readers may not be familiar with and defines some of the more general descriptive terms.
For example:
Raceme: a group of flowers arranged along an unbranched stem, each floret having a distinct stalk.

Climatic Zones

Each entry lists the climatic zones in which the flowers can be grown. The climatic zones are outlined on the maps on pages 588–590. These maps are based on average annual minimum temperatures. Each zone covers a large area and does not take into account changes in altitude, varying rainfall, soil conditions or microclimates. Therefore these zonings should be used as a guide only, with the understanding that most species will adapt to slighter warmer (one zone above) or slighter cooler (one zone below) conditions than those listed in the entries. Readers should refer to the hardiness maps to find the zone they are in, and then check with their local garden center to ensure that species are suited to cultivation in that specific area.

Floral Anatomy

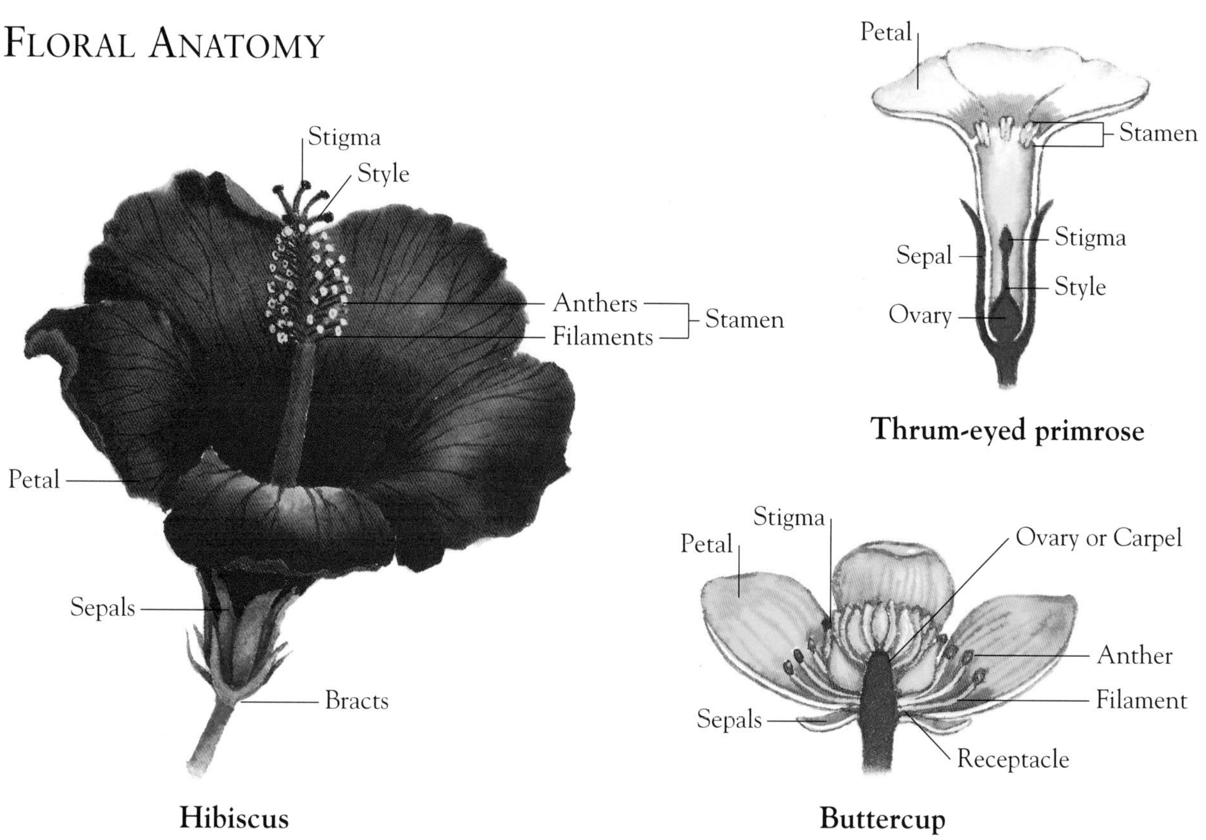

Inflorescence

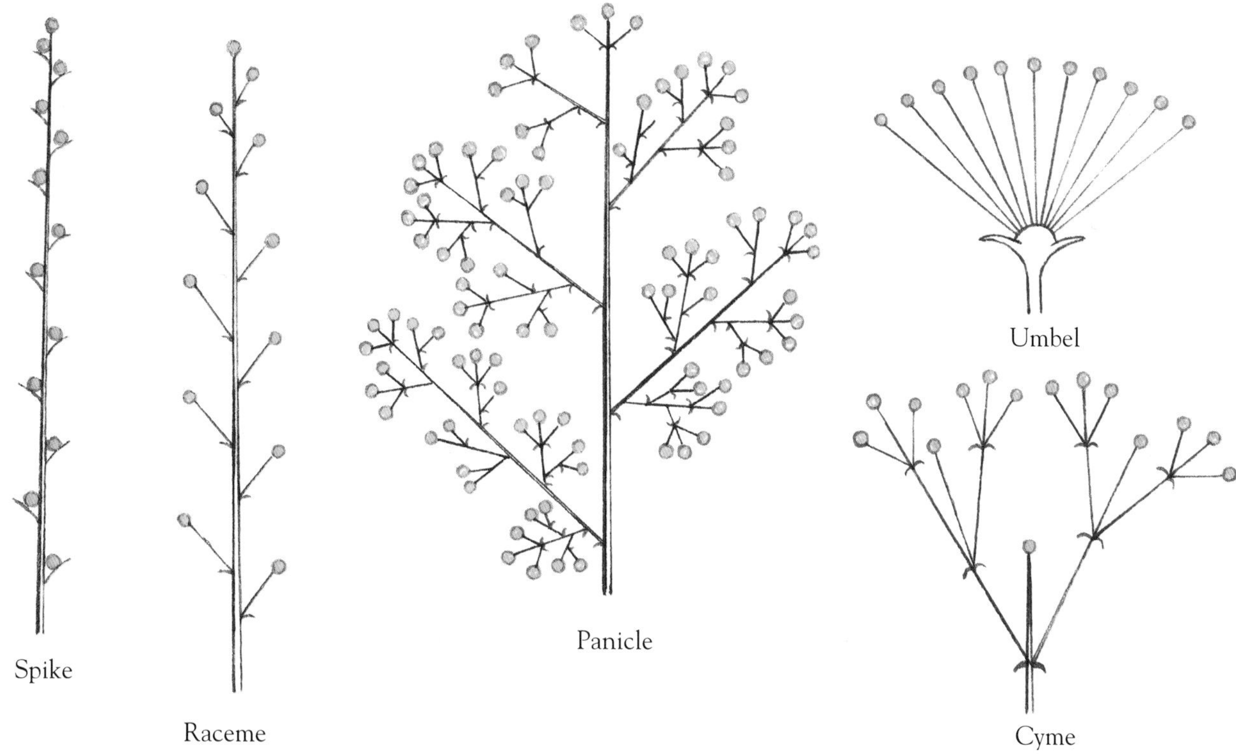

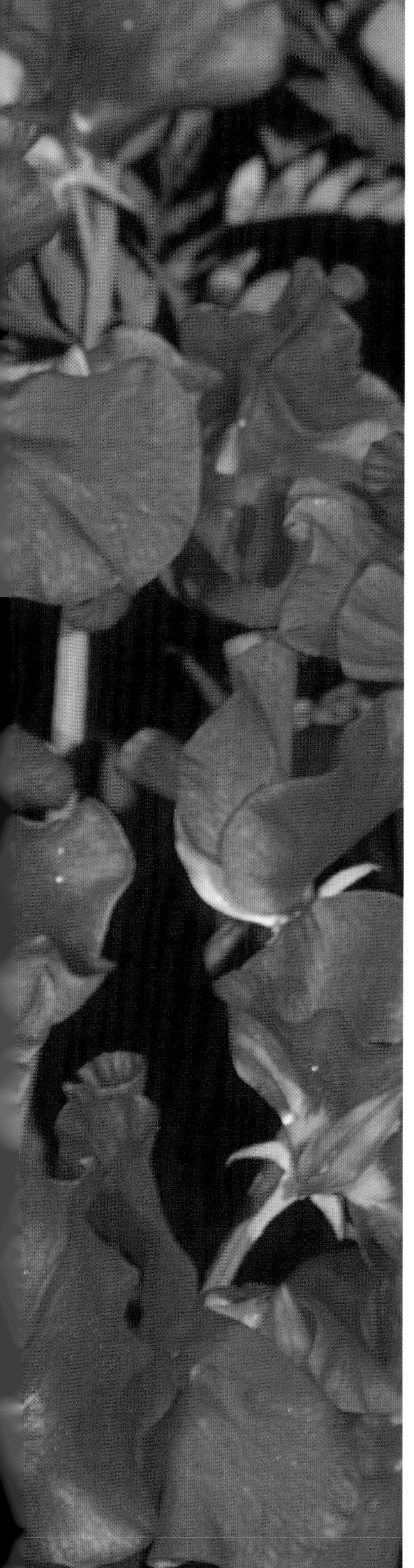

SECTION ONE

Orange-Red Flowers

Annuals *312*

Bulbs *316*

Climbers *320*

Perennials *326*

Shrubs *334*

Trees *342*

Alonsoa warscewiczii
MASK FLOWER ○

Family: SCROPHULARIACEAE
Origin: Peru.
Flowering time: Summer.
Climatic zone: 6, 7, 8, 9, 10.
Dimensions: Up to 2 feet (600 mm) high.
Description: This subtropical plant produces its small, individual flowers in terminal racemes. It is usually well-branched which shows off its bright, flat flowers, whose petals curl slightly outwards at the extremities. Mask flower may be grown in any well-drained soil, outdoors as an annual or in a greenhouse.
Varieties/cultivars: There is a compact form *A. compacta* growing to 12 inches (300 mm) high.

Alonsoa warscewiczii

Amaranthus caudatus
KISS-ME-OVER-THE-GARDEN-GATE (U.S.A.), LOVE-LIES-BLEEDING (U.K.), TASSEL-FLOWER ○

Family: AMARANTHACEAE
Origin: Tropical Africa, South America.
Flowering time: Summer.
Climatic zone: 6, 7, 8, 9, 10.
Dimensions: Up to 3 feet (1 meter) high.
Description: This tall, annual plant is eye-catching with its minute, red flowers clustered in dense, pendant tails which are sometimes more than 15 inches (400 mm) long. Grow in any well-drained garden soil but add compost or well-rotted manure prior to planting. Best suited to large spaces where it can be displayed as a feature. It needs plenty of sunshine.
Varieties/cultivars: 'Viridis' (green flowers).

Amaranthus caudatus

Amaranthus tricolor

Amaranthus tricolor
JOSEPH'S-COAT, FOUNTAIN PLANT ○

Family: AMARANTHACEAE
Origin: Tropical Africa.
Flowering time: Summer.
Climatic zone: 9, 10.
Dimensions: Up to 4 feet (over 1 meter) high.
Description: Joseph's-coat, as its name indicates, has multi-colored foliage which is most striking in massed plantings. The flowers are red and, although tiny, appear in dense spike-like clusters hidden among the foliage which is flushed or striped with many shades of yellow, orange, and red. Protect from snails while seedlings are young, and water well during hot weather.
Varieties/cultivars: 'Splendens' (red foliage, red flowers), var. *salicifolius* (narrow leaves).

Antirrhinum majus
COMMON SNAPDRAGON, TOAD'S MOUTH ○

Family: SCROPHULARIACEAE
Origin: Southwestern Europe.
Flowering time: Late summer–autumn.
Climatic zone: 6, 7, 8, 9, 10.
Dimensions: Up to 3 feet (1 meter) high.
Description: Snapdragon is usually classed as an annual, but may persist as a short-lived perennial. Its tall stems, well-clothed with foliage, are topped by racemes of showy, tubular flowers. The strong stems and long-lasting flowers make snapdragon ideal for tall floral arrangements. Although old-fashioned, it is still popular in the garden because of its height and versatility. The dwarf varieties available in segregated or mixed colors make it an excellent massing or border flower. Plant seedlings in an open, sunny position in moderately rich and well-drained soil.
Other colors: White, cream, yellow, pink, purple.
Varieties/cultivars: 'Tetraploid', 'Guardsman', 'Floral Carpet' (dwarf), 'Little Darling' (semidwarf).

Antirrhinum majus

Dorotheanthus bellidiformis

Dorotheanthus bellidiformis syn. *Mesembryanthemum criniflorum*

LIVINGSTONE DAISY ○

Family: AIZOACEAE
Origin: South Africa.
Flowering time: Early summer–autumn.
Climatic zone: 6, 7, 8, 9, 10.
Dimensions: Up to 3 inches (75 mm) high.
Description: A dwarf plant, Livingstone daisy is frost-tender, preferring warmer weather. It has succulent foliage, a mat-forming habit, and short, spreading, flat, daisy-like flowers up to 2 inches (50 mm) in diameter. The original flower was rosy-red with white centers but the plant is now available in mauve, orange, and yellow, usually with a ring of white near the center. The colors are iridescent and the flowers make an excellent annual border in hot, dry climates. In dull or wet conditions, they will close, as they also do at night. It tolerates poor, dry soil, but prefers a well-drained, sunny site.
Other colors: See Description.
Varieties/cultivars: 'El Cerrito'.

Eschscholzia californica

CALIFORNIAN POPPY ○

Family: PAPAVERACEAE
Origin: United States (west coast).
Flowering time: Summer–autumn.
Climatic zone: 6, 7, 8, 9, 10.
Dimensions: Up to 12 inches (300 mm) high.
Description: Californian poppy, the official floral emblem of California, is a hardy annual or short-lived perennial that seeds prolifically, so it is wise to locate it where it can spread without interference. The brilliant open flowers,

Eschscholzia californica

which are complemented by the fine, fern-like, gray-green foliage, fold at dusk, but make a vivid show in strong sunlight. They are not suitable for indoor decoration. The plant tolerates a wide range of soils, but dislikes continued dampness.
Other colors: Creamy-white, yellow, gold, pink.
Varieties/cultivars: Among many varieties are 'Alba', 'Crocea', 'Rosea', 'Mission Bells', 'Ballerina', 'Double Mixed'.

Mirabilis jalapa

FOUR-O'CLOCK, MARVEL-OF-PERU ◑

Family: NYCTAGINACEAE
Origin: Central South America.
Flowering time: Summer.
Climatic zone: 6, 7, 8, 9, 10.
Dimensions: Up to 3 feet (1 meter) high.
Description: This is a perennial plant which may be grown as an annual. It is soft-wooded, of bushy habit, and produces terminal flowers. It is called four-o'clock because its flowers open in the late afternoon and may even remain open through the night. The fragrant flowers, which cover the outside of the plant, are tubular and flare out to about 1 inch (25 mm) across. They seed prolifically. The foliage is easily bruised but recovers quickly from damage. Plant in full sun, in light, well-drained soil. Water regularly or they will droop in hot weather. Feed monthly from spring through summer.
Other colors: Pink, white, yellow.

Mirabilis jalapa

Papaver nudicaule

Papaver nudicaule

ICELAND POPPY ○

Family: PAPAVERACEAE
Origin: Sub-arctic region in Europe, Asia, North America.
Flowering time: Late winter–early spring.
Climatic zone: 5, 6, 7, 8, 9, 10.
Dimensions: Between 10 and 18 inches (250–450 mm) high.
Description: Iceland poppies make a distinctive floral display, with their cup-shaped flowers on naked, hairy stems. They like a sunny aspect where they are protected from the wind. The showy, papery flowers emanate from pairs of boat-shaped, hairy sepals. Poppies are very suitable for mass planting as well as for harvesting as cut flowers. They may be picked in bud to open later indoors. Iceland poppies prefer cool climates and light, well-drained soil. The plants should be sustained on complete fertilizer, but should not be allowed to produce flowers too early.
Other colors: White, cream, yellow, pink.
Varieties/cultivars: 'Spring Song', 'Coonara', 'Artists Glory', 'Rimfire'.

Papaver rhoeas

Papaver rhoeas

FLANDERS POPPY, SHIRLEY OR CORN POPPY (U.K.) ○

Family: PAPAVERACEAE
Origin: Europe, Asia.
Flowering time: Summer.
Climatic zone: 4, 5, 6, 7, 8, 9, 10.
Dimensions: Up to 3 feet (1 meter) high.
Description: This is the common European poppy, seen often among the fields of wheat (corn) in Europe where it is regarded as a weed. In cultivation, it becomes a hardy, colorful annual with wiry stems and sparse foliage. The short-lived flowers are borne singly at the top of each stem well above the foliage; they are mostly single red, with very noticeable black stamens. Removing the spent blooms encourages flowering. Shirley poppies like full sun, rich soil, and good drainage. Seed may be sown directly into the ground after adequate preparation. They are best displayed in the landscape as a mass planting or at the back of a perennial border.
Other colors: White, pink, and bicolors.

Penstemon x *gloxinioides*

PENSTEMON ○ ◑

Family: SCROPHULARIACEAE
Origin: Hybrid.
Flowering time: Spring–summer.
Climatic zone: 5, 6, 7, 8, 9, 10.
Dimensions: Up to 3 feet (1 meter) high.
Description: Penstemon is a hardy perennial which may be grown as an annual. It produces several sturdy stems from the base, with flowers covering the terminal racemes. The plant is stiff and erect and lends charm to the cottage garden. As a vase flower, it is long-lasting and because of its long stems, is a favorite in large flower arrangements and bouquets. Penstemons require full sun or at least four hours of sunlight daily. They may be propagated by cuttings in late summer. Penstemon prefers a loose, gravelly soil with excellent drainage. Ensure there is some wind protection.
Other colors: Pink, mauve, blue, white.

Penstemon x *gloxinioides*

Salpiglossis sinuata

PAINTED-TONGUE (U.K.), VELVET TRUMPET FLOWER ○

Family: SOLANACEAE
Origin: Chile, Peru.
Flowering time: Summer.
Climatic zone: 4, 5, 6, 7, 8, 9, 10.
Dimensions: Up to 2 feet (600 mm) high.
Description: This is a hardy annual which grows into a many-branched, rather slender plant, bearing brightly-colored flowers each 2 inches (50 mm) in diameter. Most colors have a herringbone marking on the petal, but this is not as noticeable with the reds and purples. Its profusion of blooms makes *Salpiglossis* ideal for cutting and indoor use. Good drainage is important as root rot is a problem. Add plenty of well-rotted compost to the ground prior to planting.
Other colors: Yellow, mauve, cream.

Salvia splendens

Salvia splendens

SCARLET SAGE ○ ◑

Family: LABIATAE
Origin: Brazil.
Flowering time: Summer, autumn, winter.
Climatic zone: 4, 5, 6, 7, 8, 9, 10.
Dimensions: Up to 2 feet (600 mm) high.
Description: *Salvias*, with their strong, upright, shrubby growth habit, provide a vivid display of scarlet flowers. They are best used in borders or in association with perennials where a focal point is required. *Salvias* flower about four months after sowing and in cool climates require a heated glasshouse for germination. They need a sunny location and are tolerant of a wide range of soils.
Other colors: White, pink, dark-purple.
Varieties/cultivars: 'Blaze of Fire', 'Salmon Pigmy', 'White Fire', 'Purple Blaze', 'Tom Thumb' (dwarf).

Salpiglossis sinuata cultivar

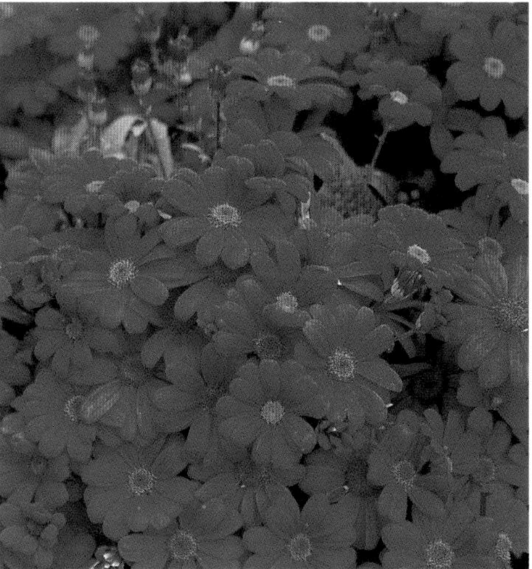
Senecio x *hybridus* cultivar

Senecio x *hybridus*
CINERARIA ◑

Family: COMPOSITAE
Origin: Hybrid.
Flowering time: Late winter–spring.
Climatic zone: 9, 10.
Dimensions: Up to 3 feet (1 meter) high.
Description: Cineraria is a perennial, but is best grown as an annual. It is slow to develop from seed, but the floral display makes the wait worthwhile. The flower clusters are up to 12 inches (300 mm) across and are composed of numerous daisy-like flowers, about 2 inches (50 mm) wide, many having a white circle towards the center. The color range, though wide, does not include yellow or gold. The plant requires protection from full sun, frosts, and strong wind. Apart from its use as a mass bedding display, cineraria may be potted to provide vivid color indoors. This is especially so in cold climates where it does best under glass.
Other colors: Brown, pink, blue, purple, bicolors.
Varieties/cultivars: 'Stellata', 'Multiflora', 'Californian Giant', 'Grandiflora Nana', 'Prized Mixed', 'Exhibition', 'Berliner Market'.

Ursinia anthemoides
DILL LEAF ○

Family: COMPOSITAE
Origin: South Africa.
Flowering time: Summer.
Climatic zone: 4, 5, 6, 7, 8, 9, 10.
Dimensions: Up to 12 inches (300 mm) high.
Description: This charming low-

Ursinia anthemoides

growing annual is similar to arcotis, except for its delightfully fine, feathery foliage. The flowers are prolific and daisy-like, with purple centers and bright yellow-orange petals. Seeds for this annual should be sown in late winter or spring in average soil with good drainage. In cold climates, sow under glass. Over-rich soil encourages foliage production at the expense of flowers. Choose a sunny position and water daily until germination, which is usually rapid. When established, the plants require little or no maintenance. Dill leaf is an excellent border specimen.
Other colors: Various shades of orange.
Varieties/cultivars: Some hybrid forms.

Zinnia elegans
ZINNIA ○

Family: COMPOSITAE
Origin: Mexico.
Flowering time: Summer.
Climatic zone: 5, 6, 7, 8, 9, 10.
Dimensions: Up to 2½ feet (750 mm) high.
Description: Zinnias prefer a warm, sheltered position in the garden, where they can enjoy full sun and protection

Zinnia elegans cultivar

from the wind. Their tall, erect stems with clasping foliage can often be brittle. The showy, single or double, daisy-like flowers, which are about 4 inches (100 mm) across, make a striking display in the garden as well as being suitable for cutting. Zinnias take twelve weeks to flower from seed and in cooler climates should be sown later than in warmer ones. The plants are subject to fungal diseases in unusually wet periods.
Other colors: White, yellow, rose-pink, apricot, lavender, purple.
Varieties/cultivars: Many cultivars available including 'Happy Talk' (unusual petals), 'Envy' (lime-green), 'Lilliput' (2½ inches (30 mm) wide — pompom), 'Thumbelina' (dwarf).

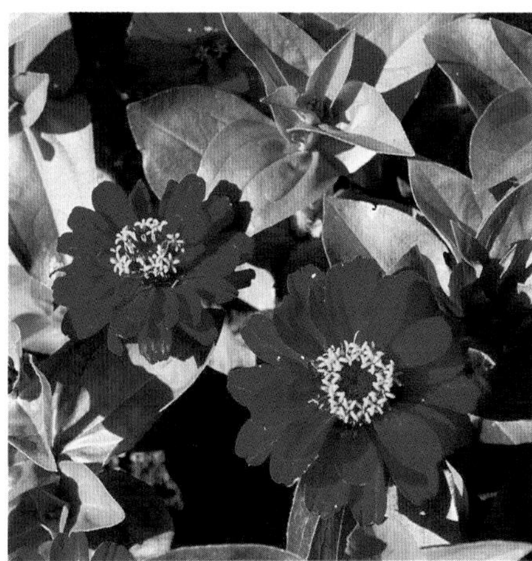
Zinnia haageana 'Dazzler'

Zinnia haageana
PERSIAN CARPET, MEXICAN ZINNIA (U.S.A.), CHIPPENDALE DAISY ○

Family: COMPOSITAE
Origin: Mexico.
Flowering time: Summer.
Climatic zone: 5, 6, 7, 8, 9, 10.
Dimensions: Up to 2 feet (600 mm) high.
Description: This is a warm-climate bedding plant, producing masses of flowers above deep-green, spear-shaped leaves. The blooms are 2½ inches (60 mm) wide and the layers of ray florets are bright red, with yellow to orange tips. Since the stems are soft, the flowers are not suitable for floral work. The plant flowers for over three months in the garden. Moderately rich soils and shelter from winds are essential.
Other colors: Bicolors.
Varieties/cultivars: 'Old Mexico', 'Persian Carpet', 'Dazzler'.

Canna indica

Canna indica
INDIAN-SHOT, CANNA ○

Family: CANNACEAE
Origin: Central and South America.
Flowering time: Summer.
Climatic zone: 9, 10.
Dimensions: Up to 5 feet (approx. 2 meters) high.
Description: Indian-Shot was first introduced into Europe in 1846 by a French consular agent who planted his "souvenirs" in a garden near Paris. The leaves of this versatile plant were formerly used for wrapping food and its seeds for ammunition and rosary beads. Often seen gracing public parks, it makes a lofty statement amidst lower shrubs. Indian-Shot forms a lush backdrop against a wall and with its small tubular flowers looks especially effective with the foreground planted with zinnia and salvia. It prefers fertile, deep soil in full sun and should be watered regularly. It is one parent of many popular garden hybrids known as *Canna* x *generalis*.

Crocosmia masonorum

Crocosmia masonorum
MONTBRETIA (U.K.), GOLDEN SWAN ○

Family: IRIDACEAE
Origin: South Africa.
Flowering time: Summer.
Climatic zone: 7, 8, 9.
Dimensions: Up to 4 feet (approx. 1 meter) high.
Description: As the common name "golden swan" suggests, this plant has a graceful, arching quality. Its stems of bright orange flowers bend like the neck of a bird. It is a good companion plant with *Gladiolus* as its foliage and growth habit are similar, and they require the same conditions — full sunlight and a well-drained position in deeply prepared soil. The flowers are ideal for cut flower arrangements.

Dahlia hybrids

Dahlia hybrids
DAHLIA ○

Family: COMPOSITAE
Origin: Hybrid.
Flowering time: Summer–autumn.
Climatic zone: 3, 4, 5, 6, 7, 8, 9, 10.
Dimensions: Up to 6 feet (2 meters) high.
Description: Dahlias, which were cultivated by the Aztecs, were introduced into Europe in 1789. A favorite of the Empress Josephine of France, these members of the daisy family were reserved for the royal gardens. Grow them in large beds with their sisters, aster and chrysanthemum, and use the dwarf varieties for borders. Dahlias are much favored by florists during their flowering season. They prefer moist soil, well-dug and fertilized. These sun worshippers were termed "water-pipe" by the Mexicans.
Other colors: Red, orange, pink, purple, white, yellow.
Varieties/cultivars: Single, anemone flowered, collerette, paeony flowered, decorative, ball, pompom, cactus and semi-cactus.

Gloriosa rothschildiana
CLIMBING LILY, GLORY LILY ◑

Family: LILIACEAE
Origin: Tropical Africa.
Flowering time: Spring–summer, northern hemisphere; spring–autumn, southern hemisphere.
Climatic zone: 9, 10.
Dimensions: Up to 5 feet (approx. 2 meters) high.
Description: This is a spectacular lily, which climbs using fingertip tendrils at the tops of its leaves. The bright yellow and red flame-like petals turning to orange and claret curve backwards while the flower stalk itself arches down. A tropical plant, it needs plenty of water and leaf mold. A well-drained but moisture-retaining potting mix is beneficial. Plant it as a backdrop to orchids or train it along a trellis or wall that is partially shaded and protected from the winds. Prune it to ground level when the plant dies back.

Gloriosa rothschildiana

Haemanthus multiflorus

Haemanthus multiflorus
FIREBALL LILY, BLOOD LILY, SCARLET STARBURST (U.S.A.) ◑

Family: AMARYLLIDACEAE
Origin: Tropical and southern Africa.
Flowering time: Spring–summer.
Climatic zone: 9.
Dimensions: Up to 18 inches (450 mm) high.
Description: This exotic member of the amaryllis family has broad leaves and deep-red flowers, followed by scarlet berries. Unable to withstand frost, it is best grown in clumps, in warm but shady nooks. In colder climates, it prefers greenhouse conditions. Ginger lily (*Hedychium gardnerianum*) can be used as a companion for color accent and perfume. The neck of the bulb should be planted just below the surface of well-drained soil. Flower spikes last for one to two weeks.
Other colors: White, orange.

Hippeastrum puniceum
BARBADOS LILY, GIANT AMARYLLIS ○ ◑

Family: AMARYLLIDACEAE
Origin: South America.
Flowering time: Spring, northern hemisphere; spring–summer, southern hemisphere.
Climatic zone: 9,10.
Dimensions: Up to 3 feet (1 meter) high.
Description: These exotic specimens make ideal pot plants. Up to three or four red trumpet-like blooms are borne on long stems, the strap-like leaves appearing after the flowers. In tropical climates they can be grown outdoors, but in cooler climates they must be grown indoors near a sunny window. The bulb should be two-thirds buried in potting mixture and moved into the sunlight when it sprouts. Feed monthly with weak liquid fertilizer. This lily may be induced to flower in mid-winter.
Other colors: White, purple, orange.

Hippeastrum puniceum

Lachenalia aloides
CAPE COWSLIP, SOLDIERS ○

Family: LILIACEAE
Origin: South Africa.
Flowering time: Spring.
Climatic zone: 9, 10.
Dimensions: 9–12 inches (225–300 mm) high.
Description: When these hardy plants are mass-planted, their bright flowers look like marching soldiers. Because of their size, lachenalias are especially suited to borders and rock gardens, providing good cut flowers which retain their color even after drying. The foliage is spotted at the base and attractive. The plants may also be grown in pots or hanging baskets and like a seaside environment. Lachenalias attract birds and are almost disease- and pest-free. They grow in any good garden loam. In very cold climates, a greenhouse environment is preferred.
Other colors: Red, orange, white, blue, pink.

Lachenalia aloides

Lapeirousia cruenta syn. *Anomatheca cruenta*
FLAME FREESIA, PAINTED PETALS (U.S.A.) ○

Family: IRIDACEAE
Origin: South Africa.
Flowering time: Late spring–summer, northern hemisphere; spring, southern hemisphere.
Climatic zone: 9, 10.
Dimensions: Up to 10 inches (250 mm) high.
Description: These pretty ornamental flowers look well in rock gardens and as pot plants and provide good blooms for cut floral arrangements. Grow them in pots of sandy soil or well-drained pockets in sheltered or warm situations. In cold climates, they prefer a greenhouse. The bright coral-red blooms on long spikes will flower for extensive periods. They resemble miniature gladioli and plants will often self-sow. Divide the bulbs every few years to prevent overcrowding. If placed in a woodland setting, they can be allowed to naturalize.
Other colors: Blue-purple, yellow, white.

Lapeirousia cruenta

Lilium pardalinum

Lilium pardalinum
PANTHER OR LEOPARD LILY

Family: LILIACEAE
Origin: California.
Flowering time: Summer, northern hemisphere; spring–summer, southern hemisphere.
Climatic zone: 7, 8, 9, 10.
Dimensions: 4–6 feet (1.2–2 meters) high.
Description: Belonging to the Turk's Cap group, one of the two main groups of *Lilium*, this is an erect bulb with red and yellow drooping waxy flowers. The tips of the spotted petals curve back almost to the stem. This quick-growing lily bears flowers for many weeks. It does not like being overcrowded nor being disturbed once it is established, but tolerates groundcovers because they give protection to its roots. It is best planted as a feature on its own. Water well.
Other colors: Purple.

Schizostylis coccinea
KAFFIR LILY (U.K.), CRIMSON FLAG, RIVER LILY

Family: IRIDACEAE
Origin: South Africa.
Flowering time: Autumn.
Climatic zone: 8, 9.
Dimensions: Up to 2 feet (600 mm) high.
Description: Renowned for its long spikes of four to six crimson, star-shaped flowers, this lily is a vigorous grower. The flower spikes last well in floral arrangements. It can be grown successfully outdoors in northern Europe and North America though it cannot tolerate severe winters, and likes positions in or near shallow water, which makes it an ideal ornamental pond plant. A site protected from winds but affording full sun is preferable. It may be propagated by seed or root division.
Other colors: Pink.
Varieties/cultivars: 'Mrs Hegarty', 'Viscountess Byng', 'Major'.

Schizostylis coccinea 'Major'

Sparaxis tricolor
HARLEQUIN FLOWER (U.K.), VELVET FLOWER

Family: IRIDACEAE
Origin: South Africa.
Flowering time: Summer.
Climatic zone: 6, 7, 8, 9.
Dimensions: Up to 18 inches (450 mm) high.
Description: The name *sparaxis* comes from the Greek for "torn" and refers to the torn spathe , or pair of bracts, that encloses the flowers of this species. Several flowers grow on each stem. Borders, large tubs, or indoor containers are all suitable for this sun-loving plant. It will grow successfully in partial shade, but the flowers close in dull weather. Ordinary garden soil mixed with compost gives good results. Protect from frost by lifting the corms when they die down in autumn. Plant again in spring.
Other colors: Red, orange, pink, white.

Sparaxis tricolor

Sprekelia formosissima
AZTEC LILY (U.S.A.), JACOBEAN LILY (U.K.)

Family: AMARYLLIDACEAE
Origin: Mexico.
Flowering time: Summer.
Climatic zone: 9, 10.
Dimensions: Up to 12 inches (300 mm) high.
Description: These striking crimson flowers resemble fleur-de-lys, the deep-green, ribbon-like leaves developing as the flower dies. The plant was introduced into Europe by the German botanist, von Sprekelsen, in the 18th century. It can be grown in pots or the greenhouse and brought indoors for flowering. If grown in the garden it merits a feature position. Plant the bulbs in light fertile soil mixed with compost, with the neck just below ground level.

Sprekelia formosissima

Tritonia crocata
BLAZING STAR (U.K.), WEATHERCOCK, MONTBRETIA (U.K., U.S.A.) ○

Other common names: FLAME FREESIA
Family: IRIDACEAE
Origin: South Africa.
Flowering time: Spring–summer.
Climatic zone: 9.
Dimensions: Up to 18 inches (450 mm) high.
Description: A showy herbaceous perennial, *Tritonia* bears orange or yellow, bell-shaped flowers for several weeks. Suited to pot-planting, borders or massed plantings with freesias or other bulbs. It is called *Tritonia*, meaning weathercock, because of the variable directions of the stamens. Although there are about fifty species, this is the only one commonly cultivated. A hardy grower, it likes a sunny situation in ordinary garden soil and should be treated like its near relative, the gladiolus. In cold climates, a greenhouse environment is preferred.
Other colors: Red, pink, yellow.

Tritonia crocata

Vallota speciosa

Tulipa hybrid cultivars

Tulipa hybrid cultivars
TULIP ○

Family: LILIACEAE
Origin: Turkey.
Flowering time: Spring.
Climatic zone: 5, 6, 7, 8, 9.
Dimensions: 6–30 inches (150–750 mm) high.
Description: The tulip was first introduced into Europe in 1554 by the Austrian Ambassador to the Sultan of Turkey. By 1634 the tulip craze had swept the Netherlands. Fortunes were made and lost and rare bulbs commanded high prices. Tulips provide magnificent color in massed plantings. In cooler climates they can be grown indoors in pots and make pretty window displays. Bulbs should be grown in slightly alkaline, rich, well-drained soil. They respond well to fertilizing and are sensitive to windy areas.
Other colors: Red, white, pink, yellow.

Vallota speciosa
SCARBOROUGH LILY, GEORGE LILY ○

Family: AMARYLLIDACEAE
Origin: South Africa.
Flowering time: Summer.
Climatic zone: 9, 10.
Dimensions: Up to 2 feet (600 mm) high.
Description: Clusters of scarlet, trumpet-shaped blooms accompany leaves up to 2 feet (600 mm) long. Planting the lily in clumps with white amaryllis provides dramatic contrast. It is well-suited to pot-planting or in garden beds where full sun is available. In colder climates, the protection of a greenhouse or warm window sill is necessary. It thrives in deeply dug, well-drained soil which has been fertilized.
Other colors: White.
Varieties/cultivars: *V. alba*.

Climbers

Berberidopsis corallina
CHILEAN CORAL VINE, CORAL PLANT (U.K.) ○

Family: FLACOURTIACEAE
Origin: Coastal forests of Chile.
Flowering time: Summer.
Climatic zone: 8, 9.
Description: The leaves of this scrambling, twining shrub are oblong, 2–3 inches long (50–70 mm), glossy dark-green, and sharply-toothed. Crimson rounded flowers hang in drooping clusters, and are followed by small berries. It is not an easy plant to grow, but it will do best in a cool, lime-free soil with protection from wind and frost. Severe winters can damage or kill it. Unless trained onto a trellis or frame, this evergreen plant will grow as a sprawling mound.

Berberidopsis corallina

Bougainvillea x *buttiana* 'Scarlet O'Hara' syn. 'San Diego' (U.S.A.)
BOUGAINVILLEA ○

Family: NYCTAGINACEAE
Origin: Hybrid.
Flowering time: Summer.
Climatic zone: 9, 10.
Description: This is one of the most spectacular tropical vines in cultivation, its vivid color being due to the three prominent bracts that surround the small, insignificant flowers. The strong branches have sharp spines. The plant requires sun, heat, and good drainage. Do not overwater. Hard pruning is necessary to control the size of the vine and to promote flowering. Although an evergreen in warm climates, it can become semideciduous or deciduous in

Bougainvillea x *buttiana*

cooler zones, but only the mature plant can withstand even moderate cold. Usually grown on a sunny wall, bougainvillea can be kept in pots if limited in size, and it can also be trained to a "standard" tree shape.

Campsis grandiflora syn. *C. chinensis*
TRUMPET VINE, TRUMPET CREEPER (U.K.) ○

Family: BIGNONIACEAE
Origin: China.
Flowering time: Summer.
Climatic zone: 7, 8, 9.
Description: Sprays of brilliant orange-red, trumpet-shaped flowers open out to five rounded lobes. *Campsis* is a strong, deciduous vine with heavy, woody growth, and with aerial rootlets which cling to rough surfaces. In hot climates, hard pruning in winter will promote new vigorous growth for the following year. In cooler climates, pruning is unnecessary. Grow in full sun and give average watering to produce a quick-growing vine. It can withstand salty winds and is a good choice for coastal areas.

Campsis radicans
COMMON TRUMPET CREEPER ○

Family: BIGNONIACEAE
Origin: Southeastern United States.
Flowering time: Midsummer–late summer.
Climatic zone: 5, 6, 7, 8, 9.
Description: A larger and more vigorous vine than *Campsis grandiflora*, this plant will quickly cover a brick, stone, or timber wall. Its attractive foliage has nine to eleven toothed leaflets, and flowers are 3 inch (75 mm) long, orange tubes. Use it for large-scale effects, and quick summer screens, but keep it under control as it can become top-heavy. A cold winter can kill the stem tips, but new growth appears quickly in spring.
Other colors: Yellow.
Varieties/cultivars: 'Flava'.

Campsis grandiflora

Campsis radicans

Clerodendrum splendens
GLORY-BOWER ○ ◑

Family: VERBENACEAE
Origin: Tropical West Africa.
Flowering time: Spring and autumn.
Climatic zone: 9, 10.
Description: Scarlet flowers hang in large clusters on this evergreen shrubby scrambler. Shiny, corrugated, leathery leaves up to 6 inches (150 mm) long give it an attractive appearance. It may be short-lived if not given good drainage and protection from the wind. To grow as a climber, it will need to be tied and trained to a trellis or wire frame, but can be grown as a mounded shrub. Use it where a light vine is required; it will not become large or invasive. In cold climates, a greenhouse is necessary.

Clerodendrum splendens

Distictis buccinatoria syn. *Phaedranthus buccinatorius*
MEXICAN BLOOD TRUMPET, BLOOD-RED TRUMPET VINE ○ ◑

Family: BIGNONIACEAE
Origin: Mexico.
Flowering time: Bursts of flower throughout the year.
Climatic zone: 9, 10.
Description: The trumpet-shaped, waxy flowers, 4 inches (100 mm) long, have flaring lobes. They are crimson red, with a scarlet sheen and an orange-yellow throat, and are conspicuous because they stand out beyond the foliage. This is a very vigorous vine with rough, leathery, oval leaflets, and needs annual pruning to keep it under control. It will attach itself by tendrils to walls, fences, and sheds. For a quick-growing, dense, evergreen cover, this is a good choice, especially with the added bonus of spectacular flowers. In a cold climate, a greenhouse environment is essential.

Distictis buccinatoria

Eccremocarpus scaber

Eccremocarpus scaber
CHILEAN GLORY FLOWER ○

Family: BIGNONIACEAE
Origin: Chile.
Flowering time: Late summer and early autumn.
Climatic zone: 8, 9.
Dimensions: Up to 10 feet (3 meters) high.
Description: This charming climber is rather delicate in appearance, with dainty foliage and bright orange-red, tubular flowers. By no means a vigorous grower, it requires a deep, rich, and well-drained soil, and a sunny, open position. Encourage the young plant to grow on a trellis, and water and feed it frequently, especially during summer. In cool climates, where frosts are a problem, it can be grown as an annual.
Other colors: Yellow, carmine.
Varieties/cultivars: *E. s. aureus*, *E. s. carmineus*.

Kennedia rubicunda

Kennedia rubicunda
DUSKY CORAL PEA ○

Family: LEGUMINOSAE
Origin: Eastern Australia.
Flowering time: Spring and early summer.
Climatic zone: 9, 10.
Description: An excellent evergreen plant for a quick screen on a fence or trellis, the dusky coral pea is also a very good groundcover. It needs sun and warmth, and once established is drought-tolerant. The oval leaves are in groups of three, tough and leathery, with the new growth an interesting silky brown. The red pea-shaped flowers hang down, usually in pairs, and are 1½ inches (40 mm) long. This is a hardy and vigorous vine, but not invasive.

Lapageria rosea
CHILEAN BELLFLOWER, CHILE-BELLS ○

Family: PHILESIACEAE
Origin: Chile.
Flowering time: Late spring–autumn.

Lapageria rosea

Climatic zone: 8, 9.
Description: One of the most strikingly beautiful flowers, the Chilean bellflower is a highly prized climbing plant for cool districts. A cool mountain zone with rich soil is its preference. The roots should be well mulched to retain moisture and keep an even temperature. The growth is slender, never dense, and the vine needs support to grow up against a wall. Given the right conditions, this is a beautiful plant with trumpet-shaped, waxy flowers, 2 inches (50 mm) long. It is the national flower of Chile.
Other colors: White.
Varieties/cultivars: *L. r.* var. *albiflora.*

Lathyrus grandiflorus
TWO-FLOWERED PEA, EVERLASTING PEA ○

Family: LEGUMINOSAE
Origin: Southern Europe.
Flowering time: Midsummer.

Lathyrus grandiflorus

Climatic zone: 7, 8, 9.
Description: With smaller leaves than *L. latifolius*, but larger flowers, this hardy, herbaceous, climbing perennial is a popular plant for cut flowers. It is easily grown and long-lived if given adequate water and fertilizer. After it dies down each year, a good mulch over the roots is advisable, and it will produce new shoots from the root clump in spring. It prefers cool conditions, but a sunny position. The flowers, although not fragrant, are charming and useful in floral arrangements.

Lonicera sempervirens
TRUMPET HONEYSUCKLE, CORAL HONEYSUCKLE ○ ◑ ●

Family: CAPRIFOLIACEAE
Origin: Southeastern United States.
Flowering time: Summer.
Climatic zone: 7, 8, 9.
Description: This robust, fast-growing climber is evergreen in mild climates, and will tolerate a shady position. Rich orange-scarlet flowers with yellow inside appear at the ends of branchlets, usually in groups of six. The upper leaves are joined in pairs. The flowers are not fragrant but are large, 2 inches (50 mm) long, and rich in color. Good soil and cool roots will result in a handsome vine which should be thinned out occasionally. A support should be provided for its twining habit.
Other colors: Yellow.
Varieties/cultivars: 'Sulphurea'.

Lonicera sempervirens

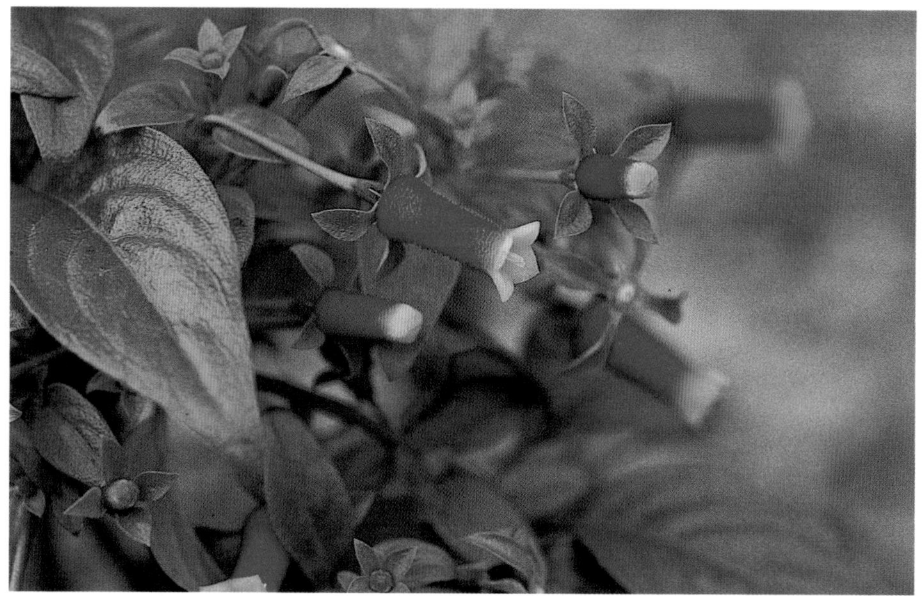
Manettia bicolor

Manettia bicolor syn. *M. inflata*
FIRECRACKER PLANT, FIRECRACKER FLOWER (U.K.) ○ ◑

Family: RUBIACEAE
Origin: Paraguay, Uruguay.
Flowering time: Spring, summer, autumn.
Climatic zone: 9, 10.
Description: An evergreen, small, dainty twiner, *Manettia* is an easily managed little plant. The 1 inch (25 mm) long, waxy, tubular flowers are yellow-tipped, and the lower half is covered with bright scarlet bristles. The flowers give a delightful sprinkling of color for many months. It is useful as cover for pillars, and to produce light shade over pergolas. Rich soil and a sheltered position are preferred, and it can be grown among shrubs for protection from cool winters. In cold climates, a greenhouse environment is essential.

Passiflora coccinea
RED PASSIONFLOWER (U.K.), SCARLET PASSIONFLOWER ○

Family: PASSIFLORACEAE
Origin: Venezuela–Brazil.
Flowering time: Summer.
Climatic zone: 9, 10.
Description: The startlingly beautiful flowers gave the name to this genus of tendril-climbers. It was believed that features of the flower were representations of the suffering of Jesus Christ. The red passionflower has shiny, wide scarlet petals, 4 inches (100 mm) across. The very free-blooming habit in summer makes it desirable as a cover over pergolas or on fences or, in a cooler climate, it can be grown in large pots and brought indoors in the winter months. It may not flower until two or three years old, but removing old wood in the winter will promote flowering.

Passiflora coccinea

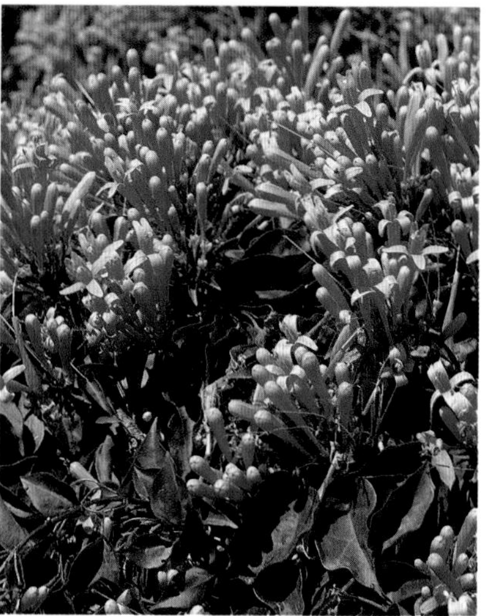
Pyrostegia venusta

Pyrostegia venusta
FLAME VINE, FLAMING TRUMPET, APRICOT BELLS ○ ◑

Other common names: GOLDEN SHOWER
Family: BIGNONIACEAE
Origin: Brazil, Paraguay.
Flowering time: Winter, spring.
Climatic zone: 9, 10.
Description: In full flower, the flame vine has clusters of slender-tubed flowers hanging like a dense curtain from a woody, evergreen vine. It is an exceptionally vigorous grower, and will cover high walls or roof tops. It produces its best growth when planted in a very sunny position. A strong support is necessary, as new growth drapes over the previous growth, and eventually the vine becomes very thick and dense. It will tolerate wind and mild frost when established, and is improved with regular watering. Adaptable to a greenhouse in cooler areas.

Quisqualis indica

Quisqualis indica
RANGOON CREEPER ○ ◑

Family: COMBRETACEAE
Origin: Burma to the Philippines and New Guinea.
Flowering time: Summer.
Climatic zone: 9, 10.
Description: The slender, dainty flower tubes of the rangoon creeper are 3 inches (75 mm) long, and change from white to pink and crimson. The delicious and unusual fragrance resembles apricots, and is very pervasive at night. Support is needed to train this shrubby vine up over a wall or fence, and it can make climbing stems up to 3 feet (1 meter) long each year. Although it will tolerate some shade, a warm protected site is best. Plant it near an open window to gain the benefit of its distinctive perfume.

Rosa 'Albertine'
ALBERTINE ROSE ○

Family: ROSACEAE
Origin: Cultivar.
Flowering time: Summer.
Climatic zone: 5, 6, 7, 8, 9.
Description: Grown as a rather lax shrub, or trained as a climber, this popular rose has loosely double, large, and richly-fragrant, coppery-pink blooms. The flowers are in clusters of six to ten, and are carried on upright stems 6 inches (150 mm) above the prostrate branches. It is a very useful plant as a groundcover, to cover low walls, or to train up pillars. It is sufficiently vigorous to train up house walls and even over sheds or out-house buildings. Prune after flowering.

Rosa 'Albertine'

Rosa 'Bloomfield Courage'
BLOOMFIELD COURAGE ○

Family: ROSACEAE
Origin: Cultivar.
Flowering time: Midsummer.
Climatic zone: 5, 6, 7, 8, 9.
Description: A trailing plant which can grow stems 10 to 12 feet (3 to 4 meters) long in one season, this rose can be used as a good groundcover, even in fairly poor soil. As it has a habit of taking root from the stems which are in contact with the soil, it can spread over a wide area. It is often grafted to a tall standard to produce a weeping standard rose. The flowers, which are single, deep-red with white centers and yellow stamens, and are about 1½ inches (40 mm) across, hang in clusters.

Rosa 'Bloomfield Courage'

Rosa 'Excelsa'
EXCELSA ROSE ○

Family: ROSACEAE
Origin: Cultivar.
Flowering time: Spring.
Climatic zone: 6, 7, 8, 9.
Description: The small, bright crimson flowers on this supple-stemmed climber are double, and produced in great abundance in springtime. It will grow up to 12 to 15 feet (4 to 5 meters), and is often grafted onto the top of a tall stem to create a weeping standard rose. It also

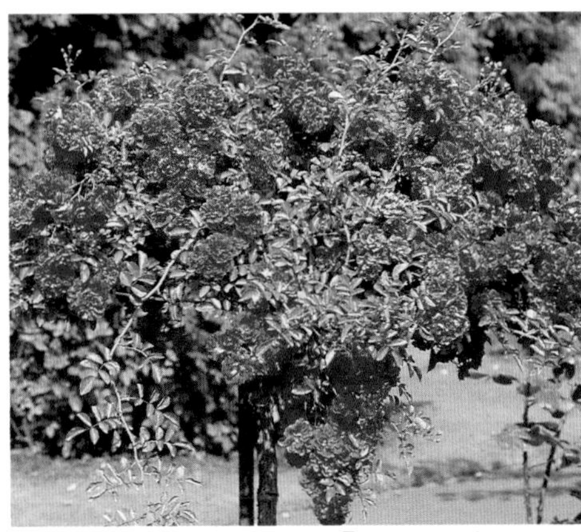
Rosa 'Excelsa'

makes an excellent groundcover, or can be grown over a tree stump, or low wall, or trained up a post or pillar. Pruning in the winter is needed to remove old wood and selectively shorten some of the branches.

Tecomaria capensis
CAPE HONEYSUCKLE ○ ◑

Family: BIGNONIACEAE
Origin: South Africa.
Flowering time: Autumn and winter.
Climatic zone: 9, 10.
Description: Best used as a clipped hedge, this *Tecomaria* is a rambling, scrambling, shrubby plant with evergreen foliage. It is easily grown in warm districts, but needs to be controlled. New growth comes from the base each year, so the width increases quite significantly. It can be used to cover a bank, or be trained up through a wire frame as a free-standing hedge, or supported against a fence or wall. The orange flowers are prolific, but are reduced with regular clipping.
Other colors: Orange-yellow, pink, yellow.

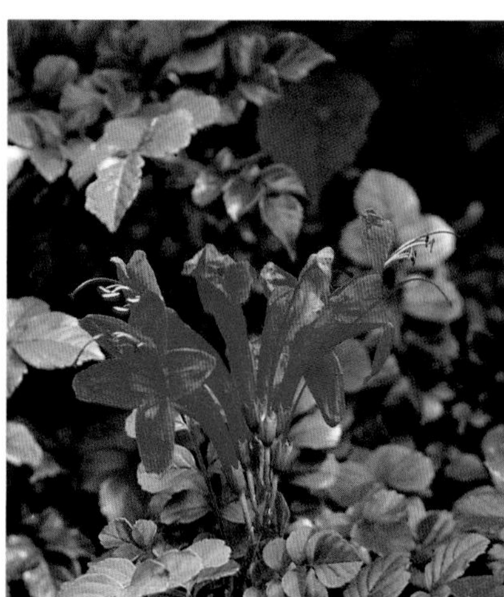

Tecomaria capensis

Thunbergia alata
ORANGE CLOCK VINE, BLACK-EYED SUSAN VINE (U.S.A.) ○

Family: ACANTHACEAE
Origin: Tropical Africa.
Flowering time: Late summer–autumn.
Climatic zone: 5, 6, 7, 8, 9, 10.
Description: This well-known twining perennial vine has toothed, triangular leaves on little winged stems. The slender stems and light appearance are deceptive. It is able to cover a shed or a sloping bank very quickly. The funnel-shaped orange flowers are a colorful addition to a dreary corner. It is easily kept under control if grown as an annual (especially in cooler districts). It prefers a sunny position and foliage will be thicker and more attractive if adequate water is provided.
Other colors: Creamy-yellow, white.

Thunbergia alata

Tropaeolum speciosum
FLAME CREEPER ○

Family: TROPAEOLACEAE
Origin: Chilean Andes.
Flowering time: Summer.
Climatic zone: 7, 8, 9, 10.
Description: From five to seven leaflets make up the small circular leaves of this climbing perennial herb. The fleshy tubers produce new growth each year. The curious-looking flowers have a scarlet spur and yellow petals, and look like little, tailed balloons. This is a very pretty summer-flowering twiner, and should have support to hold it in place. Wire frames can be used, which will be quickly covered, or it can be grown in a hanging basket for summer display. In cold areas, it will flower in spring under glass.

Tropaeolum speciosum

Tropaeolum tricolorum

Tropaeolum tricolorum
CLIMBING NASTURTIUM, TRICOLORED INDIAN CRESS ○

Family: TROPAEOLACEAE
Origin: Chile.
Flowering time: Spring–summer.
Climatic zone: 9.
Description: Unusual, beautiful flowers appear on this herbaceous climbing perennial. It has a fast-growing habit, with the fleshy roots producing new growth in the spring. The flowers are about 1½ inches (40 mm) wide with little "stemmed" petals which give an open, delicate appearance. They are vivid scarlet with yellow at the base. The vine itself likes the sun, but the roots should be kept cool and moist, and protected from temperature changes. Neutral to acid soil is essential. Severe winters can kill this plant.

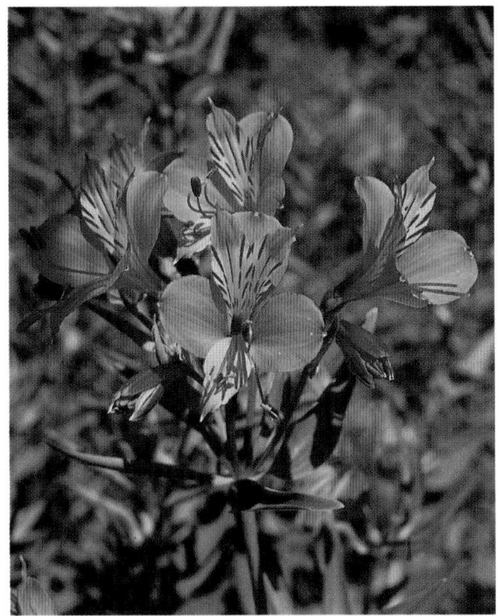

Alstroemeria aurantiaca

Alstroemeria aurantiaca
PERUVIAN LILY, CHILEAN LILY 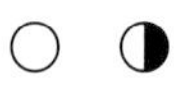

Family: ALSTROEMERIACEAE
Origin: South America.
Flowering time: Summer.
Climatic zone: 8, 9.
Dimensions: Up to 3 feet (1 meter) high.
Description: Although the Peruvian lily is quite hardy, it is both drought- and frost-susceptible, and requires well-drained, moist soil and shelter. Its showy flowers are valued as pot specimens and for cut flower arrangements. It can be naturalized under trees or grown in cool greenhouse conditions, but it is best in an open, sunny, sheltered site. Propagate it from root division in autumn after the rapid root increase of summer, or propagate from seed. Peruvian lily is a handsome companion for agapanthus and scabiosa in a sheltered border.
Other colors: Pink, yellow.
Varieties/cultivars: 'Dover Orange', 'Moerhaim Orange', 'Lutea'.

Anigozanthos manglesii
KANGAROO-PAW ○

Family: HAEMODORACEAE
Origin: Western Australia.
Flowering time: Late spring–summer.
Climatic zone: 9.
Dimensions: Up to 6 feet (2 meters) high.
Description: *A. manglesii* is an easy species of kangaroo paw to grow. Although it is susceptible to cold, high humidity, and fungal disease, it is worth growing for its unusual and exotically colored flowers and its red woolly stems. It prefers sandy, well-drained soil and requires manure and plenty of water in spring. With its narrow strap-like foliage and interesting flowers it makes an impressive show. It is a good cut flower, fresh or dried.
Other colors: Yellow, green, pink.

Anigozanthos manglesii

Aquilegia canadensis
COMMON COLUMBINE, CANADIAN COLUMBINE (U.K.) ○ ◑

Family: RANUNCULACEAE
Origin: North America.
Flowering time: Early summer.
Climatic zone: 3, 4, 5, 6, 7, 8, 9.
Dimensions: Up to 18 inches (450 mm) high.
Description: Aquilegias are one of the loveliest of perennials for the spring border. *C. canadensis* has yellow petals with red sepals and spurs and looks well planted with the strong blue of *cynoglossum* and the white of *Anemone sylvestris*. It prefers a well-drained, sandy loam and liquid fertilizer during its growth period. In hot climates a semi-shaded aspect is preferable and plants will be short-lived if allowed to become waterlogged. It self-sows modestly in cold climates and is a good cut flower.

Aquilegia hybrids
COLUMBINE 

Family: RANUNCULACEAE
Origin: U.K.
Flowering time: Early summer.
Climatic zone: 3, 4, 5, 6, 7, 8.

Aquilegia hybrids

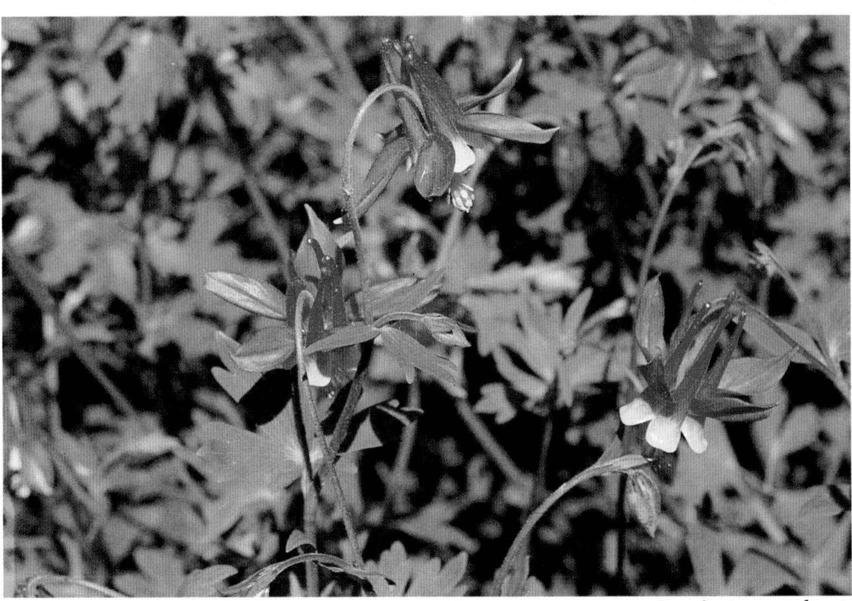

Aquilegia canadensis

Dimensions: Up to 2½ feet (750 mm) high.
Description: Aquilegias come in myriad colors and in single and double varieties. Their foliage is dainty and rather like coarse maidenhair fern. The taller cultivars are most suited to the herbaceous border and the smaller ones for rockeries. Some aquilegias are propagated by root division in spring; others are best left to self-sow, which they do profusely in cool, moist conditions. They are frost-resistant, but drought-susceptible, and are best grown in well-drained, sandy loam. They look attractive if left to naturalize under deciduous trees, and are good as cut flowers.
Other colors: Pink, blue, white, yellow, purple.
Varieties/cultivars: 'Snow Queen', 'Nora Barlow', 'McKana Hybrids', 'Laudham Strain'.

Astilbe x *arendsii*
ASTILBE, FALSE SPIREA ○ ◑

Family: SAXIFRAGACEAE
Origin: Hybrid.
Flowering time: Summer.
Climatic zone: 4, 5, 6, 7, 8, 9.
Dimensions: Up to 4 feet (approx. 1 meter) high.
Description: Astilbes are seen at their best in partial shade. Naturalized under trees and beside ponds they are spectacular. However, they will grow in the herbaceous border provided they have rich, moist soil. Their foliage is as pretty as their feathery flowers and often has a coppery-pink tinge. The plants are best propagated from root division in autumn and early spring. Astilbes are heavy feeders, so fertilize well in spring and summer. Cut back in autumn and divide every three years. They are a showy cut flower.
Other colors: White, pink.
Varieties/cultivars: 'Feuer', 'Bressingham Charm'.

Astilbe x *arendsii*

Astilbe x *crispa*
GOATSBEARD ◑

Family: SAXIFRAGACEAE
Origin: Hybrid.
Flowering time: Summer.
Climatic zone: 5.
Dimensions: Up to 10 inches (250 mm) high.
Description: *Astilbe* x *crispa*, with its salmon-pink, feathery flowers, is an excellent choice for rockeries, especially those surrounding small ponds. It is also lovely when grown edging pathways beneath established deciduous trees. Its requirements are moist soil and semishade. As plants reproduce rapidly, division every few years is advisable. Propagate from root division in autumn and early spring.
Varieties/cultivars: 'Perkeo', 'Peter Pan', 'Gnome', and several others.

Astilbe x *crispa*

Centaurea dealbata 'Steenbergii'
WILD CORNFLOWER ○

Family: COMPOSITAE
Origin: Caucasus.
Flowering time: Summer.
Climatic zone: 4, 5, 6, 7, 8.
Dimensions: Up to 3 feet (900 mm) high.
Description: *Centaurea dealbata* 'Steenbergii' is valuable in the herbaceous border, both for its foliage and its flowers. Its leaves are lobed and silvery-white on the underside, and its thistle-like flowers are a rich crimson.

Centaurea dealbata 'Steenbergii'

The plant looks showy when grown with *Lavandula angustifolia* and *Catananche caerulea*. It requires a light, dry but fertile soil, and may need to be staked. Propagate it by root division in spring or sow in autumn or spring. As a cut flower, it forms a splash of color indoors.
Other colors: Pink, purple.

Centranthus ruber
RED VALERIAN (U.K.), JUPITER'S BEARD ○

Family: VALERIANACEAE
Origin: Mediterranean region.
Flowering time: Summer.
Climatic zone: 7, 8, 9.
Dimensions: 2–3 feet (600–900 mm) high.
Description: Red valerian is an herbaceous perennial which grows pleasantly bushy. It thrives in any well-drained soil and needs little attention apart from the cutting back of spent flowers. Often used for dry situations where other plants do not do well, it self-sows profusely and can become a problem if not contained. Propagate it from seed in spring or soft tip cuttings. Red valerian looks well planted with *Veronica spicata* and *Iberis sempervirens*, and is a good cut flower.

Centranthus ruber

Clivia miniata

Clivia miniata
KAFFIR LILY

Family: AMARYLLIDACEAE
Origin: South Africa.
Flowering time: Spring.
Climatic zone: 9, 10.
Dimensions: 1½–2 feet (450–600 mm) high.
Description: The Kaffir lily can be naturalized beneath large trees. With shelter from hot summer sun and winter frosts, good drainage, and plenty of compost, it will reward you with a dazzling floral display in spring. In cold climates it needs to be grown under glass. This is followed by a crop of deep crimson berries from late summer into winter. It needs to be kept moist in spring and summer, but needs drier conditions in autumn and winter. Propagation is by root division after spring flowering. Large clumps provide a showy effect. It is an excellent cut flower and pot specimen.
Varieties/cultivars: 'Grandiflora'.

Dianthus deltoides
MAIDEN PINK

Family: CARYOPHYLLACEAE
Origin: Europe.
Flowering time: Late spring.
Climatic zone: 4, 5, 6, 7, 8, 9.
Dimensions: Up to 10 inches (250 mm) high.
Description: Maiden pink, with its spreading habit and neat mat-like appearance, makes an excellent groundcover, border edging, and rockery plant. It requires very well-drained alkaline soil and good air

Dianthus deltoides

circulation, so do not mulch. Propagation is by cuttings in late summer, root division or seed in spring. Extend flowering by cutting back spent flowers and prune the flowering stems in autumn. As long as they do not crowd it out, it looks lovely grown with *Bellis perennis*, *Myosotis scorpioides* and *Cerastium tomentosum*. This is an excellent cut flower.
Other colors: Pink, white with crimson eye.
Varieties/cultivars: 'Albus' and some others.

Euphorbia griffithii 'Fireglow'

Euphorbia griffithii 'Fireglow'
FIREGLOW

Family: EUPHORBIACEAE
Origin: Cultivar.
Flowering time: Early summer.
Climatic zone: 5, 6, 7, 8, 9.
Dimensions: Up to 3 feet (1 meter) high.
Description: Fireglow is one of the hardier euphorbias. It is perennial, with attractive veined foliage, and produces masses of rich orange flowers for about 2 months in early summer. The color is actually in the bracts, not the petals. It prefers semishade and is easy to grow in any moderately fertile, well-drained soil. Propagation is by cuttings or root division. Care should be taken to avoid contact with the sticky, milky substance exuded by all euphorbias when cut. At best it is an irritant, at worst poisonous.

Gaillardia x *grandiflora*
BLANKET FLOWER

Family: COMPOSITAE
Origin: Hybrid.
Flowering time: Summer.
Climatic zone: 4, 5, 6, 7, 8, 9.
Dimensions: 1–3 feet (300–900 mm) high.
Description: Gaillardias come in dazzling shades of red and yellow and are particularly showy if planted en masse. They tend to get a bit untidy, so if this is a problem, choose the more compact dwarf variety, 'Goblin'. They are fussy about soil in that they need it to be exceptionally well-drained in autumn and winter. Any summer dryness can be counteracted with mulch. Liquid manure is beneficial at the budding stage. Propagation is by root division in autumn or spring. Gaillardias are good cut flowers.
Other colors: Yellow, deep crimson, bicolors.
Varieties/cultivars: 'Burgundy', 'Copper Beauty', 'Dazzler', 'Yellow Queen'.

Gaillardia x *grandiflora*

Gazania x *hybrida*

Gazania x *hybrida*

GAZANIA, TREASURE FLOWER ○

Family: COMPOSITAE
Origin: Hybrid.
Flowering time: Summer.
Climatic zone: 8, 9, 10.
Dimensions: Up to 12 inches (300 mm) high.
Description: Gazanias are available in trailing and clumping varieties, the trailing form being especially useful in rockery and terraced situations. They prefer light (even poor), well-drained soil in full sun and benefit from a dressing of blood and bone in spring. Propagation is by stem cuttings or seedlings in autumn. Gazanias are salt-resistant, so are good in coastal areas, but they are very frost-susceptible and in frost-prone regions should be lifted and stored over winter. The flowers, with their habit of closing in the late afternoon, have no value when picked.
Other colors: White, cream, yellow, pink, green.
Varieties/cultivars: 'Freddie', 'Sunbeam'.

Geum quellyon syn. *G. chiloense*

AVENS ○ ◑

Family: ROSACEAE
Origin: Chile.
Flowering time: Summer.

Geum quellyon 'Prince of Orange'

Climatic zone: 5, 6.
Dimensions: Up to 2 feet (600 mm) high.
Description: This is a charming old fashioned perennial with pinnate, hairy, coarsely toothed leaves and tall stems topped by panicles of brilliant red flowers. Ideal as part of an herbaceous border, it can be grown successfully in any moderately rich soil with good drainage, and will propagate easily from seed.
Other colors: Yellow, orange.
Varieties/cultivars: 'Lady Stratheden', 'Mrs. Bradshaw', 'Prince of Orange', 'Red Wings', 'Starkers Magnificent'.

Heuchera sanguinea

Heuchera sanguinea

CORAL BELLS ○ ◑

Family: SAXIFRAGACEAE
Origin: Southwestern United States, Mexico.
Flowering time: Summer.
Climatic zone: 4, 5, 6, 7, 8, 9.
Dimensions: Up to 2 feet (600 mm) high.
Description: In 1885, several plants of coral bells survived a journey from Mexico to England and were later hybridized. *H. sanguinea* is at home in shaded rock gardens. Mix it in with white primula and dark-blue campanula in borders. Mulched, well-drained soil encourages it to flower freely.
Varieties/cultivars: Many cultivars are available.

Kniphofia uvaria and hybrids

RED-HOT-POKER, TORCH LILY ○

Family: LILIACEAE
Origin: Hybrid.
Flowering time: Spring–autumn.
Climatic zone: 6, 7, 8, 9.
Dimensions: 2–4 feet high.
Description: Red-hot-pokers, with their brightly colored, torch-like flowers erupting from large clumps of grass-like foliage, make handsome specimen plants and are a showy feature in the summer border. They need well-drained, sandy loam with the addition of compost or animal manure. Mulch to protect the crown from freezing in cold climates and to retain moisture during the flowering season. Propagation is by root division in late winter or early spring.
Other colors: Yellow (without *uvaria*).
Varieties/cultivars: 'Yellow Hammer', 'Buttercup', 'Mount Etna', 'Royal Standard' (all of hybrid origin).

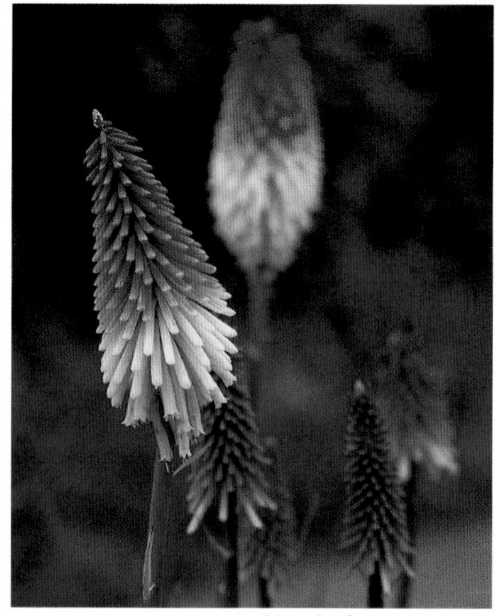

Kniphofia uvaria

Lobelia cardinalis

CARDINAL-FLOWER ○ ◑

Family: LOBELIACEAE
Origin: Eastern North America.
Flowering time: Summer.
Climatic zone: 4, 5, 6, 7, 8, 9.
Dimensions: 3–6 feet (1–2 meters) high.
Description: The cardinal flower is suitable for both the sheltered border and the cottage garden. It is sun-tolerant but will also grow in partial shade. It needs constantly moist, well-mulched, and well-drained soil, and in colder climates protection against prolonged cold and damp is essential. It can be propagated by root division and cuttings in spring. Cardinal flower looks well planted with *Artemesia lactiflora* and *Astilbe arendsii*. Its flowers are short-lived.
Other colors: White.
Varieties/cultivars: 'Alba', 'Angel Song', 'Arabella's Vision', 'Twilight Zone'.

Lobelia cardinalis

Lobelia laxiflora

PEACH-LEAVED LOBELIA, TORCH LOBELIA ○

Family: LOBELIACEAE
Origin: Arizona to Mexico and Colombia.
Flowering time: Summer.
Climatic zone: 9, 10.
Dimensions: From 3 feet (1 meter) high.
Description: This is a tall, shrubby

Lobelia laxiflora

member of the genus *Lobelia* with a spread equal to its height. Place it among other sun-loving, evergreen shrubs or near a wall where it will be protected from frosts. Do not plant it near gross feeders, as it likes rich, moist, well-drained soil. The red and yellow flowers, 1 inch (30 mm) across, are in terminal leafy spikes. Propagation is by seed or cuttings.

Lupinus 'Russell Hybrid'

RUSSELL HYBRID LUPIN ○ ◑

Family: LEGUMINOSAE
Origin: Hybrids.
Flowering time: Summer.
Climatic zone: 5, 6, 7, 8, 9.
Dimensions: 3 feet (1 meter) high.
Description: Lupins are among the showiest of the herbaceous perennials. They form handsome clumps, their gray-green foliage a perfect backdrop for their own abundantly colored blooms

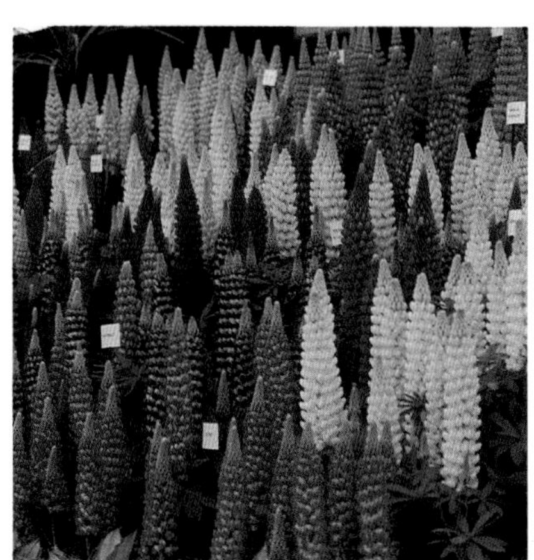

Lupinus 'Russell Hybrid'

and for companion plantings of *Papaver orientale*, *Phlox paniculata*, *Penstemon gloxinioides*, and *Baptista australis*. They prefer a light, neutral, sandy soil and plenty of water. Propagate them from seed sown direct in autumn or by division in early spring. Lupins are good cut flowers.
Other colors: White, cream, yellow, pink, blue, lilac, purple.
Varieties/cultivars: 'Betty Astell', 'Lilac Time', 'Fireglow', 'Gladys Cooper'.

Lychnis chalcedonica

Lychnis chalcedonica

MALTESE-CROSS 

Family: CARYOPHYLLACEAE
Origin: Northern Russia.
Flowering time: Summer.
Climatic zone: 4, 5, 6, 7, 8.
Dimensions: Up to 3 feet (1 meter) high.
Description: *Lychnis chalcedonica* adds vibrant color to the herbaceous border or cottage garden. It is hardy, a prolific seeder, and looks very well planted with the blues and purples of some varieties of salvia, and *Nepeta* x *faassenii*, offset by splashes of white from *Achillea*. It thrives in any well-drained, moist soil, but appreciates extra mulch and water in spring and summer. Propagation is by seed in spring or by division in late winter. Regular picking keeps the plant under control and prolongs flowering.
Other colors: White, rose-pink.
Varieties/cultivars: 'Alba', 'Flora Plena'.

Monarda didyma

Monarda didyma
BEE BALM, OSWEGO TEA ○ ◑

Family: LABIATAE
Origin: North America.
Flowering time: Summer.
Climatic zone: 4, 5, 6, 7, 8, 9.
Dimensions: 2–3 feet (up to 1 meter) high.
Description: *Monarda didyma* is a delight. Its colors are superb, its fragrance overwhelming, attracting bees and butterflies in profusion. It looks as well in the herbaceous border as the herb garden, particularly if care is taken with color combinations. It requires only average, well-drained soil, but benefits from good mulching and plenty of water in dry conditions, especially if planted in full sun. Its leaves can be used for potpourri. Propagate from seed or by division in spring. It is susceptible to powdery mildew.
Other colors: White, pink, mauve, purple.
Varieties/cultivars: 'Blue Stocking', 'Cambridge Scarlet', 'Snow Maiden', 'Croftway Pink'.

Paeonia officinalis 'Rubra Plena'
COMMON PEONY ○ ◑

Family: PAEONIACEAE
Origin: Cultivar.
Flowering time: Late spring.
Climatic zone: 5, 6, 7, 8, 9.
Dimensions: Up to 3 feet (1 meter) high.
Description: Once established, peonies will grow for decades in the cool-climate garden. They require well-drained, deep, fertile soil, enriched with plenty of animal manure, and ample water during the flowering period. They also need protection from strong winds and, in warmer areas, extra shade. Propagation is by tuber division in early autumn, but take care to disturb established clumps as little as possible. Prune by removing spent flower stems when foliage yellows. Picked at the bud stage, peonies are excellent cut flowers.

Paeonia officinalis 'Rubra Plena'

Papaver orientale
ORIENTAL POPPY ○

Family: PAPAVERACEAE
Origin: Southwestern Asia.
Flowering time: Early summer.
Climatic zone: 4, 5, 6, 7, 8, 9.
Dimensions: 3–4 feet (approx. 1 meter) high.
Description: The oriental poppy is a long-time favorite for the herbaceous border and cottage garden. Its large, open blooms, often darkly blotched at the base, come in dazzling colors and more than compensate for its foliage, which becomes very untidy after flowering. This is best disguised by surrounding poppies with perennials like *Stokesia laevis*, *Veronica virginica*, and *Anemone* x *hybrida*. Oriental poppy requires well-drained, deep loam with a good dressing of manure in early spring. Propagation is by division in spring or by seed. It is a good cut flower.
Other colors: Pink, rose, white, yellow.
Varieties/cultivars: 'China Boy', 'Mrs Perry', 'Grossfurst', 'Perry's White', 'Princess Victoria Louise', 'Harvest Moon'.

Papaver orientale 'Harvest Moon'

Pelargonium x *domesticum*
MARTHA WASHINGTON GERANIUM (U.S.A.), REGAL OR SHOW GERANIUM (U.K.) ○

Family: GERANIACEAE
Origin: Hybrids.
Flowering time: Spring–summer.
Climatic zone: 9, 10.
Dimensions: 18 inches (450 mm) high.
Description: *Pelargonium* x *domesticum* is larger in habit than *P.* x *hortorum* and has a shorter flowering season. Its foliage is evergreen and pleasantly aromatic when bruised, and its flowers are deeply colored and ruffled. In the northern hemisphere, it is often grown as a showy greenhouse pot specimen. It requires well-drained, light soil with a dressing of complete fertilizer in late winter to encourage flowering. Do not overwater. It is susceptible to frost and fungal disease. Remove spent flowers to prolong blooming.
Other colors: White, pink, mauve, purple.
Varieties/cultivars: 'Axminster', 'Mrs G. Morf', 'Hula', 'Carefree', 'Annie Hawkins'.

Pelargonium x *domesticum*

Pelargonium x *hortorum*
ZONAL GERANIUM ○

Family: GERANIACEAE
Origin: Hybrids.
Flowering time: Late spring–autumn.
Climatic zone: 9, 10.
Dimensions: 6 inches–3 feet (450 mm–1 meter) high.
Description: *Pelargonium* x *hortorum* is a shrubby evergreen perennial, valuable for its variable foliage as well as its flowers, which come in single, semidouble and double form. It likes well-drained, neutral, light soil and dislikes excess water. Water only in dry weather. To keep the plant thick and encourage flowering, prune regularly. Propagation is by cuttings in summer in cold climates, and year-round elsewhere. It is a good cut flower, but is susceptible to frost and fungal disease.
Other colors: White, pink, salmon, mauve.
Varieties/cultivars: 'Dagata', 'Rubin', 'Highland Queen', 'Henri Joignot'.

Pelargonium x *hortorum*

Penstemon barbatus
BEARDLIP PENSTEMON, PENSTEMON (U.K.) ○

Family: SCROPHULARIACEAE
Origin: South western United States, Mexico.
Flowering time: Summer–autumn.
Climatic zone: 4.
Dimensions: 2–3 feet (600–900 mm) high.
Description: Beardlip penstemon, formerly known as *Chelone barbatus*, takes its name from its flowers' bearded throat and lip. The species appears in several colors, but the scarlet-flowered one is the most popular. It is not particularly hardy and requires well-drained, fertile soil and shelter from wind. Excess water in winter will kill it. Propagation is from cuttings in late summer or seed sown under glass in spring. The plant needs hard pruning to ground level in spring, just as new growth begins. Beardlip penstemon is good for planting on wild, sheltered slopes.
Other colors: Pink, purple, lavender.
Varieties/cultivars: 'Carnea'.

Penstemon barbatus

Penstemon x *gloxinioides* 'Firebird'
PENSTEMON, GLOXINIA PENSTEMON ○ ◑

Family: SCROPHULARIACEAE
Origin: Hybrid.
Flowering time: Summer–autumn.
Climatic zone: 8, 9.
Dimensions: 2 feet (600 mm) high.
Description: *Penstemon* x *gloxinioides* 'Firebird' is similar to *P. barbatus*, but its flower is larger and unbearded, and it flowers more abundantly. Well-drained soil and a sheltered position are necessary for good growth, and it benefits from winter mulching. Partial shade will give the plant a longer life and weekly application of soluble fertilizer will extend its flowering. It is at its best in the herbaceous border with perennials like *Anthemis sancti-johannis*, *Helenium autumnale* and *Lavandula stoechas*.

Penstemon x *gloxinioides* 'Firebird'

Pentas lanceolata

Pentas lanceolata
EGYPTIAN STAR-CLUSTER ○ ◑

Family: RUBIACEAE
Origin: East Africa–southern Arabia.
Flowering time: Summer.
Climatic zone: 9, 10.
Dimensions: 2–5 feet (600–1500 mm) high.
Description: *Pentas lanceolata* is ideal for the sunny subtropical garden, preferring wet summers, warm winters, and no frost. In cooler climates, it can be grown under greenhouse conditions and it lends itself to pot cultivation. It requires well-drained, sandy soil with the addition of plenty of organic mulch. It is fast-growing, with a shrubby habit. To keep its shape and induce constant flowering, prune it lightly and regularly. Propagation is from seed or, more commonly, from tip cuttings taken in spring to autumn and grown in humid conditions.
Other colors: White, pink, rose, lilac.
Varieties/cultivars: 'Coccinea'.

Physalis alkekengi syn. *P. franchetii*
BLADDER CHERRY, CHINESE LANTERN (U.K.) ○ ◑

Family: SOLANACEAE
Origin: Southeastern Europe–Japan.
Flowering time: Summer–autumn.
Climatic zone: 3, 4, 5, 6, 7, 8, 9, 10.
Dimensions: Up to 2 feet (600 mm) high.
Description: *Physalis* is a hardy, creeping perennial, grown largely for its showy, berry-bearing calyx that becomes brightly colored and inflated after flowering. It requires well-drained soil and plenty of summer water. Because of its creeping habit, it can be useful as a groundcover, particularly the dwarf cultivar 'Nana'. Propagation is by seed or by root division in autumn or early spring. The dried calyces make handsome winter decoration and the berries are edible.
Varieties/cultivars: 'Gigantea', 'Orbiculare', 'Monstrosa', 'Nana'.

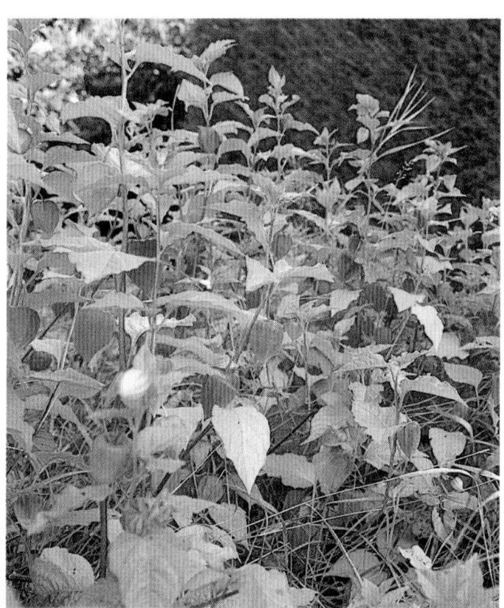
Physalis alkekengi

Potentilla atrosanguinea
RUBY CINQUEFOIL ○

Family: ROSACEAE
Origin: Himalayas.
Flowering time: Summer, northern hemisphere; spring, southern hemisphere.
Climatic zone: 5, 6, 7, 8, 9.
Dimensions: Up to 18 inches (450 mm) high.
Description: A very useful plant for a small garden, ruby cinquefoil is compact and colorful, its strawberry-like blooms flowering for many months. It looks effective in a border, when complementing *Gypsophila* and *Alyssum*. This pretty perennial will thrive in moderately moist soil of average

Potentilla atrosanguinea

fertility, providing it has full sun. This reason alone makes it a good choice for small, suburban gardens. Propagate it by division or seed in spring.
Other colors: Yellow.
Varieties/cultivars: 'Gibson's Scarlet', 'California'.

Potentilla nepalensis
NEPAL CINQUEFOIL ○

Family: ROSACEAE
Origin: Himalayas.
Flowering time: Summer, northern hemisphere; spring, southern hemisphere.
Climatic zone: 5, 6, 7, 8, 9.
Dimensions: Up to 18 inches (450 mm) high.
Description: This is a tufted herbaceous perennial which is a good front of border plant. The deep-green, serrated leaves accompany rose-red flowers with darker centers. It will flower profusely for many months during the spring or summer. Plant it in a border among phlox and primula for a pretty, cottage-garden look. It will flourish in ordinary soil in full sun, and is a good choice in a garden where the soil has been neglected.
Varieties/cultivars: 'Miss Wilmott', 'Roxana'.

Potentilla nepalensis 'Roxana'

Verbena x *hybrida*
ROSE VERVAIN, COMMON VERBENA (U.K.) ○

Family: VERBENACEAE
Origin: Hybrid.
Flowering time: Summer–autumn.
Climatic zone: 9, 10.
Dimensions: Up to 2 feet (600 mm) high.
Description: This pretty, spreading, border or groundcover plant will bloom for long periods. Densely packed flower heads set amid dark-green leaves give an effective display. There are many named varieties in a wide choice of colors. Usually grown as an annual, verbena will develop a compact habit if new shoots are pinched out. Remove dead flower heads to prolong the blooming period. Lower growing varieties look attractive, spilling over rock edges or walls. Grow the plant from seed or cutting.
Varieties/cultivars: 'Lawrence Johnston'.

Verbena x *hybrida* 'Lawrence Johnston'

Bauhinia galpinii syn. *B. punctata*
RED BAUHINIA (U.S.A.), ORCHID TREE, BUTTERFLY TREE ○

Family: LEGUMINOSAE
Origin: Tropical Africa.
Flowering time: Summer.
Climatic zone: 9, 10.
Dimensions: 6 feet (2 meters) high.
Description: During summer this shrub is a mass of brick-red flowers. The mid-green leaves have the appearance of a butterfly, hence the common name. For best results grow red bauhinia in a well-drained acid soil. A mulch of cow manure or a handful of complete plant food applied around the tree in early spring will ensure a good flower display. After flowering, the shrub is covered in masses of brown pea-like pods the seeds from which can be used for propagation.

Bauhinia galpinii

Begonia x *corallina*

Begonia x *corallina*
CORAL BEGONIA ○ ◑

Family: BEGONIACEAE
Origin: Hybrid.
Flowering time: Spring–autumn.
Climatic zone: 9, 10.
Dimensions: 8–10 feet (2–3 meters) high.
Description: A pretty free-flowering shrub having coral-red flowers and attractive foliage, coral begonia is an ideal shrub for a herbaceous garden. It can also be grown in a large tub on a patio or verandah. In cold climates, a greenhouse is required. A sheltered position is a must. Its main requirement is a well-drained soil that is enriched with animal manure or compost.

Other colors: Pink, white.

Calliandra tweedii
RED TASSEL FLOWER, FLAME BUSH, RED POWDERPUFF ○ ◑

Family: LEGUMINOSAE
Origin: Brazil.
Flowering time: Summer and again in autumn.
Climatic zone: 9, 10.
Dimensions: 6 feet (2 meters) high.
Description: This dense shrub is covered in numerous short branches and finely divided dark-green, fern-like foliage. The large rich-red flowers have a pompom-like appearance. Red tassel flower prefers a well-drained soil, but is adaptable to other soil types. Apply a mulch of manure or compost in spring. Where summers are hot keep well-watered. In cold climates a glasshouse is required. Prune, if necessary, after flowering has finished in autumn. This shrub makes an ideal feature plant.

Calliandra tweedii

Callistemon citrinus 'Endeavour'

Callistemon citrinus 'Endeavour'
CRIMSON BOTTLEBRUSH ○ ◑

Family: MYRTACEAE
Origin: Cultivar.
Flowering time: Spring.
Climatic zone: 9, 10.
Dimensions: 5 feet (approx. 2 meters) high.
Description: A hardy shrub in milder climates, crimson bottlebrush thrives in a wide range of soil types including sandy loam, clay and wet, soggy soil. Large, crimson, bottlebrush-like flowers cover it in spring. Pruning should be carried out if necessary as soon as the flowers fade and before new growth develops. Fertilize around the shrub with either an organic mixture or a mulch of cow manure. Crimson bottlebrush may be used in a shrub border or on its own as a specimen plant.

Callistemon citrinus 'Western Glory'

Callistemon citrinus 'Western Glory'
BOTTLEBRUSH ○

Family: MYRTACEAE
Origin: Cultivar.
Flowering time: Spring–summer.
Climatic zone: 9, 10.
Dimensions: 6–13 feet (2–4 meters) high.
Description: This bushy, medium-sized shrub, which has large spikes of deep mauve-pink flowers, can be used as a specimen shrub or screen plant in a warm climate garden. The flowers last quite well when picked and brought indoors for decoration. This bottlebrush will grow in any well-drained garden soil. Mulch around the base with cow manure or compost in spring. This will not only feed the plant, but keep the soil moist. Water well during summer.

Callistemon viminalis
WEEPING OR DROOPING BOTTLEBRUSH ○ ◑

Family: MYRTACEAE
Origin: Eastern Australia.
Flowering time: Summer and again in autumn.
Climatic zone: 9.
Dimensions: 20 feet (6 meters) high.
Description: An outstanding feature plant, this large shrub has an attractive weeping habit and during spring and autumn is covered in a profusion of bright-red flower spikes. The new leaf growth is an attractive bronze color.

Callistemon viminalis

Weeping bottlebrush is tolerant of most soils and makes an excellent screen plant. It prefers a mild climate but will tolerate some frost. Organic fertilizer applied in late spring and plenty of summer water speeds growth. It makes an excellent cut flower.
Varieties/cultivars: 'Captain Cook', 'Hannah Ray', 'Gawler', 'King's Park Special'.

Calycanthus floridus

Calycanthus floridus
COMMON SWEET SHRUB (U.S.A.), CAROLINA ALLSPICE (U.K.), STRAWBERRY SHRUB ○ ◑

Family: CALYCANTHACEAE
Origin: North America.
Flowering time: Spring–summer.
Climatic zone: 5, 6, 7, 8, 9.
Dimensions: 8–10 feet (2–3 meters) high.
Description: This is a hardy, deciduous shrub which prefers a position in partial shade, though in cold climates full sun is necessary to ensure flowering. When flowering, it is covered in attractive reddish-brown flowers. The soil should be rich and well-drained with compost or leaf mold added to it each other spring. Pruning out the old wood after flowering has finished helps to maintain this shrub's atttractive appearance. Common sweet shrub looks delightful when planted in a shrub border next to white flowering shrubs.

Cantua buxifolia
FLOWER-OF-THE-INCAS ○ ◑

Family: POLEMONIACEAE
Origin: Peru.
Flowering time: Spring–summer.
Climatic zone: 9, 10.
Dimensions: 6–10 feet (2–3 meters) high.
Description: A sparse, evergreen shrub, *Cantua buxifolia* has beautiful pendulous clusters of bright-rose or pale-red funnel-shaped flowers with an elongated tube. For best results, plant it in well-drained soil enriched with well-rotted compost or leaf mold. It requires at least half-sun and some protection from heavy frosts. In cooler climates, plant *Cantua buxifolia* against a warm sunny wall. Do not prune — this will ruin its shape.

Cantua buxifolia

Cestrum fasciculatum 'Newellii'
RED CESTRUM ○

Family: SOLANACEAE
Origin: Cultivar.
Flowering time: Spring–summer.
Climatic zone: 7, 8, 9.
Dimensions: 6–8 feet (2–3 meters) high.
Description: 'Newellii' is a seedling variant. The spectacular, bright orange-red, pitcher-shaped tubular flowers cover it in spring and summer. Grow it at the back of a shrub border or among other screening shrubs. The soil should be well-drained but enriched with organic matter such as compost or manure. A good soil will ensure quick growth. It can be easily propagated from cuttings taken in autumn or winter. In colder areas it can be grown on a sunny wall or in a conservatory.

Cestrum fasciculatum 'Newellii'

Chaenomeles japonica
DWARF FLOWERING QUINCE, JAPONICA, JAPANESE QUINCE (U.K.) ○ ◑ ●

Family: ROSACEAE
Origin: Japan.
Flowering time: Spring.
Climatic zone: 5, 6, 7, 8.
Dimensions: 3 feet (1 meter) high.
Description: Dwarf flowering quince is a low, spiny, deciduous shrub that spreads wider than its height. Bright orange-red flowers cover the plant before the leaves appear or just as they unfold. The hard, round apple-shaped yellow fruits are delightfully fragrant and make excellent jam or jelly. It is a very hardy shrub which will tolerate full shade or sun, and will thrive in any free-draining garden soil. It can be grown in city conditions, as it is tolerant of pollution. It is often used in hedges or in a shrub border.
Varieties/cultivars: 'Alpina'.

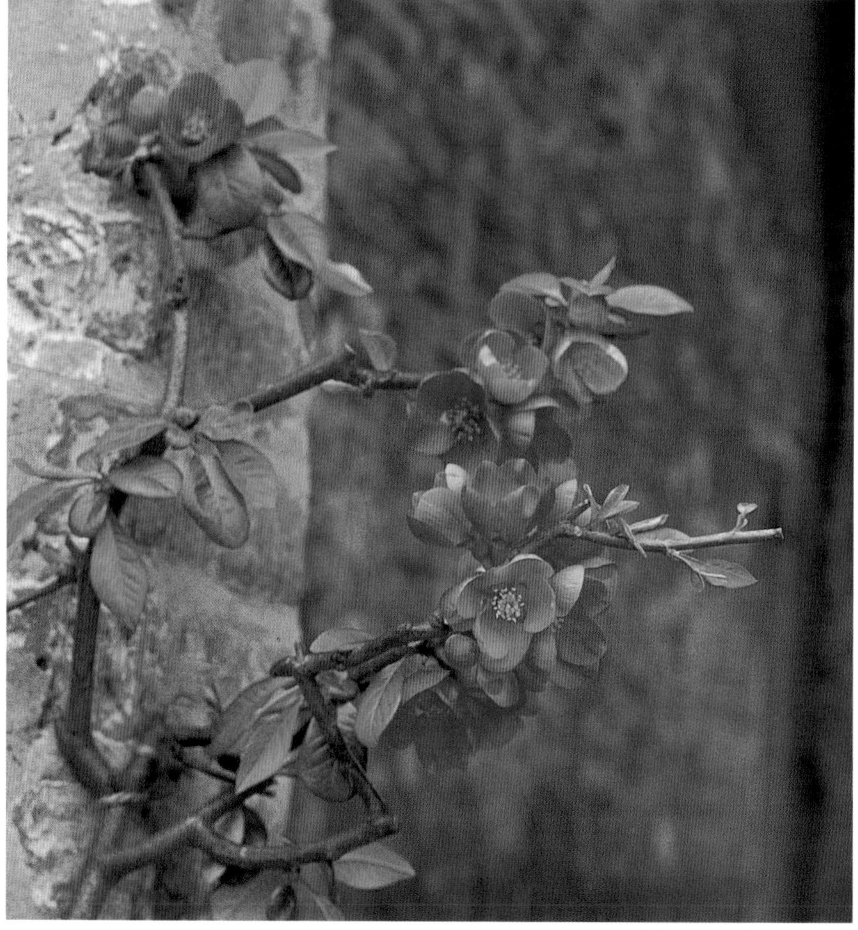

Chaenomeles japonica

Chaenomeles speciosa

JAPONICA, COMMON FLOWERING QUINCE (U.S.A.), FLOWERING OR JAPANESE QUINCE (U.K.) ○ ◑ ●

Family: ROSACEAE
Origin: China.
Flowering time: Spring.
Climatic zone: 5, 6, 7, 8.
Dimensions: 6–10 feet (2–3 meters) high.
Description: A delightful deciduous shrub, flowering quince has a wide, spreading, rounded habit with dark, glossy green foliage. When grown in milder climates it is only partly deciduous. The 2-inch (50 mm) wide flowers are scarlet to blood-red. Yellowish-green fruit, which makes excellent jam, follows the flowers. This hardy shrub will grow in any soil type as long as it is well-drained. Mulching with manure or compost in late winter ensures a good flower display.
Other colors: Deep crimson, pink and white, pink, white, orange, buff-coral, creamy-salmon, orange-red, creamy-apricot.
Varieties/cultivars: Numerous cultivars have been developed from this species.

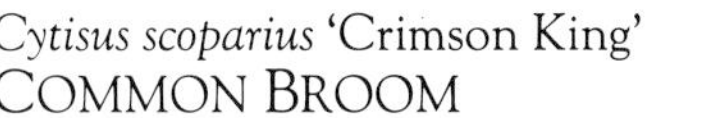

Chaenomeles speciosa 'Umbilicata'

Chorizema cordatum

HEART-LEAF FLAME PEA, FLAME PEA, CORAL PEA ○ ◑

Family: LEGUMINOSAE
Origin: Western Australia.
Flowering time: Late spring and summer.
Climatic zone: 9, 10.
Dimensions: 3–6 feet (1–2 meters) high.
Description: An attractive low-growing shrub, flame pea is used in rockeries as a specimen plant in hot climates. In colder areas, a greenhouse may be necessary. The small red and orange pea-shaped flowers, which are very bright, attractive, and abundant, cover the plant for nearly six months. The leaves are heart-shaped. Its main requirement is a well-drained, sandy soil. It is frost- and drought-resistant. Flame pea is easily propagated from seed, but these should be soaked in water that is near boiling point before they are sown.

Chorizema cordatum

Cytisus scoparius 'Crimson King'

COMMON BROOM ○

Family: LEGUMINOSAE
Origin: Hybrid.
Flowering time: Spring.
Climatic zone: 6, 7, 8, 9.
Dimensions: 4–9 feet (1–3 meters) high.
Description: 'Crimson King', a cultivar of *Cytisus scoparius* has magnificent true red flowers. It is extremely easy to cultivate, but prefers a well-drained soil. In warmer climates, pruning it back by at least half its height after flowering ensures a thicker shrub. In cool areas, pruning should be limited to avoid dieback. This is an ideal plant for a shrub or perennial border and looks magnificent if planted near white flowering plants. It is easily propagated from cuttings taken in early spring.

Cytisus scoparius 'Crimson King'

Euphorbia milii

Euphorbia milii
CROWN-OF-THORNS ○

Family: EUPHORBIACEAE
Origin: Madagascar.
Flowering time: Summer.
Climatic zone: 9, 10.
Dimensions: 3 feet (1 meter) high.
Description: Crown-of-thorns is a spiny, succulent shrub with brown, almost leafless stems and long, straight, tapering spines. The leaves are very sparse and appear at the ends of branches. The flowers themselves are inconspicuous but are surrounded by showy, bright scarlet bracts. In warm climates, the best location for the crown-of-thorns is in a large rockery or against a wall. A greenhouse location is essential in cold climates. Its needs are a hot position and a well-drained soil.

Feijoa sellowiana
FEIJOA, PINEAPPLE GUAVA (U.S.A.), FRUIT SALAD TREE ○

Family: MYRTACEAE
Origin: Brazil.
Flowering time: Summer.
Climatic zone: 8, 9, 10.
Dimensions: 5–20 feet (2–6 meters) high.
Description: This attractive ornamental shrub is grown for its crimson-and-white flowers and edible fruit. The leaves are gray-green with a white, felty underside. The dark-green fragrant fruits ripen in winter and, when mature, fall on the ground. They can be eaten raw or used in jam. Feijoa likes a well-drained soil but requires ample summer water for good fruit production. The fragrant petals can be eaten and look delightful sprinkled over the top of a salad. Not suited to areas where winters are severe.
Varieties/cultivars: 'Variegata', 'Gigantea', 'Coolidgei'.

Fuchsia magellanica
MAGELLAN FUCHSIA, COMMON FUCHSIA (U.K.) ○ ◑ ●

Family: ONAGRACEAE
Origin: Southern Chile, Argentina.
Flowering time: Summer–autumn.
Climatic zone: 7, 8, 9.
Dimensions: 6–10 feet (2–3 meters) high.
Description: This is a free-flowering shrub with long, arching branches and an abundance of pendant flowers. The flower sepals are bright crimson and the petals are purplish-blue. It can be used in a shrub border or as a hedge plant. The nodding flowers are very rich in honey, making this a valuable bird-attracting plant in the garden. It is easily propagated from cuttings taken in late summer or spring. For best results plant in a rich, free-draining soil.
Other colors: Scarlet and deep violet; white and mauve; white and pink.
Varieties/cultivars: 'Alba', 'Riccardo, 'Variegata', 'Gracilis'.

Fuchsia magellanica 'Gracilis'

Hibiscus schizopetalus
FRINGED HIBISCUS, JAPANESE HIBISCUS ○

Family: MALVACEAE
Origin: Tropical East Africa.
Flowering time: Spring–summer.
Climatic zone: 9, 10.
Dimensions: 5–10 feet (approx. 1½–3 meters) high.
Description: Fringed hibiscus is a pretty shrub with slender stems which usually require supporting. The orange-red pendant flowers have fringed, backward curving petals with long stamens projecting beyond them. Fringed hibiscus requires a warm, sheltered position and a rich, well-drained soil. It can be trained on a wall or trellis. In spring cut away any

Feijoa sellowiana

Hibiscus schizopetalus

unwanted growth, and shorten the stems and branches to within 5 inches (125 mm) of the base. It can be grown in a large pot or tub. In cool climates, it grows best in a greenhouse.

Lechenaultia formosa

LECHENAULTIA ○ ◑

Family: GOODENIACEAE
Origin: Western Australia.
Flowering time: Spring and summer.
Climatic zone: 9.
Dimensions: 11 inches (300 mm) high.
Description: This prostrate shrub is covered in small grayish-green leaves and an abundance of vermilion-red flowers in spring. It is variable in form and also flower color which can vary from white, yellow, pink, rose to any combination of these. Its main requirement is an extremely well-drained sandy soil. A rockery, especially one on a sloping site, is an ideal position, but in cooler climates a greenhouse is necessary.
Other colors: See description.
Varieties/cultivars: 'Scarlet O'Hara'.

Lechenaultia formosa 'Scarlet O'Hara'

Leonotis leonurus

LION'S EAR ○

Family: LABIATAE
Origin: South Africa.
Flowering time: Late summer–autumn.
Climatic zone: 9, 10.
Dimensions: 4–7 feet (approx. 1–2 meters) high.
Description: *Leonotis* is a pretty, square-stemmed plant with downy, dull-green leaves and showy spikes of orange-scarlet flowers. The name *Leonotis*, from *leon* (lion) and *otos* (ear), was given because the flower looks like a lion's ear. This fast-growing plant thrives in well-drained soil. A mulch of manure or compost in spring will ensure good flower production. Pruning can be carried out if required after the flowers have finished.

Leonotis leonurus

Leucospermum reflexum

ROCKET PINCUSHION ○

Family: PROTEACEAE
Origin: South Africa.
Flowering time: Spring.
Climatic zone: 9.
Dimensions: 6–10 feet (2–3 meters) high.
Description: This eye-catching shrub has downy, bluish-gray leaves and large orange-red flowerheads about 4 inches (100 mm) across. Good drainage is essential for the plant's success. It should not be planted where there is a heavy clay subsoil, as the excessive moisture retained will eventually rot the roots, causing plant collapse. During wet spring weather the new shoots will often rot and collapse. This is not a disease and does not occur when the weather is dry and hot.

Leucospermum reflexum.

Mussaenda frondosa
MUSSAENDA ○

Family: RUBIACEAE
Origin: Tropical Africa, Asia, Pacific islands.
Flowering time: Summer.
Climatic zone: 9, 10.
Dimensions: 3–6 feet (1–2 meters) high.
Description: The orange-yellow flowers of this shrub are actually quite inconspicuous, but they are surrounded by large white bracts which stay on the plant for a long time after the flowers have fallen. The combination of the soft-green leaves and the white bracts is very striking. Mussaenda thrives in warm coastal districts where the soil is free-draining. Plant it in a shrub border or use as a specimen plant. In colder climates, a greenhouse location is necessary. Feed it in early spring and water well during the summer months.

Mussaenda frondosa

Odontonema strictum syn. *Thyrsacanthus, Justicia coccinea*
RED JUSTICIA, FIERY SPIKE ○

Family: ACANTHACEAE
Origin: Tropical America.
Flowering time: Autumn.

Odontonema strictum

Climatic zone: 9, 10.
Dimensions: 8 feet (2–3 meters) high.
Description: A favorite plant for hot-climate gardens, it has large, glossy green leaves and spectacular scarlet flowers which open irregularly. It is often grown on patios in a large pot. Red justicia's main cultivation requirements are a rich soil, preferably with leaf mold added, and ample summer water. It is easily propagated from spring cuttings.

Protea grandiceps

Protea spp.
PROTEA ○

Family: PROTEACEAE
Origin: South Africa.
Flowering time: Depends on the species, but generally winter.
Climatic zone: 9, 10.
Dimensions: 2–10 feet (approx. 1–3 meters) high.
Description: There are many species of proteas. The flowers of *Protea pulchra* vary from deep ruby-red to salmon and pink. *Protea neriifolia* 'Taylors Surprise' has brilliant salmon-red flowers and *Protea nana* is renowned for its bright rosy-crimson to orange-red flowers. Proteas strongly resent over-rich soils and thrive in rather poor slightly acid soil that contains a lot of rubble or sand. Add sulfur to the soil if it is too alkaline. Avoid using phosphates. Do not overwater.
Other colors: Pink, white, green, cream.

Punica granatum
POMEGRANATE ○

Family: PUNICACEAE
Origin: Southwest Asia.
Flowering time: Summer.
Climatic zone: 8, 9.
Dimensions: 10–20 feet (3–6 meters) high.
Description: The new spring leaves of this large deciduous shrub are coppery in color before changing to a deep, shiny green. In autumn they turn a bright yellow. The orange-red flowers have a wrinkled appearance. The fruit needs a long hot summer before it develops properly. Pomegranate's main requirements are a hot position and a well-drained soil. It can be grown very successfully in large pots or tubs, or against a sunny wall. Feed with a complete plant food in spring.
Other colors: Scarlet-red, ruby-red, reddish-salmon.
Varieties/cultivars: 'Pleniflora', 'Spanish Ruby', 'Nana', 'Nana Plena', 'De Regina', 'Albo-plena'.

Punica granatum

Rhododendron x *gandavense*

Rhododendron x *gandavense*
GHENT AZALEA, DECIDUOUS AZALEA, MOLLIS AZALEA ○ ◑

Family: ERICACEAE
Origin: Hybrid.
Flowering time: Spring.
Climatic zone: 6, 7, 8, 9.
Dimensions: 5 feet (approx. 2 meters) high.
Description: This is a mixed race of hybrids, the result of crossing between *R. luteum* and several other species. Many are in the orange-red color range. The flowers are lightly perfumed and the shrub is slightly more twiggy than other deciduous azaleas. Ghent azaleas like a cool, acid soil which has been enriched with organic matter, preferably peat. They will grow in full sun in cool climates, but in temperate climates prefer partial shade.
Other colors: Pink, yellow.
Varieties/cultivars: There are numerous cultivars throughout the world.

Rhododendron Knap Hill

Rhododendron Knap Hill
DECIDUOUS AZALEA ○ ◑

Family: ERICACEAE
Origin: Hybrid.
Flowering time: Spring.
Climatic zone: 6, 7, 8, 9.
Dimensions: 3–9 feet (1–3 meters) high.
Description: Knap Hill hybrids originated in England in the early 1900s. They are valued for their orange-red color range. The leaves color in autumn before they drop. They like cool to cold climates and will grow in full sun in colder climates but perform just as well or better in dappled shade. A mulch of leaf mold or cow manure, applied around the base of the shrubs in spring, will keep the shallow roots moist and cool during summer.
Other colors: Yellow, gold, orange, scarlet, pink, white.
Varieties/cultivars: Numerous cultivars are available throughout the world.

Telopea speciosissima
NEW SOUTH WALES WARATAH ○ ◑

Family: PROTEACEAE
Origin: Australia (N.S.W.).
Flowering time: Spring.
Climatic zone: 9, 10.
Dimensions: 10 feet (3 meters) high.
Description: Very large, red flowers (3–6 inches, 80–150 mm in diameter) appear on this shrub during spring. The flowers are followed by long brown pods. Waratahs tend to respond to cultivation provided that the soil is acid and rainfall high. They always look more magnificent in a garden than in the wild. For best results feed only with organic fertilizers and prune rather hard to shape them after flowering. Waratahs attract birds to the garden as well as making superb feature plants. Keep well watered during summer.
Varieties/cultivars: 'Braidwood Brilliant'.

Telopea speciosissima

Brachychiton acerifolium
ILLAWARRA FLAME TREE, FLAME BOTTLE TREE (U.K.) ○

Family: STERCULIACEAE
Origin: Eastern Australia (coastal slopes).
Flowering time: Late spring–early summer.
Climatic zone: 9, 10.
Dimensions: 35–45 feet (11–14 meters) high.
Description: This tree is erratic in its flowering habit, but the blooms, which appear as a cloud of scarlet on bare wood, are a sight worth waiting for. Sometimes only one side of the tree will produce flowers. Good flowering seems to follow a dryish winter. It is mostly evergreen, but is deciduous on the flowering branches. The Illawarra flame tree flourishes in warm, coastal districts and is a popular garden tree. It does not suffer from any special pest or disease problems.

Brachychiton acerifolium

Callistemon viminalis 'Hannah Ray'
BOTTLEBRUSH ○

Family: MYRTACEAE
Origin: Cultivar
Flowering time: Spring and autumn, southern hemisphere; summer, northern hemisphere.
Climatic zone: 8, 9, 10.
Dimensions: 13 feet (4 meters) high x 6 feet (2 meters) wide.
Description: A cultivar of the weeping bottlebrush, this delightful, small, evergreen tree flowers for long periods and, like most bottlebrushes, will grow in very variable soil conditions, from poorly drained to well drained. Its long, brush-like, crimson flowers attract honey-eating birds. Young foliage is a pink color which later turns to green. Sawflies, which in some areas cluster on leaves and branches in warmer months, may be removed by hand.

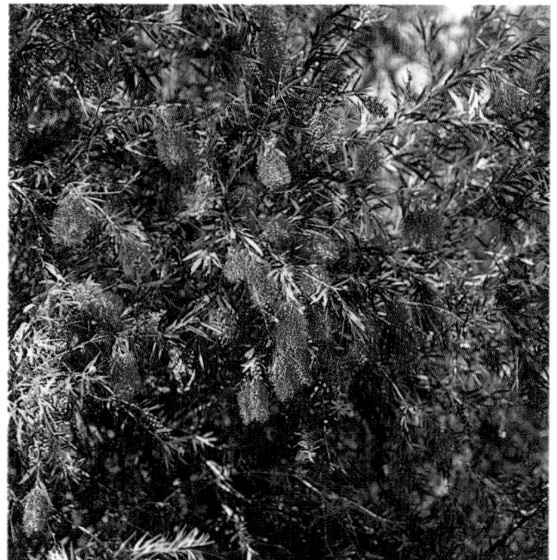
Callistemon viminalis 'Hannah Ray'

Ceratonia siliqua
CAROB BEAN, LOCUST ○

Family: CAESALPINACEAE
Origin: Eastern Mediterranean.
Flowering time: Spring, northern hemisphere; spring–autumn, southern hemisphere.
Climatic zone: 6, 7, 8, 9.
Dimensions: 15–30 feet (5–10 meters) high.
Description: This compact-growing tree is grown chiefly for the generous shade it affords in hot climates, and for the edible beans which follow the flowers in autumn, and which St. John the Baptist is believed to have eaten in the wilderness. Although slow growing in its native lands, it is more vigorous in cultivation. The leaves are dark green and leathery in texture, while the reddish flowers appear in small clusters close to the branches. Ideal for growing in hot and dry conditions, well-drained soil produces the best results. A male and female plant are required to produce the edible pods.

Ceratonia siliqua

Crataegus laevigata 'Paulii' syn. *C. oxyacantha* 'Paul's Scarlet'
DOUBLE RED HAWTHORN, MIDLAND HAWTHORN (U.K.), SCARLET THORN ○

Family: ROSACEAE
Origin: Cultivar
Flowering time: Spring–early summer.
Climatic zone: 5, 6, 7, 8, 9.
Dimensions: 16–20 feet (5–6 meters) high.
Description: A hardy little tree-cum-shrub, English hawthorn is smothered in gorgeous scarlet flowers in spring. Often used in the landscape as a hedge, the leaves turn yellow in autumn, and its dense, thorny growth gives protection even in winter when the leaves have dropped. It prefers a limestone soil, performs best in a cool climate, and is problem-free.

Crataegus laevigata 'Paulii'

Delonix regia
ROYAL POINCIANA (U.S.A.), PEACOCK FLOWER, FLAME TREE ○

Other common names: FLAMBOYANT TREE
Family: CAESALPINACEAE
Origin: Madagascar.
Flowering time: Summer.
Climatic zone: 9, 10.

Delonix regia

Dimensions: 40–50 feet (12–15 meters) high x 50–65 feet (15–20 meters) wide.
Description: Flamboyant by name, flamboyant by nature, *Delonix regia* flowers only in the warmest of climates or in a warm microclimate, when suddenly the whole canopy of the tree is covered in showy bunches of red flowers. Grown as a beautiful shade tree, the canopy often spreads to twice the width of the height. Leaves are similar to those of the blue-flowering jacaranda — lacy and bright green, almost evergreen. This tree is widely planted in Florida and tropical towns in Australia.
Other colors: Cream (rare).

Erythrina x *sykesii* syn. *E. indica, E. variegata*
COMMON CORAL TREE, SYKES'S CORAL TREE (U.K.) ○

Family: LEGUMINOSAE
Origin: Hybrid.
Flowering time: Late winter–early spring, northern hemisphere; mid-winter–late spring, southern hemisphere.
Climatic zone: 9, 10.
Dimensions: 40–60 feet (12–18 meters) high.
Description: Belonging to a large genus of over 100 species, the common coral tree is a familiar sight in both northern and southern hemispheres. Its brilliant red flowers are a welcome sight in winter as they appear on bare branches, the leaves following later. Sharp, fat prickles cover trunk and branches. A tree of generous proportions, with a wide canopy and a short trunk, it flourishes in coastal districts. It is often planted as a shade tree in large gardens, and in parks and car parks. It may also be grown in pots in a frost-free greenhouse though it does not flower in containers.
Other colors: White.
Varieties/cultivars: 'Alba', var. *orientalis*.

Erythrina x *sykesii*

Eucalyptus ficifolia
RED-FLOWERING GUM, SCARLET-FLOWERING GUM ○

Family: MYRTACEAE
Origin: Western Australia (southern coast).
Flowering time: Summer, northern hemisphere; late spring–summer, southern hemisphere.
Climatic zone: 9, 10.
Dimensions: 15–40 feet (8–12 meters) high.
Description: If planted in full sun with excellent drainage, this small tree will reward you with masses of fluffy, red flowers each year. Large gum nuts (the fruits), which follow, hang on the tree for a long time, and can be used as dried arrangements for the house. One of the most popular small eucalypts, it has found its way into coastal gardens of both hemispheres. It needs a sheltered position and mild winter climate.
Other colors: Color is variable.

Eucalyptus ficifolia

Eucalyptus leucoxylon 'Rosea'
WHITE IRONBARK ○

Family: MYRTACEAE
Origin: Cultivar.
Flowering time: Winter–late spring.
Climatic zone: 9, 10.
Dimensions: 30–45 feet (10–15 meters) high.
Description: White ironbark, which is a winter-flowerer, is popular in many home gardens and parks for its abundant, pretty rose-pink flowers and contrasting handsome bark. Its long-stalked buds with their pointed caps which are found in groups of three, make the tree readily identifiable. Although the bark is mainly smooth and yellowish, the tree is nevertheless classed as an ironbark rather than a smoothbark, because of the fibrous, persistent bark near the base. A medium-sized eucalypt, white ironbark adapts well to most soils and conditions.

Eucalyptus leucoxylon 'Rosea'

Euphorbia pulcherrima

Malus 'Profusion'

Euphorbia pulcherrima
CHRISTMAS STAR, POINSETTIA (U.K.) ○

Other common names: MEXICAN FLAMELEAF
Family: EUPHORBIACEAE
Origin: Tropical Mexico and Central America.
Flowering time: Winter–spring, northern hemisphere; late autumn–late spring, southern hemisphere.
Climatic zone: 9, 10.
Dimensions: 10–12 feet (3–4 meters) high.
Description: Brilliant red bracts surround the insignificant flowers of this world-popular plant. Grown outdoors, it needs a warm, sheltered position. Short days and long dark nights are necessary for good flowering. Commercial growers simulate these conditions in glasshouses to produce flowers over a very long period. Plant potted specimens outdoors in warm climates when the flowers have died. Cut back most of the stem after flowering and tip-prune a few weeks after new shoots appear. The stems are brittle and the milky sap is poisonous.
Other colors: Cream, pale pink.
Varieties/cultivars: 'Henrietta Eck', 'Annette Hegge' (dwarf).

Malus 'Profusion'
ORNAMENTAL CRAB APPLE, RED CRAB APPLE, FLOWERING CRAB APPLE (U.K.) ○

Family: ROSACEAE
Origin: Hybrid.
Flowering time: Early summer.
Climatic zone: 4, 5, 6, 7, 8, 9.
Dimensions: 6–20 feet (2–6 meters) high.
Description: As its name suggests, this delightful, small crab apple is one of the most free-flowering of all the crab apples, producing flowers when just a yearling. It belongs to a group of M. *niedzwetkyana* hybrids. Like most crab apples it is very hardy and is happy in most soils, given adequate humus. Mass-plant it or use along a driveway or pathway for a spectacular display of flower color in spring, and of brilliant crab apples in autumn.

Metrosideros excelsa
POHUTUKAWA (N.Z.), NEW ZEALAND CHRISTMAS TREE ○

Family: MYRTACEAE
Origin: New Zealand.
Flowering time: Summer, northern hemisphere; late spring–summer, southern hemisphere.
Climatic zone: 9, 10.
Dimensions: 30–60 feet (10–18 meters) high.
Description: *Metrosideros* is very much at home clinging to soil at the beach edge. This evergreen revels in salt-laden, windy, and exposed sites, and sports eye-catching, fluffy red flowers in time for Christmas in the southern hemisphere. It requires a cool, prolonged

Metrosideros excelsa

winter to flower well, and needs plenty of space to develop a wide crown from the short, stout trunk. It makes a good hedge or windbreak and will stand heavy pruning. Grow new plants from cuttings or seed.
Other colors: Creamy yellow.
Varieties/cultivars: 'Aurea'.

Prunus campanulata
TAIWAN CHERRY, BELL-FLOWER CHERRY, FORMOSAN CHERRY ○

Family: ROSACEAE
Origin: Taiwan and Ryuku Archipelago.
Flowering time: Late winter–early spring.
Climatic zone: 9.
Dimensions: 20–30 feet (6–8 meters) high.
Description: Pretty, carmine, bell-shaped flowers hang in small clusters from this deciduous, ornamental tree before the leaves appear. One of the reddest-flowered cherries, it is for a warm climate only. It is seldom grown in areas with late frosts, which damage the blossom and foliage. Its single trunk and wide canopy make for a splendid garden tree under which can be grown plants that enjoy dappled shade in summer and sun in winter.

Prunus campanulata

Prunus persica 'Magnifica'
DOUBLE RED-FLOWERING PEACH ○

Family: ROSACEAE
Origin: Cultivar.
Flowering time: Spring.
Climatic zone: 5, 6, 7, 8, 9.
Dimensions: 10–20 feet (3–6 meters) high.
Description: One of the best red-flowering cultivars, this tree comes into blossom in late spring. It has large, double, bright rosy-red flowers. In wet climates the disease peach leaf curl is a

Prunus persica 'Magnifica'

problem. Spray with bordeaux mixture each spring when flower buds swell or color up, to kill over-wintering fungus, or prune back the branches to about half their length immediately after flowering. Plant this tree to provide a canopy of color over spring-flowering shrubs and perennials.

Spathodea campanulata
WEST AFRICAN TULIP TREE, FOUNTAIN TREE, FLAME-OF-THE-FOREST ○

Family: BIGNONIACEAE
Origin: West Africa.
Flowering time: Early spring–late summer.
Climatic zone: 9, 10.
Dimensions: 30–60 feet (9–18 meters) high.
Description: Bold in every way, this tree will take your breath away at first sight. Handsome, evergreen, compound

Spathodea campanulata

leaves support the magnificent, scarlet-orange flowers that are borne in spikes just above them. The display lasts a long time as flowers open one after the other instead of en masse. The tree develops a broad dome. It thrives in warm coastal areas, but should be protected from strong, salt-laden winds. Plant it in fertile soil with good drainage. It can be easily grown from seed sown in spring in the glasshouse.

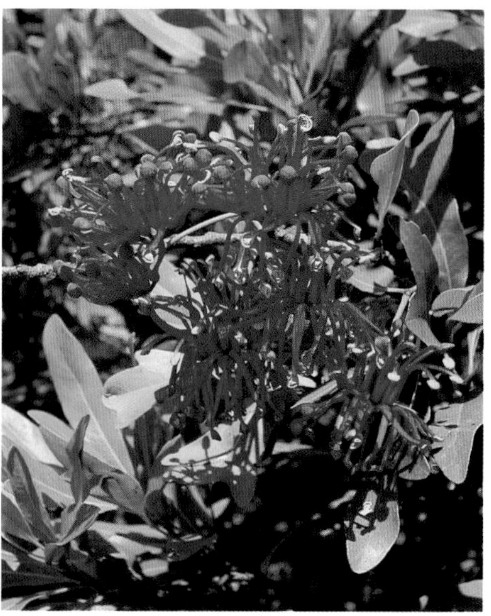

Stenocarpus sinuatus

Stenocarpus sinuatus
QUEENSLAND FIREWHEEL TREE ○

Family: PROTEACEAE
Origin: Australia (Queensland and N.S.W.).
Flowering time: Early autumn–mid-winter, southern hemisphere.
Climatic zone: 8, 9, 10.
Dimensions: 30–100 feet (10–30 meters) high.
Description: Not grown nearly as much as it deserves in Australia, it is often planted as a street tree in California, where it is well appreciated. Beautiful and interesting at every stage of its development, there is no other flower quite like this one, aptly described as a "wheel". The "spokes", or flower buds, arranged around a central hub, split open to expose the golden stamens within. A slow-growing, slender tree, it reaches in cultivation only half the height it attains in its native habitat. This evergreen can be grown in warm areas only.

SECTION TWO

Pink Flowers

Annuals 348

Bulbs 356

Climbers 358

Perennials 362

Shrubs 378

Trees 388

Agrostemma githago
CORN COCKLE

Family: CARYOPHYLLACEAE
Origin: Mediterranean region.
Flowering time: Summer.
Climatic zone: 3, 4, 5, 6, 7, 8, 9.
Dimensions: Up to 3 feet (1 meter) high.
Description: This is an erect, slender plant with narrow, grayish, hairy foliage. The rosy pink to magenta-colored flowers are on single stems and open flat to 2 inches (50 mm) wide. The corn cockle is still considered to be a weed in grain-growing areas where its flowers are prominent in the fields. In cultivation it is hardy, but it is of no use in floral work, as the flower folds towards evening. It needs a sunny, well-drained position.
Other colors: White, rose-purple, lilac-pink.
Varieties/cultivars: 'Milas' (flowers are 3 inches (75 mm) wide, 'Purple Queen'.

Agrostemma githago

Begonia semperflorens
WAX BEGONIA

Family: BEGONIACEAE
Origin: Brazil.
Flowering time: Spring–summer–autumn.
Climatic zone: 4, 5, 6, 7, 8, 9, 10.
Dimensions: Up to 12 inches (300 mm) high.
Description: This is a tender summer annual or perennial which flowers continuously in warmth. The flowers, though small — up to 1 inch (25 mm) wide — are produced in clusters on a stiff, succulent stem. Begonias are used for borders or massed bedding with contrasting colors of foliage and flowers. The leaves may be deep bronze to bright green according to variety. Plant in rich, well-drained soil, but allow soil to dry out a little between waterings.
Other colors: White, red.
Varieties/cultivars: 'Thousand Wonders', 'Comet'.

Begonia semperflorens

Bellis perennis
COMMON OR LAWN DAISY, ENGLISH DAISY

Family: COMPOSITAE
Origin: Europe–western Asia.
Flowering time: Spring–summer.
Climatic zone: 6, 7, 8, 9.
Dimensions: Up to 4 inches (100 mm) high.
Description: This is the original daisy. The flowers are up to 1 inch (25 mm) wide, and are double in form. They are formed on a single stem and protrude from the basal leaves, which are shiny green and in the form of a rosette. The plant may be used as an attractive edging in cooler gardens. It will not stand continued hot sun. Although usually grown as an annual, it may be perennial. Rich, moist soil conditions are essential for success.
Other colors: White, rosy-red.
Varieties/cultivars: 'Montrosa' (larger heads of flowers, red), 'Rosea' (rose-pink), 'Prolifera' (secondary heads on the stem).

Callistephus chinensis
CHINA ASTER

Family: COMPOSITAE
Origin: China, Japan.
Flowering time: Summer–early autumn.
Climatic zone: 4, 5, 6, 7, 8, 9.
Dimensions: Up to 2 feet (600 mm) high.
Description: This is one of the best garden plants for floral art. The stiff stems may branch to form up to six flowers on each. The flowers, up to 5 inches (125 mm) wide, are many-petaled and double. The plant is subject to wilt which may weaken it considerably and suddenly. For healthy asters, ensure

Bellis perennis cultivar

that soil is light and sandy. Add lime if pH levels are acid.
Other colors: White, blue, violet.
Varieties/cultivars: 'Princess' (larger than average flowers), 'King' (more branches), 'Seven Dwarfs' (low variety).

Callistephus chinensis

Celosia cristata
CRESTED CELOSIA ○

Family: AMARANTHACEAE
Origin: Tropical Asia.
Flowering time: Summer.
Climatic zone: 5, 6, 7, 8, 9, 10.
Dimensions: Up to 2 feet (600 mm) high.
Description: This erect plant forms upright flowers which look like woolly feathers in terminal spikes. Their vibrant colors make them a good summer annual for hot and dry conditions. The leaves may also be variegated in red and gold colors. The flowers, in their crested shape, may be up to 6 inches (150 mm) wide and brilliant in color. They are very suitable for large displays in parks. Celosia thrives in rich, well-drained soil that is kept constantly moist.
Other colors: Yellow, orange, red, and occasionally, white and purple.
Varieties/cultivars: 'Forest Fire', 'Golden Triumph' 'Fairy Fountain' (dwarf, mixed colors, 12 inches (300 mm) high).

Celosia cristata

Clarkia unguiculata

Clarkia unguiculata syn. *Clarkia elegans*
CLARKIA (U.K.), GARLAND FLOWER ○

Family: ONAGRACEAE
Origin: California.
Flowering time: Summer.
Climatic zone: 4, 5, 6, 7, 8, 9, 10.
Dimensions: Up to 2 feet (600 mm) high.
Description: This erect, hardy annual produces many flowers on stiff stems. The rose-pink flowers have four petals, widening at the outer edge, and up to 2 inches (50 mm) across when open. The cut flowers are good for indoor decoration. Excellent for poor, sandy soils — in fact, avoid using too much humus as flowers will be overwhelmed by foliage.
Other colors: Red, lavender, salmon, purple.
Varieties/cultivars: Single and double cultivars available.

Cleome hassleriana syn. *C. pungens*, *C. spinosa*
SPIDER FLOWER ○

Family: CAPPARIDACEAE
Origin: West Indies, Brazil–Argentina.
Flowering time: Summer.
Climatic zone: 4, 5, 6, 7, 8, 9, 10.
Dimensions: Up to 5 feet (1–1½ meters) high.
Description: In the right climate, this annual can be a commanding background to lower-growing annuals. The long, clawed petals, and extended stamens of the flowers, give them their spider-like appearance. The flowers are clustered to form large heads up to 5 inches (125 mm) across, in pale pink, almost white colors, with overtones of deeper pink and mauve. Cleome is a good flower for large, open areas such as parks and needs plenty of space, as each plant is quite wide. Warm conditions are essential. Water well.

Cleome hassleriana

Clarkia amoena
GODETIA ○

Family: ONAGRACEAE
Origin: Western North America, Chile.
Flowering time: Summer.
Climatic zone: 4, 5, 6, 7, 8, 9.
Dimensions: Up to 2 feet (600 mm) high.
Description: A delightful annual from California, previously classified as Godetia, this plant has graceful spikes of showy, pale pink or lavender to white flowers, measuring 2 inches (50 mm) across. Foliage is lance-shaped and toothed. The slender, erect habit of this annual makes it an ideal cut flower or useful pot plant for a cool greenhouse. Plant it in an open, sunny position in well-drained, humus-rich soil and ensure adequate water during spring growth and the summer flowering period.

Clarkia amoena

Cosmos bipinnatus
COMMON OR GARDEN COSMOS ◑

Family: COMPOSITAE
Origin: Mexico.
Flowering time: Summer–autumn.

Cosmos bipinnatus

Climatic zone: 4, 5, 6, 7, 8, 9, 10.
Dimensions: Up to 6 feet (2 meters) high.
Description: Cosmos is a tall annual, well suited as a background in a cottage garden. The plant produces many flowers which are suitable for use indoors. The foliage is fern-like, providing an attractive background for the flowers, which are flat, open, and up to 2½ inches (65 mm) wide with yellow centers. Cosmos will thrive in most soils, preferring light, dry conditions.
Other colors: Red, white, deep mauve.
Varieties/cultivars: 'Mammoth Single', 'Bright-lights' (double flowers), 'Alba'.

Dianthus chinensis syn. *D. sinensis*
CHINA PINK, INDIAN PINK ○

Family: CARYOPHYLLACEAE
Origin: Eastern Asia.
Flowering time: Summer–autumn in cooler climates.
Climatic zone: 6, 7, 8, 9, 10.
Dimensions: Up to 18 inches (450 mm) high.
Description: This is a semi-hardy annual or short-lived perennial and may behave as a biennial. The semi-double flowers, which are up to 2 inches (50 mm) wide, have attractive, tooth-edged petals. They may be on single stems or loosely clustered and are only faintly fragrant. A neutral to limey soil is important and it should also be light, sandy and well-drained.
Other colors: White, lilac, red.
Varieties/cultivars: *D. c.* var. *Heddewigii*

Dianthus chinensis var. *Heddewigii*

Gomphrena globosa
GLOBE AMARANTH ○

Family: AMARANTHACEAE
Origin: Tropical Asia.
Flowering time: Midsummer–early autumn.
Climatic zone: 4, 5, 6, 7, 8, 9, 10.
Dimensions: Up to 18 inches (450 mm) high.
Description: This very low-growing, dense, annual plant likes a warm, dry climate. It is tough and needs no special soil conditions. It has a rounded, bushy habit, the flowers borne on slender stalks that protrude slightly from the edge of the foliage. The tight, clover-like flower heads are up to 1 inch (25 mm) in diameter. When cut, the flowers last well and are suitable for small arrangements and posies; they also dry well. Mulch in summer.
Other colors: Red, white, orange, purple. Variegated flowers are sometimes seen.
Varieties/cultivars: 'Rubra'.

Gomphrena globosa

Impatiens balsamina
COMMON OR GARDEN BALSAM 

Family: BALSAMINACEAE
Origin: India–Malaya.
Flowering time: Summer.
Climatic zone: 4, 5, 6, 7, 8, 9, 10.
Dimensions: Up to 12 inches (300 mm) high.
Description: This is a tender annual that thrives in warm shade. The stiff stems are somewhat brittle and may easily suffer wind damage. The flowers are single or double and up to 2 inches (50 mm) wide. They are long-lasting on the plant and quickly replaced, but they have no value as a cut flower. Choose a good fertile soil that does not dry out and pinch back to encourage more bushy growth.

Other colors: Scarlet, yellow, white, purple. May be occasionally striped.
Varieties/cultivars: Double-flowered types are often called 'Camellia-flowered'.

Impatiens balsamina cultivar

Impatiens walleriana

BUSY LIZZY, PATIEN LUCY, SULTANA

Family: BALSAMINACEAE
Origin: Tanzania, Mozambique.
Flowering time: Warm months, but may flower all year.
Climatic zone: 5, 6, 7, 8, 9, 10.
Dimensions: Up to 2 feet (600 mm) high.
Description: This brittle-stemmed perennial is often grown as an annual. It thrives in warm, shaded areas where it is possible for it to flower most of the year. The flowers are up to 2 inches (50 mm) wide on single stems, and open flat. They have four petals, which are broad at the edge and curve slightly downwards. It is possible to use this plant for tubs and baskets and also to bring it indoors as a house plant. Water well in hot weather, and mulch with well-rotted compost for good results.
Other colors: Red, purple, orange, white.
Varieties/cultivars: There are double forms, also 'Nana' (dwarf-growing), and 'Variegata' (foliage variegated white).

Impatiens walleriana cultivar

Lathyrus odoratus cultivar

Lathyrus odoratus

SWEET PEA ○

Family: LEGUMINOSAE
Origin: Southern Italy, Sicily.
Flowering time: Summer–early autumn.
Climatic zone: 6, 7, 8, 9, 10.
Dimensions: Climbing plant to 6 feet (2 m) high.
Description: The sweet pea, with its delightful fragrance, is one of the most popular of plants, both for background planting in the garden and as a cut flower for floral use. Up to seven of the large, pea-like blooms, which are about 2 inches (50 mm) wide, are borne on a long, stiff stem. They appear in various shades of both bright and subtle colors. Being a tendril-climber, sweet pea needs the support of wires, strings, or a lattice. Add lime, and blood and bone to the soil prior to planting, and water well until plants are established.
Other colors: White, purple, red.
Varieties/cultivars: There are many cultivars of the above, some with large flowers, and very long stems. 'Bijou' is a dwarf variety, also used for bedding. Some varieties are early flowering and heat resistant.

Lavatera trimestris

ANNUAL MALLOW ○

Family: MALVACEAE
Origin: Mediterranean region, Portugal.
Flowering time: Early spring–autumn.
Climatic zone: 4, 5, 6, 7, 8, 9, 10.
Dimensions: Up to 3 feet (1 meter) tall.
Description: This plant likes well-drained soil and flowers best in the cooler months in a warm climate. The leaves are slightly hairy and almost round in shape with clear, ribbed veins. The flowers, which are mostly solitary on the outside of the plant, are as large as the leaf — up to 4 inches (100 mm) wide — and open flat.
Other colors: Shades of red and white.
Varieties/cultivars: 'Loveliness' (satiny, rose-pink), 'Splendens' (rose-red and occasionally white), 'Silver Cup'.

Lavateria trimestris 'Silver Cup'

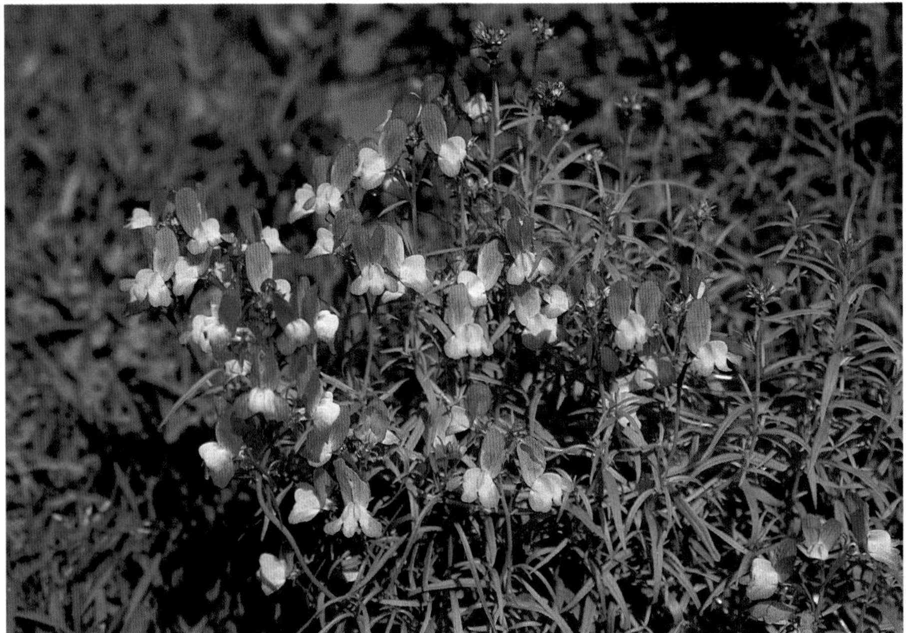
Linaria maroccana

Linaria maroccana
TOADFLAX, BABY SNAPDRAGON, FAIRY FLAX ○

Family: SCROPHULARIACEAE
Origin: Morocco.
Flowering time: Spring.
Climatic zone: 6, 7, 8, 9, 10.
Dimensions: 12–18 inches (300–450 mm) high.
Description: This low-growing annual is mostly used as a border plant near other low-growing annuals. It should be densely planted to make a show of the delicate, small flowers, which are about 1 inch (25 mm) long and ½ inch (15 mm) wide and look like miniature snapdragons with a long spur. They are found only in soft, pastel shades and most of them have a yellow-spotted throat. Any well-drained soil will suffice, but take care not to overwater.
Other colors: Red, purple, and occasionally dark-blue.
Varieties/cultivars: 'Excelsior', 'Fairy Bouquet' (dwarf).

Linum grandiflorum
SCARLET FLAX ○

Family: LINACEAE
Origin: North Africa.
Flowering time: Summer.
Climatic zone: 6, 7, 8, 9, 10.
Dimensions: Up to 18 inches (450 mm) tall.
Description: This is a slender and gracefully erect plant, which is very tolerant and produces wide, open flowers at the stem tips. It may grow in poor soil but prefers a moderately fertile one and will flower throughout the season. It will not persist in extremes of heat. Flowers are up to 1½ inches (40 mm) wide.
Other colors: Scarlet, purple, red.
Varieties/cultivars: 'Coccineum' (scarlet), 'Caeruleum' (bluish-purple), 'Roseum' (rose pink), 'Rubrum' (deep-red).

Linum grandiflorum

Lunaria annua
HONESTY, MOONWORT, MONEYPLANT ◑

Other common names: SATINFLOWER, PENNY FLOWER, SILVER DOLLAR
Family: CRUCIFERAE
Origin: Mediterranean region.
Flowering time: Spring–summer.
Climatic zone: 7, 8, 9, 10.
Dimensions: Up to 3 feet (900 mm) high.
Description: Although this plant is grown principally for its dried seed casing, it does bear an attractive head of small purplish-pink flowers. When these flowers fall and the seed pods appear, it presents quite a different appearance. The seed pods are flat, broadly oval to almost circular, 1½–2½ inches (40–60 mm) long. When ripe, the walls of the pod fall away to reveal a central silvery membrane which glows with a pearly lustre. In this silvery pearly form, the plant lasts indefinitely indoors and is an excellent decoration. Most soils are suitable providing drainage is adequate.
Other colors: White.
Varieties/cultivars: 'Alba', 'Variegata'.

Lunaria annua

Malcolmia maritima
VIRGINIA STOCK ○

Family: CRUCIFERAE
Origin: Greece, Albania.
Flowering time: Early summer–autumn.
Climatic zone: 6, 7, 8, 9, 10.
Dimensions: Up to 10 inches (250 mm) high.
Description: Virginia stock is a hardy annual for cool to warm climates. The plant is low-growing and bushy which makes it ideal as an annual border for taller annuals and perennials. It is a good bedding plant for massing between shrubs. The flowers, which are only ¾ inch (19 mm) wide, are found in clusters in terminal racemes. Their sweet

Malcolmia maritima

fragrance is reminiscent of stock. Matures quickly if planted in a warm, sunny position, in rich, well-drained soil.
Other colors: Red, purple, white.

Matthiola incana
STOCK, BROMPTON STOCK, GILLYFLOWER ○

Family: CRUCIFERAE
Origin: Mediterranean region.
Flowering time: Spring.
Climatic zone: 7, 8, 9.
Dimensions: Up to 2½ feet (750 mm) high.
Description: Stock is much sought after. With its excellent, lasting qualities, good color range, and delightful fragrance, it is ideal for floral decoration. Varieties produce long (up to 18 inches (450 mm)) stems of tight, either single or double flowers. The single flowers have the stronger perfume, but the doubles are more showy. Individual flowers are only 1 inch (25 mm) wide but there are many of them on strong upright stems. The plant may be grown as either an annual or a biennial. The soil should be enriched with lime and plenty of organic matter before planting. Water well for good results.
Other colors: White, yellow, purple, red.
Varieties/cultivars: 'Perfection', 'Hi-double' (Trisomic), 'Giant Column' (tall heads of flowers), 'Austral' (slightly dwarf to 18 inches (450 mm)), 'Dwarf' (up to 12 inches (300 mm) high).

Matthiola incana cultivar

Petunia x *hybrida*
PETUNIA ○

Family: SOLANACEAE
Origin: Hybrid.
Flowering time: Summer.
Climatic zone: 6, 7, 8, 9, 10.
Dimensions: Up to 18 inches (450 mm) high.
Description: The petunia in any one of its many forms is the most universally known and widely used annual in the world. It is an asset anywhere with bright summer colors in all shades. The flowers are up to 4 inches (100 mm) wide, rather flat, but sometimes fringed and frilled on the edges. They are often striped in lines from the center or in contrasting-colored circles. They may also have contrasting vein markings. The plants have soft stems and may trail, which makes them attractive in hanging baskets or bowls in good sunlight. Fertile soil and a sunny position are essential.
Other colors: All colours, including white, yellow, and mixtures of these.
Varieties/cultivars: 'Bonanza', 'Dazzler', 'Color Parade', 'Giant Victorious', 'Fringed', and many others.

Petunia x *hybrida* cultivar

Phlox drummondii
ANNUAL PHLOX, DRUMMOND PHLOX, TEXAN PRIDE ○

Family: POLEMONIACEAE
Origin: Texas.
Flowering time: Summer.
Climatic zone: 6, 7, 8, 9, 10.
Dimensions: Up to 18 inches (450 mm) high.
Description: This is a popular summer annual which grows readily in sunny situations. The separate flowers are up to 1½ inches (35 mm) wide and make a vivid show because they are closely clustered. All colors are available as well as fringed bicolors or contrasting centers. Generally phlox is not used as a cut flower, but lasts well enough to be used in small posies or bowls. Light, dry, and well-drained soils give the best results. Take care not to overwater.
Other colors: All colors and mixtures.
Varieties/cultivars: 'Compact' (dwarf form), 'Twinkle' (star-like), 'Bright Eyes', 'Derwent'.

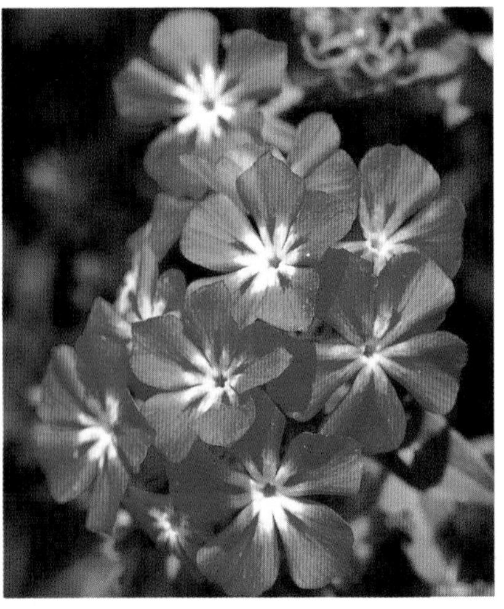

Phlox drummondii

Portulaca grandiflora
ROSE MOSS, SUN MOSS, WAX PINK ○

Other common names: SUN PLANT, GARDEN PORTULACA
Family: PORTULACACEAE
Origin: Brazil–Argentina.
Flowering time: Midsummer.
Climatic zone: 6, 7, 8, 9, 10.
Dimensions: Up to 5 inches (125 mm) high.
Description: Portulacas have soft, succulent stems and a trailing habit, and can be used as groundcover or a border. The flowers, which are about 1½ inches (35 mm) wide, and may be single or double, are borne on short stems and are found in bright, clear colors with, occasionally, tiny, contrasting-colored centers. They open in the heat of the day and close at night or in cloudy conditions. Portulacas prefer hot, dry climates.
Other colors: White, yellow, red, purple.
Varieties/cultivars: 'Sunglow', 'Sunnybank'.

Portulaca grandiflora cultivar

Schizanthus pinnatus
BUTTERFLY FLOWER, POOR MAN'S ORCHID ◑

Family: SOLANACEAE
Origin: Chile.
Flowering time: Spring–summer.
Climatic zone: 7, 8, 9.
Dimensions: Up to 3 feet (approx. 1 meter) high.
Description: This lovely, soft-stemmed plant forms an erect, dense, compact mass of pale-green foliage which is ferny in appearance and attractive. It prefers a cool, sheltered position and produces masses of small flowers up to 1 inch (25 mm) wide in pastel tonings with vein-like markings and a contrasting-colored rim. The flowers have an upper and lower lip shaped like a small orchid. They are very decorative in hanging baskets, but are not ideal for picking. Plant in semishade in rich, moist, and well-drained soil. Pinch back new growth to encourage more blooms. Depending on the climate, this plant suits either a summer garden bed or a greenhouse.
Other colors: White, red, mauve, cream.
Varieties/cultivars: 'Dwarf Bouquet', 'Giant Hybrid', 'Hit Parade'.

Silene pendula
NODDING CATCHFLY ○

Family: CARYOPHYLLACEAE
Origin: Mediterranean region–Caucasus, southern U.S.S.R.
Flowering time: Summer.
Climatic zone: 6, 7, 8, 9.
Dimensions: Up to 18 inches (300 mm) high.
Description: This hardy annual is not freely grown. It forms a bushy, densely-leaved plant which bears clusters of small flowers up to 1 inch (25 mm) wide.

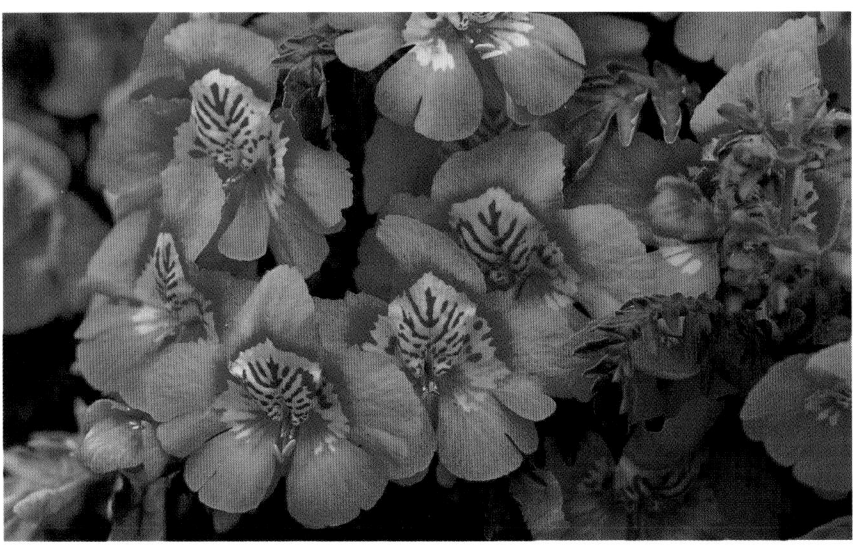

Schizanthus pinnatus

The flower heads are not dense and although delicate in appearance, they are hardy. Can be grown successfully in a wide range of soils, providing drainage is good.
Other colors: Carmine, occasionally white.
Varieties/cultivars: 'Ruberrima Bonnettii', 'Compacta'.

Silene pendula

Viola x *wittrockiana*
PANSY, HEARTSEASE, LADIES' DELIGHT ○

Family: VIOLACEAE
Origin: Hybrid.
Flowering time: Spring–winter.
Climatic zone: 6, 7, 8, 9.
Dimensions: Up to 9 inches (225 mm) high.
Description: Pansies are one of the best known of the annual, flowering plants. The foliage spreads to about 12 inches (30 mm) wide, from which single-stemmed flowers appear face-up. They are available in all shades, in separate colors or with contrasting marks and veining. The flat flowers have four petals in opposite, overlapping pairs. They are suitable for posies or small vases and bloom for a long period. Pansies often have a very velvety texture, and prefer semishaded conditions and a moderately rich, moist soil.
Other colors: Purple, blue, maroon, red, yellow, orange, white.
Varieties/cultivars: 'Can Can', 'Roggli', 'Swiss Giants', 'Jumbo'.

Viola x *wittrockiana* cultivar

Xeranthemum annuum
EVERLASTING, ANNUAL EVERLASTING, IMMORTELLE ○

Family: COMPOSITAE
Origin: Southeastern–central Europe.
Flowering time: Summer.
Climatic zone: 7, 8, 9, 10.
Dimensions: Up to 2 feet (600 mm) high.
Description: This very hardy annual will grow in poor soil, produce many single-stemmed flowers typically daisy-like in shape, but with shiny, papery petals and a firm seed center. The flowers cover the bushes although, individually, they are only up to 1½ inches (40 mm) wide. They are very useful as cut flowers and dry well also.
Other colors: White, mauve, purple.
Varieties/cultivars: 'Ligulosum'.

Xeranthemum annuum

Amaryllis belladonna

Cyclamen neapolitanum

Amaryllis belladonna
BELLADONNA LILY, NAKED LADY ○

Family: AMARYLLIDACEAE
Origin: South Africa.
Flowering time: Summer–autumn.
Climatic zone: 8, 9, 10.
Dimensions: Up to 3 feet (1 meter) high.
Description: Named after a shepherdess in Greek mythology, this legendary plant has numerous fragrant trumpet-shaped flowers borne on long stems. Strap-shaped leaves usually appear after the plant blooms. If left undisturbed in a sheltered position, bulbs will multiply and give a massed display. It is suitable for borders along a gravel drive or against sunny fences. Cut flowers add elegance indoors. Water well when buds appear. Belladonna lily can be cultivated in pots for indoor display.
Varieties/cultivars: 'Rubra'.

Anemone nemorosa
WOOD ANEMONE, FAIRY'S WINDFLOWER ◑

Family: RANUNCULACEAE
Origin: Europe including U.K.
Flowering time: Spring.
Climatic zone: 5, 6, 7, 8.

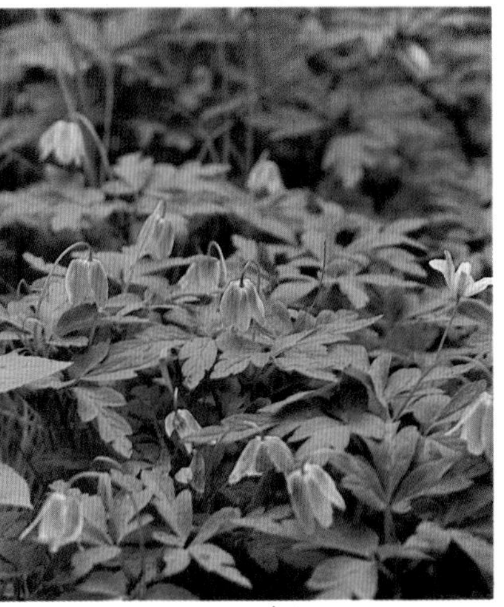

Anemone nemorosa

Dimensions: Up to 12 inches (300 mm) high.
Description: This pretty, pink perennial is a delightful flower to associate with ferns and primroses and will spread rapidly in woodland settings. The flowers are solitary with 6 sepals. Moist soil in a protected position suits it best. It will do well near water features in the garden.
Other colors: Blue, white.
Varieties/cultivars: 'Wilkes white', 'Flore Pleno'.

Cyclamen neapolitanum syn. *C. hederifolium*
ROCK CYCLAMEN, COMMON CYCLAMEN (U.K.), SOWBREAD ◑

Family: PRIMULACEAE
Origin: Southern Europe.
Flowering time: Late summer–autumn.
Climatic zone: 7, 8, 9.
Dimensions: Up to 4 inches (100 mm) high.
Description: Rock cyclamen, with its unusual rose or white petals turned backwards to resemble shuttlecocks, was used in ancient times as an ingredient in love potions. Most of the flowers are produced before the deep green and silver leaves fully expand, the first flowers appearing in late summer before any leaf shows. This cyclamen will flower for up to eight weeks. A pretty addition to a fernery it can also be grown indoors in pots. Use fertilizer sparingly. Some bulbs have been known to produce for over 100 years. Allow it to colonize in light shade beneath trees or in garden pockets. Avoid excessive use of water.
Other colors: White, purple, red.

Lilium rubellum
LILY ○

Family: LILIACEAE
Origin: Japan.
Flowering time: Early–midsummer.
Climatic zone: 6, 7, 8, 9.
Dimensions: Up to 2 feet (600 mm) high.
Description: This oriental hybrid produces clusters of fragrant, pink flowers. It can be planted among herbaceous perennials or in lightly wooded areas. Water settings can be enhanced by including it among stones or pebbles. Adaptable to most good,

well-drained soils, it prefers an open sunny position. Light frosts will not affect it adversely, but it is sensitive to drought and excessive feeding. Large tubs of lilies look particularly effective at the entrance to a house or by the gate.

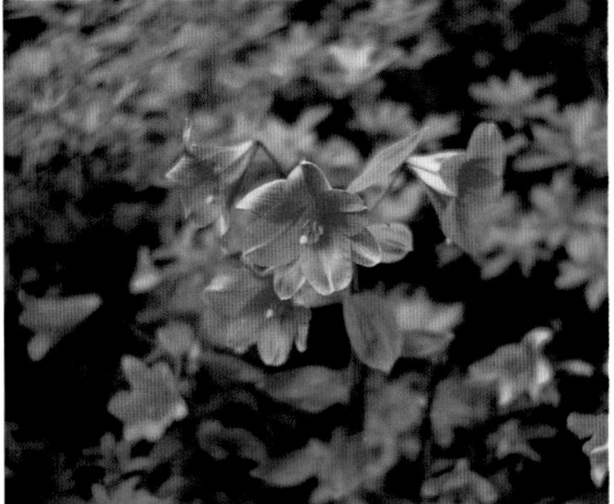

Lilium rubellum

Nerine bowdenii
SPIDER LILY ○

Family: AMARYLLIDACEAE
Origin: South Africa.
Flowering time: Autumn.
Climatic zone: 7, 8, 9.
Dimensions: Up to 18 inches (450 mm) high.
Description: A hardy grower with eight or more tubular flowers produced on long stems, spider lily is ideally suited for planting in rock gardens, near water, in tubs on patios or verandahs. The graceful spider-like flowers enhance trees when grown at their base. After bulbs have been planted they should be left undisturbed for several years until clumps form. They benefit from an application of general fertilizer in spring. Maintain adequate moisture.
Other colors: Red.
Varieties/cultivars: 'Pink Beauty', 'Hera', 'Fenwick's Variety'.

Nerine bowdenii

Oxalis adenophylla
MOUNTAIN SOURSOP, WOOD SORREL (U.S.A.), OXALIS ◑

Family: OXALIDACEAE
Origin: Chile and Argentina.
Flowering time: Summer, outdoors; winter, indoors.
Climatic zone: 8, 9.
Dimensions: Up to 4 inches (100 mm) high.
Description: *Oxalis* is often overlooked as a garden flower because of its weed reputation. *O. adenophylla* is not a weed, but a pretty, long-flowering perennial adaptable to rock gardens, pot culture, and window boxes. Softly colored, gray-green crinkled leaves accompany pale lilac/pink flowers. Although termed wood sorrel, this is not one for making soup from. Like many of the 800 species of *Oxalis*, this plant has a sour juice when extracted. Grow it in a cool situation in neutral or slightly alkaline soil. It can be grown indoors in winter.
Other colors: Red, purple, yellow, white.

Oxalis adenophylla

Primula malacoides
FAIRY PRIMROSE ◑

Family: PRIMULACEAE
Origin: China.
Flowering time: Spring.
Climatic zone: 8.
Dimensions: Up to 18 inches (450 mm) high.
Description: Associated with the arrival of spring, this plant will thrive in wooded situations or in the vicinity of water gardens and is a versatile plant for pots, edges, borders, rock gardens, and window boxes. *P. malacoides* flowers in various shades of rose and lavender to pure white. It prefers a moist, cool position with some sun. In colder climates, a greenhouse is essential. Propagation is by seed or division.
Other colors: White, red, purple.

Primula malacoides

Rhodohypoxis baurii
ROSE GRASS ○

Family: HYPOXIDACEAE
Origin: South Africa.
Flowering time: Spring–summer.
Climatic zone: 8, 9.
Dimensions: Up to 4 inches (100 mm) high.
Description: A rhizomatous, herbaceous perennial, rose grass derived its botanical name from the Greek 'rhodon' meaning rose. The tufted foliage is hairy and masses of rose-colored flowers show pale undersides. This small, slow-growing plant is an attractive rock garden addition. A sheltered, sunny site is best. The corm-like rhizome should be located in lime-free and moist, well-drained garden soil. An easy plant to look after, it is seldom attacked by garden pests.
Other colors: White.
Varieties/cultivars: 'Apple Blossom', 'Platypetala'.

Rhodohypoxis baurii

Antigonon leptopus
CORAL VINE, CORALLITA, MOUNTAIN ROSE ○ ◑

Other common names: QUEEN'S WREATH
Family: POLYGONACEAE
Origin: Mexico.
Flowering time: Mid-summer–autumn.
Climatic zone: 9, 10.
Description: Fast-growing, *Antigonon* climbs trees, fences, or trellises by attaching itself with small, strong tendrils. Flower sprays are numerous and make a spectacular display in summer. Treat it as a perennial in cooler districts, or in very hot zones where it may burn if planted in a windy exposed position. It can be used as a groundcover for sloping banks or sunny hillsides, or as a cover over a pergola. The arrow or heart-shaped leaves are an attractive addition to the bright floral display.
Other colors: White, red.

Antigonon leptopus

Bauhinia corymbosa
CLIMBING BAUHINIA ○

Family: LEGUMINOSAE
Origin: South East Asia.
Flowering time: Spring and autumn.
Climatic zone: 9, 10.
Description: Orchid-like flowers with red stamens appear on this evergreen plant in spring and autumn. The typical *Bauhinia* leaves, folded in half, are small and dainty and have reddish, hairy stems. A warm and sunny spot with rich soil will help this rather slow-developing vine to reach maximum growth. Some support will be necessary to train this sprawling plant as a climber. A warm climate plant, it needs full sun, good drainage, and a protected position. It is well worth growing for its attractive appearance all year.

Bauhinia corymbosa

Clematis montana 'Rubens'
PINK ANEMONE CLEMATIS (U.S.A.), TRAVELLER'S JOY ○ ◑

Family: RANUNCULACEAE
Origin: Himalayas – western China.
Flowering time: Spring–summer.
Climatic zone: 5, 6, 7, 8, 9.
Description: Pink anemone clematis has a dainty, fragrant flower with four petals in the shape of a cross. The flowers are rose-pink, fading to light pink, and are about 2 inches (50 mm) across. This deciduous vine is thin-stemmed and needs support during its spring–summer growing period when it is covered with a mass of blooms. In cold climates it flowers in early summer. It likes a warm sunny position, but does not like direct sun on the soil over the roots. Protect it by putting plenty of compost round its roots. It is best left unpruned, but if pruning is necessary, remove unwanted stems during the growing season.

Clematis montana 'Rubens'

Lonicera x *americana*
HONEYSUCKLE ○

Family: CAPRIFOLIACEAE
Origin: Hybrid.
Flowering time: Summer.
Climatic zone: 7, 8, 9.
Description: A vigorous, deciduous climber, this honeysuckle has large clusters of fragrant, yellowish-white flowers that are tinged with pink when in bud. Leaves are broad, and pointed at the tip. May be pruned after flowering, or in winter, to prevent it from becoming too prolific. Well-drained, moist soil and a sunny or partially shaded position give best results.

Lonicera x *americana*

Mandevilla sanderi
BRAZILIAN JASMINE, DIPLADENIA (Aust.), CHILEAN JASMINE (U.K.) ○ ◑

Family: APOCYNACEAE
Origin: Brazil.
Flowering time: Almost all year.
Climatic zone: 9, 10.
Description: Unlike the white *Mandevilla*, this beautiful little vine does not have fragrant flowers, but its clear pink, 3-inch (75-mm) blooms continue nearly all year provided conditions are warm enough. Grow as a tub plant with a trellis or wire support, or train over a lattice or trellis. Protect it from harsh sun, and provide rich soil and ample water for a delightful patio plant. In very warm zones, Brazilian jasmine can be grown in full shade, but filtered light is best. In cool areas, it does well as a greenhouse or house plant.

Mandevilla sanderi

Mandevilla splendens syn. *Dipladenia splendens*
CHILEAN JASMINE ○ ◑

Family: APOCYNACEAE
Origin: Southeastern Brazil.
Flowering time: Most of the year.
Climatic zone: 9, 10.
Description: Magnificent, clear pink flowers are scattered over this lovely vine almost all year long in warm climates. In cooler areas, a greenhouse is often necessary. It is evergreen, and although it will reach 20 feet (6 meters) if grown in the best position in the ground, it is usually treated as a container plant for patios. Twining stems will climb on to a trellis or wire support. A slender pole or frame is required for container growing, or it can be pruned to a low shrubby shape. Protect it from harsh sun and give regular water and deep compost for best results.

Mandevilla splendens

Pandorea jasminoides 'Rosea'
BOWER OF BEAUTY, BOWER PLANT ○ ◑

Family: BIGNONIACEAE
Origin: Cultivar.
Flowering time: Summer–autumn.
Climatic zone: 9, 10.
Description: An evergreen, quick-growing climber, *Pandorea* has attractive, glossy, compound leaves with five to nine leaflets. The trumpet-shaped flowers are 2 inches (50 mm) long, and are pinkish-white streaked with pink or red inside the throat. Protect it from strong winds and give it adequate support for maximum cover over a fence, or train it to climb up a pillar. It is not tolerant of cold or frost, so in colder areas a greenhouse is required. It does best with regular watering and good soil. The shiny leaves make it a handsome plant when the flowers have finished.

Pandorea jasminoides 'Rosea'

Pelargonium peltatum cultivar

Rosa 'Cecile Brunner'
PINK CLIMBING ROSE, CLIMBING CECILE BRUNNER (U.K.) ○

Family: ROSACEAE
Origin: Hybrid.
Flowering time: Summer.
Climatic zone: 5, 6, 7, 8, 9.
Description: The beautifully shaped shell-pink miniature flowers of 'Cecile Brunner' are often found among the red-colored new growth of the leaves. The plant has a tendency to be shrubby, but it can reach up to 15 feet (5 meters) or more. Give it plenty of room to spread, as the bright green foliage is attractive and will disguise an ugly corner. Even when it has become wide and thick, it still has a rather open, airy appearance. The flowers have a light, delicate fragrance.

Rosa 'Cecile Brunner'

Pelargonium peltatum
IVY GERANIUM, IVY-LEAVED GERANIUM (U.K.) ○ ◑

Family: GERANIACEAE
Origin: Eastern South Africa.
Flowering time: All year.
Climatic zone: All zones.
Description: Widely grown for its continual flowering habit and range of brightly colored flowers, the ivy geranium can tolerate sunny conditions, or partial shade. It is treated as an annual in cold districts, when it is grown just for the summer months. It can be used in hanging baskets, window boxes, pots, tubs, or can be tied to and trained up a lattice or wire frame to cover a fence or wall. The ivy-like, pointed, five-lobed leaves are shiny and attractive and ivy geranium is one of the most adaptable and versatile light trailing plants.
Other colors: White, red, purple.
Varieties/cultivars: Many including 'Amethyst', 'Galilee', 'Gardenia', 'Gloire d'Orleans', 'The Pearl'.

Podranea ricasoliana
PORT ST. JOHN CREEPER, PINK TECOMA ○

Family: BIGNONIACEAE
Origin: South Africa.
Flowering time: Summer.
Climatic zone: 9, 10.
Description: The flowers appear above the leaves on this lovely climber, and almost cover the plant. It is evergreen with glossy deep-green leaves divided into seven to eleven leaflets. The flowers are trumpet-shaped, 2 inches (50 mm) long, with rounded lobes, and are produced in large clusters. Support is needed to hold the plant against a wall or fence, or it can be allowed to grow into a wide, flowing shrub which will "lean" against a fence. It is tolerant of wind and will withstand a light frost, but in cold climates a greenhouse is essential.

Podranea ricasoliana

Rosa 'Dorothy Perkins'

Rosa 'Dorothy Perkins'
PINK CLIMBING ROSE, PINK RAMBLER (U.K.) ○

Family: ROSACEAE
Origin: Hybrid.
Flowering time: Summer.
Climatic zone: 5, 6, 7, 8, 9.
Description: This is a beautiful little rose which has lost some popularity, due to its short blooming period and susceptibility to mildew. The non-recurrent flowers are small, dainty, double, and rosette-like. Bright pink, slightly fragrant, they are produced prolifically during early summer. Because of its vigorous growth and long, arching habit, it is often used for grafting onto a tall stem to create a weeping standard rose. The tiny buds are favorites for old-fashioned posies or small flower arrangements.

Tecomanthe hillii
PINK TRUMPET VINE ◑

Family: BIGNONIACEAE
Origin: Australia (Northeastern coast).
Flowering time: Summer.
Climatic zone: 9, 10.
Description: Rosy flowers marked with purplish lines make the pink trumpet vine an unusual climber. It has a vigorous twining habit, and dark-green pinnate leaves with prominent veins. The flowers are borne in drooping clusters, and are bell-shaped. Fairly humid conditions are preferred, so it is most successful in hotter climates. In other areas, a greenhouse may be necessary. It is a very showy climber on a fence or trellis in a semishaded position.

Wisteria floribunda 'Rosea'
PINK WISTERIA ○

Family: LEGUMINOSAE
Origin: Cultivar.
Flowering time: Late spring–early summer.
Climatic zone: 4, 5, 6, 7, 8, 9.
Description: 'Rosea' is the pink form of the commonly grown Japanese wisteria. Superbly fragrant, pea flowers hang in profusion in long sprays. The flowers open progressively from the base to the tip of the spray. It differs from the Chinese wisteria in the number of leaflets (fifteen to nineteen), and in its longer flower sprays. It usually blooms a few weeks later. It is best grown over a pergola where its spectacular beauty can be seen to advantage. It needs pruning during the summer growing season, and shaping during the winter.

Wisteria floribunda 'Rosea'

Tecomanthe hillii

Acanthus mollis 'Latifolius'

Acanthus mollis 'Latifolius'
BEAR'S-BREECH, OYSTER PLANT ○ ◑ ●

Family: ACANTHACEAE
Origin: Cultivar.
Flowering time: Summer.
Climatic zone: 6, 7, 8, 9.
Dimensions: Up to 4½ feet (over 1 meter) high.
Description: *Acanthus mollis* is much desired as a border and specimen plant, both for its handsome, deeply-cut and glossy foliage and its showy flowers on spikes up to 18 inches (450 mm) long. Given a sheltered, sunny position, it flowers profusely and likes a moderately rich, well-drained loam. *Acanthus* is slow to establish but forms a large clump once settled. It is propagated by seed sown in spring, or by root division in autumn or spring. Prune it by removing spent flowers and leaves. It attracts snails.
Other colors: White, lilac, purple.

Alcea rosea syn. *Althaea rosea*
HOLLYHOCK ○

Family: MALVACEAE
Origin: Eastern Mediterranean region.
Flowering time: Summer.
Climatic zone: 4, 5, 6, 7, 8, 9.
Dimensions: 5–9 feet (2–3 meters) high.
Description: Hollyhocks are at their best when grown as a backdrop to a profuse summer border, and given the shelter and support of a wall. They will stand sentinel to delphiniums, foxgloves, zinnias, rudbeckias, and all the other dazzling blooms of summer. They require fairly rich, well-drained soil, and plenty of water in dry periods. Short-lived, they are often treated as biennials. To promote longer life, remove flower stalks at the base as soon as the flowers fade. Hollyhocks are subject to attack by red spider and rust. They are attractive in mixed flower arrangements.
Other colors: White, purple, red, yellow.
Varieties/cultivars: 'Chater's Improved', 'Summer Carnival', 'Begonia Flowered'.

Alcea rosea

Antennaria dioica
CAT'S FOOT, PUSSY TOES (U.S.A.), MOUNTAIN EVERLASTING ○

Family: COMPOSITAE
Origin: Eurasia.
Flowering time: Late spring.
Climatic zone: 4, 5, 6, 7, 8.
Dimensions: Up to 6 inches (150 mm) high.

Antennaria dioica

Description: *Antennaria dioica* is a useful mat-forming rockery plant because of its creeping, fast-growing habit. Its flowers are small, tubular and borne in terminal clusters, and the foliage is tufted and woolly in appearance. Although the plant grows as well in rich, moist soils as in dry, sandy conditions, it nevertheless needs good drainage. It is propagated by seed in autumn or spring or by division and looks well planted with *Achillea* x *lewisii* (King Edward). It has no particular value as a cut flower.
Other colors: White, rose-red.
Varieties/cultivars: 'Minima', 'Rosea', 'Rubra'.

Armeria pseudarmeria

Armeria pseudarmeria
THRIFT, PLANTAIN THRIFT ○

Family: PLUMBAGINACEAE
Origin: Portugal.
Flowering time: Summer.
Climatic zone: 6, 7, 8, 9.
Dimensions: 1½–2 feet (450–600 mm) high.
Description: Plantain thrift is a relatively tall variety of *Armeria* and is therefore more useful in the herbaceous border than the lower-growing common thrift, *A. maritima*. With its round flower heads borne on stiff stalks and its grass-like, tufted foliage, it is easy to grow in most soils, but thrives in well-drained, sandy loam. Removing spent blooms prolongs flowering. Easily propagated by division of clumps in autumn, plantain thrift makes a long-lasting pot specimen in cool conditions and is a good cut flower.
Other colors: White, red.
Varieties/cultivars: 'Bees Ruby'.

Aster novae-angliae

Aster novae-angliae
NEW ENGLAND ASTER (U.S.A.), MICHAELMAS DAISY (U.K.), EASTER DAISY (Aust.) ○

Family: COMPOSITAE
Origin: Eastern North America.
Flowering time: Late summer–autumn.
Climatic zone: 4, 5, 6, 7, 8, 9.
Dimensions: 3–5 feet (nearly 2 meters) high.
Description: *Aster novae-angliae* brings a wonderful splash of color to the autumn garden. It is equally lovely as a late-flowerer in the summer border or grown in the smaller space of a city garden. Its foliage is dense and grayish-green; the flowers are large, and clustered on strong, hairy stems. It prefers well-mulched, moist, fertile soil that is well-drained and benefits from complete fertilizer in spring and summer. It has an unhappy habit of closing at night. Use it as a cut flower in indoor decorating.
Other colors: Blue, purple.
Varieties/cultivars: 'Alma Potschke', 'Barr's Pink', 'Harrington Pink', 'Ryecroft Purple'.

Aster novi-belgii 'Patricia Ballard'
NEW YORK ASTER (U.S.A.), MICHAELMAS DAISY (U.K.), EASTER DAISY (Aust.) ○

Family: COMPOSITAE
Origin: Cultivar.
Flowering time: Late summer–autumn.
Climatic zone: 5, 6, 7, 8, 9.
Dimensions: Up to 3 feet (900 mm) high.
Description: What color the New York aster brings to the autumn garden! Plant it against a backdrop of autumn leaves and scarlet berry colors and highlight it by the white of the Japanese windflower. It prefers well-composted, moist, and well-drained soil. Fertilizer in spring and summer, and plenty of water in dry periods are essential. Prune it by cutting spent flower stems to ground level. New York aster provides good cut flowers.

Aster novi-belgii 'Patricia Ballard'

Astrantia maxima

Astrantia maxima syn. *A. helleborifolia*
MASTERWORT ○ ◑

Family: UMBELLIFERAE
Origin: Caucasus, Turkey.
Flowering time: Summer.
Climatic zone: 4, 5, 6, 7, 8, 9.
Dimensions: Up to 2 feet (600 mm) high.
Description: Masterwort, with its tall stems, numerous delicate flowers, and interesting foliage, is best suited to wild or cottage gardens. The flowers may be cut and dried for use in floral arrangements. Any ordinary garden soil suits masterwort, but it needs adequate water in summer. Propagate it by root division or by seed.

Aubrieta deltoidea
FALSE ROCK CRESS, AUBRIETA (U.K.) ○ 

Family: CRUCIFERAE
Origin: Southern Greece, Sicily.
Flowering time: Spring–early summer.
Climatic zone: 5, 6, 7, 8, 9.
Dimensions: Up to 6 inches (150 mm) high.
Description: Aubrieta is a cheerful, profusely flowering rockery or border-edging plant. Its flowers appear in loose clusters, held above the foliage. They come in both single and double forms. Its grayish-green, downy leaves form a spreading mat which can be invasive if not trimmed back. Propagation is by seed sown in spring or by cuttings. Well-drained, light soil is required for best results where summers are mild.
Other colors: Mauve, lilac, purple, blue, white.
Varieties/cultivars: Several cultivars include 'Borsch's White', 'Gloriosa', 'Greencourt Purple', 'Mrs. Rodewald', 'Purple Gem', 'Variegata'.

Aubrieta deltoidea cultivar

Begonia x *semperflorens-cultorum*

Begonia x *semperflorens-cultorum* syn. *B. semperflorens*, *B. cucculata* var. *hookeri*
WAX BEGONIA ◑

Family: BEGONIACEAE
Origin: Hybrid.
Flowering time: Summer.
Climatic zone: 3, 4, 5, 6, 7, 8, 9, 10.
Dimensions: Up to 18 inches (450 mm) high.
Description: A useful perennial with fleshy foliage and showy clusters of pink flowers, *Begonia* requires a rich, moist soil and semishaded conditions. Protection from summer midday sun is essential. Often grown as a summer bedding plant among annuals and other perennials, it likes plenty of water during summer and several applications of liquid plant food to encourage good flower production. It is not difficult to propagate from stem or leaf cuttings in spring or summer, or raise from seed.
Other colors: Red, pink, white, doubles and singles, bronze and purple foliage.
Varieties/cultivars: Many cultivars are available including 'Carmen', 'Flamingo', 'Galaxy', 'Indian Maid', 'Linda', 'Organdy'.

Bergenia cordifolia
HEARTLEAF BERGENIA, SAXIFRAGE, MEGASEA (U.K.) ○ ◑ ●

Family: SAXIFRAGACEAE
Origin: Siberia.
Flowering time: Late winter–spring.
Climatic zone: 3, 4, 5, 6, 7, 8, 9, 10.
Dimensions: 12–18 inches (300–450 mm) high.

Bergenia cordifolia hybrid cultivar

Description: Heartleaf bergenia takes its name from its large, heart-shaped leaves which are thick, fleshy, and evergreen, making a very attractive groundcover or border edging, especially in damp and shaded positions. The flowers are in large clusters on sturdy stems and, in mild climates, bloom in winter. Remove spent flower heads to prolong flowering. Bergenia will grow in any soil but thrives with organic mulch and plenty of water during dry spells. Propagate by root division from autumn to spring.
Other colors: White, red, lilac.
Varieties/cultivars: 'Purpurea', 'Perfecta'.

Bergenia x *schmidtii*

Bergenia x *schmidtii*
BERGENIA, MEGASEA ○ ◑

Family: SAXIFRAGACEAE
Origin: Hybrid.
Flowering time: Late winter–late spring.
Climatic zone: 4, 5, 6, 7, 8, 9.
Dimensions: 9–18 inches (225–450 mm) high.
Description: This useful and hardy perennial has large, thick, almost leathery leaves and a showy display of pink flowers borne in nodding flower heads. It really thrives in moderately rich and well-drained soil, but can survive in less favorable conditions, including rocky and poor soils. Plant it in light shade, or in full sun if moisture is provided.

Centaurea hypoleuca 'John Coutts'

Centaurea hypoleuca 'John Coutts'
PINK CORNFLOWER ○

Family: COMPOSITAE
Origin: Cultivar.
Flowering time: Summer.
Climatic zone: 4, 5, 6, 7, 8, 9.
Dimensions: 1½–2 feet (450–600 mm) high.
Description: The pink cornflower, with its deep rose-colored and fringed ray flowers, looks stunning in a massed border display. Its lobed leaves, green on the surface and whitish underneath, are also attractive. It prefers dry, well-drained soil and an open position. Propagate by dividing established clumps in autumn or spring. The cut flowers are attractive in floral decorations.

Chelone lyonii
PINK TURTLEHEAD ◑

Family: SCROPHULARIACEAE
Origin: Southeastern United States.
Flowering time: Summer–autumn.
Climatic zone: 4, 5, 6, 7, 8, 9.

Dimensions: Up to 3 feet (1 meter) high.
Description: *C. lyonii* is most desirable in the summer garden for both its dark, glossy foliage, and its slightly hooded, rosy-pink flowers borne on a terminal spike. It prefers partial shade and moist, humus-enriched soil. Propagate it from seed sown in spring or root division in autumn or spring.

Chelone lyonii

Coronilla varia
CROWN VETCH ○

Family: LEGUMINOSAE
Origin: Central and southern Europe.
Flowering time: Summer.
Climatic zone: 4, 5, 6, 7, 8, 9, 10.
Dimensions: Up to 18 inches (450 mm) high.
Description: This sprawling perennial can be invasive in the garden. It is ideal as a groundcover for steep, sunny banks or in borders. The long tricolored flowers of pink, rose, and white are pea-shaped. These dense clusters are most attractive against their ferny foliage which closes up at night. Fast-growing, crown vetch will cover mounds or building rubble and control erosion if the soil is dry. Propagation is by seed.
Varieties/cultivars: 'Aurea', 'Penngift'.

Coronilla varia

Darmera peltata syn. *Peltiphyllum peltatum, Saxifraga peltatum*
UMBRELLA PLANT, INDIAN RHUBARB ○ ◑

Family: SAXIFRAGACEAE
Origin: California, Oregon.
Flowering time: Spring.
Climatic zone: 6, 7, 8, 9.
Dimensions: Up to 4 feet (over 1 meter) high.
Description: This moisture-loving perennial has pale pink flowers that form clusters on sturdy stems about 2 feet (600 mm) high. The leaves are lotus-like and borne at the top of stems growing between 3 and 4 feet (approx. 1 meter) high. It is a suitable plant for moist areas beside ponds or streams but, because it can become very invasive, it is unsuitable for small gardens. The Californian Indians ate the peeled leaf stalks, hence the name "Indian rhubarb". Propagate it by root division or seed.
Other colors: White.
Varieties/cultivars: 'Nanum' (dwarf).

Darmera peltata

Dianthus barbatus

Dianthus barbatus
SWEET WILLIAM ○

Family: CARYOPHYLLACEAE
Origin: Southern Europe and Mediterranean region.
Flowering time: Summer.
Climatic zone: 6, 7, 8, 9.
Dimensions: Up to 16 inches (400 mm) high.
Description: Once known as the divine flower of Jupiter and Zeus, this perennial will bloom for six to ten weeks. Sweetly scented flowers are single or double and occur in a variety of colors. It is suitable for borders, edges, or potted on garden steps and decks. Related to the carnation and pinks family, *Dianthus* likes an open sunny position in sandy loam. Generous colorful heads will result from an application of lime and compost when planting.
Other colors: Red, purple, white.
Varieties/cultivars: 'Giant white', 'Dunnets dark crimson', Dwarf mixed.

Dianthus caryophyllus
CARNATION, CLOVE PINK ○

Family: CARYOPHYLLACEAE
Origin: Central Europe.
Flowering time: Summer.
Climatic zone: 7, 8, 9.
Dimensions: Up to 2 feet (600 mm) high.
Description: *Dianthus caryophyllus*, known and used as a garland flower from the time of the Norman conquest, and referred to as "the divine flower" by the ancient Greeks, is the parent of modern carnations. Commonly referred to now as "the perpetual", carnation is a perennial with multi-petaled flowers, that blooms all year round. A wide choice of colors is available. There are also border carnations available, which flower only once a year and have a bushier growth than the perpetuals. Plant carnations in light, sandy soil mixed with compost and lime. Stakes are required for support when plants grow tall. Carnations dislike wet, sunless winters so need a greenhouse environment in these areas.
Other colors: Red, yellow, white.
Varieties/cultivars: 'Dwarf Pygmy Mixed', 'Enfant de Nice', 'Giant Chabaud'.

Dianthus caryophyllus hybrid

Dianthus plumarius
COMMON PINK, GRASS PINK, COTTAGE PINK ○

Family: CARYOPHYLLACEAE
Origin: Eastern and central Europe.
Flowering time: Early summer.
Climatic zone: 5, 6, 7, 8, 9.
Dimensions: Up to 18 inches (450 mm) high.
Description: *D. plumarius* is thought to be the parent of the old-fashioned and modern pinks. Similar to carnations in their foliage, pinks have simpler flowers and share a wide color range. Use them as borders in beds of carnations or sweet William. Their fragrant perfume adds an old-fashioned touch to gardens. Plant cuttings in light, sandy soil mixed with compost and lime. Provide them with a sunny position protected from wind, and water regularly. They make pretty posies indoors.
Other colors: White, red, purple.

Dianthus plumarius

Dianthus x *allwoodii*
ALLWOOD PINK ○

Family: CARYOPHYLLACEAE
Origin: Hybrid.
Flowering time: Spring–summer.
Climatic zone: 7, 8, 9.
Dimensions: Up to 18 inches (450 mm) high.
Description: Allwood pink is a hybrid whose flowers are fringed or plain-petaled and can be single, double, or semidouble. The petals spray outwards in a delicate formation from their tubular base, and are found in shades of pink, red and white, or combinations of these. Planted in front of delphiniums, they produce a cottage garden effect. Allwood pink is easy to grow in any garden soil, but requires good drainage. Alkaline soil, provided with additional humus, gives best results. Prolong the flowering period by removing spent flowers.
Other colors: White, red.
Varieties/cultivars: 'Doris', 'Lilian', 'Robin', 'Timothy'.

Dianthus x *allwoodii* 'Doris'

Dicentra eximia 'Bountiful'

Dicentra eximia

FRINGED BLEEDING HEART, WILD BLEEDING HEART ○ ◑

Family: FUMARIACEAE
Origin: Eastern United States.
Flowering time: Spring–summer.
Climatic zone: 3, 4, 5, 6, 7, 8, 9, 10.
Dimensions: Approx. 12 inches (300 mm) high.
Description: Fern-like foliage and rose-purple, heart-shaped blooms that bees love make this a useful border perennial. *D. eximia* is equally at home in sun or shade, providing the soil is moist. It is a good choice for corners of the garden needing a little color. Open borders, ferneries, and rock gardens will also suit it if the soil is rich, moist, and has had humus added. Propagate by root division in early spring.
Other colors: White, red.
Varieties/cultivars: 'Alba', 'Luxuriant', 'Bountiful'.

Dicentra spectabilis

Dicentra spectabilis

COMMON BLEEDING-HEART, DUTCHMAN'S BREECHES ◑ ●

Family: FUMARIACEAE
Origin: Japan, Korea, China.
Flowering time: Spring–early summer.
Climatic zone: 3, 4, 5, 6, 7, 8, 9.
Dimensions: Up to 2 feet (600 mm) high.
Description: The outstandingly elegant, heart-shaped flowers droop from arching, horizontal stems. White petals glisten at the tip of each "heart" like tears. A Japanese-style garden would suit this plant to perfection. Feature *D. spectabilis* against a cool rock wall where it will not have to compete to show its splendor. It should be planted in light sun or shade in cool, rich, well-drained soil, and protected from slugs. Lifted plants can easily be grown in a warm greenhouse.
Other colors: White.
Varieties/cultivars: 'Alba'.

Digitalis x *mertonensis*

Digitalis x *mertonensis*

MERTON FOXGLOVE ◑

Family: SCROPHULARIACEAE
Origin: Hybrid.
Flowering time: Summer.
Climatic zone: 6, 7, 8, 9, 10.
Dimensions: Up to 3 feet (1 meter) high.
Description: This hybrid of *D. purpurea* is a favorite of bees and smaller insects which shelter in the drooping, rose-pink blooms. Foxglove forms a good backdrop for beds of annuals, and looks well with most cottage garden favorites. This hybrid requires frequent division in spring to maintain its perennial character. An easy plant to grow in ordinary well-drained garden soil, it benefits from an application of compost in spring.

Dodecatheon meadia

COMMON SHOOTING-STAR ◑

Family: PRIMULACEAE
Origin: Eastern United States.
Flowering time: Spring–early summer.
Climatic zone: 4, 5, 6, 7, 8, 9.
Dimensions: Up to 18 inches (450 mm) high.
Description: A member of the primrose family, *D. meadia* has up to twenty rose-purple, reflexed flowers resembling shooting-stars. The yellow or purple anthers form a dart-like tip, giving the blooms their starry appearance. The foliage dies down when flowering has finished. The plant is suited to wild gardens, rock gardens, and shaded borders, and is easily grown in rich, sandy soil with plenty of organic matter. Good drainage is needed, as is moisture during the growing season. Propagate this plant by division or seed.
Other colors: Red, purple, white.
Varieties/cultivars: 'Album'.

Dodecatheon meadia

Eremurus robustus

Eremurus robustus
FOXTAIL LILY, DESERT CANDLES ○

Family: LILIACEAE
Origin: Turkestan.
Flowering time: Summer.
Climatic zone: 7, 8, 9.
Dimensions: Up to 10 feet (3 meters) high.
Description: This lofty plant, with soft-pink, closely packed flowers borne on long spikes, is a stately herbaceous perennial which can be companion-planted with delphiniums and irises. The leaves of some species of this lily are eaten in Afghanistan as a vegetable. The tubers are octopus-shaped and need to be planted 6–8 inches (150–200 mm) deep, resting on sand. Well-drained soil in an open, sunny position suits this spectacular plant best.

Filipendula palmata syn. *F. multijuga*
SIBERIAN MEADOWSWEET ◑

Family: ROSACEAE
Origin: Siberia.
Flowering time: Summer.
Climatic zone: 4, 5, 6, 7, 8, 9.
Dimensions: Up to 2½ feet (750 mm) high.
Description: A graceful perennial with large seven-lobed leaves and showy flat heads of pinkish-purple flowers. A useful addition to a mixed floral border, it has a spreading habit and requires plenty of space to give a good display. Likes moderately rich, moist soil. Can be propagated either by division, or from seed. It benefits from an application of compost in the spring.

Filipendula palmata syn. *F. multijuga*

Filipendula rubra 'Venusta'

Filipendula rubra
QUEEN-OF-THE-PRAIRIE ◑

Family: ROSACEAE
Origin: Eastern United States.
Flowering time: Summer.
Climatic zone: 3, 4, 5, 6, 7, 8, 9.
Dimensions: Up to 5 feet (approx. 2 meters) high.
Description: Peach-pink flowers form airy clusters on this tall, feathery border plant. Related to the rose, it needs plenty of space in a shaded part of the garden. Plant it in filtered sun under large trees or among ferns and orchids. *F. rubra* looks attractive planted behind pink and white peonies in a bed. It is easy to grow in very moist garden soil, especially if humus has been added to help retain moisture. Propagate it by division of the clumps in early spring.
Other colors: Deep pink.
Varieties/cultivars: 'Venusta'.

Geranium x *magnificum*
CRANESBILL ○ ◑

Family: GERANIACEAE
Origin: Hybrid.
Flowering time: Summer.
Climatic zone: 4, 5, 6, 7, 8, 9.
Dimensions: Up to 2 feet (600 mm) high.
Description: A most successful cross between G. *ibericum* and G. *platypetalum*, this clump-forming perennial is superior to either of its parents. The wide and deeply-lobed foliage grows vigorously, while the showy violet flowers have reddish stems and bloom in profusion, measuring 1½ inches (30 mm) in diameter. It likes well-drained, moderately-rich soil and can be incorporated into a mixed bed of perennials, or grown in a large container.

Geranium x *magnificum*

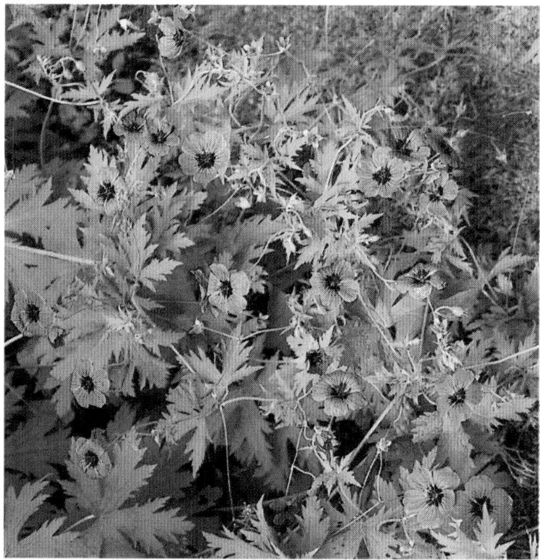

Geranium psilostemon

Geranium psilostemon

ARMENIAN CRANESBILL

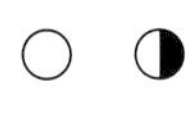

Family: GERANIACEAE
Origin: Turkey, Caucasus.
Flowering time: Spring–summer.
Climatic zone: 5, 6, 7, 8, 9.
Dimensions: Up to 3 feet (900 mm) high.
Description: With its brilliant magenta flowers, black-spotted at the base, and its deeply-lobed leaves, Armenian cranesbill makes an eye-catching border plant. It forms large clumps in full sun, and also looks well placed among other herbaceous perennials against a stone wall, or along pathways, or in woodland areas. It flowers freely in any light, well-drained soil, in full sun where summers are cool, but appreciates partial shade in hot areas. Propagate it by seed, cuttings, or division.
Other colors: Blue-purple.

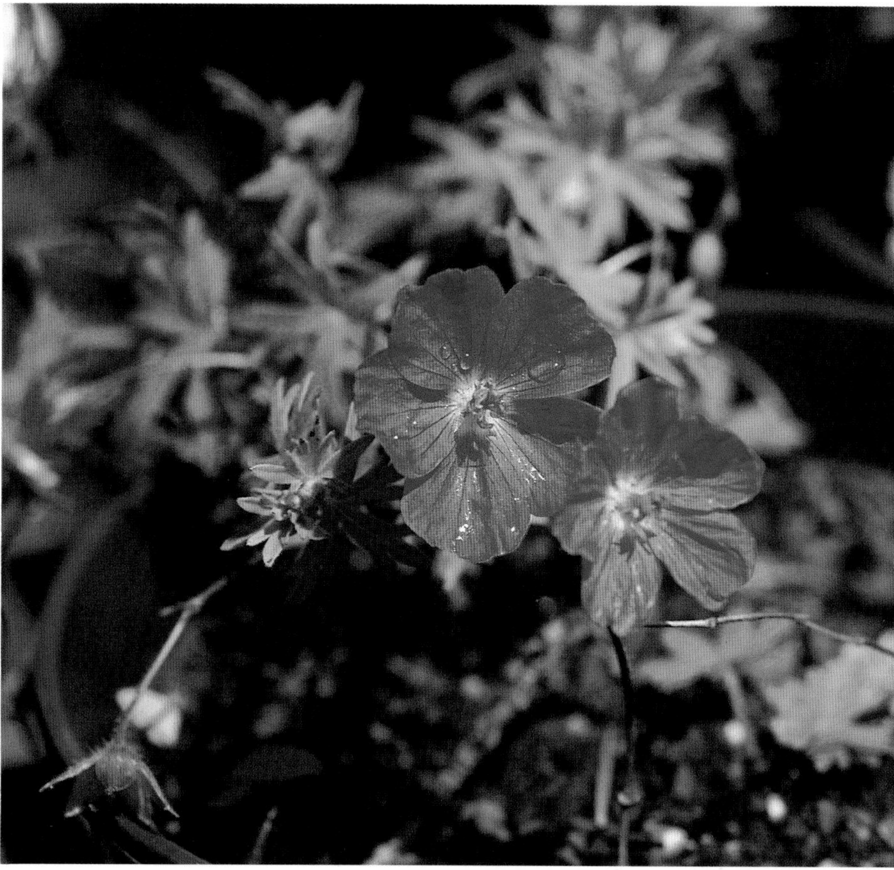

Geranium sanguineum

Geranium sanguineum

BLOODY CRANESBILL ○ ◑

Family: GERANIACEAE
Origin: Europe, western Asia.
Flowering time: Spring–summer.
Climatic zone: 4, 5, 6, 7, 8, 9, 10.
Dimensions: Up to 18 inches (450 mm) high.
Description: An invaluable and highly adaptable plant, with flowers ranging from pale pink to reddish-purple, bloody cranesbill will tolerate full sun even in hot, dry summers. It is a good choice for open borders and sloping sites, and can also be planted among large boulders, on mounds, and in rock garden pockets. Grow it in fertile, well-drained soil, mulch and water it well in summer, and give it fertilizer. Its dwarf variety, *G. sanguineum* var. *lancastrense*, forms flat carpets of large, rosy flowers.
Other colors: White, purplish-red.
Varieties/cultivars: 'Album', 'Shepherd's warning', *G. s.* var. *lancastrense*.

Gypsophila repens 'Rosea'

Gypsophila repens 'Rosea'

CREEPING BABY'S BREATH, FAIRY GRASS ○

Family: CARYOPHYLLACEAE
Origin: Central and southern European mountains.
Flowering time: Spring–summer.
Climatic zone: 3, 4, 5, 6, 7, 8, 9.
Dimensions: Up to 8 inches (200 mm) high.
Description: Dense mats of this dainty-flowered creeper soften sloping sites. The masses of pale pink flowers bloom profusely throughout spring and summer. It is an effective groundcover grown near paved areas or cascading over walls. Plant it in fertile, well-drained soil in a sunny position and water regularly. Apply complete fertilizer in spring and trim after flowering. Gathered in bunches, creeping baby's breath is excellent for small floral arrangements.
Other colors: White.

Helleborus orientalis
LENTEN ROSE, HELLEBORE ◑

Family: RANUNCULACEAE
Origin: Greece, Turkey.
Flowering time: Late winter–spring.
Climatic zone: 4, 5, 6, 7, 8, 9.
Dimensions: Approx. 18 inches (450 mm) high.
Description: The hellebores, whose name is derived from the Greek "elein" (to injure) and "bora" (food), have been known and used since ancient times. Although the plants are poisonous, they have been used medicinally. Lenten rose is the easiest species of *Helleborus* to grow and is a popular addition to gardens. Each stem carries several cup-shaped flowers, often speckled inside. The plant grows well among trees or shrubs as a low-maintenance groundcover. Moist soil is essential.
Other colors: Pale yellow, white, green, red, maroon.
Varieties/cultivars: Several cultivars are available.

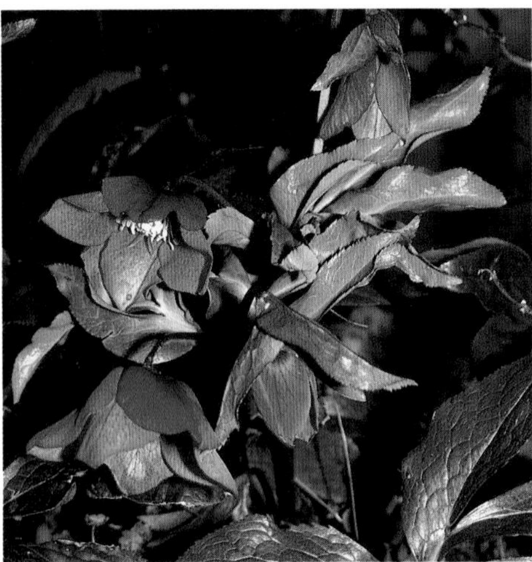

Helleborus orientalis

Heterocentron elegans syn. *Schizocentron elegans, Heeria elegans*
SPANISH SHAWL ◑

Family: MELASTOMATACEAE
Origin: Mexico, Guatemala, Honduras.
Flowering time: Summer.
Climatic zone: 9, 10.
Dimensions: Up to 2 inches (50 mm) high.
Description: This perennial is shy of the sun despite its tropical origins. The stems are prostrate, with trailing or cascading branches which can reach out to 3 feet (1 meter) across. Oval or heart-

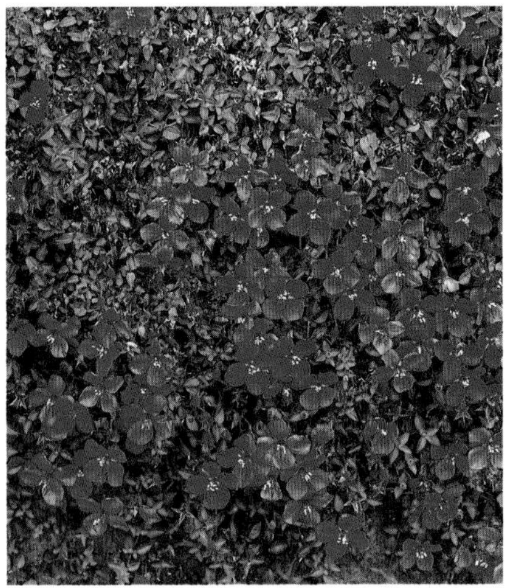

Heterocentron elegans

shaped, bright green leaves accompany profuse pink flowers. Needing filtered sunlight, spanish shawl is a groundcover suited to shady edges, near ferns or in cool rock garden pockets. It prefers rich, moist, well-drained soil in a protected position. Propagation is by seed or root division. It is susceptible to drought and frost.

Incarvillea delavayi

Incarvillea delavayi
HARDY GLOXINIA, PRIDE OF CHINA ○

Family: BIGNONIACEAE
Origin: China.
Flowering time: Summer.
Climatic zone: 5, 6, 7, 8, 9.
Dimensions: Up to 2 feet (600 mm) high.
Description: This is a showy perennial with large clusters of flared, trumpet-shaped flowers. Its bright purplish-pink blooms have yellow throats and together with the fern-like leaves make a good display in a sunny position in a temperate garden. It grows well in borders, rock gardens, or pots. Light soils suit it best and it needs good drainage or the roots will rot. Although it is easily propagated by seed, the seedlings take about two years to flower. In colder zones, provide winter protection. Apply a complete fertilizer in late winter.

Liatris spicata

Liatris spicata
GAY FEATHER, BLAZING STAR ○

Family: COMPOSITAE
Origin: Eastern and central United States.
Flowering time: Summer–autumn.
Climatic zone: 3, 4, 5, 6, 7, 8, 9.
Dimensions: Up to 5 feet (approx. 2 meters) high.
Description: This herbaceous perennial produces tall spikes of rose-lilac flowers like fluffy feather dusters; the grass-like leaves grow in tufts. A quick-growing plant, gay feather is ideal for a mixed border and looks attractive with *Dianthus* x *allwoodii* in the foreground. It likes an open, sunny position and light or ordinary garden soil. Water it regularly and apply a complete fertilizer in spring. Cut it back after flowering. This plant is seldom attacked by pests or diseases.
Varieties/cultivars: *L. s. montana*, *L. s. m.* 'Kobold'.

Lychnis coronaria

Lychnis coronaria

ROSE CAMPION, DUSTY MILLER ○ ◑

Family: CARYOPHYLLACEAE
Origin: Southern Europe.
Flowering time: Summer.
Climatic zone: 4, 5, 6, 7, 8, 9.
Dimensions: Up to 2 feet (600 mm) high.
Description: Rose campion has wheel-like, cerise-pink flowers on pale stems. The foliage has fine, silvery hairs. A gray groundcover can be created by removing the flowers. It is a good, but short-lived, border plant, the seedlings flowering within a year. Growing either as a biennial or perennial, it likes alkaline, moist, well-drained soil and a position in sun or partial shade.
Other colors: White.
Varieties/cultivars: 'Alba', 'Abbotswood Rose', *L. c.* var. *oculata*.

Lychnis viscaria syn. *Viscaria vulgaris*

GERMAN CATCHFLY ○

Family: CARYOPHYLLACEAE
Origin: Europe.
Flowering time: Spring–summer.
Climatic zone: 4, 5, 6, 7, 8, 9.
Dimensions: Up to 18 inches (450 mm) high.
Description: The purplish-pink flowers form in clusters on top of the sticky stems that have given the common name, German catchfly, to this plant. The stickiness protects the plants from insects, particularly ants. It likes moist, sandy soil, and an open position. Propagate it by division in autumn or by sowing seed in spring. Double-flowered varieties are available.
Other colors: White, red, purple.
Varieties/cultivars: 'Splendens', 'Splendens Plena', 'Alba', 'Zulu'.

Lychnis viscaria

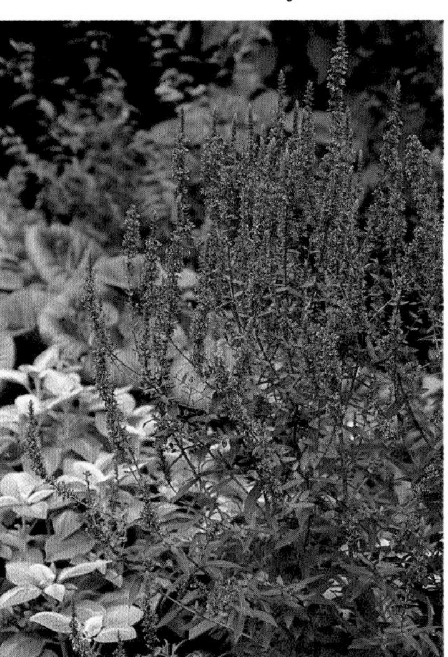

Lythrum salicaria

Lythrum salicaria

PURPLE LOOSESTRIFE ○ ◑

Family: LYTHRACEAE
Origin: Asia, Europe, North Africa.
Flowering time: Summer.
Climatic zone: 3, 4, 5, 6, 7, 8, 9.
Dimensions: Up to 4 feet (over 1 meter) high.
Description: The name *Lythrum* is from the Greek word for "blood", alluding to the color of the flowers. These are vibrant magenta-pink and borne in whorls around the stems, the leaves being willow-like. Marsh-loving, it is ideal planted beside ponds, near streams, or in damp places in the garden, but it also flowers freely in ground that is not especially wet.
A valuable and widely grown plant, it has been used for tanning leather and in treating dysentery and blindness.
L. salicaria may be invasive, but the cultivars are not.
Other colors: Red, violet.
Varieties/cultivars: 'Happy', 'Robert', 'Dropmore Purple', 'Firecandle', 'Morden's Gleam', 'Morden's Pink', 'Purple Spires'.

Malva alcea 'Fastigiata'

Malva alcea

MALLOW, HOLLYHOCK MALLOW ○ ◑

Family: MALVACEAE
Origin: Europe.
Flowering time: Summer–autumn.
Climatic zone: 5, 6, 7, 8, 9.
Dimensions: Up to 4 feet (over 1 meter) high.
Description: The flowers of hollyhock mallow are a delicate pink, and the downy, heart-shaped leaves add to the plant's ornamental value in borders and beds. Related to the hibiscus, which is also a member of the mallow family, *M. alcea* is like a smaller version of this flower, which is probably why some consider it to be inferior. Flowers are borne in terminal spikes, and occur in great profusion. It is easy to grow in any garden soil, but prefers it dry. Propagate by dividing it in spring.
Other colors: Purple.
Varieties/cultivars: 'Fastigiata'.

Malva moschata

MUSK MALLOW, MUSK ROSE ○ ◑

Family: MALVACEAE
Origin: Europe, North Africa.
Flowering time: Summer–autumn.
Climatic zone: 4, 5, 6, 7, 8, 9, 10.
Dimensions: Up to 3 feet (1 meter) high.
Description: The handsome pink flowers of musk mallow appear mostly at the top of the stems. Its leaves emit a musky fragrance when bruised. Musk mallow makes an attractive ornamental border plant among hollyhocks and lupins in cottage gardens. Drought-tolerant, it does well in most soils, but prefers a well-drained position. Propagate it from seed in spring. Musk mallow has medicinal properties.
Other colors: White.
Varieties/cultivars: 'Alba'.

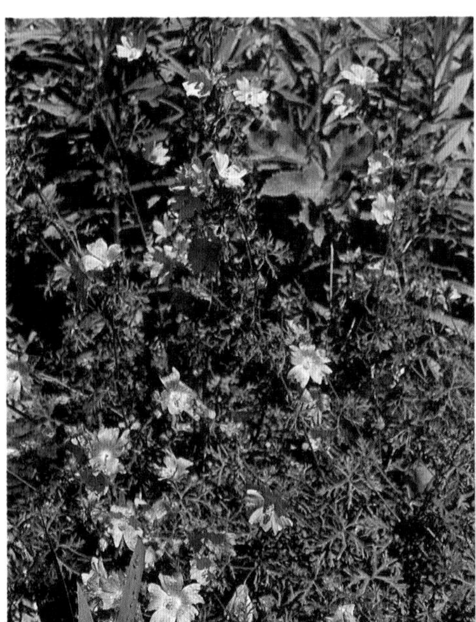

Malva moschata

Oenothera speciosa

SHOWY PRIMROSE, EVENING PRIMROSE ○

Family: ONAGRACEAE
Origin: Southern United States, Mexico.
Flowering time: Summer.
Climatic zone: 5, 6, 7, 8, 9.
Dimensions: Up to 18 inches (450 mm) high.
Description: Like most evening primroses, showy primrose has flowers that open during the day. They are shallowly basin-shaped and fragrant, fading to a soft rose color, and look attractive at the front of a border or in a large rock garden. Because of its spreading habit, the plant is a good choice for a wild garden and is easy to grow in a sunny spot, in sandy or loamy soil.

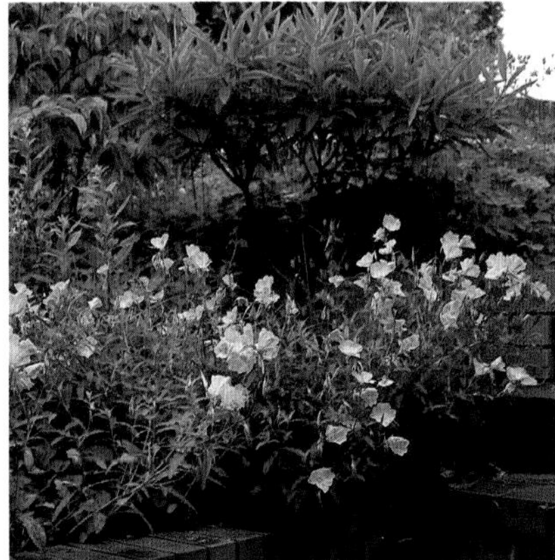

Oenothera speciosa

Paeonia officinalis

COMMON PEONY ○ ◑

Family: PAEONIACEAE
Origin: Southern Europe.
Flowering time: Early summer.
Climatic zone: 3, 4, 5, 6, 7, 8, 9.
Dimensions: Up to 3 feet (1 meter) high.
Description: An extremely hardy perennial, common peony grows well only in frosty areas, but needs a position where the early morning sun will not damage the flowers after frost. The solitary, crimson flowers are saucer-shaped with yellow stamens and red filaments. It grows well in fertile, well-drained soil and must be well-watered in dry weather. A plant known to the ancients, peony was said to cure lunacy, nightmares, and nervous disorders. Ideal for low maintenance gardens, they are also excellent cut flowers.
Other colors: Red, white.
Varieties/cultivars: 'Rubra Plena', 'Alba Plena'.

Phlox subulata

GROUND PINK, MOSS PINK, MOSS PHLOX (U.K.) ○ ◑

Family: POLEMONIACEAE
Origin: Northeastern United States.
Flowering time: Late spring, northern hemisphere; summer, southern hemisphere.
Climatic zone: 3, 4, 5, 6, 7, 8.
Dimensions: Up to 6 inches (150 mm) high.
Description: Introduced into England in the early part of the eighteenth century, ground pink is an old, easy-to-grow favorite. An evergreen creeper, it forms a thick carpet and produces dense flowers which are ¾ inch (20 mm) wide with slightly notched petals. A profuse flowerer, this alpine phlox suits rock

Paeonia officinalis

Phlox subulata 'Alexander's Surprise'

gardens and sloping sites and looks attractive planted to give a spill-over effect over rocks or down stone walls. It prefers average, well-drained garden soil. Prune the stems severely after flowering to promote denser growth. Propagate it from seeds, cuttings or division of the roots.
Other colors: White, red, lavender-blue.
Varieties/cultivars: 'Alba', 'Brilliant', 'Temiscaming', 'G. F. Wilson', 'Alexander's Surprise', 'Oakington Blue Eyes', 'Red Wings', 'White Delight'.

Plectranthus Sp.
CANDLE PLANT ◑ ●

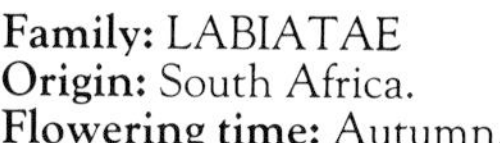

Family: LABIATAE
Origin: South Africa.
Flowering time: Autumn.

Plectranthus Sp.

Climatic zone: 9, 10.
Dimensions: Up to 2 feet (600 mm) high.
Description: This plant is a most useful groundcover for shady areas, where its long branches frequently send down roots at each leaf node. The profuse spires of flowers are pale mauve when they open, fading to white, and the attractive, oval leaves are green above and deep-purple on the underside. Candle plant does not tolerate dry conditions, growing best in moist soil with plenty of leaf mold. It propagates very easily from cuttings and makes a fine hanging basket, house, or greenhouse plant.

Polygonum bistorta 'Superbum'
COMMON EUROPEAN BISTORT, EASTER LEDGES, SNAKEWEED (U.S.A.) ○ ◑

Family: POLYGONACEAE
Origin: Cultivar.
Flowering time: Summer.
Climatic zone: 3, 4, 5, 6, 7, 8, 9.
Dimensions: Up to 3 feet (1 meter) high.
Description: The pink flowers of this perennial appear in dense, robust spikes about 6 inches (150 mm) long, on stems well above the foliage. Its large, paddle-like leaves make it a handsome plant even when not in flower. Given the right position, it may bloom twice during the summer. Mass-plant it in long borders beside driveways and paths, or near fruit trees to attract the bees. It likes moist soil in a shaded position, although where summers are cool it will grow in full sun.

Polygonum bistorta 'Superbum'

Polygonum capitatum

Polygonum capitatum
FLEECE FLOWER, JAPANESE KNOT-FLOWER ○ ●

Family: POLYGONACEAE
Origin: Himalayas.
Flowering time: Spring–autumn.
Climatic zone: 9, 10.
Dimensions: Up to 6 inches (150 mm) high.
Description: This vigorous and quick-growing perennial has attractive, pink, globular flowers and dark-green leaves with V-shaped bands. Its low, spreading habit makes it a useful groundcover, but pruning may be necessary to control its spread. An easy-to-grow plant, it is tolerant of a wide range of soils and conditions and is seldom bothered by pests or diseases. Plant cuttings or seed in full sun or shade.

Primula japonica

Primula japonica
JAPANESE PRIMROSE ◑

Family: PRIMULACEAE
Origin: Japan.
Flowering time: Late spring–early summer.
Climatic zone: 5, 6, 7, 8, 9.
Dimensions: Up to 16 inches (400 mm) high.
Description: Primula has strong stems bearing whorled tiers of glistening flowers which look spectacular mass-planted under trees or around shrubs. A moisture-lover, it grows well near ponds and streams and in damp and partially shady problem areas in the garden. Plant it in humus-enriched soil and provide constant moisture. It does not like hot, dry summers. *Astilbe* species, which need similar conditions, make ideal companion plants.
Other colors: White, red, purple, lavender.
Varieties/cultivars: 'Miller's Crimson', 'Postford's White'.

Prunella grandiflora 'Rosea'
SELF-HEAL, HEART-OF-THE-EARTH (U.S.A.), LARGE-FLOWERED SELF-HEAL (U.K.) ○ ◑

Family: LABIATAE
Origin: Cultivar.
Flowering time: Summer.
Climatic zone: 5, 6, 7, 8, 9.
Dimensions: Up to 12 inches (300 mm) high.
Description: A member of the mint family, self-heal is said to heal wounds, and cure headaches and sore throats. The parent species has been a common pasture plant in Europe and U.K. for centuries. The two-lipped tubular flowers appear in dense spikes on erect stems well above the foliage. It appreciates damp and shady places in rock or wild gardens. A hardy perennial, it thrives in full sun in cool climates, but in warmer areas it needs partial shade. Plant it in moist, humus-enriched soil. Propagate by division.

Prunella grandiflora 'Rosea'

Saponaria ocymoides
ROCK SOAPWORT ○

Family: CARYOPHYLLACEAE
Origin: Central and southern Europe.
Flowering time: Spring–summer.
Climatic zone: 3, 4, 5, 6, 7, 8.
Dimensions: Up to 8 inches (200 mm) high.
Description: With its masses of bright, showy flowers growing in loose clusters, this vigorous alpine rock plant looks graceful near steps or trailing over edges or rock walls. Rock soapwort thrives in a sunny position, in sandy soil with good drainage. It can be propagated from cuttings, from seed in early spring, or by division of rootstock in early spring or autumn. 'Rubra Compacta' has deeper pink flowers and a more compact form.
Other colors: Red, white.
Varieties/cultivars: 'Alba', 'Rubra', 'Rubra Compacta', 'Splendens'.

Saponaria ocymoides

Saponaria officinalis
BOUNCING BET, SOAPWORT ○

Family: CARYOPHYLLACEAE
Origin: Europe, Asia.
Flowering time: Summer.
Climatic zone: 3, 4, 5, 6, 7, 8, 9.
Dimensions: Up to 3 feet (1 meter) high.
Description: With its bright pink clusters of flowers often borne in profusion, soapwort is well suited to both wild and cottage gardens. Grow it in sandy, well-drained soil; in moist, fertile soil it tends to be invasive, so choose a position where its growth can be checked if necessary. Soapwort gets its name from the fact that if its leaves are bruised and swished in water, they form a lather. It was used in ancient times as a soap and also for its medicinal properties.
Other colors: Red, white.
Varieties/cultivars: 'Rubra Plena', 'Rosea Plena', 'Alba Plena'.

Saponaria officinalis 'Rosea Plena'

Saxifraga moschata 'Peter Pan'

Saxifraga moschata and hybrids
MOSSY SAXIFRAGE ○ ◑ ●

Family: SAXIFRAGACEAE
Origin: Southern Spain, Italy, Balkans.
Flowering time: Spring.
Climatic zone: 3, 4, 5, 6, 7, 8.
Dimensions: Up to 6 inches (150 mm) high.
Description: Mossy saxifrage is a quick-growing perennial which forms a low mound and is ideal in rock garden pockets, in courtyards, or under trees and shrubs. The leaves are fan-shaped and deeply lobed; the flowers are only ½–1 inch (12–24 mm) wide. There are several cultivars, some of which are hybrids with allied species. Many of these perennials prefer positions either shaded from midday sun or in complete shade. Moist, gritty soil with lime suits them best. Propagate them by seed, root division or cuttings.
Other colors: Scarlet, yellow, white.
Varieties/cultivars: 'Cloth of Gold', 'Triumph', 'Peter Pan'.

Scabiosa caucasica

Scabiosa caucasica
PINCUSHION FLOWER, COMMON SCABIOUS, BORDER SCABIOUS ○

Family: DIPSACACEAE
Origin: Caucasus.
Flowering time: Summer, northern hemisphere; spring–summer, southern hemisphere.
Climatic zone: 4, 5, 6, 7, 8, 9.
Dimensions: Up to 2½ feet (750 mm) high.
Description: Introduced into Britain in 1591, pincushion flower blooms for a long time and the cut flowers are excellent in floral arrangements. The flowers are flat, 2–3 inches (50–70 mm) wide, and similar to the daisy in appearance. Grow it in a border in full sun, in well-drained, limy soil. It resents being moved; if this is necessary, move it in the spring. Propagate it by root division in winter. If the plants become sickly try another cultivar.
Other colors: Lavender, lavender-blue, white.
Varieties/cultivars: 'Moorheim Blue', 'Bressingham White', 'Loddon White', 'Clive Greaves', 'Miss Willmott'.

Sedum maximum 'Atropurpureum'
ICE PLANT, GREAT STONECROP ○ ◑

Family: CRASSULACEAE
Origin: Cultivar.
Flowering time: Summer–autumn.
Climatic zone: 4, 5, 6, 7, 8, 9, 10.
Dimensions: Up to 2 feet (600 mm) high.
Description: The spectacular flowers and foliage make this a good plant in a border or rock garden. The thick, fleshy leaves, green at first and turning a deep claret color later, look dramatic with the pink flowers. Plant it where this effect will brighten a bare part of the garden in autumn. It is easy to grow if it has good drainage, particularly in winter. For best results, plant it in average soil, in sun or partial shade.

Sedum maximum 'Atropurpureum'

Sedum spectabile

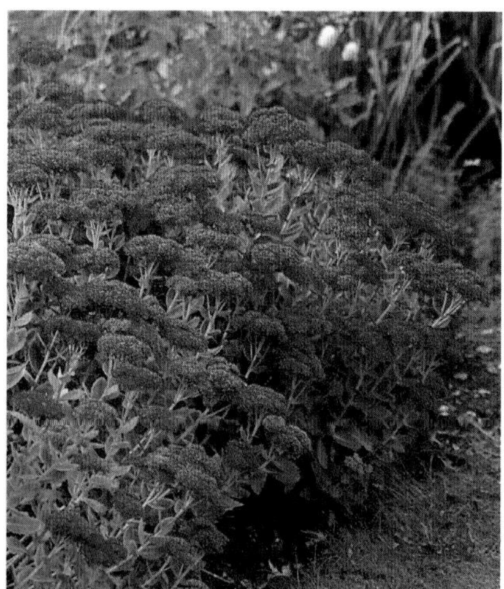

Sedum spectabile 'Autumn Joy'

Sedum spectabile
LIVE-FOR-EVER, SHOWY STONECROP (U.S.A.), ICE PLANT (U.K.) ○ ◑

Family: CRASSULACEAE
Origin: Korea–central China.
Flowering time: Late summer–autumn.
Climatic zone: 4, 5, 6, 7, 8, 9, 10.
Dimensions: Up to 2 feet (600 mm) high.
Description: Much loved by butterflies and bees, ice plant is grown for its showy, plate-like heads of starry, pink flowers, borne in clusters on sturdy stems. The oval, succulent leaves help the plant withstand long dry periods. Good drainage is necessary, particularly in winter, for robust, freely blooming plants. An excellent plant in a border or rock garden, it is easy to grow in average soil, in either sun or partial shade. Apply complete fertilizer in spring and propagate by seed, division, cuttings, or from the leaves themselves.
Other colors: Red, rose-salmon, white.
Varieties/cultivars: 'Brilliant', 'Meteor', 'Autumn Joy', 'Iceberg', 'September Ruby', 'Stardust', 'Variegatum'.

Sedum spectabile 'Autumn Joy'
WILD THYME, MOTHER OF THYME ○ ◑

Family: CRASSULACEAE
Origin: Cultivar.
Flowering time: Summer.
Climatic zone: 4, 5, 6, 7, 8, 9, 10.
Dimensions: Up to 2 feet (600 mm) high.
Description: The salmon-pink aging to rusty-red flowers of this plant form in clusters resembling broccoli heads. Bees and butterflies love them. A compact perennial which is ideally suited to borders, it is easy to grow in average soil. Good drainage is essential, particularly in winter. Propagation is by division, cuttings, or leaves.

Sidalcea malviflora
CHECKERBLOOM, PRAIRIE MALLOW ○ ◑

Family: MALVACEAE
Origin: Oregon–California, Mexico.
Flowering time: Summer.
Climatic zone: 5, 6, 7, 8, 9, 10.
Dimensions: Up to 3 feet (1 meter) high.
Description: This graceful, long-flowering, herbaceous perennial has spikes of pink flowers resembling a small hollyhock. The spikes may need staking if the plant becomes too tall. Fast-growing, it is a good choice for wild or cottage gardens and in sunny, slightly unruly gardens is a good companion plant for delphiniums and gypsophila. Easily grown in average, well-drained soil with some moisture, it likes full sun in colder climates and partial shade in hot areas. Propagate it by seed or root division.
Other colors: Red.
Varieties/cultivars: 'Loveliness', 'Brilliant', 'Croftway Red', 'Sussex Beauty', 'William Smith', 'Rose Green', 'Elsie Heugh'.

Sidalcea malviflora

Thalictrum aquilegifolium
KING-OF-THE-MEADOW, COLUMBINE MEADOWRUE ○ ◑

Family: RANUNCULACEAE
Origin: Eastern and central Europe–northern Asia.
Flowering time: Early summer, northern hemisphere; spring, southern hemisphere.
Climatic zone: 5, 6, 7, 8, 9,10.
Dimensions: Up to 3 feet (1 meter) high.
Description: With its fluffy heads of tassel-like, pink flowers and decorative ferny foliage, king-of-the-meadow makes a handsome border plant. It is unusual in that the male and female flowers bloom on separate plants, the male being the more showy. King-of-the-meadow provides a good foil for larger-flowered plants. Easy to grow in moist, well-drained soil enriched with humus, it needs shade in hot summers. Water regularly, protect it from the wind, and apply complete fertilizer in late winter.
Other colors: White, purple, mauve.

Thalictrum aquilegifolium

Thalictrum delavayi

Thalictrum delavayi syn.
T. dipterocarpum

MEADOWRUE, LAVENDER SHOWER ○ ◑

Family: RANUNCULACEAE
Origin: Western China.
Flowering time: Summer, northern hemisphere; spring, southern hemisphere.
Climatic zone: 5, 6, 7, 8, 9.
Dimensions: Up to 5 feet (over 1 meter) high.
Description: The delicate branching stems of this meadowrue produce numerous gracefully hanging, mauve-pink blooms with yellow anthers. The ferny foliage resembles maidenhair, giving the plant a delicate, oriental look. It forms a good backdrop to annuals or among other perennials. For best results, mulch the plant annually with compost or well-rotted manure. Care is needed when cultivating the soil around the plant, as new growth, which emerges near the parent plant, may be easily severed. It is easy to grow in moist, well-drained soil and should be divided in early spring.
Other colors: White, rose-purple, mauve.
Varieties/cultivars: 'Album', 'Purple Cloud', 'Hewitt's Double'.

Thymus praecox arcticus syn. *T. drucei*

MOTHER OF THYME, WILD THYME ○ ◑

Family: LABIATAE
Origin: Europe.
Flowering time: Spring–summer.
Climatic zone: 4, 5, 6, 7, 8, 9.
Dimensions: Up to 4 inches (100 mm) high.
Description: Mother of thyme is a prostrate, evergreen groundcover. One of the carpet-forming thymes, it is very useful in the rock garden and needs little attention. It can also be placed among paving stones and around paths, emitting a pungent aroma when walked on. The flowers are two-lipped, small, and tubular, appearing in terminal spikes. Plant it in fertile, sandy soil and prune if it becomes invasive. It is propagated by root division or cuttings. This herb can be used in cooking.
Other colors: White, red.
Varieties/cultivars: 'Albus', 'Coccineus', 'Annie Hall', 'Pink Chintz'.

Thymus praecox arcticus

Tradescantia x *andersoniana* syn.
T. virginiana

WIDOW'S TEARS, COMMON SPIDERWORT ○ ◑

Family: COMMELINACEAE
Origin: Hybrid.
Flowering time: Spring–summer.
Climatic zone: 5, 6, 7, 8, 9.

Tradescantia x *andersoniana* 'Carmine Glow'

Dimensions: Up to 2 feet (600 mm) high.
Description: Related to the American wandering Jew, this free-flowering perennial produces attractive clumps. The blooming period is long, though the flowers themselves are short-lived. The clumps may become untidy unless pruned in autumn. Plant it in well-drained soil, in partial shade in hotter areas, and in full sun in cooler climates. Divide it in spring.
Other colors: Many colors.
Varieties/cultivars: Great variety of cultivars available.

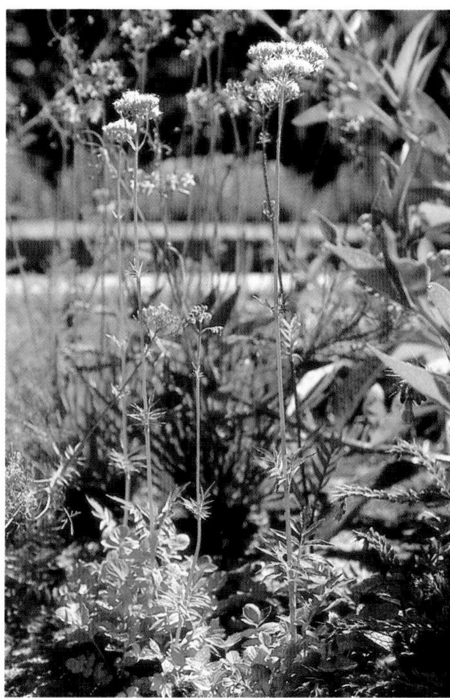

Valeriana officinalis

Valeriana officinalis

COMMON VALERIAN ○

Family: VALERIANACEAE
Origin: Europe, Asia.
Flowering time: Summer.
Climatic zone: 5, 6, 7, 8, 9.
Dimensions: Up to 4 feet (approx. 1 meter) high.
Description: Valerian is an ancient plant with medicinal uses. The aromatic roots have a great attraction for cats. A good border plant, it produces numerous pink flowers in fragrant clusters. It may be prey to aphids. Easy to grow, it prefers very moist, well-drained soil in full sun. Propagate it by seed or division.
Other colors: White, lavender.

Abelia schumannii

Abelia schumannii
SCHUMANN'S ABELIA

Family: CAPRIFOLIACEAE
Origin: Western China.
Flowering time: Summer–autumn.
Climatic zone: 7, 8, 9.
Dimensions: 4–6 feet (1–2 meters) high.
Description: In the northern hemisphere, Schumann's abelia is semi-deciduous but in the southern hemisphere it is evergreen. The new leaves are purplish at first, changing later to a mid-green. Attractive rosy-pink flowers cover the plant for a long period. Plant it in a shrub border or use as a screen plant. Mulch with manure or feed with a complete plant food in early spring. It is not fussy about soil type, but it needs a well-drained position.

Abelia x *grandiflora*
GLOSSY ABELIA

Family: CAPRIFOLIACEAE
Origin: Hybrid.
Flowering time: Summer–autumn.
Climatic zone: 6, 7, 8, 9.
Dimensions: 3–6 feet (1–2 meters) high.
Description: A fast-growing semi-evergreen shrub, glossy abelia is widely used as a hedge or screen plant. It carries its pink and white flowers over a long period; after these have fallen the reddish-brown calyxes remain attractive for months. The leaves are dark-green and glossy. The shrub will grow in any type of free-draining soil in a sheltered site. It can be pruned after flowering if required. Cut back into the old wood so that new arching branches can be formed.
Varieties/cultivars: 'Prostrata'.

Abelia x *grandiflora*

Abutilon 'Tunisia'

Abutilon 'Tunisia'
CHINESE LANTERN, FLOWERING MAPLE (U.K.)

Family: MALVACEAE
Origin: Cultivar.
Flowering time: Summer.
Climatic zone: 9, 10.
Dimensions: 4–6 feet (1–2 meters) high.
Description: Chinese lantern is a spectacular shrub having large, fuchsia-pink flowers similar in appearance to the old-fashioned hollyhock. Prune it back to at least two-thirds of the current year's growth each winter to maintain bushy growth. Fertilize in spring with a complete plant food or mulch around the plant with manure or compost. Ample summer water is required. Chinese lantern makes an excellent background shrub for a perennial border or can be used as a feature plant. It can also be grown in a large tub.

Andromeda polifolia
BOG ROSEMARY

Family: ERICACEAE
Origin: Europe, northern Asia, North America.
Flowering time: Spring–summer.
Climatic zone: 2, 3, 4, 5, 6, 7.

Andromeda polifolia

Dimensions: 12 inches (300 mm) high.
Description: This is an extremely pretty shrub having clusters of delicate, urn-shaped, pale-pink flowers. As the common name suggests, it will only grow in moist and cool soil which must be acidic. Adding peat to the soil and using it as a mulch around the shrub provides perfect conditions. Summer heat and dry soil will kill the plant. It may become straggly with age, but this can be overcome by an occasional heavy pruning after flowering has finished.

Bauera rubioides
DOG ROSE, RIVER ROSE, WIRY BAUERA

Family: BAUERACEAE
Origin: Australia.
Flowering time: Spring–summer.
Climatic zone: 9.
Dimensions: 3 feet (900 mm) high.
Description: This semi-prostrate, heath-like shrub, with its small, dainty, pale-pink flowers, blooms for a long period. Dog rose will grow in full sun, but prefers a shaded position and damp, acidic, well-drained soil. A mulch of leaf

Bauera rubioides

mold around the plant will keep the soil moist and cool. This delicate shrub is suited to a cottage garden or rockery, but in cold climates, it needs to be grown under glass. Fertilize in spring with manure, compost or organic fertilizer. Dog rose does not appreciate artificial fertilizers.

Boronia floribunda
PINK BORONIA ◑ ●

Family: RUTACEAE
Origin: Australia (N.S.W.).
Flowering time: Spring.
Climatic zone: 9.
Dimensions: 3 feet (900 mm) high.
Description: Pink boronia is a very free-flowering, small shrub, bearing fragrant, pale-pink, star-like flowers. The small leaves are a soft, light-green. Plant it near a doorway or window so that the strong fragrance can be appreciated. In very cold areas, it needs to be grown under glass. The main requirements of pink boronia are good drainage and a sandy soil. Apply a heavy mulch of leaf litter under which the surface roots can remain cool. Feed in spring with well-rotted compost, cow manure, or an organic fertilizer.

Boronia floribunda

Callistemon citrinus 'Pink Clusters'
BOTTLEBRUSH ○ ◑

Family: MYRTACEAE
Origin: Cultivar.
Flowering time: Spring.
Climatic zone: 9, 10.
Dimensions: 10–11 feet (3–4 meters) high.
Description: This pretty cultivar has very light-green young leaves which turn darker as they age. The pink flower spikes are 3 inches (80 mm) long.

Callistemon citrinus 'Pink Clusters'

Although the main flowering period is spring, there are always one or two flowers on the shrub throughout the year. Use in the garden as a specimen shrub or at the back of a shrub border. A warm climate plant, crimson bottlebrush likes well-drained soil. Mulch with manure or compost in spring, or feed with blood and bone.

Calluna vulgaris and cultivars
HEATHER ○ ◑

Family: ERICACEAE
Origin: Europe, Asia Minor.
Flowering time: Depends on the cultivar but always summer–autumn.
Climatic zone: 5, 6, 7, 8, 9.
Dimensions: 18 inches (450 mm) high. Height of cultivars differs.
Description: Many varieties of heather are cultivated in gardens, and vary in their shades of pink, flowering time, and habit. The flowers are valued for indoor decoration. They are all easily-grown

Calluna vulgaris 'Anne Marie'

plants, tolerant of lime-free soils and even, moist positions. Although tolerant of some shade, they flower better in full sun. Pruning, if necessary, can be carried out after flowering finishes. Heather combines well with old-fashioned plants in a cottage garden scheme.
Other colors: Red, white, mauve, purple, crimson.
Varieties/cultivars: There are many different cultivars throughout the world.

Camellia japonica 'Drama Girl'

Camellia japonica and cultivars
JAPANESE CAMELLIA, COMMON CAMELLIA ○ ◑

Family: THEACEAE
Origin: China, Korea, Japan.
Flowering time: Winter–spring.
Climatic zone: 7, 8, 9.
Dimensions: 20 feet (6.0 meters) high.
Description: There are hundreds of different cultivars of this plant in every shade of pink imaginable. Flower shape includes single, double, semi-double, and formal double. The leaves are a shiny dark-green. Camellias like moist, but free-draining, acid soil. The root systems are shallow, so mulch around the plant with peat or leaf mold to encourage acid conditions and to keep the soil damp. Lack of water, especially during summer, will cause the buds to drop.
Other colors: Many different shades of pink, red and white, and combinations of these.
Varieties/cultivars: There are many different cultivars throughout the world.

Camellia sasanqua 'Plantation Pink'

Camellia sasanqua cultivars

SASANQUA CAMELLIA ○ ◑

Family: THEACEAE
Origin: Japan.
Flowering time: Autumn–spring.
Climatic zone: 7, 8, 9.
Dimensions: 6–10 feet (2–3 meters) high.
Description: A similar-looking plant to *Camellia japonica*, *C. sasanqua* is hardier and has a more open habit. There are several cultivars of this plant in various shades of pink. In cold areas it requires protection near a wall, but as it ages it becomes more tolerant of cold. The soil should be acidic and moist but free-draining. A mulch is essential to protect the surface roots. Use pine leaves, peat, or leaf mold.
Other colors: Color range is from white through to red with combinations of these.
Varieties/cultivars: There are several different cultivars throughout the world.

Cercis chinensis

CHINESE REDBUD (U.S.A.), CHINESE JUDAS TREE (U.K.) ○

Family: LEGUMINOSAE
Origin: China.
Flowering time: Spring.
Climatic zone: 7, 8, 9.
Dimensions: 15 feet (5 meters) high.
Description: Chinese redbud is a pretty, deciduous shrub with large round, but pointed, glossy green leaves. In spring it is clothed in clusters of bright pink flowers. Although it is a hardy shrub which is easily grown under average conditions, it does not transplant readily. The soil should be well-drained and mulched every spring with manure or compost, or alternatively fed with a small amount of complete plant food. Pruning is not necessary.

Cercis chinensis

Cotinus coggyria

VENETIAN SUMACH (U.S.A.), SMOKE TREE (U.K.), SMOKEBUSH ○ ◑

Family: ANACARDIACEAE
Origin: Central and southern Europe.
Flowering time: Summer.
Climatic zone: 5, 6, 7, 8, 9.
Dimensions: 10–15 feet (3–5 meters) high.
Description: A pretty, deciduous shrub, smoke tree is grown for its lovely autumn color and profusion of fawny-pink feathery flower-stalks which eventually turn a smoky-gray. The flower stalks persist for months and actually do look like clouds of smoke. Smoke tree is easy to grow in any ordinary garden soil that is not too rich or moist.
Other colors: Purple. The leaves of some cultivars are also purple or red.
Varieties/cultivars: 'Purpureus', 'Royal Purple', 'Foliis Purpureis', 'Flame'.

Cotinus coggyria

Dais cotinifolia

Dais cotinifolia

POMPOM TREE ○

Family: THYMELAEACEAE
Origin: South Africa.
Flowering time: Spring.
Climatic zone: 9, 10.
Dimensions: 10–20 feet (3–6 meters) high.
Description: The bark of this shrub is the strongest fiber known to the Africans who use it as a thread. The whole bush is covered for at least a month in attractive pompom-like heads of pinkish-lilac flowers measuring about 2 inches (50 mm) across. The smooth leaves are a bluish-green. Plant in a well-drained soil that is enriched annually with cow manure or compost. Pruning, if necessary, can be carried out after flowering.

Daphne cneorum

Daphne cneorum

ROSE DAPHNE (U.S.A.), GARLAND FLOWER (U.K.) ○ ◑

Family: THYMELIACEAE
Origin: Central and southern Europe.
Flowering time: Spring.
Climatic zone: 4, 5, 6, 7, 8.

Dimensions: 12 inches (300 mm) high.
Description: Garland flower is a popular plant on account of its fragrant, rose-pink flowers which are borne in clusters on prostrate branches. It is an ideal shrub for a rock garden or as a border to a large shrubbery. Garland flower requires a cool, lime-free soil which must be friable and well-drained. Before planting, dig in copious amounts of leaf mold or peat. Do not use chemical fertilizers. A mulch of leaf mold or cow manure annually will suffice and will not harm the plant.
Other colors: White.
Varieties/cultivars: 'Eximea', 'Alba', 'Variegata', 'Major'.

Deutzia scabra 'Flore Pleno'
SNOWFLOWER ○ ◑

Family: SAXIFRAGACEAE
Origin: Cultivar.
Flowering time: Summer.
Climatic zone: 5, 6, 7, 8, 9.
Dimensions: Up to 6 feet (2 meters) high.
Description: This pretty, deciduous shrub has a compact shape with arching branches of dull green foliage, and abundant clusters of white flowers that are suffused with rose-purple on the outside. Adaptable to a wide range of soils and conditions, this shrub benefits from a light pruning after flowering to maintain its shape. It makes an excellent addition to a cottage garden.

Deutzia scabra 'Flore Pleno'

Erica canaliculata
TREE HEATH, PURPLE HEATH ○ ◑

Family: ERICACEAE
Origin: South Africa.
Flowering time: Late winter–early summer.
Climatic zone: 8, 9, 10.
Dimensions: 4–6 feet (1–2 meters) high.
Description: A hardy shrub which, in flower, becomes entirely covered in pale pink or white bells. It forms a neat bush and looks most delightful when planted at the back of a perennial border. Since an acid soil is essential for success, dig in copious amounts of peat or leaf mold, and add a handful of sulfur before planting. Tree heath is easily propagated from self-rooted layers or late summer cuttings.

Erica canaliculata

Erica carnea and cultivars
HEATH, SPRING HEATH, WINTER HEATH ○

Family: ERICACEAE
Origin: Central Europe.
Flowering time: Winter–spring. Different cultivars flower at different times during this period.
Climatic zone: 5, 6, 7, 8, 9.
Dimensions: 8–12 inches (200–300 mm) high and twice this wide.
Description: The delightful urn-shaped, rosy-red flowers are about 3 inches (75 mm) long, but there are innumerable cultivars available in a wide range of shades. Cultivars can be planted so that one of them is in flower from late autumn to late spring. *Erica carnea* and its cultivars prefer an acid soil, too much lime can actually retard growth. Bush mold, decayed oak leaves, or peat worked into the soil will provide the desired conditions. Heath makes an ideal cut flower.
Other colors: A wide range through the white-pink-purple spectrum.
Varieties/cultivars: Numerous cultivars have been developed from this species.

Erica carnea cultivars

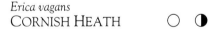

Erica vagans 'Mrs D. F. Maxwell'

Erica vagans
CORNISH HEATH ○ ◑

Family: ERICACEAE
Origin: Southwestern Europe.
Flowering time: Summer–autumn.
Climatic zone: 6, 7, 8, 9.
Dimensions: 1–3 feet (300–900 mm) high.
Description: A small, hardy shrub which produces an abundance of purplish-pink flowers, Cornish heath can be used in a rockery or in the front of a shrub border. The main requirements for healthy growth are an acid, well-drained but moist soil. This can be provided by digging leaf mold or peat into the soil before planting and by sprinkling a handful of sulfur around the plant. Picking the flowers for indoor decoration helps to keep the bush more compact.
Other colors: White, shades of pink and red.
Varieties/cultivars: There are numerous cultivars of this shrub.

Erica tetralix 'Con Underwood'

Erica tetralix and cultivars
CROSS-LEAVED HEATH

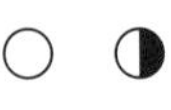

Family: ERICACEAE
Origin: Northern and western Europe.
Flowering time: Summer–autumn.
Climatic zone: 6, 7, 8, 9.
Dimensions: 12–18 inches (300–450 mm) high.
Description: *Erica tetralix* has dainty, urn-shaped, soft-pink flowers and grayish-green foliage. There are several different cultivars and many of them are in different shades of pink. An acid, moist soil is essential for success with this plant. Add peat or leaf mold to the soil when planting, or as a mulch to provide the necessary acidity. A handful of sulfur sprinkled around the plant is also beneficial. This is an ideal shrub for a rockery. It also makes a pretty groundcover.
Other colors: White, shades of pink and red.
Varieties/cultivars: There are numerous cultivars of this shrub.

Erica x *darleyensis*
DARLEY HEATH

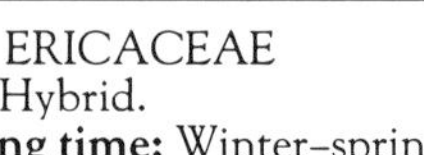

Family: ERICACEAE
Origin: Hybrid.
Flowering time: Winter–spring.
Climatic zone: 6, 7, 8, 9.
Dimensions: 4 feet (approx. 1 meter) high.
Description: When in flower this hardy hybrid, with its compact, cushion-like habit, is smothered with numerous small, rosy-pink bells. It looks like a natural companion when planted with *Erica carnea*. It is as lime-tolerant as *E. carnea*, but thrives when mulched with leaf mold or peat. Plant it in a cottage garden or use at the front of a shrub border. The cut flowers last for a long time indoors.
Other colors: Magenta, red, white, shades of pink.
Varieties/cultivars: There are several cultivars of this species.

Erica x *darleyensis* 'Darley Dale'

Fuchsia x *hybrida*
FUCHSIA

Family: ONAGRACEAE
Origin: Hybrids.
Flowering time: Spring, summer, autumn.
Climatic zone: 7, 8, 9, 10.
Dimensions: 2 feet (600 mm) high.
Description: There are hundreds of different cultivars of fuchsias throughout the world, many of them in the pink color range. These delightful plants will flower freely for many months. When cut back severely in autumn in cooler areas, they will burst forth with new shoots the following spring. Fuchsias like a rich, well-drained soil. A mulch of manure or a handful of complete plant food in early spring will ensure a good flower display. They are very suited to pot culture.
Other colors: Red, purple, blue, white, violet, and combinations of these.
Varieties/cultivars: Numerous cultivars are available.

Fuchsia x *hybrida*

Grevillea rosmarinifolia

Grevillea rosmarinifolia
ROSEMARY GREVILLEA

Family: PROTEACEAE
Origin: Eastern Australia.
Flowering time: Throughout the year.
Climatic zone: 9, 10.
Dimensions: 4 feet (approx. 2 meters) high.
Description: This pretty shrub has thin green leaves and flowers which vary from red to creamy pink mainly in spring and summer. Some flowers remain throughout the year. Plant rosemary grevillea where it can be seen from a window, as it is very attractive to birds. It can be heavily pruned to make a formal hedge if required. It requires a greenhouse environment in cool climates. Its main requirements are a well-drained soil and applications of organic fertilizer. Propagation can be carried out from cuttings taken in early spring.
Other colors: Red and dark pink.
Varieties/cultivars: 'Jenkinsii', 'Olympic Flame'.

Hibiscus rosa-sinensis cultivars
ROSE-OF-CHINA, CHINESE HIBISCUS

Family: MALVACEAE
Origin: Southern China.
Flowering time: Spring–summer.

Hibiscus rosa-sinensis

Climatic zone: 9, 10.
Dimensions: 6–10 feet (2–3 meters) high.
Description: This is a beautiful flowering shrub with literally hundreds of different cultivars, many of which grow in various shades of pink. They make beautiful feature plants or can be grown in a shrub border. In cool climates, a greenhouse environment is essential. Bushes should be pruned back to near half height each winter to maintain a good shape and to produce a better display of flowers the following year. A well-drained soil and regular applications of plant food during spring and summer are their main requirements.
Other colors: White, orange, red.
Varieties/cultivars: There are numerous cultivars.

Justicia carnea
PINK JACOBINIA, BRAZILIAN-PLUME FLOWER, KING'S-CROWN ○ ◑

Other common names: PINK ACANTHUS
Family: ACANTHACEAE
Origin: Brazil.
Flowering time: Summer–autumn.
Climatic zone: 9, 10.
Dimensions: 5 feet (approx. 2 meters) high.
Description: Pink jacobinia has large, deeply veined, dark-green leaves and big cone-shaped flower heads. Each flower head consists of many rosy-pink flowers. It is a fast-growing shrub which becomes straggly and unattractive unless it is drastically pruned every spring. It is often grown as an indoor plant. For best results, plant in a rich, well-drained soil and feed every spring with a complete plant food. It is easily propagated from early spring cuttings.

Justicia carnea

Kalmia latifolia

Kalmia latifolia
MOUNTAIN LAUREL, CALICO BUSH ◑

Family: ERICACEAE
Origin: Eastern North America.
Flowering time: Summer.
Climatic zone: 4, 5, 6, 7, 8, 9.
Dimensions: 7–15 feet (2–5 meters) high.
Description: This is one of the most beautiful and valued evergreen shrubs for a cold-climate garden. The delightful shell-pink, saucer-shaped flowers are crinkled at the edges. An acid, lime-free soil is an essential requirement. It will not grow in heavy clay soils nor in areas which have hot, dry summers. Plant it in soil that has been heavily enriched with leaf mold or peat and apply a mulch of this around the shrub.

Kolkwitzia amabilis
BEAUTYBUSH ○

Family: CAPRIFOLIACEAE
Origin: Western China.
Flowering time: Spring–summer.
Climatic zone: 5, 6, 7, 8, 9.
Dimensions: 8–12 feet (2.4–4 meters) high.
Description: Beautybush is an extremely attractive, erect shrub. The bell-like flowers are pink with a yellow throat. It is useful for a cottage garden. Although not fussy about soil type, it appreciates a handful of complete plant food sprinkled around its base in late winter. Do not prune unless absolutely necessary. Pruning will not only spoil the shape but will prevent flowering for a season as flowers are produced on the previous year's growth.

Kolkwitzia amabilis

Lantana camara

Lantana camara
COMMON LANTANA, RED SAGE, YELLOW SAGE (U.K.) ○

Family: VERBENACEAE
Origin: Tropical America.
Flowering time: Summer–autumn, but in warmer climates there are some flowers on the shrub throughout the year.
Climatic zone: 9, 10.
Dimensions: 3 feet (1 meter) high.
Description: A prickly-stemmed shrub, lantana has dull-green, strangely-scented leaves which are rough to the touch. It is valued for its yellow flowers ageing to red or white which stay on the plant for a long period. The flowers are followed by shining black, berry-like seeds that are relished by birds. It will thrive when planted near the coast or in areas that experience drought. Grow common lantana in a sandy, free-draining soil. It needs to be pruned in spring to prevent legginess.
Other colors: White, cream, lilac, orange yellow.
Varieties/cultivars: There are several cultivars throughout the world.

Leptospermum scoparium and cultivars

TEA TREE, MANUKA ○ ◑

Family: MYRTACEAE
Origin: Australia, New Zealand.
Flowering time: Spring–summer.
Climatic zone: 8, 9, 10.
Dimensions: 3–6 feet (1–2 meters) high, depending on the cultivar.
Description: Tea trees are attractive evergreen shrubs bearing white, red, or pink flowers. They are very suited to coastal planting as the majority of them often thrive where not much else will grow. All the cultivars of leptospermum like a slightly acid soil of a sandy nature, and an open sunny position, but they can become accustomed to dappled shade. Prune lightly after flowering if they become too straggly. The cut flowers are pretty indoors.
Other colors: Various shades of white, red, pink.
Varieties/cultivars: Numerous cultivars are available.

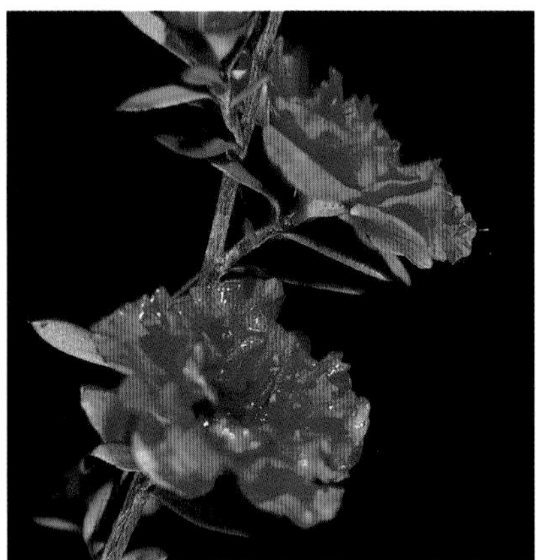

Leptospermum scoparium 'Sunraysia'

Lonicera tatarica

TATARIAN HONEYSUCKLE ○ ◑

Family: CAPRIFOLIACEAE
Origin: Central Asia, Russia.
Flowering time: Spring.
Climatic zone: 4, 5, 6, 7, 8.
Dimensions: 8–10 feet (2–3 meters) high.
Description: An old-fashioned, bushy honeysuckle which has multitudes of fragrant, soft-pink flowers during spring, followed by red berries. This species is variable and the flowers are often rich pink. The leaves are oval. It makes an ideal background shrub in a cottage garden. If it becomes too leggy it can be pruned after flowering has finished.

Lonicera tatarica

Tatarian honeysuckle is not fussy about soil type as long as the drainage is good.
Other colors: White, red.
Varieties/cultivars: 'Alba', 'Arnold Red', 'Hack's Red', 'Sibirica'.

Luculia gratissima

LUCULIA, PINK SIVA ○ ◑

Family: RUBIACEAE
Origin: Himalayas, India.
Flowering time: Late autumn–late winter.
Climatic zone: 9, 10.
Dimensions: 4–6 feet (1–2 meters) high.
Description: Luculia is one of the most beautiful winter-flowering shrubs. Fragrant clusters of soft-pink flowers cover the bush. The large leaves are light-green with a slightly downy underside. Plant near a window or door where the beautiful fragrance can be appreciated. Luculia flowers last well when picked and brought indoors. A well-drained soil and ample summer water are essential. Prune moderately after flowering — severe pruning can lead to the death of the plant.

Luculia gratissima

Melaleuca decussata

TOTEM POLES, CROSS-LEAVED HONEY-MYRTLE ○ ◑

Family: MYRTACEAE
Origin: Australia (S.A., Vic.).
Flowering time: Spring–summer.
Climatic zone: 9, 10.
Dimensions: 6–11 feet (2–4 meters) high.
Description: This rounded shrub, with fine, stiff, narrow gray-green leaves, has mauve-pink bottlebrush-like flowers that quickly fade to white. They are very attractive to birds. It is an adaptable shrub which will survive wet or dry conditions. *Melaleuca* can be used as a specimen shrub or as a windbreak or hedge. Feed annually with cow manure or compost. Alternatively, apply a handful of blood and bone around the plant in spring.

Melaleuca decussata

Nerium oleander and cultivars

OLEANDER, ROSE-BAY (U.S.A.) ○

Family: APOCYNACEAE
Origin: Southern Europe, North Africa, Japan.
Flowering time: Summer–autumn.
Climatic zone: 9, 10.
Dimensions: 4–15 feet (1–5 meters) high.
Description: Oleander is an extremely hardy shrub which will tolerate heat, drought, and salt. However, in cool climates, it needs to be grown under glass. The large, open-faced pink or white flowers stay on the plant throughout summer. There are few shrubs which flower for so long a period. The dark-green leaves are in pairs or whorls of three around the stem. All parts of this plant are poisonous, so keep children and pets from eating it. Do not burn the leaves. The many cultivars of this plant have

Nerium oleander

become much more popular than the species itself.
Other colors: White, yellow, buff, red.
Varieties/cultivars: Several cultivars have been developed throughout the world.

Paeonia suffruticosa and cultivars
TREE PEONY, MOUNTAIN PEONY (U.S.A.) ○ ◑

Family: PAEONIACEAE
Origin: China.
Flowering time: Early summer.
Climatic zone: 6, 7, 8, 9.
Dimensions: Up to 6 feet (2 meters) high.
Description: The tree peony and its cultivars are among the finest of all spring-flowering shrubs. The large, shaggy-petalled flower heads are 6–8 inches (150–200 mm) wide. Flower color of the species is pink to white, each petal having a maroon splash at the base. Whilst tree peony and its cultivars are frost-hardy, the new growth is susceptible to late-spring frosts so it should be given protection. Tree peonies grow best in a neutral to acid, humus-rich soil, with shelter from strong winds.
Other colors: White, red.
Varieties/cultivars: 'Godaishu', 'Hodai', 'Kumagai', 'Sakurajishi', 'Taiyo'.

Paeonia suffruticosa

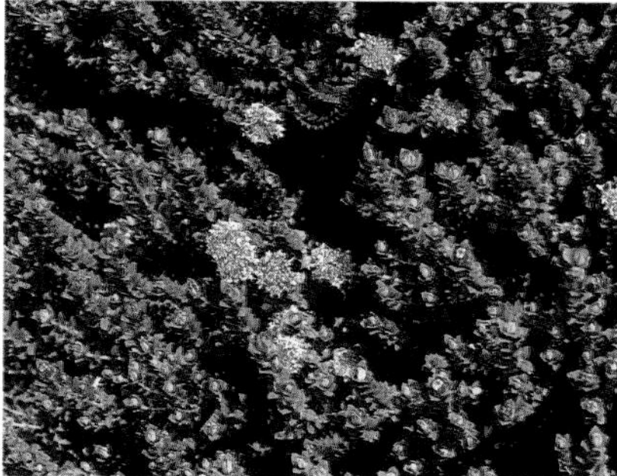

Pimelea ferruginea

Pimelea ferruginea
PINK RICE FLOWER ○ ◑

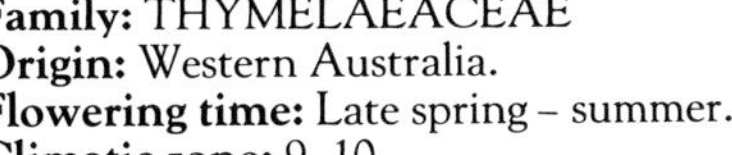

Family: THYMELAEACEAE
Origin: Western Australia.
Flowering time: Late spring – summer.
Climatic zone: 9, 10.
Dimensions: 1–3 feet (100–900 mm) high.
Description: A neat, rounded shrub with small, glossy green leaves, pink rice flower has a profusion of pink flowers borne in terminal heads during spring. It is an ideal plant for use in a rockery. Salt-tolerant, it is a useful shrub for beachside planting. It likes a well-drained soil. Very little fertilizer or pruning is required to maintain this shrub.

Protea cynaroides

Protea cynaroides
GIANT PROTEA, KING PROTEA (U.K.) ○

Family: PROTEACEAE
Origin: South Africa.
Flowering time: Winter–summer.
Climatic zone: 9, 10.
Dimensions: 2–6 feet (1–2 meters) high.
Description: Giant protea is the most spectacular of all the proteas. The beautiful flower heads of soft silvery pink are 8–12 inches (200–300 mm) across. In the right position the shrub will flower for nine months of the year. In some cold areas, a greenhouse is required. All proteas strongly resent over-rich soils and will thrive in rather poor, slightly acid soil that contains a lot of rubble or sand. Add sulfur to the soil if it is too alkaline. Avoid using phosphates. Do not overwater.

Protea neriifolia

Protea neriifolia
OLEANDER-LEAF PROTEA ○

Family: PROTEACEAE
Origin: South Africa.
Flowering time: Spring–winter.
Climatic zone: 9, 10.
Dimensions: 4–6 feet (1–2 meters) high.
Description: One of the most popular proteas, *P. neriifolia* has deep rose-pink flowers 5 inches (125 mm) long and 3 inches (75 mm) wide. The tips of the petals are black and furry. The long leaves are a soft green. Grow proteas in soil that is not too rich. A poor, slightly acid soil that contains a lot of rubble or sand is ideal. Add sulfur to the soil if it is too alkaline. Avoid using phosphates. Do not overwater, especially in winter. A greenhouse may be necessary in cold climates.
Other colors: Salmon-red.
Varieties/cultivars: 'Taylors Surprise', 'Snow Crest'.

Rhaphiolepis x *delacourii*
PINK INDIAN HAWTHORN ○

Family: ROSACEAE
Origin: Hybrid.
Flowering time: Spring and autumn.
Climatic zone: 8, 9.
Dimensions: 6 feet (2 meters) high.
Description: This is a charming shrub which has a neat rounded habit and glossy-green leaves. The rose-pink flowers are borne in terminal branching clusters. Pink Indian hawthorn is a slow-growing shrub, but a worthwhile addition to the garden. It is used for hedges and in shrub borders. It is not fussy about soil type, but appreciates a handful of complete plant food around its base in late winter.
Other colors: Crimson.
Varieties/cultivars: 'Coates Crimson'.

Rhaphiolepis x *delacourii*

Rhododendron indicum
INDIAN AZALEA ○ ◑

Family: ERICACEAE
Origin: Southern Japan.
Flowering time: Winter–spring.
Climatic zone: 8, 9.
Dimensions: 3–8 feet (1–2 meters) high.
Description: This species is the origin of most of the garden forms developed by hybridizing with the allied species. It is a small, dense, evergreen bush. The funnel-shaped flowers are single or in pairs. There are hundreds of different cultivars, many of which are in the pink color range. Indian azaleas require an acid, well-drained soil enriched with leaf mold or compost. Mulching around the plant is also important as the roots are very shallow.
Other colors: White, red, orange, purple.
Varieties/cultivars: There are numerous cultivars of this species.

Rhododendron indicum 'Alphonse Andersen'

Rhododendron Kurume Group
KURUME AZALEA ○ ◑

Family: ERICACEAE
Origin: Japan.
Flowering time: Spring.
Climatic zone: 6, 7, 8.
Dimensions: Can reach 4 feet (over 1 meter) high.
Description: Kurume azaleas originated from the Kurume province in Japan so they can withstand more cold than *R. indicum*. They are evergreen, with small, rounded leaves. Although the flowers are smaller than other azaleas, they are produced in such profusion that they completely cover the bush. Plant in an acid, well-drained soil which has been enriched with leaf mold or compost. Mulching around the base of the plant is important, as the roots are very shallow.
Other colors: Orange, red, purple, white.
Varieties/cultivars: There are numerous hybrids and varieties of this species.

Rhododendron Kurume Group 'Fairy Queen'

Rhododendron spp.
RHODODENDRON, AZALEA ○ ◑

Family: ERICACEAE
Origin: Japan, China, Himalayas, Burma.
Flowering time: Winter–spring.
Climatic zone: 5, 6, 7, 8, 9.
Dimensions: 1–10 feet (up to 3 meters) high.
Description: The genus rhododendron is one of the largest, numbering over 800 species, which range from tiny, prostrate plants to large shrubs. The flowers vary through the whole color spectrum. The majority of the species like a sheltered position and an acid, well-drained soil that has been enriched with leaf mold or compost. A mulch around the shallow, fibrous roots is essential to keep them cool and moist.
Other colors: White, red, yellow, purple, blue.
Varieties/cultivars: There are numerous cultivars.

Rhododendron spp.

Ribes sanguineum
FLOWERING CURRANT (U.K.), AMERICAN CURRANT ○ ◑

Family: GROSSULARIACEAE
Origin: Western North America.
Flowering time: Spring.
Climatic zone: 6, 7, 8.
Dimensions: 5–12 feet (2–4 meters) high.
Description: An ornamental and pretty, deciduous shrub, flowering currant can be used as a feature shrub or in a shrub border of a cottage garden. During spring it is covered in hanging flower heads, 3–4 inches (75–100 mm) long, of rosy-pink flowers which are followed by black berries with a waxy, white patina which makes them look gray from a distance. The leaves have a characteristically pungent smell. Flowering currant is an easily grown

Ribes sanguineum

shrub, thriving in any soil. Prune after flowering. It can be propagated from layering, cuttings, or seeds.
Other colors: White, red, crimson.
Varieties/cultivars: 'King Edward VII', 'Splendens', 'Album', 'Albescens', 'Carneum'.

Robinia kelseyi
ALLEGHENY MOSS LOCUST (U.S.A.) ○ ◑

Family: LEGUMINOSAE
Origin: South Allegheny Mountains (U.S.A.).
Flowering time: Spring, southern hemisphere; summer, northern hemisphere.
Climatic zone: 6, 7, 8, 9.
Dimensions: 8–10 feet (2–3 meters) high.
Description: This graceful shrub or small tree with slender branches and elegant foliage has slightly fragrant rose-pink flowers hanging in clusters. Allegheny moss locust makes a perfect feature shrub. A sheltered position is essential as the branches are very brittle and easily broken by wind. It is excellent in dry, inland areas, as it will withstand near-drought conditions.

Robinia kelseyi

Rondeletia amoena
YELLOW-THROAT RONDELETIA ○ ◑

Family: RUBIACEAE
Origin: West Indies.
Flowering time: Summer.
Climatic zone: 9, 10.
Dimensions: 6-10 feet (2–3 meters) high.
Description: Yellow-throat rondeletia is a bushy evergreen shrub, with large, handsome, rather leathery leaves. The salmon-pink, fragrant, tubular flowers are borne in terminal clusters and have a golden beard at the throat. It is useful as a screen or feature shrub, and will grow in any well-drained garden soil. However, in cold climates it grows best in a greenhouse. Prune, if required, to just above the lower leaves on the branches as the flowers finish.

Rondeletia amoena

Spiraea japonica
JAPANESE SPIRAEA, PINK MAY ○ ◑

Family: ROSACEAE
Origin: Japan.
Flowering time: Summer.
Climatic zone: 5, 6, 7, 8, 9.

Spiraea japonica 'Ruberrima'

Dimensions: 4–6 feet (1–2 meters) high.
Description: This hardy deciduous shrub, valued for its flattened heads of pink flowers, is a popular landscape or feature plant. Japanese spiraea is easily grown in any type of garden soil as long as it is well-drained. Removing some of the older, less productive branches at the base each year after flowering will encourage the growth of new, vigorous wood. The cut flowers last well indoors.
Other colors: Red, white, crimson.
Varieties/cultivars: 'Alpina', 'Atrosanguinea', 'Bullata', 'Fastigiata', 'Little Princess', 'Ruberrima', var. *albiflora*.

Weigela florida cultivar

Weigela florida and cultivars
WEIGELA, APPLE BLOSSOM (U.S.A.)

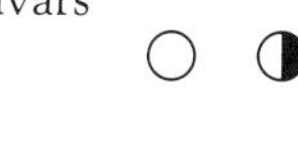

Family: CAPRIFOLIACEAE
Origin: Japan, Korea, northern China.
Flowering time: Spring–summer.
Climatic zone: 5, 6, 7, 8, 9.
Dimensions: 7–10 feet (2–3 meters) high.
Description: This is a pretty, deciduous shrub with cane-like branches covered in funnel-shaped, rose-pink flowers which are pale-pink inside. There are many attractive hybrids of this plant. Weigela will grow in any garden soil and should be pruned only after flowering has finished as flowers are borne on the current season's growth. Grow in a shrub border or as a feature plant.
Other colors: White, red, crimson, rosy-crimson.
Varieties/cultivars: There are numerous varieties throughout the world.

Aesculus x *carnea* 'Briottii' syn. *A. rubicunda*
RED HORSE CHESTNUT ○

Family: SAPINDACEAE
Origin: Hybrid.
Flowering time: Late spring–early summer.
Climatic zone: 4, 5, 6, 7, 8, 9.
Dimensions: Up to 40 feet (13 meters) high.
Description: This strikingly beautiful horse chestnut tree has an attractive rounded shape and a profusion of large heads of deep pink blooms during its flowering period. It can be grown from seed, and should be planted where there is plenty of space to allow its shape to develop. Like most horse chestnuts it is quite slow growing, and unless rich, moist soil is provided the foliage will burn and growth will be retarded.

Aesculus x *carnea* 'Briottii'

Albizia julibrissin
MIMOSA TREE (U.S.A.), PERSIAN SILK TREE ○

Family: LEGUMINOSAE
Origin: Western Asia–Japan.
Flowering time: Late spring–early summer.
Climatic zone: 9, 10.
Dimensions: 16–20 feet (5–6 meters) high x 25–27 feet (7–8 meters) wide.
Description: Soft, feathery green leaves combined with pretty, fluffy, pink-and-cream flowers belie the toughness of this small, deciduous tree. Once established, it thrives in hot, dry areas, in light sandy soils. Typical of the Leguminosae family, it closes its leaves at night to conserve moisture. A fast grower, it is particularly suitable to plant in a new garden as a screen or splendid shade tree. Much smaller and bushier is *A. j.* 'Rosea'. Both are easily grown from seed.
Other colors: White.
Varieties/cultivars: 'Alba', 'Rosea'.

Albizia julibrissin

Bauhinia x *blakeana*
HONG KONG ORCHID TREE, BUTTERFLY TREE ○

Family: LEGUMINOSAE
Origin: Hybrid.
Flowering time: Winter, northern hemisphere; late summer–late spring, southern hemisphere.
Climatic zone: 9, 10.
Dimensions: 15–25 feet (5–7 meters) high.
Description: Floral emblem of Hong Kong, this tree deserves that honor, for there are not many months when it is not actually producing flowers. An evergreen, growing almost as wide as it does high, it produces a dense, leafy canopy offering welcome shade in hot climates. The fragrant and exotic orchid-like flowers do not produce the bean pods common to its genus (which can look rather messy), for it is a sterile hybrid. Grow it from cuttings. Prune to shape it while young and prune after each flush of flowers. Hong Kong orchid tree grows well in California and Florida.

Bauhinia x *blakeana*

Bixa orellana
LIPSTICK TREE, ANNATTO TREE ○

Family: BIXACEAE
Origin: Tropical America.
Flowering time: Summer.
Climatic zone: 9, 10.
Dimensions: 10–30 feet (3–10 meters) high.
Description: An evergreen tree for very warm climates only, bixa is normally bushy in habit but can be trained by careful pruning into a single-stemmed, small tree. Quick-growing, it makes a handsome screen or hedging plant. The flowers form at the tips of branches, and are followed by red-brown spiny fruit. To enjoy summer-long fragrant flowering, trim after the fruits deteriorate, then allow new buds to form. Water well in dry weather. Bixa can be grown from seed.

Bixa orellana

Brachychiton discolor
QUEENSLAND LACEBARK, PINK FLAME TREE (U.K.), HAT TREE ○

Other common names: WHITE KURRAJONG (Aust.)
Family: STERCULIACEAE
Origin: Australia (northern N.S.W., Queensland, and Northern Territory coastal regions).
Flowering time: Late spring–early autumn.

Climatic zone: 9, 10.
Dimensions: 20–65 feet (6–20 meters) high.
Description: The Queensland lacebark is widely grown as a shade tree in hot, dryish climates, including California, South Africa, and the Mediterranean. Although normally evergreen, it loses some leaves in cooler regions. The leaves are variable in shape, smooth above and woolly beneath. In a good year, the flowers are spectacular and when they fall, forming a carpet beneath the tree, they create a picture of mirrored beauty. Lacebark prefers deep soils and high rainfall. It is commonly planted as a street tree.

Brachychiton discolor

Calodendrum capense
CAPE CHESTNUT ○

Family: RUTACEAE
Origin: South Africa (coast to tropics).
Flowering time: Late spring–mid-summer in southern hemisphere.
Climatic zone: 8, 9, 10.
Dimensions: 30–45 feet (9–15 meters) high.
Description: An extremely beautiful and adaptable tree, Cape chestnut grows in a range of climates from warm temperate to tropical. Sprays of highly perfumed, mottled pink flowers that cover the canopy seem to be orchid look-alikes. Because it is slow to flower from seed, it is best grown as a grafted plant. Given a good start in fertile soil, it grows fairly quickly, but slows down later, seldom reaching more than 30 feet (10 meters) in the garden. It needs plenty of water in dry weather. Cape chestnut is evergreen in warm climates, but semideciduous in frost areas.

Calodendrum capense

Camellia reticulata and cultivars
NET VEIN CAMELLIA, NETTED CAMELLIA ○ ◑

Family: THEACEAE
Origin: Yunnan, western China.
Flowering time: Late autumn and early spring, southern hemisphere; spring, northern hemisphere.
Climatic zone: 8, 9.
Dimensions: 6–35 feet (2–10 meters) high.
Description: Really a large shrub, *Camellia reticulata* grows to tree proportions in the wild. Its flowers are larger than other camellias and very free-forming, and although its growth is not as compact as in *C. japonica*, the new cultivars are producing denser growth. Easily grown in tubs or for use as tall, background plants, reticulatas are long-lived, requiring only good drainage and a fairly acid soil. Like all camellias and azaleas, their roots are shallow-surfaced, so constant mulching is very beneficial. Reticulatas perform well in full sun, protected from winds.
Other colors: Red, coral, crimson, dark purple-red, white.
Varieties/cultivars: 'Pagoda', 'Letitia', 'Buddha', 'Franci L', 'Howard Asper', 'Purple Gown', 'Tali Queen'.

Camellia reticulata cultivar

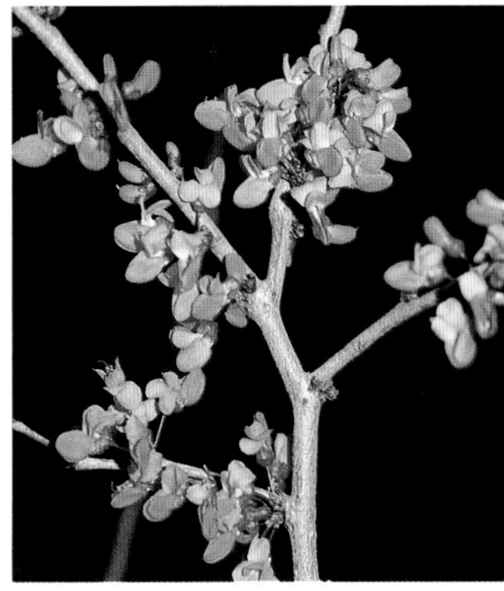

Cercis canadensis

Cercis canadensis
EASTERN REDBUD, AMERICAN JUDAS TREE (U.K.) ○ ◑

Family: LEGUMINOSAE
Origin: Southeastern Canada, eastern United States, northeastern Mexico.
Flowering time: Spring.
Climatic zone: 4, 5, 6, 7, 8, 9.
Dimensions: 20–40 feet (6–12 meters) high.
Description: Related to the Judas tree, with similar, but heart-shaped leaves and narrower growth habit, the eastern redbud is a beautiful feature of the spring landscape in the eastern and central states of America. One of the first trees to bloom after winter, numerous clusters of stemless flowers are borne on mature branches, often coming straight out of the wood. It quickly grows into a small, round-headed tree in cultivation. Although not fussy as to soil, it must have good drainage and plenty of water in dry, hot summers. It is deciduous.
Other colors: White.
Varieties/cultivars: 'Alba', 'Plena'.

Cercis siliquastrum
JUDAS TREE, LOVE TREE (U.S.A.) ○

Family: LEGUMINOSAE
Origin: Southern Europe, western Asia.
Flowering time: Early–late spring.
Climatic zone: 7, 8, 9.
Dimensions: 20–30 feet (6–9 meters) high.
Description: This was the tree from which Judas Iscariot supposedly hanged himself after betraying Christ. Like all *Cercis* species, it grows into a delightful small tree, smothering itself with rosy-colored blossom in spring. Typical of the genus, the pea-shaped flowers appear on all parts of the bare wood, even straight out of the trunk. The leaves are kidney-shaped. Most adaptable, it will flourish in heat and drought, is resistant to light frost and will grow in coastal gardens. It is deciduous.
Other colors: White.
Varieties/cultivars: 'Alba'.

Cercis siliquastrum

Cornus florida 'Rubra'
PINK-FLOWERING DOGWOOD ○ ◑

Family: CORNACEAE
Origin: Cultivar.
Flowering time: Spring.
Climatic zone: 5, 6, 7, 8, 9.
Dimensions: 13–40 feet (4–12 meters) high.
Description: Pink-flowering dogwood is one of the most beautiful sights of spring when it flowers on bare wood from upturned twigs. The actual flowers are small and greenish in color, surrounded by four, showy, rosy-pink bracts. A second treat arrives with autumn as the scarlet-colored fruit ripens and the leaves become crimson. Happiest in cool, moist climates, it develops into a small, wide-canopied tree. It needs excellent drainage in acid soil but must not be allowed to dry out. Mulch regularly.

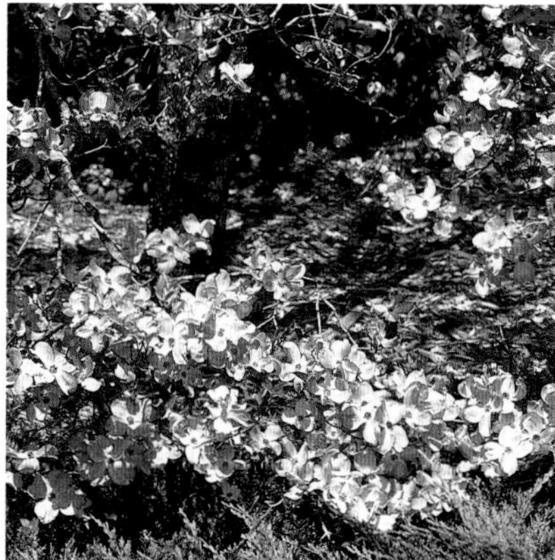

Cornus florida 'Rubra'

Dombeya x *cayeuxii*
MEXICAN ROSE, PINK BALL DOMBEYA, CAPE WEDDING FLOWER ○

Family: BYTTNERIACEAE
Origin: Hybrid.
Flowering time: Late autumn–spring.
Climatic zone: 9, 10.
Dimensions: 15–30 feet (4–9 meters) high.
Description: The parents of this hybrid are *D. burgessiae* and *D. wallichii*. The hanging clusters of shell-pink flowers are somewhat like those of a viburnum and the leaves are poplar-shaped and large. A good fill-in plant for a warm corner position or background situation, it develops a shrubby growth habit. It is easily grown from cuttings in spring and is widespread in many climates including those of Florida, India, Africa, and Australia.

Dombeya x *cayeuxii*

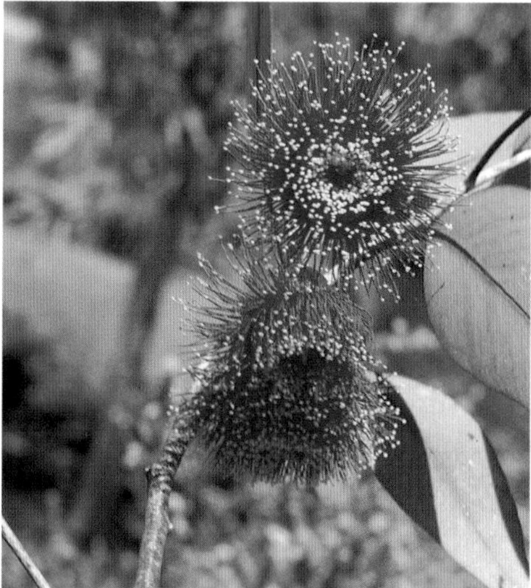

Eucalyptus caesia

Eucalyptus caesia
GUNGUNNA, GUNGURRU (Aust.) ○

Family: MYRTACEAE
Origin: Southwestern Western Australia.
Flowering time: Winter–mid-spring in southern hemisphere.
Climatic zone: 9, 10.
Dimensions: Up to 27 feet (8 meters) high.
Description: One of the most delightful small eucalypts, it develops an open, somewhat sprawling, tree-like habit when cultivated. It is admired for the showy stamens of the flowers which appear on branches covered in a whitish waxy patina. Very decorative, mealy-covered, urn-shaped gumnuts form later which hang for months, and make interesting indoor dried arrangements. Gungunna will not tolerate bad drainage or a prolonged humid atmosphere. Grown from seed, it should be pruned lightly for more compact growth.
Varieties/cultivars: 'Silver Princess'.

Magnolia campbellii
CHINESE TULIP TREE, PINK TULIP TREE, CAMPBELL MAGNOLIA ○

Family: MAGNOLIACEAE
Origin: Himalayas.
Flowering time: Spring.
Climatic zone: 7, 8, 9.
Dimensions: 40–160 feet (12–50 meters) high.
Description: Probably seen at its

maximum height only in its native habitat, the Chinese tulip tree is very slow-maturing, and takes about 12–15 years to come into flower. Plant it for your children to enjoy! Its maximum height in the U.K. is 60 feet (18 meters). The flowers sit on bare wood and are large, pink, and waxy. Large velvety leaves follow, their color in autumn complementing the spikes of scarlet seeds. This tree grows best in frost-free areas.
Other colors: White, purple.
Varieties/cultivars: *M. c.* var. *mollicomata.*

Magnolia campbellii

Malus floribunda
JAPANESE CRAB APPLE ○

Family: ROSACEAE
Origin: Japan, China.
Flowering time: Spring.
Climatic zone: 5, 6, 7, 8, 9.
Dimensions: 16–25 feet (5–7 meters) high.
Description: Although some crab apples are inclined to bloom only every two years, *M. floribunda* is renowned for its reliability in flowering every year. The backs of the petals are a rosy color and the insides white — which produces a delightful sight when rosy buds are opening among already-opened, white flowers. Beautiful fruits, yellow with a reddish flush, develop in autumn, although in the U.K. this species fruits poorly and the very small 'apples' are not usually brightly colored. The crab apple prefers a moist climate with long winters. Protect it from strong winds but allow it plenty of root space.
Other colors: Purplish-red.
Varieties/cultivars: 'Gibb's Golden Gage', 'Indian Magic', 'Indian Summer', 'Liset', 'Makamik', 'Mary Potter', 'Robinson'.

Malus floribunda

Malus ioensis 'Plena'
PRAIRIE CRAB (U.S.A.), BECHTEL CRAB APPLE ○

Family: ROSACEAE
Origin: Cultivar.
Flowering time: Late spring–early summer.
Climatic zone: 2, 3, 4, 5, 6, 7, 8, 9.
Dimensions: 20–30 feet (6–9 meters) high.
Description: This is arguably the most beautiful of the flowering crab apples, but is not a strong grower. *M. ioensis* 'Plena' is a double-flowered bud-mutant (that is, produced by a mutation in one of the buds) of *M. ioensis*, discovered by Bechtel, an Illinois nurseryman. Flowers are abundant and sweetly perfumed, opening later than those of most crab apples, which is useful if you want to prolong spring flowering. Fruit is seldom seen, but the leaves color in autumn to vivid shades of yellow, orange, and crimson. It can be susceptible to juniper rust.

Malus ioensis 'Plena'

Malus spectabilis 'Plena'

Malus spectabilis 'Plena'
CHINESE CRAB APPLE, DOUBLE FLOWERED CHINESE CRAB APPLE ○

Family: ROSACEAE
Origin: Cultivar.
Flowering time: Mid–late spring.
Climatic zone: 4, 5, 6, 7, 8, 9.
Dimensions: 16–30 feet (5–9 meters) high.
Description: This is possibly a natural hybrid of Chinese origin. It is unknown as a native tree growing in the wild. Flowers of *M. s.* 'Plena' are semidouble, rose-pink when in bud, opening to blush-pink, then fading to white. They are faintly perfumed. Its beauty when flowering, plus its vigorous growth habit, make this tree a valuable addition to any cool, moist, elevated garden in regions with longish winters. A row of crab apples lining a driveway or footpath, in blossom or in fruit, is a breathtaking sight.

Malus x *purpurea* 'Eleyi'
PURPLE CRAB APPLE ○

Family: ROSACEAE
Origin: Hybrid.
Flowering time: Late spring.
Climatic zone: 4, 5, 6, 7, 8, 9.
Dimensions: 20–25 feet (6–7 meters) high.
Description: Flowers of M. x *p.* 'Eleyi' are a pretty rosy-magenta in bud, opening to a paler shade. Purplish-red fruits persist into late autumn. It is a deciduous tree. Trees and shrubs with reddish to purplish leaves are best used with discretion for they can easily dominate a garden landscape. *Malus* x *p.* 'Eleyi', can be beautifully integrated with plants that have silvery-gray foliage. Try planting it with willow-leaved pear (*Pyrus salicifolia*) as did Vita Sackville-West in her famous White Garden at Sissinghurst. For best results, plant in well-drained, rich soil and mulch annually with well-rotted compost or manure. Water well in summer.

Malus x *purpurea* 'Eleyi'

Prunus mume 'Geisha'
JAPANESE APRICOT ○

Family: ROSACEAE
Origin: Cultivar.
Flowering time: Early–late spring, northern hemisphere; winter, southern hemisphere.
Climatic zone: 7, 8, 9.
Dimensions: 20–27 feet (6–8 meters) high.
Description: The semidouble, rosy-red flowers of *P. m.* 'Geisha' appear in clusters on one- and two-year-old wood in winter or spring. Being on very short stalks, they appear as solid branches of color. The small, deciduous tree, which develops a broadly rounded crown, is ideal for planting bulbs beneath. Plant it against a warm wall in cold areas.

Prunus mume 'Geisha'

Prunus persica
PEACH, WILD PEACH ○

Family: ROSACEAE
Origin: China.
Flowering time: Spring.
Climatic zone: 5, 6, 7, 8, 9.
Dimensions: 10–25 feet (3–7 meters) high.
Description: Many varieties have been bred from this species, first found growing in the wild in China. Rose-pink flowers appear, followed by round, edible fruits. Unfortunately the tree is subject to borer attack and peach leaf curl (a fungus disease). In parts of Australia the fruit is attacked by fruit fly, and must be treated as the fruit begin to ripen. Keep the tree vigorous by regular feeding and watering, and spray the leaves with a fungicide at bud-swell stage. If you only want flowers, it is advisable to grow one of the many cultivars.
Other colors: White, rosy-red, white-and-red stripes.
Varieties/cultivars: 'Alba Plena', 'Alba Plena Pendula', 'Foliis Rubis', 'Klara Mayer', 'Lilian Burrows', 'Magnifica', 'Rosea Plena', 'Versicolor'.

Prunus persica

Prunus 'Amanogawa' syn. *P. serrulata erecta*
JAPANESE FLOWERING CHERRY ○

Family: ROSACEAE
Origin: Hybrid.
Flowering time: Late spring, northern hemisphere; mid–late spring, southern hemisphere.
Climatic zone: 5, 6, 7, 8, 9.
Dimensions: 13–20 feet (4–6 meters) high.
Description: Unlike most Japanese flowering cherries, which either spread their branches wide to form a flattened crown or develop a broad vase shape, *P.* 'Amanogawa' develops into a narrow, upright form. Given its narrow habit, this cherry is best used as a background tree or in a narrow space. Semidouble, blush-pink, fragrant flowers appear in erect clusters on this deciduous tree. Do not prune it. Cherries, badly pruned, can die from producing excess gum.

Prunus 'Amanogawa'

Prunus serrulata 'Shimidsu Sakura'

JAPANESE FLOWERING CHERRY ○

Family: ROSACEAE
Origin: Cultivar.
Flowering time: Mid–late spring.
Climatic zone: 5, 6, 7, 8, 9.
Dimensions: 10–13 feet (3–4 meters) high.
Description: Pink buds opening to pure white, hanging clusters of flowers adorn this small, deciduous tree from mid- to late spring. Considered one of the most beautiful of the flowering cherries, it develops wide-spreading, gracefully arching branches to form a broad, flattened crown. Green leaves color brilliantly in autumn. It prefers a cool, moist climate on elevated soils.

Prunus serrulata 'Shimidsu Sakura'

Prunus subhirtella

Prunus subhirtella and cultivars

HIGAN CHERRY, ROSEBUD CHERRY ○

Family: ROSACEAE
Origin: Hybrid.
Flowering time: Spring.
Climatic zone: 6, 7, 8, 9.
Dimensions: 20–30 feet (6–9 meters) high.
Description: The tiny, pink flowers of the natural hybrid *P. subhirtella* are not as beautiful as in the cultivated varieties. Slender branches carry small, green leaves which color well in autumn and then drop. As with all flowering cherries, avoid pruning, but if it becomes necessary prune in summer. For showier flowers and smaller growth, plant the cultivars.
Other colors: Deep to light pink, single and double.
Varieties/cultivars: 'Pendula', 'Pendula Rosea', 'Pendula Rubra', 'Autumnalis', 'Fukubana'.

Prunus subhirtella 'Autumnalis'

Prunus subhirtella 'Autumnalis'

WINTER SPRING, WINTER CHERRY (U.K.) ○

Family: ROSACEAE
Origin: Cultivar.
Flowering time: Autumn, winter, spring.
Climatic zone: 6, 7, 8, 9.
Dimensions: 20–30 feet (6–9 meters) high.
Description: Other cherries may be much more showy, displaying beautiful, hanging clusters of flowers, but this cultivar has the advantage of flowering over an extended period. In a mild winter it can begin to flower in autumn and continue intermittently into spring. The modest clusters of flowers cling to small shoots that grow straight out of the trunk. As with all deciduous cherries, it performs best in a cool, moist climate.

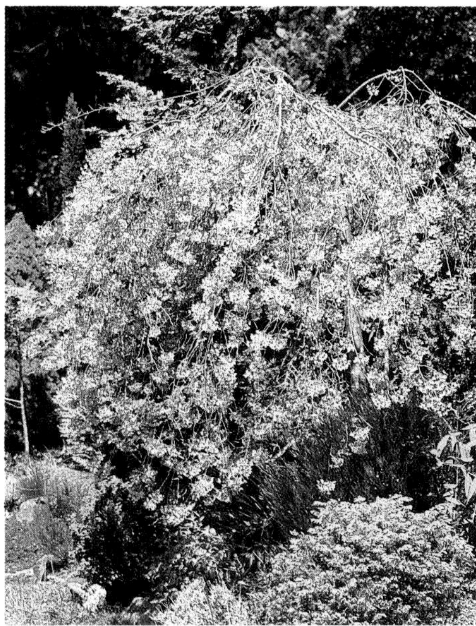

Prunus subhirtella 'Pendula Rosea'

Prunus subhirtella 'Pendula Rosea'

WEEPING CHERRY, SPRING CHERRY ○

Family: ROSACEAE
Origin: Cultivar.
Flowering time: Spring, northern hemisphere; late spring, southern hemisphere.
Climatic zone: 6, 7, 8, 9.
Dimensions: 6–10 feet (2–3 meters) high.
Description: Fountains of delightful, dainty, pink, single flowers cascade from the canopy of this weeping small tree each spring. They are a rich pink when in bud, fading later to blush pink. Beautiful, slender, arching branches give the tree the appearance of a miniature weeping willow. It can provide an avenue of color, or be grown as an individual against a background of evergreen trees. Often grown as a small standard, this tree makes an ideal specimen in a small garden. Very little pruning is necessary.

Prunus x *amygdalo-persica* 'Pollardii'

FLOWERING ALMOND ○

Family: ROSACEAE
Origin: Hybrid.
Flowering time: Spring, southern hemisphere.
Climatic zone: 6, 7, 8, 9.
Dimensions: 10–20 feet (3–6 meters) high.
Description: A cross between a peach and an almond, this Australian-raised hybrid quickly grows into a robust, small tree. Single, soft rose-pink flowers appear in profusion each spring, well before the leaves unfurl. If cut while still in bud, the flowers will open indoors, lasting a week in water. It is reasonably resistant to the peach leaf curl which attacks so many flowering peaches. Fruits are almond-shaped. The green leaves do not produce good autumn coloring.

Prunus x *amygdalo-persica* 'Pollardii'

Prunus x *blireana*

DOUBLE ROSE CHERRY, FLOWERING CHERRY PLUM ○

Family: ROSACEAE
Origin: Hybrid.
Flowering time: Spring, northern hemisphere; early spring, southern hemisphere.
Climatic zone: 6, 7, 8, 9.
Dimensions: 8–17 feet (2–5 meters) high.
Description: Flowering cherry plum is a cross between *P. cerasifera* 'Atropurpurea' and *P. mume* 'Alphandii'. It is a small, compact, deciduous tree, bearing semidouble, rose-pink, fragrant flowers. These appear en masse and are much in

Prunus x *blireana*

demand for use in floral art and as an indoor cut flower. The tree has coppery-purple leaves, and as with all trees and shrubs with reddish leaves, in a small garden it may overpower other plants. In a larger setting, plant as an avenue.
Other colors: Pale pink flowers, pale reddish-purple leaves.
Varieties/cultivars: 'Moseri'.

Prunus x *yedoensis*

JAPANESE FLOWERING CHERRY, YOSHINO CHERRY ○

Family: ROSACEAE
Origin: Hybrid.
Flowering time: Spring, northern hemisphere.
Climatic zone: 6, 7, 8, 9.

Prunus x *yedoensis*

Dimensions: 27–40 feet (8–12 meters) high.
Description: This beautiful deciduous tree has long been cultivated in Japan and is the principal park and street cherry tree grown in that country. Thought to be a cross between *P. subhirtella* and *P. speciosa*, it has a short main trunk, and forms a flattish, broad-domed shape. Almond-scented, blush-pink flowers appear in profusion each spring. Ideal for cool and temperate climates, it thrives in well-drained, moderately rich soil that is well watered in summer. Incorporate plenty of well-rotted compost prior to planting.
Other colors: White, pale pink.
Varieties/cultivars: 'Ivensii', 'Shidare Yoshino', 'Akebono'.

Rhododendron arboreum

Rhododendron arboreum

TREE RHODODENDRON ○ 

Family: ERICACEAE
Origin: Himalayas.
Flowering time: Mid-winter–spring, northern hemisphere.
Climatic zone: 8, 9.
Dimensions: 20–50 feet (6–15 meters) high.
Description: Parent to many sturdy hybrids, this tall species rhododendron was first discovered in the Himalayas in 1820 and is the first known tree rhododendron. It injected a rich, red color into the breeding program. Regal-looking flower clusters open atop rosettes of handsome, evergreen leaves which droop down at flowering time to display the blooms. It prefers a cool, moist climate and acid soils, and needs regular mulching.
Other colors: White.
Varieties/cultivars: 'Blood Red', 'Roseum', 'Sir Charles Lemon', 'Cornubia', 'Gill's Triumph', 'Glory of Penjerrick'.

Robinia hispida
ROSE ACACIA (U.K.), BRISTLY LOCUST, MOSS LOCUST ○

Family: LEGUMINOSAE
Origin: Southeastern United States.
Flowering time: Late spring, northern hemisphere; early summer, southern hemisphere.
Climatic zone: 5, 6, 7, 8, 9.
Dimensions: 4–7 feet (1–2 meters) high.
Description: Although really a shrub, *R. hispida* is often grafted onto the standard rootstock of *R. pseudoacacia*, to form a small tree. Fragrant, pea-shaped flowers of a charming rose-pink color hang in clusters, partly hidden by the green, fern-like foliage. Plant where its slightly drooping branches can hang over a wall to best display the flowers. If grown as a shrub, it tends to sucker, but does not outgrow its welcome. As its stems are very brittle, if grown on a standard, plant it in a wind-protected spot, preferably against a sunny wall. Buy grafted stock, or propagate shrubs from suckers or root cuttings.
Varieties/cultivars: var. *macrophylla* 'Superba'.

Robinia hispida 'Macrophylla'

Tamarix aphylla
ATHEL TREE, EVERGREEN TAMARISK ○

Family: TAMARICACEAE
Origin: India, northwest Africa, eastern Mediterranean.
Flowering time: Late summer–early autumn.
Climatic zone: 8, 9.
Dimensions: 30–40 feet (10–12 meters) high.
Description: This tree has tiny whitish pink flowers which appear along slender ½ inch (12 mm) spikes in summer. It is valuable for its ability to survive under hot, dry conditions. An evergreen, it is a perfect specimen for the hot and arid places in Australia, Africa, and the U.S.A. Once established, it can withstand the heat and a rainfall of less than 5 inches (125 mm) per year. It is also a useful tree for seaside planting, withstanding salt-laden winds and providing shelter for less hardy plants. Good drainage is essential. It resents being moved.

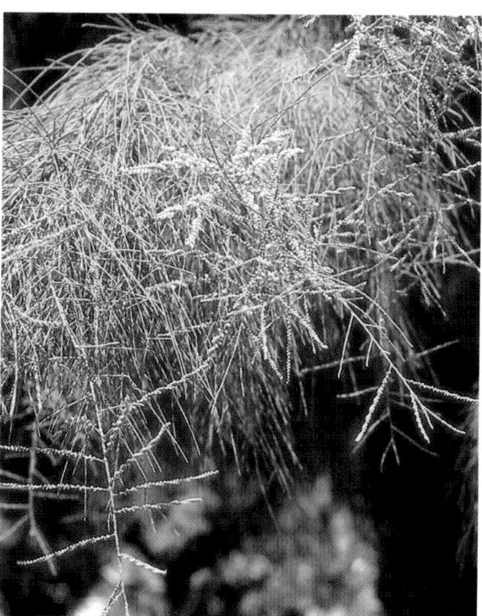

Tamarix aphylla

Tamarix parviflora
TAMARISK ○

Family: TAMARICACEAE
Origin: Yugoslavia, Greece, Turkey, Crete.
Flowering time: Spring.
Climatic zone: 6, 7, 8, 9.
Dimensions: 10–15 feet (3–5 meters) high.
Description: All tamarisks are useful plants in low rainfall areas. *T. parviflora*, although not showy, is a picture in spring when masses of tiny, pale-pink flowers festoon the fine, bare branches. These are followed by feathery foliage. An excellent plant to use in a subtle landscape design, it provides shelter for less hardy plants in a seaside location or in a hot, dry situation. Good drainage is essential and if not provided, plants can become infested by borer. With its open, irregular shape and no main trunk, it is shrub-like in appearance.

Tamarix parviflora

Virgilia capensis syn. *V. oroboides*
KEURBOOM, VIRGILA ○ ◑

Family: LEGUMINOSAE
Origin: South Africa.
Flowering time: Spring–early summer.
Climatic zone: 9, 10.
Dimensions: 27–33 feet (8–10 meters) high.
Description: One of the fastest-growing trees in cultivation, it enjoys a good but brief life, often dying after about fifteen years. Like fast-growing wattles, it makes a good "nurse" plant, protecting slower-growing species close by and filling in areas where privacy is needed. It is an erect evergreen that lives longer in cool rather than hot areas and prefers light, well-drained soils with adequate water in hot summers. Trim the plant back each year to keep it more compact and vigorous.

Virgilia capensis

SECTION THREE

Purple-Blue Flowers

Annuals 398

Bulbs 402

Climbers 408

Perennials 414

Shrubs 436

Trees 450

Ageratum houstonianum
COMMON AGERATUM, FLOSSFLOWER ○ ◑

Family: COMPOSITAE
Origin: Mexico.
Flowering time: Summer–autumn.
Climatic zone: 5, 6, 7, 8, 9, 10.
Dimensions: 18 inches (450 mm) high.
Description: The flower heads are borne in dense terminal clusters of many flowers, each one of which is ¼ inch (6 mm) in diameter, but the entire head is up to 2 inches (50 mm) wide and looks like a single flower. The flower heads, which are mainly blue to lavender, are soft and fluffy and, especially in the dwarf varieties, can cover the top of the plant. Ageratum makes an excellent border plant because of its contrasting color and dense habit. The taller types can be cut and last well indoors. Sow seedlings in spring in any well-drained soil.
Other colors: Pink, white.
Varieties/cultivars: 'Blue Angel', 'Lilac Angel', 'Blue Blazer', 'White Angel', 'Blue Mink'.

Ageratum houstonianum 'Blue Mink'

Borago officinalis
BORAGE, TALEWORT ○ ◑

Family: BORAGINACEAE
Origin: Mediterranean region.
Flowering time: Summer.
Climatic zone: 4, 5, 6, 7, 8, 9, 10.
Dimensions: Up to 2 feet (600 mm) high.
Description: This is a plant grown principally as a culinary herb. Both the leaves and the very attractive soft-blue flowers may be used as a garnish or to flavor drinks. It is a quick-growing annual with stiff but soft, hairy, gray-green foliage. The flowers form in a terminal head up to ¼ inch (18 mm) wide, and are also hairy, giving the plant a soft, clouded appearance. Bees are attracted to the flowers which may be crystallized, used in potpourri, or as a cake decoration; the leaves may be shredded and used in salads. Plant in full sun or semishade in moderately rich, well-drained soil.
Other colors: Purple, white.

Borago officinalis

Centaurea cyanus

Centaurea cyanus
CORNFLOWER, BLUEBOTTLE, BLUE BONNETS ○ ◑

Other common names: BATCHELOR'S-BUTTON, RAGGED SAILOR
Family: COMPOSITAE
Origin: Southern and eastern Europe.
Flowering time: Summer–autumn.
Climatic zone: 5, 6, 7, 8, 9.
Dimensions: Up to 2 feet (600 mm) high.
Description: A very useful floral plant, grown as an annual, it has bright blue flowers on stiff upright stems which make it ideal for florist work. The flowers are up to 1½ inches (40 mm) wide in a tight head. It is hardy and flowers best in early summer before it is too hot. It is not a leafy plant but produces many flower stems. Choose a sunny or lightly shaded position and ensure that the soil is light but rich with organic matter. Water well while buds are forming.
Other colors: White, lavender, pink.
Varieties/cultivars: 'Alba'.

Consolida orientalis syn. *Delphinium orientale*
LARKSPUR ○

Family: RANUNCULACEAE
Origin: Southern Europe–western Asia, North Africa.
Flowering time: Summer.
Climatic zone: 5, 6, 7, 8, 9.
Dimensions: Up to 3 feet (1 meter) high.
Description: With its tall, strong-stemmed, many-flowered spikes, this larkspur is an attractive garden plant. It is a favorite with florists for use as background in floral arrangements with its even, blue flowers. Flower spikes are up to 12 inches (300 mm) long and covered in small blooms 1½ inches (30 mm) wide. It is excellent for bedding as a background to other shorter annuals. Although hardy, it does not tolerate hot, dry conditions. For a good display sow seeds or seedlings in clumps in slightly alkaline soil — add lime if the soil is acid. Feed weekly while buds are forming.
Other colors: Violet, pink, white.
Varieties/cultivars: 'Rainbow' mixed may produce other colors.

Consolida orientalis

Delphinium consolida syn. *Consolida regalis*

DELPHINIUM ○

Family: RANUNCULACEAE
Origin: Southern and central Europe–western Asia.
Flowering time: Summer–autumn.
Climatic zone: 5, 6, 7, 8, 9.
Dimensions: Up to 7 feet (2 meters) high.
Description: The majestic tall flower spikes of this Delphinium species make it the most-prized of these useful perennials. The flowers are soft and blue/purple in color, while the kidney-shaped foliage is mid green. Ideal for an old-fashioned flower garden, it should be positioned towards the back. Plant in deep, rich and slightly alkaline soil and provide some shelter from strong winds as the tall flower spikes are prone to collapse if not protected.
Other colors: Pink, mauve, lilac, white.

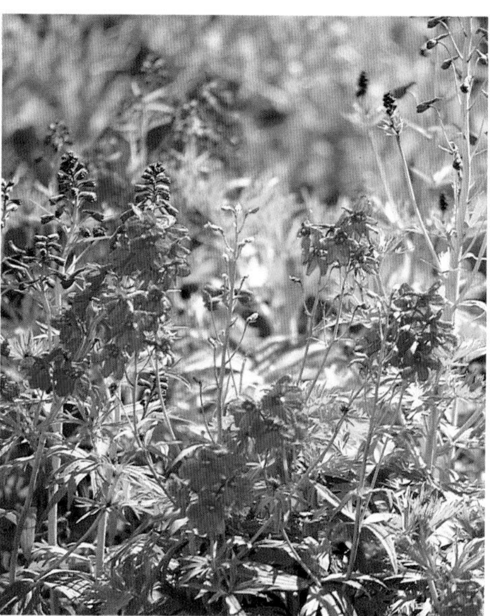

Delphinium consolida

Eustoma grandiflorum syn. *Lisianthus russellianus*

LISIANTHUS, PRAIRIE GENTIAN ○

Family: GENTIANACEAE
Origin: Central southern United States.
Flowering time: Summer.
Climatic zone: 6, 7, 8, 9.
Dimensions: Up to 3 feet (1 meter) high.
Description: This flower is shaped like an upturned bell, flaring at the edges and blotched at the base, being some 2 inches (50 mm) wide. It is long-lasting as a cut flower, and useful as an indoor flowering pot plant in a well-lit situation. The foliage is pale-green, dull, and not impressive. It is hardy, tolerating a wide range of conditions.
Other colors: White, pink, lavender, dark purple.
Varieties/cultivars: 'Yodel Pink', 'Yodel Blue', 'Yodel White' (all compact to 18 inches (450 mm) high).

Eustoma grandiflorum

Exacum affine

PERSIAN VIOLET ◑

Family: GENTIANACEAE
Origin: South Yemen.
Flowering time: Spring–autumn.
Climatic zone: 9, 10.
Dimensions: Up to 10 inches (250 mm) high.
Description: This is a low-growing, compact plant, suitable for borders in sheltered areas in warm climates. It needs partial shade because the stems and leaves are tender and will not tolerate frost. The tiny flowers, lavender with yellow centers, are about ½ inch (13 mm) wide and cover the plant profusely. They have a sweet perfume. Its compact habit makes it an ideal plant for small containers. It will live and flower indoors or under shelter in good light for three to four months. It does not like to be overwatered. It is a short-lived perennial usually grown as an annual. It is well-suited to a greenhouse in cold climates.
Other colors: White, pink.

Exacum affine

Limonium sinuatum

Limonium sinuatum

STATICE, SEA LAVENDER, SEA PINK ○

Family: PLUMBAGINACEAE
Origin: Mediterranean region–Portugal.
Flowering time: Spring–summer.
Climatic zone: 6, 7, 8, 9, 10.
Dimensions: Up to 18 inches (450 mm) high.
Description: Its strong, wiry stems and many-colored flowers, added to its lasting qualities when picked, make statice popular with florists and for indoor arrangements. The tiny flowers are only ⅜ inch (9 mm) wide, but are tightly clustered to give good color. They are dry and papery when in full bloom and are borne on winged branches. The plant is biennial but is mostly grown as an annual. The foliage is in a rosette at the base of the plant and of minor importance. Valued for its tolerance to low rainfall and also to seaspray, it is excellent in both seaside and country gardens. Apply a general fertilizer when buds are forming, to encourage a good floral display.
Other colors: Dark-red, yellow, pink, white.

Lobelia erinus

COMMON LOBELIA, EDGING LOBELIA ○

Family: LOBELIACEAE
Origin: South Africa.
Flowering time: All seasons, excluding frost.
Climatic zone: 5, 6, 7, 8, 9, 10.
Dimensions: Up to 6 inches (150 mm) high.
Description: This is a wiry-stemmed bushy plant but some types have a trailing habit. Although short in stature with small flowers, it gives a mass of color when in bloom. Individual flowers, which are barely ½ inch (13 mm) wide, are deep-blue and often have a white eye. When grown with multicolored annuals, their rich color forms a vivid contrast. The stems are slender but when the plants are grown closely together they form a continuous color border. The trailing varieties are used effectively in hanging baskets in cool but light situations. Best results are obtained if planted in rich, moist soil.
Other colors: Pale blue, white, purple, red, cream.
Varieties/cultivars: 'String of Pearls' (mixed variety), 'Basket Lobelia' (trailing).

Lobelia erinus

Lupinus hartwegii

LUPIN, ANNUAL LUPIN, HAIRY LUPIN ○

Family: LEGUMINOSAE
Origin: Mexico.
Flowering time: Summer–autumn.
Climatic zone: 7, 8, 9.
Dimensions: Up to 2½ feet (750 mm) high.
Description: This is a tall, upright, strong-growing annual, with a long flowering period. The foliage is compact and stiff and produces flower stems up to 18 inches (450 mm) high, making lupin an ideal cut flower. The long-lasting flowers are about 1 inch (25 mm) long and cover the stems densely in pastel shades of blue, pink, and white. All the foliage and the flowers are covered with soft, silky hairs. A fertile, moist soil ensures best results. Full sun and good drainage are essential.
Varieties/cultivars: 'Pixie' (dwarf form, growing 8 inches (200 mm) high).

Lupinus hartwegii

Nemophila menziesii

Nemophila menziesii

BABY-BLUE-EYES ◑

Family: HYDROPHYLLACEAE
Origin: California.
Flowering time: Summer.
Climatic zone: 5, 6, 7, 8, 9.
Dimensions: Up to 8 inches (200 mm).
Description: While this plant grows only to a low height, it spreads well and has dainty fern-like foliage. On the tips of the stems are many bright blue flowers with white centers, saucer-like in shape, up to 1½ inches (40 mm) wide. The outstanding blue with white shows prominently in the garden when baby-blue-eyes is planted closely in groups. It is not suitable for picking, but is attractive in hanging baskets in a cool situation.
Other colors: White, blue-margined white, and brownish-purple margined white.
Varieties/cultivars: 'Alba', 'Peter Blue' (veined purple), 'Crambeoides', 'Atomaria', 'Disoidalis'.

Nierembergia hippomanica

CUPFLOWER ○ ◑

Family: SOLANACEAE
Origin: Argentina.
Flowering time: Summer–autumn.
Climatic zone: 6, 7, 8, 9, 10.
Dimensions: Up to 15 inches (380 mm) high.
Description: This plant is usually grown as an annual, but is a shrubby perennial in mild winters. It is hardy and withstands strong sunlight. The flowers though small, up to 1 inch (25 mm) wide, are numerous and tightly packed. They are shaped like a tiny cup, yellow in the center and violet on the rim. Cupflower is useful for hanging baskets, but has no picking value. Easy to cultivate in a wide range of soils and conditions, in full sun or semishade.
Varieties/cultivars: 'Violacea', 'Purple Robe'.

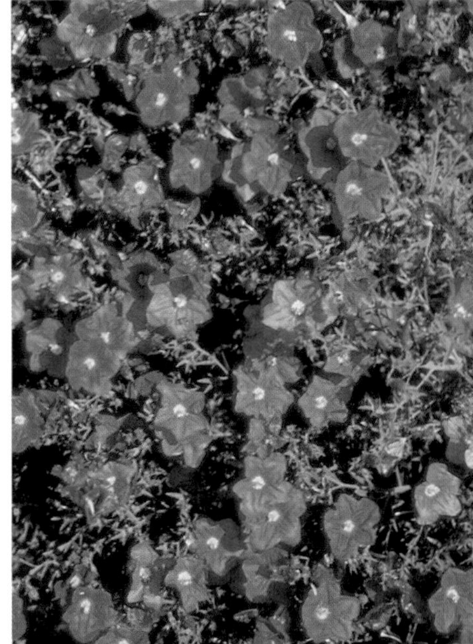

Nierembergia hippomanica

Nigella damascena
LOVE-IN-A-MIST, DEVIL-IN-THE-BUSH, WILD FENNEL ○

Family: RANUNCULACEAE
Origin: Southern Europe, North Africa.
Flowering time: Summer–autumn.
Climatic zone: 5, 6, 7, 8, 9.
Dimensions: Up to 18 inches (450 mm) high.
Description: Bright green, lace-like foliage gives an attractive background to the small flowers scattered on the surface. The flowers may be white, light blue, rose-pink, mauve, or purple, and are up to 1½ inches (40 mm) wide. Both the flowers and the globe-shaped dried seed pods keep well when cut. The plant is hardy and has a long flowering season. Choose a sunny position and ensure that soil is well-drained.

Nigella damascena

Salvia patens
GENTIAN SAGE ○

Family: LABIATAE
Origin: Mexico.
Flowering time: Summer.
Climatic zone: 5, 6, 7, 8, 9,10.
Dimensions: Up to 3 feet (1 meter) high.
Description: This is a hardy plant usually grown as an annual, but may persist as a perennial especially if old flower heads are cut back. The flower spike is upright and protrudes from the foliage, which is dull green and hairy. When grown closely, 12 inches (300 mm) apart, the plant makes an attractive hedge or background for other annuals. Flowers are bright blue, up to 3 inches (75 mm) long, and flower spikes are up to 12 inches (300 mm) long. Plant in a sunny but sheltered position and enrich the soil with plenty of well-rotted manure or compost prior to planting.
Other colors: White.
Varieties/cultivars: 'Alba'.

Salvia patens

Torenia fournieri
WISHBONE FLOWER, BLUEWINGS ○  ●

Family: SCROPHULARIACEAE
Origin: Vietnam.
Flowering time: Summer.
Climatic zone: 6, 7, 8, 9.
Dimensions: Up to 12 inches (300 mm) high.
Description: These low-growing, rather tender plants need to be grown closely together to give a massed border effect. The flowers are 1½ inches (35 mm) long and 1 inch (25 mm) wide with four petals, three of them purple and the largest pale blue, all with yellow spots in the throat. They are attractive in hanging baskets but no use as a cut flower. Warm, humid conditions and a rich, moist soil are essential. In the right climate it can be grown in full sun or shade.
Other colors: White, also with yellow spots in the throat.
Varieties/cultivars: 'Alba'.

Torenia fournieri

Viola tricolor
JOHNNY-JUMP-UP, PANSY, HEARTSEASE  

Family: VIOLACEAE
Origin: Europe, Asia.
Flowering time: Spring–autumn.
Climatic zone: 6, 7, 8, 9.
Dimensions: Up to 12 inches (300 mm) high.
Description: *Viola tricolor* is the true wild species pansy which varies in size and color. One plant produces many tiny flowers in two tones of blue to purple, often bicolored. Flowers are usually borne singly and are from ¾ inch (19 mm) to 4 inches (100 mm) wide. It is useful for planting over naturalized bulbs and also in pots and baskets. Rich, moist soil and a sunny to semishaded position are ideal for pansies.

Viola tricolor

Allium aflatunense

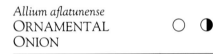

Allium aflatunense
ORNAMENTAL ONION ○ ◑

Family: LILIACEAE
Origin: Central Asia–China.
Flowering time: Spring.
Climatic zone: 6, 7, 8.
Dimensions: Up to 2½ feet (750 mm) high.
Description: This plant, which belongs to the leek, chive, garlic and shallot family, produces large, beautiful flowers. It is one of the larger varieties and can be featured in mixed borders naturalized in grass, woodland and rock gardens. This Asian variety produces large round heads of purple star-like flowers and has attractive strap-like leaves. Clumps can be lifted and divided in early autumn.

Anemone coronaria
WINDFLOWER, POPPY-FLOWERED ANEMONE ○ ◑ ●

Family: RANUNCULACEAE
Origin: Mediterranean.
Flowering time: Spring.
Climatic zone: 8, 9.
Dimensions: Up to 18 inches (450 mm) high.
Description: During the Crusades, soil

Anemone coronaria 'St. Brigid'

from the Holy Land was taken to Pisa as ship's ballast to bury dead soldiers. The following spring, the area was carpeted with anemones. The flowers were called "blood drops of Christ" and spread across Europe. These anemones will grow abundantly in full sun or partial shade. Provide well-drained sandy soil rich in humus. Both single and double blooms are available and look pretty in borders or massed under trees.
Other colors: Red, white, mauve, yellow.
Varieties/cultivars: 'St. Brigid'.

Babiana stricta
BABOON FLOWER (U.K.), BABOONROOT, WINE CUPS ○

Family: IRIDACEAE
Origin: South Africa.
Flowering time: Spring.

Babiana stricta

Climatic zone: 9, 10.
Dimensions: Up to 8 inches (200 mm) high.
Description: These plants were named by early settlers to South Africa when they discovered baboons eating the corms. The plants produce about six purple flowers, not unlike freesias, on each stem. They are well-suited to growing in pots, tubs, or window boxes. This species will adapt equally well to naturalizing in woodlands and lawns. Full sun is needed and successful growth depends on the bulbs being planted deeply in sandy soil. The same procedure applies if planting in pots. A greenhouse environment is necessary in cold climates.
Other colors: Mauve, cream, red, white, yellow.

Chionodoxa luciliae

Chionodoxa luciliae
GLORY-OF-THE-SNOW ◑

Family: LILIACEAE
Origin: Turkey.
Flowering time: Spring.
Climatic zone: 4, 5, 6, 7, 8, 9.
Dimensions: Up to 6 inches (150 mm) high.
Description: This small, colorful bulb is at its best when clustered under deciduous trees and shrubs. It is one of the early flowers of spring, hence the common name, glory-of-the-snow. Naturalize it in wooded areas or rock gardens. This plant will tolerate shade and can be grown indoors in pots or window boxes. Plant in well-drained soil mixed with organic matter. Apply fertilizer when flowering has finished. This flower is a good choice for a blue garden.
Other colors: Pink and white.
Varieties/cultivars: 'Rosea', 'Zwanenburg', 'Pink giant'.

Crocus tommasinianus

Colchicum cilicicum 'Byzantinum'

Colchicum cilicicum 'Byzantinum'
AUTUMN CROCUS ◑

Family: LILIACEAE
Origin: Cultivar.
Flowering time: Autumn.
Climatic zone: 4, 5, 6, 7, 8, 9.
Dimensions: Up to 12 inches (300 mm) high.
Description: Autumn crocus are best planted in a nook by themselves with a groundcover. The funnel-shaped flowers of rose-pink and purple shoot out of the ground without any leaves. Their lush, coarse foliage appears in spring. Crocus prefer well-composted, well-drained soil. This perennial will flourish in an open sunny situation. To divide the plants, lift and move them while they are dormant before flowering. Replant immediately, as the root growth is active at that time. As it is a woodland species, it should not be allowed to dry out too much.
Other colors: White, pink, purple.

Crocus speciosus
AUTUMN CROCUS ◑

Family: IRIDACEAE
Origin: Turkey, Iran, Crimea, Caucasus.
Flowering time: Autumn.
Climatic zone: 5, 6, 7, 8, 9.
Dimensions: Up to 6 inches (150 mm) high.
Description: This is an easily grown corm producing violet flowers. Naturalize in grassy areas or under trees. This plant is also adaptable to rock gardens and pot-planting. As with most corms, it looks best when massed generously, rather than used as a small feature. There are many other species available offering a good color selection. Plant in organic mulch in well-drained soil. Water regularly from when flowers first appear to when the leaves die back. Fertilize weekly during the growing period.
Other colors: White, lavender, blue, yellow.

Crocus tommasinianus
WINTER CROCUS ○

Family: IRIDACEAE
Origin: Yugoslavia–Hungary.
Flowering time: Winter–spring.
Climatic zone: 5, 6, 7, 8, 9.
Dimensions: Up to 5 inches (130 mm) high.
Description: Affectionately known as "Tommies" by many gardeners, these crocus pop up everywhere, even among pebbles. Landscape usage is very flexible. They can be planted in rock gardens, borders, and pots. Although easy to grow, these crocus do like definite cold in winter. Provide light- to medium-rich soil in a sunny open position. If naturalizing in a lawn, do not mow once buds emerge from the soil.
Varieties/cultivars: 'Whitewell purple', 'Ruby giant'.

Crocus speciosus

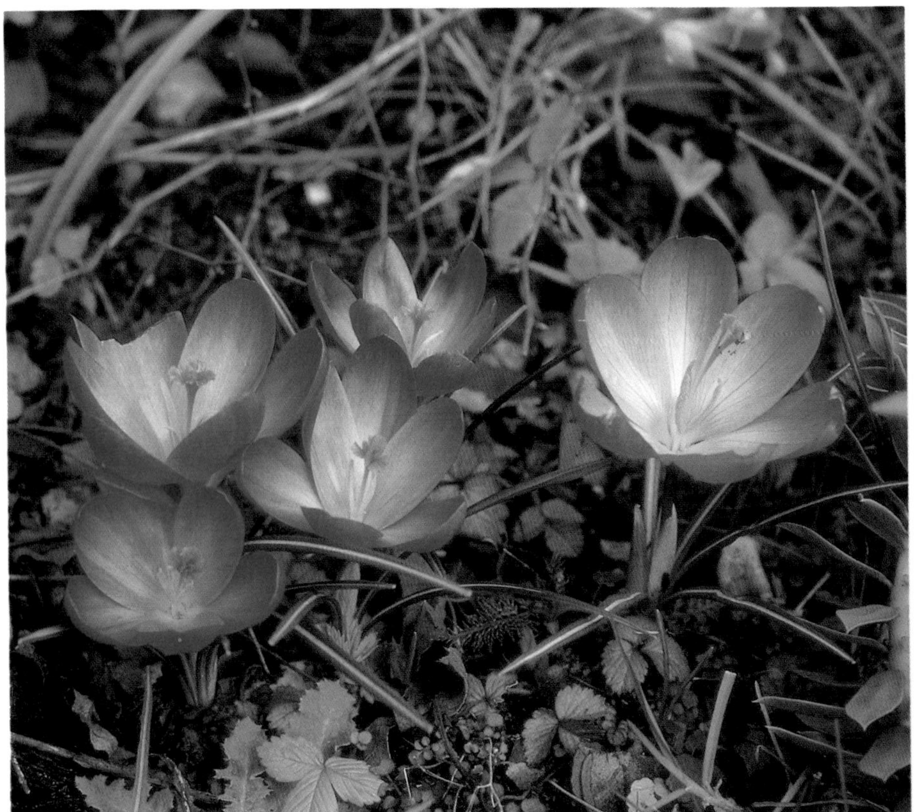

Crocus vernus 'Enchantress'

Crocus vernus and cultivars
DUTCH CROCUS, SPRING CROCUS ○ ◑

Family: IRIDACEAE
Origin: Mediterranean region.
Flowering time: Spring.
Climatic zone: 3, 4, 5, 6, 7, 8, 9.
Dimensions: Up to 8 inches (200 mm) high.
Description: Originally the purple or white crocus found growing wild on alpine slopes, it is now cultivated to produce free-flowering bulbs. It can be planted in clumps in lawns, under trees, and in beds or window boxes. It looks attractive indoors in blue delft pots to accentuate the "Dutch touch". For selective planting, grow it in rock walls, gravel pathways, or between paving stones. Crocus is not very particular about soil types, but needs good drainage. A sunny location is necessary in cold climates to open the flowers, but in hot areas, filtered sun is best.
Other colors: Pale lilac, mauve, white, deep purple, golden-yellow.
Varieties/cultivars: 'Yellow Giant', 'Dutch Yellow', 'Negro Boy', 'Striped Beauty', 'Haarlem Gem', 'Enchantress'.

Cyclamen persicum

Cyclamen persicum
FLORIST'S CYCLAMEN, COMMON CYCLAMEN ◑

Family: PRIMULACEAE
Origin: Eastern Mediterranean.
Flowering time: Winter–spring.
Climatic zone: 9.
Dimensions: Up to 12 inches (300 mm) high.
Description: This plant needs special attention if grown from seed or tuber-corms. Mainly used as a potted specimen it does well in a warm but not hot position. It must be grown under glass in colder climates. Fragrant strains are available and there is a wide choice of colors. Grow in pots of gritty compost with leaf mold and add pieces of chalk or limestone in the drainage area. Excessive temperatures will lead to failure. This species needs plenty of light (though not more than four hours of direct sunlight per day) and a slightly moist atmosphere and does not tolerate high temperatures. Wet soil will cause the buds and leaf base to rot.
Other colors: White, pink, purple, red.
Varieties/cultivars: Many cultivars are available.

Dierama pulcherrimum

Dierama pulcherrimum
WANDFLOWER, FAIRY FISHING ROD, FAIRY BELLS ○ ◑

Family: IRIDACEAE
Origin: South Africa.
Flowering time: Spring–summer.
Climatic zone: 8, 9.
Dimensions: Up to 5 feet (approx. 2 meters) high.
Description: A delightful plant, it has long fishing-rod stems which arch with the weight of hanging flowers. The graceful, arching growth merits a front row position in a border. The fairy quality of this flower enhances cottage gardens. A hardy grower, it requires sun in temperate climates but needs shade in the tropics. The soil should be moist, fertile, and well-drained.
Other colors: White, pink, purple, red.
Varieties/cultivars: 'Blackbird', 'Jay', 'Kingfisher'.

Endymion hispanicus hybrid

Endymion hispanicus and hybrids syn. *Scilla hispanica, S. campanulata*

SPANISH BLUEBELL, GIANT BLUEBELL ◑

Family: LILIACEAE
Origin: Spain and Portugal–central Italy.
Flowering time: Spring.
Climatic zone: 5, 6, 7, 8, 9.
Dimensions: Up to 18 inches (450 mm) high.
Description: Bluebells look pretty planted in borders, edges, rock gardens or under deciduous trees and shrubs. They blend well with lily-of-the-valley and a carpet of alyssum. They will naturalize rapidly if planted in woodland settings. Bluebells can also be grown in containers indoors. Plant the bulbs in autumn in deep, fertile soil in a lightly shaded or sunny position. Water regularly in winter and spring but keep them dry once foliage turns yellow.
Other colors: Pink, white.

Fritillaria meleagris

SNAKE'S-HEAD FRITILLARY (U.K.), BLOODY WARRIOR, LEOPARD LILY ○

Other common names: CHECKERED LILY, GUINEA FLOWER
Family: LILIACEAE
Origin: U.K., central Europe, Scandinavia.
Flowering time: Spring.
Climatic zone: 4, 5, 6, 7, 8, 9.
Dimensions: Up to 18 inches (450 mm) high.
Description: This is an old-fashioned favorite that lasts for years and is easy to grow. It looks well in rock gardens. The solitary and delicate bell-shaped flower belies its fierce common names. Leopard lily is a corruption of leper lily, so-named because the flower resembled the warning bell of lepers. The checkered bells add a distinctive contrast to a garden. Plant in deep humus-rich soil, in a sunny position. It is native to damp European meadows.
Other colors: Orange, white, green, purple, yellow.
Varieties/cultivars: 'Alba'.

Fritillaria meleagris

Hyacinthus orientalis

DUTCH HYACINTH, COMMON HYACINTH ○

Family: LILIACEAE
Origin: Mediterranean region.
Flowering time: Winter–spring.
Climatic zone: 5, 6, 7, 8, 9.
Dimensions: Up to 18 inches (450 mm) high.
Description: Hyacinths are best suited to formal settings because of their stiff stems and dense flower spikes. They have heavily perfumed, waxy, bell-shaped flowers and do well indoors. They can also be grown most effectively if planted in groups in the garden. They can be susceptible to fungal conditions in soil that is too wet, the bulbs becoming soft and rotten. All garden hyacinths are derived from *H. orientalis*. Some varieties have double blooms. For an exotic touch they can be grown indoors in water in special hyacinth glasses.
Other colors: White, yellow, pink, mauve, purple.
Varieties/cultivars: *H. o. albulus*.

Hyacinthus orientalis

Ipheion uniflorum

TRITELEIA, SPRING STARFLOWER ◑

Family: LILIACEAE
Origin: Peru.
Flowering time: Spring–summer.
Climatic zone: 7, 8, 9.
Dimensions: Up to 8 inches (200 mm) high.
Description: *Ipheion* is well suited to massing at the front of borders or rock gardens. This prolific plant produces numerous solitary flowers. The perfumed blooms are funnel-shaped, with white, pale mauve, or lilac petals. The grassy leaves emit a faint onion-like odor when pressed. *Ipheion* multiplies rapidly in a sunny position in well-drained soil. Bulbs should be left undisturbed for several years until clumps form. They will flower for up to eight weeks and need little attention.

Ipheion uniflorum

Iris reticulata

Iris reticulata
SPANISH IRIS

Family: IRIDACEAE
Origin: Central Turkey, Caucasus, Iran, Iraq.
Flowering time: Spring.
Climatic zone: 6, 7, 8, 9.
Dimensions: Up to 18 inches (450 mm) high.
Description: Spanish iris is a violet-scented beauty with grassy leaves and deep-blue or purple flowers. In some areas it is best grown in a cool greenhouse. It is suitable for rock gardens, the front of borders and will grow well in pots. Iris likes sandy light soil in a sunny position protected from wind. The best results are achieved if bulbs are lifted after flowering. They should be stored in dry sand. It is important to keep the bulbs as dry as possible during their dormant period.
Other colors: Yellow.
Varieties/cultivars: There are many cultivars available.

Iris xiphioides
ENGLISH IRIS

Family: IRIDACEAE
Origin: Spain, the Pyrenees.
Flowering time: Spring–summer.
Climatic zone: 6, 7, 8, 9.
Dimensions: Up to 18 inches (450 mm) high.
Description: Early botanists thought that this plant was an English native. Although it flourished for centuries near Bristol, it had been brought from Spain by merchant seamen. It blooms in various shades of blue, except for one white form. This blue and gold beauty makes a colorful addition to the rose garden and flowers for up to eight weeks. Iris, which was named after the goddess of the rainbow, is an excellent cut flower. It requires cool, moist soil in a sunny area protected from strong wind.

Iris xiphioides

Iris xiphium
SPANISH IRIS

Family: IRIDACEAE
Origin: Spain, Portugal, southern France.
Flowering time: Early summer.
Climatic zone: 6, 7, 8, 9.
Dimensions: Up to 2 feet (600 mm) high.
Description: *I. xiphium* is a parent of the dutch iris. The flowers have petals the standards and falls of which are often of different colors. Use it in borders or in a sunny corner against a fence or trellis. Their eye-catching beauty makes them ideal for indoor floral arrangements and ornamental pot plants. Plant in fertile soil using plenty of organic matter and protect from winds.
Other colors: White, yellow, orange, bronze.
Varieties/cultivars: Several cultivars are available.

Iris xiphium 'Franz Hals'

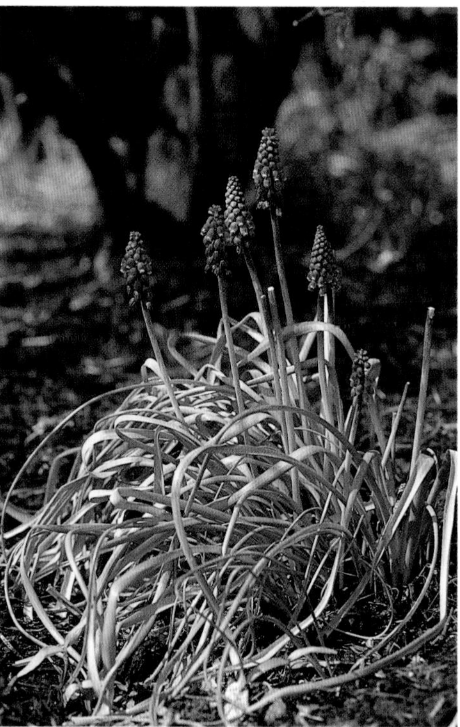
Muscari armeniacum

Muscari armeniacum
GRAPE HYACINTH

Family: LILIACEAE
Origin: Asia Minor.
Flowering time: Spring.
Climatic zone: 4, 5, 6, 7, 8, 9.
Dimensions: Up to 8 inches (200 mm) high.
Description: The dense heads of rich blue fragrant flowers suit borders and edges. Several varieties of these grape-shaped flowers are available. They make good companions for yellow violas and white primula. They will readily naturalize when planted in grass or lightly wooded areas, and are good plants for potting indoors. Cultivate in well-rotted compost and water regularly.
Other colors: Mauve, white.
Varieties/cultivars: 'Blue spike', 'Cantab'.

Puschkinia scilloides
STRIPED SQUILL  

Family: LILIACEAE
Origin: Eastern Turkey, Caucasus, Lebanon.
Flowering time: Spring.
Climatic zone: 4, 5, 6, 7, 8, 9.
Dimensions: Up to 6 inches (150 mm) high.

Puschkinia scilloides

Description: These dainty powder-blue flowers with deep-blue stripes blend well with violas and rock garden plants. They need to be placed where they complement other plants, as they are not very showy on their own. Easy to grow in sandy soil enriched with humus, they will take full sun or partial shade. The bulbs need not be disturbed for several years. If flowering diminishes, they will need to be relocated in new soil.

Scilla bifolia

BLUEBELL, TWIN-LEAF SQUILL ○ ◑

Family: LILIACEAE
Origin: Southern Europe–Turkey.
Flowering time: Spring.
Climatic zone: 5, 6, 7, 8, 9.
Dimensions: Up to 6 inches (150 mm) high.
Description: These hardy bulbs are adaptable to most cool soils and positions. *Scillas* are good carpet plants in beds of early-flowering tulips. They are easy to grow, will rapidly increase, and are suitable for borders, edges, pots, and in clumps under deciduous trees.

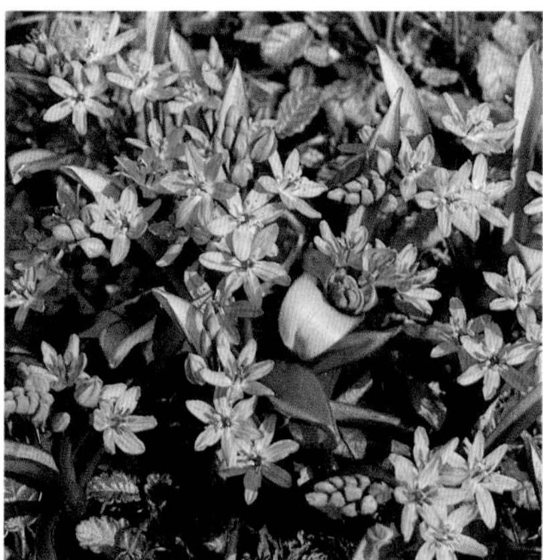

Scilla bifolia

Plant in rich, sandy soil in sun or partial shade. They will benefit from an occasional top dressing of good soil or old manure. Divide small bulblets from older bulbs in autumn to accelerate their spread.

Scilla peruviana

CUBAN LILY, PERUVIAN SCILLA, PERUVIAN LILY (U.K.) ○ ◑

Family: LILIACEAE
Origin: Southern Europe.
Flowering time: Early summer.
Climatic zone: 8, 9.

Scilla peruviana

Dimensions: Up to 18 inches (450 mm) high.
Description: Cuban lily is a showy bulb featuring clusters of fifty or more flowers. It can be massed in beds, planted as a backdrop to annuals, or used as a border along fences, and as an edge between garden beds. This species is easy to grow in rich, sandy soil in sun or partial shade. Divide the bulbs for extra plantings in autumn. At this time, they will also benefit from an occasional top dressing of old manure or good soil.

Scilla sibirica

SIBERIAN SCILLA, SPRING SQUILL (U.K.) ○

Family: LILIACEAE
Origin: Turkey, Iran, Caucasus.
Flowering time: Spring.
Climatic zone: 3, 4, 5, 6, 7, 8.
Dimensions: Up to 6 inches (150 mm) high.
Description: As its origins suggest, this dainty species is hardy. The deep-blue, drooping flowers produce three to five blooms to a stem. *Scilla* is ideal for rock gardens or planted under azaleas and camellias. Intersperse it with other bulbs where it can form a carpet. If rich, sandy soil is provided, it will rapidly increase. Top dress with good soil, compost, or old manure. Divide the plant when dormant to cover a large area quickly.
Varieties/cultivars: 'Spring Beauty', 'Atrocaerulea'.

Scilla sibirica

Akebia quinata

Akebia quinata
AKEBIA, FIVE-LEAFED AKEBIA ○ ◑

Family: LARDIZABALACEAE
Origin: China, Korea, Japan.
Flowering time: Spring.
Climatic zone: 4, 5, 6, 7, 8, 9.
Description: Akebia's unusual purplish-brown flowers are often the subject of much comment. They appear in spring on short stems, are often freely produced, and are quite fragrant. This is a fast-growing vine, but not invasive. The attractive leaves, in clusters of five, make a handsome cover for fences or pergolas, and it will tolerate a shady position. It is evergreen in warm zones. If it becomes too thick or unmanageable, cut it back to a few small, branching canes, and it will soon become green and dense again.

Clematis 'Barbara Jackman'
BARBARA JACKMAN CLEMATIS, LARGE-FLOWERED CLEMATIS ○

Family: RANUNCULACEAE
Origin: Cultivar.
Flowering time: Early summer.
Climatic zone: 5, 6, 7, 8, 9.
Description: A popular cultivar, this clematis has purple flowers, not as dark as those of C. x *jackmanii*, and about 4–5 inches (100–125 mm) across. Clematis needs plenty of compost and protection from heat around the roots. It can be grown beside a sheltering shrub, and if grown in pots or large containers, needs a climbing support and a deep mulch as well as shade for the containers to prevent the whole root system from becoming overheated.

Clematis 'Barbara Jackman'

Clematis x *jackmanii*
CLEMATIS, LARGE-FLOWERED CLEMATIS ○

Family: RANUNCULACEAE
Origin: Hybrid.
Flowering time: Summer.
Climatic zone: 5, 6, 7, 8, 9.
Description: One of the early hybrids of this magnificent genus, this clematis has a profusion of 4–5 inch (100–125 mm), rich purple flowers. Later hybrids have larger, but not as many, flowers. Rich soil, full sun, and cool roots are the requirements for these vines. This one flowers on new season's growth, so severe pruning is necessary in the winter, or when leaves drop. Lime

Clematis x *jackmanii*

may be needed in the soil, as it is not tolerant of very acid soil.
Varieties/cultivars: Many, including 'Rubra', 'Henry', 'Mrs Cholmondeley', 'The President'.

Clytostoma callistegioides
VIOLET TRUMPET VINE, ARGENTINE TRUMPET VINE ○ ◑

Family: BIGNONIACEAE
Origin: Brazil, Argentina.
Flowering time: Late spring–summer.
Climatic zone: 9, 10.
Description: Lavender streaked with violet is the color of the large funnel-shaped flowers, which appear in pairs at the ends of long, drooping stems. Although evergreen, this strong-growing climber may be semideciduous in cooler zones. Tendrils help it to climb a fence or a wall, but some support is required. A sunny position with rich soil and regular watering suits this very attractive and colorful vine, but it will also tolerate a semishaded site, as long as it is a warm one. A greenhouse is necessary for cold climates.

Clytostoma callistegioides

Cobaea scandens
CUP-AND-SAUCER VINE, CUP-AND-SAUCER CREEPER (U.K.), CATHEDRAL BELLS ◑

Family: POLEMONIACEAE
Origin: Mexico–northern Chile.
Flowering time: Spring, summer, autumn.
Climatic zone: 5, 6, 7, 8, 9, 10.
Description: *Cobaea* is a fast-growing, vigorous climber with most unusual

Cobaea scandens

flowers. They are large and bell-shaped, up to 2 inches (50 mm) long, opening yellow-green and changing to purple. They have a slight resemblance to a cup sitting on a saucer. A branched tendril at the end of the group of leaflets is the means of support to hold this vine against a wall. Grow it in a warm, semishady position and protect it from wind. It needs good soil, deep mulch, and regular watering. It can be grown as an annual.

Distictis laxiflora
VANILLA TRUMPET VINE ○

Family: BIGNONIACEAE
Origin: Mexico.
Flowering time: Most of the year.
Climatic zone: 9, 10.
Description: Less rampant than many of the trumpet vines, *Distictis laxiflora* has two or three leaflets, the leaves giving this evergreen climber an attractive appearance for the short time that the flowers are not present. The

Distictis laxiflora

flowers are vanilla-scented and about 3½ inches (80 mm) long. They open as a violet color and fade to lavender and white. This is a hot climate plant and needs a greenhouse in colder areas.

Hardenbergia comptoniana
LILAC VINE (U.S.A.), WILD SARSAPARILLA, NATIVE WISTERIA (Aust.) ○ ◑

Family: LEGUMINOSAE
Origin: Western Australia.
Flowering time: Late winter–spring.
Climatic zone: 9.
Description: Violet-blue pea-flowers are massed in graceful sprays on this evergreen climber. Grow it over a low mesh fence, or trail it over the wall of a raised garden bed. It is an easily controlled vine, growing to about 10 feet (3 meters), or a groundcover, when it grows quite flat and spreading. Choose a sunny, well-drained position with minimum water. A wire frame in a container makes a good base for a pillar shape, but it can be trained into any shape. A warm climate plant, it needs to be grown under glass in other areas.

Hardenbergia comptoniana

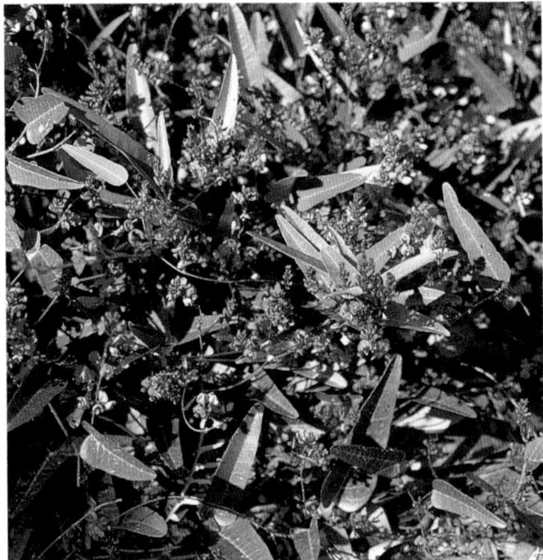

Hardenbergia violacea

Ipomoea purpurea

Hardenbergia violacea

PURPLE CORAL PEA, NATIVE SARSAPARILLA (Aust.), WILD SARSAPARILLA ○

Family: LEGUMINOSAE
Origin: Eastern and southern Australia.
Flowering time: Spring.
Climatic zone: 9.
Description: Masses of small purple-blue flowers on slender, wiry stems make a glorious display in spring. This twining vine has long, oval, and pointed leaves, and will endure harsh, dry conditions. Plant it in full sun in well-drained soil. It will be happy to creep over banks and trees, or it can be trained as a vine. The denser and coarser texture of this species makes it more tolerant of wind and very sunny positions than the lilac vine, and it is faster growing.
Other colors: White, pink.

Ipomoea purpurea

MORNING GLORY ○ ◑

Family: CONVOLVULACEAE
Origin: Tropical America.
Flowering time: Summer.
Climatic zone: 4, 5, 6, 7, 8, 9, 10.
Description: A vigorous, twining climber, morning glory has broadly ovate leaves and large open purple flowers that bloom in profusion during summer. Easy to cultivate in a wide range of soils and conditions, it can become a pest in warmer climates as it tends to take a stranglehold on the garden. In cooler climates treat as an annual planting in spring after the chance of frost has passed. Young shoots can be trained to cover a trellis or column.
Other colors: Pink, blue.

Ipomoea tricolor

MORNING GLORY ○

Family: CONVOLVULACEAE
Origin: Tropical America.
Flowering time: Summer–autumn.
Climatic zone: 4, 5, 6, 7, 8, 9, 10.
Description: This is the popular morning glory cultivated as an annual in gardens all over the world. In warm zones it is a perennial climber. The flower buds are red and open to large, purplish-blue blooms 4 inches (100 mm) across. It is an excellent plant for climbing fences, or growing over arches, or in pots on a terrace or patio. Kept restricted in root space, there is a tendency for earlier flowering. The flowers last only one day, fading to a lighter color in the afternoon.
Other colors: Scarlet, white.
Varieties/cultivars: 'Heavenly Blue', 'Alba', 'Rose Marie', 'Scarlet O'Hara'.

Kennedia nigricans

BLACK CORAL PEA ○ ◑

Family: LEGUMINOSAE
Origin: Western Australia.
Flowering time: Summer.
Climatic zone: 9, 10.
Description: A vigorous evergreen twiner, *Kennedia nigricans* has black-purple flowers with a yellow blotch on the top petal. They are most unusual and distinctive, and are followed by flat, hairy pods. The vine is tolerant of a shady position, but prefers a warm site with very good drainage. Being quite

Kennedia nigricans

Ipomoea tricolor

drought-tolerant when established, it is worth growing in an awkward spot to give a good fence cover or groundcover. A hot climate plant, it needs greenhouse protection in colder areas.

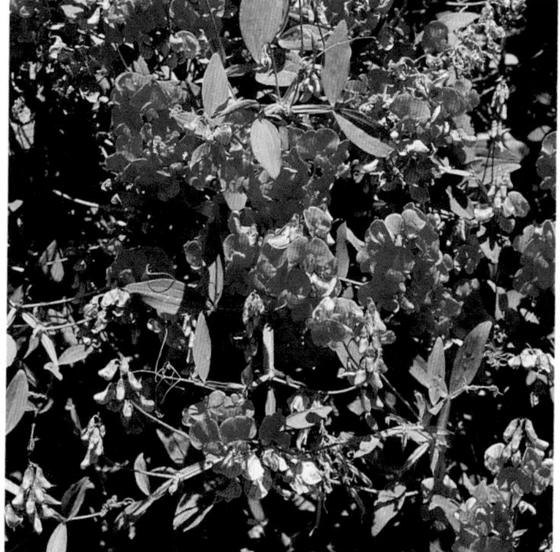

Lathyrus latifolius

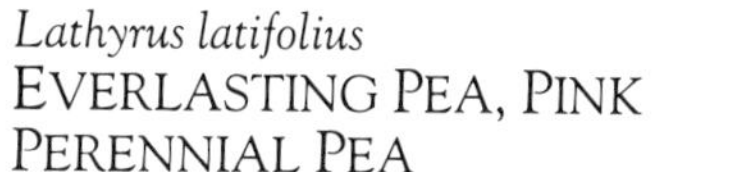

Lathyrus latifolius

EVERLASTING PEA, PINK PERENNIAL PEA ○

Family: LEGUMINOSAE
Origin: Southern Europe.
Flowering time: Summer.
Climatic zone: 5, 6, 7, 8, 9.
Description: Many new shoots come from the base of this perennial climber each year. It is happy in most conditions, including windy sites near the sea, and will grow up to 10 feet (3 meters) high. The large attractive sprays of flowers are held on long, upright stems. The vine looks beautiful trained over a summerhouse, porch, or trellis, but needs a sunny position. Although quick-growing, it is not featured as often as it deserves. Mulch well and prune off all old growth at the end of summer.

Lonicera japonica var. *repens* syn. *L. j.* var. *flexuosa*, *L. j.* 'Purpurea'

JAPANESE HONEYSUCKLE ○ ◑

Family: CAPRIFOLIACEAE
Origin: Japan, China, Korea.
Flowering time: Summer.
Climatic zone: 6, 7, 8, 9.
Description: The white flowers of this well-known climber are tinged with purple on the outside. An evergreen or semideciduous, this Japanese honeysuckle has highly fragrant flowers which appear in summer, growing in pairs. A vigorous vine, it can quickly cover a fence, and should be planted in a warm, sheltered position. It will tolerate quite cool conditions if grown under trees or given some protection from frost. It does not seem to be fussy about soil, and will thrive almost anywhere.

Lonicera japonica var. *repens*

Passiflora caerulea

BLUE-CROWN PASSION FLOWER, BLUE PASSION FLOWER, COMMON PASSION FLOWER (U.K.) ○ ◑

Family: PASSIFLORACEAE
Origin: Western and central South America.
Flowering time: Summer.
Climatic zone: 8, 9.
Description: This is the best *Passiflora* for growing in frosty districts, although it is happy in warm areas. A slender, but strong-growing vine, which will quickly climb up a tree or over a fence, it needs either plenty of space, or regular pruning. The flowers are white with a central fringe of blue, white, and purple, and are followed by orange-colored fruit which is not edible. This species was often used as root stock on which the edible types of passionfruit were grafted.

Passiflora caerulea

Petrea volubilis

Petrea volubilis

QUEEN'S WREATH, PURPLE WREATH ○

Family: VERBENACEAE
Origin: Mexico–Panama, West Indies.
Flowering time: Winter–spring.
Climatic zone: 9, 10.
Description: Rough, brittle leaves on this wiry-stemmed twiner contrast with the beauty of the rich-colored, five-lobed petals. The lilac calyx remains on the plant for a long time and finally falls, spinning like a tiny top. A hot climate is necessary for this evergreen vine. Rich soil and ample water will give best foliage. It is a delightful climber which is easy to control and will never be invasive. It can combine with another light climber with white flowers, to give a two-colored effect.

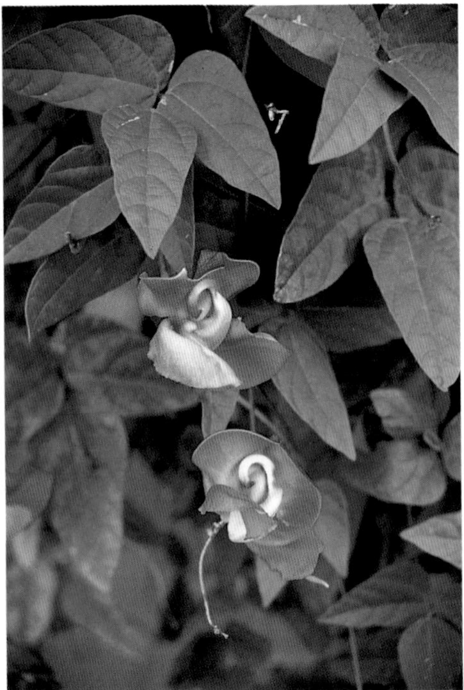

Phaseolus caracalla

Phaseolus caracalla syn. *Vigna caracalla*
SNAIL FLOWER, CORKSCREW FLOWER ○ ◑

Family: LEGUMINOSAE
Origin: Tropical South America.
Flowering time: Spring or summer.
Climatic zone: 5, 6, 7, 8, 9, 10.
Description: This relative of the scarlet runner bean is an equally vigorous grower and has masses of curious flowers with a delightful fragrance. The flowers are coiled like snails and fleshy, with creamy, purple colors. Quick-growing, this deciduous twiner can be pruned back to ground level in late autumn and will soon cover a fence in the following spring. It does best in rich soil and prefers a sheltered position. The dense, lush foliage needs a wire support to help it attain an upright growth. In cooler climates, it is best grown as an annual.

Sollya heterophylla
AUSTRALIAN BLUEBELL CREEPER ○ ◑

Family: PITTOSPORACEAE
Origin: Western Australia.
Flowering time: Summer–autumn.
Climatic zone: 9.
Description: This vine's slender twining stems will gradually cover a fence without ever becoming a problem. Clusters of tiny, bell-shaped, bright-blue flowers hang in delicate little sprays in spring and summer, and are followed by purple berries. Tolerant of semishade, it is a good groundcover, or will twine around a post or pergola. Best foliage is obtained when it is given sheltered conditions, with ample water and good drainage. The narrow, glossy green leaves are attractive, and make this evergreen vine a good choice for container-growing. In cold climates, it will grow well in a greenhouse.
Other colors: Pink, white.

Sollya heterophylla

Thunbergia grandiflora
SKY FLOWER, CLOCK VINE, BLUE TRUMPET VINE ○ ◑

Family: ACANTHACEAE
Origin: Northern India–southern China.
Flowering time: Summer, autumn.
Climatic zone: 9, 10.
Description: Rough, toothed leaves cover this woody twiner with vigorous growth. The bell-shaped flowers, 2 inches or more across (50–60 mm), are a clear periwinkle blue with a white throat. The flowers are single, appear in the leaf axils, and are slightly pendant. This is a showy, robust climber which needs good soil and adequate summer water to look its best. It is not tolerant of frost, although if grown in a sheltered position it will survive quite cool conditions. A greenhouse is ideal for cooler zones.

Thunbergia grandiflora

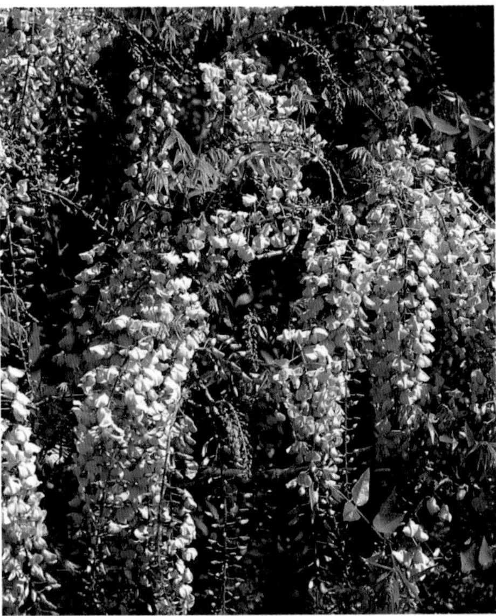

Wisteria floribunda

Wisteria floribunda syn. *W. multijuga*
JAPANESE WISTERIA ○

Family: LEGUMINOSAE
Origin: Japan.
Flowering time: Early summer.
Climatic zone: 4, 5, 6, 7, 8, 9.
Description: The fragrant pea-shaped flowers on this lovely vine appear at the same time as the new leaves. The flower sprays are in shades of violet-blue, and hang in clusters 18 inches (450 mm) long. The display lasts longer than in other species as the flowers at the base of the spray open first, followed gradually by those nearer the tip. The attractive, glossy leaves are made up of between thirteen and nineteen leaflets. It is a vigorous climber and needs a strong support for the dense canopy produced in the summer time.
Varieties/cultivars: 'Rosea', 'Violacea Plena', 'Macrobotrys', 'Alba'.

Wisteria floribunda 'Macrobotrys'

Wisteria floribunda 'Macrobotrys' syn. *W. multijuga*

JAPANESE WISTERIA, LONG JAPANESE WISTERIA ○

Family: LEGUMINOSAE
Origin: Cultivar.
Flowering time: Spring–early summer.
Climatic zone: 5, 6, 7, 8, 9.
Description: Honey-scented violet-purple flowers hang in enormous sprays, up to 3 feet (900 mm) long, on this tall-climbing woody vine. Each flower is about 1 inch (25 mm) long. They appear either before or with the glossy green leaves which have thirteen to nineteen leaflets. The flowering season is very short, and flowers are followed by long, soft-green, velvety pods. For an eye-catching display, grow this wisteria over a tall pergola, or arbor, which the blossoms can cascade down. Water well during flowering to hold the blossoms.

Wisteria floribunda 'Violacea Plena'

DOUBLE JAPANESE WISTERIA ○

Family: LEGUMINOSAE
Origin: Cultivar.
Flowering time: Spring.
Climatic zone: 5, 6, 7, 8, 9.
Description: Both the flowering and the growth habit distinguish this cultivar from its parent plant. The small, tight, flower clusters hang in sprays 6–8 inches (150–200 mm) long, but they are double flowers and held in a fairly tightly packed group. The dense, bushy growth is more shrub-like, and can be trained into a shrub or small tree if pruned during summer. It will need support on which to climb when used as a vine. Loamy acid soil is best, with plenty of water at flowering time.

Wisteria floribunda 'Violacea Plena'

Wisteria sinensis

CHINESE WISTERIA ○ 

Family: LEGUMINOSAE
Origin: China.
Flowering time: Spring–early summer.
Climatic zone: 5, 6, 7, 8, 9.
Description: This wisteria is an early spring favorite. The slightly fragrant, lilac flowers are in drooping clusters from 8–12 inches (200–300 mm) in length, and tend to open nearly the full length of the cluster at one time. A very vigorous deciduous vine, it will develop a trunk like a tree, but with constant pruning in summer it can be trained as a weeping standard tree, or it can become a gnarled-trunked shrub. Velvety, bean-like pods are attractive decoration among the leaves when the flowers are finished.
Other colors: White.
Varieties/cultivars: *Wisteria sinensis* 'Alba'.

Wisteria sinensis

Aconitum carmichaelii

Aconitum carmichaelii syn. *A. fischeri*
AZURE MONKSHOOD ◑

Family: RANUNCULACEAE
Origin: Eastern Asia.
Flowering time: Late summer–autumn.
Climatic zone: 3, 4, 5, 6, 7, 8, 9.
Dimensions: Up to 4 feet (approx. 1 meter) high.
Description: Azure monkshood is one of the most popular of the garden monkshoods. The dramatic blue hoods of the flowers extend into a spur-like visor and are borne on long stems. These may need staking. A showy border plant, it needs a position in partial shade and does not like to be disturbed. Plant it in rich, moist, well-drained soil. As the juice is highly poisonous, it is not wise to plant monkshood in a garden used by small children.

Aconitum napellus
COMMON MONKSHOOD ◑

Family: RANUNCULACEAE
Origin: Europe, Asia.
Flowering time: Summer.
Climatic zone: 3, 4, 5, 6, 7, 8, 9.
Dimensions: Up to 5 feet (approx. 2 meters) high.
Description: Common monkshood has brilliant green foliage and tall spikes of helmet-like flowers in a rich violet-blue. It is a useful cottage garden plant, and suitable as a background border. It grows best in cool-climate gardens, in deep, rich, moist soil that has adequate drainage. The foliage dies back in winter. Despite the fact that all parts of the plant are poisonous, common monkshood was regarded as a valuable ingredient in medieval potions.
Other colors: White, pink.
Varieties/cultivars: 'Album', 'Carneum'.

Aconitum napellus

Aconitum x *bicolor*
HYBRID MONKSHOOD, WOLFBANE ○ ◑

Family: RANUNCULACEAE
Origin: Hybrid.
Flowering time: Summer.
Climatic zone: 3, 4, 5, 6, 7, 8, 9.
Dimensions: 3–4 feet (approx. 1 meter) high.
Description: This dramatic old-fashioned favorite gives a wonderful display of violet-blue and white, helmet-shaped flowers that are borne in a terminal raceme. The foliage is mid-green in color. Ideal for an herbaceous border, monkshood should be grown in semishade in rich, moist soil with good drainage. The plant may require staking when it reaches its full height.
Other colors: Deeper violet blue, blue and white.

Aconitum x *bicolor*

Adenophora confusa
LADYBELLS ○ ◑

Family: CAMPANULACEAE
Origin: Eastern Asia.
Flowering time: Mid–late summer.
Climatic zone: 4, 5, 6, 7, 8, 9.
Dimensions: Up to 3 feet (1 meter) high.
Description: Ladybells is a charming plant with tall, slender stems and large, dark-purple, bell-shaped flowers, measuring up to ¾ inch (18 mm) in length. Plant it in either full sun or semishade in well-drained, moderately rich soil. It can even be grown in rather poor soils providing there is adequate moisture and good drainage. It makes a very pretty addition to a mixed bed of summer-flowering annuals and perennials.

Adenophora confusa

Agapanthus praecox syn. *A. umbellatus*
AGAPANTHUS, AFRICAN LILY, BLUE AFRICAN LILY ○ ◑

Family: AMARYLLIDACEAE
Origin: South Africa.
Flowering time: Summer.

Agapanthus praecox

Climatic zone: 8, 9.
Dimensions: 2–3 feet (600–900 mm) high.
Description: Agapanthus is a useful and hardy specimen, which looks most attractive as a border or background plant. It forms a large clump of strap-like leaves and produces tall stems in summer, topped by large, globular flower heads in various shades of blue to purple. Full sun or semishade suits it best, and it will grow in most soil conditions providing reasonable drainage is provided. The clumps can be divided during winter to produce new plants.
Other colors: White.
Varieties/cultivars: Many varieties and cultivars are available.

Ajuga reptans
COMMON BLUE BUGLEWEED, BUGLE, COMMON BUGLE ○ ◑

Family: LABIATAE
Origin: Europe–Southwestern Asia.
Flowering time: Spring–summer.
Climatic zone: 4, 5, 6, 7, 8, 9.
Dimensions: 8–12 inches (200–300 mm) high.
Description: This is a spreading perennial groundcover with oval, dark-green leaves and spikes of blue flowers. Cultivars have variegated cream, pink, and burgundy foliage. A quick-growing plant, it is attractive in rock gardens, under large trees, or between pavers. Plant it in a sunny or semishaded position and water regularly. It will tolerate poor and heavy soils. Cut back the dead flower heads. Propagate it by its free-rooting stems or by seed in spring. An infusion of the plant was used for centuries to cure coughs, bruises and hemorrhages.
Other colors: White, pink.
Varieties/cultivars: 'Burgundy Glow', 'Alba', 'Atropurpurea', 'Delight', 'Multicolor', 'Pink Elf', 'Variegata'.

Amsonia tabernaemontana

Amsonia tabernaemontana
BLUE STAR, WILLOW AMSONIA ○ ◑

Family: APOCYNACEAE
Origin: Central and eastern United States.
Flowering time: Summer.
Climatic zone: 4, 5, 6, 7, 8, 9.
Dimensions: Up to 2 feet (600 mm) high.
Description: The very pale, small, star-like flowers of this perennial form in clusters at the top of the tall, leaved stems. It is suited to partially shaded or sunny herbaceous borders and in the right position will become quite bushy. If growth is sparse and open, cut back the plant to half its size to encourage denser growth. It looks attractive planted with campanulas; *C. lactiflora* 'Alba' complements it well. Blue star is easy to grow in any moist, ordinary garden soil and can be propagated by division in spring or autumn. It is often sold as *A. salicifolia*.

Ajuga reptans

Anchusa azurea

Anchusa azurea syn. *A. italica*
ITALIAN BUGLOSS ○

Family: BORAGINACEAE
Origin: Caucasus–central Europe.
Flowering time: Late spring–early summer.
Climatic zone: 4, 5, 6, 7.
Dimensions: 3–5 feet (approx. 1–2 meters) high.
Description: This delightful wild plant is a relative of the herb borage, and has lance-shaped, gray-green foliage and small, round, bright blue flowers. It likes an open, sunny position and can be grown in a wide range of soils, as long as drainage is good and water is provided during hot summer weather.
Varieties/cultivars: 'Loddon Royalist', 'Morning Glory'.

Aquilegia caerulea
ROCKY MOUNTAIN COLUMBINE ○ ◑

Family: RANUNCULACEAE
Origin: Rocky Mountains, North America.
Flowering time: Late spring–early summer.
Climatic zone: 4, 5, 6, 7, 8, 9.
Dimensions: Up to 2 feet (600 mm) high.
Description: *A. caerulea*, with its soft lavender-blue and creamy white blooms, is the state flower of Colorado. Plant it in sun or partial shade and leave undisturbed so that the seeds drop and colonies form. Moist soils that neither dry out in summer nor become waterlogged in winter suit it best.

Aquilegia caerulea

Arisaema triphyllum

Arisaema triphyllum
JACK-IN-THE-PULPIT, INDIAN TURNIP ◑ ●

Family: ARACEAE
Origin: North America.
Flowering time: Spring–summer.
Climatic zone: 4, 5, 6, 7, 8, 9.
Dimensions: Up to 2½ feet (750 mm) high.
Description: A cool fernery or rock garden is the ideal position for *Arisaema*, with its purplish-green hooded spathe. Plant it in rich, moist humus soil in a sheltered, partially shaded site, and give it plenty of water in summer. Propagate by offsets or by seed. The North American Indians used the turnip-shaped, acrid root to cure headaches, and also as a contraceptive.
Varieties/cultivars: *A. t. stewardsonii*, *A. t. zebrinum*.

Aster thomsonii
ASTER, THOMSON'S ASTER (U.K.) 

Family: COMPOSITAE
Origin: Western Himalayas.
Flowering time: Summer–autumn.
Climatic zone: 7, 8, 9.
Dimensions: Up to 2 feet (600 mm) high.
Description: This is one of the lavender-blue group of asters which has produced many hybrids. The daisy-like flowers are profuse and the almost heart-shaped leaves are serrated. Plant it in sunny, open borders where the soil will not dry out during the growing season. Protect it from wind and stake it if necessary. This is a good plant for cut

Aster thomsonii 'Nana'

floral arrangements. The dwarf form, 'Nana', grows to a height of about 15 inches (375 mm).
Varieties/cultivars: 'Nana'.

Aster x *frikartii*
ASTER

Family: COMPOSITAE
Origin: Hybrid.
Flowering time: Summer–autumn.
Climatic zone: 5, 6, 7, 8, 9.
Dimensions: Up to 3 feet (1 meter) high.
Description: These vibrant lavender-blue daisies with yellow centers provide a constant source of flowers for floral arrangements. A fragrant perennial plant that is well suited to cottage gardens, it will grow quite quickly into an attractive clump. Plant it in full sun along pathways and low fences or beside a front gate. It likes fertile, well-drained soil, and may be prone to mildew in humid areas.

Aster x *frikartii*

Astilbe chinensis 'Pumila'
ASTILBE, DWARF FALSE GOATSBEARD

Family: SAXIFRAGACEAE
Origin: Cultivar.
Flowering time: Summer.
Climatic zone: 4, 5, 6, 7, 8, 9.
Dimensions: Up to 12 inches (300 mm) high.
Description: This handsome perennial is a good choice for the front of borders. The densely clustered, mauve-pink flowers and attractive foliage contrast well with white daisies or silver-gray artemisia. 'Pumila' tolerates drier soils than other astilbes and, being a gross feeder, needs an extra application of fertilizer during summer. Easy to grow in any ordinary, moist garden soil, it reproduces quickly and should either be given plenty of space to spread or be divided every three years.

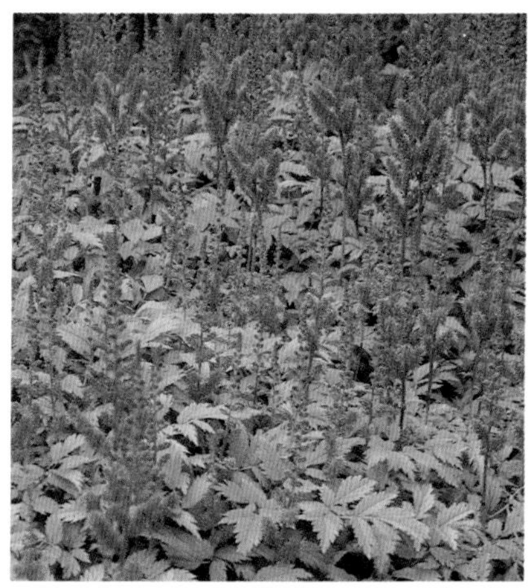
Astilbe chinensis 'Pumila'

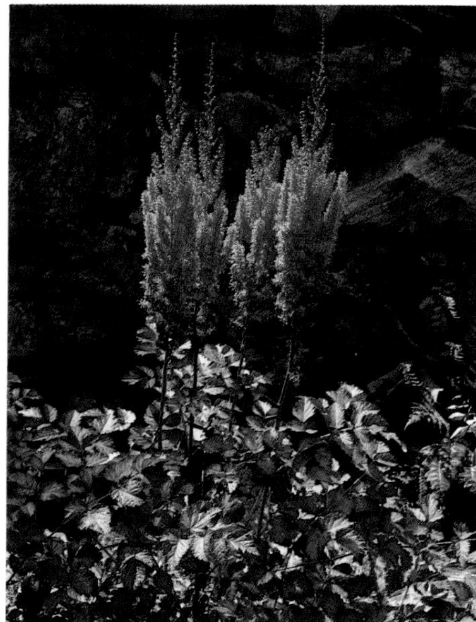
Astilbe taquetii 'Superba'

Astilbe taquetii 'Superba'
ASTILBE, FALSE GOATSBEARD 

Family: SAXIFRAGACEAE
Origin: Cultivar.
Flowering time: Late summer.
Climatic zone: 5, 6, 7, 8, 9.
Dimensions: Up to 4 feet (approx. 1 meter) high.
Description: Long, feathery spikes of magenta or reddish-purple flowers accompany bronze-green foliage. A single plume may have hundreds of florets and the overall effect is spectacular. 'Superba' suits borders and rock gardens and particularly the surrounds of rock pools. A deep, rich, moisture-retaining soil with a liberal application of humus is the ideal environment for it. This cultivar is more drought-tolerant than some strains.

Baptisia australis

Baptisia australis syn. *B. exaltata*
WILD INDIGO, FALSE INDIGO ○ ◑

Family: LEGUMINOSAE
Origin: Eastern United States.
Flowering time: Spring–summer, northern hemisphere; summer, southern hemisphere.
Climatic zone: 4, 5, 6, 7, 8, 9.
Dimensions: Up to 5 feet (over 1 meter) high.
Description: Wild indigo has numerous deep purplish-blue, pea-like flowers borne in terminal racemes.These are followed by attractive seed pods. Resembling lupins, they are attractive in indoor floral arrangements. The plant likes an open, sunny position in sandy loam which has had compost added, and is useful for the drier parts of borders or in wild gardens. Cut it back after flowering. This plant was used in ancient times to cure infections.

Brunnera macrophylla syn. *Anchusa myosotidiflora*
SIBERIAN BUGLOSS (U.S.A.), FORGET-ME-NOT (U.K.), ANCHUSA (U.K.) ◑

Family: BORAGINACEAE
Origin: Western Caucasus.
Flowering time: Spring.
Climatic zone: 4, 5, 6, 7, 8, 9.
Dimensions: Up to 18 inches (450 mm) high.
Description: The branching, starry, blue flowers of Siberian bugloss resemble forget-me-nots. A member of the borage family, this woodland species has rough, heart-shaped leaves and hairy stems. Grow it in open woodland areas, under trees and shrubs, or in borders. Tolerant of soil types, it can survive in dry, shady positions, but prefers partial shade in moist soil.
Varieties/cultivars: 'Variegata'.

Brunnera macrophylla

Campanula carpatica
CARPATHIAN HAREBELL ○ ◑

Family: CAMPANULACEAE
Origin: Carpathian mountains.
Flowering time: Spring–summer.
Climatic zone: 4, 5, 6, 7, 8, 9.
Dimensions: Up to 12 inches (300 mm) high.
Description: Carpathian harebell grows in clumps. The large (2 inches (50 mm) wide), deep-blue flowers are bell-shaped and the leaves are oval. A quick-growing plant, it is useful for groundcover in rock gardens or on sloping sites. Plant it in fertile, moist soil protected from summer sun and water it liberally. Propagate it by division or from cuttings.
Other colors: Many shades from white to sky-blue.
Varieties/cultivars: 'Loddon Fairy', 'Riverslea', 'White Star'.

Campanula cochleariifolia syn. *C. pusilla*
BELLFLOWER ◑

Family: CAMPANULACEAE
Origin: European mountains.
Flowering time: Summer.

Campanula cochleariifolia

Campanula carpatica

Climatic zone: 6, 7, 8, 9.
Dimensions: Up to 6 inches (150 mm) high.
Description: This is another easy-to-grow campanula which is useful for edging beds or planting in rock garden pockets. The solitary, drooping bells appear in great profusion during summer. In larger areas such as sloping sites, plant several different varieties and colors of campanula together to form an effective display. It likes moist, fertile soil protected from summer sun. It is propagated by division or seed.
Other colors: White.
Varieties/cultivars: 'Alba', 'Oakington Blue', 'Miranda'.

Campanula garganica

Campanula garganica
BELLFLOWER ○ ◑

Family: CAMPANULACEAE
Origin: Italy, Greece.
Flowering time: Summer–autumn, northern hemisphere; spring–autumn, southern hemisphere.
Climatic zone: 5, 6, 7, 8, 9.
Dimensions: Up to 4 inches (100 mm) high.
Description: This sprawling, low-growing evergreen is often grown in rock gardens or as a groundcover. Wheel-shaped flowers are borne on long, slender stems, and the leaves are kidney-shaped and coarsely toothed. Flowering begins early in the season and may continue in a sporadic fashion until autumn. Plant it in partial shade in warmer climates, and in full sun in cooler zones. Ordinary garden soil is suitable, but this plant benefits from the addition of compost. Do not allow the soil to dry out.

Campanula glomerata

Campanula glomerata
CLUSTERED BELLFLOWER, DANESBLOOD BELLFLOWER ○ ◑

Family: CAMPANULACEAE
Origin: Europe–western Asia.
Flowering time: Summer.
Climatic zone: 3, 4, 5, 6, 7, 8, 9.
Dimensions: Up to 3 feet (1 meter) high.
Description: This is one of the taller types of *Campanula*. The individual funnel-shaped blooms are rich violet, large, and showy. They form in clusters at the top of stems that are about 1–2 feet (300–600 mm) high and are suitable for floral arrangements. *C. glomerata* is useful in shaded rockeries and is also popular in a border. It grows well in ordinary garden soil. A double-flowered form is available and a variety with deep-violet flowers growing in large clusters.
Other colors: White, violet.
Varieties/cultivars: Several varieties and cultivars are available including *C. g.* var. *dahurica*.

Campanula latifolia
GIANT BELLFLOWER ○ ◑

Family: CAMPANULACEAE
Origin: Europe–western Asia, Siberia.
Flowering time: Summer.
Climatic zone: 4, 5, 6, 7, 8.
Dimensions: Up to 4 feet (approx. 1 meter) high.
Description: Now growing widely across Europe to the mountains of Kashmir, giant bellflower, with its numerous, showy, violet-colored, bell-shaped flowers, makes a fine border plant once established. Self-seeding, it will create a good summer display if allowed to colonize. Although tall, giant bellflower seldom requires staking. It is at home in shady, moist areas but, depending on the climate, will grow in a sunny or semishaded position, in ordinary garden soil. The cultivar 'Macrantha' has purple flowers that are wider than those of giant bellflower.
Other colors: White.
Varieties/cultivars: 'Alba', 'Brantwood', 'Macrantha'.

Campanula latifolia

Campanula medium

Campanula medium
CANTERBURY-BELLS ○

Family: CAMPANULACEAE
Origin: Southern Europe.
Flowering time: Summer.
Climatic zone: 7, 8, 9.
Dimensions: Up to 3 feet (1 meter) high.
Description: These flowers are said to have been named in honor of St. Thomas à Becket because they resemble the horse bells used by pilgrims visiting his shrine at Canterbury Cathedral. A hardy, quick-growing biennial with blue bell-shaped flowers, they make an excellent border plant that will flower from six to nine weeks. Plant the seeds in soil mixed with fertilizer and compost. An application of lime will benefit growth. It likes a sunny position sheltered from wind.
Other colors: White, pink, mauve.
Varieties/cultivars: *C. m. calycanthema.*

Campanula persicifolia

Campanula persicifolia
PEACH-LEAVED BELLFLOWER ○ ◑

Family: CAMPANULACEAE
Origin: Europe, Asia.
Flowering time: Summer.
Climatic zone: 4, 5, 6, 7, 8, 9.
Dimensions: Up to 3 feet (1 meter) high.
Description: Once used medicinally, this evergreen, perennial border plant produces excellent blue, bell-shaped flowers suitable for cutting. Remove spent blooms to encourage a second flowering. It likes moist, ordinary garden soil and a position in partial shade or full sun, depending upon the climate.
Other colors: White.
Varieties/cultivars: 'Alba'.

Campanula poscharskyana
SERBIAN BELLFLOWER ○ ◑

Family: CAMPANULACEAE
Origin: Western Yugoslavia.
Flowering time: Summer–autumn.
Climatic zone: 4, 5, 6, 7, 8, 9.
Dimensions: Up to 6 inches (150 mm) high.
Description: Serbian bellflower produces masses of lilac flowers which create a dense carpet of color. Its sprawling habit makes it a good choice for a sloping site or a well-drained rock garden; it is also suited to wild gardens,

Campanula poscharskyana

where it can ramble unhindered. One of the easier campanulas to grow, it is drought-resistant. Plant it in ordinary garden soil in sun or partial shade.
Varieties/cultivars: 'E. K. Toogood'.

Campanula portenschlagiana syn. *C. muralis*
DALMATIAN BELLFLOWER ○ ◑

Family: CAMPANULACEAE
Origin: Yugoslavia.
Flowering time: Spring–summer.
Climatic zone: 5, 6, 7, 8, 9.
Dimensions: Up to 6 inches (150 mm) high.
Description: This little alpine is easier to grow than many other campanulas. The deep bluish-purple, bell-shaped flowers look attractive in rock garden pockets, in rock walls, or edging garden beds. Woodland drifts are also suitable sites for this plant. Its masses of dark-green, heart-shaped leaves make it a good groundcover, but the foliage may be susceptible to slugs. Plant in well-drained, gritty soil in sun or partial shade.
Other colors: White.

Campanula portenschlagiana

Campanula rotundifolia
HAREBELL OF ENGLAND, BLUEBELL OF SCOTLAND ○

Family: CAMPANULACEAE
Origin: Northern temperate and arctic regions.
Flowering time: Summer.
Climatic zone: 3, 4, 5, 6, 7, 8, 9.
Dimensions: Up to 12 inches (300 mm) high.
Description: One of the more easily grown alpine campanulas, harebell is not unlike *C. cochleariifolia* in form. The nodding bells of bright blue flowers grow in a loose cluster on thread-like stems. It is best planted in open areas, and in wild gardens, or shrubberies, where it will quickly establish itself and self-seed. This little sun-lover is at home in the Scottish Highlands, where it grows wild.
Other colors: White.
Varieties/cultivars: 'Alba'.

Campanula rotundifolia

Catananche caerulea
CUPID'S-DART, BLUE SUCCORY ○

Family: COMPOSITAE
Origin: Portugal–Italy.
Flowering time: Summer.
Climatic zone: 6, 7, 8, 9, 10.
Dimensions: Up to 2 feet (600 mm) high.
Description: A romantic flower, as its common name implies, cupid's dart was once used as an ingredient in love potions. A cornflower-like plant, the mauve heads are protected by silver, papery bracts. The leaves are hairy. Apart from its garden value, the flowers, which rustle when touched, are

Catananche caerulea

excellent for dried floral arrangements. A drought-tolerant plant, it is easy to grow in a sunny position in ordinary garden soil, but good drainage is essential, and wet soil in winter may kill it.

Centaurea montana
MOUNTAIN BLUET, PERENNIAL CORNFLOWER, MOUNTAIN CORNFLOWER (U.K.) ○

Other common names: KNAPWEED (U.K.)
Family: COMPOSITAE
Origin: European mountains.
Flowering time: Mid-spring–early summer.
Climatic zone: 3, 4, 5, 6, 7, 8, 9.
Dimensions: 1½–2 feet (450–600 mm) high.
Description: Mountain bluet is one of the most popular of the perennial *Centaurea* species. Its flowers are thistle-like, with large, deeply fringed, marginal florets. It has a long blooming period,

Centaurea montana

and needs only average, well-drained soil. It looks attractive at the front of a cottage garden border. Propagate it by root division in spring. It is a good cut flower for mixed spring arrangements.
Other colors: White, pink, red.
Varieties/cultivars: 'Alba', 'Rosea', 'Rubra'.

Cheiranthus mutabilis

Cheiranthus mutabilis
WALLFLOWER, CHANGEABLE WALLFLOWER ○

Family: CRUCIFERAE
Origin: Canary Islands, Madeira.
Flowering time: Late spring–early summer.
Climatic zone: 8, 9.
Dimensions: Up to 12 inches (300 mm) high.
Description: A perennial cousin of the commonly grown wallflower, this species has attractive gray-green foliage and masses of slightly fragrant flowers which open yellow but age lilac-purple. It likes full sun, and soil that is either neutral or slightly alkaline, with excellent drainage. Take care not to overwater. Feed it well during summer to extend the flowering season.
Varieties/cultivars: *C. m.* var. *variegatus*.

Clematis heracleifolia

Clematis heracleifolia
TUBE CLEMATIS

Family: RANUNCULACEAE
Origin: China.
Flowering time: Summer.
Climatic zone: 4, 5, 6, 7, 8, 9.
Dimensions: Up to 4 feet (approx. 1 meter) high.
Description: This is a woody-based clematis suited to the herbaceous border. The blue, narrowly bell-shaped flowers resemble the hyacinth and are fragrant. It likes full sun to partial shade and moist, fertile soil, which should not be allowed to become either too wet or too dry. If the soil is light and sandy, apply peat moss, compost, or leaf mold generously before planting. It is advisable to mulch in spring.
Varieties/cultivars: 'Wyevale', 'Davidiana'.

Convolvulus sabatius syn. *C. mauritanicus*
GROUND MORNING GLORY (U.S.A.), BINDWEED

Family: CONVOLVULACEAE
Origin: North Africa.
Flowering time: Summer.
Climatic zone: 8, 9, 10.
Dimensions: Up to 12 inches (300 mm) high.
Description: This perennial, evergreen, trailing plant has widely funnel-shaped, satiny, violet or blue flowers with white throats. It is an attractive basket plant for a greenhouse or a rambler in sheltered rock gardens, and looks particularly effective spilling over rock walls. Plant it as rooted cuttings in ordinary garden soil mixed with compost and a complete fertilizer and water it well.
Other colors: Pink.

Convolvulus sabatius

Cynoglossum nervosum

Cynoglossum nervosum
GREAT HOUND'S TONGUE BLUE HOUND'S TONGUE

Family: BORAGINACEAE
Origin: Himalayas.
Flowering time: Summer.
Climatic zone: 5, 6, 7, 8, 9.
Dimensions: Up to 2 feet (600 mm) high.
Description: The small, intensely blue flowers of this hound's tongue are borne on tall, branching stems and resemble forget-me-nots. The long, thin, hairy leaves easily identify it as a member of the borage family. Use it in borders or rock gardens where the soil is not very rich, as very fertile soil may cause the stems to fall over. This is a plant which will thrive in full sun and average, well-drained soil. Propagate it by division or seed in spring.

Delphinium elatum hybrids
DELPHINIUM, CANDLE LARKSPUR

Family: RANUNCULACEAE
Origin: Hybrids.
Flowering time: Summer, northern hemisphere; spring–summer, southern hemisphere.
Climatic zone: 4, 5, 6, 7, 8, 9.
Dimensions: Up to 6 feet (2 meters) high.
Description: The name *Delphinium* comes from the Greek word for "dolphin" which the flower buds were thought to resemble. The stately, candle-like flowers on their tall stems make these hybrids most striking in a border. Grow them in moist soil in full sun, and fertilize them regularly. Protect them from the wind, staking if necessary. They are susceptible to pests and mildew and the juice of the plants is poisonous.
Other colors: Red, pink, white, cream.
Varieties/cultivars: Many hybrid cultivars are available.

Delphinium elatum

Dianella caerulea
FLAX LILY

Family: LILIACEAE
Origin: Eastern and southern Australia.
Flowering time: Early spring and summer.
Climatic zone: 9, 10.
Dimensions: Up to 4 feet (approx. 1 meter) high.
Description: This is an attractive,

Dianella caerulea

fibrous-rooted perennial which spreads by means of underground rhizomes. The foliage appears at various intervals and is tough and flax-like. The flowers are up to ½ inch (12 mm) wide, starry, six-petaled and blue or whitish with a central cone of yellow stamens, carried in large, airy panicles. They are followed by pretty, deep-blue berries. Flax lily can be grown in most soils and conditions, but must be watered well in summer. The rhizomes can be easily divided to create new plants.

Digitalis purpurea

COMMON FOXGLOVE ◑

Family: SCROPHULARIACEAE
Origin: Western Europe and U.K.
Flowering time: Spring–summer.
Climatic zone: 5, 6, 7, 8, 9.
Dimensions: Up to 4 feet (approx. 2 meters) high.
Description: Foxglove is a good choice for a high backdrop to a border. It likes shade and blends well with ferns and campanulas. Although loved by cottage gardeners, it is considered a noxious weed in some countries. This plant possesses an important medicinal compound, digitalin, which is extracted from the leaves and used for certain heart conditions. In the past, herbalists prescribed foxglove for fevers and liver complaints. With its masses of bell-shaped flowers, this biennial will bloom for six to ten weeks. Plant it in a shady position in humus-rich soil.
Other colors: Yellow, white, pink, red, purple.
Varieties/cultivars: 'Alba', 'Excelsior', 'Shirley'.

Digitalis purpurea

Echinops ritro 'Veitch's Blue'

Echinops ritro

GLOBE THISTLE ○

Family: COMPOSITAE
Origin: Eastern Europe–western Asia.
Flowering time: Summer.
Climatic zone: 3, 4, 5, 6, 7, 8, 9, 10.
Dimensions: Up to 4 feet (approx. 1 meter) high.
Description: This is a handsome, old-world, thistle-like plant which is useful in hardy borders. The blue flowers and the white, woolly foliage can be cut and used in dried floral arrangements. A bold and showy plant, it associates well with phlox in the garden, but needs plenty of space and a moderately sunny position. It prefers ordinary garden soil and may need to be staked if the soil is too moist or fertile. Propagate by division or seed.
Varieties/cultivars: 'Taplow Blue', 'Veitch's Blue'.

Erinus alpinus

SUMMER STARWORT, FAIRY FOXGLOVE (U.K.) ○ ◑

Family: SCROPHULARIACEAE
Origin: European Alps, Pyrenees.
Flowering time: Spring–summer.
Climatic zone: 3, 4, 5, 6, 7, 8, 9.
Dimensions: Up to 6 inches (150 mm) high.
Description: Rock crevices or confined spaces in a wall are ideal environments for this little alpine. When planted in rock garden pockets it will form a close-tufted, evergreen mound. Starry, rosy-purple flowers are borne in profusion on terminal sprays. Mix the seed with moist loam or peat and place it in cracks of walls or rocks to germinate. Well-drained soil in full sun or half-shade will ensure good results.
Other colors: White, pink.
Varieties/cultivars: *E. a.* var. *albus*, 'Dr. Hanaele', 'Mrs. Boyle'.

Erinus alpinus

Eryngium x *zabelii*

ZABEL ERYNGO, SEA HOLLY (U.K.) ○

Family: UMBELLIFERAE
Origin: Hybrids.
Flowering time: Summer.
Climatic zone: 6, 7, 8, 9.
Dimensions: Up to 2½ feet (750 mm) high.
Description: These hybrids are thistle-like plants with blue flowers. The flowers can be dried for use in floral arrangements. Plant them in well-drained, sandy soil that is moderately fertile, and provide plenty of space for growth. They are difficult to transplant. In ancient times they had many medicinal uses.

Eryngium x *zabelii*

Gentiana acaulis syn. G. *excisa*

STEMLESS GENTIAN, TRUMPET GENTIAN (U.K.) ○ ◑

Family: GENTIANIACEAE
Origin: European mountains.
Flowering time: Spring.
Climatic zone: 5, 6, 7, 8, 9.
Dimensions: Up to 4 inches (100 mm) high.
Description: This is one of the best known of the gentians that grow in the alpine meadows in Europe, and needs similar conditions if it is to thrive in the garden. If the environment is right and not too warm, stemless gentian produces a glorious carpet of vivid blue flowers that enhance garden edges and rock garden pockets, or it can be planted in drifts. It needs cool, moist, light, well-drained soil. If it produces leaves but no flowers, it needs to be moved to a warmer position.

Gentiana acaulis

Gentiana asclepiadea

WILLOW GENTIAN ◑ ●

Family: GENTIANIACEAE
Origin: European Alps, Apennines.
Flowering time: Late summer–autumn.
Climatic zone: 5, 6, 7, 8, 9.
Dimensions: Up to 2 feet (600 mm) high.
Description: One of the more reliable and easy-to-grow perennial gentians, it produces flowers of a deep purple-blue, which bloom year after year on long arching stems. Planted in shaded borders or in rock gardens, willow gentian will freely reproduce from seed. It is best grown in acid, humus-rich soil that is kept moist and cool, emulating the mountain conditions of its native habitat. As a rule, gentians do not appreciate root disturbance so a thriving colony should be left alone.
Other colors: White.
Varieties/cultivars: G. *a.* var. *alba*.

Gentiana asclepiadea

Hesperis matronalis

DAME'S ROCKET, DAME'S VIOLET ○ ◑

Family: CRUCIFERAE
Origin: Europe–central Asia.
Flowering time: Summer.
Climatic zone: 5, 6, 7, 8, 9.
Dimensions: Up to 3 feet (1 meter) high.
Description: Known to cooks as "garden rocket", the acrid leaves are eaten like cress in salads in some countries. The purple, mauve or lilac-purple flowers resemble phlox, and have a lovely fragrance which is given out only at night. In modern gardens, it is a short-lived perennial and needs to be replaced with seedlings. It likes moist, well-drained soil and is longer lived in poorer soils.
Other colors: White.
Varieties/cultivars: 'Alba'.

Hesperis matronalis

Hosta fortunei

FORTUNE'S PLANTAIN LILY, PLANTAIN LILY ◑

Family: LILIACEAE
Origin: Japan.
Flowering time: Summer.
Climatic zone: 3, 4, 5, 6, 7, 8, 9.
Dimensions: Up to 2 feet (600 mm) high.
Description: This spectacular plant has striking foliage and handsome spikes of mauve or violet flowers. This lily is ideal for special positions where fine foliage effects are desired — stone planter boxes, by a garden seat, in shady borders, or reflected in a water feature. The clumps will improve with age and should be left undisturbed. Plant it in rich humus soil that does not dry out. Avoid full sun as it may burn the leaves. Divide in spring to propagate it. Cultivars differ in the markings and color of foliage.
Other colors: White.
Varieties/cultivars: 'Aurea-marginata', 'Albopicta'.

Hosta fortunei

Hosta sieboldiana

Hosta sieboldiana
SIEBOLD PLANTAIN LILY, PLANTAIN LILY

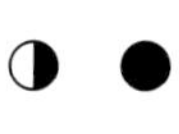

Family: LILIACEAE
Origin: Japan.
Flowering time: Summer.
Climatic zone: 3, 4, 5, 6, 7, 8, 9.
Dimensions: Up to 18 inches (750 mm) high.
Description: The large, striking leaves which seem almost to be stitched or quilted are an outstanding feature of this lily. The lilac flowers with deeper stripes rise on a slender stem that is generally shorter than the foliage. Place this plant in a key position near a water feature, flanking shady steps, or beside a garden seat. In summer it prefers cool, moist soil, but wet soil in winter may damage the leaves. It is susceptible to slugs and snails.

Hosta ventricosa
BLUE PLANTAIN LILY, PLANTAIN LILY

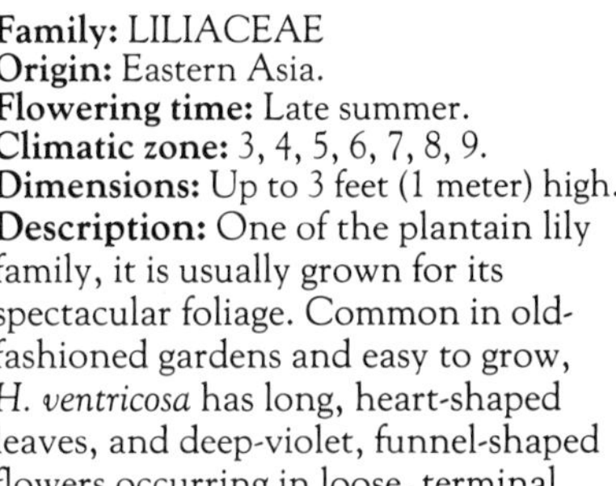

Family: LILIACEAE
Origin: Eastern Asia.
Flowering time: Late summer.
Climatic zone: 3, 4, 5, 6, 7, 8, 9.
Dimensions: Up to 3 feet (1 meter) high.
Description: One of the plantain lily family, it is usually grown for its spectacular foliage. Common in old-fashioned gardens and easy to grow, *H. ventricosa* has long, heart-shaped leaves, and deep-violet, funnel-shaped flowers occurring in loose, terminal clusters. This is a drought- and frost-tender perennial suited to borders. It prefers shade, and soil that is moist in summer. Increase it by division in spring or autumn.

Hosta ventricosa

Iris germanica
TALL BEARDED IRIS

Family: IRIDACEAE
Origin: Southern Europe.
Flowering time: Summer, northern hemisphere; spring, southern hemisphere.
Climatic zone: 4, 5, 6, 7, 8, 9.
Dimensions: Up to 2½ feet (750 mm) high.
Description: This is one of the species from which most bearded irises have been bred. Tall, it is best suited to growing in separate beds or in groups among shrubs. The flowers are deep purple with a yellow beard and a pretty effect can be achieved by planting it in a circular bed or as a backdrop along a sunny wall. It likes very well-drained, fertile soil mixed with plenty of organic matter, and protection from wind. Water it freely during its growing period.
Other colors: Orange with yellow, cream.
Varieties/cultivars: 'Ola Kala', 'Rippling Waters', 'Starshine', 'Velvet Vista'.

Iris germanica 'Velvet Vista'

Iris kaempferi 'Garry Gallant'

Iris kaempferi syn. *I. ensata*
JAPANESE WATER IRIS, JAPANESE IRIS

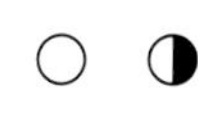

Family: IRIDACEAE
Origin: Japan, China.
Flowering time: Spring.
Climatic zone: 5, 6, 7, 8, 9.
Dimensions: Up to 3 feet (1 meter) high.
Description: This moisture-loving iris is well suited to waterside planting. Some of the cultivars are very colorful, some double-flowered, blotched, stippled, or striped. It makes a good companion plant with primula in a damp border that is free of lime. Plant it at the water's edge, but not below the water surface. Japanese iris will also grow well in ordinary garden soil, providing it has plenty of moisture throughout the growing season. It will die back completely during winter, when dead leaves should be removed.
Other colors: White, pink, red.
Varieties/cultivars: Several cultivars are available.

Iris pumila

Iris pumila
DWARF BEARDED IRIS ○

Family: IRIDACEAE
Origin: Central Europe–Turkey, southern U.S.S.R.
Flowering time: Spring.
Climatic zone: 4, 5, 6, 7, 8, 9.
Dimensions: Up to 8 inches (200 mm) high.
Description: This broad-leafed dwarf iris flowers earlier than the taller flag irises, and looks most effective planted in rock garden pockets or massed at the front of borders. It is short-stemmed and the leaves grow longer after the plant has flowered. Most of the dwarf bearded irises are cultivars and a good selection of colors is available. Irises rarely need mulching. Propagate by division. They are prone to iris borer.
Other colors: White, yellow.
Varieties/cultivars: 'Blue Denim', 'Pogo'.

Iris sibirica
SIBERIAN IRIS ○ ◑

Family: IRIDACEAE
Origin: Central Europe–Lake Baikal, U.S.S.R.
Flowering time: Summer.
Climatic zone: 4, 5, 6, 7, 8, 9.
Dimensions: Up to 4 feet (approx. 1 meter) high.
Description: The parent species of several cultivars and hybrids, *I. sibirica* is a moisture-lover which will form large clumps at the edge of ponds. The flowers are lilac-blue to blue-purple with a purple-veined, white basal patch. It grows best in slightly moist soil but will still do well in conditions that are less than ideal.
Other colors: White, pearly-gray.
Varieties/cultivars: 'Caesar', 'Caesar's Brother', 'White Swirl', 'Snow Queen', 'Mrs Rowe', 'Perry's Blue', 'Cambridge Blue'.

Iris sibirica 'Cambridge Blue'

Jasione perennis
SHEPHERD'S SCABIOUS (U.S.A.), SHEEP'S-BIT (U.K.) ○ ◑

Family: CAMPANULACEAE
Origin: Europe.
Flowering time: Spring–summer.
Climatic zone: 6, 7, 8.
Dimensions: Up to 12 inches (300 mm) high.
Description: This low-growing perennial is ideally suited to sunny rock garden pockets. It has a dense rosette of leaves and lilac-blue flower heads composed of many tiny florets which resemble pincushions. The heads are borne on erect stems. Plant it in winter in light, open soil in a sunny or semishaded position. Apply complete fertilizer in early spring and propagate it by root division in winter.

Limonium latifolium
BORDER SEA LAVENDER ○

Family: PLUMBAGINACEAE
Origin: Southeastern Europe–U.S.S.R.
Flowering time: Summer–autumn.
Climatic zone: 4, 5, 6, 7, 8, 9, 10.
Dimensions: Up to 2 feet (600 mm) high.

Limonium latifolium

Jasione perennis

Description: This member of the plumbago family is resistant to salt spray. It has rosettes of large leaves topped by long stems packed with masses of deep lavender-blue flowers. Bunches may be gathered and dried for semipermanent floral arrangements. It is easy to grow in sunny positions in light, sandy, moist soil, and is a good choice for the gardens of holiday houses which cannot be constantly maintained.
Varieties/cultivars: 'Violetta', 'Chilwell Beauty'.

Linum perenne syn. *L. sibiricum*
PERENNIAL FLAX ○

Family: LINACEAE
Origin: Europe.
Flowering time: Summer.
Climatic zone: 6, 7, 8, 9.
Dimensions: Up to 2 feet (600 mm) high.
Description: Perennial flax is a hardy border plant with gray-green leaves and clusters of pale blue, saucer-shaped flowers. The roots generally throw up numerous stems. It likes ordinary, well-drained soil, a sunny position, and regular watering. Apply a complete fertilizer in spring. Propagate it by seed in spring.

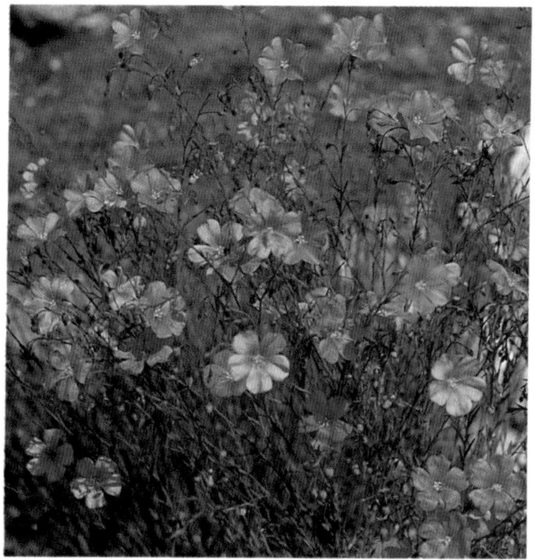
Linum perenne

Lobelia x *gerardii*
LOBELIA ○

Family: CAMPANULACEAE
Origin: Hybrid.
Flowering time: Summer.
Climatic zone: 5, 6, 7, 8, 9, 10.
Dimensions: Up to 3 feet (1 meter) high.
Description: This is a less commonly

Lobelia x *gerardii*

grown hybrid Lobelia, whose ancestry is uncertain due to back-breeding. In general it is a robust plant with leafy stems and a striking display of violet-purple flowers appearing in terminal racemes. The flowering period is spread over many weeks as the axillary branches are later to bloom. It prefers moderately rich and well-drained soil, with a good mulch of organic matter to protect the roots in winter. Makes a beautiful cut flower.
Other colors: Pink.
Varieties/cultivars: 'Surprise'.

Mazus reptans
TEAT FLOWER ○

Family: SCROPHULARIACEAE
Origin: Himalayas.
Flowering time: Spring.
Climatic zone: 6, 7, 8, 9.
Dimensions: Up to 9 inches (225 mm) high.
Description: This low-growing perennial forms a dense carpet and is well suited to sloping sites and rock gardens. Plant several close together near large rocks where the prostrate stems can form mats. The flowers are light purplish-blue with white, yellow and purple markings on the lower lips. It adapts to most soil types, but likes a moist soil and an open, sunny position. It is frost-resistant, but susceptible to drought.

Mazus reptans

Meconopsis betonicifolia syn. *M. baileyi*
HIMALAYAN BLUE POPPY, TIBETAN POPPY ○ ◑

Family: PAPAVERACEAE
Origin: Himalayas.
Flowering time: Early summer.
Climatic zone: 6, 7, 8, 9.
Dimensions: Up to 4 feet (approx. 1 meter) high.
Description: The satiny, rich-blue, poppy-like flowers of Tibetan poppy are borne in groups of three or four at the tops of strong, slim stems. A cold-climate species, this herbaceous perennial from the Himalayan mountains needs deep, cool, fertile, moist soil in semishade or full sun. Protect it from the wind, water it regularly, and apply a complete fertilizer in the spring. Propagation is by seed in autumn.

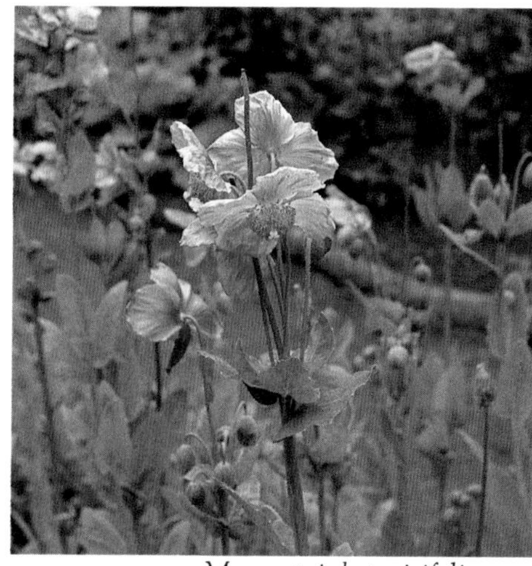
Meconopsis betonicifolia

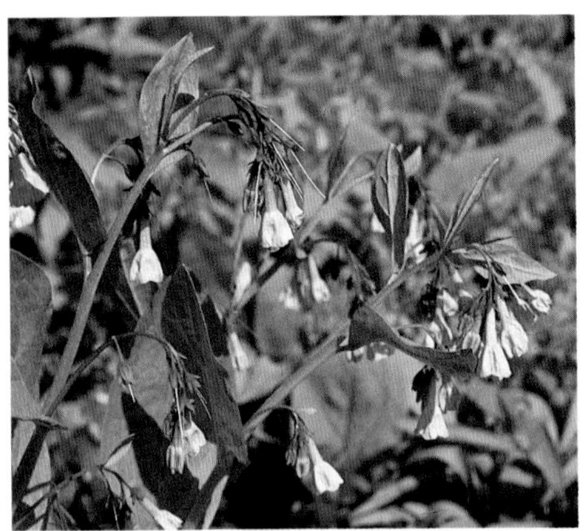

Mertensia virginica

Mertensia virginica
VIRGINIA BLUEBELLS ◑

Family: BORAGINACEAE
Origin: Central eastern and southeastern United States.
Flowering time: Late spring.
Climatic zone: 4, 5, 6, 7, 8, 9.
Dimensions: Up to 18 inches (450 mm) high.
Description: This pretty perennial has pale blue-green foliage and long, tubular, purple-blue flowers in drooping clusters. It needs cool soil that is rich in organic matter and that is kept moist, especially in the warm weather when the foliage dies back after flowering. Mulch the soil well with rotted compost.
Other colors: White, pink.
Varieties/cultivars: 'Alba', 'Rubra'.

Myosotis sylvatica
FORGET-ME-NOT ◑

Family: BORAGINACEAE
Origin: Europe.
Flowering time: Spring.
Climatic zone: 5, 6, 7, 8, 9.
Dimensions: Up to 12 inches (300 mm) high.

Myosotis sylvatica 'Royal Blue'

Description: This bushy biennial makes a good indoor winter pot plant. If using in borders it will spread rapidly and needs to be checked. It is best used with spring bulbs in pots, and under deciduous trees and shrubs where it will self-sow many seedlings each season. Cottage gardens are an ideal environment for it. Forget-me-not will grow in ordinary garden soil and thrives in rich, limed, sandy loam.
Varieties/cultivars: 'Royal Blue'.

Nepeta x *faassenii*
CATMINT ○

Family: LABIATAE
Origin: Hybrid.
Flowering time: Summer.
Climatic zone: 4, 5, 6, 7, 8, 9, 10.
Dimensions: Up to 18 inches (450 mm) high.

Nepeta x *faassenii*

Description: When the leaves of catmint are bruised, the aroma has a curious fascination for some cats, who chew the plant, roll on it, and eventually become quite intoxicated. This useful edging plant has aromatic spikes of small, mauve flowers and silver-gray leaves. It likes warm, sandy, well-drained soil and is easily grown and propagated from seeds in spring or by root division.

Omphalodes verna
CREEPING FORGET-ME-NOT, BLUE-EYED MARY ●

Family: BORAGINACEAE
Origin: Central southern Europe.
Flowering time: Spring.
Climatic zone: 5, 6, 7, 8, 9.
Dimensions: Up to 8 inches (200 mm) high.
Description: Creeping forget-me-not forms a clearblue groundcover when planted in woodland or under large trees and shrubs. The erect stems bear clusters of forget-me-not-like flowers in loose sprays. The plant thrives in neutral or slightly alkaline soil, provided it is cool, moist, and well-drained, and enriched with organic matter. It likes full shade and in the right position will flower for several months. Propagation is by seed in spring or by root division in spring or autumn.
Other colors: White.
Varieties/cultivars: 'Alba'.

Omphalodes verna

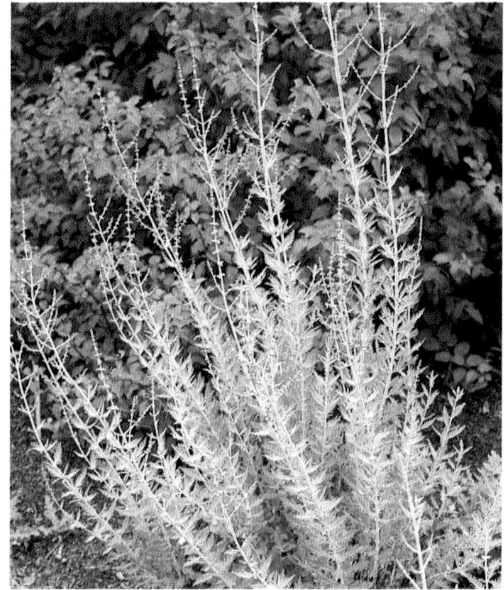
Perovskia atriplicifolia

Perovskia atriplicifolia
AZURE SAGE ○

Family: LABIATAE
Origin: Western Himalayas, Afghanistan.
Flowering time: Summer.
Climatic zone: 6, 7, 8, 9, 10.
Dimensions: Up to 5 feet (approx. 2 meters) high.
Description: Although this plant is a member of the mint family, it has a strong, sage-like aroma when bruised. With its attractive blue flowers it makes a good companion plant with globe thistle in an open border. In full sun it forms a very attractive, upright plant, but in shaded situations it is inclined to sprawl. Cut it back to ground level each spring to promote strong new growth and good flowering. Azure sage is easy to grow in well-drained soil and is propagated by cuttings in late summer.

Platycodon grandiflorus
BALLOON FLOWER, CHINESE BELLFLOWER (U.S.A.) ○

Family: CAMPANULACEAE
Origin: Eastern Asia.
Flowering time: Late summer.
Climatic zone: 4, 5, 6, 7, 8, 9.
Dimensions: Up to 3 feet (1 meter) high.
Description: This compact, clump-forming, herbaceous plant sends up numerous leafy flower stems. The balloon-like buds open to form wide, cup-shaped flowers. It is an easy plant to grow provided it has a sunny position in an enriched, loamy soil. It makes an attractive picture when planted in combination with fuchsias. Propagation is either by division or from seed in spring.
Other colors: White, pink.
Varieties/cultivars: 'Mariesii', 'Mother of Pearl', 'Capri'.

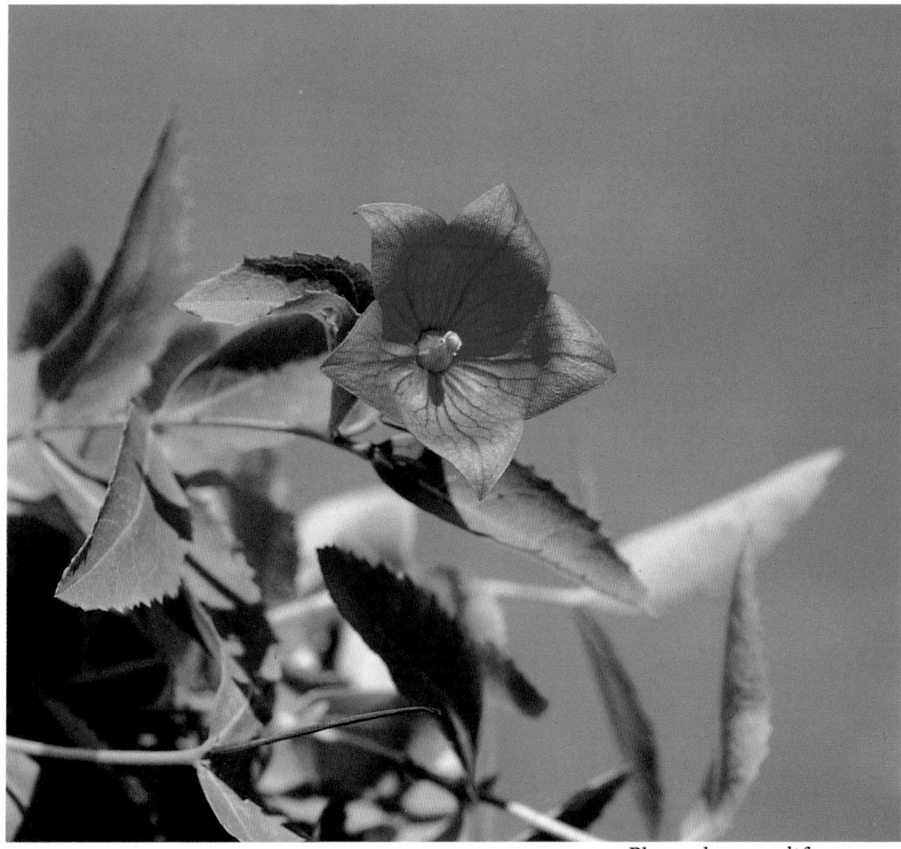
Platycodon grandiflorus

Platycodon grandiflorus 'Mariesii'
DWARF BALLOON FLOWER ○

Family: CAMPANULACEAE
Origin: Cultivar.
Flowering time: Summer.
Climatic zone: 4, 5, 6, 7, 8, 9.
Dimensions: Up to 18 inches (450 mm) high.
Description: This smaller growing cultivar of *Platycodon grandiflorus* was introduced into England from Japan and is now the form of balloon flower most widely grown in gardens. It is a vigorous perennial, forming quite large clumps after two or three years. The flowers last well both on the plant and when picked. It is easily propagated by lifting the clumps after a few years and carefully dividing them, replanting the separated pieces immediately.
Other colors: White.

Platycodon grandiflorus 'Mariesii'

Polemonium caeruleum

JACOB'S-LADDER ○ ◑

Family: POLEMONIACEAE
Origin: Northern hemisphere.
Flowering time: Summer.
Climatic zone: 4, 5, 6, 7, 8, 9.
Dimensions: 2–3 feet (600–900 mm) high.
Description: The neatly divided leaflets, arranged in opposite pairs resembling the rungs of a ladder, give this plant its common name. The blooms are arranged in loose clusters of small, silky, bell-shaped flowers, with prominent orange stamens. It is an easily grown plant, though often short-lived unless divided in spring and replanted. Alternatively, it can be easily increased by seed.
Other colors: White.
Varieties/cultivars: 'Richardsonii', 'Dawn Flight', 'Sapphire'.

Polemonium caeruleum

Polemonium reptans

DWARF JACOB'S-LADDER, CREEPING POLEMONIUM ○ ◑

Family: POLEMONIACEAE
Origin: Eastern United States.
Flowering time: Spring–summer.
Climatic zone: 4, 5, 6, 7, 8, 9.
Dimensions: 8–12 inches (200–300 mm) high.
Description: This is an early flowering species which has branching stems and leaves divided into six or seven pairs. The pendant, cup-shaped flowers are carried in loose terminal clusters. This

Polemonium reptans

plant has a spreading rather than creeping habit, and prefers rich and moist well-drained soils and a protected position. It is frost-resistant but sensitive to drought. It can be propagated by seed or division.

Pulmonaria officinalis

LUNGWORT, SPOTTED DOG, SOLDIERS AND SAILORS (U.K.) ◑ ●

Family: BORAGINACEAE
Origin: Central Europe.
Flowering time: Spring.
Climatic zone: 4, 5, 6, 7, 8, 9.
Dimensions: Up to 12 inches (300 mm) high.
Description: The tubular flowers of this species are purple-pink at first but become shades of purple and then violet-blue as they mature. The large, bristly, heart-shaped leaves are irregularly spotted with white and were thought by ancient herbalists to cure spots on the lung. This plant is not particular about soil type, but prefers moist conditions. It is usually propagated by division in late winter.
Other colors: White.

Pulsatilla vulgaris syn. *Anemone pulsatilla*

PASQUE FLOWER ○ ◑

Family: RANUNCULACEAE
Origin: Europe and western U.S.S.R.
Flowering time: Spring.

Pulsatilla vulgaris

Pulmonaria officinalis

Climatic zone: 3, 4, 5, 6, 7, 8, 9.
Dimensions: 8–12 inches (200–300 mm) high.
Description: Pasque flower is an attractive rock garden plant with ferny leaves and nodding flowers on erect, hairy stems. Its common name was given because it comes into bloom round about Easter in the northern hemisphere. Well-drained garden soil suits it best and it is propagated by seed.
Other colors: Pink, mauve.

Salvia farinacea 'Blue Bedder'

Salvia farinacea
MEALY-CUP SAGE ○ ◑

Family: LABIATAE
Origin: Texas, New Mexico.
Flowering time: Summer–early autumn.
Climatic zone: 7, 8, 9.
Dimensions: 3–4 feet (approx. 1 meter) high.
Description: A slightly frost-tender member of the salvia genus, this species makes an excellent display in the summer border. The flowers are borne on long, graceful spikes, somewhat resembling lavender but much larger, and the aromatic leaves are long and narrow. Propagate the plant by division, or sow the seeds in spring. It is advisable to plant out in the garden after the risk of frost has passed
Other colors: White.
Varieties/cultivars: 'Blue Bedder', 'Alba'.

Salvia officinalis

Salvia officinalis and cultivars
COMMON SAGE ○ ◑

Family: LABIATAE
Origin: Southern Europe.
Flowering time: Summer.
Climatic zone: 6, 7, 8, 9.
Dimensions: Up to 3 feet (1 meter) high.
Description: Common sage has strongly aromatic, gray-green leaves and bluish-purple flowers. It has been cultivated for centuries as a culinary herb. The cultivar 'Purpurascens' is commonly called purple-leafed sage because both new stems and foliage are suffused with purple. 'Tricolor' is very distinctive with its gray-green leaves splashed with creamy white and suffused with purple and pink. Sage will grow in any free-draining garden soil. The leaves can be used fresh for cooking and in salads, or picked and dried for later use.
Other colors: White.
Varieties/cultivars: 'Alba', 'Icterina', 'Purpurascens', 'Tricolor'.

Salvia pratensis
MEADOW CLARY ○ ◑

Family: LABIATAE
Origin: Europe and North Africa.
Flowering time: Summer.
Climatic zone: 5, 6, 7, 8, 9.
Dimensions: 2–3 feet (approx. 1 meter) high.
Description: This sturdy plant forms a good basal clump of leaves below long spikes of violet-blue flowers. The leaves, slightly spotted with red, are rather coarse and the flower stems are square in shape. Like most members of the salvia genus, it prefers warm and dryish conditions and does not tolerate heavy frosts. It should be cut back after flowering and can be propagated from cuttings.
Other colors: White, pink.
Varieties/cultivars: 'Baumgartenii', *S. p. tenorii.*

Salvia pratensis

Salvia x *superba*

Salvia x *superba*
VIOLET SAGE ○

Family: LABIATAE
Origin: Hybrid.
Flowering time: Summer–early autumn.
Climatic zone: 5, 6, 7, 8, 9.
Dimensions: 2–3 feet (up to 1 meter) high.
Description: The violet-red bracts which surround the crimson-purple flowers of this species persist after the flowers themselves have finished, providing a long and colorful display. The small, green leaves on the upright stems are aromatic. It is a useful plant for a mixed border and the flowers are excellent for cutting and drying. It grows well in ordinary garden soil and can be propagated by seed.
Varieties/cultivars: 'Lubeca', 'East Friesland'.

Stachys byzantina syn. *S. lanata*, *S. olympica*

LAMB'S EARS, LAMBS' TONGUES, DONKEY'S EARS (U.S.A.) ○ ◑

Family: LABIATAE
Origin: Southwestern Asia–Turkey.
Flowering time: Summer.
Climatic zone: 5, 6, 7, 8, 9.
Dimensions: Up to 18 inches (450 mm) high.
Description: This is an excellent groundcover with its dense mats of woolly, gray leaves. It thrives in full sun or part shade and often succeeds in poor soil. The spikes of small purple flowers are half-hidden by silver bracts. Propagation is by division.
Varieties/cultivars: 'Silver Carpet' (non-flowering), 'Cotton Boll'.

Stachys byzantina

Stachys macrantha syn. *S. grandiflora*, *Betonica macrantha*

BIG BETONY (U.S.A.), GRAND WOUNDWORT (U.K.) ○ ◑

Family: LABIATAE
Origin: The Caucasus.
Flowering time: Summer.
Climatic zone: 4, 5, 6, 7, 8, 9.
Dimensions: Up to 2 feet (600 mm) high.
Description: The dark-green, downy leaves of this plant have an unusual wrinkled or corrugated appearance. From the dense clumps of leaves, erect flower stems emerge with three or four whorls of hooded blooms of a purplish-mauve color. Garden forms exist which have deeper and richer violet flowers and there are also those with pink and white blooms. It is easily propagated by

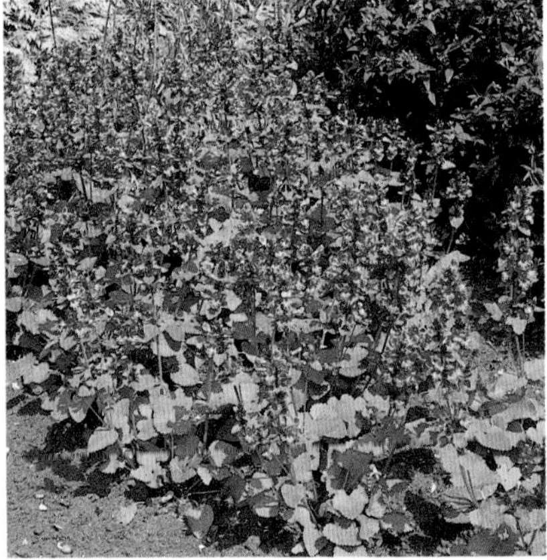

Stachys macrantha

division in early spring. Plant in well-drained soil.
Other colors: Pink, white
Varieties/cultivars: 'Superba', 'Robusta'.

Stokesia laevis

STOKES' ASTER ○ ◑

Family: COMPOSITAE
Origin: Southeastern United States.
Flowering time: Summer–autumn.
Climatic zone: 5, 6, 7, 8, 9.
Dimensions: 18 inches (450 mm) high.
Description: From a basal rosette of plain, green leaves, the flower stems emerge with a cornflower-like bloom set off by a collar of green leaves (or bracts). The blue flowers can often be up to 4 inches (100 mm) across with paler centers. They last well on the plant and are also good for picking. The plants thrive in any good, well-drained soil, and are usually propagated by division in late winter.
Other colors: Pink, white.
Varieties/cultivars: 'Blue Star', 'Alba', 'Rosea'.

Teucrium fruticans

MINT GERMANDER, SHRUBBY GERMANDER ○ ◑

Family: LABIATAE
Origin: Western Mediterranean region and Portugal.
Flowering time: Summer–autumn.
Climatic zone: 8, 9, 10.
Dimensions: 4 to 7 feet (1–2 meters) high.

Teucrium fruticans

Stokesia laevis

Description: Mint germander is an easily cultivated, evergreen shrub with attractive gray-green oval leaves, slightly curled at the edges. It flowers over a long period. It is a dense shrub and can be clipped to shape, making it ideal for hedges. A quick grower in any good garden soil, even the slightly alkaline, it is also useful for seaside planting, tolerating warm, dry conditions. In cooler areas, it grows well against a sunny wall, or in a container on a patio. It can be propagated from cuttings taken in late summer, or from seed.

Teucrium marum

Teucrium marum syn. *Micromeria corsica*

CATNIP, CAT THYME ○

Family: LABIATAE
Origin: Yugoslavia and Mediterranean islands.
Flowering time: Summer.
Climatic zone: 7, 8, 9, 10.
Dimensions: 6–12 inches (150–300 mm) high.
Description: This is an adaptable plant, growing well in most types of soil providing it is well-drained. It is frost-resistant and will tolerate drought. The gray-green, oval leaves on wiry stems have an aromatic odor. It can sometimes be an unfortunate addition to a garden as cats are said to be inordinately fond of it, tearing it to pieces and rolling on its neighbors! It can be grown in a rockery and propagated by seed or cuttings.

Tricyrtis formosana

Tricyrtis formosana

TOAD LILY

Family: LILIACEAE
Origin: Taiwan.
Flowering time: Early autumn.
Climatic zone: 5, 6, 7, 8, 9.
Dimensions: 2–3 feet (600–900 mm) high.
Description: Toad lilies, so called because of their spotted flowers, have shiny, dark leaves and upright flower stems that branch into heads of mauve-white flowers having yellow, purple-spotted throats. Grow them in a soil that does not dry out and that contains plenty of organic matter. They do well in a shady position, although a little dappled sunshine will hasten the development of flowers. Propagation is by seeds or offsets.
Other colors: Reddish-purple.
Varieties/cultivars: *T. f. stolonifera.*

Veronica austriaca teucrium

SPEEDWELL, BLUE SPEEDWELL, HUNGARIAN SPEEDWELL (U.S.A.) ○ ◑

Family: SCROPHULARIACEAE
Origin: Europe.
Flowering time: Summer.
Climatic zone: 4, 5, 6, 7, 8, 9.
Dimensions: 1–2 feet (300–600 mm) high.
Description: This charming perennial has slender spikes of lavender-blue flowers and narrow, deep-green leaves on slender stems. A useful plant for borders or rockeries, it likes a sunny or semishaded position and a fertile, well-drained soil. Cut it back in autumn to encourage strong growth the following spring, and divide clumps every four years to produce new, healthy plants. Feed it with a liquid fertilizer in spring to encourage good flower production.
Other colors: Various shades of blue.
Varieties/cultivars: 'Blue Fountain', 'Crater Lake Blue', 'Trehane', 'Pavane', 'Shirley Blue', 'Knallblau'.

Veronica austriaca teucrium 'Knallblau'

Veronica spicata

Veronica spicata

SPIKE SPEEDWELL, CAT'S TAIL SPEEDWELL (U.K.) ○ ◑

Family: SCROPHULARIACEAE
Origin: Europe and Asia.
Flowering time: Summer–early autumn.
Climatic zone: 4, 5, 6, 7, 8, 9.
Dimensions: 18 inches (450 mm) high.
Description: This is a valuable plant for the front of a border as it makes a fine display. It forms a compact tussock of leaves from which arise the numerous dense spikes of flowers. It is easy to grow in most soil types, provided they are well-drained. Over the years it has been successfully crossed with other species to produce many attractive garden varieties. The best method of propagation is by division.
Other colors: Pink, white.
Varieties/cultivars: 'Sarabande', 'Icicle', 'Blue Fox', 'Red Fox', 'Blue Peter', 'Snow White'.

Veronica spicata var *incana*

Veronica spicata var. *incana* syn. *V incana* ○

GRAY SPIKE SPEEDWELL (U.K.), WOOLLY SPEEDWELL (U.S.A.)

Family: SCROPHULARIACEAE
Origin: Northern Asia and U.S.S.R.
Flowering time: Summer.
Climatic zone: 4, 5, 6, 7, 8, 9.
Dimensions: 12–18 inches (300–450 mm) high.
Description: Gray speedwell is a more-or-less evergreen plant that is easy to grow in average garden soil provided it receives ample sunshine. The deep blue flowers are carried in terminal spikes, and the leaves are silvery-gray and slightly toothed. This plant makes a good show in the garden and has a long flowering period. The best method of propagation is by division, either in autumn or in spring.
Other colors: Pink.
Varieties/cultivars: 'Barcarolle', 'Minuet'.

Vinca minor

LESSER PERIWINKLE (U.K.), RUNNING MYRTLE ◑ ●

Family: APOCYNACEAE
Origin: Europe and western Asia.
Flowering time: Spring–summer.
Climatic zone: 5, 6, 7, 8, 9.
Dimensions: Prostrate to 4 inches (100 mm) high.
Description: A hardy, trailing plant with small, dark-green, shiny leaves, dwarf periwinkle spreads rapidly over the soil surface, rooting at every node to form new plants. This is a most useful plant for covering the ground in shaded areas under trees. The flower color is somewhat variable, but always in shades of blue, purple, and white. There are several cultivars, including two with variegated foliage. It is easily propagated by simply cutting the rooted stems and planting them elsewhere. Vinca grows well in most well-drained soils.
Other colors: Pink, white.
Varieties/cultivars: 'Alba', 'Bowles Variety', 'Rosea'.

Vinca minor

Viola cornuta

Viola cornuta

HORNED VIOLET 

Family: VIOLACEAE
Origin: Pyrenees.
Flowering time: Late spring–autumn.
Climatic zone: 5, 6, 7, 8, 9.
Dimensions: Up to 8 inches (200 mm) high.
Description: This dainty little edging or rock garden plant is a short-lived perennial which prefers a semishaded position in ordinary garden soil. The evergreen leaves form a compact tuft and violet-colored flowers are held on long stalks. The flowering period can be prolonged if the dead flowers are removed regularly. Once established, this viola will spread well to form an attractive groundcover. It is closely related to pansies and violets.
Other colors: White.

Viola hederacea

WILD VIOLET, AUSTRALIAN NATIVE VIOLET, IVY-LEAVED VIOLET ◑ ●

Family: VIOLACEAE
Origin: Southeastern Australia.
Flowering time: Spring–autumn.
Climatic zone: 8, 9, 10.
Dimensions: Prostrate to 4 inches (100 mm) high.
Description: This dense mat-forming plant with kidney-shaped leaves spreads on long runners that bind the soil or cascade over banks. A good groundcover plant for either sandy or clay soils, it prefers a moist and semisheltered position. One plant will cover up to 1 square yard

Viola hederacea

(approximately 1 square meter) of soil. It is tolerant of some frost and snow provided that winters are not too severe. It is also moderately tolerant of limy soil.
Other colors: White.
Varieties/cultivars: 'Baby Blue'.

Viola labradorica 'Purpurea'
LABRADOR VIOLET ◑ ●

Family: VIOLACEAE
Origin: Cultivar.
Flowering time: Spring–summer.
Climatic zone: 3, 4, 5, 6, 7, 8, 9.
Dimensions: 4 inches (100 mm) high.
Description: This little violet is an attractive groundcover all year round due to the deep purple-green of its leaves. It makes a useful color contrast in the garden, especially if near plants with lime-yellow foliage. The flowers are a pretty lavender-blue, but without any perfume. It spreads easily in most soils, rooting at the nodes, and is usually propagated by division during autumn or winter.

Viola labradorica 'Purpurea'

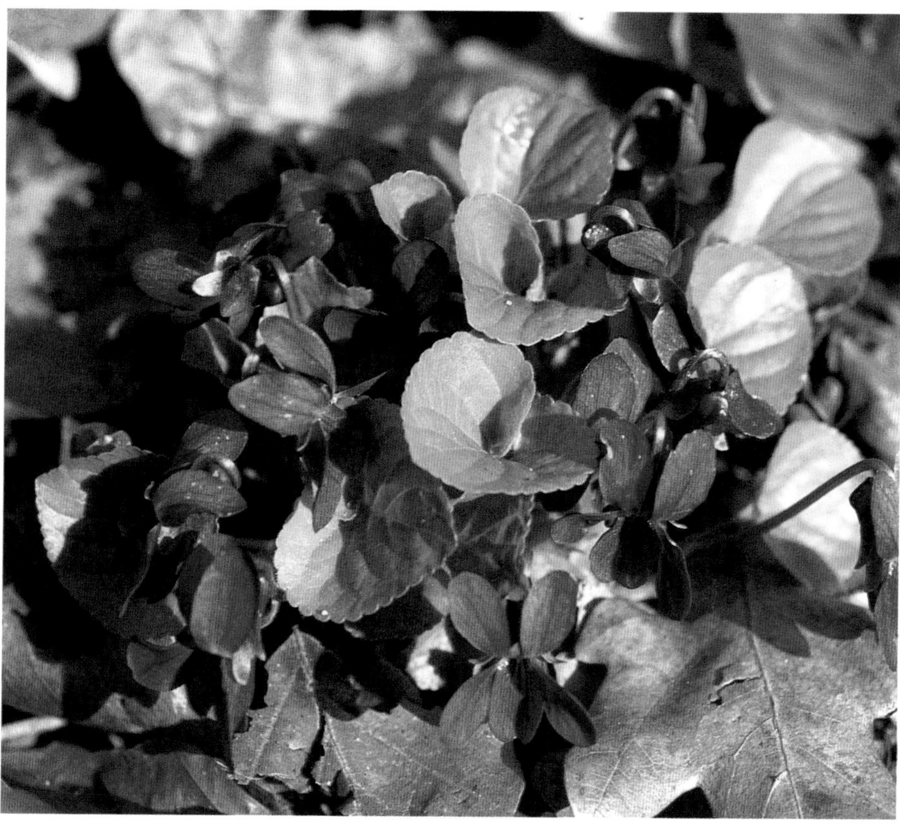

Viola odorata

Viola odorata
COMMON VIOLET, SWEET VIOLET (U.K.) ◑ ●

Family: VIOLACEAE
Origin: Europe, North Africa, Asia.
Climatic zone: 6, 7, 8, 9.
Dimensions: 6 inches (150 mm) high.
Description: For the size of this little perennial, the flowers are relatively large, being up to 1 inch (25 mm) across. Their perfume is sweet and quite strong. The plant spreads by runners and it can be divided in autumn and spring. It often self-sows. It is an easily grown groundcover, which likes moist, moderately rich soil. There are now many garden forms.
Other colors: White, pink, apricot.
Varieties/cultivars: 'Marie Louise', 'Princess of Wales', 'Czar', 'Royal Robe'.

Wahlenbergia gloriosa
ROYAL BLUEBELL ○ ◑

Family: CAMPANULACEAE
Origin: Southeastern Australia.
Flowering time: Late spring–summer.
Climatic zone: 8, 9.
Dimensions: Prostrate, spreading up to 3 sq. feet (1 sq. meter).
Description: This is a very showy creeper which spreads quite rapidly by suckering. It is a hardy, frost-resistant plant although it does not withstand severe winters. It grows best in a loamy soil with plenty of moisture. It looks spectacular when mass-planted, but it can also be grown successfully and looks attractive in a tub or large pot. Its flower is the floral emblem of the Australian Capital Territory.

Wahlenbergia gloriosa

Brunfelsia australis

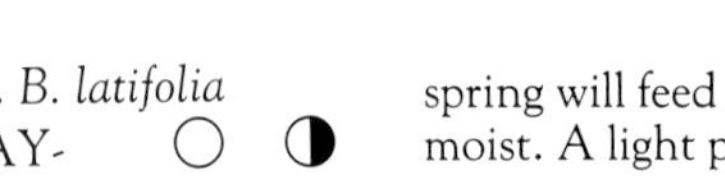

Brunfelsia australis syn. *B. latifolia*
YESTERDAY-TODAY-AND-TOMORROW ○ ◑

Family: SOLANACEAE
Origin: Central America.
Flowering time: Spring–summer.
Climatic zone: 9, 10.
Dimensions: 3–6 feet (1–2 meters) high.
Description: The common name is derived from the flowers which, over a period of three days, change from violet-blue, fading to lavender and eventually to white. The phlox-like flowers are very fragrant and the leaves are grayish-green. In cold climates, yesterday-today-and-tomorrow is grown in greenhouses or indoors. It likes a warm, sheltered position and benefits from a light pruning after flowering. Feed in early spring with a complete plant food.

Brunfelsia calycina
DWARF BRUNFELSIA, YESTERDAY-TODAY-AND-TOMORROW ○ ◑

Family: SOLANACEAE
Origin: South America.
Flowering time: Spring–summer.
Climatic zone: 9, 10.
Dimensions: 3–4 feet (approx. 1 meter) high.
Description: Compact, with slender, semi-glossy green foliage, dwarf brunfelsia makes a pretty feature shrub. The fragrant violet flowers virtually cover the plant and fade to white as they age. The shrub requires a warm, sheltered position and well-drained soil. A mulch of manure or compost in

Brunfelsia calycina

spring will feed it and keep the roots moist. A light pruning after flowering encourages more compact growth.
Varieties/cultivars: 'Eximea', *B. c.* var. *floribunda.*

Buddleia alternifolia
FOUNTAIN BUDDLEIA, ALTERNATE-LEAFED BUDDLEIA ○ ◑

Family: LOGANIACEAE
Origin: China.
Flowering time: Early summer.
Climatic zone: 5, 6, 7, 8, 9.
Dimensions: 10–20 feet (3–6 meters).

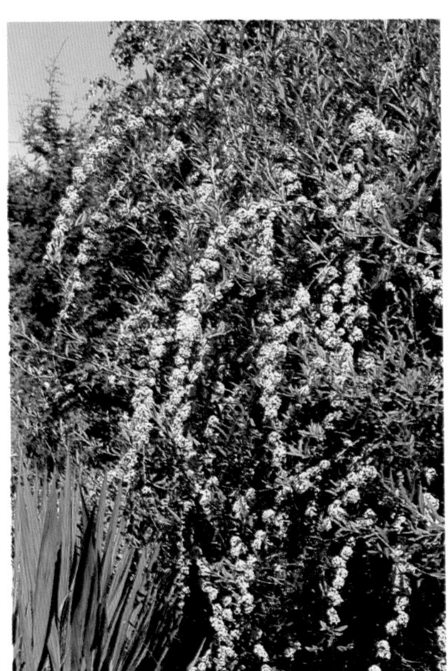
Buddleia alternifolia

Description: A large shrub with gracefully arching branches bearing long, narrow leaves, fountain buddleia produces an abundance of fragrant, lilac-purple flowers that weigh the branches down. Pruning, if required, should be carried out after flowering has finished, as flowers appear on the previous year's growth. Fountain buddleia is popular in cottage gardens and makes a good screen plant. It will grow in any well-drained garden soil. Apply a handful of complete plant food in early spring.
Other colors: Mauve-pink.
Varieties/cultivars: 'Argentea', 'Hever Castle'.

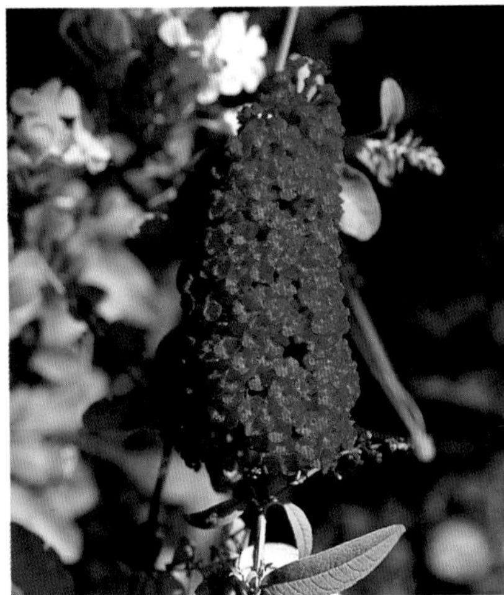
Buddleia davidii

Buddleia davidii
BUTTERFLY BUSH, BUDDLEIA ○ ◑

Family: LOGANIACEAE
Origin: China.
Flowering time: Summer.
Climatic zone: 5, 6, 7, 8, 9.
Dimensions: 10 feet (3 meters) high.
Description: Butterfly bush is a very worthy addition to gardens because of its hardiness, attractiveness to butterflies, and its tolerance of a wide range of soils, temperatures, and environments. Its rapid growth makes it useful for screen plantings. The gray-green foliage is attractive and complements the mauve spikes of the flower heads. Pruning in winter is essential to control the shape of the bush.
Other colors: Rich red-purple, white.
Varieties/cultivars: 'Royal Red', 'White Bouquet', 'Ile de France'.

Callicarpa bodinieri var. *giraldii*

Callicarpa bodinieri var. *giraldii*
CHINESE BEAUTYBERRY, BEAUTY BERRY (U.K.) ○

Family: VERBENACEAE
Origin: Western China.
Flowering time: Summer.
Climatic zone: 6, 7, 8, 9.
Dimensions: 6 feet (2 meters) high.
Description: This is a handsome shrub valued for its downy foliage and rosy-lilac flowers, which are followed by clusters of shining bluish-lilac fruits. Use it as a background plant for a shrub border. Easily grown, Chinese beautyberry will thrive in any well-drained soil that does not dry out. A sunny aspect is essential. Pruning is not necessary unless the plant becomes straggly, when it can be cut back heavily in late winter. Chinese beautyberry can be propagated from cuttings or seed.

Calluna vulgaris
LING, HEATHER, SCOTCH HEATHER ○ ◑

Family: ERICACEAE
Origin: Europe, western Asia, Morocco, the Azores.
Flowering time: Spring and summer.
Climatic zone: 5, 6, 7, 8, 9.
Dimensions: 12 inches (450 mm) high.
Description: Heather is loved for its evergreen foliage and profusion of small, bell-like, purplish-pink, nodding flowers and is a good shrub to use in front of borders or as a groundcover in a small

Calluna vulgaris

garden. It will grow in poor soil as long as it is well-drained and acidic. Cultivate around the plant with care as the roots are very close to the surface. A mulch of leaf mold or peat is beneficial. Pruning can be carried out after flowering to keep the plants compact.
Other colors: White, mauve, crimson, pink.
Varieties/cultivars: There are numerous cultivars of heather throughout the world.

Caryopteris incana
BLUEBEARD, BLUE SPIRAEA (U.K.) ○

Family: VERBENACEAE
Origin: Japan, Korea, China.
Flowering time: Late summer–autumn.

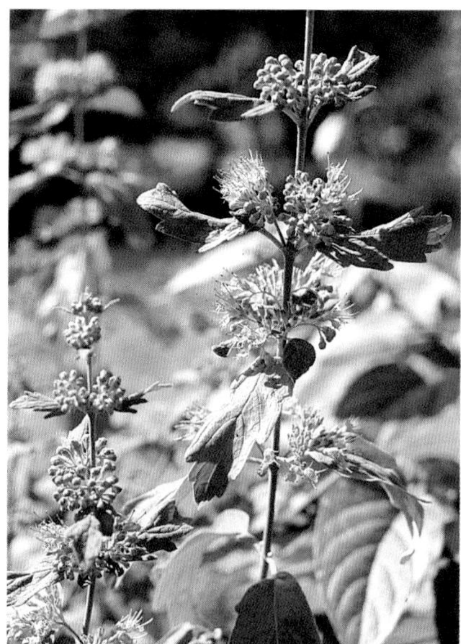

Caryopteris incana

Climatic zone: 5, 6, 7, 8, 9.
Dimensions: 3 feet (1 meter) high.
Description: This small shrub has an abundance of grayish-green, aromatic leaves. The axillary clusters of violet-blue flowers appear at the tips of the shoots. A valued shrub because it flowers when few other blue-flowering shrubs are in bloom, bluebeard will thrive in a moisture-retentive but well-drained loamy soil. Because flowers are produced on the new wood, prune during winter.

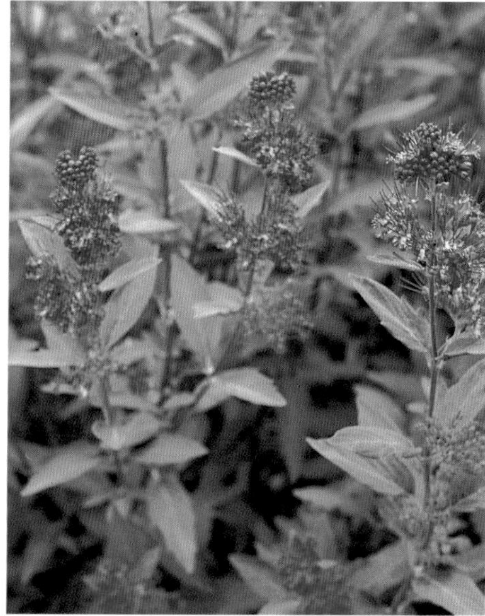

Caryopteris x *clandonensis*

Caryopteris x *clandonensis*
BLUEBEARD, BLUE SPIRAEA (U.K.) ○

Family: VERBENACEAE
Origin: Hybrid.
Flowering time: Summer–autumn.
Climatic zone: 5, 6, 7, 8, 9.
Dimensions: 2 feet (600 mm) high.
Description: This pretty plant is also known as *Caryopteris* x *clandonensis* 'Arthur Simmonds' after the man who first raised it. The bright blue flowers appear among the aromatic, dull green, downy foliage. A hardy shrub, it will grow in almost any soil and is an ideal subject for mass-planting. Pruning during winter will encourage more flowers the next season. Apply mulch, manure, compost, or a handful of complete plant food in early spring.
Other colors: Lilac-blue.
Varieties/cultivars: 'Ferndown', 'Heavenly Blue', 'Blue Mist', 'Kew Blue'.

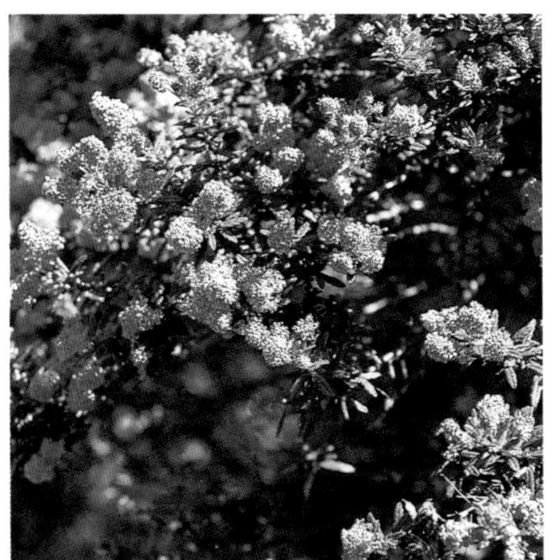
Ceanothus 'Pacific Beauty'

Ceanothus cultivars
CALIFORNIA LILAC, WILD LILAC (U.S.A.), BUCKBRUSH (U.S.A.) ○

Family: RHAMNACEAE
Origin: Cultivars.
Flowering time: Spring–summer.
Climatic zone: 7, 8, 9.
Dimensions: 3–12 feet (1–4 meters) high, depending on the cultivar.
Description: There are many different cultivars of *Ceanothus* in a wide variety of shades of blue. Varying in size from small, prostrate plants to vigorous, tall shrubs, when in bloom, they are almost entirely covered with flowers. These showy plants will thrive in any well-drained soil, and are excellent shrubs for seaside plantings. Prune after flowering has finished.
Other colors: Lavender, violet and various shades of blue.
Varieties/cultivars: There are numerous cultivars of *Ceanothus*.

Ceanothus impressus
CEANOTHUS, CALIFORNIAN LILAC, SANTA BARBARA CEANOTHUS ○

Other common names: WILD LILAC (U.S.A.), BUCKBRUSH (U.S.A.)
Family: RHAMNACEAE
Origin: California.
Flowering time: Spring.
Climatic zone: 8, 9.
Dimensions: 6–10 feet (2–3 meters) high.
Description: *Ceanothus impressus* is a dense, compact shrub, which, during spring, is completely covered in deep-blue flowers. The impressed vein pattern of the foliage is distinctive, dark green marked with pale green. Use ceanothus in a shrub border or as a feature plant. It is semideciduous in colder climates, but tends to remain evergreen in temperate climates. Plant it in well-drained soil and feed with a complete plant food during spring. It can be pruned when it has finished flowering.

Ceanothus impressus

Ceanothus thyrsiflorus var. *repens*
CREEPING BLUE BLOSSOM, CALIFORNIAN LILAC, SANTA BARBARA CEANOTHUS ○ ◑

Other common names: WILD LILAC (U.S.A.), BUCKBRUSH (U.S.A.)
Family: RHAMNACEAE
Origin: California.
Flowering time: Summer.
Climatic zone: 8, 9.
Dimensions: 3 feet (900 mm) high.
Description: This shrub, prostrate when young and then gradually building up into a mound-shaped bush, produces generous quantities of sky-blue flowers. Use creeping blue blossom in the front of a shrub border or in a rockery. Plant it in well-drained soil that is enriched annually with manure or compost or, alternatively, apply a handful of complete plant food. Pruning, if necessary, should be done just after flowering. The plant is easily propagated from cuttings taken in early spring or late summer.

Ceanothus thyrsiflorus var. *repens*

Ceanothus x *veitchianus*
CALIFORNIA LILAC, WILD LILAC (U.S.A.), BUCKBRUSH (U.S.A.) ○

Family: RHAMNACEAE
Origin: Hybrid.
Flowering time: Early summer.
Climatic zone: 7, 8, 9.
Dimensions: 10 feet (3 meters) high.
Description: An evergreen hybrid,

Ceanothus x *veitchianus*

California lilac forms a bushy, many-branched shrub with small oval leaves and clusters of deep-blue flowers. The flowers appear at the tips of the branches towards the end of the previous year's growth. Plant California lilac in a sheltered position, as it has a tendency to produce growth quickly during the first couple of years and then die off equally quickly if it is damaged by prolonged frost.

Ceratostigma griffithii

Ceratostigma griffithii

CERATOSTIGMA, BURMESE PLUMBAGO, HARDY PLUMBAGO (U.K.) ○

Family: PLUMBAGINACEAE
Origin: Himalayas, Burma.
Flowering time: Summer.
Climatic zone: 8, 9.
Dimensions: 2 feet (600 mm) high.
Description: A beautiful shrub, ceratostigma makes a delightful, hardy feature shrub, producing an abundance of deep-blue flowers over a long period. The leaves often turn conspicuously red in autumn. It likes full sun, a sheltered site, and a well-drained soil, and during spring should be mulched with manure or compost. Alternatively, apply a handful of complete plant food. Regular feeding will ensure a good flower display. Propagation can be carried out easily from cuttings or by root division.

Ceratostigma willmottianum

CERATOSTIGMA, CHINESE PLUMBAGO, HARDY PLUMBAGO (U.K.) ○

Family: PLUMBAGINACEAE
Origin: Western China.
Flowering time: Late summer.

Ceratostigma willmottianum

Climatic zone: 8, 9.
Dimensions: 2–3 feet (600–900 mm) high, 3–4 feet (approx. 1 meter) wide.
Description: Ceratostigma is a loose, open bush with distinctive sharp-angled stems. Red autumn foliage and bright blue tubular flowers make a colorful show for a large part of the year. It can be used at the front of a border or as an informal low hedge. It is hardy and tolerates a wide range of soils. Annual pruning is required.

Cistus x *purpureus*

PURPLE ROCK ROSE, ORCHID ROCK ROSE, SUNROSE (U.K.) ○

Family: CISTACEAE
Origin: Hybrid.
Flowering time: Summer.
Climatic zone: 8, 9, 10.
Dimensions: 3–4 feet (over 1 meter) high.
Description: The showy purple flowers of purple rock rose have a darker blotch on each petal and a yellow "eye". The gray-green leaves are nearly stalkless. It is an ideal plant for the seaside and hot, dry areas, but will grow in cool areas if given a warm position and well-drained soil. It will not tolerate overwet soil or severe frost. During spring, feed it with a complete plant food.

Cistus x *purpureus*

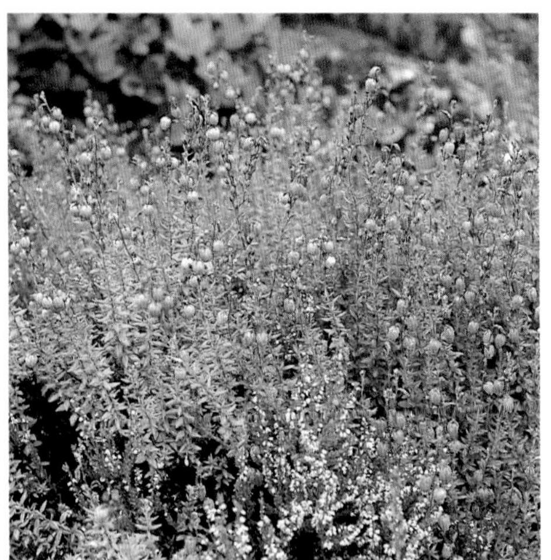
Daboecia cantabrica

Daboecia cantabrica and cultivars
IRISH HEATH, ST. DABEOC'S HEATH, CONNEMARA HEATH ◑

Family: ERICACEAE
Origin: Western Europe.
Flowering time: Early summer–early autumn.
Climatic zone: 5, 6, 7, 8.
Dimensions: 12–18 inches (300–450 mm) high.
Description: These low-growing shrubs are popular for their long flowering period. There are several cultivars in various shades of purple, which can be used in rockeries or mass-planted. They thrive in cold climates in a free-draining, acidic soil. To ensure that the soil is acid, mulch around the plants with peat to a depth of about 1 foot (300 mm). Irish heath are easily propagated from seed or autumn cuttings.
Other colors: White, rich pink.
Varieties/cultivars: There are several cultivars of this shrub.

Daphne mezereum
DAPHNE, FEBRUARY DAPHNE, MEZEREON (U.K.) ◑

Family: THYMELAEACEAE
Origin: Central and southern Europe, Asia Minor, Siberia.
Flowering time: Spring.
Climatic zone: 5, 6, 7, 8.
Dimensions: 3 feet (1 meter) high.
Description: A deciduous shrub, daphne is loved for its sweet-smelling, purple-red flowers. These cover the previous year's shoots and are followed by scarlet fruits, which are poisonous. Daphne's survival seems to depend on a cold winter. It likes a well-drained, alkaline soil. Daphne does not like chemical fertilizers — a mulch of cow manure or leaf mold annually will suffice.
Other colors: White, rose-pink.
Varieties/cultivars: 'Alba', 'Grandiflora', 'Rosea'.

Daphne mezereum

Daphne odora
DAPHNE ◑

Family: THYMELAEACEAE
Origin: China.
Flowering time: Late winter–spring.
Climatic zone: 7, 8, 9.
Dimensions: 3 feet (900 mm) high x 4 feet (approx. 1 meter) wide.
Description: Daphne, though often difficult to grow, is worthy of a place in the garden because of its wonderful perfume. These small, evergreen, compact bushes require special conditions of good drainage and rich, crumbly, slightly acidic soils. At their flowering peak, the bushes are covered with dense heads of up to thirty star-shaped flowers which are rose-purple in bud and paler within. They are happy growing in association with rhododendrons or in containers as a focal point.
Other colors: Pink, white.
Varieties/cultivars: 'Alba', 'Aureomarginata', 'Rubra'.

Daphne odora

Disanthus cercidifolius
DISANTHUS ◑

Family: HAMAMELIDACEAE
Origin: Japan, South-east China.
Flowering time: Autumn.
Climatic zone: 5, 6, 7, 8, 9.
Dimensions: 6–10 feet (2–3 meters) high.
Description: This large and beautiful deciduous shrub has slender branches and heart-shaped, thick leaves which turn from green to glorious shades of red and orange in autumn. The dark purple flowers have thin, spidery petals and are borne in pairs on short stalks. Best grown in cool, moist, and slightly acid soil, it should be located in a sheltered position and pruned lightly to keep the growth habit dense.

Disanthus cercidifolius

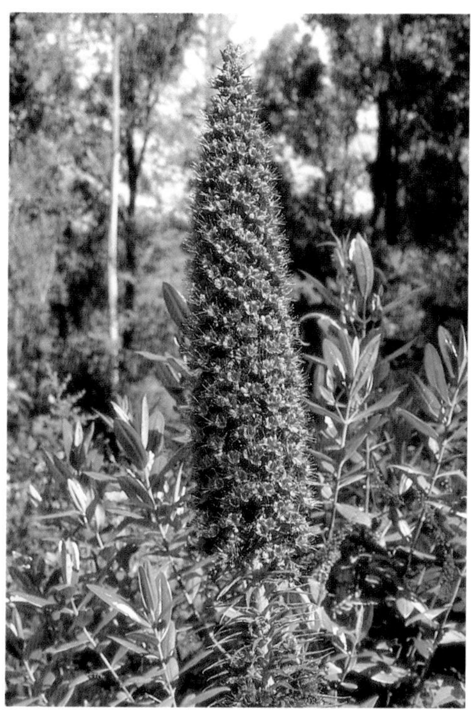
Echium fastuosum

Echium fastuosum
VIPER'S BUGLOSS, PRIDE OF MADEIRA (U.K.) ○

Family: BORAGINACEAE
Origin: Canary Islands.
Flowering time: Spring–summer.
Climatic zone: 9, 10.
Dimensions: 4 feet (approx. 1 meter) high.
Description: Viper's bugloss is a soft-wooded shrub which is sometimes classed as a woody perennial. The dense branches bear a great profusion of lance-shaped, gray-green, hairy leaves. These develop central spikes up to 12 inches (300 mm) long, tightly packed with long-stamened, blue or purple flowers. Viper's bugloss will thrive near the seaside in a hot, sunny position. It needs a well-drained soil and tends to flower more profusely in poor and fairly dry soils. Cut off the older rosettes after flowering.

Eupatorium megalophyllum
SHRUB AGERATUM, MIST FLOWER, EUPATORIUM (U.K.) ○ ◑

Family: COMPOSITAE
Origin: Southern Mexico.
Flowering time: Late spring.

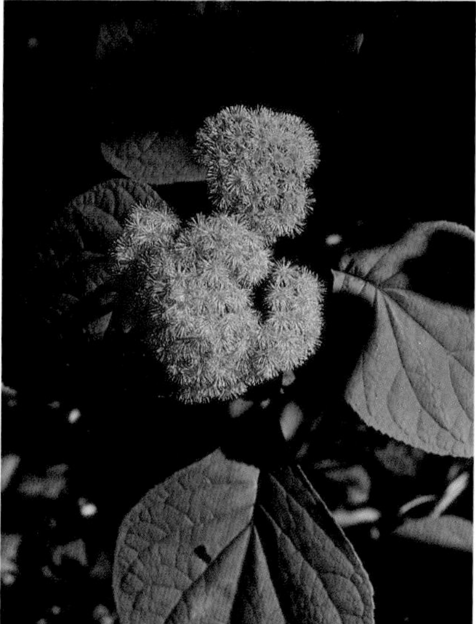
Eupatorium megalophyllum

Climatic zone: 9, 10.
Dimensions: 6 feet (2 meters) high.
Description: Eupatorium requires temperatures above 32°F (0°C) and consequently is not commonly seen in northern hemisphere gardens. The plant looks like an overgrown ageratum, but is distinguished from it by its furry foliage with dense clusters of mauve flowers in late spring. The size of eupatoriums gives scale to a shrub border. They are an attractive companion plant to rondeletias.

Felicia amelloides
BLUE MARGUERITE, BLUE DAISY, AGATHAEA, FELICIA ○

Family: COMPOSITAE
Origin: South Africa.
Flowering time: Early summer and intermittently through into autumn.
Climatic zone: 9, 10.
Dimensions: 20 inches (500 mm) high.
Description: This is a hardy, evergreen shrub with a compact form which becomes covered with a profusion of bright blue, daisy-like flowers with yellow centers. It is a very useful fill-in plant, and will complement a perennial border. It likes full sun and good drainage, and a moderate pruning after flowering helps maintain its shape. It differs from *F. angustifolia*, its near relative, in its leaf arrangement.

Felicia amelloides

Felicia angustifolia

Felicia angustifolia
FELICIA (U.K.), KINGFISHER DAISY ○ ◑

Family: COMPOSITAE
Origin: South Africa.
Flowering time: Spring.
Climatic zone: 9, 10.
Dimensions: 3 feet (1 meter) high.
Description: A very free-flowering small shrub, felicia has daisy-like, light-purple flowers which cover the bright green foliage for a few weeks during spring. Because of its spreading and trailing habit, it makes a good groundcover or rockery plant. It is a hardy plant which will thrive in any well-drained garden soil. A light pruning after flowering encourages more flowers the following season. Feed in early spring with a handful of complete plant food.

Hebe hulkeana
NEW ZEALAND LILAC, VERONICA ○ ◑

Family: SCROPHULARIACEAE
Origin: New Zealand.
Flowering time: Spring–summer.
Climatic zone: 8, 9.
Dimensions: 3 feet (1 meter) high.
Description: This is one of the most beautiful species of *Hebe* in cultivation. It is a small shrub, with a loose, open growth and glossy green leaves. It bears large clusters of delicate, lilac-blue flowers. It is easily grown in any type of soil, but dislikes drying out during summer. A mulch of manure or compost will keep the soil moist, as well as providing food. New Zealand lilac may need pruning every second winter to maintain a good shape.

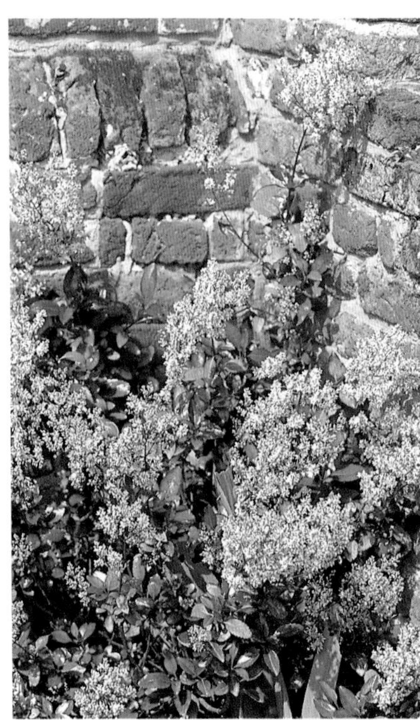
Hebe hulkeana

Hebe speciosa 'La Seduisante'

Hebe speciosa 'La Seduisante'
SPEEDWELL HEBE, SHRUBBY VERONICA (U.K.) ○ ◑

Family: SCROPHULARIACEAE
Origin: Cultivar.
Flowering time: Summer.
Climatic zone: 8, 9.
Dimensions: 3 feet (1 meter) high.
Description: This French cultivar has bright rosy-purple flowers, and interesting, dark-green leaves that are purple underneath. It makes a lovely feature plant as it looks attractive even when not in flower. Mulch around the plant with manure or compost to prevent the shallow roots from drying out during summer. It can be pruned after flowering if it loses its shape.

Hebe x *andersonii*
SPEEDWELL HEBE, SHRUBBY VERONICA (U.K.) ○ ◑

Family: SCROPHULARIACEAE
Origin: Hybrid.
Flowering time: Summer–autumn.

Hebe x *andersonii*

Climatic zone: 8, 9.
Dimensions: 4–6 feet (1–2 meters) high.
Description: This vigorous shrub has leaves 4–6 inches (100–150 mm) long and 5-inch (125-mm) long spikes of soft lavender-blue flowers which fade to white. There is also a variegated form which has creamy-white margins along the leaves. It is a fast-growing shrub which makes an excellent screen plant. Before planting, enrich the soil with manure or compost and mulch around it to protect the shallow roots. Speedwell hebe can be lightly pruned after flowering to encourage a denser habit.
Varieties/cultivars: Cultivars include 'Variegata', 'Anne Pimm'.

Hebe x *andersonii* 'Anne Pimm'
SPEEDWELL HEBE, SHRUBBY VERONICA (U.K.) ○ ◑

Family: SCROPHULARIACEAE
Origin: Hybrid.
Flowering time: Summer–autumn.
Climatic zone: 8, 9.
Dimensions: 4–6 feet (1–2 meters) high.
Description: This vigorous shrub has leaves 4–6 inches (100–150 cm) long, mid-green and flushed with reddish-purple underneath when young. The soft lavender-purple flowers are borne on long spikes, making a most attractive display over many weeks. It is a fast-growing shrub, which makes an excellent screen plant. Incorporate plenty of compost into the soil prior to planting, and mulch well to protect the shallow roots. Lightly prune after flowering to encourage a denser habit.

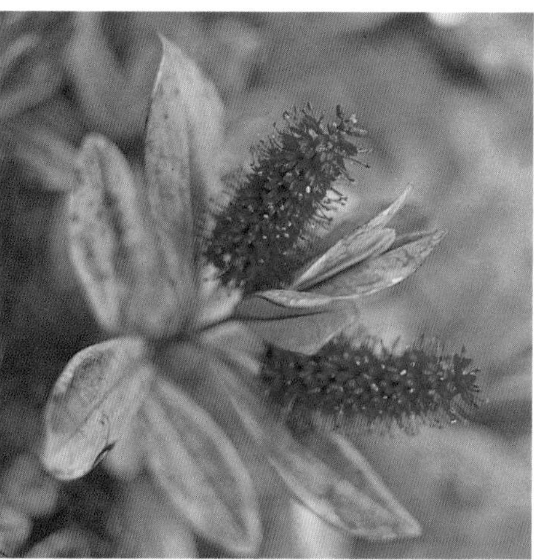
Hebe x *andersonii* 'Anne Pimm'

Hebe x *franciscana* 'Blue Gem'

Hebe x *franciscana* 'Blue Gem'
SPEEDWELL HEBE, SHRUBBY VERONICA (U.K.) ○ ◑

Family: SCROPHULARIACEAE
Origin: Cultivar.
Flowering time: Summer.
Climatic zone: 8, 9.
Dimensions: 3 feet (1 meter) high.
Description: This compact shrub produces dense racemes of bright blue flowers. It is one of the hardiest hebes, and its resistance to salt-laden winds makes it a popular shrub for seaside plantings. It is often used for low hedges. Plant it in soil that has been enriched with manure or compost. This will provide food as well as keep the soil moist. It can be pruned to shape during winter.

Heliotropium arborescens
CHERRY-PIE, HELIOTROPE ○ ◑

Family: BORAGINACEAE
Origin: Peru.
Flowering time: Spring–summer.
Climatic zone: 9, 10.
Dimensions: 6 feet (2 meters) high.
Description: Cherry-pie is a pretty shrub with wrinkled, hairy leaves and branched spikes crowded with fragrant, violet or lilac flowers. Powerfully scented, these flowers are used in the manufacture of perfume. It will adapt to any well-drained soil and should be fed in spring with a handful of complete plant food. Water it well during the summer months.

Heliotropium arborescens

Hibiscus syriacus

Hibiscus syriacus
ROSE-OF-SHARON, SYRIAN HIBISCUS, MALLOW ○

Other common names: BLUE HIBISCUS
Family: MALVACEAE
Origin: Eastern Asia.
Flowering time: Late summer–autumn.
Climatic zone: 5, 6, 7, 8, 9.
Dimensions: 8 feet (over 2 meters) high.
Description: A hardy, deciduous shrub, rose-of-Sharon is valued for its late summer and autumn flowers, which vary greatly in color. Although predominantly blue and purple, there are often two or more shades in the same flower. One of its common names is Syrian hibiscus, but it has never been found growing wild in that country.
Other colors: Red, white, rose, carmine, pink.
Varieties/cultivars: There are numerous varieties throughout the world.

Hovea chorizemifolia
HOLLY-LEAF HOVEA ◑ ●

Family: LEGUMINOSAE
Origin: Western Australia.
Flowering time: Spring.
Climatic zone: 9.
Dimensions: 22 inches (600 mm) high.
Description: An erect, sparsely branched, small shrub with holly-like leaves and deep-purple pea flowers, this very pretty shrub is not often found in cultivation. It needs excellent drainage and some overhead shade to grow successfully. The roots must be kept cool with a mulch of leaf litter or well-rotted compost. It can be easily propagated from seed.

Hovea chorizemifolia

Hydrangea macrophylla and cultivars
COMMON HYDRANGEA, BIGLEAF HYDRANGEA (U.S.A.), FLORIST'S HYDRANGEA (U.K.) ○ ◑ ●

Other common names: HORTENSIA (U.S.A.)
Family: HYDRANGEACEAE
Origin: Japan.
Flowering time: Spring–summer.
Climatic zone: 7, 8, 9, 10.
Dimensions: 3–6 feet (1–2 meters) high.
Description: Hydrangeas are popular plants because of their hardy nature and beautiful flower colors; the various shades of blue available depend on the cultivar. The color of the flower generally depends on the soil. An alkaline soil produces pink flowers while an acid soil produces blue flowers. To maintain the blue color of the flowers add aluminum sulfate annually to the soil (1 tablespoon per square meter), or keep the soil mulched with peat moss or oak leaves.
Other colors: Pink, red, mauve.
Varieties/cultivars: There are numerous cultivars throughout the world.

Indigofera australis
AUSTRALIAN INDIGO   

Family: LEGUMINOSAE
Origin: Australia.
Flowering time: Spring.
Climatic zone: 9, 10.
Dimensions: 6 feet (2 meters) high.
Description: This open, spreading plant, which grows to 6 feet (2 meters) wide, is covered in sprays of purple, pea-like flowers in spring. Australian indigo

Hydrangea macrophylla

Indigofera australis

flowers just as well in full sun as in the shade, and will grow in most soils except those which are very wet. Prune it after the flowers have finished, to maintain a good shape. It is easily propagated from seed or cuttings.
Varieties/cultivars: 'Signata'.

Lavandula angustifolia syn.
L. officinalis, L. spica, L. vera
ENGLISH LAVENDER, COMMON LAVENDER (U.K.) ○

Family: LABIATAE
Origin: Mediterranean region.
Flowering time: Summer.
Climatic zone: 6, 7, 8, 9.
Dimensions: 3 feet (1 meter) high.
Description: What garden is complete without the fragrance of lavender? The beautiful lavender-blue spikes of flowers attract bees to the garden and the leaves have a similar scent to the flowers. Plant it along the side of a path where the perfume can be appreciated. English lavender will thrive in a sandy soil and is a handy shrub for seaside gardens. Prune it after flowering to maintain a compact shape. It is easily propagated from cuttings taken in late summer.
Other colors: Pink, white, violet.
Varieties/cultivars: There are several varieties of this shrub.

Lavandula dentata
FRENCH LAVENDER, SPANISH LAVENDER, TOOTHED LAVENDER ○

Family: LABIATAE
Origin: Spain and Balearic Islands.
Flowering time: Summer.
Climatic zone: 8, 9.
Dimensions: 3 feet (1 meter) high.
Description: *Lavandula dentata* is a popular, hardy, garden plant, grown for its silvery leaves and its wonderful perfume. It is distinguished by a gray, toothed leaf and a mauve spike of aromatic flowers, both of which are used for potpourri. It is tolerant of a wide range of soils, providing drainage is good, and grows well near the sea. Pruning is essential to maintain its shape and prevent it from becoming woody. Lavender requires full sun.

Lavandula dentata

Lavandula stoechas
FRENCH LAVENDER, TOPPED LAVENDER ○

Family: LABIATAE
Origin: Mediterranean region, Portugal.
Flowering time: Summer.
Climatic zone: 7, 8, 9.
Dimensions: Up to 2 feet (600 mm) high.
Description: This is a small, intensely aromatic shrub with narrow, grayish-green leaves. The dark-purple flowers are borne in dense, terminal heads. It can be used as a low, fragrant hedge along the side of a path or as a border around a cottage garden. The main requirements of French lavender are a warm, sunny position and a sandy, well-drained soil. Cutting off the flower heads when the flowers have finished will keep it more compact in shape.

Lavandula angustifolia

Lavandula stoechas

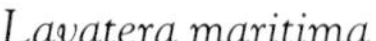
Lavatera maritima

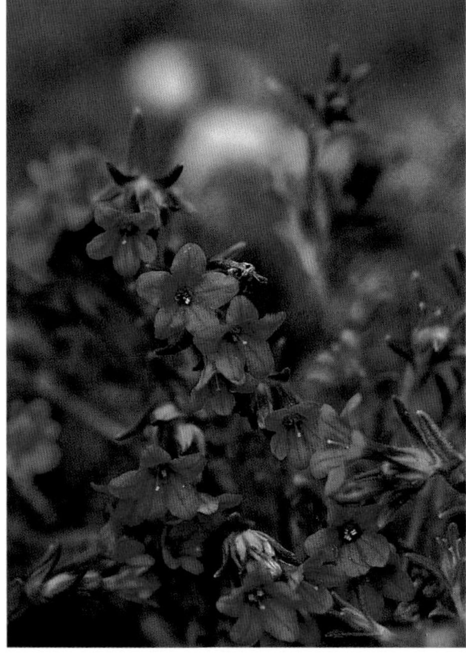

Lithospermum diffusum

Lavatera maritima

SHRUBBY MALLOW, FRENCH MALLOW, SEA MALLOW (U.K.)

Family: MALVACEAE
Origin: Southern France.
Flowering time: Summer–autumn.
Climatic zone: 8, 9.
Dimensions: 4–6 feet (up to 2 meters) high.
Description: This elegant shrub has unusual grayish, downy stems and leaves. The large saucer-shaped flowers are pale lilac with purple veins and eye, and remain on the plant for a long period. It makes an ideal feature shrub, but to be grown successfully it must be given a warm, sheltered position, preferably against a wall. Mulch it annually with well-rotted manure or compost or apply a handful of complete plant food.

Lechenaultia biloba

BLUE LECHENAULTIA

Family: GOODENIACEAE
Origin: Western Australia.
Flowering time: Spring.
Climatic zone: 9, 10.
Dimensions: 16 inches (400 mm) high.
Description: This straggly plant, though short-lived in cultivation, is most desirable because of its intense blue flowers. It needs excellent drainage to survive, and is best used in the garden trailing over rocks or walls, or as an informal groundcover.
Varieties/cultivars: 'White Flash'.

Lechenaultia biloba

Lithospermum diffusum

LITHOSPERMUM, HEAVENLY BLUE

Family: BORAGINACEAE
Origin: Southern Europe.
Flowering time: Spring–summer.
Climatic zone: 8, 9.
Dimensions: 3–4 inches (75–100 mm) high.
Description: This prostrate shrub forms a large mat which becomes covered in lovely blue flowers. It is valued for its long flowering period, and for its usefulness as a rockery plant and a groundcover. Old plants tend to die out in bad winters, especially in poorly drained soils, but if they are cut back a little after flowering they seem to be more durable. Add peat or leaf mold to the soil to keep it acidic, as lithospermum dislikes lime.
Other colors: White.
Varieties/cultivars: 'Album', 'Grace Ward', 'Heavenly Blue'.

Mackaya bella

MACKAYA

Family: ACANTHACEAE
Origin: South Africa.
Flowering time: Summer.
Climatic zone: 9, 10.
Dimensions: 4–6 feet (approx. 1–2 meters) high.
Description: An extremely pretty shrub, mackaya is valued for its 5-inch-long (125 mm), oblong leaves and large, spotted, lilac flowers. It makes an elegant feature shrub in warm climates. It is not fussy about soil type, but likes a sheltered position. Feed it in early spring by mulching with manure or compost, or, alternatively, apply a handful of complete plant food. Propagation is carried out from cuttings taken in early spring.

Mackaya bella

Oxypetalum caeruleum

Michelia figo
PORT WINE MAGNOLIA, BANANA SHRUB (U.K.), FRUIT SALAD MAGNOLIA

Family: MAGNOLIACEAE
Origin: China.
Flowering time: Spring–summer.
Climatic zone: 9, 10.
Dimensions: 10–15 feet (3–5 meters) high.
Description: An attractive, evergreen shrub, port wine magnolia has a neat, rounded appearance. The young shoots are brown and hairy, and the elliptic, dark-green leaves are smooth and shiny. The purplish-colored flowers, initially enclosed in brown bracts, are strongly scented, emitting their perfume throughout the garden. This is a perfect shrub to plant near a doorway or window so that the perfume can be appreciated. It is easy to grow and its main requirement is a neutral to acid soil that does not dry out.

Michelia figo

Oxypetalum caeruleum
TWEEDIA

Family: ASCLEPIADACEAE
Origin: South America, West Indies.
Flowering time: Summer–autumn.
Climatic zone: 9, 10.
Dimensions: 3 feet (1 meter) or more high.
Description: This is a weak-stemmed, small, spreading sub-shrub with grayish-green leaves which are covered in a soft down. The terminal clusters of starry, sky-blue flowers cover the plant from summer to autumn, but in warm climates there are generally flowers on the plant throughout the year. It is pretty planted in the sunny foreground of shrubberies, or included in an annual or perennial garden. Tweedia is a short-lived plant, but it is easily raised from seed or cuttings.

Plumbago auriculata

Plumbago auriculata syn. *P. capensis*
CAPE LEADWORT, PLUMBAGO (U.K.)

Family: PLUMBAGINACEAE
Origin: South Africa.
Flowering time: Early summer–autumn.
Climatic zone: 9, 10.
Dimensions: 4–8 feet (approx. 1–2 meters) high.
Description: A slender-stemmed, rambling shrub with neat, evergreen leaves and large trusses of sky-blue, phlox-like flowers, plumbago is a favorite in warm climate gardens. It clambers over other shrubs, makes attractive hedges, sprawls down banks, or becomes a good wall shrub. Given a sunny position with no frost, plumbago will flower off and on throughout the year. Plant it in a well-drained soil, enriched with manure or compost.

Polygala myrtifolia var. *grandiflora*

Polygala myrtifolia var. *grandiflora*
BLUE CAPS, MILKWORT (U.K.) ○ ◑

Family: POLYGALACEAE
Origin: South Africa.
Flowering time: Winter–autumn.
Climatic zone: 9, 10.
Dimensions: 4–8 feet (approx. 1–2 meters) high.
Description: The prolonged flowering period of this shrub is its greatest asset. The rich-purple, "sweet pea" like flowers are produced in clusters near the end of the shoots. It will tolerate dappled shade, but under these conditions flowers only for short periods. Blue caps will thrive in any soil type. It should be fed during early spring with a complete plant food. Pruning during this season will encourage more compact growth.

Prostanthera rotundifolia
ROUND-LEAF MINTBUSH, MINTBUSH (U.K.) ○

Family: LABIATAE
Origin: Eastern Australia.
Flowering time: Spring.
Climatic zone: 9.
Dimensions: 6 feet (2 meters) high.
Description: This outstanding but fairly short-lived shrub is covered in heavy masses of purple flowers during spring. The leaves are small and round.

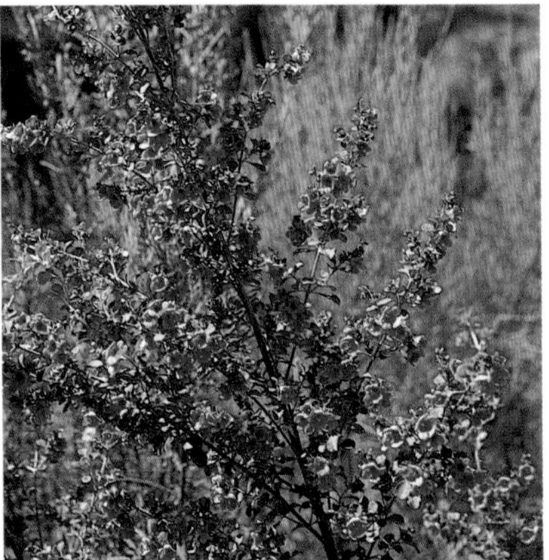
Prostanthera rotundifolia

Use it as a specimen shrub, or as a background shrub in herbaceous borders. The main requirement of the round-leaf mintbush is perfect drainage. Light pruning after flowering will keep it more compact.

Rosmarinus lavandulaceus
PROSTRATE ROSEMARY ○

Family: LABIATAE
Origin: Southern Spain, North Africa.
Flowering time: Spring–summer.
Climatic zone: 9, 10.
Dimensions: 1 foot (300 mm) high.
Description: This evergreen shrub forms a large, dense, mat which becomes thickly studded with clusters of blue, fragrant flowers. The green leaves have a pale downy underside and are very fragrant. Prostrate rosemary should be planted along the tops of walls or banks where it can cascade down the side. It needs a mild winter climate and does not tolerate frosts. It is a useful plant for seaside gardens.

Rosmarinus lavandulaceus

Rosmarinus officinalis
COMMON ROSEMARY ○

Family: LABIATAE
Origin: Mediterranean coastal regions.
Flowering time: Late spring–early summer.
Climatic zone: 7, 8, 9, 10.
Dimensions: 3–6 feet (1–2 meters) tall.
Description: Rosemary, though more commonly known for its culinary and medicinal uses, is a worthwhile addition

Rosmarinus officinalis

to a garden because of its dark-green foliage and delicate lavender flowers. This plant requires heavy pruning to prevent bare woody growth. It makes a very suitable hedging plant.
Varieties/cultivars: 'Blue Lagoon'.

Strobilanthes anisophyllus

Strobilanthes anisophyllus
GOLDFUSSIA ○ ◑

Family: ACANTHACEAE
Origin: South East Asia.
Flowering time: Summer–autumn.
Climatic zone: 8, 9, 10.
Dimensions: 2–3 feet (up to 1 meter) high.
Description: A bushy shrub, goldfussia produces an abundance of purple, narrow, lance-shaped leaves. The small groups of long, tubular, lavender flowers with bell-shaped mouths appear between the leaves and stems. In colder climates it is often grown as an indoor plant. Best results are achieved if this shrub is given well-drained soil and regular spring applications of plant food.

Syringa vulgaris 'Charles Joly'
COMMON LILAC, EUROPEAN LILAC, ENGLISH LILAC ○

Family: OLEACEAE
Origin: Cultivar.
Flowering time: Late spring–early summer.

Syringa vulgaris 'Charles Joly'

Climatic zone: 4, 5, 6, 7, 8.
Dimensions: 4–10 feet (1–3 meters) high.
Description: Lilac is loved for its highly perfumed flowers. There is probably no other shrub or tree that has given rise to so many cultivars as *Syringa vulgaris*, the parent of 'Charles Joly'. 'Charles Joly' has dark purplish-red flowers which appear later in spring than most other lilac varieties. During winter, cut the tops of the more vigorous stems to produce side shoots, as this new growth carries next season's flowers. Lilac likes a slightly limy, well-drained soil.

Tibouchina urvilleana
LASIANDRA, GLORY BUSH (U.K.), SPIDER FLOWER ○

Other common names: PRINCESS FLOWER (U.S.A.)
Family: MELASTOMATACEAE
Origin: Tropical America.
Flowering time: Summer–autumn.
Climatic zone: 9, 10.
Dimensions: 4–15 feet (approx. 1–5 meters) high.
Description: A handsome but straggly shrub, glory bush has very showy, large, vivid purple flowers and large velvety leaves. Its shape can be improved by pruning after flowering. Pinching the new shoots will also promote a denser bush. Even though glory bush needs full sun, its roots must be kept cool. This can be achieved by placing a mulch of leaf litter, compost, or manure around the base in late winter and again in early summer. Neutral to acid soil is essential for rich-green leaves and free-flowering.

Tibouchina urvilleana

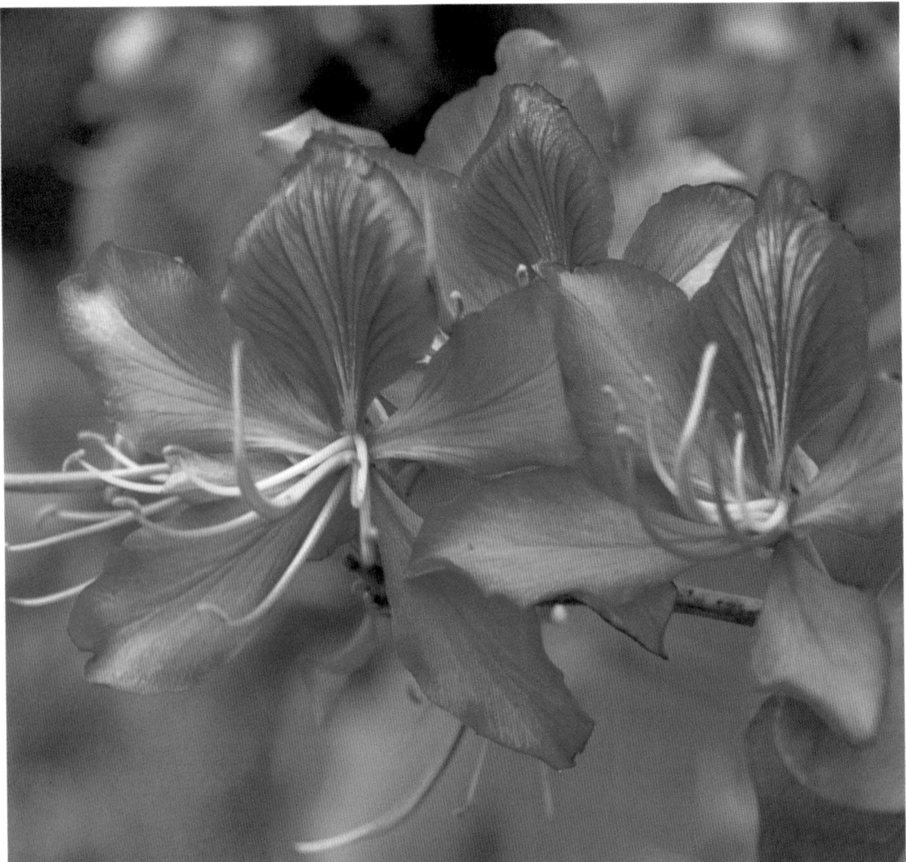

Bauhinia variegata

Bauhinia variegata
BUTTERFLY TREE, ORCHID TREE, MOUNTAIN EBONY ○

Family: CAESALPINACEAE
Origin: Pakistan–Burma, China.
Flowering time: Spring, northern hemisphere; mid-spring–early summer and intermittently autumn, southern hemisphere.
Climatic zone: 9, 10.
Dimensions: 16–27 feet (5–8 meters) high.
Description: Bauhinias are easily identified by their showy, orchid-like flowers and bilobed leaves. *Variegata* in this case refers to the mixed streaks of color in the flowers which are about 2 inches (50 mm) across and usually rosy-purple, but the colors vary somewhat when the plant is grown from seed. The tree grows in warm districts. If cultivated in cooler climates, it develops a rather straggly canopy and becomes semideciduous. It enjoys rich, well-drained soils and a position in full sun, protected from cold or salty winds.
Other colors: White.
Varieties/cultivars: *B. v.* var. *candida*.

Jacaranda mimosifolia

Jacaranda mimosifolia
JACARANDA, FERN TREE ○

Family: BIGNONIACEAE
Origin: Northwestern Argentina.
Flowering time: Late spring.
Climatic zone: 9, 10.
Dimensions: 40–50 feet (12–15 meters) high.
Description: One of the loveliest trees of all time, jacarandas in flower, in a good year, are a breathtaking sight. A whole street planted in jacarandas appears misty blue. The drier the winter, the better they flower. Jacarandas develop a broad dome of lacy, soft green-colored leaves which, although deciduous, can remain on the tree until late winter. Given full sun and good drainage, jacarandas add immense charm to any garden in warm areas. They are excellent shade trees.

Lagerstroemia indica 'Heliotrope Beauty'

Lagerstroemia indica
CREPE MYRTLE ○

Family: LYTHRACEAE
Origin: India, South East Asia, China.
Flowering time: Late summer–early autumn.
Climatic zone: 9, 10.
Dimensions: 20–30 feet (6–9 meters) high.
Description: Many cultivars have been bred from the species, often much

smaller in habit. *L. indica* is a charming, deciduous tree, happiest in warm-climate gardens. Clusters of crinkly flowers are liberally borne in summer, lingering into autumn. When the leaves have dropped, the beautiful mottled bark is revealed. Many people spoil the tree's natural, graceful, spreading shape by severe pruning in the winter. In humid areas some pruning is necessary, though, for powdery mildew attacks the leaves if the tree is not pruned or treated each year.
Other colors: White, pink, lavender, red, bicolors.
Varieties/cultivars: 'Eavsii', 'Heliotrope Beauty', 'Matthewsii', 'Newmannii', 'Petites' (Californian series).

Melia azedarach var. *australasica*
WHITE CEDAR, CHINABERRY ○

Family: MELIACEAE
Origin: Orient, South East Asia, Australia.
Flowering time: Mid–late spring, southern hemisphere.
Climatic zone: 9, 10.
Dimensions: 30–50 feet (10–15 meters) high.
Description: Rapid adaptability to a wide range of soils and climates has made this species a very popular garden tree. The woolly sprays of flowers are lilac in color, followed by oval, orange-yellow berries during winter. This variety has naturalized on much of the east coast of Australia, from N.S.W. to Queensland, and is in cultivation in many other parts of the country. The main species has adapted to many areas of the United States and is relatively pest-free. In coastal parts of Australia, however, this particular variety, which is deciduous, is attacked by white cedar caterpillars in autumn, which can be controlled by trapping them at night in a hessian bag wrapped around the tree trunk.

Paulownia tomentosa syn. *P. imperialis*
EMPRESS OR PRINCESS TREE, ROYAL PAULOWNIA, FORTUNE'S PAULOWNIA ○

Other common names: MOUNTAIN JACARANDA
Family: BIGNONIACEAE
Origin: Central China, Korea.
Flowering time: Spring, southern and northern hemispheres.
Climatic zone: 7, 8, 9.
Dimensions: 50 feet (15 meters) high.
Description: This beautiful, deciduous tree, named after a Russian princess, has a single trunk with a broad, spreading crown. Large, heart-shaped leaves are covered in downy hairs. The trumpet-like flowers, borne in upright clusters, are violet-blue, paling to white at the base which is marked with violet and yellowish streaks and spots. Severe winters may damage dormant flower buds. Easily grown from seed, paulownia likes a well-drained soil with ample water in summer. This tree is often mistaken for catalpa, a close relative.

Paulownia tomentosa

Melia azedarach

SECTION FOUR

White Flowers

Annuals *454*

Bulbs *456*

Climbers *464*

Perennials *472*

Shrubs *488*

Trees *518*

Asperula odorata syn. *Galium odoratum*

WOODRUFF ○ ◑ ●

Family: RUBIACEAE
Origin: Caucasus.
Flowering time: Spring–summer.
Climatic zone: 6, 7, 8, 9, 10.
Dimensions: Up to 12 inches (300 mm) high.
Description: This leafy plant sprawls and is useful for filling gaps among shrubs and perennials. As an annual it also has its own place in summer beds and borders. The masses of tiny, tubular, white flowers are ⅜ inch (9 mm) long and borne in tight, terminal clusters. Beneath each flower is a leafy bract which persists after the flower has died. In hot climates, woodruff prefers shade and ample moisture, but in general it is hardy. The flowers are not suitable for floral work.

Asperula odorata

Chrysanthemum parthenium syn. *Matricaria eximia*

FEVERFEW, MAYWEED ○ ◑

Family: COMPOSITAE
Origin: Southeastern Europe–Caucasus.
Flowering time: Summer–autumn.
Climatic zone: 4, 5, 6, 7, 8, 9.
Dimensions: Up to 3 feet (1 meter) high.
Description: Small, white daisy-like flowers cover this plant in profusion. It is useful for floral work and flowers for many weeks in cooler climates. *Chrysanthemum parthenium* is a herb which can be used as an insect repellant and medicinally for headaches. It is excellent as a border for a vegetable garden. Good soil preparation is vital. Add some dolomite, well-rotted cow manure, and an all-purpose fertilizer prior to planting. Best results when planted in full sun.
Varieties/cultivars: 'Golden Feather', 'White Stars', 'Selaginoides', 'Aureum'.

Chrysanthemum parthenium

Euphorbia marginata

SNOW-ON-THE-MOUNTAIN, GHOSTWEED ○ ◑

Family: EUPHORBIACEAE
Origin: Central United States.
Flowering time: Summer.
Climatic zone: 6, 7, 8, 9.
Dimensions: Up to 3 feet (1 meter) high.
Description: This plant forms a good background hedge for lower annuals, or a tall border for a shrubbery. The flowers are tiny, up to ¼ inch (7 mm) and greenish white. They are almost concealed by clusters of showy, white and green bracts. The lower leaves are bright green; those nearing the top are white-margined. Snow-on-the-mountain is a very decorative plant and in much demand for floral work. Valued for its ease of cultivation in a wide range of soils and conditions, in either full sun or partial shade.

Euphorbia marginata

Gypsophila elegans

Gypsophila elegans

ANNUAL BABY'S BREATH ○

Family: CARYOPHYLLACEAE
Origin: Caucasus, Iran, Turkey.
Flowering time: Summer–autumn.
Climatic zone: 4, 5, 6, 7, 8, 9.
Dimensions: Up to 18 inches (450 mm) high.
Description: Although this rather slim annual has a delicate appearance, it is

tough. Its stems are stiff and upright and the leaves are small and sparse. The tiny flowers (¼ inch (6 mm) wide) which appear on many-branched stems are usually white and move with the lightest wind. Baby's breath is very popular with florists for use in bunches of mixed flowers and table decorations. It lasts well and is grown as a hardy annual. Well-drained, slightly alkaline soil is preferred. After the first flush of flowers fade, trim back to allow new blooms to be produced.
Other colors: Rose, purple, pink.
Varieties/cultivars: 'Carminea', 'Grandiflora Alba', 'Purpurea', 'Rosea'.

Iberis umbellata
GLOBE CANDYTUFT, ANNUAL CANDYTUFT ○

Family: CRUCIFERAE
Origin: Mediterranean region.
Flowering time: Summer–autumn.
Climatic zone: 5, 6, 7, 8, 9.
Dimensions: Up to 16 inches (400 mm) high.
Description: This is an erect, many-branched annual which prefers cool but sunny climates. The flower clusters, which are up to 2 inches (50 mm) wide, are carried just above the foliage, often in abundance. They are shaped like a pincushion and may be cut for decoration. Plant in full sun in any moderately rich, well-drained soil.
Other colors: Pink, mauve, violet, purple-red.
Varieties/cultivars: 'Atropurpurea', 'Cardinal', 'Lavender', 'Lilac', 'Rosea'.

Iberis umbellata

Lobularia maritima syn. *Alyssum maritimum*
SWEET ALYSSUM ○ ◑

Family: CRUCIFERAE
Origin: Mediterranean region.
Flowering time: Spring–autumn.
Climatic zone: 5, 6, 7, 8, 9.
Dimensions: Up to 6 inches (150 mm) high.
Description: This low-growing annual is very popular with gardeners because it grows easily, readily produces viable seeds, and thus may persist for many years. The small plants grow closely together to form a continuous edging of color. The flowers, though tiny, form tight clusters, and have a honeyed perfume that attracts bees. It is excellent for window boxes or hanging baskets. This adaptable annual can be grown in virtually any well-drained soil, thriving in full sun or partial shade.
Other colors: Pink, purple.
Varieties/cultivars: 'Rosie O'Day', 'Royal carpet'.

Lobularia maritima

Moluccella laevis
BELLS-OF-IRELAND, MOLUCCA BALM, SHELL-FLOWER ○ ◑

Family: LABIATAE
Origin: Turkey–Syria.
Flowering time: Summer–autumn.
Climatic zone: 6, 7, 8, 9, 10.
Dimensions: Up to 2 feet (600 mm) high.
Description: The tiny flowers of this plant are ½ inch (6 mm) wide and are enclosed in cup or shell-shaped, bright green calyces which form conspicuous spikes. The profusion of the flower spikes is a feature of the plant, which is prized by florists and home decorators. Plant in spring in moderately rich soil, and water and feed sparingly during the main growing period.

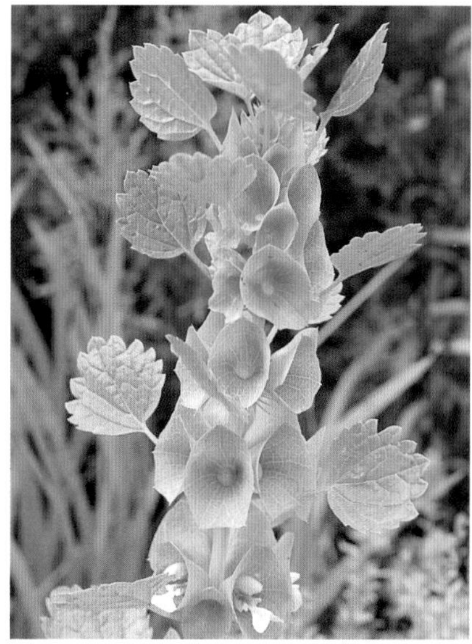

Moluccella laevis

Nicotiana alata
FLOWERING TOBACCO ◑

Family: SOLANACEAE
Origin: South America.
Flowering time: Spring, summer, autumn.
Climatic zone: 6, 7, 8, 9, 10.
Dimensions: Up to 3 feet (1 meter) high.
Description: This soft-foliaged short-lived perennial grown as an annual forms an ideal background in cottage gardens and perennial borders. It produces many stems about 12 inches (300 mm) long, terminating in fragrant, outward-pointing flowers. These are tubular, up to 4 inches (100 mm) long, and about 2 inches (50 mm) wide at the mouth. Flowering tobacco seeds readily. This fragrant annual likes average garden soil with good drainage.
Other colors: Cream-yellow, rose-red, green, pink, maroon, purple.
Varieties/cultivars: 'Nana' (dwarf form to 18 inches (450 mm) high), 'Rubelle' (red).

Nicotiana alata

Allium triquestrum

Convallaria majalis

Allium triquestrum
TRIQUESTROUS GARLIC

Family: ALLIACEAE
Origin: Mediterranean region.
Flowering time: Spring.
Climatic zone: 8, 9, 10.
Dimensions: Up to 18 inches (450 mm) high.
Description: Numerous small, white flowers which occur in terminal umbels create a pretty spring display. The stem is erect, while the slender mid-green foliage is linear. Adaptable to most soils, it prefers a protected, sunny position and requires regular watering in summer if the conditions are hot and dry. Pretty in a cottage garden landscape, or as a potted specimen on a sunny verandah or balcony.

Cardiocrinum giganteum
GIANT LILY

Family: LILIACEAE
Origin: Himalayas, southeastern Tibet.
Flowering time: Summer.
Climatic zone: 7, 8, 9.
Dimensions: Up to 10 feet (3 meters) high.
Description: Giant lily is a magnificent plant for a damp position in an open woodland area. The tall, robust stem produces many drooping, long, white flowers, like those of a trumpet lily. Because of its heart-shaped leaves, and the size of the plant, it merits a special place in the garden. The bulbs usually take more than a year to settle down before they flower; it takes five to seven years from seeding to flowering. After flowering, the main bulb dies, but produces small offset bulbs which can be lifted.

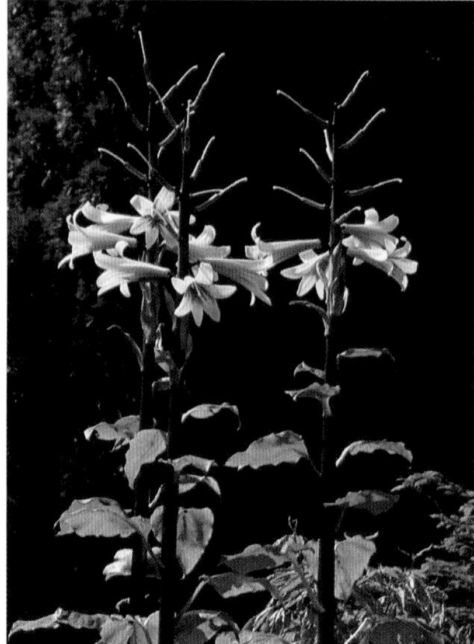

Cardiocrinum giganteum

Convallaria majalis
LILY-OF-THE-VALLEY

Family: LILIACEAE
Origin: Northern temperate zone.
Flowering time: Spring.
Climatic zone: 4, 5, 6, 7, 8.
Dimensions: 6–8 inches (150–200 mm) high.
Description: Lily-of-the-valley is a favorite with many gardeners because of its sweet perfume. The delicate, waxy, bell-shaped flowers appear with the broad leaves, and the foliage persists through the summer. It likes a rich soil full of humus and, once established, should not be disturbed for a number of years until the clump becomes overcrowded. In good conditions, the flowers are followed by scarlet berries. The rhizomes should be planted in early winter.
Other colors: Pink, beige.
Varieties/cultivars: 'Everest', 'Fortune's Giant', 'Variegata'.

Crinum x *powellii* 'Album'
CRINUM

Family: AMARYLLIDACEAE
Origin: Hybrid.
Flowering time: Summer.
Climatic zone: 8, 9.
Dimensions: Up to 4 feet (1.2 meters) high.

Description: A tender hybrid, crinum produces six to eight large white flowers on each long stem. This handsome plant is a rich feeder and needs plenty of water. Suited to water landscapes near ponds, among ferns and trees, it can be temperamental if moved and may not flower for a season after being lifted. If left alone it will produce a clump of striking-looking flowers. Propagate from the offset bulbs which will take two to three years to flower. Crimum also does well grown in pots in a greenhouse.
Other colors: Pink.

Crinum x *powellii* 'Album'

Crocus biflorus
SCOTCH CROCUS ○

Family: IRIDACEAE
Origin: Italy–Caucasus and Iran.
Flowering time: Spring.
Climatic zone: 5, 6, 7, 8, 9.
Dimensions: Up to 4 inches (100 mm) high.
Description: Scotch crocus is a pretty addition to the rock garden. The closed, white petals of the flower are striped in purple and open to reveal the delicate, yellow-throated center. When flowering in small clumps it resembles a bouquet. Plant it near gates and pathways where visitors can admire its beauty. It may be naturalized in lawns, which should not be mown until the foliage dies down. This species needs a cold winter.
Other colors: Violet, blue.
Varieties/cultivars: *C. b. adamii*, *C. b. weldonii*.

Crocus biflorus weldonii

Crocus niveus
AUTUMN CROCUS, CROCUS (U.K.) ○

Family: IRIDACEAE
Origin: Southern Greece.
Flowering time: Autumn.
Climatic zone: 6, 7, 8, 9.
Dimensions: Up to 6 inches (150 mm) high.

Crocus niveus

Description: Autumn crocus provides delicate color in a bare season. Emerging from light groundcovers, its delicacy is accentuated. It is a useful addition to herb gardens which often die back in autumn. Plant in a sunny spot with warm, well-drained soil where it can self-sow, naturalize it in lawns, but do not mow the grass until the foliage dies back. Definite cold is required in winter.
Other colors: Pale lilac.

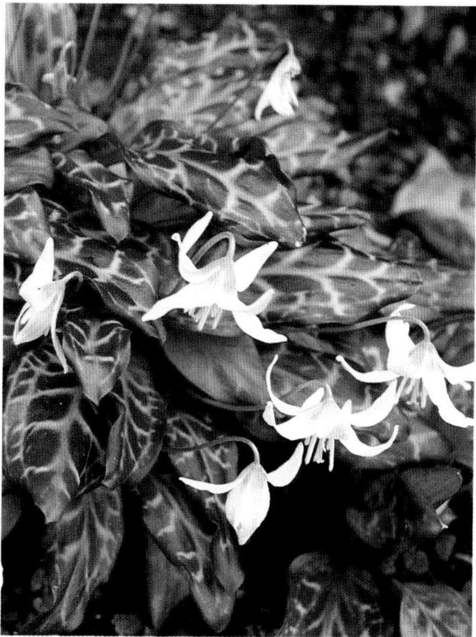

Erythronium dens-canis 'White Splendour'

Erythronium dens-canis 'White Splendour'
DOG-TOOTH VIOLET ◑

Family: LILIACEAE
Origin: Cultivar.
Flowering time: Spring.
Climatic zone: 5, 6, 7, 8.
Dimensions: Up to 6 inches (150 mm) high.
Description: Called "dog-tooth" because of its small, tooth-shaped bulb, this violet will flower for up to three weeks. Plant it in rock garden pockets and at the front of shady borders. A beautiful and graceful specimen, it is quite hardy and adapts to woodlands and wet areas. If planted in open positions, it will multiply rapidly. Clumps need to be divided every three to four years. It can be grown successfully indoors in containers and should be watered well.

Erythronium revolutum 'White Beauty'

COAST FAWN LILY, AMERICAN TROUT-LILY, DOG-TOOTH VIOLET (U.K.) ◑

Family: LILIACEAE
Origin: California.
Flowering time: Spring.
Climatic zone: 6, 7, 8, 9.
Dimensions: Up to 6 inches (150 mm) high.
Description: This is one of the finest trout-lilies from America, with its cream flowers accompanying faintly mottled foliage. It establishes itself well in a damp position. Plant it in rock gardens or at the front of shaded borders. When planted in open places it may increase very quickly. Avoid transplanting it as *Erythronium* does not like being moved. Indoor cultivation in pots is possible if it is given rich, moist soil and is well maintained.
Other colors: Pink.

Erythronium revolutum 'White Beauty'

Eucharis grandiflora

AMAZON LILY ◑

Family: AMARYLLIDACEAE
Origin: South America.
Flowering time: Spring–summer.
Climatic zone: 9, 10.
Dimensions: Up to 2 feet (600 mm) high.
Description: "Eucharis" is Greek for pleasing or graceful, a word which describes the beauty of these fragrant white flowers. Four to six snow-white blooms, up to 5 inches (120 mm) across, droop from a long stem. Amazon lily is a glasshouse plant in temperate areas, but can be grown outdoors in semishade in warmer zones. The easiest and most effective way to grow this plant is by planting several bulbs together in a large pot. The bulbs need a constant mild temperature and frequent watering.

Freesia x *hybrida*

Freesia x *hybrida*

FREESIA ○

Family: IRIDACEAE
Origin: Hybrid.
Flowering time: Spring–late summer, northern hemisphere; spring, southern hemisphere.
Climatic zone: 9, 10.
Dimensions: Up to 2 feet (600 mm) high.
Description: Freesias are highly popular flowers especially for the cut-flower market. Most of the present-day hybrids have been derived from *F. refracta* and *F. armstrongii*. The highly perfumed, trumpet-shaped flowers open successively in branched spikes. Greenhouse cultivation is preferable in very cold climates. Outdoors they can be naturalized in grass and wooded areas or planted in pots and window boxes. Freesias have been heavily hybridized, but the older cultivars seem to have a stronger scent. Many colors are available.
Other colors: Yellow, orange, pink, blue.
Varieties/cultivars: 'Snow Queen', 'Orange Favourite', 'Pink Giant', 'Sapphire'.

Galanthus elwesii

GIANT SNOWDROP ○ ◑

Family: AMARYLLIDACEAE
Origin: Western Turkey.
Flowering time: Winter–spring.
Climatic zone: 4, 5, 6, 7, 8.
Dimensions: Up to 8 inches (200 mm) high.

Galanthus elwesii

Eucharis grandiflora

Description: *G. elwesii* is one of the largest flowers in the genus. The white drops have green patches at the base and tip and two wing-like petals on either side. Naturalize them in wooded areas, under trees, in rock gardens, and in pots. They prefer partial shade and cool, slightly moist soil with a mulch of well-rotted manure or compost in autumn.

Galanthus nivalis
SNOWDROP ◑ ●

Family: AMARYLLIDACEAE
Origin: Europe and western Asia.
Flowering time: Winter.
Climatic zone: 4, 5, 6, 7, 8.
Dimensions: 4–8 inches (100–200 mm) tall.
Description: The common snowdrop is one of the earliest bulbs to bloom, its delicate, bell-shaped flowers appearing in mid-winter. The pure white petals are tipped with bright green. Snowdrop prefers cool, moist soil, and should be planted in shade, except in the coldest districts where partial sun is of some benefit to open the flowers. It looks best when grown in clumps scattered through beds and borders, or when allowed to naturalize at the base of trees or in the lawn.
Varieties/cultivars: 'Atkinsii', 'S. Arnott'.

Galanthus nivalis

Galtonia candicans
SUMMER HYACINTH (U.K.), CAPE HYACINTH ○

Family: LILIACEAE
Origin: South Africa.
Flowering time: Summer.
Climatic zone: 7, 8, 9.
Dimensions: Up to 4 feet (approx. 1 meter) high.

Galtonia candicans

Description: Summer hyacinth has numerous showy, fragrant, bell-shaped, white flowers on a single stem. It is well-suited to herbaceous borders and seaside gardens, especially with red-hot-pokers or agapanthus as companions. Plant the bulbs in well-rotted compost about 6 inches (150 mm) deep, in a sunny, open position protected from wind, and water regularly during spring and summer. The plants can be propagated by offsets from the bulbs in late winter, and should not be lifted until they become crowded.

Leucojum aestivum
GIANT SNOWFLAKE, SUMMER SNOWFLAKE (U.K.) ○ ◑

Family: AMARYLLIDACEAE
Origin: Europe.
Flowering time: Spring.
Climatic zone: 4, 5, 6, 7, 8.
Dimensions: Up to 2 feet (600 mm) high.
Description: *Leucojum*, from the Greek for "white violet", probably alludes to the perfume of the giant snowflake. The nodding, bell-like, white blooms, with a green spot near the apex, appear in clusters of between two and five to a stem. Plant between shrubs, in borders among ferns, in rock gardens, or under deciduous trees. A sunny, moist position is best. The bulbs should be planted in very moist soil with plenty of compost and leaf mold. Giant snowflake can be grown indoors in containers.
Varieties/cultivars: 'Gravetye'.

Leucojum aestivum 'Gravetye'

Leucojum vernum
SPRING SNOWFLAKE (U.K.), SNOWFLAKE ○ ◑

Family: AMARYLLIDACEAE
Origin: Southern Europe.
Flowering time: Late winter–early spring.
Climatic zone: 4, 5, 6, 7, 8.
Dimensions: 6–10 inches (150–250 mm) high.
Description: The dainty quality of this plant belies its hardiness. Similar to its sister *L. aestivum*, it is suitable for growing in rock gardens, under deciduous trees, or in containers indoors. The large, usually solitary, fragrant blooms bear a yellow or green spot at the apex of each petal. Like *L. aestivum*, it too has a preference for a damp location. Plant it in humus-rich, sandy, well-drained soil. Once planted, the bulbs need not be disturbed for several years. Propagate by separating offset bulbs when the plant is dormant.

Leucojum vernum

Lilium auratum

Lilium auratum
GOLDEN-RAYED LILY ◑

Family: LILIACEAE
Origin: Japan.
Flowering time: Summer.
Climatic zone: 7, 8, 9.
Dimensions: Up to 5 feet (approx. 2 meters) high.
Description: This lily created a sensation when introduced into Europe from Japan in the mid-19th century. The spectacular flowers can measure up to 12 inches (300 mm) across, and sometimes individual stems will bear 20–30 buds. The large, white, fragrant flowers have golden bands from throat to petal edge and have purplish-red flecks. Give this lily a special place of its own. It likes acid to neutral, not alkaline soil, but is not easy to keep growing for more than a few years.
Other colors: Yellow, orange, red, pink, purple.

Lilium candidum
MADONNA LILY (U.K.), ANNUNCIATION LILY ○ ◑

Family: LILIACEAE
Origin: Mediterranean region.
Flowering time: Summer.
Climatic zone: 7, 8, 9.
Dimensions: Up to 4 feet (approx. 1 meter) high.
Description: This elegant lily is sweetly perfumed. Grown by the Cretans and Egyptians, it was portrayed on vases and other artifacts around 1750 BC. It was popular in monasteries in the Middle Ages, and in Renaissance art was associated with the Virgin, as the name Madonna lily suggests. The immaculate white flowers are carried on long stems, and it prefers to be undisturbed once it is established. This lovely lily merits a special place of its own in the garden. It can also be planted among herbaceous perennials. It requires plenty of moisture.

Lilium candidum

Lilium formosanum

Lilium formosanum
FORMOSAN LILY ○

Family: LILIACEAE
Origin: Taiwan.
Flowering time: Summer–autumn.
Climatic zone: 7, 8, 9.
Dimensions: Up to 7 feet (approx. 2 meters) high.
Description: This is a tender species susceptible to virus disease. Cultivated in the Orient, it is best grown in a greenhouse environment or among ferns in a sheltered position. If planted close to a house, the fragrance from the trumpet-shaped flowers will waft in through open windows. The long, white blooms are stained purplish-red on the outside and grow horizontally from the top of leafy stems. Most lilies benefit from a light groundcover to shade their roots. This also protects new shoots as they emerge from the soil.

Lilium longiflorum

Lilium longiflorum
TRUMPET LILY, EASTER LILY 

Family: LILIACEAE
Origin: Japan.
Flowering time: Summer.
Climatic zone: 8, 9.
Dimensions: Up to 3 feet (1 meter) high.
Description: These traditional white, trumpet-shaped lilies are used extensively in garden landscapes. They are popular with the cut-flower trade and for church floral decorations. Providing they are not overcrowded, they associate well with other herbaceous perennials. At no time should the bulbs be allowed to dry out. Sun and shade are required in equal amounts, so plant them against a garden wall which receives early morning sun and afternoon shade. Trumpet lilies can also be cultivated in well-drained pots which are kept well watered.
Varieties/cultivars: *L. l.* var. *eximium.*

Lilium regale 'Album'

Lilium regale
REGAL LILY ○

Family: LILIACEAE
Origin: Western China.
Flowering time: Summer.
Climatic zone: 5, 6, 7, 8, 9.
Dimensions: 3–6 feet (1–2 meters) high.
Description: A popular lily discovered in China by E. H. Wilson in 1904, these fragrant funnel-shaped flowers have rose-purple markings on the outside, with a white throat blending to yellow. The large flower clusters are extremely useful for garden display. Use as a majestic backdrop to a lower front bed and border, but do not overcrowd them. *L. regale* is quite hardy and should be grown in full sun in moist but well-drained soil. It becomes soft if overfed.
Varieties/cultivars: 'Album'.

Lilium speciosum var. *album*

Lilium speciosum var. *album*
JAPANESE LILY, PINK TIGER LILY ○ ◑

Family: LILIACEAE
Origin: Japan.
Flowering time: Summer–autumn.
Climatic zone: 7, 8, 9.
Dimensions: 3–5 feet (1–1.5 meters) high.
Description: The long stems of this lily carry 6–10 white flowers with strongly-reflexed petals with crimson spots. The large, drooping flowers are 4–6 inches (100–150 mm) across, and are perfumed. Plant Japanese lily in clumps in full sun or partial shade in leafy glades near trees. It may also be cultivated in large, movable tubs. If the position is too hot, move the tub to a cooler area in summer. This exotic, fragrant lily enhances any garden setting. Keep the soil it is in moist and well-drained.

Narcissus poeticus
POET'S NARCISSUS ○ ◑

Family: AMARYLLIDACEAE
Origin: Spain–Greece.
Flowering time: Spring.
Climatic zone: 5, 6, 7, 8, 9.
Dimensions: Up to 18 inches (450 mm) high.
Description: *Narcissus poeticus* is named after the mythological youth who fell in love with his own reflection in a pool and became a flower. Fragrant, starry white blooms blend well with early-flowering perennials. Grow the bulbs at random under trees and in wild gardens. The cut flowers are excellent for use indoors where their perfume lingers. Bulbs will grow in full sun or part shade. Plant in light, crumbly, well-drained soil to which has been added some compost. Water regularly during the growing period and fertilize when buds appear.
Other colors: Yellow.
Varieties/cultivars: 'Actaea', 'Queen of Narcissi'.

Narcissus poeticus 'Actaea'

Narcissus tazetta 'Paper White'

Narcissus tazetta 'Paper White'
WHITE NARCISSUS ○ ◑

Family: AMARYLLIDACEAE
Origin: Cultivar.
Flowering time: Later winter–early spring.
Climatic zone: 7, 8, 9.
Dimensions: 18 inches (450 mm) high.
Description: An exquisite member of the polyanthus narcissus group, white narcissus has star-like flowers with pure white petals. It flowers quite early, bringing life to the garden before the main flush of spring. The best results are achieved by planting the bulbs in autumn in deep, rich, well-drained soil, and by making sure that the ground is lightly damp — never wet — during the cool winter. Choose a sunny position, except in warmer climates where the shade of a deciduous tree is beneficial. Never cut back the greenery after flowering, and remember to divide the clumps every four years. Often grown indoors in cool climates.
Varieties/cultivars: 'Paper White Grandiflora'.

Ornithogalum thyrsoides
WONDER FLOWER, CHINCHERINCHEE (U.K.) ○

Family: LILIACEAE
Origin: South Africa.
Flowering time: Summer.
Climatic zone: 9, 10.
Dimensions: Up to 18 inches (450 mm) high.
Description: Wonder flower is a splendid bloomer, producing masses of cream or yellow buds opening from the base of the conical head. When cut it will last for several weeks even without water. Cultivate it as a border plant, in a cool greenhouse, or in pots on sunny window ledges. This species is tender and needs good drainage to prevent rot. Use a compost of sandy loam and leaf mold, and water well once the plant is established. Give it fertilizer when the buds appear.

Ornithogalum thyrsoides

Ornithogalum umbellatum

Ornithogalum umbellatum
STAR-OF-BETHLEHEM ○

Family: LILIACEAE
Origin: Europe, U.K., North Africa.
Flowering time: Late spring–early summer.
Climatic zone: 5, 6, 7, 8.
Dimensions: Up to 8 inches (200 mm) high.
Description: A seemingly delicate, but quite hardy, little perennial, star-of-Bethlehem will spread rapidly when naturalized. The flowers, twelve to twenty in a cluster, open late in the morning and close late in the afternoon. A pretty effect can be achieved by planting it under trees or shrubs or in a wild garden. Considered in parts of North America as an invasive garden pest, it is used by some herbalists as a remedy for sadness or depression. Allow it free range in an open, sunny area.

Polianthes tuberosa
TUBEROSE ○

Family: AGAVACEAE
Origin: Central America.
Flowering time: Summer–autumn.
Climatic zone: 9, 10.
Dimensions: Up to 3 feet (1 meter) high.
Description: Tuberose is easy to grow where the summers are long and warm. A favorite with brides for bouquets and headdresses, it is also cultivated widely in France for the perfume industry. The exquisite fragrance is produced from white, single or double flowers. Plant tuberose in the garden in rich soil near open windows and doors. The tubers will not flower in the second year and are usually discarded after flowering. Offsets can be planted when frosts have finished. This is a good pot plant for greenhouses in colder climates.
Varieties/cultivars: 'The Pearl' (double).

Polianthes tuberosa 'The Pearl'

Watsonia hybrids
BUGLE LILY ○

Family: IRIDACEAE
Origin: South Africa.
Flowering time: Summer–autumn, northern hemisphere; spring–summer, southern hemisphere.
Climatic zone: 9, 10.
Dimensions: Up to 6 feet (2 meters) high.
Description: A colorful and showy plant for high borders and wild gardens, *Watsonia* thrives in warmer areas, but dislikes the cold. Like its relative the *Gladiolus*, it will form clumps and is easy to grow in the right environment. It appreciates plenty of water and sun, and rich, but well-drained soil. Popular as cut flowers, *Watsonia* hybrids offer a profusion of colors. Deciduous and evergreen hybrids are available, the former being the hardier as they can be lifted and rested. *Watsonia* is a good greenhouse plant in cold climates.
Other colors: Red, orange, pink, purple.

Watsonia hybrids

Zantedeschia aethiopica
ARUM LILY (U.K.), LILY OF THE NILE ○

Family: ARACEAE
Origin: South Africa.
Flowering time: Spring–late summer, northern hemisphere; summer, southern hemisphere.
Climatic zone: 9, 10.
Dimensions: Up to 4 feet (approx. 1 meter) high.
Description: This perennial water-plant is suited to ponds, marshy areas, and damp sites in the garden. It was called "pig lily" by the early settlers in South Africa when they found porcupines (which they called pigs) eating the fleshy roots. The flower, because of its interesting bracts, is widely cultivated for the cut flower market, and is often seen in church floral arrangements. Plant arum lily tubers in permanently damp soil or in very shallow water. It needs generous feeding and will flower profusely.

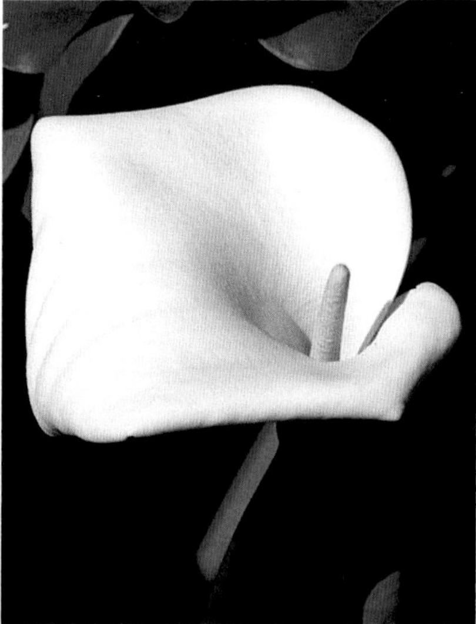
Zantedeschia aethiopica

Zephyranthes candida
WIND FLOWER (U.K.), RAIN LILY, ZEPHYR LILY ○ ◑

Family: AMARYLLIDACEAE
Origin: Argentina, Uruguay.
Flowering time: Autumn.
Climatic zone: 8, 9, 10.
Dimensions: Up to 12 inches (300 mm) high.
Description: This dainty perennial looks like a crocus. When massed in rock gardens and edges the white, star-like flowers provide a showy display, and planted in a warm, sheltered border against a wall the plant will multiply rapidly. Suited to pot-planting in temperate climates, it needs well-drained soil enriched with organic matter. Water well during the flowering period and apply a complete fertilizer when buds first appear.

Zephyranthes candida

Aristolochia elegans
CALICO DUTCHMAN'S PIPE

Family: ARISTOLOCHIACEAE
Origin: Brazil.
Flowering time: Summer.
Climatic zone: 7, 8, 9, 10.
Description: A most attractive evergreen vine that can grow to 10 feet (3 meters) in the right conditions. The woody, twining stems are covered with large, heart-shaped leaves while the reddish-purple flowers are marked with white and yellow. The vine also carries interesting fruit, in basket-like pods. Plant in a sheltered, semi-shaded position in rich, moist soil with plenty of organic matter added. Will not withstand frost, or drought conditions.

Aristolochia elegans

Beaumontia grandiflora

Beaumontia grandiflora
HERALD'S-TRUMPET, EASTER-LILY VINE ○ ◑

Family: APOCYNACEAE
Origin: India.
Flowering time: Spring.
Climatic zone: 9, 10.
Description: An arching, semi-twining, evergreen vine, *Beaumontia* will spread to 30 feet (10 meters). Its large, dark-green leaves are smooth and shiny, and its white, fragrant, trumpet-shaped flowers, 5 inches (125 mm) long, somewhat resemble Easter lilies. Prune after flowering to promote new shoots. The flowering shoots grow on old wood, so avoid removing all old wood. It appreciates deep, rich soil and plenty of fertilizer. A warm wall with strong support for climbing is the most suitable position.

Clematis armandii
EVERGREEN CLEMATIS, ARMAND CLEMATIS ○ ◑

Family: RANUNCULACEAE
Origin: Central and western China.
Flowering time: Spring.
Climatic zone: 7, 8, 9.
Description: One of the most beautiful, evergreen, flowering climbers, this clematis has the same requirements as other woodland plants. It needs deep, rich soil, shaded from the sun, but is able to take hot sunny conditions on the upper canopy. Severe winters will kill it. The pure white flowers, 2 inches (50 mm) across, are clustered three to a stalk. They are perfumed with a fragrance like honey and almonds, and gradually change color from white to rose-pink. As the blooms are on old wood, prune lightly after flowering, and when the vine becomes too dense, prune out old and dead wood.
Varieties/cultivars: 'Apple Blossom' (rose pink), 'Snowdrift' (white).

Clematis armandii 'Snowdrift'

Clematis montana
ANEMONE CLEMATIS ○ ◑

Family: RANUNCULACEAE
Origin: Himalayas, China.
Flowering time: Spring.
Climatic zone: 5, 6, 7, 8, 9.
Description: Vigorous, hardy, and easy to grow, anemone clematis blooms magnificently in early spring. The flowers are white when they open and change to delicate pink. Prune the vine after flowering, as flowers appear on old wood. For heavy pruning, selectively remove some branches to thin out the vine and reduce its overall size. This lovely deciduous climber tolerates warmer conditions than most clematis, but prefers cool or mountain climates. Plant it where the roots will remain in shade, but where it can reach up to the sun.
Varieties/cultivars: 'Rubens' (rose pink), 'Tetrarose' (rose pink, more vigorous than 'Rubens').

Clematis montana

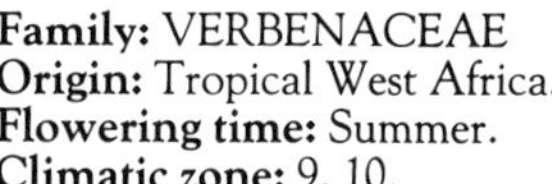

Clerodendrum thomsonae
BLEEDING-HEART VINE ○

Family: VERBENACEAE
Origin: Tropical West Africa.
Flowering time: Summer.
Climatic zone: 9, 10.
Description: This eye-catching flower is a crimson tube encased in a large, white calyx with very long white stamens. The blooms hang in forking clusters from this delicate, evergreen vine, which requires frost-free conditions and a warm, sheltered, humid position. Suitable for container growing, it can be grown successfully as an indoor plant. Prune regularly to obtain a compact plant. Feed and water it well until it is established, then reduce the feeding and watering to mature the wood and induce flowering.

Clerodendrum thomsonae

Hoya australis
AUSTRALIAN WAX PLANT, PORCELAIN FLOWER (U.S.A.) ◑

Family: ASCLEPIADACEAE
Origin: Northern and eastern Australia.
Flowering time: Summer.
Climatic zone: 9, 10.
Description: The very fragrant, long-stalked, waxy-white flowers of *H. australis* form a dome-shaped cluster about 4 inches (100 mm) across. The leaves are thick, textured, and look attractive all year round. This strong-growing vine climbs by twining stems and can be trained ontò a frame. It makes a good pot plant, but needs support and requires a warm, moist, shaded position.

Hoya australis

Hoya carnosa
COMMON WAX PLANT, WAXFLOWER

Family: ASCLEPIADACEAE
Origin: Southern China–northern Australia.
Flowering time: Early summer–autumn.
Climatic zone: 9, 10.
Description: Common wax plant is one of the most highly prized of small climbing plants. It twines by using aerial roots. Its fleshy, waxy leaves hang sparsely from the firm stems of this lovely vine which has fragrant star-shaped waxy, white flowers with deep-pink centers. As the flowers emerge from the same stalk each year, cutting or pruning will reduce the blooms for the following year. It thrives in a pot in a sunny or shady position, but must have well-drained soil, and does not seem to mind being in a too-small container.
Varieties/cultivars: Variegated form.

Hoya carnosa

Hydrangea petiolaris syn. *H. anomala* var. *petiolaris*

CLIMBING HYDRANGEA ○ ◑

Family: SAXIFRAGACEAE
Origin: Japan, Taiwan.
Flowering time: Summer.
Climatic zone: 5, 6, 7, 8, 9.
Description: Climbing hydrangea is a vigorous, deciduous vine which grows well only in cooler climates. Its flat, white flowers are borne on long stems and form clusters about 6–10 inches (150–250 mm) across. The attractive, heart-shaped leaves are 2–4 inches (50–100 mm) wide. A sturdy climber, the vine attaches itself to upright surfaces by aerial rootlets, but grown without support, it can be trained as a shrub if pruned annually to remove the long stems.

Hydrangea petiolaris

Jasminum grandiflorum

SPANISH JASMINE ○ ◑

Family: OLEACEAE
Origin: South East Asia.
Flowering time: Spring, summer, autumn.
Climatic zone: 7, 8, 9.
Description: Spanish jasmine grows very rapidly. The leaves are made up of five to seven leaflets, and the large, single flowers, which are intensely fragrant, are pink in the bud and open to white. Although each flower lasts only a short time, the vine bears flowers for several months. The long, arching branches can be cut to maintain a shrubby growth, or can be retained and trained onto walls or pergolas. Spanish jasmine always has a light, open, lacy appearance.

Jasminum grandiflorum

Jasminum nitidum syn. *J. ilicifolium*

ANGEL-WING JASMINE, STAR JASMINE (U.K.) ○ ◑

Family: OLEACEAE
Origin: South Pacific.
Flowering time: Spring, summer.
Climatic zone: 9, 10.
Description: Angel-wing jasmine's windmill-like, fragrant white flowers are 1 to 1½ inches (25–40 mm) long, and are grouped in small sprays. The buds have a purplish color, and open out to bright-white, flat-topped flowers. With its attractive, glossy leaves this evergreen vine makes a good specimen for a container plant. It can be grown as a shrub or a climber, but it will need to be trained if it is to climb up a post or over a wall. Suited to warm conditions only, it is attractive all year round.

Jasminum polyanthum

PINK JASMINE, CHINESE JASMINE, SWEET-SCENTED JASMINE ○ ◑

Family: OLEACEAE
Origin: Western China.
Flowering time: Early spring–late summer.
Climatic zone: 8, 9, 10.
Description: Grown in sun or shade this jasmine can become invasive if not kept under control. The pink buds open to white flowers in a great burst in the springtime, giving out an exceptionally pervasive perfume. This magnificent display lasts for about a month. A vigorous climber, pink jasmine will build up a thick layer of dense, twiggy growth, with new foliage appearing on the surface. A strong support is necessary and, occasionally, very hard pruning. Branches will take root where they make contact with the soil. It will not survive severe winters.

Jasminum polyanthum

Jasminum nitidum

Jasminum sambac

Mandevilla laxa syn. *M. suaveolens*

CHILEAN JASMINE, HUG ME TIGHT, MANDEVILLA ○ ◑

Family: APOCYNACEAE
Origin: Bolivia, Argentina, Peru.
Flowering time: Summer.
Climatic zone: 8, 9.
Description: A vigorous grower in warm climates, Chilean jasmine prefers the shelter of surrounding foliage in cooler climates, and will happily use shrubs or trees to climb through or up to get to the sun. It also grows well on a sheltered wall. The white, intensely fragrant flowers are funnel-shaped and appear in sprays during summer. They tend to be at the tops of the long, arching, slender branches. The vine is widely grown in mild climates, but needs to have its size or spread reduced if it is to be kept under control. Rich, sandy loam and regular water are essential. It cannot withstand severe winters.

Jasminum sambac

ARABIAN JASMINE, PIKAKE ○ ◑

Family: OLEACEAE
Origin: India.
Flowering time: Spring, summer, autumn.
Climatic zone: 9, 10.
Description: An evergreen, shrubby vine up to 8 feet (2.4 meters) high, this is a very versatile plant. With support and training it can grow as a climber or it can be pruned to form a compact shrub, and is also excellent as a container plant. The white, intensely-perfumed flowers appear in tight clusters at the ends of branchlets, and are used for the flavoring in jasmine tea. The leaves are shiny, pointed and very decorative. Jasmine has a long flowering period, but can only be grown in warm conditions.
Varieties/cultivars: 'Grand Duke of Tuscany'.

Lonicera japonica 'Halliana'

HALL'S HONEYSUCKLE, JAPANESE HONEYSUCKLE ○ ◑

Family: CAPRIFOLIACEAE
Origin: Cultivar.
Flowering time: Spring and summer.
Climatic zone: 4, 5, 6, 7, 8, 9.
Description: This honeysuckle has white flowers which turn yellow as they age. They are very fragrant and their nectar is enjoyed by both birds and children! It is a very quick-growing vine, and will cover a fence or a shed in one good growing season. It needs to be controlled, or it will find its way to the top of adjoining trees. Its evergreen habit makes it useful for the quick disguising of old sheds.

Mandevilla laxa

Lonicera japonica 'Halliana'

Pandorea jasminoides
BOWER PLANT, BOWER-OF-BEAUTY ○ ◑

Family: BIGNONIACEAE
Origin: Australia (Queensland, N.S.W.).
Flowering time: Summer–autumn.
Climatic zone: 9, 10.
Description: An attractive, fast-growing, evergreen climber, this *Pandorea* will tolerate coastal conditions or cooler inland conditions. It is a very useful, versatile climber, and produces a mass of trumpet shaped white flowers with pink throats, standing out from the shiny, dark-green leaves. Protection from strong wind and frost will be needed, but in a sheltered position it will withstand occasional cold nights. Good soil and summer water give best results.
Varieties/cultivars: 'Rosea' (pink), 'Alba' (pure white).

Pandorea jasminoides

Pandorea pandorana
WONGA-WONGA VINE   

Family: BIGNONIACEAE
Origin: Southern and eastern Australia–New Guinea.
Flowering time: Throughout the year.
Climatic zone: 9, 10.
Description: Small, cream flowers with purple or maroon-striped throats are produced in abundance on this shiny, evergreen vine. The foliage is attractive all year, and the vine is fast-growing. Rich soil will help it become established, and it is happy in either a sunny or shady position. Pruning is advisable after flowering to tidy up the branchlets, and to induce further compact growth. Without support the vine can become a sprawling shrub, but needs pruning if a rounded shape is required. A warm climate plant, it cannot tolerate frost.

Pandorea pandorana

Passiflora edulis
PASSION FRUIT, PURPLE GRANADILLA, PASSION FLOWER ○

Family: PASSIFLORACEAE
Origin: Brazil–northern Argentina.
Flowering time: Summer.
Climatic zone: 9, 10.
Description: Passion fruit's attractive white and green flowers with a purple zoned center are partially hidden by the dense foliage. The flowers are followed by thick-skinned, purple fruit which is edible, and which falls to the ground when ripe. Tolerant of occasional very light frost only, this very quick-growing vine can be used for covering fences, pergolas, or be trained through lattice or wire frames. Excellent drainage and regular summer watering will produce good fruit. Passion fruit is often a relatively short-lived vine.
Varieties/cultivars: *P. e.* var. *flavicarpa* (yellowish fruits).

Passiflora edulis

Polygonum aubertii syn. *Fallopia aubertii*
SILVER FLEECE VINE, SILVER LACE VINE, RUSSIAN VINE (U.K.) ○

Family: POLYGONACEAE
Origin: Western China–Tibet.
Flowering time: Late summer.
Climatic zone: 4, 5, 6, 7, 8, 9.
Description: A rapid grower, silver lace vine can quickly cover an area of 100 square feet (9 square meters), with its heart-shaped, glossy leaves. It is covered with masses of small, creamy-white flowers in long sprays in summer. Grow it to provide quick cover for fences or arbors, or as groundcover. It is not fussy about soil, and is tolerant of coastal conditions. Although it is evergreen in mild climates, it may be deciduous in cooler areas. Prune it hard to control its size; it can become invasive.

Polygonum aubertii

Rosa banksiae 'Alba Plena'
BANKS' ROSE, LADY BANKS' ROSE, BANKSIA ROSE (Aust.) ○

Family: ROSACEAE
Origin: Cultivar.
Flowering time: Summer.
Climatic zone: 8, 9.
Description: Double, white flowers cover this popular, thornless rose in summer. It is a vigorous plant, resistant to many of the diseases that plague most

roses. In a sheltered position on a sunny wall this old favorite will grow in quite cool climates. Prune old growth regularly to help reduce the many stems rising from the base, and make the vine easier to control. If space permits, allow it to flow, sprawl, and climb to fill a wide space.

Rosa banksiae 'Alba Plena'

Rosa laevigata
CHEROKEE ROSE ○

Family: ROSACEAE
Origin: China.
Flowering time: Summer.
Climatic zone: 7, 8, 9.
Description: The single, fragrant, white flowers of this beautiful old rose grow up to 5 inches (125 mm) wide, have prominent yellow stamens, and are followed by bright red hips. Although this rose was common in the temperate zones of China, surprisingly, it was found in the southern states of the United States, where it is now the state flower of Georgia. Trained up a pillar, or over a pergola, this delightful rose will be evergreen in mild climates. It is not tolerant of cold zones.

Rosa laevigata

Rosa wichuraiana

Rosa wichuraiana
MEMORIAL ROSE ○

Family: ROSACEAE
Origin: Japan, China, Korea, Taiwan.
Flowering time: Summer.
Climatic zone: 6, 7, 8, 9.
Description: This nearly prostrate, semi-evergreen, rambler has long, horizontal branches and can be trained as an upright vine. Individual, fragrant flowers are 2 inches (50 mm) across and are held in clusters above the foliage. Train it over old trees, or stumps, or use it to cover sloping banks. Because the branches root if left in contact with soil, the vine makes a good groundcover.
Varieties/cultivars: Many hybrid cultivars have been developed from this hardy plant.

Solanum jasminoides, 'Album'
POTATO CREEPER, POTATO VINE, JASMINE NIGHTSHADE (U.K.) ○

Family: SOLANACEAE
Origin: Cultivar.
Flowering time: Summer–autumn.
Climatic zone: 8, 9.
Description: The potato creeper is a quick-growing, evergreen climber, popular in warm climates. It is not fussy about soil, but requires a warm, sunny position. Severe winters will kill it. The dainty foliage and clusters of white flowers make a delightful contrast with the stems which become strong and woody over the years. Some support is needed to help the vine climb a wall or fence, or it can be trailed over a low wall or fence. Try it as a container plant, either spilling over the edges, or trained up a slender frame.

Solanum jasminoides, 'Album'

Stephanotis floribunda

Stephanotis floribunda
MADAGASCAR ○ ◑
JASMINE, CHAPLET FLOWER, CLUSTERED WAXFLOWER

Family: ASCLEPIADACEAE
Origin: Madagascar.
Flowering time: Late spring–early autumn.
Climatic zone: 9, 10.
Description: The delightful fragrance of this beautiful trumpet-shaped flower has made it a highly prized bloom for floral arrangements, especially wedding bouquets. The flowers hang in clusters of eight to ten from late spring to early autumn. Rich, free-draining soil is required and although the roots should be in a shady, cool position, the vine needs to be able to climb up in the sunlight. This is a light climber which will enhance an archway or patio, or can be grown in a container. In cool climates, this makes a good house or greenhouse plant.

Thunbergia grandiflora 'Alba'

Thunbergia grandiflora 'Alba'
BENGAL CLOCK ○ ◑
VINE, SKYFLOWER, TRUMPET VINE (U.K.)

Family: ACANTHACEAE
Origin: Cultivar.
Flowering time: Summer–autumn.
Climatic zone: 9, 10.
Description: This white variety of the skyflower is perhaps not quite so vigorous a grower as *Thunbergia grandiflora*, but it will cover a fence or pergola and give good shade. The flowers are slightly drooping, and hang singly or in small clusters. An attractive, evergreen vine, it needs a sheltered position protected from wind and frost if grown in cooler climates. In hot, inland districts, a semishaded position is tolerated. Prune gently to reduce the size; heavy pruning will result in few flowers the following year.

Trachelospermum asiaticum
JAPANESE STAR ○ ◑ ●
JASMINE

Family: APOCYNACEAE
Origin: Japan, Korea.
Flowering time: Summer.
Climatic zone: 8, 9.
Description: Creamy-yellow flowers and smaller, darker leaves distinguish this vine from the Chinese star jasmine. Generally it is a tidier vine, more easily held to a flat surface. The sweetly-scented flowers appear for several months, but not in such profusion as on the Chinese jasmine. Although it is a vigorous climber, it is slow to start, and needs well-drained, rich soil, with regular watering in summer. Tolerant of cool conditions, it will withstand quite heavy shade. However, it cannot withstand severe winters.

Trachelospermum asiaticum

Trachelospermum jasminoides
STAR JASMINE, CHINESE STAR JASMINE, CONFEDERATE JASMINE ○ ◑ ●

Family: APOCYNACEAE
Origin: Southern China, Japan.
Flowering time: Spring, early summer.
Climatic zone: 9.
Description: Wiry stems with their milky sap will develop into a sturdy trunk after many years. The very fragrant, star-shaped flowers are borne in profusion during spring and early summer. Glossy dark-green foliage makes an excellent background for the bright white blossoms. Support is necessary to grow this vine as a climber, but it will enhance a wall or fence, and is also excellent as a groundcover, a spill-over, or pruned to a small shrub. It can also be trained up a slender pole as a container plant. In cool climates, a greenhouse is preferred.
Varieties/cultivars: 'Variegatum' (variegated leaf color).

Trachelospermum jasminoides

Wisteria floribunda 'Alba' syn. *W. f.* 'Longissima Alba'
JAPANESE WISTERIA ○

Family: LEGUMINOSAE
Origin: Cultivar.
Flowering time: Early summer.
Climatic zone: 4, 5, 6, 7, 8, 9.
Description: The clusters of white flowers on this vigorous, deciduous vine appear at the same time as the early leaves. The flowers begin opening at the base of the cluster and gradually continue opening towards the tip, thus prolonging the blooming period, but not making quite such a spectacular display as those of *W. floribunda*. Developing a dense canopy, it will quickly cover a pergola, fence, or wall, or it can be trained up the face of a building. Regular pruning is required during the summer to remove long, arching branches, and to restrict the overall size.

Wisteria floribunda 'Alba'

Wisteria sinensis 'Alba'
CHINESE WISTERIA ○

Family: LEGUMINOSAE
Origin: Cultivar.
Flowering time: Late spring.
Climatic zone: 5, 6, 7, 8, 9.
Description: The white flowers of Chinese wisteria appear before the leaves, and the 12 inch (300 mm) long clusters open from base to tip at the same time. The flowering period is short, but the masses of flowers with their slight fragrance make a wonderful display. Annual pruning in winter to reduce size, as well as regular summer pruning, is necessary to control this vigorous vine. Cold winters may damage flower buds. Grow only grafted or layered plants or cuttings, as seedlings may not bloom for many years.

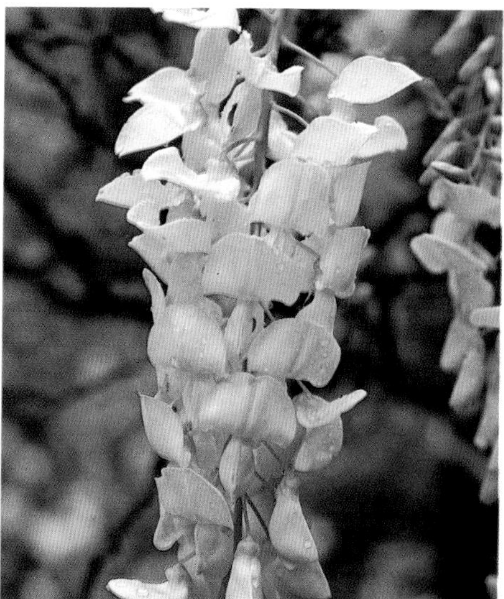
Wisteria sinensis 'Alba'

Wisteria venusta syn. *W. brachybotrys* 'Alba'
SILKY WISTERIA, JAPANESE WISTERIA ○

Family: LEGUMINOSAE
Origin: Japan.
Flowering time: Spring.
Climatic zone: 5, 6, 7, 8, 9.
Description: Large, white, long-stalked flowers are carried on 6-inch-long (150 mm) sprays. Such a spectacular display of massed blossoms makes this one of the best of the white wisterias. Silky hairs on the surface of the leaflets give the species its name. The leaves have nine to thirteen broad leaflets. Trained to a tree shape, this plant will bloom profusely, and is a magnificent specimen, especially when it becomes old. It needs constant pruning if it is to develop tree proportions, but looks beautiful, even when bare-branched in the winter.

Wisteria venusta

Achillea ageratifolia

Achillea ageratifolia
YARROW ○

Family: COMPOSITAE
Origin: Greece.
Flowering time: Summer.
Climatic zone: 5, 6, 7, 8, 9, 10.
Dimensions: Up to 6 inches (150 mm) high.
Description: A handsome, low-growing, spreading shrub, it has a covering of grey-green foliage, and masses of small, white, daisy-like flowers with yellow centers. Plant it in an open, sunny position in light, well-drained soil that has been enriched with plenty of organic matter. It is easily propagated either by division during autumn or spring, or by cuttings.

Achillea millefolium
COMMON YARROW, MILFOIL ○

Family: COMPOSITAE
Origin: Europe, Caucasus, Himalayas, Siberia.
Flowering time: Summer.
Climatic zone: 3, 4, 5, 6, 7, 8, 9, 10.
Dimensions: 2 feet (600 mm) high.
Description: This plant, with its invasive roots, spreads quickly and can be a troublesome weed if it infests a lawn. Each root produces a clump of feathery, dark-green leaves and the strong, wiry stems produce a white flower head. It is strongly resistant to both cold and drought and will grow in all types of soil, particularly sandy soils near the sea. Propagation is easy by division in spring or autumn.
Other colors: Pink, red.
Varieties/cultivars: 'Cerise Queen', 'Red Beauty', 'Fire King'.

Achillea millefolium

Actaea rubra
RED BANEBERRY, RED COHOSH (U.S.A.) ◑ ●

Family: RANUNCULACEAE
Origin: North America.
Flowering time: Spring.
Climatic zone: 3, 4, 5, 6, 7, 8.
Dimensions: 18 inches to 2 feet (450–600 mm) high.
Description: The two main features of this plant are its stems of small, white flowers in spring and its clusters of glistening scarlet berries in autumn. The berries are poisonous, hence the name baneberry. Although adaptable and very hardy, it grows best in cool, shaded positions in moist and fertile soils. The clumps of green, coarse, ferny leaves contrast well with other foliage. Propagation is by division, or from seeds which take many months to germinate.
Varieties/cultivars: *A. r.* var. *album*, *A. r.* var. *neglecta*.

Actaea rubra var. *album*

Anaphalis cinnamomea
PEARLY EVERLASTING ◑

Family: COMPOSITAE
Origin: India, Burma.
Flowering time: Late summer.
Climatic zone: 5, 6, 7, 8, 9, 10.
Dimensions: Up to 2½ feet (750 mm) high.
Description: This attractive herbaceous perennial forms a wide clump of downy grey-green leaves and in summer is covered with globular clusters of white flowers. An adaptable plant which can be grown with success in a wide range of soils and conditions, it prefers a semishaded, protected position and good soil drainage. It can be propagated either by seed or by division.

Anaphalis cinnamomea

Anaphalis nubigena

Anaphalis nubigena
PEARLY EVERLASTING 

Family: COMPOSITAE
Origin: Himalayas.
Flowering time: Summer.

Climatic zone: 4, 5, 6, 7, 8, 9.
Dimensions: 8–12 inches (200–300 mm) high.
Description: This tufted plant has silvery-gray, woolly leaves with inrolled margins. The little starry, daisy-like flowers are on wide branching stems above the foliage. They are excellent for cutting and can be successfully dried. The plant quickly makes a large clump if grown in any good garden soil in an open position, but will droop if the roots are allowed to dry out. It can be propagated from seed but is usually divided in spring.

Anaphalis triplinervis

Anaphalis triplinervis
PEARLY EVERLASTING

Family: COMPOSITAE
Origin: Himalayas.
Flowering time: Late summer–autumn.
Climatic zone: 3, 4, 5, 6, 7, 8, 9.
Dimensions: Up to 18 inches (450 mm) high.
Description: This is a tufted plant which forms a clump of silver-gray foliage. This later becomes buried beneath the wide sprays of crisp, white daisies which are excellent for cutting and drying. To dry them, hang the cut flower heads upside down. An ideal plant for the edge of a border, pearly everlasting makes a pleasing combination with pink flowers. It is an easy plant to grow, but will not tolerate drought.
Varieties/cultivars: 'Summer Snow'

Androsace lanuginosa

Androsace lanuginosa
ROCK JASMINE ○

Family: PRIMULACEAE
Origin: Himalayas.
Flowering time: Summer.
Climatic zone: 4, 5, 6, 7, 8.
Dimensions: Up to 4 inches (100 mm) high.
Description: This low-growing, tussock-forming alpine perennial has trailing stems of silvery foliage in rosettes. The white to pale pink flowers occur in dense terminal clusters. It is an excellent rock garden plant in the right conditions, due to showy flowering and cascading habit. It prefers well-composted, well-drained soils and an open, sunny position. Cuttings can be taken in spring.

Anemone sylvestris
SNOWDROP ANEMONE, SNOWDROP WINDFLOWER ◑ ●

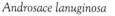

Family: RANUNCULACEAE
Origin: Europe–Siberia.
Flowering time: Late spring–summer.
Climatic zone: 3, 4, 5, 6, 7, 8.
Dimensions: 18 inches (450 mm) high.
Description: In light soil, this anemone spreads freely and quickly but is more restrained in heavier clay soils. The erect to somewhat nodding white flowers are pleasantly fragrant and set off by a group of yellow stamens in the center. The blooms are followed by clusters of woolly seed heads. It is best propagated by seed, although the clumps formed in light soil can be easily divided.
Varieties/cultivars: 'Grandiflora'.

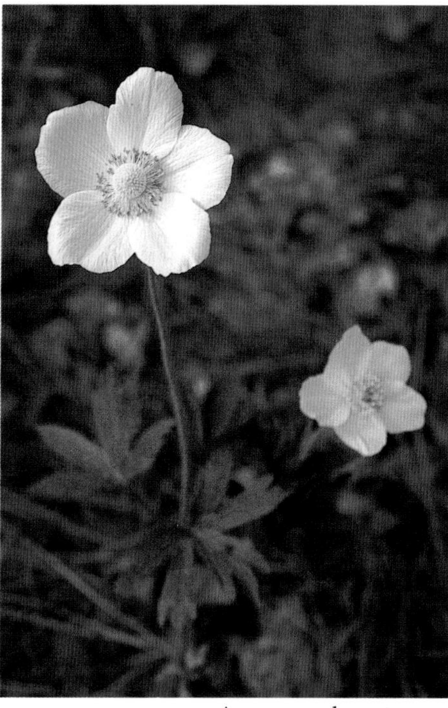

Anemone sylvestris

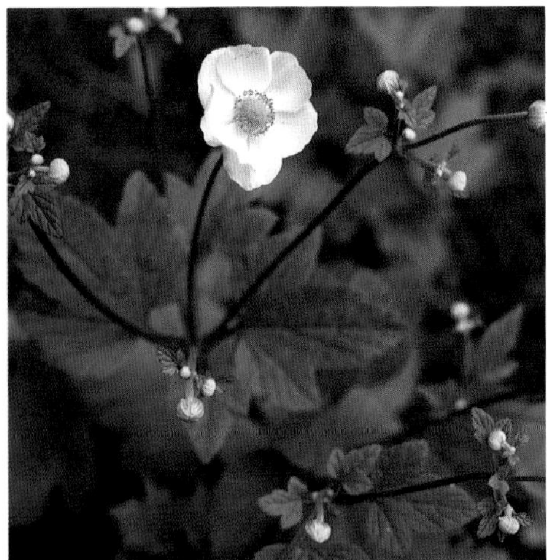

Anemone vitifolia 'Robustissima'

Anemone vitifolia 'Robustissima'
JAPANESE ANEMONE

Family: RANUNCULACEAE
Origin: Himalayas–China.
Flowering time: Late summer–autumn.
Climatic zone: 5.
Dimensions: 2–3 feet (approx. 1 meter) high.
Description: The Japanese anemone, a delight in the autumn garden when the summer blooms are fading, has showy flowers borne on longish stem clusters. The plant grows in clumps which are slow to develop in their first year, but then spread rapidly and prefer to remain undisturbed. It prefers rich, well-drained soil, with ample water in dry conditions, especially if it is grown in full sun. It makes an attractive show planted with Michaelmas daisies and old-fashioned autumn climbing roses. Japanese anemone is a good cut flower.

Anemone x *hybrida*
JAPANESE ANEMONE, JAPANESE WINDFLOWER

Family: RANUNCULACEAE
Origin: U.K.
Flowering time: Late summer–autumn.
Climatic zone: 5, 6, 7, 8, 9.
Dimensions: Up to 4 feet (over 1 meter) high.
Description: This is one of the most elegant and beautiful of the autumn perennials, with its rounded blooms produced on ascending branching stems over a period of many weeks. Once established, the plant can spread quite rapidly, making fine clumps of trifoliate dark-green leaves. Derived from the species *A. hupehensis*, which is pink-flowered, there are now many shades of color in this garden hybrid, the single white being one of the most popular. This anemone prefers good soil and moist conditions.
Other colors: Deep pink, rosy pink, red.
Varieties/cultivars: 'Honorine Jobert', 'Queen Charlotte', 'Whirlwind', 'Margarete', 'Lorelei'.

Anemone x *hybrida*

Arabis caucasica
ROCK CRESS

Family: CRUCIFERAE
Origin: Caucasus.
Flowering time: Late spring–summer.
Climatic zone: 4, 5, 6, 7, 8, 9.
Dimensions: 6–10 inches (150–250 mm) high.
Description: The most widely grown rock cress, this vigorous trailing plant is suited to a spacious walled garden which will allow it plenty of room. It will also grow on a sunny bank and does best in poor soil and an open position. Cut it back after flowering. The cuttings will easily take root in a pot or in the ground, or the plant can also be divided. The leaves are grayish-green and the flowers slightly scented.
Varieties/cultivars: 'Flore Pleno', and a variegated leaf form.

Arabis caucasica

Arabis procurrens
ROCK CRESS 

Family: CRUCIFERAE
Origin: Southeastern Europe.
Flowering time: Spring.
Climatic zone: 4, 5, 6, 7, 8, 9.
Dimensions: Up to 12 inches (300 mm) high.
Description: Rock cress is one of the more showy species in this group of low-

Arabis procurrens

growing members of the mustard family. The flowers are quite large for the size of the plant, and are borne on slender heads. The foliage spreads at ground level by a series of short runners. Ideal for rock gardens, the plant thrives in poor soils and dry conditions, but needs a well-drained position. Plant it in either full sun or partial shade.

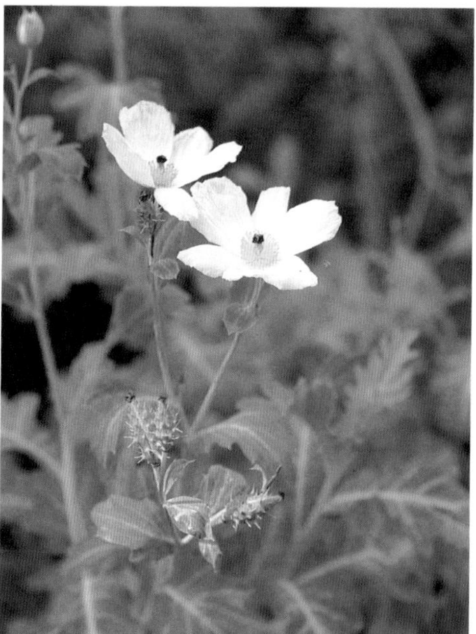
Argemone glauca

Argemone glauca
PRICKLY POPPY ○

Family: PAPAVERACEAE
Origin: North America.
Flowering time: Summer.
Climatic zone: 9, 10.
Dimensions: Up to 2 feet (600 mm) high.
Description: These exquisite, soft white poppy flowers have bright yellow stamens that exude a sticky sap. The prickly stems are unpleasant to touch except with gloves. The plant is ideal for borders or mixed beds of annuals and likes full sun and warm weather. The soil should be light and well-drained. The seeds can be sown in summer and the seedlings transplanted in autumn for flowering the following year.

Armeria maritima
THRIFT, COMMON THRIFT (U.K.), SEA PINK ○

Family: PLUMBAGINACEAE
Origin: Northern hemisphere (mainly coastal and mountainous areas).
Flowering time: Summer.
Climatic zone: 3, 4, 5, 6, 7, 8.
Dimensions: 6–12 inches (150–300 mm) high.
Description: This is a useful edging or front-of-the-border plant with rich green, grass-like foliage. Erect and rigid stems bear individual flower heads in the shape of a globe, each made up of many small flowers. It prefers a light, open soil and grows particularly well near the sea as indicated by its name, sea pink. Propagation can be by seed or, better still, by division or cuttings taken in early autumn.
Other colors: Pink, red, purple.
Varieties/cultivars: 'Alba', 'Grandiflora', 'Purpurea', 'Rubra', 'Splendens'.

Artemisia lactiflora
CHINESE MUGWORT, WHITE MUGWORT, GHOSTPLANT (U.S.A.) ○ ◑

Family: COMPOSITAE
Origin: China, India.
Flowering time: Late summer–autumn.
Climatic zone: 4, 5, 6, 7, 8.
Dimensions: 4–5 feet (1.5 meters) high.
Description: This strong-growing plant is useful in the background of a garden bed as a foil for more brightly colored subjects. It has jagged, green leaves and conspicuous sheaves of tiny, creamy-white flowers which are long-lasting and suitable for cutting. Because of their color, the flowers tend to look "dirty" when placed near white flowers or silver foliage and are better when grouped with yellow or blue flowers. It prefers a moist and fertile soil.

Artemisia lactiflora

Armeria maritima 'Alba'

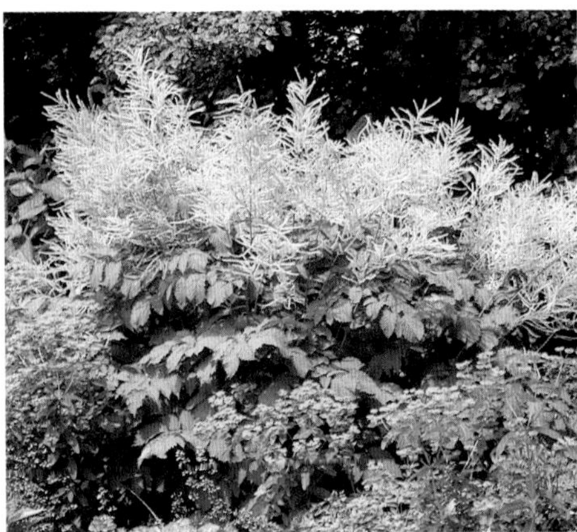

Aruncus dioicus

Boltonia asteroides

Aruncus dioicus

GOATSBEARD ○ ◑

Family: ROSACEAE
Origin: Northern hemisphere.
Flowering time: Summer.
Climatic zone: 3, 4, 5, 6, 7, 8, 9.
Dimensions: 4–7 feet (1.2–2 meters) high.
Description: Goatsbeard is a handsome plant which forms a massive clump of fernlike foliage from which arise large plumes of minute creamy-white flowers. It can be used successfully as an isolated specimen, but is also good for general use, especially as a companion to shrub roses. It is easy to grow in most soils, but prefers moist conditions. Propagate by division or seed.
Varieties/cultivars: 'Kneiffii'.

Boltonia asteroides

WHITE BOLTONIA, FALSE CHAMOMILE, FALSE STARWORT (U.S.A.) ○ ◑

Family: COMPOSITAE
Origin: North America.
Flowering time: Autumn.
Climatic zone: 4, 5, 6, 7, 8, 9.
Dimensions: 5–6 feet (2 meters) high.
Description: This is an easily grown plant in most types of soil and ideal as a background plant. Massed heads of tiny, daisy-like flowers are produced in such vast quantities that the plants may need staking for support when in bloom. The pale-green leaves are quite small and insignificant. It is propagated by division in winter and is somewhat susceptible to mildew in warm, moist conditions.
Other colors: Pink, purple.
Varieties/cultivars: 'Snowbank'.

Campanula persicifolia 'Alba'

PEACH-LEAVED BELLFLOWER, PAPER BELLFLOWER (U.K.) ○ ◑

Family: CAMPANULACEAE
Origin: Cultivar.
Flowering time: Summer.
Climatic zone: 4, 5, 6, 7, 8, 9.
Dimensions: 2–3 feet (1 meter) high.
Description: This is a popular perennial which forms wide clumps of dense, narrow leaves and strong but slender stems bearing large, cup-shaped flowers. Being evergreen, it makes a useful groundcover throughout the year. It flowers over a long period and is good for cutting. It can be grown from seed, or propagated by root division in autumn or spring.

Campanula persicifolia 'Alba'

Cerastium tomentosum

SNOW-IN-SUMMER ○ ◑

Family: CARYOPHYLLACEAE
Origin: Italy and Sicily.
Flowering time: Summer.
Climatic zone: 5, 6, 7, 8, 9.
Dimensions: 4–6 inches (100–150 mm) high.
Description: A delightful groundcover plant, snow-in-summer spreads quickly in a sunny or lightly shaded spot. Its silvery-white foliage and white flowers give it its common name. It will grow in most soils, even sand, and is useful for retaining soil on steep banks as it puts down roots from each stem. Because it is invasive, it is not recommended for small gardens or choice spots. It is easily divided at any time except mid-winter.

Cerastium tomentosum

Chrysanthemum frutescens

PARIS DAISY, MARGUERITE DAISY ○

Family: COMPOSITAE
Origin: Canary Islands.
Flowering time: Spring–autumn and winter.
Climatic zone: 9, 10.
Dimensions: 3 feet (1 meter) high.
Description: This shrub-like evergreen perennial is of great value in the garden as it is covered in a mass of flowers for a long period if the spent blooms are removed. It has neatly divided, light-green foliage and does well in most garden soils, provided it gets plenty of water in summer. It makes a good specimen for planting in large

Chrysanthemum frutescens

containers and can be easily propagated from cuttings taken in spring or autumn.
Other colors: Pink, yellow.
Varieties/cultivars: 'Coronation', 'Mary Wootton'.

Chrysanthemum leucanthemum
OX-EYE DAISY, COMMON DAISY ○ ◑

Family: COMPOSITAE
Origin: Europe, Asia.
Flowering time: Early to late summer.
Climatic zone: 3, 4, 5, 6, 7, 8, 9, 10.

Chrysanthemum leucanthemum

Dimensions: 2 feet (600 mm) high.
Description: This is the common, white field daisy which can be quite attractive when mass-planted, although it often becomes a nuisance in gardens. The flower heads, usually solitary, are on a long, sturdy stalk which rarely needs staking for wind protection. The cut flowers last quite well indoors. This hardy perennial reseeds easily and so spreads rapidly.
Varieties/cultivars: 'Maistern'.

Chrysanthemum x *superbum*

Chrysanthemum x *superbum* syn. *C. maximum*
SHASTA DAISY ○ ◑

Family: COMPOSITAE
Origin: Hybrid.
Flowering time: Summer.
Climatic zone: 5, 6, 7, 8, 9.
Dimensions: 3 feet (1 meter) high.
Description: A robust plant, shasta daisy is coarser in all its parts than most other chrysanthemums. The daisy flowers it produces are large, up to 5 or 6 inches (130–150 mm) across, and last well when cut. It is one of the easiest plants to cultivate in almost any position, although it does best in full sun. It is available in single and double forms and there are now several cultivars. Plant it out in autumn, and lift and divide the clumps every two years.
Varieties/cultivars: 'Wirral Supreme', 'Aglaia', 'Fiona Coghill', 'September Snow', 'Mayfield Giant'.

Crambe cordifolia

Crambe cordifolia
HEARTLEAF CRAMBE, SEA KALE ○

Family: CRUCIFERAE
Origin: Caucasus.
Flowering time: Early summer.
Climatic zone: 5, 6, 7, 8, 9.
Dimensions: 6 feet (2 meters) high.
Description: This is a massive plant with bold basal leaves, gray-green in color and often deeply lobed or cut. The intricately branched flowering stems carry clouds of tiny, white flowers, rather strongly scented. It is a most effective plant for a large garden, given well-drained, slightly alkaline soil and a position preferably in full sunshine. It is sometimes attacked by the caterpillars of the cabbage white butterfly. Propagate it from root cuttings in late winter or early spring.
Varieties/cultivars: 'Grandiflora'.

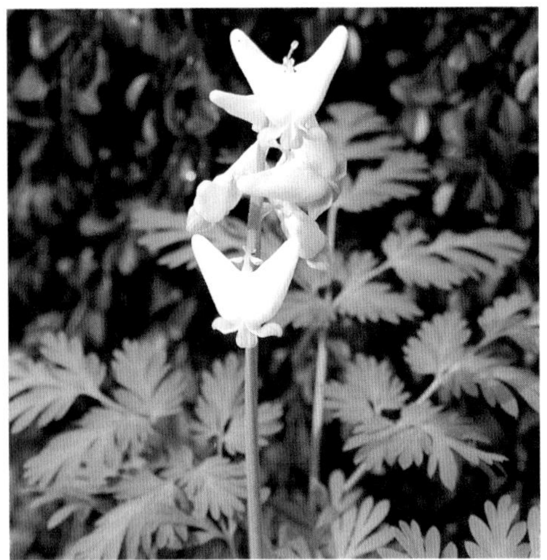

Dicentra cucullaria

Dicentra cucullaria
DUTCHMAN'S-BREECHES, WHITE EARDROPS ○ ◑

Family: FUMARIACEAE
Origin: Eastern United States.
Flowering time: Late spring.
Climatic zone: 4, 5, 6, 7, 8, 9.
Dimensions: 8 inches (200 mm) high.
Description: This is a graceful, stemless plant with numerous feathery basal leaves. The pendant flowers, on their slender, arching stalks, are divided into two spurs, giving the bloom a forked appearance similar to the trousers worn by Dutch peasants, hence the common name. It prefers a rich, well-drained soil and is frost-resistant, but drought-tender. It can be propagated by seed or division.

Dictamnus albus
GAS PLANT, BURNING BUSH, DITTANY (U.K.) ○ ◑

Family: RUTACEAE
Origin: Eastern Europe.
Flowering time: Summer.
Climatic zone: 3, 4, 5, 6, 7, 8, 9.
Dimensions: 2–3 feet (up to 1 meter) high.
Description: A bushy perennial with simple upright stems, this plant is not extensively cultivated but is worth growing for the tangy lemon perfume of its leaves and its elegant flowers. It grows best in a fertile soil in a sunny position. The volatile oil from this plant will ignite if a lighted match is held near the developing seed pods on a windless day. The ripe seed pods explode violently in warm, dry weather and the seeds can take up to a year to germinate.
Other colors: Red, purple.
Varieties/cultivars: 'Purpureus', 'Rubrus'.

Dictamnus albus

Dianthus arenarius
PRUSSIAN PINK, GRASS PINK (U.K.) ◑

Family: CARYOPHYLLACEAE
Origin: Eastern Europe.
Flowering time: Summer.
Climatic zone: 4, 5, 6, 7, 8, 9.

Dianthus arenarius

Dimensions: 8–12 inches (200–300 mm) high.
Description: A useful mat-forming plant with masses of single, heavily fringed, white flowers with a greenish eye. This species prefers a semishaded position and a slightly gritty soil that has been enriched with a potassium-rich fertilizer. Make sure that plenty of water is supplied, especially during the warm summer months. Prussian pink is easily grown from either seed or cuttings.

Dietes vegeta syn. *Moraea iridioides*
AFRICAN IRIS ○ ◑

Family: IRIDACEAE
Origin: South Africa.
Flowering time: Summer.

Dietes vegeta

Climatic zone: 9, 10.
Dimensions: Up to 2 feet (600 mm) high.
Description: The glorious lily-like flowers of this species appear in profusion on long, slender stems during the warm weather. Even when the plant is not in flower, the evergreen, sword-like foliage, in large clumps, is most attractive and makes an excellent feature. In its native environment, African iris is found growing in semishade under spreading trees. It can withstand extremely dry conditions, prefers light and well-drained soils, and is often grown as a low hedge. Once established it will readily self-seed.

Dimorphotheca ecklonis syn. *Osteospermum ecklonis*
WHITE VELDT DAISY, SAILOR BOY DAISY ○

Family: COMPOSITAE
Origin: South Africa.
Flowering time: Summer–autumn.
Climatic zone: 9.
Dimensions: Up to 3 feet (1 meter) high.
Description: In a frost-free climate, this plant grows into a vigorous, upright, shrubby bush. It prefers a light, well-drained soil and is able to withstand periods of dryness. The petals of the daisy-like flower, white on top and purple underneath, close at night time. The long, narrow, light-green leaves are lightly toothed around the margin. It is easily propagated from cuttings and can also be grown from seed.
Varieties/cultivars: var. *prostrata*, 'Whirligig', 'Pink whirls'.

Dimorphotheca ecklonis

Epilobium glabellum

Epilobium glabellum
FIREWEED, WILLOW HERB ○ ◑

Family: ONAGRACEAE
Origin: New Zealand.
Flowering time: Summer.
Climatic zone: 8, 9, 10.
Dimensions: Up to 15 inches (375 mm) high.
Description: The shining, light-green leaves of this little alpine perennial form attractive clumps which gradually expand, but are never a nuisance. The tumbled masses of funnel-shaped flowers are followed by fluffy seed heads. As it comes from the rocky subalpine and alpine slopes, it needs an open, well-drained soil that is reasonably fertile. It can be propagated by division during spring.
Other colors: Yellow, pink.
Varieties/cultivars: 'Sulphureum'.

Epimedium x *youngianum* 'Niveum'
SNOWY BARRENWORT ◑

Family: BERBERIDACEAE
Origin: Hybrid cultivar.
Flowering time: Spring.
Climatic zone: 5, 6, 7, 8, 9.
Dimensions: 6–12 inches (150–300 mm) high.

Epimedium x *youngianum* 'Niveum'

Description: This perennial is valued for its delicate-looking, but leathery-textured, leaves made up of heart-shaped leaflets on wiry stems. They are light green with pink veins in spring, turning to reddish-bronze in autumn. The flowers, borne in pendulous white clusters, composed of eight sepals and four petals, are excellent for cutting. It grows well in cool and temperate areas in light shade and moist soil that is well-nourished. The clumps may be divided in autumn or spring.

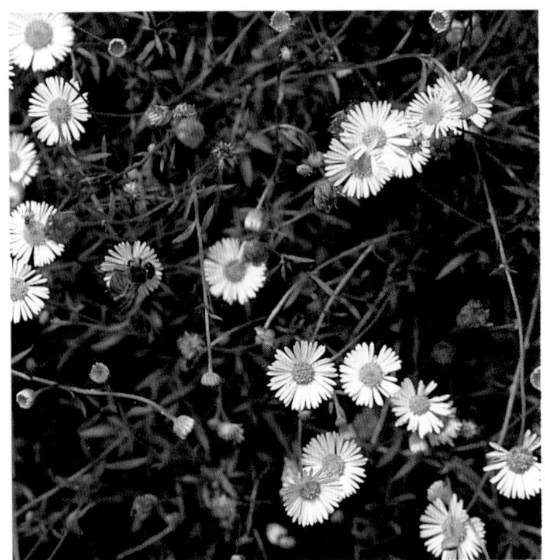

Erigeron mucronatus

Erigeron mucronatus syn.
E. karvinskianus
BONYTIP FLEABANE, ○ ◑
MEXICAN FLEABANE (U.K.),
BABY'S TEARS (Aust.)

Family: COMPOSITAE
Origin: Mexico–Venezuela.
Flowering time: Spring–summer and autumn.
Climatic zone: 8, 9, 10.
Dimensions: 8 inches (200 mm) high.
Description: This attractive little plant self-seeds vigorously and will fill up many a bare space with endless clouds of little white and pink daisies. It is excellent around steps or in gaps in brick or stone paving. It also spreads by means of underground runners. It dies down in winter but will reappear in spring. It seems to do best in light, well-drained, sandy soil of low fertility, especially in areas near the sea.

Eryngium bourgatii
MEDITERRANEAN ○
ERYNGO (U.S.A.), SEA HOLLY

Family: UMBELLIFERAE
Origin: Pyrenees.
Flowering time: Summer.
Climatic zone: 6, 7, 8, 9, 10.
Dimensions: 2 feet (600 mm) high.
Description: This is an eye-catching plant because of its unusual foliage. The leaves are crisp and curly, gray-green in color with white veins, and form a basal rosette. The blue-green, thistle-like flowers are protected by silvery-white bracts tipped with spines. It thrives in full sun and well-drained, sandy soil that is moderately fertile. The flower heads are most useful for dried floral arrangements. Seed in spring or root cuttings in late winter are the best means of propagation.

Eryngium bourgatii

Filipendula vulgaris 'Flore Pleno'

Filipendula vulgaris 'Flore Pleno' syn.
F. hexapetala 'Flore Pleno'
DOUBLE-FLOWERED ○ ◑
DROPWORT, MEADOWSWEET

Family: ROSACEAE
Origin: Eastern Europe, Siberia.
Flowering time: Summer.
Climatic zone: 4, 5, 6, 7, 8, 9.
Dimensions: Up to 2 feet (600 mm) high.
Description: This plant has finely divided foliage like that of the carrot and produces double, creamy-white flowers in a loose raceme. It will tolerate reasonably dry conditions and will grow well in either full sun or partial shade. It makes an excellent border subject when mixed with other plants of a different texture. It is usually propagated by division in autumn or spring.

Fragaria chiloensis
CHILOE STRAWBERRY, ○ ◑
BEACH STRAWBERRY

Family: ROSACEAE
Origin: Western North and South America from Alaska to Chile.
Flowering time: Spring.
Climatic zone: 5, 6, 7, 8, 9.
Dimensions: Up to 6 inches (150 mm) high.
Description: This is a low, spreading, groundcover plant which sends out stems, or runners, after it has finished flowering and fruiting. The attractive leaves are green and glossy above and pale bluish-white beneath. The fruit is large, firm and dark-red, this plant being one of the parents of our dessert strawberries. It prefers a position in cool, moist, fertile soil open to sunshine.

Fragaria chiloensis

Gypsophila paniculata

Gillenia trifoliata
INDIAN-PHYSIC, BOWMAN'S-ROOT (U.S.A.)

Family: ROSACEAE
Origin: Eastern North America.
Flowering time: Summer.
Climatic zone: 4, 5, 6, 7, 8, 9.
Dimensions: 3 feet (1 meter) high.
Description: Indian-physic is a dainty and refined perennial with wiry, reddish stems and leaves divided into three parts. It forms a clump from which it sends up stems of small white flowers in airy clusters. After the petals fall, the red calyces persist and remain decorative until the seeds ripen. It can be grown in full sun except in very hot regions, and any type of soil that is not too dry seems to suit it. Propagate it by division of the clumps in spring.

Gypsophila paniculata
BABY'S-BREATH, CHALK PLANT

Family: CARYOPHYLLACEAE
Origin: Central Europe– central Siberia.
Flowering time: Summer.
Climatic zone: 3, 4, 5, 6, 7, 8, 9.
Dimensions: Up to 3 feet (1 meter) high.
Description: A wide-spreading plant up to 3 feet (1 meter) in diameter, baby's-breath produces dense tufts of intricately branched, erect stems covered in a froth of tiny star-like flowers. It prefers a neutral or slightly alkaline soil and resents disturbance of the roots once established. The plant's cloud-like appearance makes a dramatic contrast with other more striking subjects in the garden. It can be grown from seed.
Other colors: Pink.
Varieties/cultivars: 'Bristol Fairy', 'Flamingo', 'Rosy Veil'.

Gillenia trifoliata

Helleborus corsicus

Helleborus corsicus syn. *H. lividus corsicus, H. argutifolius*
CORSICAN HELLEBORE

Family: RANUNCULACEAE
Origin: Corsica, Sardinia.
Flowering time: Winter–spring.
Climatic zone: 6, 7, 8, 9.
Dimensions: 2–3 feet (up to 1 meter) high.
Description: This handsome, evergreen perennial produces large, three-part leaves, serrated at the edges, during its first year. From the top of a short leafy stem the flower stalk develops in the second year. The single, upright spike bears a cluster of fifteen to twenty cup-shaped flowers of an unusual pale green, which last for many months. It is ideal for growing under deciduous trees in a moist, fertile soil. Propagate it from seed or by division, but exercise care with division; the roots are brittle.

Helleborus foetidus

Helleborus foetidus

STINKING HELLEBORE, SETTERWORT, BEAR'S FOOT

Family: RANUNCULACEAE
Origin: Western Europe.
Flowering time: Winter–spring.
Climatic zone: 6, 7, 8, 9.
Dimensions: Up to 3 feet (1 meter) high.
Description: This plant has handsome, deeply divided, dark-green leaves which form a compact clump. The flowers are airy clusters at the end of the stems, thimble-shaped and of a pale green color edged with maroon. The plant has tough roots that penetrate the soil for a considerable depth. The shiny foliage makes an excellent foil for silver-leaved plants, and the masses of blooms stay fresh for some time. The plant self-seeds readily.

Helleborus lividus

MAJORCA HELLEBORE

Family: RANUNCULACEAE
Origin: Majorca.
Flowering time: Early spring.
Climatic zone: 9.
Dimensions: 12 inches (300 mm) high.
Description: This perennial has leathery leaves divided into three parts and overlaced with gray-white markings and purple beneath. The clusters of flowers appear on leafy stems in the second year and are yellowish-green flushed purplish-pink and delicately scented. The fragrance is most noted when the plant is grown under cover. Best grown under glass in cold climates.

Helleborus lividus

Helleborus niger

Helleborus niger

CHRISTMAS ROSE, BLACK HELLEBORE

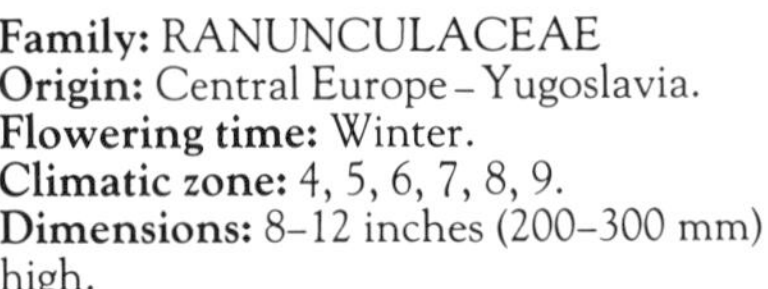

Family: RANUNCULACEAE
Origin: Central Europe – Yugoslavia.
Flowering time: Winter.
Climatic zone: 4, 5, 6, 7, 8, 9.
Dimensions: 8–12 inches (200–300 mm) high.
Description: The leathery leaves are evergreen and the single flowers, up to 3 inches (75 mm) across, are pure white, becoming pinkish as they age. The name black hellebore refers to the color of the roots. It thrives best in heavy, moist soils in either full or partial shade. This plant has been in cultivation since the Middle Ages and is a welcome sight after Christmas in the northern hemisphere.
Other colors: Pink.
Varieties/cultivars: 'Louis Cobbett', 'Altifolius', 'Praecox'.

Iberis sempervirens

PERENNIAL CANDYTUFT

Family: CRUCIFERAE
Origin: Mediterranean region.
Flowering time: Spring.
Climatic zone: 7, 8, 9.
Dimensions: Up to 12 inches (300 mm) high.
Description: This makes a fine edging plant or can be planted among rocks. Usually evergreen, it becomes covered in a mass of flattish white flower clusters. To avoid the formation of a noticeable space in the center of the plant after flowering, the stems should be lightly cut back. It prefers a sunny position but will stop flowering if allowed to dry out. It is easily propagated by division or from seed.
Varieties/cultivars: 'Little Gem', 'Plena'.

Iberis sempervirens

Lamium maculatum

SPOTTED DEAD NETTLE

Family: LABIATAE
Origin: Most of Europe – Russia and Turkey.
Flowering time: Early summer.
Climatic zone: 5, 6, 7, 8, 9.
Dimensions: 6–8 inches (150–200 mm) high.
Description: This useful groundcover plant has white flowers and attractively marked foliage. The mid-green leaves with their silver stripe will form a carpet under trees and in shaded areas. The semi-prostrate stems send out runners which will put down roots and these can be easily cut off and replanted elsewhere. It will thrive in poor soils and

Lamium maculatum 'White Nancy'

is useful for planting under hedges and for covering steep banks.
Other colors: Mauve-pink.
Varieties/cultivars: 'Beacon Silver', 'White Nancy', 'Roseum'.

Leontopodium alpinum
EDELWEISS ○

Family: COMPOSITAE
Origin: Central Europe.
Flowering time: Summer.
Climatic zone: 4, 5, 6, 7, 8.
Dimensions: 6 inches (150 mm) high.
Description: This well-known alpine plant from the European mountains produces small, low tufts of gray, furry leaves. It has clustered heads of small flowers, each surrounded by a collar of grayish-white, felted bracts. It is grown more for its romantic associations than its beauty. It needs well-drained soil in a sunny spot and resents the winter wet, which may cause it to rot. It can be grown readily from seed.

Leontopodium alpinum

Macleaya cordata

Macleaya cordata syn. *Bocconia cordata*
PLUME POPPY ○ ◑

Family: PAPAVERACEAE
Origin: China, Japan.
Flowering time: Summer.
Climatic zone: 4, 5, 6, 7, 8, 9.
Dimensions: 7 feet (2 meters) high.
Description: This tall perennial combines handsome foliage with delightful, small white flowers that appear in masses of feathery plumes. The gray-green leaves, not unlike those of the culinary fig, are gray-white and downy underneath. At its best in reasonably moist soils, it is deciduous, self-supporting in spite of its height, and spreads by suckering roots. In hot areas, some shade is necessary. It should be planted in autumn or spring, divided in spring, or grown from root cuttings in late winter.

Minuartia verna syn. *Arenaria verna* var. *caespitosa*
IRISH MOSS, SPRING SANDWORT (U.K.)  

Family: CARYOPHYLLACEAE
Origin: European and Rocky Mountains.
Flowering time: Late spring.
Climatic zone: 4, 5, 6, 7, 8.
Dimensions: 2 inches (50 mm) high.
Description: This alpine perennial produces dense, mosslike clumps and, in sufficient sunshine, small starry flowers. It grows well in ordinary soil but with the addition of leaf mold it will thrive. It tolerates full shade and partial sun.
Varieties/cultivars: 'Aurea'.

Minuartia verna

Paeonia lactiflora 'Lady Alexander Duff'

Paeonia lactiflora and hybrids
CHINESE PEONY

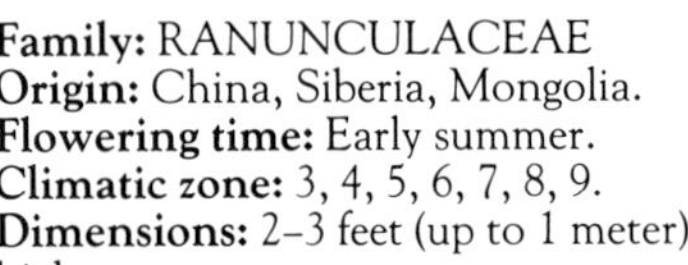

Family: RANUNCULACEAE
Origin: China, Siberia, Mongolia.
Flowering time: Early summer.
Climatic zone: 3, 4, 5, 6, 7, 8, 9.
Dimensions: 2–3 feet (up to 1 meter) high.
Description: This species, which has large, white, fragrant flowers, is the parent of many garden peony hybrids. These cultivars offer great variety in shape and color and are easy to grow given the right conditions. They need deep, fertile, neutral to slightly alkaline soil, well-drained, but moisture-retentive. A sunny position suits best, with an annual mulch over the crowns to keep them cool and moist during hot weather. They resent disturbance. Propagate by root division in autumn, but only when essential.
Other colors: Pink, crimson, scarlet.
Varieties/cultivars: 'Whitleyi Major', 'The Bride', 'Solange', 'Sarah Bernhardt', 'The Moor', 'Victoria', 'Duchesse de Nemours', 'Bunker Hill', 'Pink Delight', 'Lady Alexander Duff'.

Pachysandra terminalis
JAPANESE SPURGE

Family: BUXACEAE
Origin: China, Japan.
Flowering time: Spring.
Climatic zone: 4, 5, 6, 7, 8, 9.
Dimensions: Up to 12 inches (300 mm) high.
Description: This is a widely grown, evergreen groundcover with handsome, spoon-shaped leaves of a glossy dark green, and spikes of small, scented flowers. It does well in moist, well-drained soil in shaded areas. Too much exposure to the sun tends to turn the foliage yellow. It spreads quickly by underground stems and is vigorous and tough enough for planting in public places. Propagate by division in spring.
Varieties/cultivars: 'Variegata'.

Pachysandra terminalis

Phlox paniculata

Phlox paniculata and cultivars
PERENNIAL PHLOX, GARDEN PHLOX, BORDER PHLOX (U.K.)

Family: POLEMONIACEAE
Origin: Eastern North America.
Flowering time: Late summer.
Climatic zone: 4, 5, 6, 7, 8, 9.
Dimensions: 2–3 feet (up to 1 meter) high.
Description: The many cultivars of this species are easy to grow and provide masses of long-lasting color in border gardens. A sunny position is best, in a fairly rich soil with applications of liquid fertilizer during the growing period. The dense flower heads are fragrant and useful for cutting. The plants are prone to the fungal disease powdery mildew and to spider mites. Propagate it from root cuttings in winter or by division in spring.
Other colors: Pink, red, pale-blue, violet, salmon.
Varieties/cultivars: 'Mars', 'Purple King', 'Leo Schlageter', 'Mount Fuji', 'September Schnee', and others.

Physostegia virginiana 'Summer Snow'

Physostegia virginiana 'Summer Snow'
FALSE DRAGONHEAD, OBEDIENT PLANT

Family: LABIATAE
Origin: Cultivar.
Flowering time: Late summer–early autumn.
Climatic zone: 4, 5, 6, 7, 8, 9.
Dimensions: Up to 4 feet (over 1 meter) high.
Description: This is an easy-to-grow, herbaceous perennial with leafy, upright stems, and spikes of tubular white flowers. The individual flowers have hinged stalks and will remain in any position they are moved to, hence the name obedient plant. The leaves are long and tapered, and toothed around the margins. It thrives in any fertile soil, but the soil must not be allowed to dry out. Propagation is best by the division of established plants in spring.

Polygonatum x *hybridum*

Polygonatum x *hybridum*

SOLOMON'S-SEAL, DAVID'S HARP 

Family: LILIACEAE
Origin: Hybrid.
Flowering time: Late spring.
Climatic zone: 5, 6, 7, 8, 9.
Dimensions: 2 feet (600 mm) high.
Description: This plant likes being left undisturbed to allow the rhizomes to spread. A woodland plant, it looks particularly attractive when associated with ferns and hostas. The broad, green leaves are attractive and the dainty tubular flowers, carried one or two at a time, are fragrant. The leaves turn a buttery yellow in autumn. Any good garden soil will suit, provided it contains organic matter and is cool and moisture-retentive.
Varieties/cultivars: 'Flore Pleno'.

Potentilla tridentata

CINQUEFOIL, THREE-TOOTHED CINQUEFOIL ○ ◑

Family: ROSACEAE
Origin: North America.
Flowering time: Summer.
Climatic zone: 5, 6, 7, 8.
Dimensions: 6–10 inches (150–200 mm) high.
Description: This plant has trifoliate, evergreen, leathery leaflets, quite shiny on the upper surface. It is easy to grow in most types of soils provided they are well-drained, but it will not tolerate extra-dry conditions. Although not a particularly showy plant, it flowers for a prolonged period. It looks its best at the front of a border or in a rockery, and the stems can be cut back after flowering. Propagate it by seed or division in spring.

Potentilla tridentata

Rheum alexandrae

RHUBARB (not culinary) 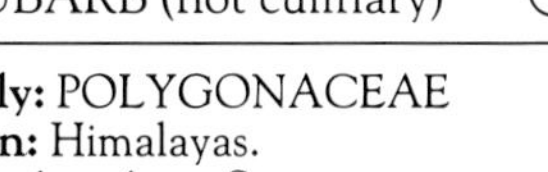

Family: POLYGONACEAE
Origin: Himalayas.
Flowering time: Summer.
Climatic zone: 5, 6, 7, 8, 9.
Dimensions: 3 feet (1 meter) high.
Description: This is a curious species that scarcely resembles a rhubarb as growing all the way down the stems are straw-colored bracts which sheath the flowers and look like tiles on a house. The bracts protect the flowers and ripening seeds. The leaves are oval, dark shining green, and prominently ribbed. A fine plant, it is difficult to cultivate unless the climate is moist and cool. Propagation is by division, or by sowing seeds in spring.

Rheum alexandrae

Rodgersia podophylla

Rodgersia podophylla

BRONZE LEAF, RODGERS' FLOWER  

Family: SAXIFRAGACEAE
Origin: China, Japan.
Flowering time: Summer.
Climatic zone: 5, 6, 7, 8, 9.
Dimensions: 3–4 feet (approx. 1 meter) high.
Description: This plant, with its superb ornamental foliage, is very suitable for moist garden situations or beside water. The large, divided leaves are bronze when young, then turn green, and finally take on dark coppery tones as they mature in summer. The fluffy flowers are carried on arching stems well above the foliage. Strong winds can damage the foliage, so the plant should be given a sheltered position where it will form large colonies in time.

Romneya coulteri

Saxifraga stolonifera

Romneya coulteri

CALIFORNIA TREE POPPY, MATILIJA POPPY ○

Family: PAPAVERACEAE
Origin: California.
Flowering time: Summer–autumn.
Climatic zone: 8, 9, 10.
Dimensions: Up to 8 feet (over 2 meters) high.
Description: Although a somewhat difficult plant to establish as it resents any root disturbance, the flowers make it well worth the effort. These are silky and crinkled, up to 6 inches (150 mm) wide, and sweetly fragrant. They contrast well with the green-gray, deeply divided foliage. The plant prefers a warm and well-drained position in normal garden soil, even slightly alkaline. It can be propagated by root cuttings, but disturbing the roots in this way can unfortunately result in the death of the parent plant.

Saxifraga stolonifera syn. *S. sarmentosa*

STRAWBERRY GERANIUM (U.K.), MOTHER OF THOUSANDS, CREEPING SAILOR ◑ ●

Family: SAXIFRAGACEAE
Origin: Eastern Asia.
Flowering time: Summer.
Climatic zone: 8, 9, 10.
Dimensions: Up to 18 inches (450 mm) high.
Description: This plant has long, prostrate stems which send out roots and then develop rosettes of round and toothed, glossy leaves. These are veined, marbled, and colored a strawberry pink underneath. Delicate, small, white flowers are borne on loose panicles, standing above the foliage. It makes a useful and most decorative basket or pot plant, as well as a good groundcover provided it is given room to spread in a warm, sheltered spot. It can be propagated from seed in spring or by division in summer.
Varieties/cultivars: 'Tricolor'.

Shortia galacifolia

OCONEE-BELLS ◑ ●

Family: DIAPENSIACEAE
Origin: Eastern North America.
Flowering time: Summer.
Climatic zone: 4, 5, 6, 7, 8, 9.
Dimensions: Up to 6 inches (150 mm) high.
Description: The small, delicate, white blooms of oconee-bells resemble frilled bells. They emerge from their low foliage on slender, leafless stalks and have a nodding habit. The plant is not an easy one to grow, and once established should not be moved. It is an excellent choice for a rock garden. Grow it in cool, moist, well-drained, acid soil enriched with humus. Use peat moss as humus in clay-loam soils to make them acid. Propagate by division in early spring.

Smilacina racemosa

FALSE SPIKENARD, FALSE SOLOMON'S SEAL ◑ ●

Family: LILIACEAE
Origin: North America.
Flowering time: Late spring.
Climatic zone: 3, 4, 5, 6, 7, 8, 9.

Smilacina racemosa

Shortia galacifolia

Dimensions: Up to 3 feet (1 meter) high.
Description: This plant has erect to ascending stems of fresh green leaves and spikes of fluffy, creamy-white flowers, deliciously lemon-scented. As the flowers age they become tinged with pink and can be followed by red berries. The plant makes a good combination with ferns and primulas. It prefers shaded conditions in a lime-free soil and, with consistent moisture, is not difficult to grow. Propagate it by division in spring.

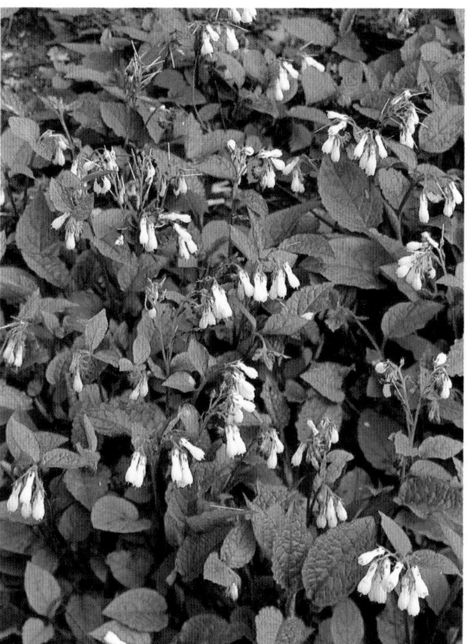

Symphytum grandiflorum

Symphytum grandiflorum
GROUND-COVER COMFREY, CREEPING COMFREY (U.K.)

Family: BORAGINACEAE
Origin: Caucasus.
Flowering time: Spring.
Climatic zone: 5, 6, 7, 8, 9.
Dimensions: Up to 12 inches (300 mm) high.
Description: This perennial herb makes an excellent groundcover, spreading by means of underground stems. The dark-green leaves are broad and hairy, and make a close carpet on the soil. The buds arise on hooked stems and open to tubular, cream flowers. The plant prefers moist, but not boggy, soil, and is easy to grow. Propagation is usually by division in spring or autumn.
Varieties/cultivars: 'Variegatum'.

Trillium grandiflorum

Trillium grandiflorum
WAKE ROBIN, SNOW TRILLIUM, TRINITY FLOWER

Other common names: WOOD LILY (U.K.)
Family: LILIACEAE
Origin: Eastern North America.
Flowering time: Spring–early summer.
Climatic zone: 5, 6, 7, 8, 9.
Dimensions: 12–18 inches (300–450 mm) high.
Description: This woodland plant has undeniable appeal, but is often difficult to grow among other plants in a border. Each erect stem bears three leaves, three calyx lobes, and three petals — hence the names "trillium" and "trinity". The foliage dies down in summer and the plant can be lifted and divided then. It likes moist but well-drained soil, enriched with plenty of leaf mold, which must never be allowed to dry out.
Other colors: Pink.
Varieties/cultivars: 'Roseum'.

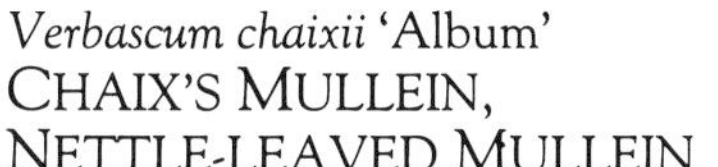

Verbascum chaixii 'Album'
CHAIX'S MULLEIN, NETTLE-LEAVED MULLEIN

Family: SCROPHULARIACEAE
Origin: Southern and central Europe.
Flowering time: Summer.
Climatic zone: 5, 6, 7, 8, 9.
Dimensions: 3 feet (1 meter) high.
Description: This variety has delightful, pure white flowers with rose-colored stamens, borne on showy spikes which rise from large basal leaves which are gray and hairy and often up to 12 inches (300 mm) long. An easy plant to grow, it likes a light, sandy, well-drained soil. It looks well combined with other plants in a border or wild garden, and is attractive with campanulas and as a contrast to rounded gray shrubs. It can be propagated by seed in spring.

Verbascum chaixii 'Album'

Yucca filamentosa

Yucca filamentosa
ADAM'S-NEEDLE

Family: AGAVACEAE
Origin: Southeastern United States.
Flowering time: Late summer.
Climatic zone: 5, 6, 7, 8, 9.
Dimensions: 5 feet (over 1 meter) high.
Description: The grayish-green leaves of this semidesert plant are almost bayonet-like and have thread-like hairs along their margin — representing the needle and thread. The tall, beautiful flower spikes rising from these basal leaves are deliciously fragrant in the evening. The sharp outlines of this plant make it a useful specimen when landscaping. It does best in well-drained, sandy loam and can be propagated by seeds or offsets.
Varieties/cultivars: 'Variegata', 'Golden Sword'.

Abeliophyllum distichum

Adenandra uniflora

Abeliophyllum distichum
KOREAN ABELIALEAF, WHITE FORSYTHIA ○

Family: OLEACEAE
Origin: Korea.
Flowering time: Spring.
Climatic zone: 5, 6, 7, 8, 9.
Dimensions: 3–5 feet (approx. 1–2 meters) high.
Description: Korean abelialeaf is a very pretty, slow-growing, deciduous shrub with arching stems. The white, bell-like flowers appear in early spring, covering leafless stems. Plant it in a shrub border or use it at the back of a perennial garden. It is easy to grow in most garden soils. Pruning should be carried out as soon as the flowers have finished, as flowers appear on wood from the previous year. New growth can be stimulated by removing old wood to the ground.

Adenandra uniflora
ADENANDRA, ENAMEL FLOWER ○ ◑

Family: RUTACEAE
Origin: South Africa.
Flowering time: Spring–summer.
Climatic zone: 8, 9, 10.
Dimensions: 3 feet (1 meter) high.
Description: This is a bushy, evergreen shrub with small, tapering leaves and numerous white flowers which have a rose-pink rib down the center of each petal and purplish-brown anthers. Adenandra looks pretty when grown in the front of a shrub border. It is a hardy shrub which, because of its naturally compact shape, does not require pruning. It will tolerate most garden soils. In spring apply a handful of complete plant food around the base of the plant.

Aesculus parviflora
DWARF HORSE CHESTNUT (U.S.A.), BOTTLEBRUSH BUCKEYE (U.K.) ○ ◑

Family: HIPPOCASTANACEAE
Origin: Southeastern United States.
Flowering time: Summer.
Climatic zone: 4, 5, 6, 7, 8, 9.
Dimensions: 8–12 feet (2–4 meters) high.

Aesculus parviflora

Description: Bottlebrush buckeye is a spreading, suckering, free-flowering, deciduous shrub. The white flowers have very showy, dark-pink anthers and the leaves color attractively during autumn. Plant it as a specimen plant or in a shrub border, giving it plenty of room so that its spreading shape can be appreciated. It is not suitable for a small garden as suckers can spread widely creating thickets up to 20 feet (6 meters) across. It will thrive in almost any garden soil. A mulch of manure or compost around the roots in spring will provide food and keep the roots moist.

Arctostaphylos uva-ursi

Arctostaphylos uva-ursi
BEARBERRY, RED BEARBERRY, KINNIKINNICK (U.S.A.) ○

Family: ERICACEAE
Origin: North America, Europe, Asia, circumpolar.
Flowering time: Spring.
Climatic zone: 2, 3, 4, 5, 6, 7, 8, 9.
Dimensions: Up to 6 inches (150 mm) high.
Description: Bearberry is an interesting, creeping, mountain or cold climate shrub. Its white, bell-shaped flowers are tinged with pink, and are followed by red berries. The prostrate stems are often up to 7 feet (2 meters) long. Because of its dense foliage it makes a good groundcover for large banks. Bearberry needs a well-drained, acid soil and, because it is salt-tolerant, will grow in sandy soils near the sea.

Ardisia crispa

Aronia arbutifolia

Ardisia crispa syn. *A. crenulata, A. crenata*
CORALBERRY, SPICEBERRY, CORAL ARDISIA ◑ ●

Family: MYRSINIACEAE
Origin: Southeastern Asia.
Flowering time: Summer.
Climatic zone: 9, 10.
Dimensions: 3 feet (1 meter) high.
Description: This is a popular small shrub for shady situations and for use as an indoor plant. The fragrant, star-shaped, white flowers appear in terminal clusters and are followed by a heavy crop of scarlet berries, which remain on the plant throughout autumn and winter. The glossy, dark-green leaves have wavy margins. Coralberry requires a hot climate and a well-drained soil. In colder climates, it thrives as an indoor pot plant.

Aronia arbutifolia
RED CHOKEBERRY ○

Family: ROSACEAE
Origin: Eastern North America.
Flowering time: Spring–summer.
Climatic zone: 5, 6, 7, 8.
Dimensions: 6–8 feet (2–3 meters) high.
Description: This deciduous shrub has white flowers, tinted with pink, which are followed in autumn by masses of small, round berries that remain on the plant for a long period. The long, glossy green leaves with their gray undersides turn red in autumn. The plant will thrive in normal to acid soil. It increases freely by suckers which can easily be divided.
Varieties/cultivars: 'Erecta'.

Aronia melanocarpa
BLACK CHOKEBERRY ○

Family: ROSACEAE
Origin: Eastern North America.
Flowering time: Spring.
Climatic zone: 5, 6, 7, 8, 9.
Dimensions: 2–3 feet (up to 1 meter) high.
Description: Black chokeberry is a low-growing shrub which is covered in white flowers during spring. These are followed by lustrous, deep purple-black berries. It looks most striking at the back of a herbaceous border or planted with low-growing asters. Black chokeberry requires a free-draining soil.

Aronia melanocarpa

Azalea indica 'Alba Magna'

Azalea indica 'Alba Magna'

INDIAN AZALEA, EVERGREEN AZALEA ○ ◑

Family: ERICACEAE
Origin: Cultivar.
Flowering time: Spring.
Climatic zone: 6, 7, 8, 9.
Dimensions: 6 feet (2 meters) high.
Description: A beautiful evergreen shrub, Indian azalea is covered in a profusion of large, white flowers during spring. It requires a well-drained, acid soil which should be enriched with leaf mold, compost, or peat before planting. Azaleas have a very shallow root system, which should not be allowed to dry out during summer. Drying out can be prevented by mulching the root area.

Bouvardia longiflora

WHITE BOUVARDIA ○

Family: RUBIACEAE
Origin: Mexico.
Flowering time: Summer–autumn.

Bouvardia longiflora

Climatic zone: 9, 10.
Dimensions: 3–5 feet (approx. 1–2 meters) high.
Description: This pretty shrub has terminal heads of long, fragrant, white, jasmine-like flowers, and glossy green leaves. Plant white bouvardia near a doorway, window, or garden seat where the perfume can be appreciated. It will grow in any well-drained soil and should be pruned lightly after flowering has finished. Apply a handful of complete plant food in early spring.
Varieties/cultivars: There are numerous varieties throughout the world.

Buddleia davidii 'White Bouquet'

BUTTERFLY BUSH ○ ◑

Family: LOGANIACEAE
Origin: Cultivar.
Flowering time: Summer–autumn.
Climatic zone: 5, 6, 7, 8, 9.
Dimensions: 6–10 feet (2–3 meters) high.
Description: The fragrant, white flowers of this shrub have yellow eyes and are borne in large clusters which attract butterflies, hence the common name. Butterfly bush is a strong shrub with long, slender, dark-green leaves which are felted underneath. It grows well near the sea. A rapid grower, especially in sheltered sites, it likes good drainage. A yearly prune during winter produces a nicely shaped bush.

Buddleia davidii 'White Bouquet'

Calliandra portoricensis

WHITE TASSEL FLOWER, SNOWFLAKE ACACIA, WHITE POWDER PUFF ○

Family: LEGUMINOSAE
Origin: Southern Mexico–Panama, West Indes.
Flowering time: Spring–autumn.
Climatic zone: 9, 10.
Dimensions: 8–12 feet (approx. 2–4 meters) high.
Description: Admired for its fern-like foliage and long flowering period, this handsome shrub produces fragrant, fluffy white flowers that resemble flakes of snow. Unless grown where there are

Calliandra portoricensis

hot, dry summers, it tends to produce an abundance of foliage and odd-shaped flowers. Plant it in well-drained soil that has been enriched with leaf mold or compost. An occasional spring pruning will keep the shrub in good shape.

Calocephalus brownii

Calocephalus brownii
CUSHION BUSH, SKELETON PLANT ○

Family: COMPOSITAE
Origin: Australia.
Flowering time: Summer.
Climatic zone: 9, 10.
Dimensions: Up to 3 feet (1 meter) high.
Description: Cushion bush is a round, silvery, mound-like shrub with silvery-white, multi-branched stems and minute leaves which clasp the stem. The small, greenish-yellow flowers are insignificant compared with the foliage. Cushion bush grows in any soil and suits rockeries where its silvery appearance contrasts with other green shrubs. Alternatively, it is an ideal plant for a gray or white garden scheme. It is often found growing naturally on sandy and rocky seashores. Prune it after flowering has finished to maintain its bushy habit.

Carissa grandiflora
NATAL PLUM, AMATUNGULA (U.S.A.) ○

Family: APOCYNACEAE
Origin: South Africa.
Flowering time: Throughout the year.
Climatic zone: 9, 10.
Dimensions: Up to 15 feet (5 meters) high.
Description: A bushy shrub covered in long spines, natal plum is often used for

Carissa grandiflora

hedging. It has oval leaves and pretty, fragrant, white flowers which are 2 inches (50 mm) wide. The flowers are followed by egg-shaped berries, tasting similar to cranberries, which can be eaten fresh or made into a sauce. Natal plum is easy to grow and will thrive if given ample amounts of summer water. Mulching around its roots will help to keep the soil moist.

Carpenteria californica
CALIFORNIAN MOCK ORANGE ○

Family: PHILADELPHACEAE
Origin: California.
Flowering time: Summer.
Climatic zone: 8, 9, 10.
Dimensions: 6–8 feet (2–3 meters) high.
Description: A beautiful, bushy

Carpenteria californica

evergreen, this shrub has long, smooth, narrow leaves which are bright green above and rather downy underneath. The fragrant flowers with their creamy-white central stamens are about 2½ inches (62 mm) across and borne in terminal clusters. Californian mock orange requires a moist but well-drained soil, otherwise the foliage will burn during summer. Add plenty of compost or manure to the soil and keep it mulched with this.
Varieties/cultivars: 'Ladham's Variety'.

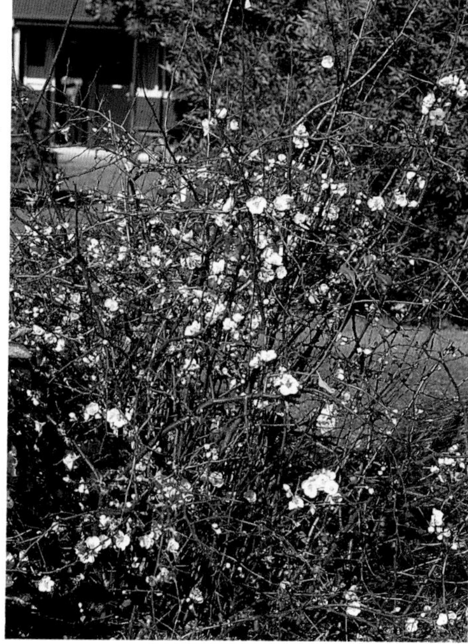

Chaenomeles speciosa 'Nivalis'

Chaenomeles speciosa 'Nivalis'
FLOWERING QUINCE, JAPONICA, JAPANESE QUINCE (U.K.) ○ ◑

Family: ROSACEAE
Origin: China.
Flowering time: Spring.
Climatic zone: 5, 6, 7, 8, 9.
Dimensions: 6–10 feet (2–3 meters) high.
Description: This deciduous shrub has spiny, smooth branches and oval leaves which may turn shades of red, orange, or yellow during autumn. 'Nivalis' is valued for its large, pure-white flowers which appear before the leaves in early spring. It makes a delightful feature plant or can be used with evergreen shrubs in a border. Flowering quince is easy to grow in any garden soil. Apply a handful of complete plant food in late winter to ensure a good flower display.

Chamelaucium uncinatum
GERALDTON WAXFLOWER ○

Family: MYRTACEAE
Origin: Western Australia.
Flowering time: Late spring–summer.
Climatic zone: 9, 10.
Dimensions: 9 feet (3 meters) high.
Description: Geraldton waxflower is a spreading, open shrub with fine foliage. The terminal sprays of dainty, waxy-textured flowers are white but can vary in color to pink or purple. The flowers are ideal for indoor decoration as they will last for a long time when picked. The shrub requires a sandy soil that contains some lime. It resents root disturbance so care should be taken not to cultivate in close proximity to it.
Other colors: Dark plum.
Varieties/cultivars: 'University'.

Chamelaucium uncinatum

Choisya ternata
MEXICAN ORANGE BLOSSOM ○ ◑

Family: RUTACEAE
Origin: Mexico.
Flowering time: Spring.
Climatic zone: 7, 8, 9, 10.
Dimensions: 6–8 feet (2–3 meters) high.
Description: A compact, evergreen shrub, the dark-green, glossy leaves of Mexican orange blossom make a striking contrast with the abundant clusters of crisp, white, fragrant flowers. The leaves have an interesting aroma when crushed. Plant it near a door or window so that the delightful perfume can be appreciated. It is an adaptable shrub, growing just as well in full sun as in partial shade. It likes a well-drained, humus-rich soil, but can be damaged by prolonged frosty winters.

Choisya ternata

Cistus ladanifer
CRIMSON SPOT ROCK ROSE, GUM CISTUS, CRIMSON SPOT SUNROSE (U.K.) ○

Other common names: GUM SUNROSE (U.K.)
Family: CISTACEAE
Origin: Southwestern Europe.
Flowering time: Summer.
Climatic zone: 7, 8, 9.
Dimensions: Up to 6 feet (2 meters) high.
Description: This erect species has lance-shaped leaves, and interesting, fragrant, white flowers with a yellow center and a purple blotch on each petal. The flowers are at least 3½ inches (85 mm) across. Crimson spot rock rose is a very hardy plant that will withstand salt winds and drought, although it may be killed by severe winters. It will thrive if given a well-drained, shady soil and a very hot, sunny position in the garden. Plant it alone, as a feature plant, or in a herbaceous garden.
Other colors: Pure white.
Varieties/cultivars: 'Albiflorus', 'Maculatus'.

Cistus salviifolius
ROCK ROSE, SAGE-LEAVED SUNROSE (U.K.) ○

Family: CISTACEAE
Origin: Southern Europe.
Flowering time: Summer.
Climatic zone: 7, 8, 9.
Dimensions: 3 feet (1 meter) high.
Description: This pretty, low-growing shrub, with its sage-like, grayish-green leaves, has white flowers with a yellow center. Plant it in a large rockery or at the front of a shrub border. It looks

Cistus salviifolius

Cistus ladanifer

interesting when planted either with dark-green shrubs or as part of a white and gray garden theme. Rock rose will thrive if given a well-drained, sandy soil and full sun in the hottest part of the garden. It can be killed by severe winters.
Varieties/cultivars: 'Prostratus'.

Clerodendrum trichotomum

Clerodendrum trichotomum
HARLEQUIN GLORY BOWER 

Family: VERBENACEAE
Origin: China, Japan.
Flowering time: Summer–autumn.
Climatic zone: 5, 6, 7, 8, 9.
Dimensions: 8–12 feet (3–4 meters) high.
Description: Throughout summer, this attractive shrub is covered in fragrant, white flowers which are enclosed in maroon calyces. The flowers are followed by bright-blue berries still surrounded by the colorful calyces, hanging among the large leaves in their autumn tonings. It makes an interesting feature shrub, looking as wonderful when in flower as when covered with berries. Plant it in well-drained soil that has been previously enriched with manure or compost.

Clethra alnifolia
SWEET PEPPERBUSH, SUMMER SWEET CLETHRA, SPIKED ALDER (U.S.A.) ○ ◑

Family: CLETHRACEAE
Origin: Eastern United States.
Flowering time: Summer.
Climatic zone: 4, 5, 6, 7, 8, 9.
Dimensions: 6–9 feet (2–3 meters) high.
Description: This hardy, deciduous shrub has long leaves and is covered in a profusion of very fragrant, terminal spikes of white flowers in summer. It should be planted close to a door or window so that the delicious perfume can be appreciated. It is very easy to grow and will thrive in a moist, neutral to acid soil. Keep the soil around the base of the plant mulched with manure or compost. This will not only feed the shrub, but keep the soil moist.
Other colors: Pink.
Varieties/cultivars: 'Pink Spires', 'Rosea', 'Paniculata'.

Clethra alnifolia

Cleyera japonica

Cleyera japonica
SASAKI ○

Family: THEACEAE
Origin: Japan, China, Korea, Taiwan.
Flowering time: Spring.
Climatic zone: 8, 9.
Dimensions: 6–10 feet (2–3 meters) high.
Description: This slow-growing shrub has a distinctive growth habit. The branches spread rigidly and are very densely covered in dark-green, shining leaves. In spring, it can be covered in a profusion of small, white flowers. Some of the leaves may turn red in winter, even though it is an evergreen. It likes sandy loam and responds to regular fertilizing in spring.

Convolvulus cneorum
SILVERBUSH ○

Family: CONVOLVULACEAE
Origin: Southeastern Europe.
Flowering time: Spring–summer.
Climatic zone: 7, 8, 9, 10.
Dimensions: Up to 3 feet (1 meter) high.
Description: The white flowers of this compact, little evergreen shrub look at first like partly opened umbrellas, but when fully open are about 2 inches (50 mm) across. The slender, silvery-gray foliage is covered in silky hairs. Silverbush makes a good non-invasive shrub in large rock gardens or can be included in a herbaceous border. It will thrive in a sunny position in sandy, well-drained soil, but may be killed by severe winters. Fertilize it with a handful of complete plant food in early spring.

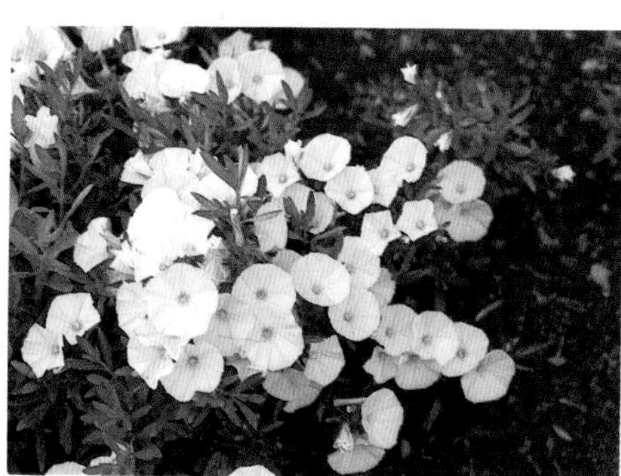

Convolvulus cneorum

Cornus alba

Cornus sanguinea

Cornus alba
RED-BARKED DOGWOOD, TARTARIAN DOGWOOD ○ ◑

Family: CORNACEAE
Origin: Eastern Asia.
Flowering time: Early summer.
Climatic zone: 3, 4, 5, 6, 7, 8, 9.
Dimensions: 6–10 feet (2–3 meters) high.
Description: The white flowers of tartarian dogwood appear in profusion during early summer. An added feature is the deep-red, twiggy branches which add some color to the garden during the winter months. The oval leaves may color well in autumn. There are many different varieties of this plant, the majority of them having variegated leaves. Tartarian dogwood will grow well in either wet or dry soil.
Varieties/cultivars: There are numerous cultivars throughout the world. Flower color is generally white, but the color of the branches ranges from black-purple to bronze.

Cornus sanguinea
COMMON DOGWOOD, BLOOD-TWIG DOGWOOD ○ ◑

Family: CORNACEAE
Origin: Europe, southwestern Asia.
Flowering time: Summer.
Climatic zone: 4, 5, 6, 7, 8, 9.
Dimensions: 4–6 feet (1–2 meters) high.
Description: Grown throughout England as a hedgerow plant, this attractive, hardy shrub has dark-reddish stems and oval leaves that turn a rich purple in autumn. The off-white, scented flowers are followed in autumn by large clusters of black fruits. Plant it in a shrub border or with evergreen plants in an informal hedge. Prune it every second spring to encourage new shoots.

Cornus stolonifera syn. *C. sericea*
RED OSIER, DOGWOOD ○ ◑

Family: CORNACEAE
Origin: North America.
Flowering time: Spring.
Climatic zone: 3, 4, 5, 6, 7, 8, 9.
Dimensions: 6 feet (2 meters) high.
Description: This is a rampant, suckering, hardy shrub which forms a dense thicket of purplish-red, upright branches. The off-white flowers are followed by white berries. It thrives in wet soil and is often used for hedges, especially on large estates. It can be pruned heavily in late winter if required. Mulch around the base of the plant with manure, compost, or grass clippings to keep the soil moist.
Varieties/cultivars: 'Flaviramea'.

Cornus stolonifera

Cornus stolonifera 'Flaviramea'

Cornus stolonifera 'Flaviramea' syn. *C. sericea* 'Flaviramea'
YELLOWTWIG, DOGWOOD ○ ◑

Family: CORNACEAE
Origin: Cultivar.
Flowering time: Spring.
Climatic zone: 3, 4, 5, 6, 7, 8, 9.
Dimensions: 4–6 feet (1–2 meters) high.
Description: The white flowers of this low, spreading, deciduous shrub are produced in clusters and are followed by small, round, black berries. It has shining, bright greenish-yellow bark and looks particularly attractive when planted with the red-stemmed species, *C. sanguinea*. This hardy shrub will thrive in moist or wet conditions. If planted in ordinary garden soil, make sure the area around the base of the plant is continually mulched to keep the moisture in the soil, and supply ample water in the summer.

Correa alba
WHITE CORREA, AUSTRALIAN FUCHSIA ○ ◑

Family: RUTACEAE
Origin: Eastern Australia, Tasmania.
Flowering time: Winter.

Correa alba

Climatic zone: 9, 10.
Dimensions: 5 feet (approx. 2 meters) high.
Description: This rounded shrub has circular leaves with a waxy bloom. The white flowers are valued for providing winter color when, in most places, other flowers are scarce. Although this is the main flowering period there are usually some flowers on the plant throughout the year. They attract nectar-feeding birds. It is very salt-resistant and therefore suitable for seaside planting. The soil should be well drained and fed with an organic fertilizer in early spring.

Cyrilla racemiflora
LEATHERWOOD, SWAMP CYRILLA ○

Family: CYRILLACEAE
Origin: Southeastern United States, West Indies, eastern South America.
Flowering time: Summer.
Climatic zone: 6, 7, 8, 9, 10.
Dimensions: 10–15 feet (3–5 meters) high.
Description: The white flowers of this pretty shrub are borne in whorls of slender racemes at the base of the current year's shoots. The lance-shaped leaves may turn crimson in autumn. The shrub looks most attractive in a woodland garden. It requires an acid soil. Mulching around the base with oak leaves or peat will keep the soil acidic. It is easily propagated from cuttings taken in summer, or by seed.

Cyrilla racemiflora

Cytisus x *kewensis*
KEW BROOM ○

Family: LEGUMINOSAE
Origin: Hybrid.
Flowering time: Early summer.
Climatic zone: 6, 7, 8, 9.
Dimensions: 12 inches (300 mm) high.
Description: This is a deciduous, semiprostrate, mat-forming hybrid which was raised at Kew Gardens in England. The small trifoliate leaves are slightly hairy on the edges and underneath. The creamy-white flowers are produced in abundance, making a most magnificent display. Plant it in large rockeries, on banks, or at the front of shrub borders. Kew broom likes a free-draining soil.

Cytisus x *kewensis*

Cytisus 'Snow Queen'

Cytisus 'Snow Queen'
BROOM, WHITE BROOM ○

Family: LEGUMINOSAE
Origin: Cultivar.
Flowering time: Spring.
Climatic zone: 6, 7, 8, 9.
Dimensions: 3–4 feet (approx. 1 meter) high.
Description: White broom looks magnificent when covered in its masses of white flowers in spring. These look impressive especially if near plants with dark-green foliage. Plant it at the front of a shrub border, or at the back of a herbaceous border. The main requirement of white broom is well-drained soil.

Cytisus x *praecox*
WARMINSTER BROOM ○

Family: LEGUMINOSAE
Origin: Hybrid.
Flowering time: Early summer.
Climatic zone: 6, 7, 8, 9.
Dimensions: 3–4 feet (approx. 1 meter) high.
Description: This extremely pretty plant has a dainty, loose habit. When in bloom it becomes a tumbling mass of creamy white as the long, thin stems hang down with the sheer weight of the flowers. It makes a delightful feature plant and fits in well with herbaceous plants in a border. Plant it in well-drained soil and fertilize it in spring with a handful of complete plant food.
Other colors: Golden yellow.
Varieties/cultivars: 'Alba', 'Allgold', 'Gold Spear', 'Hollandia'.

Cytisus x *praecox*

Daphne odora 'Alba'
FRAGRANT DAPHNE, WINTER DAPHNE ○ ◑

Family: THYMELAEACEAE
Origin: Cultivar.
Flowering time: Winter–spring.
Climatic zone: 7, 8, 9.
Dimensions: 3 feet (1 meter) high.
Description: An attractive shrub, fragrant daphne has a spreading habit and smooth, showy, deep-green leaves. The extremely fragrant flowers are in tight clusters, each composed of thirty to forty flowers. The shrub requires a cool soil which must be crumbly and well-drained. Before planting, dig in leaf mold or peat. Do not use chemical fertilizers. A mulch of leaf mold annually will suffice to feed the plant and will not harm it.

Daphne x *burkwoodii* 'Albert Burkwood'
BURKWOOD DAPHNE ○ 

Family: THYMELAEACEAE
Origin: Hybrid.
Flowering time: Summer.
Climatic zone: 5, 6, 7, 8, 9.
Dimensions: Up to 3 feet (1 meter) high.
Description: This is a useful, low-growing, semi-evergreen shrub for the front border. In summer the stem tips are crowned with clusters of fragrant white flowers which age to pink. Burkwood daphne thrives in a neutral to limy soil. Do not use chemical fertilizer as, like other daphnes, it is easily killed with such kindness. A mulch of leaf mold or manure applied around the plant in spring is all that is required.

Daphne odora 'Alba'

Daphne x *burkwoodii* 'Albert Burkwood'

Datura suaveolens

Datura suaveolens syn. *Brugmansia suaveolens*
ANGEL'S-TRUMPET ○ ◑

Family: SOLANACEAE
Origin: Mexico.
Flowering time: Summer.
Climatic zone: 9, 10.
Dimensions: 6–10 feet (2–3 meters) high.
Description: This large shrub has flannel-like leaves and bears large, hanging, trumpet-shaped, fragrant flowers during summer. It makes an eye-catching specimen shrub. Quick-growing, it flourishes in warm temperate to tropical climates, but withstands cold if it is cut back to near ground level during winter. In spring, new shoots will burst forth and flower during the first season. Angel's-trumpet is often grown in conservatories in cold climates.

Deutzia gracilis

Deutzia gracilis
SLENDER DEUTZIA ○

Family: PHILADELPHACEAE
Origin: Japan.
Flowering time: Early summer.
Climatic zone: 4, 5, 6, 7, 8, 9.
Dimensions: Up to 4 feet (approx. 1 meter) high.
Description: This elegant, deciduous shrub maintains a bushy form and has yellow-gray bark on its hollow stems. It is excellent in cool-climate gardens, where its many-flowered heads of pure-white flowers are a delight in the summer. Prune it immediately after it has finished flowering.

Deutzia scabra

Deutzia scabra
FUZZY DEUTZIA ○

Family: PHILADELPHACEAE
Origin: Japan, China.
Flowering time: Early summer.
Climatic zone: 5, 6, 7, 8, 9.
Dimensions: Up to 8 feet (approx. 3 meters) high.
Description: This widely cultivated deciduous shrub has produced some well-known cultivars including those with double flowers. The species produces abundant spikes, up to 5 inches (125 mm) long, of star-shaped flowers, which may show a faint flush of pink on the outside of the petals. Arising from the base, the branches are erect, arching canes, with the upper twigs coppery-green and furry and the older wood peeling in small shreds. The shrub should be pruned immediately after flowering by removing the oldest canes at the base.
Varieties/cultivars: 'Candidissima', 'Pride of Rochester'.

Deutzia x *lemoinei*
LEMOINE DEUTZIA ○

Family: PHILADELPHACEAE
Origin: Hybrid.
Flowering time: Early summer.
Climatic zone: 4, 5, 6, 7, 8, 9.
Dimensions: Up to 7 feet (2 meters) high.
Description: This hybrid from *D. gracilis* and *D. parviflora* was produced by Victor Lemoine of Nancy in France. A many-branched, deciduous shrub, it grows erect and has narrow leaves, up to 4 inches (100 mm) long, which are sharply toothed. The pure-white flowers are very numerous and, though individually only ¾ inch (18 mm) wide, they appear in spikes up to 4 inches (100 mm) long. Annual pruning after flowering is advisable to encourage strong growth.

Deutzia x *lemoinei*

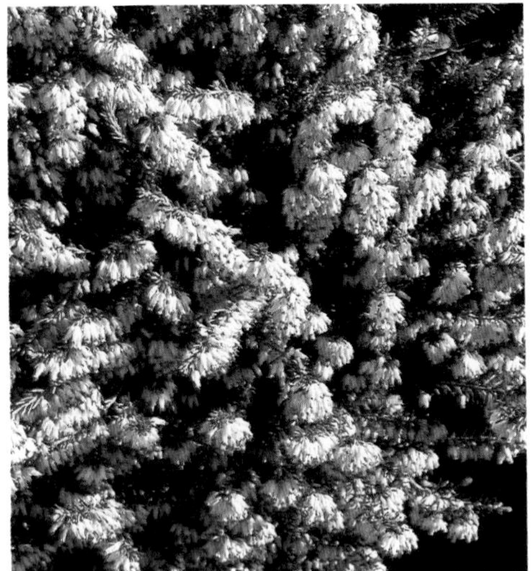
Erica carnea 'Springwood White'

Erica carnea 'Springwood White'
WINTER HEATH ○

Family: ERICACEAE
Origin: Cultivar.
Flowering time: Midwinter–early spring.
Climatic zone: 5, 6, 7.
Dimensions: Up to 1 foot (300 mm) high.
Description: Considered the finest white cultivar of Erica, this is a low, spreading shrub with masses of showy, urn-shaped flowers. Hardy and easy to cultivate, plant it in an open, sunny position in moderately rich, well-drained soil that is slightly acidic. It is ideal for grouping with dwarf rhododendrons and conifers which like the same growing conditions. Prune back immediately after flowering to maintain a neat shape.

Escallonia bifida syn. *E. montevidensis*
ESCALLONIA ○

Family: ESCALLONIACEAE
Origin: Uruguay, southern Brazil.
Flowering time: Summer–mid-autumn.
Climatic zone: 8, 9.
Dimensions: 13 feet (4 meters) high.
Description: The most beautiful of the white-flowered escallonias is this handsome evergreen shrub with a loose, open habit. It sometimes attains a tree-like form. The sweetly honey-scented flowers are star-shaped, ½ inch (12 mm) wide, and attached to the stem by a bell-shaped receptacle. Its shoots are hairless but sometimes slightly sticky, and its elliptic or spatula-shaped leaves, up to 3 inches (75 mm) long, are sprinkled on their undersides with small resinous dots. Easy to cultivate, this shrub flowers generously over a long period and is suitable for seaside conditions. In colder climates, the protection of a wall is necessary as the shrub may be killed by severe winters.

Escallonia bifida

Exochorda racemosa
PEARLBUSH ○

Family: ROSACEAE
Origin: China.
Flowering time: Spring.
Climatic zone: 5, 6, 7, 8, 9.
Dimensions: Up to 15 feet (5 meters) high.
Description: This is a deciduous shrub of considerable beauty, much prized for its showy display of paper-white flowers, which coincides with lilac flowering time. Its buds in racemes are said to look like a string of pearls. The five petals of the open flowers spread to 1½ inches (35 mm) wide with many stamens arranged around the rim of the green center. Grown in slightly acid soil, the shrub needs to have the oldest branches pruned back to the base in late winter.

Exochorda racemosa

Fothergilla gardenii

Fothergilla gardenii
DWARF FOTHERGILLA ○

Family: HAMAMELIDACEAE
Origin: Southeastern United States.
Flowering time: Spring.
Climatic zone: 5, 6, 7, 8, 9.
Dimensions: 3 feet (1 meter) high.
Description: An attractive and unusual spring-bloomer, this small, deciduous shrub deserves greater popularity. The masses of flower spikes are without petals and appear as erect dish-mop heads of fragrant, white stamens measuring 1 inch (25 mm) long. These

bloom before the leaves unfold. In autumn, the leaves are a brilliant display of orange-crimson color. Plant the bush among other favorites in the shrub garden, preferably with an evergreen as a background so that the fluffy flower heads can be seen at their best.

Fothergilla major

Fothergilla major syn. *F. monticola*
WITCH ELDER, FOTHERGILLA, MOUNTAIN SNOW ○

Family: HAMAMELIDACEAE
Origin: Southeastern United States.
Flowering time: Spring.
Climatic zone: 5, 6, 7, 8, 9.
Dimensions: 6 feet (2 meters) high.
Description: The genus name honors John Fothergill, an eighteenth-century English physician and friend of Benjamin Franklin, who introduced many American plants into cultivation in England. Witch elder is a shrub with either an open, spreading habit or a rounded habit. Its roundish or heart-shaped leaves, becoming brilliant scarlet or crimson in autumn, make it one of the finest of the autumn coloring plants. In spring, it also offers a conspicuous show of terminal heads, up to 2 inches (50 mm) long, the petalless flowers relying on the spikes of stamens for their display. A lime-free soil will ensure continuous good growth.

Gardenia jasminoides 'Florida'
FLORIST'S GARDENIA ○ ◑

Family: RUBIACEAE
Origin: Cultivar.
Flowering time: Spring–summer.
Climatic zone: 9, 10.
Dimensions: Up to 5 feet (approx. 2 meters) high.
Description: Growing in warm

Gardenia jasminoides 'Florida'

climates, gardenias are cherished for their perfume, their white perfection, and their long flowering period. The glossy green leaves, up to 4 inches (100 mm) long, are also attractive all year. The solitary flowers stand clear of the top-most leaves and open from bright green buds in a spiral of overlapping petals to a width of 2½ inches (60 mm). The plants thrive in a slightly acid soil and should be planted near a doorway, window, or outdoor sitting area, where their perfume can be appreciated. Florists use the flowers because of their perfume and longevity.

Gardenia jasminoides 'Magnifica'
LARGE FLOWERED GARDENIA, FLORIST'S GARDENIA ○ ◑

Family: RUBIACEAE
Origin: Cultivar.
Flowering time: Spring–summer.
Climatic zone: 9, 10.
Dimensions: Up to 8 feet (approx. 2 meters) high.
Description: This cultivar is a larger shrub than *G. jasminoides* 'Florida', being both taller and wider. Its leaves are also larger, 4½ inches (112 mm) long, more lustrous, and a brighter green. Most of the twenty large, unfurling petals of the flowers spread out to measure 4½ inches (112 mm) wide, but some remain unopened and stand erect in the center. Their perfume is heady. Among the choicest of evergreen flowering shrubs, this gardenia adds distinction to shrub beds and borders. A hot-climate plant, plenty of water and an acid fertilizer are essential.

Gardenia jasminoides 'Magnifica'

Gardenia jasminoides 'Prostrata'

Gardenia jasminoides 'Prostrata' syn. 'Radicans'
DWARF GARDENIA, FLORIST'S GARDENIA ○ ◑

Family: RUBIACEAE
Origin: Cultivar.
Flowering time: Spring–summer.
Climatic zone: 9, 10.
Dimensions: 12 inches (300 mm) high.
Description: This low, broad-spreading cultivar is an excellent small-scale groundcover. The lower branches often self-layer. The leaves are narrow and small, about 1½ inches (35 mm) long, and a bright, glossy green. The fragrant flowers are semidouble, about 1½ inches (35 mm) wide, with somewhat twisted petals. The miniature flower makes a perfect buttonhole. As well as being an excellent border shrub, this evergreen makes a very effective, low, informal hedge if enough shrubs are planted close together. A hot, humid summer is its main requirement, but plenty of water and regular feeding with an acid plant food is necessary for good flowering. It is also a good container plant, so a greenhouse environment will enable it to cope with cold climates.

Gaultheria procumbens

Gaultheria shallon

Gaultheria procumbens
WINTERGREEN, CHECKERBERRY ◑

Family: ERICACEAE
Origin: Eastern United States.
Flowering time: Spring.
Climatic zone: 3, 4, 5, 6, 7, 8, 9.
Dimensions: 6 inches (150 mm) high.
Description: Wintergreen is found growing naturally in acid soils in dry and moist woodlands over areas that are vastly different climatically. Spreading by means of rhizomes, the stems of this prostrate, creeping shrub stand erect with the foliage crowded near the top. The evergreen leaves are up to 2 inches (50 mm) long. About ⅓ inch (8 mm) long, the waxy, white, bell-shaped flowers are solitary and hang from the leaf axils. The highly decorative, bright scarlet fruits are spicy and aromatic and much sought after as winter food by deer, grouse, and partridges.

Gaultheria shallon
SALAL, SHALLON ◑

Family: ERICACEAE
Origin: Western United States.
Flowering time: Early summer.
Climatic zone: 6, 7, 8, 9.
Dimensions: Up to 5 feet (approx. 2 meters) high.
Description: This plant forms a pleasing ornamental, open shrub. It has many hairy stems with broad, ovate leaves which measure up to 5 inches (125 mm) long and are hairless when mature. The felted blooms, which can be tinged with pink, are about ½ inch (12 mm) long and are suspended like bells in terminal clusters of slender racemes. They are followed by edible, purple fruits which turn black when mature. Esteemed for its attractive leaves, flowers, and fruit, this shrub is a good choice in a lightly shaded shrub border or woodland garden, although it can be very invasive when grown in moist, acid soil.

Genista monosperma
WHITE BROOM, WHITE WEEPING BROOM, BRIDAL VEIL BROOM ○

Family: LEGUMINOSAE
Origin: Spain, Portugal, North Africa.
Flowering time: Spring.
Climatic zone: 9, 10.
Dimensions: Up to 10 feet (3 meters) high.
Description: Somewhat straggly, this deciduous shrub has rush-like, wide-spreading, pendant branches that are silky-haired when young. When they appear, the leaves are sparse, up to ¾ inch (18 mm) long, narrow, and also covered with silky hairs. The very fragrant flowers, each about ½ inch (12 mm) wide, are scattered abundantly along the branches in short racemes. They, too, have a silky-haired covering. Dry, well-drained, alkaline soils with poor fertility best simulate the conditions of their native habitat. Annual pruning and thinning out of the oldest branches is recommended.

Genista monosperma

Grevillea banksii 'Alba'
BANKS' WHITE GREVILLEA ○

Family: PROTEACEAE
Origin: Cultivar.
Flowering time: Spring–early summer.
Climatic zone: 9, 10.
Dimensions: Up to 13 feet (4 meters) high.
Description: This upright, many-branched shrub has leaves of dark green with silky hairs giving a white appearance to their undersides. The leaves can measure up to 12 inches (300 mm) long. The flowers are produced in profusion, with forty to eighty crowded on an erect, terminal, cylindrical head up to 4 inches (100 mm) long. This white form of the red-flowering species has the same

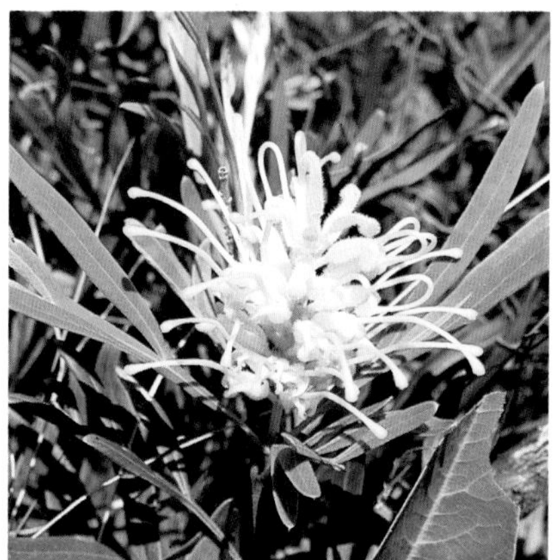

Grevillea banksii 'Alba'

reputation as the red for blooming intermittently after the main flowering period is over. Thriving in a sunny position, it is a very hardy and rewarding plant. It attracts birds.

Hakea acicularis

Hakea acicularis syn. *H. sericea*
BUSHY NEEDLEWOOD, SILKY HAKEA ○

Family: PROTEACEAE
Origin: Southeastern Australia.
Flowering time: Winter–spring.
Climatic zone: 9, 10.
Dimensions: 9 feet (3 meters) high.
Description: Care should be taken when positioning this shrub in the garden as its stiff, needle-like leaves, which spread in all directions, have sharp points which can prick the unwary. However, planted as an impenetrable hedge, this species would have few equals. The perfumed flowers, which sometimes show a tinge of pink, appear mostly as small clusters in the upper leaf axils and are a dainty foil to the leaves. The prominent, woody fruits, measuring up to 1½ inches (35 mm) long, persist on the plant, unopened, for several years unless disturbed by fire or injury. It is easy to grow in well-drained soil.

Hebe albicans

Hebe albicans
NEW ZEALAND LILAC, SHRUBBY VERONICA (U.K.) ○

Family: SCROPHULARIACEAE
Origin: New Zealand.
Flowering time: Summer–autumn.
Climatic zone: 7, 8, 9.
Dimensions: Up to 3 feet (1 meter) high.
Description: This is a splendid dwarf, evergreen shrub with a dense, rounded shape. The gray-green leaves arranged opposite one another on the stem give way at the top to the flower heads. Here, numerous 1 inch (25 mm) long spikes of flowers cover the plant throughout its long flowering period. Hardy in most soils which are well drained, this is another species that can tolerate difficult locations near the sea. Pruning is not needed.

Hebe diosmifolia

Hebe diosmifolia
VERONICA ○ ◑

Family: SCROPHULARIACEAE
Origin: New Zealand.
Flowering time: Summer.
Climatic zone: 6, 7, 8, 9.
Dimensions: Up to 3 feet (1 meter) high.
Description: A small, neat shrub, this species has glossy green foliage and flat clusters of small white flowers, tinged with palest lilac. Like most veronicas it thrives in rich, well-drained soil if planted in an open, sunny position. It can withstand both frosts and drought conditions and can be easily propagated by cuttings taken at any time of the year.

Hebe odora

Hebe odora syn. *H. buxifolia*
WHITE SPEEDWELL, SHRUBBY VERONICA ○

Family: SCROPHULARIACEAE
Origin: New Zealand mountains.
Flowering time: Spring–summer.
Climatic zone: 8, 9.
Dimensions: Up to 6 feet (2 meters) high.
Description: Of the one hundred species of *Hebe*, all but a few are natives of New Zealand. This plant is a small, erect, evergreen shrub with polished green leaves less than 1 inch (25 mm) long. The flowers grow on 1–2-inch (25–50 mm) terminal spikes. When *H. odora* is in full bloom, the profusion of flowers almost hides the leaves. Very ornamental, this species is also invaluable for seaside and industrial estate planting.

Hebe salicifolia

Hebe salicifolia
KOROMIKO, SHRUBBY VERONICA ○

Family: SCROPHULARIACEAE
Origin: New Zealand, southern Chile.
Flowering time: Summer.
Climatic zone: 7, 8, 9.
Dimensions: Up to 15 feet (5 meters) high.
Description: With the specific name meaning "leaves like a *Salix* (or willow)" it is no surprise to find this evergreen species has narrow leaves up to 6 inches (150 mm) long, tapering to a point at the tips. They usually have toothed margins. The flower spikes are slender and cylindrical and are sometimes more than 6 inches (150 mm) long. The small, white, individual blooms can be tinged with pale to darker lilac. This is a shrub which is ideally suited to seaside areas and, as with the other *Hebe* species, is one of the easiest plants to maintain in the garden. It is a parent of many hardy hybrids. It does not, however, tolerate prolonged winter cold.

Hibiscus mutabilis
COTTON ROSE, CONFEDERATE ROSE, ROSE COTTON ○

Other common names: ROSE OF SHARON
Family: MALVACEAE
Origin: Southeastern China.
Flowering time: Autumn.
Climatic zone: 9, 10.
Dimensions: Up to 13 feet (4 meters) high.
Description: *Mutabilis*, meaning "to change", indicates the change in flower color, from white when they emerge to deep-red as they age. This transition means that the shrub is liberally clothed in flowers of white and red, as well as all the intervening shades of pink. The long-stalked leaves are also distinctive. They are wider than they are long, about 7 inches (175 mm) across, with three to seven coarsely toothed, shallow triangular lobes, and both they and the young stems are thickly covered with yellowish hairs. It needs protection from frost and wind, and enjoys full sun and a well-drained soil.

Hibiscus mutabilis

Hydrangea arborescens 'Grandiflora'

Hydrangea arborescens
TREE HYDRANGEA, SMOOTH HYDRANGEA ○

Family: HYDRANGEACEAE
Origin: Southeastern United States.
Flowering time: Summer.
Climatic zone: 4, 5, 6, 7, 8, 9.
Dimensions: Up to 5 feet (approx. 2 meters) high.
Description: This ornamental, deciduous shrub has a somewhat loose and straggling growth. Its leaves are large and egg-shaped. Its flattish flower clusters are up to 6 inches (150 mm) across, consisting of masses of small, fertile flowers and a dappling of a few large, showy, sterile ones on the outer edges. *H. arborescens* 'Grandiflora', known as Hills of Snow, is very popular and the more commonly cultivated form. An annual prune after flowering will keep this shrub compact. The cut blooms are very decorative in vases.
Varieties/cultivars: 'Grandiflora'.

Hydrangea quercifolia

Hydrangea quercifolia
OAK-LEAVED HYDRANGEA ○ ◑

Family: HYDRANGEACEAE
Origin: Southeastern United States.
Flowering time: Summer.
Climatic zone: 5, 6, 7, 8, 9.
Dimensions: Up to 6 feet (2 meters) high.
Description: This beautiful deciduous shrub is an elegant inclusion in an open woodland garden or positioned in light shade. Many cultivate it for its bold, handsome foliage. The leaves are 8 inches (200 mm) long, with three to five deep lobes, whitish on their undersides when newly opened, and changing in autumn to produce a spectacular display of bronzy-purple. The flower clusters are in 12-inch-long (300 mm) pyramids of long-stalked, showy, sterile blooms, as well as smaller, fertile ones. They age to a rosy-purple. It requires a humus-rich soil and may be damaged by severe winters.

Itea virginica

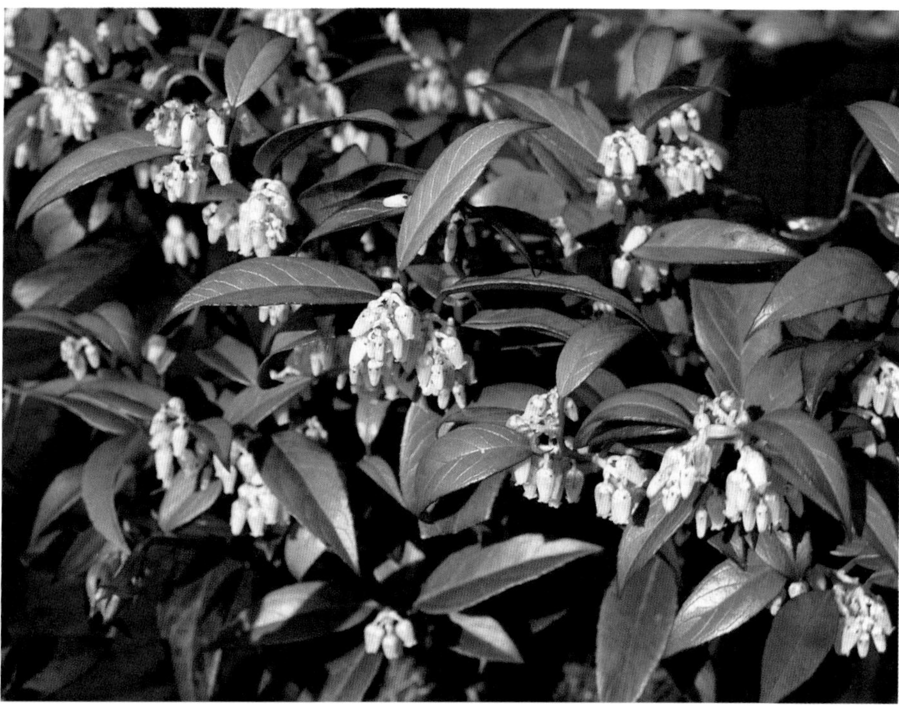

Leucothoe axillaris

Itea virginica
VIRGINIA WILLOW, SWEETSPIRE ○ ◑

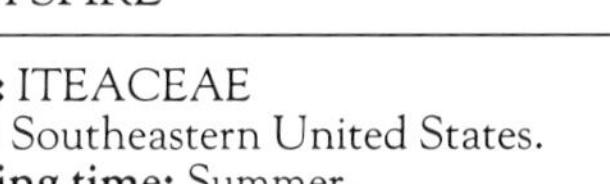

Family: ITEACEAE
Origin: Southeastern United States.
Flowering time: Summer.
Climatic zone: 5, 6, 7, 8, 9.
Dimensions: Up to 10 feet (3 meters) high.
Description: A native of wet woods and swamps of the coastal region, this deciduous shrub branches into many slender stems which support its handsome leaves. Up to 4 inches (100 mm) long, with finely toothed margins, they turn beautiful shades of red in autumn. The small, fluffy, creamy-white flowers, which are tinged with green, are sweetly fragrant and produced in great profusion in semi-erect racemes measuring up to 6 inches (150 mm) long. Humus-rich soil is preferred and the protection of a wall or sheltered corner is desirable.

Leucothoe axillaris syn. *L. catesbaei*
COAST LEUCOTHOE ◑

Family: ERICACEAE
Origin: Southeastern United States.
Flowering time: Summer.
Climatic zone: 5, 6, 7, 8, 9.
Dimensions: Up to 6 feet (2 meters) high.
Description: Named after Leucothoë, a legendary princess of Babylon who was believed to have been changed into a shrub by the god Apollo, this excellent evergreen shrub is generally similar to *L. fontanesiana*. It is, however, a native of moist woodlands of the coastal plain. The flower heads, which are about 3 inches (75 mm) long, are crowded with broad, urn-shaped flowers. The leaves are bluntly pointed and only sparsely toothed. This shrub likes moist, acid soil.

Leucothoe fontanesiana
DROOPING LEUCOTHOE ○ ◑

Family: ERICACEAE
Origin: Eastern United States.
Flowering time: Early summer.
Climatic zone: 5, 6, 7, 8, 9.
Dimensions: Up to 6 feet (2 meters) high.
Description: This is an attractive and useful evergreen shrub for lightly shaded garden areas, and open woodlands where naturalistic effects are sought. Its native habitat is along banks of mountain streams. The flowers, which are small, urn-shaped, and drooping, appear in clusters up to 4 inches (100 mm) long, all along the graceful, arching stems. The stems, reddish when young, support lance-like, leathery leaves which, in the cold months and especially in exposed positions, become tinged with deep reds and bronzy-purples. An acid, peaty soil is necessary which is moist but well-drained.

Leucothoe fontanesiana

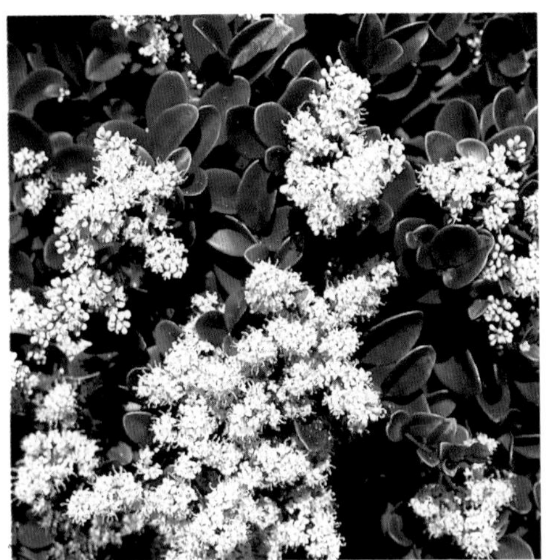

Ligustrum japonicum 'Rotundifolium'

Ligustrum japonicum
JAPANESE PRIVET, JAPANESE TREE PRIVET ○

Family: OLEACEAE
Origin: Japan, Korea.
Flowering time: Late summer–autumn.
Climatic zone: 7, 8, 9.
Dimensions: Up to 10 feet (3 meters) high.
Description: Sometimes assuming a tree-like form, this dense, evergreen shrub has shiny olive-green leaves over 4 inches (100 mm) long. The flowers are small and are borne in large clusters up to 6 inches (150 mm) long, on the terminal shoots. Many people find their scent unpleasant. These plants make an effective hedge, screen, or background. They can be clipped into formal shapes or left as a natural wall of greenery, and thrive even when neglected or grown in poor soils.
Varieties/cultivars: 'Rotundifolium'.

Ligustrum lucidum
CHINESE PRIVET ○

Family: OLEACEAE
Origin: Japan, Korea, China.
Flowering time: Late summer–autumn.
Climatic zone: 7, 8, 9.
Dimensions: Up to 30 feet (9 meters) high.
Description: Occasionally seen as a beautiful, symmetrical tree with an attractive, fluted trunk, this evergreen can also be clipped as a hedge. It has large, glossy green, pointed leaves, up to 6 inches (150 mm) in length, and large, handsome clusters of flowers with petals as long as the corolla tubes that support them. All privets have some unwelcome characteristics. The scent of the flowers is offensive to some people, and the roots are "hungry" and impoverish nearby soil.
Varieties/cultivars: 'Excelsum Superbum', 'Tricolor'.

Ligustrum lucidum

Ligustrum ovalifolium

Ligustrum ovalifolium
CALIFORNIA PRIVET (U.S.A.), OVAL LEAF PRIVET (U.K.), HEDGING PRIVET (U.K.) ○

Family: OLEACEAE
Origin: Japan.
Flowering time: Summer.
Climatic zone: 5, 6, 7, 8, 9.
Dimensions: Up to 13 feet (4 meters) high.
Description: This favorite hedge plant grows erect and stiff, but possesses the fine twiggy growth so essential for the formation of a good, dense hedge. It can be grown successfully in poor soils and remains semi-evergreen, except in very severe winters when it becomes deciduous. The short-stalked flowers appear in profuse clusters, up to 4 inches (100 mm) long. Many people dislike their smell. The leaves, which are glossy green and pointed, are up to 2½ inches (62 mm) long.
Varieties/cultivars: 'Aureum', 'Argenteum'.

Lonicera nitida 'Aurea'

Lonicera nitida
BOX-LEAF HONEYSUCKLE

Family: CAPRIFOLIACEAE
Origin: Western China.
Flowering time: Spring.
Climatic zone: 7, 8, 9.
Dimensions: Up to 6 feet (2 meters) high.
Description: This twiggy, evergreen shrub is a vigorous grower, stands clipping well, and makes a dense, compact hedge. The tiny, sweetly fragrant flowers appear in pairs from the leaf axils, and are followed by bluish-purple berries, ¼ inch (6 mm) wide. The leaves are small, thick, glossy, oval to rounded in shape, and up to ½ inch (12 mm) long. When training it as a hedge, establish a good basic framework when the plant is young by regular pruning. Grow in well-drained but moist soil.
Varieties/cultivars: Several cultivars are available.

Loropetalum chinense
FRINGE FLOWER, LOROPETALUM ○

Family: HAMAMELIDACEAE
Origin: China.
Flowering time: Spring.
Climatic zone: 8, 9, 10.

Loropetalum chinense

Dimensions: Up to 12 feet (4 meters) high.
Description: This neat-foliaged, evergreen shrub grows well among azaleas and other shrubs which have the same well-drained, acid soil requirements. The showy flowers consist of four soft, strap-shaped petals about 1 inch (25 mm) long, freely produced in clusters of six to nine to give a fringed appearance to the shrub. The leaves are rough to the touch, egg-shaped, and up to 2 inches (50 mm) long. A warm, sheltered position is necessary for this shrub. It does not tolerate severe winter weather. It appreciates an application of lime-free compost.

Magnolia stellata
STAR MAGNOLIA ○ ◑

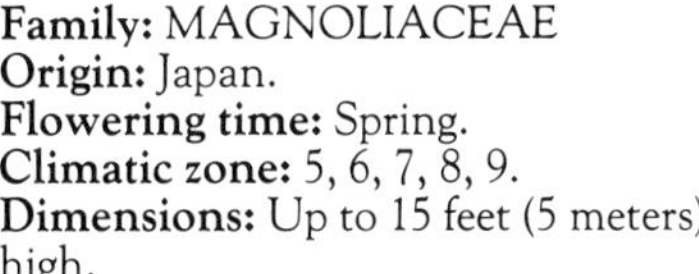

Family: MAGNOLIACEAE
Origin: Japan.
Flowering time: Spring.
Climatic zone: 5, 6, 7, 8, 9.
Dimensions: Up to 15 feet (5 meters) high.
Description: Slow-growing and deciduous, this shrub is distinctive and charming. With its many spreading branches, it grows wider than it does high and is prized for its brilliant spring floral display. The fragrant, star-like flowers burst open on bare branches. They comprise up to twenty-one petals and sepals, which look alike and are narrow, strap-shaped, 1½ inches (35 mm) long, and bend backwards with age. The leaves are broadly oval to

Magnolia stellata

oblong and up to 5 inches (125 mm) long. Plant in fertile, well-drained soil with plenty of humus.
Other colors: Pink, purplish-pink.
Varieties/cultivars: 'Rosea', 'Rubra'.

Melaleuca armillaris
HONEY MYRTLE, BRACELET HONEY MYRTLE ○

Family: MYRTACEAE
Origin: Eastern Australia.
Flowering time: Spring–summer.
Climatic zone: 9, 10.
Dimensions: Up to 17 feet (approx. 5 meters) high.
Description: This is a hardy, fast-growing, evergreen, bushy shrub, or

Melaleuca armillaris

small tree, which often grows wider than it does tall. Narrow, 1-inch-long (25 mm) leaves, thickly covering the many fine stems, form a dense, impenetrable barrier, making this an excellent choice for a windbreak or screen. The flowers are arranged in a spike up to 2½ inches (60 mm) long. Their conspicuous stamens give the whole flower the appearance of a "bottlebrush". The woody, capsular fruit with their seeds remain on the plant for several years. It grows well in most soils and will tolerate lime.

Melaleuca incana

Melaleuca incana
GRAY HONEY MYRTLE ○

Family: MYRTACEAE
Origin: Western Australia.
Flowering time: Late spring–early summer.
Climatic zone: 9, 10.
Dimensions: Up to 10 feet (3 meters) high.
Description: The Latin word *incana* meaning "quite gray", refers to the color of the foliage of this attractive and useful evergreen shrub. The twenty to forty tiny flowers are densely crowded onto spikes up to 1 inch (25 mm) long. The leaves are small, up to ½ inch (12 mm) long, and their soft, white, hairy covering extends also to the twigs supporting them. These leaves assume a grayish-purple tinge in winter. This species requires an extremely well-drained situation in open, light soil.

Melaleuca linariifolia 'Snowstorm'

Melaleuca linariifolia 'Snowstorm'
SNOW-IN-SUMMER ○

Family: MYRTACEAE
Origin: Cultivar.
Flowering time: Late spring–summer.
Climatic zone: 9, 10.
Dimensions: Up to 5 feet (approx. 2 meters) high.
Description: This is a registered dwarf form of the well-known evergreen tree species. As its cultivated name indicates, at flowering time the display of flowers covers the plant so profusely that the fine, narrow leaves are not visible. The flower head is a slender spike containing thirty to forty-five flowers massed along its 2½-inch (60-mm) length. The light perfume is reminiscent of honey. The bark is thick, spongy, white, and papery, and the 1 inch (25 mm) long, leaves contain sweet-smelling oil glands. This shrub will thrive even in exposed positions in seaside gardens.

Murraya paniculata syn. *M. exotica*
MOCK ORANGE, ORANGE JESSAMINE ○ ◑

Family: RUTACEAE
Origin: South East Asia.
Flowering time: Spring and intermittently.
Climatic zone: 9, 10.
Dimensions: Up to 10 feet (3 meters) high.
Description: This evergreen, ornamental shrub is highly esteemed in gardens or containers in the tropics and subtropics. The blooms, deliciously scented, open to a trumpet shape, about 1 inch (25 mm) across, in clusters of ten to twenty. The decorative oval fruit ripens to a bright red. The plant often flowers several times a year. The leaves are a bright, shining green, with three to nine leaflets, each up to 2 inches (50 mm) long, and, because this species belongs to the same family as *Citrus*, they emit a sweet smell when handled. This shrub requires lots of water and a humus-rich soil.

Murraya paniculata

Myoporum parvifolium

Myoporum parvifolium
CREEPING MYOPORUM ○

Family: MYOPORACEAE
Origin: Eastern Australia.
Flowering time: Spring.
Climatic zone: 9, 10.
Dimensions: Up to 10 inches (250 mm) high.
Description: This prostrate, evergreen shrub makes an excellent mat-forming plant, spreading readily to 3 feet (1 meter) and sending down roots as its trailing stems proceed. Tiny, white, star-like flowers are borne all along the stems. The rich green of the foliage of this hardy plant is also a feature. The leaves are narrow, fleshy, and thickly produced. Fine-, medium-, and broad-leaved as well as purple-stemmed forms are available. Well-drained soil in a sunny position gives the best results.

Myrtus communis

Myrtus communis
COMMON MYRTLE ○

Family: MYRTACEAE
Origin: Western Asia.
Flowering time: Summer.
Climatic zone: 8, 9, 10.
Dimensions: Up to 15 feet (5 meters) high.
Description: Esteemed since classical times as a symbol of love and peace, myrtle is often traditionally included in the bride's bouquet, from which cuttings are grown, to be kept as carefully tended plants throughout life. This dense, leafy, evergreen shrub has leaves that are glossy, spicily aromatic, elliptic to lance-shaped, and nearly 2 inches (50 mm) long. The four petals of the solitary flowers spread wide to ¾ inch (18 mm) across, to display a profusion of long stamens. The fruit is ½ inch (12 mm) long and ripens to bluish-black. Although fairly hardy, it grows best against a sunny, sheltered wall. In cooler climates, myrtle should be kept in a greenhouse in winter.
Varieties/cultivars: 'Flore Pleno', 'Microphylla', 'Tarentina', 'Variegata'.

Nandina domestica

Nandina domestica

SACRED BAMBOO, HEAVENLY BAMBOO

○ ◑ ●

Family: BERBERIDACEAE
Origin: India–eastern Asia.
Flowering time: Spring.
Climatic zone: 7, 8, 9.
Dimensions: Up to 8 feet (approx. 2 meters) high.
Description: Somewhat like a bamboo in appearance, this evergreen shrub is grown in gardens and tubs for its ornamental qualities. Much of its beauty lies in the delicate tracery of the fine leaflets on leaves which can be up to 1½ feet (450 mm) long and which may assume brilliant shades of red to purple in autumn. The flowers, while not showy, are produced in terminal, pyramidal clusters, 12 inches (300 mm) long. The fruits, considered by some to be the most attractive feature of the plant, ripen to a handsome, rich red. It prefers a sheltered position away from cold winds and may be damaged by severe winters. Plant in humus-rich, neutral to acid soil.
Varieties/cultivars: 'Nana Compacta'.

Olearia x *haastii*

NEW ZEALAND DAISYBUSH

○

Family: COMPOSITAE
Origin: Hybrid.
Flowering time: Late summer.
Climatic zone: 7, 8, 9.
Dimensions: Up to 10 feet (3 meters) high.
Description: A wild hybrid between two New Zealand species, this shrub is one of the hardiest and, at the same

Olearia x *haastii*

time, the most floriferous and popular of the daisybushes. It is a many-branching, rounded shrub with small, crowded, oblong to egg-shaped leaves which are glossy green with white-felted undersides. The individual flower heads, about ⅓ inch (8 mm) across with yellow centers, are in flattish, long-stalked clusters up to 3½ inches (85 mm) in diameter. Ideally suited for hedges and thriving in seaside gardens, this shrub will withstand some frost. Well-drained but moist soil in a reasonably sunny position is required.

Osmanthus delavayi

DELAVAY OSMANTHUS

○ ◑

Family: OLEACEAE
Origin: Western China.
Flowering time: Spring.
Climatic zone: 7, 8, 9.
Dimensions: Up to 8 feet (approx. 2 meters) high.
Description: Introduced into Europe

Osmanthus delavayi

by Abbé Delavay as recently as 1890, this shrub is one of China's gems. It is a beautiful, fairly slow-growing, evergreen shrub densely covered with small, lustrous green, ovate leaves about 1 inch (25 mm) long. The freely produced tubular flowers are fragrant and jasmine-like, arising in small clusters from the leaf axils. The berry-like fruits, about ½ inch (12 mm) long, ripen in summer to a bluish-black. Although reasonably hardy, the shrub likes protection from the fiercest sun, and does not survive severe winters. Humus-rich, well-drained soil in a sheltered site is preferred.

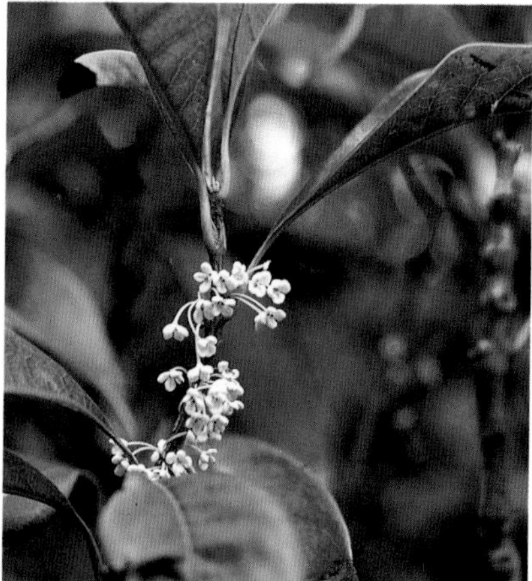

Osmanthus fragrans

Osmanthus fragrans

SWEET OSMANTHUS, FRAGRANT TEA OLIVE, SWEET OLIVE

Family: OLEACEAE
Origin: Himalayas–China.
Flowering time: Summer.
Climatic zone: 8, 9.
Dimensions: Up to 25 feet (8 meters) high.
Description: This evergreen shrub is grown for the beautiful, rich fragrance of its bell-shaped flowers. In its native lands, it has been cultivated for many centuries as an ornamental. Its dried flowers make a scented tea and, it is said, are used to keep clothes insect-free. It can be found in the garden in mild climates and in greenhouses in colder regions. The leaves are oval or oblong, up to 4 inches (100 mm) long, and finely toothed on the margins. A dense shrub, it can be trained as an espalier or small tree, or clipped as a hedge. Semishade and rich, acid soil suit it best.

Philadelphus coronarius

Philadelphus coronarius

Common Mock Orange, Sweet Mock Orange ○

Family: SAXIFRAGACEAE
Origin: Europe, southwestern Asia.
Flowering time: Early summer.
Climatic zone: 4, 5, 6, 7, 8, 9.
Dimensions: Up to 10 feet (3 meters) high.
Description: A deciduous shrub, sweet mock orange gives a splendid display of spring blossom. These very fragrant flowers, each about 1½ inches (35 mm) across, open wide to display four distinct, rounded petals and appear in five-to-seven-flowered heads at the ends of the many erect stems. The narrow leaves measure up to 3 inches (75 mm) long, have toothed margins, and change from a dark green to dull yellow in autumn. This very commonly cultivated species is particularly suited to dry soils.
Varieties/cultivars: 'Aureus', 'Variegatus'.

Philadelphus mexicanus

Mexican Mock Orange ○

Family: SAXIFRAGACEAE
Origin: Southern Mexico, Guatemala.
Flowering time: Late spring.
Climatic zone: 9, 10.
Dimensions: Up to 6 feet (2 meters) high.
Description: Mexican mock orange is an evergreen shrub whose numerous slender branches arise from the base and arch outwards to form a loose, rounded shape. It is included in gardens for its spring floral display. The sweetly perfumed flowers measure about 1½ inches (35 mm) across and occur singly or in clusters of three on small shoots from the upper branches. The softly textured leaves are up to 2½ inches (60 mm) across and somewhat furry, as are the new stems. Requiring little in the way of cultivation, these shrubs respond to pruning immediately after flowering.

Philadelphus mexicanus

Philadelphus x *lemoinei*

Philadelphus x *lemoinei*

Lemoine Mock Orange ○

Family: SAXIFRAGACEAE
Origin: Hybrid.
Flowering time: Late spring.
Climatic zone: 5, 6, 7, 8, 9.
Dimensions: Up to 6 feet (2 meters) high.
Description: This is one of an array of hybrids bred during the nineteenth century by Victor Lemoine in France. Its parents are *P. coronarius* and *P. microphyllus*. The profusion of 1-inch-wide (25 mm) flowers, with their many golden-yellow anthers standing out against the white of the petals, and with their sweet fragrance, are this deciduous shrub's main attraction. They are produced on short stalks in terminal clusters of from three to five flowers. The leaves are up to 3 inches (75 mm) long. Any well-drained garden soil in a sunny position will ensure a rewarding display of flowers.
Varieties/cultivars: 'Avalanche', 'Boule d'Argent', 'Innocence', 'Manteau d'Hermine'.

Philadelphus x *virginalis*

Philadelphus x *virginalis*

Virginal Mock Orange ○

Family: SAXIFRAGACEAE
Origin: Hybrid.
Flowering time: Spring.
Climatic zone: 5, 6, 7, 8, 9.
Dimensions: Up to 10 feet (3 meters) high.
Description: This deciduous hybrid shrub is understandably popular, producing displays of double or semidouble blooms of superb quality. The flowers are generally large, up to 2 inches (50 mm) in diameter, and occur in abundance in clusters of five to seven on the many erect shoots. The rich fragrance of the flowers, which is likened to orange blossom, makes them an excellent inclusion in bridal bouquets. The leaves are up to 3 inches (75 mm) long with a coarsely toothed margin. Well-drained soil and a sunny position are preferred.
Varieties/cultivars: 'Virginal'.

Physocarpus opulifolius

Physocarpus opulifolius
COMMON NINEBARK ○ ◑

Family: ROSACEAE
Origin: Eastern North America.
Flowering time: Spring.
Climatic zone: 3, 4, 5, 6, 7, 8, 9.
Dimensions: Up to 10 feet (3 meters) high.
Description: The name common ninebark refers to the shedding and peeling bark seen on all species of *Physocarpus*. These deciduous shrubs are closely related to spiraeas although they are less showy in bloom. They thrive in almost any open position, are hardy, vigorous, and remarkably free from pests and diseases. The small flowers, which are sometimes tinged with pink, form profuse clusters, nearly 2 inches (50 mm) wide, along the many arching stems. The leaves are three-lobed and about 3 inches (75 mm) long. Moderately fertile, well-drained soil in a sunny or partially shaded position will ensure best results.
Varieties/cultivars: 'Intermedius', 'Luteus'.

Pieris formosa
HIMALAYAN ANDROMEDA, LILY-OF-THE-VALLEY SHRUB ◑ ●

Family: ERICACEAE
Origin: Himalayas.
Flowering time: Spring–early summer.
Climatic zone: 7, 8, 9.
Dimensions: Up to 10 feet (3 meters) high.
Description: Attractive throughout the year, this is a magnificent evergreen shrub whose large leaves are leathery and a lustrous green, with a fine-toothed margin. When new they are attractively copper-tinted. The flowers, resembling lily-of-the-valley flowers, are clustered together into large panicles which hang from the terminal shoots. The presentation of attractive flowers and foliage in a compact form makes this a highly decorative shrub. However, some consider it is surpassed by the cultivar 'Forrestii', whose young growth is brilliant red. A rich, lime-free soil and a cool, moist, sheltered position are essential for best results. This shrub may be damaged by prolonged, frosty winters.
Varieties/cultivars: 'Forrestii'.

Pieris formosa

Pieris japonica
JAPANESE PIERIS, JAPANESE PEARL FLOWER, JAPANESE ANDROMEDA ◑ ●

Family: ERICACEAE
Origin: Japan.
Flowering time: Spring.
Climatic zone: 5, 6, 7, 8, 9.
Dimensions: Up to 10 feet (3 meters) high.
Description: Somewhat hardier than *P. formosa*, this is another very attractive evergreen shrub which, under favorable conditions, can reach a height of 30 feet (9 meters) but mostly does not exceed shrub dimensions. Its narrow leaves, up to 4 inches (100 mm) long, with a coppery tinge when young, mature to a dark, lustrous green. The pitcher-shaped flowers, individually up to ¼ inch (6 mm) long, are displayed in spreading clusters of eight or ten drooping racemes which measure about 6 inches (150 mm) long. The buds for these sprays appear in autumn. Plant in neutral to acid, peaty soil and provide shelter from cold winds.
Other colors: Pink.
Varieties/cultivars: 'Bert Chandler', 'Pygmaea', 'Variegata', Daisen', 'Christmas Cheer'.

Pieris japonica 'Bert Chandler'

Prunus glandulosa 'Alba Plena'

Prunus glandulosa 'Alba Plena'
DOUBLE WHITE DWARF FLOWERING ALMOND, CHINESE BUSH CHERRY ○

Family: ROSACEAE
Origin: Cultivar.
Flowering time: Spring.
Climatic zone: 4, 5, 6, 7, 8, 9.
Dimensions: Up to 4 feet (over 1 meter) tall.
Description: Double white dwarf flowering almond, with its many slender, erect shoots, forms a neat, bushy shrub. It is grown for its spring display of large double flowers which are produced in such profusion that they bend the stems with their weight. Sprays of blossom are often cut for house decoration. The leaves, opening after the flowers, are up to 4 inches (100 mm) long and provide good autumn color. This shrub requires a warm sheltered position and can be pruned hard after flowering.

Plumbago auriculata 'Alba'

Pyracantha coccinea

Plumbago auriculata 'Alba' syn. *P. capensis* 'Alba'
PLUMBAGO, CAPE PLUMBAGO LEADWORT ○ ◑

Family: PLUMBAGINACEAE
Origin: Cultivar.
Flowering time: Summer, autumn.
Climatic zone: 9, 10.
Dimensions: Up to 10 feet (3 meters) tall.
Description: This is the white-flowering cultivar of the blue-flowering species. It is an upright, straggling, and partly climbing, evergreen shrub which responds well to pruning and is most effective against a wall or as a hedge. The flowers appear almost continually in warm, sunny conditions. They are in rounded clusters with five spreading petals at the top of a slender tube. Viscous glands at the base of the flowers make them very sticky to the touch. The 4-inch-long (100 mm) leaves are dull green. Well-drained soil and a partially shady or sunny site suit this warm-climate plant. It spreads rapidly from suckers.

Pyracantha coccinea
SCARLET FIRETHORN, COMMON FIRETHORN (U.K.) ○

Family: ROSACEAE
Origin: Southern Europe–western Himalayas.
Flowering time: Spring–early summer.
Climatic zone: 6, 7, 8, 9.
Dimensions: Up to 15 feet (5 meters) high.
Description: The rich red fruits, formed in dense clusters in autumn and winter, and the thorny branches, have given the name "scarlet firethorn" to this shrub. The creamy-white flowers, looking like those of a hawthorn but smaller, appear in profusion, and are followed by the fruits, each about ⅓ inch (8 mm) wide. The evergreen leaves, which are about 1½ inches (37 mm) long, are narrow and oval with finely-toothed margins. This is an excellent shrub to grow in fertile, moist, well-drained soil.
Varieties/cultivars: 'Lalandei'.

Sambucus nigra

Sambucus nigra
ELDER, EUROPEAN ELDER ○

Family: CAPRIFOLIACEAE
Origin: Europe, western Asia, North Africa.
Flowering time: Summer.
Climatic zone: 5, 6, 7, 8, 9.
Dimensions: 10–30 feet (3–9 meters) high.
Description: European elder has been cultivated over a long period in history. It is a familiar large, deciduous shrub and is sometimes seen as a smallish tree with a rugged, fissured bark. It has attractive leaves with from five to seven leaflets, each up to 4 inches (100 mm) long. In autumn the leaves may change from their summer mid-green to bright yellow or dull purple. The flowers appear as flattened heads, up to 7 inches (175 mm) across, of masses of sweetly fragrant blooms. The fruits are glossy black and, with the flowers, are used in country wine-making. Moisture-retentive but well-drained soil creates ideal growing conditions.
Varieties/cultivars: 'Albovariegata', 'Aurea', 'Lanciniata', 'Purpurea'.

Serissa foetida
SERISSA ○ ◑

Family: RUBIACEAE
Origin: South East Asia.
Flowering time: Autumn.
Climatic zone: 9, 10.
Dimensions: Up to 3 feet (1 meter) high.
Description: Outdoors, in frost-free regions, this useful shrub is seen in shrubberies, rock gardens, and borders, commonly growing broader than it does tall. The attractive, small flowers, pink in bud, solitary or in small clusters, open to ½ inch (12 mm) across with petals that are hairy on the insides. In warm situations, serissa flowers for most of the year. The leaves are elliptic, up to 1 inch (25 mm) long, and dark green, with an unpleasant odor when crushed. In cooler climates they make good container plants in greenhouses where they grow well with minimum care.
Varieties/cultivars: 'Variegata'.

Serissa foetida

Skimmia japonica 'Fragrans'

Skimmia reevesiana

Skimmia japonica
JAPANESE SKIMMIA ○ ◑

Family: RUTACEAE
Origin: Japan.
Flowering time: Spring.
Climatic zone: 7, 8, 9.
Dimensions: Up to 5 feet (approx. 2 meters) high.
Description: Among the most satisfactory broadleaf evergreens for shady areas, this shrub is also excellent for industrial or city areas and seaside gardens. Skimmias are slow-growing and compact, spreading wider than they are tall. The four-petaled, fragrant, white flowers appear in large panicles above the foliage. They are also grown for their decorative red fruits, about ¼ inch (6 mm) in diameter, which follow the flowers and last on the plants throughout winter. There are male and female flowers on different plants. Fruits are only produced if both sexes are planted together, one male to three females. Humus-rich soil is preferred.
Varieties/cultivars: 'Foremanii', 'Fragrans', 'Rubella', 'Rogersii'.

Skimmia reevesiana
SKIMMIA ●

Family: RUTACEAE
Origin: China, Taiwan, Philippines.
Flowering time: Late spring.
Climatic zone: 7, 8, 9.
Dimensions: Up to 2 feet (600 mm) high.
Description: This dwarf shrub forms a low, compact mound. It is slow-growing and because it withstands polluted air better than most evergreens, it is excellent for city gardens. It is also good planted beneath trees as it thrives in shade. The leaves are elliptic, up to 4 inches (100 mm) long, and dark green. The fragrant flowers are bisexual (unlike those of Japanese skimmia), small, about ½ inch (12 mm) wide, and are borne in a dense head up to 3 inches (75 mm) long. They are followed by oval, matte, crimson-red fruits which remain on the plant all winter.
Varieties/cultivars: 'Variegata'.

Spiraea cantoniensis 'Flore Pleno'
MAY, REEVES SPIRAEA ○

Family: ROSACEAE
Origin: Southeastern China.
Flowering time: Spring.
Climatic zone: 7, 8, 9.
Dimensions: Up to 5 feet (approx. 2 meters) high.
Description: The generic name comes from the Greek *speira* meaning a wreath, which appropriately describes this shrub when it is in full flower with its branches garlanded with clusters of blooms. These clusters, up to 2 inches (50 mm) wide, are rounded and contain twenty to twenty-five diminutive flowers. They grow in such profusion along the length of the arching stems that the stems can be bent to the ground. The narrow leaves, up to 2½ inches (60 mm) long, are dark green with irregularly toothed margins. Pruning, immediately after flowering, is essential.
Varieties/cultivars: 'Lanceata'.

Spiraea cantoniensis 'Flore Pleno'

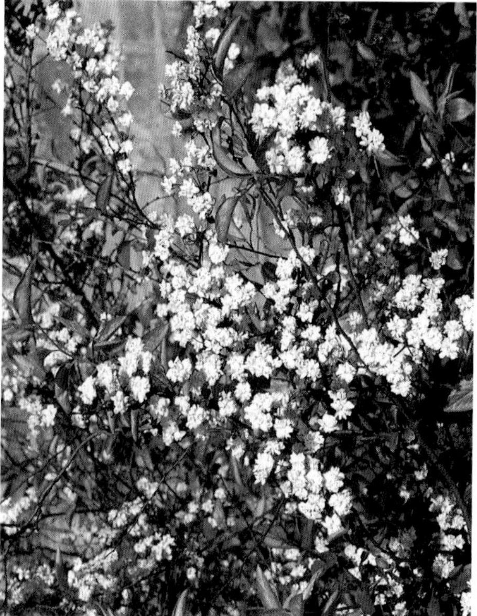

Spiraea prunifolia

Spiraea prunifolia syn. *S. p.* 'Plena'
BRIDAL-WREATH ○

Family: ROSACEAE
Origin: Japan.
Flowering time: Spring.
Climatic zone: 4, 5, 6, 7, 8, 9.
Dimensions: Up to 6 feet (2 meters) high.
Description: This popular plant is only known in cultivation and was first introduced into Europe from Japan in about 1845. It is a dense shrub with many slender, arching branches and grows almost as broad as it does high. The flowers are double and almost ½ inch (12 mm) across. They are borne in tight, button-like, stalkless clusters along the branches. The young shoots are slightly hairy, and the elliptic leaves, which open after the flowers, are up to 2 inches (50 mm) long. Autumn interest is provided by the orange and red foliage. Prune after flowering.

Spiraea thunbergii

Spiraea x *arguta*

Spiraea thunbergii

THUNBERG SPIRAEA ○

Family: ROSACEAE
Origin: China.
Flowering time: Spring–summer.
Climatic zone: 5, 6, 7, 8, 9.
Dimensions: Up to 6 feet (2 meters) high.
Description: Generally the earliest of the spiraeas to bloom, its pure white flowers often smother the arching branches of this graceful, deciduous shrub. It has a dense twiggy habit, often broader than it is tall, with slender downy stems. The leaves, which are narrow and shiny, about 1 inch (25 mm) long with a toothed margin, turn in autumn to shades of orange and scarlet. The flowers occur in numerous, but small, stalkless clusters of two to five flowers. Late frosts are a hazard to the early flowers of this popular shrub. Remove dead flower heads and stems if unsightly.

Spiraea x *arguta*

BRIDAL WREATH (U.K.), GARLAND SPIRAEA ○

Family: ROSACEAE
Origin: Hybrid.
Flowering time: Late spring.
Climatic zone: 4, 5, 6, 7, 8, 9.
Dimensions: Up to 6 feet (2 meters) high.
Description: One of the most effective and free-flowering of the spiraeas, bridal wreath is a hybrid of *S. thunbergii* and *S. multiflora*. It is a dense-growing, deciduous shrub with graceful, slender branches and, in habit, resembles *S. thunbergii*. However, its leaves are broader and it blooms later in spring so that its flowers are not so subject to damage by late frosts. To maintain a tidy appearance, prune this shrub hard immediately after flowering. Alternatively, if large flowers are desired, remove dead flower heads and stems only if unsightly. Otherwise, it is very easy and rewarding to grow.

Spiraea x *vanhouttei*

VANHOUTTE SPIRAEA ○

Family: ROSACEAE
Origin: Hybrid.
Flowering time: Summer.
Climatic zone: 4, 5, 6, 7, 8, 9.
Dimensions: Up to 8 feet (approx. 2 meters) high.
Description: A hybrid from *S. cantoniensis* and *S. trilobata*, this deciduous shrub, slender and vigorous with beautifully arching branches, is one of the most commonly cultivated spiraeas. The leaves are coarsely toothed, up to 1½ inches (35 mm) long, sometimes with three to five lobes, and blue-green in color. They show off the great numbers of many-flowered clusters of blooms which smother the stems. This showy shrub may also produce good autumn color in the leaves and makes an excellent hedge. Prune after flowering by removing dead stems and flower heads.

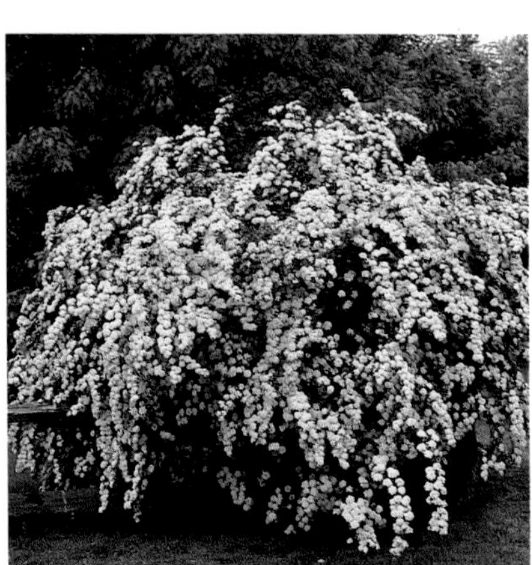

Spiraea x *vanhouttei*

Styrax americanus

Styrax americanus

SNOWBELL ○

Family: STYRACACEAE
Origin: Southeastern United States.
Flowering time: Early summer.
Climatic zone: 6, 7, 8, 9.
Dimensions: Up to 9 feet (3 meters) high.
Description: Not the easiest of plants to grow, this deciduous shrub, with its refined and graceful habit, combines well with other trees and shrubs in a mixed border. The leaves on the ascending branches are narrow, bright green, minutely toothed, and up to 3½ inches (85 mm) long. Its flowers are bell-shaped, up to ½ inch (12 mm) long, and hang by hairy stalks, either solitary or in clusters of up to four. Egg-shaped fruits about ⅓ inch (8 mm) long follow. A sandy, porous soil enriched with compost will ensure the best results. Protect from strong, cold winds. This shrub may be damaged by severe winters.

Symphoricarpos albus 'Laevigatus'

SNOWBERRY, WAXBERRY ○ ◑ ●

Family: CAPRIFOLIACEAE
Origin: Cultivar.
Flowering time: Summer–autumn.

Symphoricarpos albus 'Laevigatus'

Climatic zone: 3, 4, 5, 6, 7, 8, 9.
Dimensions: Up to 4 feet (approx. 1 meter) high.
Description: Having clusters of small, bell-shaped flowers, this deciduous shrub is mainly grown for its abundant display of fruits which appear in late summer and autumn and are retained for a long period. The fruits are round, white berries about ½ inch (12 mm) in diameter and are prized by floral arrangers for winter decoration. The shrubs, with slender, erect, downy shoots, form dense thickets of upright stems. The leaves are about 1 inch (25 mm) long. Snowberries will grow in shade, and in city and seaside environments.

Syringa vulgaris 'Madame Lemoine'
LILAC ○ ◑

Family: OLEACEAE
Origin: Cultivar.
Flowering time: Early summer.
Climatic zone: 4, 5, 6, 7, 8, 9.
Dimensions: Up to 15 feet (5 meters) high.
Description: This horticultural cultivar of the common lilac is grown, as are all lilacs, for its deliciously perfumed flowers. These cover the plant in great panicles, up to 8 inches (200 mm) long, of multiple blooms. The flowers are creamy-yellow in bud, opening to pure white. The leaves are heart-shaped and up to 5 inches (125 mm) long. Grow in fertile, moist soil.

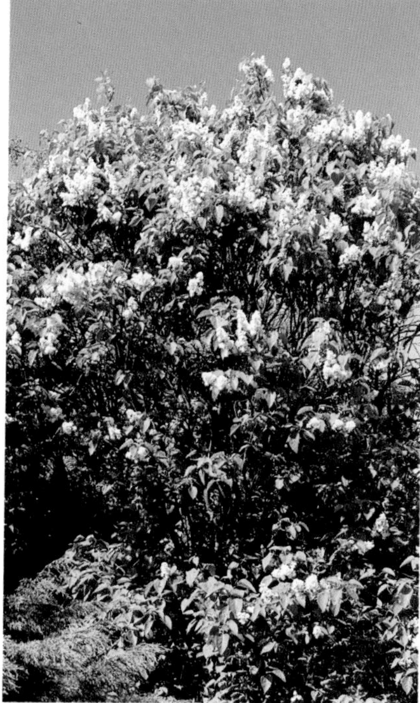

Syringa vulgaris 'Madame Lemoine'

Teucrium chamaedrys
WALL GERMANDER ○

Family: LABIATAE
Origin: Central and southern Europe–southwestern Asia.
Flowering time: Late summer.
Climatic zone: 6, 7, 8, 9.
Dimensions: Up to 12 inches (300 mm) high.
Description: A small, erect shrub, well suited to a sunny border, *T. chamaedrys* has toothed, glossy, deep-green leaves and tiny, tubular flowers which are pale to deep rosy-purple and appear in terminal whorls. Plant in well-drained soil in a sunny position.

Vaccinium corymbosum
SWAMP BLUEBERRY, HIGHBUSH BLUEBERRY ○

Family: ERICACEAE
Origin: Eastern North America.
Flowering time: Early summer–mid summer.
Climatic zone: 3, 4, 5, 6, 7, 8, 9.
Dimensions: Up to 12 feet (4 meters) high.
Description: While showy autumn leaves and attractive berries are notable features of this deciduous shrub, the flowers, in clusters of small, urn-shaped blooms, are also attractive. When they open, the leaves are half-grown. The leaves are bright green and when mature are about 3 inches (75 mm) long. With autumn, they turn brilliant shades of bronze and scarlet. The comparatively large berries, about ⅓ inch (8 mm) in diameter, are black with a "blue" bloom and are sweet and edible. Larger fruits are produced on commercial cultivars. For best results, plant in a moist, acid, peaty soil.
Varieties/cultivars: 'Early Blue', 'Grover', 'Jersey', 'Pemberton'.

Vaccinium corymbosum

Teucrium chamaedrys

Viburnum carlesii

Viburnum dentatum

Viburnum carlesii
KOREAN VIBURNUM ○ ◑

Family: CAPRIFOLIACEAE
Origin: Korea.
Flowering time: Spring.
Climatic zone: 4, 5, 6, 7, 8, 9.
Dimensions: Up to 5 feet (approx. 2 meters) high.
Description: Since W. R. Charles, a British diplomat, discovered this deciduous plant in Korea, it has become one of the most popular of shrubs. It is a rounded bush whose leaves, downy on both sides, look dull until autumn comes, when they turn shades of yellow and red. The buds are pink and the flowers exquisitely fragrant. Supported by a rose-pink tube, the petals are pure white on the inside. The flower heads, produced in profusion, are hemispherical, about 3 inches (75 mm) across, and appear with the new leaves. A hardy plant, it prefers fertile, well-drained soil.

Viburnum dentatum
ARROWWOOD ○

Family: CAPRIFOLIACEAE
Origin: Eastern United States.
Flowering time: Late spring.
Climatic zone: 2, 3, 4, 5, 6, 7, 8, 9.
Dimensions: Up to 15 feet (5 meters) high.
Description: The common name of this deciduous shrub refers to the strong, straight basal shoots which the American Indians are said to have used for making arrows. The leaves are oval, up to 3 inches (75 mm) long, and coarsely toothed, with hairs on both surfaces. In autumn they may become shining red. Produced in long-stemmed clusters measuring about 3 inches (75 mm) in diameter, the flowers are small with long, protruding stamens. The egg-shaped fruits are blue-black. A sunny position and well-drained soil are preferred.

Viburnum farreri syn. *V. fragrans*
FRAGRANT VIBURNUM ○

Family: CAPRIFOLIACEAE
Origin: Northern China.
Flowering time: Winter.
Climatic zone: 6, 7, 8.
Dimensions: Up to 10 feet (3 meters) high.
Description: With its very fragrant flowers opening well in advance of its foliage, this shrub is a most valuable, deciduous, winter-flowering plant. The leaves are up to 4 inches (100 mm) long, elliptic, and toothed, with conspicuous, parallel veins. The flowers are produced in somewhat rounded clusters up to 2 inches (50 mm) wide, and retain a blush of pink after opening from pink buds. Hardy, this plant prefers a fertile, well-drained, sunny position.
Varieties/cultivars: 'Candidissimum', 'Nanum'.

Viburnum farreri 'Candidissimum'

Viburnum japonicum

Viburnum japonicum
JAPANESE VIBURNUM ○

Family: CAPRIFOLIACEAE
Origin: Japan.
Flowering time: Spring.
Climatic zone: 8, 9.
Dimensions: Up to 25 feet (8 meters) high.
Description: Sometimes seen as a small tree, this handsome evergreen shrub has glossy, leathery, dark-green leaves up to 6 inches (150 mm) long. The paler undersides are spotted and the leaf margins near the tips may be toothed. On mature plants, the small, fragrant flowers are borne in dense, rounded clusters. Small numbers of red fruits are produced and are particularly sparse on young specimens. Japanese viburnum has conspicuous, warty young shoots and relatively flat flower clusters. Plant in a sunny position in well-drained soil. It may be killed or damaged by severe winters and needs a sheltered site.

Viburnum macrocephalum 'Sterile'
CHINESE SNOWBALL ○

Family: CAPRIFOLIACEAE
Origin: Cultivar.
Flowering time: Late spring.
Climatic zone: 6, 7, 8, 9.

Viburnum macrocephalum 'Sterile'

Dimensions: Up to 12 feet (4 meters) high.
Description: Chinese snowball is a semi-evergreen shrub which will lose all its leaves in a severe winter. Its leaves are finely toothed, up to 4 inches (100 mm) long, and furry on both surfaces. The flowers give a spectacular display of open-faced, sterile blooms in large, globular heads up to 6 inches (150 mm) across, reminiscent of the sterile forms of *Hydrangea macrophylla*. There is some doubt as to whether the wild form, with fertile flowers, is still in cultivation. This cultivar thrives in a sunny, well-drained location.

Viburnum odoratissimum
SWEET VIBURNUM ○

Family: CAPRIFOLOACEAE
Origin: China.
Flowering time: Summer.
Climatic zone: 6, 7, 8, 9, 10.
Dimensions: Up to 13 feet (4 meters) high.
Description: This viburnum is a delightful, fragrant, deciduous tree which appears quite ordinary until in flower when it is covered with dense, terminal clusters of small, white flowers. Plant in an open, sunny position in medium to light, well-drained soil, and mulch around the base well with organic matter to keep the ground cool in summer. This viburnum cannot withstand very dry summers or extremely cold winters, and should be positioned with some thought to protection from strong winds.

Viburnum odoratissimum

Viburnum plicatum

Viburnum plicatum syn. *V. tomentosum* 'Plicatum'
JAPANESE SNOWBALL ○ ◑

Family: CAPRIFOLIACEAE
Origin: China, Japan.
Flowering time: Late spring.
Climatic zone: 4, 5, 6, 7, 8, 9.
Dimensions: Up to 10 feet (3 meters) high.
Description: This is the finest of the snowball bushes and rates very highly among the hardy ornamental shrubs. It is deciduous, with wide-spreading, arching branches. Its leaves, egg-shaped and toothed on the margins, are up to 4 inches (100 mm) long and hairy on their undersides. They color in the autumn. The conspicuous, sterile flowers are arranged in globular heads measuring up to 3 inches (75 mm) across. They are produced in a double row along the length of each stem of the previous year's growth and persist for several weeks. Make this a feature plant as it is hardy and prefers a reasonably sunny, well-drained site.
Varieties/cultivars: *V. p.* var. *tomentosum*, *V. p. t.* 'Lanarth', *V. p. t.* 'Mariesii', *V. p. t.* 'Pink Beauty', *V. p. t.* 'Rowallane'.

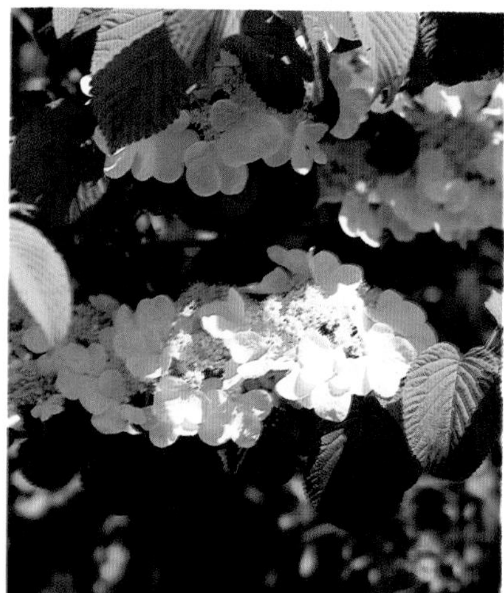

Viburnum plicatum var. *tomentosum* 'Mariesii'

Viburnum plicatum var. *tomentosum* 'Mariesii'
DOUBLEFILE VIBURNUM ○ ◑

Family: CAPRIFOLIACEAE
Origin: Cultivar.
Flowering time: Summer.
Climatic zone: 4, 5, 6, 7, 8, 9.
Dimensions: Up to 8 feet (approx. 2 meters) high.
Description: A cultivar of *V. plicatum* var. *tomentosum*, the original wild species of *Viburnum*, 'Mariesii' has a much stronger tiered habit than its parent and is very free-flowering, making it a most desirable addition to the garden. Plant 'Mariesii' in a well-drained, reasonably sunny position.

Viburnum rhytidophyllum

Viburnum rhytidophyllum

LEATHERLEAF VIBURNUM ○ ◑

Family: CAPRIFOLIACEAE
Origin: China.
Flowering time: Late spring–early summer.
Climatic zone: 5, 6, 7, 8, 9.
Dimensions: Up to 15 feet (approx. 5 meters) high.
Description: The hardiest of the evergreen viburnums, this shrub, which becomes as broad as it is tall, is thickly covered with narrow leaves up to 7 inches (175 mm) long. These are distinctive because of their much-wrinkled upper surfaces and the dense felting of yellowish hairs on the undersurfaces. The flowers, which individually measure ¼ inch (6 mm) across, are yellowish-white and are gathered into large, flat clusters up to 8 inches (200 mm) wide. The red, oval fruits become black when mature. Plant in well-drained soil.

Viburnum sieboldii

SIEBOLD VIBURNUM ○ ◑

Family: CAPRIFOLIACEAE
Origin: Japan.
Flowering time: Early spring.
Climatic zone: 7, 8, 9.
Dimensions: Up to 30 feet (9 meters) high.
Description: One of the most handsome viburnums, this deciduous shrub has a shapely, rounded form. The elliptic leaves are coarsely toothed, up to 6 inches (150 mm) long, with conspicuous veins, and while the upper surfaces are glossy, the undersides are hairy. Numerous small, creamy-white flowers are produced in rounded, open clusters up to 4 inches (100 mm) long. The distinctive oval fruits are pink, maturing to blue-black. The new leaves of spring and fallen leaves of autumn emit an objectionable smell when crushed. Plant in well-drained soil. Propagate from seed when ripe, or by layering in late winter.

Viburnum sieboldii

Viburnum tinus

Viburnum tinus

LAURUSTINUS ○ ◑

Family: CAPRIFOLIACEAE
Origin: Southeastern Europe.
Flowering time: Late autumn–early spring.
Climatic zone: 7, 8, 9.
Dimensions: Up to 10 feet (3 meters) high.
Description: This shrub is a most popular evergreen. Its dense, bushy habit, with foliage growing from ground level, makes it an excellent informal hedge. Its glossy, oval, dark-green leaves, up to 4 inches (100 mm) long, thickly cover the stems. This valuable winter-flowering shrub can have its long flowering period extended if there are spells of mild weather. The flowers, each ¼ inch (6 mm) wide, emerge from pink buds in flat clusters about 4 inches (100 mm) across. The plant tolerates light shade and grows well in seaside locations. It may be damaged or killed by severe winters.
Varieties/cultivars: 'Eve Price', 'Variegatum', *V. t.* var. *hirtulum*, *V. t.* var. *lucidum*.

Viburnum x *burkwoodii*

BURKWOOD VIBURNUM

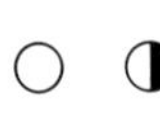

Family: CAPRIFOLIACEAE
Origin: Hybrid.
Flowering time: Spring.
Climatic zone: 5, 6, 7, 8, 9.
Dimensions: Up to 6 feet (2 meters) high.
Description: This upright shrub is semi-evergreen to evergreen. It is a more vigorous grower than its parent,

V. *carlesii*, from which it inherits its fragrant, pink-budded, white flowers. Rounded, and measuring up to 3 inches (75 mm) across, the beautiful flower heads open after the new leaves. The egg-shaped leaves are slightly toothed, up to 4 inches (100 mm) long, and a shiny, rich green on the upper surface, with grayish-brown felting on the underside. The fruits are red, maturing to black. Hardy, it prefers a well-drained but not dry soil. It is well-suited to training up a wall, where it may grow up to 10 feet (3 meters) high.
Varieties/cultivars: 'Chenaultii', 'Park Farm Hybrid'.

Viburnum x *burkwoodii*

Viburnum x *carlcephalum*

Viburnum x *carlcephalum*
FRAGRANT SNOWBALL ○ ◑

Family: CAPRIFOLIACEAE
Origin: Hybrid.
Flowering time: Spring.
Climatic zone: 5, 6, 7, 8, 9.
Dimensions: Up to 10 feet (3 meters) high.
Description: Fragrant snowball is a splendid, compact, deciduous shrub producing large, rounded flower heads up to 5 inches (125 mm) across. The flowers are very fragrant and open from pink buds. The broad leaves are up to 4 inches (100 mm) long, shiny green on the upper surface and covered with fine hairs on the undersides. After hot summers they color to rich shades of orange and crimson in autumn. A robust grower, plant from autumn to spring in well-drained soil.

Vitex agnus-castus 'Alba'

Vitex agnus-castus 'Alba'
CHASTE TREE ○

Family: VERBENACEAE
Origin: Cultivar.
Flowering time: Summer.
Climatic zone: 8, 9, 10.
Dimensions: Up to 20 feet (6 meters) high.
Description: Chaste tree is an ornamental, deciduous shrub which can withstand sea winds in warmer regions. The fragrant flowers are small and tubular and grow in spikes up to 7 inches (175 mm) long, clustered at the ends of the erect stems. The shrub's velvety appearance is due to the short gray hairs on the undersurface of the dark-green leaves. The new shoots are also hairy, and they and the leaves are strongly aromatic when bruised. The leaves consist of five or seven narrow leaflets up to 4 inches (100 mm) in length. Plant in autumn or spring against a wall in a sunny position. Fertile, well-drained soil is preferred.

Zenobia pulverulenta

Zenobia pulverulenta syn. *Z. speciosa*
ZENOBIA, ANDROMEDA ○ ◑

Family: ERICACEAE
Origin: Southeastern United States.
Flowering time: Early summer.
Climatic zone: 5, 6, 7, 8, 9.
Dimensions: To 6 feet (2 meters) high.
Description: Named after Zenobia, a queen of ancient Syria, this single species of *Zenobia* is a beautiful deciduous or semi-evergreen, small shrub. The narrow leaves, up to 3 inches (75 mm) long, are covered by a conspicuous gray bloom which is more noticeable when they are young. The flowers are fragrant and bell-shaped, resembling a large lily-of-the-valley. About ½ inch (12 mm) long, they appear on whitish stems in drooping clusters. Zenobia requires a lime-free, moist soil and is an excellent companion plant for *Pieris*, *Leucothoe* and *Rhododendron*.
Varieties/cultivars: *Z. p.* var. *nuda*.

Aesculus hippocastanum
COMMON HORSE CHESTNUT ○

Family: HIPPOCASTANACEAE
Origin: Northern Greece, Albania, Bulgaria.
Flowering time: Late spring–early summer.
Climatic zone: 3, 4, 5, 6, 7, 8, 9.
Dimensions: 60–120 feet (20–36 meters) high.
Description: Horse chestnut is one of the finest of all the deciduous broadleaf trees, with its handsome canopy of huge, radiating leaves, bright green in spring and turning yellow in autumn. Its wonderful spikes of white flowers flecked with red, sit up like candles in spring. In autumn children use the seeds to play the game of "conkers". The leaves create such a dense shade that nothing much will grow beneath the tree. Slow-growing, it is not fussy regarding soil type.
Other colors: Crimson.
Varieties/cultivars: 'Baumannii', *A.* x *carnea* 'Briotii'.

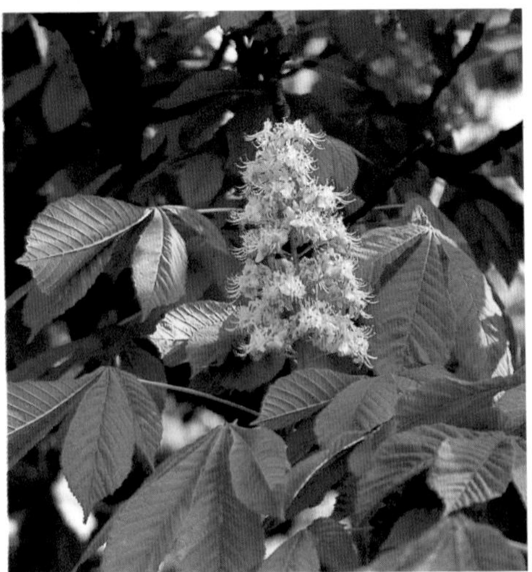
Aesculus hippocastanum

Amelanchier arborea
SHADBLOW (U.S.A.), SERVICEBERRY, JUNE-BERRY (U.K.) ○ ◑

Family: ROSACEAE
Origin: Eastern North America.
Flowering time: Spring, northern hemisphere.
Climatic zone: 4, 5, 6, 7, 8, 9.
Dimensions: 30–50 feet (10–17 meters) high.
Description: The most vigorous and tallest-growing of the amelanchiers, *A. arborea* is similar to the much smaller *A. canadensis*, but its pure white, star-shaped flowers are larger and hang more loosely. Deciduous, toothed leaves appear in spring from pointed buds. In summer, bunches of edible black berries hang among the foliage. Autumn changes the color of the foliage to subtle reds, oranges, and browns. This tree requires lime-free soil, with plenty of water in dry spells. It is susceptible to rust and fire-blight disease in some areas.

Amelanchier arborea

Amelanchier laevis
ALLEGHENY SERVICEBERRY (U.S.A.), SHADBLOW (U.S.A.), SHADBUSH (U.K.) ○ ◑

Family: ROSACEAE
Origin: Eastern North America.
Flowering time: Spring, northern hemisphere.
Climatic zone: 4, 5, 6, 7, 8, 9.
Dimensions: 20–35 feet (6–11 meters) high.
Description: Masses of pure white, star-shaped, fragrant flowers hanging in slender, nodding clusters bedeck this pretty tree in spring. Tender young leaves emerging as a delicate pink turn to a rich red color in autumn. In summer, birds love the clusters of sweet edible berries, which start as purplish black and later turn to red. *A. laevis* forms a more tree-like shape than most amelanchiers and pruning is rarely necessary. Give it extra water during dry spells. Plant it in a lime-free soil in a moist situation.

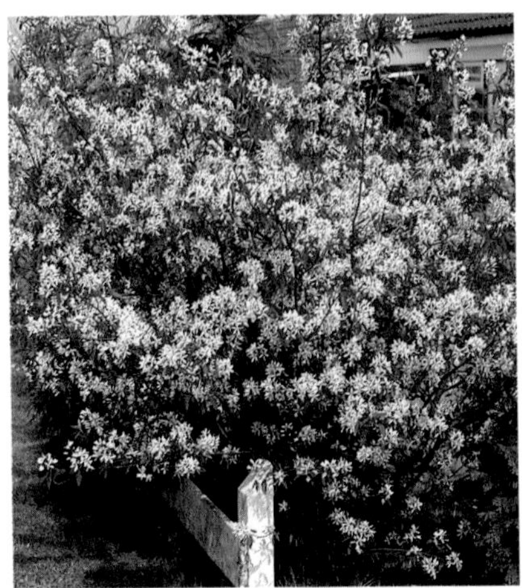
Amelanchier laevis

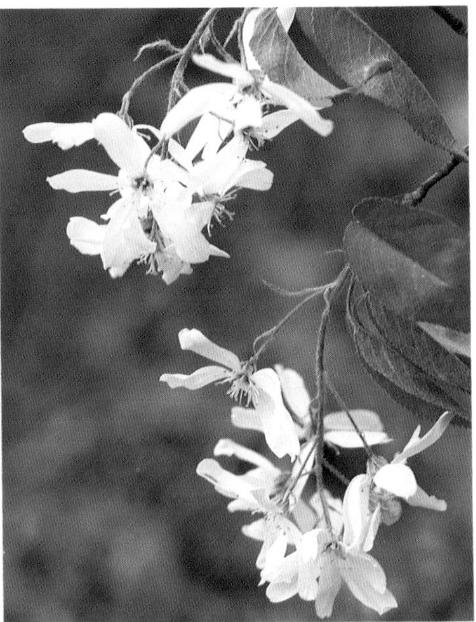
Amelanchier x *lamarkii*

Amelanchier x *lamarkii*
SHADBUSH ○ ◑

Family: ROSACEAE
Origin: Northern Europe.
Flowering time: Spring.
Climatic zone: 4, 5, 6, 7, 8, 9.
Dimensions: Up to 25 feet (8 meters).
Description: A most attractive deciduous tree, often confused with *A. canadensis*, however distinguished by the new foliage growth which is coppery-red and covered with silken hairs. The small white flowers appear in profusion, making a dramatic, if short-lived, display. It prefers a well drained, slightly acid soil and a sheltered position. Although frost resistant, it cannot withstand long periods without water.

Arbutus menziesii

Arbutus menziesii

MADRONE (U.K.), MADRONA, OREGON LAUREL ○ ◑

Family: ERICACEAE
Origin: British Columbia–California.
Flowering time: Spring, northern hemisphere; late winter and spring, southern hemisphere.
Climatic zone: 7, 8, 9.
Dimensions: 25–100 feet (7–30 meters) high.
Description: Often called the Californian version of the strawberry tree, this magnificent tree adds drama and beauty to gardens in many climates. In its native habitat it grows to large proportions, but in gardens it rarely exceeds 30 feet (10 meters). It bears clusters of small, white flowers similar to those of heather, which belongs to the same family. In autumn, handsome, round fruits change color from yellow to orange to red amid rich green leaves. This species can tolerate some lime though it prefers neutral to acid conditions and should be planted in any moderately rich, well-drained soil. Excellent in that it can tolerate hot, dry conditions.

Arbutus unedo

STRAWBERRY TREE ○

Family: ERICACEAE
Origin: Mediterranean region and southwestern Eire.
Flowering time: Autumn to early winter, southern hemisphere; late autumn, northern hemisphere.
Climatic zone: 7, 8, 9.
Dimensions: 20–25 feet (6–8 meters) high.
Description: Every part of this tree is attractive — its almost translucent-petaled flowers which look like lily-of-the-valley, the red, round fruits that follow, and the rich red stringy bark of the trunk and branches. All three delights can be enjoyed in autumn when the tree is covered in fragrant, white flowers, blooming amid the previous year's fruit. Easily grown, this evergreen is perfect for small gardens. Enrich soil with some well-rotted compost or cow manure prior to planting, and ensure that drainage is adequate. It can be damaged by severe winters.
Other colors: Pink.

Arbutus unedo

Callistemon salignus

WHITE BOTTLEBRUSH, WILLOW BOTTLEBRUSH ○

Family: MYRTACEAE
Origin: Australia (southern Queensland–Tasmania).
Flowering time: Mid-spring–summer.

Callistemon salignus

Climatic zone: 8, 9.
Dimensions: 27–40 feet (8–12 meters) high.
Description: This is one of the hardiest of the bottlebrushes and will grow in both hemispheres. The leaves, soft, downy, and pink when new, turn green at maturity and are aromatic when crushed. The flowers are actually a pale creamy-yellow and bloom in abundance. New shoots emerge from the flowering tips, which may be pruned to encourage bushier growth and longer life. These evergreen bottlebrushes grow in most soils, dry or wet.
Other colors: Pink.

Catalpa bignonioides

Catalpa bignonioides

SOUTHERN CATALPA (U.S.A.), INDIAN BEAN TREE (U.K.) ○

Family: BIGNONIACEAE
Origin: Southeastern United States.
Flowering time: Spring.
Climatic zone: 5, 6, 7, 8, 9.
Dimensions: 30–40 feet (9–12 meters) high.
Description: Big, bold, and beautiful, southern catalpa is unfortunately not very long-lived. This exotic-looking, rounded tree on a sturdy trunk is much admired for its wonderful clusters of fragrant, white flowers spotted with yellow, and its huge, heart-shaped leaves. Its rapid growth makes it a most desirable tree for new gardens. Because it needs a lot of space, it is best planted in large gardens. It will tolerate wet and dry conditions and withstand frost. Its leaves, though attractive, have an unpleasant smell.
Varieties/cultivars: 'Aurea' (yellow-tinted foliage).

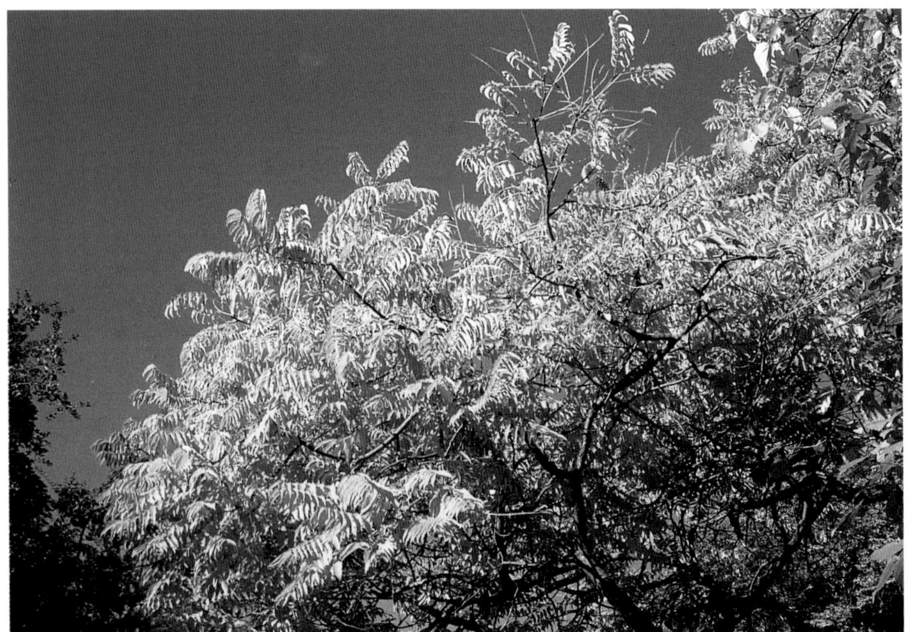
Cedrela sinensis

Cedrela sinensis syn. *Toona sinensis*
CHINESE CEDAR, CHINESE TOON ○

Family: MELIACEAE
Origin: Northern and western China.
Flowering time: Summer, northern hemisphere.
Climatic zone: 6, 7, 8, 9.
Dimensions: 20–70 feet (6–21 meters) high.
Description: Given the right conditions, this deciduous tree is perfect for the larger garden. A fast-grower, it will, if carefully pruned, develop a single trunk and rounded canopy. Its huge leaves, made up of numerous leaflets, are pinkish, onion-flavored, and edible when young, turning to green in summer and yellow in autumn. Flowers hang in 12-inch (300-mm) long clusters. It needs hot summers, complete protection from winds, and excellent drainage, and is found in such diverse places as wilderness areas in Victoria, Australia, and the streets of Paris.

Chionanthus retusus
CHINESE FRINGE TREE ○

Family: OLEACEAE
Origin: China.
Flowering time: Summer.
Climatic zone: 6, 7, 8, 9.
Dimensions: 10–20 feet (3–6 meters) high.
Description: This superb deciduous tree, often shrub-like, is covered with white, fine-petaled flowers during summer. It is an ideal choice for the cool, temperate garden because of its size and its tolerance of a wide range of soils. Chinese fringe tree prefers a sunny aspect with protection from the wind.

Chionanthus virginicus
OLD-MAN'S-BEARD, FRINGE TREE (U.K.) ○

Family: OLEACEAE
Origin: Gulf and lower Atlantic states of United States.
Flowering time: Late spring.
Climatic zone: 5, 6, 7, 8, 9.
Dimensions: 10–30 feet (3–9 meters) high.

Chionanthus retusus

Description: *Chionanthus* is derived from Greek words meaning snowflower. Pure white, fragrant flowers in loosely branched clusters grow at the end of branches produced from the previous year's growth. Later, dark-blue fruits ripen on the female trees. The fringe tree, with its single trunk and spreading canopy, makes an ideal shade tree. In autumn, the leaves turn yellow and often remain on the tree, especially in milder areas. Rather slow-growing — 8 feet or so (about 2 meters) in 20 years — it likes rich, moist soils on a wind-sheltered site, in a cool, humid climate.

Chionanthus virginicus

Citharexylum spinosum
FIDDLEWOOD ○

Family: VERBENACEAE
Origin: West Indies, Central America.
Flowering time: Mid-summer–mid-winter.
Climatic zone: 9, 10.
Dimensions: 16–40 feet (5–12 meters) high.
Description: *C. spinosum* is conspicuous

Citharexylum spinosum

among green trees in late winter when its own leaves turn a beautiful shade of apricot before some of them drop. Creamy-colored spikes of deliciously perfumed flowers appear in warm weather. New leaves are a glossy, bright green. Happy in most soils, it needs plenty of mulch and water in hot, dry weather. A fast-grower, it responds well to fertilizer and to pruning, which makes it an ideal plant for hedging. Plant it near the house in large containers so that the perfume, especially at night, can be enjoyed.

Clethra arborea

Clethra arborea

LILY-OF-THE-VALLEY TREE ○

Family: CLETHRACEAE
Origin: Madeira.
Flowering time: Late spring, southern hemisphere; late summer, northern hemisphere.
Climatic zone: 9, 10.
Dimensions: 10–20 feet (3–6 meters) high.
Description: Would that this delightful, small, evergreen tree could be grown in a wider range of climates. The nodding clusters of flowers resemble those of lily-of-the-valley, hence its name. Its glossy, elliptic leaves, 2–5 inches (50–130 mm) long, are similar to those of the rhododendron but serrated. It enjoys a mild, coastal climate and humus-rich, lime-free soils. If it is growing where autumns are always hot, dry, and long, giving time for the tender wood to harden, it may survive brief, light frosts. It develops into a multi-stemmed tree, unlike other *Clethra* which are shrub-like.
Varieties/cultivars: 'Flore-pleno' (double-flowered form).

Cornus capitata

STRAWBERRY TREE, EVERGREEN DOGWOOD, BENTHAM'S CORNEL ○

Family: CORNACEAE
Origin: Himalayas, western China.
Flowering time: Summer.
Climatic zone: 8, 9.
Dimensions: 20–30 feet (6–10 meters) high.
Description: One of the many beautiful dogwoods, this small, slow-growing, evergreen species is happiest in the mildest of climates. The actual flowers are quite small, but are surrounded by four to six cream-colored bracts which are what really attract the eye. These splendid "flowers" are followed by strawberry-shaped fruits, 1–1½ inches (25–40 mm) wide, which turn from yellow to crimson. The young shoots harden into sprays of dull green, leathery leaves.

Cornus capitata

Cornus florida

Cornus florida

FLOWERING DOGWOOD (U.K.), EASTERN DOGWOOD ○

Family: CORNACEAE
Origin: Eastern United States (south of Massachusetts).
Flowering time: Late spring–early summer, northern hemisphere; late spring, southern hemisphere.
Climatic zone: 5, 6, 7, 8, 9.
Dimensions: 13–30 feet (4–9 meters) high.
Description: *C. florida* is a spectacular sight when in full flower. Petal-like bracts surround the tiny, greenish flowers, which are carried on upturned twigs along horizontal branches. Very often the canopy spreads wider than the height of the tree, the main trunk dividing at an early stage of growth. The flowers are followed in autumn by scarlet fruits and red to purplish leaves. It needs excellent drainage, but will not tolerate drought conditions.
Other colors: Red, pink.
Varieties/cultivars: 'Pleniflora', *C. f.* var. *rubra*.

Cornus kousa

Cornus kousa

JAPANESE DOGWOOD, KOREAN DOGWOOD ○ ◑

Family: CORNACEAE
Origin: Japan, Korea, China.
Flowering time: Early summer.
Climatic zone: 5, 6, 7, 8, 9.
Dimensions: 16–20 feet (5–6 meters) high.
Description: This small, deciduous tree is mostly grown for its summer display of white, showy bracts. It has a preference for acid soils and summer moisture. Its distinctive strawberry-like fruit in late summer and its bright autumn foliage are added features. Its size makes it suitable for small gardens.
Other colors: Pink.
Varieties/cultivars: 'Chinensis', 'Rubra'.

Crataegus crus-galli

COCKSPUR THORN, COCKSPUR HAWTHORN ○

Family: ROSACEAE
Origin: Northeastern United States and adjacent Canada.
Flowering time: Spring.
Climatic zone: 5, 6, 7, 8, 9.
Dimensions: 13–30 feet (4–9 meters) high.
Description: Cockspur thorn lights up each spring as small clusters of tiny rose-like flowers decorate this attractive, deciduous tree. The orange to scarlet foliage provides a foil for the crimson berries in autumn. It develops a small trunk which branches low down. Formidable, sharp thorns (up to 4 inches (100 mm) in length) cover the branches, making it an ideal barrier plant, although it will not stand much clipping. It grows best in cool climates in limy soils, and tolerates drought and pollution. In disease-prone areas, check for fireblight regularly.

Crataegus crus-galli

Crataegus phaenopyrum

WASHINGTON THORN ○

Family: ROSACEAE
Origin: Southeastern United States.
Flowering time: Spring, northern hemisphere; late spring–early summer, southern hemisphere.
Climatic zone: 5, 6, 7, 8, 9.
Dimensions: 20–30 feet (6–9 meters) high.
Description: Often described as the best of the hawthorns, *C. phaenopyrum* is deciduous and easy to grow. Profuse, pear-like blossom sits well clear of the foliage in spring, and is followed by numerous clusters of bright red "berries" in autumn. Orangy-red foliage at this time produces what looks like a tree on fire! Its single, short trunk and shapely canopy make it an excellent small shade tree, and its very sharp, slender thorns 2–2½ inches (50–65 mm) long make it a good barrier plant. It prefers cool climates and deep, rich soils.

Crataegus phaenopyrum

Crataegus x *lavallei*

LAVALLE THORN ○

Family: ROSACEAE
Origin: Hybrid.
Flowering time: Mid-spring, northern hemisphere; late spring, southern hemisphere.
Climatic zone: 5, 6, 7, 8, 9.
Dimensions: 16–25 feet (5–7 meters) high.
Description: The hardy hawthorns are all reliable for their show of spring flowers and autumn color. *C. lavallei* is no exception. Pretty, white flowers,

Crataegus x *lavallei*

marked with a red disk, produce brick-red fruits in autumn which hang on into winter. Autumn leaf coloration varies from reddish-brown to purplish-red. Sparse, stout, dark-red thorns 2 inches (50 mm) in length on the branches make it a suitable small barrier tree, or it can be grown as a small shade tree if the lower branches are cut away from the trunk to form a partial standard. Deciduous, though in mild climatic conditions only a percentage of the foliage falls in winter.

Davidia involucrata

Davidia involucrata
HANDKERCHIEF TREE, DOVE TREE ○ ◑

Family: DAVIDIACEAE
Origin: Southwestern China.
Flowering time: Late spring–early summer.
Climatic zone: 6, 7, 8, 9.
Dimensions: 40–50 feet (12–15 meters) high.
Description: This deciduous tree is named after the nineteenth-century plant collector and missionary, Abbé Armand David. The common name refers to the conspicuous white bracts which flutter in the breeze like handkerchiefs waving. The floral display, which begins just as the tree's foliage opens, lasts for several weeks. The tree is welcome in the garden because it tolerates a wide range of climates.

Dombeya tiliacea
NATAL CHERRY, WEDDING FLOWER ○

Family: BYTTNERIACEAE
Origin: South Africa (frost-free areas of Eastern Cape, Natal, Transvaal).
Flowering time: Autumn–winter, northern hemisphere; autumn–spring, southern hemisphere.
Climatic zone: 9, 10.
Dimensions: 13–25 feet (4–7 meters) high.
Description: Like all dombeyas, this is a small tree for tropical to subtropical areas only. In autumn it becomes weighed down by what look like huge clusters of cherry blossom. These perfumed flowers later fade to a pale brown, becoming papery and persistent. Although the tree is evergreen, some of the dark-green leaves turn yellow or red in autumn. The mature tree is slim, with a rounded crown. Grow it in fertile, well-drained soils, in a warm, wind-sheltered position.
Other colors: Rose-pink.
Varieties/cultivars: 'Dregiana'.

Dombeya tiliacea

Eucalyptus citriodora
LEMON-SCENTED GUM ○

Family: MYRTACEAE
Origin: Australia (tropical Queensland).
Flowering time: Winter, southern hemisphere.
Climatic zone: 9, 10.
Dimensions: 30–65 feet (10–20 meters) high.
Description: Tall, slender, and graceful describes this popular, ornamental, evergreen eucalypt. Its elevated canopy makes this tree a marvellous feature in parks and gardens when planted in small groups. Its smooth, pale gray-pink to white bark is then really appreciated. The flowers are pretty, and its rough leaves give off a strong lemon scent when the breeze blows or when they are crushed. Grow it in well-drained sites, but give it water in dry spells. Do not spoil its shape by lopping. In cold climates it is often grown as a greenhouse pot plant for its scented foliage.

Eucalyptus citriodora

Eucalyptus scoparia

Eucalyptus scoparia
WALLANGARRA WHITE GUM, WILLOW GUM ○

Family: MYRTACEAE
Origin: Australia (N.S.W. and Queensland border).
Flowering time: Late spring–summer, southern hemisphere.
Climatic zone: 9, 10.
Dimensions: 30–40 feet (10–12 meters) high.
Description: One of the loveliest eucalypts, willow gum is grown widely in hot climates as an evergreen, ornamental, shade, or screen tree. Graceful, willowy leaves cover the slender canopy. It has attractive white flowers, and the smooth bark is a wonderful, subtle medley of white and creamy-yellow, often daubed with areas of blue and pink which intensify in color when wet. Plant it in coarse, well-drained soils, giving plenty of water in dry weather.

Eucryphia lucida
LEATHERWOOD ○ ◑

Family: EUCRYPHIACEAE
Origin: Australia (Tasmania).
Flowering time: Summer, northern hemisphere; late summer–early autumn, southern hemisphere.
Climatic zone: 8, 9.
Dimensions: 10–30 feet (3–9 meters) high.
Description: Native to rainforest areas of Tasmania, this slender evergreen tree is popular with bees. Leatherwood honey has a very distinctive, strong, and pungent flavor. The beautiful, delicate-looking, fragrant flowers with numerous stamens have been likened to small, single camellias, and cover the crown in abundance. Not easy to cultivate unless conditions are just right, it enjoys cool, moist conditions. It will not endure harsh, drying winds or frosty winters. *Lucida*, Latin for bright and shiny, refers to the glossy leaves.

Eucryphia lucida

Eugenia smithii syn. *Acmena smithii*
LILLY PILLY ○ ◑

Family: MYRTACEAE
Origin: East coast of Australia (Cape Howe to Cape York).
Flowering time: Late spring–summer, southern hemisphere.
Climatic zone: 9, 10.
Dimensions: 25–30 feet (7–10 meters) high.
Description: If you live in a warm climate, this evergreen tree will certainly enhance your garden. Everything comes in abundance; indeed, the Greek word *acmena* means buxom. Glossy green leaves, numerous fluffy flowers, followed by clusters of white to purplish, edible fruits keep this plant looking good all year. Prune it to form a hedge or screening plant, or allow it to grow as a tree, pruning to a single trunk. It likes well-drained soils, and plenty of water in hot, dry weather.

Eugenia smithii

Franklinia alatamaha

Franklinia alatamaha
FRANKLIN TREE ○

Family: THEACEAE
Origin: Georgia, United States.
Flowering time: Late summer–autumn.
Climatic zone: 6, 7, 8, 9, 10.
Dimensions: Up to 30 feet (9 meters) high.
Description: This tree, discovered close to the mouth of the Alatamaha River in 1765, was named in honor of Benjamin Franklin. It has not been seen in the wild since 1803, so all known specimens are the result of the original collection of seeds. This history makes it an interesting tree, but it is also highly ornamental. Given a hot continental summer, the 3-inch (75-mm) wide, open, cup-shaped flowers with their conspicuous yellow stamens are produced in profusion. In autumn, the large, lustrous, green leaves, 6 inches (150 mm) long, turn crimson before they fall. It requires an acid soil and cannot tolerate cold winters.

Fraxinus ornus
MANNA ASH (U.K.), FLOWERING ASH ○

Family: OLEACEAE
Origin: Southern Europe–Turkey.
Flowering time: Late spring–early summer.

Fraxinus ornus

Climatic zone: 5, 6, 7.
Dimensions: 20–65 feet (6–20 meters) high.
Description: Manna ash is grown in southern Italy and Sicily for its sap which hardens to a sugary substance called manna and is used medicinally. The tree is readily distinguished from other ashes by the showy clusters of fragrant flowers opening in late spring just after the new leaves have appeared. In its native habitat it is found growing in mixed woods, thickets, and rocky places, so the ideal place for this deciduous tree is in similar positions in large gardens for a natural effect.

Gordonia axillaris
GORDONIA, FALSE CAMELLIA ○ ◑

Family: THEACEAE
Origin: Taiwan, southern China, Vietnam.
Flowering time: Late autumn–early winter.
Climatic zone: 8, 9, 10.
Dimensions: 30 feet (10 meters) high.
Description: Gordonia, a close relative of the camellia, is an evergreen tree which is slow to establish. It is noted for its showy, solitary, white flowers, with their prominent stamens. The flowering cycle can last from two to three months, the fallen blooms producing a showy carpet beneath the tree. Gordonias respond equally well to full sun or dappled shade, but tolerate nothing more than light frosts — severe winters can kill them. Its soil requirements are similar to those of camellias — a light, well-drained, acid soil enriched with well-rotted compost to encourage rapid growth. The two can be grown successfully together.

Gordonia axillaris

Hakea laurina
PINCUSHION HAKEA, SEA URCHIN ○

Family: PROTEACEAE
Origin: Western Australia.
Flowering time: Autumn–winter, southern hemisphere.
Climatic zone: 9, 10.
Dimensions: 10–20 feet (3–6 meters) high.
Description: Its curious and beautiful flowers are the main attraction of this pretty hakea. The globular flower clusters, with their protruding, creamy-colored styles, look like round pincushions when fully opened. Sprays, attached to branches, make good cut flowers in autumn and winter. Give this evergreen tree a sunny, well-drained position in a dry atmosphere similar to that of its native home in Western Australia and its adopted home in California. It grows fairly quickly into a small, low-branching tree. Prune it lightly after flowering.

Hakea laurina

Hakea salicifolia syn. *H. saligna*
WILLOW-LEAVED HAKEA ○

Family: PROTEACEAE
Origin: Australia (coastal N.S.W. and Queensland).
Flowering time: Spring–early summer, southern hemisphere.
Climatic zone: 9, 10.
Dimensions: 10–20 feet (3–6 meters) high.
Description: Unlike most hakeas, which need well-drained soils, the willow-leaved hakea will grow in wetter conditions, often being found in good soils near permanent, running streams in its native habitat. It will tolerate some frost and is most useful in the home garden as a quick-growing, evergreen, screen plant. It has attractive, white flowers borne in showy, dense clusters. Tip-prune it regularly to keep the screen or hedge dense, but do wait until the flowers have finished. Hakeas form decorative, woody fruits after flowering, so you have to decide whether to keep these or prune the plant.
Varieties/cultivars: 'Fine Leaf'.

Hakea salicifolia

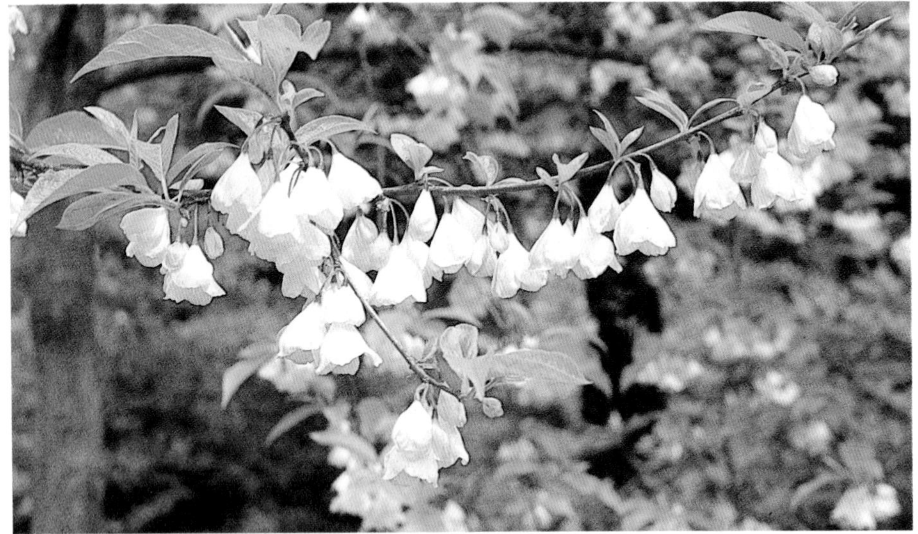

Halesia carolina

Halesia carolina syn. *H. tetraptera*

SILVER-BELL TREE, SNOWDROP TREE (U.K.), CAROLINA SILVERBELL ○ ◑

Family: STYRACACEAE
Origin: Southeastern United States.
Flowering time: Spring.
Climatic zone: 5, 6, 7, 8, 9.
Dimensions: 10–30 feet (3–9 meters) high.
Description: Halesias enjoy similar conditions to rhododendrons and azaleas — moist, rich, well-drained, lime-free soil. Requiring filtered sun and protection from strong winds, these plants would revel in a light, woodland setting. Easily grown, they are hardy in cold winter areas. Train them to a single stem whilst young or the plants will become too bushy. You have plenty of time for they grow slowly — about 12 feet (4.5 meters) in 15 years. In late spring, an excellent display of pendulous clusters of white, bell-shaped flowers appear just before the new leaves begin to open. The leaves turn yellow in autumn.

Hoheria glabrata

HOUHERIA ○ ◑ ●

Family: MALVACEAE
Origin: New Zealand (North Island).
Flowering time: Summer (northern hemisphere); late summer (southern hemisphere).
Climatic zone: 8, 9.
Dimensions: Up to 30 feet (9 meters) high.
Description: Native to the North Island of New Zealand, the Latin name *Hoheria* is derived from the Maori name "houhere". *H. glabrata* has pale green, oval leaves with serrated margins, and fragrant white trumpet-shaped flowers occurring in terminal clusters. Grows best in organically rich, well-drained soil and is frost resistant, but drought tender. Useful as a screen or background plant, it can be propagated either by seed or from cuttings.

Liriodendron tulipifera

TULIP TREE, WHITEWOOD, YELLOW POPLAR ○

Family: MAGNOLIACEAE
Origin: Southeastern United States.
Flowering time: Early summer.
Climatic zone: 4, 5, 6, 7, 8, 9.
Dimensions: 50–200 feet (15–60 meters) high.
Description: This magnificent tree,

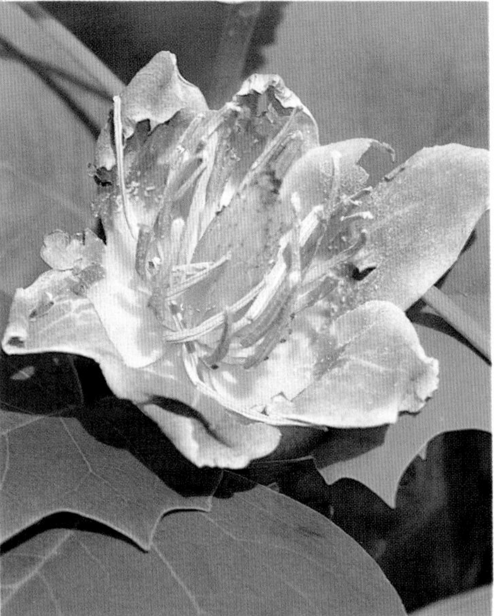

Liriodendron tulipifera

Hoheria glabrata

which grows huge and fast on a straight trunk, can be grown in the very large garden. The handsome leaves differ markedly from any other broadleaf, looking rather like a maple leaf with the middle lobe cut off. One cultivar develops leaves that are almost rectangular. The flowers resemble tulips. Carried on the branchlet tips, these are greenish-yellow with a band of orange, and often only appear when the tree is twenty to twenty-five years old. Tulip tree prefers deep, crumbly soils and a cool, wet spring season. Deciduous, with yellow leaves in autumn, it withstands pollution.
Varieties/cultivars: 'Fastigiatum' (narrow tree, for limited space), 'Aureo-marginatum' (variegated foliage).

Magnolia grandiflora
BULL BAY MAGNOLIA (U.K.), SOUTHERN MAGNOLIA (U.S.A.) ○

Family: MAGNOLIACEAE
Origin: Florida–Texas, North Carolina, United States.
Flowering time: Mid-summer.
Climatic zone: 7, 8, 9, 10.
Dimensions: 80 feet (25 meters) high.
Description: This is a slow-growing, broad-domed, evergreen tree, with dark, glossy green leaves and spectacular, solitary, bowl-shaped white flowers. Its size, longevity, and grandeur make it very suitable for use in large-scale landscapes, such as parklands, avenues, and malls. It prefers a well-drained, sandy loam which is slightly acid. Summer moisture is essential, and frost protection is necessary when the tree is young. Prune to shape the tree and raise the crown in its early years.
Varieties/cultivars: Several cultivars are available.

Magnolia grandiflora

Malus baccata 'Jackii'

Malus baccata hybrids and cultivars
SIBERIAN CRAB APPLE ○

Family: ROSACEAE
Origin: Eastern Asia.
Flowering time: Mid–late spring.
Climatic zone: 2, 3, 4, 5, 6, 7, 8, 9.
Dimensions: 15–40 feet (5–12 meters) high.
Description: Any plant that can grow in Siberia is tough. Siberian crab apple is a beautiful tree, smothered in fragrant, white blossom in spring, and later by yellow to red fruits which remain after the leaves have dropped. It has been used by breeders since the end of the eighteenth century to yield a fair number of hybrids and cultivars. A most successful cultivar, 'Manchuria', is the first of all the crab apples to flower. The species plant is resistant to apple scab and is long-lived. It does best in cool, moist climates, and is deciduous.
Varieties/cultivars: There are many cultivars available.

Malus 'Golden Hornet'
ORNAMENTAL CRAB APPLE ○

Family: ROSACEAE
Origin: Cultivar.
Flowering time: Mid-spring.
Climatic zone: 4, 5, 6, 7, 8, 9.
Dimensions: 13–25 feet (4–7 meters) high.
Description: Ornamental crab apple has white to palest pink flowers in spring, followed by delightful yellow fruits (¾ inch (20 mm) across) which hang on the tree into winter. Heavy crops weigh down its slender branches, creating a graceful, weeping appearance. Delicious jelly can be made from the apples. Like all other crabs, they are best pruned only when young, in this

Malus 'Golden Hornet'

case to a single trunk. Thereafter flowering and fruiting are better if the tree is left undisturbed. This deciduous tree does best in cool, moist climates and good soils.

Malus 'John Downie'
ORNAMENTAL CRAB APPLE ○

Family: ROSACEAE
Origin: Cultivar.
Flowering time: Spring.
Climatic zone: 4, 5, 6, 7, 8, 9.
Dimensions: 13–20 feet (4–6 meters) high.
Description: This crab apple is grown for its luscious fruit, which are good for eating straight off the tree or for making jam. The white flowers in spring are followed by a generous crop of bright orange and red fruits in autumn, which, if not picked, remain through the winter. Do not crowd this pretty deciduous tree among other trees. It prefers a cool, moist climate and good soils.

Malus 'John Downie'

Melaleuca linariifolia

Melaleuca linariifolia
FLAXLEAF PAPERBARK, SNOW IN SUMMER

Family: MYRTACEAE
Origin: Australia (Queensland and N.S.W.).
Flowering time: Late spring, northern hemisphere; late spring–summer, southern hemisphere.
Climatic zone: 9, 10.
Dimensions: 16–30 feet (5–9 meters) high.
Description: A hot climate tree, snow in summer certainly lives up to its name when a cloudburst of white flowers envelops it all at once. The flowers, though otherwise similar to the bottlebrush, differ in that the stamens are joined together in groups. Birds find the honey attractive. Often developing several trunks, it is a good foil tree, and its flaky bark makes it team well with shrubby plants. It will grow in any soil, and has needle-like, evergreen leaves.

Melaleuca quinquenervia
BROAD-LEAVED PAPERBARK, PAPERBARK (U.K.), CAJEPUT TREE, SWAMP TEA TREE

Family: MYRTACEAE
Origin: Australia (east coast from Cape York to Shoalhaven).
Flowering time: Spring–late summer and intermittently.

Melaleuca quinquenervia

Climatic zone: 9, 10.
Dimensions: 27–75 feet (8–23 meters) high.
Description: So good is this tree at adaptation, it is planted worldwide for many purposes. It will grow in dry or wet ground, and in some countries it is used to stabilize swampy ground. Unfortunately, it has become too successful in Florida, where it threatens to overtake the Everglades. Its fluffy, cream flowers are similar to those of the bottlebrush, except that the stamens of *Melaleuca* are united in bundles. White, flaky bark contrasts with the dark-green leaves, with their five parallel veins. An evergreen, it is best grown from seed or semihardwood cuttings in large home gardens as a background plant.
Varieties/cultivars: 'McMahon's Golden'.

Michelia doltsopa
MICHELIA, WONG-LAN

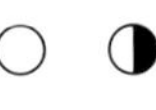

Family: MAGNOLIACEAE
Origin: Eastern Himalayas–western China.
Flowering time: Winter–spring.
Climatic zone: 8, 9, 10.
Dimensions: 20–40 feet (6–12 meters) high.
Description: This neat, pyramid-shaped tree, with its rich green leaves is popular in many home gardens. The large, showy white flowers are fragrant and measure 4 inches (100 mm) across, with 12–16 narrow petals. Plant it as an individual in a lawn or use it as a background tree. Do not plant it too near the house, because perfume from the flowers, although pleasant at first, can become rather overpowering. Fast-growing and easy to grow in mild climates, it likes a rich, well-drained soil. Sow this evergreen from seed in spring.

Michelia doltsopa

Oxydendrum arboreum
SOURWOOD, SORREL TREE (U.K.)

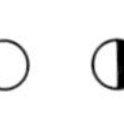

Family: ERICACEAE
Origin: Southeastern United States.
Flowering time: Mid-summer–late summer.

Oxydendrum arboreum

Climatic zone: 5, 6, 7, 8, 9.
Dimensions: 20–50 feet (6–15 meters) high.
Description: Sourwood is worth growing for its brilliant coloring in autumn, when its leaves turn a fiery red before they fall. Slender heads of fragrant flowers droop from the tips of shoots in summer, attracting birds and bees to their honeyed nectar. Belonging to the same family as rhododendrons, it enjoys similar conditions — moist, acid soil with other trees nearby, in a light glade, for example. It can be grown from seed, cuttings, or layers, but is slow-growing and dislikes polluted air.

Photinia x *fraseri* 'Robusta'
RED-LEAF PHOTINIA ○

Family: ROSACEAE
Origin: Hybrid.
Flowering time: Spring–early summer, southern hemisphere; late spring–summer, northern hemisphere.

Photinia x *fraseri* 'Robusta'

Climatic zone: 4, 5, 6, 7, 8.
Dimensions: 13–16 feet (4–5 meters) high.
Description: This handsome, evergreen shrub has white, bitter-smelling flowers which fade to brown. Carried in clusters 5–6 inches (120–150 mm) across, they appear above the upper leaves. Fleshy, green fruits follow, ripening to red in autumn. It has showy foliage — the new leaves are a shiny, coppery-red which then mature to a deep green; older leaves turn crimson in autumn before they fall. Tolerant of regular clipping which induces plenty of new growth, photinias are often used as hedging plants, or as a background foil.
Varieties/cultivars: 'Red Robin', 'Americanum'.

Plumeria rubra

Plumeria rubra syn. *P. acutifolia*
FRANGIPANI, GRAVEYARD TREE (Asia) ○

Family: APOCYNACEAE
Origin: Central America, Mexico, Venezuela.
Flowering time: Summer–autumn, northern and southern hemispheres; most of year in tropical areas.
Climatic zone: 9, 10.
Dimensions: 10–27 feet (3–8 meters) high.
Description: You can often smell this wonderful tree before you see it, so pervasive is its perfume. Glorious flowers, carried on stubby branches, cover the tree in bloom. It can be grown successfully only in warmer gardens in full sun, protected from the wind. Cuttings taken from hardened stem tips about 4–6 inches (100–150 mm) long are planted in early spring. The stems contain a milky sap. Deciduous, it is often planted as a street tree in tropical countries.

Prunus cerasifera and cultivars
CHERRY PLUM, MYROBALAN CHERRY ○

Family: ROSACEAE
Origin: Southeastern Europe–central Asia.
Flowering time: Late winter–early spring.
Climatic zone: 4, 5, 6, 7, 8, 9.
Dimensions: 15–30 feet (5–9 meters) high.
Description: Flowering cherry plums really are a study in themselves, with so many beautiful varieties and cultivars bred from the species. One of the more notable ones is 'Pissardii', first noticed in the Shah of Persia's garden by the French gardener Pissardt. Its flowers are

Prunus cerasifera

white to blush-pink and the foliage is purple. A further development from America produced 'Pissardii Thundercloud', with pink flowers and deep, smoky, purplish-red foliage. Others are listed below. All are deciduous, easy to grow, and do best in full sun. Their dark-colored foliage can be used, sparingly, for contrast in the garden.
Varieties/cultivars: 'Festeri' and 'Nigra' (single pale pink), 'Vesuvius' (white to blush-pink), 'Elvins', 'Rosea' (salmon-pink flowers, bronze-green foliage).

Prunus cerasifera 'Elvins'
CHERRY PLUM ○

Family: ROSACEAE
Origin: Cultivar.
Flowering time: Spring.
Climatic zone: 4, 5, 6, 7, 8, 9.
Dimensions: 10–13 feet (3–4 meters) high.
Description: 'Elvins', developed in Victoria in about 1940, is a small tree that can enhance many small gardens in cool to temperate climates. Each spring it appears as a froth of pure white flowers which, though enchanting, have a very brief life. This deciduous tree has a mass of slender shoots spreading out from a short trunk. Plant it with other blossom trees for an outstanding spring show.

Prunus cerasifera 'Elvins'

Prunus dulcis syn. *P. amygdalus*
ALMOND, COMMON ALMOND ○

Family: ROSACEAE
Origin: Western Asia.
Flowering time: Late winter–early spring.
Climatic zone: 7, 8, 9.
Dimensions: 20–30 feet (6–9 meters) high.
Description: Almonds, which are among the very first trees to blossom, are followed soon after by the peach trees. Plant them together for an extended blooming period. The species almond is a spreading, deciduous tree, extensively grown in Sicily for commercial purposes. It grows well in a dryish climate in well-drained soils. It has been crossed with *P. persica* to produce the cultivar 'Pollardii'. Often flowering in late winter, it needs protection from inclement weather. The almond looks wonderful against a

Prunus dulcis

backdrop of large evergreens which also provide protection.
Varieties/cultivars: *P. d.* var. *praecox*, 'Macrocarpa' (large, very pale pink to white flowers), 'Roseoplena' (double pale pink flowers).

Prunus lusitanica
PORTUGAL LAUREL ○ ◑

Family: ROSACEAE
Origin: Spain, Portugal.
Flowering time: Early summer.
Climatic zone: 7, 8, 9.
Dimensions: 13–40 feet (4–12 meters) high.
Description: Suitable for clipping, Portugal laurel makes an elegant round-

Prunus lusitanica

topped tree, or a formal or informal hedge or screen. Evergreen and elegant all year with glossy green foliage, there comes a bonus in spring as slender, long heads of cream, fragrant flowers appear, followed in summer by red berries that turn purplish-black. It withstands poor, chalky soils, and looks most effective in large gardens lining a driveway or screening off unattractive areas.
Varieties/cultivars: 'Variegata', 'Myrtifolia'.

Prunus mume 'Alba Plena'
JAPANESE APRICOT (U.K.) ○

Family: ROSACEAE
Origin: Cultivar.
Flowering time: Early spring.
Climatic zone: 7, 8, 9, 10.
Dimensions: 10–27 feet (3–8 meters) high.
Description: Japanese apricot flowers at

Prunus mume 'Alba Plena'

the same time as many of the almonds, but needs more protection from the elements. If planted in a cold-climate garden, place it against the warmest-facing wall. The pure white, semidouble flowers decorating this deciduous tree each winter are at their best after a summer of good sunshine. Cool, moist soil conditions are preferred, however a rich and well-drained soil that is watered consistently should produce good flowering results.

Prunus serrulata hybrids and cultivars

JAPANESE FLOWERING CHERRY ○

Family: ROSACEAE
Origin: Japan, China, Korea.
Flowering time: Mid–late spring.
Climatic zone: 6, 7, 8, 9.
Dimensions: 13–27 feet (4–8 meters) high.
Description: The many cultivars bred from this species are mostly wide, flat-topped, small trees. Most of them flower in mid-spring, producing extremely beautiful clusters of flowers hanging from long stalks. The shiny trunks are often marked by horizontal scars and the leaves color yellow through red in autumn. Give these wide-spreading, deciduous cultivars plenty of space for best effect. They need a moist, elevated site.
Varieties/cultivars: 'Shirotae' (Mt. Fuji), 'Snow Goose' (masses of pure white flowers), 'Shimidsu Sakura' (large, double white flowers pink-tinged in bud), 'Shirofugen', 'Purpurea' (white flowers, rich purple foliage), 'Kiku-shidare Sakura' (double, clear, deep-pink flowers), 'Tai Haku', 'Fugenzo', 'Autumn Glory' (pale blush flowers), 'Ojochin', 'Ichiyo'.

Prunus subhirtella 'Alba'

WHITE SPRING, WEEPING SPRING CHERRY ○

Family: ROSACEAE
Origin: Cultivar.
Flowering time: Spring.
Climatic zone: 6, 7, 8, 9.

Prunus subhirtella 'Alba'

Dimensions: 3–10 feet (1–3 meters) high.
Description: Graceful at any time, this little tree is a most glorious sight in spring when it is smothered in cascades of hanging flowers. The pink buds open to a single white flower. Plant white spring in a lawn or at a focal point in the garden where it is shown at its best. Deciduous, its leaves color attractively in autumn. It likes a cool climate.

Prunus 'Ukon'

Prunus serrulata 'Mt. Fuji'

Prunus 'Ukon' syn. *P. serrulata luteovirens*

JAPANESE FLOWERING CHERRY (U.K.), GREEN JAPANESE FLOWERING CHERRY ○

Family: ROSACEAE
Origin: Japan.
Flowering time: Mid-spring.
Climatic zone: 6, 7, 8, 9.
Dimensions: 15–30 feet (5–9 meters) high.
Description: The most unusual coloring of the flowers sets this Japanese flowering cherry apart from the others. In mid-spring the flower buds appear lime-green in color, opening to reveal pale greenish-yellow to white petals, with a hint of rose along the central rib. When leaves appear, they are a pale bronze-green which soon turns to green. Later in autumn they become a rusty-purple color. Like all cherries, this tree is deciduous, needing a moist, elevated, cool site.

Pyrus calleryana

Pyrus calleryana

CALLERY PEAR, CHINESE WILD PEAR, BRADFORD PEAR (U.K.) ○

Family: ROSACEAE
Origin: Central and southeastern China.
Flowering time: Spring.
Climatic zone: 6, 7, 8, 9.
Dimensions: 25–30 feet (7–9 meters) high.
Description: Trouble-free and unfussy, this species grows in the wilds of China as a medium-sized, deciduous tree. Pyramidal in outline, it forms a dense, much-branched canopy and lives to a great age. Frothy sprays of attractive white flowers appear each spring, followed by small, brown fruits on slender stalks. The leaves are glossy green, turning to red in autumn. Callery pear needs full sun and occasional pruning to thin out dense, thorny branches. It tolerates lime soils and thrives even when neglected.
Varieties/cultivars: 'Bradford', 'Chanticleer'.

Pyrus salicifolia 'Pendula'

WILLOW-LEAVED PEAR (U.K.), WEEPING SILVER PEAR ○

Family: ROSACEAE
Origin: Cultivar.
Flowering time: Early spring.
Climatic zone: 5, 6, 7, 8, 9.
Dimensions: 15–20 feet (5–6 meters) high.
Description: Many pears grow rather too large and unruly for the average garden, but this little deciduous tree is perfect for many landscape situations. Tightly packed, small flowers in flat heads appearing in spring are followed by small, brown, inedible fruits. Long, grayish leaves, covered in a silvery down, hanging from slender, drooping branches, make this tree a perfect foil for more somber-colored plants. Planted in a white garden among flowering perennials, it adds a graceful harmony. It revels in full sun in cool-climate gardens, and is not fussy as to soil conditions.

Pyrus salicifolia 'Pendula'

Pyrus ussuriensis

USSURIAN PEAR, CHINESE PEAR, MANCHURIAN PEAR ○

Family: ROSACEAE
Origin: Northeastern China–eastern U.S.S.R., Korea, northern Japan.
Flowering time: Spring.
Climatic zone: 5, 6, 7, 8, 9.

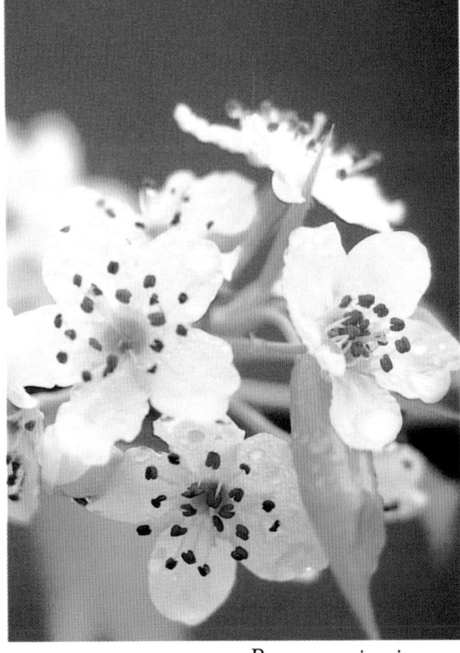

Pyrus ussuriensis

Dimensions: 40–50 feet (12–15 meters) high.
Description: Eventually growing to about 50 feet (15 meters) in height, Ussurian pear develops a broad crown on a straight trunk. It is a perfect deciduous tree for a large country garden where informality is the keynote. Flat heads of pretty, white flowers, often tinged pink in the bud, appear in spring and are followed by yellowish, round fruits. These can become a nuisance if they fall on a public footpath. The broad, shiny, green leaves turn reddish in autumn. Like all pears it needs full sun. This species is resistant to fireblight disease.

Robinia pseudoacacia

BLACK LOCUST (U.K.), FALSE ACACIA, COMMON ACACIA ○

Family: LEGUMINOSAE
Origin: Eastern and central United States.
Flowering time: Early summer, northern hemisphere; mid–late spring, southern hemisphere.
Climatic zone: 3, 4, 5, 6, 7, 8, 9.
Dimensions: 40–65 feet (12–20 meters) high.
Description: Now at home in many countries of both hemispheres, this tree thrives in dry soils, but casts only a light shade from its open canopy. Zig-zag branches carry bright green leaves — and thorns! Its delightful, fragrant, pea-like flowers are borne in clusters, partially hidden by foliage. Fast-growing, it is valued for its durable timber. The leaves arrive late and fall early, providing sun and shade when most needed.
Varieties/cultivars: 'Frisia', 'Inermis'.

Robinia pseudoacacia

Rothmannia globosa syn. *Gardenia globosa*

TREE GARDENIA ◑

Family: RUBIACEAE
Origin: South Africa.
Flowering time: Spring.
Climatic zone: 9, 10.
Dimensions: 9–12 feet (3–4 meters) high.
Description: A close relative of the gardenia, this evergreen tree with its upright stems forms a small multi-branched dome. It is covered with small, bell-shaped, cream flowers in spring, followed by black, round, woody seed capsules which remain on the tree. Rothmannias like only mild climates and survive best in acid soils with summer moisture. They are usually grown for their sweet fragrance.

Rothmannia globosa

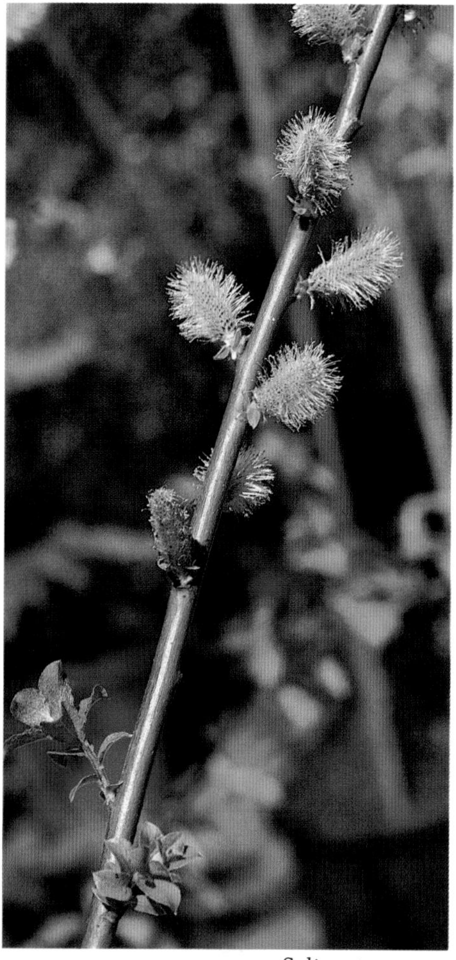

Salix caprea

Salix caprea

GOAT WILLOW, SALLOW, PUSSY WILLOW ○

Family: SALICACEAE
Origin: Europe–southwestern Asia.
Flowering time: Late winter–mid-spring.
Climatic zone: 5, 6, 7, 8, 9.
Dimensions: 27–33 feet (8–10 meters) high.
Description: Like all willows, goat willow likes water. It is a small, shrubby, deciduous tree, loved for its pretty, furry catkins. Male and female catkins grow on separate trees. Female catkins are silky and silvery. Male catkins are larger, and silky-white, turning to yellow. More graceful and needing less space is the cultivar 'Pendula'. The male tree produces ornamental yellow catkins. 'Pendula' is usually grafted onto the species as a standard trunk about 6½ feet (2 meters) tall. Plant it near water or in boggy ground.
Varieties/cultivars: See description.

Sophora japonica

Sophora japonica
JAPANESE PAGODA TREE, CHINESE SCHOLAR TREE ○

Family: LEGUMINOSAE
Origin: China, Korea, Japan.
Flowering time: Late summer.
Climatic zone: 5, 6, 7, 8, 9.
Dimensions: 40–70 feet (12–21 meters) high.
Description: Admired for its beautiful foliage, the Japanese pagoda tree has bright leaves and clusters of flowers which later form pods. The leaves of this shapely tree stay fresh-looking into winter. Grow it from seed in well-drained soil and protect the young plants from frost. The cultivar, 'Pendula', is grafted onto a standard *Sophora japonica* and develops drooping, contorted branches. It tolerates pollution.
Varieties/cultivars: See description.

Sorbus alnifolia
KOREAN MOUNTAIN ASH, WHITEBEAM (U.K.) ○

Family: ROSACEAE
Origin: Eastern Asia.
Flowering time: Late spring.
Climatic zone: 6, 7, 8, 9.
Dimensions: 30–50 feet (9–15 meters) high.
Description: All year round there is something to enjoy on this comely tree. In spring, the abundant, flat-topped heads of white flowers become delightful, tiny, pinkish-orange berries which remain hanging on the tree. In autumn, the broad leaves turn to a beautiful orange-brown, and in winter, the beautiful gray bark is the tree's eye-catching feature. Plant it with other deciduous trees for glorious autumn color, or against dark-green evergreens for dramatic effect. Easily grown from seed, it performs best in cool, elevated sites, and must be given extra water during hot, dry spells.

Sorbus alnifolia

Sorbus aria

Sorbus aria
WHITEBEAM (U.K.) ○

Family: ROSACEAE
Origin: Southern and central Europe, U.K.
Flowering time: Spring.
Climatic zone: 6, 7, 8, 9.
Dimensions: 25–45 feet (8–14 meters) high.
Description: If you first see this tree in spring, you can be forgiven for thinking that it is in flower, for as the leaves open, in an upright position, they show only the silvery-white, hairy undersides. The flowers follow, in heavily scented clusters. Bunches of abundant red fruits and russet-colored foliage glow in autumn. It prefers well-drained, lime soils and with its silvery foliage will brighten a dull corner in the garden. It makes a good coastal tree and can withstand pollution. In some areas it is attacked by leaf skeletonizers.
Varieties/cultivars: 'Chrysophylla' (yellow leaves), 'Decaisneana' (large leaves), 'Lutescens', (hairy, gray-green leaves), 'Pendula' (small, weeping tree; leaves small and narrow).

Sorbus aucuparia

Sorbus aucuparia
COMMON MOUNTAIN ASH (U.K.), ROWAN TREE, EUROPEAN MOUNTAIN ASH ○

Family: ROSACEAE
Origin: Europe, western Asia, North Africa.
Flowering time: Summer.
Climatic zone: 3, 4, 5, 6, 7, 8, 9.
Dimensions: 20–50 feet (6–15 meters) high.
Description: The common mountain ash has ash-like leaves, made up of small leaflets and contrasting with the dramatic display of bright red berries which appear after the large clusters of cream flowers. Thriving on acid soils, but short-lived on chalky soils, it prefers a well-drained site, with plenty of mulch and water in warm, dry spells. It can be susceptible to borer in the U.S.A. In autumn the leaves produce a range of color from yellow through to red, before they fall.
Varieties/cultivars: 'Cardinal Royal', 'Asplenifolia', 'Beissneri', 'Edulis', 'Fastigiata','Sheerwater Seedling', 'Xanthocarpa'.

Sorbus domestica

Sorbus domestica
SERVICE TREE, TRUE SERVICE TREE ○

Family: ROSACEAE
Origin: Southern and central Europe, North Africa, western Asia.
Flowering time: Late spring.
Climatic zone: 5, 6.
Dimensions: 33–60 feet (10–18 meters) high.
Description: This deciduous tree is distinguished from the rowans by its scaly bark, often used in tanning, and by its more open and wider-spreading branches. The pretty, feathery foliage colors later than that of other service trees and the attractive, rounded or pear-shaped berries turn from green to brown in autumn. Larger than those of the common rowan, they are edible only after a frost and are used in alcoholic beverages. The winter buds of this tree are shiny and sticky. Demanding no special conditions, it is an easy tree to grow.

Stewartia pseudocamellia
STEWARTIA ◑

Family: THEACEAE
Origin: Japan.
Flowering time: Summer.
Climatic zone: 7, 8, 9.
Dimensions: Up to 35 feet (12 meters) high.
Description: A spreading deciduous tree that is valued for its foliage, flowers, and attractive flaking bark. The large but delicate, single white flowers resemble camellias and require similar conditions that is, a well-drained, acid soil with plenty of mulch to keep the roots cool, and extra water in warm, dry spells. Planted in semishade with azaleas and camellias it will give a fine show of summer flowers for some weeks, long after the azaleas and camellias have finished. Autumn brings more interest as the foliage turns brilliant shades of red and orange.

Stewartia pseudocamellia

Styrax japonica
JAPANESE SNOWDROP TREE, JAPANESE SNOW-BELL TREE (U.K.) ○ ◑

Family: STYRACACEAE
Origin: Japan, Korea, China, Taiwan, Philippines.
Flowering time: Late spring–summer.
Climatic zone: 5, 6, 7, 8, 9.
Dimensions: 10–25 feet (3–8 meters) high.
Description: This graceful little tree, when in bloom, is profusely covered with snowdrop-like, waxy, fragrant flowers. Plant it on a bank or terrace where you can look up at the flowers. Another delight is the pinkish-orange fissuring appearing between ridges in the trunk. The wide-spreading, horizontal branches carry bright, glossy green leaves through the summer, which turn yellow and red in autumn. A slow-grower, this deciduous tree likes cool gardens and well-drained but moist, lime-free soils.
Varieties/cultivars: 'Fargesii'.

Styrax japonica 'Fargesii'

Syzygium jambos

Syzygium jambos
ROSE APPLE, JAMBU, MALABAR PLUM ○

Family: MYRTACEAE
Origin: Tropical South East Asia, Indonesia, naturalized in West Indies.
Flowering time: Spring–autumn.
Climatic zone: 9, 10.
Dimensions: 30–40 feet (9–12 meters) high.
Description: The glossy green leaves of this evergreen are bright crimson when young, and its showy, fluffy flowers, which bloom for months, are followed by pretty, fragrant, creamy-yellow fruits, tinged with rosy-pink. Insects are attracted to the nectar-bearing flowers, and flavorsome jams and jellies can be made from the fruits. When mature, jambu forms a broad dome on a short trunk, casting a welcome, dense shade. It needs no special attention.

SECTION FIVE

Yellow Flowers

Annuals 538

Bulbs 542

Climbers 548

Perennials 552

Shrubs 568

Trees 582

Calceolaria x *herbeohybrida*
SLIPPERWORT ○

Family: SCROPHULARIACEAE
Origin: Hybrid.
Flowering time: Late spring–midsummer.
Climatic zone: 7, 8, 9.
Dimensions: Up to 18 inches (450 mm) high.
Description: A dramatic, giant-flowering hybrid available in various shades of yellow, orange, and red, spotted and blotched in many combinations. The flowers are borne in terminal trusses, are pouch-shaped, and can reach 2 inches (50 mm) across. In the right conditions this hybrid can be treated as a biennial. Plant in moderately rich, acid soil and ensure that drainage is good. Care must be taken not to overwater as it resents waterlogged root conditions. The best display is achieved by group planting which also suits its preference for slightly crowded root conditions.

Calceolaria x *herbeohybrida*

Calendula officinalis
POT MARIGOLD ○

Family: COMPOSITAE
Origin: Southern Europe.
Flowering time: Summer–autumn.
Climatic zone: 4, 5, 6, 7, 8, 9.
Dimensions: 1–2 feet (300–600 mm) high.
Description: This hardy and fast-growing annual blooms over many months, bringing a real splash of color to the garden, with its bright and showy, yellow-orange flowers. Sow seeds in early spring, when frosts have finished, in an open position, in moderately rich and well-drained soil. Keep the seedlings well-watered during the growing period (10 weeks) and, once they are established, mulch with well-rotted manure to keep weeds down and encourage good flower production. If the seeds are allowed to ripen on the flower and fall, they will germinate the following season.

Calendula officinalis

Coreopsis tinctoria
GOLDEN COREOPSIS, CALLIOPSIS ○

Family: COMPOSITAE
Origin: North America.
Flowering time: Summer.
Climatic zone: 6, 7, 8, 9, 10.
Dimensions: Up to 2 feet (600 mm) high.
Description: This self-seeding, very hardy annual has flat, daisy-like flowers which appear at the tops of the stems. The flowers are up to 2 inches (50 mm) wide, yellow-petaled with a red-brown center, and the foliage is fern-like. Because they are so brightly colored and their stems are so long (up to 18 inches (450 mm)), coreopsis are popular with both florists and home decorators. Easily grown in most soils and conditions, it may require some support when flowering.
Varieties/cultivars: 'Nana' (dwarf), also double-flowered form.

Helianthus annuus
ANNUAL SUNFLOWER, EVERLASTING, COMMON SUNFLOWER ○

Family: COMPOSITAE
Origin: North America, Mexico.
Flowering time: Summer–autumn.
Climatic zone: 6, 7, 8, 9, 10.
Dimensions: Up to 10 feet (3 meters) high.
Description: One of the tallest of the annuals, sunflowers need to be grown in special open, sunny situations to be seen at their best. The bright yellow flowers, which may be 12 inches (300 mm) across, are borne on long, hairy stems, and face the sun. Because of their size, they are seldom used in the home, but are very suitable for large-scale

Coreopsis tinctoria

arrangements in foyers and other large spaces in buildings. Both humans and birds love the mature seeds, which are not only nutritious, but also produce a valuable oil. Sunflowers will grow in any soil, but really thrive in ground that has been enriched with plenty of organic matter. Full sun and some protection from strong wind is important.
Other colors: Wine-red.
Varieties/cultivars: 'Purpureus'. Also dwarf forms to 3 feet (1 meter) high.

Helianthus annuus

Helichrysum bracteatum
STRAWFLOWER, EVERLASTING ○

Family: COMPOSITAE
Origin: Australia.
Flowering time: Summer–autumn.
Climatic zone: 5, 6, 7, 8, 9, 10.
Dimensions: Up to 3 feet (1 meter) high.
Description: This very hardy plant is a short-lived perennial, but is usually grown as an annual. Its long stems, up to 18 inches (450 mm) high, are topped with brightly colored, paper-textured flowers that last many weeks on the plant. They are very useful for floral work, particularly as a dried specimen, when they are truly everlasting. Choose a warm, sunny, and sheltered position, and water regularly for a good flower display.
Varieties/cultivars: 'Monstrosum' (large size flowers).

Helichrysum bracteatum

Hunnemania fumariifolia
MEXICAN TULIP POPPY, GOLDEN CUP ○

Family: PAPAVERACEAE
Origin: Mexico.
Flowering time: Summer–autumn.
Climatic zone: 4, 5, 6, 7, 8, 9, 10.
Dimensions: Up to 2 feet (600 mm) high.
Description: The foliage of this sun-loving plant is slightly gray and feathery, making a soft background for the bright yellow, cup-shaped flowers. Up to 3 inches (75 mm) wide, these are borne on upright stems about 12 inches (300 mm) long. The petals curve inwards slightly towards the center of the flower. The soil should be moderately rich, but well-drained. It can withstand very dry summers.

Hunnemania fumariifolia

Layia platyglossa syn. *L. elegans*
TIDY TIPS ○

Family: COMPOSITAE
Origin: California.
Flowering time: Summer–autumn.
Climatic zone: 4, 5, 6, 7, 8, 9.
Dimensions: Up to 2 feet (600 mm) high.
Description: This is an attractive garden flower for sunny situations and, although it thrives in dry climates, it does not respond in temperatures continuously over 95°F (35°C). It prefers much cooler weather. The flower stems are up to 12 inches (300 mm) long, and the individual, daisy-like flowers have a clear yellow center, a ring of yellow florets with white tips. Flowers may be up to 2 inches (50 mm) wide. Moist, rich soil and full sun will yield good results.

Layia platyglossa

Limnanthes douglasii

Limnanthes douglasii

MEADOW FOAM, POACHED EGG PLANT ◑

Family: LIMNANTHACEAE
Origin: North America.
Flowering time: Late spring–summer; summer–autumn.
Climatic zone: 4, 5, 6, 7, 8, 9.
Dimensions: Up to 12 inches (300 mm) high.
Description: This low-growing plant may be used in rock gardens, or at the front of borders, preferably in moist conditions. It will not tolerate dry heat in summer. The flowers are up to 1 inch (25 mm) wide, have broadly notched petals which are yellow with a broad white tip. These show above a bed of dense fern-like foliage. Rather sensitive to cultivate, meadow foam likes open sun, but cool, moist soil. Sow in autumn or in spring.
Varieties/cultivars: 'Sulphurae'.

Mentzelia lindleyi

BLAZING STAR, BARTONIA (U.K.) ○

Family: LOASACEAE
Origin: California.
Flowering time: Summer–autumn.
Climatic zone: 5, 6, 7, 8, 9.
Dimensions: Up to 2 feet (600 mm) high.
Description: This annual has broadly-cut, toothed leaves. The flowers open flat and are the clearest shiny yellow, with slightly darker stamens. The fragrant, single-stemmed flowers are up to 2½ inches (60 mm) wide. A most versatile plant, it thrives in most soils, preferring full sun in cooler climates and good drainage.

Mentzelia lindleyi

Nemesia strumosa

NEMESIA ○

Family: SCROPHULARIACEAE
Origin: South Africa.
Flowering time: Spring.
Climatic zone: 4, 5, 6, 7, 8, 9.
Dimensions: Up to 12 inches (300 mm) high.
Description: While the individual flowers of nemesia are small (1 inch (25 mm) wide), they are produced in great quantity to give a vivid display of color. They appear on top of leafy stems. Grown closely together, the

Nemesia strumosa cultivar

plants form a wonderful flowering border. The flowers mature quickly, but do not persist in hot climates (i.e. in temperatures over 85°F (30°C)). They are short-lived when picked and cannot be used in floral decoration. For beautiful blooms add lots of manure or fertilizer to the soil before planting. Choose a sunny position and ensure that drainage is good.
Other colors: Pale blue.
Varieties/cultivars: 'Compacta', 'Carnival', 'Blue Gem'.

Sanvitalia procumbens
CREEPING ZINNIA ○

Family: COMPOSITAE
Origin: Mexico, Guatemala.
Flowering time: Summer.
Climatic zone: 5, 6, 7, 8, 9, 10.
Dimensions: Up to 6 inches (150 mm) high.
Description: This is a sprawling groundcover or trailing plant which produces clusters of bright, daisy-like flowers in midsummer. Even though the flowers are only 1 inch (25 mm) in diameter, the spreading capacity of the plant and the masses of flowers produced makes it highly suitable for use in hanging baskets in a warm situation. Seeds should be sown directly where the plant is to grow, as creeping zinnia does not transplant well. The soil should be moderately rich with good drainage.

Sanvitalia procumbens

Tagetes erecta
AFRICAN MARIGOLD, AZTEC MARIGOLD, AMERICAN MARIGOLD ○

Family: COMPOSITAE
Origin: Mexico.
Flowering time: Summer–autumn.
Climatic zone: 4, 5, 6, 7, 8, 9, 10.

Tagetes erecta cultivar

Dimensions: Up to 3 feet (1 meter) high.
Description: These tall, attractive, summer-flowering plants are among the most popular in the yellow color range. They are easily grown in average warm conditions. Each plant produces abundant, pompom-like flowers for up to two months. The stems are up to 18 inches (450 mm) long and bear large, densely petaled double flowers up to 6 inches (150 mm) wide. Not very demanding, it grows in any fertile garden soil. Water well during the growing period.
Other colors: Cream, orange, orange-red.
Varieties/cultivars: Many cultivars including 'Jubilee', 'Golden Girl', 'African Queen'.

Tagetes patula
FRENCH MARIGOLD ○

Family: COMPOSITAE
Origin: Mexico, Guatemala.
Flowering time: Late summer–autumn.
Climatic zone: 4, 5, 6, 7, 8, 9, 10.
Dimensions: Up to 2 feet (600 mm) high.
Description: While the French marigold likes the sun, it prefers cooler conditions than its so-called African namesake. The plant is bushy and produces many flowers of a smaller size (up to 3 inches (75 mm) wide), which are useful for floral work and home decoration. They are usually yellow to orange with darker reddish marks towards the center, and are borne singly on short stems. Plant in an open, sunny location. Water and feed it regularly in the growing period.
Other colors: Clear orange, clear red.
Varieties/cultivars: 'Honeycomb', 'Gypsy', 'Petite Yellow', 'Petite Orange', 'Queen Sophia', 'Freckle Face', 'Cinnabar', 'Tiger Eyes'.

Tagetes patula cultivar

Tropaeolum majus cultivar

Tropaeolum majus
NASTURTIUM, INDIAN CRESS ◑

Family: TROPAEOLACEAE
Origin: South America (cool mountain areas).
Flowering time: Summer.
Climatic zone: 4, 5, 6, 7, 8, 9.
Dimensions: Trailing or climbing, to 10 feet (3 meters) long. Dwarf types to 12 inches (300 mm) high.
Description: Nasturtium is a climbing or trailing plant with long stems, which may be supported on a trellis or wire fence or allowed to hang from baskets. It has unusually shaped flowers, 2½ inches (60 mm) wide with five petals opening out and curving slightly backwards. The largest petal lengthens to a spur which bears nectar. The leaves are large, flat, and are edible with a pleasant, sharp flavor. The plant prefers a sheltered position where it may persist for years. It seeds prolifically and the seeds too are edible when soft and green. They are used as a substitute for capers. Moderate to poor soils are preferable — too much fertilizer encourages foliage growth at the expense of the flowers.
Other colors: Orange to ruby-red.
Varieties/cultivars: Dwarf cultivars are 'Jewel', 'Cherry Rose', 'Whirly Bird', 'Alaska', which are all compact and non-trailing. 'Gleam' types are semitrailing and used as groundcover.

Calochortus venustus

Calochortus venustus
MARIPOSA LILY ○

Family: LILIACEAE
Origin: North America and Mexico.
Flowering time: Early summer, northern hemisphere; summer, southern hemisphere.
Climatic zone: 7, 8, 9.
Dimensions: Up to 18 inches (450 mm) high.
Description: Mariposa lily is an American wildflower with one to three bowl-shaped flowers per stem, with patches of deep red on the stem. The flower color is very variable. The leaves are sparse and grass-like, hence the name *Calochortus*, which is Greek for "beautiful grass". Plant it in rock or native gardens and among pebble paths. It is a good choice for a newly established garden, where the soil is not too rich, but it does not like manure, frosty conditions, or very wet areas. It can be grown in pots on a sunny deck.
Other colors: White, cream, pinkish-purple, red.

Crocus chrysanthus and cultivars
WINTER CROCUS ○ ◑

Family: IRIDACEAE
Origin: Yugoslavia to Turkey.
Flowering time: Late winter to spring.
Climatic zone: 5, 6, 7, 8, 9.
Dimensions: Up to 4 inches (100 mm) high.
Description: The native form is yellow. This variable plant has produced many cultivars and is a favorite with alpine and cold climate gardeners. It provides a spectacular display in rock gardens, outdoor pots and indoor pans. Crocus forms clumps and needs little attention. Pre-cooled bulbs should be planted in semishaded areas. In their native element they thrive in enriched soils and sunny or lightly shaded positions. If plenty of water is provided a few bulbs will quickly spread and become a colorful colony in the garden.
Other colors: Blue, gold, cream, white.
Varieties/cultivars: 'Blue Pearl', 'E. A. Bowles', 'Cream Beauty', 'Warley', 'Zwanenburg Bronze'.

Crocus chrysanthus and cultivars

Eranthis hyemalis

Eranthis hyemalis
WINTER ACONITE ○ ◑

Family: RANUNCULACEAE
Origin: France–Bulgaria.
Flowering time: Spring.
Climatic zone: 3, 4, 5, 6, 7, 8.
Dimensions: 4 inches (100 mm) high.
Description: Related to the buttercup, these hardy plants are best naturalized. Nestling at the base of large trees or around shrubs, they will produce flowers for up to four weeks. Propagation is by offsets from the tubers or by seed. Both seeds and tubers need to be soaked overnight in warm water. Plant them in generous clusters in compost for a good spring display. Mice may be a problem in some areas.
Varieties/cultivars: *E.* x *tubergenii.*

Eucomis comosa syn. *E. punctata*
PINEAPPLE LILY ○

Family: LILIACEAE
Origin: South Africa.
Flowering time: Late summer–autumn.
Climatic zone: 7, 8, 9, 10.
Dimensions: Up to 2½ feet (750 mm) high.
Description: Dozens of flowers mass on the thick stem to form a spike, capped by a pineapple-like tuft of leaves. The name *Eucomis* comes from the Greek for "beautiful topknot". The flowers turn green with age and will bloom for several months. These sun-lovers make beautiful plants for a sheltered border. They also do well in cool greenhouses. Plant in rich, composed soil near a sunny wall protected from the wind.

Eucomis comosa

When planted the tops of the bulbs should be well below the soil surface to give frost protection in winter. Water well in summer.
Other colors: Purple, cream.

Fritillaria imperialis 'Lutea Maxima'

Fritillaria imperialis
CROWN IMPERIAL

Family: LILIACEAE
Origin: Iran–Kashmir.
Flowering time: Early spring.
Climatic zone: 5, 6, 7, 8, 9.
Dimensions: Up to 3 feet (1 meter) high.
Description: This bulb is noted for its eye-catching flower-head. At the top of an erect stem is a crown of bell-shaped flowers surrounded by a rosette of shiny leaves. *Fritillaria* has a regal form and is happy in full sun or partial shade. It requires rich, well-drained soil. Leave the bulbs undisturbed in the ground.
Varieties/cultivars: 'Lutea Maxima'.

Fritillaria pudica

Fritillaria pudica

YELLOW FRITILLARY, YELLOW BELL ○ ◑

Family: LILIACEAE
Origin: Western North America.
Flowering time: Spring.
Climatic zone: 6, 7, 8, 9.
Dimensions: Up to 9 inches (225 mm) high.
Description: Yellow fritillary is not unlike golden snowdrop. Plant it in open woodland, in rock garden pockets, and along paths and driveways. Providing it has good sunlight, perfect drainage, and very little humus, it will produce abundant offset bulbs, which should be dug up, divided, and replanted every second or third year. The bulbs should be replanted as soon as they are dug up as they can dry out very rapidly. Bunches of these yellow bells make very pretty spring floral arrangements indoors.

Gladiolus hybrids

GLADIOLI ○

Family: IRIDACEAE
Origin: Hybrid.
Flowering time: Summer.
Climatic zone: 7, 8, 9, 10.
Dimensions: Up to 3 feet (1 meter) high.
Description: There are over 200 species of gladioli which take their name from their sword-like leaves, the Latin *gladius* meaning sword. Miniature to giant varieties are available, with an almost endless range of forms and colors. They require some attention because of their susceptibility to virus and fungal disease which can spread and ruin the corms. They are best planted en masse in garden beds in good sun, protected from wind, and the smaller varieties make splendid pot plants. Gladioli are widely cultivated commercially for the cut flower trade.
Other colors: Red, white, purple, pink, lilac.
Varieties/cultivars: There are many varieties and cultivars available.

Gladiolus 'Georgette'

Hypoxis longifolia

STAR GRASS ○

Family: AMARYLLIDACEAE
Origin: South Africa.
Flowering time: Autumn.
Climatic zone: 9, 10.
Dimensions: Up to 12 inches (300 mm) high.
Description: A low-growing, spreading groundcover, *H. longifolia* is distinguished by its long, slender, glossy leaves and brilliant yellow, star-like flowers. The underside of the yellow petals is green. Grown from large tubers, it is a warm climate plant preferring a warm, sunny position in moderately rich, slightly acid soil that has good drainage. Protect from wet winter weather and frosts. Every four years the plants should be lifted and separated.

Hypoxis longifolia

Iris danfordiae

WINTER IRIS ○

Family: IRIDACEAE
Origin: Turkey.
Flowering time: Winter–spring.
Climatic zone: 6, 7, 8, 9.
Dimensions: Up to 4 inches (100 mm) high.
Description: The short stems of this iris make it ideal for rock gardens, where the honey-scented, bright yellow blooms will flower for many weeks. Plant the bulbs 4 inches (100 mm) deep in well-drained soil enriched with compost. Although hardy, they need a sunny, protected position and regular fertilizing.

Iris danfordiae

Ixia maculata

Ixia maculata

AFRICAN CORN LILY ○

Family: IRIDACEAE
Origin: South Africa.
Flowering time: Spring–summer.
Climatic zone: 8, 9.
Dimensions: Up to 18 inches (450 mm) high.
Description: A tender corm, *Ixia maculata* produces brilliant and graceful corn-colored flowers. Each long stem carries numerous blooms opening successively from the base up. The corm multiplies quickly in warmer climates and is a good choice for sunny edges and borders, where light to medium, well-drained soil is available. In colder climates, it can be successfully cultivated in a greenhouse. If pot-planting outdoors, put six to twelve corms in a large pot. *Ixia* is a very pretty plant, producing good cut flowers.

Narcissus bulbocodium

HOOP-PETTICOAT DAFFODIL ○ 

Family: LILIACEAE
Origin: Spain, Portugal, France, Northwestern Africa .
Flowering time: Spring.
Climatic zone: 5, 6, 7, 8.
Dimensions: Up to 6 inches (150 mm) high.
Description: Hoop-petticoat daffodil has almost cylindrical leaves which are longer than the flower stems. The flowers are shades of bright yellow, with very large trumpets and six very small, narrow petals. Plant the bulbs in naturalized settings where they can be left undisturbed. The informal nature of the flower and its brilliant color make it an interesting inclusion in the spring garden.

Narcissus bulbocodium

Narcissus (daffodil)

Narcissus (daffodil)

DAFFODIL, NARCISSUS ○ ◑

Family: AMARYLLIDACEAE
Origin: Southern Europe–Asia.
Flowering time: Spring.
Climatic zone: 5, 6, 7, 8, 9.
Dimensions: Up to 18 inches (450 mm) high.
Description: This is one of the biggest and most popular genera for gardeners. *Narcissus* was named after the celebrated youth who fell in love with his own image. The daffodil, with its trumpet-shaped corona surrounded by six tepals, may be naturalized, planted in clumps between shrubs, or grown in pots. Praised by poets and gardeners alike, it is beautiful indoors and out.
Other colors: White, pink.
Varieties/cultivars: The many cultivars include 'King Alfred', 'Mount Hood', 'Romance', 'Mrs. R. O. Backhouse'.

Narcissus (Tazetta hybrids)

JONQUIL ○ ◑

Family: AMARYLLIDACEAE
Origin: Southern Europe, Algeria.
Flowering time: Late spring.
Climatic zone: 6, 7, 8.
Dimensions: 18 inches (450 mm) high.
Description: Jonquil is like a bunch-flowered narcissus, but with rush-like, dark green leaves. Strongly fragrant, they tend to flower earlier than daffodils. They are seen at their best in drifts under deciduous trees or naturalized in lawn areas. Jonquils are an old, familiar, hardy favorite in all gardens. Cool, moist, and well-drained soil conditions are essential for healthy growth. In warmer districts, wait until the ground has cooled in autumn before planting. Incorporate plenty of well-rotted compost.

Narcissus (Tazetta hybrids)

Ranunculus asiaticus

RANUNCULUS, TURBAN FLOWER ○

Family: RANUNCULACEAE
Origin: Southwestern Asia and Crete.
Flowering time: Late spring, early summer.
Climatic zone: 6, 7, 8, 9.
Dimensions: Up to 18 inches (450 mm) high.
Description: The small claw-like tubers of ranunculus are planted and then lifted in order to promote optimum flowering. Ranunculus display solitary, open, single or double flowers on erect stems. The flowers are surrounded by a mass of segmented foliage. They are most suited to being mass-planted in full sun or used in a perennial border. They are also very attractive as cut flowers. Cool, moist soil conditions are important, and bulbs will rot if planted during warm weather. The soil should be well-drained and rich in organic matter.
Other colors: White, pink, red, copper, bronze.

Sternbergia lutea

YELLOW AUTUMN CROCUS (U.K.), WINTER DAFFODIL, LILIES-OF-THE-FIELD ○

Family: AMARYLLIDACEAE
Origin: Mediterranean Europe–Turkey, Iran, and adjacent U.S.S.R.
Flowering time: Autumn.
Climatic zone: 6, 7, 8, 9.
Dimensions: Up to 6 inches (150 mm) high.
Description: These golden-yellow flowers, which resemble crocuses and are believed by some to be the biblical "lilies-of-the-field", flourish in rocky mountain areas. They are ideal grown indoors in pots, or outdoors in rock garden pockets, or naturalized in lawns.

Ranunculus asiaticus

Sternbergia lutea

Provided they have good sun and regular watering, they need little attention. The bulbs should be planted in sandy, well-drained soil which has had an application of compost. Lift and divide them in summer to propagate.

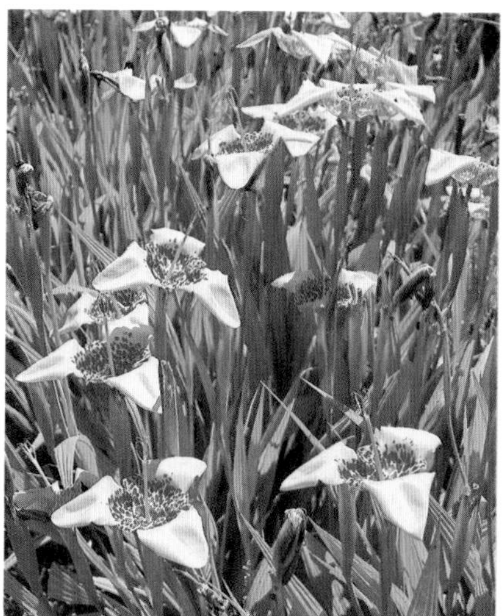

Tigridia pavonia

Tigridia pavonia

JOCKEY'S CAP LILY, MEXICAN TIGER FLOWER, PEACOCK TIGER FLOWER (U.K.) ○

Family: IRIDACEAE
Origin: Mexico, Guatemala.
Flowering time: Summer.
Climatic zone: 8, 9, 10.
Dimensions: Up to 18 inches (450 mm) high.
Description: These spectacular flowers look like large butterflies and can measure up to 6 inches (150 mm) across. Resting on tall, gladiolus-like stems, they are most effective planted en masse in drifts or clumps. In warmer areas, the clumps should not be disturbed for three to four years after planting. In colder climates they should be lifted annually in autumn and replanted in spring. Plant in moist, fertile soil in a sunny position protected from the wind. Water regularly.
Other colors: Red.

Triteleia ixioides syn. *Brodiaea ixioides, B. lutea*

TRITELEIA ○

Family: LILIACEAE
Origin: California, Oregon.
Flowering time: Summer.
Climatic zone: 7, 8, 9.
Dimensions: 12–18 inches (300–450 mm) high.
Description: This plant produces clusters of starry, yellow flowers boldly veined with purplish-brown and having six, widely expanding petal lobes. It likes a sunny, open position with light to medium, well-drained soil. It will grow in sandy or gritty soils and is useful for newly established gardens where soils are still being built up. Frosts do not bother it, but it dislikes drought, so plenty of water is needed. It does well in borders and pots.

Triteleia ixioides

Allamanda cathartica

Allamanda cathartica
ALLAMANDA, GOLDEN ALLAMANDA ○

Family: APOCYNACEAE
Origin: Guyana.
Flowering time: Summer, autumn.
Climatic zone: 9, 10.
Description: A warmth-loving, tropical vine with clear, bright yellow flowers and strong, vigorous shoots, the allamanda will decorate posts, pillars, and fences with its glossy green foliage. Rich soil, good drainage, and ample water will ensure a handsome appearance. This lovely evergreen vine is only suitable for warm tropical conditions, but makes a good addition to a warm greenhouse.
Varieties/cultivars: 'Hendersonii' (orange-yellow), 'Nobilis' (clear yellow), 'Schottii' (yellow, striped with brown).

Bignonia capreolata
TRUMPET FLOWER, CROSS VINE ○

Family: BIGNONIACEAE
Origin: Southeastern United States.
Flowering time: Spring.

Bignonia capreolata

Climatic zone: 8, 9, 10.
Description: This evergreen climber will grow as high as 45–50 feet (12 meters). The tendrils at the end of the branchlets cling by tiny hooks and disks, and the funnel-shaped flowers, 2 inches (50 mm) wide, are orangey-yellow, and hang in clusters. With rich, moist soil, and good drainage, this vigorous vine will quickly spread to become large and shrubby, unless trained and tied to achieve a climbing habit. It cannot withstand heavy frosts.
Other colors: Red.
Varieties/cultivars: 'Atrosanguinea'.

Billardiera longiflora

Billardiera longiflora
PURPLE APPLEBERRY (Aust.) ○

Family: PITTOSPORACEAE
Origin: Southeastern Australia.
Flowering time: Summer–autumn.
Climatic zone: 8, 9, 10.
Description: An evergreen climber suited to moist forest conditions, the purple appleberry is a slight vine with narrow, dark-green leaves. The flowers are pale greenish-yellow with purple shading and are followed by shiny purple-blue berries which remain hanging from the slender branches for a long period. Support is needed to control its wandering habit, and it can be grown in a container up a wire or trellis. It needs well-drained soil and protection from the wind.

Clematis tangutica
GOLDEN CLEMATIS ○

Family: RANUNCULACEAE
Origin: Central Asia.
Flowering time: Summer–autumn.
Climatic zone: 5, 6, 7, 8, 9.
Description: An unusual clematis, this deciduous climber with finely divided foliage becomes a graceful, elegant vine of up to 20 feet (7 meters) high. The flowers are bell-shaped with golden-yellow petal-like sepals, 2 inches (50 mm) long and stalks 3–4 inches (75–100 mm) long. It is a vigorous vine, very hardy and free-flowering. Golden clematis needs a sunny position, but its roots must be kept cool.
Varieties/cultivars: 'Gravetye'.

Clematis tangutica

Gelsemium sempervirens
CAROLINA JASMINE, CAROLINA JESSAMINE ○ ◑

Family: LOGANIACEAE
Origin: Southeastern United States, Mexico–Guatemala.
Flowering time: Late winter–spring.

Gelsemium sempervirens

Climatic zone: 9, 10.
Description: The strong, slender branches of this dainty little evergreen vine bear small, funnel-shaped flowers about 1 inch (30 mm) across. They are bright yellow and slightly fragrant among narrow leaves. The vine looks attractive climbing up a trellis, lattice, or archway. It also makes a useful groundcover but should be kept away from children as the plant is poisonous. A hot climate plant, a greenhouse environment is essential in cooler areas.

Hibbertia scandens
SNAKE VINE, GOLDEN GUINEA VINE ○ ◑

Family: DILLENIACEAE
Origin: Australia (Queensland, N.S.W.).
Flowering time: Spring, summer, autumn.
Climatic zone: 9, 10.
Description: The shiny leaves are attractive all year on this fast-growing, but non-invasive climber. It is a versatile plant which can be grown as a groundcover, as a container plant, as a trailer over a wall or low fence, or as a climber. Clear, rich yellow flowers 2 inches (50 mm) across are scattered over the vine from spring to summer. It tolerates some shade but prefers a sunny position. Very well-drained, sandy soil is essential. This is a warm climate plant which requires a greenhouse in cool areas.

Lonicera caprifolium

Lonicera caprifolium
SWEET HONEYSUCKLE ○ ◑

Family: CAPRIFOLIACEAE
Origin: Europe, western Asia.
Flowering time: Late spring–early summer.
Climatic zone: 5, 6, 7, 8, 9.
Description: Sweet honeysuckle is a vigorous and hardy deciduous climber with attractive foliage and masses of showy flowers that are white to deep creamy yellow, sometimes tinged with pink. The flowers are followed by orange berries. Plant in rich, well-drained soil that retains moisture well, and choose either a sunny or semishaded position offering some support to the young shoots to encourage climbing.
Other colors: Reddish-purple.
Varieties/cultivars: 'Pauciflora'.

Lonicera hildebrandiana

Hibbertia scandens

Lonicera hildebrandiana
GIANT BURMESE HONEYSUCKLE 

Family: CAPRIFOLIACEAE
Origin: Burma, Cambodia, southern China.
Flowering time: Summer.
Climatic zone: 9, 10.
Description: Everything about this honeysuckle is big. Huge, highly-perfumed flowers 6–7 inches (150–175 mm) long changing from cream to orange-yellow hang from strong, sturdy stems. The leaves are large and glossy, up to 6 inches (150 mm) long. It grows best in good soil with plenty of water. A very vigorous climber, it needs plenty of space to grow, or regular pruning and thinning out of older branches to control its size. The stems become thick and woody when mature.

Lonicera periclymenum
WOODBINE, HONEYSUCKLE (U.K.) ○

Family: CAPRIFOLIACEAE
Origin: Europe, western Asia, North Africa.
Flowering time: Summer.
Climatic zone: 4, 5, 6, 7, 8, 9.
Description: A handsome climber, honeysuckle has showy clusters of fragrant, creamy flowers with pink or crimson buds. It likes temperate conditions, a moderately rich soil with good drainge, and an open, sunny position. Provide plenty of support to display this climber to best advantage. It is an excellent choice for covering a wall or trellis.
Varieties/cultivars: 'Belgica', 'Serotina'.

Lonicera periclymenum

Macfadyena unguis-cati syn. *Bignonia* and *Doxantha unguis-cati*
CAT'S-CLAW CREEPER ○

Family: BIGNONIACEAE
Origin: Argentina–Mexico.
Flowering time: Spring.
Climatic zone: 9, 10.
Description: This is the vine to choose when there is no support or frame available. A vigorous climber, it will cling to any surface with its dainty, claw-like tendrils. It does no damage to the surface, and can be peeled off if necessary, and grown again. Trumpet-shaped flowers, 3 inches (75 mm) wide, stand out from the evergreen foliage to form a brilliant yellow curtain in spring. Warm zones will produce rampant growth which is difficult to control. It is better grown in cooler climates. It needs a lot of sun to flower freely.

Macfadyena unguis-cati

Rosa banksiae
BANKS' ROSE, LADY BANKS' ROSE, BANKSIA ROSE (Aust.) ○

Family: ROSACEAE
Origin: Southern China.
Flowering time: Spring, summer.
Climatic zone: 7, 8, 9.
Description: Many thornless stems, up to 20 feet (6 meters) long, make a wide base on this shrubby climber. Tiny, double, buff-yellow blooms which are delicately fragrant appear in spring or summer. A strong pergola or other support is required, or its overall size can be reduced by regular pruning and thinning. Although evergreen in warm and moderate climates, it is deciduous where the winters are cold. Because its stems are thornless, it is an excellent choice for growing over arbors or planting near paths.
Varieties/cultivars: 'Lutea' (golden yellow), 'Lutescens' (creamy yellow), 'Alba Plena' (double white).

Rosa 'Mermaid'
MERMAID ROSE ○

Family: ROSACEAE
Origin: Hybrid.
Flowering time: Early–late summer.
Climatic zone: 7, 8, 9.
Description: This is a popular climbing rose with large, single, open flowers, and a dense ring of yellow stamens. The flowers appear on the previous year's wood, so pruning should be selective, some old and some new wood should be retained each year. A strong-growing evergreen it will climb up into trees and hang in great festoons from the branches, or it can be tied to fences or pergolas where the lovely blooms can be seen more easily. It does not tolerate severe cold.

Rosa 'Mermaid'

Rosa banksiae

Senecio macroglossus

Senecio macroglossus
KENYA IVY, CAPE IVY (U.K.), WAX VINE (U.K.) ○ ◑

Family: COMPOSITAE
Origin: South Africa (East Cape Province).
Flowering time: Winter.
Climatic zone: 8, 9, 10.
Description: As the name implies, the thick, waxy, young leaves are shaped like ivy, but, unexpectedly, the flowers are long-stalked, daisy-like, 2 inches (50 mm) wide, and in considerable numbers so they are quite showy. It is a handsome climber when growing over a low wall, or trained up a pillar. A warm and rather dry position suits it best. Protect from frost when it is young, but it becomes a little more tolerant of cold when mature. Try it in a hanging basket where the glossy leaves will look interesting all year, with the bonus of flowers in winter. In cold areas, it makes a perfect house or greenhouse plant.
Varieties/cultivars: 'Variegatum'.

Solandra maxima syn. *S. guttata*, *S. grandiflora*
GOLDEN CUP VINE, CUP OF GOLD ○ ◑

Family: SOLANACEAE
Origin: Mexico.
Flowering time: Late winter and spring.
Climatic zone: 9, 10.
Description: This rampant, evergreen vine will grow 40 feet (12 meters) high or more and grows superbly even in quite poor soils. It is tolerant of salt spray and windy positions. With good soil and adequate water it needs plenty of space.

Solandra maxima

The huge, golden flowers up to 8 inches (200 mm) across are produced sporadically in winter and spring. It needs a very strong support and can cover a fence very quickly. Too heavy and thick-stemmed to be controlled by pruning, it is not suitable for a small garden. As this is a hot climate plant, a greenhouse is essential in cold areas.

Stigmaphyllon ciliatum
BRAZILIAN GLORY VINE, GOLDEN VINE, GOLDEN CREEPER (U.K.) ○

Other common names: BUTTERFLY VINE (U.K.)
Family: MALPIGHIACEAE

Stigmaphyllon ciliatum

Origin: Tropical America.
Flowering time: Summer, autumn.
Climatic zone: 9, 10.
Description: The unusual flowers on this delightful climber hang in small clusters. The petals are fringed and appear to be on little stems, giving the golden-yellow blooms a lacy appearance. Its fast-growing, twining habit makes it useful for covering fences, lattices, or frames, or it can be used as a groundcover. The heart-shaped leaves are glossy and attractive all year. If grown in the cooler zones, this plant needs a greenhouse, but it prefers a warm, humid climate.

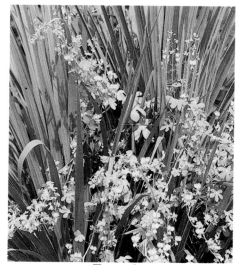

Tropaeolum peregrinum

Tropaeolum peregrinum
CANARY-BIRD FLOWER, CANARY CREEPER ◑

Family: TROPAEOLACEAE
Origin: Peru.
Flowering time: Late summer and autumn.
Climatic zone: 5, 6, 7, 8, 9, 10.
Description: The canary creeper is a smooth-stemmed, much-branched climber, which will reach a height of 10–15 feet (3–4 meters). The flowers are bright yellow, frilled and fringed, and have a green spur holding the nectar. Ample water is needed and a frame or support to hold this graceful plant with its somewhat succulent growth. It is happy in partial shade, and should be given space to grow by itself. It does not seem to be at its best with competition from other climbers. In frost-free areas it grows as a short-lived perennial, otherwise it is treated as an annual.

Achillea filipendulina
FERN LEAF YARROW ○

Family: COMPOSITAE
Origin: Caucasus, Iran, Afghanistan.
Flowering time: Summer.
Climatic zone: 4, 5, 6, 7, 8, 9.
Dimensions: 3 feet (1 meter) high.
Description: This is a most distinctive plant whose stout, leafy, erect stems bear feathery, finely divided, green leaves. The flower heads, like a yellow plate, are up to 5 inches (125 mm) across, and the foliage has a strong, spicy odor. It is a very useful perennial in borders, the flowers lasting for a long time. They can also be successfully dried. The plant needs good drainage, but the soil should be reasonably moisture-retentive. Propagate it by division in spring.
Varieties/cultivars: 'Gold Plate', 'Canary Bird', 'Sungold', 'Parker's Variety'.

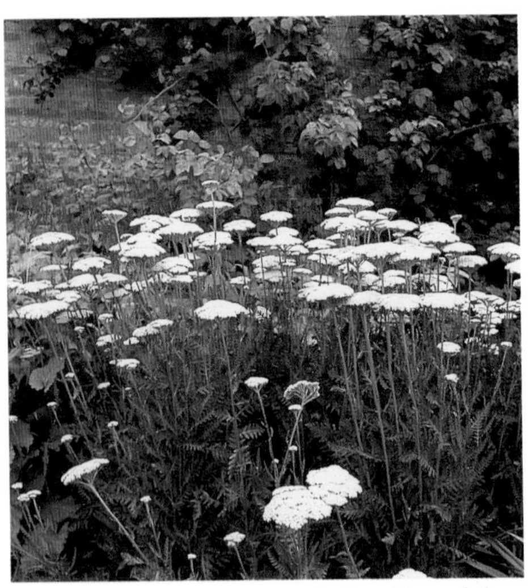
Achillea filipendulina

Achillea tomentosa
YARROW ○

Family: COMPOSITAE
Origin: Central Europe–western Asia.
Flowering time: Summer–early autumn.
Climatic zone: 4, 5, 6, 7, 8, 9.
Dimensions: 4–6 inches (100–150 mm) high.
Description: Found on dry, sunny slopes in sandy or stony soils, this mat-forming plant is very easy to grow. It is well-suited to a rock garden or herbaceous border. The leaves are silver-gray and hairy and, if bruised, emit an aromatic fragrance. The flower heads appear in flattened clusters on

Achillea tomentosa

long stalks and can be used for dried floral arrangements. They should be picked, tied in bunches, and hung downwards in a sheltered place. In this way they will keep their form and color. Propagate woolly yarrow by division.
Varieties/cultivars: 'Maynard Gold'.

Adonis amurensis
AMUR ADONIS, PHEASANT'S EYE ○ ◑

Family: RANUNCULACEAE
Origin: Japan, Manchuria.
Flowering time: Early spring.
Climatic zone: 4, 5, 6, 7, 8, 9.
Dimensions: 8–12 inches (200–300 mm) high.
Description: This is a pretty plant for the front of the border, with anemone-like flowers and much-divided, ferny leaves. A well-drained, fertile soil suits it best, but it should be kept consistently moist. Plant it in autumn and propagate it by division, or seed sown immediately after gathering. Germination is slow. Grow amur adonis in clumps a little distance from other plants with hungry roots.
Varieties/cultivars: 'Fukujukai', 'Nadeshiku', 'Pleniflora', 'Yatsubusa'.

Adonis amurensis 'Yatsubusa'

Alchemilla mollis
LADY'S-MANTLE ○ ◑

Family: ROSACEAE
Origin: Eastern Europe–Turkey.
Flowering time: Early summer.
Climatic zone: 4, 5, 6, 7, 8, 9.
Dimensions: 18 inches (450 mm) high.
Description: Both the leaves and the flowers of this perennial have a special beauty, making it popular with many gardeners. The soft-green leaves are rounded and downy, with radiating veins prolonged into gentle, toothed scallops. They hold drops of water like pearls. The flowers are a froth of tiny lime-green stars produced in feathery sprays which last for weeks. Lady's-mantle is the ideal foil for white or blue flowers. It can be propagated by division or seed and often self-sows if the soil remains moist.

Alchemilla mollis

Alyssum saxatile syn. *Aurinia saxatile*
BASKET-OF-GOLD, GOLD DUST ALYSSUM ○

Family: CRUCIFERAE
Origin: Central and southeastern Europe.
Flowering time: Spring.
Climatic zone: 4, 5, 6, 7, 8, 9, 10.
Dimensions: 8–12 inches (200–300 mm) high.
Description: This bushy rock-garden plant flourishes in almost any soil, provided it is well-drained and not too

Alyssum saxatile

moist. Above the gray-green leaves the branched clusters of flowers are produced in profusion and, if allowed to cascade over a wall, can be most eye-catching. Water it only during dry periods and cut back quite hard after flowering to prevent it becoming woody and straggly. It is easily propagated by seed in spring or cuttings in late summer.
Varieties/cultivars: 'Citrinum'.

Angelica archangelica

Angelica archangelica
ANGELICA, ARCHANGEL, WILD PARSNIP ○ ◑

Family: UMBELLIFERAE
Origin: Syria.
Flowering time: Summer.
Climatic zone: 5, 6, 7, 8, 9.
Dimensions: 6½ feet (2 meters) high.
Description: Angelica is a biennial herb with yellow flowers and soft green leaves. It was said to have been given to mankind by the Archangel Michael as protection against the plague. The stems can be cooked with sugar and eaten as candied fruit. The leaves may be dried to make a tea. It may be placed among shrubs or in the herb garden. Plant it in fertile, moist, well-dug soil and protect it from the wind.

Anthemis sancti-johannis
SAINT JOHN'S CHAMOMILE ○

Family: COMPOSITAE
Origin: Bulgaria.
Flowering time: Summer.
Climatic zone: 5, 6, 7, 8, 9.
Dimensions: 1–3 feet (up to 1 meter) high.
Description: These large and beautiful daisy-like flowers, up to 2 inches (50 mm) wide, make a great splash in the garden against the elegantly lobed foliage. Nowadays the true species is rarely seen because it has cross-pollinated so prolifically with the species *A. tinctoria*. Clump-forming, it grows best in a sunny position in a well-drained soil and should be divided and replanted each spring to keep it growing vigorously. It can be grown from seed or cuttings.

Anthemis sancti-johannis

Anthemis tinctoria
GOLDEN MARGUERITE, OX-EYE CHAMOMILE ○

Family: COMPOSITAE
Origin: Europe.
Flowering time: Late summer.
Climatic zone: 4, 5, 6, 7, 8, 9.
Dimensions: Up to 3 feet (1 meter) high.
Description: This showy garden plant produces a basal clump of leaves like parsley, above which masses of daisy flowers are produced for many weeks. They were once used by the French to make a fine yellow dye. For garden purposes, the original species has been much surpassed by a vast number of improved hybrids. It does not require a

Anthemis tinctoria

very rich soil, but needs a fairly open position. Propagate it by division in spring or autumn.
Varieties/cultivars: 'Moonlight', 'Golden Dawn', 'Perry's Variety'.

Arctotis x *hybrida* syn. *Venidio-arctotis*
AFRICAN DAISY (U.K.), AURORA DAISY ○

Family: COMPOSITAE
Origin: Hybrid.
Flowering time: Summer.
Climatic zone: 8, 9, 10.
Dimensions: 1–2 feet (300–600 mm) high.
Description: The numerous hybrids of this daisy vary in height, leaf shape, and color. The beautifully colored daisy flowers open only in full sunlight and the plants do best in an open, sunny position in rich, damp soil. They respond well to organic feeding and regular watering and dislike very cold weather and wet conditions. In cold climates, a greenhouse is desirable. They can be lifted and grown indoors as pot plants in winter. Keep them bushy by pinching out the growing points. They can be grown from seed.
Other colors: White, pink, red, bronze, purple.
Varieties/cultivars: Many cultivars are available.

Arctotis x *hybrida*

Artemisia stellerana

Artemisia stellerana
BEACH WORMWOOD (U.K.), DUSTY MILLER, OLD WOMAN ○

Family: COMPOSITAE
Origin: Northeastern Asia.
Flowering time: Summer.
Climatic zone: 5, 6, 7, 8, 9.
Dimensions: Up to 2 feet (600 mm) high.
Description: Beach wormwood has dense heads of yellow flowers and chrysanthemum-like silvery-gray foliage which makes it an attractive perennial planted among beds of summer flowers. Unlike other *Artemisia*, it can withstand humid conditions. In general, poor, sandy soils suit it better than rich ones, but they must be well-drained and in a sunny position. Many of the *Artemisia* group are used medicinally or, like the herb tarragon, in cooking.

Buphthalmum salicifolium
YELLOW OX-EYE DAISY ○ ◑

Family: COMPOSITAE
Origin: Central Europe.
Flowering time: Summer.
Climatic zone: 4, 5, 6, 7, 8, 9.
Dimensions: Up to 2 feet (600 mm) high.

Buphthalmum salicifolium

Description: This perennial prefers limy soils which are not too fertile. When in flower it is often staked but looks better when allowed to flop and make a large mass of narrow, dark-green leaves under the stems of the brightly colored daisy flowers. It is both drought- and frost-resistant and forms a clump about 2 feet (600 mm) wide. It can be increased by seed but is usually propagated by division in autumn or spring.

Caltha palustris

Caltha palustris
MARSH MARIGOLD, KING CUP, COWSLIP (U.S.A.) ○ ◑

Family: RANUNCULACEAE
Origin: Northern temperate zone.
Flowering time: Spring.
Climatic zone: 3, 4, 5, 6, 7, 8, 9.
Dimensions: Up to 18 inches (450 mm) high.
Description: This moisture-loving plant is found in nature in marshy meadows and beside streams. In cultivation, it will grow in any wet soil, but prefers a sunny site. It makes a clump of shining, rounded leaves with brownish yellow branching stems covered with single flowers filled with rich yellow stamens. This perennial looks best when planted beside water, such as an ornamental pond. Propagate it by division or by seed.
Varieties/cultivars: 'Flore Pleno' (double).

Canna x generalis
INDIAN SHOT (U.K.), CANNA LILY ○

Family: CANNACEAE
Origin: Hybrid.
Flowering time: Summer–autumn.

Canna x generalis

Climatic zone: 5, 6, 7, 8, 9, 10.
Dimensions: Up to 5 feet (approx. 2 meters) high.
Description: These cultivated varieties are all hybrids obtained by crossing three distinct canna species. They are most decorative plants, both for flowers and foliage, and suit both summer bedding and pot planting. The three-petaled tubular flowers appear on terminal racemes and are most striking. The leaves vary from pale- to dark-green to bronze and claret shades. They require enriched soil, a sunny site, and copious water during dry weather. Dead blooms should be continuously removed to ensure a long flowering period. They should be cut down to ground level in winter and the rhizomes can then be divided. Protect against frost. In cold areas, they should be lifted in autumn and replanted in spring.
Other colors: Pink, white, red, orange, speckled.
Varieties/cultivars: Many cultivars are available including 'Eureka', 'The President', 'King Humbert', 'Wyoming', 'Copper Giant', 'Bonfire', 'Brilliant', 'Coq d'Or', 'America', 'Striped Beauty'.

Centaurea macrocephala
YELLOW HARDHEAD, GLOBE CENTAUREA, YELLOW KNAPWEED (U.K.) ○

Family: COMPOSITAE
Origin: Caucasus.
Flowering time: Summer.
Climatic zone: 3, 4, 5, 6, 7, 8, 9.
Dimensions: 3 feet (1 meter) high.
Description: A well-grown plant of this species may produce between twenty

Centaurea macrocephala

and thirty stems topped with golden flowers enclosed in brown calyxes which look like a fur coating. The rough, oblong leaves are stemless, giving the plant a very dense appearance. The flowers make excellent specimens for drying. Fertile, moist but well-drained soils seem to suit them best, although they are easy to grow in most garden soils.

Cephalaria gigantea
GIANT SCABIOUS ○ ◑

Family: DIPSACACEAE
Origin: Siberia.
Flowering time: Summer.
Climatic zone: 5, 6, 7, 8, 9.
Dimensions: Up to 6 feet (2 meters) high.
Description: This quite large perennial is best used as a background plant as it tends to be rather ungainly. It has dark-green, divided leaves and wiry stems ending in the large scabious-like flowers. The blooms are excellent for cutting purposes. It is a hardy plant needing only a normal, fertile soil to give good results. Propagate it from seed or by division in spring.

Cephalaria gigantea

Cheiranthus cheiri

Cheiranthus cheiri
WALLFLOWER ○

Family: CRUCIFERAE
Origin: Southern Europe.
Flowering time: Early spring–early summer, northern hemisphere; summer, southern hemisphere.
Climatic zone: 7, 8, 9.
Dimensions: Up to 16 inches (400 mm) high.
Description: In ancient times, maidens carried these flowers during festivals and the Elizabethans called them gilloflowers, or "yellow flowers". These popular perennials, grown as annuals or biennials, look pretty against a sunny wall in a cottage garden. Although the old-fashioned yellow and brown wallflowers are still the favorites, there are now many different colors to choose from. Flowering for several weeks, the plants are suited to beds and borders in a sunny position, protected from the wind.
Other colors: Many varied colors including red.
Varieties/cultivars: 'Harpur Crewe', 'Rufus'.

Chelidonium majus
GREATER CELANDINE, SWALLOW-WORT ○

Family: PAPAVERACEAE
Origin: Europe, Asia.
Flowering time: Late spring–late summer.
Climatic zone: 5, 6, 7, 8, 9.
Dimensions: 2 feet (600 mm) high.
Description: This rather weedy plant is best suited to a wild garden. It forms a basal rosette of quite attractive, coarsely-toothed and lobed foliage. In its second year, erect branching stems of small flowers rise from the rosette. These stems, when broken, emit a

Chelidonium majus

bright yellow, somewhat caustic juice. It self-sows readily but dislikes boggy locations and over-wet conditions. There is a semi-double-flowered form which also self-sows readily.
Varieties/cultivars: 'Flore Pleno'.

Coreopsis lanceolata
TICKSEED, LANCE COREOPSIS ○ ◑

Family: COMPOSITAE
Origin: Eastern United States.
Flowering time: Summer.
Climatic zone: 5, 6, 7, 8, 9.
Dimensions: 2–3 feet (up to 1 meter) high.
Description: This is a short-lived perennial which thrives in any well-drained soil. If the soil is too fertile, it tends to produce more foliage than flowers. Dead flowers should be removed to keep the plant flowering constantly. Any position in the garden usually suits it, but it does not like to be disturbed and needs regular but restrained watering. It can be propagated by division in spring or autumn.
Varieties/cultivars: 'Sunray', 'Baby Sun'.

Coreopsis lanceolata

Coreopsis verticillata

Dietes bicolor

Coreopsis verticillata
THREADLEAF COREOPSIS, TICKSEED ○ ◑

Family: COMPOSITAE
Origin: Southeastern United States.
Flowering time: Summer–autumn.
Climatic zone: 4, 5, 6, 7, 8, 9.
Dimensions: 2 feet (600 mm) high.
Description: This species is distinctive because of its foliage which is finely divided into thread-like segments. The daisy-like flowers, 1–2 inches (30–40 mm) wide, are produced in great profusion over a number of months, and are useful for cutting. It is easy to grow and will withstand dry conditions for a long period. Once established, it increases quite readily to form wide clumps. The usual method of propagation is by division.
Varieties/cultivars: 'Golden Shower', 'Moonbeam', 'Zagreb'.

Dietes bicolor
FORTNIGHT LILY ◑

Family: IRIDACEAE
Origin: South Africa.
Flowering time: Summer.
Climatic zone: 9, 10.
Dimensions: Up to 12 inches (300 mm).
Description: Fortnight lily forms a spectacular clump of arching, slender, green leaves and showy, yellow flowers with brown blotches on three of the six petals. The flower, resembling iris in shape, is borne on graceful stems. Drought-resistant, it prefers a rich and well-drained soil and a semishaded position. It can be planted as a low-growing hedge which, when established, will annually self-seed to create a thick, lush clump.

Digitalis grandiflora

Digitalis grandiflora
YELLOW FOXGLOVE ○ ◑

Family: SCROPHULARIACEAE
Origin: Southern and central Europe–western Turkey.
Flowering time: Summer.
Climatic zone: 4, 5, 6, 7, 8, 9.
Dimensions: 2–3 feet (up to 1 meter) high.
Description: This clump-forming perennial has broad, slightly hairy leaves and produces tall flower spikes of showy blooms arranged on only one side of the spike. It prefers moist but well-drained soils, rich in organic matter. All species of the *Digitalis* genus are poisonous, but they are worthy garden subjects. Yellow foxglove can be easily propagated by seed.

Doronicum cordatum syn. *D. columnae*
LEOPARD'S-BANE ○ ◑

Family: COMPOSITAE
Origin: Eastern Europe.
Flowering time: Late spring.

Doronicum cordatum

Climatic zone: 4, 5, 6, 7, 8, 9.
Dimensions: 1–2 feet (300–600 mm) high.
Description: An easy-to-grow perennial with heart-shaped, serrated leaves and short stems of daisy-like flowers, leopard's-bane flowers in spring with the daffodils. Partial shade is needed in hot climates, where it may become dormant. It does best in a moist soil even during its dormant period. Slugs and snails are particularly partial to the new shoots. The flowers are excellent for cutting and often a second crop is produced in autumn. Dividing the roots in spring will produce new plants.
Varieties/cultivars: 'Miss Mason', 'Madame Mason', 'Spring Beauty', 'Magnificum'.

Doronicum plantagineum
LEOPARD'S-BANE ○ ◑

Family: COMPOSITAE
Origin: Western Europe.
Flowering time: Spring.
Climatic zone: 4, 5, 6, 7, 8, 9.
Dimensions: 2 feet (600 mm) high.
Description: The hairy, kidney-shaped leaves of this perennial are slightly toothed and the upper ones clasp the stem. It makes a lovely contrast in the garden when planted with euphorbias and honesty (*Lunaria*). Easy to grow, it likes moist and fertile soil and the flower stems are excellent for picking. A number of hybrids have now been produced, and this species is largely passed over by gardeners in favor of the new cultivars. It can be propagated by division.
Varieties/cultivars: 'Harpur Crewe', 'Excelsum'.

Epimedium perralderianum
ALGERIAN BARRENWORT ○ ◑ ●

Family: BERBERIDACEAE
Origin: Algeria.
Flowering time: Spring.
Climatic zone: 5, 6, 7, 8, 9.
Dimensions: 12 inches (300 mm) high.
Description: This spreading perennial has very attractive foliage, the shiny, rich-green leaves being bronze-tinted

Doronicum plantagineum

Epimedium perralderianum

when young. It forms wide clumps, with the little brown-spurred flowers appearing on wiry stems just above the leaves. Like all epimediums it can be used in the front of a border or as a groundcover under trees. It retains its leaves throughout the year. It is best propagated by division after flowering.
Varieties/cultivars: 'Fronleiten'.

Euphorbia characias var. *wulfenii*

Euphorbia characias var. *wulfenii*
POISON SPURGE (U.S.A.) ○

Family: EUPHORBIACEAE
Origin: Eastern Mediterranean region.
Flowering time: Late winter–late spring.
Climatic zone: 8, 9.
Dimensions: 4 feet (over 1 meter) high.
Description: This is a handsome and eye-catching plant in the garden because of its unusual color. The tall, imposing flower stems are clothed in gray-green leaves and topped with yellowish-green flowers. These decorative parts are really bracts, the flowers themselves being small and insignificant. When cut, the stems exude a milky sap which is poisonous and may irritate the skin. It prefers a relatively dry position and makes an effective color contrast with bronze foliage. Propagate it by seed in early spring or soft cuttings in summer.

Gaillardia aristata

Gaillardia aristata
BLANKET FLOWER ○

Family: COMPOSITAE
Origin: Central–northwestern United States.
Flowering time: Summer.
Climatic zone: 4, 5, 6, 7, 8, 9.
Dimensions: 2–3 feet (up to 1 meter) high.
Description: Blanket flower is a very showy perennial, although it is often not long-lived, especially if the soil becomes overly wet. It blooms in the first year from seed and is a parent of most of the garden forms grown today. The plant tends to be sticky and aromatic and the large, daisy-shaped flowers are excellent for cutting. It is easily raised from seed, but the many named hybrids are propagated from root cuttings. Over-fertilizing may cause the plant to collapse.
Other colors: Red, orange.
Varieties/cultivars: 'Croftway Yellow', 'Wirral Flame', 'The King', 'Ipswich Beauty', 'Mandarin', 'Dazzler'.

Gerbera jamesonii
BARBERTON DAISY, AFRICAN DAISY, TRANSVAAL DAISY ○ ◑

Family: COMPOSITAE
Origin: South Africa.
Flowering time: Spring–summer.
Climatic zone: 9, 10.
Dimensions: 18 inches (450 mm) high.
Description: From clumps of dark-green, lobed, and rather coarse leaves arise single, strong flower stems. The perfect shape of the bloom makes it look almost artificial. As a cut flower, it lasts a long time in water. Not particularly easy to grow, Barberton daisy prefers neutral to slightly alkaline soil that is well-drained. It can be propagated by division in autumn if the young plants are protected from frost. If grown from seed, the seed must be very fresh.
Other colors: White, red, orange, pink.
Varieties/cultivars: Many semidouble and double varieties.

Gerbera jamesonii

Hedychium gardnerianum
FALSE GINGER LILY, KAHILI GINGER ○ ◑

Family: ZINGIBERACEAE
Origin: India.
Flowering time: Late summer–autumn.
Climatic zone: 9, 10.
Dimensions: Up to 4 feet (approx. 1 meter) high.
Description: Growing from a large rhizome, the tall stems have paddle-shaped leaves for most of their length and are topped with an exotic flower head composed of many orchid-like flowers. The perfume is very pronounced and spicy. It is rather like a canna lily and responds to similar treatment of cutting the flowering stems back to ground level in winter. It requires a moist soil enriched with organic matter. The rhizomes can be divided in winter.

Hedychium gardnerianum

Helianthus angustifolius

Helianthus angustifolius
SUNFLOWER, SWAMP SUNFLOWER ○

Family: COMPOSITAE
Origin: Southeastern United States.
Flowering time: Late summer–autumn.
Climatic zone: 6, 7, 8, 9.
Dimensions: 5 feet (approx. 2 meters) high.
Description: This is an easily grown perennial with coarse, hairy leaves and stiff, upright flower stems. It prefers a moist, fairly fertile soil, but even when it is planted at the back of a border, the roots can be invasive. For this reason it should be divided at least every three years. It is closely related to the Jerusalem artichoke. It can be used as a cut flower and is propagated by division in autumn.

Helenium autumnale

Helenium autumnale

SNEEZEWEED, FALSE SUNFLOWER ○

Family: COMPOSITAE
Origin: Eastern and central northern North America.
Flowering time: Late summer–autumn.
Climatic zone: 3, 4, 5, 6, 7, 8, 9.
Dimensions: 5 feet (approx. 2 meters) high.
Description: This plant is usually so covered with flowers that it requires staking. It is very useful as a background plant, but the strong colors need to be softened by grouping it with good greenery and some creamy-white flowers. It is the parent plant to several horticultural varieties. It grows in almost any soil, provided it is well-drained. Propagation is by division in autumn or spring.
Other colors: Red, orange, bronze.
Varieties/cultivars: 'Riverton Beauty', 'Riverton Gem', 'Bruno', 'Crimson Beauty', 'Wyndley', 'Coppelia'.

Helianthus x *multiflorus*

PERENNIAL SUNFLOWER ○ ◑

Family: COMPOSITAE
Origin: Hybrid.
Flowering time: Late summer.
Climatic zone: 4, 5, 6, 7, 8, 9.
Dimensions: 3–6 feet (1–2 meters) high.
Description: This robust and very showy perennial performs best in moist, well-drained soils. It is a thin-leafed plant producing tall, branched flowering stems which should be cut back after flowering to the basal clump. The wide daisy-like flowers are yellow with a large central disk. It is a plant that spreads quickly and requires regular division. It is best planted at the back of the border and will need staking. There are now many cultivars and they are propagated easily by division.
Varieties/cultivars: 'Loddon Gold', 'Soleil d'Or', 'Miss Mellish', 'Triomphe de Gard'.

Helianthus x *multiflorus*

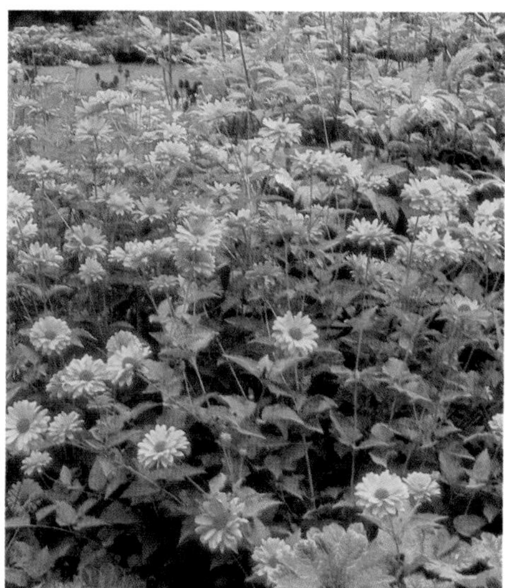

Heliopsis helianthoides var. *scabra*

Heliopsis helianthoides var. *scabra*

ORANGE SUNFLOWER, ROUGH HELIOPSIS, OX-EYE ○

Family: COMPOSITAE
Origin: Eastern North America.
Flowering time: Late summer.
Climatic zone: 4, 5, 6, 7, 8, 9.
Dimensions: Up to 4 feet (over 1 meter) high.
Description: Like most of the sunflower-type plants, this is a long-lasting perennial giving strong color to border plantings. The flowers range from single to fully double and are produced quite prolifically. It is a reasonably compact plant with very rough stems and leaves and is easily grown in most types of soil. Several garden varieties have been bred from the species. It is propagated by division in spring.
Other colors: Orange.
Varieties/cultivars: 'Light of Loddon', 'Orange King', 'Patula', 'Summer Sun', 'Gold Greenheart'.

Hemerocallis x *hybrida*

Hemerocallis x *hybrida*
DAYLILY 

Family: LILIACEAE
Origin: Hybrids.
Flowering time: Spring–summer.
Climatic zone: 4, 5, 6, 7, 8, 9.
Dimensions: Up to 3 feet (1 meter) high.
Description: The elegance and charm of these plants and the range of flower colors make them an asset in any garden. Easy to grow and tolerant, they thrive in any good soil, preferably a moist one, and although each flower only lasts a day or two, the blooms open successively over a long period. The clumps of arching leaves are attractive and many turn bright yellow in autumn. The plant can be divided at any time, although spring is best, as the new growth appears.
Other colors: White, red, pink, bronze, violet, orange.
Varieties/cultivars: 'Black Cherry', 'Diva', 'Bride Elect', 'Green Magic', 'Pink Damask', 'Royal Crown'.

Iris pseudacorus
YELLOW FLAG, YELLOW IRIS ○ ◑

Family: IRIDACEAE
Origin: Europe, western Asia.
Flowering time: Summer.
Climatic zone: 4, 5, 6, 7, 8, 9.
Dimensions: 4 feet (over 1 meter) high.
Description: This is an aquatic iris that thrives in water or in boggy ground beside streams and ponds. It colonizes quite rapidly and large clumps can make a stunning picture, especially when associated with blue flowers. The graceful, slender foliage is attractive, and there is a variegated form with yellow-striped leaves turning green in summer. This flower is the Fleur de Lys of heraldry. It is propagated by division.
Varieties/cultivars: 'Golden Fleece', 'Variegata'.

Iris pseudacorus

Ligularia stenocephala
ROCKET LIGULARIA  

Family: COMPOSITAE
Origin: Northern China.
Flowering time: Summer.
Climatic zone: 4, 5, 6, 7, 8, 9.
Dimensions: 4–6 feet (up to 2 meters) high.
Description: In its natural habitat, this perennial is found in damp mountain meadows and forests and therefore needs a deep, fertile, and moist soil. The dark-green leaves are elegant, decorative, and deeply lobed and extend up the almost black-colored stems. The spikes of daisy-like flowers look quite imposing, especially when planted near water. Hot sun can wilt the large leaves and slugs and snails are fond of them. Propagation is by division in spring.
Varieties/cultivars: 'The Rocket'.

Linum flavum
GOLDEN FLAX, YELLOW FLAX (U.K.) ○

Family: LINACEAE
Origin: Central and southeastern Europe.
Flowering time: Summer.
Climatic zone: 5, 6, 7, 8, 9.
Dimensions: 1–2 feet (300–600 mm) high.
Description: This woody-based species forms mounds of spoon-shaped leaves in rosettes, above which rise the wiry stems of satiny-textured flowers. Flowering will be prolonged if the faded blooms are regularly removed. It requires a well-drained soil in an open position and makes a very satisfactory rock garden plant. The usual method of propagation is by seed in spring or by cuttings in summer.
Varieties/cultivars: 'Compactum'.

Ligularia stenocephala 'The Rocket'

Linum flavum

Lysimachia punctata

YELLOW LOOSESTRIFE, CIRCLE FLOWER ○ ◑

Family: PRIMULACEAE
Origin: Southeastern Europe.
Flowering time: Summer.
Climatic zone: 4, 5, 6, 7, 8, 9.
Dimensions: 3 feet (1 meter) high.
Description: This plant is best grown in a wild garden as it spreads readily and the underground rhizomes can be very invasive. It prefers moist or wet soils and usually looks good when planted near water. The spikes of brightly colored flowers, in whorls around the leaf axils, last for a considerable period without any maintenance. The clumps need to be reduced regularly, and it is propagated by division.

Lysimachia punctata

Meconopsis cambrica

Meconopsis cambrica

WELSH POPPY ○ ◑

Family: PAPAVERACEAE
Origin: Western Europe.
Flowering time: Late spring.
Climatic zone: 6, 7, 8, 9.
Dimensions: 18 inches (450 mm) high.
Description: This delightful little plant forms clumps of ferny leaves, the papery flowers swaying above them on fine stems. It blooms for a long period and seeds readily so that the plant soon naturalizes itself. Although it seems to flourish in most conditions, it prefers a well-drained soil, rich in humus. There is a double-flowered form which does not self-seed as readily. Welsh poppy is one of the easiest of the *Meconopsis* genus to grow.
Other colors: Orange.
Varieties/cultivars: *M. c.* var. *aurantiaca*, 'Flore Pleno'.

Mimulus guttatus

COMMON MONKEY FLOWER ◑

Family: SCROPHULARIACEAE
Origin: Western North America.
Flowering time: Summer–autumn.
Climatic zone: 5, 6, 7, 8, 9.
Dimensions: Up to 2 feet (600 mm) high.
Description: Cool conditions are essential for this plant, although it is widely grown throughout America. The 2 inches (50 mm) long flowers are tubular, expanding to five rounded petal lobes at the mouth. Basically yellow, each flower has a red-spotted throat. Several flowers are borne on a single stem which makes the plant useful for pot culture, especially as it will flourish indoors. The soft leaves may be eaten in salads. Ideal for damp, partially shady corners.

Mimulus guttatus

Oenothera fruticosa

Papaver alpinum

Oenothera fruticosa
COMMON SUNDROPS, EVENING PRIMROSE ○

Family: ONAGRACEAE
Origin: Eastern United States.
Flowering time: Summer.
Climatic zone: 5, 6, 7, 8, 9.
Dimensions: 18 inches (450 mm) high.
Description: The foliage is small, narrow, and pointed and forms dark clumps, over which the stiff stems of the flowers appear. The flowers are reddish in bud before they open out into silky, cup-shaped, yellow blooms. Unlike some of the evening primroses, which belong to the same genus, these flowers remain open all day. It is a suitable plant for edging purposes or for rock garden pockets. Propagate it by seed, division, or by cuttings. It is sometimes confused with *O. tetragona*, a very closely related species.
Varieties/cultivars: 'Yellow River', 'William Cuthbertson'.

Papaver alpinum
ALPINE POPPY ○ ◑

Family: PAPAVERACEAE
Origin: European alps.
Flowering time: Summer.
Climatic zone: 5, 6, 7, 8, 9.
Dimensions: 6 inches (150 mm) high.
Description: The rock garden is the place for this tiny, tufted perennial with pretty four-petaled, bowl-shaped flowers. If conditions are ideal, it will often seed itself and grow in unlikely spots, especially gravel paths. It forms a close-growing, compact plant with much-segmented leaves. It needs open, well-drained soil. With a little attention, it makes an excellent pot plant. Propagate it from seed which should be fresh.
Other colors: White, red.

Phlomis russeliana
BORDER JERUSALEM SAGE ○ ◑

Family: LABIATAE
Origin: Turkey.
Flowering time: Summer.
Climatic zone: 5, 6, 7, 8, 9.
Dimensions: 3 feet (1 meter) high.
Description: This is a plant for a warm, well-drained position in the garden. The finely wrinkled, sage-like leaves are evergreen, and the hooded flowers are formed in whorls around the stem. It is excellent in gardens by the seaside or in a border of gray-leaved plants. It will tolerate even strongly alkaline soils, but needs protection in cold winters. It can be propagated by seed or by division.

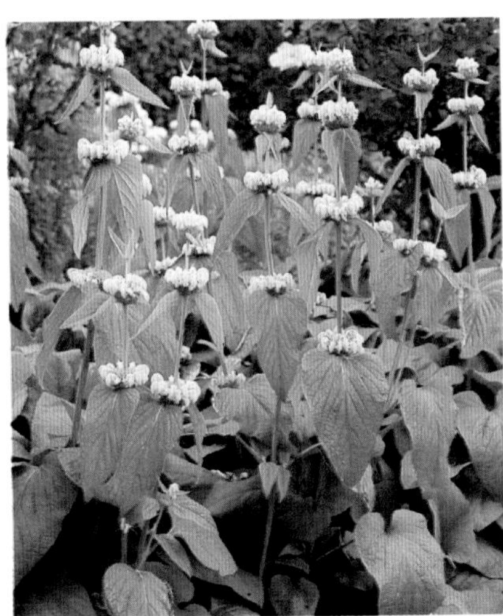

Phlomis russeliana

Potentilla eriocarpa
CINQUEFOIL ○

Family: ROSACEAE
Origin: Himalayas.
Flowering time: Spring–autumn.
Climatic zone: 4, 5, 6, 7, 8, 9.
Dimensions: Up to 2 inches (50 mm) high.
Description: This matt-forming groundcover spreads to 12 inches (300 mm) in width, with a dense covering of hairy, gray-green foliage and a dramatic display of showy, bright yellow flowers over many weeks. Position in an open, sunny location in well-drained, moderately rich soil. It grows extremely well in rocky soil, making a delightful addition to the rock garden.

Potentilla eriocarpa

Primula veris
COWSLIP, COWSLIP PRIMROSE (U.S.A.) ◑ 

Family: PRIMULACEAE
Origin: Europe–western Asia.
Flowering time: Spring.
Climatic zone: 5, 6, 7, 8, 9.
Dimensions: 8–12 inches (200–300 mm) high.
Description: As this species grows wild

Primula veris

in cool, fresh meadows and open woodlands, it prefers a moist, well-drained soil, but will not tolerate dryness. The broad and wrinkled leaves form a basal rosette, and the erect stems bear drooping, bell-shaped flowers with a pleasant fragrance. It can be propagated by division in autumn or spring or from chilled, fresh seed. In ancient times an infusion of the roots and flowers was believed to have a sedative effect.
Other colors: White, pink, red, purple.
Varieties/cultivars: 'Alba', 'Aurea', 'Caerulea'.

Primula vulgaris

COMMON PRIMROSE, ENGLISH PRIMROSE (U.S.A.)

Family: PRIMULACEAE
Origin: Europe–western Asia.
Flowering time: Spring.
Climatic zone: 5, 6, 7, 8, 9.
Dimensions: 6 inches (150 mm) high.
Description: Common primrose is one of the best-known wildflowers in Europe, where it sometimes forms carpets of yellow in sheltered and shaded areas. It prefers moist, humus-rich soil, as found in woodland surroundings. The rough and wrinkled green leaves form a rosette from which the flower stems arise. This species has given rise to a number of garden varieties. It is very useful in planters or rockeries, and the clumps can be divided in autumn.
Other colors: White, red, purple, pink.
Varieties/cultivars: *P. v.* var. *sibthorpii*, 'Alba Plena'.

Primula vulgaris

Primula x *polyantha* 'Barrowby Gem'

Primula x *polyantha* syn. *P.* x *tommasin*, *P.* x *variabilis*

POLYANTHUS

Family: PRIMULACEAE
Origin: Hybrids.
Flowering time: Late winter–spring.
Climatic zone: 5, 6, 7, 8, 9.
Dimensions: Up to 9 inches (225 mm) high.
Description: These popular plants are chiefly derived from *P. veris* and *P. vulgaris*. They have coarse green leaves and bunched flower heads in a variety of colors. They will grow in practically any soil, but grow best when the soil is kept moist and decayed animal manure is dug in. After flowering, they should not be left in a hot, dry place, but dug up and replanted in cool shade. Protect them from attack by slugs and snails. They can be divided after flowering.
Other colors: White, cream, pink, red, blue.
Varieties/cultivars: 'Garryarde Guinevere', 'Pacific Giants', 'Barrowby Gem'.

Ranunculus acris 'Flore Pleno'

Ranunculus acris 'Flore Pleno'
DOUBLE MEADOW BUTTERCUP, BACHELOR'S BUTTONS ○ ◑

Family: RANUNCULACEAE
Origin: Cultivar.
Flowering time: Late spring.
Climatic zone: 5, 6, 7, 8, 9.
Dimensions: 3 feet (1 meter) high.
Description: Derived from the common European meadow buttercup, this attractive plant forms wiry, branching stems with neat, shining, and fully double flowers. It often flowers twice in a season and is a non-invasive, clump-forming perennial. Propagation is by division in autumn or spring. This plant is poisonous.

Rudbeckia fulgida
CONEFLOWER, BLACK-EYED SUSAN ○ ◑

Family: COMPOSITAE
Origin: Eastern United States.
Flowering time: Summer–autumn.
Climatic zone: 3, 4, 5, 6, 7, 8, 9.
Dimensions: 2 feet (600 mm) high.
Description: A sturdy and hardy plant with rough, narrow leaves and tall stems of flowers, it looks best in bold groups. The flowers last for a long time and are suitable for cutting. It will tolerate light frosts and most garden conditions, and does exceptionally well on heavy soils but needs plenty of water during summer. Propagation is mainly by division in spring or by sowing seed.
Varieties/cultivars: *R. f.* var. *speciosa*, *R. f.* var. *sullivantii* 'Goldsturm', *R.f.* var. *deamii*.

Rudbeckia fulgida var. *deamii*.

Rudbeckia hirta
BLACK-EYED SUSAN, CONEFLOWER, GLORIOSA DAISY ○

Family: COMPOSITAE
Origin: Eastern North America.
Flowering time: Summer.
Climatic zone: 5, 6, 7, 8, 9, 10.
Dimensions: Up to 3 feet (1 meter) high.
Description: Originally a short-lived perennial, black-eyed Susan is now mostly grown as a hardy annual. It is grown widely for its continuous flowering and ability to stand up to hard conditions. The flowers may be 4–6 inches (100–150 mm) in diameter

Rudbeckia hirta

and mostly in shades of deep yellow to orange, but always with a contrasting black center. Given its height, the plant is best situated towards the rear of a border, in association with others of complementary tones. It looks spectacular mass-planted in parks and other large areas. Indoors it is also very useful for floral work. It is easily grown from seed and thrives in warm, sunny situations. Grows well in most soils and conditions, providing drainage is good.
Other colors: See Description.
Varieties/cultivars: 'Gloriosa', 'Marmalade', 'Gold Flame'.

Rudbeckia nitida
BLACK-EYED SUSAN, CONEFLOWER ○ ◑

Family: COMPOSITAE
Origin: Southeastern United States.
Flowering time: Late summer.
Climatic zone: 5, 6, 7, 8, 9.
Dimensions: 4 feet (over 1 meter) high.
Description: The single daisy flowers with their green central cone have a certain freshness in their appearance even on a hot summer's day. This plant is good in a large garden, but can be blown about by wind so some support is necessary. The rounded, lance-shaped leaves are attractive and the flowers are excellent for cutting. If grown on light soils, it needs plenty of organic matter added. Propagate it by division or cuttings in spring.
Varieties/cultivars: 'Herbstsonne', 'Goldquelle'.

Santolina chamaecyparissus
LAVENDER COTTON ○ ◑

Family: COMPOSITAE
Origin: Mediterranean region.
Flowering time: Spring–summer.
Climatic zone: 6, 7, 8, 9, 10.
Dimensions: 1–2 feet (300–600 mm) high.
Description: The finely dissected and heavily felted foliage forms attractive mounds of silvery white, making this a most useful plant in garden borders. The leaves have a strong, aromatic odor when bruised, and the button flowers, on almost leafless stems, are useful for picking and drying. It does best in an open situation in well-drained soil. This plant is evergreen but should be cut back hard, almost to ground level in spring, to prevent it from becoming straggly. It can be propagated by stem cuttings in the summer.
Varieties/cultivars: 'Weston'.

Santolina chamaecyparissus

Rudbeckia nitida

Senecio cineraria syn. *Cineraria maritima, Senecio maritimus*
DUSTY-MILLER (U.K.), SEA RAGWORT, SILVER CINERARIA ○

Family: COMPOSITAE
Origin: Mediterranean region.
Flowering time: Summer.
Climatic zone: 7, 8, 9.
Dimensions: 2 feet (600 mm) high.
Description: The jagged, lobed leaves of this plant are felted in a silvery gray color making it a useful foil for other colors in a garden border. Like so many gray-leaved plants it grows exceptionally well near the seaside and can survive dry conditions, but not frost. Weak and exhausted growth should be removed after flowering and the plant regularly trimmed. The small, rayed flower heads appear in compound corymbs. Propagation is by cuttings or clump division in autumn, and also by seed.
Varieties/cultivars: 'White Diamond', 'Hoar Frost', 'Dwarf Silver'.

Senecio cineraria syn. *Cineraria maritima*

Sisyrinchium striatum

Sisyrinchium striatum
SATIN FLOWER ○ ◑

Family: IRIDACEAE
Origin: Southern Chile.
Flowering time: Summer.
Climatic zone: 7, 8, 9, 10.
Dimensions: 2 feet (600 mm) high.
Description: The gray-green, sword-like leaves of satin flower grow in clumps similar to bearded iris and from them arise the slender spikes of flowers. The flowers fade in the afternoon. When grown in an open, well-drained location, it will freely set seed. It is usually propagated from seed.
Varieties/cultivars: 'Aunt May'.

Solidago canadensis
GOLDEN ROD ○

Family: COMPOSITAE
Origin: North America.
Flowering time: Summer.
Climatic zone: 4, 5, 6, 7, 8, 9.
Dimensions: Up to 5 feet (approx. 2 meters) high.
Description: This species is one of the parents of the many hybrid forms of golden rod available today. It forms wide clumps and has narrow, downy leaves and broad, pyramidal clusters of flowers. A very easily grown plant, it is useful at the back of the border, but it can be quite invasive and spreads seed prolifically. The garden cultivars are less weedy and more acceptable. It grows in any good garden soil, and was once used medicinally as a poultice and a tonic. Propagate it by division.
Varieties/cultivars: 'Golden Wings', 'Goldenmosa', 'Lesdale', 'Cloth of Gold', 'Lemore', 'Golden Thumb'.

Solidago canadensis

Thalictrum speciosissimum syn. *T. flavum glaucum*
YELLOW MEADOW RUE ○ ◑

Family: RANUNCULACEAE
Origin: Europe, temperate Asia.
Flowering time: Summer.
Climatic zone: 5, 6, 7, 8, 9.
Dimensions: Up to 5 feet (approx. 2 meters) high.
Description: The handsome foliage is blue-green in color and delicately lobed and divided. The tiny flowers are formed in dense panicles on tall stems. This is a most useful plant in the garden especially in blue-and-yellow color schemes. It will grow in most types of soil, but requires good watering during dry weather and may need support to hold the flower heads high. It becomes dormant in winter and can be divided or else propagated from seed.
Varieties/cultivars: 'Illuminator'.

Thalictrum speciosissimum

Trollius europaeus
GLOBEFLOWER 

Family: RANUNCULACEAE
Origin: Europe–Caucasus, Canada.
Flowering time: Late spring–summer.
Climatic zone: 3, 4, 5, 6, 7, 8, 9.
Dimensions: 2 feet (600 mm) high.
Description: This is a plant for moist, boggy soils, good for growing in a

Trollius europaeus

sunken garden or beside an ornamental pond. The leaves form a basal clump which gradually increases with age. In high altitudes it can take full sun, but it usually requires some protection. The flowers, which are single and solitary, are mildly fragrant. There are now a number of hybrid cultivars available. It is propagated by division in autumn or spring.
Varieties/cultivars: 'Superbus', 'Canary Bird', 'Orange Princess', 'Empire Day', 'Lemon Queen', 'Fire Globe'.

Trollius x *cultorum* 'Golden Queen'
GLOBEFLOWER ○ ◑

Family: RANUNCULACEAE
Origin: Hybrid
Flowering time: Summer.

Trollius x *cultorum* 'Golden Queen'

Climatic zone: 4, 5, 6, 7, 8, 9.
Dimensions: 2–3 feet (up to 1 meter) high.
Description: This garden form is distinct from the true species which is now claimed not to be in cultivation. The formation of the flower is a little different from other globeflowers as the inside is filled with slender, petal-like orange stamens. It requires moist, well-drained soil that is well nourished, and looks splendid beside a green lawn or a stretch of water. Propagate it by division in autumn.

Uvularia grandiflora

Uvularia grandiflora
MERRYBELLS, MOUNTAIN MERRYBELLS, BELLWORT ◑

Family: LILIACEAE
Origin: Eastern North America.
Flowering time: Late spring.
Climatic zone: 4, 5, 6, 7, 8, 9.
Dimensions: Up to 2 feet (600 mm) high.
Description: This dainty woodland plant, closely related to Solomon's seal, has a thick, creeping rootstock. The narrowly oval to oblong leaves on arching stems are half unrolled as the pretty bell-shaped flowers hang from the stem. When they have faded, the leaves straighten out and remain fresh throughout summer. It needs a moist, slightly acid soil, with protection from the wind. It is easily propagated by division of the rhizomes in autumn.
Varieties/cultivars: 'Pallida'.

Verbascum phoeniceum

Verbascum phoeniceum hybrids
MULLEIN ○ ◑

Family: SCROPHULARIACEAE
Origin: Hybrids.
Flowering time: Summer.
Climatic zone: 6, 7, 8, 9.
Dimensions: 3–6 feet (1–2 meters) high.
Description: These lovely perennial hybrids are useful garden plants with a wide range of colors. From a rosette of large, gray-felted leaves, a tall flower spike arises bearing masses of small flowers. Mullein look best when grown in large numbers and at the back of a border with delphiniums and lupins. They thrive in well-drained, even poor, dry soil. Some plants may need staking if exposed to the wind. Cut them back after flowering and divide in autumn or spring.
Other colors: White, pink, mauve, bronze.
Varieties/cultivars: 'Bridal Bouquet', 'Miss Willmott', 'C. L. Adams', 'Cotswold Queen', 'Gainsborough'.

Abutilon megapotamicum

Abutilon megapotamicum
BRAZIL FLOWERING MAPLE, BRAZILIAN LANTERN FLOWER ◑

Family: MALVACEAE
Origin: Brazil.
Flowering time: Summer and autumn.
Climatic zone: 9, 10.
Dimensions: Up to 6 feet (2 meters) tall.
Description: This evergreen plant with its drooping stems and pendulous flowers looks attractive in a hanging basket or spilling over the edge of a large container or retaining wall. The leaves are arrow-shaped, slender, and up to 4 inches (100 mm) long. Each flower, with its yellow petals and purple anthers, is suspended by a slender stem holding a bell-shaped red calyx from which the petals unfurl to a diameter of 1 inch (25 mm). It dislikes cold climates, where a greenhouse is essential.
Varieties/cultivars: 'Variegatum'.

Abutilon x *hybridum* 'Golden Fleece'
FLOWERING MAPLE ○

Family: MALVACEAE
Origin: Hybrid.
Flowering time: Summer–autumn.
Climatic zone: 9, 10.
Dimensions: Up to 7 feet (approx. 2 meters) high.
Description: This charming, warm-climate shrub is generally grown for its pendulous, bell-shaped, golden yellow flowers and handsome, long-stalked, maple-like leaves. The best position is against a warm, sunny, and sheltered wall where well-drained, moderately rich soil will help produce an abundance of flowers in summer. Water well in summer and pinch back to encourage branching and increased flower display. *Abutilon* can also be trained around a column if the conditions are warm and sheltered.
Other colors: Orange, crimson, orange-yellow, creamy yellow, yellow with purple veins.
Varieties/cultivars: 'Ashford Red', 'Boule de Neige', 'Canary Bird', 'Fireball', 'Nabob', 'Orange Glow', 'Souvenir de Bob', 'Emperor', 'Vesuvius', 'Tunisia'.

Abutilon x *hybridum* 'Golden Fleece'

Banksia robur

Banksia robur

SWAMP BANKSIA, BROAD-LEAVED BANKSIA ○ ◑

Family: PROTEACEAE
Origin: Australia (Queensland, N.S.W.).
Flowering time: Winter–spring.
Climatic zone: 9, 10.
Dimensions: Up to 7 feet (2 meters) tall.
Description: In its swampy native habitat, this unusual shrub, with its coarse, wide-spreading branches, grows broader (9 feet (3 meters)) than it does tall. The flowers are in dense, erect spikes, or "brushes", 6 inches (150 mm) long, yellowish-green at first, deepening to bronze-green with black stigmas. The large, elliptic leaves, 10 inches (250 mm) long, with sharp, irregular teeth on the margins, are smooth and dark green on the upper surface and rusty-red and furry on the undersurface. Prefers well-drained, heavy soil that is slightly acid.

Berberis darwinii

BARBERRY (U.K.), DARWIN BARBERRY ○ ◑ ●

Family: BERBERIDACEAE
Origin: Chile.
Flowering time: Early spring.
Climatic zone: 7, 8, 9.
Dimensions: Up to 10 feet (3 meters) high.
Description: First discovered in Chile in 1835 by Charles Darwin on the voyage of the *Beagle*, this early-flowering species is one of the finest of all flowering shrubs. The orange-yellow flowers numbering from ten to thirty, are arranged in drooping flower heads up to 4 inches (100 mm) long. It is a densely-branched shrub with the new growth arching outwards. The leaves are holly-like, three-pointed and spiny-toothed up to ¾ inch (18 mm) long, and a rich glossy green. Dark-blue-purple waxy berries make a fine autumn and winter display. A sheltered position is preferred together with well-drained soil to ensure good results.

Berberis darwinii

Berberis thunbergii 'Crimson Pygmy'

Berberis thunbergii 'Crimson Pygmy'

BARBERRY, JAPANESE BARBERRY ○ ◑

Family: BERBERIDACEAE
Origin: Japan.
Flowering time: Spring.
Climatic zone: 4, 5, 6, 7, 8, 9.
Dimensions: Up to 2 feet (600 mm) high.
Description: Also known as 'Atropurpurea Nana' and 'Little Favorite', this dwarf cultivar was raised in Holland in 1942. The pale yellow flowers form in small clusters and are followed by bright red berries which persist all winter. The rich reddish-purple color of the foliage intensifies as winter approaches. This charming compact shrub is excellent in rock gardens and, with its thorns, makes an impenetrable low hedge. Hardy, it needs a well-drained soil.

Buddleia globosa

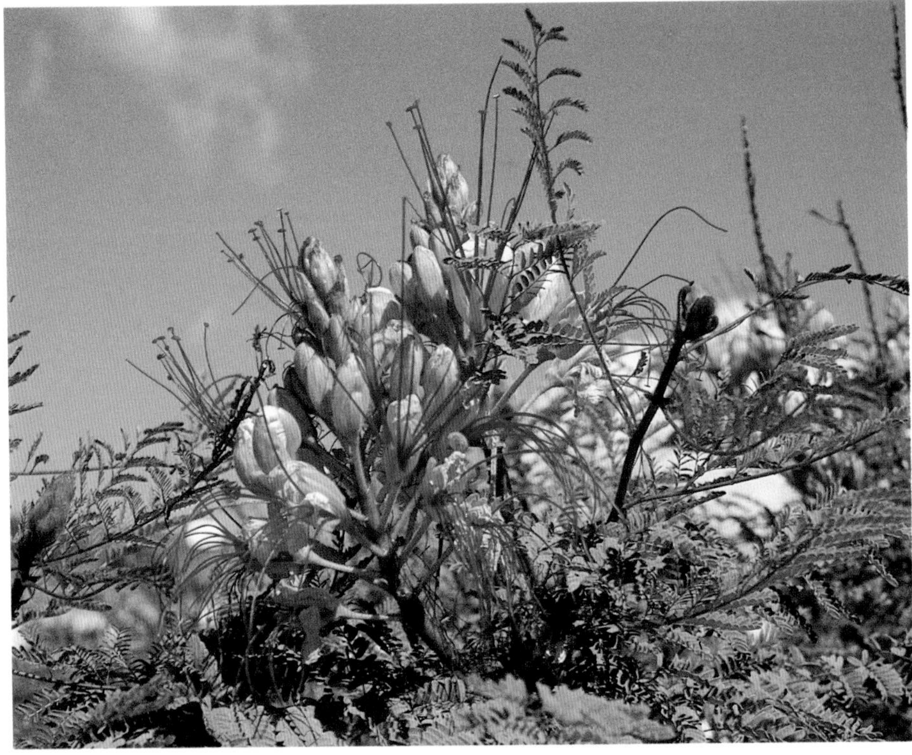

Caesalpinia gilliesii

Buddleia globosa

GOLDEN HONEY BALLS, GLOBE BUDDLEIA (U.K.), ORANGE BALL TREE ○

Family: LOGANIACEAE
Origin: Chile, Peru.
Flowering time: Summer.
Climatic zone: 7, 8, 9.
Dimensions: Up to 15 feet (5 meters) high.
Description: This is a striking, wide-spreading, semi-evergreen shrub which is deciduous if the winter is severe. The common names describe the tight ball-like clusters of flowers which are arranged in loose clusters at the tips of the stems. They have a pronounced honey fragrance and flower for several weeks. The handsome, lance-shaped leaves, up to 8 inches (200 mm) long, are dark-green and wrinkled above, with felted, tawny hairs on their undersides. Plant in well-drained soil in a sunny position.
Varieties/cultivars: 'Lemon Ball'.

Caesalpinia gilliesii

BIRD-OF-PARADISE BUSH ○

Family: CAESALPINACEAE
Origin: Argentina.
Flowering time: Summer.
Climatic zone: 9, 10.
Dimensions: Up to 10 feet (3 meters) high.
Description: This is a non-prickly, straggly, evergreen shrub or small tree. The flowers, crowded thirty or forty together in racemes up to 5 inches (125 mm) long, consist of rich yellow petals from which bright red, showy stamens protrude. The cluster of stamens can be as long as 3 inches (75 mm). The new shoots are sticky and hairy and the numerous small, dainty leaflets make the foliage appear very feathery and graceful. An open, sunny position with well-drained soil fertilized with a complete plant food will ensure good results for this warm climate plant.

Cassia artemisioides

SILVER CASSIA ○

Family: CAESALPINACEAE
Origin: Australia.
Flowering time: Early spring–summer.
Climatic zone: 9, 10.
Dimensions: Up to 4 feet (over 1 meter) high.
Description: Compact and bushy, this attractive, evergreen shrub has beautiful silvery gray shoots and feathery foliage. The leaves are finely divided into six or eight narrow leaflets. The abundant bright yellow flowers, each about ½ inch (12 mm) in diameter, form flower heads 6 inches (150 mm) long, arising in the leaf axils. The seed pods are flat and about 3 inches (75 mm) long. Excellently adapted to hot dry conditions, this plant requires full sun and exceptionally well-drained, open, sandy soil.

Cassia artemisioides

Chimonanthus praecox syn. *C. fragrans*

WINTERSWEET ○

Family: CALYCANTHACEAE
Origin: China.
Flowering time: Winter.
Climatic zone: 7, 8, 9.
Dimensions: Up to 8 feet (2.4 meters) high.
Description: This deciduous shrub spreads as wide as it grows tall. The bare stems of the previous year produce

Chimonanthus praecox

exceedingly fragrant flowers during the winter months. They open to 1 inch (25 mm) across, the outer petals being a translucent greenish-yellow and the inner ones stained a purplish-brown. Cutting the flowered stems to bring the perfume indoors, is also an effective method of pruning. The short-stalked, ovalish, dark-green leaves are up to 6 inches (150 mm) long. A good wall shrub, it prefers a sheltered, sunny position in well-drained, humus-rich soil.
Varieties/cultivars: 'Grandiflorus', 'Luteus'.

Colutea arborescens
BLADDER SENNA ○ ◑

Family: LEGUMINOSAE
Origin: Southeastern Europe.
Flowering time: Early summer.
Climatic zone: 6, 7, 8, 9.
Dimensions: Up to 12 feet (4 meters) high.
Description: This deciduous shrub sometimes naturalizes too readily to be included with selected plantings, but it will succeed in many inhospitable situations as long as the soil is not too wet and the position is not too shaded. The leaves, which are up to 6 inches (150 mm) long, consist of seven to thirteen leaflets each 1 inch (25 mm) long. The bright yellow flowers are about ¾ inch (18 mm) long and are arranged in racemes of three to eight flowers. The papery and inflated bladder-like pods are about 3 inches (75 mm) long and are sometimes flushed with red. Grow it in well-drained soil.

Colutea arborescens

Corylopsis veitchiana

Corylopsis veitchiana
WINTERHAZEL 

Family: HAMAMELIDACEAE
Origin: China.
Flowering time: Spring.
Climatic zone: 7, 8, 9, 10.
Dimensions: Up to 6½ feet (2 meters) high.
Description: A bushy, rounded, deciduous shrub, this species has slender, pointed leaves and showy catkin-like racemes of fragrant primrose-yellow flowers which create a dense display. For good results this shrub requires humus-rich, slightly acid soil and should be positioned in a semishaded, protected site. It can be propagated either from ripe seed cuttings, or by layering in spring.

Corylopsis spicata

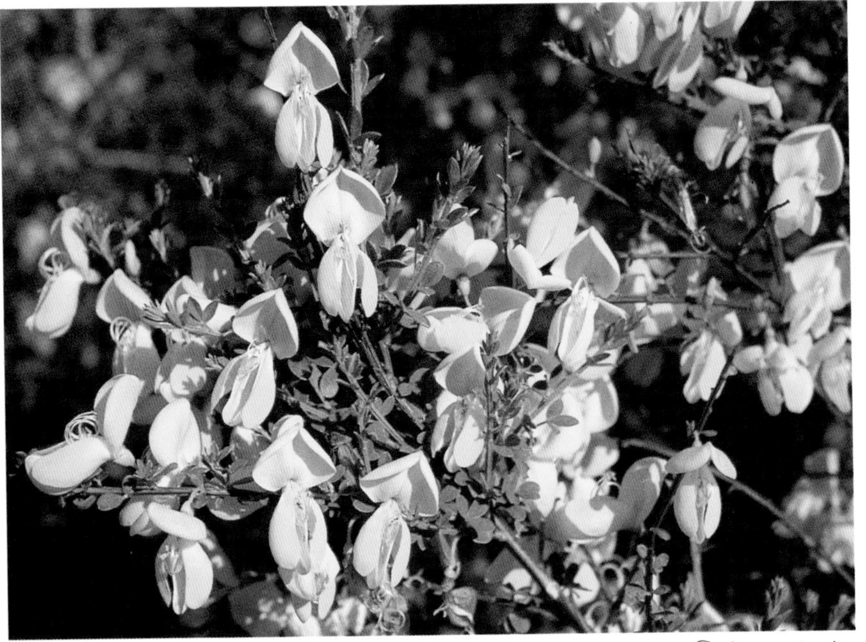

Cytisus scoparius

Corylopsis spicata
SPIKE WINTER HAZEL ○

Family: HAMAMELIDACEAE
Origin: Japan.
Flowering time: Spring.
Climatic zone: 5, 6, 7, 8, 9.
Dimensions: Up to 8 feet (2.4 meters) high.
Description: Spike winter hazel is a wide-spreading shrub with a subtle display of bright yellow blooms, sometimes appearing in late winter. The open, cup-shaped flowers are produced in pendant spikes up to 2 inches (50 mm) long of six to twelve flowers with hairy calyxes. The stamens are much the same length as the petals and the anthers are purple. The rounded leaves are about 4 inches (100 mm) long with grayish-green, hairy undersides supported by 1 inch (25 mm) long densely hairy stalks. Humus-rich, acid to neutral soil is preferred.

Cytisus scoparius syn. *Sarothamnus scoparius*
COMMON BROOM, SCOTCH BROOM ○

Family: LEGUMINOSAE
Origin: Western and central Europe.
Flowering time: Late spring–early summer.
Climatic zone: 6, 7, 8, 9.
Dimensions: Up to 10 feet (3 meters) high.
Description: Freely naturalizing, this shrub grows in great numbers in many areas, where its glowing flowers can turn a whole hillside golden. It is a deciduous, erect shrub with many evergreen branches. The leaf usually consists of three leaflets about ½ inch (12 mm) long. The profuse flowers are produced singly or in pairs, and measure about 1 inch (25 mm) long. Many cultivars are available, with flower colors ranging from cream to shades of yellow with splashes of reds and browns. Although hardy, it prefers a well-drained, sunny site.
Varieties/cultivars: 'Andreanus', 'Cornish Cream', 'Golden Sunlight', 'Sulphureus', 'Firefly'.

Cytisus x *spachianus*
YELLOW BROOM, CANARY ISLAND BROOM (U.K.) ○ ◑

Family: LEGUMINOSAE
Origin: Hybrid.
Flowering time: Winter–spring.
Climatic zone: 9, 10.
Dimensions: Up to 6 feet (2 meters) high.
Description: This tender, evergreen shrub has deep-green foliage with silky down beneath and rich yellow, fragrant, pea-shaped flowers in slender racemes. Often grown as a pot plant under the name *Genista fragrans*, this species prefers a light, well-drained, slightly acid soil and plenty of water during spring and summer. Intolerant of severe winters.
Other colors: Brown, crimson, orange, scarlet, deep yellow, pale cream.
Varieties/cultivars: 'Andreanus', 'Cornish Cream', 'Dorothy Walpole', 'Firefly', 'Lady Moore', 'Lord Lambourne'.

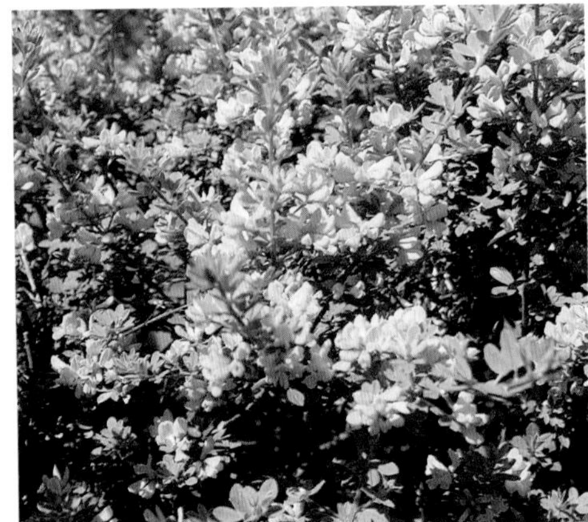

Cytisus x *spachianus*

Enkianthus campanulatus
ENKIANTHUS, RED-VEIN BELL FLOWER, REDVEIN ENKIANTHUS ○ ◑

Family: ERICACEAE
Origin: Japan.
Flowering time: Early summer.

Enkianthus campanulatus

Climatic zone: 4, 5, 6, 7, 8, 9.
Dimensions: Up to 12 feet (4 meters) high.
Description: This erect, deciduous shrub is an excellent companion for rhododendron, because they both require lime-free soil. The bell-shaped flowers, up to ½ inch (12 mm) long, are yellow to yellow-orange and streaked with red. Five to fifteen flowers form flower heads, which appear in great profusion and last on the shrub for about three weeks. The elliptic leaves, which are about 3 inches (75 mm) long with bristly, toothed margins, appear before the flowers open, and turn gold and red in autumn. The cut flowers are useful for floral decoration. Lime-free loamy soil which is well-drained is preferred.

Euryops pectinatus
GRAY EURYOPS ○

Family: COMPOSITAE
Origin: South Africa.
Flowering time: Spring–summer.
Climatic zone: 8, 9, 10.
Dimensions: Up to 5 feet (approx. 2 meters) high.
Description: In a warm, sunny position and well-drained soil, this half-hardy evergreen shrub will flower for months and provide constant color in the garden. The daisy-like flowers, 2 inches (50 mm) across and borne in great numbers on erect, 6-inch-long (150 mm) stems, are clustered towards the end of the branches. The leaves are up to 3 inches (75 mm) long and deeply lobed, and both leaves and stems are densely felted with gray or white hairs. Cutting the flower heads for indoor decoration provides sufficient pruning for this plant. In cooler climates, this plant makes an attractive pot plant for a greenhouse or patio.

Euryops pectinatus

Forsythia viridissima
GOLDEN-BELLS, SPRING BELLS (U.K.), FORSYTHIA ○

Family: OLEACEAE
Origin: Eastern China.
Flowering time: Spring.
Climatic zone: 5, 6, 7, 8, 9.
Dimensions: Up to 10 feet (3 meters) high.
Description: Golden-bells is normally the last forsythia to flower. The flowers, which consist of four strap-shaped petals, cover the length of the erect, square stems in clusters of up to six. Each bright yellow flower is 1¼ inches (30 mm) wide. The leaves are lance-like, up to 6 inches (150 mm) long, and turn purple-red before they fall. Easy to grow, forsythia is effective planted in large masses with an evergreen background. Well-drained soil in a sunny position is necessary for good flower production.
Varieties/cultivars: 'Bronxensis', 'Koreana'.

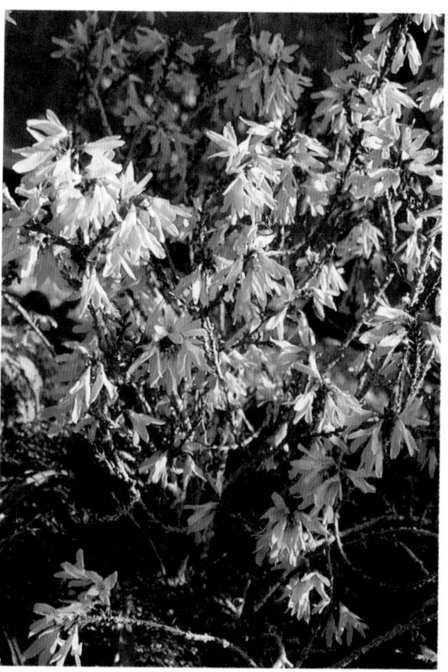

Forsythia viridissima 'Bronxensis'

Forsythia x *intermedia*

Forsythia x *intermedia*
GOLDEN-BELLS, SPRING BELLS (U.K.), FORSYTHIA ○

Family: OLEACEAE
Origin: Hybrid.
Flowering time: Spring.
Climatic zone: 5, 6, 7, 8, 9.
Dimensions: Up to 10 feet (3 meters) high.
Description: This hybrid (derived from *F. suspensa* and *F. viridissima*) and its cultivated varieties are regarded as being among the most beautiful of the forsythias. So many clusters of flowers appear along the length of each stem that it seems to be a solid block of color. The flower, with its four strap-shaped petals, is about 1 inch (25 mm) wide. The branches are arching or spreading and the oblong or oval leaves, up to 5 inches (125 mm) long, are toothed or sometimes divided into three. Plant in any well-drained garden soil. Pruning every few years encourages a neater, more compact shape.
Varieties/cultivars: 'Primulina', 'Spectabilis', 'Vitellina'.

Fremontodendron californicum

Genista hispanica

Fremontodendron californicum syn. *Fremontia californicum*
FLANNEL BUSH, FREMONTIA (U.K.) ○

Family: STERCULIACEAE
Origin: California, Arizona.
Flowering time: Spring–summer.
Climatic zone: 8, 9.
Dimensions: Up to 20 feet (6 meters) high.
Description: Previously named *Fremontia*, this evergreen shrub is excellent as a single specimen, in groups, or espaliered. The flowers, which open flat, are up to 2¼ inches (56 mm) across and although they are produced singly from the leaf axils, they are numerous. The thick, dull green leaves are covered on their undersides with irritant hairs which easily rub off and can be painful if they get into eyes. Each leaf is up to 3 inches (75 mm) long and more or less three-lobed, with three veins radiating from the heart-shaped base. This shrub thrives in dry conditions.

Genista hispanica
SPANISH GORSE ○

Family: LEGUMINOSAE
Origin: Southwestern Europe.
Flowering time: Early summer.
Climatic zone: 7, 8, 9.
Dimensions: Up to 2 feet (600 mm) high.
Description: Closely allied to *Cytisus*, this small, deciduous shrub grows as a rounded, prickly mound with intertwining, prominently spined branches and hairy shoots. The stalkless leaves are less than ½ inch (12 mm) long and densely covered with silky hairs on the undersides. The flowers, about ⅓ inch (8 mm) long, are in crowded clusters of up to twelve and are produced so abundantly that they completely cover the shrub for up to two months. This plant is easy to grow in soils that are dry and infertile, although it can be damaged or killed by severe winters.

Genista tinctoria
DYER'S GREENWEED ○

Family: LEGUMINOSAE
Origin: Mediterranean Europe, Caucasus, Turkey.
Flowering time: Summer–early autumn.
Climatic zone: 3, 4, 5, 6, 7, 8, 9.
Dimensions: Up to 2 feet (600 mm) high.
Description: This shrub is hardy and has naturalized in many areas on poor, gravelly soils. Typically, it has many upright branches which are spineless. The pea-shaped flowers are produced in great profusion in long, terminal racemes over a long period. The narrow, oblong pods are often slightly hairy like the leaves, which are nearly ½ inch (12 mm) long. This is the best known and hardiest of the genistas, but some of its cultivars are more attractive for planting in gardens.
Varieties/cultivars: *G. t.* var. *prostrata*, 'Plena', 'Royal Gold'.

Genista tinctoria var. *prostrata*

Hamamelis mollis
CHINESE WITCH HAZEL ○ ◑

Family: HAMAMELIDACEAE
Origin: Western China.
Flowering time: Winter.
Climatic zone: 5, 6, 7, 8, 9.
Dimensions: 10–20 feet (3–6 meters) high.
Description: This slow-growing, deciduous shrub or tree is perhaps the

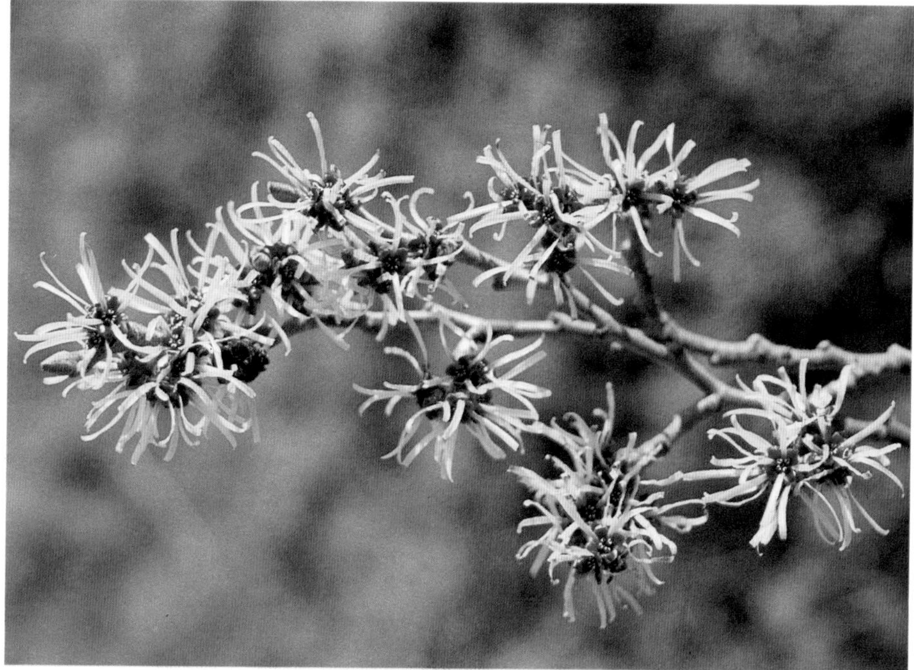
Hamamelis mollis

finest witch hazel in bloom and certainly the most popular. It is distinguished from the other species by the soft hair on its young shoots and the undersides of its leaves. It has large, rounded leaves to 6 inches (150 mm) long. The fragrant flowers consist of four narrow, strap-shaped petals which emerge crumpled from the buds. When fully open, they are ¾ inch (18 mm) long, reddish at the base, and a welcome sight in the cold months.
Varieties/cultivars: 'Pallida'.

Hamamelis virginiana

Hamamelis virginiana
WITCH HAZEL ○ ◑

Family: HAMAMELIDACEAE
Origin: Eastern North America.
Flowering time: Autumn.
Climatic zone: 4, 5, 6, 7, 8, 9.
Dimensions: Up to 20 feet (6 meters) high.
Description: This deciduous shrub flowers as the leaves drop in autumn. The fragrant flowers have four strap-shaped petals which are up to ¾ inch (18 mm) long, and arranged in clusters. The leaves are oval, 6 inches (150 mm) long, coarsely toothed, and turn golden yellow before they fall. This large shrub, which is the source of commercial witch hazel, is occasionally seen as a small, broad-domed tree.

Hypericum calycinum
SHRUBBY ST. JOHNS WORT, AARON'S BEARD, ROSE OF SHARON ○ ◑

Family: HYPERICACEAE
Origin: Southeastern Bulgaria, Turkey.
Flowering time: Summer–autumn.
Climatic zone: 6, 7, 8, 9.
Dimensions: 1–2 feet (300–600 mm) high.
Description: This semi-evergreen, dwarf shrub is one of the finest of the hypericums. Spreading by stems that can take root where they touch the ground, it forms a dense mat which makes it an excellent groundcover, but it can become a nuisance if allowed to spread unchecked. The flowers, which appear over the whole of a long summer season, are up to 4 inches (100 mm) wide, occur singly or in pairs, and have numerous stamens. The leaves are oblong and up to 4 inches (100 mm) long. The plant thrives in either sun or partial shade, and in dry soils.

Hypericum calycinum

Hypericum kalmianum

Hypericum kalmianum

KALM ST. JOHNS WORT, SHRUBBY ST. JOHNS WORT ○

Family: HYPERICACEAE
Origin: Northeastern North America.
Flowering time: Summer.
Climatic zone: 4, 5, 6, 7, 8, 9.
Dimensions: Up to 3 feet (1 meter) high.
Description: This dense, compact, evergreen shrub exists as a native over large areas of the eastern United States and is a popular garden inclusion. The stems are pale green when young, and when mature are often gnarled with pale brown, flaky bark. Its leaves, up to 2½ inches (60 mm) long, are narrowly oblong. The flowers, almost stalkless, open wide to 2 inches (50 mm) across to display five rounded petals and a show of stamens. They appear in the axils of the leaves as solitary flowers or in groups of two or three. Plant in a sunny position, in well-drained soil.

Hypericum x *moseranum* 'Tricolor'

Hypericum x *moseranum*

GOLD FLOWER, SHRUBBY ST. JOHNS WORT ○

Family: HYPERICACEAE
Origin: Hybrid.
Flowering time: Summer.
Climatic zone: 7, 8, 9.
Dimensions: Up to 2 feet (600 mm) high.
Description: Raised in France in 1887 from *H. calycinum* and *H. patulum*, this low-growing shrub does not, however, spread by rooting stems like *H. calycinum*. With its numerous arching, reddish branches it is an excellent dwarf shrub for rock gardens. The flowers, solitary or in clusters of up to five in number, are 2½ inches (60 mm) across, with conspicuous reddish anthers, and are borne over a long summer. The egg-shaped leaves, up to 2¼ inches (54 mm) long, are grayish on their undersides. Cut back to ground level if winters are harsh. A sunny, well-drained site is preferred.
Varieties/cultivars: 'Tricolor'.

Illicium anisatum

Illicium anisatum syn. *I. religiosum*, *I. japonicum*

JAPANESE STAR ANISE   

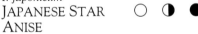

Family: ILLICIACEAE
Origin: China, Japan, Taiwan.
Flowering time: Spring.
Climatic zone: 8, 9.
Dimensions: Up to 25 feet (8 meters) high.
Description: Related to the magnolia, this outstanding evergreen shrub thrives in conditions congenial to Rhododendron. It is slow-growing and aromatic and is often found in Buddhist cemeteries or near temples, where its wood is used in incense. Its lustrous, oval leaves, which are also aromatic, are thick, fleshy, deep-green, and up to 4 inches (100 mm) long. The many-petaled flowers are pale yellow, about 1 inch (25 mm) across, and appear even on young plants. This species is poisonous, and needs a sheltered site in cooler climates.
Varieties/cultivars: 'Variegatum'.

Itea ilicifolia

Itea ilicifolia
HOLLY-LEAF SWEETSPIRE

Family: SAXIFRAGACEAE
Origin: Western China.
Flowering time: Late summer.
Climatic zone: 7, 8, 9.
Dimensions: Up to 9 feet (3 meters) high.
Description: This handsome evergreen shrub has holly-like, spiny-toothed, broad leaves up to 4 inches (100 mm) long, which are a rich, glossy green on the upper surface and paler beneath. The pale greenish-yellow flowers, which are produced in arching, trailing, slender, catkin-like racemes up to 12 inches (300 mm) long, cover the plant in late summer. These shrubs can be used in much the same manner as hollies — in groups, as single specimens, as hedges, or combined with other plants in the shrub garden. Plant in well-drained, humus-rich soil in sun or partial shade. A sheltered position is preferred, especially in cooler climates.

Jasminum humile 'Revolutum'
YELLOW JASMINE, SHRUBBY YELLOW JASMINE, ITALIAN JASMINE

Family: OLEACEAE
Origin: Cultivar.
Flowering time: Summer–autumn.
Climatic zone: 7, 8, 9.
Dimensions: Up to 10 feet (3 meters) high.
Description: Although rather sprawling in habit, this beautiful evergreen shrub forms a more or less rounded shape. Its deep-green leaves with three to seven leaflets, the terminal one being the longest and measuring up to 2½ inches (60 mm) long, form a splendid background for the deep-yellow, sometimes fragrant flowers. On a long tube, the spreading petals, measuring ¾ inch (18 mm) across, are arranged in clusters of six to twelve or more. This shrub is an ideal plant for a sunny, protected situation such as against a wall. It does not tolerate severe winters. Well-drained but moist soil is preferred.

Jasminum humile 'Revolutum'

Jasminum mesnyi

Jasminum mesnyi syn. *J. primulinum*
PRIMROSE JASMINE

Family: OLEACEAE
Origin: Western China.
Flowering time: Spring.
Climatic zone: 8, 9, 10.
Dimensions: Up to 3 feet (1 meter) high.
Description: Sometimes included among the climbing plants, this very attractive evergreen shrub has weak stems which emerge from the base and, arching outwards, scramble over any support. The flowers of deep-yellow open to 1½ inches (35 mm) across on a slender tube ½ inch (12 mm) long. They are often semidouble and are produced in succession over a long spring season on the 1- and 2-year-old outer stems for a length of 3 feet (1 meter) or more. The leaves, which grow opposite one another on the stems, consist of three leaflets and are up to 4 inches (100 mm) long. Well-drained, moist soil is preferred. This plant may be killed by severe winters.

Kerria japonica 'Pleniflora'

Kerria japonica 'Pleniflora' syn. 'Flore Pleno'
KERRIA, JEW'S MALLOW, BACHELORS BUTTONS (U.K.)

Family: ROSACEAE
Origin: Cultivar.
Flowering time: Spring.
Climatic zone: 5, 6, 7, 8, 9.
Dimensions: Up to 6 feet (2 meters) high.
Description: A cultivar of the only species of *Kerria*, this deciduous, suckering shrub has been a favorite in gardens since its introduction into Europe in 1834. Long, slender, cane-like stems from the previous year support the flowers, which are clear golden-yellow, up to 1¾ inches (42 mm) across, and which open to show their petals and numerous stamens. The egg-shaped leaves, which are about 4 inches (100 mm) long with double-toothed margins, are bright green, smooth on the upper surface, and hairy on the underside. They turn yellow in autumn. Grow in any well-drained soil. It tolerates both sun and partial shade.

Lantana camara 'Drap d'Or'
COMMON LANTANA, YELLOW SAGE (U.K.)

Family: VERBENACEAE
Origin: Cultivar.
Flowering time: Year round.
Climatic zone: 9, 10.
Dimensions: Up to 6 feet (2 meters) high.
Description: Deep golden-yellow flowers and a more compact growth habit distinguish this cultivated variety from other *Lantana* species. Otherwise it has similar characteristics — the crushed leaves give off the familiar pungent smell, the stems are prickly, and the foliage is covered in short hairs. The leaves are oval, wrinkled, up to 5 inches (125 mm) in length, with toothed margins. The small flowers are arranged in flattish clusters of twenty to thirty, measuring up to 2 inches (50 mm) across. The black fruits which follow are mostly sterile (and do not present the same problem as the non-cultivated lantanas whose readily germinating seeds are widely dispersed by birds).

Lantana camara 'Drap d'Or'

Laurus nobilis
SWEET BAY, BAY LAUREL

Family: LAURACEAE
Origin: Mediterranean region.
Flowering time: Late spring.
Climatic zone: 7, 8, 9.
Dimensions: Up to 20 feet (6 meters) high.
Description: In cultivation since 1562, this is the true laurel that the ancients made into wreaths for poets and crowns for triumphant heroes. Because it stands

Laurus nobilis

clipping well it is today often grown beside doorways and trimmed to shape. Although in the wild it can reach a height of 40 feet (12 meters), in a cultivated garden it is well suited to large containers. The evergreen leaves are narrow, up to 5 inches (125 mm) long, a rich dark-green, and are the bay leaves much esteemed by cooks the world over. Small clusters of fragrant, yellowish flowers are followed by small berries which ripen to purplish-black. Plant in spring in moderate soil in a sunny or partially shady position. It is tolerant of some frost but may be damaged by severe winters.
Varieties/cultivars: 'Angustifolia'.

Lindera benzoin
SPICE BUSH

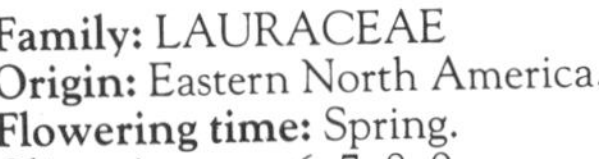

Family: LAURACEAE
Origin: Eastern North America.
Flowering time: Spring.
Climatic zone: 6, 7, 8, 9.

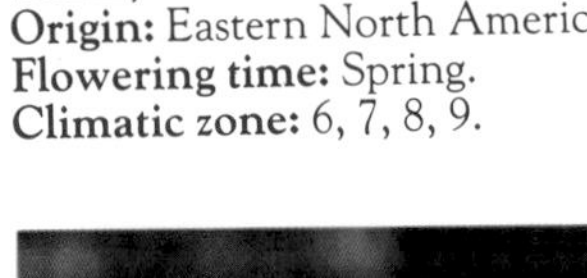

Lindera benzoin

Dimensions: Up to 15 feet (5 meters) high.
Description: Of compact habit, this is a magnificent deciduous, tall shrub. Its long leaves are aromatic when bruised. Bright green in summer, the leaves in autumn may turn a glorious butter-yellow with rich pink tints. The small flowers are petalless, their calyces being yellow-green. The berry-like fruits are red. Plant in partial shade or full sun in moist soil.

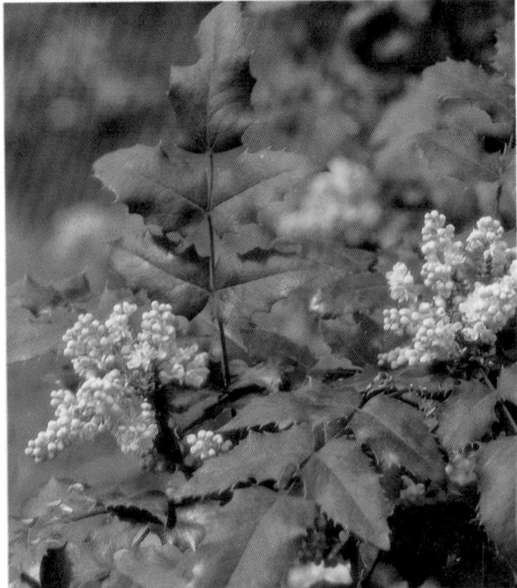
Mahonia aquifolium

Mahonia aquifolium
OREGON GRAPE, HOLLY MAHONIA

Family: BERBERIDACEAE
Origin: Northwestern North America.
Flowering time: Spring.
Climatic zone: 6, 7, 8, 9.
Dimensions: Up to 4 feet (approx. 1 meter) high.
Description: This very beautiful evergreen shrub looks attractive planted under deciduous trees. The showy flowers are produced in dense, golden-yellow clusters of racemes up to 3 inches (75 mm) long. Masses of attractive blue-black berries follow with their covering of purple bloom. The handsome leaves, up to 10 inches (250 mm) long, consist of five to nine oblong leaflets each up to 3 inches (75 mm) long with shallow-toothed margins. In autumn bronze and purple tints are added to their rich, glossy green. Grow in humus-rich, well-drained soil.
Varieties/cultivars: 'Atropurpureum', 'Moseri'.

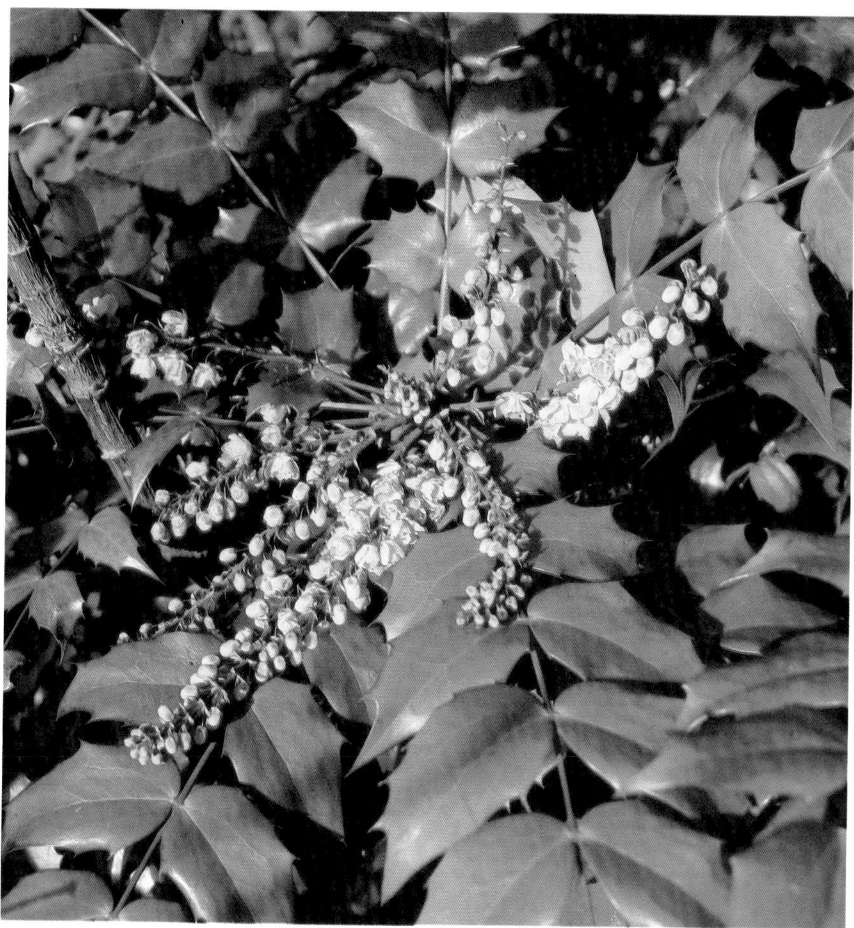

Mahonia bealei

Mahonia bealei
LEATHERLEAF MAHONIA ○ ◑

Family: BERBERIDACEAE
Origin: China.
Flowering time: Late winter–late spring.
Climatic zone: 6, 7, 8, 9.
Dimensions: Up to 8 feet (approx. 2 meters) high.
Description: The hardiest of the Asian mahonias and, with M. *aquifolium* and M. *repens*, the most cold-resistant, this popular evergreen shrub has stout, upright stems. The fragrant, lemon-yellow flowers are clustered into erect racemes up to 6 inches (150 mm) long. The fruits are a waxy bluish-black. The leaves are stiff, leathery, semi-glossy, deep green and up to 1½ feet (450 mm) long, with nine to fifteen round to oval leaflets each up to 4 inches (100 mm) in length. There are a few large, spiny teeth on the margins. It is adaptable to both sun and partial shade as long as a humus-rich soil is provided.

Ochna serrulata

Ochna serrulata syn. *O. atropurpurea*
BIRD'S EYE BUSH, MICKEY-MOUSE PLANT, CARNIVAL BUSH ○

Family: OCHNACEAE
Origin: South Africa.
Flowering time: Summer.
Climatic zone: 9.
Dimensions: Up to 10 feet (3 meters) high.
Description: Often known as O. *multiflora*, this evergreen shrub has leathery, elliptic leaves which are up to 2 inches (50 mm) long and have sharply toothed margins and prominent midribs. The bronze-colored spring foliage is followed by the fragrant flowers, resembling yellow buttercups, about ¾ inch (18 mm) wide, which are freely produced at the ends of the many lateral shoots. The fruits which quickly follow are kidney-shaped and bright green at first, maturing to a glossy black. Their curious appearance is heightened by the enlarged, bright crimson, waxy receptacles to which they are attached. Hardy, it is easy to propagate as seedlings are freely produced.

Phlomis fruticosa
JERUSALEM SAGE ○

Family: LABIATAE
Origin: Southwestern Europe.
Flowering time: Summer.
Climatic zone: 7, 8, 9.
Dimensions: Up to 4 feet (approx. 1 meter) high.
Description: Jerusalem sage is a small, broad, evergreen shrub excellent for a sunny position in well-drained soil. Its many branches are densely hairy, as are the ovalish, wrinkled leaves, which are up to 4 inches (100 mm) long. The hairs on their upper surface are green, while those on the undersides are more dense and white or yellowish. The flowers, which are dusky yellow and more than 1 inch (25 mm) long, form rounded clusters at the tops of the stems. Pruning the spent flower heads will increase flowering and maintain the bush's compact shape.

Phlomis fruticosa

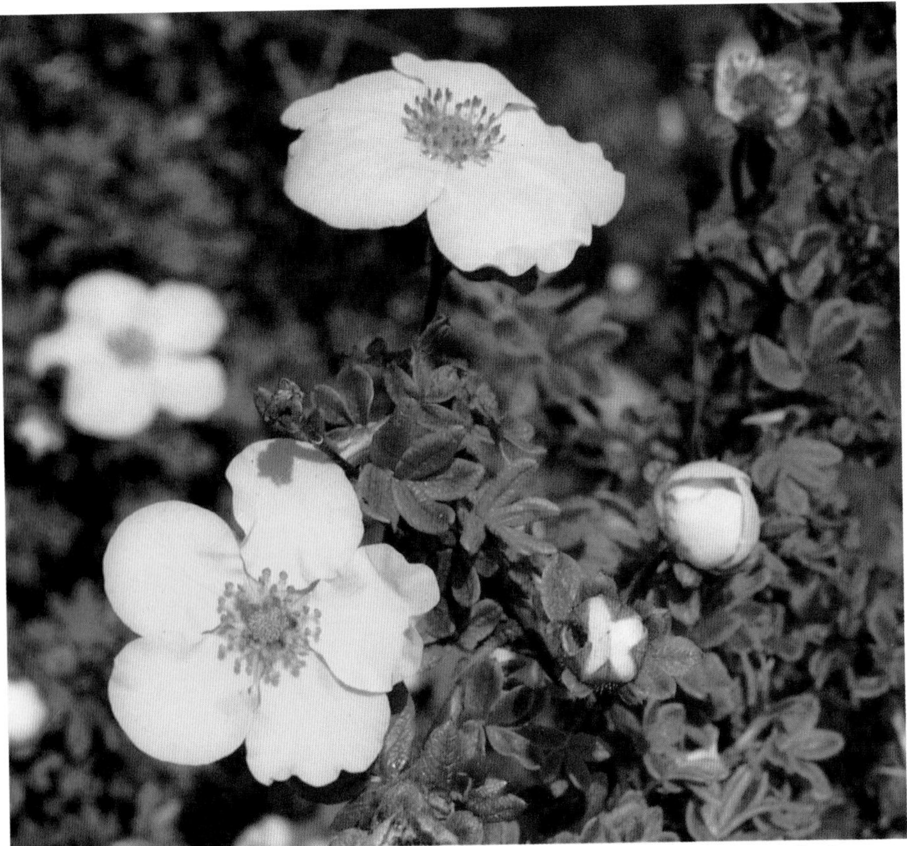

Potentilla fruticosa

Potentilla fruticosa

SHRUBBY CINQUEFOIL ○

Family: ROSACEAE
Origin: Northern temperate zone, mountains further south.
Flowering time: Summer.
Climatic zone: 2, 3, 4, 5, 6, 7, 8, 9.
Dimensions: Up to 3 feet (1 meter) high.
Description: Usually a rounded bush growing as wide as it does tall, this deciduous shrub is hardy, thrives in any soil, and has flowers like small, single roses which are displayed over a long summer season. Its erect stems bear hairy green to grey leaves divided into five to seven leaflets up to 1 inch (25 mm) long. The open-faced, bright yellow flowers, up to 2 inches (50 mm) in diameter, are numerous and showy. This shrub is the parent of several hybrids as well as producing many cultivated varieties.
Other colors: White, red, orange, cream.
Varieties/cultivars: Many cultivars are available, including 'Grandiflora', 'Katherine Dykes', 'Vilmoriniana', 'Berlin Beauty', 'Klondyke', 'Longacre'.

Reinwardtia indica syn. *R. trigyna*, *Linum trigynum*

YELLOW FLAX ○

Family: LINACEAE
Origin: Northern India.
Flowering time: Winter–spring.
Climatic zone: 9, 10.
Dimensions: Up to 3 feet (1 meter) high.
Description: The most commonly cultivated of the few species of *Reinwardtia*, yellow flax is a splendid small, evergreen shrub for warm, sunny, and preferably humid locations and, in warm greenhouses, makes an attractive pot plant. The bright golden-yellow, nearly circular flowers are about 2 inches (50 mm) in diameter and open wide above a slender tube. They fall quickly, but are produced in abundance over a long period. The soft, thin, narrow leaves, about 3 inches (75 mm) long, are bright green. The plant should be pruned to shape in early spring.

Reinwardtia indica

Ribes odoratum

YELLOW FLOWERING CURRANT, BUFFALO CURRANT (U.K.) ○ ◑

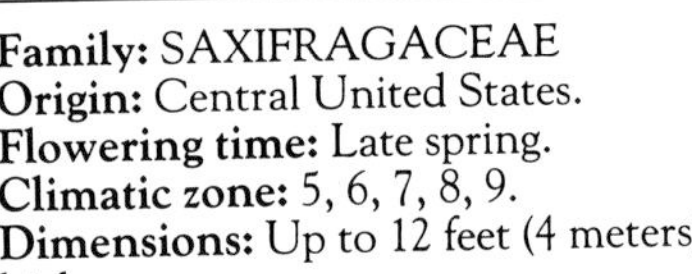

Family: SAXIFRAGACEAE
Origin: Central United States.
Flowering time: Late spring.
Climatic zone: 5, 6, 7, 8, 9.
Dimensions: Up to 12 feet (4 meters) high.
Description: Closely related to the fruiting currants and gooseberries, this ornamental, deciduous shrub is charming in bloom, when its numerous clove-scented, bright yellow, tubular flowers emerge in drooping, hairy racemes of up to ten. The racemes are 2 inches (50 mm) long. Small, smooth, black, edible fruits follow. The leaves are three- or five-lobed, smooth, though at first hairy, and measure up to 3 inches (75 mm) in length and width. They color to scarlet in autumn. Pruning after flowering produces a compact shape. A well-drained but moist soil and a sunny or partially shaded position are preferred.

Ribes odoratum

Senecio greyi

Senecio greyi

GROUNDSEL, SHRUBBY GROUNDSEL ○

Family: COMPOSITAE
Origin: New Zealand.
Flowering time: Summer.
Climatic zone: 7, 8, 9.
Dimensions: Up to 6 feet (2 meters) high.
Description: Considered by some the loveliest of the New Zealand *Senecio* species, this very popular wide-spreading, evergreen shrub brings soft shades of white-gray to the garden, with the young shoots, undersides of the leaves, and leaf stalks all densely covered in a felt of white hairs. The bright yellow, daisy flower heads, up to 1 inch (25 mm) wide, are arranged in broad clusters up to 6 inches (150 mm) long. The oblong leaves are up to 4 inches (100 mm) long. This shrub is ideal for seaside planting, but cannot tolerate severe winters.

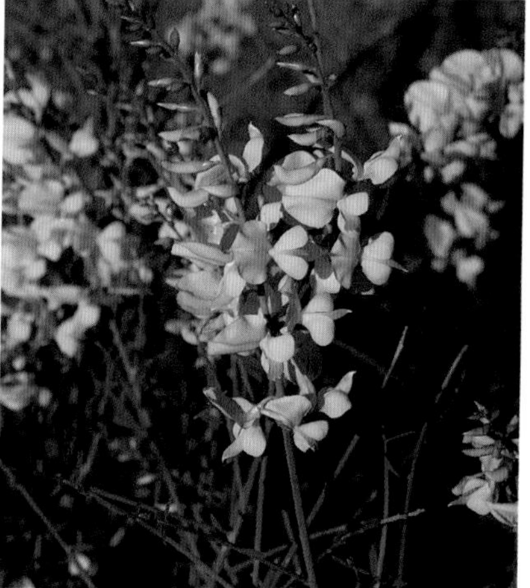

Spartium junceum

Spartium junceum

SPANISH BROOM, WEAVER'S BROOM ○

Family: LEGUMINOSAE
Origin: Southwestern Europe.
Flowering time: Summer–autumn.
Climatic zone: 8, 9.
Dimensions: Up to 8 feet (approx. 2 meters) high.
Description: Closely related to *Cytisus* and *Genista*, this single species of *Spartium* is a wonderful seaside shrub thriving in well-drained soils in a sunny situation. The fragrant flowers measure 1 inch (25 mm) long and wide, and look like small, golden-yellow sweet peas arranged in showy, loose, terminal racemes up to 1½ feet (450 mm) long. Because its leaves are small and inconspicuous on the erect, rush-like, green stems, the shrub seems almost leafless. Prune in early spring to keep it shapely. The shrub is tolerant of moderate frost but not severe winters.

Ulex europaeus

COMMON GORSE, FURZE, WHIN ○

Family: LEGUMINOSAE
Origin: Western Europe–southern Scandinavia.
Flowering time: Late winter–late spring.
Climatic zone: 6, 7, 8, 9.
Dimensions: Up to 6 feet (2 meters) high.
Description: Closely resembling the related *Cytisus*, this fiercely spiny, evergreen shrub has been known to produce flowers over the whole year, but only in dry, sandy soil in full sun and in a mild climate. The brilliant yellow pea flowers are up to ¾ inch (18 mm) long, almond-scented, and form loose to dense clusters at the ends of the branches. Young plants have three leaflets, but on older specimens the leaves are scale-like or represented by spines. Naturalized in many areas, sometimes to the point of being a pest, gorse grows well in association with heather. It is suitable for clipping as a hedge.
Varieties/cultivars: 'Plenus'.

Ulex europaeus

Acacia baileyana

Acacia baileyana
COOTAMUNDRA WATTLE, BAILEY WATTLE, BAILEY ACACIA ○

Family: LEGUMINOSAE
Origin: Australia, N.S.W.
Flowering time: Winter–spring.
Climatic zone: 9, 10.
Dimensions: 20–40 feet (6–12 meters) high.
Description: One of the most popular and widely grown of the acacias, Cootamundra wattle is smothered in golden balls of small, fluffy, fragrant flowers in winter. Its bluish or silvery-gray leaves consist of many, divided leaflets, producing a soft, feathery appearance. It can be grown successfully in most soils and conditions, providing drainage is excellent. Like all wattles it is fast-growing which makes it a valuable plant for new gardens for use as a screen or a shade tree. Another asset in landscaping is its role as a "nurse" plant — it fills in space and protects much slower-growing plants. In cold areas, it needs to be grown under glass. Tip-prune it after flowering, to prolong its life.
Varieties/cultivars: 'Purpurea'.

Acacia dealbata
SILVER WATTLE, MIMOSA ○

Family: LEGUMINOSAE
Origin: Eastern Australia.
Flowering time: Spring.
Climatic zone: 8, 9, 10.
Dimensions: 33–66 feet (10–20 meters) high.
Description: In the wild, silver wattle grows by permanent creeks. With its profuse flower heads of highly fragrant flowers it is a favorite in France for the perfume industry. After blooming, the tree takes on a hazy pink hue, as masses of pods hang among the silvery, feathery foliage. Fast-growing and evergreen, it is best grown in a very large, natural garden, near a running creek. It is easily grown from seed in spring, but the seed must be soaked in freshly boiled water which is allowed to cool slowly for 24 hours before sowing.

Acacia dealbata

Acacia longifolia
SYDNEY GOLDEN WATTLE, SALLOW WATTLE ○

Family: LEGUMINOSAE
Origin: Eastern and southern Australia.
Flowering time: Spring.
Climatic zone: 9, 10.
Dimensions: 10–20 feet (3-6 meters) high.
Description: At home in many warm, temperate climates, this evergreen tree is used extensively in California as a street tree, while in South Africa it has reached almost weed proportions. Profuse, fragrant fingers of fluffy flowers appear each spring. Beautiful, fast-growing, and resistant to salt spray, it will bind soil when planted on a bank, or very quickly create a screen for a new garden. *Acacia longifolia* var. *sophorae* is a much smaller, spreading form which will bind sand in beach gardens. Grow new plants from seed in spring, soaking them in warm water for 12 hours before planting.
Varieties/cultivars: *A. l.* var. *sophorae*.

Acacia longifolia

Acer platanoides
NORWAY MAPLE ○

Family: ACERACEAE
Origin: Scandinavia, western Europe, western Asia.
Flowering time: Early spring.
Climatic zone: 3, 4, 5, 6, 7, 8, 9.
Dimensions: 50–100 feet (15–30 meters) high.
Description: Found over large areas in its natural habitat, this tree is also extensively cultivated. Attractive clusters of yellow flowers appear just before the fine, green leaves, which turn yellow briefly in autumn before falling. One of the fastest-growing of the maples, it prefers cool, moist gardens in areas high above sea level, but will withstand pollution. Because it produces a dense canopy, not much will grow beneath this tree. Plant it where shade is required, perhaps in a paved area with garden seats.
Varieties/cultivars: 'Crimson King', 'Drummondii', 'Dissectum', 'Erectum', 'Faasen's Black', 'Reitenbachii', 'Schwedleri', 'Goldsworth Purple', 'Laciniatum', 'Lorbergii'.

Acer platanoides

Azara lanceolata

Azara lanceolata
AZARA ○ ◑

Family: FLACOURTIACEAE
Origin: Chile.
Flowering time: Midsummer.
Climatic zone: 8, 9.
Dimensions: Up to 20 feet (6 meters) high.
Description: This is a neat and pretty evergreen tree covered in slender, dark green, glossy foliage. The strongly fragrant flowers are mustard-yellow, and followed by pretty, pale mauve berries. To achieve good results position in a warm, sheltered site in rich, moist soil that is slightly acid. Mulch well around the base, and ensure there is a good supply of water during summer. Avoid planting close to other species, as the roots produce a growth inhibitor.

Banksia serrata
RED HONEYSUCKLE, SAW BANKSIA ○

Family: PROTEACEAE
Origin: Eastern Australia.
Flowering time: Summer.
Climatic zone: 9, 10.
Dimensions: Up to 30 feet (9 meters) high.
Description: Banksias are a useful shrub in poor, sandy, coastal soil and are salt-resistant. The spikes of golden flowers, which look like erect cylinders, are about 6 inches (150 mm) long. The fruits are woody seed cells. The shiny

Banksia serrata

leaves are leathery, narrow, and up to 6 inches (150 mm) long, with closely toothed margins. Plant in acid, well-drained, sandy to loamy soil.

Caesalpinia ferrea syn. *Poinciana ferrea*
BRAZILIAN IRONWOOD, LEOPARD TREE ○

Family: CAESALPINACEAE
Origin: Eastern Brazil.
Flowering time: Spring.
Climatic zone: 9, 10.
Dimensions: 33–50 feet (10–15 meters) high.
Description: The beautiful mottling of the trunk, caused by peeling bark, gives this tree the name leopard. In spring,

Caesalpinia ferrea

the top of the tree is lit up with vivid yellow blossoms, and its soft, feathery foliage, reddish at first but bright green when mature, adds a touch of elegance. Ideal in the subtropical garden, it is a fairly fast grower, making a good shade tree, but needing plenty of room. It grows well in coastal areas, but not the dry inland. Grow it from seed that has been soaked for several hours in warm water.

Caragana arborescens

Caragana arborescens
SIBERIAN PEA TREE, PEA SHRUB ○

Family: FABACEAE
Origin: Siberia, Mongolia.
Flowering time: Late spring, northern hemisphere.
Climatic zone: 3, 4, 5, 6, 7, 8, 9.
Dimensions: 15–20 feet (5–6 meters) high.
Description: The deciduous Siberian pea tree was first introduced into England in the mid-eighteenth century and has since been used as a hedge or windbreak in dry, exposed areas. The attractive yellow flowers appear in clusters from buds of the previous year. This tree is best planted in either autumn or winter, and will grow well in most soils and conditions providing drainage is adequate. Being such an adaptable plant it is often used for grafting other desirable varieties.
Varieties/cultivars: 'Lorbergii', 'Nana', 'Pendula'.

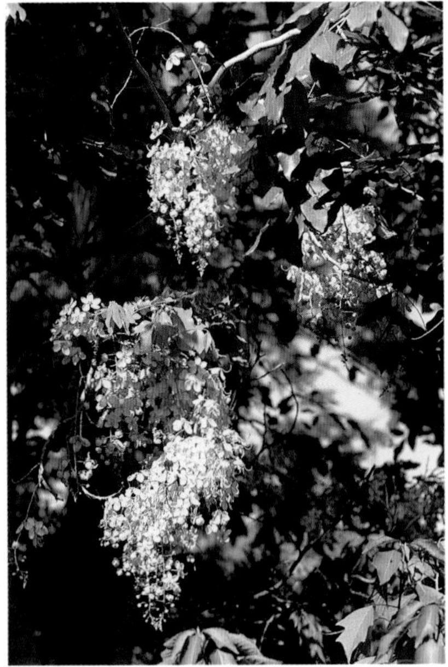
Cassia fistula

Cassia fistula
GOLDEN-SHOWER (U.K.), INDIAN LABURNUM, PUDDING-PIPE TREE ○

Family: CAESALPINACEAE
Origin: Tropical India, Burma, Sri Lanka.
Flowering time: Late summer–early autumn.
Climatic zone: 9, 10.
Dimensions: 20–33 feet (6–10 meters) high.
Description: Showy, large, drooping clusters of clear yellow, fragrant flowers adorn this lovely tree for weeks on end, enhanced by the pretty, fresh-green leaves. The name "pudding-pipe" refers to the long, brown, rather ugly seed pods that hang from the branches. The seeds may be sown in spring after soaking them in warm water for 24 hours to soften their outer coating. Easy to grow in warmer gardens, pudding-pipe tree needs to be protected from frost and cold winds in borderline climates. It thrives in well-drained soils in warm, coastal environments with good rainfall. It sheds its leaves for short periods.

Cornus mas
CORNELIAN CHERRY ○

Family: CORNACEAE
Origin: Central and southern Europe.
Flowering time: Late winter–spring.
Climatic zone: 4, 5, 6, 7, 8, 9.
Dimensions: 17–27 feet (5–8 meters) high.
Description: Cornelian cherry bears profuse clusters of tiny, yellow flowers on naked branches at the end of winter, and produces pretty, bright-red, edible fruits in summer. In autumn, the leaves may turn reddish-purple before falling. Not many other trees will tolerate the conditions this tree does — dry, chalky soils, pollution, exposed situations — and also resist pests and diseases. Often shrubby in habit, cornelian cherry should be pruned to train it as a single trunk. Grow this tree from semihardwood cuttings in late summer.
Varieties/cultivars: 'Aurea', 'Elegantissima', 'Variegata'.

Cornus mas

Genista aetnensis
MOUNT ETNA BROOM ○

Family: LEGUMINOSAE
Origin: Sicily, Sardinia.
Flowering time: Summer, northern hemisphere; late spring–mid-summer, southern hemisphere.
Climatic zone: 8, 9.
Dimensions: 17–20 feet (5–6 meters) high.
Description: Imagine a landscape of black and yellow. That is Mount Etna in summer, when the broom is in full flower on the lava-blackened slopes. Loose clusters of fragrant, clear yellow, pea-shaped flowers weigh down the slender branches of this graceful, little deciduous tree. The silky, downy, sparse leaves appear somewhat silvery. This

Genista aetnensis

broom prefers a well-drained position and tolerates chalky soil; in some areas it is subject to fungal die-back. Grow it in spring from seed that has been soaked for 24 hours in warm water. It requires no pruning.

Grevillea robusta
SILK OAK (U.S.A.), SILKY OAK ○

Family: PROTEACEAE
Origin: Australia (coastal N.S.W. and Queensland).
Flowering time: Spring, northern hemisphere; late spring–early summer, southern hemisphere.
Climatic zone: 9, 10.

Grevillea robusta

Dimensions: 40–145 feet (12-44 meters) high.
Description: Silky oak is widely grown — as a garden tree, a street tree, a pot plant, indoors and outdoors, and as a rootstock for grafting other grevilleas. Largest of all the grevilleas, it can grow rapidly to 65 feet or more (over 20 meters) in southern hemisphere gardens, and even higher in parts of the northern hemisphere. It has yellowy orange, toothbrush-shaped clusters of spider-like flowers and deeply-lobed, feathery leaves, somewhat silvery underneath. The tree prefers warm, moist soils. Normally evergreen, it tends to become deciduous if affected by cold and drought. Protect it from frost when young. It can be grown from seed.

Harpephyllum caffrum

Harpephyllum caffrum
KAFFIR PLUM ○  

Family: ANACARDIACEAE
Origin: Southeastern Africa.
Flowering time: Mid–late summer.
Climatic zone: 8, 9, 10.
Dimensions: 33–40 feet (10–12 meters) high.
Description: Give this handsome, evergreen tree plenty of space to develop its wide canopy. The young leaves appear reddish and shiny and can be mistaken for flowers from a distance. They later become dark-green and lustrous giving the tree a rather somber appearance. Delicious jams and jellies are made from the bright, red fruits, which develop from the rather pale, greenish-yellow flowers. Plant it as a shade tree in large coastal gardens where the rainfall is high. It grows easily from large stem cuttings, 12–24 inches (300–600 mm) long in late spring.

Hymenosporum flavum

Hymenosporum flavum
NATIVE FRANGIPANI, AUSTRALIAN FRANGIPANI, SWEET-SHADE (U.K.) ○

Family: PITTOSPORACEAE
Origin: Australia (northern N.S.W. and Queensland).
Flowering time: Late spring–early summer.
Climatic zone: 9, 10.
Dimensions: 20–66 feet (6–20 meters) high.
Description: In a sunny, open space in the garden, this delightful, evergreen tree grows only a fraction of the height it attains in its natural habitat, where it has to fight for light. The sprays of scented yellow flowers are tubular, with five open lobes. The tree needs to be carefully positioned, because both flowers and leaves are borne towards the end of the thinnish, brittle branches. Because its branching is open and irregular, it throws little shade. Protect it from the wind by planting it either against a fence or wall, or behind a shrubbery. It enjoys warm, coastal areas and free-draining soil.

Koelreuteria paniculata
VARNISH TREE (U.S.A.), GOLDEN RAIN TREE (U.K.), PRIDE OF CHINA TREE ○

Other common names: WILLOW PATTERN PLATE TREE
Family: SAPINDACEAE
Origin: Northern China, Korea.
Flowering time: Early summer.
Climatic zone: 5, 6, 7, 8.
Dimensions: 20–50 feet (6–15 meters) high.
Description: Golden rain tree grows in a wide range of climates and soils, tolerating drought, but disliking the coastal garden with its salt-laden winds. Its large, drooping clusters of yellow

Koelreuteria paniculata

flowers are followed by long, reddish, papery pods which hang on the tree into winter, and its large, feathery leaves color well in the autumn. Developing a wide canopy when mature, it grows rapidly in warmer climates, but in cooler regions takes about 20 years to attain a height of 18 feet (5 meters). Propagate it from seed or root cuttings.
Varieties/cultivars: 'Fastigiata', 'September' (flowers in late summer).

Laburnum anagyroides

Laburnum anagyroides
COMMON LABURNUM ○

Family: LEGUMINOSAE
Origin: Central and southern Europe.
Flowering time: Early summer.
Climatic zone: 6, 7, 8, 9.
Dimensions: Up to 20 feet (6 meters).
Description: This charming, small, deciduous tree has a spreading shape and large, drooping clusters of bright yellow, pea-like flowers. It likes cool-climate gardens, and although it can be grown successfully in most soil types, one that is deep and moist will bring the best results. In country gardens do not position it where stock can eat it, as all parts of the plant are poisonous.

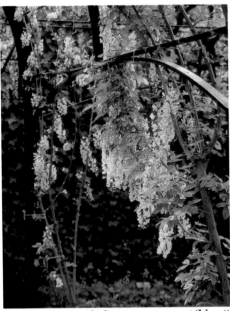

Laburnum x watereri 'Vossii'

Laburnum x watereri 'Vossii'
LABURNUM, GOLDEN CHAIN TREE, WATERER'S LABURNUM ○

Family: LEGUMINOSAE
Origin: Hybrid.
Flowering time: Late spring–early summer.
Climatic zone: 6, 7, 8, 9.
Dimensions: 20–30 feet (6–9 meters) high.
Description: This beautiful tree bears long, drooping sprays of yellow, pea-shaped flowers, and has attractive, soft foliage which consists of three leaflets on a common stalk. An avenue of laburnum, flowering vividly yellow in the spring, is an enchanting spectacle. Laburnum is deciduous and grows in almost any position in regions where the winters are cold and the atmosphere moist. All parts of the plant are poisonous so fence off from stock.

Parkinsonia aculeata

Parkinsonia aculeata
MEXICAN PALO VERDE (U.S.A.), JERUSALEM THORN (U.K.) ○

Family: LEGUMINOSAE
Origin: Tropical America.
Flowering time: Spring.
Climatic zone: 9, 10.
Dimensions: 20–27 feet (6–8 meters) high.
Description: Growing rapidly in its early years, this elegant little tree is for the tropical garden only. Its large clusters of yellow flowers, slightly scented, are followed by seed pods which look like a short string of beads. The soft, green, gracefully drooping branches, with their sparse foliage, cast a delicate tracery of shadow, but carry sharp thorns about 1 inch (25 mm) long. Jerusalem thorn grows well in coastal gardens or in frost-free inland gardens and tolerates alkaline soil and drought. Propagate it from seed.

Tamarindus indica
TAMARIND ○

Family: CAESALPINACEAE
Origin: Tropical Africa, Abyssinia, India.
Flowering time: Summer, then intermittently.
Climatic zone: 10.
Dimensions: 50–80 feet (15–25 meters) high.
Description: In India, it is believed that bad spirits take possession of anyone who sleeps beneath the dense canopy of the tamarind, so dense that nothing grows below it. Abundant, orchid-like flowers, with a delicate scent, fall to create carpets of pale yellow. A hot-climate, adaptable tree, it grows slowly, tolerating semi-arid conditions, but preferring deep, moist soils. Grow it from seed or buy a grafted specimen for quicker flowering. It is best suited to large, coastal or country gardens. The pulp from the large seed pods is used in curries and drinks.

Tamarindus indica

GLOSSARY

ACID SOIL: has a pH of less than 6, turning litmus paper red.
ALKALINE SOIL: has a pH of more than 8, turning litmus paper blue.
ANNUAL: a plant grown from seed that flowers, fruits, then dies within one year or season.
AXIL: the angle or point between a leaf and stem or branch.
BIENNIAL: a plant completing its life cycle in the space of two years.
BRACT: a modified leaf, often at the base of a flower.
BUD: a more or less immature shoot arising from the leaf axil.
CALYX: the outer ring of the flower, consisting of sepals.
CANE: a slender woody stem that is often hollow. Bamboo and most berry fruits produce canes.
CONIFER: a plant that bears its primitive flowers and seeds in cones.
COROLLA: a collective term for sepals and petals.
CORYMB: similar to a raceme, but with the stalks of the lower florets longer than the upper ones, creating a flattened or convex head.
CULTIVAR: a selected plant form introduced into cultivation, which has some horticultural value.
DECIDUOUS: a plant which loses its leaves every year, generally referring to shrubs or trees.
DIVISION: a propagating method where perennials are separated by digging up and dividing the roots and top growth into clumps that can be replanted.
DOUBLE FLOWER: a flower with more than twice the usual number of petals, usually formed from stamens.
ELLIPTIC: describing the shape of a leaf, being in outline the shape of an ellipse.
ESPALIER: a plant which has been trained to lie flat against a wall or trellis featuring a central trunk with opposite pairs of horizontal stems.
EPIPHYTE: a plant which grows on another, using it for support without actually being parasitic, e.g. many orchids.
FAMILY: a natural grouping of plant genera with certain essential characteristics in common.
FLORET: an individual small flower that forms part of a larger cluster of flowers, e.g. daisy.
GENUS: a group of species which have common features and characteristics.
GRAFTING: a propagating method where a section of one plant is inserted into the rootstock of another.
GREENHOUSE: a structure surfaced with glass or plastic sheeting which provides a sheltered environment for growing plants.
HARDENING OFF: a method of gradually acclimatizing plants into a new temperature situation, usually after being reared in a greenhouse before transplanting into the garden.
HARDY: being able to withstand extremes of cold and frost, or harsh, dry conditions. Varies from zone to zone.
HUMUS: dark brown material produced after composting vegetable and animal matter.
HYBRID: the progeny of a cross between two different species.
INFLORESCENCE: the arrangement of flowers of a plant.
LANCEOLATE: describing the shape of a leaf, being like the head of a lance, tapering at each end.
LATERAL: a stem or shoot arising from a leaf axil of a larger stem.
LEADER: a shoot at the end of a main stem.
LINEAR: very narrow.
LOAM: a moderately fertile soil composed of clay, sand, and humus with a texture that is neither too sandy nor too heavy. Good loam will retain moisture and be rich in humus.
MULCH: a layer of organic material laid at ground level to help reduce weed growth and conserve soil moisture.
NATURALIZED: plants growing in areas or countries where they do not naturally occur, often escapees from gardens.
ORGANIC: material derived from living organisms. In horticulture referring to soil additives of natural origins, i.e. animal manure, compost from decayed plant remains.
OVATE: describing the shape of a leaf, being oval or egg-shaped in outline.
PANICLE: a many-branched inflorescence.
PERENNIAL: a plant living for more than two years.
PINNATE: a compound leaf with leaflets arranged along either side of a common stalk.
PISTIL: the female section of the flower.
RACEME: a group of flowers arranged along an unbranched stem, each floret having a distinct stalk.
RHIZOME: an underground creeping root system from which shoots and roots develop.
ROOTSTOCK: the root and base of a plant onto which sections of another plant can be grafted.
ROSETTE: a group of leaves arranged in an overlapping, circular fashion.
RUNNER: aerial stems from which roots grow, forming a new plant.
SEPAL: a unit of the calyx protecting the petals.
SESSILE: used of flowers and leaves without individual stalks.
SINGLE FLOWER: a simple flower form with one ring of petals.
SPADIX: a spiked inflorescence in which the axis is fleshy.
SPATHE: a large bract, sometimes pair of bracts, enclosing the spadix.
SPECIES: a collection of individual plants essentially alike when grown in the same conditions. In horticulture and botany it is used as a form of classification.
SPIKE: similar to a raceme but having stalkless florets.
SPORE: a specialized reproductive cell usually formed asexually: the reproductive unit of ferns and fungi.
STAMEN: the male part of the plant, consisting of filament, anther, and pollen.
SUCKER: a shoot arising from the root system or base of a plant.
SYN: a plant name that has been set aside in favor of a new name.
TENDRIL: a spiralling slender shoot by which some climbing plants cling for support.
TERMINAL: at the apex or tip.
TRIFOLIATE: a leaf divided into three leaflets.
TUBER: a fleshy root or stem that stores nutrients for later use.
UMBEL: a rounded, often flattened head of flowers, the stalks of which all arise together from the tip of a stem.
UNISEXUAL: a flower of only one sex.
VAR: a variant species.
WEEPING: a shrub or tree whose branches hang in a pendulous, drooping fashion.
WHORL: a group of three or more structures encircling an axis.
X: denoting a hybrid species

Plant Hardiness Zone Maps

These maps of the United States, Canada and Europe are divided into ten zones. Each zone is based on a 10°F (5.6°C) difference in average annual minimum temperature. Some areas are considered too high in elevation for plant cultivation and so are not assigned to any zone. There are also island zones that are warmer or cooler than surrounding areas because of differences in elevation; they have been given a zone different from the surrounding areas. Many large urban areas, for example, are in a warmer zone than the surrounding land. Plants grow best within an optimum range of temperatures. The range may be wide for some species and narrow for others. Plants also differ in their ability to survive frost and in their sun or shade requirements.

The zone ratings indicate conditions where designated plants will grow well and not merely survive. Many plants may survive in zones warmer or colder than their recommended zone range. Remember that other factors, including wind, soil type, soil moisture, humidity, snow and winter sunshine, may have a great effect on growth.

Some nursery plants have been grown in greenhouses and they might not survive in your garden, so it's a waste of money, and a cause of heartache, to buy plants that aren't right for your climate zone.

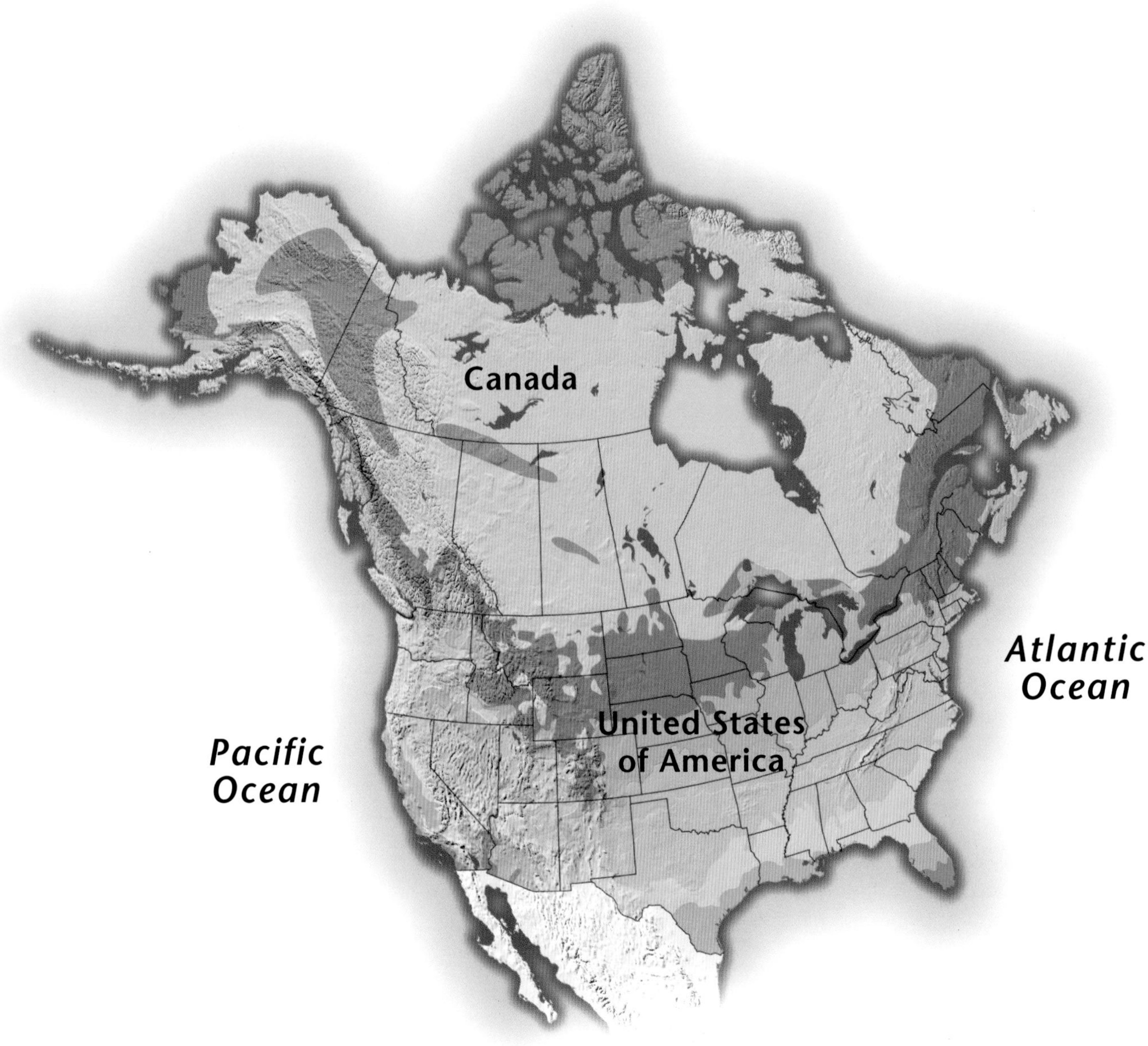

Average annual minimum temperature °F (°C)

Zone 1	Below -50°F (Below -45°C)
Zone 2	-50° to -40°F (-45° to -40°C)
Zone 3	-40° to -30°F (-40° to -34°C)
Zone 4	-30° to -20°F (-34° to -29°C)
Zone 5	-20° to -10°F (-29° to -23°C)
Zone 6	-10° to 0°F (-23° to -18°C)
Zone 7	0° to 10°F (-18° to -12°C)
Zone 8	10° to 20°F (-12° to -7°C)
Zone 9	20° to 30°F (-7° to -1°C)
Zone 10	30° to 40°F (-1° to 4°C)

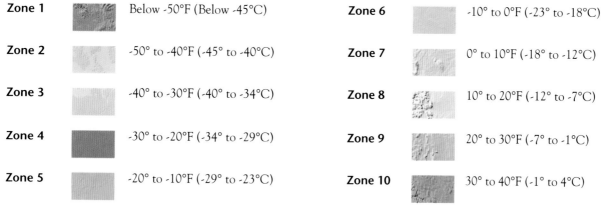

Australia and New Zealand

These maps divide Australia and New Zealand into seven climate zones which, as near as possible, correspond to the USDA climate zones used in the United States, Britain and Europe and in this book. The zones are based on the minimum temperatures usually, or possibly, experienced within each zone. Over the year, air temperatures heat then cool the soil and this is important to plants. Some cannot tolerate cold or even cool temperatures, while others require a period of low temperatures to grow properly. Although this book is designed primarily for cool-climate gardens, the information in it can be adapted for gardens in hotter climates.

In this book, the ideal zones in which to grow particular plants are indicated and when you read that a plant is suitable for any of the zones 7 through to 13, you will know that it should grow successfully in those zones in Australia and New Zealand. There are other factors that affect plant growth, but temperature is one of the most important.

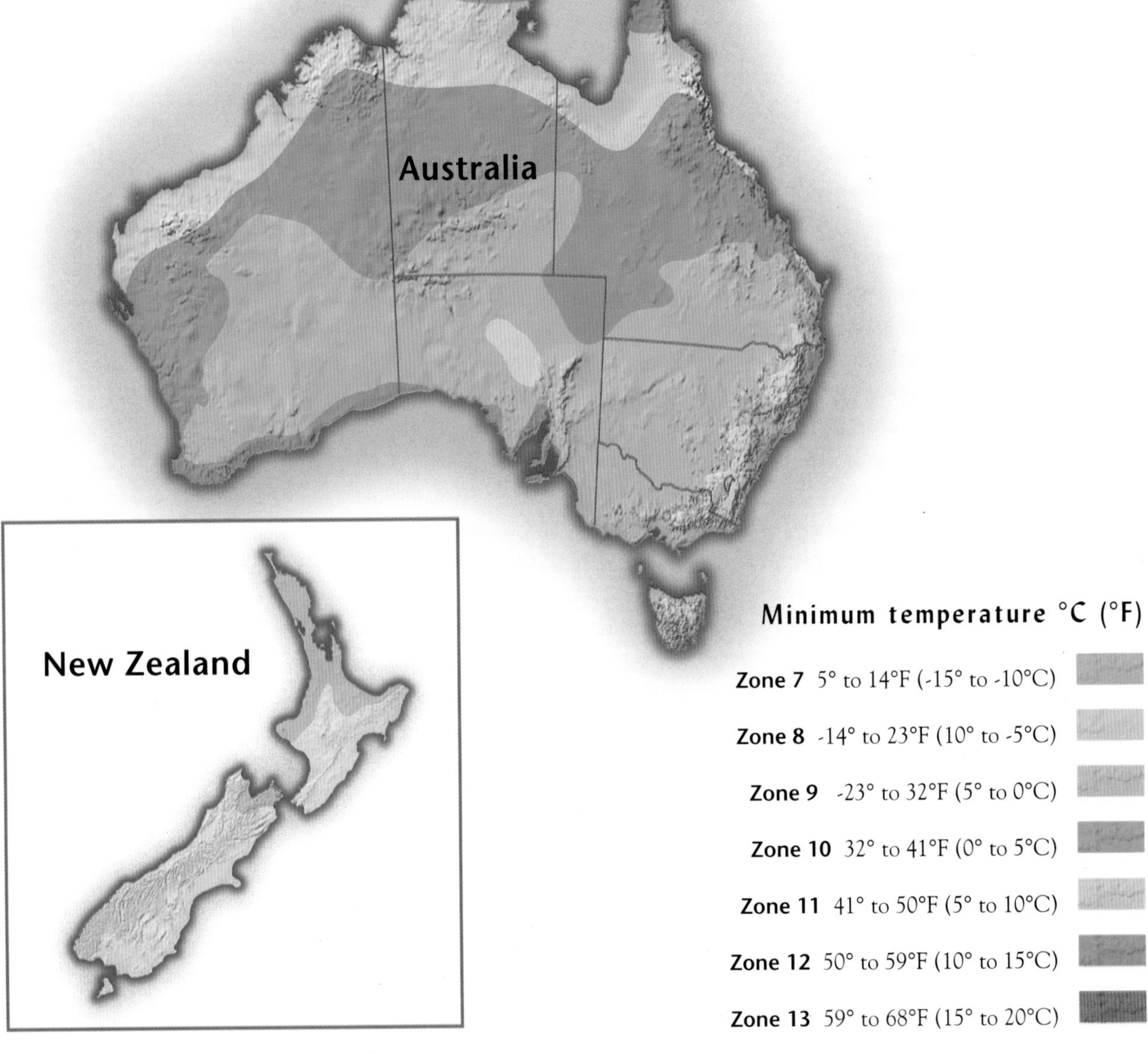

Index

Page references in *italics* indicate photos and illustrations
Page references in **bold** indicate main references

A

Abelia
  glossy 127, 142, 187, 205, **378**, *378*
  Schumann's **378**, *378*
Abelia
  schumannii **378**, *378*
  x *grandiflora* 127, 142, 187, 205, **378**, *378*
Abeliophyllum distichum **488**, *488*
Abutilon
  hybrids 238, **378**, *378*, **568**, *568*
  megapotamicum **568**, *568*
Acacia **582**, *582*
  rose **393**, *393*
Acacia
  baileyana **582**, *582*
  dealbata **582**, *582*
  longifolia **582**, *582*
Acalypha hispida 238
Acanthaceae 325, 340, 362, 383, 412, 446, 449, 470
Acanthus 256
Acanthus spp. 260
  mollis 122, **362**, *362*
Acer spp. *271*, *304*
  buergerianum 285
  japonicum 284
  palmatum 258, 282, *282*, *284*, *301*
  platanoides 285, **582**, *582*
  rubrum *250*, 285
Aceraceae 582
Achillea spp. 84, 88, 102, 255
  ageratifolia **472**, *472*
  filipendulina 139, 143, 152, 161, **552**, *552*
  Galaxy series 27
  millefolium **472**, *472*
  tomentosa 138, 194, **552**, *552*
Acmena smithii **524**, *524*
Aconitum
  carmichaelii 194, **414**, *414*
  napellus **414**, *414*
  x *biclor* 194, **414**, *414*
Acorus spp.
  calamus 255
  gramineus 255, *275*
Actaea
  alba 194
  pachypoda 157
  rubra **472**, *472*
Actinidia spp. 288
Adam's needle 152, 161, **487**, *487*
Adenandra uniflora **488**, *488*
Adenophora confusa **414**, *414*
Adiantum spp. *223*
  ethiopicum 264
  pedatum 243
Adonis amurensis **552**, *552*
Aegopodium podagraria 153
Aeschynanthus hybrids 238
Aesculus
  hippocastanum **518**, *518*
  parviflora **488**, *488*
  x *carnea* 'Briottii' syn. *A. rubicunda* **388**, *388*
Agapanthus 253, **414–15**, *415*
Agapanthus praecox syn. *A. umbellatus* 253, **414–15**, *415*
Agavaceae 462, 487
Agave *38*, *165*, 248
Agave spp.
  parryi 248–9
Ageratum houstonianum 37, 172, 187, 199, **398**, *398*
Ageratums 20, 37, 125, 171, 172, 187, 199, **398**, *398*
  shrubs **441**, *441*
Aglaeonema spp. 212, *212*
Agrostemma githago **348**, *348*
Aizoaceae 313
Ajuga 41, 123, *133*, 150, 155, 157, 194, **415**, *415*
Ajuga reptans 41, 123, 150, 155, 157, 194, *252*, 261, **415**, *415*
Akebia **408**, *408*
Akebia quinata **408**, *408*
Albizia julibrissin **388**, *388*
Alcea rosea 19, 21, 22, 93, 96, 126, 132, 141–2, 151, **362**, *362*
Alchemilla mollis 42, 140–1, 152, 177, 194, 260, **552**, *552*
Allamanda cathartica **548**, *548*
Allegheny moss locust **387**, *387*
Allegheny pachysandra 150, 197
Alliaceae 456
Allium spp. 63, 134
  aflatunense **402**, *402*
  caeruleum 253
  christophii 203
  giganteum 161
  karataviense *264*
  moly 60
  triquestrum **456**, *456*
Almond **530**, *530*
  flowering **392**, *392*, **509**, *509*
Aloe spp.
  vera 221, *221*
Alonsoa warscewiczii **312**, *312*
Alstroemeria spp.
  aurantiaca **326**, *326*
  aurea 194
Alstroemeriaceae 326
Alyssum *16*, 105, *105*, **455**, *455*
Alyssum spp. *16*, 105, *105*, **455**, *455*
  saxatile **552–3**, *553*
Amaranthaceae 312, 349–50
Amaranthus
  caudatus 21, 130, 161, 176, 186, 199, **312**, *312*
  tricolor 17, 122, *251*, **312**, *312*
Amaryllidaceae 317–19, 328, 356–7, 414–15, 456–9, 461, 463, 544, 546–7
Amaryllis 30, 31, 177, 231, 239
  giant **317**, *317*
Amaryllis spp.
  belladonna 257, **356**, *356*
Amelanchier
  arborea **518**, *518*
  laevis **518**, *518*
  x *lamarckii* 277, **518**, *518*
Ampelopsis brevipedunculata 288
Amsonia spp. 127
  tabernaemontana 194, **415**, *415*
Anacardiaceae 380, 584
Anaphalis
  cinnamomea **472**, *472*
  nubigena **472–3**, *472*
  triplinervis 194, **473**, *473*
Anchusa
  azurea 73, 194, 252, **416**, *416*
  myosotidiflora **418**, *418*
Andromeda **509**, *509*, **517**, *517*
Andromeda polifolia **378**, *378*
Andropogon spp.
  virginicus 138–9
Andropsace languinosa **473**, *473*
Anemone
  grape-leaved 194
  Japanese 24, 37, 42, 73, *73*, 103, 152, 246, **474**, *474*
  pink **358**, *358*
  snowdrop **473**, *473*
  wood 27, **356**, *356*
Anemone
  blanda 55, 60, 61, 203
  coronaria **402**, *402*
  nemorosa 27, **356**, *356*
  pulsatilla **430–1**, *430*
  sylvestris *275*, **473**, *473*
  tomentosa 'Robustissima' 194
  vitifolia 'Robustissima' **474**, *474*
  x *hybrida* 24, 37, 42, 73, 103, 152, **474**, *474*
Angelica 159, 242, **553**, *553*
Angelica spp.
  archangelica 242, **553**, *553*
  atropurpurea 159
Anigozanthos manglesii **326**, *326*
Anise 144
  Japanese star **576**, *576*
Annuals **16–21**, 64–7, 312–15, 348–55, 398–401, 454–5, 538–41
  arranging 18–19
  beds and borders 129–32
  buying 52, 54
  containers 20, *170*, 174–7
  cut flowers 21, 135
  easy to grow 152
  garden challenges 21
  indoors 105
  life cycle 16
  nutrient needs 88
  planting **56–8**
  reseeding 21
  root system 12
  scented gardens 20–1, 144–5, **266–7**, *266–7*
  types 17
  weeds 98
  wintering 104–5
Anomatheca **317**, *317*
Antennaria dioica 150, **362**, *362*
Anthemis
  sancti-johannis **553**, *553*
  tinctoria **553**, *553*
Anthurium spp. 238
Antigonon leptopus **358**, *358*
Antirrhinum majus 37, 102, 135, 182, 199, 255
Aphids 92, 93, 189, 222, *223*
Apocynaceae 359, 384–5, 415, 434, 464, 467, 470–1, 491, 529, 548
Appleberry, purple **548**, *548*

Apricot, Japanese **392**, *392*, **530–1**, *530*
Aquilegia spp. 22, 93, 96, 103, 126, 157, 247, *252*
caerulea **416**, *416*
canadensis 27, 101, **326**, *326*
x *hybrida* 141, 194, **326–7**, *326*
Arabis spp. 22
caucasica 27, 70, 72, 102, 138, 155, 204, **474**, *474*
procurrens **474–5**, *475*
Araceae 416, 463
Aralia, Japanese 243
Araucaria heterophylla 274
Arborvitae 287
Arbutus
menziesii **519**, *519*
unedo **519**, *519*
Archangel, yellow 156, 204, **553**, *553*
Arctostaphylos uva-ursi **488**, *488*
Arctotis x *hybrida* **553**, *553*
Ardisia crispa **489**, *489*
Arenaria
montana 204
verna **483**, *483*
Argemone glauca **475**, *475*
Argyranthemum spp. 257
frutescens 18, 194
Arisaema triphyllum 127, 157–8, **416**, *416*
Aristolochia elegans **464**, *464*
Aristolochiaceae 464
Armeria
maritima 84, 102, 123, 152, 194, 257, **475**, *475*
pseudameria **362**, *362*
Aronia
abutifolia **489**, *489*
melonocarpa **489**, *489*
Arrowwood **514**, *514*
Artemisia 49, 246, *249*, 266
Silver King 248
Artemisia spp.
absinthium 144, 161, 248–9
lactiflora **475**, *475*
ludoviciana 248–9
'Powis Castle' 248
stelleriana 248, **554**, *554*
Arum italicum 30, 203, 244
'Marmoratum' 245
Aruncus dioicus 27, 102, 158, **476**, *476*
Asarum europaeum 122, 124, 150, 155, 157–8
Asclepiadaceae 447, 465, 470
Asclepias spp. 142
incarnata 159
tuberosa 26, 139, 143, 152, 161, 195
Ash 271
flowering **524–5**, *524*
mountain 277, 285, **534**, *534*
Asperula odorata **454**, *454*
Aspidistra elatior 'Variegata' 245
Asplemium nidus 212
Aster 68, 71, 96, 97, 102–3, 127, 143, 153, *177*, 253
China 21, 135, 199, **348–9**, *348*
Frikart's 102, 195, **417**, *417*
New England 15, *15*, 26, 110, 120, 139, 141, 143, 152, 159, *174*, 195, **363**, *363*
New York 93, **363**, *363*
Stoke's 198, **432**, *432*
Thomson's **416–17**, *417*
Aster 15
novae-angliae 15, *15*, 26, 110, 139, 141, 143, 152, 159, *174*, 195, **363**, *363*
novi-belgii 93, 120, 257, **363**, *363*
thomsonii **416–17**, *417*
x *frikartii* 102, 195, **417**, *417*
Astilbe spp. *257*
chinensis var. *pumila* 195, **417**, *417*
taquetti 'Superba' **417**, *417*
x *arendsii* 51, 143, 157, 195, **327**, *327*
x *crispa* **327**, *327*
Astilbes *35*, 51, 71, 85, 101, 104, *105*, 120, 127, 143, 157, 195, 257, *257*, *274*, 276–7, **327**, *327*
dwarf 195, **417**, *417*
Astrantia major 141, 158, 195, **363**, *363*
Astrophytum myriostigma 237
Athel tree **393**, *393*
Aubrieta deltoides 141, 161, 195, **363**, *363*
Aucuba 271, *301*
Aurinia saxatile 27, 141, 155, 161, 187, 195, **552–3**, *553*
Australian indigo **444–5**, *445*
Avens **329**, *329*
Azalea
indica 'Alba Manga' **490**, *490*
Azaleas 126, 167, 173, 246–7, 257, *257*, 271, 273, 282, 286, 295, **341**, *341*, **386**, *386*
evergreen **490**, *490*
Indian **386**, *386*, **490**, *490*
Kurume **386**, *386*
Azara lanceolata **583**, *583*

B

Babiana stricta **402**, *402*
Baboon flower **402**, *402*
Baby-blue-eyes 133, 172, 201, **400**, *400*
Baby's breath 37, 96, 97, 102, 118, 132, 134–5, 140–1, 153, 196, 247, **454–5**, *454*, **481**, *481*
creeping **369**, *369*
Baby's tears 264
Balloon flowers 96, 97, 127, 152–3, *153*, 198, **429**, *429*
dwarf **429**, *429*
Balsam, garden 21, 201, **350–1**, *351*
Balsaminaceae 350–1
Bamboo 245, 268, *268*, 292–3, 295
heavenly 186, **507**, *507*
medium-sized 243
Bambusa spp.
multiplex 268
ventricosa 268
vulgaris 268, *268*
Banana, Japanese 243
Baneberry 157, 194, **472**, *472*
Banksia
saw **583**, *583*
swamp **569**, *569*
Banksia
robur **569**, *569*
serrata **583**, *583*
Baptisia australis 42, 59, 72, 104, 125, 127, 139, 143, 152, 161, **418**, *418*
Barberry **569**, *569*
Darwin **569**, *569*
Japanese **569**, *569*
Barrenwort
Algerian **557**, *557*
American 150, 156
snowy **479**, *479*
Bartonia **540**, *540*
Basil 144, 297
Basket-of-gold 27, 141, 155, 161, 187, 195, **552–3**, *553*
Bauera rubioides **378–9**, *378*
Baueraceae 378–9
Bauhinia
climbing **358**, *358*
red **334**, *334*
Bauhinia
corymbosa **358**, *358*
galpinii syn. *B. punctata* **334**, *334*
variegata **450**, *450*
x *blakeana* **388**, *388*
Bay 242, 293, 296, **578**, *578*
Bearberry **488**, *488*
Bear's breech 122, **362**, *362*
Beaumontia grandiflora **464**, *464*
Beauty bush 257, **383**, *383*
Beautyberry, Chinese **437**, *437*
Beds 26, 30, **128–32**, 246–7, *278*, *296*
Bee balm 15, 26, 71, 96, 102, 110, *120*, 143, 144, *144*, 158, *277*, **331**, *331*
Beech 282
Beefsteak plant 260
Beetroot *242*
Begoniaceae 334, 348, 364
Begonia spp. 238
rex 220
Semperflorens-cultorum hybrid 18, 157, 176, 199, 233, *233*, **348**, *348*, **364**, *364*
Tuberhybrida hybrids 183
x *corallina* **334**, *334*
Begonias 66, 156, 182, 238, 250, *250*, 276
coral **334**, *334*
fibrous 178
Reiger 231
rex 220
tuberous 29, 74, 105, *107*, 111, 176, 178, 183
wax 18, 88, 105, 122, 157, 176, 199, 233, *233*, **348**, *348*, **364**, *364*
Belamcanda chinensis 101, 122, 126–7
Belladonna delphinium 141
Bellflowers *24*, 70, 97, 102, 125, *128*, *140–1*, 153, 177, *177*, 252, **418–19**, *418–19*
Chilean **322** *322*
clustered **419**, *419*
Dalmatian 141, 150, 195, **420**, *420*
giant **419**, *419*
peach-leaved 141, **420**, *420*, **476**, *476*
red-vein **572–3**, *573*
Serbian **420**, *420*
tussock 25
Bellis perennis 18, 178, 199, **348**, *348*
Bells of Ireland *123*, **455**, *455*
Berberidaceae 479, 507, 557, 569, 578–9
Berberidopsis corallina **320**, *320*
Berberis *spp.*
darwinii **569**, *569*
thunbergii 250, 261, **569**, *569*
Bergamot *see* Bee balm
Bergenia spp. 37, 44, 157, 176, 187, 276
cordifolia 131, 177, 195, **364**, *364*
x *schmidtii* **364**, *364*
Bergenias 37, 157, 176, 187, **364**, *364*
heart-leaved 131, 177, 195, **364**, *364*
Betonica macrantha **432**, *432*
Betony **432**, *432*

Biennials **17**, *22*, 131–2, *151*
  planting 58
  reseeding 21
Bignonia
  capreolata **548**, *548*
  unguis-cati **550**, *550*
Bignoniaceae 320–1, 323, 325, 345, 359–61, 370, 409, 450–1, 468, 519, 548, 550
Billardiera longiflora **548**, *548*
Bindweed 98, **422**, *422*
Bird-of-Paradise bush **570**, *570*
Bird's eye bush **579**, *579*
Bistort **373**, *373*
Bixa orellana **388**, *388*
Bixaceae 388
Black-eyed Susan 19, 133, 135, *137*, 161, 202, 288, *288*, **325**, *325*, **564–5**, *565*
Black locust tree *285*, **533**, *533*
Bladder sienna **571**, *571*
Blanket flowers 22, 102, 127, 135, 139, 143, 152, *152*, 161, 196, 200, **328**, *328*, **558**, *558*
Blazing star **319**, *319*, **540**, *540*
Bleeding heart 27, 120, 153, *153*, 155, 157, 196, **367**, *367*
  fringed **367**, *367*
  vine **465**, *465*
Blue caps **448**, *448*
Blue-eyed Mary 204, **428**, *428*
Bluebeard **437**, *437*
  hybrid 205
Bluebells *34*, 43, *126*, 253, **407**, *407*
  Australian creeper **412**, *412*
  royal **435**, *435*
  Scotland, of **420**, *420*
  Spanish 31, 60, *61*, 125, 203, **405**, *405*
  Virginia 27, **428**, *428*
Blueberry, swamp **513**, *513*
Bluestem, little 139
Bocconia cordata **483**, *483*
Boltonia 42, 102, 123, 127, 143, 152, **476**, *476*
Boltonia asteroides 42, 102, 123, 143, 152, **476**, *476*
Bonsai 281, *281*, **282–3**, *282–3*, *295*
  maintenance 283
  shaping 282, *282*
  style and effects 281–2
  suitable plants 282–3
Borage *121*, 252, **398**, *398*
Boraginaceae 398, 416, 418, 422, 428, 430, 441, 443, 446, 487
Borago officinalis 252, **398**, *398*
Borders 26, 30, **128–32**, 246–7, 278–9
  edging 148
Boronia, pink **379**, *379*
Boronia floribunda **379**, *379*
Botrytis blight 96
Bottlebrush **335**, *335*, 342, *342*, **379**, *379*
  buckeye **488**, *488*
  crimson **335**, *335*
  weeping or drooping **335**, *335*
  white or willow **519**, *519*
Bougainvillea **320**, *320*
Bougainvillea spp. 238
  x *buttiana* **320**, *320*
Bouteloua spp.
  curtipendula 139
Bouvardia **490**, *490*
Bouvardia longiflora **490**, *490*
Bower of beauty **359**, *359*, **468**, *468*
Box 185, 205
Boxwood 265, 271, 273, 280, *280*, 282, 287, *292*, 296
Brachychiton
  acerfolium **342**, *342*
  discolor **388–9**, *389*
Brachyscome iberidifolia 199
Bracteantha bracteatum 21, 64, 199
Brassica oleracea 199
Brazilian glory vine **551**, *551*
Bridal-wreath **511–12**, *511–12*
Brodiaea ixioides **547**, *547*
Bromeliads 171, *229*, *243*
Bronze leaf 261, **485**, *485*
Broom **337**, *337*, **572**, *572*
  Canary Island **572**, *572*
  Kew **495**, *495*
  Mt Etna **584**, *584*
  Spanish **581**, *581*
  Warminster **496**, *496*
  weaver's **581**, *581*
  weeping **500**, *500*
Broomsedge 138–9
Browallia 172, 178, 183, 199
Browallia speciosa 172, 178, 183, 199
Brugmansia suaveolens **497**, *497*
Brunfelsia
  australis syn. *B. latifolia* **436**, *436*
  calycina **436**, *436*
Brunnera macrophylla 27, 120, 157–8, 195, **418**, *418*
Buckbrush **438–9**, *438*
Buddleia spp.
  alternifolia 248–9, **436**, *436*
  davidii 127, 142, **436**, *436*, **490**, *490*
  globosa **570**, *570*
Bugleweed **415**, *415*
Bulbs 12, 16, 19, 22, **28–31**, *110*, *276*, 316–19, 356–7, 402–7, 456–63, 542–7
  arranging 30–1
  buying 52, 55
  containers 31, *170*, 177–9
  corms 29, 74
  cuttings 134
  easy to grow 152–3
  forcing 31, 231–2
  growth, 28–9
  indoors **231–2**, *232*
  multiple plantings 178
  multiplication **74–5**
  naturalizing 62–3, 139
  nutrient needs 89
  planting **60–3**
  rhizomes 29, 75
  seasonal 63
  seeds 75
  storage 106–7, *107*, 179
  tender 105–7
  true 29
  tubers 29, 74–5
  winter chilling 63, 178
Buphthalmum salicifolium **554**, *554*
Burning bush 127
Burro's tail 220
Bush germander 252
Buttercups 255, **564**, *564*
Butterflies 174, **142–3**, *143*
Butterfly bush *120*, 127, 142, 174, **436**, *436*, **490**, *490*
  fountain 248, **436**, *436*
Butterfly flower **354**, *354*
Butterfly tree **334**, *334*, **388**, *388*, **450**, *450*
Butterfly weed 26, 139, 143, 152, 161, 174, 195
Buxaceae 484
Buxus spp. 185, 280, *280*, 282
  sempervirens 205, *287*, *293*
Buying plants **52–5**
  healthy plant checklist 53
  plant list, planning your 116
Byttneriaceae 390, 523

C

Cabbage, ornamental 199, 242
Cabbage tree *243*
  New Zealand 243
Cachepots 181
Cacti 214, *214*, 234, 237, *237*, 265, *265*, 267, 271, 292
  bishop's cap 237
  Christmas 229, 239
  feather 237
  golden barrel 265, *265*
  old man 237
  wax vine 237, 239
Caesalpinaceae 342–3, 450, 570, 583–4
Caesalpinia
  ferrea **583**, *583*
  gilliesii **570**, *570*
Caladiums 29, 105, 111, 156, *245*
Calceolaria x *herbeohybrida* **538**, *538*
Calendula officinalis 21, 132, 135, 153, 161, 199, 255, **538**, *538*
Calendulas 175
Calico Dutchman's pipe **464**, *464*
Calliandra
  portoricensis **490–1**, *490*
  tweedii **334**, *334*
Callicarpa bodinieri var. *giraldii* **437**, *437*
Calliopsis 137
Calliopsis tinctoria 137
Callistemon spp.
  citrinus **335**, *335*, **379**, *379*
  salignus **519**, *519*
  viminalis **335**, *335*, 342, *342*
Callistephus chinensis 21, 135, 199, **348–9**, *348*
Calluna vulgaris 150, 205, **379**, *379*, **437**, *437*
Calocephalus brownii **491**, *491*
Calochortus venustus **542**, *542*
Calodendrum capense **389**, *389*
Caltha palustris 27, 85, 159, **554**, *554*
Calycanthaceae 335, 570–1
Calycanthus floridus **335**, *335*
Camellia spp. 257, 282, 286–7
  japonica 205, *301*, **379**, *379*
  reticulata **389**, *389*
  sasanqua 170, 205, *293*, 294, **380**, *380*
Camellias 167, 170, 173, 205, 246–7, 256–7, 271, *271*, 282, 286–7, 295
  false **525**, *525*
  Japanese **379**, *379*
  net vein **389**, *389*
  sasanqua 170, 205, 294, **380**, *380*
Campanula spp. 70, 97, 102, 125, 153, 247
  carpatica 195, **418**, *418*
  cochleariifolia syn. *C. pusilla* **418–19**, *418*
  garganica **419**, *419*
  glomerata **419**, *419*
  latifolia **419**, *419*
  medium 131, **419**, *419*
  persicifolia 141, 252, **420**, *420*, **476**, *476*
  portenschlagiana 141, 150, 195, **420**, *420*
  poscharskyana **420**, *420*
  rotundifolia **420**, *420*
Campanulaceae 414, 418–20, 426–7, 429, 435, 476
Campsis spp. 127
  grandiflora syn. *C. chinensis* **320**, *320*
  radicans **320**, *320*

Canary-bird flower **551**, *551*
Candytuft 41, 246
annual 21, 132, 135, 201, **455**, *455*
perennial 27, 85, 102, 131, 197, **482**, *482*
Canna
indica **316**, *316*
x *generalis* 134, 153, **554**, *554*
Cannaceae 316, 554
Cannas 29, 30, 75, 105, 106, 134, 153
Indian-shot **316**, *316*
Canterbury bells 131, 253, **419**, *419*
Cantua buxifolia **336**, *336*
Cape cowslip **317**, *317*
Capparidaceae 349
Caprifoliaceae 322, 358, 378, 383–4, 387, 411, 467, 504, 510, 512–17, 549–50
Capsicum spp.
annuum 238
dwarf 250
Caragana arborescens **583**, *583*
Cardinal flower 27, 132, 139, 158, 197, **330**, *330*
red-spiked 41
Cardiocrinum giganteum **456**, *456*
Cardoon 248, *248*, 253
Carissa grandiflora **491**, *491*
Carnations 247, 257, 257, **366**, *366*
Carnival bush **579**, *579*
Carnivorous plants 237, *237*
Carob bean tree **342**, *342*
Carpenteria californica **491**, *491*
Caryophyllaceae 328, 330, 348, 350, 354–5, 366, 369, 371, 374, 454–5, 476, 478, 481, 483
Caryopteris
incana **437**, *437*
x *clandonensis* 125, 205, **437**, *437*
Cassia, silver **570**, *570*
Cassia
artemisioides **570**, *570*
fistula **584**, *584*
Cast-iron plant 245
Castor bean 130, 132
Catalpa bignonioides **519**, *519*
Catananche caerulea 42, 85, 161, 195, **420–1**, *421*
Catharanthus roseus 18, 123, 161, 183, 199
Catmint 102, 140–1, 145, *145*, 152, 253, **428**, *428*
Catnip **433**, *433*
Cat's-claw creeper **550**, *550*
Cat's foot **362**, *362*
Cattails 159
Ceanothus spp. **438**, *438*
impressus **438**, *438*
thyrsiflorus var. *repens* **438**, *438*
x *veitchianus* **438–9**, *438*
Cedar 248, 274
Chinese **520**, *520*
white **451**, *451*
Cedrela sinensis **520**, *520*
Cedrus spp. *274*
atlantica 'Glauca Pendula' 248
Celandine **555**, *555*
Celosia 17, 64, 157, 199, 261
crested **349**, *349*
Celosia spp. 17
cristata 157, 199, **349**, *349*
Centaurea spp.
cyanus 21, 120, 133, 135, 137, 153, 161, 172, 200, 252, **398**, *398*
dealbata 102, **327**, *327*
hypoleuca 141, 195, **364**, *364*
macrocephala **554–5**, *555*
montana **421**, *421*
Centranthus ruber 141, 143, 145, 152, 161, 195, **327**, *327*
Cephalaria gigantea **555**, *555*
Cephalocereus senilis 237
Cerastium tomentosum 70, 141, 102, 155, 161, 204, 264, **476**, *476*
Ceratonia siliqua **342**, *342*
Ceratostigma
griffithii **439**, *439*
plumbaginoides 195
willmottianum **439**, *439*
Cercis
canadensis **389**, *389*
chinensis **380**, *380*
siliquastrum **390**, *390*
Cestrum fasciculatum 'Newellii' **336**, *336*
Cestrums 267, **336**, *336*
Chaenomeles spp.
japonica **336**, *336*
speciosa **337**, *337*, 491, *491*
Chamaedorea
elegans 236
erumpens 236
Chamaemelum nobile 150
Chamelaucium uncinatum **492**, *492*
Chamomile 276
ox-eye **553**, *553*
Roman 150
St John's **553**, *553*
Chard 242
ruby 141, 250
Chaste tree **517**, *517*
Checkerbloom **376**, *376*
Cheiranthus
cheiri **555**, *555*
mutabilis **421**, *421*
Chelidonium majus **555**, *555*
Chelone spp. 27, 158
glabra 139
lyonii 195, **364–5**, *365*
obliqua 257
Chenille plant 238
Cherry
bladder **333**, *333*
Cornelian **584**, *584*
double rose **392**, *392*
flowering 126, 256–7, **392–3**, *392–3*
higan **393**, *393*
Japanese flowering **392**, *392*, 531, *531*
myrobalan **529**, *529*
Natal **523**, *523*
plum **529–30**, *529–30*
Taiwan **345**, *345*
weeping **393**, *393*
weeping or white spring **531**, *531*
winter **393**, *393*
Chervil 297
Chestnut
cape **389**, *389*
Children's play areas 301
Chilean glory flower **321**, *321*
Chimonanthus praecox 266, **570–1**, *571*
Chinese evergreens 212, *212*
Chionanthus
retusus **520**, *520*
virginicus **520**, *520*
Chionodoxa luciliae **402**, *402*
Chives *122*, 297
Chlorophytum comosum 221
Choisya ternata 266, *301*, **492**, *492*
Chokeberry **489**, *489*
Chorizema cordatum **337**, *337*
Chrysanthemum spp. 37, 238
coccineum 71
frutescens **476–7**, *477*
leucanthemum **477**, *477*
parthenium **454**, *454*
x *morifolium* 68, 71, 93, 96, 100, *100*, 110
x *superbum* **477**, *477*
Chrysanthemums 24, 37, 238
Cigar plant 238
Cimicifuga racemosa 123, 157
Cineraria **315**, *315*, **565**, *565*
Cinquefoil **485**, *485*, **562**, *562*
Nepal **333**, *333*
ruby **333**, *333*
shrubby **580**, *580*
Cistaceae 439, 392–3
Cistus 277
ladanifer **492**, *492*
salviifolius **492–3**, *492*
x *purpureus* **439**, *439*
Citharexylum spinosum **520–1**, *520*
Citrus spp. 238, 293, 296
Clarkia **349**, *349*
Clarkia
amoena **350**, *350*
unguiculata syn. *C. elegans* **349**, *349*
Clay soil 34, *34*
Clematis 126, *126*, 186, 246, 257, 288, **358**, *358*
anemone **465**, *465*
Barbara Jackson **408**, *408*
evergreen **464**, *464*
golden **548**, *548*
large flowered **408–9**, *408*
sweet autumn 288
tube **422**, *422*
Clematis spp. 288
armandii 246, **464**, *464*
'Barbara Jackson' **408**, *408*
heracleifolia **422**, *422*
maximowicziana 288
montana 246, **358**, *358*, **465**, *465*
tangutica **548**, *548*
x *jackmanii* **408–9**, *408*
Cleome spp. 23, 132–3, 151, 153, 176
hasslerana 21, 133, 153, 200, 257, **349**, *349*
Clerodendrum spp.
splendens **321**, *321*
thomsoniae 186, **465**, *465*
trichotomum **493**, *493*
Clethra
alnifolia **493**, *493*
arborea **521**, *521*
Clethraceae 493, 521
Cleyera japonica **493**, *493*
Climate **38–9**
controlling 284
microclimates 42, 45, 184, 226–8
Climbing plants 100–3, 246, 320–5, 358–61, 408–13, 464–71, 548–51
Clivia 238
Clivia miniata 238, **328**, *328*
Clytostoma callistegioides **409**, *409*
Cobaea scandens 133, 186, **409**, *409*
Codiaeum variegatum 171, *243*
Coffea arabica 238
Coffee plant 238
Colchicum
autumnale 28, 31, 257
cilicicum 'Byzantinum' **403**, *403*
speciosum 60, 203
Coleus 13, 18, 105, 122, 156, *157*, 176, 178, 202, 233, 245

Color 116, 124–5, **242**
blue *124*, 125, 172, **252–3**, *252–3*
combinations 118, 121–2, **258–61**, *258–61*
containers 166, 171–2, 182
contrasts and compliments 120
cream 255
green **242–5**, *242–5*, 258, 292
pink 125, **256–7**, *256–7*
purple *124*, **252–3**, *252–3*
red 125, *125*, **250–1**, *250–1*
silver and gray **248–9**, *248–9*
variegated **244–5**, *244–5*
white 125, *125*, **246–7**, *246–7*
yellow and orange 125, *125*, **254–5**, *254–5*
Columbine *13*, 22, 68, 93, 96, 103, 126, 157, 247, *252*, 253, **326**, *326*
hybrid 141, 194, **326–7**, *326*
Rocky Mountain **416**, *416*
wild 27, 101
Colutea arborescens **571**, *571*
Combretaceae 324
Comfrey, ground-cover **487**, *487*
Commelinaceae 377
Compositae 315–16, 327–9, 348–50, 355, 362–4, 370, 398, 416–17, 420–1, 423, 432, 441–2, 454, 472–3, 475–7, 479–80, 483, 491, 507, 538, 541, 551–60, 564–6, 573, 581
Compost 88–9
cold 91
containers, for 169, **193**
hot 90–1
houseplants 216
mulching with 84
using **90–1**
Comus sericea 271
Coneflowers 13, *14*, 42, *42*, *43*, 85, 101, 120, *120*, 127, 143, **564**, *564*
'Goldsturm' 69
orange *26*, 139, *142*, 143, 152, 161, 198
Persian 102
purple 24, 26, 68, 93, *138*, 139, 143, 152, 161
Consolida
ambigua 21, 57, 102, 131, 135, 153, 172, 200
orientalis **398**, *398*
regalis **399**, *399*
Containers **164–5**, 174–9, 294–5, **295**
annuals 20, *170*, 174–7
bulbs 31, *170*, 177–9
caring for **188–93**
clay and terracotta 165, *164–5*, 174, 180 , 185
compost 169, **193**
drainage 166, 168, 173, 182, 277, 295
fertilizing 169, 175, 182, *192–3*
getting started **170–3**
grasses 179, *179*
hanging baskets **182–3**, *182–3*, 295, *295*
houseplants *see* Houseplants
metal 166, *166*
mixes 168–9, 174, 187, 214–15, 218
moveable nature 172
perennials 27, 58, 174, 177
plastic and fiberglass 165–6, 174, 180
problems 189
seeds, for 64–5
self-watering pots 190
size 164–5, 170–1
things to avoid 167
watering 175, 190–1
window boxes **180–1**, *180–1*, 297, *297*
wood 166, *166*, 180
Convallaria majalis 37, 138, 145, 150, 155, 195, **456**, *456*
Convolvulaceae 410, 422, 493
Convolvulus
cneorum **493**, *493*
sabatius syn. *C. mauritanicus* **422**, *422*
tricolor 64, 200
Coral bells 22, 37, 59, 97, 120, 123, 141, 196, **329**, *329*
Coral pea
black **410–11**, *410*
purple **410**, *410*
Coral tree **343**, *343*
Coralberry **489**, *489*
Cordyline australis 243, *243*
Cordylines 243, *243*, 258
Coreopsis 36, 84, 88, 96, 97, 102, 122, 127, 153, 200
golden **538**, *538*
lance **555**, *555*
thread-leaved 120, 141, 152, 161, **556**, *556*
Coreopsis spp. 84, 88, 96, 102, 127, 153
lanceolata **555**, *555*
tinctoria 21, 200, **538**, *538*
verticullata 25, 120, 141, 152, 161, **556**, *556*
Corn 13
Corn cockle **348**, *348*
Cornaceae 390, 494, 521–2, 584
Cornflower 21, 120, 126, 133, *127*, 135, 137, 153, 161, 172, 200, 252–3, **327**, *327*, **364**, *364*, **398**, *398*
mountain perennial **421**, *421*
Cornus spp.
alba 251, 277, **494**, *494*
capitata **521**, *521*
florida 293, **390**, *390*, 521, *521*
kousa 285, **522**, *522*
mas **584**, *584*
sanguinea **494**, *494*
stolonifera **494**, *494*
Coronilla varia **365**, *365*
Correa, white **494–5**, *495*
Correa alba **494–5**, *495*
Corylopsis
spicata **572**, *572*
veitchiana **571**, *571*
Cosmos 13, *16*, 21, 23, 37, *43*, 123, 131, 135, *135*, 151, 200, *246*, 257, **350**, *350*
Cosmos
bipinnatus 21, 37, 135, **350**, *350*
sulphureus 123, 135, 200
Cotinus coggyria 205, 285, **380**, *380*
Cotoneaster 127, 251
Cowslip **554**, *554*
Crab apple 126–7, **344**, *344*, **527**, *527*
Chinese **391**, *391*
Japanese **391**, *391*
ornamental **527**, *527*
prairie **391**, *391*
purple **392**, *392*
Siberian **527**, *527*
Crambe, heart-leaf **477**, *477*
Crambe cordifolia **477**, *477*
Cranesbill 42, *42*, *49*, 70, 126, 141, 150, 152, **368**, *368*
Armenian **369**, *369*
bloody **369**, *369*
endres 196
Crassula argentea 220
Crassulaceae 375–6
Crataegus spp. 282
crus-galli 285, **522**, *522*
laevigata **342**, *342*
phaenopyrum **522**, *522*
x *lavallei* **522–3**, *522*
Creeping Jenny 204
Crimson starglory 288
Crinum **456–7**, *457*
Crinum x *powellii* 'Album' **456–7**, *457*
Crocosmia 178, 203
'Lucifer' 250
masonorum **316**, *316*
x *crocosmilflora* 203
Crocus 22, 28–9, 31, *31*, 60, 62, 63, *63*, 126, 138–9, *139*, 153, 155, 276
autumn **403**, *403*, **457**, *457*, **546–7**, *547*
Dutch 31, **404**, *404*
fall 28, 31
Scotch **457**, *457*
showy autumn 60, *106*, 203, 257
spring-blooming 231, **404**, *404*
winter **403**, *403*, **542**, *542*
Crocus spp. 31, 60
biflorus **457**, *457*
chrysanthus 247, **542**, *542*
niveus **457**, *457*
speciosus **403**, *403*
tommasinianus 31, **403**, *403*
vernus hybrids 31, **404**, *404*
Crotons 171, *243*
Crowbars 79
Crown imperial *28*, 31, 93, 203, **543**, *543*
Crown-of-thorns 238, **338**, *338*
Crown vetch **365**, *365*
Cruciferae 352–3, 363, 421, 424, 455, 474–5, 477, 482, 552–3, 555
Cultivars 15, *79*, 80
Cup-and-saucer vine 133, 186, **409**, *409*
Cup of gold **551**, *551*
Cupflower **400**, *400*
Cuphea ignea 238
Cupid's dart 42, 85, 161, 195, **420–1**, *421*
Cupressus macrocarpa 242
Currant, flowering **386–7**, *387*, **580**, *580*
Curry plant 264
Cushion bush **491**, *491*
Cushion spurge 42, 126, 141, 161
Cuttings **72–3**, 219–20, **219**, 233
annuals 135
bulbs 134
cutting garden 26, 30, **134–5**, *134–5*
root *73*, 233
stem *72*
Cyclamen 28, 31, 55, 203, 209, 219, *227*, 231, 238, 276, **404**, *404*
rock **356**, *356*
Cyclamen spp. 31, 55
hederifolium 28, 203, 257, 276
neapolitanum syn. *C. hederifolium* **356**, *356*
persicum 209, 219, 231, 238, **404**, *404*
Cynara spp.
cardunculus 248, 253
Cynoglossum
amabile 252
nervosum **422**, *422*
Cyperus papyrus 297
Cypress 263, 271, 274
Monterey *242*
summer 122
Cypressus spp. 274
Cyrilla racemiflora **495**, *495*
Cyrillaceae 495

Cyrtostachys renda 273
Cytisus **496**, *496*
scoparius **337**, *337*, **572**, *572*
x *kewensis* **495**, *495*
x *praecox* **496**, *496*
x *spachianus* **572**, *572*

D

Daboecia cantabrica **440**, *440*
Daffodils 22, *27*, 28–31 *28*, *30–1*, 38, 55, *55*, 60, *61*, 63, 74, 134, 138, *139*, 145, 152–3, 178, *178*, 187, 204, 231, 254–5, 258, 276, **546**, *546*
hoop-petticoat **545**, *545*
Dahlia *23*, 26, 29, 30, 74, 96, 97, 101, 102, *102*, 105, 106, *107*, 110–11, 153, 179, 203, 247, 250, 255, 257, 261, **316**, *316*
hybrids 134, **316**, *316*
Dais cotinoifolia **380**, *380*
Daisy 13, *28*, *174*, **477**, *477*
African **553**, *553*, **558**, *558*
Barberton **558**, *558*
English 18, 178, 199, **348**, *348*
gloriosa 18, **564–5**, *565*
kingfisher **442**, *442*
Livingstone **313**, *313*
marguerite 257, 266, 297, **441**, *441*, **476–7**, *477*
Mexican 271
ox-eye **477**, *477*, **554**, *554*
painted 71
paper *22*
Paris **476–7**, *477*
shasta 68, 122, 138, 141, *141*, 143, 152, 197, **477**, *477*
Swan River 199
white veldt **479**, *479*
Daisybush, New Zealand **507**, *507*
Dame's rocket 247, **424**, *424*
Dandelions 98, 99
Daphne spp. 266
cneorum 205, 257, **380–1**, *380*
mezereum **440**, *440*
odora **440**, *440*, **496**, *496*
x *burwoodii* **496**, *496*
Daphne **440**, *440*, **496**, *496*
Burkwood **496**, *496*
rose 205, 257, **380–1**, *380*
Darmera peltata **365**, *365*
Datura suaveolens **497**, *497*
Davidia involucrata **523**, *523*
Davidiaceae 523
Daylilies *25*, 41, 42, 45, 70, 71, 96, 120, 145, 150, 152–4, 196, 250, 254–5, 258, 277, **560**, *560*
'Stella de Oro' 25, 27, 177
Dead nettle 245, *245*, **482–3**, *483*
Deadheading 16
Delonix regia **342–3**, *343*
Delosperma cooperi 204
Delphinium spp.
consolida **399**, *399*
elatum hybrids **422**, *422*
orientalis **398**, *398*
x *belladonna* 141
x *elatum* hybrids 196
Delphiniums *22*, 26, 68, *68*, 85, 88, 93, 96, 97, 102, 110, 120, 125, 132, 134, 138, *141*, 252–3, *260*, *270*, 271, **399**, *399*
cultivars 252
hybrid 196, **422**, *422*
Dendranthema x *grandiflorum* 196
Deschampsia caespitosa 138
Design **118–27**, 242
bloom time, consideration of 120
color *see* Color
combinations 118, **258–61**, *258–61*
compatible plants 120
contemporary and avant-garde **302–5**, *302–5*
contrasts and compliments 120
fillers **133**
height and habits 122–3, *122*
quick and easy flowers 150–1
rules 118
seasonal **126–7**
sketching 116–117, *117*
texture and form 122, *122–3*
Deutzia 205, 257, **497**, *497*
Deutzia
gracilis 205, **497**, *497*
scabra 'Flore Pleno' **381**, *381*, **497**, *497*
x *elegantissima* 257
x *lemoinei* **497**, *497*
Dianella caerulea **422–3**, *423*
Dianthus spp. 37, 70, 72, 88, 97, 123, 250, 257
arenarius **478**, *478*
barbatus 17, 22, 135, 144–5, **366**, *366*
caryophyllus **366**, *366*
chinensis 18, 144–5, **350**, *350*
deltoides 138, 150, **328**, *328*
gratianopolitanus 141, 143, 145, 155, 161, 196
plumarius 196, **366**, *366*
x *allwoodii* **366**, *366*
Diapensiaceae 486
Dicentra spp. 120, 153, 276
cucullaria **478**, *478*
exemia 155, 157, **367**, *367*
spectabilis 27, 196, **367**, *367*
Dicksonia antarctica 243
Dictamnus spp.
albus 59, 71, 141, **478**, *478*
purpureus 138
Dieffenbachia amoena 220
Dierama pulcherrimum 257, **404**, *404*
Dietes
bicolor **556**, *556*
vegata **478–9**, *478*
Digging *see* Soil
Digitalis spp. 101, 102, 105, 122, 126, 132
grandiflora **556**, *556*
purpurea 17, 19, 21, *21*, 22, 58, 93, 131, *293*, **423**, *423*
x *mertonensis* **367**, *367*
Dill 144
Dilleniaceae 549
Dill leaf **315**, *315*
Dimorphotheca ecklonis **479**, *479*
Dionaea muscipula 237
Dipladenia splendens **359**, *359*
Dipsacaceae 375, 555
Disanthus **440**, *440*
Disanthus cercidifolius **440**, *440*
Diseases **95–7**, 189
bacterial 96–7, *97*
controlling 97, 223–5
fungal 96, *96–7*
fungi 96
houseplants 222–5
managing disease 223
signs and symptoms chart 224–5
identifying 95–6
infectious 96–7
nematodes 97
viruses 97
Distinctis
buccinatoria **321**, *321*
laxiflora **409**, *409*
Division **71–2**, *71*, 221
Dodecatheon meadia **367**, *367*
Dogwood 126, 271, 285, **390**, *390*, **494**, *494*
evergreen **521**, *521*
flowering **521**, *521*
Japanese **522**, *522*
red-barked **494**, *494*
red osier **494**, *494*
yellowtwig **494**, *494*
Dombeya
tiliacea **523**, *523*
x *cayeuxii* **390**, *390*
Doronicum
cordatum **556–7**, *557*
orientale 196
plantagineum **557**, *557*
Dorotheanthus bellidiformis **313**, *313*
Doxantha unguis-cati **550**, *550*
Dracaena spp. 220
Dropseed, prairie 139
Dropwort, double-flowered **480**, *480*
Dryopteris filix-mas 243
Dumbcane 220
Dusky coral pea **322**, *322*
Dusty miller 13, 18, 122, 172, 198, 248, *248*, **553**, *553*, **565**, *565*
Dutchman's-breeches **478**, *478*
Dyer's greenweed **574**, *574*

E

Eccremocarpus scaber **321**, *321*
Echeveria spp. 248–9
Echinacea spp. 85, 101, 143
purpurea 24, 26, 68, 93, 120, 139, 143, 152, 161
Echinocactus grusonii 265, *265*
Echinops ritro 152, 161, 196, **423**, *423*
Echium fatuosum **441**, *441*
Edelweiss **483**, *483*
Egyptian star-cluster **332**, *332*
Elaeagnus spp. *275*
Elder **510**, *510*
Elm 271, 274
Elodea canadensis 179
Empress tree **451**, *451*
Enamel flower **488**, *488*
Endymion hispanicus **405**, *405*
Enkianthus campanulatus **572–3**, *573*
Epilobium glabellum **479**, *479*
Epimedium, red 155, 157
Epimedium spp. 156
perralderianum **557**, *557*
x *rubrum* 155, 157
x *youngianum* **479**, *479*
Eranthis
cilicicus 55
hyemalis 55, **543**, *543*
Eremurus robustus 257, **368**, *368*
Erica spp.
canaliculata **381**, *381*
carnea **381**, *381*, **498**, *498*
tetralix **382**, *382*
vagans **381**, *381*
x *darleyensis* **382**, *382*
Ericaceae 341, 378–9, 381–3, 386, 394, 437, 440, 488, 490, 498, 500, 503, 509, 513, 517, 519, 528–9, 572–3
Erigeron
mucronatus **480**, *480*
speciousus 143, 196
Erinus alpinus **423**, *423*
Eryngium spp. 71
amethystinum 125, 161, 196
bourgatii **479**, *479*
giganteum 253
x *zabelii* **423**, *423*

- *Erysimum* spp. 255
  - *cheiri* 18, 145, 200
- *Erythrina* x *sykesii* **343**, *343*
- *Erythronium*
  - *dens-canis* 'White Splendor' **457**, *457*
  - *revolutum* 257, **458**, *458*
- Escallonia 498
- *Escallonia bifida* **498**, *498*
- *Eschscholzia californica* 21, 51, 57, 122, *136*, 137, 153, 200, 254, **313**, *313*
- Espalier 280, 294, *294*
- *Eucalyptus* 271, 285
  - *caesia* **390**, *390*
  - *citriodora* **523**, *523*
  - *ficifolia* **343**, *343*
  - *leucoxylon* 'Rosea' **343**, *343*
  - *scoparia* **524**, *524*
- *Eucharis grandiflora* **458**, *458*
- *Eucomis cormosa* syn. *E. punctata* **543**, *543*
- *Eucryphia lucida* **524**, *524*
- Eucryphiaceae 524
- *Eugenia smithii* **524**, *524*
- *Euonymus* spp.
  - *alata* 127
  - *fortunei* 288–9, 293
- *Eupatorium* spp. 127
  - *maculatum* 132, 139, 158–9
  - *megalophyllum* **441**, *441*
  - *rugosum* 139, 143
- *Euphorbia* spp. *122*
  - *characias* subsp. *wulfenii* 260, **557**, *557*
  - *epithymoides* 42, 126, 141, 161
  - *griffithii* 'Fireglow' **328**, *328*
  - *marginata* 200, **454**, *454*
  - *milii* 238, **338**, *338*
  - *pulcherrima* 231, 238, **344**, *344*
- Euphorbiaceae 328, 338, 344, 454, 557
- *Euryops pectinatus* **573**, *573*
- *Eustoma grandiflorum* 18, **399**, *399*
- Everlasting **355**, *355*, **362**, *362*
  - pearly **472–3**, *472–3*
- *Exacum affine* 209, **399**, *399*
- *Exochorda racemosa* **498**, *498*
- Exposure **42–3**
  - eastern 42
  - northern 43
  - south-facing sites 42
  - sun and shade 43, 114, 120, **156–7**
  - west-facing sites 42

F

- Fabaceae 583
- *Fagus* spp. 282
- Fairy's fishing rod 257, **404**, *404*
- *Fallopia aubertii* **468**, *468*
- False indigo, blue 42, 59, 60, 72, 104, 125, 127, 139, 143, 152, 161, **418**, *418*
- *Fatsia japonica* 243
- Feijoa **338**, *338*
- *Feijoa sellowiana* **338**, *338*
- Felicia 297, **441–2**, *441–2*
- *Felicia*
  - *amelloides* 252, *252*, **441**, *441*
  - *angustifolia* **442**, *442*
- Fennel 242, 256
- Ferns 43, 138, 156, 173, 234, 264, 295
  - beech 159
  - Bird's nest 212
  - Boston *182*
  - maidenhair *223*, 243, 264
  - male 243
  - ostrich 243
  - royal 159
  - soft shield 243
  - soft tree 243
  - tree 243, 296
- Fertilizing 50, 84, **88–91**, *90*
  - bonsai 283
  - containers, for 169, 175, 182, **192–3**
  - houseplants 216–17, 230–1
  - liquid 90
  - organic 89
- Fescues 139
  - blue 125, 153, 248
- *Festuca* spp. 139
  - *cinerea* 125, 153
  - *glauca* 248
- Feverfew 21, *119*, 122, 172, 202, **454**, *454*
- *Ficus* spp. 282
  - *benjamina* 212, *212*, 218
- Fiddlewood **520–1**, *520*
- Fig 282, 297
  - weeping 212, *212*, 218
- *Filipendula*
  - *palmata* **368**, *368*
  - *rubra* 132, 139, 158, 196, **368**, *368*
  - *vulgaris* **480**, *480*
- Fillers **133**
- Firecracker plant 250, **323**, *323*
- Fireglow **328**, *328*
- Firethorn, scarlet **510**, *510*
- Fireweed **479**, *479*
- Firewheel tree, Queensland **345**, *345*
- Flacourtiaceae 320, 583
- Flame creeper **325**, *325*
- Flame tree
  - Illawarra **342**, *342*
  - pink **388–9**, *389*
- Flame vine **323**, *323*
- Flamingo flowers 238
- Flannel bush **574**, *574*
- Flat areas 40
- Flax 245
  - golden or yellow **560**, *560*, 580, *580*
  - New Zealand 243, 250, 271
  - perennial **427**, *427*
  - scarlet **352**, *352*
- Fleabane
  - daisy 143, 196
  - Mexican **480**, *480*
- Fleece vine, silver **468**, *468*
- Fleeceflowers *123*, 158
- Flower-of-the-Incas **336**, *336*
- Flowering tobacco *12*, 21, 125, 144–5, *144*, 157, 161, 176, 187, 202, 246–7, **455**, *455*
- Foamflowers 43, 150, 155, 157, 198
- Foliage **13**, *13*, 122, **134**, 171, 296
  - discolored 95–6
  - fragrant 144
  - green garden design **242**, *242*, 292
  - variegated 244–5, *244–5*
  - white 246
- Forget-me-not 13, 17, *17*, 21, *30*, *34*, 58, *121*, 123, 157, 172, 252–3, *253*, *262*, **418**, *418*, **428**, *428*
  - Chinese 252
  - creeping **428**, *428*
- Forks 78–9
  - broadforks 79
- Forsythia 30, 108, 126, **488**, *488*, **573**, *573*
- *Forsythia*
  - *viridissima* **573**, *573*
  - x *intermedia* **573**, *573*
- Fothergilla **499**, *499*
  - dwarf 273, **498–9**, *498*
- *Fothergilla*
  - *gardenii* 273, **498–9**, *498*
  - *major* **499**, *499*
- Four-o'clocks 16, 18, 21, 66, 145, 187, 201, 262, **313**, *313*
- Foxglove 17, 19, 21, *21*, 22, 58, 93, 95, 101, 102, 105, *111*, 122, 126, 131, 132, *132*, *140*, 247, 260, 276, **423**, *423*, **556**, *556*
  - fairy **423**, *423*
  - Merton **367**, *367*
- *Fragaria* spp. 187
  - *chiloensis* **480**, *480*
- Fragrance **144–5**
  - scented gardens 20–1, **266–7**, *266–7*
- Frangipani **529**, *529*, 585, *585*
- Franklin tree **524**, *524*
- *Franklinia alatamaha* **524**, *524*
- *Fraxinus ornus* **524–5**, *524*
- *Freesia* x *hybrida* **458**, *458*
- Freesias 247, 267, **458**, *458*
  - flame **317**, *317*
- *Fremontodendron californicum* **574**, *574*
- Fringe flower **504–5**, *505*
- Fringe tree **520**, *520*
  - Chinese **520**, *520*
- *Fritillaria*
  - *imperialis* 31, 93, 203, **543**, *543*
  - *meleagris* 203, *262*, **405**, *405*
  - *pudica* **544**, *544*
- Frost 65, 277
- Fruit 13, 141, 184, *184*, 186, 278, 294, *294*, 296
- Fumariaceae 367, 478
- Fungus gnats 222
- *Fuschia*
  - *magellanica* **338**, *338*
  - x *hybrida* 183, 187, 205, **382**, *382*
- Fuschias 173, 183, 187, 205, 250, 295–7, **382**, *382*
  - Australian **494–5**, *495*
  - Magellan **338**, *338*

G

- *Gaillardia*
  - *aristata* **558**, *558*
  - *pulchella* 135, 161, 200
  - x *grandiflora* 22, 102, 127, 139, 143, 152, 161, 196, **328**, *328*
- *Galanthus* spp. 28, 31, 55
  - *elwesii* **458–9**, *458*
  - *nivalis* 60, 203, **459**, *459*
- *Galium* spp.
  - *odoratum* 150, 155, 158, **454**, *454*
- *Galtonia candicans* 247, **459**, *459*
- Garden mums 68, 71, 72, 93, 96, 100, *100*, 110, 138, 196, *250*
- Garden planning 44–5, **114–17**, *114–17*
  - color *see* Color
  - containers 170–2, 184
  - deciding where to plant 114
  - design *see* Design
  - foundation planting **131**, *272–3*
  - landscaping *see* Landscaping
  - month by month **108–11**
  - plant list 116
  - problems 114–15, 148–61, *274–7*
  - senses *see* Senses
  - site map 45, *45*, 116
  - size of garden 115

Garden styles 115–16
balcony 172–3, **184–7**, *184*, 294–5, *295*
beds 26, 30, **128–32**, 246–7, 278, 296
bog garden 27
borders 25, 30, **128–32**, 246–7
cottage 25, **140–5**, *140–5*
courtyards and patios **185–7**, *185*, 300–1
cutting garden 26, 30, **134–5**, *134–5*
decks 173, 296, 300–1, *300*
dish and bottle 235
formal 24–5, *115*, 116, 130
front 296–7
hanging baskets **182–3**, *182–3*
informal *115*, 116, 130–1
Japanese **302–4**, *302–4*
meadow 26–7, **136–9**, *136–9*, *151*, 154
night 267
rock garden 27, 154–5
roof 173, 184, *184*, 295–6, *295*
scented 30
seaside 276–7, *276*
terrariums 234–5
tropical 243, *243*
urban **292–7**, *292–7*, 302–3
water 179, *179*, 142, 186, 269, *269*, 293, *293*, 303–4
window boxes **180–1**, *180–1*, 297, *297*
woodland 27, 31, *128*
Gardener's garters 245
Gardenia 238, 246–7, 266, **499**, *499*
dwarf **499**, *499*
tree **533**, *533*
Gardenia spp. 238, 246–7, 266
augusta 187, 205
globosa **533**, *533*
jasminoides 238, **499**, *499*
Garlic, triquestrous **456**, *456*
Gas plant 59, 71, 138, 141, **478**, *478*
Gaultheria
procumbens **500**, *500*
shallon **500**, *500*
Gaura 102
Gaura lindheimeri 102
Gay feather **370**, *370*
Gazania
hybrids 18, 45, **329**, *329*
rigens 176, 187, 200
Gelsemium sempivirens **548–9**, *548*
Genista
aetnensis **584**, *584*
hispanica **574**, *574*
monosperma **500**, *500*
tinctoria **574**, *574*
Gentian 252
stemless **424**, *424*
trumpet **424**, *424*
willow **424**, *424*
Gentiana spp. 252
acaulis syn. *G. excisa* **424**, *424*
asclepiadea **424**, *424*
Gentianaceae 399, 424
Geraniaceae 331–2, 360, 368–9
Geranium spp. 41, 42, 70
endressi 196
macrorrhizum 71
psilostemon **369**, *369*
sanguineum 126, 141, 150, 152, **369**, *369*
x *magnificum* **368**, *368*
Geraniums 13, *14*, 18, 20, 41, 105, 144, 177, 181, 186, *187*, 233, *233*, 235, 239
bigroot 71
ivy 183, **360**, *360*
Martha Washington **331**, *331*
rose 266
strawberry 150, **486**, *486*
zonal 18, *67*, **332**, *332*
Gerbera *250*
Gerbera jamesonii **558**, *558*
Geum quelyon syn. *G. chiloense* **329**, *329*
Gillenia trifoliata **481**, *481*
Ginger, European 122, 124, 150, 155, 157–8
Gladioli 28–30, 74, 105, *106*, 110–11, 122, 134, 178, **544**, *544*
Gladiolus spp. **544**, *544*
x *hortulanus* 134
Glechoma hederacea 'Variegata' 245
Gleditisia triacanthos var. *inermis* 285
Globe amaranth 21, 64, 161, 201, 256, **350**, *350*
Globeflower **566–7**, *567*
Gloriosa rothschildiana **316**, *316*
Glory-bower **321**, *321*
bleeding 186
harlequin **493**, *493*
Glory bush **449**, *449*
Glory-of-the-snow **402**, *402*
Gloxinias 239, **370**, *370*
miniature 234
Goat's beard 27, 102, 158, **327**, *327*, 476, *476*
false **417**, *417*
Godetia **350**, *350*
Golden-bells **573**, *573*
Golden cup vine **551**, *551*
Golden honey balls **570**, *570*
Golden rain tree 285, **585**, *585*
Golden rod **566**, *566*
Golden-shower **584**, *584*
Golden swan **316**, *316*
Goldenrods 123, 132, *279*
Goldfussia **449**, *449*
Gomphrena globosa 21, 64, 161, 201, *256*, **350**, *350*
Goodeniaceae 339, 446
Gooseberry, Chinese *see* Kiwi fruit
Gordonia **525**, *525*
Gordonia axillaris **525**, *525*
Gorse **581**, *581*
Spanish **574**, *574*
Goutweed 153
Grammagrass, side oats 139
Grass *160*, 277, 292
containers, for 179, *179*
fountain 153
Japanese silver 245
lawn 264
meadow garden 138, 154
mondo 243, 264
ornamental 70, 127, 153, 245, 271
prairie cord 138
Red Baron blood grass 251, *279*
star **544**, *544*
switch 138
variegated 244–5, *245*, 261
zebra 245
Graveyard tree **529**, *529*
Grecian windflower 55, 60, 61, 203
Grevillea, Bank's **500–1**, *501*
Grevillea
banksii **500–1**, *501*
robusta 274, **584–5**, *584*
rosmarinifolia **382**, *382*
Grossulariaceae 386–7
Groundcovers *148*, **149–50**, *150*
Groundsel **581**, *581*
Growth **13–15**, 28–9
stunted 95–6
Gungunna **390**, *390*
Gunnera manicata 243
Gypsophila spp.
elegans 132, 135, **454–5**, *454*
paniculata 37, 96, 102, 118, 140–1, 153, 196, **481**, *481*
repens 'Rosea' **369**, *369*

H

Haemanthus multiflorus **317**, *317*
Haemodoraceae 326
Hairgrass, tufted 138
Hakea
pincushion **525**, *525*
willow-leaved **525**, *525*
Hakea
acicularis **501**, *501*
laurina **525**, *525*
salicifolia syn. *H. saligna* **525**, *525*
Halesia carolina syn. *H. tetraptera* **526**, *526*
Hamamelidaceae 440, 498–9, 504–5, 571–2, 574–5
Hamamelis spp. 266
mollis **574–5**, *575*
virginiana **575**, *575*
Hand pruners 81, *81*
Handkerchief tree **523**, *523*
Hanging baskets **182–3**, *182–3*
Hardenbergia
comptoniana **409**, *409*
violacea **410**, *410*
Hardening off **57**
Hardiness zones **38**
Harebell
Carpathian 195, **418**, *418*
England, of **420**, *420*
Harlequin flower **318**, *318*
Harpephyllum caffrum **585**, *585*
Hawthorn 282
double red **342**, *342*
pink Indian **386**, *386*
thornless cockspur 285
Heart-leaf pea **337**, *337*
Heartsease **355**, *355*, **401**, *401*
Heath **381–2**, *381–2*
Irish **440**, *440*
winter **498**, *498*
Heather 150, 205, **379**, *379*
Scotch **437**, *437*
Hebe 265
speedwell **442–3**, *442–3*
Hebe
albicans **501**, *501*
diosmifolia **501**, *501*
hulkeana **442**, *442*
odora syn. *H. buxifolia* **501**, *501*
salicifolia **502**, *502*
speciosa **442**, *442*
x *andersonii* **442–3**, *442–3*
x *franciscana* **443**, *443*
Hedera spp. 219
helix 182, 235, 244–5, 288–9
Hedges *115*, 116, 274, 286–7, 296
Hedychium gardnerianum **558**, *558*
Helenium spp. 255, 261
autumnale 72, 139, 196, **559**, *559*
'Waldtraut' *254*
Helen's flower 255
Helianthemum nummularium 204
Helianthus spp. 102
angustifolius **558**, *558*
annuus 132, 135, 153, 161, 255, **538–9**, *539*
petiolatum 20
x *multiflorus* 139, 161, **559**, *559*
Helichrysum
bracteatum **539**, *539*
frutescens 21
italicum 264
petiolatum 182, 201

Heliopsis helianthoides var. *scabra* **559**, *559*
Heliotrope 18, 105, 145
cherry-pie **443**, *443*
Heliotropium arborescens 18, 105, 145, **443**, *443*
Hellebores *27*, 156, *272*
black **482**, *482*
Corsican **481**, *481*
Majorca **482**, *482*
stinking **482**, *482*
Helleborus spp. 156, *272*
corsicus **481**, *481*
foetidus **482**, *482*
lividus **482**, *482*
niger **482**, *482*
x *orientalis* 27, 68, 101, 126, 157, 196, **370**, *370*
Helxine 264
Hemerocallis spp. 42, 45, 196, 255
hybrids 145, 150, 152, 254, **560**, *560*
Hens-and-chickens 205
Herald's-trumpet **464**, *464*
Herbs 100, 131, 173, 181, *181*, 183, 184, 186, 242, 266, 276, 278, 293, 296–7. *See also by name*
Hesperis matronalis **424**, *424*
var. *albiflora* 247
Heterocentron elegans **370**, *370*
Heuchera spp. 22, 37, 59, 120, 196, 250
'Palace Purple' 126
sanguinea 97, 123, 141, **329**, *329*
Hibbertia scandens **549**, *549*
Hibiscus
Chinese **382–3**, *383*
fringed **338–9**, *338*
Norfolk Island 274
Syrian **444**, *444*
Hibiscus spp. 238
mutabilis 262, **502**, *502*
rosa-sinensis 230, 238, **382–3**, *383*
schizopetalus **338–9**, *338*
syriacus **444**, *444*
Hills 40–1, **154–5**, *154–5*, **276**, *276*. *see also* Terraces
Hippeastrum
hybrids 30, 177, 239
puniceum **317**, *317*
Hippocastanaceae 488, 518
Hoes 80, 99, *99*
Hoheria glabrata **526**, *526*
Holly 127, 271, 274, *274*, 287
sea *see* Sea holly
Holly-leaf sweetspire **577**, *577*
Hollyhocks 19, 21, 22, *22*, 93, 96, 126, 132, 141–2, 151, *254*, 271, **362**, *362*
Honesty 17, 21, 105, 157, 201, *268*
Honey locusts 43
Honeysuckle 126, 141, 288, **358**, *358*, **583**, *583*
box-leaf **504**, *504*
Cape **325**, *325*
giant Burmese **549**, *549*
Hall's **467**, *467*
Japanese **411**, *411*, **467**, *467*
sweet **549**, *549*
Tatarian **384**, *384*
trumpet **322**, *322*
woodbine **550**, *550*
Hops 288
Horse chestnut **388**, *388*, **518**, *518*
dwarf **488**, *488*
Hosta spp. 27, *41*, 43, *43*, 70, 101, *118*, 122, *123*, 124, 138, *151*, 153, 155–7, 177, 197, 243, 244, *244*, *246*, 256, 261, *261*, 276–7
crispula 245
fortunei 156, 245, *275*, *301*, **424**, *424*
'Gold Standard' 23
hybrids 150, 155, 157, 197
'Moonlight' 245
'Shade Fanfare' 245
sieboldiana 156, 261, **425**, *425*
undulata var. *univittata* 245, 261
ventricosta *275*, **425**, *425*
Hot and dry sites 277
Houheria **526**, *526*
Hound's tongue **422**, *422*
Houseplants **208–13**, *208–13*
buying 208–10
cacti 237, *237*
caring for **214–21**
bulbs **231–2**, *232*
flowering plants **230–1**, *230*
carnivorous plants 237, *237*
container mixes 168–9, 174, 187, 218
creative displays **234–7**, *234–7*
exposure 208–9, 226–7
fertilizing 216–17, 230–1
flowering habits 209–10
grooming and pruning 218–19
herbicides, homemade 223
hormones 221
humidity 212–13, 227–8
hydroponics **236**
inside out and outside in **232–3**
light factors 210–11, 214, 228–9
fluorescent lights 228–9
high-intensity discharge lights (HID) 229
light bulbs 229
light levels 212–13
placing plants 211
selecting plants 208–9
symptoms of problems 212
living with **226–9**, *226–9*
microclimates 226–8
orchids 236–7, *236*
palms 236
pests and diseases **222–3**
potting and repotting 217–18, *218*
propagating 219–21
sensitive plants 237
temperature 213, 227
topiaries 235, *235*
watering 214–15
overwatering 215
vacations, during 216
water-quality 216
Hovea, holly-leaf **444**, *444*
Hovea chorizemifolia **444**, *444*
Howea forsterana 236
Hoya
australis **465**, *465*
carnosa 237, 239, **465**, *465*
Humulus lupulus 288
Hunnemania fumariifolia **539**, *539*
Hyacinth 22, 28–31, *28*, *30–1*, 134, 145, *168*, 178, 203, 231–2, 247, 253, *259*, 296, **405**, *405*
bean 133
cape **459**, *459*
Dutch **405**, *405*
grape 31, 38, 60, 62, *62*, 134, 138, 204, **406**, *406*
Hyacinthoides spp. 126
hispanicus 31, 60, 125, 203
Hyacinthus orientalis 134, 145, 203, **405**, *405*
Hybrids 15, 68
Hydrangea 127, 252, 256, 265, 271, 287, *287*, **444**, *444*
climbing 246, 289, **466**, *466*
oak-leaved **502**, *502*
tree **502**, *502*
Hydrangea spp.
anomala var. *petiolaris* 289
arborescens **502**, *502*
macrophylla 252, **444**, *444*
petiolaris 246, **466**, *466*
quercifolia 287, **502**, *502*
Hydrangeaceae 444, 502
Hydrophyllaceae 400
Hydroponics **236**
Hymenosporum flavum **585**, *585*
Hypericaceae 575–6
Hypericum
calycinum **575**, *575*
kalmianum **576**, *576*
x *moseranum* **576**, *576*
Hypoestes phyllostachya 171, 234
Hypoxidaceae 357
Hypoxis longifolia **544**, *544*
Hyssop 252

I

Iberis
sempervirens 27, 41, 85, 102, 131, 197, **482**, *482*
umbellata 21, 132, 135, 201, **455**, *455*
Ice plant **375–6**, *375–6*
Iceplant, hardy 204
Ilex spp. 127, 274, 287
Illiciaceae 576
Illicium anisatum **576**, *576*
Impatiens 18, 64, 105, 120, 156–7, *156*, 176–7, *183*, 187, 197, *254*, 296, **351**, *351*
New Guinea type 105, 197
Impatiens spp. 176, 197
balsamina 21, 201, **350–1**, *351*
wallerana 18, 157, *183*, 197, **351**, *351*
Imperata cylindrica 'Red Baron' 251
Incarvillea delavayi **370**, *370*
Indian bean tree **519**, *519*
Indian-physic **481**, *481*
Indigofera australis **444–5**, *445*
Indoor gardens *see* Containers, Houseplants
Insects *see* Pests
beneficial 94, 142–3
insecticides 94–5
Ipheion uniflorum **405**, *405*
Ipomoea spp. 57, 101
alba 132, 145, 187
purpurea 288, **410**, *410*
tricolor 21, 132, *295*, **410**, *410*
Iresine spp. 260
Iridaceae 316–19, 402–4, 406, 425–6, 457–8, 463, 478–9, 542, 544–5, 547, 556, 560, 566
Iris 12, 23, *27*, *41*, *43*, 70, 96, 100, 122, 126, 151, 153, 253, 255, *258*, 261, *261*, 271, *292*
African **478–9**, *478*
bearded 29, 75, *75*, 141, 145, 255
blue flag 138, 159
crested 157, 197
cultivars 252
Dalmatian 245
dwarf bearded **426**, *426*
English **406**, *406*
Japanese 27, *135*, 255, **425**, *425*
reticulated 31, 155, 178, 203, 231
Siberian *23*, 24, 125, 138, 152, 158, 178, 204, **426**, *426*
Spanish **406**, *406*
tall bearded **425**, *425*
winter **544**, *544*
yellow flag 159, 255, **560**, *560*

Iris
cristata 157, 197
danfordiae **544**, *544*
ensata 27, 255, **425**, *425*
germanica **425**, *425*
kaempferi **425**, *425*
maculata **545**, *545*
pallida 'Variegata' 244–5
pseudacorus 159, 255, **560**, 560
pumilla **426**, *426*
reticulata 31, 155, 178, 203, 231, **406**, *406*
sibirica 24, 125, 138, 152, 158, 178, 204, **426**, *426*
versicolor 138, 159
xiphioides **406**, *406*
xiphium **406**, *406*
Ironbark, white **343**, *343*
Ironweed 102
Ironwood, Brazilian **583**, *583*
Italian arum *30*, 203, 244, 245
Italian bugloss 194, 252, **416**, *416*
Itea
ilicifolia **577**, *577*
virginica **503**, *503*
Iteaceae 503
Ivy *44*, 186, 219, *235*, 244, 271, *272*, 294–5
Boston 289
cape **551**, *551*
English 123, 183, 235, 245, 288–9
Kenya **551**, *551*
Swedish 219
variegated 244–5, *244*

J

Jacaranda **450**, *450*
Jacaranda mimosifolia **450**, *450*
Jack-in-the-pulpit 127, 157–8, **416**, *416*
Jacobina, pink **383**, *383*
Jacob's ladder 252–3, **430**, *430*
dwarf **430**, *430*
Jade plant 220
Japanese beetles *92*, 93, 189, *189*
Japanese spurge **484**, *484*
Japonica **491**, *491*
Jasione perennis **426**, *426*
Jasmine 187, 239, 246, 271
Arabian **467**, *467*
Brazilian **359**, *359*
Carolina **548–9**, *548*
Chilean 187, **359**, *359*, 467, *467*
Chinese **466**, *466*
Chinese star **471**, *471*
Confederate 246
Japanese star **470**, *470*
Madagascar **470**, *470*
orange 239
pink **466**, *466*
primrose **577**, *577*
rock **473**, *473*
Spanish **466**, *466*
star 186–7, **466**, *466*, **471**, *471*
yellow **577**, *577*
Jasminum spp. 187, 239
grandiflorum **466**, *466*
humile 'Revolutum' **577**, *577*
mesnyi **577**, *577*
nitidum syn. *J. ilicifolium* **466**, *466*
polyanthum **466**, *466*
sambac **467**, *467*
Jerusalem cherry 239
Joe-Pye weeds 127, 132, 139, 158–9
Johnny-jump-ups 176, **401**, *401*
Jonquil 254–5, **546**, *546*
Joseph's coat 17, 122, *251*, **312**, *312*
Judas tree **380**, *380*, **389–90**, *389–90*
Juniper 263, 282–3, 286–7
creeping 154
dwarf 277
Juniperus spp. 282, 286
horizontalis 154
virginiana 263, 274, *293*
Justicia carnea **383**, *383*
Justicia, red **340**, *340*

K

Kalanchoe blossfeldiana 239
Kalmia latifolia 177, 257, **383**, *383*
Kangaroo-paw **326**, *326*
Kennedia
nigricans **410–11**, *410*
rubicunda **322**, *322*
Kerria, Japanese 273, *273*, **577**, *577*
Kerria japonica 273, *273*, **577**, *577*
Keurboom **393**, *393*
King cup **554**, *554*
Kiwi fruit 288
Knapweed 141, 195, **554–5**, *555*
Kniphofia
cultivars 255
hybrids 85
uvaria 23
Kochia scoparia 122
Koelreuteria paniculata 285, **585**, *585*
Kolkwitzia amabilis 257, **383**, *383*
Koromiko **502**, *502*

L

Labiatae 314, 331, 339, 373–4, 377, 401, 415, 428–9, 431–3, 445, 448–9, 455, 482–4, 513, 562, 579
Lablab purpureus 133
Laburnum anagyroides **585**, *585*
Lacebark, Queensland **388**, *388*
Lachenalia aloides **317**, *317*
Ladybells **414**, *414*
Lady's-mantle 42, 140–1, 152, 194, 276, **552**, *552*
Lagerstroemia indica 265, **450–1**, *450*
Lagunaria patersonii 274
Lamb's ears 122, 125, *140*, 150, 153, 155, *160*, 161, 198, 246, 248–9, *249*, 256, 264, *264*, **432**, *432*
Lamiastrum galeobdolon 156
Lamium, spotted 102, 123, 150, 155–7, 177, **482–3**, *483*
Lamium
galeobdolon 204
maculatum 102, 123, 150, 155–7, 177, 245, **482–3**, *483*
Landscaping **270–83**
bonsai 281, *281*, **282–3**, *282–3*
concealment 277
espalier 280
feature plants 272
foundation planting 272–3
framework of plants 272
outdoor living areas **300–1**
plant form 270–2, 285–6
pleaching 281, *281*
pollarding 281, *281*
problems 274–7
shrubs, with **286–7**, *286–7*
special plant effects 280
topiary 235, *235*, 244, 280–1, *280*
trees, with **284–5**, *284–5*
vines, with **288–9**, *288–9*
Lantana 177, *235*, **383**, *383*, **578**, *578*
Lantana spp. 235
camara 177, 235, **383**, *383*, **578**, *578*
montevidensis 235
Lapageria rosea **322**, *322*
Lapeirousia cruenta **317**, *317*
Lardizabalaceae 408
Larkspur
candle **422**, *422*
rocket 21, 57, 102, 131, 135, 153, 172, **398**, 398
Lasiandra **449**, *449*
Lathyrus spp.
grandiflorus **322**, *322*
latifolius **411**, *411*
odoratus 88, 133, 135, 145, 153, 187, 201, 267, 289, **351**, *351*
Lauraceae 578
Laurel
bay **578**, *578*
mountain 177, 257, **383**, *383*
Oregon **519**, *519*
Portugal **530**, *530*
Laurus nobilis 242, **578**, *578*
Laurustinus **516**, *516*
Lavandula spp. 235
angustifolia 15, 145, 187, 248, *278*, **445**, *445*
dentata **445**, *445*
stoechas **445**, *445*
Lavatera spp. 257
maritima **446**, *446*
trimestris **351**, *351*
Lavender 13, 85, *119*, *128*, 140, 144–5, *145*, 187, 235, 252, 265–6, 277, 286, 293
English 15, *24*, 248, **445**, *445*
French **445**, *445*
sea 39, *39*, **426–7**, *426*
Spanish **445**, *445*
Lavender cotton 102, 177, 246, 248–9, 253, 256, **565**, *565*
Lawns 296. *see also* Grass
bulbs in 31
time-saving tips 149–50
Layering **70–1**, *70*
Layia platyglossa syn. *L. elegans* **539**, *539*
Leadwort 195
Leafminers 92, 93
Leatherwood **495**, 495, **524**, *524*
Lechenaultia **339**, 339, **446**, *446*
Lechenaultia
biloba **446**, *446*
formosa **339**, *339*
Leguminosae 322, 330, 334, 337, 343, 351, 358, 361, 365, 380, 387–90, 394, 400, 409–13, 418, 444–5, 471, 490–1, 495–6, 500, 533–4, 571–2, 574, 581–2, 584–5
Lemon balm 13, 144, 187, *242*, 245, 297
Lenten rose 27, 68, 101, 126, 157, 196, **370**, *370*
Leonotis leonurus **339**, *339*
Leontopodium alpinum **483**, *483*
Leopard's-bane 196, **556–7**, *557*
Leptospermum scoparium **384**, *384*
Lettuce *242*
Leucanthemum x *superbum* 68, 122, 138, 141, 143, 152, 197

Leucojum
  aestivum 30, 55, 60, 134, **459**, *459*
  vernum **459**, *459*
Leucospermum reflexum **339**, *339*
Leucothoe
  coast **503**, *503*
  drooping **503**, *503*
Leucothoe
  axillaris syn. *L. catesaei* **503**, *503*
  fontanesiana **503**, *503*
Liatris spicata 122, 126, 139, 152, 197, **370**, *370*
Licorice plant *20*, 201
Ligularia 41, 158, 255, 277
  rocket **560**, *560*
Ligularia spp. 118
  dentata 41, 158, *293*
  stenocephala **560**, *560*
Ligustrum
  japonicum **504**, *504*
  ludicum **504**, *504*
  ovalifolium **504**, *504*
Lilac 253, **449**, *449*, 513, *513*
  California **438–9**, *438*
  New Zealand **442**, *442*, 501, *501*
  vine **409**, *409*
  wild **438–9**, *438*
Liliaceae 316–19, 329, 356–7, 368, 402–3, 405–7, 422–5, 433, 456–62, 485–7, 542–5, 547, 560, 567
Lilies *24*, 28–9, *29*, 30, 37, 75, 88, 100, *106*, *120*, 125, 152, 187, 204, 246–7, *256*, *270*, 271, **356–7**, *357*
  African **414–15**, *415*
  African corn **545**, *545*
  Amazon **458**, *458*
  arum 243, **463**, *463*
  Asiatic hybrid 123, *129*, 134
  Aztec **318**, *318*
  Barbados **317**, *317*
  belladonna 257, **356**, *356*
  blackberry 101, 122, 126–7
  bugle **463**, *463*
  bulbils 75
  calla 29
  canna 261, 297, **554**, *554*
  checkered 203, *262*
  climbing **316**, *316*
  coast fawn **458**, *458*
  crimson flag **318**, *318*
  Cuban **407**, *407*
  day *see* Daylily
  false ginger **558**, *558*
  fireball **317**, *317*
  flax **422–3**, *423*
  Formosan **460**, *460*
  fortnight **556**, *556*
  foxtail **368**, *368*
  giant **456**, *456*
  golden-rayed **460**, *460*
  Japanese **461**, *461*
  jockey's cap **547**, *547*
  Kaffir **328**, *328*
  leopard **405**, *405*
  Madonna 30, **460**, *460*
  Mariposa **542**, *542*
  oriental hybrids 134, 145
  panther **318**, *318*
  Peruvian 194, **326**, *326*
  pineapple **543**, *543*
  pink tiger **461**, *461*
  rain **463**, *463*
  regal 145, **461**, *461*
  scaling technique 75
  Scarborough **319**, *319*
  spider 257, **357**, *357*
  summer 247
  tiger 255
  toad **433**, *433*
  torch 23, 85, *160*, **329**, *329*
  trout 257, **458**, *458*
  trumpet hybrids 134, *134*, 145, **460**, *460*
  Turk's cap 261
  zephyr **463**, *463*
Lilium spp. 37, 179, 254
  auratum **460**, *460*
  candidum 30, 247, **460**, *460*
  formosanum **460**, *460*
  hybrids 141, 145, 152, 187, 204
  longiflorum **460**, *460*
  pardalinum **318**, *318*
  regale 247, **461**, *461*
  rubellum **356–7**, *357*
  speciosum var. *album* **461**, *461*
Lilly pilly **524**, *524*
Lily leek 60
Lily-of-the-valley 37, 138, 145, 150, *150*, 155, 195, 246–7, **456**, *456*
  shrub **509**, *509*
  tree **521**, *521*
Lilyturf 245, 276
  creeping 150, 197
Limnanthaceae 540
Limnanthus douglasii **540**, *540*
Limonium spp. 39, *39*
  latifolium **426–7**, *426*
  sinuatum 21, 201, **399**, *399*
Linaria spp. *19*
  maroccana **352**, *352*
Linden, silver 285
Lindera benzoin **578**, *578*
Lime tree *281*, 296
Linaceae 352, 427, 560, 580
Linden spp. *281*
Linum
  flavum **560**, *560*
  grandiflorum **352**, *352*
  perenne syn. *L. sibiricum* **427**, *427*
  trigynum **580**, *580*
Lion's ear **339**, *339*
Lipstick tree **388**, *388*
Lipstick vine 238
Liquidambar 271, 274
Liquidambar styraciflua 274
Liriodendron tulipifera **526–7**, *526*
Liriope spp.
  muscari 245, 276
  spicata 150, 197
Lisianthus **399**, *399*
Lisianthus russellianus **399**, *399*
Lithospermum **446**, *446*
Lithospermum diffusum **446**, *446*
Loasaceae 540
Lobelia 123, 125, 183, 246, **400**, *400*, 427, *427*
  edging 130, 157, 172, 177, 201
  great blue 102, 159
  peach-leaved **330**, *330*
Lobelia
  cardinalis 27, 41, 132, 139, 158, 197, **330**, *330*
  erinus 125, 130, 157, 172, 177, 183, **400**, *400*
  laxiflora **330**, *330*
  syphilitica 102, 159
  x *gerardii* **427**, *427*
Lobeliaceae 330, 400
Lobularia maritima 21, 105, 123, 125, 130, 133, 144–5, 153, 172, 181, 183, 201, 246, **455**, *455*
Loganiaceae 436, 490, 548–9, 570
Lonicera spp. 126, 288
  caprifolium **549**, *549*
  hildebrandiana **549**, *549*
  japonica **411**, *411*, **467**, *467*
  nitida **504**, *504*
  periclymenum **550**, *550*
  sempervirens **322**, *322*
  tatarica **384**, *384*
  x *americana* **358**, *358*
Loosestrife 49, *120*, *141*, 158, 255, 277, **371**, *371*, **561**, *561*
Loropetalum chinense **504–5**, *505*
Love-in-a-mist 13, 21, 153, 172, 202, 252, **401**, *401*
Love-lies-bleeding 21, *104*, 130, 161, 176, 186, 199, **312**, *312*
Luculia, pink siva 266, **384**, *384*
Luculia gratissima 266, **384**, *384*
Lunaria annua 17, 21, 105, 157, 201, 268, **352**, *352*
Lungwort 27, 43, 122, 156, **430**, *430*
Lupines 13, *25*, 50, 138, 140–1, 143, 253, **400**, *400*
  Carolina 139
  Russell 257, **330**, *330*
Lupinus spp. 13, *25*, 50, 138, 253, **330**, *330*
  polyphyllus 140–1, 143
Lychnis spp.
  chalcedonica **330**, *330*
  coronaria 140–1, **371**, *371*
  viscaria **371**, *371*
Lycoris squamigera 134
Lysimachia
  nummularia 204
  punctata 158, 255, **561**, *561*
Lythraceae 371, 450–1
Lythrum salicaria 277, **371**, *371*

M

Macfadyena unguis-cati **550**, *550*
Mackaya **446**, *446*
Mackaya bella **446**, *446*
Macleaya cordata **483**, *483*
Madagascar periwinkle 18, 123, 161, 199
Madrone **519**, *519*
Magnolia 126, 187
  Bull Bay **527**, *527*
  Campbell **390–1**, *391*
  lily 257
  port wine 266, **447**, *447*
  saucer 285
  southern **527**, *527*
  star **505**, *505*
Magnolia spp. 187
  campbellii **390–1**, *391*
  grandiflora **527**, *527*
  lilliflora 257
  stellata **505**, *505*
  x *soulangiana* 285
Magnoliaceae 390–1, 447, 505, 526–8
Mahonia
  aquifolium *275*, **578**, *578*
  bealei **579**, *579*
Maidenhair 243, 264
Malcomia maritima 201, **352–3**, *353*
Mallow **351**, *351*, **444**, *444*
  hollyhock **371**, *371*
  Jew's **577**, *577*
  musk **372**, *372*
  prairie **376**, *376*
Malpighiaceae 551
Maltese-cross **330**, *330*
Malus spp. **344**, *344*, **527**, *527*
  baccata **527**, *527*
  floribunda **391**, *391*
  ioensis 'Plena' **391**, *391*
  spectabilis 'Plena' **391**, *391*
  x *purpurea* 'Eleyi' **392**, *392*
Malva
  alcea **371**, *371*
  moschata **372**, *372*

Malvaceae 338, 351, 362, 371–2, 376, 378, 382–3, 444, 446, 502, 526, 568
Mammillaria plumosa 237
Mandevilla
  laxa **467**, *467*
  sanderi **359**, *359*
  splendens **359**, *359*
  suaveolens 187, **467**, *467*
Mandevillas 186, **467**, *467*
Manettia bicolor syn. *M. inflata* **323**, *323*
Manuka **384**, *384*
Maple *43*, 271, 304
  flowering 238, **378**, *378*, **568**, *568*
  full-moon *284*
  Japanese 258, 282–3, *282*, *284*, 295
  Norway 285, **582**, *582*
  red *250*
  trident 285
Marguerite 18, 194, 252, **553**, *553*
Marigolds 13, 16, *17*, 37, 58, 67, 130, 153, *175*, 176, 181, 202, *254*, 266, 271
  African **541**, *541*
  American **541**, *541*
  Aztec **541**, *541*
  dwarf 18, 171, 271
  French **541**, *541*
  marsh 27, 85, 159, **554**, *554*
  pot 21, *121*, 132, *133*, 135, 153, *160*, 161, 199, 254–5, **538**, *538*
Maskflower **312**, *312*
Masterwort 141, 158, 195, **363**, *363*
Matricaria eximia **454**, *454*
Matteuccia struthiopteris 243
Matthiola
  bicornis 187, *187*
  incana 135, 145, 178, 181, 201, **353**, *353*
  longipetala subsp. *bicornis* 21, 144, 181
Mattocks 79, *79*
Mazus reptans 204, **427**, *427*
Meadow clary **431**, *431*
Meadow foam **540**, *540*
Meadowrue **377**, *377*
Meadowsweet **480**, *480*
  Siberian **368**, *368*
Mealybugs 222
Meconopsis
  betonicifolia syn. *M. baileyi* **427**, *427*
  cambrica **561**, *561*
Mediterranean gardens 277, 278, 293
Melaleuca
  armillaris **505**, *505*
  decussata **384**, *384*
  incana **505**, *505*
  linariifolia **506**, *506*, **528**, *528*
  quinquenervia 274, **528**, *528*
Melastomataceae 370, 449
Melia azedarach var. *australasica* **451**, *451*
Meliaceae 451, 520
Melianthus major 367
Melissa officinalis 144, 187, *242*, 245
Mentha spp. 183
  suaveolens 'Variegata' 245
Mentzelia lindleyi **540**, *540*
Merrybells 157, 198, **567**, *567*
Mertensia virginica 27, 43, **428**, *428*
Mesembryanthemum criniflorum **313**, *313*
Metrosideros excelsa **344–5**, *344*
Mexican orange blossoms 266
Michelia
  doltsopa **528**, *528*
  figo 266, **447**, *447*
Micromeria corsica **433**, *433*
Mignonette 144, 181
Mildew 96, *96*
Milkweed 142
  swamp 159
Milkwort **448**, *448*
Mimosa pudica 237
Mimosa tree **388**, *388*
Mimulus
  guttatus **561**, *561*
  x *hybridus* 176, 201, 277
Mina lobata 288
Mint 183, 242, 297
  variegated apple 245
Mint germander **432–3**, *432*
Mintbush **448**, *448*
Minuartia verna **483**, *483*
Mirabilis jalapa 16, 18, 21, 66, 145, 187, 262, **313**, *313*
Miscanthus sinensis 245
Mites 222
Mock orange **506**, *506*, **508**, *508*
  Californian **491**, *491*
  Lemoine **508**, *508*
  Mexican **508**, *508*
  virginal **508**, *508*
Moluccella laevis **455**, *455*
Monarda spp.
  'Cambridge Scarlet' 261
  didyma 15, 26, 71, 96, 102, 110, 143, 144, 158, **331**, *331*
Mondo grass 243, 264
Monkey flower 176, 201, 277
Monkshood 194, **414**, *414*
  azure **414**, *414*
  hybrid **414**, *414*
Moonflower 132, 145, 187, 246, *246*
Moraea iridioides **478–9**, *478*
Morning glory 21, 57, 101, 132, 288, **410**, *410*
  dwarf 64, 200
  ground **422**, *422*
Morus spp. *281*
Mosaic 97, *97*
Mosses 234, 264–5
  Irish **483**, *483*
  Spanish 264
Mother-of-thyme 150, 205, **376–7**, *376–7*
Mountain sandwort 204
Mugwort **475**, *475*
Mulberry *281*
Mulching **84–5**, *84–5*, 98, 99, 104, *111*, 191
Mulleins 21, 37, 104, 122, 132, 248, **567**, *567*
  nettle-leaved 141, 161, 199, **487**, *487*
Murraya spp. 266, 296
  paniculata 239, 266, **506**, *506*
Musa basjoo 243
Muscari spp. 31
  armeniacum 60, 62, *62*, 134, 204, **406**, *406*
Mussaenda frondosa **340**, *340*
Myoporaceae 506
Myoporum parvifolium **506**, *506*
Myosotis spp. 17, *17*, 252, *253*
  sylvatica 21, 58, 157, 172, 201, **428**, *428*
Myrrhis odorata 187
Myrsiniaceae 489
Myrtaceae 335, 338, 342–4, 379, 384, 390, 392, 505–6, 519, 523–4, 528, 535
Myrtle 235, 296, **506**, *506*
  crepe 265, **450–1**, *450*
  honey **505**, *505*
Myrtus communis 235, **506**, *506*

N

Names **15**
Nandina domestica 186, 251, *275*, **507**, *507*
Narcissus 31, 267, **546**, *546*
  poet's **461**, *461*
  white **461**, *461*
Narcissus spp. 60, 254–5, **546**, *546*
  asturiensis 55
  bulbocodium 55, **545**, *545*
  hybrids 187, 134, 145, 152, 204
  poeticus **461**, *461*
  tazetta **461**, *461*, **546**, *546*
  triandrus 55
Nasturtium 13, 19, 21, *118*, 183, 187, 203, 255, 271, **541**, *541*
  climbing **325**, *325*
Needlewood, bushy **501**, *501*
Nemesia *108*, **540–1**, *540*
Nemesia strumosa **540–1**, *540*
Nemophila menziesii 133, 172, 201, **400**, *400*
Nepeta spp. 102, *253*
  mussinii 197
  x *faassenii* 102, 140–1, 145, 152, **428**, *428*
Nephrolepsis exaltata 182
Nerine bowdenii 257, **357**, *357*
Nerium oleander **384–5**, *385*
Nicotiana spp. 176, 187, 202, 267
  alata 21, 125, 157, 145, 161, 247, **455**, *455*
  sylvestris 144
Nierembergia hippomanica **400**, *400*
Nigella damascena 21, 153, 172, 202, 252, **401**, *401*
Ninebark, common **509**, *509*
Nutrients 88–9
  adding **50–1**
Nuts 13
Nyctaginaceae 313, 320
Nymphaea spp. 255
Nymphoides peltata 255
Nyssa sylvatica 258

O

Oak 271
  pin 274
  silky 274, **584–5**, *584*
Obedient plant 71, 139, 152, 158, 198, **484**, *484*
Ochna serrulata syn. *O. atropurpurea* **579**, *579*
Ochnaceae 579
Oconee-bells **486**, *486*
Odontonema stricutum **340**, *340*
Oenothera
  fruticosa **562**, *562*
  speciosa 150, 197, **372**, *372*
  tetragona 42, 45, 127, 139, 161
Oleaceae 449, 466–7, 488, 504, 507, 513, 520, 524–5, 573, 577
Oleander **384–5**, *385*
Olearia x *haastii* **507**, *507*
Olive, sweet 239
Omphalodes verna 204, **428**, *428*
Onagraceae 338, 349–50, 372, 382, 562
Onions 63, 134, 161
  ornamental **402**, *402*
Ophiopogon spp. *243*
  japonicus *275*, 293
  planiscarpus 'Nigrescens' 261
Opuntia humifusa 197
Orange blossom, Mexican **492**, *492*

Orchid tree, Hong Kong **388**, *388*
Orchids 209, 239
  Dendrobium hybrids 236
  houseplants 236–7, *236*
  moth 230, 237
  Phalaenopsis hybrids 236–7
Organic matter **35**, *35*
Ornamental kale 17
Ornithogalum
  thyrsoides **462**, *462*
  umbellatum **462**, *462*
Osmanthus 239, 266, **507**, *507*
Osmanthus
  delavayi **507**, *507*
  fragrans 239, 266, **507**, *507*
Osmunda spp. 159
Osteospermum ecklonis **479**, *479*
Oswego tea *see* Bee balm
Our Lord's Candle 248
Oxalidaceae 357
Oxalis spp. 239
  adenophylla **357**, *357*
Oxydendrum arboreum 127, **528–9**, *529*
Oxypetalum caeruleum **447**, *447*

P

Pachysandra 155
  Allegheny 150, 197
  Japanese 150, 276
Pachysandra spp.
  procumbens 150, 197
  terminalis 150, 155, 276, **484**, *484*
Paeonia spp. 37
  lactiflora 141, 145, 152, 197, 257, **484**, *484*
  officinalis **331**, *331*, **372**, *372*
  suffruticosa 22, **385**, *385*
Paeoniaceae 331, 372, 385
Pagoda tree, Japanese 127, 285, **534**, *534*
Palms 236, *236*, 258, 271, 295–6
  bamboo 236
  chusan 243
  date 236
  kentia 236
  parlor 236
  sealing wax *273*
  small 236
  windmill 243
Pandorea
  jasminoides **359**, *359*, **468**, *468*
  pnadorana **468**, *468*
Panicum virgatum 138
Pansies *16*, 17, 18, *27*, 45, *131*, *133*, 135, 172, *172*, 176, 178, 183, 203, *250*, *259*, **355**, *355*, **401**, *401*
Papaver spp. 96, 101
  alpinum **562**, *562*
  nudicaule 202, 254–5, **313**, *313*
  orientale 73, 111, 141, 197, **331**, *331*
  rhoeas 21, 137, 153, 202, **314**, *314*
Papaveraceae 313–14, 331, 427, 475, 483, 486, 539, 555, 561–2
Paperbark
  broad-leaved 274, **528**, *528*
  flaxleaf **528**, *528*
Papyrus 297
Parsley 142, 297
Parthenocissus
  quinquefolia 289
  tricuspidata *270*, 289
Pasque flower 198, **430–1**, *430*
Passiflora spp. 219, 239, 288–9
  caerulea **411**, *411*
  coccinea **323**, *323*
  edulus **468**, *468*
Passifloraceae 323, 411, 468
Passion fruit **468**, *468*
Passionflowers 219, 239, 288–9, **468**, *468*
  blue crown **411**, *411*
  red **323**, *323*
Paths and paving 116, *119*, *130*, *161*, 297
Patrinia 42, 104, 141
Patrinia scabiosifolia 42, 104, 141
Paulownia tomentosa syn. *P. imperialis* **451**, *451*
Pea, everlasting **411**, *411*
Pea tree, Siberian **583**, *583*
Peach **392**, *392*
  double red-flowering **345**, *345*
Pear
  callery **532**, *532*
  Chinese **532**, *532*
  Manchurian **532–3**, *532*
  Ussurian **532–3**, *532*
  willow-leaved or weeping silver **532**, *532*
Pearl flower, Japanese **509**, *509*
Pearlbush **498**, *498*
Pelargonium spp. 105, 181, 182, 186, *187*, 233, 235, 239
  crispum 144
  graveolens 266
  peltatum 183, **360**, *360*
  tomentosum 144
  x *domesticum* **331**, *331*
  x *hortorum* 18, **332**, *332*
Pennisetum alopecuroides 153
Penstemon 197, **314**, *314*
  beardlip **332**, *332*
  gloxinia **332**, *332*
Penstemon spp.
  barbatus **332**, *332*
  digitalis 197
  x *gloxinioides* **314**, *314*, **332**, *332*
Pentas lanceolata **332**, *332*
Peonies 13, 23, 24, 37, 59, 70, 71, 96, 97, 102–3, 110, 118, 125–7, 134, 138, 140–1, 145, 151–2, 197, 256–7, **331**, *331*, **372**, *372*
  Chinese **484**, *484*
  tree 22, **385**, *385*
Pepper, ornamental 238
Pepperbush, sweet **493**, *493*
Peppercorn tree 274
Perennials **22–7**, *109*, 326–33, 362–77, 414–35, 472–87, 552–67
  arranging 24–7
  beds and borders 129
  buying 53–5
  containers 27, 58, 174, 177
  easy to grow 152–3
  nutrient needs 88–9
  planting **58–61**, *58*, *59*
  propagating **68–73**
  root system 12
  seasonal change 23–4
  seeds 68–70
  weeds 98
Periwinkle 155, 180, 203, 245
  lesser **434**, *434*
  Madagascar *see* Madagascar periwinkle
Perovskia atriplicifolia 161, **429**, *429*
Persian nepeta 197
Pests **92–5**, 189
  controlling 94–5, 223–5
  indoor plants 223–5, 233
  wildlife 93
Petrea volubilis **411**, *411*
Petunias *12*, 13, 16, *17*, *20*, *41*, *44*, 66, 132, 172, 177, 181–3, *182*, 186, 202, 246, 295, 296
  x *hybrida* 145, 202, **353**, *353*
Phaedranthus **321**, *321*
Phalaenopsis hybrids 230
Phalaris arundinacea var. *picta* 245
Phaseolus
  caracalla **412**, *412*
  coccineus 19, 132
Pheasant's eye **552**, *552*
Philadelphaceae 491, 497
Philadelphus
  coronarius **508**, *508*
  Mexicanus **508**, *508*
  x *lemoinei* **508**, *508*
  x *virginalis* **508**, *508*
Philesiaceae 322
Phlomis 277
  fruticosa **579**, *579*
  russeliana **562**, *562*
Phlox 110, *128*, *138*
  annual 16, 202
  creeping 102, 123, 150, 155, 205
  garden 72, 73, 96, 110, *110*, 141, 143, 145, 197, **484**, *484*
  moss 155
  night 181
Phlox
  drummondii 202, **354**, *354*
  paniculata 72, 73, 96, 110, 141, 143, 145, 197, **484**, *484*
  stolonifera 102, 123, 150, 155, 205
  subulata 102, 155, **372–3**, *373*
Phoenix roebelinii 236
Phormium tenax 243, *301*
  'Purpureum' 261
  'Variegatum' 245
Phormiums, variegated 243, 258
Photinia **529**, *529*
Photinia x *fraseri* **529**, *529*
Photosynthesis 14–15
Phyllostachys spp. 243, *303*
Physalis alkekengi syn. *P. franchetii* **333**, *333*
Physocarpus opulifolius **509**, *509*
Physostegia virginiana 71, 139, 152, 158, 198, **484**, *484*
Picea spp. 282, 287
  abies 274
  pungens 'Glauca' 248, *248*
Pieris
  formosa **509**, *509*
  japonica 293, **509**, *509*
Piggyback plants 221
Pimelea ferruginea **385**, *385*
Pincushion flower 101, 102, 125, 143, 198, **375**, *375*
  rocket **339**, *339*
Pine 271, 282
  dwarf mugo 286
  Mexican weeping 268
  Monterey 268
  Norfolk Island 274
Pinks 37, 70, 72, 88, 97, 123, *249*, 257
  allwood **366**, *366*
  cheddar 141, 143, 145, 155, 161, 196
  China 18, 144–5, 200, **350**, *350*
  cottage 196, **366**, *366*
  maiden 138, 150, *150*, **328**, *328*
  moss 102, **372–3**, *373*
  Prussian **478**, *478*
  sea 257
Pinus spp. 274, *303*
  mugo 282, 286
  parvifolia 282
  patula 268
  radiata 268
Pitcher plants 237

Pittosporaceae 412, 548, 585
Plane tree, oriental 274
Plant anatomy 12–13, **308–9**, *308–9*
Plant bugs 93, *93*
Planting
choosing plants **52–5**
time **56–63**
Platanus orientalis 274
Platycodon grandiflorus 96, 127, 152–3, 198, **429**, *429*
'Mariesii' **429**, *429*
Pleaching 281, *281*
Plectranthus spp. **373**, *373*
australis 219
Pleioblastus variegatus 245
Plum
kaffir **585**, 585
Malabar **535**, 535
Natal **491**, *491*
Plumbaginaceae 362, 399, 426–7, 439, 447, 475, 510
Plumbago **439**, *439*,
Cape Leadwort **447**, *447*, **510**, *510*
Plumbago auriculata syn. *P. capensis* **447**, *447*, **510**, *510*
Plumeria rubra 266, **529**, *529*
Poached egg plant **540**, *540*
Podranea ricasoliana **360**, *360*
Pohutukawa **344**, *344*
Poinciana, royal **342–3**, *343*
Poinciana ferrea **583**, *583*
Poinsettia 229, *229*, 231, 238, **344**, *344*
Poison spurge **557**, *557*
Polemoniaceae 336, 354, 372–3, 409, 430, 484
Polemonium
caeruleum 252–3, **430**, *430*
reptans **430**, *430*
Polianthes tuberosa 30, **462**, *462*
Polka dot plant 171, 234
Pollarding 281, *281*
Pollination 13
Polyanthus **563**, *563*
Polygala myrtufolia var. *grandiflora* **448**, *448*
Polygalaceae 448
Polygonaceae 358, 373, 468, 485
Polygonatum
odoratum 27, 145, 157–8, 198
x *hybridum* **485**, *485*
Polygonum spp. *123*
aubertiii **468**, *468*
bistorta 'Superbum' **373**, *373*
capitatum **373**, *373*
Polystichum setiferum 243
Pomegranate **340**, *340*
Pompom tree **380**, *380*
Poplar 274, **526–7**, *526*
Poppies 13, 16, 96, 97, 101, *101*, 111, *121*, 138, *246*, 257, *260*
alpine **562**, *562*
California 21, *39*, 51, 57, 122, *136*, 137, 153, *153*, 200, 254, **313**, *313*
California tree **486**, *486*
corn 21, *127*, 137, 153, 202, **314**, *314*
Himalayan blue **427**, *427*
Iceland 202, 254–5, **313**, *313*
Mexican tulip **539**, *539*
oriental 73, 111, *140*, 141, 197, **331**, *331*
plume **483**, *483*
prickly **475**, *475*
Welsh **561**, *561*
Populus spp. 274
Porcelain ampelopsis 288
Port St. John creeper **360**, *360*
Portaluca
grandiflora 21, 133, 153, 182, 202, **354**, *354*
oleracea 99
Portulacaceae 354
Potato creeper **469**, *469*
Potentilla spp.
atrosanguinea **333**, *333*
eriocarpa **562**, *562*
fruticosa **580**, *580*
nepalensis **333**, *333*
tridentata **485**, *485*
Prairie gentian 18, **399**, *399*
Prickly pear 197
Primrose 24, *24*, 27, *27*, *31*, 41, *41*, *43*, *159*, 172, **563**, *563*
cape 220, 239
cowslip **562–3**, *563*
drumstick 158
English 68, 141, 198
evening **372**, *372*
fairy **357**, *357*
Japanese 41, 85, *133*, 198, **374**, *374*
polyanthus *22*, *61*, 198
Primula spp. 27, 41
denticulata 158
japonica 41, 85, 198, **374**, *374*
malacoides **357**, *357*
veris **562–3**, *563*
vulgaris 141, 198, **563**, *563*
x *polyantha* 198, **563**, *563*
Primulaceae 356–7, 367, 374, 404, 473, 561–3
Primulas *176*, *246*, 271, 277
candelabra 255
Privet
California **504**, *504*
Chinese **504**, *504*
Japanese **504**, *504*
Prostanthera rotundifolia **448**, *448*
Protea
giant **385**, *385*
oleander-leaf **385**, *385*
Protea spp. **340**, *340*
cynaroides **385**, *385*
neriifolia **385**, *385*
Proteaceae 339–41, 345, 382, 385, 500–1, 525, 569, 583–4
Prunella grandiflora 'Rosea' **374**, *374*
Pruning **100–3**
cutting back 101–2
deadheading 101, *101*, 182
disbudding 101
houseplants 218–19, *219*
pinching 100–1, *100*, 182
spring and summer trimming 102
Prunus spp.
'Amonogawa' syn. *P. erecta* **392**, *392*
campanulata **345**, *345*
cerasifera **529–30**, *529–30*
dulcis **530**, *530*
glandulosa **509**, *509*
lusitanica **530**, *530*
mume **392**, *392*, **530–1**, *530*
persica **345**, *345*, **392**, *392*
serrulata **393**, *393*, **531**, *531*
'Ukon' **531**, *531*
x *amygdalo-persica* 'Pollardi' **392**, *392*
x *blireana* **392**, *392*
x *subhirtella* 257, **393**, *393*, **531**, *531*
x *yedoensis* **392**, *392*
Pulmonaria spp. 43, 122, 156
officinalis **430**, *430*
saccharata 27, 141, 157, 205
Pulsatilla vulgaris 198, **430–1**, *430*
Punica granatum **340**, *340*
Punicaceae 340
Pushkinia scilloides **406–7**, *407*
Pussy willow **533**, *533*
Pyracantha spp. 287
coccinea **510**, *510*
Pyracanthas 287
Pyrostegia venusta **323**, *323*
Pyrus
calleryana **532**, *532*
salicifolia 'Pendula' **532**, *532*
ussuriensis **532–3**, *532*

Q

Queen-of-the-prairie 132, 139, 158, 196, **368**, *368*
Queen's wreath **411**, *411*
Quercus palustris 274
Quince, flowering 271, **337**, *337*, **491**, *491*
dwarf **336**, *336*
Quisqualis indica **324**, *324*

R

Ragwort, sea **565**, *565*
Rainfall 86
Rakes 79, *79*
Ranunculaceae 326–7, 356, 358, 370, 376–7, 398–9, 401–2, 408, 414, 416, 422, 430–1, 464–5, 472–4, 481–2, 484, 543, 546, 548, 552, 554, 564, 566–7
Ranunculus *108*, **546**, *546*
Ranunculus spp. 255
acris **564**, *564*
asiaticus **546**, *546*
lingua 255
Recycling materials 297, *297*
Red hot pokers 255, 261, **329**, *329*
Redbud
Chinese **380**, *380*
eastern **389**, *389*
Reinwardtia indica syn. *R. trigyna* **580**, *580*
Reproduction **13**
Reseda odorata 144, 181
Rhamnaceae 438–9
Rhaphiolepis x *delacourii* **386**, *386*
Rheum
alexandrae **485**, *485*
palmatum 'Atrosanguineum' 251
Rhizomes 12, **29**, 98
Rhododendron spp. 257, *257*, 282, 286, *286*, **386**, *386*
arboreum **392**, *392*
indicum **386**, *386*
Knap Hill **341**, *341*
Kurume Group **386**, *386*
x *gandavense* **341**, *341*
Rhododendrons *34*, 126, 167, 256–7, 271, 286
tree **392**, *392*
Rhodohypoxis baurii **357**, *357*
Rhubarb 242, **485**, *485*
Ribes
odoratum **580**, *580*
sanguineum **386–7**, *387*
Rice flower, pink **385**, *385*
Rice-paper plant 243
Ricinus communis 130, 132, 251, 261
Robinia
hispida **393**, *393*
kelseyi **387**, *387*
pseudoacacia 43, *242*, 258, 285, **533**, *533*

Rock cress 22, 102, 141, *141*, 161, 195, **363**, *363*, **474–5**, *475*
wall 27, 70, 72, 102, 138, 155, 204, **474**, *474*
Rocket larkspur 21, 57, 200
Rodgersia 41
Rodgersia
pinnata 41
podophylla 261, **485**, *485*
Romneya coutleri **486**, *486*
Rondeletia, yellow-throat **387**, *387*
Rondeletia amoena **387**, *387*
Root system **12**, 14, 221
fibrous 12, *12*
lateral 14
radicle 14
taproot 12, *12*, 98
Rosa spp. 187, 257, 286, **324**, *324*
banksiae **468–9**, *469*, **550**, *550*
climbing **360–1**, *360–1*
'Lady Waterlow' *289*
laevigata **469**, *469*
rugosa 251
wichuraiana **469**, *469*
Rosaceae 324, 329, 333, 336–7, 342, 344–5, 360–1, 368, 386–7, 391–4, 468–9, 476, 480–1, 485, 489, 491, 498, 509–12, 518, 522–3, 527, 529–32, 534–5, 550, 552, 562, 577, 580
Rose apple **535**, *535*
Rose campion *39*, *121*, 140–1, **371**, *371*
Rose grass **357**, *357*
Rose mallow *24*, *141*, 257
Rose moss 21, 133, 153, 182, 202, **354**, *354*
Rose-of-Sharon **444**, *444*, **574**, *574*
Rosemary 187, 233, 235, 242, 277, 296–7, **448–9**, *448*
bog **378**, *378*
grevillia **382**, *382*
prostrate **448**, *448*
Roses *22*, *24*, *39*, 125–6, *126*, 141, *144*, *170*, 187, 246, 250, 256–7, *256*, 266, 271, 286, *286*, 293
Albertine **324**, *324*
Banks' **468–9**, *469*, **550**, *550*
Bloomfield Courage **324**, *324*
Cherokee **469**, *469*
Christmas **482**, *482*
climbing 289, *289*, **360–1**, *360–1*
cotton **502**, *502*
dog **378–9**, *378*
Excelsa **324**, *324*
'Iceberg' 247, *247*
memorial **469**, *469*
mermaid **550**, *550*
Mexican **390**, *390*
minature *219*
rock 277, **492**, *492*
crimson spot **492**, *492*
purple **439**, *439*
sun 204
white 246
Rosmarinus
lavandulaceus **448**, *448*
officinalis 187, 233, 235, 242, **448–9**, *448*
Rotary tillers 80–1
Rothmannia globosa **533**, *533*
Rowan **534**, *534*
Rubiaceae 323, 332, 340, 384, 387, 454, 490, 499, 510, 533
Rudbeckia spp. 85, 101, 143, 261
fulgida 69, 139, 143, 152, 161, 198, **564**, *564*
hirta 18, 19, 135, 161, 202, **564–5**, *564*
nitida **565**, *565*
Rue 125, 144, 248, **566**, *566*
Rushes 138
Russelia equiesetiformis 250
Ruta graveolens 125, 144
'Jackman's Blue' 248
Rutaceae 379, 389, 478, 488, 492, 494–5, 506, 511

S

Sage *51*, 88, 102, *104*, 161, 186, 248, 253, 271, 277, **383**, *383*, **431**, *431*
azure **429**, *429*
Bethlehem 141, 157, 205, 276
gentian **401**, *401*
Jerusalem **562**, *562*, **579**, *579*
mealy-cup 18, 172, 176, 202, 252, *115*, *120*, 123, **431**, *431*
Russian *160*, 161
scarlet 18, 202, **314**, *314*
violet 42, 125, 152, 161, 198, 250, 256, **431**, *431*
St John's wort **575–6**, *575–6*
Saintpaulia spp. 209, 218–19, *218*, 220, 230, 239
Salal **500**, *500*
Salicaceae 533
Salix caprea **533**, *533*
Salpiglossis sinuata **314**, *314*
Salvia spp. *41*, 88, 102, 186
farinacea 18, 123, 172, 176, 202, 252, **431**, *431*
officinalis 125, 161, 248, 250, **431**, *431*
patens **401**, *401*
pratensis **431**, *431*
splendens 18, 202, **314**, *314*
x *superba* 42, 152, 161, 198, **431**, *431*
Sambucus spp.
nigra **510**, *510*
racemosa 258
Sandy soil 34, *34*
Santolina spp. 246, 253
chamaecyparissus 102, 177, 248–9, **565**, *565*
Sanvitalia procumbens 21, 161, 177, 202, **541**, *541*
Sapindaceae 388, 585
Saponaria spp. 102
ocymoides 205, **374**, *374*
officinalis **374**, *374*
Sarothamnus scoparius **572**, *572*
Sarracenia spp. 237
Sasaki **493**, *493*
Satin flower **566**, *566*
Saxifraga
moschata 'Peter Pan' **375**, *375*
stolonifera 150, **486**, *486*
Saxifragaceae 327, 329, 364–5, 374, 381, 417, 466, 485–6, 508, 577, 580
Saxifrage, mossy **375**, *375*
Scabiosa caucasica 101, 102, 125, 143, 198, **375**, *375*
Scabious
giant **555**, *555*
Shepherd's **426**, *426*
Scales 222, *223*
Scarlet runner bean 19, 132
Schinus molle 274
Schizachyrium spp.
scoparium 139
Schizanthus pinnatus **354**, *354*
Schizocentron elegans **370**, *370*
Schizostylis coccinea **318**, *318*
Schlumbergera bridgesii 229, 239
Scilla
bifolia **407**, *407*
hispanicus **405**, *405*
peruviana **407**, *407*
sibirica 31, 60, *60*, 62, 125, 204, 231, **407**, *407*
Screens **132–3**, 272–3, *272*, 280, 294
shrubs 287
Scrophulariaceae 312, 314, 332, 352, 364–5, 367, 401, 423, 427, 433–4, 442–3, 487, 501–2, 538, 540–1, 556, 561, 567
Sea holly 71, *140*, 277, **423**, *423*, **480**, *480*
amethyst 125, 161, 196
Sea kale **477**, *477*
Sea urchin **525**, *525*
Seaside gardens 276–7, *276*
Seasonal garden design **126–7**
fall 127
month by month **108–11**
spring 126
summer 126–7
winter 127
Sedges 138, 292
Sedum spp. 152
maximum 'Atropurpureum' **375**, *375*
morganianum 220
spectabile 72, 143, 161, 198, 257, **376**, *376*
spurium 155, 161, 205
Sedums *51*, *102*, 152, *160*, 198, 264
'Autumn Joy' 101, **376**, *376*
two-row 155
Seedlings 67, 69, 70
Seeds 13–14, 176
bulbs 75
saving 67
sowing 57–8, 66, 69–70
indoors **64–7**
Selaginella 264
Selenicereus grandiflorus 267
Self-heal **374**, *374*
Sempervirum tectorum 205
Senecio
cineraria 18, 172, 198, 248, **565**, *565*
greyi **581**, *581*
macroglosus **551**, *551*
viravira 248
x *hybridus* **315**, *315*
Senses
sight **262–3**, *262–3*
smell **266–7**, *266–7*
sound **268–9**, *268–9*
touch **264–5**, *264–5*
Sensitive plants 237
Serissa foetida **510**, *510*
Service tree **535**, *535*
Serviceberry **518**, *518*
Shadbush **518**, *518*
Shade 43, 114, 120, **156–7**, 275–6
trees for 285
Shooting star, common **367**, *367*
Shortia galacifolia **486**, *486*
Shovels 78, *79*
Shrubs 334–41, 378–87, 436–48, 488–517, 568–81
dwarf or miniature 287
landscaping with **286–7**, *286–7*
Siberian bugloss 27, 73, 120, 157–8, 195, **418**, *418*
Sidalcea malviflora **376**, *376*
Silene pendula **354–5**, *355*
Silty soil 34–5, *34*
Silver-bell tree **526**, *526*
Silverbush **493**, *493*
Sinningia hybrids 234, 239

Sisyrinchium striatum **566**, 566
Skimmia **511**, *511*
Skimmia
japonica **511**, *511*
reevesiana **511**, *511*
Sky flower 252, **412**, *412*, **470**, *470*
Slipperwort **538**, 538
Slopes 41, **154–5**, *154–5*, 276
Slugs and snails 93, 93, 110, 157, 189, *189*
Smilacina racemosa 157–8, 198, 255, **486–7**, 486
Smoke tree 205, 285, **380**, 380
Snailflower **412**, *412*
Snake vine **549**, 549
Snakeroot
black 123, 157
white 139, 143
Snapdragons 13, 17, 21, 37, 102, 135, 177, 182, 199, 255, **312**, *312*
Sneezeweed 72, 120, 139, *139*, 196, 255, *255*, **559**, 559
Snowball **514–15**, *515*, **517**, *517*
Snowbell **512**, *512*
Snowberry **512–13**, *513*
Snow-in-summer 70, 102, 141, 155, 161, 204, 264, **476**, 476, **506**, 506
Snow-on-the-mountain 200, **454**, 454
Snowdrop tree **526**, 526
Japanese **535**, 535
Snowdrops 28, 31, 55, 60, 138, 203, 247, 276, **459**, 459
anemone **473**, 473
giant **458–9**, 458
Snowflake
spring **459**, 459
summer 30, 55, 60, 134, 204, **459**, 459
Snowflower **381**, *381*
Soapwort 102, **374**, *374*
rock 205, **374**, *374*
Soil **34–7**, 114
bonsai, for 283
composition 34
containers 168–9, 188
depth 35–6
double-digging 49, 49
fertility 36–7
moisture, testing for 49, 84, 214–15
nutrients, adding **50–1**
organisms 36, 36
pH 37, 96
preparation **48–9**, 150, 155
seeds 65
structure 35
testing 50–1, 108, 111
texture 34–5
wet sites 158–9
Solanaceae 314, 333, 336, 353–4, 400, 436, 455, 469, 497, 551
Solandra maxima **551**, *551*
Solanum spp.
jasminoides **469**, 469
pseudocapsicum 239
Soleirolia soleirolii 264
Solenostemon scutellarioides 18, 202
Solidago spp. 123, 132
canadensis **566**, 566
Sollya heterophylla **412**, *412*
Solomon's plume 157, 198
Solomon's seal 27, 145, 157, 198, **485**, *485*
false 255, **486–7**, 486
Sophora japonica 127, 285, **534**, 534
Sorbus spp. 277
alnifolia **534**, *534*
americana 285
aria **534**, *534*
aucuparia **534**, *534*
domestica **535**, *535*
Sorrel tree **528–9**, *528*
Soursop, mountain **357**, *357*
Sourwood 127, **528–9**, *528*
Spades 78
Spanish shawl **370**, *370*
Sparaxis tricolor **318**, *318*
Spartina pectinata 138
Spartium junceum **581**, *581*
Spathodea campanulata **345**, *345*
Speedwell **433**, *433*, **501**, *501*
gray spike **434**, *434*
rock 187, 205, 252
spike 39, 72, 152, 199, 252, **433**, *433*
Spice bush **578**, *578*
Spider flower 257, 271, **349**, *349*, **449**, *449*
Spider mites 92, 93
Spider plants 221
Spiderwort 102–3, 158, 198, **377**, *377*
Spike gayfeather 122, 126, 139, 152, 197, *279*
Spiraea **511**, *511*
blue **437**, *437*
garland **512**, *512*
Japanese **387**, *387*
Thunberg **512**, *512*
Vanhoutte **512**, *512*
Spiraea spp.
cantoniensis 247, **511**, *511*
japonica **387**, *387*
prunifolia **511**, *511*
thunbergii **512**, *512*
x *arguta* **512**, *512*
x *vanhouttei* **512**, *512*
Sporobolus heterolepsis 139
Sprekelia formosissima **318**, *318*
Spruce 271, 280, 282, 287
Colorado 248
Norway 274
Squill
Siberian 31, 60, 60, 62, 125, *157*, 204, 231, **407**, 407
striped **406–7**, *407*
twin-leafed **407**, *407*
Stachys
byzantina 122, 125, 150, 153, 155, 161, 198, 246, 248–9, *249*, 256, 264, *264*, **432**, *432*
macrantha **432**, *432*
Staking **102–3**, *102*
Standards 235, *242*
Star-of-Bethlehem **462**, *462*
Star of Persia 203
Starflower, spring **405**, *405*
Starwort, summer **423**, *423*
Statice 21, 201, **399**, 399
Stenocarpus sinuatus **345**, *345*
Stephanotis 187, 239
Stephanotis floribunda 187, 239, **470**, *470*
Sterculiaceae 342, 388–9, 574
Sternbergia 55
Sternbergia spp. 55
lutea **546–7**, *547*
Stewartia **535**, *535*
Stewartia pseudocamellia **535**, *535*
Stock 13, 135, 145, *145*, 178, 181, 201, **353**, *353*
evening-scented 181
night-scented 21, 144, 187, *187*
Virginia 201, **352–3**, *353*
Stokesia laevis 198, **432**, *432*
Stolons 12
Stonecrop
great **375**, *375*
showy 72, *142*, 143, **376**, *376*
two-row 205
Strawberries 187, 205, 296
barren 150, 205
beach **480**, 480
Strawberry tree **519**, *519*
Strawflowers 21, 64, 199, **539**, 539
Streptocarpus hybrids 220, 239
Strobilanthes anisophyllus **449**, *449*
Stugmaphyllon ciliatum **551**, *551*
Styracaceae 512, 526, 535
Styrax
americanus **512**, *512*
japonica **535**, *535*
Succulents 234, 237, *237*, 265, 271, 292
Sun 43, 114, 120
Sundrops 42, 45, 127, 139, 161, **562**, 562
showy 150, 197
Sunflowers 13, 19, 21, 102, 132, *132*, 135, *138*, 139, 153, 161, *254*, 255, 261, **538–9**, *539*, 558–9, *558–9*
false **559**, 559
Mexican 21, 132, 135, 202
orange **559**, *559*
Swallow-wort **555**, *555*
Sweet alyssum 21, 123, 125, 130, 133, 144–5, 153, 172, 181, 183, 201, *246*, **455**, *455*
Sweet cicely 187
Sweet peas 88, 133, 135, 145, *145*, 153, 187, 201, *254*, 267, 289, **351**, *351*
Sweet William 17, 22, 135, 144–5, 200, **366**, 366
Sweet woodruff 12, 150, 155, 158, **454**, *454*
Symphoricarpos albus **512–13**, *513*
Symphytum grandiflorum **487**, *487*
Syringa spp.
meyeri 'Superba' 257
vulgaris **449**, *449*, **513**, *513*
Syzygium jambos **535**, *535*

T

Tagetes spp. 37, 67, 153, 202
erecta **541**, *541*
patula **541**, *541*
tenufolia 'Lemon Gem' 181
Tamariacaceae 395
Tamarisk **393**, 393
Tamarix
aphylla **393**, 393
parvifolia **393**, 393
Tanacetum parthenium 21, 173, 202
Tassel flower **334**, *334*, **490–1**, 490
Taxus spp. 280, 287
baccata 280
Tea tree **384**, *384*
Teat flower **427**, *427*
Tecomanthe hillii **361**, *361*
Tecomaria capensis **325**, *325*
Telopea speciosissima **341**, *341*
Terraces 155, 276, *276*
Terrariums 234–5
Tetrapanax papyrifer 243
Teucrium spp.
chamaedrys **513**, *513*
fruticans 252, **432–3**, *432*
marum **433**, *433*
Thalictrum
aquilegifolium **376**, *376*
delavayi syn. *T. dipterocarpum* **377**, *377*
speciosissimum syn. *T. flavum glaucum* **566**, 566

Theaceae 379–80, 389, 493, 524–5, 535
Thelypteris spp. 159
Thermopsis caroliniana 139
Thistle
  Canada 98
  globe 152, 161, 196, **423**, *423*
  ornamental *127*
Thorn
  cockspur **522**, *522*
  lavalle **522–3**, *522*
  Washington **522**, *522*
Thornless honey locust tree 285
Three-veined everlasting 194
Thrift 25, 84, 102, 123, 152, *155*, 194, **362**, *362*, **475**, *475*
Thrips 93, *93*
Thrysacanthus **340**, *340*
Thuja spp. 287
  occidentalis 297
Thunbergia spp.
  alata 133, 288, *288*, **325**, *325*
  grandiflora 252, **412**, *412*, **470**, *470*
Thyme 140, 242, *242*, 276, 296–7
Thymeleaceae 380–1, 385, 440, 496
Thymus spp. 242, *242*
  praecox arcticus syn. *T. drucei* **377**, *377*
  serpyllum 150, 205
Tiarella spp. 43
  cordifolia 150, 155, 157, 198
Tibouchina urvilleana **449**, *449*
Tidy tips **539**, *539*
Tiger flower, Mexican **547**, *547*
Tigridia pavonia **547**, *547*
Tilia tomentosa 285
Tillandsia usneoides 264
Time-saving tips **148–53**
  quick and easy flowers 150–3
Tithonia rotundiflora 21, 132, 135, 202
Toadflax *19*, **352**, *352*
Tolmeia menziesii 221
Tools **78–83**, *101*
  buying 81–3
  caring for 83
  handles *81*
Toona sinensis **520**, *520*
Topiaries 280–1, *280*, *292*
  houseplants 235, *235*, 244
Topography **40–1**
  exposure 42–3
Torenia fournieri 18, 172, 176, 178, 202, **401**, *401*
Totem poles **384**, *384*
Touch-me-not 237
Trachechelospermum
  asiaticum **470**, *470*
  jasminoides 186–7, *275*, **471**, *471*
Trachycarpus fortunei 243
Tradescantia spp. 103
  x *andersoniana* 102, 158, 198, **377**, *377*
Training **100–3**, *110*
  staking 102–3, *102*
  vines *235*, 288–9
Transplanting **56–7**, *56*, *67*
Treasure flower 18, 45, 176, 187, 200, **329**, *329*
Trees 342–5, 388–95, 450–1, 518–35, 582–5
  deciduous or evergreen **271–2**
  landscaping with **284–5**, *284–5*
  shade 285
  specimen 285
  street 285
Tricyrtis formosana **433**, *433*
Trillium grandiflorum **487**, *487*
Trinity flower **487**, *487*
Triteleia **405**, *405*, **547**, *547*
Triteleia ixioides **547**, *547*
Tritonia crocata **319**, *319*
Trollius
  europaeus **566–7**, *567*
  x *cultorum* 158, **567**, *567*
Trompe d'oeil 263, *263*
Tropaeolaceae 325, 541, 551
Tropaeolum spp.
  majus 21, 183, 187, 203, 255, **541**, *541*
  peregrinum **551**, *551*
  speciosum **325**, *325*
  tricolorum **325**, *325*
Trowels 79
Trumpet flower **548**, *548*
  velvet **314**, *314*
Trumpet vine 127, 252, **320**, *320*, **470**, *470*
  blood-red **321**, *321*
  blue **412**, *412*
  vanilla **409**, *409*
  violet **409**, *409*
Tuberose 30, **462**, *462*
Tulip tree **526–7**, *526*
  Chinese **390–1**, *391*
  West African **345**, *345*
Tulipa spp. 255, *293*
  batalinii 231
  hybrids 134, 204, **319**, *319*
  kaufmanniana 204
  tarda 231
Tulips 13, *16*, 22, *24*, 28–31 *28*, *30*, *38*, *61*, 74, *74*, *121*, 134, *134–5*, 138, *173*, *174*, 177–8, *178*, 204, 231, *231*, 246, 250, 255, 259, *261*, *262*, **319**, *319*
  hybrid 63, *63*, *128*, 204
  Kaufmannia 204
Turtlehead 27, 139, 158, *159*, 195, 257, **364–5**, *365*
Tussock bellflower *see* Bellflowers
Tweedia **447**, *447*
Two-flowered pea **322**, *322*
Typha latifolia 159

U

Ulex europaeus **581**, *581*
Ulmus parvifolia 274
Umbelliferae 363, 423, 480, 553
Umbrella plant **365**, *365*
Ursinnia anthemoides **315**, *315*
Uvularia grandiflora 157, 198, **567**, *567*

V

Vaccinium corymbosum **513**, *513*
Valerian 141, 143, 145, 152, 161, 195, **327**, *327*, **377**, *377*
Valeriana officinalis **377**, *377*
Valerianaceae 327, 377
Valleys 41
Vallora speciosa **319**, *319*
Vancouveria hexandra 150
Venidio-arctotis **553**, *553*
Venus fly-traps 237, *237*
Verbascum spp. 37, 104, 122, 132
  bombycirerum 21
  chaixii 141, 161, 199, **487**, *487*
  olympicum 248
  phoeniceum hybrids **567**, *567*
Verbena *38*, *51*, 250, 253, **333**, *333*
  garden 18, 161, 182
  purple *18*
Verbena x *hybrida* 18, 161, 182, **333**, *333*
Verbenaceae 321, 333, 383, 411, 437, 465, 493, 517, 520–1, 578
Vernonia spp. 102
Veronica **442**, *442*, **501**, *501*
  shrubby **442–3**, *442–3*, **501–2**, *501–2*
Veronica spp.
  austriaca teucrium **433**, *433*
  prostrata 187, 205, 252
  spicata 72, 152, 199, 252, **433–4**, *433–4*
Vervain, rose **333**, *333*
Viburnum spp. 287
  carlesii **514**, *514*
  dentatum **514**, *514*
  farreri syn. *V. fragrans* **514**, *514*
  japonicum **514**, *514*
  macrocephalum **514–15**, *515*
  odoratissimum **515**, *515*
  opulus 277
  plicatum syn. *V. tomentosium* **515**, *515*
  rhytidophyllum **516**, *516*
  sieboldii **516**, *516*
  tinus **516**, *516*
  x *burkwoodii* **516–17**, *517*
  x *carlcephalum* **517**, *517*
Viburnums 127, 246–7, 271, 287
  Burkwood **516–17**, *517*
  doublefile **515**, *515*
  fragrant **514**, *514*
  Japanese **514**, *514*
  Korean **514**, *514*
  leatherleaf **516**, *516*
  siebold **516**, *516*
  sweet **515**, *515*
Vigna caracalla **412**, *412*
Vinca 183, 271
Vinca
  major 155, 181, 203, 245
  minor **434**, *434*
Vines *131*, 132, 235, *235*, 295
  landscaping with **288–9**, *288–9*
Viola
  cornuta **434**, *434*
  hederacea **434–5**, *435*
  labradorica 27, **435**, *435*
  odorata 15, 120, 199, **435**, *435*
  tricolor 176, **401**, *401*
  x *wittrockiana* 18, 135, 172, 183, 203, **355**, *355*
Violaceae 355, 401, 434–5
Violas *133*, 246
Violet 24, 142, 253, 260, **435**, *435*
  African 168, 209, 218–19, *218*, 220, 230, 239
  dog-tooth **457–8**, *457–8*
  horned **434**, *434*
  Labrador 27, **435**, *435*
  Persian 209, **399**, *399*
  sweet 12, 15, 120, 199, **435**, *435*
  wild **434–5**, *435*
Viper's bugloss **441**, *441*
Virgilia capensis syn. *V. oroboides* **393**, *393*
Virginia creeper *270*, 289, 294
Viscaria vulgaris **371**, *371*
Visual tricks 263, *263*
Vitex agnus-castus **517**, *517*

W

Wahlenbergia gloriosa **435**, *435*
Waldsteinia fragariodes 150, 205
Wall germander **513**, *513*
Wall plants **294**, *294*
Wallflowers 18, *29*, 145, 200, 255, *261*, 267, **421**, *421*, **555**, *555*
Wandering Jew 219
Wandflower **404**, *404*

Waratah (New South Wales) **341**, *341*
Water lilies 179, 186, 255, 277
Watering **86–7**, *86–7*, 104, 114
bonsai 283
conservation of water 87, 191, **160–1**
containers 175, 179, **190–1**
houseplants 214–16
overwatering 215
vacations, during 216
water-quality 216
time-saving tips 149
Watsonia hybrids **463**, *463*
Wattle **582**, *582*
Wax plant, Australian **465**, *465*
Wax vine **551**, *551*
Waxflower **465**, *465*
Geraldton **492**, *492*
Weeding **98–9**, *108*
control of weeds 98–9, 137, *137*
hoeing and tilling 99, *99*
mowing 99
pulling and digging 98, 99, *99*
time-saving tips 149
Weigela 257, **387**, *387*
Weigela florida 256–7, **387**, *387*
Wet sites **158–9**, *158–9*, 277
Whitebeam **534**, *534*
Whiteflies 222, *222*
Wildlife 269
Willow 277
goat **533**, *533*
Virginia **503**, *503*
Willow blue star 194, **415**, *415*
Wind 268, 274–5. *see also* Exposure
Windflower **402**, *402*, **473**, *473*
Japanese **474**, *474*
Window boxes **180–1**, *180–1*, 297, *297*
Winter, preparing for **104–7**, 111
Winter aconite 55, **543**, *543*
Winter sweet 266
Wintergreen **500**, *500*
Winterhazel **571**, *571*
spike **572**, *572*
Wishbone flower 18, 172, 176, 178, 202, **401**, *401*
Wisteria 126, 246, 252, 265, *270*, 271, 288–9, 289, 293
Chinese **413**, *413*, **471**, *471*
Japanese **412–13**, *412–13*, **471**, *471*
pink **361**, *361*
silky **471**, *471*
Wisteria spp. 265, *270*, 271, 288–9, *289*
floribunda **361**, *361*, **412–13**, *412–13*, **471**, *471*
sinensis 246, 252, **413**, *413*, **471**, *471*
venusta syn. *W. brachybotrys* **471**, *471*
Witch hazel 266, **575**, *575*
Chinese **574–5**, *575*
Wolfbane **414**, *414*
Wonder flower **462**, *462*
Wormwood 13, 144, 161, 248
beach 248, **553**, *553*
'Lambrook Silver' 248

X

Xeranthemum annuum **355**, *355*

Y

Yarrow 13, *42*, 49, *49*, 71, 84, 88, 102, *160*, 194, 255, **472**, *472*, **552**, *552*
fern-leaved 139, 143, 152, 161, **552**, *552*
Galaxy series 27
woolly 138
Yellow bell **544**, *544*
Yesterday-today-and-tomorrow **436**, *436*
Yew 280, *280*, 287
Yucca spp.
filamentosa 152, 161, **487**, *487*
rigida 248–9
whipplei 248–9
Yuccas 126, 186, 248

Z

Zaluzianskya capensis 245
Zantedeschia
aethiopica 29, 243, **463**, *463*
elliottiana 244
Zebrina pendula 219
Zenobia **517**, *517*
Zenobia pulverulenta syn. *Z. speciosa* **517**, *517*
Zephyranthes candida **463**, *463*
Zingiberaceae 558
Zinnia 18, 21, 37, 64, 203, *116*, 135, **315**, *315*
creeping 21, 161, 177, 202, **541**, *541*
Mexican **315**, *315*
narrow-leaved 21, 176
Zinnia spp. 37, 203
angustifolia 21, 176
elegans 21, 135, 250, **315**, *315*
haageana 250, **315**, *315*

Credits and Acknowledgments

Photographs have been supplied by the following libraries and individual photographers:

Addington Turf & Horticultural Consultants; Allan Armitage; Heather Angel; Ardea; The Art Archive; Auscape; Australian Picture Library; A-Z Botanical; Nan Barbour; Gillian Beckett; Bruce Coleman Ltd; Geoffrey Burnie; John Callahan; Leigh Clapp; Corel Corp.; Michael Dirr; Thomas Eltzroth; Derek Fell; Garden Picture Library; Getty Images; Denise Greig; Ivy Hansen; Harry Smith Collection; Hemera Studio; Holt Studios International; Andrew Larson; Robert E. Lyons; Stirling Macoboy; Cheryl Maddocks; S. & O. Mathews; Clive Nichols; Oxford Scientific Films; Jerry Pavia; Joanna Pavia; PhotoDisc; photolibrary.com; Photos Horticultural; Lee Reich; G. R. "Dick" Roberts; Rodale Stock Images; Tony Rodd; Lorna Rose; Susan Roth; Anita Sabarese; John J. Smith; David Wallace; Mel Watson; Weldon Owen; Ron West; Gerry Whitmont; James Young.

Illustrations are by:

Artville; Anne Bowman; Tony Britt-Lewis; Mike Gorman; Helen Halliday; Angela Lober; David Mackay; Stuart McVicar; Nicola Oram; Oliver Rennert; Edwina Riddell; Barbara Rodanska; Jan Smith; Kathie Smith; Sharif Tarabay; Genevieve Wallace.